Introductory Mathematical Analysis

For Business, Economics, and the Life and Social Sciences

Second Custom Edition for St. John's University

Taken from:
Introductory Mathematical Analysis for Business, Economics, and the Life and Social Sciences, Thirteenth Edition
by Ernest F. Haeussler, Jr., Richard S. Paul, and Richard J. Wood

Cover Art: Courtesy of Photodisc, Stockbyte, Glow Images/Getty

Taken from:

Introductory Mathematical Analysis for Business, Economics, and the Life and Social Sciences, Thirteenth Edition
by Ernest F. Haeussler, Jr., Richard S. Paul, and Richard J. Wood
Copyright © 2011, 2008, 2005 by Pearson Education, Inc.
Published by Prentice Hall
Upper Saddle River, New Jersey 07458

Pearson Learning Solutions, 501 Boylston Street, Suite 900, Boston, MA 02116
A Pearson Education Company
www.pearsoned.com

Printed in the United States of America

4 5 6 7 8 9 10 v092 17 16 15

000200010271303059

TF

ISBN 10: 1-256-72643-5
ISBN 13: 978-1-256-72643-2

Contents

Preface

The thirteenth edition of *Introductory Mathematical Analysis for Business, Economics, and the Life and Social Sciences* continues to provide a mathematical foundation for students in a variety of fields and majors. It begins with precalculus and finite mathematics topics such as functions, equations, mathematics of finance, matrix algebra, linear programming, and probability. Then it progresses through both single variable and multivariable calculus, including continuous random variables. Technical proofs, conditions, and the like are sufficiently described but are not overdone. Our guiding philosophy led us to include those proofs and general calculations that shed light on how the corresponding calculations are done in applied problems. Informal intuitive arguments are often given as well.

Approach

Introductory Mathematical Analysis for Business, Economics, and the Life and Social Sciences takes a unique approach to problem solving. As has been the case in earlier editions of this book, we establish an emphasis on algebraic calculations that sets this text apart from other introductory, applied mathematics books. The process of calculating with variables builds skill in mathematical modeling and paves the way for students to use calculus. The reader will not find a "definition-theorem-proof" treatment, but there is a sustained effort to impart a genuine mathematical treatment of real world problems. Emphasis on developing algebraic skills is extended to the exercises, in which many, even those of the drill type, are given with general coefficients.

In addition to the overall approach to problem solving, we aim to work through examples and explanations with just the right blend of rigor and accessibility. The tone of the book is not too formal, yet certainly not lacking precision. One might say the book reads in a relaxed tone without sacrificing opportunities to bring students to a higher level of understanding through strongly motivated applications. In addition, we have refined the organization over many editions to present the content in very manageable portions for optimal teaching and learning.

Changes for the Thirteenth Edition

In the thirteenth edition we have tried to make the elementary notions in the early chapters pave the way for their use in more advanced topics. Our early treatment of summation notation, discussed in further detail below, is but one example. In Section 1.3, inequalities are introduced and we point out that $a \leq b$ is equivalent to "there exists a non-negative number s such that $a + s = b$". The idea is not deep but the pedagogical point is that *slack variables*, key to implementing the simplex algorithm in Chapter 7, should be familiar and not distract from the rather technical material in linear programming. For yet another example, we mention absolute value of Section 1.4. It is common to note that $|a - b|$ provides the distance from a to b. In Example 4e of Section 1.4 we point out that "x is less than σ units from μ" translates as $|x - \mu| < \sigma$. In Section 1.4 this is but an exercise with the notation, as it should be, but the point here is that later, in Chapter 9, μ will be the mean and σ the standard deviation of a random variable. Again we have separated, in advance, a simple idea from a more advanced one. In problem 12 of Problem 1.4, we ask the student to set up $|f(x) - L| < \epsilon$, an expression that an instructor of a more advanced class might wish to use in Chapter 10 on Limits.

We have tried to increase the internal consistency of the book and expanded our use of pointing back, for review purposes, when new work benefits from doing so. We have also improved the pointing forward to relevant exercises that is provided by the *Now Work Problem N* elements. We have increased the number of these and tried to improve the pairings of worked examples and suggested problems.

Several organizational improvements were implemented in the thirteenth edition. To summarize the changes in Chapter 1 a new section on Sequences was added the section on Functions of Several Variables, formerly in Chapter 17, was moved to Chapter 2 and rewritten to suit that placement. A section on Perpetuities was added to Chapter 5. The sections on Area and Area between Curves in Chapter 14 were combined into a single section and adapted considerably. There are also many other improvements to the text involving less than complete revision of a section.

- **Section 1.6, Arithmetic and Geometric Sequences:** The section on Sequences provides several pedagogical advantages. The very definition is stated in a fashion that paves the way for the more important and more basic definition of function in Chapter 2. In summing the terms of a sequence we are able to practice the use of Summation Notation introduced in the preceding section. The most obvious benefit though is that "Sequences" allows us a better organization in the Annuities section of Chapter 5. Both the present and the future values of an annuity are obtained by summing (finite) geometric sequences. Later in the text, sequences arise in the definition of the number e in Chapter 4, in Markov Chains in Chapter 9, and in Newton's Method in Chapter 12, so that a helpful unifying reference is obtained.

  In the course of summing the terms of a finite sequence, it is natural to raise the possibility of summing the terms of an infinite sequence. This is a nonthreatening environment in which to provide a first foray into the world of limits. We simply explain how certain infinite geometric sequences have well-defined sums and phrase the results in a way that will create a toehold for the formal introduction of limits in Chapter 10. These particular infinite sums enable us to introduce the idea of a perpetuity, first informally in the sequence section, and then again in more detail in a further new section on Perpetuities in Chapter 5.

- **Section 2.8, Functions of Several Variables:** The introduction to functions of several variables, which appeared at the beginning of Chapter 17 in the previous edition, has been relocated and reworked to appear in Chapter 2. Functions of Several Variables is a topic that should appear long before Calculus. Once we have done some calculus there are particular ways to use calculus in the study of Functions of Several Variables, but these aspects should not be confused with the basics that we use throughout the book. For example, "a-sub-n-angle-r" and "s-sub-n-angle-r" studied in the Mathematics of Finance, Chapter 5, are perfectly good functions of two variables.

- **Section 5.6, Perpetuities:** The new Section 1.6 further enables us to introduce Perpetuities in the Finance chapter. "Perpetuity" is a nice, practical, example of a fairly profound mathematical idea that will appeal to commerce students.

- **Section 14.9, Area:** It was thought that the two earlier sections on area were somewhat repetitive. The first, called simply "Area", dealt with the important special case of the second, "Area between Curves", in which the lower curve is the x-axis. We believe that by combining these sections we have gained some unification and economy of presentation, with no sacrifice of detail.

- **Leontieff's Input-Output Analysis (in Section 6.7):** In the section on Leontieff's Input-Output Analysis we have separated various aspects of the total problem. We begin by describing what we now call the Leontieff matrix A as an encoding of the input and output relationships between sectors of an economy. Since this matrix can often be assumed to be constant, for a substantial period of time, we begin by assuming that A is a given. The simpler problem is then to determine the production X which is required to meet an external demand D for an economy whose Leontieff matrix is A. We provide a careful account of this as the solution of $(I-A)X = D$. Since A can be assumed to be fixed while various demands D are investigated, there is *some* justification to compute $(I-A)^{-1}$ so that we have $X = (I-A)^{-1}D$. However, use of a matrix inverse should not be considered an essential part of the solution. Finally, we explain how the Leontieff matrix can be found from a table of data that might be available to a planner.

- **Birthday Probability (in Section 8.4):** New to "Probability" is a treatment of the classic problem of determining the probability that at least 2 of n people have their birthday on the same day. While this problem is given as an example in many texts, the recursive formula that we give for calculating the probability as a function of n is not a common feature. It is reasonable to include it in this edition because recursively defined sequences appear explicitly in our new section "Sequences".

- **Sign Charts for a Function (in Chapter 10):** The sign charts that we introduced in the 12th edition now make their appearance in Chapter 10. Our point is that these charts can be made for any real-valued function of a real variable and their help in graphing a function begins prior to the introduction of derivatives. Of course we continue to exploit their use in Chapter 13 "Curve Sketching" where, for each function f, we advocate making a sign chart for each of f, f', and f'', interpreted for f itself.

- **Exercise Update:** Approximately 20% have been either updated or written completely new.

- **Updated feature names:** Labeling improvements were made to a few features to clarify their pedagogical use for instructors and students. *Mathematical Snapshots* at the end of chapters are now referred to as *Explore & Extend*, *Principles in Practice* exercises next to examples are now referred to as *Apply It* exercises, and the *Pointer* notes in the margin are now named *To Review*.

Hallmark Features and Pedagogy

- **Applications:** An abundance and variety of applications for the intended audience appear throughout the book; students continually see how the mathematics they are learning can be used. These applications cover such diverse areas as business, economics, biology, medicine, sociology, psychology, ecology, statistics, earth science, and archaeology. Many of these real-world situations are drawn from literature and are documented by references, sometimes from the Web. In some, the background and context are given in order to stimulate interest. However, the text is self-contained, in the sense that it assumes no prior exposure to the concepts on which the applications are based. (See, for example, page 340, Example 2 in 7.7)

- *Apply It*: The *Apply It* exercises, formerly called *Principles in Practice*, provide students with further applications. Located in the margins, these additional exercises give students real-world applications and more opportunities to see the chapter material put into practice. An icon indicates *Apply It* problems that can be solved using a graphing calculator. Answers to *Apply It* problems appear at the end of the text and complete solutions to these problems are found in the Solutions Manuals. (See, for example, page 376, Apply It 1 in 8.3)

- *Now Work Problem N*: Throughout the text we have retained the popular *Now Work Problem N* feature. The idea is that after a worked example, students are directed to an end of section problem (labeled with a blue exercise number) that reinforces the ideas of the worked example. This gives students an opportunity to practice what they have just learned. Because the majority of these keyed exercises are odd-numbered, students can immediately check their answer in the back of the book to assess their level of understanding. The complete solutions to these exercises can be found in the Student Solutions Manual. (See, for example, page 466, Example 7 in 10.1)

- *Cautions*: Throughout the book, cautionary warnings are presented in very much the same way an instructor would warn students in class of commonly-made errors. These *Cautions* are indicated with an icon to help students prevent common misconceptions. (See, for example, page 495, Example 2 in 11.1)

- **Definitions, key concepts, and important rules and formulas** are clearly stated and displayed as a way to make the navigation of the book that much easier for the student. (See, for example, page 495, Definition of Derivative in 11.1)

- *Explore & Extend* **Activities,** formerly called *Mathematical Snapshots,* are strategically placed at the end of the chapter to bring together multiple mathematical concepts studied in the previous sections within the context of a highly relevant and interesting application. These activities can be completed in or out of class either individually or within a group. (See, for example, page 574, in Chapter 12)

- **Review Material:** Each chapter (except Chapter 0) has a review section that contains a list of important terms and symbols, a chapter summary, and numerous review problems.

In addition, key examples are referenced along with each group of important terms and symbols. (See, for example, page 572, in Chapter 12)

■ **Back-of-Book Answers:** Answers to odd-numbered problems appear at the end of the book. For many of the differentiation problems, the answers appear in both "unsimplified" and "simplified" forms. (Of course "simplified" is in any event a subjective term when applied to mathematical expressions that tends to presuppose the nature of subsequent calculations with such expressions.) This allows students to readily check their work. (See, for example, page AN-22, in Answers for 11.4)

■ **Markov Chains:** In Section 9.3, on Markov Chains, we noticed that considerable simplification to the problem of finding steady state vectors is obtained by writing state vectors as columns rather than rows. This does necessitate that a transition matrix $\mathbf{T} = [t_{ij}]$ have $t_{ij} =$ probability that next state is i given that current state is j but avoids artificial transpositions later. (See page 445)

■ **Sign Charts:** In Chapter 13 on Curve Sketching, the use of *sign charts* is greatly expanded as compared to other books. In particular, a sign chart for a first derivative is always accompanied by a further line interpreting the results for the function that is to be graphed. Thus, on an interval where we record "+" for f we also record "/" for f and on an interval where we record "−" for f we also record "\" for f. The resulting strings of such elements, say /\/, with further embellishments that we describe in the text, provide a very preliminary sketch of the curve in question. We freely acknowledge that this is a blackboard technique used by many instructors, but it appears too rarely in textbooks. (See, for example, page 578, first sign chart in Chapter 13)

Examples and Exercises

Most instructors and students will agree that the key to an effective textbook is in the quality and quantity of the examples and exercise sets. To that end, more than 850 examples are worked out in detail. Some of these examples include a *strategy* box designed to guide students through the general steps of the solution before the specific solution is obtained (See pages 639–640, 14.3 example 4). In addition, an abundant number of diagrams (almost 500) and exercises (more than 5000) are included. Of the exercises, approximately 20% have been either updated or written completely new. In each exercise set, grouped problems are given in increasing order of difficulty. In most exercise sets the problems progress from the basic mechanical drill-type to more interesting thought-provoking problems. The exercises labeled with a blue exercise number correlate to a "Now Work Problem N" statement and example in the section.

Based on the feedback we have received from users of this text, the diversity of the applications provided in both the exercise sets and examples is truly an asset of this book. Many real-world type problems with accurate data are included. Students do not need to look hard to see how the math they are learning is applied to everyday or work-related situations. A great deal of effort has been put into producing a proper balance between the drill-type exercises and the problems requiring the integration and application of the concepts learned. (see pages 125–126, Explore and Extend for Chapter 2; 172, Explore and Extend for Chapter 3; 787–788, Example 1 in 17.8 on Lines of Regression)

Technology

In order that students appreciate the value of current *technology*, optional graphing calculator material appears throughout the text both in the exposition and exercises. It appears for a variety of reasons: as a mathematical tool, to visualize a concept, as a computing aid, and to reinforce concepts. Although calculator displays for a TI-83 Plus accompany the corresponding technology discussion, our approach is general enough so that it can be applied to other graphing calculators. In the exercise sets, graphing calculator problems are indicated by an icon. To provide flexibility for an instructor in planning assignments, these problems are typically placed at the end of an exercise set.

Course Planning

One of the obvious assets of this book is that a considerable number of courses can be served by it. Because instructors plan a course outline to serve the individual needs of a particular class and curriculum, we will not attempt to provide detailed sample outlines. The Table of Contents has now been divided into three parts to aid in course preparation but this does not designate any change in the flow from one chapter to the next.

Part I: College Algebra includes Chapters 0–4 and includes core precalculus topics.

Part II: Finite Mathematics covers Chapters 5–9 and has a wide variety of topics from which instructors can often pick and choose.

Part III: Calculus is the topic of the remaining Chapters 10–17.

Below are some additional notes to consider when creating a syllabus or outlining your course.

- **Two Semester Courses:** Schools that have two academic terms per year tend to give business students a term devoted to Finite Mathematics and a term devoted to Calculus. For these schools we recommend Chapters 1 through 9 for the first course, starting wherever the preparation of the students allows, and Chapters 10 through 17 for the second—deleting most optional material.

- **Three Quarter or Three Semester Courses:** For the **first course**, a program that allows three quarters of Mathematics for well-prepared Business students can start a first course with Chapter 1 and choose such topics as are of interest, up to and including Chapter 9. A **second course** on Differential Calculus will use Chapter 10 on Limits and Continuity, followed by the three "differentiation chapters", 11 through 13 inclusive. Here, Section 12.6 on Newton's Method can be omitted without loss of continuity while some instructors may prefer to review Chapter 4 on Exponential and Logarithmic Functions prior to their study as differentiable functions. Finally, Chapters 14 through 17 inclusive could define a **third course** on Integral Calculus with an introduction to Multivariable Calculus. In an applied course it is well to stress the use of tables to find integrals and thus the techniques of "parts" and "partial fractions", in 15.1 and 15.2 respectively, should be considered optional. Chapter 16 is certainly not needed for Chapter 17 and Section 15.7 on Improper Integrals can be safely omitted if Chapter 16 is not covered.

Supplements

- The *Student Solutions Manual* includes worked solutions for all odd-numbered problems and all *Apply It* problems. ISBN 0-321-64530-8 | 978-0-321-64530-2

- The *Instructor's Solution Manual* has worked solutions to all problems, including those in the *Apply It* exercises and in the *Explore & Extend* activities. It is downloadable from the Instructor's Resource Center at www.pearsonhighered.com/irc.

- *TestGen*®(www.pearsoned.com/testgen) enables instructors to build, edit, and print, and administer tests using a computerized bank of questions developed to cover all the objectives of the text. TestGen is algorithmically based, allowing instructors to create multiple but equivalent versions of the same question or test with the click of a button. Instructors can also modify test bank questions or add new questions. The software and testbank are available for download from Pearson Education's online catalog and from the Instructor's Resource Center at www.pearsonhighered.com/irc.

Acknowledgments

We express our appreciation to the following colleagues who contributed comments and suggestions that were valuable to us in the evolution of this text (professors marked with an asterisk reviewed the thirteenth edition):

E. Adibi, *Chapman University*
R. M. Alliston, *Pennsylvania State University*
R. A. Alo, *University of Houston*
K. T. Andrews, *Oakland University*
M. N. de Arce, *University of Puerto Rico*
E. Barbut, *University of Idaho*
G. R. Bates, *Western Illinois University*
*S. Beck, *Navarro College*
D. E. Bennett, *Murray State University*
C. Bernett, *Harper College*
A. Bishop, *Western Illinois University*
P. Blau, *Shawnee State University*
R. Blute, *University of Ottawa*
S. A. Book, *California State University*
A. Brink, *St. Cloud State University*
R. Brown, *York University*
R. W. Brown, *University of Alaska*
S. D. Bulman-Fleming, *Wilfrid Laurier University*
D. Calvetti, *National College*
D. Cameron, *University of Akron*
K. S. Chung, *Kapiolani Community College*
D. N. Clark, *University of Georgia*
E. L. Cohen, *University of Ottawa*
J. Dawson, *Pennsylvania State University*
A. Dollins, *Pennsylvania State University*
*T. J. Duda, *Columbus State Community College*
G. A. Earles, *St. Cloud State University*
B. H. Edwards, *University of Florida*
J. R. Elliott, *Wilfrid Laurier University*
J. Fitzpatrick, *University of Texas at El Paso*
M. J. Flynn, *Rhode Island Junior College*
G. J. Fuentes, *University of Maine*
L. Gerber, *St. John's University*
T. G. Goedde, *The University of Findlay*
S. K. Goel, *Valdosta State University*
G. Goff, *Oklahoma State University*
J. Goldman, *DePaul University*
*E. Greenwood, *Tarrant County College, Northwest Campus*
J. T. Gresser, *Bowling Green State University*
L. Griff, *Pennsylvania State University*
*R. Grinnell, *University of Toronto at Scarborough*
F. H. Hall, *Pennsylvania State University*
V. E. Hanks, *Western Kentucky University*
R. C. Heitmann, *The University of Texas at Austin*
J. N. Henry, *California State University*
W. U. Hodgson, *West Chester State College*
B. C. Horne, Jr., *Virginia Polytechnic Institute and State University*
J. Hradnansky, *Pennsylvania State University*
P. Huneke, *The Ohio State University*
C. Hurd, *Pennsylvania State University*

J. A. Jiminez, *Pennsylvania State University*
W. C. Jones, *Western Kentucky University*
R. M. King, *Gettysburg College*
M. M. Kostreva, *University of Maine*
G. A. Kraus, *Gannon University*
J. Kucera, *Washington State University*
M. R. Latina, *Rhode Island Junior College*
*L. N. Laughlin, *University of Alaska, Fairbanks*
P. Lockwood-Cooke, *West Texas A&M University*
J. F. Longman, *Villanova University*
I. Marshak, *Loyola University of Chicago*
D. Mason, *Elmhurst College*
F. B. Mayer, *Mt. San Antonio College*
P. McDougle, *University of Miami*
F. Miles, *California State University*
E. Mohnike, *Mt. San Antonio College*
C. Monk, *University of Richmond*
R. A. Moreland, *Texas Tech University*
J. G. Morris, *University of Wisconsin-Madison*
J. C. Moss, *Paducah Community College*
D. Mullin, *Pennsylvania State University*
E. Nelson, *Pennsylvania State University*
S. A. Nett, *Western Illinois University*
R. H. Oehmke, *University of Iowa*
Y. Y. Oh, *Pennsylvania State University*
J. U. Overall, *University of La Verne*
A. Panayides, *William Patterson University*
D. Parker, *University of Pacific*
N. B. Patterson, *Pennsylvania State University*
V. Pedwaydon, *Lawrence Technical University*
E. Pemberton, *Wilfrid Laurier University*
M. Perkel, *Wright State University*
D. B. Priest, *Harding College*
J. R. Provencio, *University of Texas*
L. R. Pulsinelli, *Western Kentucky University*
M. Racine, *University of Ottawa*
N. M. Rice, *Queen's University*
A. Santiago, *University of Puerto Rico*
J. R. Schaefer, *University of Wisconsin–Milwaukee*
*S. Sehgal, *The Ohio State University*
W. H. Seybold, Jr., *West Chester State College*
G. Shilling, *The University of Texas at Arlington*
S. Singh, *Pennsylvania State University*
L. Small, *Los Angeles Pierce College*
E. Smet, *Huron College*
J. Stein, *California State University, Long Beach*
M. Stoll, *University of South Carolina*
T. S. Sullivan, *Southern Illinois University Edwardsville*
E. A. Terry, *St. Joseph's University*
A. Tierman, *Saginaw Valley State University*
B. Toole, *University of Maine*
J. W. Toole, *University of Maine*

D. H. Trahan, *Naval Postgraduate School*

J. P. Tull, *The Ohio State University*

L. O. Vaughan, Jr., *University of Alabama in Birmingham*

L. A. Vercoe, *Pennsylvania State University*

M. Vuilleumier, *The Ohio State University*

B. K. Waits, *The Ohio State University*

A. Walton, *Virginia Polytechnic Institute and State University*

H. Walum, *The Ohio State University*

E. T. H. Wang, *Wilfrid Laurier University*

A. J. Weidner, *Pennsylvania State University*

L. Weiss, *Pennsylvania State University*

N. A. Weigmann, *California State University*

S. K. Wong, *Ohio State University*

G. Woods, *The Ohio State University*

C. R. B. Wright, *University of Oregon*

C. Wu, *University of Wisconsin–Milwaukee*

B. F. Wyman, *The Ohio State University*

*D. Zhang, *Washington State University*

Some exercises are taken from problem supplements used by students at Wilfrid Laurier University. We wish to extend special thanks to the Department of Mathematics of Wilfrid Laurier University for granting Prentice Hall permission to use and publish this material, and also to Prentice Hall, who in turn allowed us to make use of this material.

We again express our sincere gratitude to the faculty and course coordinators of The Ohio State University and Columbus State University who took a keen interest in this and other editions, offering a number of invaluable suggestions.

Special thanks are due to Cindy Trimble of C Trimble & Associates for her careful work on the solutions manuals. Her work was extraordinarily detailed and helpful to us. We also appreciate the care that Paul Lorczak and Gary Williams took in checking the text and exercises for accuracy.

Ernest F. Haeussler, Jr.
Richard S. Paul
Richard J. Wood

Introductory Mathematical Analysis

For Business, Economics, and the Life and Social Sciences

Chapter 1 Elementary Algebra

1.1 ARITHMETIC

Rational numbers are used to solve linear equations like $2x + 3 = 9$, but real numbers are needed to solve some polynomial equations like $x^2 + 3 = 9$.

1. BASICS OF DECIMAL NUMBERS

Real Number A number that can be expressed as either a positive or negative decimal (signed number), or 0. A number is represented by a lower case italic letter such as a.

Natural Numbers: the counting numbers, also called positive integers.

Integers: Natural numbers, their negatives, and 0. **Rational Number** Ratio of two whole numbers.

Equality $a = b$ means that a and b are names for the same number; replacing a with b does not change the truth value of a statement (**substitution property**). $a \neq b$ means a is not equal to b. Then
(a) $a = a$ (reflexive)
(b) If $a = b$ then $b = a$ (symmetric)
(c) If $a = b$ and $b = c$ then $a = c$ (transitive)

+, × We assume the student is familiar with the sum $a + b$ and product $a \times b$ or $a \cdot b$ of numbers a and b.

Parentheses (), brackets [] or braces {} (called **fences**) indicate that an expression inside is to be evaluated and treated as a single quantity. $(a + b) + c$ means add a and b first, then add this number to c. $a + (b + c)$ means calculate $b + c$ first, then add a to this number.

Powers $a^2 = a \cdot a$ (square), $a^3 = a \cdot a \cdot a$ (cube). If n is a positive integer, a^n means we multiply n copies of a. The superscript symbols 2, 3, n are called **exponents.**

Conventions The multiplication symbol may be omitted, except between two numbers. Thus $7 \times n = 7 \cdot n = 7n$, $7 \times 4 = 7 \cdot 4 = 7(4)$
Operations are performed in the order: 1. inside parentheses, 2. powers and roots, 3. multiplication division, and negation, 4. addition and subtraction. Thus $ab + ac$ means $(a \times b) + (a \times c)$.

Example 1 Evaluate (a) $3 + 4 \cdot 5^2$ (b) $(3 + 4)5^2$
Solution (a) $3 + 4 \cdot 5^2 = 3 + 4 \cdot 25 = 3 + 100 = 103$
(b) $(3 + 4)5^2 = 7 \cdot 5^2 = 7 \cdot 25 = 175$ ∎

Properties of real (or rational) numbers a, b, c. Other properties are given in §1.5.

Closure	$a + b$ and ab are real (rational) numbers.	(1)
Commutative laws	$a + b = b + a$, $ab = ba$	(2)
Associative laws	$(a + b) + c = a + (b + c)$, $(ab)c = a(bc)$	(3)
Identities	$a + 0 = 0 + a = a$, $a \cdot 1 = 1 \cdot a = a$	(4)
Inverses	Each a has a unique **negative** $-a$ such that $a + (-a) = -a + a = 0$ Each $a \neq 0$ has a unique **reciprocal** a^{-1} such that $a \cdot a^{-1} = a^{-1} \cdot a = 1$	(5)
Distributive law	$a(b + c) = ab + ac$	(6)
Zero product	$ab = 0$ if and only if $a = 0$ or $b = 0$	(7)
Zero sum	a^2 is positive unless $a = 0$. $a^2 + b^2$ is positive unless $a = 0$ and $b = 0$.	(8)

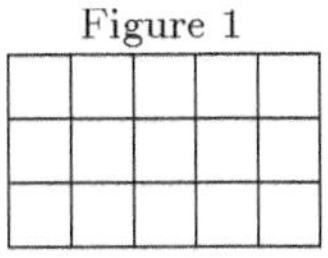

Figure 1 shows three rows of five squares is the same number as five columns of three squares, illustrating the commutative law of multiplication.

Figure 1

Figure 2

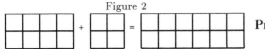

Practice 1 Which property of numbers does Figure 2 illustrate?

Remarks A set with two operations having properties (1-6) is called a **field**. Thus the real numbers are a field and the rational numbers are a field. A set with one operation having closure, associative, identity and inverse is called a **group**. The integers with addition is a group.

Because of the associative laws, we omit parentheses and write $a + b + c$ and abc.

The commutative, associative and distributive laws extend to more than three numbers. a is the negative of $-a$ and a is the reciprocal of a^{-1}: $-(-a) = a$ and $(a^{-1})^{-1} = a$.

-3 is a negative number, but $-a$ may be either positive, negative or 0.

In this book "or" means "at least one item"; we use "either...or" to mean "exactly one"

Subtraction $a - b$ means $a + (-b)$. b is the **subtrahend**. Then $-(a - b) = b - a$. $\qquad$ (9)

Division $a \div b = a/b = \frac{a}{b} = a{:}b$ means ab^{-1}. b is the **divisor**. Then $(a/b)^{-1} = b/a$ and $a^{-1} = 1/a$.
" $\div$ " is called an obelus; "/" is called a solidus; ":" is a colon.
Because 0 does not have an inverse, division by 0 can't be defined to be consistent with Properties 1-6.

Inequality $a < b$ (a less than b) means $b - a$ is positive; $a > b$ (a greater than b) means $a - b$ is positive. In particular, $a > 0$ means that a is positive and $a < 0$ means that a is negative. It follows that if a and b are real numbers, then either $a < b$, $a = b$, or $a > b$. $a \le b$ means a is less than or equal to b; $a \ge b$ means a is greater than or equal to b; a is **nonnegative** means $a \ge 0$. $\qquad$ (10)

Archimedes If $a > 0$ and $b > 0$ then there is a positive integer n such that $na > b$.

Signed Product ab is positive if a and b have like signs, and negative if they are unlike.

Calculating To add two numbers with like signs, add the unsigned numbers and restore the common sign. To add numbers with unlike signs, subtract the unsigned numbers and restore the sign of the larger.
To subtract, change the sign of the subtrahend and follow the rules for addition.
To multiply or divide, multiply or divide the unsigned numbers. If the signs are unlike, prefix a $-$.

Example 2 Calculate (a) $5 + (-7)$ (b) $5 - (-7)$ (c) $5(-7)$ (d) $(-5)(-7)$
Solution (a) 7 is larger. $5 + (-7) = -(7 - 5) = -2$
(b) $5 - (-7) = 5 + 7 = 12$
(c) $5(-7) = -(5 \cdot 7) = -35$ (d) $(-5)(-7) = 5 \cdot 7 = 35$ $\qquad$ ∎

Digits The decimal number $x = abcd.efg$ has the value
$1000a + 100b + 10c + d + e/10 + f/100 + g/1000$
$= 10^3 a + 10^2 b + 10c + d + 10^{-1}e + 10^{-2}f + 10^{-3}g$
where each letter is one of the digits 0, 1, 2, 3, 4, 5, 6, 7, 8 or 9. We use 0 to push other digits into the desired column.

10^3 thousands	10^2 hundreds	10 tens	1 units	decimal point	10^{-1} tenths	10^{-2} hundredths	10^{-3} thousandths
a	b	c	d	.	e	f	g

Writing Cardinal numbers indicate quantity: $0 = $ zero, $1 = $ one, $2 = $ two, $3 = $ three, $4 = $ four, $5 = $ five, $6 = $ six, $7 = $ seven, $8 = $ eight, $9 = $ nine, $10 = $ ten, $11 = $ eleven, $12 = $ twelve, $13 = $ thirteen, $14 = $ fourteen, $15 = $ fifteen, $16 = $ sixteen, $17 = $ seventeen, $18 = $ eighteen, $19 = $ nineteen. Multiples of 10 also have names: $20 = $ twenty, $30 = $ thirty, $40 = $ forty, $50 = $ fifty, $60 = $ sixty, $70 = $ seventy, $80 = $ eighty, $90 = $ ninety, $100 = $ hundred, $1000 = $ thousand. Also, $2 = $ pair, $12 = $ dozen, $20 = $ score, $100 = $ centum, $144 = $ gross, $1000 = $ chiliad, $10000 = $ myriad. Adjectives include binary (2), decimal (10), vicenary (20), sexigesimal (60). (Ordinal numbers are with sequences below.) $\qquad$ (11)

Numbers less than 100 written with two words need a hyphen: 35 is thirty-five.
A decimal point becomes "and": 407.23 is four hundred seven and twenty-three hundredths; read it as four hundred seven point two three.
Spell out a number beginning a sentence. See Large Prefix, Small Prefix in §1.4.

Figure 3

Numerals less than 1 get a leading 0 if the quantity could exceed 1, or in medical records to reinforce the decimal point and avoid overdosing by a factor of 10 or 100. Figure 3 is 1 of 10 from Beth Israel Hospital. A leading 0 is not used for interest or probability.

Numbers greater than 9999 are grouped by threes by commas, going left from the decimal point. The next groups from the decimal are the number of thousands, millions, billions and trillions. Decimals are grouped by threes by spaces going right.

Example 3 An astronomical unit is 149,597,870.691 kilometers. Write this in English.
Solution Working left from the decimal we have 870 units, 597 thousand, 149 million. Hence one hundred forty-nine million, five hundred ninety-seven thousand, eight hundred seventy and six hundred ninety-one thousandths. ∎

Add, Subtract To add more than two single-digit numbers:

First number is total.
Total plus next number is new total. $\qquad$ (∗)
If any number remains, repeat (∗).

To add $2 + 7 + 6 + 5$, the successive totals are 2, $2 + 7 = 9$, $9 + 6 = 15$, $15 + 5 = 20$.
To add multidigit numbers, we place them vertically so the units are in the same column and add from right to left. Figure 1.3.7 is an addition table. Because 17 units $= 1$ ten $+ 7$ units, etc., when the total for a column exceeds 9, we carry the tens digit to the column to the left, as indicated by the superscripts.

$$\begin{array}{r} {}^1 1 {}^1 5\ 8 \\ +2\ 4\ 9 \\ \underline{6\ 3\ 0} \\ 1\ 0\ 0\ 7 \end{array}$$

In subtraction, we may borrow from the column or columns to the left. The example below shows we borrowed 1 ten from 40 tens.

$$\begin{array}{r} {}^{39}\\ 4\!\!\!/\,0\,{}^1 7 \\ -2\ 4\ 9 \\ \underline{1\ 5\ 8} \end{array}$$

Practice 3 What is the fewest numbers we can add to generate a 2-digit carry?

Multiplication by Natural Number is equivalent to repeated addition:
$3 \times 17 = (1 + 1 + 1)17 = 17 + 17 + 17$ and $a + a = 2a$.

The integer n is **even** (French: pair) if it is twice an integer; otherwise n is **odd**.

Multiply by 10 If there is no decimal point, append a 0 at the right. If the decimal point is at the right, remove it and append a 0. Otherwise move the decimal point 1 place right. To multiply by 100, multiply by 10 twice; etc. $\qquad$ (12)

Divide by 10 If the decimal point is at the left, insert a 0 to its right. Otherwise move the decimal point (if there is none, insert one at the right) 1 place left. To divide by 100, divide by 10 twice.
Proof From the distributive law and $x = abcd.efg$,

$$10x = 10000a + 1000b + 100c + 10d + e + f/10 + g/100 = abcde.fg \text{ and}$$

$$x/10 = 100a + 10b + c + d/10 + e/100 + f/1000 + g/10000 = abc.defg. \qquad ∎$$

Practice 4 $\pi \approx 3.14$. Calculate (a) 1000π (b) $\pi/100$.

Multiplying $a \times b$. Ignoring any decimal points, place a above b so the units, tens, etc. are in the same column. Multiply a by the units digit of b and align right. (Figure 1.3.8 is a multiplication table.) Multiply a by the tens digit of b and shift left one column. Multiply a by the hundreds digit of b and shift left two columns, etc. Add these products. The number of decimal places in the product is the sum of the number of places in a and b.

Example 4 Multiply 4.07 by 7.3.

Solution

$$
\begin{array}{r}
407 \\
\underline{73} \\
1221 \\
\underline{2849} \\
29711
\end{array}
$$

407×3

407×7 tens. Shift left one.

The number of decimal places is $2 + 1 = 3$. Hence the product is 29.711. ■

Fractions In the fraction $\frac{a}{b}$ (built-up) or $\frac{a}{b}$ (case), a/b (shilling) or $\%$ (special), a is the **numerator** and b is the **denominator**. (a and b used to be called the terms of the fraction, hence *lowest terms* below.) a/b is **proper** if (ignoring sign) $a < b$, otherwise **improper**. Mixed numbers: an integer plus a proper fraction with the plus omitted, for example $\pi \approx 3\frac{14}{100}$; avoid, because $a\frac{b}{c} = \frac{ab}{c}$. Write fractions with a hyphen unless the numerator or denominator has one: $\frac{2}{3}$ is two-thirds.

Decimal to Fraction If there are n digits after the decimal point, delete any leading zeros; the remaining digits form the numerator. The denominator is 1 followed by n zeros. For example, $.002307 = \frac{2307}{1000000}$.

Equivalent The symbol $\Leftrightarrow$ between statements means they are equivalent: both are true or both are false. (13)

Comparing Fractions If a, b, c, d are positive,

then $\frac{a}{b} < \frac{c}{d} \Leftrightarrow ad < bc$, $\frac{a}{b} = \frac{c}{d} \Leftrightarrow ad = bc$, $\frac{a}{b} > \frac{c}{d} \Leftrightarrow ad > bc$

Practice 5 Compare $\frac{3}{7}$ to $\frac{4}{9}$.

Operations with Fractions
Example

(a) To reduce $\frac{a}{b}$ to **lowest terms**, cancel common factors of a and b: $\frac{6}{8} = \frac{3 \cdot \cancel{2}}{4 \cdot \cancel{2}} = \frac{3}{4}$

(b) Add or subtract with common (same) denominator: $\frac{3}{5} + \frac{4}{5} = \frac{3+4}{5} = \frac{7}{5}$

(c) To add or subtract otherwise, multiply each term by $\frac{a}{a} = 1$ to make a common denominator: $\frac{6}{5} - \frac{4}{3} = \frac{6}{5} \cdot \frac{3}{3} - \frac{4}{3} \cdot \frac{5}{5} = \frac{18-20}{15} = -\frac{2}{15}$

(d) Subtract mixed numbers: borrow 1 unit if necessary: $5\frac{1}{2} - 3\frac{2}{3} = 5\frac{3}{6} - 3\frac{4}{6} = 4\frac{9}{6} - 3\frac{4}{6} = 1\frac{5}{6}$

(e) Mixed number to fraction, make a common denominator: $2\frac{5}{8} = 2 \cdot \frac{8}{8} + \frac{5}{8} = \frac{16+5}{8} = \frac{21}{8}$

(f) Multiply by multiplying numerators and denominators: $\frac{3}{4} \cdot \frac{4}{5} = \frac{3 \cdot \cancel{4}}{\cancel{4} \cdot 5} = \frac{3}{5}$

(g) Multiply mixed numbers by converting to fractions: $1\frac{2}{3} \cdot 3\frac{1}{2} = \frac{5}{3} \cdot \frac{7}{2} = \frac{35}{6}$

(h) Divide by inverting the divisor and multiplying: $\frac{1}{2} \div \frac{2}{3} = \frac{1}{2} \cdot \frac{3}{2} = \frac{3}{4}$

Proof (a) $\frac{cf}{df} = \frac{c}{d}$ because $(cf)d = (df)c$ (b) $\frac{a+b}{c} = (a+b)c^{-1} = ac^{-1} + bc^{-1} = \frac{a}{c} + \frac{b}{c}$

(h) This is the definition of division. ■

English "Invert" means "turn upside-down". This is the root of "inverse".

Practice 6 Combine $\frac{3}{4} + \frac{1}{3} - 1$.

Remainder It follows from Archimedes' property (10) that for division n/d of positive integers there exist unique integers q (quotient) and r (remainder) such that $n = dq + r$, $0 \le r < d$

Practice 7 Find the quotient and remainder for the integer division $20/3$ and express $\frac{20}{3}$ as a mixed number.

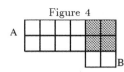
Figure 4

Visual A fraction represents a part of a whole. The area of rectangle A is $2 \times 6 = 12$ and the area of B is $2 \times 3 = 6$. The fraction of A in Figure 4 given by shaded area is $\frac{4}{12} = \frac{2}{6} = \frac{1}{3}$.

Practice 8 What part of rectangle B does the shaded area in Figure 2 represent? Give two equal fractions.

Money The U.S. uses dollars ($) and cents (¢), hundredths of a dollar. There are coins for 1¢ (penny), 5¢ (nickel), 10¢ (dime), 25¢ (quarter), 50¢ (half-dollar) and $1 (one dollar). Bills in use are $1, $5, $10, $20, $50 and $100. Coins and bills are called *cash*. If you pay more than is owed, the difference is returned as *change*.

You can deposit your money in a checking account and use checks for larger payments. A **check** is a document signed by the depositor ordering a bank to pay money to a payee. When writing a check amount in words, cents is expressed as a fraction of a dollar.   (16)

Practice 10 Write the amount $8734.28 in words for a check. ("DOLLARS" is printed on the check.)

Algorithm A prescription of a sequence of operations that leads to a goal in a finite number of steps.   (21)

Example 5 A $100 bill is tendered to pay for a $61 item. (a) How much change is due? (b) How do you give change using the smallest number of bills?
Solution (a) $100 - 61 = \$39$ change (b) Subtract the largest bill on the list not exceeding the amount due, and repeat. (Greedy algorithm) 7 bills:
$39 - 20 = 19 - 10 = 9 - 5 = 4 - 1 = 3 - 1 = 2 - 1 = 1$: $\$20 + \$10 + \$5 + \$1 + \$1 + \$1 + \$1$

2. REPEATING DECIMALS AND ROMAN NUMERALS

Pigeonhole Principle If there are d ways to be different, any set of more than d must have at least two the same.

Long Division Algorithm for n/d, $n > d > 0$. At first the quotient is empty and the remainder is as few of the left digits of n as are needed to reach or exceed d. (In Example 6 the digits 90.) (∗) Let q, $0 \le q \le 9$ be the largest digit such that $qd \le$ remainder. Append q to the quotient; subtract qd from the remainder. If n has another digit, append it to the remainder and repeat (∗); otherwise, stop.

Short Division If d is a single digit, subtract mentally and write the remainder as a superscript.
To divide by a decimal, convert to an equivalent fraction with integer denominator.

Fraction n/d to Decimal divide $n.000\ldots$ by d. Ignore the decimal point and take 0's until $\ge d$. At each step the possible remainders are $0, 1, 2, \ldots, d - 1$. If there is a remainder of 0, the decimal is **terminating**. If not, after $p \le d - 1$ steps, some remainder repeats and hence the digits of the quotient are **repeating** and p is the **period**. Indicate the **repetend** with a bar.

Example 6 Express $\frac{9}{74}$ as a decimal.
Solution

```
        .1216
74) 9.0000        90 > 74
    7 4           1 × 74
    1 60√
    1 48          2 × 74
      120
       74         1 × 74
      460
      444         6 × 74
       16√ 16 is a repeat.
```
$\frac{9}{74} = .1\ 216\ 216\ 216\ldots = .1\overline{216}$.   ■

Example 7 Express $\frac{2}{7}$ as a decimal.
Solution

```
      .2 8 5 7 1 4...
7) 2.0^6 0^4 0^5 0^1 0^3 0^2
```
Analysis $20 - 2 \times 7 = 6$, $60 - 8 \times 7 = 4$, $40 - 5 \times 7 = 5$, $50 - 7 \times 7 = 1$, $10 - 1 \times 7 = 3$, $30 - 4 \times 7 = 2$, and the cycle repeats.   ■

Terminating Decimal is rational: $2.713 = \frac{2713}{1000}$.

Repeating Decimal to Fraction Call the number x. If the repetend has 1 digit, multiply by 10; 2 digits, multiply by 100; etc. Subtract the original and the repetend is gone. Eliminate any decimal by multiplying by a power of 10. Divide by the multiplier of x to get a rational number. For a pure repeating decimal, put the repetend over p nines.

Example 8 Express as a rational number: (a) $2.7131313... = 2.7\overline{13}$, (b) $.147147...$
Solution (a) Let $x = 2.7131313...$. The repetend has 2 digits (13) so we multiply by 100.

$$
\begin{array}{rl}
100x = & 271.31313... \\
\underline{1x = } & \underline{2.71313...} \quad . \text{ Subtracting, we get} \\
99x = & 268.6. \text{ Then } 990x = 2686 \text{ so } x = \frac{2686}{990} = \frac{1343}{495}
\end{array}
$$

(b) $.147147... = \frac{147}{999} = \frac{49}{111}$ ∎

Practice 15 Find the reciprocal of $0.1454545...$ as a decimal by expressing as a fraction.

Ordering To compare decimals, compare the leftmost digits that are different. To compare fractions, convert to a common denominator or to decimals.

Practice 16 (a) Compare $1.\overline{3478}$ and $1.34\overline{7821}$
(b) Reorder from least to greatest: $\frac{1}{8}, \frac{7}{12}, \frac{4}{5}, \frac{2}{7}, \frac{5}{6}$

Roman Numerals An old system of notation still used for dates, outlines, page numbers in front matter, and drug orders in apothecary units where $\overline{ss} = \frac{1}{2}$. (22)
i = 1, v = 5, x = 10, l = 50, c = 100, d = 500, m = 1000, iv = 4, ix = 9, xl = 40, xc = 90, cd = 400, cm = 900
To read a Roman numeral: starting from the left, a group consists of a symbol or a symbol followed by one of larger value. Add the values of the groups. If a group is not on the list (e.g. ic) or is followed by a group of larger value (e.g. (ix)x), the numeral is invalid.

To convert to Roman, subtract the largest number possible on the list, use its symbol, and repeat. (This is another example of a greedy algorithm.)

Example 9 (a) Read mcdxcii (b) Write 1976 in Roman numerals.
Solution (a) m(cd)(xc)ii $= 100 + 400 + 90 + 1 + 1 = 1492$
(b) Start with 1976. Then

Subtract	1000	900	50	10	10	5	1
Remainder	976	76	26	16	6	1	0
Roman	m	mcm	mcml	mcmlx	mcmlxx	mcmlxxv	mcmlxxvi ∎

Practice Answers 1. The distributive law $2 \times 4 + 2 \times 2 = 2 \times (4+2) = 2 \times 6$
3. 11 nines give a carry of 9; a 2-digit carry needs at least 12
4. (a) $3.14 \times 1000 = 3.14 \times 10 \times 10 \times 10 = 31.4 \times 10 \times 10 = 314. \times 10 = 3140$
(b) $3.14 \div 100 = 3.14 \div 10 \div 10 = .314 \div 10 = .0314$
5. $\frac{3}{7} < \frac{4}{9}$ because $3 \cdot 9 = 27 < 7 \cdot 4 = 28$ **6.** $\frac{3}{4} + \frac{1}{3} - 1 = \frac{3}{4} \cdot \frac{3}{3} + \frac{1}{3} \cdot \frac{4}{4} - 1 \cdot \frac{12}{12} = \frac{9+4-12}{12} = \frac{1}{12}$
7. 20/3: $20 = 3q + r = 3(6) + 2$; $q = 6$, $r = 2$. Hence $\frac{20}{3} = 6\frac{2}{3}$. **8.** $\frac{4}{6} = \frac{2}{3}$
10. Eight thousand seven hundred thirty-four and $\frac{28}{100}$
15. $x = 0.145454...$, $100x = 14.545454...$, $99x = 14.4$, $x = \frac{144}{900} = \frac{8}{55}$, $1/x = \frac{55}{8} = 6.875$
16. (a) $1.34783478... > 1.34782178...$ (b) $\frac{1}{8} \approx .12, \frac{2}{7} \approx .29, \frac{7}{12} \approx .58, \frac{4}{5} = .80, \frac{5}{6} \approx .83$

Problems 1.1

OUR NATIONAL DEBT:
$6,995,659,154,368.
YOUR Family share $ 76,356.
THE NATIONAL DEBT CLOCK

1. NYTimes, Feb 8, 2004, p.BU1. See the figure. (a) Express the national debt in words. (b) How many families are there? Note: By Jun 2011 the debt was more than double.

2. Write in numerical form: nineteen billion, thirty-seven million, four hundred seven thousand, thirteen.

3. Subtract 1 from each number. Do not use a calculator. (a) $\frac{2}{3}$ (b) $-\frac{1}{4}$ (c) .763 (d) $-.451$

4. How do you give 47¢ change using the fewest coins?

5. Given $129 \times 437 = 56373$, what is $.0129 \times 4.37$?

6. Express $4.37 \div .0135$ as division by an integer.

7. Which fraction is larger: $\frac{5}{8}$ or $\frac{7}{11}$? Do not divide.

8. Write in words $\frac{17}{32}$.

In Problems 9-13, express as a fraction in lowest terms.

9. $\frac{2}{5} \times \frac{10}{3} \times \frac{6}{7}$ **10.** $\frac{3}{5} \div \frac{4}{7}$ **11.** $\frac{2}{3} + \frac{3}{4} + \frac{1}{5}$ **12.** $\dfrac{\frac{2}{3} - \frac{1}{2}}{\frac{2}{3} + \frac{1}{2}}$ **13.** $3\frac{2}{5} \times 1\frac{1}{4}$

14. Find the reciprocal of $1\frac{5}{8}$.

15. Convert each number to rational form or state that it is irrational.
(a) 5.02 (b) 5.020202... (c) 5.02002000200002... (d) 0.71621212121... (e) 0.125

16. Convert each fraction to a repeating decimal: (a) $\frac{5}{41}$ (b) $\frac{11}{74}$ (c) $\frac{3}{13}$

17. Express as repeating decimals by converting to rationals: (a) $0.\overline{2} \times 0.\overline{3}$ (b) $1 \div 0.\overline{2}$ (c) $0.\overline{1}^2$

18. (a) Which fractions can be expressed as terminating decimals? (b) Find a rule for the number of decimal places.

Problems 19 and 20 deal with Roman numerals.

19. Write CDLIX (a) as a decimal number (b) in English.

20. Write 1944 in (a) Roman numerals (b) English

21. NYTimes, Nov 7, 2010, Education Life, p.31: Under a particular set of rules, numbers were drawn in the boxes and circles. Work out the rules and find the missing number.

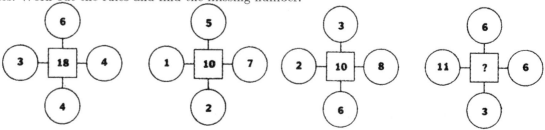

1.2 EQUATIONS AND SERIES

1. EQUATIONS

Terminology If two or more expressions are added or subtracted, each is called a **term** and the result is a **sum** or **difference**. If two or more expressions are multiplied, each is called a **factor** and the result is a **product**. As a verb, factor means to express as a product or power. If a dividend is divided by a divisor, the result is a **quotient**. The product of all the factors of a term *except* those specified, like factors being grouped by exponents, is the **coefficient**: in ax^2y^3, the coefficient of x^2 is ay^3; the coefficient of x^2y^3 is a; the coefficient of ax^2y^3 is 1.   (4)

A division bar is a fence: $(x+y)^3 + \dfrac{a+b}{c-d}$ has just two terms, $(x+y)^3$ and $\dfrac{a+b}{c-d}$.

Practice 1 Write $\dfrac{a+b}{c-d}$ on one line.

Example 1 Use the distributive law to factor $28xz + 60xy$.

Solution 4 and x are factors of each term. Then

$$28xz + 60xy = 4x\left(\frac{28xz}{4x} + \frac{60xy}{4x}\right) = 4x(7z + 15y)$$ ■

Practice 2 Use the distributive law to combine $x + 3x$.

Equation A *variable* is a symbol that may be replaced by a number. An equation is a statement of equality between two **members** which may have variables. An equation that is true whenever both sides are defined is an **identity**. One that is true for *all* real values of the variables is **unconditional**. One that is true for some values but not for others is **conditional; solve** means to find these **solutions**, which are said to *satisfy* the equation. One that is never true is **impossible**. Equations are **equivalent** if they have the same solutions. (5)

Practice 3 Classify each equation:

(a) $x + 1 = x$ (b) $x + 1 = 1$ (c) $x + 1 = 1 + x$ (d) $x/x = 1$

By the substitution property, the following give an equivalent equation:
Both sides of an equation may be increased or decreased by equal numbers. (6)
Both sides of an equation may be multiplied or divided by equal nonzero numbers. (7)
If we add the negative of a number in the equation, we have *transposed* the number.

Remark If we multiply $x = 2$ by itself we get $x^2 = 4$ which has -2 and 2 as solutions.

Solving Linear Equations
(a) Remove any fractions by multiplying each term by the same nonzero number (7).
(b) Remove any parentheses (distributive law).
(c) Move all terms in the required variable to the left and all other terms to the right (6). If the required variable appears without a power, the equation is linear; go to (d). If the equation becomes $0 = 0$, it is an identity. If the equation becomes 0 equals a nonzero number, there is no solution. Which of these cases applies may depend on other variables.
(d) Factor the required variable from its terms (distributive law).
(e) Divide by the coefficient of the required variable if the coefficient is not 0 (7).

Example 2 Solve for x: $5x - 3 = 2x + 9$
Solution
Subtract $2x$ from each side (a) $3x - 3 = 9$

Add 3 to each side (a) $3x = 12$

Divide each side by 3 (b) $x = 4$ ∎

Example 3 Solve for y: $\dfrac{7y}{5} - y = \dfrac{1}{2}$

Solution Multiply each term by $5 \cdot 2$ to eliminate both denominators.
$\dfrac{7y}{5} \cdot 5 \cdot 2 - y \cdot 5 \cdot 2 = \dfrac{1}{2} \cdot 5 \cdot 2$ so $14y - 10y = 5$ or $4y = 5$ and $y = \dfrac{5}{4}$ ∎

Example 4 Solve for t: $\dfrac{t - 2x}{a} = \dfrac{3(t - y)}{z}$
Solution
(1) Multiply by az (a and z are not 0) $z(t - 2x) = 3a(t - y)$

(2) Distribute $zt - 2zx = 3at - 3ay$

(3) Subtract $3at$, add $2zx$ $zt - 3at = 2zx - 3ay$

(4) Factor t $(z - 3a)t = 2zx - 3ay$

(5) Divide if $z - 3a \neq 0$ $t = \dfrac{2zx - 3ay}{z - 3a}$

If $z - 3a = 0$, we have an identity if $2zx - 3ay = 0$, and no solution otherwise.   ∎

Prime y' is a quantity related to, but different from y. Similar to subscripts.

Example 5 A calculus technique called implicit differentiation gives
$2x - y - xy' + 2yy' = 0$. Solve for y'.
Analysis This equation is linear in y'; transpose the non-y' terms to the right, then factor y' on the left.
Solution $2yy' - xy' = y - 2x$ so $y'(2y - x) = y - 2x$ and $y' = (y - 2x)/(2y - x)$ ∎

Proof A **postulate** is a statement assumed to be true. A **theorem** is a statement proved true by using definitions, postulates, previous theorems and rules of logic. A **corollary** is a by-product of another theorem. (17)

Verify means to show a result is true in a particular case. It is not a proof.

Zero, Negative Powers If $a \neq 0$ and n is a positive integer, $a^0 = 1$ and $a^{-n} = 1/a^n$.

Operations with Integer Powers (a) $a^m a^n = a^{m+n}$ (b) $a^m/a^n = a^{m-n} = 1/a^{n-m}$
(c) $(ab)^m = a^m b^m$ (d) $(a^m)^n = a^{mn}$, $ab \neq 0$ (8)

Proof Let m and n be positive.
(a) m factors of a followed by n factors of a gives $m+n$ factors of a.
(b) $a^n a^{m-n} = a^{n+(m-n)} = a^m$
(c) By the commutative law, we can rewrite $(ab)(ab)\cdots(ab)$ so the m factors of a appear first. For negative exponents, use reciprocals.
(d) n sets of m factors gives mn factors. ∎

Practice 4 Write without multiplication or division: (a) $2 \cdot 2 \cdot 2 \cdot 2 \cdot 2$ (b) $\dfrac{1}{x \cdot x \cdot x}$

Inequalities (a) If $a < b$ then $a+c < b+c$. (b) If $a < b$ and $c > 0$, then $ac < bc$. If $a < b$ and $c < 0$, then $ac > bc$. Multiplication by a negative reverses an inequality.
(c) If $0 < a < b$ then $a^n < b^n$ for any positive integer n. (d) If $0 < r < 1$, then $1/r > 1$.
Proof (a) $(b+c)-(a+c) = b-a > 0$ (b) $bc - ac = (b-a)c$. If c is positive this is a product of positive numbers and is positive; if c is negative, the product is negative.
(c) $a^2 = aa < ab < bb = b^2$, etc. (d) $\dfrac{1}{r} - 1 = \dfrac{1}{r} - \dfrac{r}{r} = \dfrac{1-r}{r}$ is a quotient of positives. ∎

Example 2 (continued) Solve for x: $5x - 3 > 2x + 9$
Solution $3x - 3 > 9$, $3x > 12$. Because 3 is positive, $x > 4$. ∎

Double Inequality $a < x < b$ means $a < x$ and $x < b$, i.e. x is between a and b.

Function When a dependent variable is expressed explicitly in terms of one or more independent variables, which may be listed in parentheses, such as $y = y(x) = x^2 + 1$ or $c = c(a,b) = a^2 + b^2$.

Absolute Value The absolute value of a number is just the unsigned number: $|-9| = 9$. The rule for a variable x is:
If $x \geq 0$ then $|x| = x$ and if $x < 0$ then $|x| = -x$. (9)
If $x \geq y$ then $|x-y| = x-y$ and if $x < y$ then $|x-y| = y-x$.
If $k > 0$, then (i) $|x| \leq k \Leftrightarrow -k \leq x \leq k$ and (ii) $|x| \geq k \Leftrightarrow x \leq -k$ or $x \geq k$.

Practice 5 Calculate $|3 - \pi| + |4 - \pi|$.

Example 6 Prove that (a) $|x|^2 = x^2$, (b) $|xy| = |x||y|$ (c) $\left|x/y\right| = |x|/|y|$ (d) $|-x| = |x|$
Solution Both members have the same magnitude, and both are positive. ∎

Set A well-defined collection of **elements**. Two sets are **equal** if they consist of the same elements. A set may be defined by a property or an unordered list in braces with no repetitions: $\{1,3,5\} = \{5,1,3\}$; $\{\ \}$ is the **empty set**. $x \in A$ means that x is an element of set A or x has the property. The **complement** of A consists of all elements not in A. (10)

Ellipsis (...) means that a pattern is followed. $Z^+ = \{1,2,3,...\}$ indicates the set of positive integers, $\{...,-3,-2,-1\}$ the negative integers, and $\{1,2,3,...,9\} = \{1,2,3,4,5,6,7,8,9\}$. The dots are raised for sums: $1 + 2 + 3 + \cdots + 9$.
An equation like $\frac{1}{3} = .333...$ means that we can make the difference between the two sides as small (close to 0) as we want by going sufficiently far and stopping.
$\frac{1}{3} - .3 = \frac{1}{3} - \frac{3}{10} = \frac{10}{30} - \frac{9}{30} = \frac{1}{30}$, $\frac{1}{3} - .33 = \frac{1}{3} - \frac{33}{100} = \frac{100}{300} - \frac{99}{300} = \frac{1}{300}$, etc.
If 999... is not allowed, different decimals are unequal.

Practice 6 We say $\frac{5}{6} = .833...$. Evaluate $\frac{5}{6} - .83$.

2. SERIES

Counting A set A is **finite** if it is empty or for some positive integer m its elements can be labeled with 1, 2, 3, ..., m. The **cardinality** of A is the number of elements in A. $C = \{a, b, c\}$ is finite because we can label its elements a_1, b_2, c_3. (Read a-sub-1, b-sub-2. The subscripts are ranks here, but have other uses, as in Property 15.) C has cardinality 3.

A set is **infinite** if it is not finite. B is a **subset** of A if every element of B is an element of A, and is a **proper subset** if $B \neq A$. A subset of a finite set is finite. Any infinite set can be matched with a proper subset.　　　　(13)

Practice 7 Show that the set $\{-2, -1, 0, 1, 2, 3\}$ is finite.

Bounded A set A of numbers is **bounded** if there are numbers c (lower bound) and d (upper bound) such that $c \leq x \leq d$ for each x in A. A finite set $A = \{a_1, ..., a_m\}$ is bounded and has a smallest element (minimum) $a_j = \mathbf{min}(a_1, ..., a_m) = \min(A)$ and a largest element (maximum) $a_i = \mathbf{max}(a_1, ..., a_m) = \max(A)$; that is, there are members of the set that are lower and upper bounds.　　　　(14)

An infinite set may be unbounded, and even a bounded set may not have a maximum or a minimum. c is the **greatest lower bound** (glb) if c is greater than any other lower bound; d is a **least upper bound** (lub) if d is less than any other upper bound.

To find the maximum of a finite set:

> First number is max.
> Larger of max and next number is new max.　　　　(∗)
> If any number remains, repeat (∗).

To find $\max(2, 7, 6, 5)$, the successive maxima are 2, $\max(2, 7) = 7$, $\max(7, 6) = 7$, $\max(7, 5) = 7$.

Practice 8 Give an example of a bounded set that does not have a maximum. Find its least upper bound.

Sum, Product of Real Numbers Let x_n and y_n denote the truncation of x and y to n decimal places. If x and y are positive then $x + y$ is the lub of $x_1 + y_1$, $x_2 + y_2$, ..., xy is the lub of $x_1 y_1$, $x_2 y_2$, ..., $1/y$ is the glb of $1/y_1$, $1/y_2$, ... and $x/y = x \cdot 1/y$.　　　　(15)

Example 7 Illustrate the product $.333... \times .666...$.
Solution $.33 \times .66 = .2178$, $.333 \times .666 = .221778$, $.3333 \times .6666 = .22217778$. Evidently, if there are n threes and sixes, the product consists of $n - 1$ twos, a 1, $n - 1$ sevens and an 8. An upper bound is clearly $.222...$ and any smaller number will eventually be exceeded.∎

Series Let a_1, a_2, ... be numbers. $s = a_1 + a_2 + a_3 + a_4 + \cdots$, means we can make the difference between s and the partial sums $s_1 = a_1$, $s_2 = a_1 + a_2$, $s_3 = a_1 + a_2 + a_3$, ... as small as we like by taking sufficiently many terms. A **sequence** is a list labeled with the integers. We say the series and the sequence $(s_1, s_2, s_3, ...)$ **converges** to s. If the terms are not approaching 0 or the partial sums are unbounded, the series **diverges** (does not exist).

The sequence is **increasing** if $a_{n+1} \geq a_n$ for all n, and is **decreasing** if $a_{n+1} \leq a_n$ for all n.

Mathematical Induction If a_1 has a certain property, and whenever *some* a_n has the property then following member a_{n+1} has the property, then a_n has the property for *all n*.

Completeness A bounded set of real numbers has a greatest lower bound and a least upper bound. An increasing or decreasing sequence that is bounded converges.　　　　(16)

Ordinal number refers to a sequence: a_1 is first, a_2 is second, a_3 is third, a_4 is fourth, ..., a_{21} is twenty-first, ..., a_n is nth, ... Ordinals are also used to write fractions, except for one-half ($\frac{1}{2}$) and one-quarter ($\frac{1}{4}$): $3\frac{9}{74}$ is three and nine seventy-fourths. Sequences of 2, 3, 4, or n elements (a_1, a_2), (a_1, a_2, a_3), (a_1, a_2, a_3, a_4), $(a_1, ..., a_n)$ are called ordered **pairs, triples, quadruples**, or n-tuples

Arithmetic Sequence (arithmetic progression) $a = (a_1, a_2, a_3, \ldots)$: the difference of any two consecutive terms is a constant d. Thus

$$a_2 = a_1 + d, \; a_3 = a_1 + 2d, \; \ldots, \; a_n = a_1 + (n-1)d = \ell$$

Geometric Sequence a: the ratio of any two consecutive terms is a constant r. Thus

$$a_2 = a_1 r, \; a_3 = a_1 r^2, \; \ldots, \; a_n = a_1 r^{n-1}.$$

Example 8 Classify the sequences as (i) arithmetic, geometric or neither; find a_n; (ii) increasing or decreasing (iii) bounded or unbounded;
(a) 3, 6, 12, 24, ... (b) 12, 10, 8, 6, ... (c) $\frac{1}{2}, \frac{1}{3}, \frac{1}{4}, \frac{1}{5}, \ldots$
Solution (a) $6/3 = 2$, $12/6 = 2$, $24/12 = 2$ constant ratio so geometric sequence, $a_n = 3 \cdot 2^{n-1}$; increasing; unbounded
(b) $10 - 12 = -2$, $8 - 10 = -2$, $6 - 8 = -2$ constant difference so arithmetic sequence, $a_n = 12 - 2(n-1) = 14 - 2n$; decreasing; unbounded
(c) $\frac{1}{3} - \frac{1}{2} = -\frac{1}{6}$ but $\frac{1}{4} - \frac{1}{3} = \frac{1}{12}$, $\frac{1}{3}/\frac{1}{2} = \frac{2}{3}$ but $\frac{1}{4}/\frac{1}{3} = \frac{3}{4}$, neither, $a_n = \frac{1}{n+1}$; decreasing; bounded.

Practice 9 Which sequence (a) 3, 6, 12, 24, ... (b) 12, 10, 8, 6, ... (c) $\frac{1}{2}, \frac{1}{3}, \frac{1}{4}, \frac{1}{5}, \ldots$ of Example 8 has a limit? What is the limit?

Example 9 Find the sum of an arithmetic sequence
$$s_n = a + (a + d) + \cdots + [a + (n-1)d]$$
Solution Also, $s_n = [a + (n-1)d] + \cdots + (a + d) + a.$ \hfill Adding the two forms,
$$2s_n = [2a + (n-1)d] + \cdots + [2a + (n-1)d] = n[2a + (n-1)d],$$
$$\boxed{s_n = \tfrac{1}{2}n[2a + (n-1)d] = \tfrac{1}{2}n(a + \ell)}$$
∎

Practice 10 Find the sum of the first n integers $1 + 2 + 3 + \cdots + n$.

Example 10 For the geometric sequence $a = (1, -1, 1, -1, \ldots)$, find a formula for a_n and $s_n = a_1 + a_2 + \cdots + a_n$.
Solution $a_1 = 1 = (-1)(-1) = (-1)^2$, $a_2 = -1 = (-1)(-1)(-1) = (-1)^3$, $a_3 = 1 = (-1)^4$.
$a_n = (-1)^{n+1}$. $s_1 = 1 = \tfrac{1}{2}(1+1)$, $s_2 = 1 + (-1) = 0 = \tfrac{1}{2}(1-1)$,
$s_3 = 1 + (-1) + 1 = 1 = \tfrac{1}{2}(1+1)$. $s_n = \tfrac{1}{2}(1 + (-1)^{n+1})$
∎

Bad Math Let $s = 1 + 2 + 4 + 8 + \cdots$. Then $2s = 2 + 4 + 8 + \cdots$ and $2s - s = s = -1$. What is wrong is that s does not have any meaning; the partial sums 1, $1 + 2 = 3$, $1 + 2 + 4 = 7$, $1 + 2 + 4 + 8 = 15$, ... are not getting closer to any number. Good math takes more work.

Practice 11 Use the distributive law to explain how to multiply by .99 by doing an easy subtraction.

Graph shows the relation between two quantities using horizontal and vertical distances.

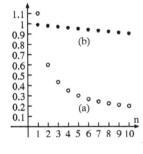

Example 11 Calculate the first four terms of (a) $a_n = \dfrac{10 + n}{10n}$ and (b) $b_n = .99^n$. Both sequences are positive and decreasing, so they converge; does either converge to 0? The figure shows ten terms of a_n open and b_n solid.

Solution (a) $a_1 = \dfrac{10+1}{10 \cdot 1} = \dfrac{11}{10} = 1.10$, $a_2 = \dfrac{10+2}{10 \cdot 2} = \dfrac{12}{20} = 0.60$, $a_3 = \dfrac{13}{30} = 0.43$,
$a_4 = \dfrac{14}{40} = 0.35$. $a_n = \dfrac{1}{n} + \dfrac{1}{10} > \dfrac{1}{10}$ is not approaching 0.

(b) To multiply by .99, we subtract one-hundredth of what we have.

$$.9900$$
$$\underline{-.0099}$$
$$.99^2 = .9801$$
$$\underline{-.0098}$$
$$.99^3 = .9703$$
$$\underline{-.0097}$$
$$.99^4 = .9606$$

Because we subtract less each time, it's hard to be sure we get close to 0. We look at powers of the reciprocal 1.01.

To multiply by 1.01, we add one-hundredth of what we have (Property 12).

$$1.0100$$
$$\underline{+.0101}$$
$$1.01^2 = 1.0201$$
$$\underline{+.0102}$$
$$1.01^3 = 1.0303$$
$$\underline{+.0103}$$
$$1.01^4 = 1.0406$$

Because we add more than .01 each time, in n steps we will add at least $.01n$ so $1.01^n > 1 + .01n$.

Hence $.99^n < \dfrac{1}{1 + .01n}$ can be made as close to 0 as we like. ∎

Remark The next example shows that powers of any proper fraction approach 0.

Example 12 Bernoulli's inequality: If $1 + a > 1$ and n is an integer > 1 then $(1+a)^n > 1 + na$. It follows that if $|r| = 1/(1+a) < 1$, then $|r|^n < 1/(1+na)$ is arbitrarily small for n sufficiently large.

Solution Using the distributive law twice, and $a^2 > 0$,
$(1+a)^2 = (1+a)(1+a) = 1 + 2a + a^2 > 1 + 2a$. Suppose $(1+a)^n > 1 + na$ for some n. Then $(1+a)^{n+1} = (1+a)^n(1+a) > (1+na)(1+a) = 1 + na + a + a^2 > 1 + (n+1)a$. By mathematical induction, $(1+a)^n > 1 + na$ for all n. ∎

Practice 12 What values of n guarantee $.8^n < .01$?

Geometric Series If $r \neq 1$, $a + ar + ar^2 + \cdots + ar^{n-1} = \dfrac{a - ar^n}{1 - r}$ (First term minus term after last over 1 minus ratio.)
If $|r| < 1$, then r^n approaches 0 as the integer n increases, and $a + ar + ar^2 + \cdots = \dfrac{a}{1 - r}$.
(First term over 1 minus the ratio.) If $|r| \geq 1$, the series diverges.   (18)

Proof   Let $S_n = a + ar + ar^2 + \cdots + ar^{n-1}$ By the distributive law

$$rS_n = ar + ar^2 + \cdots + ar^{n-1} + ar^n$$ Subtracting, we get

$$S_n - rS_n = a - ar^n \text{ so } S_n(1-r) = a - ar^n \text{ and } S_n = \frac{a}{1-r} - \frac{ar^n}{1-r}. \text{ If } |r| < 1, \text{ we can}$$

make r^n and $\dfrac{ar^n}{1-r}$ as small as we want. Hence S_n is arbitrarily close to $\dfrac{a}{1-r}$. ∎

Example 13 (Life Science) A patient takes 60 mg of a drug every 4 hours, at which time $\frac{2}{3}$ of the previous dose has been eliminated. What will the eventual accumulation of the drug be?

Solution The body retains $\frac{1}{3}$ of the previous dose, $\frac{1}{3}$ of $\frac{1}{3} = \left(\frac{1}{3}\right)^2$ of the dose before that, $\left(\frac{1}{3}\right)^3$ of the one before that, etc. Including the current dose, the accumulation factor is the

geometric series $1 + \frac{1}{3} + \left(\frac{1}{3}\right)^2 + \left(\frac{1}{3}\right)^3 + \cdots = \dfrac{1}{1 - \frac{1}{3}} = \dfrac{1}{\frac{2}{3}} = \frac{3}{2}$. The eventual accumulation is

$\frac{3}{2} \cdot 60 = 90$ mg. If an initial (loading) dose of 90 mg is given, after the first 60 mg (maintenance) dose, the amount in the body is $\frac{1}{3} \cdot 90 + 60 = 90$ mg again. ∎

Example 13 (Business) Suppose the people of a town spend 80% of their income in town; the rest is spent out of town or saved. What is the total effect of a resident receiving a $1000 tax refund?

Solution   Let $y_0 = 1000$. The resident spends $y_1 = .8y_0$. The recipients spend $y_2 = .8y_1 = .8^2 y_0$. Those in turn spend $y_3 = .8y_2 = .8^3 y_0$, etc. The total receipts is the geometric series

$$y_0 + .8y_0 + .8^2 y_0 + .8^3 y_0 + \cdots = y_0/(1 - .8) = y_0/.2 = 5y_0 = 5000$$

The income multiplier is 5 times the refund. ∎

Multinomial is a sum of terms. A multinomial with 1, 2, or 3 terms is called a **monomial**, **binomial**, or **trinomial**.

Polynomial P is comprised of terms a, ax^n or $ax^n y^m$ where $a \neq 0$ and m and n are positive integers; the **degrees** of these terms are 0, n and $n+m$. Here a, m, n each represent a single number (**constants**) while x and y represent arbitrary numbers (**variables**). The degree of P is that of the term of greatest degree. If P has degree 1, 2, or 3 it is **linear**, **quadratic**, or **cubic**. P is **homogeneous** if all terms have the same degree. (19)

Example 14 Describe: (a) $5x^3 - 7$ (b) $2x^2 - xy/2 - 8y^2$ (c) $2x - 3y + \pi$ (d) $4x^2/y$
Solution (a) cubic binomial (b) homogeneous quadratic trinomial ($xy/2 = \frac{1}{2}xy$)
(c) linear trinomial (d) not a polynomial ∎

Practice 13 Write the most general homogeneous polynomial of degree 2 in x and y. Use a, b, ... as coefficients.

Example 15 (a) Let A denote $x = 2$ and $y = 3$. A implies B: $xy = 6$, but B is not equivalent to A since B is also true when $x = 1$ and $y = 6$. Use the zero sum Property (8) to write a single equation that is equivalent to A.
(b) Let C denote $x = 2$ or $y = 3$. C does not imply $xy = 6$. Use the zero product Property (7) to write a single equation equivalent to C.
Solution (a) $x - 2 = 0$ and $y - 3 = 0$ is equivalent to $(x-2)^2 + (y-3)^2 = 0$
(b) $x - 2 = 0$ or $y - 3 = 0$ is equivalent to $(x-2)(y-3) = 0$ ∎

Irrational Number is a real number that is not rational. Its digits neither terminate nor repeat, but may have a pattern, such as .123456789101112..... An **algebraic number** of degree d is the root of a polynomial equation of degree d (and no lower) with integer coefficients. **Surds**, numbers that can be constructed from the integers in a finite number of arithmetic operations including root taking, such as the rational numbers and roots of quadratic equations, are algebraic. However, the roots of $x^5 - x - 1 = 0$ are algebraic though they are not surds. $\approx$ means "approximately equal". (20)

History Euclid IX.35 is the sum of a finite geometric series. The Pythagoreans discovered the irrationality of $\sqrt{2}$. Euclid's Definition V.5: $a = b$ if whenever $\frac{n}{m} < a < \frac{n+1}{m}$ for integers m and n, then $\frac{n}{m} < b < \frac{n+1}{m}$. If m is a power of 10, this is equivalent to saying they are the same decimal. π is the ratio of the circumference of a circle to its diameter. A Chinese author c.500 gave π as 3 chang, 1 chin 4 tsun 1 fen 5 li 9 hao 2 miao 7 hu, using decimal lengths. An inscription in India from 876 uses decimal numbers with 0 as placeholder. The earliest use of actual decimal fractions was by al-Kashi c.1430 who gave $\pi \approx 3.1415926535898732$. He used a space instead of a dot, which wasn't used consistently until c.1600. At that time the negative of 5 began to be written -5; 1600 years earlier, the Chinese used red ink for positive numbers, black for negative. The rules for working with decimal numbers were first published by Stevin in 1585. (21)

Practice 14 (a) Which group properties: closure, identity, inverse, do the irrationals under addition have? (b) Are the roots of $\frac{1}{3}x^2 + \frac{2}{5}x - \frac{1}{4} = 0$ algebraic numbers?

Why do we need real numbers? 2000 years ago, Euclid found the following related reasons: 1. To solve equations. If a polynomial P(x) has negative and positive values, then some value of x (a root) makes P(x) $= 0$. 2. Completeness (Property 16).

Roots If $a > 0$ then $x^2 = a$ has two solutions called the **square roots** of a. The positive solution is designated $\sqrt{a}$; the other solution is $-\sqrt{a}$. We may say $x = \pm\sqrt{a}$. Also, $\sqrt{0} = 0$. If $a < 0$, then $\sqrt{a^2} = -a$. For all a, we have $\sqrt{a^2} = |a|$.

In general, the nth root of a, $\sqrt[n]{a} = a^{1/n}$, is the unique solution of $x^n = a$ if n is odd, and the nonnegative solution of $x^n = a$ if $a \geq 0$. $a^{m/n} = (a^{1/n})^m = (a^m)^{1/n}$ when m/n is in lowest terms, where $a \geq 0$ if n is even.
It follows that if $0 < a < b$ then $a^{1/n} < b^{1/n}$ for any positive integer n. (22)

Example 16 Compare $\sqrt{5}$ and $\frac{7}{3}$.

Solution $\frac{7}{3} = \sqrt{\frac{49}{9}} > \sqrt{\frac{45}{9}} = \sqrt{5}$ ∎

Negation of a statement has the opposite truth value and is usually formed by adding *not*: Four is a perfect square (true); four is not a perfect square (false). (23)

Proof by Contradiction A statement is true if its negation leads to a contradiction.

Example 17 If $k^2 < n < (k+1)^2$ for integers n and k, prove that $\sqrt{n}$ is irrational.

Solution Suppose $\sqrt{n} = a/b$ for the smallest possible denominator, so $a^2 = nb^2$. Then

$k < \sqrt{n} = a/b < k+1$, so $bk < a < b(k+1)$, and $0 < a - bk < b$. Then we can get a smaller denominator:

$$\frac{a}{b} = \frac{a(a-bk)}{b(a-bk)} = \frac{a^2 - abk}{b(a-bk)} = \frac{nb^2 - abk}{b(a-bk)} = \frac{b(nb-ak)}{b(a-bk)} = \frac{nb-ak}{a-bk}$$

This contradiction shows that $\sqrt{n}$ cannot be rational. ∎

Practice Answers 1. $(a+b)/(c-d)$ **2.** $x + 3x = x(1+3) = 4x$ **3.** (a) $x+1 = x \Leftrightarrow 1 = 0$, impossible (b) $x+1 = 1$ $\Leftrightarrow x = 0$ conditional (c) $x+1 = 1+x \Leftrightarrow 0 = 0$ unconditional (d) $z/x = 1$ identity; true if $x \neq 0$
4. (a) $2 \cdot 2 \cdot 2 \cdot 2 \cdot 2 = 2^5$ (b) $1/(x \cdot x \cdot x) = x^{-3}$
5. Because $3 < \pi < 4$, $|3 - \pi| + |4 - \pi| = (\pi - 3) + (4 - \pi) = 1$
6. $\frac{5}{6} - .83 = \frac{5}{6} - \frac{83}{100} = \frac{5}{6} \cdot \frac{50}{50} - \frac{83}{100} \cdot \frac{3}{3} = \frac{250}{300} - \frac{249}{300} = \frac{1}{300}$

7. We label the elements: -2_1, -1_2, 0_3, 1_4, 2_5, 3_6 **8.** $\{\frac{1}{2}, \frac{2}{3}, \frac{3}{4}, ...\}$ The least upper bound is 1.
9. (a) and (b) are unbounded (c) has limit 0 **10.** $\frac{1}{2}n(a + \ell) = \frac{1}{2}n(n+1)$
11. $.99x = (1 - .01)x = x - .01x$ **12.** $1/.8^n = (1 + .25)^n > 1 + .25n \geq 100$ if $.25n \geq 99$ so $n \geq 396$. This is not the smallest n. In fact, $.8^{21} = .0092$. **13.** $ax^2 + bxy + cy^2$
14. (a) not closure: $\sqrt{2}$ and $2 - \sqrt{2}$ are irrational but their sum is not; the identity 0 is not irrational; inverse: the negative of an irrational is irrational. (b) Yes: multiply by 60 to get a polynomial with integer coefficients having the same roots. **15.** (c); 0

Problems 1.2 Problems with ^{h} have hints below.

1. Factor $2a + 4abc - 2ac$

2. Factor $3abc - 3ac + 6acd$

3. Which are correct?
   (a) $x(a+b) = xa + xb$ (b) $(a+b)x = ax + bx$ (c) $\frac{x}{a+b} = \frac{x}{a} + \frac{x}{b}$ (d) $\frac{a+b}{x} = \frac{a}{x} + \frac{b}{x}$ (e) $\frac{x}{x+y} = \frac{1}{1+y}$

4. If $-5x - y - 5z = 1$ then what is $-5y - 25x - 25z$? (WSJ, Apr 9, 2011, p.C2)

Problems 5-15 deal with linear equations.
5. Solve the equation or say it is an identity: (a) $y + 3(y-4) = 4$ (b) $3x - (x+4) = 2(x-2)$ (c) $4x - 3 = 5 - 2x$

In Problems 6-11, solve the equation.
6. $3x - 5 = 0$

7. $4x + 9 = 2$

8. $\frac{2x-7}{3} = 5 - \frac{3x-2}{4}$

9. $\frac{1}{3}(2y+1) + \frac{1}{2}y = \frac{2}{5}(1 - 2y) - 4$

10. $\frac{3x+7}{2} = \frac{1+x}{3}$

11. $\frac{5y-6}{2} = y - \frac{2-y}{3}$

12. Solve $s = \frac{a - r\ell}{1 - r}$ (a) for r (b) for ℓ

13. Solve for i: $A = (p-r)/n + (p+r)i/24$

In Problems 14 and 15, solve for the primed variable.
14. $xy^2 + x^2yy' + x + yy' = 0$

15. $2xt + x^2t' + t^2 + 2xtt' + \frac{1+t'}{x+t} = 0$

16. Solve the inequality for u: $2u - 11 \leq 5u + 6$.

17. Solve the inequality for x: $5x + 7 > 31 - 3x$.

Problems 18-21 deal with max, min and absolute value.
18. (a) Find $\max(-2, (-2)^2, (-2)^3)$

(b) Find $\min(1, \frac{1}{4}x)$ if $x = 3$.

19. Express without absolute value: (a) $\left|\pi - \frac{22}{7}\right|$ (b) $\left|4 - 3\sqrt{2}\right|$

20. Midpoint. If $m = \frac{1}{2}(a+b)$ calculate $a - m$ and $m - b$.

21. (a) If 2, 3, 5, 7 are put around a circle, the sum of products of adjacent numbers is $2 \cdot 3 + 3 \cdot 5 + 5 \cdot 7 + 7 \cdot 2 = 70$. Reorder the numbers to get the maximum sum. (b) If $a \leq b \leq c \leq d$, what order maximizes the sum?

22. State whether the sequence is arithmetic (give d), geometric (give r), or neither:
(a) $.1, .02, .004, .008$ (b) $3, 7, 15, 31$ (c) $7, 11, 15, 19$

Problems 23-25 deal with arithmetic sequences and series.

23. A man swims 3 laps on day 1, and 2 additional laps on each succeeding day, until the day he swims 23 laps. (a) Which day is this? (b) Find the total number of laps swum.

24. The first three alkanes are: methane $H\overset{H}{\underset{H}{C}}H$ or CH_4, ethane $H\overset{HH}{\underset{HH}{CC}}H$ or C_2H_6 and propane $H\overset{HHH}{\underset{HHH}{CCC}}H$ or C_3H_8. Find the formula for the nth member. The next names are butane, pentane, etc.

25. A straight slide is to have 10 equidistant supports. If the shortest is 2ft and the longest is 42ft, find the total length of the supports.

26. Evaluate (a) $\dfrac{1+3+5}{7+9+11}$ (b) $\dfrac{1+3+\cdots+(2k-1)}{(2k+1)+(2k+3)+\cdots+(4k-1)}$ (Galileo, 1615, in work on falling bodies.)

Problems 27 and 28 deal with exponents.

27. NYTimes, Apr 18, 2010, Education Life, p.30 "Any number raised to the power of zero is equal to what value?" (a) What answer were they expecting? (b) Give the correct question.

28. If P dollars is deposited and interest i is earned each period, after one period the amount is $P(1+i)$, after two periods it is $P(1+i)(1+i)$, etc. Express the amount after seventeen periods compactly.

Problems 29-41 deal with geometric series.

29. Does the geometric series have a sum? Give a reason. (a) $(\pi-2)+(\pi-2)^2+(\pi-2)^3+\cdots$
(b) $(\pi-3)+(\pi-3)^2+(\pi-3)^3+\cdots$ (c) $(\pi-4)+(\pi-4)^2+(\pi-4)^3+\cdots$ (d) $(\pi-5)+(\pi-5)^2+(\pi-5)^3+\cdots$

In Problems 30-32, sum the geometric series.

30. $1-6+6^2-\cdots-6^{149}$

31. $1-\frac{1}{3}+\frac{1}{9}-\frac{1}{27}\cdots$

32. $3+\frac{3}{2}+\frac{3}{4}+\frac{3}{8}+\cdots$

33. If $1+(4/k)+(4/k)^2+(4/k)^3+\cdots = k$, find k.

34. If the sum of a geometric series is 5 and the ratio is $\frac{1}{3}$, find the first term.

35. If R dollars is received at the end of each month for n months, and interest i could be earned elsewhere, the present value is $P = R[1/(1+i)+1/(1+i)^2+\cdots+1/(1+i)^n]$. Simplify P.

36. If R dollars is deposited at the end of each month earning interest i, the amount at the end of n months is $F = R[1+(1+i)+(1+i)^2+\cdots+(1+i)^{n-1}]$. Simplify F.

37. Zeno's paradox. Achilles is 100 yards behind a tortoise but runs 10 times as fast. When Achilles has covered the 100 yards, the tortoise has gone 10 yards; when Achilles has covered the 10 yards, the tortoise has gone 1 yard, etc. Zeno was troubled because the total distance to overtake can be expressed as an infinite series. How far does Achilles go?

38. (a) Find the accumulation factor if $\frac{7}{10}$ of a drug dose is eliminated before the next dose is taken. Find the accumulation if the dose is 200 mg. (b) As of Jun 2004, the Federal Reserve required banks to keep a 10% reserve on transaction deposits (but zero on time deposits). 90% of a $100 deposit may be lent. The bank receiving that loan can lend 90% of that, etc. Find multiplier and the total effect of a $100 loan. What is the effect if the reserve requirement is raised to 20%?

39. The Talmud, Kesuboth (marriage contracts) p.68a, states that after a father's death a pool is formed with 10% of the estate for the first daughter, 10% of the remainder for the second, etc., the total to be shared equally. If there are 10 daughters, find the share of each.

Problems 40 and 41 deal with **fractals:** a small part of a figure resembles the entire figure.

40. The Sierpinski gasket. S_0 is a black triangle of area A. To get S_1, color the medial triangle (the triangle joining the midpoints of the sides) of S_0 white. To get S_2, color the medial triangle of each black triangle of S_1 white, etc. The figures show S_1, S_2, S_3 and S_4. (a) In S_4, how many white triangles are there and what is their total area? (b) Find the total area of the white triangles if the process is continued indefinitely.

Problem 40   Problem 41

41[h] A snowflake curve is formed from an equilateral triangle of area A. An equilateral triangle pointing outward is built on the middle third of each side, and the original middle third is erased. Each segment ——— is replaced with four: _Λ_. Repeat with each of the $3 \cdot 4$ segments. Repeat with each of the $3 \cdot 4^2$ segments, etc. See the figure above. At each step, there are 4 times as many segments generating triangles of $\frac{1}{9}$ the area, so the total area is $A + \frac{1}{3}A + \frac{1}{3}(\frac{4}{9})A + \frac{1}{3}(\frac{4}{9})^2 A + \cdots$. Calculate.

43. Write a simple relation if a, b, c are consecutive terms of a (a) arithmetic series (b) geometric series.

Hint 41. The geometric series starts with $\frac{1}{3}A$.

1.3 INTRODUCTION TO TECHNOLOGY

1. SUMMATION

Sums, Products Let m and n be integers, $m \le n$.
$$\sum_{i=m}^{n} x_i = \sum_{i=m}^{n} x_i = x_m + x_{m+1} + \cdots + x_n, \quad \prod_{i=m}^{n} x_i = \prod_{i=m}^{n} x_i = x_m x_{m+1} \cdots x_n$$
In words: replace i by the integers from m to n and add or multiply the results. A sum with no terms is defined to be the additive identity 0; a product with no factors is defined to be the multiplicative identity 1. The **index** i is a dummy; it can be replaced by any unused symbol without changing the meaning. If m and n are omitted, use all x_i. The index need not be a subscript, as in the geometric series $S_n = \sum_{i=0}^{n-1} ar^i$. The index need not even appear; the operation applies only to the immediately following term (Example 2). The start value is arbitrary (Example 3). $\sum$ and $\prod$ are Greek capital sigma and pi(1)

Practice 1 (a) Combine $\sum_{k=1}^{46} x_k + \sum_{j=47}^{99} x_j$ (b) How many terms are there in $\sum_{k=47}^{99} x_k$?

Example 1 Let $x_1 = 2$, $x_2 = 5$, $x_3 = -1$; $y_1 = 4$, $y_2 = 1$, $y_3 = 2$. Find (a) $\max\{x_i\}$

(b) $\min\{iy_i\}$ (c) $\sum x_i$ (d) $\sum x_i^2$ (e) $\sum x_i y_i$ (f) $\prod x_i^{y_i}$

Solution (a) $\max\{x_i\} = \max\{2, 5, -1\} = 5$

(b) $\min\{iy_i\} = \min\{1 \cdot 4, 2 \cdot 1, 3 \cdot 2\} = \min\{4, 2, 6\} = 2$

(c) $\sum x_i = x_1 + x_2 + x_3 = 2 + 5 + (-1) = 6$

(d) $\sum x_i^2 = x_1^2 + x_2^2 + x_3^2 = 2^2 + 5^2 + (-1)^2 = 30$. Note that $(\sum x_i)^2 = 6^2 = 36$

(e) $\sum x_i y_i = x_1 y_1 + x_2 y_2 + x_3 y_3 = 2(4) + 5(1) + (-1)2 = 11$

(f) $\prod x_i^{y_i} = x_1^{y_1} x_2^{y_2} x_3^{y_3} = 2^4 \times 5^1 \times (-1)^2 = 80$ ∎

Example 2 Find (a) $\sum_{i=1}^{4} r$ (b) $\sum_{i=1}^{4} i + 1$ (c) $\sum_{i=1}^{4} (i+1)$

Solution (a) $\sum_{i=1}^{4} r = r + r + r + r = 4r$ (b) $\sum_{i=1}^{4} i + 1 = 1 + 2 + 3 + 4 + 1 = 11$
(c) $\sum_{i=1}^{4} (i+1) = (1+1) + (2+1) + (3+1) + (4+1) = 2 + 3 + 4 + 5 = 14$ ∎

Alternating Series has terms alternately positive and negative.   (2)

Practice 2 Evaluate $(-1)^2$ and $(-1)^3$. Generalize.

Example 3 Express two ways without ...: (a) $\frac{1}{2^2} - \frac{1}{3^2} + \frac{1}{4^2} - \cdots - \frac{1}{87^2}$ (b) $3^2 4^3 \cdots 9^8$

Solution (a) $(-1)^k = 1$ if k is even and is -1 if k is odd. The sum is

$$\sum_{k=2}^{87} \frac{(-1)^k}{k^2} = \sum_{j=1}^{86} \frac{(-1)^{j+1}}{(j+1)^2}. \quad \text{(b)} \prod_{k=2}^{8} (k+1)^k = \prod_{k=3}^{9} k^{k-1}$$ ∎

Reversing $\sum_{k=m}^{n} f(k) = f(m) + f(m+1) + \cdots + f(n-1) + f(n)$

$$= f(n) + f(n-1) + \cdots + f(m+1) + f(m) = \sum_{k=m}^{n} f(m+n-k) \qquad (3)$$

Practice 3 Use Property 2 to evaluate the sum of the first n integers $\sum_{k=1}^{n} k$.

Distributive $\sum (ax_i + by_i) = a \sum x_i + b \sum y_i, \quad \prod x_i^a y_i^b = (\prod x_i)^a (\prod y_i)^b \qquad (4)$

Counterexample shows that a result is false in a particular case. A counterexample is a disproof.

Example 4 Find a counterexample for $\prod (x_i + y_i) = \prod x_i + \prod y_i$.
Solution Let $n = 2$, $x_1 = x_2 = y_1 = y_2 = 3$. Then $\prod (x_i + y_i) = (3+3)(3+3) = 36$
$\neq \prod x_i + \prod y_i = 3 \cdot 3 + 3 \cdot 3 = 18$ ∎

Example 5 Typical in statistics. If $y_i = a + bx_i$, $i = 1, \ldots, n$, and $\bar{x} = \frac{1}{n} \sum x_i$ and $\bar{y} = \frac{1}{n} \sum y_i$, simplify $y_i - \bar{y}$.

Solution $\bar{y} = \frac{1}{n} \sum (a + bx_i) = \frac{1}{n} \sum a + \frac{1}{n} \sum bx_i = a + b\bar{x}$. Then

$$y_i - \bar{y} = (a + bx_i) - (a + b\bar{x}) = b(x_i - \bar{x}) \qquad ∎$$

2. CALCULATING ON A TI-83

Elementary Function can be calculated in a finite number of steps using constants, one variable, $+$, $-$, $\times$, $\div$, powers and roots, logarithms, exponentials and trigonometric and inverse trigonometric functions and which produce smooth graphs. $|x| = \sqrt{x^2}$, $\sin^{-1}(\sin x)$, and $n!$ are not elementary. $\qquad (5)$

TI-83 and TI-84 graphing calculators can evaluate the elementary functions as well as the nonelementary sign and integer functions. Values are calculated to 14 digits, but the home screen displays only 10 (but see Example 6). Do not use commas inside a number. Besides the alphabet keys which must be preceded by [ALPHA], there is a convenient X key. The programming language is easy to use; the 430 page Guidebook is excellent. §1.B shows all available functions.

We use brackets for the primary function of a key: [STAT], double brackets for the second function: [[LIST]]; and use | to separate menu items after the first. Pressing [ENTER] on an empty line replays the previous entry. Press [[ENTRY]] to edit the previous entry or press repeatedly to recall earlier entries; ↑ is similar, but inserts instead of overtyping. Press [[RCL]] X to edit the value of X. We represent [STO] with → and [ENTER] with =. $\qquad (6)$

Power $4[\char`\^]3 = 64$, $4[x^2]$ displays $4^2 = 16$, $[[\sqrt{}]](4) = 2$, $10[\text{MATH}]\text{MATH} \mid {}^x\sqrt{1024} = 2$, $8[x^{-1}]$ displays $8^{-1} = .125$

Lists L_1-L_6 are the second function on keys 1-6. Lists can be typed in braces separated by commas, or generated using [[LIST]]seq(. A list may have from 1 to 999 real or complex numbers. sum(seq(creates the complete sequence, real only, subject to the 999 limit and using memory. The TI-84 [MATH]summationΣ(avoids this problem. $L_1(3)$ refers to element 3 of L_1. If L_2 has length 5, you can extend it by STOring a number to $L_2(6)$.

STOring a list to X (or any letter) puts it into LX, not X; use it from [LIST]NAMES.
Operations $\{1,2,3\} + \{4,5,6\} = \{5,7,9\}$ and $\{1,2,3\} + 4 = \{5,6,7\}$ $\qquad (7)$
seq [[LIST]]OPS | seq(expression,variable,begin,end[,increment]) returns a list. *increment* defaults to 1. If begin > end then increment must be negative.
cumsum [[LIST]]OPS | cumsum($\{$a,b,c,...$\}$) returns $\{$a,a+b,a+b+c,...$\}$
sum, prod [LIST]MATH | sum(list[,begin,end]), prod(list[,begin,end]) default is entire list.
Σ [[LIST]]MATH | summation Σ(expression,variable,begin,end) no *increment*. (TI-84 OS2.55) *variable* is a dummy.

Sequences [MODE]SEQ. In [Y=] you express u(n), v(n) in terms of n, u($n-1$), u($n-2$), v($n-1$), v($n-2$). A recursive sequence depends on previous value(s), and needs an initial value u(nMin). You specify u(nMin) as a list if using $n-2$; else as a number. You can set nMin to a nonnegative integer.

Practice 4 Write the output from seq(X^2,X,1,7,2).

Graphing The screen has 5985 pixels: 95 wide by 63 high; a 96th column is used to show the T-83 is busy. [WINDOW] controls what values are displayed: $[a,b] \times [c,d]$ means Xmin $= a$, Xmax $= b$, Ymin $= c$, Ymax $= d$. Xscl and Yscl control spacing of tick marks. Set Xres > 1 for slow functions, like solver. [ZOOM]ZStandard gives a $[-10,10] \times [-10,10]$ window. [ZOOM]Zsquare increases Xmin and Xmax by 50% so squares are square.

Graphing is done in [MODE]FUNction, PARametric, POLar, or SEQuence. Use [Y=] to enter the function to be graphed. In SEQ mode, u(n) is expressed in terms of n, u($n-1$), u($n-2$). If u($n-2$) is used, u($n$min) = {u(1),u(0)}. $\qquad$ (8)
Use [DRAW]STO to save all the elements of a graph in a graphics database which can be saved on a computer. [STAT PLOT] graphs polygons with coordinates in two lists.

To fix ERR: INVALID DIM, turn off StatPlots. If you move the cursor on a graph, the value of X is available on the home screen.

Tables [TABLE] shows x-values, and y-values of one or two defined functions.
[STAT]EDIT shows up to three defined lists.

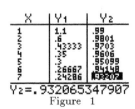
$Y_2 = .932065347907$
Figure 1

Example 6 Use a TI-83 table to display the first seven terms of the sequences $a_n = (10 + n)/10n$ and $b_n = .99^n$ of Example 1.2.15.
Solution Press Y= to get the function editor and define $Y_1 = (10+X)/(10X)$ and $Y_2 = .99 \char`^ X$. Press [TBLSET] and set TblStart$\doteq$1, ΔTbl=1. Then [TABLE] gives the display in Figure 1. The highlighted value is displayed to 12 digits at the bottom.

Method 2. [MODE]SEQ, nMin=1, u(n)=(10+n)/(10n), v(n)=v($n-1$).99, v(nMin)=.99 gives the table with headings n, u(n), v(n) but only 10 digits at the bottom. $\qquad$ ∎

Remark Go to the top of a column and press [ENTER] to edit the function.

Practice 5 Evaluate $\sqrt{2}$ on a TI-83 to 12 digits.

Example 7 A device has a useful life of 10 years and is expected to save $1000 the first year, $950 the second, ..., $550 the fifth year (uniform gradient). If interest is 7%, the present value of the savings is PV $= 1000/1.07 + 950/1.07^2 + \cdots + 550/1.07^{10}$. Express PV in summation notation and evaluate.

Solution PV $= \displaystyle\sum_{k=1}^{10} (1050 - 50k)/1.07^k = \text{sum(seq}((1050-50X)/1.07\char`^ X,X,1,10)) = \$5637.80$

Practice 6 Express the first 100 terms of $60 + 60(\frac{1}{3}) + 60(\frac{1}{3})^2 + \cdots$ in sigma notation starting with 1, and sum on a TI-83.

Example 8 (Example 1) Let $x_1 = 2$, $x_2 = 5$, $x_3 = -1$; $y_1 = 4$, $y_2 = 1$, $y_3 = 2$.

Find (a) max$\{x_i\}$ (b) min$\{iy_i\}$ (c) $\sum x_i$ (d) $\sum x_i^2$ (e) $\sum x_i y_i$ (f) $\prod x_i^{y_i}$

Solution Store (x_i) and (y_i) in lists: $\{2,5,-1\} \to L_1$, $\{4,1,2\} \to L_2$ (a) max(L_1) = 5

(b) min($\{1,2,3\}L_2$) = 2 (c) sum(L_1) = 6 (d) sum(L_1^2) = 30 (e) sum($L_1 \times L_2$) = 11

(f) prod($L_1 \char`^ L_2$) = 80 $\qquad$ ∎

Remark For two arguments max(1,2) = 2. For more than two: max($\{1,2,3\}$) = 3.

Example 9 Suppose L_1 contains the test scores of 50 students numbered 1-50. Find *which* student(s) have the highest score.
Solution seq(X,X,1,50)$\to L_2$. From [LIST]OPS | SortD(L_1,L_2), then [STAT]EDIT shows which items in L_2 correspond to the largest in L_1. $\qquad$ ∎

Multiplication, Division 2π and $5(1+2)$ are treated as implied multiplication. When you press $\times$ and $\div$, the TI-83 shows $*$ and $/$.

Solidus Warning Mathematically, all factors after the solidus ($/$) belong to the denominator, so $1/2x$ means $\frac{1}{2x}$, but the TI-83 and Excel (below) treat this as $\frac{1}{2}x$. Use parentheses around a denominator.

TI-83 Order of Operations: 1. Functions before the argument eg $\sqrt{(}$, sin(, not(2. Functions after the argument eg ^{2}, $^{-1}$, ! 3. other powers and roots 4. negation 5. nPr and nCr 6. multiplication, division 7. addition, subtraction 8. relations eg $>$ 9. and 10. or, xor. Within a level, from left to right.

Entering Formulas These need parentheses: a numerator with more than 1 term, a denominator with more than 1 term or factor, a radical or exponent with any operation. When working with fractions, put mixed numbers in parentheses and follow with [MATH]MATH | $\triangleright$frac. Functions are entered the way they are written; the TI-83 provides (. For negative numbers use [(−)], not [−]. For powers use [^]. For square roots use $[\![\sqrt{\ }]\!]$. For other roots use a fraction exponent in parentheses.

Example 10 Evaluating formulas on a TI-83.

Formula	TI-83	Result	Formula	TI-83	Result
(a) $\dfrac{2.47+3.86}{5.91+7.23}$	$(2.47+3.86)\div(5.91+7.23)=$	0.4817	(b) $\sqrt{4.1\times3.8}$	$[\![\sqrt{\ }]\!]4.1\times3.8)=$	3.94715
(c) $1\frac{2}{3}\div2\frac{3}{4}$	$(1+2/3)\div(2+3/4)\triangleright$frac $=20/33$		(d) 4^{2^3}	$4\hat{\ }(2\hat{\ }3)=$	65536
(e) 2^{-3}	$2\hat{\ }[(-)]3=$	0.125	(f) -3^2	$\boxed{(-)}3[x^2]=$	-9
(g) $\sqrt[5]{42}$	$5[\text{MATH}]^x\sqrt{\ }42=$	2.11179	(h) $8^{5/3}$	$8\hat{\ }(5\div3)=$	32
(i) $(-8)^{5/3}$	$([(-)]8)\hat{\ }(5\div3)=$	-32			∎

solver finds a value of a variable that makes a formula 0.

Example 11 Use solver to find the positive root of $x^3=3x+1$.
Solution [MATH]MATH | Solver displays EQUATION SOLVER Eqn: 0=. Type X^3−3X−1 and [ENTER]. Set X=1. bound change −1E99 to 0. Move back to X and [ALPHA][[SOLVE]] gives X=1.8793. ∎

Matrix is a rectangular array used for storing the coefficients and constants of a linear system of equations. rref solves a system of n equations in at least n unknowns for the first n unknowns. Used in §1.6.

Applications Finance and Science Tools come preloaded, and many more are available. You run them with [APPS]. Used first in §1.4.

3. EXCEL

Excel A spreadsheet program that allows you to enter numbers and formulas into a computer in rows (1, 2, 3, ...) and columns (A, B, C, ...). The intersection of a row and column is a **cell**. (9)

A *range* like H4:J6 specifies all the cells within the rectangle that has H4 in the upper-left corner and J6 in the lower-right corner (H4, H5, H6, I4, I5, I6, J4, J5, and J6). Our text separates successive selections from menus, dialog box tabs, etc. by a vertical bar.

	A	B	C	D
1				
2	XXXX	XXXX	XXXX	
3	XXXX	XXXX	XXXX	
4				

Figure 2

Practice 12 Give the reference for the marked cells in Figure 2.

Formulas in Excel begin with = (but not if part of another formula) and may contain numbers, functions and cell references. Excel uses $*$ for multiplication, $/$ for division, $\hat{\ }$ (shift-6) for exponentiation, ABS(x) for $|x|$, SQRT(x) for $\sqrt{x}$, and & for joining text strings.

To copy a formula in a cell, move the cursor near its lower left corner (*fill handle*) and the fat $+$ becomes thin. If you drag right, any column reference increases; if you drag down, any row reference increases. Prevent a reference from changing by preceding either or both with a $. [A1]=1/8 means select A1, type =1/8 and press Enter.

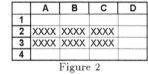
fat thin

To move a formula in a cell, move the cursor near the right edge and drag. *Moving* a formula does not change references in a formula, but does change references to the cell.

Practice 13 Write an Excel formula to evaluate $S_n = \dfrac{a - ar^n}{1 - r}$ if $[A1] = a = 60$, $[A2] = r = \frac{1}{3}$, $[A3] = n = 10$.

	A	B	C
1	0.33333	60	=60
2	89.9985	20	=B1*A$1
3		6.6667	=B2*A$1
4		2.2222	=B3*A$1
5		0.7407	=B4*A$1
6		0.2469	=B5*A$1
7		0.0823	=B6*A$1
8		0.0274	=B7*A$1
9		0.0091	=B8*A$1
10		0.003	=B9*A$1

Figure 3

Example 12 Sum 10 terms of the geometric series with first term 60 and ratio $\frac{1}{3}$.

Solution Enter the ratio $[A1]=1/3$ and the first term $[B1]=60$. The second term is the first times the ratio: $[B2]=B1*A\$1$. Drag B2 by the fill handle down to B10. When the formula is copied to B3, one row down, the reference B1 changes to B2 but the \$ prevents A\$1 from changing, so we get $[B3]=B2*A\$1$.

Column C in Figure 3 shows the formulas from column B. $[A2]=SUM(B1:B10)$ gives 89.9985.

In Example 15 we sum a large number of terms without putting them on the sheet. ∎

Practice 14 What does the formula $=\$A3+B\$5$ become if it is copied three rows down and one column right?

Example 13 Suppose A1:B50 contains the names and test scores of 50 students. Find which student(s) has the highest score.

Solution Select A1:B50. Then DATA | Sort | By column B, Descending. OK. Row 1 now has the highest scorer and score. ∎

Excel Order of Operations: (range), space (intersection), (comma) union, - (negation), % (percentage), ^ (exponentiation), * or / (multiplication or division), + or - (addition or subtraction), & (text operator), = < > <= >= <> (comparison operators)

Warning In Excel, $=-3^2$ gives 9; Example 14(e).

Example 14 Evaluating formulas in Excel.

Formula	Excel	Result	Formula	Excel	Result
(a) $\dfrac{2.47 + 3.86}{5.91 + 7.23}$	=(2.47 + 3.86)/(5.91 + 7.23)	0.4817	(b) $\sqrt{4.1 \times 3.8}$	=SQRT(4.1*3.8)	3.94715
(c) 4^{2^3}	=4^(2^3)	65536	(d) 2^{-3}	=2^(-3)	0.125
(e) -3^2	= -(3^2)	-9	(f) $\sqrt[5]{42}$	=42^(1/5)	2.11179
(g) $8^{5/3}$	= 8^(5/3)	32	(h) $(-32)^{1/5}$	=(-32)^.2	-2
(i) $(-8)^{5/3}$	= ((-8)^(1/3))^5	-32	(j) $1\frac{2}{3} \div 2\frac{3}{4}$	=(1 2/3)/(2 3/4)	20/33

In (j) the cell is formatted as a 2-digit fraction. ∎

Array is a rectangle of contiguous cells or a list of constants (not cells or formulas) in braces using commas to separate columns and semicolons to separate rows. Although {3,4,5} is used in mathematics for a set, an Excel array is ordered. When we ask Excel to perform an operation with an array, it operates with each entry separately. TRANSPOSE(x) turns rows 1, 2,... into columns 1, 2,..., and vice-versa. (15)

ROW function If $m \le n$ are positive integers, =ROW(\$m:\$n) creates in memory the array {m,m+1,...,n}. For example, =ROW(\$3:\$7) creates the array {3,4,5,6,7} (actually {3;4;5;6;7}). Use subtraction to create an array with 0 or negative entries; for example ROW(\$1:\$5) − 2 creates {−1,0,1,2,3}. Multiply by d to create an array whose entries differ by d.

Practice 15 Write an Excel formula to create the array (a) {1,2,...,100} (b) {0,1,...,99} (c) {3, 6, 9, ..., 240}

Example 15 A device has a useful life of 10 years and is expected to save \$1000 the first year, \$950 the second, ..., \$550 the fifth year (uniform gradient). If interest is 7%, the present value of the savings is $PV = 1000/1.07 + 950/1.07^2 + \cdots + 550/1.07^{10}$. Express PV in summation notation and evaluate in Excel.

Figure 4

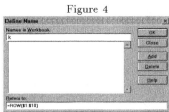

Solution $PV = \sum_{k=1}^{10} (1050 - 50k)/1.07^k$. To use a formula for the index, Define Name (Ctrl+F3). See Figure 4. Names in workbook k, **Refers to** =ROW(\$1:\$10) $\boxed{OK}$ which creates the array $\{1,2,...,10\}$ in memory. In any cell type =SUM((1050−50*k)/1.07^k) and press Ctrl-Shift-Enter. If you don't define k, replace k with its definition: =SUM((1050−50*ROW(\$1:\$10))/1.07^ROW(\$1:\$10)) Excel gives 5637.80. ∎

Practice 16 Express the first 100 terms of $60 + 60(\frac{1}{3}) + 60(\frac{1}{3})^2 + \cdots$ in sigma notation starting with 1, and sum in Excel.

Like Arrays Excel combines two arrays x and y having the same dimensions element by element. If A1:B2 = {3,1;4,1} = $\begin{bmatrix} 3 & 1 \\ 2 & 1 \end{bmatrix}$ and D1:E2 = {2,7;1,8} = $\begin{bmatrix} 2 & 7 \\ 1 & 8 \end{bmatrix}$, and we select a 2×2 range, such as G1:H2, type =A1:B2+D1:E2, and press Ctrl+Shift+Enter (**array-enter**) we get $\begin{bmatrix} 5 & 8 \\ 5 & 9 \end{bmatrix}$.

Unlike Arrays x and y having different dimensions can be combined if by replicating x and y they can be extended to the same size. If x = {1;2} = $\begin{bmatrix} 1 \\ 2 \end{bmatrix}$ and y = {3,4,5} = $\boxed{3 \ 4 \ 5}$ then select a rectangle having 2 rows and 3 columns, array-enter =x+y to get

$$\begin{bmatrix} 1 & 1 & 1 \\ 2 & 2 & 2 \end{bmatrix} + \begin{bmatrix} 3 & 4 & 5 \\ 3 & 4 & 5 \end{bmatrix} = \begin{bmatrix} 1+3 & 1+4 & 1+5 \\ 2+3 & 2+4 & 2+5 \end{bmatrix} = \begin{bmatrix} 4 & 5 & 6 \\ 5 & 6 & 7 \end{bmatrix},$$

but $\{1,2\} + \{3,4,5\}$ gives $\{4,6,\#N/A\}$.

Names A selected cell or array can be named by typing a name in the Name Box just above column A and pressing Enter.

Formula Bar Large area to the right of name box shows the formula in a selected cell.

Example 16 (Example 1) Let $x_1 = 2$, $x_2 = 5$, $x_3 = -1$; $y_1 = 4$, $y_2 = 1$, $y_3 = 2$. Use Excel functions to find (a) $\max\{x_i\}$ (b) $\min\{iy_i\}$ (c) $\sum x_i$ (d) $\sum x_i^2$ (e) $\sum x_i y_i$ (f) $\prod x_i^{y_i}$

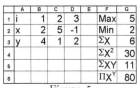

	A	B	C	D	E	F	G
1	i	1	2	3		Max	5
2	x	2	5	-1		Min	2
3	y	4	1	2		ΣX	6
4						ΣX²	30
5						ΣXY	11
6						ΠXᵞ	80

Figure 5

Solution Enter the labels and values in A1:F3 as shown in Figure 5. To get ΣX in F3, type SX, then select the S in the formula bar and Format | Cells | Font and type SYMBOL. To get ΣX^2 in F4, type SX2. Change the S to Σ. Then select the 2 and Format | Cells and check the superscript box. Similarly for F5. To get $\prod X^Y$ in F6, type PXY. Then select the P and Format | Cells | Font | Symbol | OK; select the Y and Format | Cells | superscript.
Select B1:D1 and type I in the name box. Select B2:D2 and type X in the name box. Select B3:D3 and type Y in the name box. To get $\max\{x_i\}$ in G1, enter =MAX(X). To get $\min\{iy_i\}$ in G2 type =MIN(I)*Y). Here I*Y = {1,2,3}*{4,1,2} creates the array {4,2,6} in memory. Because we are summing numbers that are not on the sheet, we must array-enter.
To get $\sum x_i$ in G3, enter =SUM(X). To get $\sum x_i^2$ in G4 array-enter =SUM(X^2). Excel squares each entry. To get $\sum x_i y_i$ in G5, array-enter =SUM(X*Y). Excel multiplies the first entry of X by the first entry of Y, the second entry of X by the second entry of Y, etc. To get $\prod x_i^{y_i}$ in G6, array-enter =PRODUCT(X^Y). ∎

Text Function TEXT(*value,format*) Converts *value* to text using *format*, such as number ("##"), day ("ddd"), or month ("mmm"), or "general" (to 11 digits).

Time If a cell's contents look like one of Excel's date (e.g. 3/4/04) or time formats (e.g. 8:50 pm), Excel stores it as a serial date number. A serial date number is the number of days since 12/31/1899 (including Feb 29, 1900) with time expressed as fractions of a day.

Example 17 What day is 100 days after Nov 24, 2011?
Solution =TEXT("11/24/11"+100,"ddd mmm d yyy") gives Sat Mar 3 2012. ∎

Graphing Use Chart Wizard for curves (xy-scatter) and also surfaces.

Table is a rectangular arrangement as in range A1:D3 of Figure 5. If we look in the row headed x and the column headed "2" we find $x_2 = 5$. (17)

Example 18 Make addition and multiplication tables for the integers 1-9. See Figures 6-7.
Solution [B1]=1, [C1]=2. Select B1:C1 and drag to J1. Type x in the name box. Click on Borders in the toolbar and put a line underneath. [A2]=1, [A3]=2. Select A2:A3 and drag to A10. Type y in the name box. Put a border on the right. [B2]=x+y. Select B2 and drag down to B10, then across to J10. Enter + A1. Select A1:J10. Optionally increase the font size to 16. Format | Column | Autofit.
Changes for the multiplication table: [B2]=x*y. Select A1 and change font to Symbol. Hold the Alt-key and type 0180 on the numeric keypad. ∎

+	1	2	3	4	5	6	7	8	9
1	2	3	4	5	6	7	8	9	10
2	3	4	5	6	7	8	9	10	11
3	4	5	6	7	8	9	10	11	12
4	5	6	7	8	9	10	11	12	13
5	6	7	8	9	10	11	12	13	14
6	7	8	9	10	11	12	13	14	15
7	8	9	10	11	12	13	14	15	16
8	9	10	11	12	13	14	15	16	17
9	10	11	12	13	14	15	16	17	18

Figure 6

×	1	2	3	4	5	6	7	8	9
1	1	2	3	4	5	6	7	8	9
2	2	4	6	8	10	12	14	16	18
3	3	6	9	12	15	18	21	24	27
4	4	8	12	16	20	24	28	32	36
5	5	10	15	20	25	30	35	40	45
6	6	12	18	24	30	36	42	48	54
7	7	14	21	28	35	42	49	56	63
8	8	16	24	32	40	48	56	64	72
9	9	18	27	36	45	54	63	72	81

Figure 7

Solver the powerful Excel add-in, must be installed before you use it the first time.

Example 19 Use Solver to find the positive root of $x^3 = 3x + 1$.
Solution Select A1 and type x in the name box. Select B1 and enter =x^3−3*x−1. Tools | Solver. For Target cell, select B1; Equal to Value of 0; By changing cells A1; Subject to constrain Add A1>=0; OK Solver found a solution OK. In A1 is 1.879385. ∎

4. OTHER TECHNOLOGY

Typing Math in Word When you come to a formula, start Equation Editor with Insert | Object | Microsoft Equation 3.0. (Not found in a Typical installation. Use Control Panel Add/Remove Programs.) You are presented with a screen containing a single slot indicated by a dashed rectangle. Slots demarcate the components of an equation. In a fraction, the numerator is one slot and the denominator is another. You move from slot to slot with the arrow and tab keys, filling in the slots to create your equation.

You start in Math style where variables are in italics, function names are roman, and proper spaces are inserted. Symbols and templates can be accessed from their respective palettes; the most common have keyboard shortcuts (below). Templates for fences such as parentheses, brackets and braces expand to accommodate what they enclose. You can change the size of other templates, but to select them you must hold the control key. Press ENTER only when you want to create a new slot beneath the current one. For example, to create $\binom{n}{r}$, type: Ctrl+(, n, ENTER, r.

When your equation is complete, press the Esc key to return to Word. To edit an existing equation, either zoom then double click, or select, Edit | Equation object | open, then zoom.

Equation Editor keystrokes
Text mode: Ctrl+Shift+e   Math mode: Ctrl+Shift+=
Superscript (high) Ctrl+h, Subscript (low) Ctrl+l, Joint Ctrl+j
Parentheses, braces, brackets: Ctrl+9 or 0, Ctrl+{ or }, Ctrl+[or]
Absolute value: Ctrl+| Integral: Ctrl+I   Thin space (before dx): Ctrl+space
Characters Ctrl+k: i (∞) a($\rightarrow$) d (∂) <($\leq$) >($\geq$) t($\times$) e($\in$) E($\notin$) c($\subset$)
Templates Ctrl+t: f (fraction) r (square root) n (nth root) s (summation) p (product) u (underscript)
Next character Greek: Ctrl+g, a for α, q for θ. Next character bold roman: Ctrl+b
Overbar $\bar{x}$: Ctrl+Shift+hyphen. vector $\vec{x}$: Ctrl+Alt+Hyphen. overdot $\dot{x}$: Ctrl+Alt+.
For other characters or templates you use a palette. With a keyboard, press the F2 function key, use $\rightarrow$ to select a palette, $\downarrow$ to open it and $\rightarrow$ to select, then ENTER. The top row contains characters; the bottom row, templates.

Example 20 Type in Word
"The quadratic formula is $x = \dfrac{-b \pm \sqrt{b^2 - 4ac}}{2a}$ and $\lim_{a \to 0} x = -\dfrac{c}{b}$."

Solution Type "The quadratic formula is " then start Equation Editor. (In the instructions below, keystrokes except ordinary typing are separated by | . "Tab" and "Esc" are on the keyboard.

x= | Ctrl+f |-b | click on ± from the 4th symbol palette | Ctrl+r | b | Ctrl+h | 2 | Tab |-4ac | Tab | Tab | 2a | Esc and type "and ".
Start again Ctrl+t | u | lim | Tab | a | Ctrl+k | a | 0 | Tab | x=−f | Ctr+t | f | c | Tab | b | Esc and type the period. ∎

Evaluating Formulas in Word To evaluate $\sqrt[5]{42}$, press Ctrl+F9 to show a pair of braces designating a field code, type =42^(1/5). Press F9 to evaluate and Alt+F9 to see the result 2.11. To get 5 decimals, press Alt+F9 to show the codes and add \# followed by the codes "#.######" in quotes. Press F9 and Alt+F9 to see 2.11179. For large numbers you get 14 digits followed by 0's to a maximum of 65 digits. Word cannot do SQRT or transcendental functions like SIN.

Scientific Calculators have more functions on the keypad than graphic calculators. On the classic style, such as a TI-30Xa, unary operators such as $\sqrt{x}$ follow the number and don't need parentheses; on the algebraic style, unary operators come before the number and need parentheses. The styles are the same for binary operators like ×. (19)

Windows Scientific Calculator (Start | Programs | Accessories | Calculator. First use: View | Scientific) Has 32-digit precision. Functions act on display like a classic calculator. Right-clicking a key gives an explanation and a keyboard equivalent. You can enter exponents to 9999. Results can have higher exponents but beyond 99999 may take a very long time. It has no button for fractions, combinations or polar coordinates.

CAS A Computer Algebra System can be used to do numerical calculations to any number of digits, and symbolic calculations in algebra and calculus. Scientific Workplace front end for Maple is easy to use but is sometimes wrong. Derive is harder to use but is always right if you do Manage | Branch | Real). Derive is implemented in the TI-89 and TI-92 graphics calculators. Mathematica is sometimes wrong, but only it could evaluate $1/(1^2 + 1) + 1/(2^2 + 1) + 1/(3^2 + 1) + \cdots$ exactly.

Google the Web search engine, has a 15-digit calculator and understands units. 4^2^3 gives 4^(2^3)=65536 and 0^0 gives 1.

Practice Answers 1. (a) $\sum_{k=1}^{99}$ (b) $99 - 46 = 53$

2. $(-1)(-1) = 1$, $[(-1)(-1)](-1) = 1(-1)$. If n is even then $(-1)^n$ is a product of pairs each 1 so the product is 1. If n is odd, the product has one additional factor of -1, so the product is -1.

3. $\sum_{k=1}^{n} k = \sum_{k=1}^{n} (n + 1 - k) = \frac{1}{2}[\sum_{k=1}^{n} k + \sum_{k=1}^{n} (n + 1 - k)] = \frac{1}{2}\sum_{k=1}^{n}(n + 1) = \frac{1}{2}n(n + 1)$

4. $\{1\ 9\ 25\ 49\}$ **5.** 1.41421356237 **6.** $\sum_{i=1}^{100} 60(\frac{1}{3})^{i-1}$ on the TI-83 = sum(seq(60(1/3)^(X−1),X,1,100)) = 90.

12. A2:C3 **13.** =(A1 − A1∗A2^A3)/(1 − A2) **14.** =$A6+C$5

15. (a) =ROW($1:$100) (b) =ROW($1:$100) − 1 (c) =3∗ROW($1:$80)

16. $\sum_{i=1}^{100} 60(\frac{1}{3})^{i-1}$ in Excel = SUM(60∗(1/3)^(ROW($1:$100)−1)) gives 90.

Problems 1.3

Problems 1-8 deal with indices and sigma notation.

1. In the sum $1 + 2x + 3x^2 + \cdots + kx^{k-1}$, write the terms before and after the ellipsis ($\cdots$).

2. Which sums are equal to $\sum_{n=3}^{10} (n + 5)$? (a) $\sum_{n=7}^{14} (n + 9)$ (b) $\sum_{n=7}^{14} (n + 1)$ (c) $\sum_{n=1}^{8} (n + 7)$

3. Write each sum using index j. (a) The first 50 terms of $\frac{1}{2} - \frac{1}{4} + \frac{1}{8} - \frac{1}{16} + \cdots$ (b) $7^2 - 8^2 + 9^2 - \cdots + 53^2$.

4. Find the nth term and the sum of n terms of the series $2 + 2 \cdot 3 + 2 \cdot 3^2 + 2 \cdot 3^3 + \cdots$. Has the series a sum?

5. For $\sum_{k=10}^{49} (103 - 2k)$ find the first term a, the common difference d, the numbers of terms n, and the sum s.

6. If $\sum x_i = 13$ and $\sum y_i = 25$, find $\sum (3x_i + 2y_i)$.

7. Let $x_1 = 2$, $x_2 = -5$, $x_3 = 4$, $x_4 = -8$; $y_1 = -3$, $y_2 = -8$, $y_3 = 10$, $y_4 = 6$. Calculate

(a) $\sum x_i$, (b) $\prod y_i$, (c) $\sum x_i y_i$, (d) $\sum x_i^2$, (e) $(\sum x_i)^2$

8. Express $\sum_{i=1}^{30} x_i - \sum_{i=1}^{14} x_i$ as a single sum.

Problems 9-19 are for a TI-83.

9. Write $7^2 + 8^2 + \cdots + 53^2$ (a) using sigma notation with index k and (b) calculate.

10. (a) Write a formula for the first 100 terms of $1(\frac{1}{3}) + 2(\frac{1}{3})^2 + 3(\frac{1}{3})^3 + \cdots$ for a TI-83. (b) Calculate the answer. (c) Sum the series algebraically.

In Problems 12-17, write a TI-83 formula and evaluate the expression.

12. $\sqrt{7.2 + 3.5(2.6)^4}$

13. $\dfrac{1}{4.7 + 3.6^{1 + \sqrt{2}}}$

14. $17.5^{-1.3}$

15. $\dfrac{1}{1 + \sqrt{2}} + \dfrac{1}{1 + \sqrt{3}}$

16. $1.2^{2.3^{0.86}}$

17. $(\sqrt{2} - 3)^{3/5}$

18. Let $y_{k+2} - y_{k+1} - 2y_k = 0$, $y_0 = 9$, $y_1 = -12$. Rewrite in the form u(n) = and find u_6.

19. Use sorted lists to find which term of $a_n = n^{12}/2^n$ is largest.

Problems 20-33 are for Excel.

20. Let $y_{k+2} - y_{k+1} - 2y_k = 0$, $y_0 = 9$, $y_1 = -12$. Use Excel to get y_2 to y_6.

21. (a) Write a formula for the first 100 terms of $1(\frac{1}{3}) + 2(\frac{1}{3})^2 + 3(\frac{1}{3})^3 + \cdots$ in Excel assuming I is defined as =ROW($1:$100). (b) Calculate the answer. (c) Sum the series algebraically.

22. Write out the array =10*ROW($13:$19)+5

23. Write $7^2 + 8^2 + \cdots + 53^2$ (a) using sigma notation with index k and (b) calculate using Excel.

24. The formula =A$5+$B6 is typed in cell C9. What does it become when copied to cell E15?

25. A sheet has the names of cars in A1:A7, miles driven in B1:B7, gallons of gas used in C1:C7. Find the car with the worst gas mileage.

26. Give the result of the formula as Excel would if entered properly: (a) ={4,5}*{6,7} (b) ={4,5}*{6;7}

In Problems 27-32, write an Excel formula, starting with =, and evaluate.

27. $\dfrac{1}{4.7 + 3.6^{1 + \sqrt{2}}}$

28. $\sqrt{7.2 + 3.5(2.6)^4}$

29. $\dfrac{1}{1 + \sqrt{2}} + \dfrac{1}{1 + \sqrt{3}}$

30. $17.5^{-1.3}$

31. $(\sqrt{2} - 3)^{3/5}$

32. $1.2^{2.3^{0.86}}$

33. Use Excel TEXT to find the date of 104th day of the current year.

1.4 PERCENT, UNITS, AVERAGE, PROPORTION

We encounter percents and unit conversions when we compare prices or products.

1. SCIENTIFIC NOTATION

Significant Digits (sd) of the approximate numbers used in practical calculations are those that are not trailing zeros in an integer (5400 has 2 sd) or leading zeros after the decimal point in a fraction (.0045 has 2 sd). 54.00 has 4 sd. A decimal indicates that trailing zeros are significant: 5400. lb has 4 sd.

Scientific Notation A nonzero number x in the form $\pm a \times 10^c$ where $1 \le a < 10$ and c is an integer. 10^0 is seldom written. All digits in the *significand* a are significant.

Engineering notation uses $\pm a \times 10^c$ where $1 \le a < 1000$ and c is a multiple of 3.

Practice 1 For which numbers x in scientific notation is the exponent c positive? negative?

Calculator uses floating point notation (ordinary decimals) for x if $|x| > 1$ and the integer part fits the display, or $0 < |x| < 1$ and a significant digit will display. Use scientific notation to make it show more significant digits if $0 < x < .1$. (1)

Large Prefixes 10^3 = thousand = kilo (k), 10^6 = million = mega (M), 10^9 = billion = giga (G), 10^{12} = trillion = tera (T), 10^{15} = peta (P), 10^{18} = exa (E). The stress is always on the prefix: kilo′meter.

Small Prefixes $10^{-2} = $ centi (c), $10^{-3} = $ milli (m), $10^{-6} = $ micro (μ), $10^{-9} = $ nano (n), $10^{-12} = $ pico(p), $10^{-15} = $ femto (f), $10^{-18} = $ atto (a)
μg, mg, and kg represent microgram, milligram and kilogram masses.

In the binary computer world, kilobyte might be $2^{10} = 1024$ or just 1000 bytes, so in 1999 the ISO adopted:
$2^{10} = 1024 = $ kibi (Ki), $2^{20} = 1,048,576 = $ mebi(Mi), $2^{30} = 1,073,741,824 = $ gibi (Gi)

Practice 2 (a) Express the Stefan-Boltzmann constant 5.6704×10^{-8} in engineering notation. (b) Interpret the unit mN/m.

Example 1 (a) In 1998, the US government spent \$1,652,200,000,000. Express this number in scientific notation. (b) The Stefan-Boltzmann constant is $5.6704 \times 10^{-8} \, \text{W} \cdot \text{m}^{-2} \cdot \text{K}^{-4}$. Express as an ordinary decimal.
Solution (a) Move the decimal point 12 places left to get a number between 1 and 10; compensate by using a positive exponent: 1.6522×10^{12}.
(b) The negative exponent tells us to move the point 8 places left: .000000056704. ∎

Operations To multiply or divide, operate on the significands and add or subtract the exponents (Property 1.2.18). To add or subtract, give all numbers the lowest power of 10. Any case may need a final move.

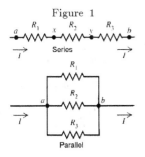

Figure 1

Series

Parallel

Ohm's Law (1827) $E = IR$ for electric current I amperes (A) where E volts (V) is the potential difference between two ends of a resistance of R ohms (Ω). See Figure 1. If resistors are connected in series, the voltage drop from a to b is the sum of the voltage drops, and the current is constant:

$$E = E_1 + E_2 + E_3, \quad IR = IR_1 + IR_2 + IR_3 \text{ so } R = R_1 + R_2 + R_3.$$

If resistors are connected in parallel, we add currents and the voltage drop is constant:

$$I = I_1 + I_2 + I_3, \quad E/R = E/R_1 + E/R_2 + E/R_3 \text{ so } 1/R = 1/R_1 + 1/R_2 + 1/R_3 \qquad (2)$$

Symbols All variables are numbers. I is the number of amperes in the current.

Example 2 (a) A current of 27.0 μA flows through a resistance of 3.00 MΩ. Find the voltage. (b) Subtract $2 \times 10^{-12} - 4 \times 10^{-18}$.
Solution (a) $E = IR = (27.0 \times 10^{-6}) \times (3.00 \times 10^{6}) = 81.0$ V
(b) Increase -18 to -12 and move the decimal 6 places right
$2. \times 10^{-12} - 4. \times 10^{-18} = 2.000000 \times 10^{-12} - 0.000004 \times 10^{-12} = 1.9999996 \times 10^{-12}$ ∎

Not a Product To enter 1.6522×10^{12} on a calculator use $1.6522⟦EE⟧12$. In Excel or Scientific Workplace, use 1.6522E12. The maximum exponent on a calculator is 99; in Excel it is 307.
To display 4sd: TI-83 [MODE] change from normal to SCI, from FLOAT to 3.
In Excel Format | Cells | Number | Custom | Type #.000E$-$##.
Do not allow a long formula to break at $\times$ as you would for a product.

2. ROUNDING
Keep full precision until the very end, then round. If the first digit dropped is less than 5, the last retained digit is unchanged. If the first digit dropped is greater than 5, or is 5 followed by a nonzero digit, the last retained digit is increased by 1. If the digit being dropped is 5 with nothing after it, there are two ways to round. The first is more likely to preserve the sum of a set of rounded numbers. (3)

Original: $0.5 + 1.5 + 2.5 + 3.5 + 4.5 + 5.5 + 6.5 + 7.5 + 8.5 + 9.5 = 50$
round to an even digit $0 + 2 + 2 + 4 + 4 + 6 + 6 + 8 + 8 + 10 = 50$
4/5: always round up $1 + 2 + 3 + 4 + 5 + 6 + 7 + 8 + 9 + 10 = 55$

Round to even (Banker's Rounding) is specified by IEEE Standard 754, NIST, and used by BASIC.
A calculator, Excel, and IRS Pub. 17: Increase amounts from 50¢ to 99¢. Sign is ignored.

An approximate number in scientific notation has a maximum error of 5 units is the first missing digit. When an approximation is given as a rational number $\frac{n}{d}$ such as $\pi \approx \frac{22}{7}$, we assume there is no better approximation with same or smaller d. Then the error $< 1/d^2$.

Example 3 Express 23,700 in scientific notation and give the smallest and largest number it could represent if the number of significant digits (sd) is (a) 3, (b) 4
Solution (a) 2.37×10^4; from 23650 to 23750
(b) 2.370×10^4; from 23,695 to 23,705
Number words or larger units could be used: for 4 sd we could write 23.70 thousand, or 23.70 km for 23 700 m. ∎

Example 4 Express 1/234567 as a decimal to 8 sd.
Solution A TI-30 displays 0.000004263. To display additional significant digits, switch to scientific notation: 4.263174274E−6 and write 0.0000042631743 after rounding 4274 to 43. The TI-83 in NORMAL mode switches to scientific notation for numbers $< .001$. ∎

Standard Rule To add (or subtract) approximate numbers, express the largest in scientific notation and the others with the same exponent. After adding, round to the minimum number of decimal places in the significands. See Error (Property 9). When multiplying, dividing or extracting roots, use as many sd as in the factor with the minimum number of sd. Consider exact numbers as having many decimal places or sd. Units are treated as algebraic quantities.

Figure 2

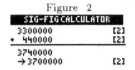

Figure 3

Example 5 Calculate (a) the sum and (b) the product of 3.3×10^6 and 4.4×10^5. (c) Compare the possible range of the product with the implied range of the answer.

Solution (a) $3.3 \times 10^6 + 4.4 \times 10^4 = 3.3 \times 10^6 + 0.44 \times 10^6 = (3.3 + 0.44) \times 10^6 = 3.74 \times 10^6$
$\approx 3.7 \times 10^6$ (3.3 has only 1 decimal place).
Figure 2 shows the problem using TI-83 APPS | Sci Tools | SIG-FIG CALCULATOR

(b) $(3.3 \times 10^6) \times (4.4 \times 10^5) = (3.3 \times 4.4) \times (10^6 \times 10^5) = 14.52 \times 10^{11} = 1.5 \times 10^{12}$

(c) $(3.35 \times 4.45 - 3.25 \times 4.35) \times 10^{11} = 0.77 \times 10^{11}$ vs $(1.55 - 1.45) \times 10^{12} = 1.0 \times 10^{11}$ ∎

Rectangular Box of length ℓ, width w, height h has area $= 2\ell w + 2\ell h + 2wh$, volume $= \ell wh$. See Figure 3. A selection of area and volume formulas is given in §1.A. (4)

Example 6 The edges of a rectangular box measure 28 in by 49.5 in by 106 in. Find with appropriate precision (a) the volume V and (b) the total surface area.
Solution (a) $V = \ell wh = 28$ in $\times 49.5$ in $\times 106$ in $= 146{,}916$ in$^3 \approx 1.5 \times 10^5$ in^3 since the first factor is correct to 2 sd. The volume could be as large as $28.5 \times 49.55 \times 106.5 = 150{,}396$ so a more precise answer such as 1.47×10^5 would be incorrect.

(b) There are 3 pairs of equal areas of total

$2(28$ in $\times 49.5$ in $+ 28$ in $\times 106$ in $+ 49.5$ in $\times 106$ in$) = 2(1386 + 2968 + 5247)$in^2
$= 19{,}202$ in$^2 = 1.92 \times 10^3$ in^2

since the first two terms are correct to 2 sd and hence the nearest hundred. ∎

Decimal to Fraction If a display is equal to a fraction having denominator up to 4 digits: On the TI-83: [MATH]MATH | ▷ Frac. In Excel, Format the cell to fraction.
For an approximation with a given denominator, subtract the integer part, multiply by the desired denominator, round to an integer to get the numerator. (5)

Exact vs Rounded When solving word problems, give a rounded answer with suitable units; in other problems give an exact answer.

Example 7 (a) Solve $x^2 = 21$. (b) Find the side of a square whose area is 21 in^2 to the nearest $\frac{1}{16}$ inch.
Solution (a) $x = \pm\sqrt{21}$

(b) $x = \sqrt{21} \approx 4.582$. Subtract 4 and multiply by 16 to get $9.32 \approx 9$. Hence $4\frac{9}{16}$ in. ∎

3. PERCENT

Percent A way of expressing decimals: $n\% = \frac{n}{100}$. Thus $7\% = \frac{7}{100} = .07$. Percent is always percent of some number (the **base**). Beware of percents when the base is not given! A liquid solute is given as a percentage of the volume, and percent alcohol is half the proof, but a solid solution is given in grams per 100 ml. To convert to percent, multiply by $1 = 100\%$. For smaller fractions we have per mil (per thousand): $n\%_0 = \frac{n}{1000}$, and ppm (parts per million).

$$(6)$$

Visual Figure 4, from NYTimes, Oct 5, 2003, shows ages 0 to 17 (24%), 18 to 64 (64%) and 65+ (12%) in New York City

12%
64%
24%
Figure 4

Example 8 (a) How much alcohol is there in a 6 oz drink of 80 proof vodka? (b) How much glucose is there in 750ml of a 5% glucose solution?

Solution (a) The vodka is 40% alcohol. $6\,\text{oz} \times .4 = 2.4\,\text{oz}$ (b) $750\text{ml} \times \dfrac{5\text{g}}{100\text{ml}} = 37.5\text{g}$ ∎

Equivalents

$\frac{1}{2} = .5 = 50\%$	$\frac{1}{3} = .333\ldots = 33\frac{1}{3}\%$	$\frac{1}{4} = .25 = 25\%$	$\frac{1}{5} = .2 = 20\%$
$\frac{1}{6} = .166\ldots = 16\frac{2}{3}\%$	$\frac{1}{8} = .125 = 12\frac{1}{2}\%$	$\frac{1}{9} = .111\ldots = 11\frac{1}{9}\%$	$\frac{1}{10} = .1 = 10\%$
$\frac{1}{12} = .083\ldots = 8\frac{1}{3}\%$	$\frac{1}{20} = .05 = 5\%$	$\frac{2}{3} = .666\ldots = 66\frac{2}{3}\%$	$\frac{3}{4} = .75 = 75\%$
$\frac{2}{5} = .4 = 40\%$	$\frac{3}{5} = .6 = 60\%$	$\frac{4}{5} = .8 = 80\%$	

$$(7)$$

Practice 5 (a) Convert $\frac{5}{12}$ to percent. Round to 1 decimal place. (b) Express $3\frac{1}{3}\%$ exactly as a fraction. (c) Express $\sqrt{1\%}$ in percent. (Roots are used to find average percent changes; see Example 21.)

Interest is a fee paid for the use of another's money that depends on the amount and time used. The **profit** or **markup** on an item is the difference between its selling price p and its cost c. **Tax** on income, profits, sales, etc. is money paid to the government.

Example 9 Find the selling price p when the cost is $35 if the markup 20% is based (a) on cost (b) on price.
Solution (a) markup $= p - 35 = .2 \times 35 = 7$ so $p = 35 + 7 = \$42$

(b) markup $= p - 35 = .2p$ so $1p - .2p = .8p = 35$ and $p = 35/.8 = \$43.75$ ∎

Example 10 Since Aug 2009, NYC sales tax is 8.875% with 4/5 rounding. A toaster costs $35.82. Find the total cost.
Solution Total cost $=$ toaster $+$ tax $= 100\% + 8.875\% \overset{\text{mental}}{=} 108.875\%$ of $35.82 or

$1.08875 \times 35.82 \overset{\text{calculator}}{=} 38.999 = \$39$ ∎

Percent Change $=$ (new $-$ base)/base.

Example 11 Find the percent change if the size of a can is (a) increased from 8 oz to 12 oz (b) decreased from 12 oz to 8 oz.
Solution (a) $(12 - 8)/8 = 4/8 = .50 = 50\%$ increase

(b) $(8 - 12)/12 = -4/12 = -.33 = 33\%$ decrease ∎

Practice 7 What percent discount is "Buy four get one free"?

Chain of Changes can't be added or subtracted because the bases are different. Add each change to, or subtract from 100%, then convert to a decimal and multiply. Subtract 1 or from 1 and convert back to percent. The order of the changes does not matter because multiplication is commutative.

Example 12 A merchant marks up his goods 45%, then sells them at "25% off". Find the actual markup.
Solution The marked price is $100\% + 45\% = 145\%$ of cost. The selling price is $100\% - 25\% = 75\%$ of the marked price, which is $1.45 \times .75 = 1.0875$ times cost. The profit is $.0875 = 8.75\%$ of cost. ∎

Practice 8 A store offers successive discounts of 5%, 10% and 20%. Find the equivalent single discount.

Percent Difference $= |x_1 - x_2| / |\frac{1}{2} x_1 + x_2|$ where x_1 and x_2 are two values, neither of which is "first" or "true".

Practice 9 NYTimes, Oct 26, 2003, p.BU 11, reports that 9.2% and 10.5% of mothers with 4 boys and 4 girls are divorced or separated. Find the percentage difference.

Writing "Y is 60% *higher than* X" means "Y is 160% as *high as* X".
Do not use "twice as low" when you mean "half as high".
Use "out of" instead of "of" to indicate subtraction rather than multiplication of percents. When stating a change, give the *to* figure first to prevent misreading as a range: The price rose to $25 from $23. Or insert a comma: The price will rise by $3, to $23.

Practice 10 (a) NYTimes, Jun 13, 2003, p.W1: "The government is selling 25 percent of its 45.8 percent stake in Maruti. After the sale, the government's stake will drop to some 20 percent of the company." Clearly the government is selling more than a quarter of its shares. Rewrite the first sentence.

(b) NYTimes, May 27, 2008, p.F1: "The cost of repairing damage to those schools has ranged from 10 to 100 times below repair costs for other schools." Rewrite.

Error Absolute error = measurement − true.
Relative error = absolute error/true = (measured − true)/true.
The absolute error in a sum or difference is the sum of the absolute errors.

Product, Quotient The relative error in a (a) product or (b) quotient is the sum of the relative errors. For n operations with equal errors, the maximum error is multiplied by n, but the expected error is multiplied by $\sqrt{n}$. (9)

Proof Let a and b be the errors in A and B, and the relative errors a/A and b/B are small.
(a) $\dfrac{(A+a)(B+b) - AB}{AB} = \dfrac{aB + bA - ab}{AB} = \dfrac{a}{A} + \dfrac{b}{B} - \dfrac{a}{A} \cdot \dfrac{b}{B} \approx \dfrac{a}{A} + \dfrac{b}{B}$ since $\dfrac{a}{A} \cdot \dfrac{b}{B}$ is smaller than either factor (b) $\left(\dfrac{A+a}{B+b} - \dfrac{A}{B}\right)\Big/\dfrac{A}{B} = \dfrac{B(A+a)}{A(B+b)} - 1 = \dfrac{aB - bA}{A(B+b)} \approx \dfrac{aB - bA}{AB} = \dfrac{a}{A} - \dfrac{b}{B}$. The maximum error is when $\dfrac{a}{b} < 0$. ∎

Example 13 Gravitational acceleration g is measured in lab experiment as 9.62 m/sec² while the true value is 9.81 m/sec². Find (a) the absolute error AE and (b) the relative error RE.
Solution (a) AE $= 9.62 - 9.81 = -0.19$ m/sec²
(b) RE $= -0.19/9.81 = -.0194 = -1.94\%$ (pure number) ∎

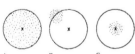

Precision is measured by the number of sd in repeated measurements. **Accuracy** is measured by the deviation from the true value as illustrated by the X in Figure 5. A is accurate but imprecise; B is precise but inaccurate; C is accurate and precise.

A   B   C
Figure 5

± Notation Because the uncertainty is not always a half unit, physicists use $m \pm \sigma$ where σ is the standard error. This means there is a 65% chance the true value is between $m - \sigma$ and $m + \sigma$. CODATA 2006 gives the Stefan-Boltzman constant as $5.670400(40) \times 10^{-8}$ which is short for $(5.670400 \pm .000040) \times 10^{-8}$. Medical tables use $m \pm 2\sigma$ which include 95% of the population. $\pm$ is also used when there are no significant digits. The difference $2.33 \times 10^5 - 2.3 \times 10^5 = .03 \times 10^5$ is swamped by the possible error $\pm.05 \times 10^5$. We may write $(3 \pm 5) \times 10^3$ or just the magnitude $\pm 10^3$.

Practice 11 Use $\pm$ notation to express 240V if voltage can vary by as much as 10%.

4. UNITS

Unit The dimension of a physical quantity, such as length, is expressed as a multiple of a standard quantity, called a unit. If a unit is named after a person, the symbol is capitalized but the word is not: 10 hertz = 10 Hz. "in" gets a period where it could be a word (Example 19), but other abbreviations do not. To convert between different units, express an equation relating the units as a **unit fraction** (fraction of value 1) and multiply so the units cancel. Use §1.A.

To calculate with mixed units, convert to the smaller unit. To convert from decimal to mixed units (compound number) subtract the integer part and convert the decimal part.

Prime $15'6''$ denotes 15 minutes 6 seconds of angle or 15 feet 6 inches of length, depending on context.

Spaces Write a space between a numeral and a symbol except for variables, superscripts, percent, and KB (kilobyte) and MB (megabyte): 3 ft but $3'$. Use parentheses if a number has more than one term. Numbers attached to SI units are grouped by spaces; those less than 1 always get a leading 0.

Writing Units denote a measure, not a count, and take a singular verb: "Seven feet *is* underwater", not *are*.

Use *less* and *amount* for things you measure, *fewer* and *number* for things you count: NYTimes, Oct 14, 2006, p.C6: Lighter jets mean less fuel and one fewer flight attendant. Also: the amount of fuel, the number of attendants.

With percent, it depends on position: "Less than 35% of voters support the measure" but "There were 35% fewer voters this year".

A 3-inch square has area $3\,\text{in} \times 3\,\text{in} = 9\,\text{in}^2$.

Practice 12 Write the perimeter of a triangle whose sides are 1 ft, 2 ft, and $\sqrt{3}$ ft.

Example 14 (a) Convert 675oz to lb and oz. (b) A man's height is $6'1''$. Convert to cm. (c) NYC law requires every apartment to have at least one room of area at least $150\,\text{ft}^2$. Convert to m^2. (d) Convert 15 mi/hr to ft/sec.

Solution (a) $675\text{oz} \times \dfrac{1\text{lb}}{16\text{oz}} = 42.1875\text{lb} = 42\text{lb} + .1875 \times \dfrac{16\text{oz}}{1\text{lb}} = 42\text{lb}3\text{oz}$

(b) $6\,\text{ft} \times \dfrac{12\,\text{in}}{1\,\text{ft}} + 1\,\text{in} = 73\,\text{in} \times \dfrac{2.54\,\text{cm}}{1\,\text{in}} = 185.4 \approx 185\,\text{cm}$

(c) $150\,\text{ft}^2 \times \left(\dfrac{12\,\text{in}}{1\,\text{ft}} \times \dfrac{2.54\,\text{cm}}{1\,\text{in}} \times \dfrac{1\,\text{m}}{100\,\text{cm}}\right)^2 = 13.935 \approx 13.9\,\text{m}^2$

(d) $\dfrac{15\,\text{mi}}{\text{hr}} \times \dfrac{1\,\text{hr}}{3600\,\text{sec}} \times \dfrac{5280\,\text{ft}}{1\,\text{mi}} = 22\,\dfrac{\text{ft}}{\text{sec}}$

Practice 13 Convert 1 mi to km.

Example 15 (Business) If \$1 buys .95 euro, and apples cost 4.15 euro per kilogram, convert to dollars per pound.

Solution $\dfrac{4.15\,\text{euro}}{\text{kg}} \times \dfrac{.4536\,\text{kg}}{1\,\text{lb}} \times \dfrac{1\,\text{dollar}}{.95\,\text{euro}} = 1.982 = \$1.98$ ∎

Example 15 (Life Science) A bottle of tablets is labeled "Gantrisin 0.5g". A patient needing 1500mg gets how many tablets?

Solution $1500\text{mg} \times \dfrac{1\text{g}}{1000\text{mg}} \times \dfrac{1\,\text{tablet}}{0.5\text{g}} = 3$ tablets ∎

Motion speed = rate = change in distance/time taken

acceleration = change in speed/time taken   (10)

These are *average* speed and acceleration. Calculus deals with *instantaneous* speed and acceleration. *Velocity* is used as a synonym for *speed*; technically it is speed in a specified direction.

Practice 14 A car accelerates uniformly from 0 to 60 mph in 5.5 seconds. Find the acceleration in ft/sec^2.

Force, Mass, Pressure 1 pound of force (lbf) accelerates a 1 pound mass (1 lbm = .45359 kg by definition) with the acceleration of gravity, 9.80665 m/s². 1 newton (N) of force accelerates a 1 kg mass at 1 m/s², so it takes 9.81N to lift 1kg. Pressure is force divided by area, for example, pounds per square inch (psi).

Work, Power Work = force in direction of motion × distance. Power = work/time.
Efficiency of a device is the ratio of work output to work input. (11)

Example 16 Convert 1 newton to pounds of force, and then to ounces.

Solution $1 \text{ N} = \dfrac{1 \text{ kg-m}}{\text{s}^2} \times \dfrac{1 \text{ lbm}}{.45359 \text{ kg}} \times \dfrac{1 \text{ lbf}}{1 \text{ lbm} \times 9.80665 \text{ m/s}^2} = .22809 \text{ lbf} \times \dfrac{16 \text{ ozf}}{1 \text{ lbf}} = 3.60 \text{ ozf}$

Practice 15 Use Example 16 to convert a standard atmosphere of 101.3 kPa to pounds/in². 1 Pa = 1 N/m².

Example 17 (a) How much work must be done to lift a 25kg object 4m? (b) How much work must be done to lift a 50lb object 13ft if the machine is 85% efficient?
Solution (a) work = force × distance = $25 \times 9.81 \times 4 = 981$ N · m = 981J

(b) $.85 = $ output/input $= 50\text{lb} \times 13\text{ft/input}$, input $= 50\text{lb} \times 13\text{ft}/.85 = 764.7 \approx 760\text{ft-lb}$ ∎

Excel (You must install Analysis Toolpak) CONVERT(*num,from,to*), where *from* and *to* are text, can change units within each category (italics denote SI base unit): time (yr, day, hr, mn, *sec*), distance (*m*, mi, Nmi (nautical mile) in, ft, yd, ang (angstrom), Pica (actually point = $\frac{1}{72}$in), liquid measure (tsp, tbs, oz, cup, pt, qt, gal, l NOT L), mass (*kg*, sg (slug), lbm, u (atomic mass unit), ozm), force (N, dyn, lbf), pressure (Pa, atm, mmHg), energy (J, e (erg), c (thermodynamic calorie), cal, eV (electron volt), HPh, Wh, flb, BTU), power (HP, W), temperature (C, F, *K*), and magnetism (T (tesla), ga (gauss)). The other SI base units are electric current (ampere), substance (mole) and luminous intensity (candela). To convert compound units, nest the CONVERTs. For units in the denominator, reverse *from* and *to*.

TI-83 APPS | Sci Tools | Unit Converter has length (fm (femtometer, formerly fermi), A, mm, cm, m, km, Mil, in, ft, yd, fath, rd, mi, Nmi, ltyr), area (cm², m², ha, km², in², ft², yd², acre, mi²), volume (cm³, mL, L, m³, tsp, tbsp, in³, ozuk, cup, pt, qt, gal, galuk, ft³), time (ns, μs, ms, s, min, h, day, week, yr), temperature (°C, K, °F, °R), velocity (m/s, km/h, ft/s, mi/h, knot), mass (u, g, kg, lbm, slug, ton, mton), force/weight (dyne, N, kgf, lbf, tonf), pressure (Pa, kPa, bar, mmH₂O, mmHg, inH₂O, inHg, lb/in², atm), energy/work (eV, erg, J, ft-lbf, cal, l-atm, Btu, kwh), power (W, ft-lb/s, cal/s, Btu/min, hp). There are 15 constants, e.g. Avogadro. Press EXPT [ZOOM] to paste the value to the home screen.

Google has easier-to-use conversion. Put the word *in* followed by the name of a unit at the end. In most cases you can use the long name as well as the SI name.

Example 14 (continued) Do Example 14 using Excel and   Google.
Solution (a) =CONVERT(6+1/12,"ft","cm") → 185.4   6 ft 1 inch in cm

(b) =CONVERT(CONVERT(150,"ft","m"),"ft","m") → 13.935 150 ft^2 in m^2

(c) =CONVERT(CONVERT(15,"mi","ft"),"sec","hr")→22   15 mi/h in ft/s   ∎

Figure 6

Example 14 (concluded) Do Example 14 using TI-83 Unit Converter.
Solution Start with APPS | Sci Tools | Unit Converter. QUIT after each part to select a different category. (a) length 73 in cm → 1.8542 E2 cm See Figure 6.
(b) area 150 ft² cm² → 1.393546 E1 m²
(c) velocity 15 mi/h ft/s → 2.2E1 ft/s   ∎

Example 18 A person's BMI (Body Mass Index) is their weight in kilograms divided by the square of their height in meters. (a) Express this as a formula. (b) Find the formula in lb and inches.

Solution (a) BMI is a pure number. weight in kilograms = weight/kg and height in inches is height/in. Hence BMI = weight/kg/(height/m)^2.

(b) BMI = weight/kg · .4536kg/lb/(height/m · .0254 m/in)^2 = 703 × weight/lb/(height/in)^2

Example 19 A dollar bill measures $2\frac{5}{8}$ in. by $6\frac{1}{8}$ in. Find its area.

Solution Area of rectangle

$$= \text{length} \times \text{width} = 2\tfrac{5}{8} \times 6\tfrac{1}{8} = (2 \cdot \tfrac{8}{8} + \tfrac{5}{8}) \times (6 \cdot \tfrac{8}{8} + \tfrac{1}{8}) = \tfrac{21}{8} \cdot \tfrac{49}{8} = \tfrac{1029}{64} = 16\tfrac{5}{64} \text{in}^2$$

On a TI-83: (2+5/8)(6+1/8) = 16.078125. Then − 16[MATH]MATH | ▷ Frac = 5/64.

TI-84 with OS2.55: (2+5/8)(6+1/8) ▷ Frac = 16 ⊔ 5/64

In Excel: =2 5/8*6 1/8 gives 16.078125. We apply the fraction format # ??/?? to get 16 5/64. For proper fractions, use a leading 0. ∎

Practice 16 How many pieces $2'5''$ can be cut from a $20'$ board?

5. AVERAGE AND PROPORTION

Average x: If each of finitely or infinitely many numbers is replaced by x, the net effect is the same. (12)

Arithmetic Mean of numbers x_1, x_2, ..., x_n is $\bar{x} = (x_1 + x_2 + \cdots + x_n)/n$. It is the most common type of average.

Weighted Mean If there are m numbers equal to x_1 and n numbers equal to x_2, then $\bar{x} = (mx_1 + nx_2)/(m+n)$. We extend this to any numbers with $m + n \neq 0$. If m and n are percentages, the denominator is 1.

Harmonic Mean of positive numbers x_1, x_2, ..., x_n is $x_H = \dfrac{n}{\frac{1}{x_1} + \frac{1}{x_2} + \cdots + \frac{1}{x_n}}$ or

$\dfrac{1}{x_H} = \left(\dfrac{1}{x_1} + \dfrac{1}{x_2} + \cdots + \dfrac{1}{x_n}\right)/n$

Root Mean Square (RMS) of x_1, x_2, ..., x_n is $x_R = \sqrt{(x_1^2 + x_2^2 + \cdots + x_n^2)/n}$ or $x_R^2 = (x_1^2 + x_2^2 + \cdots + x_n^2)/n$

Geometric Mean of positive numbers x_1, x_2, ..., x_n is $x_G = \sqrt[n]{x_1 x_2 \cdots x_n}$ or $\ln x_G = (\ln x_1 + \ln x_2 + \cdots + \ln x_n)/n$ where $\ln x$ is the natural logarithm of x.

Unless the x_i are equal

$$\min(x_1, x_2, ..., x_n) < \text{harmonic mean} < \text{geometric mean} < \text{arithmetic mean} < \text{RMS} < \max(x_1, x_2, ..., x_n)$$

Excel $\bar{x}$ is =AVERAGE(x1,x2,...), x_H is =HARMEAN(x1,x2,...), x_G is =GEOMEAN(x1,x2,...)

TI-83 can do weighted mean: [LIST]MATH | mean(*list,freqlist*).

Period of a repetitive or wave motion is the time per cycle. The reciprocal of period (s) is frequency (Hz) so velocity = wavelength × frequency: $v = \lambda f$ (13)

Practice 17 Saturn's orbit is nearly a circle of radius 1.427×10^9km and has a period of 10759 days. Find its speed in km/s.

Example 20 (a) From nhtsa.gov. A manufacturer produces 130 thousand light trucks getting 22 mpg (mi/gal), 120 thousand getting 20 mpg, and 100 thousand getting 16 mpg. Find the CAFE (Corporate Average Fuel Economy) (b) Electric work is E^2t/R. If $E = 100$ V for 1 s and 200 V for 1 s, find the average voltage x V.

Solution (a) We replace each mpg by a single mpg x so the total gallons used is the same, assuming each truck travels 1 mile.

$$130 \times \frac{1\,\text{mi}}{22\,\text{mi/gal}} + 120 \times \frac{1\,\text{mi}}{20\,\text{mi/gal}} + 100 \times \frac{1\,\text{mi}}{16\,\text{mi/gal}} = 130 \times \frac{1}{x} + 120 \times \frac{1}{x} + 100 \times \frac{1}{x} = \frac{350}{x}$$

$x = 350/(130/22 + 120/20 + 100/16) = 19.27$ mpg, a weighted harmonic mean.

(b) work $= 100^2/R + 200^2/R = x^2/R + x^2/R$, $100^2 + 200^2 = 2x^2$,
$x = \sqrt{(100^2 + 200^2)/2} = 158$, the RMS ∎

Example 21 (a) A company's sales increased by 15% in 1997, by 20% in 1998, and decreased by 10% in 1999. Find the average rate of growth of the company over the 3-year period (compound annual growth rate CAGR) (b) Of Jmart's competitors, A is 15% larger, B is 20% larger, and C is 10% smaller. Find the average size of the competitors.
Analysis (a) is a chain of changes; multiply. (b) all are based on Jmart; add.
Solution (a) If x is the average rate of growth, then

$$(1 + .15)(1 + .20)(1 - .1) = (1 + x)(1 + x)(1 + x), \ (1 + x)^3 = 1.15 \times 1.20 \times .90,$$

$$1 + x = \sqrt[3]{1.15 \times 1.2 \times .9} = 1.0749 \text{ and so } x = .0749 = 7.49\%$$

On a calculator: $(1.15 \times 1.2 \times .9)\hat{\ }(1/3) =$ (b) If x is the average excess of a competitor, $.15 + .20 - .10 = x + x + x$, $3x = .25$, $x = .0833 = 8.33\%$ ∎

Example 22 Of the silicon atoms found in nature, 92% have mass number 28, 5% have mass number 29, and 3% have mass number 30. Find the average (atomic weight) A_r.
Solution The weighted mean $A_r = .92 \times 28 + .05 \times 29 + .03 \times 30 = 28.1$ ∎

Ratio of two numbers a and b written $a{:}b$ is the fraction a/b, $b \neq 0$. If a and b are quantities, they must be expressed in the same units.

Proportion: an equality of two or more ratios. $a{:}b{:}c{:}\cdots = A{:}B{:}C{:}\cdots$ means $a/A = b/B = c/C = \cdots$. Sometimes :: is used instead of = , as in $2{:}3 :: 10{:}15$.
If $a/A = b/B$ is a proportion, then $Ab = aB$: the product of the means equals the product of the extremes.

The geometric mean of a and b is called the **mean proportion** because if $a{:}x = x{:}b$, then $x^2 = ab$, $x = \sqrt{ab}$.

Example 23 Find the ratio of each pair: (a) 6 pounds to 12 ounces (b) 3 square yards to 6 square feet.
Solution (a) 6 lb $= \dfrac{16 \text{ oz}}{1 \text{ lb}} = 96$ oz. The ratio is $96{:}12 = 8{:}1$.
(b) 3 yd^2 $= 3$ yd$^2 \times \left(\dfrac{3 \text{ ft}}{1 \text{ yd}}\right)^2 = 27$ ft^2. The ratio is $27{:}6 = 9{:}2$. ∎

Example 24 A $30''$ line is divided in the ratio $2{:}3$; find the length of each part.
Solution $2 + 3 = 5$. The first part is $\frac{2}{5}$ of the whole $= \frac{2}{3} \times 30 = 12''$. The second part is $\frac{3}{5} \times 30 = 18''$. ∎

Practice 19 Solve the proportion $x{:}13 = 4{:}9$.

Variation Direct: If x varies **directly** as y, or x is directly proportional to y, then $x = ky$ or $k = x/y = x_2/y_2$.

Inverse: If x varies **inversely** as y, or x is inversely proportional to y, then $x = k/y$ or $k = xy = x_2 y_2$.

Joint: If x varies **jointly** with y and z, then $x = kyz$ or $k = x/yz = x_2/y_2 z_2$.   (15)
k is the **constant of proportionality.**

Measure If corresponding lengths of similar figures have ratio s, their areas have ratio s^2 and their volumes have ratio s^3.

Joint Variation If x varies directly with y when z is constant and x varies directly with z when y is constant, then x varies jointly with y and z.
Proof $\dfrac{x}{x_2} = \dfrac{x(y, z)}{x(y_2, z_2)} = \dfrac{x(y, z)}{x(y_2, z)} \cdot \dfrac{x(y_2, z)}{x(y_2, z_2)} = \dfrac{y}{y_2} \cdot \dfrac{z}{z_2}$, or $\dfrac{x}{yz} = \dfrac{x_2}{y_2 z_2}$ ∎

Temperature The Fahrenheit scale sets the freezing point of water at 32°F and the boiling point at 212°F. The Celsius scale sets 0°C at the freezing point and 100°C at the boiling point. A gas at 0°C will lose 1/273.15 of its volume for a 1°C drop in temperature. At this rate, its volume would be 0 at −273.15°C, absolute zero. The Kelvin or absolute temperature, Celsius temperature + 273.15, must be used for ratio calculations. No degree symbol is used with K. (16)

Remark In medical shorthand, the degree symbol denotes hours, hence q4° means "every four hours".

History Fahrenheit invented the mercury thermometer in 1714. Celsius invented his scale in 1742; Kelvin his scale in 1848, which is independent of any particular substance. The mean body temperature is 98.2°F, not 98.6°F. Wunderlicht (1868) reported 37°C; it was mistakenly treated as 37.0°C.

Practice 21 (a) Criticize (Schaum's Earth Science, 2ed, p.70): The surface temperature of the sun is 6000K. This is equivalent to $6000 - 273 = 5727$°C. (b) A Carnot engine uses hot and cold temperatures H and K; its efficiency is $E = 1 - K/H$. Find E if H and K are the boiling and freezing points of water.

Example 25 Translate each statement into an equation using k as the constant of proportionality. Abbreviate each variable by its initial. Use subscripts for two variables of the same kind. (a) The period of a simple pendulum is proportional to the square root of its length. (b) A blackbody's radiation is proportional to its area and the 4th power of its temperature.
(c) The force of attraction between two bodies varies directly as the product of the masses and inversely as the square of the distance between them (inverse-square law).
Solution (a) $p = k\sqrt{\ell}$

(b) $R = kAT^4$. k is the Stefan-Boltzmann constant times a fraction.
(c) $F = km_1 m_2/d^2$. k is the universal gravitational constant. ∎

Practice 22 Translate Newton's second law of motion: Acceleration is directly proportional to force on a body and inversely proportional to its mass.

Solving Proportions Replace the variables with the first set of values to determine k. Then use k and the given values of the second set to determine the missing value. The values in a set can be any units but corresponding values in the two sets must have the same units.

Example 26 The kinetic energy of a body is proportional to its mass and the square of its speed. An 8 lb body moving at 4 ft/sec has 2 ft-lb of kinetic energy. Find the energy of a 3 ton truck moving at 60 mph.
Solution $3 \text{ tons} \times \dfrac{2000 \text{ lb}}{1 \text{ ton}} = 6000 \text{ lb}$ and $\dfrac{60 \text{ mi}}{\text{hr}} \times \dfrac{5280 \text{ ft}}{1 \text{ mi}} \times \dfrac{1 \text{ hr}}{3600 \text{ sec}} = 88 \text{ ft/sec}$. Then
$E = kwv^2$, where $k = \dfrac{E}{wv^2} = \dfrac{2}{8 \times 4^2} = \dfrac{1}{64}$ so $E = \frac{1}{64} \times 600 \times 88^2 = 726{,}000$ ft-lb. ∎

Example 27 If 8 workers take 12 days to make 16 tanks, how long will it take 15 workers to make 50 tanks?
Solution The number of days is directly proportional to the number of tanks and inversely proportional to the number of workers.
$d = km/w$, $k = dw/m = 12 \times 8/16 = 6$. $d = 6 \times 50/15 = 20$ days ∎

Percent Change in Proportion Write the equation with subscripts 1 and with subscripts 2 and divide to eliminate k.

Example 28 By what percent x must a pendulum be lengthened to increase its period by 3%?
Solution From Example 25(a), $p_1 = k\sqrt{\ell_1}$ and $p_2 = k\sqrt{\ell_2}$ so
$\dfrac{p_2}{p_1} = \dfrac{k\sqrt{\ell_2}}{k\sqrt{\ell_1}} = \sqrt{\dfrac{\ell_2}{\ell_1}} = \sqrt{1+x} = 1.03$. Thus $1 + x = 1.03^2$ so $x = 1.03^2 - 1 = .0609 \approx 6.1\%$

Practice Answers 1. $c > 0$ if $|x| > 1$; $c < 0$ if $|x| > 1$ **2.** (a) 56.704×10^{-9} (b) millinewton per meter

5. (a) $\frac{5}{12} = \frac{5}{12} \cdot 100\% = 41\frac{2}{3}\% \approx 41.7\%$ (b) $3\frac{1}{3}\% = 3\frac{1}{3} \times \frac{1}{100} = \frac{10}{3} \times \frac{1}{100} = \frac{1}{30}$ (c) $\sqrt{1\%} = \sqrt{.01} = .1 = 10\%$

6. Eight thousand seven hundred thirty-four and $\frac{28}{100}$

7. You pay $\frac{4}{5} = 80\%$ of the regular price; the discount is 20%.

8. You pay $.95 \times .90 \times .80 = .684$ of the original. The discount is $.316 = 31.6\%$

9. $|9.2 - 10.5|/\frac{1}{2}|9.2 + 10.5| = 1.3/9.85 = .1319 = 13.2\%$

10. (a) The government is selling 25 percent *out* of its 45.8 percent stake in Maruti.

(b) ... has ranged from 1% to 10% of repair costs for other schools.

11. (240 ± 24)V or $240(1 \pm 10\%)$V but not 240V $\pm 10\%$ (one cannot add 240 V and 10%)

12. $(3 + \sqrt{3})$ft **13.** $1 \text{ mi} \times \dfrac{5280 \text{ ft}}{1 \text{ mi}} \times \dfrac{12 \text{ in}}{1 \text{ ft}} \times \dfrac{2.54 \text{ cm}}{1 \text{ in}} \times \dfrac{1 \text{ m}}{100 \text{ cm}} \times \dfrac{1 \text{ km}}{1000 \text{ km}} = 1.609344$ km exactly

14. $\dfrac{60\text{mi}}{\text{hr}} \times \dfrac{5280\text{ft}}{1\text{mi}} \times \dfrac{1\text{hr}}{3600\text{s}} = \dfrac{60\text{mi}}{\text{hr}} \times \dfrac{22\text{ft/s}}{15\text{mi/hr}} = 88\text{ft/s}$. $88\text{ft/s} \div 5.5\text{s} = 16\text{ft/s}^2$

15. $101.3\,\text{kPa} \times \dfrac{1000\,\text{N/m}^2}{1\,\text{kPa}} \times \dfrac{.224809\,\text{lbf}}{1\,\text{N}} \times \left(\dfrac{0.254\,\text{m}}{1\,\text{in}}\right)^2 = 14.59\,\text{psi}$ **16.** $20 \div (2+5/12) = 8.275$. 8 pieces.

17. circumference $= 2\pi r$. $2\pi \times 1.427 \times 10^9 \text{km}/(107592 \text{ d} \times \dfrac{24\text{hr}}{1\text{d}} \times \dfrac{3600\text{s}}{1\text{hr}}) = 9.645\text{km/s}$

19. $x/13 = 4/9$, $x = 4 \times 13/9 = \frac{52}{97}$

21. (a) 6000K has at most 2sd. The equivalent is 5700°C. (b) $1 - 273.15/373.15 = 26.8\%$

22. $a = kF/m$. Units chosen so $k = 1$. Then $F = ma$.

Problems 1.4 Problems with ^{h} have hints below; those with ^{T} use technology. Appendix 1.A has geometry formulas.

1. Find the volume of a USPS Priority Mail Flat Rate box with inside dimensions $11\frac{7}{8}'' \times 13\frac{5}{8}'' \times 3\frac{3}{8}''$.

2. The front, side, and bottom faces of a rectangular box have areas 15 in^2, 35 in^2, and 21 in^2. Find the volume.

Problems 3-6 deal with scientific notation.

3. The belladonna dosage prescribed by homeopaths for bronchitis is known as 30C: one drop of belladonna extract is dissolved in 99 drops of a water/alcohol solution. Then 1 drop of the new solution is diluted by 99 drops of liquid, and so on, 30 times. (a) Express the final concentration of belladonna in scientific notation. (b) Compare with 1 drop $(.05 \text{ cm}^3)$ dissolved in all the oceans of the world $(1.4 \times 10^9 \text{ km}^3)$. (c) To get the "weaker" 6X dosage, 1 drop is dissolved in 9, and the process is performed 6 times. Express this in terms of C.

4. Write as a decimal: (a) 1.3×10^4 (b) 8.3×10^{-7} (c) 1.27×10^3 (d) 6.14×10^{-2}

5. Write in scientific notation: (a) 52.60 (b) 0.0061 (c) 172,000 (3 sd) (d) 172,000 (4 sd)

6. Subtract, assuming both numbers are exact: $3.1 \times 10^{-5} - 2.5 \times 10^{-8}$.

Problems 8-11 deal with precision.

8. The sides of a rectangular box measure 6.5 cm by 31.4 cm by 115 cm. Find with appropriate precision (a) the volume and (b) the total surface area.

9. One rectangle is 2.4×10^3 cm by 1.5×10^2 cm and another is 3.0×10^3 cm by 1.2×10^2 cm. Each has area approximately 3.6×10^5 cm^2. Find a bound on the difference d cm^2.

10. For a temperature of 1.8 °C, calculate T^{-1}, where T is absolute temperature, to the proper number of digits.

11. A side of a square is approximately 345 cm. How accurately must it be measured to determine to the nearest integer (a) its perimeter in cm and (b) its area in cm^2?

12. WSJ, Jul 10, 2010, p.A2. A strong signal near a cell tower could be 10 billionths of a watt; a signal of 10 quadrillionths of a watt could be enough to complete a call. Express the strengths using prefixes.

Problems 13-26 deal with percent.

13. If the output of a machine remains constant, how much is input decreased if efficiency is increased by 25%?

14. A copper ore is 4.5% copper. How much ore is needed to yield 90lb of copper?

15. NYTimes, Jul 1, 2008, p.F2. For apricots, a cup of fresh halves is 86% water with 74 calories, and a half-cup of dried fruit is $x\%$ water with 212 calories. Find x (the Times had 76%).

16. A store gives markdowns of 40%, 10% and 10%. Find the equivalent single markdown.

17. Macy's ad, Oct 10, 2010. Take off an additional 40% for a total savings of 80%. Find the original discount.

18. A tourist get a 25% premium when he converts US dollars to Canadian, and loses 25% when he converts back. Find his net gain or loss.

19. (a) If profit is 20% of cost, what percent of selling price is it? (b) If profit is 20% of selling price, what percent of cost is it?

20[h] A can of tuna is changed from 7 oz to 6 oz. (a) What is the percent change? (b) If the price of a can remains the same, what is the percent change in the unit price?

21[T](a) On Mar 2, 2008, the MTA reduced the bonus on Metrocards from 20% to 15%. What is the effective percent fare increase? (b) Use technology to find the smallest multiple of 5¢ not less than $7.00 such that the amount plus the bonus gives a whole dollar amount.

22. The period of a pendulum is given as $2\pi\sqrt{\ell/g}$ but is really $4M\sqrt{\ell/g}$ where M depends on the angular displacement β and is 1.598142 when $\beta = 30°$. Find (a) the relative error $(4M - 2\pi)/4M = 1 - \pi/2M$ and (b) the error in a day.

23. From Schaum's Heat Transfer (1998), p.234: Water at $20°$ is heated by a $15\,\text{cm} \times 15\,\text{cm}$ plate at $52°\text{C}$. The heat transmitted is found to be $420\,\text{W}$ and $556\,\text{W}$ in Problems 8.2 and 8.3! Find the percentage difference.

24. From NYTimes, Aug 8, 2006, p.F1. The tsunami-causing earthquake of Dec 2004 decreased the gravity at the earth's surface by as much as 0.0000015 percent, meaning that a 150-lb person would experience a weight loss of one-nth of an ounce. Find n to the nearest 5000.

25. Good Housekeeping, Jan 2010, p.101: On an electric stove, use a pan that matches the burner size. Putting a 6" pan on an 8" burner wastes x percent of the energy because the heat dissipates into the air. Find x.

26. How many milliliters of a 4% solution of boric acid can be made from 5g of boric acid?

Problems 27-30 deal with averages.

27. A and B went on a 3-day trip. Each day A bought 20 gallons of gas and B bought $60 worth. If the prices per gallon were $2.90 on day 1, $3.00 on day 2 and $3.10 on day 3, find the average price per gallon for each.

28. The value of a mutual fund increased 30% in 1997, 25% in 1998, 15% in 1999 and decreased 20% in 2000. Find the average rate of growth for the 4 years.

29. Due to extreme demand, voltage was cut to $100\,\text{V}$ from noon to 2PM, $110\,\text{V}$ from 2-4PM, and was $120\,\text{V}$ from 4-6PM. Find the RMS voltage for the afternoon.

30. Use a weighted mean to find the student's GPA for the semester.

Grade	4	3.5	3	2.5	2
Credits	3	4	3	3	2

31. Two weights on opposite sides of a fulcrum balance if they have the same product of weight and distance (moment). An object is weighed on a balance with unequal arms. It balances w_1 on one side and w_2 on the other. Find and name the true weight w.

Problems 32-44 deal with unit conversions.

32. Which is the best buy (lowest unit cost) on cooking oil: 1 pint for 89¢, 24 ounces for $1.29, 1 gallon for $5.99?

33. Blue light has a wavelength $\approx 4500\text{Å} = 4.5 \times 10^{-7}\text{m}$. Find its frequency. The speed of light $= 3.0 \times 10^8\text{m/s}$.

34. (a) $20\,\text{lb}$ bond paper is the weight of 1 ream (500 sheets) of $17\,\text{in}$ by $22\,\text{in}$ (basic size). Express in g/m^2.
   (b) 20 lb bond = 50 lb book = 28 lb cover = 46 lb tag = 42 lb index. 30 lb wrapping paper is $49\,\text{g/m}^2$. Which category is it?

35. NYTimes, Sep 29, 2009, p.A1. The average price farmers received for milk in July was $11.30 for 100 pounds; the average retail price was $2.91 a gallon. If milk weighs $64.4\,\text{lb/ft}^3$, find the percent markup based on cost.

36. A bottle of elixir is labeled "20 mEq per 15 ml". How many milliliters will contain 25 mEq?

In Problems 37 and 38, a cubic foot of water weighs 62.4 lb.

37. NYTimes, Aug 26, 2008. The darkness of the deep ocean is matched by the intense pressure. Four miles down, it amounts to nearly five tons per square inch. Find a more precise value for the pressure.

38. From NYTimes, Jul 28, 2002, RE LI 8: If you have a 200-ft well, an x horsepower pump should provide 7 gallons per minute. Find x. (1 hp = 33,000 ft-lb/min).

39. PCWorld, Jan 2009, p.17: An average black-ink cartridge contains 8ml of ink and costs \$10. If you bought a gallon of the stuff over the life of your printer, you'd have paid about x dollars. Find x.

40. NYTimes, Mar 16, 2007, p.A17. Mars has deposits of ice covering an area the size of Texas so thick they would blanket the planet in 36 feet of water if they were liquid. Find the average thickness in miles. (The maximum thickness is 2.3 mi.) The area of Texas is 269,000 mi; Mars is a sphere of radius 2110 mi.

41. NYTimes, Mar 4, 2007, p.A16: "A trillion gallons of water sitting behind the dam is enough to cover the state of Kentucky to a depth of three inches." (a) Kentucky has area 40409 mi^2; find the correct depth. (b) Convert the volume to acre-feet used by conservationists.

42. (a) Which computer chip is faster: a 40 nanosecond cycle or a 40 megahertz speed? (hertz = cycle/second)
(b) Each square on an electrocardiogram represents $\frac{1}{5}$ second. Find a patient's heart rate in beats/minute if there are n squares in a beat.

43. In the US, fuel economy is measured in miles per gallon (mpg) so higher is better; in the EU, economy is measured in liters per 100 km, so lower is better. (a) Convert 7.3 L/100 km to the US standard. Use 1 mi = 1.6093 km, 1 qt = .9464 L. (b) NYTimes Magazine, Dec 14, 2008, p.56: The move from 10 to 11 mpg saves more than the leap from 35 to 50 mpg. Illustrate with 10000 miles.

44. Good Housekeeping, Mar 2010, p.207. Campbells egg noodles. x feet in every 11oz can of noodle soup. Assume the noodles fill $\frac{1}{5}$ the can and their cross-section is a 0.1in square. Find x.

45[h] The recommended Dubois formula for body surface area in m^2 when the height h is in cm and the weight w in kg is $\sqrt{hw/3600}$. Modify the formula for BSA in m^2 with h in inches and w in pounds.

Problems 46-53 deal with ratio and proportion.

46. The force of wind on a sail varies jointly as the area of the sail and the square of the wind speed. When the wind speed is 15 mph, there is a 1 lb force on a square foot of sail. Find the force of a 45 mph wind on a sail of 20 square yards.

47. R varies inversely as the square of S. When S is multiplied by 4, how does R change?

48. If 2 workers can test 6 samples in 4 hours, how many workers are needed to test 18 samples in 8 hours?

49. The life of a lightbulb varies inversely as the 13th power of the voltage. (Electronics Engineers' Handbook 1997, p.15.3) If a bulb lives 750 hr at 130V, how long will it last at 120V?

50[h] Graham's law. At a given temperature, the rate of diffusion of a gas is inversely proportional to the square root of its molecular mass. H_2 has mass 2.02 and Ne has mass 20.2. If $\frac{2}{3}$ of the H_2 escapes from a container in 6 hours, how long will it take $\frac{1}{2}$ the Ne to escape from a similar container?

51. Hooke's law. The elongation of a spring is proportional to the force, up to some limit. A 3 kg mass hanging from a spring stretches it 50 cm. Find the force to lower the mass an additional 20 cm. Use 1 kg = 9.81N.

52. Translate the equation into a statement of variation: $AS = 6$ where S is the specific heat of an element having atomic weight A (Dulong and Petit).

53. Math A Regents, Jan 2000: Sterling silver is an alloy of silver and copper in the ratio of 37:3. How much silver is in 600 g of sterling silver?

54. An estimate of the BTU/hr/°F difference needed is the area of the walls and ceiling of a room in ft^2. An air conditioner of how many BTU/hr is needed to cool a room $9' \times 12' \times 8'$ to $70°$ if the outside temperature is $85°$?

55. Cost capacity. The cost of many types of equipment varies as the $\frac{2}{3}$ power of the capacity. If an 8000BTU air conditioner cost \$180, what should we expect to pay for a 12000BTU air conditioner with similar features?

56. Grapefruits are nearly spherical. Which is a better buy: Those with a $5''$ circumference at three for a dollar or those with a $6''$ circumference at two for a dollar? What percent more do you get for your money?

57. The cooking time of a turkey varies as the $\frac{2}{3}$ power of the weight. If a 10lb turkey takes 4.1hr, how long does an 18lb turkey take?

Hints 20. Assume the can costs \$1. **45.** The constant is *not* 3131 often given.

1.5 RATIONAL EXPONENTS AND RADICALS

Manipulating exponents is needed for solving equations and calculating derivatives and integrals.

1. MONOMIALS

Order of Operations: 1. inside parentheses (from the inside) 2. powers (from top to bottom) 3. multiplication, division, negation (from left to right) 4. addition, subtraction (from left to right). (1)

Excel, BASIC and graphics calculators evaluate powers from left to right so you must use parentheses.

Example 1 Evaluate (a) $3 + 4 \cdot 5^2$ (b) $(3 + 4)5^2$ (c) -4^{2^3}
Solution (a) $3 + 4 \cdot 5^2 = 3 + 4 \cdot 25 = 3 + 100 = 103$

(b) $(3 + 4)5^2 = 7 \cdot 5^2 = 7 \cdot 25 = 175$

(c) $-4^{2^3} = -4^8 = -65536$ ∎

Writing Don't say "squared" or "to the power"; say "square of" or "power of". "Minus five squared" can mean $-5^2 = -25$ or $(-5)^2 = 25$. Say "minus square of five" or "square of minus five" respectively.

Practice 1 Use "product of" and "quotient of" to express in English (a) $\pi r^2/4$ (b) $\pi(r/4)^2$ (c) $\pi r/4^2$

Product of Negatives: $(-)(-) = +$, (Property 1.1.11), $(-)(-)(-) = -$, $(-)(-)(-)(-) = +$, etc. That is, a product of an even number of negatives is positive, while the product of an odd number of negatives is negative. It follows that no real number is the square root or even root of a negative number. (3)

Exponents In a^x, a is the **base** and x is the **exponent**. n is a positive integer.

0 If $a \neq 0$, $a^0 = 1$. $0^x = 0$ if $x > 0$. 0^0 is not defined.

a^n $a^n = a \cdot a \cdots a$ with n factors, for any a and $a^{-n} = 1/a^n$ if $a \neq 0$.

$(-1)^n = 1$ if n is even and $(-1)^n = -1$ if n is odd.

$a^{1/n}$ If n is odd $a^{1/n} = \sqrt[n]{a}$ is the unique real root of $x^n = a$. Thus $(\sqrt[n]{a})^n = a$ and $\sqrt[n]{b^n} = b$. If n is even and $a \geq 0$, $a^{1/n} = \sqrt[n]{a}$ is the positive root of $x^n = a$, so $(\sqrt[n]{a})^n = a$, $a \geq 0$ and $\sqrt[n]{b^n} = |b|$.

$a^{m/n}$ $= (a^{1/n})^m = (a^m)^{1/n}$ when m/n is in lowest terms and $a^{-m/n} = 1/a^{m/n}$, where $a \geq 0$ if n is even.

$a\hat{\ }b\hat{\ }c$ is not defined; specify $(a\hat{\ }b)\hat{\ }c$ or $a\hat{\ }(b\hat{\ }c)$.

Practice 3 Solve $a^b = 1$.

Radical The symbol $\sqrt[n]{a}$; n is the **index**. If $n = 2$, n is omitted (square root): $\sqrt{a} = a^{1/2}$. If $n = 3$ we have a cube root: $\sqrt[3]{a} = a^{1/3}$. (4)
$\sqrt{a+b} = \sqrt{(a+b)}$: the bar is a fence called a vinculum; see Example 19(b).

Practice 4 Write the cube root of $1 - x$ (a) using exponents (b) using radicals.

Any equation in powers is equivalent to one in roots. Memorize the table of powers and roots: (5)

Power	$2^2 = 4$	$3^2 = 9$	$4^2 = 16$	$5^2 = 25$	$6^2 = 36$	$7^2 = 49$	$8^2 = 64$	$9^2 = 81$	$10^2 = 100$	$11^2 = 121$
Root	$4^{1/2} = 2$	$9^{1/2} = 3$	$16^{1/2} = 4$	$25^{1/2} = 5$	$36^{1/2} = 6$	$49^{1/2} = 7$	$64^{1/2} = 8$	$81^{1/2} = 9$	$100^{1/2} = 10$	$121^{1/2} = 11$

Power	$2^3 = 8$	$3^3 = 27$	$4^3 = 64$	$5^3 = 125$	$2^4 = 16$	$3^4 = 81$	$2^5 = 32$	$2^6 = 64$	$2^7 = 128$
Root	$8^{1/3} = 2$	$27^{1/3} = 3$	$64^{1/3} = 4$	$125^{1/3} = 5$	$16^{1/4} = 2$	$81^{1/4} = 3$	$32^{1/5} = 2$	$64^{1/6} = 2$	$128^{1/7} = 2$

Example 2 Evaluate (a) $27^{-1/3}$, (b) $(-27)^{-1/3}$, (c) $(-27)^{-2/3}$

Solution (a) $27^{-1/3} = \dfrac{1}{27^{1/3}} = \dfrac{1}{\sqrt[3]{27}} = \dfrac{1}{3}$

(b) $(-27)^{-1/3} = \dfrac{1}{\sqrt[3]{-27}} = -\dfrac{1}{3}$

(c) $(-27)^{-2/3} = \dfrac{1}{(\sqrt[3]{-27})^2} = \dfrac{1}{(-3)^2} = \dfrac{1}{9}$

Analysis It is true that $a^{m/n} = (a^m)^{1/n}$ so there are 6 possible orders to evaluate (c). The parts of the exponent we chose were: sign, denominator (root), numerator (power). Doing the power first gives bigger numbers:
$$(-27)^{-2/3} = ((-27)^2)^{-1/3} = (729)^{-1/3} = (\sqrt[3]{729})^{-1} = 9^{-1} = \tfrac{1}{9}$$ ∎

Example 3 Evaluate $x = (-64)^{8/6}$.

Solution Bad: $(-64)^{8/6} = [(-64)^{1/6}]^8$ doesn't exist.

Good: $(-64)^{8/6} = (-64)^{4/3} = [(-64)^{1/3}]^4 = (-4)^4 = 256$ ∎

Exponent Laws	Example	English	(6)
$a^x \cdot a^y = a^{x+y}$	$2^3 \cdot 2^{-5} = 2^{-2}$	To multiply expressions with the same base, keep the base and add exponents.	
$a^x/a^y = a^{x-y}$	$2^3/2^{-5} = 2^8$	To divide expressions with the same base, keep the base and subtract exponents.	
$1/a^y = a^{-y}$	$1/2^{-5} = 2^5$	To move a factor between numerator and denominator, negate its exponent.	
$(a^x)^y = a^{xy}$	$(2^3)^{-5} = 2^{-15}$	To raise a power to a power, multiply the exponents.	
$(ab)^x = a^x b^x$	$(2z)^3 = 2^3 z^3 = 8z^3$	To raise a product to a power, raise each factor to the power.	
$(a/b)^x = a^x/b^x$	$(2/z)^3 = 2^3/z^3 = 8/z^3$	To raise a quotient to a power, raise each factor to the power.	
$\sqrt[n]{ab} = \sqrt[n]{a}\sqrt[n]{b}$	$\sqrt{9z^2} = \sqrt{9}\sqrt{z^2} = 3|z|$	Root of a product = product of roots	
$\sqrt[n]{a/b} = \sqrt[n]{a}/\sqrt[n]{b}$	$\sqrt[3]{27/8} = \sqrt[3]{27}/\sqrt[3]{8} = \tfrac{3}{2}$	Root of a quotient = quotient of roots	

Proof (Part) Let $x = m/q$, $y = n/q$, m, n, q integers. Then $a^{m/q} = b$ means $a^m = b^q$ and $a^{n/q} = c$ means $a^n = c^q$. Thus $(bc)^q = b^q c^q = a^m a^n = a^{m+n}$ and so $a^x a^y = a^{m/q} a^{n/q} = bc = a^{(m+n)/q} = a^{x+y}$ ∎

Example 4 Simplify $(-1)(-1)^2 \cdots (-1)^n$.
Solution To multiply expressions with base -1 we add the exponents $1 + 2 + \cdots + n = \tfrac{1}{2}n(n+1)$. Because the exponent is complex, we write $(-1)^{[\tfrac{1}{2}n(n+1)]}$.

Simplify Numbers An expression involving products and quotients of roots or rational exponents of rational numbers is **simple** if it is the product of a rational number and the smallest possible root of the smallest possible integer. To simplify:
(1) split off the integer part of the exponent,
(2) factor nth powers and remove from the radical,
(3) multiply by a unit fraction to make the denominator a power and remove from radical
(4) multiply by a unit fraction.
Expressions can be added or subtracted if their simplified radicals are equal.

Practice 5 Factor 2500 completely.

Example 5 Simplify (a) $x = \tfrac{4}{3}8^{-6/5}$ (b) $\dfrac{28}{\sqrt{12}}$ (c) $\sqrt[3]{2500}$ (d) $\sqrt[5]{2500}$ (e) $\dfrac{\sqrt{3}}{\sqrt[3]{4}}$.

Solution $\overset{1}{=}$ shows step a. (a) $x = \tfrac{4}{3}(2^3)^{-6/5} = \tfrac{4}{3}2^{-18/5} \overset{1}{=} \tfrac{4}{3}2^{-20/5}2^{2/5} = \tfrac{4}{3}\cdot\tfrac{1}{16}2^{2/5} = \tfrac{1}{12}2^{2/5}$

(b) $\dfrac{28}{\sqrt{12}} \overset{3}{=} \dfrac{28}{\sqrt{4\cdot3}}\cdot\dfrac{\sqrt{3}}{\sqrt{3}} = \dfrac{28\sqrt{3}}{2\cdot3} = \tfrac{14}{3}\sqrt{3}$ (c) $\sqrt[3]{5^4\cdot2^2} \overset{2}{=} \sqrt[3]{5^3\cdot5\cdot2^2} = 5\sqrt[3]{20}$

(d) $\sqrt[5]{2500}$ is simple because no power in $2500 = 5^4\cdot2^2$ is at least 5.

(e) $\dfrac{\sqrt{3}}{\sqrt[3]{4}} \dfrac{3}{2^{2/3}} \cdot \dfrac{3^{1/2}}{2^{1/3}} \cdot \dfrac{2^{1/3}}{2^{1/3}} = \frac{1}{2}3^{1/2}2^{1/3} = \frac{1}{2}3^{3/6}2^{2/6} = \frac{1}{2}\sqrt[6]{3^3 2^2} = \frac{1}{2}\sqrt[6]{108}$ ∎

Note $\dfrac{1}{\sqrt{2}} = \dfrac{1}{\sqrt{2}} \cdot \dfrac{\sqrt{2}}{\sqrt{2}} = \dfrac{\sqrt{2}}{2}$ but do *not* write $\dfrac{1}{\sqrt{\pi}}$ as $\dfrac{\sqrt{\pi}}{\pi}$ or $\dfrac{1}{\sqrt{x}}$ as $\dfrac{\sqrt{x}}{x}$; π and x are not integers.

Example 6 Simplify $y = 2\sqrt{75} + 10\sqrt{\frac{1}{12}}$.

Solution Because $12 = 2^2 \cdot 3$, we use $3/3$ in step 4.

$$y = 2\sqrt{25 \cdot 3} + \sqrt{\frac{1}{12} \cdot \frac{3}{3}} = 2\sqrt{25}\sqrt{3} + 10\frac{\sqrt{3}}{\sqrt{36}} = 2 \cdot 5\sqrt{3} + 10 \cdot \frac{1}{6}\sqrt{3} = \left(10 + \frac{5}{3}\right)\sqrt{3} = \frac{35}{3}\sqrt{3}$$

Simplify Expressions Use the rules from left to right to eliminate parentheses and repeated bases. Change radicals to exponents to combine.

Restrictions (1) $a/0$ and (2) 0^n if $n \leq 0$, are not defined; (3) $x^{m/n}$ if x is negative and n is even, is not real.

Warning If the rules say A→B, watch for differences for 0 and negative values of x.

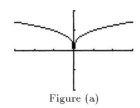

Figure (a)

value of x	value of A	value of B	Remedy	See
$x = 0$	not defined	defined	Add: $x \neq 0$	Example 7
$x = 0$	defined	not defined	none: can't simplify	Example 9
$x < 0$	not defined	defined	Add: $x > 0$ or $x \geq 0$	Example 8(b)
$x < 0$	doesn't change sign	changes sign	Use absolute value	Example 8(a)

Example 7 Simplify $\sqrt[3]{x}\sqrt[4]{x}/\sqrt{x}$.

Solution $\dfrac{\sqrt[3]{x}\sqrt[4]{x}}{\sqrt{x}} = \dfrac{x^{1/3}x^{1/4}}{x^{1/2}} = x^{\frac{1}{3}+\frac{1}{4}-\frac{1}{2}} = x^{\frac{4}{12}+\frac{3}{12}-\frac{6}{12}} = x^{1/12}$, $x \neq 0$

Analysis We changed radicals to exponents. We multiplied and divided like bases by adding and subtracting exponents. Because the original is not defined at 0 and the final is, we added the restriction. ∎

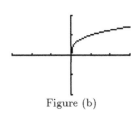

Figure (b)

Practice 6 Simplify $\sqrt{5x}\sqrt{10x}$.

Example 8 Simplify (a) $y = (x^{2/3})^{1/2}$ (b) $z = (x^{1/2})^{2/3}$ (c) Graph y, z, and $w = x^{1/3}$ in separate $[-3, 3] \times [-2, 2]$ windows.
Solution (a) y is defined for all numbers, is always positive: $y = |x|^{2/3 \cdot 1/2} = |x|^{1/3}$
(b) z is defined for positive numbers and 0. $z = x^{1/2 \cdot 2/3} = x^{1/3}$, $x \geq 0$ (c) w is negative for negative numbers; positive for positive numbers. See Figures (a), (b) and (c). ∎

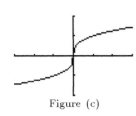

Figure (c)

Practice 7 How do $y' = (x^{-2/3})^{-1/2}$, $z' = (x^{-1/2})^{-2/3}$, $w' = (x^{-1})^{-1/3}$ differ from y, z, w in Example 8?

Example 9 Simplify (a) $\sqrt{x^2 - x^4}$ (b) $\sqrt{x^4 - x^2}$

Solution (a) $\sqrt{x^2(1 - x^2)} = |x|\sqrt{1 - x^2}$

(b) $\sqrt{x^2(x^2 - 1)} \neq |x|\sqrt{x^2 - 1}$: the left member is defined at 0, the right member is not. ∎

Practice 8 Classify as conditional, identity or unconditionally true:
(a) $\sqrt{x^2} = x$ (b) $\sqrt{x^3} = x\sqrt{x}$ (c) $\sqrt{x^4} = x^2$ (d) $\sqrt{x^5} = x^2\sqrt{x}$ (e) $\sqrt{x^6} = x^3$

Two Protocols At times we want only positive exponents; at times we use negative exponents to avoid division.

Example 10 Simplify $\dfrac{x^2 y^{-3}}{z^4 w^{-5}}$ (a) using only positive exponents and (b) without using division.

Solution (a) Move negative exponents, get $\dfrac{x^2 w^5}{y^3 z^4}$, $w \neq 0$.

(b) Move the denominator, get $x^2 y^{-3} z^{-4} w^5$, $w \neq 0$. ∎

Example 11 Simplify $\left(\dfrac{x^{-4}}{4y^6}\right)^{-1/2}$.

Analysis We (1) raise a quotient to a power, (2) raise a power to a power, (3) move factors, (4) use the table.

Solution $\left(\dfrac{x^{-4}}{4y^6}\right)^{-1/2} = \dfrac{(x^{-4})^{-1/2}}{(4y^6)^{-1/2}} = \dfrac{x^2}{4^{-1/2}|y|^{-3}} = 4^{1/2}x^2|y|^3 = 2x^2|y|^3,\ x \neq 0,\ y \neq 0$ ∎

Example 12 Simplify $xy\sqrt{y/x}$ by eliminating repeated variables. Explain why $x^{1/2}y^{3/2}$ is not correct.

Solution $\sqrt{y/x}$ is defined when x and y have the same sign so $xy > 0$. Hence

$$xy\sqrt{y/x} = \sqrt{x^2y^2 \cdot y/x} = \sqrt{xy^3},\ x \neq 0$$

$x^{1/2}y^{3/2}$ is defined only if both x and y are positive. ∎

Single-Power Equations Let u be an expression in x. To solve $u^n = a$, use the definition of $a^{1/n}$. To solve $u^{n/m} = a$, use either $(u^n)^{1/m} = a$ or $(u^{1/m})^n = a$. If n is even there will be two solutions. (8)

Example 13 Solve the odd-power equation for x: (a) $x^3 + 8 = 0$ (b) $(x+1)^{3/2} - 64 = 0$
Solution (a) $x^3 = -8 \Rightarrow x = (-8)^{1/3} = -2$
(b) $(x+1)^{3/2} = 64 \Rightarrow x + 1 = 64^{2/3} = 16,\ x = 15$ ∎

Example 14 Solve the even-power equation for x:
(a) $\sqrt{x^2+1} = 5$ (b) $(x-3)^{2/3} = 16$ (c) $x^6 - 8 = 0$

Solution (a) $\sqrt{x^2+1} = 5 \Rightarrow x^2 + 1 = 5^2 = 25,\ x^2 = 24,\ x = \pm\sqrt{24} = \pm\sqrt{4\cdot 6} = \pm 2\sqrt{6}$

(b) $[(x-3)^{1/3}]^2 = 16 \Rightarrow (x-3)^{1/3} = \pm\sqrt{16} = \pm 4,\ x - 3 = (\pm 4)^3 = \pm 64,$

$x = 64 + 3 = 67$ or $x = -64 + 3 = -61$

(c) $x^6 = 8,\ (x^2)^3 = 2^3,\ x^2 = 2,\ x = \pm\sqrt{2}$ ∎

Warning Don't distribute powers or roots over sums or differences:

$(x+1)^{3/2} \neq x^{3/2} + 1,\ \sqrt{x^2+1} \neq x + 1,\ (x-3)^{1/3} \neq x^{1/3} - 3^{1/3}$

Practice 9 Which step in the following solution is wrong: (a) $x - x^2 = 1$ (b) $x \neq 0$ so $1 - x = 1/x$ (c) $x + 1/x = 1$ (d) $x + 1/x = x - x^2$ (e) $1/x = -x^2$ (f) $x^3 = -1$ (g) $x = -1$

Technology works with a finite subset of the real numbers and may not obey the order of operations or even basic arithmetic. (2)
(a) $3 + 4*5$ in Windows Calculator, Standard view gives $(3+4)*5 = 35$. (Scientific view gives 23.)

(b) In Excel, TI-83, 4^3^2 gives $(4^3)^2 = 4096$. Scientific Workplace won't evaluate. Derive and Google give $4^{(3^2)} = 262144$.

(c) In Excel, $=-5^2$ gives $(-5)^2 = 25$.

(d) In Excel, $=.5-.4-.1=0$ gives FALSE. On a TI-83, $3(1/3) - .99 - .01=0$ gives FALSE, but if two numbers a and b differ by less than a unit in the 13th digit, $a - b$ is set to 0.

(e) In Excel and TI-83, $=1+1E-15=1$ and $=1E15+1=1E15$ give TRUE.

(f) In Excel, $=0^0$ gives #NUM!; on a TI-83 0^0 gives ERR: DOMAIN, but in Windows Scientific Calculator $0\boxed{y^x}0 = 1$ and in Google 0^0 gives 1.
In the sequence $.01^{1/2}$, $.001^{1/3}$, $.0001^{1/4}$, ..., the base and exponent approach 0, but each term and the limit is .1.

Practice 10 On your calculator find the smallest integer n such that $1 \times 10^n + 1 - 1 \times 10^n$ gives 0.

2. BINOMIALS AND TRINOMIALS

Distributive $a(b + c + \cdots) = ab + ac + \cdots$

Basic Learn the first three rules in English. (9)

(a) $(x + y)(x - y) = x^2 - y^2$: The product of the sum and difference of the same two numbers is the square of the first minus the square of the second.

(b) $(x + y)^2 = x^2 + 2xy + y^2$ and $(x - y)^2 = x^2 - 2xy + y^2$: The square of a binomial is the square of the first term plus twice the product plus square of the second term.

(c) $(x + y + z)^2 = x^2 + y^2 + z^2 + 2xy + 2xz + 2yz$: The square of a sum is the sum of the squares plus the sum of twice each product of two terms.

(d) $(x + y)^3 = x^3 + 3x^2y + 3xy^2 + y^3$ and $(x - y)^3 = x^3 - 3x^2y + 3xy^2 - y^3$

Example 15 Simplify (a) $\sqrt{2}(\sqrt{6} + \sqrt{18})$ (b) $(3 - \sqrt{7})^2$ (c) $(2\sqrt{a} + \sqrt{3})(2\sqrt{a} - \sqrt{3})$
(d) $(\sqrt{2} + \sqrt{5})^3$

Solution (a) $\sqrt{2}(\sqrt{6} + \sqrt{18}) = \sqrt{2}\sqrt{6} + \sqrt{2}\sqrt{18} = \sqrt{12} + \sqrt{36} = \sqrt{4 \cdot 3} + 6 = 2\sqrt{3} + 6$

(b) $(3 - \sqrt{7})^2 = 3^2 - 2 \cdot 3\sqrt{7} + (\sqrt{7})^2 = 9 - 6\sqrt{7} + 7 = 16 - 6\sqrt{7}$

(c) $(2\sqrt{a} + \sqrt{3})(2\sqrt{a} - \sqrt{3}) = (2\sqrt{a})^2 - (\sqrt{3})^2 = 4a - 3$, $a \geq 0$

(d) Because $(\sqrt{2})^3 = (\sqrt{2})^2\sqrt{2} = 2\sqrt{2}$, and $(\sqrt{3})^3 = 3\sqrt{3}$, then $(\sqrt{2} + \sqrt{5})^3 =$
$(\sqrt{2})^3 + 3(\sqrt{2})^2\sqrt{3} + 3\sqrt{2}(\sqrt{3})^2 + (\sqrt{3})^3 = 2\sqrt{2} + 3 \cdot 2\sqrt{3} + 3\sqrt{2}(3) + 3\sqrt{3} = 11\sqrt{2} + 9\sqrt{3}$

Practice 11 Express the radical as a power and distribute: $\sqrt{u}(u^2 + u)$.

Like Terms involve the same variables raised to the same powers. To combine (add or subtract) like terms, we combine their numerical coefficients; unlike terms cannot be combined

Example 16 Distribute and combine like terms: $y = x^{-1/3}(x^3 - 2x^2) + x^{2/3}(x^2 + 3x + 4)$

Solution $y = x^{-1/3}x^3 - 2x^{-1/3}x^2 + x^{2/3}x^2 + 3x^{2/3}x + 4x^{2/3}$

$= x^{-1/3}x^{9/3} + 2x^{-1/3}x^{6/3} + x^{2/3}x^{6/3} + 3x^{2/3}x^{3/3} + 4x^{2/3}$

$= x^{8/3} + 2x^{5/3} + x^{8/3} + 3x^{5/3} + 4x^{2/3} = 2x^{8/3} + 5x^{5/3} + 4x^{2/3}$, $x \neq 0$ ∎

Conjugate of a binomial containing a square root: change the sign of one term. Use (11) or (12) for the conjugate of a binomial with a cube root.

$x^2 - y^2 = (x + y)(x - y)$ then $(\sqrt{a} - \sqrt{b})(\sqrt{a} + \sqrt{b}) = a - b$ (10)

$x^3 - y^3 = (x - y)(x^2 + xy + y^2)$ then $(a^{1/3} - b^{1/3})(a^{2/3} + a^{1/3}b^{1/3} + b^{2/3}) = a - b$ (11)

$x^3 + y^3 = (x + y)(x^2 - xy + y^2)$ then $(a^{1/3} + b^{1/3})(a^{2/3} - a^{1/3}b^{1/3} + b^{2/3}) = a + b$ (12)

The product of a binomial and its conjugate is rational.

Rationalize a numerator or denominator by using the conjugate in a unit fraction.

Make a unit fraction to rationalize a numerator or denominator.

Example 17 Rationalize the denominator: $z = \dfrac{4}{\sqrt{5} + 3\sqrt{2}}$.

Analysis $\sqrt{5} + 3\sqrt{2} = 3\sqrt{2} + \sqrt{5}$ has two conjugates: $\sqrt{5} - 3\sqrt{2}$ and $3\sqrt{2} - \sqrt{5}$; we will use the first.

Solution $z = \dfrac{4}{\sqrt{5} + 3\sqrt{2}} \cdot \dfrac{\sqrt{5} - 3\sqrt{2}}{\sqrt{5} - 3\sqrt{2}} = \dfrac{4(\sqrt{5} - 3\sqrt{2})}{(\sqrt{5})^2 - (3\sqrt{2})^2} = \dfrac{4\sqrt{5} - 12\sqrt{2}}{5 - 9(2)} = \dfrac{4\sqrt{5} - 12\sqrt{2}}{-13}$

$= \frac{12}{13}\sqrt{2} - \frac{4}{13}\sqrt{5}$ ∎

Practice 12 Simplify $\dfrac{4 - \sqrt{3}}{4 + \sqrt{3}}$.

Example 18 Solve for x: (a) $\dfrac{3}{(x+1)^2} = \dfrac{1}{(x-1)^2}$ (b) $\dfrac{3}{(x+1)^3} = \dfrac{1}{(x-1)^3}$

Analysis Multiply by $(x+1)^2$ or $(x+1)^3$ to express each as a single-power equation.

Solution (a) $\left(\dfrac{x+1}{x-1}\right)^2 = 3$. One root is $\dfrac{x+1}{x-1} = \sqrt{3}$, $x+1 = \sqrt{3}x - \sqrt{3}$,

$(\sqrt{3}-1)x = \sqrt{3}+1$, $x = \dfrac{\sqrt{3}+1}{\sqrt{3}-1} \cdot \dfrac{\sqrt{3}+1}{\sqrt{3}+1} = \dfrac{3+2\sqrt{3}+1}{3-1} = 2 + \sqrt{3}$. The other is $2 - \sqrt{3}$.

(b) $\left(\dfrac{x+1}{x-1}\right)^3 = 3$ so $\dfrac{x+1}{x-1} = 3^{1/3}$, $x+1 = 3^{1/3}x - 3^{1/3}$, $(3^{1/3}-1)x = 3^{1/3}+1$

$x = \dfrac{3^{1/3}+1}{3^{1/3}-1} \cdot \dfrac{3^{2/3}+3^{1/3}+1}{3^{2/3}+3^{1/3}+1} = \dfrac{3+2\cdot3^{2/3}+2\cdot3^{1/3}+1}{3-1} = 3^{2/3} + 3^{1/3} + 2$ ∎

Nested Radical A root of a binomial surd. In a product or quotient, absorb a binomial surd into the nested radical.

Example 19 Simplify $\tan 36° = \dfrac{\sin 36°}{\cos 36°} = \dfrac{\frac{1}{4}\sqrt{10-2\sqrt{5}}}{\frac{1}{4}(\sqrt{5}+1)}$.

Analysis After canceling $\frac{1}{4}$, square the denominator to get it inside the radical, then multiply by the conjugate.

Solution
$$\tan 36° = \dfrac{\sqrt{10-2\sqrt{5}}}{\sqrt{(\sqrt{5}+1)^2}} = \sqrt{\dfrac{10-2\sqrt{5}}{6+2\sqrt{5}}} = \sqrt{\dfrac{5-\sqrt{5}}{3+\sqrt{5}} \cdot \dfrac{3-\sqrt{5}}{3-\sqrt{5}}} = \sqrt{\dfrac{20-8\sqrt{5}}{4}} = \sqrt{5-2\sqrt{5}}$$ ∎

Unnesting a Nested Radical (Euclid X.91) Because $(\sqrt{a}+\sqrt{b})^2 = a+b+2\sqrt{ab}$, then $\sqrt{c+2\sqrt{d}} = \sqrt{a}+\sqrt{b}$ if we can find a and b such that $a+b=c$ and $ab=d$. (Like factoring $x^2 + cx + d$.) (14)

Example 20 Unnest the nested radical (a) $R = \sqrt{10+2\sqrt{21}}$ (b) $S = \sqrt{8-\sqrt{60}}$

(c) $T = \sqrt{x+3-4\sqrt{x-1}}$

Solution (a) We seek two integers whose sum is 10 and whose product is 21: 3 and 7. Then $R = \sqrt{3}+\sqrt{7}$.

(b) Because $\sqrt{60} = \sqrt{4\cdot15} = 2\sqrt{15}$, $S = \sqrt{8-2\sqrt{15}}$. Find two integers whose sum is 8 and whose product is 15: 3 and 5. Then $S = \left|\sqrt{3}-\sqrt{5}\right| = \sqrt{5}-\sqrt{3}$.

(c) Because $4 = 2\sqrt{4}$ and $4+(x-1) = x+3$, then

$$T = \sqrt{x+3-2\sqrt{4(x-1)}} = \sqrt{(2-\sqrt{x-1})^2} = \left|2-\sqrt{x-1}\right|$$ ∎

Practice 13 Simplify $Q = \sqrt{\sqrt{19}+\sqrt{3}} + \sqrt{\sqrt{19}-\sqrt{3}}$ to a single nested radical by squaring and taking the square root.

Practice Answers 1. (a) pi times the quotient of the square of r and 4 (b) pi times the square of the quotient of r and 4 (c) pi times the quotient of r and the square of 4.

3. If $a^b = 1$ then either $b = 0$ and $a \neq 0$, or $a = 1$ and any b, or $a = -1$ and b is an even integer

4. (a) $(1-x)^{1/3}$ (b) $\sqrt[3]{1-x}$ **5.** $2500 = 25 \times 10 \times 10 = 5\times5\times5\times2\times5\times2 = 5^4 \times 2^2$

6. $\sqrt{5x}\sqrt{10x} = \sqrt{50x^2} = \sqrt{25x^2\cdot2} = 5x\sqrt{2}$, $x \geq 0$

7. They are not defined at 0. On a TI-83, ⟦FORMAT⟧AxesOff to see missing pixel.

8. (a) and (e) are true if $x \geq 0$, (b) and (d) are identities, (c) is unconditionally true

9. (d) increases the degree from 2 to 3, introducing an extraneous root.

10. TI-83: $n = 14$ **11.** $\sqrt{u}(u^2 + u) = u^{1/2}(u^2 + u) = u^{1/2}u^{4/2} + u^{1/2}u^{2/2} = u^{5/2} + u^{3/2}$

12. $\dfrac{4-\sqrt{3}}{4+\sqrt{3}} \cdot \dfrac{4-\sqrt{3}}{4-\sqrt{3}} = \dfrac{16-8\sqrt{3}+3}{16-3} = \dfrac{19-8\sqrt{3}}{13} = \frac{19}{13} - \frac{8}{13}\sqrt{3}$

13. $Q^2 = (\sqrt{19}+\sqrt{3}) + 2\sqrt{19-3} + (\sqrt{19}-\sqrt{3}) = 8 + 2\sqrt{19}$ so $Q = \sqrt{8+2\sqrt{19}}$.

Problems 1.5 Problems with ^{h} have hints below; those with ^{T} use technology.

1. Which, if any, is true? (a) $\sqrt{2} + \sqrt{3} = \sqrt{5}$ (b) $\sqrt{2} + \sqrt{2} = \sqrt{8}$ (c) $\sqrt{a^2 + 9} = a + 3$ (d) $a^m \cdot a^n = a^{mn}$

2. Evaluate where possible: (a) $\frac{6}{0}$ (b) $\frac{0}{6}$ (c) $\frac{0}{0}$ (d) 0^0

3. Help the kid in the Mars Kudos granola bar ad: $4 \times 4 \div 8 + 9 + 1 \div 2 \times 3 - 4 + 6 =$

In Problems 4-9, evaluate the expression as a rational number.

4. $\sqrt{1\frac{9}{16}}$

5. $5 - 2 \cdot 3^2$

6. $16^{-3/4}$

7. $\left(\frac{1}{8}\right)^{1/3}$

8. $\left(-\frac{1}{125}\right)^{2/3}$

9. $(.01)^{-5/2}$

In Problems 10-17, simplify the number.

10. $\sqrt[3]{144}$

11. $\left(\frac{3}{20}\right)^{3/2}$

12. $2\sqrt{27} - 4\sqrt{12}$

13. $8\sqrt{3} - 6\sqrt{\frac{1}{3}}$

14. $2\sqrt{5} + 3\sqrt{20}$

15. $10\sqrt{18} + 20\sqrt{\frac{1}{2}}$

16. $\dfrac{30}{\sqrt{20}}$

17. $\sqrt{112} - \sqrt{63} + \dfrac{224}{\sqrt{28}}$

18. Simplify by eliminating repeated variables: (a) $x^2/|x|$ (b) $x^4/|x|$

19. Simplify without division or negative exponents; x will still appear twice: $x^5/\sqrt{x^6}$

20. Express using a radical: (a) $v^{3/2}$ (b) $3^{2/5}$ (c) $3^{1/2}p^{1/2}d^{-1/2}$

21. State if each equation is unconditional; if not, give a value of x where the equation is false.
(a) $|3 + x| = 3 + |x|$ (b) $|3x| = 3|x|$ (c) $|x^3| = |x|^3$ (d) $|x^{1/4}| = |x|^{1/4}$

In Problems 22 and 23, if any two are equal say which; otherwise say all different.

22. (a) $(x^2)^{3/2}$ (b) $(x^{3/2})^2$ (c) x^3 (d) $1/x^{-3}$

23. (a) x (b) $(\sqrt{x})^2$ (c) $\sqrt{x^2}$ (d) $\sqrt[3]{x^3}$

In Problems 24 and 25, simplify. Be sure to state eliminated restrictions.

24. $\sqrt{a\sqrt[3]{a}}$

25. $(8x\sqrt{x})^{2/3}$

In Problems 26–33, simplify (a) without negative exponents and (b) without division. State eliminated restrictions.

26. $(3a^2b^{-3})(5a^4b^6)$

27. $\dfrac{36x^4y^3z^2}{-12x^6yz^{-1}}$

28. $(4x^2y^{-3})^{-2}$

29. $(2a^3b)^{-4}(8a/b)^3$

30. $\dfrac{(2x^2)^3(3y^4)^2}{(5xy)^3(x^2y^2)^5}$

31. $(x^{-3/2}\sqrt{y})^2$

32. $\left(\dfrac{x^{4/3}y^{-1/2}}{x^{2/3}y^{-3/2}}\right)^2$

33. $(4a^2b^4)^{1/2}(8a^3b^2)^{1/3}$

In Problems 34 and 35, distribute and collect like terms.

34. $x^{-1/2}(x^3 + 5) + (2x^{1/2} + 1)3x^2$

35. $5x^{1/3}(4x^3 - 7) + 3x^{-2/3}(x^4 - 7x)$

36. (a) Express $\sqrt{\sqrt{\sqrt{x}}}$ with exponents. (b) $3^{1/64}$ can be evaluated on a calculator with no $\boxed{y^x}$ key by pressing 3 and $\boxed{\sqrt{}}$ several times. How many times?

In Problems 37-45, solve the single-power equation for x.

37. $x^2 - \frac{4}{9} = 0$

38. $(2x + 5)^2 = 7$

39. $(3x - 7)^3 + 8 = 0$

40. $x^4 - 81 = 0$

41. $(x - 4)^{-1/3} = 2$

42. $26 - x^{2/3} = 1$

43. $-\dfrac{1076}{x^3} + \dfrac{0.1123}{\sqrt{x}} = 0$ (to 4 digits)

44. $\dfrac{R^3}{x^2} = \dfrac{r^3}{(a - x)^2}$

45. $y = \left(1 + \dfrac{x}{m - x/2}\right)^m$

46. $\sqrt{\frac{2}{3}x + \frac{1}{3}} = 0$

Problems 47 and 48 deal with relativity. An object of rest mass m_0 is moving at speed v relative to an observer. c is the speed of light, the same to all observers.

47. The mass $m = m_0/\sqrt{1 - v^2/c^2}$. How fast must an object travel to triple its mass? Answer in terms of c.

48. The momentum is $p = m_0v/\sqrt{1 - v^2/c^2}$. Solve for v.

49. Determine which equation is an identity and give a counterexample for the other:

(a) $\sqrt{\frac{x-3}{5-x}}(5-x) = \sqrt{(x-3)(5-x)}$ (b) $\sqrt{\frac{x-3}{x-5}}(x-5) = \sqrt{(x-3)(x-5)}$

51. These expressions agree when they exist; which is different? (a) $|x|\sqrt{x^2-1}$ (b) $x^2\sqrt{1-1/x^2}$ (c) $\sqrt{x^4-x^2}$

In Problems 52-60, simplify the binomial surds.

52. $(\sqrt{6}+\sqrt{3})(\sqrt{6}-2\sqrt{3})$ **53.** $(2^{1/3}+1)^3(2^{1/3}-1)$ **54.** $\frac{1}{2}(\sqrt{10}-2)^2$

55. $\dfrac{1}{3+\sqrt{2}}$ **56.** $\dfrac{4}{\sqrt{5}+\sqrt{3}}$ **57.** $\dfrac{5-3\sqrt{2}}{3+4\sqrt{2}}$

58^h $\dfrac{1}{1+\sqrt{2}}+\dfrac{1}{\sqrt{2}+\sqrt{3}}+\cdots+\dfrac{1}{\sqrt{15}+\sqrt{16}}$ **59.** $\dfrac{5+\sqrt{5}}{\sqrt{10-2\sqrt{5}}}$ **60^h** $\dfrac{4}{1+\sqrt{2}+\sqrt{3}}$

61^T The three Excel formulas for $(-4096)^{903/1011}$ are mathematically equivalent. Explain why two give a #NUM! error; give the value of the third: (a)$=-4096\char`^(903/1011)$ (b)$=(-4096\char`^903)\char`^(1/1011)$ (c)$=(-4096\char`^(1/1011))\char`^903$

Problem 65

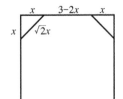

x $3-2x$ x

x $\sqrt{2}x$

62. $\sin 22.5° = \frac{1}{2}\sqrt{2-\sqrt{2}}$. Simplify $\csc 22.5° = 1/\sin 22.5°$.

In Problems 63 and 64, solve for x and simplify. The coefficient will be a binomial surd.

63. $2+\sqrt{3}x = 3+\sqrt{2}x$ **64.** $4-2x = \sqrt{3}x$

65. See the figure. If x ft is cut off each corner of a 3 ft square to get a regular octagon, then $3-2x = \sqrt{2}x$. Find x.

Problems 66-72 involve unnesting radicals.

66. Fix the error: $\sqrt{2+\sqrt{3}}+\sqrt{2-\sqrt{3}} = \sqrt{\frac{4+2\sqrt{3}}{2}}+\sqrt{\frac{4-2\sqrt{3}}{2}}$

$= \sqrt{\frac{1+2\sqrt{3}+3}{2}}+\sqrt{\frac{1-2\sqrt{3}+3}{2}} = \sqrt{\frac{(1+\sqrt{3})^2}{2}}+\sqrt{\frac{(1-\sqrt{3})^2}{2}} = \frac{1+\sqrt{3}}{\sqrt{2}}+\frac{1-\sqrt{3}}{\sqrt{2}} = \frac{2}{\sqrt{2}} = \sqrt{2}$

67. Math Mag 55:1(1982)47-48 uses $\sqrt{(9-4\sqrt{2})/7}$ as a coordinate to show how to construct a 7-gon of equal lengths of pipe and right-angle elbows. Unnest.

68. Unnest (a) $\sqrt{10+\sqrt{84}}$ (b) $\sqrt{x+\sqrt{x^2-1}}$

69. $\sin 15° = \frac{1}{4}(\sqrt{6}-\sqrt{2})$. Find and unnest $\cos 15° = \sqrt{1-\sin^2 15°}$.

70. If s is a chord in a circle of radius r, the chord of half the arc is $\sqrt{2r^2 - r\sqrt{4r^2-s^2}}$. Unnest.

Problems 71 and 72 are based on Weisstein, *Concise Encyclopedia of Math*, 2.ed

71. Simplify the distance from the center to (a) a hexagonal face of a soccer ball $\frac{1}{2}\sqrt{\frac{3}{2}(7+3\sqrt{5})}$ (p.3082)

(b) a face of a truncated cube $\frac{1}{2}\sqrt{\frac{1}{3}(17+12\sqrt{2})}$.

72^h p.814, Eq.(3) solving a dodecahedron gives as a single nested radical $x = \sqrt{50+10\sqrt{5}}-\sqrt{25+10\sqrt{5}}$ incorrectly. Find the correct value.

73. If $a_1, a_2, a_3, \ldots$ is an arithmetic sequence with difference d, and $b > 0$, then $b^{a_1}, b^{a_2}, b^{a_3}, \ldots$ is a geometric sequence. (a) What is the ratio? (b) Find $b^{\cdot 2}+b^{\cdot 5}+\cdots+b^{3.7}$. (c) Find $b^{\cdot 2}b^{\cdot 5}\cdots b^{3.7}$.

74. Let a be the error in estimating A, where a/A is small. Estimate the relative error in $\sqrt{A}$.

75. The distance traveled by a falling object varies directly as the square of the time. (a) If an object falls 144 ft in 3 sec, how far will it fall in 10 sec? (b) An object falls off a 10-story building. If it takes 3 seconds for the last 5 stories, find the total time.

76. The flow of water Q ft^3/s with a crest height h ft through a V-shaped weir having a 90° angle is Q $= 2.5h^{5/2}$. How high is the crest if water flows at 300 ft^3/s?

77. When a diatomic gas expands without gaining or losing heat (adiabatically) then $pV^{1.4} = $ constant (for monatomic, the exponent is 1.67) (a) Use subscripts 1 and 2 to eliminate the constant, as in Example 1.4.27. (b) If 22 gal of nitrogen at 5000 psi is allowed to expand to 4 times the volume, find the new pressure.

Hints 56. Rationalize each term **58.** Consider $(1+\sqrt{2})+\sqrt{3}$. **72.** Simplify x^2.

1.6 POLYNOMIALS

1. MULTIPLICATION AND DIVISION

Combine Polynomials by combining their like terms. Polynomials are **identical** if like terms have the same coefficients. In this section, $P(x)$ and $P(x, y)$ will denote polynomial functions.

Example 1 Combine (a) $P = (2x^2 - 5x + 10) + (4x^2 + 3x - 5)$

(b) $Q = (5x^2y + 2xy^2 - 4y^3) - (-3x^2y + y^3 - 10)$

Solution (a) $P = (2x^2 + 4x^2) + (-5x + 3x) + (10 - 5) = (2 + 4)x^2 + (-5 + 3)x + 5$

$= 6x^2 - 2x + 5$

(b) $Q = (5x^2y + 3x^2y) + 2xy^2 + (-4y^3 + y^3) + 10$

$= (5 + 3)x^2y + 2xy^2 + (-4 + 1)y^3 + 10 = 8x^2y + 2xy^2 - 3y^3 + 10$ ∎

Multiplying by a Monomial Use distributive law. Supply power 1. Multiply coefficients. Add powers of like bases.

Example 2 Multiply $3xy^2(x^3 + 2y)$.

Solution $3xy^2(x^3 + 2y) = 3x^1y^2 \cdot x^3 + 3xy^2 \cdot 2y^1 = 3x^{1+3}y^2 + 6xy^{2+1} = 3x^4y^2 + 6xy^3$ ∎

Multiplying Sums PQ: Multiply each term of P by each term of Q:
$$(a + b)(x + y + z) = +\begin{matrix} ax + ay + az \\ bx + by + bz \end{matrix}, \text{ 6 terms.}$$

Fundamental Principle of Counting Consider a table. If there are m ways of choosing a row and n ways of choosing a column, there are mn ways of choosing an entry. The same for any sequence of choices. (1)

Multiplying Multinomials P and Q. Multiply each term of P by each term of Q and combine like terms. Polynomials may be organized by placing the results from each term of Q in its own row and aligning like powers in columns. The degree of PQ = degree of P + degree of Q.

Example 3 Multiply $(5x^3 + 4x^2 - x + 7)(x^2 - 3x + 4)$.

Solution
$$
\begin{array}{r}
5x^3 + 4x^2 - x + 7 \\
x^2 - 3x + 4 \\
\hline
20x^3 + 16x^2 - 4x + 28 \quad \leftarrow\text{from } 4 \\
-15x^4 - 12x^3 + 3x^2 - 21x \quad\quad \leftarrow\text{from } -3x \\
5x^5 + 4x^4 - x^3 + 7x^2 \quad\quad\quad \leftarrow\text{from } x^2 \\
\hline
5x^5 - 11x^4 + 7x^3 + 26x^2 - 25x + 28
\end{array}
$$
∎

Practice 1 (a) How many coefficient multiplications are needed in Example 3(b)? How many to multiply polynomials of degree m and n?

Coefficient Let $\{x^n \mid P(x)\}$ mean "coefficient of x^n in $P(x)$"; omit $P(x)$ if there is only one function. In particular, $\{1\}$ designates the constant term. Multiplication by a binomial can be done mentally: each power in the product can be obtained at most two ways.

Example 4 Multiply $P = (x^3 + 2x^2 - 4x + 1)(3x + 5)$.

Solution $\{x^4\} = 1 \cdot 3 = 3$, $\{x^3\} = 1 \cdot 5 + 2 \cdot 3 = 11$, $\{x^2\} = 2 \cdot 5 - 4 \cdot 3 = -2$,

$\{x\} = -4 \cdot 5 + 1 \cdot 3 = -17$ $\{1\} = 1 \cdot 5 = 5$ so $P = 3x^4 + 11x^3 - 2x^2 - 17x + 5$ ∎

FOIL statement of product of binomials $(a + b)(c + d)$
$= \text{First} + \text{Outer} + \text{Inner} + \text{Last} = ac + ad + bc + bd$

Squaring Do NOT use FOIL. Learn this rule in English: (2)
The square of a sum is the sum of the squares plus the sum of twice each cross-product.

$$(x+y)^2 = x^2 + 2xy + y^2$$
$$(x+y+z)^2 = x^2 + y^2 + z^2 + 2xy + 2xz + 2yz$$

Practice 2 Expand $(2x - 3y)^2$.

Example 5 Expand (a) $p = \left(3x + \frac{4}{y}\right)^2$ (b) $q = (x^2 + 3x + 5)^2$

Solution (a) $p = (3x)^2 + 2(3x)\frac{4}{y} + \left(\frac{4}{y}\right)^2 = 9x^2 + 24\frac{x}{y} + \frac{16}{y^2}$

(b) $q = (x^2)^2 + (3x)^2 + 5^2 + 2 \cdot x^2 \cdot 3x + 2 \cdot x^2 \cdot 5 + 2 \cdot 3x \cdot 5$
$= x^4 + 9x^2 + 25 + 6x^3 + 10x^2 + 30x = x^4 + 6x^3 + 19x^2 + 30x + 25$ ∎

Division If $N(x)$ and $D(x)$ are polynomials, $D(x) \not\equiv 0$, there are unique polynomials $Q(x)$ (quotient) and $R(x)$ (remainder) such that $N(x) = D(x)Q(x) + R(x)$ where $R(x) \equiv 0$ or is of lower degree than $D(x)$.

Dividing by a Monomial In each term, divide coefficients and subtract exponents.

Example 6 Divide: $\dfrac{4x^3 - 8x^2 + 6x}{3x}$.

Solution $\dfrac{4x^3 - 8x^2 + 6x}{3x} = \dfrac{4x^3}{3x} - \dfrac{8x^2}{3x} + \dfrac{6x}{3x} = \frac{4}{3}x^2 - \frac{8}{3}x + 2,\ x \neq 0$ ∎

Division Algorithm (Long Division) for Polynomials To calculate N/D: (3)
1. Write N and D in descending powers of one of the variables common to N and D. Include missing terms with coefficient 0 in the dividend N.
2. Divide the leading term of D into leading term of N; write this term Q of the quotient above N.
3. Multiply Q by D, write the product under N, and subtract, getting a new N.
4. If the degree of N is at least the degree of D go back to step 2.
5. Any remainder is written over D and added to the quotient:

$$\frac{\text{dividend}}{\text{divisor}} = \text{quotient} + \frac{\text{remainder}}{\text{divisor}} \qquad (4)$$

Practice 3 Clear fractions in Property 4 to get a check.

Example 7 Calculate (a) $R(x) = (4x^3 - 13x - 22) \div (x - 3)$
(b) $S(x) = (7x^4 - 5x^2 + 6x + 9) \div (3x^2 + 2x)$

Solution (a)

$$
\begin{array}{r}
\frac{4x^3}{x} \quad \frac{12x^2}{x} \quad \frac{23x}{x} \qquad \leftarrow \text{Step 2}\\
\downarrow \qquad \downarrow \qquad \downarrow \\
4x^2 + 12x + 23 \\
\end{array}
$$

$$
x - 3 \,\overline{)\,4x^3 + 0x^2 - 13x - 22} \quad \leftarrow \text{Step 3}
$$
$$
\underline{4x^3 - 12x^2} \qquad\qquad \leftarrow 4x^2(x-3)
$$
$$
12x^2 - 13x - 22
$$
$$
\underline{12x^2 - 36x} \qquad \leftarrow 12x(x-3)
$$
$$
23x - 22
$$
$$
\underline{23x - 69} \leftarrow 23(x-3)
$$
$$
47
$$

$$R(x) = 4x^2 + 12x + 23 + \frac{47}{x-3}$$

(b) To avoid fractions from dividing by 3 three times, multiply N by $3^3 = 27$ and Q by $\frac{1}{27}$.

$$\frac{189x^4}{3x^2} \quad \frac{-126x^3}{3x^2} \quad \frac{-51x^2}{3x^2} \qquad \leftarrow \text{Step 2}$$
$$\downarrow \qquad \downarrow \qquad \downarrow$$

$$
\begin{array}{r}
63x^2 - 42x - 17 \\
3x^2 + 2x \overline{\big)\,189x^4 + 0x^3 - 135x^2 + 162x + 243} \quad \leftarrow \text{Step 3}\\
\underline{189x^4 + 126x^3} \qquad\qquad\qquad \leftarrow 63x^2(3x^2 + 2x)\\
-126x^3 - 135x^2 + 162x + 243 \\
\underline{-126x^3 - 84x^2} \qquad\qquad \leftarrow -42x(3x^2 + 2x)\\
-51x^2 + 162x + 243 \\
\underline{-51x^2 - 34x} \qquad\qquad \leftarrow -17(3x^2 + 2x)\\
196x + 243 \qquad S(x) = \frac{1}{27}\Big(63x^2 - 42x - 17 + \frac{196x + 243}{3x^2 + 2x}\Big) \quad \blacksquare
\end{array}
$$

Example 8 Let $P = [(x^2 + 2xy + y^2)(1 + x) - 4y^2(1 + y)]$. Find $P \div (x - y)$.
Solution Multiply and arrange the terms in descending powers of x.
$$P = (x^2 + 2xy + y^2) + (x^3 + 2x^2y + xy^2) - 4y^2 - 4y^3$$
$$= x^3 + x^2(1 + 2y) + x(2y + y^2) - (3y^2 + 4y^3)$$

$$
\begin{array}{r}
x^2 + x(1 + 3y) + (4y^2 + 3y) \qquad = x^2 + 3xy + 4y^2 + x + 3y \\
x - y \overline{\big)\,x^3 + x^2(1 + 2y) + x(2y + y^2) - (3y^2 + 4y^3)}\\
\underline{x^3 - x^2y} \qquad\qquad\qquad\qquad\qquad\\
x^2(1 + 3y) + x(2y + y^2) \qquad\qquad\\
\underline{x^2(1 + 3y) - x(y + 3y^2)} \qquad\qquad\\
x(3y + 4y^2) - y(3y + 4y^2)
\end{array}
$$

$\qquad\qquad\qquad\qquad\qquad\qquad\qquad\qquad\qquad\qquad\qquad\qquad\qquad\qquad\quad\blacksquare$

Practice 4 In Example 7(a), let $P(x) = 4x^3 - 3x - 22$. Calculate $P(3)$ and compare to the remainder.

Remainder Theorem When polynomial $P(x)$ is divided by $x - a$, the remainder $r = P(a)$.
Proof Let $Q(x)$ be the quotient. Then $P(x) = (x - a)Q(x) + r$. Now let $x = a$. $\qquad\blacksquare$

Synthetic Division of $P(x) = a_n x^n + a_{n-1} x^{n-1} + \cdots + a_1 x + a_0$ by $x - k$ or evaluate $P(k)$:
1. Write the coefficients of P in order in a horizontal row; include any zero coefficients.
2. Bring down the first coefficient a_n of P to the bottom row.
3. Multiply a_n by k, write the product below a_{n-1}; write their sum in the bottom row.
4. Multiply this sum by k, write the product below a_{n-2}; their sum in the bottom row.
5. Continue the process of steps 3 and 4 as long as possible.
6. The last number in the bottom row is the remainder $P(k)$; the rest are coefficients of the quotient.
Proof Let $a_3 x^3 + a_2 x^2 + a_1 x + a_0 = (x - k)(b_2 x^2 + b_1 x + b_0) + r$. Then $\{x^3\} = a_3 = b_2$,
$\{x^2\} = a_2 = b_1 - kb_2$, $\quad \{x\} = a_1 = b_0 - kb_1$ and $\quad \{1\} = a_0 = r - kb_0$. Thus $b_2 = a_3$,
$b_1 = a_2 + kb_2$, $b_0 = a_1 + kb_1$, and $r = a_0 + kb_0$. $\qquad\qquad\qquad\qquad\qquad\blacksquare$

Example 9 If $P(x) = 4x^3 - 13x - 22$, calculate $P(3)$ by synthetic division and compare with Example 7(a).

Solution $\boxed{3}$
$$
\begin{array}{ccccc}
4 & & 0 & -13 & -22 \\
& 3 \times 4 = 12 & 3 \times 12 = 36 & 3 \times 23 = 69 \\
\hline
4 & 12 & 23 & \boxed{47} = P(3)
\end{array}
$$

$\qquad\qquad\qquad\qquad\qquad\qquad\qquad\qquad\qquad\qquad\qquad\qquad\qquad\qquad\qquad\qquad\qquad\quad\blacksquare$

Practice 5 $P(x) = 5x^3 + 4x^2 - 3x + 11$. Find $P(x)/(x + 2)$ and $P(-2)$ by synthetic division.

Taylor Expansion By repeated division we can express $P(x)$ in powers of $x - k$. Let $\qquad$ (6)
$P(x) = b_0 + b_1(x - k) + b_2(x - k)^2 + \cdots + b_n(x - k)^n$. Divide by $x - k$. The remainder is
$P(k) = b_0$ and the quotient is $P_1(x) = b_1 + b_2(x - k) + \cdots + b_n(x - k)^{n-1}$. Divide by $x - k$
again to get b_1, etc.

Remark $P(x + k) = b_0 + b_1 x + b_2 x^2 + \cdots + b_n x^n$.

Example 9 (cont) Express $P(x) = 5x^3 + 4x^2 - 3x + 11$ in powers of $x - 3$ and $P(x + 3)$.

Solution ③

$$
\begin{array}{r|rrrr}
3 & 4 & 0 & -13 & -22 \\
  &   & 12 & 36 & 69 \\
\hline
  & 4 & 12 & 23 & 47 \\
  &   & 12 & 72 & \\
\hline
  & 4 & 24 & 95 & \\
  &   & 12 & & \\
\hline
  & 4 & 36 & &
\end{array}
$$

$P(x) = 4(x - 3)^3 + 36(x - 3)^2 + 95(x - 3) + 47$,
$P(x + 3) = 4x^3 + 36x^2 + 95x + 47$ ∎

Roots By the zero product rule, the solutions of $P(x)Q(x) = 0$ are those solving at least one of $P(x) = 0$ or $Q(x) = 0$, and by the square property the real roots of $P(x)^2 + Q(x)^2 = 0$ are those of both.

Practice 6 Write (a) the roots of (a) $(x - 2)(x + 3)(x - 4) = 0$ (b) the real roots of $P = (x - 2)^2(x + 3)^2(x - 4)^2 + (x + 3)^2(x - 4)^2(x + 5)^2$ with their multiplicities.

Factoring a Polynomial Express as a product of polynomials of as low degree as possible with real coefficients.

Factor Theorem $x = a$ is a **zero** of $P(x)$: $P(a) = 0$, if and only if $x - a$ is a factor of $P(x)$.

Identity Theorem 1. A polynomial $P(x)$ of degree n has at most n zeros. 2. If polynomials $P(x)$ and $Q(x)$ of degree $\leq n$ agree at more than n values, they are identical. (8)
Proof 1. If there were more than n factors, the degree would be greater than n.
2. If not, $P(x) - Q(x)$ would be a polynomial of degree at most n with more than n zeros.

Remark In Example 8, $x = y$ reduces the numerator to $4y^2(1 + y) - 4y^2(1 + y) = 0$.

Practice 7 If $P(x)$, $Q(x)$ are polynomials and $P(x)Q(x) \equiv 0$, either $P(x) \equiv 0$ or $Q(x) \equiv 0$.

Practice 8 $P(x, y) = 1 + 2x + 3y + 4xy$ is a polynomial in x and y of degree 2 because the term $4xy$ is of degree 2, but is of degree 1 in x and of degree 1 in y. List the terms that a polynomial of degree 5 can have that a polynomial of degree 2 in x and 3 in y cannot have.

2. INTRODUCTION TO COMPLEX NUMBERS
Complex Numbers $a + bi$ are an extension of the real number system. We use them in §1.7 to solve quadratic equations. We define

$a + bi = c + di$ if $a = c$ (real parts) and $b = d$ (imaginary parts) (10)
$(a + bi) + (c + di) = (a + b) + (c + d)i$. $(a + bi)(c + di) = (ac - bd) + (ad + bc)i$

Then $(0 + i)(0 + i) = -1 + 0i$; that is $0 + i$ is the square root of the complex number $-1 + 0i$. The associative, commutative and distributive properties hold. We shall omit 0 terms. In electricity we use j because i is used for current. See Problems 34 and 35.

TI-83 in MODE REAL gives an error for $\sqrt{(-1)}$ but $\sqrt{(-1 + 0i)} = i$.

Powers of i $i^2 = -1$, $i^3 = (i^2)i = -i$, $i^4 = 1$, $i^{-1} = \frac{1}{i} \cdot \frac{i}{i} = \frac{i}{-1} = -i$, $i^{-2} = \frac{1}{i^2} = \frac{1}{-1} = -1$,
$i^{-3} = \frac{1}{i^3} \cdot \frac{i}{i} = \frac{i}{1} = i$. $i^{4m+r} = i^r$, for any integers m and r. (11)
A TI-83 has small errors: $i\hat{\ }7 = -3\text{E}{-}13 - i$, $i\hat{\ }8 = 1 - 2\text{E}{-}13i$ but $i^{222} = 1$.

Example 10 Evaluate (a) i^{23} (b) $(2 - 3i)(3 + 4i)$ (c) $(5 - 6i)^2$

Solution (a) $i^{23} = i^{20}i^3 = (i^4)^5 i^3 = 1(-i) = -i$
(b) $(2 - 3i)(3 + 4i) = 6 + 8i - 9i + 12 = 18 - i$ (c) $(5 - 6i)^2 = 25 - 30i - 36 = -11 - 30i$

Complex Conjugate If $z = a + bi$ define $\bar{z} = a - bi$, real$(z) = a$, imag$(z) = b$. Then $z\bar{z} = (a + bi)(a - bi) = a^2 + b^2$.

Additive If z and w are complex numbers,
$$\overline{z+w} = \overline{z} + \overline{w}, \; \text{real}(z+w) = \text{real}(z) + \text{real}(w), \; \text{imag}(z+w) = \text{imag}(z) + \text{imag}(w)$$

Absolute Value $|z| = \sqrt{z\overline{z}} = \sqrt{a^2 + b^2}$ $\qquad\qquad\qquad\qquad\qquad\qquad\qquad$ (12)

Example 11 (a) If $z = -3 - 2i$, find $\overline{z}$ and $|z|$. (b) If $\overline{z} = 2 + 3i$, find z.

Solution (a) $\overline{-3 + 2i} = -3 + 2i$, $|-3 + 2i| = \sqrt{3^2 + 2^2} = \sqrt{13}$ (b) $z = \overline{(\overline{z})} = \overline{2 + 3i} = 2 - 3i$

Division $\dfrac{a+bi}{c+di} = \dfrac{a+bi}{c+di} \cdot \dfrac{c-di}{c-di} = \dfrac{ac+bd}{c^2+d^2} + \dfrac{-ad+bc}{c^2+d^2}i$ if $c + di \neq 0$, so the complex numbers form a field. The zero product property follows: $zw = 0$ if and only if $z = 0$ or $w = 0$.

Writing Treat $a + bi$ as a sum and use parentheses for a product or quotient:
$$\frac{a+bi}{c+di} = (a+bi)/(c+di)$$

Example 12 Solve for x: $3ix - 4i + 5 = (3 + i)x - 7i$.

Solution (a) $(-3 + 2i)x = -5 - 3i$, $x = \dfrac{-5-3i}{-3+2i} \cdot \dfrac{-3-2i}{-3-2i} = \dfrac{9+19i}{13} = \dfrac{9}{13} + \dfrac{19}{13}i$ $\qquad$ ∎

Square Root of a The symbol $\sqrt{a}$ designates the solution of $z^2 = a$ having a positive real part or 0 real part and positive imaginary part.

Notes 1. $\sqrt{a}$ is not continuous: $\sqrt{-1} = i$ but $\sqrt{-1 - 10^{-99}i} = -i$.

2. $\sqrt{z}\sqrt{w} = \sqrt{zw}$ may fail.

Example 13 Compare $z = \sqrt{-2}\sqrt{-32}$ and $w = \sqrt{(-2)(-32)}$

Solution $z = \sqrt{2}i \cdot \sqrt{32}i = \sqrt{64}i^2 = -8$ and $w = \sqrt{64} = 8$. $\qquad\qquad\qquad$ ∎

Example 14 Find $\sqrt{-15 - 8i}$.
Solution Because $1(-16) = -16$ and $1 + (-16) = -15$, then
$$\sqrt{-15 - 8i} = \sqrt{-15 - 2\sqrt{-16}} = 1 - \sqrt{-16} = 1 - 4i$$
On a TI-83 you enter $[\![\sqrt{}]\!](-15 - 8i)$.
In Excel you enter =IMSQRT("−15−8i") to get $1 - 4i$ as text. $\qquad\qquad\qquad$ ∎

Example 15 Find the square roots of $x + iy$.
Solution $(a + bi)^2 = a^2 - b^2 + 2abi = x + iy$ so $a^2 - b^2 = x$, $2ab = y$. Let $r = |x + iy|$. Then $r^2 = x^2 + y^2 = (a^2 - b^2)^2 + (2ab)^2 = a^4 - 2a^2b^2 + b^4 + 4a^2b^2 = a^4 + 2a^2b^2 + b^4 = (a^2 + b^2)^2$ so $a^2 + b^2 = r$. Hence $a^2 = \frac{1}{2}(r + x)$, $b^2 = \frac{1}{2}(r - x)$ and
$$\sqrt{x + iy} = \sqrt{\tfrac{1}{2}(r + x)} \pm \sqrt{\tfrac{1}{2}(r - x)}i$$ using the sign of y; the other root is the negative. $\qquad$ ∎

Example 16 Find the square roots of $2 - 3i$ and identify the principal root.

Solution $\sqrt{2 - 3i}$. $r = \sqrt{2^2 + 3^2} = \sqrt{13}$. The roots are $\sqrt{\tfrac{1}{2}(\sqrt{13} + 2)} - \sqrt{\tfrac{1}{2}(\sqrt{13} - 2)}i$ (positive real is principal) and $-\sqrt{\tfrac{1}{2}(\sqrt{13} + 2)} + \sqrt{\tfrac{1}{2}(\sqrt{13} - 2)}i$. $\qquad\qquad$ ∎

Example 17 If $r = 1/(.7 + .9i)$, show the geometric series $s = 1 + r + r^2 + \cdots$ converges and find the sum.
Solution $|r| = \dfrac{1}{\sqrt{.7^2 + .9^2}} = \dfrac{1}{\sqrt{1.3}} < 1$.
$$s = \frac{1}{1-r} = \frac{1}{1 - (.7 + .9i)} = \frac{1}{.3 - .9i} \cdot \frac{.3 + .9i}{.3 + .9i} = \frac{.3 + .9i}{.09 + .81} = \frac{1}{3} + i$$ $\qquad$ ∎

Programming is used to extend the capabilities of the TI-83. A program name is a letter followed by 0 to 7 letters or digits. The counterpart to seq($operation$,I,1,100) is For(I,1,100):operations:end. I is then 101. Operations are separated by :. For(and End are in [PRGM]CTL. Disp $value$ in [PRGM]I/O, displays one item per line, justified left for text and right for numbers. To be able to scroll lists, use Pause $value$.

Example 17 Approximate the complex series $\dfrac{1}{1+i} + \dfrac{2}{(1+i)^2} + \dfrac{3}{(1+i)^3} + \cdots$ by summing 100 terms on a TI-83.

Analysis sum(seq(X/(1+i)^X,X,1,100)) gives ERR: DATA TYPE; seq can not use complex numbers.

Solution TI-84 with OS 2.55MP: [MATH]summation Σ(X/(1+i)^X,X,1,100) $= -1-i$, the exact answer.

TI-83 and TI-84 with older OS: Write as a program, storing the partial sums and answer in S. [PRGM]NEW, Name=A then :0→S:For(X,1,100):S+X/(1+i)^X→S:End

[QUIT] the editor, then [PRGM]EXEC A puts prgmA on the home screen; add :S and press ENTER to get $-1-i$, the exact answer. ∎

Practice Answers 1. (a) One for each of the 3×4 terms. (b) $(m+1)(n+1)$. In particular, to multiply two polynomials of degree $n-1$ needs n^2 multiplications.

2. $(2x-3y)^2 = (2x)^2 - 2(2x)(3y) + (3y)^2 = 4x^2 - 12xy + 9y^2$ **3.** dividend $=$ quotient $\times$ divisor $+$ remainder

4. $P(3) = 4(3)^3 - 13(3) - 22 = 108 - 39 - 22 = 47$, the remainder

5. $\boxed{-2}$ 5   4 -3 11 $P(x)/(x+2) = 5x^2 - 6x + 9 - 7/(x+2)$

     $-2 \times 5 = -10 \, {-}2 \times -6 = 12 \, {-}2 \times 9 = -18$

     5   -6 9 $\boxed{-7}$ $P(-2) = -7$

6. (a) $2, -3, 4$ (b) $P = (x+3)^2(x-4)^2[(x-2)^2 + (x+5)^2]$; $\{\{-3, -3, 4, 4\}\}$

7. If neither $P(x) \equiv 0$ nor $Q(x) \equiv 0$, then $P(x)Q(x) = 0$ for at most $\deg(P) + \deg(Q)$ values of x.

8. $y^4, y^5, xy^4, x^3, x^3y, x^3y^2, x^4, x^4y, x^5$

Problems 1.6 Problems with ^{h} have hints below.

1. Subtract $\frac{5}{6}x^2 + \frac{1}{6}x$ from x.

2. Multiply $(5.14x + 1.82)(9.75x - 8.23)$

3. Simplify $[(a-5) + (b-5)]10 + (10-a)(10-b)$

In Problems 4-11, express as a polynomial.

4. $(\sqrt{x} + 3\sqrt{y})(\sqrt{x} - 3\sqrt{y})$

5. $(x+3)(2x^2 - 5x + 7)$

6. $(y^2 + 2y)(y^3 - 2y^2 + 1)$

7. $(x^2 - 1)(x^3 + 2)$

8. $(y+3)(2y-5) - 2(3y-2)(y+2)$

9. $2x(3x^2 - 6x + 4) - 3x[2x^2 - 4(x-1)]$

10. $\left(2xy - \frac{x}{y}\right)\left(xy^2 + \frac{2y}{x}\right)$

11. $(x-y)(x^3 + x^2y + xy^2 + y^3)$

Problems 12-18 involve squaring polynomials.

12. $(rs - 3t)^2$

13. $(x^2 - 5y)^2$

14. $(x^2 + y^2)^2 - (x^2 - y^2)^2$

15. $(2x + 3y)^2 + (2x - 3y)^2$

16. $(x + y + z + w)^2$

17. $(x^2 - 2x + 7)^2$

18. $(x^4 + x^3 + x^2 + x + 1)^2$

In Problems 19-26 perform the division.

19. $(15x^2 - 24x) \div 2x$

20. $(t^3 + 2t^2 - 3t + 1) \div t\sqrt{t}$

21. $(x^3 + x - 1) \div (x + 2)$

22. $(x^5 + 5x - 7) \div (x + 1)$

23. $(x^4 + 3x^3 - x + 1) \div (x^2 + x - 2)$

24. $(x^3 + 5x^2 - 6) \div (3x^2 - 2)$

25. $(x^4 + 4y^4) \div (x^2 + 2xy + 2y^2)$

26. $(8x^3 + y^3 + 6xy - 1) \div (2x + y)$

In Problems 27 and 28, divide by $x - k$. Find the quotient and remainder $P(k)$ by synthetic division.

27. $2x^3 - x^2 + x - 4$, $k = 1$

28. $3x^3 + 2x^2 - 4x + 5$, $k = -2$

In Problems 29 and 30, expand in powers of $x - k$ by synthetic division.

29. $x^4 - 2x - 1$, $k = 3$

30. $x^4 + 3x^2 - 14$, $k = -1$

In Problems 31 and 32, find the real roots.

31. $(4x + 3)^3(8x - 5)^2(2x + 1) = 0$

32. $(x^2 - 9)(x^3 + 8)(x^4 + 1) = 0$

Problems 33-51 deal with complex numbers.

In Problems 33-36, simplify to the form $a + bi$.

33. (a) $\left(-\frac{2}{3} + 4i\right) + \left(\frac{8}{3} - 6i\right)$ (b) $\left(4 - \frac{2}{3}i\right) - \left(6 - \frac{11}{3}i\right)$ (c) $(-4 + 2i)(6 - 3i)$

34. (a) $-5i(-i)$ (b) $-2 + 3i - 5i(6i - 4)$

35. (a) $\frac{2 - i}{2 + i}$ (b) $\frac{4}{4 - 5i}$ **36.** (a) $(3 - 2i)^3$ (b) i^{67}

37[h] Evaluate $\dfrac{1}{4x^3 + 2x}$ when (a) $x = \frac{1}{2} + \frac{1}{2}\sqrt{3}i$ (b) $x = -\frac{1}{2} + \frac{1}{2}\sqrt{3}i$.

In Problems 38 and 39, a circuit of 4Ω (ohm) resistance and 3Ω capacitive reactance is said to have an impedance of $Z = 4 - 3j \ \Omega$. Voltage E volts and current I amperes, where $E = IZ$, are also complex to represent phase shift.

38. Find I if $E = 1.6 - 0.3j$ V and $Z = 1.5 + 8j \ \Omega$.

39. If $z_1 = 10 + 20j$ and $z_2 = 15 - 15j$ are parallel impedances, find the equivalent z, where $1/z = 1/z_1 + 1/z_2$.

In Problems 40 and 41 find (a) the conjugate, (b) the absolute value.

40. $-\dfrac{1}{\sqrt{2}} + \dfrac{1}{\sqrt{2}}i$ **41.** $3 - 4i$

In Problems 42 and 43, solve for z and express in the form $a + bi$.

42. $(1 - i)z = 4 + 5i$ **43.** Solve for z: $(2 + i)z = 8 - i$

In Problems 44 and 45, sum the geometric series.

44. $5 + \dfrac{5}{2 - 3i} + \dfrac{5}{(2 - 3i)^2} + \cdots$ **45.** $1 + i + i^2 + \cdots + i^{16}$

In Problems 46 and 47, express the square root of the complex number in the form $a + bi$.

46. $\sqrt{-5 + 6i}$.   **47.** $\sqrt{55 + 22\sqrt{6}i}$

48. Sum the series $\dfrac{1^2}{3 + 4i} + \dfrac{2^2}{(3 + 4i)^2} + \dfrac{3^2}{(3 + 4i)^3} + \cdots$ by summing 100 terms on a TI-83.

Hint 37. $4x^3 + 2x = 2x(2x^2 + 1)$

1.7 POLYNOMIAL EQUATIONS

Factoring and completing the square are crucial for solving equations and finding extrema. Our factors may have radical coefficients.

1. QUADRATIC EQUATIONS

First look for common monomial factors: a product with the largest coefficient and exponents that will divide evenly into each term; then mentally divide each term by it. Next, look for the difference of two squares of the type $a^2 - b^2 = (a - b)(a + b)$.

Example 1 Factor (a) $x^5 - 3x^3$ (b) $x^5 + 3x^3$.
Solution x^3 is a factor of each term. Thus
         Divide by common factor.

(a) $x^5 - 3x^3 = x^3\left(\dfrac{x^5}{x^3} - \dfrac{3x^3}{x^3}\right) = x^3(x^2 - 3) = x^3(x - \sqrt{3})(x + \sqrt{3})$.

(b) $x^5 + 3x^3 = x^3(x^2 + 3)$ Because $x^2 + 3 > 0$, it has no factors.   ∎

Quadratic Equation in x can be put in the form $ax^2 + bx + c = 0$, $a \neq 0$.

Monic Polynomial: coefficient of highest power is 1. Let $P(x) = Q(x)R(x)$ be monic polynomials with rational coefficients. If P has integer coefficients, then so do Q and R.(1)

Monic Trinomials by product and sum:
$(x + r)(x + s) = x^2 + (r + s)x + rs = x^2 + bx + c$. Look for factors of c whose sum is b.

Example 2 Factor $p = x^2 + 6x + 8$ and find its zeros.
Solution $8 = 4 \cdot 2$ and $6 = 4 + 2$. Hence $p = (x + 4)(x + 2)$. Zeros are $x = -4$ and $x = -2$.

Product and Sum for Trinomials with integer factors. Trinomials in one variable can be written in the form $ax^2 + bx + c$ and can be factored if you can find factors of the product $a \cdot c$ whose sum is b. If $ac > 0$ and $b > 0$, start with 1 and positive (Example 3). If $ac > 0$ and $b < 0$, start with -1 and negative (Example 4). If $ac < 0$ and $b > 0$, start with -1 and positive (Example 5). If $ac < 0$ and $b < 0$, start with 1 and negative. (2)

Proof $(px + q)(rx + s) = prx^2 + (ps + qr)x + qs = ax^2 + bc + c$ where $ac = prqs$ and $b = ps + qr$ are the product and sum of the numbers ps and qr. ∎

Example 3 Factor $7x^2 + 71x + 10$ and find its zeros.
Solution Here $a = 7$ and $c = 10$, so we want numbers whose product is $7 \cdot 10 = 70$ and whose sum is 71. The numbers are 1 and 70.

$7x^2 + 71x + 10$
$= 7x^2 + x + 70x + 10$ Break up the middle term.
$= x(7x + 1) + 10(7x + 1)$ Factor each pair of terms.
$= (x + 10)(7x + 1)$ Remove the common binomial factor.

The zeros are -10 and $-\frac{1}{7}$. ∎

Example 4 Factor $16 - 26x + 3x^2$ and find its zeros.
Solution It is easier to recognize factors if we write trinomials in descending order before we factor them.
$16 - 26x + 3x^2 = 3x^2 - 26x + 16$.
Here $a = 3$ and $c = 16$, so we want numbers whose product is $3 \cdot 16 = 48$ and whose sum is -26. $(-1)(-25) = 25$ but $(-2)(-24) = 48$.

$3x^2 - 26x + 16$
$= 3x^2 - 2x - 24x + 16$ Break up the middle term.
$= x(3x - 2) - 8(3x - 2)$ Factor each pair of terms.
$= (x - 8)(3x - 2)$ Remove the common binomial factor.

The zeros are 8 and $\frac{2}{3}$. ∎

Example 5 Factor $15x^2 + 32x - 7$ and find its zeros.
Solution Here $a = 15$ and $c = -7$; we want numbers whose product is $15(-7) = -105$ and whose sum is 32. $(-1)33 = -33$, $(-2)34 = -68$ but $(-3)35 = -105$.

$15x^2 + 32x - 7$
$= 15x^2 + 35x - 3x - 7$ Break up the middle term.
$= 5x(3x + 7) - 1(3x + 7)$ Factor each pair of terms.
$= (5x - 1)(3x + 7)$ Remove the common binomial factor.

The zeros are $\frac{1}{5}$ and $-\frac{7}{3}$. ∎

Two Variables If $ax^2 + bx + c = (dx + e)(fx + g)$ then
$ax^2 + bxy + cy^2 = (dx + ey)(fx + gy)$; the same method is used.

Example 6 Factor $20x^2 - 37xy - 18y^2$.
Solution Here $a = 20$ and $c = -18$; we want numbers whose product is $20(-18) = -360$ and whose sum is -37. Check only if one number ends in 0 or 5. $3(-40) = -120$, $5(-42) = -210$, but $8(-45) = -360$.

$20x^2 - 37xy - 18y^2$
$= 20x^2 - 45xy + 8xy - 18y^2$ Break up the middle term.
$= 5x(4x - 9y) + 2y(4x - 9y)$ Factor each pair of terms.
$= (5x + 2y)(4x - 9y)$ Remove the common binomial factor. ∎

Example 7 Solve the single-power equation $(5x + 2)^2 = 13$.
Analysis Because the power is even we find two solutions using $\pm$.
Solution $5x + 2 = \pm\sqrt{13}$, $5x = -2 \pm \sqrt{13}$, $x = \frac{1}{5}(-2 \pm \sqrt{13})$ ∎

Practice 5 Solve $(3x - 4)^2 = 15$.

Completing the Square $x^2 + kx + \left(\frac{k}{2}\right)^2 = \left(x + \frac{k}{2}\right)^2$. To solve a quadratic equation: (6)

(1) Bring the x^2 and x terms to the left side, the constant to the right side.
(2) Divide by the coefficient of x^2.
(3) Add the square of half the coefficient of x to each side.
(4) Express the left side as a square; combine terms on the right.
(5) Take the square roots of both sides. If the RHS is negative, the roots are complex.
(6) Subtract the constant from both sides.

Example 8 Solve $3x^2 + 4x - 5 = 0$ by completing the square.

Solution Step 1: $3x^2 + 4x = 5$ Step 2: $x^2 + \frac{4}{3}x = \frac{5}{3}$ Step 3: $x^2 + \frac{4}{3}x + \left(\frac{2}{3}\right)^2 = \frac{5}{3} + \frac{4}{9}$

Step 4: $\left(x + \frac{2}{3}\right)^2 = \frac{19}{9}$ Step 5: $x + \frac{2}{3} = \pm\frac{1}{3}\sqrt{19}$ Step 6: $x = -\frac{2}{3} \pm \frac{1}{3}\sqrt{19}$ ∎

Practice 6 Solve $-2x^2 + 6x + 7 = 0$ by completing the square.

Quadratic Formula If $ax^2 + bx + c = 0$, $a \neq 0$, $x_\pm = \dfrac{-b \pm \sqrt{b^2 - 4ac}}{2a}$.

The sum of the roots is $-b/a$ and the product is c/a. (7)

Proof Step 1: $ax^2 + bx = -c$ Step 2: $x^2 + \frac{b}{a}x = -\frac{c}{a}$ Step 3: $x^2 + \frac{b}{a}x + \left(\frac{b}{2a}\right)^2 = \frac{b^2}{4a^2} - \frac{c}{a}$

Step 4: $\left(x + \frac{b}{2a}\right)^2 = \frac{b^2 - 4ac}{4a^2}$ Step 5: $x + \frac{b}{2a} = \frac{\pm\sqrt{b^2 - 4ac}}{2a}$ ∎

Practice 7 Find the difference of the roots of the quadratic equation $ax^2 + bx + c = 0$.

Example 9 (a) Solve $3x^2 + 4x - 5 = 0$ by the quadratic formula. (b) Check the answer by sum and product.

Solution (a) $a = 3$, $b = 4$, $c = -5$. $x = \dfrac{-4 \pm \sqrt{4^2 - 4(3)(-5)}}{2(3)} = \dfrac{-4 \pm \sqrt{76}}{6} = \dfrac{-2 \pm \sqrt{19}}{3}$

(b) $\dfrac{-2 + \sqrt{19}}{3} + \dfrac{-2 - \sqrt{19}}{3} = \dfrac{-4}{3}$ and $\dfrac{-2 + \sqrt{19}}{3} \cdot \dfrac{-2 - \sqrt{19}}{3} = \dfrac{4 - 19}{9} = \dfrac{-15}{9} = \dfrac{-5}{3}$ ∎

Example 10 Factor $3x^2 + 4x - 5$: (a) Use the results of Example 9. (b) Rearrange Example 9 to get a difference of squares.
Solution (a) The Factor Theorem gives two factors; the coefficient of x^2, a constant factor.

$3x^2 + 4x - 5 = 3\left(x - \dfrac{-2 + \sqrt{19}}{3}\right)\left(x - \dfrac{-2 - \sqrt{19}}{3}\right)$

(b) $3x^2 + 4x - 5 = 3\left(x^2 - \frac{4}{3}x - \frac{5}{3}\right) = 3\left[x^2 + \frac{4}{3}x + \left(\frac{2}{3}\right)^2 - \frac{5}{3} - \frac{4}{9}\right] = 3\left[\left(x + \frac{2}{3}\right)^2 - \frac{19}{9}\right]$

$= 3\left(x + \frac{2}{3} - \frac{1}{3}\sqrt{19}\right)\left(x + \frac{2}{3} + \frac{1}{3}\sqrt{19}\right)$ ∎

Discriminant of $ax^2 + bx + c = 0$, $a \neq 0$, is $d = b^2 - 4ac$. If $d > 0$, the roots are unequal; if $d = 0$, the roots are equal; if $d < 0$, the roots are complex. $ax^2 + bx + c$ has real factors if $d = b^2 - 4ac \geq 0$; otherwise it is irreducible. If a, b, and c are rational, then the roots are rational if and only if $\sqrt{d}$ is rational.

Example 11 Find m so that $(2m + 1)x^2 - 4mx + 3m - 1$ has equal roots.
Solution $d = b^2 - 4ac = (4m)^2 - 4(2m + 1)(3m - 1) = 16m^2 - 4(6m^2 + m - 1)$
$= 16m^2 - 24m^2 - 4m + 4 = -8m^2 - 4m + 4 = 0$ if $2m^2 + m - 1 = (2m - 1)(m + 1) = 0$,
$m = \frac{1}{2}$ or -1 ∎

Practice 7 Determine if the discriminant d of $(x - 1)^2 + (x - 2)^2 + (x - 3)^2$ is positive, negative or zero. No calculations necessary.

2. HIGHER DEGREE

Common n is a common divisor of two or more integers if it is a divisor of each; n is a common multiple if it is a multiple of each. The **greatest common divisor** (GCD) is the positive integer divisible by every common divisor; the **least common multiple** (LCM) is a divisor of every common multiple. (3)

Example 12 Find the GCD and LCM of 180, 360, and 450.
Solution $180 = 2^2 \cdot 3^2 \cdot 5$, $360 = 2^3 \cdot 3^2 \cdot 5$, $450 = 2 \cdot 3^2 \cdot 5^2$.
Taking the lowest power of each factor, GCD $= 2 \cdot 3^2 \cdot 5 = 90$.
Taking the highest power of each factor, LCM $= 2^3 \cdot 3^2 \cdot 5^2 = 1800$. ∎

TI-83 [MATH]NUM | gcd does only 2 nonnegative integers. gcd(180,gcd(360,450)) = 90 and lcm(180,lcm(360,450)) = 1800. Excel LCM and GCD can do many.

"Product Rule" binomials. In calculus, we often need to factor the derivative of a product of binomial powers.

Example 13 Factor $p = 10(2x-3)^4(4x+1)^3 + 12(2x-3)^5(4x+1)^2$ and find its zeros. p is the derivative of $(2x-3)^5(4x+1)^3$.
Solution Start by factoring the greatest common divisor of the integer coefficients 10 and 12 and the *lowest* power of each binomial. Simplify the bracket; both exponents will be 1.

$$p = 2(2x-3)^4(4x+1)^2\left[\frac{10(2x-3)^4(4x+1)^3}{2(2x-3)^4(4x+1)^2} + \frac{12(2x-3)^5(4x+1)^2}{2(3x-3)^4(4x+1)^2}\right]$$

$$= 2(2x-3)^4(4x+1)^2[5(4x+1) + 6(2x-3)] = 2(2x-3)^4(4x+1)^2[32x-13]$$

The zeros are $\frac{3}{2}$, $-\frac{1}{4}$, and $\frac{13}{32}$.

Analysis Even if the exponents are negative or fractional, the expression in brackets will be linear. ∎

Example 14 Factor $p = \frac{15}{2}(3x+1)^{3/2}(7x+2)^{-3} - 21(3x+1)^{5/2}(7x+2)^{-4}$ and find its zeros. p is the derivative of $(3x+1)^{5/2}(7x+2)^{-3}$.
Analysis If one coefficient is a fraction, make the other into a fraction: $21 = \frac{21}{1}$. To get integer coefficients, we factor a fraction whose numerator 3 is the greatest common divisor of the numerators 15 and 21, and whose denominator 2 is the least common multiple of the denominators 2 and 1. Use the lowest power of each binomial.
Solution $p = \frac{3}{2}(3x+1)^{3/2}(7x+2)^{-4}[5(7x+2) - 14(3x+1)]$

$$= \frac{3}{2}(3x+1)^{3/2}(7x+2)^{-4}[-7x-4] = -\frac{3}{2}(3x+1)^{3/2}(7x+2)^{-4}(7x+4)$$

The zeros are $-\frac{1}{3}$, $-\frac{4}{7}$. We call $-\frac{2}{7}$ a **pole** of order 4. ∎

Difference of like Powers, Sum of like Odd Powers
Pattern: in the second factor, each term has 1 less z and 1 more x.

$$z^2 - x^2 = (z-x)(z+x)$$
$$z^3 + x^3 = (z+x)(z^2 - zx + x^2)$$
$$z^3 - x^3 = (z-x)(z^2 + zx + x^2)$$
$$z^5 + x^5 = (z+x)(z^4 - z^3x + z^2x^2 - zx^3 + x^4)$$
$$z^4 - x^4 = (z-x)(z^3 + z^2x + zx^2 + x^3) = (z+x)(z^3 - z^2x + zx^2 - x^3)$$
$$z^n - x^n = (z-x)(z^{n-1} + z^{n-2}x + \cdots + x^{n-1}) \qquad \text{for any integer } n \geq 2. \qquad (4)$$
$$z^n - x^n = (z+x)(z^{n-1} - z^{n-2}x + \cdots - x^{n-1}) \qquad \text{for any even integer.}$$
$$z^n + x^n = (z+x)(z^{n-1} - z^{n-2}x + \cdots + x^{n-1}) \qquad \text{for any odd integer} \geq 3. \qquad (5)$$

Proof If $z \neq 0$ or x, the second factor is the sum of a geometric series with ratio x/z, and the term after the last is x^n/z. Thus $z^{n-1} + z^{n-2}x + \cdots + x^{n-1} = \dfrac{z^{n-1} - x^n/z}{1 - x/z} = \dfrac{z^n - x^n}{z - x}$, hence (4). By the Identity Theorem (*) also is true for these values. If n is odd, change x to $-x$ to prove (5). ∎

Practice 4 Factor $z^5 - x^5$.

Example 15 Factor (a) $w = 27a^3 - 125b^6$ (b) $z = x^3 + y^3$
Analysis We can express each as the difference of two third powers.
Solution (a) $w = (3a)^3 - (5b^2)^3 = (3a - 5b^2)[(3a)^2 + (3a)(5b^2) + (5b^2)^2]$
$= (3a - 5b^2)(9a^2 + 15ab^2 + 25b^4)$

(b) $z = x^3 - (-y)^3 = [x - (-y)][x^2 + x(-y) + (-y)^2] = (x + y)(x^2 - xy + y^2)$ ∎

Irreducible polynomial in one or more variables is one that cannot be factored into polynomials of lower degree with real coefficients. (8)

Fundamental Theorem of Algebra (Gauss 1799) Any polynomial with real coefficients can be factored into real linear and irreducible quadratic factors. This is called **factoring completely**. (9)

Example 16 Factor $x^6 - y^6$ completely.
Analysis $x^6 - y^6 = (x^2)^3 - (y^2)^3 = (x^3)^2 - (y^3)^2$. The last is best for factoring completely.

Solution $(x^3)^2 - (y^3)^2 = (x^3 - y^3)(x^3 + y^3) = (x - y)(x^2 + xy + y^2)(x + y)(x^2 - xy + y^2)$

Example 17 Use the quadratic formula to find the three cube roots of -1.
Solution If $x^3 = -1$, $0 = x^3 + 1 = (x + 1)(x^2 - x + 1)$ so $x = -1$ or

$$x = \frac{1}{2 \cdot 1}(1 \pm \sqrt{1^2 - 4 \cdot 1 \cdot 1}) = \frac{1}{2}(1 \pm \sqrt{-3}) = \frac{1}{2}(1 \pm \sqrt{3}i)$$ ∎

Remark The principal root, $-\frac{1}{2} + \frac{1}{2}\sqrt{3}i$, has the largest real part and nonnegative imaginary part. On a TI-83, $(-1)^{\hat{}}(1/3) = -1$ but $(-1 + 0i)^{\hat{}}(1/3) = .5 + .866i$.

Radical Equations Isolate a square root term and square both sides. Record any restrictions, so checking is unnecessary. Similarly, isolate $x^{m/n}$ and raise both sides to power n. Some problems can also be done by substitution; see Example 21. (10)

Example 18 Solve for x: $\sqrt[3]{1 - 3x} = 4$.
Solution Cube both sides: $1 - 3x = 64$, $-3x = 63$, $x = -21$ ∎

Example 19 Solve for p: $x = 3 + \sqrt{10 - p^2}$.

Solution $x - 3 = \sqrt{10 - p^2}$. Square: $x^2 - 6x + 9 = 10 - p^2$, so $p^2 = 1 + 6x - x^2$ and

$p = \pm\sqrt{1 + 6x - x^2}$, $3 \le x \le 3 + \sqrt{10}$ ∎

Example 20 Solve for x: $2\sqrt{x + 1} - \sqrt{2x + 3} = 1$.
Solution $x + 1 \ge 0$ so $x \ge -1$. We have $2\sqrt{x + 1} = 1 + \sqrt{2x + 3}$.

Square: $(2\sqrt{x + 1})^2 = (1 + \sqrt{2x + 3})^2$, $4(x + 1) = 1 + 2\sqrt{2x + 3} + (2x + 3)$

Collect: $2x = 2\sqrt{2x + 3}$, $x = \sqrt{2x + 3}$ Note that $x \ge 0$.

Square again. $x^2 = 2x + 3$, $0 = x^2 - 2x - 3 = (x - 3)(x + 1)$. $x = 3$. Reject $x = -1$. ∎

Substitution Many problems lead to equations that can be reduced to a quadratic equation by substituting.

Example 21 A statistics problem leads to $n - 199 = 1.28\sqrt{n}$. Solve (a) by squaring (b) by substitution.
Solution (a) $(n - 199)^2 = 1.28^2 n$. Expand: $n^2 - 398n + 39601 = 1.6384n$. Collect: $n^2 - 399.6384n + 39601 = 0$, $n = (399.6384 \pm \sqrt{399.6384^2 - 4 \times 39601})/2$ by the quadratic formula. $n_+ = 217.8944$. Reject $n_- = 181.744$ because $n - 199 \ge 0$ (b) Let $\sqrt{n} = x$, $n = x^2$. $x^2 - 199 = 1.28x$, $x^2 - 1.28x - 199 = 0$. $x = (1.28 \pm \sqrt{1.28^2 + 4 \times 199})/2$. $x_+ = 14.7612$, $n = 217.8944$. Reject $x_- = -13.4812$, $n = 181.744$. ∎

Example 22 Solve for y in terms of x: (a) $y^2 - 2xy - x^2 - 2 = 0$
(b) $(y - 3x)^2 + 3(y - 3x) - 4 = 0$
Solution (a) Complete the square on y: $0 = y^2 - 2xy + x^2 - 2x^2 - 2 = (y - x)^2 - 2x^2 - 2$,

$(y - x)^2 = 2x^2 + 2$, $y - x = \pm\sqrt{2x^2 + 2}$, $y = x \pm \sqrt{2x^2 + 2}$

(b) Let $u = y - 3x$. Then $0 = u^2 + 3u - 4 = (u + 4)(u - 1)$, $-4 = u = y - 3x$, $y = 3x - 4$ or

$1 = u = y - 3x$, $y = 3x + 1$ ∎

$x^4 + bx^2 + c$ **(biquadratic)** can be factored. If $b^2 \geq 4c$, replace c with $(\frac{1}{2}b)^2 - (\frac{1}{4}b^2 - c)$; if $b^2 < 4c$, replace bx^2 with $2\sqrt{c}x^2 - (2\sqrt{c} - b)x^2$. Then factor as the difference of squares. The first case may have linear factors.

Example 23 Factor over the reals (a) $x^4 - x^2 - 1$ (b) $x^4 + 5x^2 + 9$
Solution (a) $x^4 - x^2 - 1 = x^4 - x^2 + (-\frac{1}{2})^2 - 1 - \frac{1}{4} = (x^2 - \frac{1}{2})^2 - \frac{5}{4}$

$= (x^2 - \frac{1}{2} - \frac{1}{2}\sqrt{5})(x^2 - \frac{1}{2} + \frac{1}{2}\sqrt{5})$. Because $-\frac{1}{2} - \frac{1}{2}\sqrt{5} < 0$ and $-\frac{1}{2} + \frac{1}{2}\sqrt{5} > 0$, the first

factor can be factored and the second cannot. We get

$(x - \sqrt{\frac{1}{2} + \frac{1}{2}\sqrt{5}})(x + \sqrt{\frac{1}{2} + \frac{1}{2}\sqrt{5}})(x^2 - \frac{1}{2} + \frac{1}{2}\sqrt{5})$

(b) $x^4 + 5x^2 + 9 = x^4 + 6x^2 + 9 + (5x^2 - 6x^2) = (x^2 + 3)^2 - x^2 = (x^2 + 3 - x)(x^2 + 3 + x)$
$= (x^2 - x + 3)(x^2 + x + 3)$
Both factors are irreducible: discriminant $= (\pm 1)^2 - 12 = -11$.   ∎

Practice 9 Factor (a) $x^4 + y^4$ (b) $x^6 + y^6$

Example 24 A 4 ft board is leaning against a wall and just touches a 1×1 box in the corner. How is the board divided?
Solution See Figure 1. Because the box is square, the pieces are interchangeable; call them $2 + x$ and $2 - x$ to get an even equation. By the Pythagorean theorem, $a^2 = (2 + x)^2 - 1$.

By similar triangles, $\frac{a}{2 + x} = \frac{1}{2 - x}$ so $(2 - x)a = 2 + x$. Squaring and substituting for a^2,

$(2 - x)^2[(2 + x)^2 - 1] = (2 + x)^2$ so $(x^2 - 4)^2 = (x + 2)^2 + (x - 2)^2$,

$x^4 - 8x^2 + 16 = 2x^2 + 8,$ $x^4 - 10x^2 + 25 = 17,$ $x^2 - 5 = \pm\sqrt{17},$ $x = \pm\sqrt{5 - \sqrt{17}}$

$(\sqrt{5 + \sqrt{17}} > 2$ is too big). The pieces are $2 \pm \sqrt{5 - \sqrt{17}}$.   ∎

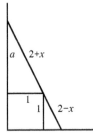

Figure 1

Example 25 Solve as a quadratic equation: (a) $x^4 - 10x^2 + 1 = 0$ (b) An interest problem with two payments of \$500 leads to $920 = 500/(1 + i/2) + 500/(1 + i/2)^2$. Find i.
Solution (a) Let $x^2 = z$, $x^4 = (x^2)^2 = z^2$, so $z^2 - 10z + 1 = 0$. By the quadratic formula,

$z = \frac{1}{2}(10 \pm \sqrt{100 - 4}) = 5 \pm 2\sqrt{6}$. Both roots are positive. Since $2 \cdot 3 = 6$ and $2 + 3 = 5$,

then $x = \pm\sqrt{5 \pm 2\sqrt{6}} = \pm(\sqrt{2} + \sqrt{3})$

(b) Let $x = 1 + i/2 > 1$; we reject the negative root. Then $920 = 500/x + 500/x^2$,

$920x^2 = 500x + 500$, $920x^2 - 500x - 500 = 0$. By the quadratic formula,

$x = \dfrac{500 + \sqrt{500^2 + 4 \cdot 920 \cdot 500}}{2 \cdot 920} = 1.05743 = 1 + \frac{1}{2}i$, $i = 2(.05743) = .11487 = 11.49\%$ ∎

Symmetric Polynomial $P(x) = a_n x^n + a_{n-1} x^{n-1} + \cdots + a_1 x + a_0$ has $a_n = a_0$, $a_{n-1} = a_1$, etc. If n is odd, then $x + 1$ is a factor. If $n = 2k$ is even, P can be reduced to a polynomial of degree k in $y = x + 1/x$.   (11)

Example 26 Factor (a) $P(x) = x^3 + 2x^2 + 2x + 1$, (b) $Q(x) = x^4 + 2x^3 - x^2 + 2x + 1$.
Solution
(a) $P(x) = x^3 + 1 + 2x(x + 1) = (x + 1)(x^2 - x + 1) + 2x(x + 1) = (x + 1)(x^2 + x + 1)$

(b) If $y = x + 1/x$, then $y^2 = x^2 + 2 + 1/x^2$. $Q(x) = x^2[(x^2 + 1/x^2) + 2(x + 1/x) - 1] =$

$x^2[(y^2 - 2) + 2y - 1] = x^2(y^2 + 2y - 3) = x^2(y - 1)(y + 3) = x^2(x + 1/x - 1)(x + 1/x + 3)$

$= (x^2 - x + 1)(x^2 + 3x + 1)$ and

$x^2 + 3x + 1 = x^2 + 3x + (\frac{3}{2})^2 + 1 - \frac{9}{4} = (x + \frac{3}{2})^2 - \frac{5}{4} = (x + \frac{3}{2} - \frac{1}{2}\sqrt{5})(x + \frac{3}{2} + \frac{1}{2}\sqrt{5})$ ∎

Rational Root Theorem If $P(x) = a_n x^n + a_{n-1} x^{n-1} + \cdots + a_1 x + a_0 = 0$, $a_0 \neq 0$, with integer coefficients has rational root in lowest terms c/d, then c is a factor of a_0 and d is a factor of a_n. A number c/d with this property is a *candidate* for a root. If $a_n = 1$, any rational root is an integer, a factor of a_0. If $a_0 = 0$, then x is a factor.

Proof $a_n(c/d)^n + a_{n-1}(c/d)^{n-1} + \cdots + a_1(c/d) + a_0 = 0$. Multiply by d^n to get   (12)

$a_n c^n + a_{n-1} c^{n-1} d + \cdots + a_1 c d^{n-1} + a_0 d^n = 0,$

$c(a_n c^{n-1} + a_{n-1} c^{n-2} d + \cdots + a_1 d^{n-1}) = -a_0 d^n$

Because c is a factor of the left side, c is a factor of $a_0 d^n$. Since c and d have no common factors, and the factors of d^n are merely repetitions of the factors of d, then c divides a_0. Similarly, d divides a_n.   ∎

Radicals If $x = n^{1/p}$ is not an integer, then x is irrational.
Proof The only possible rational roots of $x^p - n = 0$ are integers.   ∎

Practice 10 List the rational root candidates for $35x^3 + 26x^2 + 18x + 9 = 0$.

Depressed Equation If $x = a$ is a root of $P(x) = 0$ then $P(x)/(x - a) = Q(x) = 0$ is the depressed equation.   (13)

Example 27 Find all roots assuming at least one is rational: $3x^3 - 8x^2 - 17x + 14$.
Solution Let $x = \frac{1}{3}y$ to get a polynomial with integer roots:

$3(\frac{1}{3}y)^3 - 8(\frac{1}{3}y)^2 - 17(\frac{1}{3}y) + 14 = \frac{1}{9}y^3 - \frac{8}{9}y^2 - \frac{17}{3}y + 14$

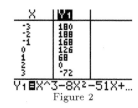

Y1◨X^3−8X²−51X+...
Figure 2

Multiply by 9 to get $y^3 - 8y^2 - 51y + 126$. Enter [Y =] as X^3−8X²−51X+126 and [TABLE] shows a root at 2. See Figure 2. Use synthetic division:

$$
\begin{array}{r|rrrr}
2 & 1 & -8 & -51 & 126 \\
  &   & 2 & -12 & -126 \\
\hline
  & 1 & -6 & -63 & \boxed{0}
\end{array}
$$

The depressed equation is $y^2 - 6y - 63 = y^2 - 6y + 9 - 72 = (y - 3)^2 - 72 = 0$ so
$y - 3 = \pm\sqrt{72} = \pm 6\sqrt{2}$, $y = 3 \pm 6\sqrt{2}$. Then $x = \frac{2}{3}$, $1 \pm 2\sqrt{2}$.   ∎

Four-Term polynomials can sometimes be factored by grouping.

Example 28 Factor $P(x) = x^3 - 2x^2 - 3x + 6$.
Solution $P(x) = x^2(x - 2) - 3(x - 2) = (x^2 - 3)(x - 2) = (x - \sqrt{3})(x + \sqrt{3})(x - 2)$ ∎

Practice Answers 4. $(z - x)(z^4 + z^3 x + z^2 x^2 + z x^3 + x^4)$

5. $3x - 4 = \pm\sqrt{15}$; $3x = 4 \pm \sqrt{15}$; $\frac{1}{3}(4 + \sqrt{15})$, $\frac{1}{3}(4 - \sqrt{15})$

6. $-2x^2 + 6x + 7 = 0$; $-2x^2 + 6x = -7$; $x^2 - 3x = -\frac{7}{2}$; $x^2 - 3x + (\frac{3}{2})^2 = \frac{7}{2} + \frac{9}{4}$; $(x - \frac{3}{2})^2 = \frac{23}{4}$

$x - \frac{3}{2} = \frac{1}{2}\sqrt{23}$ so $x = \frac{3}{2} + \frac{1}{2}\sqrt{23}$; or $x - \frac{3}{2} = -\frac{1}{2}\sqrt{23}$ so $x = \frac{3}{2} - \frac{1}{2}\sqrt{23}$ **7.** $x_+ - x_- = \sqrt{b^2 - 4ac}/a$

7. The expression is always positive, so it has no roots. Hence $d < 0$.

9. (a) $z^4 + x^4 = z^4 + 2z^2 x^2 + x^4 - 2z^2 = (z^2 + x^2)^2 - 2z^2 = (z^2 - \sqrt{2}zx + x^2)(z^2 + \sqrt{2}zx + x^2)$

(b) $x^6 + y^6 = (x^2)^3 + (y^2)^3 = (x^2 + y^2)(x^4 - x^2 y^2 + y^4) = (x^2 + y^2)(x^4 + 2x^2 y^2 + y^4 - 3x^2 y^2)$

$= (x^2 + y^2)[(x^2 + y^2)^2 - 3x^2 y^2] = (x^2 + y^2)(x^2 - \sqrt{3}xy + y^2)(x^2 + \sqrt{3}xy + y^2)$

10. The divisors of 9 are 1, 3, 9; the divisors of 35 are 1, 5, 7, 35. The candidates are $\pm 1, \pm 3, \pm 9$; $\pm\frac{1}{5}, \pm\frac{3}{5}, \pm\frac{9}{5}$; $\pm\frac{1}{7}, \pm\frac{3}{7}, \pm\frac{9}{7}$; $\pm\frac{1}{35}, \pm\frac{3}{35}, \pm\frac{9}{35}$. ($-\frac{3}{5}$ is the only root).

Problems 1.7 Problems with ^{h} have hints below.

In Problems 1-21, factor completely and find the zeros.

1. $x^4 - 7x^2$ **2.** $x^2 + 5x + 6$ **3^h** $x^2 + 2x - 8$

4. $x^2 - 9x + 14$ **5.** $2x^2 + x - 6$ **6.** $2x^2 + 13x + 6$

7. $3x^2 + 3x - 36$ **8.** $4x^2 - 8x - 60$ **9.** $2x^3 - 8x$

10. $10x^2 - 27x - 63$ **11.** $10x^2 + 19x + 6$ **12.** $6x^2 + 67x - 35$

13. $9 - 47x + 10x^2$ **14.** $10x^2 + 21x - 10$ **15.** $2x^3 - 8x^2 + 8x$

16. $x^3 + 16x^2 + 64x$ **17.** $3x^2(6x - 7)^5 + 30x^3(6x - 7)^4$

18. $\frac{2}{3}x^{-1/3}(3x + 5)^2 + 6x^{2/3}(3x + 5)$ **19.** $12(4x + 3)^2(5x - 2)^4 + 20(4x + 3)^3(5x - 2)^3$

20. $\frac{2}{3}(2x - 1)^{-2/3}(3x + 2)^{1/4} + \frac{3}{4}(2x - 1)^{1/3}(3x + 2)^{-3/4}$ **21.** $6x^2 2^x - x2^x - 2^{x+1}$

22. Express $\frac{1}{5}(a^2 - x^2)^{5/2} - \frac{1}{3}a^2(a^2 - x^2)^{3/2}$ with one fractional exponent.

In Problems 23-28, factor the polynomial in two variables into two factors.

23. $9x^2 + 21xy - 8y^2$ **24.** $9x^2 + 22xy + 8y^2$ **25.** $10x^2 - 99xy - 63y^2$

26. $16z^2 - 81w^2$ **27.** $32m^5 - n^{10}$ **28.** $x^{14} - y^7$

In Problems 29-31, solve by completing the square.

29. $2x^2 + 2x - 1 = 0$ **30.** $x^2 + x - 1 = 0$ **31.** $2x^2 - 4x - 3 = 0$

32. Factor by completing the square on a^2: $2a^2b^2 + 2a^2c^2 + 2b^2c^2 - a^4 - b^4 - c^4$. Used for area of triangle.

33^h Factor $bc(c^2 - b^2) + ca(a^2 - c^2) + ab(b^2 - a^2)$. Used for an integral.

In Problems 34-36, solve by the quadratic formula. The roots may be complex.

34. $x^2 - \sqrt{10}x + 1 = 0$ **35.** $x^2 + x + 1 = 0$ **36.** $2x^2 - 4x + 3 = 0$

37. Solve by any method: $x^2 - 13ix - 40 = 0$

38. Solve for x: $a^2 + b^2 + c^2 + x^2 = \frac{1}{2}(a + b + c + x)^2$

39. Solve for r: $1 - r + r^2 - r^3 + \cdots = r$.

40. Find the sum and product of the roots of $\sqrt{15}x^2 - \sqrt{3}x - \sqrt{5} = 0$.

In Problems 41 and 42, use the discriminant.

41. For which values of b does $2x^2 + bx + 3 = 0$ have equal roots?

42. For which values of c does $4x^2 - 5x + c = 0$ have real roots?

In Problems 43-48, factor the polynomial completely over the reals.

43. $y^4 - 6y^2x^2 + x^4$ **44.** $x^4 - 13x^2 + 36$

45^h $x^4 + 1$ **46^h** $u^4 - 4u^2 + 7$

47^h $x^8 + 1$ **48^h** $x^4 - 3x^3 + 2x^2 - 3x + 1$

49. Factor $x(x + 1)(x + 2)(x + 3) + 1$ and state a theorem about integers.

In Problems 50 and 51, find the roots of the symmetric polynomial.

50^h $x^4 - x^3 - 5x^2 - x + 1$ **51.** $x^4 + x^3 - 4x^2 + x + 1$

52. A vector with components a, b, c has magnitude $\sqrt{a^2 + b^2 + c^2}$. Find and simplify the magnitude of the vector having components $2t, 1 + t^2, 1 - t^2$.

53^h Solve for x: $\left(\frac{2x}{x + 6}\right)^{2x^2 - 9x + 4} = 1$.

In Problems 54-60, solve the radical equation for x.

54. $\sqrt[3]{4x - 3} = -3$ **55.** $\sqrt{5 + 2x} = x + 1$ **56.** $\sqrt{x} + \sqrt{p} = \sqrt{5}$

57. $5\sqrt{4 + x^2} + 4(7 - x) = 34$ **58.** $\sqrt{2x + 1} - \sqrt{x} = 1$ **59.** $y = \sqrt{\frac{x^4}{x^2 - 4}}$

In Problems 60-65, find all roots of the cubic equation assuming at least one root is rational.

60. $x^3 - 7x - 6 = 0$ **61.** $x^3 - x^2 - x - 2 = 0$ **62.** $x^3 - 2x^2 - 31x + 20 = 0$

63[h] $4x^3 - 2x^2 - 3x + 1 = 0$ **64.** $2x^3 - 7x^2 - 7x + 30 = 0$ **65.** $2x^3 + 3x^2 - 4x + 1$

In Problems 66-69, solve as a quadratic equation by making a substitution.

66. $x^2 - 6x - \sqrt{x^2 - 6x - 3} = 5$ **67.** $2^{6x} - 5 \cdot 2^{3x} + 4 = 0$ **68.** $x - 5\sqrt{x} - 6 = 0$

69. $.25/(1+j) + .9/(1+j)^2 = 1$

In Problems 70 and 71, factor by grouping.

70. $x^3 + 4x^2 - x - 4$ **71.** $x^4 + x^3 + x + 1$

72. A stone falls d ft into a well in t_1 seconds, where $d = \frac{1}{2}gt_1^2 = 16.1t_1^2$. The sound travels back in t_2 seconds, where $d = 1130t_2$ (at 70°F). If the total time $t_1 + t_2 = \sqrt{d/16.1} + d/1130 = 3.0$ seconds, find d.

73. Solve for n, the sample size for a confidence interval: $E = z\sqrt{\dfrac{1}{4n}}\sqrt{\dfrac{N-n}{N-1}}$

Hints and Notes 3. NYTimes, Aug 10, 2010, p.1 **33.** Arrange in decreasing powers of c.
45. Stumped Leibniz in 1702 **46.** Took Euler several weeks in 1742 **47.** Do $x(x+3)$ and $(x+1)(x+2)$ first.
48. symmetric **47.** Problem 45 **50.** Amer Math Monthly 114:6(2007)554-556 **53.** Practice 1.5.3
63. Used to find trig functions of multiples of 18°.

1.8 ALGEBRAIC FRACTIONS AND EQUATIONS

1. RATIONAL

Rational Expression has the form $N(x)/D(x)$ where $N(x)$ and $D(x)$ are polynomials. The coefficients need not be rational numbers. A polynomial is rational because we can write $P(x) = P(x)/1$.

Multiplication $\dfrac{A}{B} \cdot \dfrac{C}{D} = \dfrac{AC}{BD}$ **Cancellation** $\dfrac{A\cancel{C}}{B\cancel{C}} = \dfrac{A}{B}$ if $C \neq 0$. Note that $\dfrac{\cancel{C}}{B\cancel{C}} = \dfrac{1}{B}$ an empty numerator gets a 1. **Division** $\dfrac{A}{B} \div \dfrac{C}{D} = \dfrac{A}{B} \cdot \dfrac{D}{C}$ **Reciprocal** $1 \div \dfrac{C}{D} = \dfrac{D}{C}$. To divide by a fraction, multiply by its reciprocal.   (1)

Practice 1 True or false: $\dfrac{A}{B} \div \dfrac{C}{D} = \dfrac{A \div C}{B \div D}$?

Example 1 Simplify (a) $A = \dfrac{1}{2} \div \dfrac{2}{3}$ (b) $B = \dfrac{4x^2}{y} \cdot \dfrac{y^2}{10x^3}$ (c) $C = \dfrac{x^2 + 3x + 2}{6x^2 - 6} \div \dfrac{x^2 + 4x + 4}{x - 1}$

Solution (a) $A = \dfrac{1}{2} \cdot \dfrac{3}{2} = \dfrac{3}{4}$

(b) $B = \dfrac{4x^2y^2}{10x^3y} = \dfrac{2y}{5x} \cdot \dfrac{x^2y}{x^2y} = \dfrac{2y}{5x}$, $y \neq 0$

(c) $C = \dfrac{x^2 + 3x + 2}{6x^2 - 6} \cdot \dfrac{x - 1}{x^2 + 4x + 4} = \dfrac{(x+1)(x+2)}{6(x-1)(x+1)} \cdot \dfrac{x-1}{(x+2)^2} = \dfrac{1}{6(x+2)}$, $x \neq \pm 1$ ■

Practice 2 Simplify $D = \dfrac{6x - 12}{4xy + 4x} \cdot \dfrac{y^2 - 1}{2 - 3x + x^2}$.

Addition and Subtraction $\dfrac{A}{B} \pm \dfrac{C}{D} = \dfrac{A}{B} \cdot \dfrac{D}{D} \pm \dfrac{C}{D} \cdot \dfrac{B}{B} = \dfrac{AD \pm CB}{BD}$; convert the expressions to a common denominator.

LCD Least Common Denominator is the least common multiple of the denominators. To get the LCD, factor each denominator. Form a product using the highest power of a factor found in any one denominator. To add, multiply each term by a unit fraction with the factors its denominator needs to reach the LCD. If the LCD has 3 or more distinct factors, the sum may be reducible; see Example 2(a).   (2)

Practice 3 Find the LCD; do nothing else: $\dfrac{2}{x^2y^3z^5} - \dfrac{7}{x^4y^2z^3} + \dfrac{3}{x^3y^7z}$.

Example 2 Combine (a) $R = \frac{3}{10} + \frac{5}{6} - \frac{11}{45}$ (b) $S = \frac{3}{x^2} + \frac{4}{xy} - \frac{5}{y^2}$

Solution $\square$ indicates the factor of LCD missing from the denominator.

(a) $10 = 2 \cdot 5$, $6 = 2 \cdot 3$, $45 = 9 \cdot 5 = 3^2 \cdot 5$. LCD $= 2 \cdot 3^2 \cdot 5 = 90$.

$R = \frac{3}{2 \cdot 5} \cdot \frac{3^2}{\boxed{3^2}} + \frac{5}{2 \cdot 3} \cdot \frac{3 \cdot 5}{\boxed{3 \cdot 5}} - \frac{11}{3^2 \cdot 5} \cdot \frac{2}{\boxed{2}} = \frac{27 + 75 - 22}{90} = \frac{80}{90} = \frac{8}{9}$

(b) LCD $= x^2 y^2$. $S = \frac{3}{x^2} \cdot \frac{y^2}{\boxed{y^2}} + \frac{4}{xy} \cdot \frac{xy}{\boxed{xy}} - \frac{5}{y^2} \cdot \frac{x^2}{\boxed{x^2}} = \frac{3y^2 + 4xy - 5x^2}{x^2 y^2}$

Example 3 Combine $T = \frac{y-3}{(y-5)^2} + \frac{y-2}{y^2 - y - 20}$.

Solution $T = \frac{y-3}{(y-5)^2} + \frac{y-2}{(y-5)(y+4)}$. LCD $= (y-5)^2(y+4)$.

$T = \frac{y-3}{(y-5)^2} \cdot \frac{y+4}{\boxed{y+4}} + \frac{y-2}{(y-5)(y+4)} \cdot \frac{y-5}{\boxed{y-5}} = \frac{(y^2+y-12) + (y^2-7y+10)}{(y-5)^2(y+4)}$

$= \frac{2y^2 - 6y - 2}{(y-5)^2(y+4)}$

Practice 4 Combine $U = \frac{3}{y-2} - \frac{2}{y+2} - \frac{y}{y^2-4}$.

Complex Fractions have a numerator or denominator that is a fraction; otherwise the fraction is **simple**. Combine terms in numerator and denominator, factor, then invert denominator and multiply, to get a simple fraction. $\quad\quad\quad\quad\quad\quad$ (2)

Example 4 Simplify $R = \dfrac{1 - \dfrac{4}{(x-1)^2}}{\dfrac{x^2-5x+6}{x^2-1}}$.

Solution $R = \dfrac{\dfrac{1 \cdot (x-1)^2 - 4}{(x-1)^2}}{\dfrac{x^2-5x+6}{x^2-1}} = \dfrac{\dfrac{x^2+2x+1-4}{(x-1)^2}}{\dfrac{(x-3)(x-2)}{(x-1)(x+1)}} = \dfrac{x^2-2x-3}{(x-1)^2} \cdot \dfrac{(x-1)(x+1)}{(x-3)(x-2)}$

$= \dfrac{(x-3)(x+1)}{(x-1)^2} \cdot \dfrac{(x-1)(x+1)}{(x-3)(x-2)} = \dfrac{(x+1)^2}{(x-1)(x-2)}$, $x \neq -1, 3$

Practice 5 In Example 4, 3 is excluded because we canceled $x - 3$. Why is -1 excluded?

Rational Equations Multiply by the LCD to clear fractions, but exclude its zeros.

Practice 6 If $N(x)/D(x) = 0$, what simpler equation must be true?

Example 5 Solve $\frac{x}{x+2} - \frac{2}{x^2+3x+2} = \frac{1}{2}$.

Solution Because $x^2 + 3x + 2 = (x+1)(x+2)$, the LCD is $2(x+1)(x+2)$. If $x \neq -1$ or

-2, multiply to get $2(x+1)(x+2)\frac{x}{x+2} - 2(x+1)(x+2)\frac{2}{x^2+3x+2} = 2(x+1)(x+2)\frac{1}{2}$

$2x(x+1) - 2 \cdot 2 = x^2 + 3x + 2$, $2x^2 + 2x - 4 = x^2 + 3x + 2$, $0 = x^2 - x - 6 = (x-3)(x+2)$

$x = 3$ is a solution, but $x = -2$ is excluded (*extraneous*).

Practice 7 Solve $\frac{y-2}{y} = \frac{4}{y(y-2)}$.

2. RADICAL

Example 6 Combine $U = \frac{x}{\sqrt{x^2+3}} - \frac{\sqrt{x^2+3}}{x}$.

Solution LCD $= x\sqrt{x^2+3}$.

$U = \frac{x}{\sqrt{x^2+3}} \cdot \frac{x}{x} - \frac{\sqrt{x^2+3}}{x} \cdot \frac{\sqrt{x^2+3}}{\sqrt{x^2+3}} = \frac{x^2 - (x^2+3)}{x\sqrt{x^2+3}} = \frac{-3}{x\sqrt{x^2+3}}$

Example 7 (a) Evaluate $w = \dfrac{1}{\sqrt{x^2+4}+2} - \dfrac{1}{4}$ if $x = 4.537 \times 10^{-8}$. (b) Subtract, rationalize and try again.

Solution (a) A TI-83 gives 0: the first term is nearly $\frac{1}{4}$ and all significant digits are lost in subtraction.

(b) $w = \dfrac{4-(\sqrt{x^2+4}+2)}{4(\sqrt{x^2+4}+2)} = \dfrac{2-\sqrt{x^2+4}}{4(\sqrt{x^2+4}+2)} \cdot \dfrac{2+\sqrt{x^2+4}}{\sqrt{x^2+4}+2} = \dfrac{4-(x^2+4)}{4(\sqrt{x^2+4}+2)^2}$

$= \dfrac{-x^2}{4(\sqrt{x^2+4}+2)^2}$. Now a TI-83 gives -3.2163×10^{-17}. ∎

Domain of an expression is the set of values for which it is defined.

Example 8 Increase the domain of $w = \dfrac{z^{2/3}-x^{2/3}}{z-x}$ to include $z = x$. (Used in calculus.)

Analysis We express the numerator and denominator as the difference of like powers having the same base.

Solution $w = \dfrac{(z^{1/3})^2-(x^{1/3})^2}{(z^{1/3})^3-(x^{1/3})^3} = \dfrac{(z^{1/3}-x^{1/3})(z^{1/3}+x^{1/3})}{(z^{1/3}-x^{1/3})(z^{2/3}+z^{1/3}x^{1/3}+x^{2/3})}$

$= \dfrac{z^{1/3}+x^{1/3}}{z^{2/3}+z^{1/3}x^{1/3}+x^{2/3}}, \; z \neq x$ ∎

Practice 8 Simplify $\sqrt{x^2-6x+9}$.

Preserve the Domain $\sqrt{ab} \neq \sqrt{a}\sqrt{b}$ if a and b are both negative.

Example 9 Simplify $D = \sqrt{\dfrac{x+1}{x-1}} \dfrac{1}{(x+1)^2}$ (the derivative of $\sqrt{\dfrac{x-1}{x+1}}$).

Solution The domain is $x < -1$ or $x > 1$.

$D = \sqrt{\dfrac{x+1}{x-1}} \cdot \dfrac{1}{\sqrt{(x+1)^4}} = \sqrt{\dfrac{x+1}{(x-1)(x+1)^4}} = \dfrac{1}{\sqrt{(x-1)(x+1)^3}}$ ∎

Revenue $R = \text{price} \times \text{quantity} = px$ where $p = R/x$ is the **demand**. When $x = 0$, R must be 0 and p is the maximum selling price. If p is 0, then x is the maximum quantity.

Example 10 Revenue is $R = 10(\sqrt{x+4}-2) - 2x$. (a) Increase the domain of the demand to include 0, and find the maximum selling price. (b) Find the maximum quantity.

Solution (a) $p = \dfrac{10}{x}(\sqrt{x+4}-2)\dfrac{\sqrt{x+4}+2}{\sqrt{x+4}+2} - 2 = \dfrac{10}{x} \cdot \dfrac{(x+4)-4}{\sqrt{x+4}+2} - 2 = \dfrac{10}{\sqrt{x+4}+2} - 2.$

When $x = 0$, $p = \dfrac{10}{4} - 2 = .50$, the maximum price.

(b) If $p = 0$, $\dfrac{10}{\sqrt{x+4}+2} = 2$, $5 = \sqrt{x+4}+2$, $\sqrt{x+4} = 3$, $x+4 = 9$, $x = 5$, the maximum quantity. ∎

Practice Answers 1. True. $\dfrac{A}{B} \div \dfrac{C}{D} = \dfrac{A}{B} \cdot \dfrac{D}{C} = \dfrac{A}{C} \cdot \dfrac{D}{B} = \dfrac{A}{C} \div \dfrac{B}{D} = \dfrac{A \div C}{B \div D}$

2. $D = \dfrac{6(x-2)}{4x(y+1)} \cdot \dfrac{(y-1)(y+1)}{(x-1)(x-2)} = 3\dfrac{y-1}{2x(x-1)}$, $x \neq 2, y \neq -1$ **3.** $x^4y^7z^5$

4. $U = \dfrac{3}{y-2} \cdot \dfrac{y+2}{y+2} - \dfrac{2}{y+2} \cdot \dfrac{y-2}{y-2} - \dfrac{y}{y^2-4} = \dfrac{10}{y^2-4}$

5. Because $x - 1$ is a factor of the original denominator. **6.** $N(x) = 0$

7. $(y-2)^2 = 4$, $y \neq 0, 2$; $y - 2 = 2$, $y = 4$ (reject $y - 2 = -2$, $y = 0$) **8.** $\sqrt{x^2-6x+9} = \sqrt{(x-3)^2} = |x-3|$

Problems 1.8 Problems with ^{h} have hints below.

In Problems 1-4, multiply or divide and simplify. Indicate excluded values.

1. $\dfrac{25ac^2}{15a^2c} \cdot \dfrac{4ad^4}{15ab}$

2. $\dfrac{15ac^2}{7bd} \div \dfrac{4a}{14b^2d}$

3. $\dfrac{x^2 + 7x + 12}{3x^2 + 13x + 4} \cdot \dfrac{3x + 1}{x + 3}$

4. $\dfrac{y^2 - 2y + 1}{7y^2 - 7y} \div \dfrac{y^2 - 4y + 3}{35y^2}$

In Problems 5-24, express as a fraction lowest terms. Indicate excluded values.

5. $\dfrac{a}{a - 2} - \dfrac{a - 2}{a}$

6. $\dfrac{1}{42} + \dfrac{1}{86} + \dfrac{1}{129} + \dfrac{1}{301}$

7. $\dfrac{x}{x + 1} - x + 1$

8. $x - \dfrac{2}{x - 1}$

9. $\dfrac{4a}{3x + 6} + \dfrac{5a^2}{4x + 8}$

10. $\dfrac{x - 1}{x + 1} - \dfrac{2}{x^2 + x}$

11. $\dfrac{3x - 1}{2x - 4} + \dfrac{4x}{3x - 6} - \dfrac{x - 4}{5x - 10}$

12. $\dfrac{b - 1}{b^2 + 2b} + \dfrac{b}{3b + 6}$

13. $\dfrac{1}{x^2 - 4y^2} - \dfrac{1}{x^2 - 4xy + 4y^2}$

14. $\dfrac{2x + 1}{4x - 2} + \dfrac{5}{2x} - \dfrac{x + 4}{2x^2 - x}$

15. $\dfrac{\dfrac{x}{y} + \dfrac{y - x}{y + x}}{1 - \dfrac{x}{y} \cdot \dfrac{y - x}{y + x}}$

16. $\dfrac{3x^2}{x^2 - 4} + \dfrac{2}{x^2 - 4x + 4}$

17. $\dfrac{\dfrac{3}{(z + 1)^2} - \dfrac{3}{(x + 1)^2}}{z - x}$

18. $\dfrac{\dfrac{1}{x} + xy}{x + \dfrac{1}{xy}}$

19. $\dfrac{x}{x^2 - 4} + \dfrac{4}{x^2 - x - 2} - \dfrac{x - 2}{x^2 + 3x + 2}$

20. $\dfrac{1}{y^2 + 2y - 35} - \dfrac{y - 1}{y^2 - 4y - 5} + \dfrac{2}{y^2 + 8y + 7}$

21. $\left(\dfrac{1 - x^2}{1 + x^2} - \dfrac{1 - y^2}{1 + y^2}\right)^2 + \left(\dfrac{2x}{1 + x^2} - \dfrac{2y}{1 + y^2}\right)^2$

22. $\left(\dfrac{1 - x^2}{1 + x^2} + \dfrac{1 - y^2}{1 + y^2}\right)^2 + \left(\dfrac{2x}{1 + x^2} + \dfrac{2y}{1 + y^2}\right)^2$

23. $\dfrac{(x + 1/x)^6 - (x^6 + 1/x^6) - 2}{(x + 1/x)^3 + (x^3 + 1/x^3)}$

In Problems 25-29, simplify the radical expression. Indicate excluded values.

25. $\sqrt{1 + \left(\dfrac{x}{\sqrt{1 - x^2}}\right)^2}$

26. $\sqrt{1 + \left(x^3 - \dfrac{1}{4x^3}\right)^2}$

27. $\sqrt{1 - x^2} + \dfrac{1 + x^2}{\sqrt{1 - x^2}}$

28. $\dfrac{\dfrac{2}{\sqrt{x^2 + 2}} - \sqrt{x^2 + 2}}{x^2}$

29. $\left(\dfrac{x}{1 + x^3}\right)^{-1/4} \cdot \dfrac{1(1 + x^3) - x(3x^2)}{(1 + x^3)^2}$

In Problems 30 and 31, for the given revenue R $= px$, increase the domain of the demand p to include 0, and find the maximum selling price and maximum quantity.

30. R $= 30(\sqrt{x + 1} - 1) - 6x$

31. R $= 24 - x - \dfrac{192}{x + 8}$

32. Use like powers so $z = x$ is included in the domain: $\dfrac{z^{3/4} - x^{3/4}}{z - x}$.

In Problems 33-34, calculating the original expression for the given x gives 0. Rationalize to get full accuracy.

33. $(\sqrt{x^2 + 1} - 1)/x^2$ when $x = 5.6704 \times 10^{-8}$

34. $\sqrt{x^2 + x} - x$ when $x = 1.23456 \times 10^{13}$

35. If we evaluate $1/R - 1/(R + h)$ with R $= 2.09 \times 10^7$ and $h = 1.23 \times 10^{-6}$, a TI-83 gives 0. Simplify first.

36. Simplify $\dfrac{\sqrt{PQ - R^2}}{P^{3/2}}$ where P $= t^{-4} + 4t^{-2} + 4$, Q $= 4t^{-6} + 4t^{-4}$, R $= -2t^{-5} - 4t^{-3}$ (curvature of space curve)

37. (Descartes) If four circles having radii a, b, c, d are mutually tangent then $\dfrac{1}{a^2} + \dfrac{1}{b^2} + \dfrac{1}{c^2} + \dfrac{1}{d^2} = \frac{1}{2}\left(\dfrac{1}{a} + \dfrac{1}{b} + \dfrac{1}{c} + \dfrac{1}{d}\right)^2$.

If three of the radii are 1, 2, 3, find the radii of two circles tangent to these. (The circle containing them has negative radius.)

In Problems 38-45, solve the equation. Watch for extraneous solutions.

38^h $\dfrac{4}{x} - \dfrac{3}{x + 1} = 7$

39. $\dfrac{x - 1}{x} - \dfrac{x}{x + 3} = \dfrac{2x + 33}{x^3 + 3x^2}$

40. $\dfrac{x + 3}{2x + 5} = \dfrac{1}{x + 3}$

41. $\dfrac{1}{k - 2} = \dfrac{6}{k^2 - 2k}$

42. $\dfrac{b}{b + 4} - \dfrac{1}{b} = \dfrac{2}{b + 4}$

43. $\dfrac{x}{x + 8} + \dfrac{16}{x^2 - 64} = \dfrac{1}{x - 8}$

44. $\dfrac{x}{2x + 8} + \dfrac{1}{x - 4} = \dfrac{16}{x^2 - 16}$

45. $\dfrac{y}{y + 3} + \dfrac{y}{y - 3} = \dfrac{18}{y^2 - 9}$

46. $\dfrac{4}{x} + \dfrac{3}{x - 10} + \dfrac{2}{x - 6} = 0$

In Problems 47-50, solve for Y as a rational function of s. These are Laplace transforms of initial-value problems.

47. $\dfrac{8}{s} = [s^2 Y - 0s + 2] - 3[sY - 0] - 4Y$

48. $\dfrac{1}{s} = [s^2 Y - 1s - 4] - 4[sY - 1] + 3Y$

49. $\dfrac{4}{s^3} = [s^2 Y - 4s - 1] - [sY - 4] - 6Y$

50. $\dfrac{1}{s^2} = [s^2 Y - 1s - 2] - 9Y$

51. (a) Find the terms of the Balmer hydrogen sequence $a_n = \frac{\lambda}{h} = \frac{n^2}{n^2 - 4}$ for $n = 3, \ldots, 7$. (b) Show the sequence is decreasing by calculating $a_n - a_{n+1}$.

52. If $\frac{1}{1+y}$ is approximated by $1 - y$, $|y| < 1$, find the relative error.

Hint 38. Math B Regents, Jun 2004 **50.** Let $y = xt$.

1.9 WORD PROBLEMS

Starting The key to solving a word problem is to define precisely what you are looking for, often specifying units. Use your definition to translate the problem from English to algebra. Watch out for "each"; it often means two or more different items. Sketch geometric figures; learn how to make a box and a cylinder. Use dashes for hidden lines. Often it is helpful to make a word equation before you write formulas. Be sure to state your answer in English.

Practice 1 Draw and label a closed box with a square base of side x, and height h, viewed from the top right corner. Used dashed lines for the edges you cannot see.

Simple Interest $I = Prt$, where P (principal) dollars is borrowed, r is the annual rate, t is the number of years. $\hfill (1)$

Example 1 \$70,000 is invested, part at 6%, part at 8.5%. If \$5000 is earned, how much is invested at each rate?

Solution First translate "each": How much is invested at 6% and how much is invested at 8.5%. Either one can be the unknown, but you must choose; you cannot say "Let x be each." Choosing the first, we can say "Let x be the amount invested at 6%", but this is missing the units and sounds funny when you replace x by the answer. Say: x dollars is invested at 6%. Then $(70,000 - x)$ dollars is invested at 8.5%.

The relevant word equation is: interest at 6% + interest at 8.5% = total interest

$.06x + .085(70,000 - x) = 5000, \qquad .06x + 5950 - .085x = 5000, \qquad 950 = .025x,$

$x = 950/.025 = 38,000$

The answer: Invest \$38,000 at 6% and $70,000 - 38,000 = \$32,000$ at 8.5% ∎

Practice 2 Translate into algebra: There are six times as many students as there are professors. Use s for the number of students and p for the number of professors.

Example 2 A winery wishes to make 10,000 liters of 30 proof sherry (15% alcohol by volume) by mixing 20 proof white wine with 70 proof brandy. How much of each should be used?

Solution Use x liters of wine and $(10,000 - x)$ liters of brandy.

Word equation: alcohol in wine + alcohol in brandy = alcohol in sherry

$.10x + .35(10,000 - x) = .15(10,000), \qquad .10x + 3500 - .35x = 1500, \qquad 2000 = .25x,$

$x = 2000/.25 = 8000$

The answer: Use 8000 liters of wine and $10000 - 8000 = 2000$ liters of brandy. ∎

Business Terms Revenue R = selling price per unit × number of units sold = px; p is in dollars per unit unless otherwise stated. (Note: many authors use q for quantity.) C(x) is the cost of producing x units. (See Problem 27 for a nonlinear C.)

Variable cost = number of units × unit cost. The @ symbol indicates "× unit cost": 12 cases @ \$30 = \$360. The **fixed cost** is C(0). **Markup** is selling price − cost for an item. **Profit** P = revenue − cost of goods sold = R − C. A **break-even point** is where R = C. We "make a profit" if P > 0, i.e. R > C. **Objective** is a function whose value is a goal; **constraint** is a possible side condition. $\hfill (3)$

Example 3 A product has a fixed cost of \$200 per week and a unit cost of \$2. If the product sells for \$4/unit, find (a) the cost function C, (b) the revenue function R, and (c) the break-even point.

Solution x units are made and sold weekly. (a) C = fixed + variable = $200 + 2x$

(b) R = $4x$ (c) R = C so $4x = 200 + 2x$, $2x = 200$, $x = 100$ units/week ∎

Example 4 A boat can travel at 25 mph in still water. It makes a 50-mile trip upstream and back in $4\frac{1}{4}$ hours. Find the rate of the current.

Solution The rate of the current is v mph. The boat travels at $25 - v$ mph upstream and $25 + v$ mph downstream. The relevant formula is time = distance/rate.

Word equation: time upstream + time downstream = total time

$\frac{50}{25 - v} + \frac{50}{25 + v} = \frac{17}{4}$. Multiply by $4(25 - v)(25 + v)$ to clear fractions.

$4(50)(25 + v) + 4(50)(25 - v) = 17(25 - v)(25 + v)$

LHS: $(5000 + 200v) + (5000 - 200v) = 10000$. RHS: $17(625 - v^2) = 10{,}625 - 17v^2$

Hence $17v^2 = 625$, $v^2 = 625/17$, $v = \pm\sqrt{625/17} = 6.06$ (reject -6.06)

Answer: The rate of the current is 6.06 mph. ∎

Remark The total travel time for a d mile trip if the boat's speed is b mph and the current is v mph is $\frac{d}{b - v} + \frac{d}{b + v} = \frac{2bd}{b^2 - v^2}$.

Practice 3 A boat having speed b in still water is in a river having speed v. A cooler falls off as the boat is heading upstream. After 20 minutes the boat quickly turns and heads downstream. How long does it take to get back to the floating cooler?

Two Variables Sometimes it is easier to express the objective using two variables. Then we find an equation relating these variables (the constraint). Solve for the easier variable and substitute into the objective. Sometimes equations are solved numerically. In geometry problems a figure is very helpful.

Example 5 A drug company wants to fence a rectangular area against an outside wall to store liquid nitrogen. Only three sides need to be built. The budget allows for 1000 ft of fence. What dimensions will give an area of 120,000 ft^2?

Solution Let x ft of fence be perpendicular to the wall and y ft parallel. See Figure 1. The objective is the area K $= xy$ subject to the constraint $2x + y = 1000$.

Solve for y because it is easier: $y = 1000 - 2x$ and substitute in the objective, to get a function of one variable: A$(x) = x(1000 - 2x) = 1000x - 2x^2$, $0 \le x \le 500$

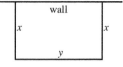

wall

A$(x) = 120{,}000 = 1000x - 2x^2$, $2x^2 - 100x + 120{,}000 = 0$,
$0 = x^2 - 500x + 60{,}000 = (x - 200)(x - 300)$
$x = 200$, $y = 1000 - 2 \cdot 200 = 600$ or $x = 300$, $y = 400$

Figure 1

Either 200 ft perpendicular and 600 ft parallel, or 300 ft perpendicular and 400 ft parallel.

Cubic Example 6 and 7 lead to cubic equations $ax^3 + bx^2 + cx + d = 0$ with at least one rational root m/n where m is a divisor of d and n is a divisor of a. If $a = 1$, any rational root is an integer. You can use a TI-83 TABLE to find it. Use synthetic division to get the quadratic factor.

Example 6 A rectangular box will be made by cutting equal squares from each corner of a sheet of cardboard 16 cm $\times$ 30 cm and folding up the sides. Find the dimensions of the box if the volume is 720 cm^3.

Solution The choice of variable is clear: The side of each square is x cm. See Figure 2; fold on the dashed lines. Since x is cut off each end, the base has length $\ell = (30 - 2x)$, width $w = (16 - 2x)$, and height $h = x$. Because ℓ and $w \ge 0$, then $0 \le x \le 8$. The volume of the box is

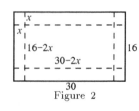

Figure 2

$\ell w h = (30 - 2x)(16 - 2x)x = (4x^2 - 92x + 480)x = 4x^3 - 92x^2 + 480x = 720$
$x^3 - 23x^2 + 120x - 180 = 0$. 〚TABLE〛 shows $x = 3$ is a root. Synthetic division shows

3	1	−23	120	−180
		3	−60	180
	1	−20	60	0

the depressed equation is $x^2 - 20x + 60 = 0$ with roots $10 \pm \sqrt{40}$ or $16.325 > 8$ and 3.675. The box is 3 cm $\times$ 24 cm $\times$ 10 cm or 3.68 cm $\times$ 22.65 cm $\times$ 8.65 cm ∎

Example 7 An open box with a square base is to contain 2000 in^3. The cost of material is 3¢/in^2 for the sides and 5¢/in^2 for the bottom. Find its dimensions if the total cost is \$32.
Solution See Figure 3. Because the box is open, we can see part of an edge. There are two variables here: the base is x in and the height is h in. The constraint is $V = x^2h = 2000$. Solve for h because it is easier: $h = 2000x^{-2}$.

Figure 3

Cost(¢) = cost of bottom + 4 × cost of a side = 5 × area of bottom + 4 × 3 × area of side
$= 5x^2 + 12xh = 5x^2 + 12x(2000x^{-2}) = 5x^2 + 24000x^{-1} = 3200$, $5x^3 + 24000 = 3200x$,
$x^3 - 640x + 4800 = 0$, $x > 0$.

TI-83: Y$_1$=X^3−640X+4800, [WINDOW] Xmin=0, Xmax=50, Xscl=10, Ymin=−10000, Ymax=10000, Yscl=1000. See Figure 4. There seems to be a root at 20. We confirm with TABLE. Use synthetic division to get the depressed equation.

Figure 4

20	1	0	−640	4800
		20	400	−4800
	1	20	−240	0

$x^2 + 20x - 240 = 0$, $x^2 + 20x + 10^2 = 240 + 100$, $x + 10 = \pm\sqrt{340} = 2\sqrt{85}$.
The base is 20 in × 20 in and the height is $2000/20^2 = 5$ in or the base is 8.44 in × 8.44 in and the height is $2000/8.44^2 = 28.08$ in. ∎

Example 8 A helicopter at point B is 2 miles offshore from the nearest point A of a straight coastline. It uses 5 gal/mi flying over water and 4 gal/mi flying over land. Its destination is point C on the coast 7 miles from A. It flies to a point D on AC, and then to C. If D is A, it uses $5(2) + 4(7) = 38$ gal. If D is C, $DC = \sqrt{2^2 + 7^2}$ miles, it uses $5\sqrt{53} = 36.4$ gal. Find D so that it uses only 34 gal.
Solution See Figure 5. If we let x be either BD or DC, then finding the other will be complicated, but both distances are easy to express in terms of AD. Let $AD = x$ mi. Then $DC = (7 - x)$ mi and $BD = \sqrt{4 + x^2}$.

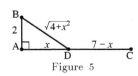

Figure 5

Gallons used over water + gallons used over land = total gallons used

$5\sqrt{4 + x^2} + 4(7 - x) = 34$ so $5\sqrt{4 + x^2} = 6 + 4x$. Square: $25(4 + x^2) = (6 + 4x)^2$,

$100 + 25x^2 = 36 + 48x + 16x^2$ so $9x^2 - 48x + 64 = 0$ and $(3x - 8)^2 = 0$. Thus $x = \frac{8}{3}$.

D should be $\frac{8}{3}$ mile from A.
Analysis Isolate the radical and square both sides. The root is double so it's a minimum. ∎

Cases One equation is valid for small values of a variable, and another for larger values.

Example 9 A smuggler has formed gold into 22 ft of edging to apply to a rectangular box with a pair of square faces, having length plus girth totaling 108″. Find the dimensions. (Length is the largest dimension, girth is the distance around the thickest part perpendicular to the length. 108″ is the maximum for USPS and UPS.)
Solution 22 ft × 12 in/1 ft = 264 in. Let x in. be a side of the square, h in. the third dimension. See Figure 3. The sum of the edges is $s = 8x + 4h$.

Figure 3 (bis)

If $x \le h$, then $h + 4x = 108$, and $h = 108 - 4x$, $108 - 4x \ge x$ so $0 \le x \le 21.6$. Then $s = 8x + 4(108 - 4x) = 432 - 8x = 264$ so $168 = 8x$ and $x = 21$.   Then $h = 108 - 4(21) = 24$ so one solution is $21'' \times 21'' \times 34''$.

If $x > h$, then length + girth = $x + (2x + 2h) = 108$, and $h = 54 - \frac{3}{2}x$, where $21.6 < x \le 36$. Then $s = 8x + 4(54 - \frac{3}{2}x) = 216 + 2x = 264$ so $2x = 48$ and $x = 24$.   Then $h = 54 - \frac{3}{2}(24) = 18$ so a second solution is $24'' \times 24'' \times 18''$. ∎

Practice 1

Practice Answers 1. Because the box is closed, we cannot see the 3 edges furthest from the upper right corner, so they are drawn dashed.
2. The number of students is six times the number of professors; $s = 6p$. (The wrong answer $6s = p$ is very common.)
3. The speed relative to the cooler is b in each direction; 20 minutes.

Problems 1.9 Problems with [h] have hints below.

0. US Supreme Court, Barber v. Thomas, Jun 7, 2010. Federal prison regulations give 54 additional days credit for each year served with good behavior; partial years are prorated. After deducting the credit for time already served, a prisoner has 298 days remaining. Assuming his good behavior continues, how many days will he actually serve?

1. A man is walking home at 3 mi/hr. His dog sees him when he is one mile away and runs at 5 mi/hr back and forth between home and the man until the man arrives home. How far did the dog travel?

Problems 2-17 involve linear equations.

2. In 1450, Gutenberg borrowed 800 guilders from Fust to finance his printing press; in 1452 he borrowed another 800 guilders. In 1455 Fust sued for 2026 guilders, principal plus simple interest. What rate was charged? (Gutenberg lost his invention and equipment; Fust published the 42-line bible in 1456.)

3. A programmer is paid $200 for each day she works but forfeits $50 for each day she takes off. At the end of 25 days she nets $4500. How many days did she work?

4. How much oil worth 28¢/qt should be mixed with oil worth 33¢/qt to make 45 qt of a mixture sold at 30¢/qt?

5[h] A 4 gallon radiator is filled with antifreeze which is 10% glycol. How much should be drained and replaced with pure glycol to get a 25% solution?

6. Tom drove 265 miles, part at 40 mph and part at 35 mph. If the trip took 7 hours, find each distance.

7. Items have a unit cost of 85¢ and the fixed costs are $280 per day. If the item can be sold for $1.10, find the break-even point.

8. A college wishing to endow a $5000 scholarship divides $80000 between investments paying 5% and 8%. How much is invested at each rate?.

9. A tank contains 200L of brine, which is 25% salt. How much water must be boiled off to get a 40% solution?

10. NYTimes, Apr 25, 2008, p.A19. One train leaves Station A at 6pm traveling at 40 miles per hour toward Station B. A second train leaves Station B at 7pm traveling on parallel tracks at 50 mph toward Station A. The stations are 400 miles apart. When do the trains pass each other?

11. An escalator of 12 steps takes 60 seconds from bottom to top. A girl walks up so that it take her 8 steps. How much time did it take?

12. Two ferries begin a trip across a river at the same time at a constant speed but from opposite sides of the river. They pass each other when they are 700 ft from one shore. They dock the same amount of time and start again. The second time they pass, they are 400 ft from the other shore. How wide is the river?

13. (CPA exam) A bank charges 10% interest and requires 8% of the loan to remain on deposit (**compensating balance**). A borrower needs $46,000. (a) How much must he borrow? (b) What is the true rate of interest?

14. Each layer of a standard DVD disc holds 133 minutes of movies. Compression ratios 2:1, 3:1, 4:1 are available with increasing loss of quality. To record a $2\frac{1}{2}$ hour movie, a recorder is started at 2:1 compression. After how many minutes can it be switched to normal mode?

15. NYTimes, Apr 19, 2009, p.Sp.1. In three starts, Wang is 0-3 with an earned run average (runs $\times$ 9/innings) of 34.50. He would need to throw $48\frac{2}{3}$ consecutive scoreless innings to reach a 3.79 ERA. How many innings has he pitched? (Given two paragraphs later.)

16. If $C(x) = \sqrt{x^2 + 1600}$ is a cost function, find the fixed cost.

17[h] A clay contains 12% water. After evaporation it contains 7% water and 50% silica. Find the original silica percentage.

18. NYTimes, Apr 20, 2008, p.BR19: Given the product of two numbers, as well as the difference between them, how do you determine the sum of their squares?

19[h] From the NYTimes, Apr 23, 2003, p.A24: 80% of breast cancer patients had the gene BPI; it was found in 57% of white patients and 89% of black patients. What fraction of patients were white?

20. The 2005 IRS tax for married filing jointly with taxable income over 59,400 but not over 119,950 is $8180 + 25\%$ of the amount over 59,400, but "do not use this to figure your tax". Instead use 25% of the whole amount minus 6670. Use a variable for the first rule and show it is equivalent to the second.

Problems 21-30 involve quadratic equations.

Problem 21

A ——x——•——$r-x$——B
$\qquad$ y

21. An underwater cable from A to B (see the figure) with a total resistance r has a leak, which may be considered a resistance y at an unknown (resistance) distance x from A. An EMF is applied at A. If the circuit is open at B, we can measure the resistance $x + y = b$. If the circuit is grounded at B, then y is in parallel with $r - x$ so we have $x + 1/[1/y + 1/(r-x)] = c$. Solve for x in terms of b, c, and r. Which root corresponds to the problem?

22[h] A line of joggers 50 ft long is jogging at a constant rate. A dog runs from the rear to the front and back again in the time it takes the joggers to run 50 ft. How far did the dog travel?

23. A vat can be filled by two pipes together in 20 minutes. The smaller alone takes 9 minutes more to fill the vat than the larger. How long does it take each pipe working alone? Interpret the negative answer too.

24. A product's cost function is $C = 80 + 4x + 0.1x^2$. If each item can be sold for \$10, find the break-even points.

25. Suppose that 240 feet of fencing will be used to enclose a rectangular field. Find the dimensions of the rectangle that will yield an area of $3500\,\text{ft}^2$.

26. A garden store wants to enclose a rectangular display of shrubs. Three sides will be built from chain-link fence costing \$20 per running foot, and the remaining side will be built from cedar fence costing \$10 per running foot. Find the dimensions of the enclosure that can be built with \$2000 worth of fence if its area is $800\,\text{ft}^2$.

27. It is required to enclose a rectangular area, partitioned into two parts by fencing parallel to two of the sides. If 360 yards of fencing are available, find the dimensions if the total area enclosed is $5400\,\text{yd}^2$.

28[h] A rectangular box with a pair of square faces has length plus girth totaling $108''$, and total surface area of $20\,\text{ft}^2$. Find the dimensions.

29. If there are w workers at a plant, each worker's output is $(100 - w)$ units per week, due to crowding, so total production is $x = w(100 - w)$, $0 \le w \le 50$. (a) Find the cost function if each worker is paid \$300/week and each unit uses \$4 of materials. (b) How much can be produced for \$19,600?

30. Four inch squares are cut from the corners of a piece of cardboard twice as long as it is wide, and folded up to make a $90\,\text{in}^3$ box. Find the dimensions of the cardboard.

Problems 31-35 involve cubic equations having at least one rational root.

31[h] A rectangular box with a pair of square faces has length plus girth totaling $108''$, and volume of $11{,}200\,\text{in}^3$. Find the dimensions.

32. A square piece of cardboard 12 inches by 12 inches will be used to make an open box by cutting a square from each corner and folding up the sides. What size square should be cut from each corner to yield a box of volume $128\,\text{in}^3$?

33. A shipper needs a closed rectangular container with a volume of 96 cubic feet and a square bottom. The heavy-duty plastic needed for the top and bottom costs \$3 per square foot, and the standard plastic for the sides costs \$2 per square foot. What dimensions yield a container costing \$288?

34. A rectangular box with a square bottom and open top is required to have a volume of 62.5 cubic inches. What dimensions yield a box with surface area of $75\,\text{in}^2$?

35. Find the dimensions of the open box with square bottom having volume $4000\,\text{in}^3$ that can be built with $1200\,\text{in}^2$ of material.

36. In Example 4, if $v = 0$ the total time is 4 hours and if $v \ge 25$ the trip upstream cannot be made. If $0 < v < 25$, calculate the total time minus 4 hours: $\dfrac{50}{25 - v} + \dfrac{50}{25 + v} - 4$. The difference is clearly positive.

Hints and Notes 5. 1 mole of nonionic solute added to 1kg water lowers the freezing point by 1.885C.
  17. The ratio of silica to all dry is constant. **19.** Assume there were 100 patients. **22.** Example 4.
  28. Example 8. **31.** Example 8.

1.10 INEQUALITIES IN ONE VARIABLE

Recall that $a < b$ means that $b - a$ is positive and $a > b$ means that $a - b$ is positive.

1. LINEAR INEQUALITIES
Equivalent Inequalities $a < b \Leftrightarrow b > a$ and $a \leq b \Leftrightarrow b \geq a$
Weak and Strict An inequality with $=$ is called weak; otherwise it is strict.
Transitivity If $a < b$ and $b < c$ then $a < c$.
Proof $b - a$ is positive and $c - b$ is positive, so the sum $(b - a) + (c - b) = c - a$ is positive.

Operations	English
(a) If $a < b$ then $a + c < b + c$	adding a positive or negative preserves an inequality
(b) If $a < b$ and $c < d$ then $a + c < b + d$. If $a < b$ and $c \leq d$ then $a + c < b + d$	
(c) If $a < b$ and $c > 0$ then $ac < bc$	multiplication by a positive preserves an inequality
(d) If $a < b$ and $c < 0$ then $ac > bc$	multiplication by a negative reverses an inequality
(e) If $0 < a < b$ and $p > 0$ then $a^p < b^p$	positive power preserves an inequality of positives
(f) If $0 < a < b$ and $p < 0$ then $a^p > b^p$	negative power reverses an inequality of positives

Proof (d) $c < 0$ so $-c > 0$, and $b - a > 0$. Then $(b - a)(-c) = ac - b > 0$ so $ac > ab$
(e) By (c), $a^2 = a \cdot a < b \cdot a \leq b \cdot b = b^2$, and similarly for any integer > 0. Let n be an integer > 0 and suppose $a^{1/n} \geq b^{1/n}$. Then $a = (a^{1/n})^n \geq (b^{1/n})^n = b$ which is a contradiction. Thus $a^{1/n} < b^{1/n}$ and so $a^{m/n} < b^{m/n}$ for any rational exponent > 0, and hence for any real exponent > 0.

Inverses (a) If $a < b$ then $c - a > c - b$ (b) If $a < b$ have the same sign, then $1/a > 1/b$.
Proof (a) $a + (c - a - b) < b + (c - a - b)$, $c - b < c - a$ (b) $\frac{1}{ab} > 0$, $a \cdot \frac{1}{ab} < b \cdot \frac{1}{ab}$, $1/b < 1/a$

Unconditional inequality is true for all values of the variables such as the triangle inequality. A **conditional** inequality not true for all numbers. We *prove* an unconditional inequality and *solve* a conditional inequality.

Number Line A horizontal line is drawn. An origin and a unit of distance is chosen. If $a > 0$, the point A, a units to the right of O is identified with a; we write A(a). If $a < 0$, we use the point $-a$ units to the left. AB $= |b - a|$ is the **distance** between A and B. If $a < b$ then A is to the left of B. The number line gets its properties from the real numbers, not conversely. (1)

Set Builder $\{x \mid \text{statement about } x\}$ means set of elements for which the statement is true.
Intervals "$a < x < b$" means "$a < x$ and $x < b$" or "x is strictly between a and b". Similarly for other chains.
Bounded intervals: $(a, b) = \{x \mid a < x < b\}$, $[a, b) = \{x \mid a \leq x < b\}$, $(a, b] = \{x \mid a < x \leq b\}$, $[a, b] = \{x \mid a \leq x \leq b\}$
Unbounded intervals: $(-\infty, b) = \{x \mid x < b\}$, $(-\infty, b] = \{x \mid x \leq b\}$, $(a, \infty) = \{x \mid x > a\}$, $[a, \infty) = \{x \mid x \geq a\}$
R $= (-\infty, \infty)$ is the set of all real numbers. a and b are **endpoints** of the interval. $\pm\infty$ means there is no endpoint; they aren't numbers.

An interval is **closed** if it contains all its endpoints; it is **open** if it contains none of its endpoints.

Closed intervals: $[a, b]$, $(-\infty, b]$, $[a, \infty)$, $(-\infty, \infty)$, $\{\}$.
Open intervals: (a, b), $(-\infty, b)$, (a, ∞), $(-\infty, \infty)$, $\{\}$.

Because $(-\infty, \infty)$ and $\{\}$ have no endpoints, they are both open and closed.
Excel Help uses $]a, b[$ for (a, b), etc. $[a, a] = \{a\}$; (a, a), $[a, a)$, $(a, a]$ are empty.

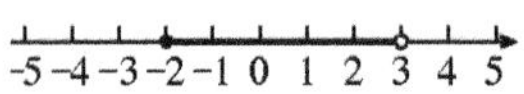

Figure 1

Example 1 Show the interval $[-2, 3)$ on a number line.
Solution See Figure 1. Use a bullet if the endpoint belongs to the interval and a hole if not.

Example 2 Solve $-3x + 2 \geq 14$ and express the solution in interval notation.
Solution Subtracting 2 from each member gives $-3x \geq 12$.
Dividing each member by -3 and reversing the inequality gives $x \leq -4$ or $(-\infty, -4]$. ∎

Practice 3 Solve $-2x + 5 < 11$ and express the solution in interval notation.

Double Inequalities If the variable appears only in the middle, solve as before. Otherwise, solve each inequality separately and take the intersection of the solutions. (4)

Example 3 Solve $7 > 5 - 2x \geq 3$.
Solution Subtract 5 to get $2 > -2x \geq -2$. Divide by -2 and reverse the inequalities: $-1 < x \leq 1$. The solution is the interval $(-1, 1]$. ∎

Example 4 Solve $8 - 3x \leq 2x - 7 < x - 13$.
Solution Solve $8 - 3x \leq 2x - 7$: $-5x \leq -15$, $x \geq 3$. Solve $2x - 7 < x - 13$: $x < -6$.
There are no numbers satisfying both inequalities; the solution is the empty set, $\emptyset$. ∎

Example 5 A firm has been buying gaskets at \$1.10 each. Manufacturing them itself will increase overhead by \$800 per month and the cost of materials and labor will be 60¢ per gasket. How many gaskets must be used each month to justify a decision to make their own?
Solution If x gaskets are used each month, the decision is justified if, in dollars,

cost of buying > cost of making, $1.10x > 0.60x + 800$, $0.50x > 800$, $x > 1600$

Making their own will be cheaper if more than 1600 gaskets are used each month. ∎

2. ABSOLUTE VALUE

Pieces Different formulas for nonoverlapping parts of the domain of a function.
Absolute Value $|x| = \begin{cases} x & \text{if } x \geq 0 \\ -x & \text{if } x < 0 \end{cases}$. TI-83: [MATH]NUM | abs(x) Excel: = ABS(x). (9)

Sign Function $\operatorname{sgn}(x) = \begin{cases} 1 & \text{if } x > 0 \\ 0 & \text{if } x = 0 \\ -1 & \text{if } x < 0 \end{cases} = (x > 0) - (x < 0)$ on a TI-83

$= \operatorname{SIGN}(x)$ in Excel. Used with absolute value: $|x| = x\operatorname{sgn}(x)$. $\operatorname{sgn}(ab) = \operatorname{sgn}(a)\operatorname{sgn}(b)$.

Example 6 Show that $\sqrt{x^2} = x$ is not always true. Give the correct formula.
Solution If $x = -3$, then $\sqrt{x^2} = \sqrt{(-3)^2} = \sqrt{9} = 3 \neq x$. Correct formula is $\sqrt{x^2} = |x|$. ∎

Example 7 Use $s = \operatorname{sgn}(x)$ to simplify (a) $|3x - 2|x||$ (b) $|2x - 3|x||$
Analysis $3 - 2s \geq 1$, $s^2 = 1$, $s|x| = x$
Solution (a) $|3x - 2|x|| = |3x - 2sx| = |3 - 2s||x| = (3 - 2s)sx = 3|x| - 2x$

(b) $|2x - 3|x|| = |-s(2x - 3|x|)| = |3x - 2|x|| = 3|x| - 2x$ ∎

Equations and Inequalities Let a be a positive constant. If $|x| = a$ then $x = a$ or $x = -a$.
If $|x| \leq a$ then $-a \leq x \leq a$. If $|x| \geq a$ then $x \leq -a$ or $x \geq a$.
If $|x| = -a$ or $|x| \leq -a$, there are no solutions. If $|x| \geq -a$, every number is a solution.
The squared relation is equivalent. (10)

Example 8 Solve $|3x - 5| = 7$.
Solution $3x - 5 = 7$, $3x = 12$, $x = 4$; or $3x - 5 = -7$, $3x = -2$, $x = -\frac{2}{3}$

Method 2: $|3x - 5|^2 = 9x^2 - 30x + 25 = 49$, $0 = 9x^2 - 30x - 24 = 3(3x^2 - 10x - 8)$
$= 3(3x + 2)(x - 4)$, $x = -\frac{2}{3}, 4$ ∎

Union If A and B are sets, then $A \cup B$ (read: A **union** B) is the set of elements belonging to A or B. For example, $\{|x| > 4\} = \{x < -4 \text{ or } x > 4\} = (-\infty, -4) \cup (4, \infty)$.

Figure 2(a)

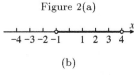

(b)

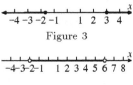

Figure 3

Example 9 Solve and graph on a number line (a) $|2x-3|<5$ (b) $|2-3x|\geq 7$

Solution See Figure 2. (a) $-5<2x-3<5$, $-2<2x<8$, $-1<x<4$, $(-1,4)$

(b) $2-3x\leq -7$, $9\leq 3x$, $3\leq x$, $[3,\infty)$; or $2-3x\geq 7$, $-5\geq 3x$, $-\frac{5}{3}\geq x$, $(-\infty,-\frac{5}{3}]$.
The solution is $(-\infty,-\frac{5}{3}]\cup[3,\infty)$. ■

Example 10 Express the set in Figure 3 as an absolute-value inequality.

Solution If the interval is (a,b), the center is $\frac{1}{2}(a+b)=\frac{1}{2}(-2+6)=2$ and the "radius" is $\frac{1}{2}(b-a)=\frac{1}{2}(6--2)=4$. Thus $|x-2|<4$. ■

Practice 12 Solve $|x|<-7$.

Example 11 Solve $\left|\frac{1}{x}-2\right|\geq 3$.

Solution $\frac{1}{x}-2\leq -3$, $\frac{1}{x}\leq -1$ or $\frac{1}{x}-2\geq 3$, $\frac{1}{x}\geq 5$. The solution is the parts of $y=1/x$ between $y=-1$ and $y=5$; we get $[-1,0)\cup(0,\frac{1}{5}]$. ■

Example 12 Solve $|x^2-x|<6$.

Solution $-6<x^2-x<6$, $-\frac{23}{4}<x^2-x+\frac{1}{4}<\frac{25}{4}$, $0\leq(x-\frac{1}{2})^2<\frac{25}{4}$, $-\frac{5}{2}<x-\frac{1}{2}<\frac{5}{2}$, $-2<x<3$. The solution is $(-2,3)$. ■

Two Absolute Values Find the zeros of each absolute value and use the definition. Note that an absolute value *equation* may have an interval solution. The graph of the sum of n absolute values of linear functions consists of two rays and $n-1$ segments.

Example 13 Solve $f(x)=|x-1|+|x-3|=2$.
Solution Critical: 1, 3.

If $x<1$, $\quad(1-x)+(3-x)=4-2x=2$, $x=1$, $\quad\quad\{\}$

If $1\leq x\leq 3$, $(x-1)+(3-x)\quad\quad\quad\quad=2$, $2=2$. $\quad[1,3]$

If $x>3$, $\quad(x-1)+(x-3)=2x-4=2$, $x=3$, $\quad\quad\{\}$

The union of these is $[1,3]$. ■

Remark "x is between a and b" is equivalent to each of the following:
(a) $|x-a|+|x-b|=|a-b|$ (b) $(x-a)(x-b)\leq 0$ (c) $0\leq(x-a)/(b-a)\leq 1$

Example 14 Solve $|x+3|>2x$.
Solution Critical: -3.

If $x\geq -3$, $\quad x+3>2x$, $3>x$, $\quad\quad\quad\quad\quad\quad\quad[-3,3)$.

If $x<-3$, $\quad-(x+3)>2x$, $-3>3x$, $-1>x$, $\quad\quad(-\infty,-3)$.

The union of these is $\quad\quad\quad\quad\quad\quad\quad\quad\quad\quad(-\infty,3)$.

Invalid (No credit): $x+3>2x$, $-x>-3$, $x<3$, $(-\infty,3)$ ■

Example 15 Solve $|3x-2|-|2x-3|\geq 4$.
Solution Critical: $\frac{2}{3},\frac{3}{2}$.

If $x\leq\frac{2}{3}$, $\quad-(3x-2)+(2x-3)\geq 4$, $-x-1\geq 4$, $-x\geq 5$, $x\leq -5$ $\quad\quad\quad\quad(-\infty,-5]$

If $\frac{2}{3}<x\leq\frac{3}{2}=\frac{15}{10}$, $(3x-2)+(2x-3)\geq 4$, $5x-5\geq 4$, $5x\geq 9$, $x\geq\frac{9}{5}=\frac{18}{10}$. $\quad\quad\{\}$

If $x>\frac{3}{2}$, $\quad(3x-2)-(2x-3)\geq 4$, $x+1\geq 4$, $x\geq 3$. $\quad\quad\quad\quad\quad\quad[3,\infty)$

The union of these is $\quad\quad\quad\quad\quad\quad\quad\quad\quad(-\infty,-5]\cup[3,\infty)$ ■

Example 16 With 3 candidates for an office, find the least number w of votes the winner (by plurality) can have if there are (a) 50 votes cast (b) n votes cast.
Solution (a) $\frac{50}{3}=16.67$, but 17 votes is not enough, since 33 votes remain so both others cannot have ≤ 16; 18 votes is the least needed.

(b) w is least if the other $n - w$ votes are split evenly between the other 2 candidates.

$\cdot$ $w \geq \frac{n-w}{2} + 1$, $2w \geq n - w + 2$, $3w \geq n + 2$. The smallest $w = \frac{n+2}{3}$ or the next integer. $\blacksquare$

Practice Answers 3. $-2x < 6$, $x > -3$, $(-3, \infty)$ **12.** $\emptyset$

Problems 1.10 Problems with ^{h} have hints or remarks below.

In Problems 0-5, solve the linear inequality. Express your answer as an interval or union of intervals.

0. $4 - 2x \leq x - 2 < 2x - 4$ **1.** $2u - 11 \leq 5u + 6$ **2.** $3 - 2y \geq 7$

3. $2x + 1 < 3 - x < 2x + 5$ **4.** $5x + 7 > 31 - 3x$ **5.** $3x + 7 > 5 - 2x \geq 13 - 6x$

Problems 6 and 7 involve statistical confidence intervals. σ is positive.

6. Solve for μ: $-1.96 \leq \frac{\bar{x} - \mu}{\sigma} \leq 1.96$ **7.** Solve for σ: $-z < \frac{s - \sigma}{\sigma/\sqrt{2n}} < z$

Problems 8-12 are applications of linear inequalities.

8. A firm has been buying belts at \$2.50 each. Making the belts themselves will increase fixed costs by \$1500 a month, but each belt will cost only \$1.70. Give the decision rule.

9. J. Amer College of Cardiology 37(2001)153-156 gives the maximal heart rate as $m = 208 - 0.7y$ where m is beats/min and y is age in years. The old formula is $m = 220 - y$. For which y does the new formula give greater values of m? (NYTimes, July 6, 2010, p.D5 announced $m = 206 - 0.88y$ for women.)

10. The current ratio of a business is the ratio of currrent assets to currrent liabilities; short term lons count for both. A firm has current assets of \$320,000 and current liabilities of \$80,000. How much can it borrow while keeping the current ratio at least 2.5?

11. On May 14, 2007 the postage for large first-class envelopes up to 16oz went from 39¢ the first ounce plus 24¢ for each additional ounce to 80¢ the first ounce or fraction, and 17¢ for each additional ounce, or fraction. Which weights cost less after the change?

12. Utility rates changed from \$5 for the first 20 kWh or less plus 6¢ for each additional kWh, to \$6 for the first 40 kWh or less plus 7¢ for each additional kWh. Which customers pay less now? Consider $(0, 40)$ and $(40, \infty)$.

13. Use absolute value to indicate that $f(x)$ and L differ by less than ϵ.

In Problems 14-22, solve the absolute-value equation or inequality.

14. $|x/4 + 5| = 6$ **15.** $|x - 2| + |x - 5| = 3$ **16.** $\frac{|x+3|}{x+3} + \frac{|x-4|}{x-4} = 0$

17. $|3x + 7| < 4$ **18.** $|2x - 5| \geq 3$ **19.** $|x + 2| + |2x - 1| \geq 5$

20. $|x - 2| < 3 - x$ **21.** $\left|\frac{1}{x} - 3\right| < 4$ **22**^{h} $|d - 620| \leq .05d$

23. Which is larger, $1 + x$ or $\frac{1}{1 - x}$ if $x < 1$?

24^h Solve $\sqrt{x + 3 - 4\sqrt{x - 1}} + \sqrt{x + 8 - 6\sqrt{x - 1}} = 1$

25. A geometric series has ratio $\frac{2x}{1 - 3x}$. For which x does the series converge?

26. $f(x) = \frac{|x|}{2 \, \text{sgn}(x) + 3x}$ uses $\text{sgn}(x)$ and $|x|$. Simplify so that only one appears.

27. John is going 60 mph on a highway passing through Pomona. He is 135 miles away now. (a) Use absolute values to give his distance from Pomona after t hours. (b) At which times will he be 15 miles from Pomona?

28. Express as a single inequality using absolute value:
(a) $2x + 3 \geq 10$ or $2x + 3 \leq -10$ (b) $2x + 3 \geq -10$ and $2x + 3 \leq 10$

Hints 10. Each side must be nonnegative and less than the sum of the other two. **22.** Math B Regents, Aug 2004 **24.** Example 1.5.20(c). (College Math J 35:3(2004)214-215)

1.R REVIEW FOR CHAPTER 1
(Property)

Operations $\text{term} + \text{term} = \text{sum}$, $\text{term} - \text{term} = \text{difference}$, $\text{factor} \times \text{factor} = \text{product}$, $\text{dividend}/\text{divisor} = \text{quotient}$
$\text{base}^{\text{exponent}} = \text{power}$, $\sqrt[\text{index}]{\text{radicand}} = \text{root}$

Arithmetic Series $a + (a+d) + \cdots + [a + (n-1)d] = \frac{1}{2}n[2a + (n-1)d]$ (Ex.1.2.13)

Geometric Series If $r \neq 1$, $a + ar + ar^2 + \cdots + ar^{n-1} = \frac{a - ar^n}{1 - r}$. If $|r| < 1$, $a + ar + ar^2 + \cdots = \frac{a}{1-r}$. (1.2.10)

Work, Speed $\text{work} = \text{force} \times \text{distance}$, $\text{power} = \frac{\text{work}}{\text{time}}$. $\text{average rate} = \frac{\text{distance}}{\text{time}}$, $\text{distance} = \text{rate} \times \text{time}$ (1.4.6)

Electric Resistance Series: $R = R_1 + R_2$ Parallel: $1/R = 1/R_1 + 1/R_2$ (1.4.1)

Mean of x_1, x_2, ..., x_n. **Arithmetic:** $\bar{x} = \frac{x_1 + x_2 + \cdots + x_n}{n}$. **Harmonic** (all positive): $x_H = \frac{n}{\frac{1}{x_1} + \frac{1}{x_2} + \cdots + \frac{1}{x_n}}$. (1.4.8)

Root Mean Square (RMS): $x_R = \sqrt{(x_1^2 + x_2^2 + \cdots + x_n^2)/n}$. **Geometric** (all positive): $x_G = \sqrt[n]{x_1 x_2 \cdots x_n}$

Exponents $a^x a^y = a^{x+y}$, $a^x \div a^y = a^{x-y}$, $(a^x)^y = a^{xy}$, $(ab)^x = a^x b^x$, $(a/b)^x = a^x/b^x$. (1.5.6)

Square of Binomial $(x + y)^2 = x^2 + 2xy + y^2$ and $(x - y)^2 = x^2 - 2xy + y^2$ (1.5.9)

Cube of Binomial $(x + y)^3 = x^3 + 3x^2 y + 3xy^2 + y^3$ and $(x - y)^3 = x^3 - 3x^2 y + 3xy^2 - y^3$

Factoring $z^2 - x^2 = (z - x)(z + x)$, $z^3 - x^3 = (z - x)(z^2 + zx + x^2)$, $z^n - x^n = (z - x)(z^{n-1} + z^{n-2}x + \cdots + x^{n-1})$

Trinomial $ax^2 + bx + c$: Find two numbers whose product is ac and whose sum is b; split the middle term. (1.6.10)

Completing the Square on $x^2 + bx$: add $(\frac{1}{2}b)^2$ to get $(x + \frac{1}{2}b)^2$; on $x^4 + a$: add $2\sqrt{a}x^2$ to get $(x^2 + \sqrt{a})^2$ (1.6.14)

Quadratic Formula If $ax^2 + bx + c = 0$, $a \neq 0$, then $x = (-b \pm \sqrt{b^2 - 4ac})/(2a)$. (1.6.15)
The sum of the roots is $-b/a$ and the product is c/a.

Rational Root Theorem If c/d is a rational root in lowest terms of $P(x) = a_n x^n + a_{n-1} x^{n-1} + \cdots + a_1 x + a_0 = 0$, $a_0 \neq 0$, with integer coefficients, then c is a factor of a_0 and d is a factor of a_n. (1.7.5)

Rational Operations $\frac{A}{B} \cdot \frac{C}{D} = \frac{AC}{BD}$, $\frac{A}{B} \div \frac{C}{D} = \frac{A}{B} \cdot \frac{D}{C}$, $\frac{A}{B} \pm \frac{C}{D} = \frac{AD \pm BC}{BD}$ (1.8.1)

Revenue $= \text{price} \times \text{quantity} = px$, **Profit** $= \text{revenue} - \text{cost}$ (1.9.3)

Intervals and Inequalities (a,b): $a < x < b$, $[a,b)$: $a \leq x < b$, $(a,b]$: $a < x \leq b$, $[a,b]$: $a \leq x \leq b$ (1.10.1)
$(-\infty, b)$: $x < b$, $(-\infty, b]$: $x \leq b$, (a, ∞): $x > a$, $[a, \infty)$: $x \geq a$

Absolute Value $|x| = \begin{cases} x & \text{if } x \geq 0 \\ -x & \text{if } x < 0 \end{cases}$. (1.10.9)

1.R Review Problems for Chapter 1 Problems with [h] have hints below.

1. NYTimes, Jul 23, 2009, p.A.25. A programming error caused a charge of $23,148,855,308,184,500 for a train ride to appear on a Visa statement. Express the amount in words.

2. How much is left if (a) a $4'3''$ board is shortened by $2'8''$? (b) A $4'3''$ elevator ride is shortened by $2'8''$?

3. (a) Sum the series $\frac{2}{3} + \frac{1}{3} + \frac{1}{6} + \frac{1}{12} + \cdots$ Express the sum of the first 40 terms (b) in sigma notation and (c) as a TI-83 formula or a single Excel statement.

4. Calculate $\sum_{i=7}^{11} \frac{i}{i+2}$ to 4 decimals.

5. The sides of a rectangular box measure 41.6 cm by 1.3 m by 2.1 m. Express the volume in cubic centimeters in scientific notation with the correct precision.

6. Ad for HP toner 2004: Change the cartridge 60% less often due to 60% more toner. Find the correct savings.

7. NYTimes, Sep 16, 2003, on the high cost of college texts: 77.6% of a book's price goes to the publisher, author and freight. Find the book store's percentage markup, based on its cost.

8. A stock's rate of return is the change in price in a year plus dividends, divided by the initial price. If a share of IBM went from $80 to $90 and paid $7 dividends in a year, find the rate of return.

9. From a full-page ad in NYTimes, Jul 16, 2003: Revenue in millions of dollars: Find the 2-year compound annual growth rate (CAGR) for each company.

	Year	2000	2001	2002
PeopleSoft		496	645	530
Oracle		1,081	896	613

10. If an electric current has one path through two resistors (series), then $R = R_1 + R_2$. If the current has two paths (parallel), $1/R = 1/R_1 + 1/R_2$. If $R_1 = 10\,\text{ohm}$ and $R_2 = 20\,\text{ohm}$, find the average resistance in (a) a series circuit (b) a parallel circuit.

11. The lift of a wing is proportional to the area and the square of the speed. If a model of area $5\,\text{ft}^2$ has 10 lb of lift at 30 mph, find the lift of a wing of area $72\,\text{ft}^2$ at 130 mph.

12. (a) A Canadian Cheerios box has a net weight of 575 g; how many ounces is this? (b) A 30 g serving provides 500 kJ; how many calories is this?

13^h A 200-lb man runs a 9-ft flight of stairs in 3 seconds. How many watts does he generate? Use $1\text{N} = .2248\text{lbf}$.

14. The volumetric coefficient of gasoline is $950 \times 10^{-6}/°\text{C}$. If gasoline costs \$3.00/gal, how much can you save buying 20 gal when the temperature is 15 °C cooler? (The temperature in underground tanks changes less.)

15. The acceleration of gravity is inversely proportional to the square of the distance from the center of the Earth above the surface, and directly proportional to the distance from the center below the surface. How far must you go to get a 1% decrease (a) above the surface (b) below the surface? Assume the Earth is a sphere of radius 3960 miles.

16. Einstein-Smoluchowsky. The average distance traveled by a diffusing molecule is proportional to the square root of time. If the average distance of a water molecule in water after 1 second is $69\mu\text{m}$, find the average distance in cm after a week.

17. 1 grain per gallon of water hardness is how many mg/L (parts per million)? 7000 grains = 1 lb.

18. (a) Convert the speed of light, 299,792,458 m/s to miles per hour. (b) A **light year** is the distance light travels in a tropical year of 365.2422 days. How many miles is this? (c) If a drawing represents an astronomical unit of 92,958,348 mi by 1 inch, how many miles would a light year be?

19. Glad clear Tall Kitchen bags are .8 mil thick. How many microns is this?

20^h If 1 lumen $= 1/683$ watt, find the efficiency of the following bulbs. (a) A GE A19 incandescent 100 watt giving 1710 lumens. (b) A T12 40 watt fluorescent giving 1250 lumens.

21. In 1774 Benjamin Franklin found the thickness of an olive oil molecule by watching a teaspoon ($\frac{1}{8}$ fluid ounce) cover a half-acre. Calculate in inches.

22. A "1 ton" air conditioner is equivalent to melting 1 ton of ice in 24 hours. Convert to BTU per hour. Melting 1 gram of ice requires 79.72 calories (heat of fusion). Note: 1 watt-hr $= 3600\text{J} = 3600/1055\text{BTU} = 3.4\text{BTU}$ but 1 watt-hr can *move* 9.7 (legal min)-13 BTU (EER).

Problems 23-57 involve algebra.

23. We wish to invest part of \$100,000 at 6% and the rest at 8%. How much should be invested at each rate to earn \$6500 annually?

24. Evaluate without a calculator: $4 - 5 \cdot 2^3$

25. Simplify $\dfrac{1}{\sqrt{2}-1} + \dfrac{2}{\sqrt{3}+1}$.

26. Simplify $\sqrt{\dfrac{18}{5}} + \dfrac{1}{5}\sqrt{40}$

27. Math B Jun 2004: The expression $\sqrt[4]{16a^6b^4}$ is equivalent to (1) $2a^2b$ (2) $2a^{3/2}b$ (3) $4a^2b$ (4) $4a^{3/2}b$. (a) Which answer did the Regents expect? (b) Write the correct answer.

28. Simplify $x + y - \sqrt{x^2 - 2xy + y^2}$.

29. Simplify $\dfrac{(-6x^{-1}y^{-2})^3}{(-2x^{-4}y^{-3})^4}$. State eliminated restrictions.

30. If $a + b = 7$ and $ab = 11$, find $(a-b)^2$.

31^h Let $x = \frac{9}{4}$ and $y = \frac{27}{8}$. Compare x^y and y^x.

32. Multiply: $(2x+1)(x^2 + x - 3)$

33. Divide: $(3x^3 - 2x^2 - x + 4) \div (x - 3)$

34. Factor $8x^2 - 18x + 9$

35. Factor $(x+1)^2 - (2x+5)^2$

36. Factor $x^3 + 8y^3$

37. Factor completely: (a) $x^4 - 4$ (b) $x^4 + 4$

38^h Factor $x^4 + x^2y^2 + y^4 - \frac{3}{2}x^2 - \frac{3}{2}y^2 + \frac{9}{16}$.

39. Simplify $\dfrac{1}{x-1} - \dfrac{1}{x^2-1} - \dfrac{1}{x-1/x}$. State eliminated restrictions.

40. Combine over a polynomial denominator: $\dfrac{1+2x}{1+x+x^2} - \dfrac{1-2x}{1-x+x^2}$

41. In Jun 2003 U-Haul trucks gave the range of a projectile: $R_b = 2R \tan^{-1}\left(\dfrac{(v^2/Rg)\sin\theta\cos\theta}{1-(v^2/Rg)\cos^2\theta}\right)$. Simplify so v and g appear only once. What are you assuming?

42. Which has a different solution: (a) $\sqrt{x} = 2$ (b) $x = 4$ (c) $x^2 = 16$ (d) $x^3 = 64$

43^h Solve for R: $a = \dfrac{2R}{R-r}$.

44^h Solve each equation for b: (a) $\dfrac{a-b}{b-c} = \dfrac{a}{a}$ (b) $\dfrac{a-b}{b-c} = \dfrac{a}{b}$ (c) $\dfrac{a-b}{b-c} = \dfrac{a}{c}$

45. Solve for x: $\dfrac{3x-2}{5} = 4 - \dfrac{1}{2}x$

46. Solve for a: $c = \sqrt{a^2 + b^2}$

47. Solve for x: $5x^2 = 13x + 6$.

48. Solve for x: $(x+2)^{-3/4} = 8$.

49. Solve for x: $\sqrt{2x-3} + x = 9$

50. Solve for x: $\dfrac{1}{x-1} = \dfrac{1}{x^2-3x+2} + \dfrac{1}{x^2-2x+1}$.

51. Solve for x (at least one root is rational): $3x^3 + 4x^2 - 13x - 14 = 0$.

In Problems 52 and 53, solve the inequality. Express your answer as an interval or union of intervals.
52. $3x - 1 > x + 3 > 2x - 3$

53. $|2x - 4| + |3x + 9| \geq 15$

54. The perimeter of a rectangle is 48 ft and the base is x ft. Find the area in terms of x.

55. An arithmetic sequence has sum $s = \dfrac{1}{2}n[2a + (n-1)d]$. (a) Solve for n. (b) Find n if $s = -3$, $a = -2$, $d = 1$.

56. Simplify the complex number $\dfrac{5-2i}{-4-3i}$

57. How far from Earth, x, in terms of Earth-moon separation d, should a satellite be positioned if it is to be in gravitational equilibrium. The moon's mass is $m = \dfrac{1}{81}m_E$. Use $F = Gm_1m_2/r^2$.

58. All 50 apartments in a building will be rented if the monthly rent is $600. For each increase of $20 in the monthly rent, one apartment will be vacant. What are the rents if the monthly revenue is to be at least $31,500?

59. Pump A can empty a pool in 3 hours; pump B can empty it in 2 hours. How long will it take working together?

60. Evaluate the nonstandard Roman numeral xcxl and write as standard.

Hints and Notes 13. NYTimes Jun 14, 2005, p.F2 reports that champion cyclist Lance Armstrong can generate 500 watts for 20 minutes.) **20.** 683 lm/W is at 555nm; the maximum for white light is ≈ 240 l/W. Hence some sources give much higher values. **31.** Express both terms as powers of $\dfrac{3}{2}$. **38.** Add and subtract x^2y^2. **43.** The mechanical advantage of a differential pulley of radii R and r. **44.** The Greek definition of some means.

1.A UNITS AND FORMULAS

SI Base Units Time: second is the duration of 9,192,631,770 ticks of a cesium-133 atom (originally 1/86,400 of mean solar day)

Length: meter is distance traveled by light in vacuum in 1/299,792,458 second (originally 1/10,000,000 of distance from equator to pole)

Mass: kilogram is mass of platinum-iridium cylinder in Paris (originally gram is mass of 1cm^3 of water at maximum density)

Current: ampere is that current in two wires 1 m apart which produces a force of 2×10^{-7} N per m length (originally the current through silver nitrate that deposits .00111800 g silver in 1 second)

Temperature: Kelvin is 1/273.16 of the temperature of the triple point of water. Celsius: add 273.15 (originally water freezes at $0\,°\text{C}$ and boils at $100\,°\text{C}$)

Substance: mole is the amount of substance having as many elementary entities (specify: atoms, ions, etc) as there are atoms in 12 g of carbon 12, ie $6.022\,141\,79(30) \times 10^{23}$ particles (Avogadro's number, CODATA 2006)

Luminous intensity: candela is light at 540×10^{12} hz that has intensity of 1/683 watt per steradian 1 lumen = 1/683 watt. Brightness: 1 nit = 1 candela/m^2.

Time 1 minute (min) = 60 seconds (sec), 1 hour (hr) = 60 min, 1 day = 24 hr, 1 week = 7 days, 52 weeks = 364 days ≈ 1 year. 10 years = 1 decade, 100 years = 1 century

1 calendar or tropical year = 365.2422 days. Leap years add 97 days/400 years = .2425 days/year. The tides slow the earth so leap seconds are sometimes added. At the last leap second (34th) on Dec 31, 2008 the clock went 23:59:59, 23:59:60, 00:00:00, 00:00:01. 1 sidereal year = 365.2564 days. There were no leap seconds in 2009, 2010 and 2011.

Calendar Days of week: Sunday, Monday, Tuesday, Wednesday, Thursday, Friday, Saturday. A year has 12 months: January (31 days), February (28), March (31), April (30), May (31), June (30), July (31), August (31), September (30), October (31), November (30), and December (31), a total of 365.

Length 1 inch (in ″) = 2.54 cm (exact), 1 foot (ft ′) = 12 in, 1 yard = 3 ft, 1 mile = 5280 ft, 1 mil = 10^{-3} in 1 dm = 10^{-1} m, 1 micron = 10^{-6} m, 1 angstrom (Å) = 10^{-10} m

Capacity is volume not in cubic units. Liquid measure: 1 gallon (gal) = 231 in^3 = 4 quarts (originally volume of cylinder height 6″, diameter 7″ ≈ 230.9 in^3. In 1706, Queen Anne simplified by using $\pi \approx \frac{22}{7}$) 1 quart = 2 pints, 1 pint = 2 cups, 1 cup = 8 ounces (fluid oz), 1 tablespoon = $\frac{1}{2}$ oz. 1 fluid dram = $\frac{1}{8}$ oz, 1 teaspoon = $\frac{1}{3}$ tablespoon. 1 liter (L) = 1000 cm^3 (originally volume of 1000 g water) 1 drop is given as $\frac{1}{20}$ ml, but tubing in common use also delivers 10, 15, or 60 drops/ml. Originally pharmacists used 1 minim = $\frac{1}{60}$ dram = $\frac{1}{480}$ oz = .0616 ml so 1ml = 16.23 minim; use 16, not 15. Dry measure: 1 bushel = 2150.42 in^3 = 4 pecks = 32 quarts

Force A newton (N) will accelerate a 1 kg mass at 1m/sec^2. 1 N ≈ 0.224809 lbf. 1 dyne = 10^{-5} N

Pressure 1 pascal (Pa) = 1 N/m^2, 1 bar = 10^5 Pa, 1 atm = 101,325 Pa = 760 torr ≈ 14.5 psi

Work 1 joule (J) = 1 N·m = 1 kg·m^2/s^2. 1 erg = 10^{-7} J

1 calorie (thermochemical) = 4.184 joule (exact) will raise the temperature of 1g water by 1°C. A food Calorie is 1000 times larger = 4.184 kJ. Specific heat in J/g°C = 4.184 × s.h. in BTU/lb°F. (Others, 4.1855J and 4.1868J are sometimes used.) 1 BTU ≈ 1055 J (depending on calorie)

Power 1 watt (W) = 1 J/s, 1 horsepower = 550 ft-lb/s, 1 hertz (Hz) = 1 cycle/s. If a current of 1 ampere dissipates 1 watt of power, the potential difference is 1 volt and the resistance is 1 ohm.

Paper sizes letter: 8.5″ × 11″, legal: 8.5″ × 14″, A4: 210mm × 297mm. Ream = 500 sheets

Miscellaneous 1 acre = $\frac{1}{640}$ mile^2, 1 are = 100 m^2, 1 hectare = 10,000 m^2, 1 ton = 2000 lb, 1 lb = 7000 grains, 1 carat = .2 g

Physical Constants have italic symbols.

Speed of light in a vacuum c = 299,792,458 m/sec (exact). Avogadro's number N_A = 6.02214×10^{23} The Earth is nearly a sphere of radius 3960 mi. 1 astronomical unit (AU) = 92,958,348 mi = 149,597,870.691 km the radius of a circular orbit having period 365.2568983 days (Gaussian year). (Until 1939, the slightly larger mean distance from earth's center to the center of the sun.)

Pound As a unit of mass, 1 lb (lbm) = .45359237 kg (US law). As a unit of weight (lbf) the pound is the weight that a mass of 1 lb has when gravity is $g = 9.80665$ m/s^2.
1 lb = 16 ounces (avoirdupois). We use 9.81 m/s^2 and 32.2 ft/s^2 in problems.
A pan balance measures mass. A spring, torsion, or electronic balance measures force; they must be calibrated with NIST (National Institute for Standards and Technology) weights.

Math Constants $\pi = 3.141\ 592\ 653\ 589\ 793\ 238\ 462\ 643\ 383\ 279\ 502\ 884\ 197...$
$e = 2.718\ 281\ 828\ 459\ 045\ 235\ 360\ 287\ 471\ 352\ 662\ 497\ 757...$
$0! = 1,\ 1! = 1,\ 2! = 2,\ 3! = 6,\ 4! = 24,\ 5! = 120,\ 6! = 720,\ 7! = 5040,\ 8! = 40{,}320,\ 9! = 362{,}880$

Geometry Parallelogram: quadrilateral having opposite sides equal and parallel.
Rectangle: parallelogram with equal (right) angles. Rhombus: parallelogram with equal sides.

Area, Volume Parallelogram has area = base × height. Equilateral triangle of side s has area $\frac{1}{4}\sqrt{3}s^2$.
Triangle has sides a, b, c, $s = \frac{1}{2}(a + b + c)$ has

area $= \frac{1}{2}$base × height $= \frac{1}{4}\sqrt{2a^2b^2 + 2a^2c^2 + 2b^2c^2 - a^4 - b^4 - c^4} = \sqrt{s(s-a)(s-b)(s-c)}$ (Hero)
Trapezoid has area = the average of the parallel sides times the distance between them.
Rectangular box of length ℓ, width w, height h has area $= 2\ell w + 2\ell h + 2wh$, volume $= \ell wh$.
Square of side s has area s^2. Cube of side s has volume s^3.
Regular tetrahedron of side s has volume $\frac{1}{12}\sqrt{2}s^3$.
Tetrahedron having mutually perpendicular edges a, b, c has volume $\frac{1}{6}abc$.
Circle of radius r has circumference $= 2\pi r$, area K $= \pi r^2$.
Sector of θ radians has arc $s = r\theta$, area $= \frac{1}{2}r^2\theta$. Segment (chord subtends θ): area $= \frac{1}{2}r^2(\theta - \sin\theta)$.
Sphere of radius r has volume V $= \frac{4}{3}\pi r^3$, area K $= 4\pi r^2$.
Spherical segment of thickness h has area $= 2\pi rh$; for one base, volume $= \pi h^2(r - \frac{1}{3}h)$.
Ellipse of semiaxes a, b has area K $= \pi ab$. Ellipsoid of semiaxes a, b, c has volume V $= \frac{4}{3}\pi abc$.
Cylinder of radius r and height h has volume V $= \pi r^2 h$, lateral area A $= 2\pi rh$ if right.
Circular cone of radius r and height h has volume V $= \frac{1}{3}\pi r^2 h$, lateral area A $= \pi r\sqrt{r^2 + h^2}$ if right.
Similar: If two angles of a triangle equal two angles of another, corresponding sides are proportional.
If lengths of similar figures have ratio s, their areas have ratio s^2 and their volumes have ratio s^3.

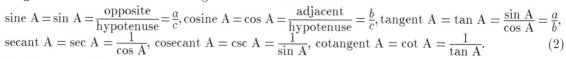

Trigonometric Functions See the figure.

sine A $=$ sin A $= \dfrac{\text{opposite}}{\text{hypotenuse}} = \dfrac{a}{c}$, cosine A $=$ cos A $= \dfrac{\text{adjacent}}{\text{hypotenuse}} = \dfrac{b}{c}$, tangent A $=$ tan A $= \dfrac{\sin A}{\cos A} = \dfrac{a}{b}$,

secant A $=$ sec A $= \dfrac{1}{\cos A}$, cosecant A $=$ csc A $= \dfrac{1}{\sin A}$, cotangent A $=$ cot A $= \dfrac{1}{\tan A}$. $\qquad$ (2)

Pythagorean Theorem: If a and b are the legs, c the hypotenuse of a right triangle, then
$c = \sqrt{a^2 + b^2}$. $\sin^2 A + \cos^2 A = 1$, $\tan^2 A + 1 = \sec^2 A$ $\qquad$ (6)

For any triangle ABC with sides a, b, c: **Law of Cosines** $b^2 = a^2 + c^2 - 2ac\cos B$ $\qquad$ (7)

Law of Sines $\dfrac{a}{\sin A} = \dfrac{b}{\sin B} = \dfrac{c}{\sin C}$ **Area** $= \frac{1}{2}ac\sin B$ $\qquad$ (8)

Angles and Circles If two lines through a point P meet a circle C, the angle between them is half the sum of the intercepted arcs if P is inside C, half the difference if P is outside C, and half the arc if P is on C. $\qquad$ (9)
Triangle Exterior angle equals sum of two remote interior angles.
Triangle Inequality Any side is less than the sum of the other two.

1.B TI-83 GRAPHING CALCULATOR

Matrices work with all keyboard operations except / and $\sqrt{}$. $\hat{}$ works for integers 1-255.
The following operations with complex numbers are supported: $+$, $-$, $\times$, $\div$, $\hat{}$, x^{-1}, $\sqrt{}$, $\sqrt[3]{}$, $\sqrt[x]{}$ x^2, LOG, 10^x, LN, e^x, abs, dec, frac, fPart, iPart, round, summation (with OS2.55), the CPX menu, test $=$, $\neq$ and lists.
It does not support matrices, trigonometric or hyperbolic functions, nDeriv, fnInt, Solver, seq, or any regression model. If Y_n has complex coefficients, $Y_n(X)$ works for real X (but not lists); GRAPH and TABLE don't.

Function limits: $\sin x, \cos x, \tan x, |x| \leq 10^{12}$; e^x, $x \leq 230.25$, $\sinh x$, $\cosh x$, $|x| \leq 230.25$; fnInt, upper$-$lower $\leq 10^5$
Default values are shown. $*$: TI-84 only. [MATH] indicates a key; [TEST] indicates a second function.
Keyboard: $[x^{-1}]$, [SIN], $[\text{SIN}^{-1}]$, [COS], $[\text{COS}^{-1}]$. [TAN], $[\text{TAN}^{-1}]$, [], $[\pi]$, $[x^2]$, $[\sqrt{}]$, $[\div]$, $[e]$, [LOG], $[10^x]$, $[\times]$, [LN], $[e^x]$, $[-]$, $[i]$, $[(-)]$

[WINDOW]
  (Func mode) WINDOW, Xmin=-10, Xmax=10, Xscl=1, Ymin=-10, Ymax=10, Yscl=1, Xres=1(-8)
    [VARS]Window | X/Y: ΔX, ΔY
  (Par mode) WINDOW, Tmin=0, Tmax=2π or 360, Tstep=$\pi/24$ or 7.5, Xmin=-10, Xmax=10, Xscl=1, Ymin=-10, Ymax=10, Yscl=1
  (Pol mode) WINDOW, θmin=0, θmax=2π, θstep=$\pi/24$, Xmin=-10, Xmax=10, Xscl=1, Ymin=-10, Ymax=10, Yscl=1
  (seq mode) WINDOW, nMin=1, nMax=10, Plotstart=1, PlotStep=1, Xmin=-10, Xmax=10, Xscl=1, Ymin=-10, Ymax=10, Yscl=1

[TBLSET] TABLE SETUP: TblStart=0, ΔTbl=1, Indpnt: Auto Ask, Depend: Auto Ask

[ZOOM] ⊘ resets T or θ min, max, step
  ZOOM, 1: Zbox, 2:Zoom in, 3:Zoom out, 4:Zdecimal$[-4.7,4.7] \times [-3.1,3.1]$ 5:Zsquare, 6:ZStandard $[-10,10]^2$⊘
    7:ZTrig$[-\frac{47}{24}\pi,\frac{47}{24}\pi] \times [-4,4]$, 8:ZInteger, 9:ZoomStat fit all data A:ZQuadrant1*, B:ZFrac1/2*, C:ZFrac1/3*,
    D:ZFrac1/4*, E:ZFrac1/5*, F:ZFrac1/8, G:Zfrac1/10
  MEMORY: 1:ZPrevious, 2:ZoomSto, 3:ZoomRcl, 4:SetFactors: ZOOMFACTORS: XFact=4, YFact=4

[FORMAT] Time Web uv vw uw (Seq mode only) RectGC/PolarGC, CoordOn/Off, GridOff/on, AxesOn/off, LabelOff/on, ExprOn/Off

[CALC]
  (Func mode) CALCULATE, 1:value, 2:zero, 3:minimum, 4:maximum, 5:intersect, d:dy/dx, 7:$\int$f(x)dx
  (Par mode) CALCULATE, 1:value, 2:dy/dx, 3:dy/dt, 4:dx/dt
  (Pol mode) CALCULATE, 1:value, 2:dy/dx, 3:dr.dθ (seq mode) CALCULATE, 1:value
[MODE] Normal Sci Eng, Float 0123456789, Radian Degree, Func Par Pol Seq, Connected Dot (default style),
  Sequential Simul, Real a+bi re$^\theta$, Full Horiz G-T, STATDIAGNOSTICS OFF ON, n/d Un/d*, SETCLOCK*
[PRGM] s:start, e:end, Δ:step (optional)
  CTL: 1:If, 2:Then, 3:Else, 4:For(var,s,e,Δ), 5:While, 6:Repeat, 7:End, 8:Pause, 9:Lbl, 0:Goto, A:IS>(, B:DS<(,
  C:Menu, D:prgm, E:Return, F:Stop, G:DelVar, H:GraphStyle
  I/O: 1:Input (without variable displays graph), 2:Prompt, 3:Disp, 4:DispGraph, 5:DispTable, 6:Output(,
  7:getKey, 8:Clrhome, 9:ClrTable, 0:GetCalc(, A:Get, B:Send
[DRAW] R:row, C:column, m: mark (optional)
  DRAW: 1:ClrDraw, 2:Line(x1,y1,x2,y2), 3:Horizontal, 4:Vertical, 5:Tangent(Y_1,x), 6:DrawF, 7:Shade(Y_L,Y_U),
  8:DrawInv, 9:Circle(x,y,r), 0:Text(R,C,"text"), A:Pen
  POINTS: 1:Pt-On(x,y,m), 2:Pt-Off(x,y,m), 3:Pt-Change(x,y),
  4:Pxl-On(R,C), 5:Pxl-Off(R,C), 6:Pxl-Change(R,C), 7:Pxl-Test(R,C)
  STO: 1:StorePic, 2:RecallPic, 3:StoreGDB, 4:RecallGDB

[STAT] XL:Xlist, YL:Ylist, f:freqlist, r:regequ, DiagnosticOn for correlation
  EDIT: 1:Edit $L_1,L_2,\ldots$, 2:SortA(, 3:SortD(, 4:ClrList, 5:SetUpEditor
  CALC: 1:1-Var Stats XL,f, 2:2-Var Stats XL,YL,f, 3:Med-Med XL,YL,f,r, 4:LinReg(ax+b) XL,YL,f,r,
  5:QuadReg XL,YL,f,r, 6:CubicReg XL,YL,f,r, 7:QuartReg XL,YL,f,r, 8:LinReg(a+bx) XL,YL,f,r,
  9:LnReg XL,YL,f,r, 0:ExpReg(ab^x) XL,YL,f,r, A:PwrReg(ax^b) XL,YL,f,r, B:Logistic XL,YL,f,r,
  C:SinReg n,XL,YL,f,r, D:Manual Linear Fit

TESTS: 1:ZTest μ when σ is known, 2:T-Test μ when σ is unknown, 3:2-SampZTest μ_1 vs μ_2, σ known
4:2-SampTTest μ_1 vs μ_2, σ unknown, 5:1-PropZtest p, 6:2-PropZtest p_1 vs p_2,
7:Zinterval confidence μ, σ known, 8:Tinterval confidence μ, σ unknown, 9:2-SampZint conf $\mu_1 - \mu_2$, σ known,
0:2-SampZint conf $\mu_1 - \mu_2$, σ known, A:1-PropZInt conf p, B:2-PropZInt conf $p_1 - p_2$,
C:χ^2-Test independence$\rightarrow$expected, D:2-SampFtest σ_1 vs σ_2, E:LinRegTTest slope vs 0, χ^2GOFTest$\rightarrow$expected$*$,
LinRegTint confidence slope, ANOVA μ_1 vs μ_2 vs μ_3

⟦LIST⟧ L:list, d:dependlist, f:freqlist, s:start, e:end, Δ:step (optional), p:pair, L:list c by columns
NAMES: 1:L_1, ..., 6:L_6, 7:RESID, 8:CNTRB$*$
OPS: 1:SortA(key,d, 2:SortD(key,d, 3:dim(, 4:Fill(, 5:seq(Y_1,X,s,e,Δ, 6:cumSum, 7:ΔList, 8:Select(L_1,L_2)
9:augment(L_1,L_2), 0:List $\triangleright$ matr(L_1,L_2,[A]) c, A:Matr $\triangleright$ list([A],L_1,L_2) or ([A],n,L_1) c, B:L
MATH: 1:min(p/L, 2:max(p/L, 3:mean(L,f, 4:median(L,f, 5:sum(L,s,e), 6:prod(L,s,e), 7:stdDev(l,f, 8:variance(L,f

[MATH] s:start, e:end, p:pair, L:list, a: operator after, b: operator between, d: display only
MATH: 1: $\triangleright$ Frac (nnnn/dddd) a, 2: $\triangleright$ Dec, 3: ^{3} a, 4: $^3\sqrt($, 5:x$\sqrt{}$ b, 6:fMin(Y_1,X,s,e), 7:fMax(Y_1,X,s,e),
8:NDeriv(Y_1,X,x), 9:fnInt(Y_1,X,s,e), 0:summationΣ(Y_1,X,s,e)$*$, A:logBASE(X,base)$*$, B:Solver
NUM: 1:abs(, 2:round(, 3:ipart(, 4:fpart(, 5:int(, 6:min(p/L, 7:max(p/L, 8:lcm(p, 9:gcd(p 0:remainder(num,den)$*$
CPX: 1:conj(, 2:real(, 3:imag(, 4:angle(, 5:abs(, 6: $\triangleright$ Rect d, 7: $\triangleright$ Polar d
PRB: 1:rand, 2:nPr b, 3:nCr b, 4:! a, 5:randint(s,e,N 6:randNorm(μ,σ,N 7:randBin(n,p,N, 8:randIntNoRep(

⟦TEST⟧ all have operator between
TEST, 1:=, 2:$\neq$, 3:>, 4:$\geq$, 5:, 6:$\leq$ LOGIC, 1:and, 2:or, 3:xor, 4:not(

[VARS]Vars: 1:Window, 2:Zoom, 3:GDB, 4:Picture, 5:Statistics, 6:Table, 7:String
Y-VARS: 1:Function, 2:Parametric, 3:Polar, 4:on/Off

⟦DISTR⟧ s:start, e:end, n: number of trials, $1 \leq n \leq 256$
DISTR: 1:normalpdf(x,μ,σ), 2:normalcdf(s,e,μ,σ), 3:invNorm(p,μ,σ), 4:invT(p,df)$*$ 5:tpdf(x,df), 6:tcdf(s,e,df),
7:χ^2pdf(x,df), 8:χ^2cdx(s,e,df), 9:Fpdf(x,numdf,dendf), 0:Fcdf(s,e,numdf,dendf), A:binompdf(n,p,[x]),
B:binomcdf(n,p,[x]), C:Poissonpdf(λ,x), D:Poissoncdf(λ,x), E:geometpdf(p,x), F:geometcdf(p,x)
DRAW: 1:ShadeNorm(s,e,μ,σ), 2:Shade_t(s,e,df), 3:Shadeχ^2(s,e,df), 4:ShadeF(s,e,numdf,dendf)

[APPS]1:Finance: Calc: 1:TVMSolver, 2:tvm_Pmt, 3:tvm_I%, 4:tvm_PV, 5:tvm_N, 6:tvm_FV, 7:npv(, 8:irr(,
9:bal, 0:ΣPrn(, A:ΣInt(, B: $\triangleright$ Nom, (C: $\triangleright$ Eff(, D:dbd(mm.ddyy), E:Pmt_End, F:Pmt_Bgn

⟦ANGLE⟧ ANGLE 1:$^\circ$, 2:$'$, 3:r, 4:$\rightarrow$DMS, 5:R$\rightarrow$Pr(x,y), 6:R$\rightarrow$Pθ(x,y), 7:P$\rightarrow$Rx(r,θ), 8:P$\rightarrow$y(r,θ)

⟦MEM⟧1:about OS, 2:MemMgmt/Del, 3:Clear Entries, 4:ClrallLists, 5:Archive, 6:UnArchive,
7:Reset RAM/ARCHIVE/ALL 8:Group GROUP/UNGROUP

⟦MATRIX⟧ NAMES EDIT r_1 row number
MATH: 1:Det, 2:T, 3:dim(, 4:Fill, 5:Identity, 6:RandM(, 7:augment([A],[B]), 8:Matr $\triangleright$ list([A],C_1,C_2),
9:List $\triangleright$ matr(L_1,L_2,[A]), 0:cumSum([A]) A:ref([A]) B:rref([A]), C:rowSwap([A],r_1,r_2), D:row+([A],r_1,r_2)
E:$*$row(x,[A],r_1), F:$*$row+(x,[A],r_1,r_2)

⟦CATALOG⟧ AsmPrgm, cosh(, cosh^{-1}(, dayOfWk(yyyy,m,d) yyyy $\geq$ 1583$*$, DiagnosticOff, DiagnosticOn,
Equ$\rightarrow$String(, expr(, GarbageCollect, getDate {y m d}$*$, getDtFmt, getTmStr, getTime {h m s}$*$, getKey,
inString(, IsClockOn, length(, sinh(, sinh^{-1}(, solve(, startTmr$*$ s 1/1/97, String$\rightarrow$Equ(, sub(, tanh(, tanh^{-1}(,
timeCnv(s (dhms)

2 Functions and Graphs

EXPLORE & EXTEND

A Taxing Experience!

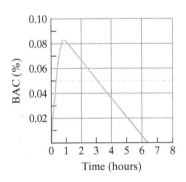

uppose a 180-pound man drinks four beers in quick succession. We know that his blood alcohol concentration, or BAC, will first rise, then gradually fall back to zero. But what is the best way to describe how quickly the BAC rises, where it peaks, and how fast it falls again?

If we obtain measured BAC values for this particular drinker, we can display them in a table, as follows:

Time (h)	1	2	3	4	5	6
BAC(%)	0.0820	0.0668	0.0516	0.0364	0.0212	0.0060

However, a table can show only a limited number of values and so does not really give the overall picture.

We might instead relate the BAC to time t using a combination of linear and quadratic equations (recall Chapter 0):

$$BAC = -0.1025t^2 + 0.1844t \qquad \text{if } t \leq 0.97$$

$$BAC = -0.0152t + 0.0972 \qquad \text{if } t > 0.97$$

As with the table, however, it is hard to look at the equations and quickly understand what is happening with BAC over time.

Probably the best description of changes in the BAC over time is a graph, like the one on the left. Here we easily see what happens. The blood alcohol concentration climbs rapidly, peaks at 0.083% after about an hour, and then gradually tapers off over the next five-and-a-half hours. Note that for almost three hours, this male drinker's BAC is above 0.05%, the point at which one's driving skills typically begin to decline. The curve will vary from one drinker to the next, but women are generally affected more severely than men, not only because of weight differences but also because of the different water contents in men's and women's bodies.

The relationship between time and blood alcohol content is an example of a function. This chapter deals in depth with functions and their graphs.

Objective

To understand what a function is and to determine domains and function values.

2.1 Functions

In the 17th century, Gottfried Wilhelm Leibniz, one of the inventors of calculus, introduced the term *function* into the mathematical vocabulary. The concept of a function is one of the most basic in all of mathematics. In particular, it is essential to the study of calculus.

In everyday speech we often hear educated people say things like "Interest rates are a function of oil prices." or "Pension income is a function of years worked." or "Blood alcohol concentration after drinking beer is a function of time." Sometimes such usage agrees with mathematical usage—but not always. We have to be careful with our meaning of the word *function* in order to make it a good mathematical tool. Nevertheless, everyday examples can help our understanding. We build the definition in the next three paragraphs.

A key idea is to realize that a **set**, as first mentioned in Section 0.1, need not have numbers as its **elements**. We can speak of a set of interest rates, a set of oil prices, a set of incomes, and so on. If X and Y are sets, in that generality, and x is an element of X and y is an an element of Y, then we write (x, y) for what we call the **ordered pair** consisting of x and y in the order displayed. Thus (y, x) is in general different from (x, y). In fact, given two ordered pairs (x, y) and (a, b), we have $(x, y) = (a, b)$ if and only if both $x = a$ and $y = b$. We will write $X \times Y$ for the set of all ordered pairs (x, y), where x is an element of X and y is an element of Y. For example, if X is the set of oil prices and Y is the set of interest rates, then an element of $X \times Y$ is a pair (p, r), where p is an oil price and r is an interest rate.

A **relation** R from a set X to a set Y is a subset of $X \times Y$. We recall from Section 0.1 that this means any element of R is also an element of $X \times Y$. If it happens that (x, y) is an element of R, then we say that x is R-related to y and write xRy. Each of $<, >, \leq$, and $\geq$ are relations from the set $(-\infty, \infty)$ of all real numbers to itself. For example, we can define $<$ as that subset of $(-\infty, \infty) \times (-\infty, \infty)$ consisting of all (a, b) such that $a < b$ is true. The use of xRy for "x is R-related to y" is inspired by the notation for inequalities. To give another example, let P and L denote, respectively, the set of all points and the set of all lines in a given plane. For an ordered pair (p, l) in $P \times L$, it is either the case that "p is on l" or "p is not on l". If we write $p \circ l$ for "p is on l", then $\circ$ is a relation from P to L in the sense of this paragraph. Returning to prices and rates, we might say that oil price p is R-related to interest rate r, and write pRr, if "there has been a time at which both the price of oil has been p and the (Fed's) interest rate has been r".

A **function** f from a set X to a set Y is a relation from X to Y with the special property that if both xfy and xfz are true, then $y = z$. (In many books it is also required that, for each x in X, there exists a y in Y, such that xfy. We will not impose this further condition.) The point is that if x is f-related to anything, then that thing is uniquely determined by x. After all, the definition says that if two things, y and z, are both f-related to x, then they are in fact the same thing, $y = z$. We write $y = f(x)$ for the unique y, if there is one, such that x is f-related to y.

With this definition we see that the notion of function is not symmetric in x and y. The notation $f : X \longrightarrow Y$ is often used for "f is a function from X to Y" because it underscores the directedness of the concept.

We now examine the putative examples from everyday speech. The relation R defined by pRr if "there has been a time at which both the price of oil has been p and the (Fed's) interest rate has been r" does *not* define a function from oil prices to interest rates. Many people will be able to recall a time when oil was $30 a barrel and the interest rate was 6% and another time when oil was $30 a barrel and the interest rate was 1%. In other words, both $(30, 6)$ and $(30, 1)$ are ordered pairs belonging to the R relation, and since $6 \neq 1$, R is not a function. Lest you think that we may be trying to do it the wrong way around, let us write R° for the relation from the set of interest rates to the set of oil prices given by $rR^\circ p$ if and only if pRr. If you can remember a time when the interest rate was 6% with oil at $30 a barrel and another time when the interest rate was 6% with oil at \$40 a barrel, then you will have both $(6, 30)$ and $(6, 40)$ in the relation $R°$. The fact that $30 \neq 40$ shows that $R°$ is also not a function.

On the other hand, suppose we bring into a testing facility a person who has just drunk five beers and test her blood alcohol concentration then and each hour thereafter for six hours. For each of the time values $\{0, 1, 2, 3, 4, 5, 6\}$, the measurement of blood alcohol concentration will produce *exactly one value*. If we write T for the set of all times beginning with that of the first test and B for the set of all blood alcohol concentration values, then testing the woman in question will determine a function $b : T \longrightarrow B$, where, for any time t in T, $b(t)$ is *the* blood alcohol concentration of the woman at time t.

It is not true that "Pension income is a function of years worked." If the value of "years worked" is 25, then the value of "pension income" is not yet determined. In most organizations, a CEO and a systems manager will retire with quite different pensions after 25 years of service. However, in this example we might be able to say that, *for each job description in a particular organization,* pension income is a function of years worked.

If \$100 is invested at, say, 6% simple interest, then the interest earned I is a function of the length of time t that the money is invested. These quantities are related by

$$I = 100(0.06)t \tag{1}$$

Here, for each value of t, there is exactly one value of I given by Equation (1). In a situation like this we will often write $I(t) = 100(0.06)t$ to reinforce the idea that the I-value is determined by the t-value. Sometimes we write $I = I(t)$ to make the claim that I is a function of t even if we do not know a formula for it. Formula (1) assigns the output 3 to the input $\frac{1}{2}$ and the output 12 to the input 2. We can think of Formula (1) as defining a *rule*: Multiply t by 100(0.06). The rule assigns to each input number t exactly one output number I, which is often symbolized by the following arrow notation:

$$t \mapsto 100(0.06)t$$

A formula provides a way of describing a rule to cover potentially infinitely many cases, but if there are only finitely many values of the input variable, as in the chapter opening paragraph, then the *rule*, as provided by the observations recorded in the table there, may not be part of any recognizable *formula*. We use the word *rule* rather than *formula* below to allow us to capture this useful generality. The following definition is sometimes easier to keep in mind than our description of a function as a special kind of relation:

Definition

A *function* $f : X \longrightarrow Y$ is a rule that assigns, to each element x of X, at most one element of Y. If an element is assigned to x in X, it is denoted by $f(x)$. The subset of X consisting of all the x for which $f(x)$ is defined is called the *domain* of f. The set of all elements in Y of the form $f(x)$, for some x in X, is called the *range* of f.

For the interest function defined by Equation (1), the input number t cannot be negative, because negative time makes no sense in this example. Thus, the domain consists of all nonnegative numbers—that is, all $t \geq 0$, where the variable gives the time elapsed from when the investment was made.

A variable that takes on values in the domain of a function $f: X \longrightarrow Y$ is sometimes called an **input** or an **independent variable** for f. A variable that takes on values in the range of f is sometimes called an **ouput** or a **dependent variable** of f. Thus, for the interest formula $I = 100(0.06)t$, the independent variable is t, the dependent variable is I, and I is a function of t.

As another example, the equation

$$y = x + 2 \tag{2}$$

defines y as a function of x. The equation gives the rule, "Add 2 to x." This rule assigns to each input x exactly one output $x + 2$, which is y. If $x = 1$, then $y = 3$; if $x = -4$, then $y = -2$. The independent variable is x and the dependent variable is y.

Not all equations in x and y define y as a function of x. For example, let $y^2 = x$. If x is 9, then $y^2 = 9$, so $y = \pm 3$. Hence, to the input 9, there are assigned not one, but *two*, output numbers: 3 and -3. This violates the definition of a function, so y is **not** a function of x.

On the other hand, some equations in two variables define either variable as a function of the other variable. For example, if $y = 2x$, then for each input x, there is exactly one output, $2x$. Thus, y is a function of x. However, solving the equation for x gives $x = y/2$. For each input y, there is exactly one output, $y/2$. Consequently, x is a function of y.

Usually, the letters f, g, h, F, G, and so on are used to name functions. For example, Equation (2), $y = x + 2$, defines y as a function of x, where the rule is "Add 2 to the input." Suppose we let f represent this rule. Then we say that f is the function. To indicate that f assigns the output 3 to the input 1, we write $f(1) = 3$, which is read "f of 1 equals 3." Similarly, $f(-4) = -2$. More generally, if x is any input, we have the following notation:

$f(x)$, which is read "f of x," and which means the output, in the range of f, that results when the rule f is applied to the input x, from the domain of f.

input
↓
$f(x)$
‾‾‾
↑
output

Thus, the output $f(x)$ is the same as y. But since $y = x + 2$, we can also write $f(x) = y = x + 2$ or more simply

$$f(x) = x + 2$$

For example, to find $f(3)$, which is the output corresponding to the input 3, we replace each x in $f(x) = x + 2$ by 3:

$$f(3) = 3 + 2 = 5$$

Outputs are also called **function values.**

For another example, the equation $g(x) = x^3 + x^2$ defines the function g that assigns the output $x^3 + x^2$ to an input x:

$$g: x \mapsto x^3 + x^2$$

In other words, g adds the cube of the input to the square of the input. Some function values are

$$g(2) = 2^3 + 2^2 = 12$$
$$g(-1) = (-1)^3 + (-1)^2 = -1 + 1 = 0$$
$$g(t) = t^3 + t^2$$
$$g(x + 1) = (x + 1)^3 + (x + 1)^2$$

The idea of *replacement* is very important in determining function values.

Note that $g(x + 1)$ was found by replacing each x in $x^3 + x^2$ by the input $x + 1$. When we refer to the function g defined by $g(x) = x^3 + x^2$, we are free to say simply "the function $g(x) = x^3 + x^2$" and similarly "the function $y = x + 2$."

Unless otherwise stated, the domain of a function $f: X \longrightarrow Y$ is the set of all x in X for which $f(x)$ makes sense, as an element of Y. When X and Y are both $(-\infty, \infty)$, this convention often refers to arithmetical restrictions. For example, suppose

$$h(x) = \frac{1}{x - 6}$$

Here any real number can be used for x except 6, because the denominator is 0 when x is 6. So the domain of h is understood to be all real numbers except 6. A useful notation for this set is $(-\infty, \infty) - \{6\}$. More generally, if A and B are subsets of a set X, then we write $A - B$ for the set of all x in X such that x is in A and x is *not* in B. We note too that the range of h is the set of all real numbers except 0. Each output of h is a fraction and the only way that a fraction can be 0 is for its numerator to be 0. While we do have

$$\frac{1}{x-6} = \frac{c}{c(x-6)} \quad \text{for all } c \neq 0$$

by the *fundamental principle of fractions* of Section 0.2, we see that 0 is not a function value for h. But if y is any nonzero real number, we can solve $\dfrac{1}{x-6} = y$ for x and get $x = 6 + \dfrac{1}{y}$ as the (unique) input for which $h(x)$ is the given y. Thus the range is $(-\infty, \infty) - \{0\}$, the set of all real numbers other than 0.

Equality of Functions

To say that two functions $f, g : X \longrightarrow Y$ are equal, denoted $f = g$, is to say that

1. The domain of f is equal to the domain of g;
2. For every x in the domain of f and g, $f(x) = g(x)$.

Requirement 1 says that an element x is in the domain of f if and only if x is in the domain of g. Thus, if we have $f(x) = x^2$, with no explicit mention of domain, and $g(x) = x^2$ for $x \geq 0$, then $f \neq g$. For here the domain of f is the whole real line $(-\infty, \infty)$ and the domain of g is $[0, \infty)$. On the other hand, if we have $f(x) = (x+1)^2$ and $g(x) = x^2 + 2x + 1$, then, for both f and g, the domain is understood to be $(-\infty, \infty)$ and the issue for deciding if $f = g$ is whether, for each real number x, we have $(x+1)^2 = x^2 + 2x + 1$. But this is true; it is a special case of item 4 in the Special Products of Section 0.4. In fact, older textbooks refer to statements like $(x+1)^2 = x^2 + 2x + 1$ as "identities," to indicate that they are true for any admissible value of the variable and to distinguish them from statements like $(x+1)^2 = 0$, which are true for some values of x.

Given functions f and g, it follows that we have $f \neq g$ if *either* the domain of f is different from the domain of g *or* there is some x for which $f(x) \neq g(x)$.

EXAMPLE 1   Determining Equality of Functions

Determine which of the following functions are equal.

a. $f(x) = \dfrac{(x+2)(x-1)}{(x-1)}$

b. $g(x) = x + 2$

c. $h(x) = \begin{cases} x+2 & \text{if } x \neq 1 \\ 0 & \text{if } x = 1 \end{cases}$

d. $k(x) = \begin{cases} x+2 & \text{if } x \neq 1 \\ 3 & \text{if } x = 1 \end{cases}$

Solution: The domain of f is the set of all real numbers other than 1, while that of g is the set of all real numbers. (For these we are following the convention that the domain is the set of all real numbers for which the rule makes sense.) We will have more to say about functions like h and k that are defined by *cases* in Example 4 of Section 2.2. Here we observe that the domain of h and the domain of k are both $(-\infty, \infty)$, since for both we have a rule that makes sense for each real number. The domains of g, h, and k are equal to each other, but that of f is different. So by requirement 1 for equality of functions, $f \neq g, f \neq h$ and $f \neq k$. By definition, $g(x) = h(x) = k(x)$ for all $x \neq 1$, so the matter of equality of g, h and k depends on their values at 1. Since $g(1) = 3$, $h(1) = 0$ and $k(1) = 3$, we conclude that $g = k$ and $g \neq h$ (and $h \neq k$).

While this example might appear to be contrived, it is typical of an issue that arises frequently in calculus.

Now Work Problem 3 ◁

APPLY IT ▷

1. The area of a circle depends on the length of the radius of the circle.

a. Write a function $a(r)$ for the area of a circle when the length of the radius is r.
b. What is the domain of this function out of context?
c. What is the domain of this function in the given context?

| EXAMPLE 2 | Finding Domains |

Find the domain of each function.

a. $f(x) = \dfrac{x}{x^2 - x - 2}$

Solution: We cannot divide by zero, so we must find any values of x that make the denominator 0. These *cannot* be inputs. Thus, we set the denominator equal to 0 and solve for x:

$$x^2 - x - 2 = 0 \qquad \text{quadratic equation}$$
$$(x - 2)(x + 1) = 0 \qquad \text{factoring}$$
$$x = 2, -1$$

Therefore, the domain of f is all real numbers *except* 2 and -1.

b. $g(t) = \sqrt{2t - 1}$ as a function $g: (-\infty, \infty) \longrightarrow (-\infty, \infty)$

Solution: $\sqrt{2t - 1}$ is a real number if $2t - 1$ is greater than or equal to 0. If $2t - 1$ is negative, then $\sqrt{2t - 1}$ is not a real number, so we must assume that

$$2t - 1 \geq 0$$
$$2t \geq 1 \qquad \text{adding 1 to both sides}$$
$$t \geq \frac{1}{2} \qquad \text{dividing both sides by 2}$$

Thus, the domain is the interval $[\frac{1}{2}, \infty)$.

Now Work Problem 7 ◁

APPLY IT ▷

2. The time it takes to go a given distance depends on the speed at which one is traveling.

a. Write a function $t(r)$ for the time it takes if the distance is 300 miles and the speed is r.
b. What is the domain of this function out of context?
c. What is the domain of this function in the given context?
d. Find $t(x), t\left(\dfrac{x}{2}\right)$, and $t\left(\dfrac{x}{4}\right)$.
e. What happens to the time if the speed is reduced (divided) by a constant c? Describe this situation using an equation.

| EXAMPLE 3 | Finding Domain and Function Values |

Let $g(x) = 3x^2 - x + 5$. Any real number can be used for x, so the domain of g is all real numbers.

a. Find $g(z)$.

Solution: Replacing each x in $g(x) = 3x^2 - x + 5$ by z gives

$$g(z) = 3(z)^2 - z + 5 = 3z^2 - z + 5$$

b. Find $g(r^2)$.

Solution: Replacing each x in $g(x) = 3x^2 - x + 5$ by r^2 gives

$$g(r^2) = 3(r^2)^2 - r^2 + 5 = 3r^4 - r^2 + 5$$

c. Find $g(x + h)$.

Solution:

$$g(x + h) = 3(x + h)^2 - (x + h) + 5$$
$$= 3(x^2 + 2hx + h^2) - x - h + 5$$
$$= 3x^2 + 6hx + 3h^2 - x - h + 5$$

Now Work Problem 31(a) ◁

CAUTION!⚠

Don't be confused by notation. In Example 3(c), we find $g(x + h)$ by replacing each x in $g(x) = 3x^2 - x + 5$ by the input $x + h$. $g(x + h)$, $g(x) + h$ and $g(x) + g(h)$ are all quite different quantities.

EXAMPLE 4   Finding a Difference Quotient

If $f(x) = x^2$, find $\dfrac{f(x + h) - f(x)}{h}$.

Solution: The expression $\dfrac{f(x + h) - f(x)}{h}$ is referred to as a **difference quotient**. Here the numerator is a difference of function values. We have

$$\frac{f(x + h) - f(x)}{h} = \frac{(x + h)^2 - x^2}{h}$$

$$= \frac{x^2 + 2hx + h^2 - x^2}{h} = \frac{2hx + h^2}{h}$$

$$= \frac{h(2x + h)}{h}$$

$$= 2x + h \quad \text{for } h \neq 0$$

The difference quotient of a function is an important mathematical concept.

If we consider the original difference quotient as a function of h, then it is different from $2x + h$ because 0 is not in the domain of the original difference quotient but it *is* in the default domain of $2x + h$. For this reason, we had to restrict the final equality.

Now Work Problem 35 ◁

In some cases, the domain of a function is restricted for physical or economic reasons. For example, the previous interest function $I = 100(0.06)t$ has $t \geq 0$ because t represents time elapsed since the investment was made. Example 5 will give another illustration.

EXAMPLE 5   Demand Function

APPLY IT ▶

3. Suppose the weekly demand function for large pizzas at a local pizza parlor is $p = 26 - \dfrac{q}{40}$.

a. If the current price is $18.50 per pizza, how many pizzas are sold each week?

b. If 200 pizzas are sold each week, what is the current price?

c. If the owner wants to double the number of large pizzas sold each week (to 400), what should the price be?

Suppose that the equation $p = 100/q$ describes the relationship between the price per unit p of a certain product and the number of units q of the product that consumers will buy (that is, demand) per week at the stated price. This equation is called a *demand equation* for the product. If q is an input, then to each value of q there is assigned at most one output p:

$$q \;\mapsto\; \frac{100}{q} = p$$

For example,

$$20 \;\mapsto\; \frac{100}{20} = 5$$

that is, when q is 20, p is 5. Thus, price p is a function of quantity demanded, q. This function is called a **demand function**. The independent variable is q, and p is the dependent variable. Since q cannot be 0 (division by 0 is not defined) and cannot be negative (q represents quantity), the domain is all $q > 0$.

Now Work Problem 43 ◁

We have seen that a function is a rule which assigns to each input in the domain exactly one output in the range. For the rule given by $f(x) = x^2$, some sample assignments are shown by the arrows in Figure 2.1. The next example discusses a rule given by a finite listing rather than an an algebraic formula.

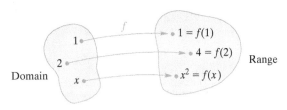

FIGURE 2.1   Some function values for $f(x) = x^2$.

EXAMPLE 6　Supply Schedule

APPLY IT ▶

4. For the supply function given by the following table, determine the weekly revenue function, assuming that all units supplied are sold.

p Price per Unit in Dollars	q Quanity Supplied per Week
500	11
600	14
700	17
800	20

The table in Apply It 4 on this page is a *supply schedule*. Such a table lists for each of certain prices p of a certain product the quantity q that producers will supply per week at that price. For each price, the table provides exactly one quantity so that it exhibits q as a function of p.

But also, for each quantity, the table provides exactly one price so that it also exhibits p as a function of q. If we write $q = f(p)$, then the table provides

$$f(500) = 11 \quad f(600) = 14 \quad f(700) = 17 \quad f(800) = 20$$

If we write $p = g(q)$, then the table also provides

$$g(11) = 500 \quad g(14) = 600 \quad g(17) = 700 \quad g(20) = 800$$

Observe that we have $g(f(p)) = p$, for all p, and $f(g(q)) = q$, for all q. We will have more to say about pairs of functions of this kind in Section 2.4. Both functions determined by this table are called **supply functions.**

Now Work Problem 53 ◁

PROBLEMS 2.1

In Problems 1–4, determine whether the given functions are equal.

1. $f(x) = \sqrt{x^2}; g(x) = x$

2. $G(x) = (\sqrt{x+1})^2; H(x) = x + 1$

3. $h(x) = \dfrac{|x|}{x}; k(x) = \begin{cases} 1 & \text{if } x \geq 0 \\ -1 & \text{if } x < 0 \end{cases}$

4. $f(x) = \begin{cases} \dfrac{x^2 - 4x + 3}{x - 3} & \text{if } x \neq 3 \\ 2 & \text{if } x = 3 \end{cases}$;

$g(x) = x - 1$

In Problems 5–16, give the domain of each function.

5. $f(x) = \dfrac{6}{x - 1}$

6. $g(x) = \dfrac{x}{5}$

7. $h(x) = \sqrt{x - 3}$

8. $K(z) = \dfrac{1}{\sqrt{z-1}}$

9. $f(z) = 3z^2 + 2z - 4$

10. $H(x) = \dfrac{x^2}{x + 3}$

11. $f(x) = \dfrac{9x - 9}{2x + 7}$

12. $g(x) = \sqrt{4x + 3}$

13. $g(y) = \dfrac{4}{y^2 - 4y + 4}$

14. $\phi(x) = \dfrac{x + 5}{x^2 + x - 6}$

15. $h(s) = \dfrac{3 - x^2}{3x^2 - 5x - 2}$

16. $G(r) = \dfrac{2}{r^2 + 1}$

In Problems 17–28, find the function values for each function.

17. $f(x) = 2x + 1; f(0), f(3), f(-4)$

18. $H(s) = 5s^2 - 3; H(4), H(\sqrt{2}), H\left(\dfrac{2}{3}\right)$

19. $G(x) = 2 - x^2; G(-8), G(u), G(u^2)$

20. $F(x) = -7x + 1; F(s), F(t + 1), F(x + 3)$

21. $\gamma(u) = 2u^2 - u; \gamma(-2), \gamma(2v), \gamma(x + a)$

22. $h(v) = \dfrac{1}{\sqrt{v}}; h(16), h\left(\dfrac{1}{4}\right), h(1 - x)$

23. $f(x) = x^2 + 2x + 1; f(1), f(-1), f(x + h)$

24. $H(x) = (x + 4)^2; H(0), H(2), H(t - 4)$

25. $k(x) = \dfrac{x - 5}{x^2 + 1}; k(5), k(2x), k(x + h)$

26. $k(x) = \sqrt{x - 3}; k(4), k(3), k(x + 1) - k(x)$

27. $f(x) = x^{4/3}; f(0), f(64), f\left(\dfrac{1}{8}\right)$

28. $g(x) = x^{2/5}; g(32), g(-64), g(t^{10})$

In Problems 29–36, find (a) $f(x + h)$ and (b) $\dfrac{f(x + h) - f(x)}{h}$; simplify your answers.

29. $f(x) = 4x - 5$

30. $f(x) = \dfrac{x}{3}$

31. $f(x) = x^2 + 2x$

32. $f(x) = 3x^2 - 2x - 1$

33. $f(x) = 3 - 2x + 4x^2$

34. $f(x) = x^3$

35. $f(x) = \dfrac{1}{x - 1}$

36. $f(x) = \dfrac{x + 8}{x}$

37. If $f(x) = 5x + 3$, find $\dfrac{f(3 + h) - f(3)}{h}$.

38. If $f(x) = 2x^2 - x + 1$, find $\dfrac{f(x) - f(2)}{x - 2}$.

In Problems 39–42, is y a function of x? Is x a function of y?

39. $9y - 3x - 4 = 0$

40. $x^4 - 1 + y = 0$

41. $y = 7x^2$

42. $x^2 + y^2 = 1$

43. The formula for the area of a circle of radius r is $A = \pi r^2$. Is the area a function of the radius?

44. Suppose $f(b) = a^2 b^3 + a^3 b^2$. (a) Find $f(a)$. (b) Find $f(ab)$.

45. Value of Business A business with an original capital of $50,000 has income and expenses each week of $7200 and $4900, respectively. If all profits are retained in the business, express the value V of the business at the end of t weeks as a function of t.

46. Depreciation If a $30,000 machine depreciates 2% of its original value each year, find a function f that expresses the machine's value V after t years have elapsed.

47. Profit Function If q units of a certain product are sold (q is nonnegative), the profit P is given by the equation $P = 1.25q$. Is P a function of q? What is the dependent variable? the independent variable?

48. Demand Function Suppose the yearly demand function for a particular actor to star in a film is $p = \dfrac{1,200,000}{q}$, where q is the number of films he stars in during the year. If the actor currently charges \$600,000 per film, how many films does he star in each year? If he wants to star in four films per year, what should his price be?

49. Supply Function Suppose the weekly supply function for a pound of house-blend coffee at a local coffee shop is $p = \dfrac{q}{48}$, where q is the number of pounds of coffee supplied per week. How many pounds of coffee per week will be supplied if the price is \$8.39 a pound? How many pounds of coffee per week will be supplied if the price is \$19.49 a pound? How does the amount supplied change as the price increases?

50. Hospital Discharges An insurance company examined the records of a group of individuals hospitalized for a particular illness. It was found that the total proportion discharged at the end of t days of hospitalization is given by

$$f(t) = 1 - \left(\frac{200}{200 + t}\right)^3$$

Evaluate (a) $f(0)$, (b) $f(100)$, and (c) $f(800)$. (d) At the end of how many days was half of the group discharged?

51. Psychology A psychophysical experiment was conducted to analyze human response to electrical shocks.[1] The subjects received a shock of a certain intensity. They were told to assign a magnitude of 10 to this particular shock, called the standard stimulus. Then other shocks (stimuli) of various intensities were given. For each one, the response R was to be a number that indicated the perceived magnitude of the shock relative to that of the standard stimulus. It was found that R was a function of the intensity I of the shock (I in microamperes) and was estimated by

$$R = f(I) = \frac{I^{4/3}}{2500} \qquad 500 \leq I \leq 3500$$

Evaluate (a) $f(1000)$ and (b) $f(2000)$. (c) Suppose that I_0 and $2I_0$ are in the domain of f. Express $f(2I_0)$ in terms of $f(I_0)$. What effect does the doubling of intensity have on response?

52. Psychology In a paired-associate learning experiment,[2] the probability of a correct response as a function of the number n of trials has the form

$$P(n) = 1 - \frac{1}{2}(1 - c)^{n-1} \qquad n \geq 1$$

where the estimated value of c is 0.344. Find $P(1)$ and $P(2)$ by using this value of c.

53. Demand Schedule The following table is called a *demand schedule*. It gives a correspondence between the price p of a product and the quantity q that consumers will demand (that is, purchase) at that price. (a) If $p = f(q)$, list the numbers in the domain of f. Find $f(2900)$ and $f(3000)$. (b) If $q = g(p)$, list the numbers in the domain of g. Find $g(10)$ and $g(17)$.

Price per Unit, p	Quantity Demanded per Week, q
\$10	3000
12	2900
17	2300
20	2000

In Problems 54–57, use your calculator to find the indicated values for the given function. Round answers to two decimal places.

54. $f(x) = 2.03x^3 - 5.27x^2 - 13.71$; (a) $f(1.73)$, (b) $f(-5.78)$, (c) $f(\sqrt{2})$

55. $f(x) = \dfrac{14.7x^2 - 3.95x - 15.76}{24.3 - x^3}$; (a) $f(4)$, (b) $f(-17/4)$, (c) $f(\pi)$

56. $f(x) = (20.3 - 3.2x)(2.25x^2 - 7.1x - 16)^4$; (a) $f(0.3)$, (b) $f(-0.02)$, (c) $f(1.9)$

57. $f(x) = \sqrt{\dfrac{\sqrt{2}x^2 + 7.31(x + 1)}{5.03}}$; (a) $f(12.35)$, (b) $f(-123)$, (c) $f(0)$

Objective

To introduce constant functions, polynomial functions, rational functions, case-defined functions, the absolute-value function, and factorial notation.

2.2 Special Functions

In this section, we look at functions having special forms and representations. We begin with perhaps the simplest type of function there is: a *constant function*.

EXAMPLE 1 Constant Functions

Let $h : (-\infty, \infty) \longrightarrow (-\infty, \infty)$ be given by $h(x) = 2$. The domain of h is $(-\infty, \infty)$, the set of all real numbers. All function values are 2. For example,

$$h(10) = 2 \qquad h(-387) = 2 \qquad h(x + 3) = 2$$

---

[1] Adapted from H. Babkoff, "Magnitude Estimation of Short Electrocutaneous Pulses," *Psychological Research*, 39, no. 1 (1976), 39–49.

[2] D. Laming, *Mathematical Psychology* (New York: Academic Press, 1983).

APPLY IT ▷

5. Suppose the monthly health insurance premiums for an individual are \$125.00.

a. Write the monthly health insurance premiums as a function of the number of visits the individual makes to the doctor.
b. How do the health insurance premiums change as the number of visits to the doctor increases?
c. What kind of function is this?

Each term in a polynomial function is either a constant or a constant times a positive integral power of x.

We call h a *constant function* because all the function values are the same. More generally, we have this definition:

A function of the form $h(x) = c$, where c is a *constant*, is called a **constant function.**

Now Work Problem 17 ◁

A constant function belongs to a broader class of functions, called *polynomial functions*. In general, a function of the form

$$f(x) = c_n x^n + c_{n-1} x^{n-1} + \cdots + c_1 x + c_0$$

where n is a nonnegative integer and $c_n, c_{n-1}, \ldots, c_0$ are constants with $c_n \neq 0$, is called a **polynomial function** (in x). The number n is called the **degree** of the polynomial, and c_n is the **leading coefficient.** Thus,

$$f(x) = 3x^2 - 8x + 9$$

is a polynomial function of degree 2 with leading coefficient 3. Likewise, $g(x) = 4 - 2x$ has degree 1 and leading coefficient -2. Polynomial functions of degree 1 or 2 are called **linear** or **quadratic functions,** respectively. For example, $g(x) = 4 - 2x$ is linear and $f(x) = 3x^2 - 8x + 9$ is quadratic. Note that a nonzero constant function, such as $f(x) = 5$ [which can be written as $f(x) = 5x^0$], is a polynomial function of degree 0. The constant function $f(x) = 0$ is also considered a polynomial function but has no degree assigned to it. The domain of any polynomial function is the set of all real numbers.

APPLY IT ▷

6. The function $d(t) = 3t^2$, for $t \geq 0$, represents the distance in meters a car will go in t seconds when it has a constant acceleration of 6 m per second.

a. What kind of function is this?
b. What is its degree?
c. What is its leading coefficient?

EXAMPLE 2   Polynomial Functions

a. $f(x) = x^3 - 6x^2 + 7$ is a polynomial (function) of degree 3 with leading coefficient 1.

b. $g(x) = \dfrac{2x}{3}$ is a linear function with leading coefficient $\dfrac{2}{3}$.

c. $f(x) = \dfrac{2}{x^3}$ is *not* a polynomial function. Because $f(x) = 2x^{-3}$ and the exponent for x is not a nonnegative integer, this function does not have the proper form for a polynomial. Similarly, $g(x) = \sqrt{x}$ is not a polynomial, because $g(x) = x^{1/2}$.

Now Work Problem 3 ◁

A function that is a quotient of polynomial functions is called a **rational function.**

EXAMPLE 3   Rational Functions

a. $f(x) = \dfrac{x^2 - 6x}{x + 5}$ is a rational function, since the numerator and denominator are each polynomials. Note that this rational function is not defined for $x = -5$.

Every polynomial function is a rational function.

b. $g(x) = 2x + 3$ is a rational function, since $2x + 3 = \dfrac{2x + 3}{1}$. In fact, every polynomial function is also a rational function.

Now Work Problem 5 ◁

Sometimes more than one expression is needed to define a function, as Example 4 shows.

EXAMPLE 4   Case-Defined Function

Let

$$F(s) = \begin{cases} 1 & \text{if } -1 \le s < 1 \\ 0 & \text{if } 1 \le s \le 2 \\ s - 3 & \text{if } 2 < s \le 8 \end{cases}$$

APPLY IT ▶

7. To reduce inventory, a department store charges three rates. If you buy 0–5 pairs of socks, the price is $3.50 per pair. If you buy 6–10 pairs of socks, the price is $3.00 per pair. If you buy more than 10 pairs, the price is $2.75 per pair. Write a case-defined function to represent the cost of buying n pairs of socks.

This is called a **case-defined function** because the rule for specifying it is given by rules for each of several disjoint cases. Here s is the independent variable, and the domain of F is all s such that $-1 \le s \le 8$. The value of s determines which expression to use.

Find $F(0)$: Since $-1 \le 0 < 1$, we have $F(0) = 1$.

Find $F(2)$: Since $1 \le 2 \le 2$, we have $F(2) = 0$.

Find $F(7)$: Since $2 < 7 \le 8$, we substitute 7 for s in $s - 3$.

$$F(7) = 7 - 3 = 4$$

Now Work Problem 19 ◁

EXAMPLE 5   Absolute-Value Function

The absolute-value function can be considered a case-defined function.

The function $|-|(x) = |x|$ is called the *absolute-value function*. Recall that the **absolute value,** of a real number x, is denoted $|x|$ and is defined by

$$|x| = \begin{cases} x & \text{if } x \ge 0 \\ -x & \text{if } x < 0 \end{cases}$$

Thus, the domain of $|-|$ is all real numbers. Some function values are

$$|16| = 16$$

$$|-\tfrac{4}{3}| = -\left(-\tfrac{4}{3}\right) = \tfrac{4}{3}$$

$$|0| = 0$$

Now Work Problem 21 ◁

In our next examples, we make use of *factorial notation*.

The symbol $r!$, with r a positive integer, is read "r **factorial.**" It represents the product of the first r positive integers:

$$r! = 1 \cdot 2 \cdot 3 \cdots r$$

We also define

$$0! = 1$$

For each nonnegative integer n, $(-)!(n) = n!$ determines a unique number so it follows that $(-)!$ is a function whose domain is the set of nonnegative integers.

EXAMPLE 6   Factorials

APPLY IT ▶

8. Seven different books are to be placed on a shelf. How many ways can they be arranged? Represent the question as a factorial problem and give the solution.

a. $5! = 1 \cdot 2 \cdot 3 \cdot 4 \cdot 5 = 120$

b. $3!(6 - 5)! = 3! \cdot 1! = (3 \cdot 2 \cdot 1)(1) = (6)(1) = 6$

c. $\dfrac{4!}{0!} = \dfrac{1 \cdot 2 \cdot 3 \cdot 4}{1} = \dfrac{24}{1} = 24$

Now Work Problem 27 ◁

EXAMPLE 7   Genetics

Suppose two black guinea pigs are bred and produce exactly five offspring. Under certain conditions, it can be shown that the probability P that exactly r of the offspring will be brown and the others black is a function of r, $P = P(r)$, where

Factorials occur frequently in probability theory.

$$P(r) = \frac{5! \left(\frac{1}{4}\right)^r \left(\frac{3}{4}\right)^{5-r}}{r!(5-r)!} \qquad r = 0, 1, 2, \ldots, 5$$

The letter P in $P = P(r)$ is used in two ways. On the right side, P represents the function rule. On the left side, P represents the dependent variable. The domain of P is all integers from 0 to 5, inclusive. Find the probability that exactly three guinea pigs will be brown.

Solution: We want to find $P(3)$. We have

$$P(3) = \frac{5! \left(\frac{1}{4}\right)^3 \left(\frac{3}{4}\right)^2}{3!2!} = \frac{120 \left(\frac{1}{64}\right)\left(\frac{9}{16}\right)}{6(2)} = \frac{45}{512}$$

Now Work Problem 35 ◁

PROBLEMS 2.2

In Problems 1–4, determine whether the given function is a polynomial function.

1. $f(x) = x^2 - x^4 + 4$

2. $f(x) = \dfrac{x^3 + 7x - 3}{3}$

3. $g(x) = \dfrac{1}{x^2 + 2x + 1}$

4. $g(x) = 2^{-3}x^3$

In Problems 5–8, determine whether the given function is a rational function.

5. $f(x) = \dfrac{x^2 + x}{x^3 + 4}$

6. $f(x) = \dfrac{3}{2x + 1}$

7. $g(x) = \begin{cases} 1 & \text{if } x < 5 \\ 4 & \text{if } x \ge 5 \end{cases}$

8. $g(x) = 4x^{-4}$

In Problems 9–12, find the domain of each function.

9. $k(z) = 26$

10. $f(x) = \sqrt{\pi}$

11. $f(x) = \begin{cases} 5x & \text{if } x > 1 \\ 4 & \text{if } x \le 1 \end{cases}$

12. $f(x) = \begin{cases} 4 & \text{if } x = 3 \\ x^2 & \text{if } 1 \le x < 3 \end{cases}$

In Problems 13–16, state (a) the degree and (b) the leading coefficient of the given polynomial function.

13. $F(x) = 7x^3 - 2x^2 + 6$

14. $g(x) = 9x^2 + 2x + 1$

15. $f(x) = \dfrac{1}{\pi} - 3x^5 + 2x^6 + x^7$

16. $f(x) = 9$

In Problems 17–22, find the function values for each function.

17. $f(x) = 8$; $f(2)$, $f(t + 8)$, $f(-\sqrt{17})$

18. $g(x) = |x - 3|$; $g(10)$, $g(3)$, $g(-3)$

19. $F(t) = \begin{cases} 2 & \text{if } t > 1 \\ 0 & \text{if } t = 1 \\ -1 & \text{if } t < 1 \end{cases}$

$F(12)$, $F(-\sqrt{3})$, $F(1)$, $F\left(\dfrac{18}{5}\right)$

20. $f(x) = \begin{cases} 4 & \text{if } x \ge 0 \\ 3 & \text{if } x < 0 \end{cases}$

$f(3), f(-4), f(0)$

21. $G(x) = \begin{cases} x - 1 & \text{if } x \ge 3 \\ 3 - x^2 & \text{if } x < 3 \end{cases}$

$G(8), G(3), G(-1), G(1)$

22. $F(\theta) = \begin{cases} 2\theta - 5 & \text{if } \theta < 2 \\ \theta^2 - 3\theta + 1 & \text{if } \theta > 2 \end{cases}$

$F(3), F(-3), F(2)$

In Problems 23–28, determine the value of each expression.

23. $6!$

24. $(3 - 3)!$

25. $(4 - 2)!$

26. $6! \cdot 2!$

27. $\dfrac{n!}{(n-1)!}$

28. $\dfrac{8!}{5!(8-5)!}$

29. Subway Ride A return subway ride ticket within the city costs $2.50. Write the cost of a return ticket as a function of a passenger's income. What kind of function is this?

30. Geometry A rectangular prism has length three more than its width and height one less than twice the width. Write the volume of the rectangular prism as a function of the width. What kind of function is this?

31. Cost Function In manufacturing a component for a machine, the initial cost of a die is $850 and all other additional costs are $3 per unit produced. (a) Express the total cost C (in dollars) as a linear function of the number q of units produced. (b) How many units are produced if the total cost is $1600?

32. Investment If a principal of P dollars is invested at a simple annual interest rate of r for t years, express the total accumulated amount of the principal and interest as a function of t. Is your result a linear function of t?

33. Sales To encourage large group sales, a theater charges two rates. If your group is less than 12, each ticket costs $9.50. If your group is 12 or more, each ticket costs $8.75. Write a case-defined function to represent the cost of buying n tickets.

34. Factorials The business mathematics class has elected a grievance committee of five to complain to the faculty about the introduction of factorial notation into the course. They decide that they will be more effective if they label themselves as members A, G, M, N, and S, where member A will lobby faculty with surnames A through F, member G will lobby faculty with surnames G through L, and so on. In how many ways can the committee so label its members?

35. Genetics   Under certain conditions, if two brown-eyed parents have exactly three children, the probability that there will be exactly r blue-eyed children is given by the function $P = P(r)$, where

$$P(r) = \frac{3!\left(\frac{1}{4}\right)^r\left(\frac{3}{4}\right)^{3-r}}{r!(3-r)!}, \qquad r = 0, 1, 2, 3$$

Find the probability that exactly two of the children will be blue-eyed.

36. Genetics   In Example 7, find the probability that all five offspring will be brown.

37. Bacteria Growth   Bacteria are growing in a culture. The time t (in hours) for the bacteria to double in number (the generation time) is a function of the temperature T (in °C) of the culture. If this function is given by[3]

$$t = f(T) = \begin{cases} \dfrac{1}{24}T + \dfrac{11}{4} & \text{if } 30 \le T \le 36 \\[2mm] \dfrac{4}{3}T - \dfrac{175}{4} & \text{if } 36 < T \le 39 \end{cases}$$

(a) determine the domain of f and **(b)** find $f(30), f(36)$, and $f(39)$.

In Problems 38–41, use your calculator to find the indicated function values for the given function. Round answers to two decimal places.

38. $f(x) = \begin{cases} 0.19x^4 - 27.99 & \text{if } x \ge 5.99 \\ 0.63x^5 - 57.42 & \text{if } x < 5.99 \end{cases}$

   (a) $f(7.98)$ **(b)** $f(2.26)$ **(c)** $f(9)$

39. $f(x) = \begin{cases} 29.5x^4 + 30.4 & \text{if } x < 3 \\ 7.9x^3 - 2.1x & \text{if } x \ge 3 \end{cases}$

   (a) $f(2.5)$ **(b)** $f(-3.6)$ **(c)** $f(3.2)$

40. $f(x) = \begin{cases} 4.07x - 2.3 & \text{if } x < -8 \\ 19.12 & \text{if } -8 \le x < -2 \\ x^2 - 4x^{-2} & \text{if } x \ge -2 \end{cases}$

   (a) $f(-5.8)$ **(b)** $f(-14.9)$ **(c)** $f(7.6)$

41. $f(x) = \begin{cases} x/(x+3) & \text{if } x < -5 \\ x(x-4)^2 & \text{if } -5 \le x < 0 \\ \sqrt{2.1x + 3} & \text{if } x \ge 0 \end{cases}$

   (a) $f(-\sqrt{30})$ **(b)** $f(46)$ **(c)** $f(-2/3)$

2.3 Combinations of Functions

Objective

To combine functions by means of addition, subtraction, multiplication, division, multiplication by a constant, and composition.

There are several ways of combining two functions to create a new function. Suppose f and g are the functions given by

$$f(x) = x^2 \quad \text{and} \quad g(x) = 3x$$

Adding $f(x)$ and $g(x)$ gives

$$f(x) + g(x) = x^2 + 3x$$

This operation defines a new function called the *sum* of f and g, denoted $f + g$. Its function value at x is $f(x) + g(x)$. That is,

$$(f + g)(x) = f(x) + g(x) = x^2 + 3x$$

For example,

$$(f + g)(2) = 2^2 + 3(2) = 10$$

In general, for any functions $f, g : X \longrightarrow (-\infty, \infty)$, we define the **sum** $f + g$, the **difference** $f - g$, the **product** fg, and the **quotient** $\dfrac{f}{g}$ as follows:

$$(f + g)(x) = f(x) + g(x)$$
$$(f - g)(x) = f(x) - g(x)$$
$$(fg)(x) = f(x) \cdot g(x)$$
$$\frac{f}{g}(x) = \frac{f(x)}{g(x)} \quad \text{for } g(x) \neq 0$$

For each of the four new functions the domain is the set of all x which belong to both the domain of f *and* the domain of g. For the quotient, we further restrict the domain to

---

[3]Adapted from F. K. E. Imrie and A. J. Vlitos, "Production of Fungal Protein from Carob," in *Single-Cell Protein II*, ed. S. R. Tannenbaum and D. I. C. Wang (Cambridge, MA: MIT Press, 1975).

exclude any value of x for which $g(x) = 0$. In each of the four combinations we have a new function from X to $(-\infty, \infty)$. For example, we have $f + g : X \longrightarrow (-\infty, \infty)$. A special case of fg deserves separate mention. For any real number c and any function f, we define cf by

$$(cf)(x) = c \cdot f(x)$$

This restricted case of product is called **scalar product.** The scalar product tends to share properties with sums (and differences) that are not enjoyed by general products (and quotients).

For $f(x) = x^2$, $g(x) = 3x$, and $c = \sqrt{2}$ we have

$$(f + g)(x) = f(x) + g(x) = x^2 + 3x$$

$$(f - g)(x) = f(x) - g(x) = x^2 - 3x$$

$$(fg)(x) = f(x) \cdot g(x) = x^2(3x) = 3x^3$$

$$\frac{f}{g}(x) = \frac{f(x)}{g(x)} = \frac{x^2}{3x} = \frac{x}{3} \quad \text{for } x \neq 0$$

$$(cf)(x) = cf(x) = \sqrt{2}x^2$$

EXAMPLE 1 Combining Functions

If $f(x) = 3x - 1$ and $g(x) = x^2 + 3x$, find

a. $(f + g)(x)$

b. $(f - g)(x)$

c. $(fg)(x)$

d. $\dfrac{f}{g}(x)$

e. $\left(\dfrac{1}{2}f\right)(x)$

Solution:

a. $(f + g)(x) = f(x) + g(x) = (3x - 1) + (x^2 + 3x) = x^2 + 6x - 1$

b. $(f - g)(x) = f(x) - g(x) = (3x - 1) - (x^2 + 3x) = -1 - x^2$

c. $(fg)(x) = f(x)g(x) = (3x - 1)(x^2 + 3x) = 3x^3 + 8x^2 - 3x$

d. $\dfrac{f}{g}(x) = \dfrac{f(x)}{g(x)} = \dfrac{3x - 1}{x^2 + 3x}$

e. $\left(\dfrac{1}{2}f\right)(x) = \dfrac{1}{2}(f(x)) = \dfrac{1}{2}(3x - 1) = \dfrac{3x - 1}{2}$

Now Work Problem 3(a)–(f) ◁

Composition

We can also combine two functions by first applying one function to an input and then applying the other function to the output of the first. For example, suppose $g(x) = 3x$, $f(x) = x^2$, and $x = 2$. Then $g(2) = 3 \cdot 2 = 6$. Thus, g sends the input 2 to the output 6:

$$2 \overset{g}{\mapsto} 6$$

Next, we let the output 6 become the input for f:

$$f(6) = 6^2 = 36$$

So f sends 6 to 36:

$$6 \overset{f}{\mapsto} 36$$

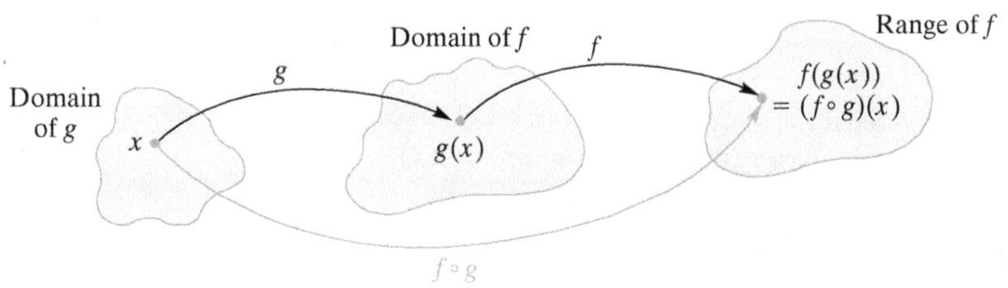

FIGURE 2.2   Composite of f with g.

By first applying g and then f, we send 2 to 36:

$$2 \overset{g}{\mapsto} 6 \overset{f}{\mapsto} 36$$

To be more general, replace the 2 by x, where x is in the domain of g. (See Figure 2.2.) Applying g to x, we get the number $g(x)$, which we will assume is in the domain of f. By applying f to $g(x)$, we get $f(g(x))$, read "f of g of x," which is in the range of f. The operation of applying g and then applying f to the result is called *composition* and the resulting function, denoted $f \circ g$, is called the *composite* of f with g. This function assigns the output $f(g(x))$ to the input x. (See the bottom arrow in Figure 2.2.) Thus, $(f \circ g)(x) = f(g(x))$.

Definition

For functions $g : X \longrightarrow Y$ and $f : Y \longrightarrow Z$, the **composite of f with g is the function $f \circ g : X \longrightarrow Z$ defined by**

$$(f \circ g)(x) = f(g(x))$$

where the domain of $f \circ g$ is the set of all those x in the domain of g such that $g(x)$ is in the domain of f.

For $f(x) = x^2$ and $g(x) = 3x$, we can get a simple form for $f \circ g$:

$$(f \circ g)(x) = f(g(x)) = f(3x) = (3x)^2 = 9x^2$$

For example, $(f \circ g)(2) = 9(2)^2 = 36$, as we saw before.

When dealing with real numbers and the operation of addition, 0 is special in that, for any real number a, we have

$$a + 0 = a = 0 + a$$

The number 1 enjoys a similar property with respect to multiplication. For any real number a, we have

$$a1 = a = 1a$$

For reference in Section 2.4, we note that the function I defined by $I(x) = x$, satisfies, for any function f,

$$f \circ I = f = I \circ f$$

where here we mean equality of functions as defined in Section 2.1. Indeed, for any x,

$$(f \circ I)(x) = f(I(x)) = f(x) = I(f(x)) = (I \circ f)(x)$$

The function I is called the *identity* function.

9. A CD costs x dollars wholesale. The price the store pays is given by the function $s(x) = x + 3$. The price the customer pays is $c(x) = 2x$, where x is the price the store pays. Write a composite function to find the customer's price as a function of the wholesale price.

CAUTION! ⚠

Generally, $f \circ g$ and $g \circ f$ are quite different. In Example 2,

$$(f \circ g)(x) = \sqrt{x+1}$$

but we have

$$(g \circ f)(x) = \sqrt{x} + 1$$

Observe that $(f \circ g)(1) = \sqrt{2}$, while $(g \circ f)(1) = 2$. Also, do not confuse $f(g(x))$ with $(fg)(x)$, which is the product $f(x)g(x)$. Here

$$f(g(x)) = \sqrt{x+1}$$

but

$$f(x)g(x) = \sqrt{x}(x+1)$$

EXAMPLE 2 Composition

Let $f(x) = \sqrt{x}$ and $g(x) = x + 1$. Find

a. $(f \circ g)(x)$

b. $(g \circ f)(x)$

Solution:

a. $(f \circ g)(x)$ is $f(g(x))$. Now g adds 1 to x, and f takes the square root of the result. Thus,

$$(f \circ g)(x) = f(g(x)) = f(x+1) = \sqrt{x+1}$$

The domain of g is all real numbers x, and the domain of f is all nonnegative reals. Hence, the domain of the composite is all x for which $g(x) = x + 1$ is nonnegative. That is, the domain is all $x \geq -1$, which is the interval $[-1, \infty)$.

b. $(g \circ f)(x)$ is $g(f(x))$. Now f takes the square root of x, and g adds 1 to the result. Thus, g adds 1 to $\sqrt{x}$, and we have

$$(g \circ f)(x) = g(f(x)) = g(\sqrt{x}) = \sqrt{x} + 1$$

The domain of f is all $x \geq 0$, and the domain of g is all reals. Hence, the domain of the composite is all $x \geq 0$ for which $f(x) = \sqrt{x}$ is real, namely, all $x \geq 0$.

Now Work Problem 7 ◁

Composition is *associative*, meaning that for any three functions f, g, and h,

$$(f \circ g) \circ h = f \circ (g \circ h)$$

EXAMPLE 3 Composition

If $F(p) = p^2 + 4p - 3$, $G(p) = 2p + 1$, and $H(p) = |p|$, find

a. $F(G(p))$

b. $F(G(H(p)))$

c. $G(F(1))$

Solution:

a. $F(G(p)) = F(2p+1) = (2p+1)^2 + 4(2p+1) - 3 = 4p^2 + 12p + 2 = (F \circ G)(p)$

b. $F(G(H(p))) = (F \circ (G \circ H))(p) = ((F \circ G) \circ H)(p) = (F \circ G)(H(p)) = (F \circ G)(|p|) = 4|p|^2 + 12|p| + 2 = 4p^2 + 12|p| + 2$

c. $G(F(1)) = G(1^2 + 4 \cdot 1 - 3) = G(2) = 2 \cdot 2 + 1 = 5$

Now Work Problem 9 ◁

In calculus, it is necessary at times to think of a particular function as a composite of two simpler functions, as the next example shows.

10. Suppose the area of a square garden is $g(x) = (x + 3)^2$. Express g as a composite of two functions, and explain what each function represents.

EXAMPLE 4 Expressing a Function as a Composite

Express $h(x) = (2x - 1)^3$ as a composite.

Solution:

We note that $h(x)$ is obtained by finding $2x - 1$ and cubing the result. Suppose we let $g(x) = 2x - 1$ and $f(x) = x^3$. Then

$$h(x) = (2x - 1)^3 = (g(x))^3 = f(g(x)) = (f \circ g)(x)$$

which gives h as a composite of two functions.

Now Work Problem 13 ◁

TECHNOLOGY ▮▮▯

Two functions can be combined by using a graphing calculator. Consider the functions

$$f(x) = 2x + 1 \quad \text{and} \quad g(x) = x^2$$

which we enter as Y_1 and Y_2, as shown in Figure 2.3. The sum of f and g is given by $Y_3 = Y_1 + Y_2$ and the composite $f \circ g$ by $Y_4 = Y_1(Y_2)$. For example, $f(g(3))$ is obtained by evaluating Y_4 at 3.

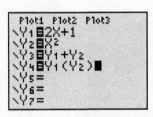

FIGURE 2.3 Y_3 and Y_4 are combinations of Y_1 and Y_2.

PROBLEMS 2.3

1. If $f(x) = x + 3$ and $g(x) = x + 5$, find the following.

(a) $(f + g)(x)$ (b) $(f + g)(0)$ (c) $(f - g)(x)$

(d) $(fg)(x)$ (e) $(fg)(-2)$ (f) $\dfrac{f}{g}(x)$

(g) $(f \circ g)(x)$ (h) $(f \circ g)(3)$ (i) $(g \circ f)(x)$

(j) $(g \circ f)(3)$

2. If $f(x) = 2x$ and $g(x) = 6 + x$, find the following.

(a) $(f + g)(x)$ (b) $(f - g)(x)$ (c) $(f - g)(4)$

(d) $(fg)(x)$ (e) $\dfrac{f}{g}(x)$ (f) $\dfrac{f}{g}(2)$

(g) $(f \circ g)(x)$ (h) $(g \circ f)(x)$ (i) $(g \circ f)(2)$

3. If $f(x) = x^2 - 1$ and $g(x) = x^2 + x$, find the following.

(a) $(f + g)(x)$ (b) $(f - g)(x)$ (c) $(f - g)\left(-\frac{1}{2}\right)$

(d) $(fg)(x)$ (e) $\dfrac{f}{g}(x)$ (f) $\dfrac{f}{g}\left(-\frac{1}{2}\right)$

(g) $(f \circ g)(x)$ (h) $(g \circ f)(x)$ (i) $(g \circ f)(-3)$

4. If $f(x) = x^2 + 1$ and $g(x) = 5$, find the following.

(a) $(f + g)(x)$ (b) $(f + g)\left(\frac{2}{3}\right)$ (c) $(f - g)(x)$

(d) $(fg)(x)$ (e) $(fg)(7)$ (f) $\dfrac{f}{g}(x)$

(g) $(f \circ g)(x)$ (h) $(f \circ g)(12{,}003)$ (i) $(g \circ f)(x)$

5. If $f(x) = 3x^2 + 6$ and $g(x) = 4 - 2x$, find $f(g(2))$ and $g(f(2))$.

6. If $f(p) = \dfrac{4}{p}$ and $g(p) = \dfrac{p - 2}{3}$, find both $(f \circ g)(p)$ and $(g \circ f)(p)$.

7. If $F(t) = t^2 + 7t + 1$ and $G(t) = \dfrac{2}{t - 1}$, find $(F \circ G)(t)$ and $(G \circ F)(t)$.

8. If $F(t) = \sqrt{t}$ and $G(t) = 2t^2 - 2t + 1$, find $(F \circ G)(t)$ and $(G \circ F)(t)$.

9. If $f(v) = \dfrac{1}{v^2 + 1}$ and $g(v) = \sqrt{v + 2}$, find $(f \circ g)(v)$ and $(g \circ f)(v)$.

10. If $f(x) = x^2 + 2x - 1$, find $(f \circ f)(x)$.

In Problems 11–16, find functions f and g such that $h(x) = f(g(x))$.

11. $h(x) = 11x - 7$

12. $h(x) = \sqrt{x^2 - 2}$

13. $h(x) = \dfrac{3}{x^2 + x + 1}$

14. $h(x) = (9x^3 - 5x)^3 - (9x^3 - 5x)^2 + 11$

15. $h(x) = \sqrt[4]{\dfrac{x^2 - 1}{x + 3}}$

16. $h(x) = \dfrac{2 - (3x - 5)}{(3x - 5)^2 + 2}$

17. Profit A coffeehouse sells a pound of coffee for \$9.75. Expenses are \$4500 each month, plus \$4.25 for each pound of coffee sold.
(a) Write a function $r(x)$ for the total monthly revenue as a function of the number of pounds of coffee sold.
(b) Write a function $e(x)$ for the total monthly expenses as a function of the number of pounds of coffee sold.
(c) Write a function $(r - e)(x)$ for the total monthly profit as a function of the number of pounds of coffee sold.

18. Geometry Suppose the volume of a sphere is $v(x) = \frac{4}{3}\pi(3x - 1)^3$. Express v as a composite of two functions, and explain what each function represents.

19. Business A manufacturer determines that the total number of units of output per day, q, is a function of the number of employees, m, where

$$q = f(m) = \dfrac{(40m - m^2)}{4}$$

The total revenue r that is received for selling q units is given by the function g, where $r = g(q) = 40q$. Find $(g \circ f)(m)$. What does this composite function describe?

20. Sociology Studies have been conducted concerning the statistical relations among a person's status, education, and income.[4] Let S denote a numerical value of status based on annual income I. For a certain population, suppose

$$S = f(I) = 0.45(I - 1000)^{0.53}$$

---

[4] R. K. Leik and B. F. Meeker, *Mathematical Sociology* (Englewood Cliffs, NJ: Prentice Hall, 1975).

Furthermore, suppose a person's income I is a function of the number of years of education E, where

$$I = g(E) = 7202 + 0.29E^{3.68}$$

Find $(f \circ g)(E)$. What does this function describe?

In Problems 21–24, for the given functions f and g, find the indicated function values. Round answers to two decimal places.

21. $f(x) = (4x - 13)^2$, $g(x) = 0.2x^2 - 4x + 3$

(a) $(f + g)(4.5)$, **(b)** $(f \circ g)(-2)$

22. $f(x) = \sqrt{\dfrac{x-3}{x+1}}$, $g(x) = 11.2x + 5.39$

(a) $\dfrac{f}{g}(-2)$, **(b)** $(g \circ f)(-10)$

23. $f(x) = x^{4/5}$, $g(x) = x^2 - 8$

(a) $(fg)(7)$, **(b)** $(g \circ f)(3.75)$

24. $f(x) = \dfrac{5}{x+3}$, $g(x) = \dfrac{2}{x^2}$

(a) $(f - g)(7.3)$, **(b)** $(f \circ g)(-4.17)$

Objective

To introduce inverse functions, their properties, and their uses.

2.4 Inverse Functions

Just as $-a$ is the number for which

$$a + (-a) = 0 = (-a) + a$$

and, for $a \neq 0$, a^{-1} is the number for which

$$aa^{-1} = 1 = a^{-1}a$$

so, given a function $f : X \longrightarrow Y$, we can inquire about the existence of a function g satisfying

$$f \circ g = I = g \circ f \tag{1}$$

where I is the identity function, introduced in the subsection titled "Composition" of Section 2.3 and given by $I(x) = x$. Suppose that we have g as above and a function h that also satisfies the equations of (1) so that

$$f \circ h = I = h \circ f$$

Then

$$h = h \circ I = h \circ (f \circ g) = (h \circ f) \circ g = I \circ g = g$$

shows that there is at most one function satisfying the requirements of g in (1). In mathematical jargon, g is uniquely determined by f and is therefore given a name, $g = f^{-1}$, that reflects its dependence on f. The function f^{-1} is read as f **inverse** and called the **inverse** of f.

The additive inverse $-a$ exists for any number a; the multiplicative inverse a^{-1} exists precisely if $a \neq 0$. The existence of f^{-1} places a strong requirement on a function f. It can be shown that f^{-1} exists if and only if, for all a and b, whenever $f(a) = f(b)$, then $a = b$. It may be helpful to think that such an f can be *canceled (on the left)*.

CAUTION!

Do not confuse f^{-1}, the inverse of f, and $\dfrac{1}{f}$, the multiplicative reciprocal of f.

Unfortunately, the nomenclature for inverse functions clashes with the numerical use of $(-)^{-1}$. Usually, $f^{-1}(x)$ is different from $\dfrac{1}{f}(x) = \dfrac{1}{f(x)}$. For example, $I^{-1} = I$ (since $I \circ I = I$) so $I^{-1}(x) = x$, but $\dfrac{1}{I}(x) = \dfrac{1}{I(x)} = \dfrac{1}{x}$.

A function f that satisfies

$$\text{for all } a \text{ and } b, \text{ if } \quad f(a) = f(b) \quad \text{then} \quad a = b$$

is called a **one-to-one** function.

Thus, we can say that a function has an inverse precisely if it is one-to-one. An equivalent way to express the one-to-one condition is

$$\text{for all } a \text{ and } b, \text{ if } \quad a \neq b \quad \text{then} \quad f(a) \neq f(b)$$

so that distinct inputs give rise to distinct outputs. Observe that this condition is not met for many simple functions. For example, if $f(x) = x^2$, then $f(-1) = (-1)^2 = 1 = (1)^2 = f(1)$ and $-1 \neq 1$ shows that the squaring function is not one-to-one. Similarly, $f(x) = |x|$ is not one-to-one.

In general, the domain of f^{-1} is the range of f and the range of f^{-1} is the domain of f.

Let us note here that the equations of (1) are equivalent to

$$f^{-1}(f(x)) = x \quad \text{for all } x \text{ in the domain of } f \tag{2}$$

and

$$f(f^{-1}(y)) = y \quad \text{for all } y \text{ in the range of } f \tag{3}$$

In general, the range of f, which is equal to the domain of f^{-1}, can be quite different from the domain of f.

EXAMPLE 1   Inverses of Linear Functions

According to Section 2.2, a function of the form $f(x) = ax + b$, where $a \neq 0$, is a linear function. Show that a linear function is one-to-one. Find the inverse of $f(x) = ax + b$ and show that it is also linear.

Solution: Assume that $f(u) = f(v)$; that is,

$$au + b = av + b \tag{4}$$

To show that f is one-to-one, we must show that $u = v$ follows from this assumption. Subtracting b from both sides of (4) gives $au = av$, from which $u = v$ follows by dividing both sides by a. (We assumed that $a \neq 0$.) Since f is given by first multiplying by a and then adding b, we might expect that the effect of f can be undone by first subtracting b and then dividing by a. So consider $g(x) = \dfrac{x - b}{a}$. We have

$$(f \circ g)(x) = f(g(x)) = a\frac{x - b}{a} + b = (x - b) + b = x$$

and

$$(g \circ f)(x) = g(f(x)) = \frac{(ax + b) - b}{a} = \frac{ax}{a} = x$$

Since g satisfies the two requirements of (1), it follows that g is the inverse of f. That is, $f^{-1}(x) = \dfrac{x - b}{a} = \dfrac{1}{a}x + \dfrac{-b}{a}$ and the last equality shows that f^{-1} is also a linear function.

Now Work Problem 1 ◁

EXAMPLE 2   Identities for Inverses

Show that

a. If f and g are one-to-one functions, the composite $f \circ g$ is also one-to-one and $(f \circ g)^{-1} = g^{-1} \circ f^{-1}$.
b. If f is one-to-one, then $(f^{-1})^{-1} = f$.

Solution:

a. Assume $(f \circ g)(a) = (f \circ g)(b)$; that is, $f(g(a)) = f(g(b))$. Since f is one-to-one, $g(a) = g(b)$. Since g is one-to-one, $a = b$ and this shows that $f \circ g$ is one-to-one. The equations

$$(f \circ g) \circ (g^{-1} \circ f^{-1}) = f \circ (g \circ g^{-1}) \circ f^{-1} = f \circ I \circ f^{-1} = f \circ f^{-1} = I$$

and

$$(g^{-1} \circ f^{-1}) \circ (f \circ g) = g^{-1} \circ (f^{-1} \circ f) \circ g = g^{-1} \circ I \circ g = g^{-1} \circ g = I$$

show that $g^{-1} \circ f^{-1}$ is the inverse of $f \circ g$, which, in symbols, is the statement $g^{-1} \circ f^{-1} = (f \circ g)^{-1}$.
b. In Equations (2) and (3), replace f by f^{-1}. Taking g to be f shows that Equations (1) are satisfied, and this gives $(f^{-1})^{-1} = f$.

◁

EXAMPLE 3   Inverses Used to Solve Equations

Many equations take the form $f(x) = 0$, where f is a function. If f is a one-to-one function, then the equation has $x = f^{-1}(0)$ as its unique solution.

Solution: Applying f^{-1} to both sides of $f(x) = 0$ gives $f^{-1}(f(x)) = f^{-1}(0)$, and $f^{-1}(f(x)) = x$ shows that $x = f^{-1}(0)$ is the only possible solution. Since $f(f^{-1}(0)) = 0$, $f^{-1}(0)$ is indeed a solution.

◁

EXAMPLE 4   Restricting the Domain of a Function

It may happen that a function f whose domain is the natural one, consisting of all elements for which the defining rule makes sense, is not one-to-one, and yet a one-to-one function g can be obtained by restricting the domain of f.

Solution: For example, we have shown that the function $f(x) = x^2$ is not one-to-one but the function $g(x) = x^2$ *with domain explicitly given as* $[0, \infty)$ is one-to-one. Since $(\sqrt{x})^2 = x$ and $\sqrt{x^2} = x$, for $x \geq 0$, it follows that $\sqrt{\ }$ is the inverse of the restricted squaring function g. Here is a more contrived example. Let $f(x) = |x|$ (with its natural domain). Let $g(x) = |x|$ *with domain explicitly given as* $(-\infty, -1) \cup [0, 1]$. The function g is one-to-one and hence has an inverse.

◁

EXAMPLE 5   Finding the Inverse of a Function

To find the inverse of a one-to-one function f, solve the equation $y = f(x)$ for x in terms of y obtaining $x = g(y)$. Then $f^{-1}(x) = g(x)$. To illustrate, find $f^{-1}(x)$ if $f(x) = (x-1)^2$, for $x \geq 1$.

Solution: Let $y = (x-1)^2$, for $x \geq 1$. Then $x - 1 = \sqrt{y}$ and hence $x = \sqrt{y} + 1$. It follows that $f^{-1}(x) = \sqrt{x} + 1$.

Now Work Problem 5 ◁

PROBLEMS 2.4

In Problems 1–6, find the inverse of the given function.

1. $f(x) = 3x + 7$

2. $g(x) = 5x - 3$

3. $F(x) = \frac{1}{2}x - 7$

4. $f(x) = (4x - 5)^2$, for $x \geq \frac{5}{4}$

5. $A(r) = \pi r^2$, for $r \geq 0$

6. $V(r) = \frac{4}{3}\pi r^3$

In Problems 7–10, determine whether or not the function is one-to-one.

7. $f(x) = 5x + 12$

8. $g(x) = (3x + 4)^2$

9. $h(x) = (5x + 12)^2$, for $x \geq -\frac{12}{5}$

10. $F(x) = |x - 9|$

In Problems 11 and 12, solve each equation by finding an inverse function.

11. $(4x - 5)^2 = 23$, for $x \geq \frac{5}{4}$

12. $2x^3 + 1 = 129$

13. **Demand Function**   The function

$$p = p(q) = \frac{1,200,000}{q} \qquad q > 0$$

expresses an actor's charge per film p as a function of the number of films q that she stars in. Express the number of films in which she stars in terms of her charge per film. Show that the expression is a function of p. Show that the resulting function is inverse to the function giving p in terms of q.

14. **Supply Function**   The weekly supply function for a pound of house-blend coffee at a coffee shop is

$$p = p(q) = \frac{q}{48} \qquad q > 0$$

where q is the number of pounds of coffee supplied per week and p is the price per pound. Express q as a function of p and demonstrate the relationship between the two functions.

15. Does the function $f(x) = 2^x$ have an inverse?

Objective

To graph equations and functions in rectangular coordinates, to determine intercepts, to apply the vertical-line test and the horizontal-line test, and to determine the domain and range of a function from a graph.

2.5 Graphs in Rectangular Coordinates

A **rectangular coordinate system** allows us to specify and locate points in a plane. It also provides a geometric way to graph equations in two variables, in particular those arising from functions.

In a plane, two real-number lines, called *coordinate axes*, are constructed perpendicular to each other so that their origins coincide, as in Figure 2.4. Their point of intersection is called the *origin* of the coordinate system. For now, we will call the horizontal line the *x-axis* and the vertical line the *y-axis*. The unit distance on the *x*-axis need not be the same as on the *y*-axis.

The plane on which the coordinate axes are placed is called a *rectangular coordinate plane* or, more simply, an *x,y-plane*. Every point in the *x,y*-plane can be labeled to indicate its position. To label point P in Figure 2.5(a), we draw perpendiculars from P to the *x*-axis and *y*-axis. They meet these axes at 4 and 2, respectively. Thus, P determines two numbers, 4 and 2. We say that the **rectangular coordinates** of P are given by the **ordered pair** $(4, 2)$. As we remarked in Section 2.1, the word *ordered* is important. In the terminology of Section 2.1, we are labeling the points of the plane by the elements of the set $(-\infty, \infty) \times (-\infty, \infty)$. In Figure 2.5(b), the point corresponding to $(4, 2)$ is not the same as that corresponding to $(2, 4)$:

$$(4, 2) \neq (2, 4)$$

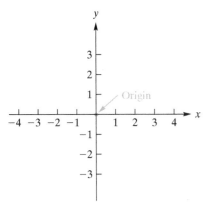

FIGURE 2.4   Coordinate axes.

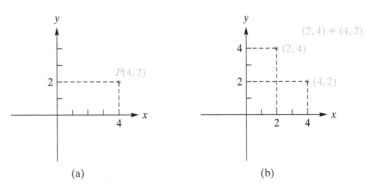

(a)   (b)

FIGURE 2.5   Rectangular coordinates.

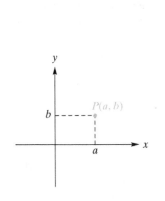

FIGURE 2.6   Coordinates of P.

In general, if P is any point, then its rectangular coordinates will be given by an ordered pair of the form (a, b). (See Figure 2.6.) We call a the *x-coordinate* of P, and b the *y-coordinate* of P. We accept that the notation for an ordered pair of real numbers is the same as that for an open interval but the practice is strongly entrenched and almost never causes any confusion.

Accordingly, with each point in a given coordinate plane, we can associate exactly one ordered pair (a, b) of real numbers. Also, it should be clear that with each ordered pair (a, b) of real numbers, we can associate exactly one point in that plane. Since there is a *one-to-one correspondence* between the points in the plane and all ordered pairs of real numbers, we refer to a point P with *x*-coordinate a and *y*-coordinate b simply as the point (a, b), or as $P(a, b)$. Moreover, we use the words *point* and *ordered pair of real numbers* interchangeably.

In Figure 2.7, the coordinates of various points are indicated. For example, the point $(1, -4)$ is located one unit to the right of the *y*-axis and four units below the *x*-axis. The origin is $(0, 0)$. The *x*-coordinate of every point on the *y*-axis is 0, and the *y*-coordinate of every point on the *x*-axis is 0.

The coordinate axes divide the plane into four regions called *quadrants* (Figure 2.8). For example, quadrant I consists of all points (x_1, y_1) with $x_1 > 0$ and $y_1 > 0$. The points on the axes do not lie in any quadrant.

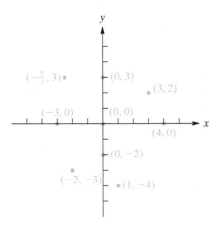

FIGURE 2.7   Coordinates of points.

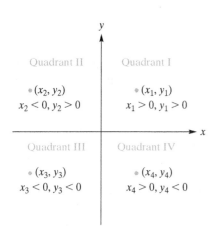

FIGURE 2.8   Quadrants.

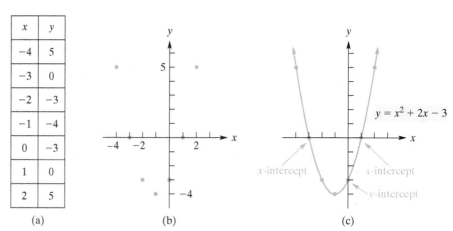

FIGURE 2.9   Graphing $y = x^2 + 2x - 3$.

Using a rectangular coordinate system, we can geometrically represent equations in two variables. For example, let us consider

$$y = x^2 + 2x - 3 \qquad (1)$$

A solution of this equation is a value of x and a value of y that make the equation true. For example, if $x = 1$, substituting into Equation (1) gives

$$y = 1^2 + 2(1) - 3 = 0$$

Thus, $x = 1, y = 0$ is a solution of Equation (1). Similarly,

$$\text{if } x = -2 \quad \text{then} \quad y = (-2)^2 + 2(-2) - 3 = -3$$

and so $x = -2, y = -3$ is also a solution. By choosing other values for x, we can get more solutions. [See Figure 2.9(a).] It should be clear that there are infinitely many solutions of Equation (1).

Each solution gives rise to a point (x, y). For example, to $x = 1$ and $y = 0$ corresponds $(1, 0)$. The **graph** of $y = x^2 + 2x - 3$ is the geometric representation of all its solutions. In Figure 2.9(b), we have plotted the points corresponding to the solutions in the table.

Since the equation has infinitely many solutions, it seems impossible to determine its graph precisely. However, we are concerned only with the graph's general shape. For this reason, we plot enough points so that we can intelligently guess its proper shape. (The calculus techniques to be studied in Chapter 13 will make such "guesses" much more intelligent.) Then we join these points by a smooth curve wherever conditions permit. This gives the curve in Figure 2.9(c). Of course, the more points we plot, the better our graph is. Here we assume that the graph extends indefinitely upward, as indicated by arrows.

The point $(0, -3)$ where the curve intersects the y-axis is called the y-*intercept*. The points $(-3, 0)$ and $(1, 0)$ where the curve intersects the x-axis are called the x-*intercepts*. In general, we have the following definition.

Often, we simply say that the y-intercept is -3 and the x-intercepts are -3 and 1.

Definition

An x-*intercept* of the graph of an equation in x and y is a point where the graph intersects the x-axis. A y-*intercept* is a point where the graph intersects the y-axis.

To find the x-intercepts of the graph of an equation in x and y, we first set $y = 0$ and then solve the resulting equation for x. To find the y-intercepts, we first set $x = 0$ and then solve for y. For example, let us find the x-intercepts for the graph of $y = x^2 + 2x - 3$. Setting $y = 0$ and solving for x gives

$$0 = x^2 + 2x - 3$$
$$0 = (x + 3)(x - 1)$$
$$x = -3, 1$$

Thus, the x-intercepts are $(-3, 0)$ and $(1, 0)$, as we saw before. If $x = 0$, then

$$y = 0^2 + 2(0) - 3 = -3$$

So $(0, -3)$ is the y-intercept. Keep in mind that an x-intercept has its y-coordinate 0, and a y-intercept has its x-coordinate 0. Intercepts are useful because they indicate precisely where the graph intersects the axes.

EXAMPLE 1   Intercepts and Graph

APPLY IT ▶

11. Rachel has saved $7250 for college expenses. She plans to spend $600 a month from this account. Write an equation to represent the situation, and identify the intercepts.

Find the x- and y-intercepts of the graph of $y = 2x + 3$, and sketch the graph.

Solution: If $y = 0$, then

$$0 = 2x + 3 \quad \text{so that} \quad x = -\frac{3}{2}$$

Thus, the x-intercept is $(-\frac{3}{2}, 0)$. If $x = 0$, then

$$y = 2(0) + 3 = 3$$

So the y-intercept is $(0, 3)$. Figure 2.10 shows a table of some points on the graph and a sketch of the graph.

Now Work Problem 9 ◁

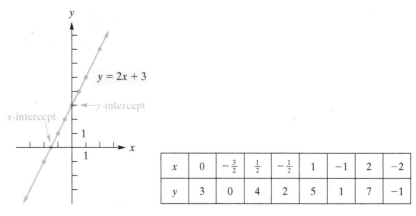

x	0	$-\frac{3}{2}$	$\frac{1}{2}$	$-\frac{1}{2}$	1	-1	2	-2
y	3	0	4	2	5	1	7	-1

FIGURE 2.10   Graph of $y = 2x + 3$.

EXAMPLE 2   Intercepts and Graph

APPLY IT ▶

12. The price of admission to an amusement park is $24.95. This fee allows the customer to ride all the rides at the park as often as he or she likes. Write an equation that represents the relationship between the number of rides, x, that a customer takes and the cost per ride, y, to that customer. Describe the graph of this equation, and identify the intercepts. Assume $x > 0$.

Determine the intercepts, if any, of the graph of $s = \dfrac{100}{t}$, and sketch the graph.

Solution: For the graph, we will label the horizontal axis t and the vertical axis s (Figure 2.11). Because t cannot equal 0 (division by 0 is not defined), there is no s-intercept. Thus, the graph has no point corresponding to $t = 0$. Moreover, there is no t-intercept, because if $s = 0$, then the equation

$$0 = \frac{100}{t}$$

has no solution. Remember, the only way that a fraction can be 0 is by having its numerator 0. Figure 2.11 shows the graph. In general, the graph of $s = k/t$, where k is a nonzero constant, is called a *rectangular hyperbola*.

Now Work Problem 11 ◁

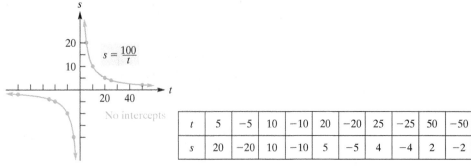

FIGURE 2.11 Graph of $s = \dfrac{100}{t}$.

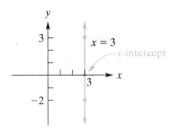

FIGURE 2.12 Graph of $x = 3$.

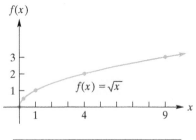

FIGURE 2.13 Graph of $f(x) = \sqrt{x}$.

EXAMPLE 3 Intercepts and Graph

Determine the intercepts of the graph of $x = 3$, and sketch the graph.

Solution: We can think of $x = 3$ as an equation in the variables x and y if we write it as $x = 3 + 0y$. Here y can be any value, but x must be 3. Because $x = 3$ when $y = 0$, the x-intercept is $(3, 0)$. There is no y-intercept, because x cannot be 0. (See Figure 2.12.) The graph is a vertical line.

Now Work Problem 13 ◁

Each function f gives rise to an equation, namely $y = f(x)$, which is a special case of the equations we have been graphing. Its **graph** consists of all points $(x, f(x))$, where x is in the domain of f. The vertical axis can be labeled either y or $f(x)$, where f is the name of the function, and is referred to as the **function-value axis**. *We always label the horizontal axis with the independent variable but note that economists label the vertical axis with the independent variable.* Observe that in graphing a function the "solutions" (x, y) that make the equation $y = f(x)$ true are handed to us. For each x in the domain of f, we have exactly one y obtained by evaluating $f(x)$. The resulting pair $(x, f(x))$ is a point on the graph and these are the only points on the graph of the equation $y = f(x)$.

The x-intercepts of the graph of a real-valued function f are all those real numbers x for which $f(x) = 0$. As such they are also known as **roots** of the equation $f(x) = 0$ and still further as **zeros** of the function f.

A useful geometric observation is that the graph of a function has at most one point of intersection with any vertical line in the plane. Recall that the equation of a vertical line is necessarily of the form $x = a$, where a is a constant. If a is not in the domain of the function f, then $x = a$ will not intersect the graph of $y = f(x)$. If a is in the domain of the function f, then $x = a$ will intersect the graph of $y = f(x)$ at the point $(a, f(a))$ and only there. Conversely, if a set of points in the plane has the property that any vertical line intersects the set at most once, then the set of points is actually the graph of a function. (The domain of the function is the set of all real numbers a with the property that the line $x = a$ does intersect the given set of points and for such an a the corresponding function value is the y-coordinate of the unique point of intersection of the line $x = a$ and the given set of points.) This is the basis of the **vertical-line test** that we will discuss after Example 7.

EXAMPLE 4 Graph of the Square-Root Function

Graph the function $f: (-\infty, \infty) \longrightarrow (-\infty, \infty)$ given by $f(x) = \sqrt{x}$.

Solution: The graph is shown in Figure 2.13. We label the vertical axis as $f(x)$. Recall that $\sqrt{x}$ denotes the *principal* square root of x. Thus, $f(9) = \sqrt{9} = 3$, not ± 3. Also, the domain of f is $[0, \infty)$ because its values are declared to be real numbers. Let us now consider intercepts. If $f(x) = 0$, then $\sqrt{x} = 0$, so that $x = 0$. Also, if $x = 0$, then $f(x) = 0$. Thus, the x-intercept and the vertical-axis intercept are the same, namely, $(0, 0)$.

Now Work Problem 29 ◁

EXAMPLE 5 Graph of the Absolute-Value Function

Graph $p = G(q) = |q|$.

APPLY IT ▶

13. Brett rented a bike from a rental shop, rode at a constant rate of 12 mi/h for 2.5 hours along a bike path, and then returned along the same path. Graph the absolute-value-like function that represents Brett's distance from the rental shop as a function of time over the appropriate domain.

Solution: We use the independent variable q to label the horizontal axis. The function-value axis can be labeled either $G(q)$ or p. (See Figure 2.14.) Notice that the q- and p-intercepts are the same point, $(0, 0)$.

Now Work Problem 31 ◁

q	0	1	−1	3	−3	5	−5
p	0	1	1	3	3	5	5

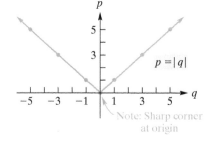

FIGURE 2.14 Graph of $p = |q|$.

TECHNOLOGY ▮▮▮▯

To solve the equation $x^3 = 3x - 1$ with a graphing calculator, we first express the equation in the form $f(x) = 0$:

$$f(x) = x^3 - 3x + 1 = 0$$

Next we graph f and then estimate the x-intercepts, either by using zoom and trace or by using the root operation. (See Figure 2.15.) Note that we defined our window for $-4 \le x \le 4$ and $-5 \le y \le 5$.

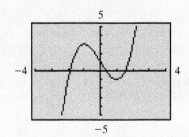

FIGURE 2.15 The roots of $x^3 - 3x + 1 = 0$ are approximately $-1.88, 0.35$, and 1.53.

Figure 2.16 shows the graph of a function $y = f(x)$. The point $(x, f(x))$ tells us that corresponding to the input number x on the horizontal axis is the output number $f(x)$ on the vertical axis, as indicated by the arrow. For example, corresponding to the input 4 is the output 3, so $f(4) = 3$.

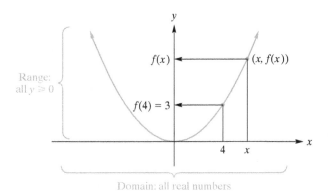

FIGURE 2.16 Domain, range, function values.

From the shape of the graph, it seems reasonable to assume that, for any value of x, there is an output number, so the domain of f is all real numbers. Notice that the set of all y-coordinates of points on the graph is the set of all nonnegative numbers. Thus, the range of f is all $y \geq 0$. This shows that we can make an "educated" guess about the domain and range of a function by looking at its graph. *In general, the domain consists of all x-values that are included in the graph, and the range is all y-values that are included.* For example, Figure 2.13 tells us that both the domain and range of $f(x) = \sqrt{x}$ are all nonnegative numbers. From Figure 2.14, it is clear that the domain of $p = G(q) = |q|$ is all real numbers and the range is all $p \geq 0$.

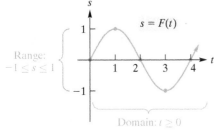

FIGURE 2.17 Domain, range, function values.

EXAMPLE 6 Domain, Range, and Function Values

Figure 2.17 shows the graph of a function F. To the right of 4, assume that the graph repeats itself indefinitely. Then the domain of F is all $t \geq 0$. The range is $-1 \leq s \leq 1$. Some function values are

$$F(0) = 0 \quad F(1) = 1 \quad F(2) = 0 \quad F(3) = -1$$

Now Work Problem 5 ◁

TECHNOLOGY ▮▮▮

Using a graphing calculator, we can estimate the range of a function. The graph of

$$f(x) = 6x^4 - 8.1x^3 + 1$$

is shown in Figure 2.18. The lowest point on the graph corresponds to the minimum value of $f(x)$, and the range is all reals greater than or equal to this minimum. We can estimate this minimum y-value either by using trace and zoom or by selecting the "minimum" operation.

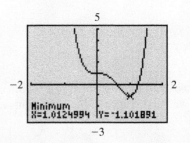

FIGURE 2.18 The range of $f(x) = 6x^4 - 8.1x^3 + 1$ is approximately $[-1.10, \infty)$.

APPLY IT ▶

14. To encourage conservation, a gas company charges two rates. You pay $0.53 per therm for 0–70 therms and $0.74 for each therm over 70. Graph the case-defined function that represents the monthly cost of t therms of gas.

EXAMPLE 7 Graph of a Case-Defined Function

Graph the case-defined function

$$f(x) = \begin{cases} x & \text{if } 0 \leq x < 3 \\ x - 1 & \text{if } 3 \leq x \leq 5 \\ 4 & \text{if } 5 < x \leq 7 \end{cases}$$

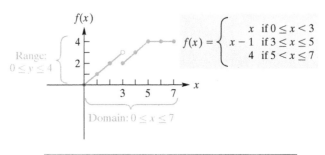

x	0	1	2	3	4	5	6	7
$f(x)$	0	1	2	2	3	4	4	4

FIGURE 2.19 Graph of case-defined function.

Solution: The domain of f is $0 \leq x \leq 7$. The graph is given in Figure 2.19, where the *hollow dot* means that the point is *not* included in the graph. Notice that the range of f is all real numbers y such that $0 \leq y \leq 4$.

Now Work Problem 35 ◁

There is an easy way to tell whether a curve is the graph of a function. In Figure 2.20(a), notice that with the given x there are associated *two* values of y: y_1 and y_2. Thus, the curve is *not* the graph of a function of x. Looking at it another way, we have the following general rule, called the **vertical-line test.** If a *vertical* line L can be drawn that intersects a curve in at least two points, then the curve is *not* the graph of a function of x. When no such vertical line can be drawn, the curve *is* the graph of a function of x. Consequently, the curves in Figure 2.20 do not represent functions of x, but those in Figure 2.21 do.

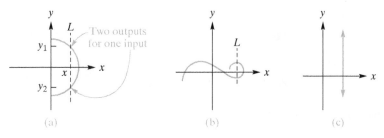

(a)   (b)   (c)

FIGURE 2.20 y is not a function of x.

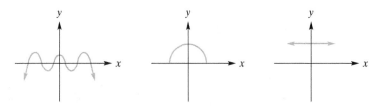

FIGURE 2.21   Functions of x.

EXAMPLE 8   **A Graph That Does Not Represent a Function of x**

Graph $x = 2y^2$.

Solution: Here it is easier to choose values of y and then find the corresponding values of x. Figure 2.22 shows the graph. By the vertical-line test, the equation $x = 2y^2$ does not define a function of x.

Now Work Problem 39 ◁

After we have determined whether a curve is the graph of a function, perhaps using the vertical-line test, there is an easy way to tell whether the function in question is one-to-one. In Figure 2.16 we see that $f(4) = 3$ and, apparently, also $f(-4) = 3$.

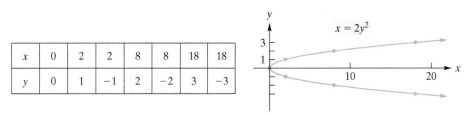

x	0	2	2	8	8	18	18
y	0	1	-1	2	-2	3	-3

FIGURE 2.22   Graph of $x = 2y^2$.

Since the distinct input values -4 and 4 produce the same output, the function is not one-to-one. Looking at it another way, we have the following general rule, called the **horizontal-line test**. If a *horizontal* line L can be drawn that intersects the graph of a function in at least two points, then the function is *not* one-to-one. When no such horizontal line can be drawn, the function is one-to-one.

PROBLEMS 2.5

In Problems 1 and 2, locate and label each of the points, and give the quadrant, if possible, in which each point lies.

1. $(-2, -5), (3, -1), \left(-\frac{1}{3}, 4\right), (1, 0)$

2. $(-4, 5), (3, 0), (1, 1), (0, -6)$

3. Figure 2.23(a) shows the graph of $y = f(x)$.
   (a) Estimate $f(0), f(2), f(4)$, and $f(-2)$.
   (b) What is the domain of f?
   (c) What is the range of f?
   (d) What is an x-intercept of f?

4. Figure 2.23(b) shows the graph of $y = f(x)$.
   (a) Estimate $f(0)$ and $f(2)$.
   (b) What is the domain of f?
   (c) What is the range of f?
   (d) What is an x-intercept of f?

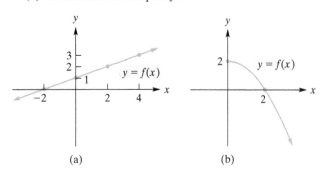

(a)   (b)

FIGURE 2.23   Diagram for Problems 3 and 4.

5. Figure 2.24(a) shows the graph of $y = f(x)$.
   (a) Estimate $f(0), f(1)$, and $f(-1)$.
   (b) What is the domain of f?
   (c) What is the range of f?
   (d) What is an x-intercept of f?

6. Figure 2.24(b) shows the graph of $y = f(x)$.
   (a) Estimate $f(0), f(2), f(3)$, and $f(4)$.
   (b) What is the domain of f?
   (c) What is the range of f?
   (d) What is an x-intercept f?

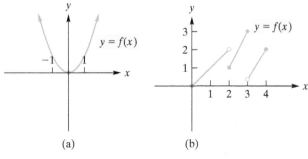

(a)   (b)

FIGURE 2.24   Diagram for Problems 5 and 6.

In Problems 7–20, determine the intercepts of the graph of each equation, and sketch the graph. Based on your graph, is y a function of x, and, if so, is it one-to-one and what are the domain and range?

7. $y = 2x$ **8.** $y = x + 1$

9. $y = 3x - 5$ **10.** $y = 3 - 2x$

11. $y = x^3 + x$ **12.** $y = \dfrac{2}{x^2}$

13. $x = 0$ **14.** $y = 4x^2 - 16$

15. $y = x^3$ **16.** $x = 3$

17. $x = -|y|$ **18.** $x^2 = y^2$

19. $2x + y - 2 = 0$ **20.** $x + y = 1$

In Problems 21–34, graph each function and give the domain and range. Also, determine the intercepts.

21. $u = f(v) = 2 + v^2$ **22.** $f(x) = 5 - 2x^2$

23. $y = h(x) = 3$ **24.** $g(s) = -17$

25. $y = h(x) = x^2 - 4x + 1$ **26.** $y = f(x) = -x^2 + x + 6$

27. $f(t) = -t^3$ **28.** $p = h(q) = 1 + 2q + q^2$

29. $s = f(t) = \sqrt{t^2 - 9}$ **30.** $F(r) = -\dfrac{1}{r}$

31. $f(x) = |3x + 2|$ **32.** $v = H(u) = |u - 3|$

33. $F(t) = \dfrac{16}{t^2}$ **34.** $y = f(x) = \dfrac{2}{x - 4}$

In Problems 35–38, graph each case-defined function and give the domain and range.

35. $c = g(p) = \begin{cases} p + 1 & \text{if } 0 \le p < 7 \\ 5 & \text{if } p \ge 7 \end{cases}$

36. $y(x) = \begin{cases} 3x & \text{if } 0 \le x < 2 \\ 10 - x^2 & \text{if } x \ge 2 \end{cases}$

37. $g(x) = \begin{cases} x + 6 & \text{if } x \ge 3 \\ x^2 & \text{if } x < 3 \end{cases}$ **38.** $f(x) = \begin{cases} x + 1 & \text{if } 0 < x \le 3 \\ 4 & \text{if } 3 < x \le 5 \\ x - 1 & \text{if } x > 5 \end{cases}$

39. Which of the graphs in Figure 2.25 represent functions of x?

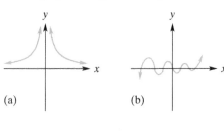

(a)   (b)

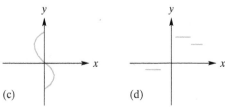

(c)   (d)

FIGURE 2.25   Diagram for Problem 39.

40. Which of the graphs in Figure 2.26 represent one-to-one functions of x?

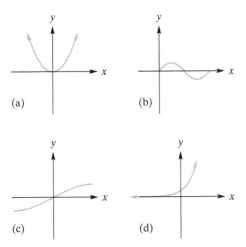

(a)   (b)   (c)   (d)

FIGURE 2.26   Diagram for Problem 40.

41. Debt Payments   Allison has charged $9200 on her credit cards. She plans to pay them off at the rate of $325 per month. Write an equation to represent the amount she owes, excluding any finance charges, after she has made x payments and identify the intercepts, explaining their financial significance if any.

42. Pricing   To encourage an even flow of customers, a restaurant varies the price of an item throughout the day. From 6:00 P.M. to 8:00 P.M., customers pay full price. At lunch, from 10:30 A.M. until 2:30 P.M., customers pay half price. From 2:30 P.M. until 4:30 P.M., customers get a dollar off the lunch price. From 4:30 P.M. until 6:00 P.M., customers get $5.00 off the dinner price. From 8:00 P.M. until closing time at 10:00 P.M., customers get $5.00 off the dinner price. Graph the case-defined function that represents the cost of an item throughout the day for a dinner price of $18.

43. Supply Schedule   Given the following supply schedule (see Example 6 of Section 2.1), plot each quantity–price pair by choosing the horizontal axis for the possible quantities. Approximate the points in between the data by connecting the data points with a smooth curve. The result is a *supply curve*. From the graph, determine the relationship between price and supply. (That is, as price increases, what happens to the quantity supplied?) Is price per unit a function of quantity supplied?

Quantity Supplied per Week, q	Price per Unit, p
30	$10
100	20
150	30
190	40
210	50

44. Demand Schedule   The following table is called a *demand schedule*. It indicates the quantities of brand X that consumers will demand (that is, purchase) each week at certain prices per unit (in dollars). Plot each quantity–price pair by choosing the vertical axis for the possible prices. Connect the points with a smooth curve. In this way, we approximate points in between the given data. The result is called a *demand curve*. From the graph, determine the relationship between the price of brand X and the amount that will be demanded. (That is, as price decreases, what happens to the quantity demanded?) Is price per unit a function of quantity demanded?

Quantity Demanded, q	Price per Unit, p
5	$20
10	10
20	5
25	4

45. Inventory   Sketch the graph of

$$y = f(x) = \begin{cases} -100x + 1000 & \text{if } 0 \le x < 7 \\ -100x + 1700 & \text{if } 7 \le x < 14 \\ -100x + 2400 & \text{if } 14 \le x < 21 \end{cases}$$

A function such as this might describe the inventory y of a company at time x.

46. Psychology   In a psychological experiment on visual information, a subject briefly viewed an array of letters and was then asked to recall as many letters as possible from the array. The procedure was repeated several times. Suppose that y is the average number of letters recalled from arrays with x letters. The graph of the results approximately fits the graph of

$$y = f(x) = \begin{cases} x & \text{if } 0 \le x \le 4 \\ \frac{1}{2}x + 2 & \text{if } 4 < x \le 5 \\ 4.5 & \text{if } 5 < x \le 12 \end{cases}$$

Plot this function.[5]

In Problems 47–50, use a graphing calculator to find all real roots, if any, of the given equation. Round answers to two decimal places.

47. $5x^3 + 7x = 3$

48. $x^2(x - 3) = 2x^4 - 1$

49. $(9x + 3.1)^2 = 7.4 - 4x^2$

50. $(x - 2)^3 = x^2 - 3$

In Problems 51–54, use a graphing calculator to find all x-intercepts of the graph of the given function. Round answers to two decimal places.

51. $f(x) = x^3 + 5x + 7$

52. $f(x) = 2x^4 - 1.5x^3 + 2$

53. $g(x) = x^4 - 1.7x^2 + 2x$

54. $g(x) = \sqrt{3}x^5 - 4x^2 + 1$

[5] Adapted from G. R. Loftus and E. F. Loftus, *Human Memory: The Processing of Information* (New York: Lawrence Erlbaum Associates, Inc., distributed by the Halsted Press, Division of John Wiley & Sons, Inc., 1976).

In Problems 55–57, use a graphing calculator to find (a) the maximum value of $f(x)$ and (b) the minimum value of $f(x)$ for the indicated values of x. Round answers to two decimal places.

55. $f(x) = x^4 - 4.1x^3 + x^2 + 10$ $1 \leq x \leq 4$

56. $f(x) = x(2.1x^2 - 3)^2 - x^3 + 1$ $-1 \leq x \leq 1$

57. $f(x) = \dfrac{x^2 - 4}{2x - 5}$ $3 \leq x \leq 5$

58. From the graph of $f(x) = \sqrt{2}x^3 + 1.1x^2 + 4$, find (a) the range and (b) the intercepts. Round values to two decimal places.

59. From the graph of $f(x) = 1 - 4x^3 - x^4$, find (a) the maximum value of $f(x)$, (b) the range of f, and (c) the real zeros of f. Round values to two decimal places.

60. From the graph of $f(x) = \dfrac{x^3 + 1.1}{3.8 + x^{2/3}}$, find (a) the range of f and (b) the intercepts. (c) Does f have any real zeros? Round values to two decimal places.

61. Graph $f(x) = \dfrac{4.1x^3 + \sqrt{2}}{x^2 - 3}$ for $2 \leq x \leq 5$. Determine (a) the maximum value of $f(x)$, (b) the minimum value of $f(x)$, (c) the range of f, and (d) all intercepts. Round values to two decimal places.

Objective

To study symmetry about the x-axis, the y-axis, and the origin, and to apply symmetry to curve sketching.

2.6 Symmetry

Examining the graphical behavior of equations is a basic part of mathematics. In this section, we examine equations to determine whether their graphs have *symmetry*. In a later chapter, you will see that calculus is a *great* aid in graphing because it helps determine the shape of a graph. It provides powerful techniques for determining whether or not a curve "wiggles" between points.

Consider the graph of $y = x^2$ in Figure 2.27. The portion to the left of the y-axis is the reflection (or mirror image) through the y-axis of that portion to the right of the y-axis, and vice versa. More precisely, if (a, b) is any point on this graph, then the point $(-a, b)$ must also lie on the graph. We say that this graph is *symmetric about the y-axis*.

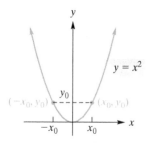

FIGURE 2.27 Symmetry about the y-axis.

> **Definition**
>
> A graph is **symmetric about the y-axis** if and only if $(-a, b)$ lies on the graph when (a, b) does.

EXAMPLE 1   *y-Axis Symmetry*

Use the preceding definition to show that the graph of $y = x^2$ is symmetric about the y-axis.

Solution: Suppose (a, b) is *any* point on the graph of $y = x^2$. Then

$$b = a^2$$

We must show that the coordinates of $(-a, b)$ satisfy $y = x^2$. But

$$(-a)^2 = a^2 = b$$

shows this to be true. Thus we have *proved* with simple algebra what the picture of the graph led us to believe: The graph of $y = x^2$ is symmetric about the y-axis.

Now Work Problem 7 ◁

When one is testing for symmetry in Example 1, (a, b) can be any point on the graph. In the future, for convenience, we write (x, y) for a typical point on the graph. This means that a graph is symmetric about the y-axis if replacing x by $-x$ in its equation results in an equivalent equation.

Another type of symmetry is shown by the graph of $x = y^2$ in Figure 2.28. Here the portion below the x-axis is the reflection through the x-axis of that portion above

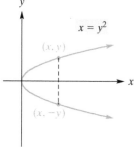

FIGURE 2.28 Symmetry about the x-axis.

the x-axis, and vice versa. If the point (x, y) lies on the graph, then $(x, -y)$ also lies on it. This graph is said to be *symmetric about the x-axis*.

> **Definition**
>
> A graph is ***symmetric about the x-axis*** if and only if $(x, -y)$ lies on the graph when (x, y) does.

Thus, the graph of an equation in x and y has x-axis symmetry if replacing y by $-y$ results in an equivalent equation. For example, applying this test to the graph of $x = y^2$, we see that $(-y)^2 = x$ if and only if $y^2 = x$, simply because $(-y)^2 = y^2$. Hence the graph of $x = y^2$ is symmetric about the x-axis.

A third type of symmetry, *symmetry about the origin*, is illustrated by the graph of $y = x^3$ (Figure 2.29). Whenever the point (x, y) lies on the graph, $(-x, -y)$ also lies on it.

> **Definition**
>
> A graph is ***symmetric about the origin*** if and only if $(-x, -y)$ lies on the graph when (x, y) does.

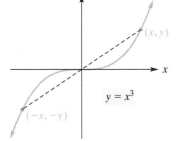

FIGURE 2.29 Symmetry about the origin.

Thus, the graph of an equation in x and y has symmetry about the origin if replacing x by $-x$ and y by $-y$ results in an equivalent equation. For example, applying this test to the graph of $y = x^3$ shown in Figure 2.29 gives

$$-y = (-x)^3$$
$$-y = -x^3$$
$$y = x^3$$

where all three equations are equivalent, in particular the first and last. Accordingly, the graph is symmetric about the origin.

Table 2.1 summarizes the tests for symmetry. When we know that a graph has symmetry, we can sketch it by plotting fewer points than would otherwise be needed.

Table 2.1 Tests for Symmetry

Symmetry about x-axis	Replace y by $-y$ in given equation. Symmetric if equivalent equation is obtained.
Symmetry about y-axis	Replace x by $-x$ in given equation. Symmetric if equivalent equation is obtained.
Symmetry about origin	Replace x by $-x$ and y by $-y$ in given equation. Symmetric if equivalent equation is obtained.

EXAMPLE 2   Graphing with Intercepts and Symmetry

Test $y = \dfrac{1}{x}$ for symmetry about the x-axis, the y-axis, and the origin. Then find the intercepts and sketch the graph.

Solution:

Symmetry   *x-axis:* Replacing y by $-y$ in $y = 1/x$ gives

$$-y = \frac{1}{x} \quad \text{equivalently} \quad y = -\frac{1}{x}$$

which is not equivalent to the given equation. Thus, the graph is *not* symmetric about the x-axis.

y-axis: Replacing x by $-x$ in $y = 1/x$ gives

$$y = \frac{1}{-x} \quad \text{equivalently} \quad y = -\frac{1}{x}$$

which is not equivalent to the given equation. Hence, the graph is *not* symmetric about the *y*-axis.

Origin: Replacing x by $-x$ and y by $-y$ in $y = 1/x$ gives

$$-y = \frac{1}{-x} \quad \text{equivalently} \quad y = \frac{1}{x}$$

which is the given equation. Consequently, the graph *is* symmetric about the origin.

Intercepts Since x cannot be 0, the graph has no *y*-intercept. If y is 0, then $0 = 1/x$, and this equation has no solution. Thus, no *x*-intercept exists.

Discussion Because no intercepts exist, the graph cannot intersect either axis. If $x > 0$, we obtain points only in quadrant I. Figure 2.30 shows the portion of the graph in quadrant I. By symmetry, we reflect that portion through the origin to obtain the entire graph.

Now Work Problem 9 ◁

EXAMPLE 3   Graphing with Intercepts and Symmetry

Test $y = f(x) = 1 - x^4$ for symmetry about the *x*-axis, the *y*-axis, and the origin. Then find the intercepts and sketch the graph.

Solution:

Symmetry *x-axis:* Replacing y by $-y$ in $y = 1 - x^4$ gives

$$-y = 1 - x^4 \quad \text{equivalently} \quad y = -1 + x^4$$

which is not equivalent to the given equation. Thus, the graph is *not* symmetric about the *x*-axis.

y-axis: Replacing x by $-x$ in $y = 1 - x^4$ gives

$$y = 1 - (-x)^4 \quad \text{equivalently} \quad y = 1 - x^4$$

which is the given equation. Hence, the graph *is* symmetric about the *y*-axis.

Origin: Replacing x by $-x$ and y by $-y$ in $y = 1 - x^4$ gives

$$-y = 1 - (-x)^4 \quad \text{equivalently} \quad -y = 1 - x^4 \quad \text{equivalently} \quad y = -1 + x^4$$

which is not equivalent to the given equation. Thus, the graph is *not* symmetric about the origin.

Intercepts Testing for *x*-intercepts, we set $y = 0$ in $y = 1 - x^4$. Then

$$1 - x^4 = 0$$
$$(1 - x^2)(1 + x^2) = 0$$
$$(1 - x)(1 + x)(1 + x^2) = 0$$
$$x = 1 \quad \text{or} \quad x = -1$$

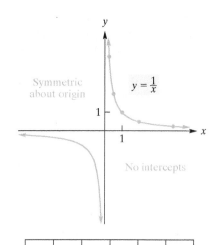

Symmetric about origin

$y = \frac{1}{x}$

No intercepts

x	$\frac{1}{4}$	$\frac{1}{2}$	1	2	4
y	4	2	1	$\frac{1}{2}$	$\frac{1}{4}$

FIGURE 2.30 Graph of $y = \dfrac{1}{x}$.

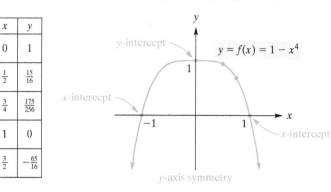

x	y
0	1
$\frac{1}{2}$	$\frac{15}{16}$
$\frac{3}{4}$	$\frac{175}{256}$
1	0
$\frac{3}{2}$	$-\frac{65}{16}$

y-intercept

$y = f(x) = 1 - x^4$

x-intercept

x-intercept

y-axis symmetry

FIGURE 2.31 Graph of $y = 1 - x^4$.

The x-intercepts are therefore $(1, 0)$ and $(-1, 0)$. Testing for y-intercepts, we set $x = 0$. Then $y = 1$, so $(0, 1)$ is the only y-intercept.

Discussion   If the intercepts and some points (x, y) to the right of the y-axis are plotted, we can sketch the *entire* graph by using symmetry about the y-axis (Figure 2.31).

Now Work Problem 19 ◁

The only *function* whose graph is symmetric about the *x*-axis is the function constantly 0.

The constant function $f(x) = 0$, for all x, is easily seen to be symmetric about the x-axis. In Example 3, we showed that the graph of $y = f(x) = 1 - x^4$ does not have x-axis symmetry. For any *function f*, suppose that the graph of $y = f(x)$ has x-axis symmetry. According to the definition, this means that we also have $-y = f(x)$. This tells us that for an arbitrary x in the domain of f we have $f(x) = y$ and $f(x) = -y$. Since for a function each x-value determines a unique y-value, we must have $y = -y$, and this implies $y = 0$. Since x was arbitrary, it follows that if the graph of a *function* is symmetric about the x-axis, then the function must be the constant 0.

EXAMPLE 4   Graphing with Intercepts and Symmetry

Test the graph of $4x^2 + 9y^2 = 36$ for intercepts and symmetry. Sketch the graph.

Solution:

Intercepts   If $y = 0$, then $4x^2 = 36$, so $x = \pm 3$. Thus, the x-intercepts are $(3, 0)$ and $(-3, 0)$. If $x = 0$, then $9y^2 = 36$, so $y = \pm 2$. Hence, the y-intercepts are $(0, 2)$ and $(0, -2)$.

Symmetry   *x-axis:* Replacing y by $-y$ in $4x^2 + 9y^2 = 36$ gives

$$4x^2 + 9(-y)^2 = 36 \quad \text{equivalently} \quad 4x^2 + 9y^2 = 36$$

which is the original equation, so there is symmetry about the x-axis.

y-axis: Replacing x by $-x$ in $4x^2 + 9y^2 = 36$ gives

$$4(-x)^2 + 9y^2 = 36 \quad \text{equivalently} \quad 4x^2 + 9y^2 = 36$$

which is the original equation, so there is also symmetry about the y-axis.

Origin: Replacing x by $-x$ and y by $-y$ in $4x^2 + 9y^2 = 36$ gives

$$4(-x)^2 + 9(-y)^2 = 36 \quad \text{equivalently} \quad 4x^2 + 9y^2 = 36$$

which is the original equation, so the graph is also symmetric about the origin.

Discussion   In Figure 2.32, the intercepts and some points in the first quadrant are plotted. The points in that quadrant are then connected by a smooth curve. By symmetry about the x-axis, the points in the fourth quadrant are obtained. Then, by symmetry about the y-axis, the complete graph is found. There are other ways of graphing the equation by using symmetry. For example, after plotting the intercepts and some points in the first quadrant, we can obtain the points in the third quadrant by symmetry about the origin. By symmetry about the x-axis (or y-axis), we can then obtain the entire graph.

Now Work Problem 23 ◁

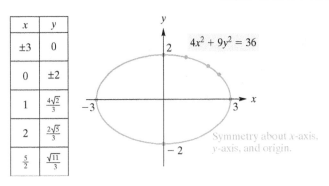

x	y
± 3	0
0	± 2
1	$\frac{4\sqrt{2}}{3}$
2	$\frac{2\sqrt{5}}{3}$
$\frac{5}{2}$	$\frac{\sqrt{11}}{3}$

$4x^2 + 9y^2 = 36$

Symmetry about x-axis, y-axis, and origin.

FIGURE 2.32   Graph of $4x^2 + 9y^2 = 36$.

This fact can be a time-saving device in checking for symmetry.

In Example 4, the graph is symmetric about the x-axis, the y-axis, and the origin. It can be shown that **for any graph, if any two of the three types of symmetry exist, then the remaining type must also exist.**

EXAMPLE 5   Symmetry about the Line $y = x$

> **Definition**
>
> A graph is **symmetric about the line** $y = x$ if and only if (b, a) lies on the graph when (a, b) does.

Another way of stating the definition is to say that interchanging the roles of x and y in the given equation results in an equivalent equation.

Use the preceding definition to show that $x^2 + y^2 = 1$ is symmetric about the line $y = x$.

Solution: Interchanging the roles of x and y produces $y^2 + x^2 = 1$, which is equivalent to $x^2 + y^2 = 1$. Thus $x^2 + y^2 = 1$ is symmetric about $y = x$.

◁

The point with coordinates (b, a) is the mirror image in the line $y = x$ of the point (a, b). If f is a one-to-one function, $b = f(a)$ if and only if $a = f^{-1}(b)$. Thus the graph of f^{-1} is the mirror image in the line $y = x$ of the graph of f. It is interesting to note that for *any* function f we can form the mirror image of the graph of f. However, the resulting graph need not be the graph of a function. For this mirror image to be itself the graph of a function, it must pass the vertical-line test. However vertical lines and horizontal lines are mirror images in the line $y = x$, and we see that for the mirror image of the graph of f to pass the vertical-line test is for the graph of f to pass the horizontal-line test. This last happens precisely if f is one-to-one, which is the case if and only if f has an inverse.

EXAMPLE 6   Symmetry and Inverse Functions

Sketch the graph of $g(x) = 2x + 1$ and its inverse in the same plane.

Solution: As we shall study in greater detail in Chapter 3, the graph of g is the straight line with slope (see Section 3.1) 2 and y-intercept 1. This line, the line $y = x$, and the reflection of $y = 2x + 1$ in $y = x$ are shown in Figure 2.33.

Now Work Problem 27 ◁

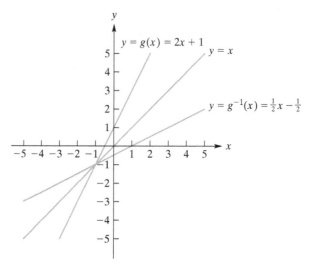

FIGURE 2.33   Graph of $y = g(x)$ and $y = g^{-1}(x)$.

PROBLEMS 2.6

In Problems 1–16, find the x- and y-intercepts of the graphs of the equations. Also, test for symmetry about the x-axis, the y-axis, the origin, and the line y = x. Do not sketch the graphs.

1. $y = 5x$

2. $y = f(x) = x^2 - 4$

3. $2x^2 + y^2x^4 = 8 - y$

4. $x = y^3$

5. $25x^2 + 144y^2 = 169$

6. $y = 57$

7. $x = -2$

8. $y = |2x| - 2$

9. $x = -y^{-4}$

10. $y = \sqrt{x^2 - 36}$

11. $x - 4y - y^2 + 21 = 0$

12. $x^2 + xy + y^3 = 0$

13. $y = f(x) = \dfrac{x^3 - 2x^2 + x}{x^2 + 1}$

14. $x^2 + xy + y^2 = 0$

15. $y = \dfrac{2}{x^3 + 27}$

16. $y = \dfrac{x^4}{x + y}$

In Problems 17–24, find the x- and y-intercepts of the graphs of the equations. Also, test for symmetry about the x-axis, the y-axis, the origin, and the line y = x. Then sketch the graphs.

17. $3x + y^2 = 9$

18. $x - 1 = y^4 + y^2$

19. $y = f(x) = x^3 - 4x$

20. $2y = 5 - x^2$

21. $|x| - |y| = 0$

22. $x^2 + y^2 = 16$

23. $9x^2 + 4y^2 = 25$

24. $x^2 - y^2 = 4$

25. Prove that the graph of $y = f(x) = 5 - 1.96x^2 - \pi x^4$ is symmetric about the y-axis, and then graph the function. (a) Make use of symmetry, where possible, to find all intercepts. Determine (b) the maximum value of $f(x)$ and (c) the range of f. Round all values to two decimal places.

26. Prove that the graph of $y = f(x) = 2x^4 - 7x^2 + 5$ is symmetric about the y-axis, and then graph the function. Find all real zeros of f. Round your answers to two decimal places.

27. Sketch the graph of $f(x) = -3x + 2$ and its inverse in the same plane.

Objective

To become familiar with the shapes of the graphs of six basic functions and to consider translation, reflection, and vertical stretching or shrinking of the graph of a function.

2.7 Translations and Reflections

Up to now, our approach to graphing has been based on plotting points and making use of any symmetry that exists. But this technique is not necessarily the preferred way. Later in this book, we will analyze graphs by using other techniques. However, some functions and their associated graphs occur so frequently that we find it worthwhile to memorize them. Figure 2.34 shows six such functions.

At times, by altering a function through an *algebraic* manipulation, the graph of the new function can be obtained from the graph of the original function by performing a *geometric* manipulation. For example, we can use the graph of $f(x) = x^2$ to graph $y = x^2 + 2$. Note that $y = f(x) + 2$. Thus, for each x, the corresponding ordinate for the

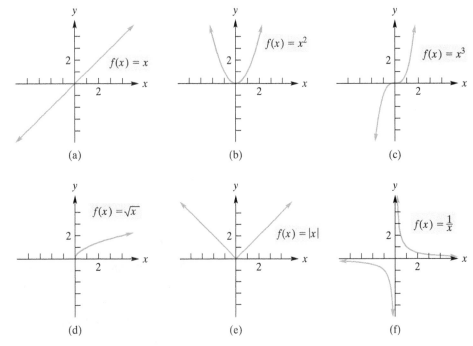

FIGURE 2.34 Functions frequently used.

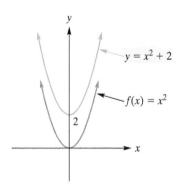

FIGURE 2.35   Graph of
$y = x^2 + 2$.

graph of $y = x^2 + 2$ is 2 more than the ordinate for the graph of $f(x) = x^2$. This means that the graph of $y = x^2 + 2$ is simply the graph of $f(x) = x^2$, shifted, or *translated*, 2 units upward. (See Figure 2.35.) We say that the graph of $y = x^2 + 2$ is a *transformation* of the graph of $f(x) = x^2$. Table 2.2 gives a list of basic types of transformations.

Table 2.2 Transformations, $c > 0$

Equation	How to Transform Graph of $y = f(x)$ to Obtain Graph of Equation
$y = f(x) + c$	shift c units upward
$y = f(x) - c$	shift c units downward
$y = f(x - c)$	shift c units to right
$y = f(x + c)$	shift c units to left
$y = -f(x)$	reflect about x-axis
$y = f(-x)$	reflect about y-axis
$y = cf(x)$ $c > 1$	vertically stretch away from x-axis by a factor of c
$y = cf(x)$ $c < 1$	vertically shrink toward x-axis by a factor of c

EXAMPLE 1   Horizontal Translation

Sketch the graph of $y = (x - 1)^3$.

Solution: We observe that $(x - 1)^3$ is x^3 with x replaced by $x - 1$. Thus, if $f(x) = x^3$, then $y = (x - 1)^3 = f(x - 1)$, which has the form $f(x - c)$, where $c = 1$. From Table 2.2, the graph of $y = (x - 1)^3$ is the graph of $f(x) = x^3$, shifted 1 unit to the right. (See Figure 2.36.)

Now Work Problem 3 ◁

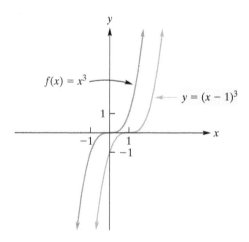

FIGURE 2.36   Graph of $y = (x - 1)^3$.

EXAMPLE 2   Shrinking and Reflection

Sketch the graph of $y = -\frac{1}{2}\sqrt{x}$.

Solution: We can do this problem in two steps. First, observe that $\frac{1}{2}\sqrt{x}$ is $\sqrt{x}$ multiplied by $\frac{1}{2}$. Thus, if $f(x) = \sqrt{x}$, then $\frac{1}{2}\sqrt{x} = \frac{1}{2}f(x)$, which has the form $cf(x)$, where $c = \frac{1}{2}$. So the graph of $y = \frac{1}{2}\sqrt{x}$ is the graph of f shrunk vertically toward

FIGURE 2.37   To graph $y = -\frac{1}{2}\sqrt{x}$, shrink $y = \sqrt{x}$ and reflect result about x-axis.

the x-axis by a factor of $\frac{1}{2}$ (transformation 8, Table 2.2; see Figure 2.37). Second, the minus sign in $y = -\frac{1}{2}\sqrt{x}$ causes a reflection in the graph of $y = \frac{1}{2}\sqrt{x}$ about the x-axis (transformation 5, Table 2.2; see Figure 2.37).

Now Work Problem 5 ◁

PROBLEMS 2.7

In Problems 1–12, use the graphs of the functions in Figure 2.34 and transformation techniques to plot the given functions.

1. $y = x^3 - 1$ **2.** $y = -x^2$ 3. $y = \dfrac{1}{x - 2}$

4. $y = -\sqrt{x - 2}$ 5. $y = \dfrac{2}{3x}$ **6.** $y = |x| - 2$

7. $y = |x + 1| - 2$ **8.** $y = -\dfrac{1}{3}\sqrt{x}$ **9.** $y = 2 + (x + 3)^3$

10. $y = (x - 1)^2 + 1$ **11.** $y = \sqrt{-x}$ **12.** $y = \dfrac{5}{2 - x}$

In Problems 13–16, describe what must be done to the graph of $y = f(x)$ to obtain the graph of the given equation.

13. $y = -2f(x + 3) + 2$ **14.** $y = 2(f(x - 1) - 4)$

15. $y = f(-x) - 5$ **16.** $y = f(3x)$

17. Graph the function $y = \sqrt[3]{x} + k$ for $k = 0, 1, 2, 3, -1, -2$, and -3. Observe the vertical translations compared to the first graph.

18. Graph the function $y = \sqrt[3]{x + k}$ for $k = 0, 1, 2, 3, -1, -2$, and -3. Observe the horizontal translations compared to the first graph.

19. Graph the function $y = kx^3$ for $k = 1, 2, \frac{1}{2}$, and 3. Observe the vertical stretching and shrinking compared to the first graph. Graph the function for $k = -2$. Observe that the graph is the same as that obtained by stretching the reflection of $y = x^3$ about the x-axis by a factor of 2.

Objective

To discuss functions of several variables and to compute function values. To discuss three-dimensional coordinates and sketch simple surfaces.

2.8 Functions of Several Variables

When we defined a *function* $f : X \longrightarrow Y$ from X to Y in Section 2.1, we did so for *sets* X and Y without requiring that they be sets of numbers. We have not often used that generality yet. Most of our examples have been functions from $(-\infty, \infty)$ to $(-\infty, \infty)$. We also saw in Section 2.1 that, for sets X and Y, we can construct the new set $X \times Y$ whose elements are ordered pairs (x, y) with x in X and y in Y. It follows that, for any three sets X, Y, and Z, the notion of a function $f : X \times Y \longrightarrow Z$ is already covered by the basic definition. Such an f is simply a rule which assigns to each element (x, y) in $X \times Y$ at most one element of Z, denoted by $f((x, y))$. There is general agreement that in this situation one should drop a layer of parentheses and write simply $f(x, y)$ for $f((x, y))$. Do note here that even if each of X and Y are sets of numbers, say $X = (-\infty, \infty) = Y$, then $X \times Y$ is definitely *not* a set of numbers. In other words, *an ordered pair of numbers is not a number.*

The *graph* of a function $f : X \longrightarrow Y$ is the subset of $X \times Y$ consisting of all ordered pairs of the form $(x, f(x))$, where x is in the domain of f. It follows that the graph of a function $f : X \times Y \longrightarrow Z$ is the subset of $(X \times Y) \times Z$ consisting of all ordered pairs of the form $((x, y), f(x, y))$, where (x, y) is in the domain of f. The ordered pair $((x, y), f(x, y))$ has its first coordinate given by (x, y), itself an ordered pair, while its second coordinate is the element $f(x, y)$ in Z. Most people prefer to replace $(X \times Y) \times Z$ with $X \times Y \times Z$, an element of which is an **ordered triple** (x, y, z), with x in X, y in Y, and z in Z. These elements are easier to read than the $((x, y), z)$, which are the "official" elements of $(X \times Y) \times Z$. In fact, we can *define* an ordered triple (x, y, z) to be a shorthand for $((x, y), z)$ if we wish.

Before going further, it is important to realize that these very general considerations have been motivated by a desire to make mathematics applicable. Many people when confronted with mathematical models built around functions, and equations relating them, express both an appreciation for the elegance of the ideas and a skepticism about their practical value. A common complaint is that in practice there are "factors" unaccounted for in a particular mathematical model. Translated into the context we are developing, this complaint frequently means that the functions in a mathematical model should involve more variables than the modeler originally contemplated. Being able to add new variables, to account for phenomena that were earlier thought to be insignificant, is an important aspect of robustness that a mathematical model should possess. If we know how to go from one variable to two variables, where the "two variables" can be construed as an ordered pair and hence a single variable of a new kind, then we can iterate the procedure and deal with functions of as many variables as we like.

For sets $X_1, X_2, \ldots, X_n$ and Y, a function $f : X_1 \times X_2 \times \cdots \times X_n \longrightarrow Y$ in our general sense provides the notion of a Y-valued function of n-variables. In this case, an element of the domain of f is an **ordered n-tuple** $(x_1, x_2, \cdots, x_n)$, with x_i in X_i for $i = 1, 2, \cdots, n$, for which $f(x_1, x_2, \cdots, x_n)$ is defined. The **graph** of f is the set of all ordered $n+1$-tuples of the form $(x_1, x_2, \cdots, x_n, f(x_1, x_2, \cdots, x_n))$, where $(x_1, x_2, \cdots, x_n)$ is in the domain of f.

Suppose a manufacturer produces two products, X and Y. Then the total cost depends on the levels of production of *both* X and Y. Table 2.3 is a schedule that indicates total cost at various levels. For example, when 5 units of X and 6 units of Y are produced, the total cost c is 17. In this situation, it seems natural to associate the number 17 with the *ordered pair* (5, 6):

$$(5, 6) \mapsto 17$$

The first element of the ordered pair, 5, represents the number of units of X produced, while the second element, 6, represents the number of units of Y produced. Corresponding to the other production situations shown, we have

$$(5, 7) \mapsto 19$$
$$(6, 6) \mapsto 18$$

and

$$(6, 7) \mapsto 20$$

No. of Units of X Produced, x	No. of Units of Y Produced, y	Total Cost of Production, c
5	6	17
5	7	19
6	6	18
6	7	20

Table 2.3

This listing can be considered to be the defintion of a function $c: X \times Y \longrightarrow (-\infty, \infty)$, where $X = \{5, 6\}$ and and $Y = \{6, 7\}$.

$$c(5, 7) = 19 \quad c(6, 7) = 20$$
$$c(5, 6) = 17 \quad c(6, 6) = 18$$

We say that the total-cost schedule can be described by $c = c(x, y)$, a function of the two independent variables x and y. The letter c is used here for both the dependent variable and the name of the rule that defines the function. Of course the range of c is the subset $\{17, 18, 19, 20\}$ of $(-\infty, \infty)$. Because negative costs are unlikely to ever make sense, we might want to refine c and construe it to be a function $c : X \times Y \longrightarrow [0, \infty)$.

Most people were acquainted with certain functions of two variables long before they ever heard of functions, as the following example illustrates.

EXAMPLE 1   Functions of Two Variables

a. $a(x, y) = x + y$ is a function of two variables. Some function values are

$$a(1, 1) = 1 + 1 = 2$$

$$a(2, 3) = 2 + 3 = 5$$

We have $a : (-\infty, \infty) \times (-\infty, \infty) \longrightarrow (-\infty, \infty)$.

b. $m(x, y) = xy$ is a function of two variables. Some function values are

$$m(2, 2) = 2 \cdot 2 = 4$$

$$m(3, 2) = 3 \cdot 2 = 6$$

The domain of both a and m is all of $(-\infty, \infty) \times (-\infty, \infty)$. Observe that if you were to define division as a function $d : (-\infty, \infty) \times (-\infty, \infty) \longrightarrow (-\infty, \infty)$ with $d(x, y) = x \div y$ then the domain of d is $(-\infty, \infty) \times ((-\infty, \infty) - \{0\})$, where $(-\infty, \infty) - \{0\}$ is the set all real numbers except 0.

◁

Turning to another function of two variables, we see that the equation

$$z = \frac{2}{x^2 + y^2}$$

defines z as a function of x and y:

$$z = f(x, y) = \frac{2}{x^2 + y^2}$$

The domain of f is all ordered pairs of real numbers (x, y) for which the equation has meaning when the first and second elements of (x, y) are substituted for x and y, respectively, in the equation. Thus, the domain of f is $(-\infty, \infty) \times (-\infty, \infty) - \{(0, 0)\}$, the set of all ordered pairs of real numbers except $(0, 0)$. To find $f(2, 3)$, for example, we substitute $x = 2$ and $y = 3$ into the expression $2/(x^2 + y^2)$. We obtain $f(2, 3) = 2/(2^2 + 3^2) = 2/13$.

EXAMPLE 2   Functions of Two Variables

a. $f(x, y) = \dfrac{x + 3}{y - 2}$ is a function of two variables. Because the denominator is zero when $y = 2$, the domain of f is all (x, y) such that $y \neq 2$. Some function values are

$$f(0, 3) = \frac{0 + 3}{3 - 2} = 3$$

$$f(3, 0) = \frac{3 + 3}{0 - 2} = -3$$

Note that $f(0, 3) \neq f(3, 0)$.

b. $h(x, y) = 4x$ defines h as a function of x and y. The domain is all ordered pairs of real numbers. Some function values are

$$h(2, 5) = 4(2) = 8$$

$$h(2, 6) = 4(2) = 8$$

Note that the function values are independent of the choice of y.

APPLY IT ▶

15. The cost per day for manufacturing both 12-ounce and 20-ounce coffee mugs is given by $c = 160 + 2x + 3y$, where x is the number of 12-ounce mugs and y is the number of 20-ounce mugs. What is the cost per day of manufacturing

a. 500 12-ounce and 700 20-ounce mugs?

b. 1000 12-ounce and 750 20-ounce mugs?

c. If $z^2 = x^2 + y^2$ and $x = 3$ and $y = 4$, then $z^2 = 3^2 + 4^2 = 25$. Consequently, $z = \pm 5$. Thus, with the ordered pair $(3, 4)$, we *cannot* associate exactly one output number. Hence $z^2 = x^2 + y^2$ does not define z as a function of x and y.

Now Work Problem 1 ◁

EXAMPLE 3   Temperature–Humidity Index

On hot and humid days, many people tend to feel uncomfortable. The degree of discomfort is numerically given by the temperature–humidity index, THI, which is a function of two variables, t_d and t_w:

$$\text{THI} = f(t_d, t_w) = 15 + 0.4(t_d + t_w)$$

where t_d is the dry-bulb temperature (in degrees Fahrenheit) and t_w is the wet-bulb temperature (in degrees Fahrenheit) of the air. Evaluate the THI when $t_d = 90$ and $t_w = 80$.

Solution: We want to find $f(90, 80)$:

$$f(90, 80) = 15 + 0.4(90 + 80) = 15 + 68 = 83$$

When the THI is greater than 75, most people are uncomfortable. In fact, the THI was once called the "discomfort index." Many electric utilities closely follow this index so that they can anticipate the demand that air-conditioning places on their systems.

Now Work Problem 3 ◁

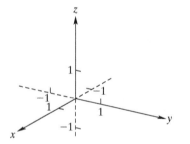

FIGURE 2.38   Three-dimensional rectangular coordinate system.

From the second paragraph in this section it follows that a function $f : (-\infty, \infty) \times (-\infty, \infty) \longrightarrow (-\infty, \infty)$, where we write $z = f(x, y)$, will have a graph consisting of ordered triples of real numbers. The set of all ordered triples of real numbers can be pictured as providing a ***three*-dimensional rectangular coordinate system**. Such a system is formed when three mutually perpendicular real-number lines in space intersect at the origin of each line, as in Figure 2.38. The three number lines are called the x-, y-, and z-axes, and their point of intersection is called the origin of the system. The arrows indicate the positive directions of the axes, and the negative portions of the axes are shown as dashed lines.

To each point P in space, we can assign a unique ordered triple of numbers, called the *coordinates* of P. To do this [see Figure 14.24(a)], from P, we construct a line perpendicular to the x, y-plane—that is, the plane determined by the x- and y-axes. Let Q be the point where the line intersects this plane. From Q, we construct perpendiculars to the x- and y-axes. These lines intersect the x- and y-axes at x_0 and y_0, respectively. From P, a perpendicular to the z-axis is constructed that intersects the axis at z_0. Thus, we assign to P the ordered triple (x_0, y_0, z_0). It should also be evident that with each ordered triple of numbers we can assign a unique point in space. Due to this one-to-one correspondence between points in space and ordered triples, an ordered triple can be

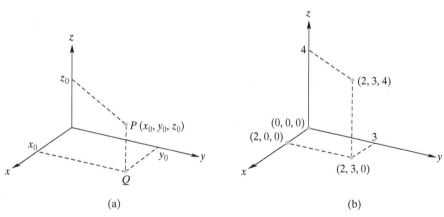

(a)   (b)

FIGURE 2.39   Points in space.

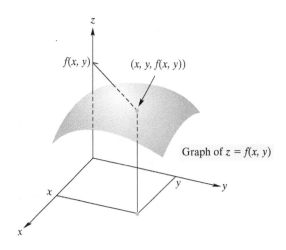

FIGURE 2.40 Graph of a function of two variables.

called a point. In Figure 14.24(b), points $(2, 0, 0)$, $(2, 3, 0)$, and $(2, 3, 4)$ are shown. Note that the origin corresponds to $(0, 0, 0)$. Typically, the negative portions of the axes are not shown unless required.

We represent a function of two variables, $z = f(x, y)$, geometrically as follows: To each ordered pair (x, y) in the domain of f, we assign the point $(x, y, f(x, y))$. The set of all such points is the *graph* of f. Such a graph appears in Figure 14.25. We can consider $z = f(x, y)$ as representing a *surface in space* in the same way that we have considered $y = f(x)$ as representing a *curve in the plane*. [Not all functions $y = f(x)$ describe aesthetically pleasing curves—in fact most do not—and in the same way we stretch the meaning of the word *surface*.]

We now give a brief discussion of sketching surfaces in space. We begin with planes that are parallel to a coordinate plane. By a "coordinate plane" we mean a plane containing two coordinate axes. For example, the plane determined by the x- and y-axes is the x, y-**plane.** Similarly, we speak of the x, z-**plane** and the y, z-**plane.** The coordinate planes divide space into eight parts, called *octants*. In particular, the part containing all points (x, y, z) such that x, y, and z are positive is called the **first octant.**

Names are not usually assigned to the remaining seven octants.

Suppose S is a plane that is parallel to the x, y-plane and passes through the point $(0, 0, 5)$. [See Figure 14.26(a).] Then the point (x, y, z) will lie on S if and only if $z = 5$; that is, x and y can be any real numbers, but z must equal 5. For this reason, we say that $z = 5$ is an equation of S. Similarly, an equation of the plane parallel to the x, z-plane and passing through the point $(0, 2, 0)$ is $y = 2$ [Figure 14.26(b)]. The equation $x = 3$ is an equation of the plane passing through $(3, 0, 0)$ and parallel to the y, z-plane [Figure 14.26(c)]. Next, we look at planes in general.

In space, the graph of an equation of the form

$$Ax + By + Cz + D = 0$$

where D is a constant and A, B, and C are constants that are not all zero, is a plane. Since three distinct points (not lying on the same line) determine a plane, a convenient

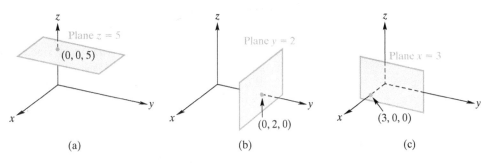

(a) (b) (c)

FIGURE 2.41 Planes parallel to coordinate planes.

way to sketch a plane is to first determine the points, if any, where the plane intersects the *x*-, *y*-, and *z*-axes. These points are called *intercepts*.

EXAMPLE 4 Graphing a Plane

Sketch the plane $2x + 3y + z = 6$.

Solution: The plane intersects the *x*-axis when $y = 0$ and $z = 0$. Thus $2x = 6$ which gives $x = 3$. Similarly, if $x = z = 0$, then $y = 2$; if $x = y = 0$, then $z = 6$. Therefore, the intercepts are $(3, 0, 0)$, $(0, 2, 0)$ and $(0, 0, 6)$. After these points are plotted, a plane is passed through them. The portion of the plane in the first octant is shown in Figure 2.42(a); note, however, that the plane extends indefinitely into space.

Now Work Problem 19 ◁

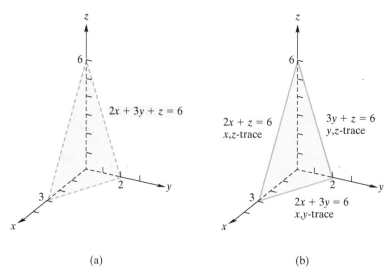

(a)   (b)

FIGURE 2.42   The plane $2x + 3y + z = 6$ and its traces.

A surface can be sketched with the aid of its **traces.** These are the intersections of the surface with the coordinate planes. To illustrate, for the plane $2x + 3y + z = 6$ in Example 4, the trace in the *x,y*-plane is obtained by setting $z = 0$. This gives $2x + 3y = 6$, which is an equation of a *line* in the *x,y*-plane. Similarly, setting $x = 0$ gives the trace in the *y,z*-plane: the line $3y + z = 6$. The *x,z*-trace is the line $2x + z = 6$. [See Figure 2.42(b).]

EXAMPLE 5 Sketching a Surface

Sketch the surface $2x + z = 4$.

Solution: This equation has the form of a plane. The *x*- and *z*-intercepts are $(2, 0, 0)$ and $(0, 0, 4)$, and there is no *y*-intercept, since *x* and *z* cannot both be zero. Setting $y = 0$ gives the *x,z*-trace $2x + z = 4$, which is a line in the *x,z*-plane. In fact, the intersection of the surface with *any* plane $y = k$ is also $2x + z = 4$. Hence, the plane appears as in Figure 2.43.

Now Work Problem 21 ◁

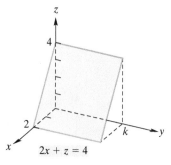

FIGURE 2.43   The plane $2x + z = 4$.

Our final examples deal with surfaces that are not planes but whose graphs can be easily obtained.

Note that this equation places no restriction on *y*.

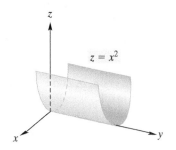

FIGURE 2.44   The surface $z = x^2$.

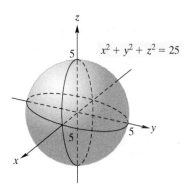

FIGURE 2.45   The surface $x^2 + y^2 + z^2 = 25$.

EXAMPLE 6   Sketching a Surface

Sketch the surface $z = x^2$.

Solution: The *x,z*-trace is the curve $z = x^2$, which is parabola. In fact, for *any* fixed value of *y*, we get $z = x^2$. Thus, the graph appears as in Figure 2.44.

Now Work Problem 25 ◁

EXAMPLE 7   Sketching a Surface

Sketch the surface $x^2 + y^2 + z^2 = 25$.

Solution: Setting $z = 0$ gives the *x,y*-trace $x^2 + y^2 = 25$, which is a circle of radius 5. Similarly, the *y,z*-, and *x,z*-traces are the circles $y^2 + z^2 = 25$ and $x^2 + z^2 = 25$, respectively. Note also that since $x^2 + y^2 = 25 - z^2$, the intersection of the surface with the plane $z = k$, where $-5 \le k \le 5$, is a circle. For example, if $z = 3$, the intersection is the circle $x^2 + y^2 = 16$. If $z = 4$, the intersection is $x^2 + y^2 = 9$. That is, cross sections of the surface that are parallel to the *x,y*-plane are circles. The surface appears in Figure 2.45; it is a sphere.

Now Work Problem 27 ◁

For a function $f : X \times Y \longrightarrow Z$, we have seen that the graph of f, being a subset of $X \times Y \times Z$, is three dimensional for numerical examples. Admittedly, constructing such a graph on paper can be challenging. There is another pictorial presentation of a function $z = f(x, y)$, for $f : (-\infty, \infty) \times (-\infty, \infty) \longrightarrow (-\infty, \infty)$ which is entirely two dimensional. Let l be a number in the range of f. The *equation* $f(x, y) = l$ has a graph in the *x, y*-plane that, in principle, can be constructed and labeled. If we repeat this contruction in the same plane, for several other values, l_i say, in the range of f then we have a set of curves, called **level curves**, which may provide us with a useful visualization of f.

There are are at least two examples of this technique that are within everyday experience for many people. For the first, consider a geographic region that is small enough to be considered planar and coordinatize it. (A city with a rectangular grid of numbered avenues and streets can be considered to be coordinatized by these.) At any given time, temperature T in degrees Farenheit is a function of place (x, y). We might write $T = T(x, y)$. On a map of the region we might connect all places that currently have a temperature of 70°F with a curve. This is the curve $T(x, y) = 70$. If we put several other curves, such as $T(x, y) = 68$ and $T(x, y) = 72$, on the same map, then we have the kind of map that appears on televised weather reports. The curves in this case are called *isotherms*; the prefix *iso* comes from the Greek *isos* meaning "equal". For the next, again referring to geography, observe that each place (x, y) has a definite altitude $A = A(x, y)$. A map of a mountainous region with points of equal altitude connected by what are called *contour lines* is called a *togographic map*, and the generic term *level curves* is particularly apt in this case.

In Chapter 7 we will encounter a number of *linear* functions of several variables. If we have $P = ax + by$, expressing profit P as a function of production x of a product X and production y of a product Y, then the level curves $ax + by = l$ are called *isoprofit lines*.

EXAMPLE 8   Level Curves

Sketch a family of at least four level curves for the function $z = x^2 + y^2$.

Solution: For any pair (x, y), $x^2 + y^2 \ge 0$, so the range of $z = x^2 + y^2$ is contained in $[0, \infty)$. On the other hand, for any $l \ge 0$ we can write $l = (\sqrt{l})^2 + 0^2$, which shows that the range of $z = x^2 + y^2$ is all of $[0, \infty)$. For $l \ge 0$ we recognize the graph of $x^2 + y^2 = l$ as a circle of radius $\sqrt{l}$ centered at the origin $(0, 0)$. If we take l to be 4, 9, 16, and 25, then our level curves are concentric circles of radii 2, 3, 4, and 5, respectively.

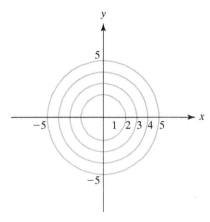

FIGURE 2.46 Level curves for $z = x^2 + y^2$.

See Figure 2.46. Note that the level "curve" $x^2 + y^2 = 0$ consists of the point $(0,0)$ and no others.

Now Work Problem 29 ◁

An example of a function of three variables is $v = v(x, y, z) = xyz$. It provides the volume of a "brick" with side lengths x, y, and z if x, y, and z are all positive.

An *ellipsoid* is a surface which in "standard position" is given by an equation of the form $\dfrac{x^2}{a^2} + \dfrac{y^2}{b^2} + \dfrac{z^2}{c^2} = 1$, for a, b, and c positive numbers called the radii. No one of the variables is a function of the other two. If two of the numbers a, b, and c are equal and the third is larger, then the special kind of ellipsoid that results is called a *prolate spheroid*, examples of which are provided by both a football and a rugby ball. In any event, the volume of space enclosed by an ellipsoid with radii a, b, and c is given by $V = V(a, b, c) = \dfrac{4}{3}\pi abc$, and this is another example of a function of three (positive) variables.

In the context of functions of several variables, it is also interesting to consider functions whose *values* are ordered pairs. For any set X, one of the simplest is the *diagonal function* $\Delta : X \longrightarrow X \times X$ given by $\Delta(x) = (x, x)$. We mentioned in Example 1(b) that ordinary multiplication is a function $m : (-\infty, \infty) \times (-\infty, \infty) \longrightarrow (-\infty, \infty)$. If we let Δ denote the diagonal function for $(-\infty, \infty)$, then we see that the composite $m \circ \Delta$ of the rather simple-minded functions Δ and m is the more interesting function $y = x^2$.

PROBLEMS 2.8

In Problems 1–12, determine the indicated function values for the given functions.

1. $f(x, y) = 4x - y^2 + 3$; $f(1, 2)$

2. $f(x, y) = 3x^2y - 4y$; $f(2, -1)$

3. $g(x, y, z) = 2x(3y + z)$; $g(3, 0, -1)$

4. $g(x, y, z) = x^2yz + xy^2z + xyz^2$; $g(3, 1, -2)$

5. $h(r, s, t, u) = \dfrac{rs}{t^2 - u^2}$; $h(-3, 3, 5, 4)$

6. $h(r, s, t, u) = ru$; $h(1, 5, 3, 1)$

7. $g(p_A, p_B) = 2p_A(p_A^2 - 5)$; $g(4, 8)$

8. $g(p_A, p_B) = p_A^2\sqrt{p_B} + 9$; $g(4, 9)$

9. $F(x, y, z) = 3$; $F(2, 0, -1)$

10. $F(x, y, z) = \dfrac{2x}{(y + 1)z}$; $F(1, 0, 3)$

11. $f(x, y) = (x + y)^2$; $f(a + h, b)$

12. $f(x, y) = x^2y - 3y^3$; $f(r + t, r)$

13. Ecology   A method of ecological sampling to determine animal populations in a given area involves first marking all the animals obtained in a sample of R animals from the area and then releasing them so that they can mix with unmarked animals. At a later date a second sample is taken of M animals, and the number of these that are marked, S, is noted. Based on R, M, and S, an estimate of the total population of animals in the sample area is given by

$$N = f(R, M, S) = \frac{RM}{S}$$

Find $f(200, 200, 50)$. This method is called the *mark-and-recapture procedure*.[6]

14. Genetics   Under certain conditions, if two brown-eyed parents have exactly k children, the probability that there will be exactly r blue-eyed children is given by

$$P(r, k) = \frac{k!\left(\frac{1}{4}\right)^r\left(\frac{3}{4}\right)^{k-r}}{r!(k - r)!} \quad r = 0, 1, 2, \ldots, k$$

Find the probability that, out of a total of four children, exactly three will be blue-eyed.

In Problems 15–18 find equations of the planes that satisfy the given conditions.

15. Parallel to the x,z-plane and also passes through the point $(0, 2, 0)$

16. Parallel to the y,z-plane and also passes through the point $(-2, 0, 0)$

17. Parallel to the x,y-plane and also passes through the point $(2, 7, 6)$

18. Parallel to the y,z-plane and also passes through the point $(96, -2, 2)$

In Problems 19–28, sketch the given surfaces.

19. $x + y + z = 1$ **20.** $2x + y + 2z = 6$

21. $3x + 6y + 2z = 12$ **22.** $2x + 3y + 5z = 1$

23. $3x + y = 6$ **24.** $y = 3z + 2$

25. $z = 4 - x^2$ **26.** $y = z^2$

27. $x^2 + y^2 + z^2 = 9$ **28.** $x^2 + 4y^2 = 1$

In Problems 29–30, sketch at least three level curves for the given function.

29. $z = 5x + 8y$ **30.** $z = x^2 - y^2$

---

[6] E. P. Odum, *Ecology* (New York: Holt, Rinehart and Winston, 1966).

Chapter 2 Review

Important Terms and Symbols

Summary

A function f is a rule that assigns at most one output $f(x)$ to each possible input x. A function is often specified by a formula that prescribes what must be done to an input x to obtain $f(x)$. To obtain a particular function value $f(a)$, we replace each x in the formula by a.

The domain of a function $f : X \longrightarrow Y$ consists of all inputs x for which the rule defines $f(x)$ as an element of Y; the range consists of all elements of Y of the form $f(x)$.

Some special types of functions are constant functions, polynomial functions, and rational functions. A function that is defined by more than one expression depending on the kind of input is called a case-defined function.

A function has an inverse if and only if it is one-to-one.

In economics, supply (demand) functions give a correspondence between the price p of a product and the number of units q of the product that producers (consumers) will supply (buy) at that price.

Two functions f and g can be combined to form a sum, difference, product, quotient, or composite as follows:

$$(f + g)(x) = f(x) + g(x)$$
$$(f - g)(x) = f(x) - g(x)$$
$$(fg)(x) = f(x)g(x)$$
$$\left(\frac{f}{g}\right)(x) = \frac{f(x)}{g(x)}$$
$$(f \circ g)(x) = f(g(x))$$

A rectangular coordinate system allows us to represent equations in two variables (in particular, those arising from functions) geometrically. The graph of an equation in x and y consists of all points (x, y) that correspond to the solutions of the equation. We plot a sufficient number of points and connect them (where appropriate) so that the basic shape of the graph is apparent. Points where the graph intersects the *x*- and *y*-axes are called *x*-intercepts and *y*-intercepts, respectively. An *x*-intercept is found by letting *y* be 0 and solving for *x*; a *y*-intercept is found by letting *x* be 0 and solving for *y*.

The graph of a function *f* is the graph of the equation $y = f(x)$ and consists of all points $(x, f(x))$ such that *x* is in the domain of *f*. From the graph of a function, it is easy to determine the domain and range.

The fact that a graph represents a function can be determined by using the vertical-line test. A vertical line cannot cut the graph of a function at more than one point.

The fact that a function is one-to-one can be determined by using the horizontal-line test on its graph. A horizontal line cannot cut the graph of a one-to-one function at more than one point. When a function passes the horizontal-line test, the graph of the inverse can be obtained by reflecting the original graph in the line $y = x$.

When the graph of an equation has symmetry, the mirror-image effect allows us to sketch the graph by plotting fewer points than would otherwise be needed. The tests for symmetry are as follows:

Symmetry about x-axis	Replace *y* by $-y$ in given equation. Symmetric if equivalent equation is obtained.
Symmetry about y-axis	Replace *x* by $-x$ in given equation. Symmetric if equivalent equation is obtained.
Symmetry about origin	Replace *x* by $-x$ and *y* by $-y$ in given equation. Symmetric if equivalent equation is obtained.
Symmetry about $y = x$	Interchange *x* and *y* in given equation. Symmetric if equivalent equation is obtained.

Sometimes the graph of a function can be obtained from that of a familiar function by means of a vertical shift upward or downward, a horizontal shift to the right or left, a reflection about the *x*-axis or *y*-axis, or a vertical stretching or shrinking away from or toward the *x*-axis. Such transformations are indicated in Table 2.2 in Section 2.7.

A function of two variables is a function whose domain consists of ordered pairs. A function of *n* variables is a function whose domain consists of ordered *n*-tuples. The graph of a real-valued function of two variables requires a three-dimensional coordinate system. Level curves provide another technique to visualize functions of two variables.

Review Problems

In Problems 1–6, give the domain of each function.

1. $f(x) = \dfrac{x}{x^2 - 6x + 5}$

2. $g(x) = x^2 + 3|x + 2|$

3. $F(t) = 7t + 4t^2$

4. $G(x) = 18$

5. $h(x) = \dfrac{\sqrt{x}}{x - 1}$

6. $H(s) = \dfrac{\sqrt{s - 5}}{4}$

In Problems 7–14, find the function values for the given function.

7. $f(x) = 2x^2 - 3x + 5;\ f(0),\ f(-2),\ f(5),\ f(\pi)$

8. $h(x) = 7;\ h(4),\ h\left(\dfrac{1}{100}\right),\ h(-156),\ h(x + 4)$

9. $G(x) = \sqrt[4]{x - 3};\ G(3),\ G(19),\ G(t + 1),\ G(x^3)$

10. $F(x) = \dfrac{x - 3}{x + 4};\ F(-1),\ F(0),\ F(5),\ F(x + 3)$

11. $h(u) = \dfrac{\sqrt{u + 4}}{u};\ h(5),\ h(-4),\ h(x),\ h(u - 4)$

12. $H(t) = \dfrac{(t - 2)^3}{5};\ H(-1),\ H(0),\ H\left(\dfrac{1}{3}\right),\ H(x^2)$

13. $f(x) = \begin{cases} -3 & \text{if } x < 1 \\ 4 + x^2 & \text{if } x > 1 \end{cases};$

$f(4),\ f(-2),\ f(0),\ f(1)$

14. $f(q) = \begin{cases} -q + 1 & \text{if } -1 \le q < 0 \\ q^2 + 1 & \text{if } 0 \le q < 5 \\ q^3 - 99 & \text{if } 5 \le q \le 7 \end{cases};$

$f\left(-\dfrac{1}{2}\right),\ f(0),\ f\left(\dfrac{1}{2}\right),\ f(5),\ f(6)$

In Problems 15–18, find (a) $f(x + h)$ and (b) $\dfrac{f(x + h) - f(x)}{h}$, and simplify your answers.

15. $f(x) = 3 - 7x$

16. $f(x) = 11x^2 + 4$

17. $f(x) = 3x^2 + x - 2$

18. $f(x) = \dfrac{7}{x + 1}$

19. If $f(x) = 3x - 1$ and $g(x) = 2x + 3$, find the following.

(a) $(f + g)(x)$ **(b)** $(f + g)(4)$ **(c)** $(f - g)(x)$

(d) $(fg)(x)$ **(e)** $(fg)(1)$ **(f)** $\dfrac{f}{g}(x)$

(g) $(f \circ g)(x)$ **(h)** $(f \circ g)(5)$ **(i)** $(g \circ f)(x)$

20. If $f(x) = -x^2$ and $g(x) = 3x - 2$, find the following.

(a) $(f + g)(x)$ **(b)** $(f - g)(x)$ **(c)** $(f - g)(-3)$

(d) $(fg)(x)$ **(e)** $\dfrac{f}{g}(x)$ **(f)** $\dfrac{f}{g}(2)$

(g) $(f \circ g)(x)$ **(h)** $(g \circ f)(x)$ **(i)** $(g \circ f)(-4)$

In Problems 21–24, find $(f \circ g)(x)$ and $(g \circ f)(x)$.

21. $f(x) = \dfrac{1}{x^2},\ g(x) = x + 1$

22. $f(x) = \dfrac{x - 2}{3},\ g(x) = \dfrac{1}{\sqrt{x}}$

23. $f(x) = \sqrt{x + 2},\ g(x) = x^3$

24. $f(x) = 2,\ g(x) = 3$

In Problems 25 and 26, find the intercepts of the graph of each equation, and test for symmetry about the x-axis, the y-axis, the origin, and $y = x$. Do not sketch the graph.

25. $y = 3x - x^3$

26. $\dfrac{x^2 y^2}{x^2 + y^2 + 1} = 4$

In Problems 27 and 28, find the x- and y-intercepts of the graphs of the equations. Also, test for symmetry about the x-axis, the y-axis, and the origin. Then sketch the graphs.

27. $y = 4 + x^2$

28. $y = 3x - 7$

In Problems 29–32, graph each function and give its domain and range. Also, determine the intercepts.

29. $G(u) = \sqrt{u + 4}$

30. $f(x) = |x| + 1$

31. $y = g(t) = \dfrac{2}{|t - 4|}$

32. $v = \phi(u) = \sqrt{-u}$

33. Graph the following case-defined function, and give its domain and range:

$$y = f(x) = \begin{cases} 2 & \text{if } x \le 0 \\ 2 - x & \text{if } x > 0 \end{cases}$$

34. Use the graph of $f(x) = \sqrt{x}$ to sketch the graph of $y = \sqrt{x - 2} - 1$.

35. Use the graph of $f(x) = x^2$ to sketch the graph of $y = -\dfrac{1}{2}x^2 + 2$.

36. Trend Equation   The projected annual sales (in dollars) of a new product are given by the equation $S = 150{,}000 + 3000t$, where t is the time in years from 2005. Such an equation is called a *trend equation*. Find the projected annual sales for 2010. Is S a function of t?

37. In Figure 2.47, which graphs represent functions of x?

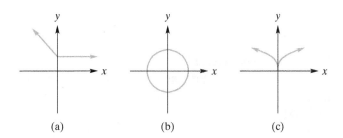

FIGURE 2.47   Diagram for Problem 37.

38. If $f(x) = (x^2 - x + 7)^3$, find **(a)** $f(2)$ and **(b)** $f(1.1)$. Round your answers to two decimal places.

39. Find all real roots of the equation

$$5x^3 - 7x^2 = 4x - 2$$

Round your answers to two decimal places.

40. Find all real roots of the equation

$$x^4 - 4x^3 = (2x - 1)^2$$

Round your answers to two decimal places.

41. Find all real zeros of

$$f(x) = x(2.1x^2 - 3)^2 - x^3 + 1$$

Round your answers to two decimal places.

42. Determine the range of

$$f(x) = \begin{cases} -2.5x - 4 & \text{if } x < 0 \\ 6 + 4.1x - x^2 & \text{if } x \ge 0 \end{cases}$$

43. From the graph of $f(x) = -x^3 + 0.04x + 7$, find **(a)** the range and **(b)** the intercepts. Round values to two decimal places.

44. From the graph of $f(x) = \sqrt{x + 5}(x^2 - 4)$, find **(a)** the minimum value of $f(x)$ **(b)** the range of f, and **(c)** all real zeros of f. Round values to two decimal places.

45. Graph $y = f(x) = x^2 + x^k$ for $k = 0$, 1, 2, 3, and 4. For which values of k does the graph have **(a)** symmetry about the y-axis? **(b)** symmetry about the origin?

46. Sketch the graph of $x + 2y + 3z = 6$.

47. Sketch the graph of $3x + y + 5z = 10$.

48. Construct three level curves for $P = 5x + 7y$.

49. Construct three level curves for $C = 2x + 10y$.

⊙ EXPLORE & EXTEND   A Taxing Experience!

O ccasionally, you will hear someone complain that an unexpected source of income is going to *bump* him or her *into the next tax bracket* with the further speculation that this will result in a *reduction in take-home earnings.* It is true that U.S. federal income tax is prescribed by case-defined functions (the cases defining what are often called *brackets*), but we will see that there are no *jumps* in tax paid as a function of income. It is an urban myth that an increase in pretax income can result in a decrease in take-home income.

   We will examine the 2008 federal tax rates for a married couple filing a joint return. The relevant document is Schedule Y-1, available at http://www.irs.gov/and partially shown in Figure 2.48.

Schedule Y-1—Use if your **2008** filing status is **Married filing jointly** or **Qualifying widow(er)**

If line 5 is:		The tax is:	of the amount
Over—	But not over—		over—
$0	$16,050	.... 10%	$0
16,050	65,100	$1,605.00 + 15%	16,050
65,100	131,450	8,962.50 + 25%	65,100
131,450	200,300	25,550.00 + 28%	131,450
200,300	357,700	44,828.00 + 33%	200,300
357,700	....	96,770.00 + 35%	357,700

FIGURE 2.48   Internal Revenue Service 2008 Schedule Y-1.

We claim that Schedule Y-1 defines a function, call it f, of income x, for $x \geq 0$. Indeed, for any $x \geq 0$, x belongs to exactly one of the intervals

$$[0, 16{,}050]$$
$$(16{,}050, 65{,}100]$$
$$(65{,}100, 131{,}450]$$
$$(131{,}450, 200{,}300]$$
$$(200{,}300, 357{,}700]$$
$$(357{,}700, \infty)$$

and as soon as the interval is determined, there is a single rule that applies to compute a unique value $f(x)$.

For example, to compute $f(83{,}500)$, tax on an income of \$83,500, observe first that 83,500 belongs to the interval $(65{,}100, 131{,}450]$ and for such an x the tax formula is $f(x) = 8{,}962.50 + 0.25(x - 65{,}100)$, since $x - 65{,}100$ is the amount over \$65,100 and it is taxed at the rate $25\% = 0.25$.

Therefore,

$$f(83{,}500) = 8{,}962.50 + 0.25(83{,}500 - 65{,}100)$$

$$= 8{,}962.50 + 0.25(18{,}400)$$

$$= 8{,}962.50 + 4{,}600$$

$$= 13{,}562.50$$

To illustrate further, we write out the entire Schedule Y-1 in our generic notation for a case-defined function.

$$f(x) = \begin{cases} 0.10x & \text{if } 0 \leq x \leq 16{,}050 \\ 1{,}605 + 0.15(x - 16{,}050) & \text{if } 16{,}050 < x \leq 65{,}100 \\ 8{,}962.50 + 0.25(x - 65{,}100) & \text{if } 65{,}100 < x \leq 131{,}450 \\ 25{,}550 + 0.28(x - 131{,}450) & \text{if } 131{,}450 < x \leq 200{,}300 \\ 44{,}828 + 0.33(x - 200{,}300) & \text{if } 200{,}300 < x \leq 357{,}700 \\ 96{,}770 + 0.35(x - 357{,}700) & \text{if } x > 357{,}700 \end{cases}$$

With these formulas, we can geometrically depict the income tax function, as in Figure 2.49.

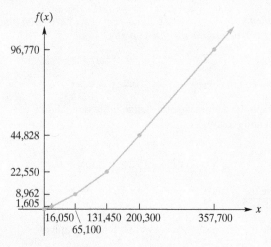

FIGURE 2.49   Income tax function.

Problems

Use the preceding income tax function f to determine the tax on the given taxable income in the year 2008.

1. \$27,000

2. \$89,000

3. \$350,000

4. \$560,000

5. Look up the most recent Schedule X at http://www.irs.gov/ and repeat Problems 1–4 for a single person.

6. Why is it significant that $f(16{,}050) = \$1605$, $f(65{,}100) = \$8962.50$ and so on?

7. Define the function g by $g(x) = x - f(x)$. Thus $g = I - f$, where I is the identity function defined in Section 2.3. The function g gives, for each pretax income x, the amount that the taxpayer gets as take-home income and is, like f, a case-defined function. Write a complete description for g, in terms of cases, as we have done for f.

8. Graph the function g defined in Problem 7. Observe that if $a < b$, then $g(a) < g(b)$. This shows that if pretax income increases, then take-home income increases, irrespective of any jumping to a higher bracket (thereby debunking an urban myth).

3

Lines, Parabolas, and Systems

For the problem of industrial pollution, some people advocate a market-based solution: Let manufacturers pollute, but make them pay for the privilege. The more pollution, the greater the fee, or levy. The idea is to give manufacturers an incentive not to pollute more than necessary.

Does this approach work? In the figure below, curve 1 represents the cost per ton[1] of cutting pollution. A company polluting indiscriminately can normally do some pollution reduction at a small cost. As the amount of pollution is reduced, however, the cost per ton of further reduction rises and ultimately increases without bound. This is illustrated by curve 1 rising indefinitely as the total tons of pollution produced approaches 0. (You should try to understand why this *model* is reasonably accurate.)

Line 2 is a levy scheme that goes easy on clean-running operations but charges an increasing per-ton fee as the total pollution amount goes up. Line 3, by contrast, is a scheme in which low-pollution manufacturers pay a high per-ton levy while gross polluters pay less per ton (but more overall). Questions of fairness aside, how well will each scheme work as a pollution control measure?

Faced with a pollution levy, a company tends to cut pollution *so long as it saves more in levy costs than it incurs in reduction costs*. The reduction efforts continue until the reduction costs exceed the levy savings.

The latter half of this chapter deals with systems of equations. Here, curve 1 and line 2 represent one system of equations, and curve 1 and line 3 represent another. Once you have learned how to solve systems of equations, you can return to this page and verify that the line 2 scheme leads to a pollution reduction from amount A to amount B, while the line 3 scheme fails as a pollution control measure, leaving the pollution level at A.

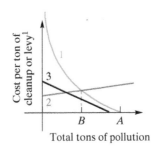

Total tons of pollution

---

[1] Technically, this is the *marginal* cost per ton (see Section 11.3).

Objective

To develop the notion of slope and different forms of equations of lines.

3.1 Lines

Slope of a Line

Many relationships between quantities can be represented conveniently by straight lines. One feature of a straight line is its "steepness." For example, in Figure 3.1, line L_1 rises faster as it goes from left to right than does line L_2. In this sense, L_1 is steeper.

To measure the steepness of a line, we use the notion of *slope*. In Figure 3.2, as we move along line L from $(1, 3)$ to $(3, 7)$, the x-coordinate increases from 1 to 3, and the y-coordinate increases from 3 to 7. The average rate of change of y with respect to x is the ratio

$$\frac{\text{change in } y}{\text{change in } x} = \frac{\text{vertical change}}{\text{horizontal change}} = \frac{7 - 3}{3 - 1} = \frac{4}{2} = 2$$

The ratio of 2 means that for each 1-unit increase in x, there is a 2-unit *increase* in y. Due to the increase, the line *rises* from left to right. It can be shown that, regardless of which two points on L are chosen to compute the ratio of the change in y to the change in x, the result is always 2, which we call the *slope* of the line.

> **Definition**
>
> Let (x_1, y_1) and (x_2, y_2) be two different points on a nonvertical line. The slope of the line is
>
> $$m = \frac{y_2 - y_1}{x_2 - x_1} \left(= \frac{\text{vertical change}}{\text{horizontal change}} \right) \tag{1}$$

 CAUTION!

Having no slope does not mean having a slope of zero.

A vertical line does not have a slope, because any two points on it must have $x_1 = x_2$ [see Figure 3.3(a)], which gives a denominator of zero in Equation (1). For a horizontal line, any two points must have $y_1 = y_2$. [See Figure 3.3(b).] This gives a numerator of zero in Equation (1), and hence the slope of the line is zero.

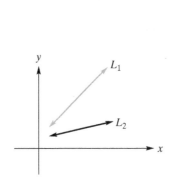

FIGURE 3.1 Line L_1 is "steeper" than L_2.

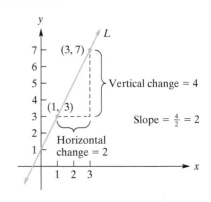

FIGURE 3.2 Slope of a line.

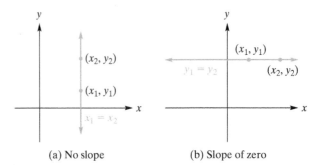

(a) No slope   (b) Slope of zero

FIGURE 3.3 Vertical and horizontal lines.

p (price)

(2, 4)

Increase of 1 unit

Decrease of $\frac{1}{2}$ unit

(8, 1)

q (quantity)

FIGURE 3.4   Price–quantity line.

This example shows how the slope can be interpreted.

APPLY IT ▶

1. A doctor purchased a new car in 2001 for \$32,000. In 2004, he sold it to a friend for \$26,000. Draw a line showing the relationship between the selling price of the car and the year in which it was sold. Find and interpret the slope.

EXAMPLE 1   **Price–Quantity Relationship**

The line in Figure 3.4 shows the relationship between the price p of a widget (in dollars) and the quantity q of widgets (in thousands) that consumers will buy at that price. Find and interpret the slope.

Solution: In the slope formula (1), we replace the x's by q's and the y's by p's. Either point in Figure 3.4 may be chosen as (q_1, p_1). Letting $(2, 4) = (q_1, p_1)$ and $(8, 1) = (q_2, p_2)$, we have

$$m = \frac{p_2 - p_1}{q_2 - q_1} = \frac{1 - 4}{8 - 2} = \frac{-3}{6} = -\frac{1}{2}$$

The slope is negative, $-\frac{1}{2}$. This means that, for each 1-unit increase in quantity (one thousand widgets), there corresponds a **decrease** in price of $\frac{1}{2}$ (dollar per widget). Due to this decrease, the line **falls** from left to right.

Now Work Problem 3 ◁

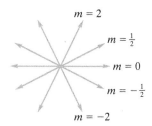

$m = 2$

$m = \frac{1}{2}$

$m = 0$

$m = -\frac{1}{2}$

$m = -2$

FIGURE 3.5   Slopes of lines.

In summary, we can characterize the orientation of a line by its slope:

Zero slope:	horizontal line
Undefined slope:	vertical line
Positive slope:	line rises from left to right
Negative slope:	line falls from left to right

Lines with different slopes are shown in Figure 3.5. Notice that *the closer the slope is to 0, the more nearly horizontal is the line. The greater the absolute value of the slope, the more nearly vertical is the line.* We remark that two lines are parallel if and only if they have the same slope or are both vertical.

Equations of Lines

If we know a point on a line and the slope of the line, we can find an equation whose graph is that line. Suppose that line L has slope m and passes through the point (x_1, y_1). If (x, y) is *any* other point on L (see Figure 3.6), we can find an algebraic relationship between x and y. Using the slope formula on the points (x_1, y_1) and (x, y) gives

$$\frac{y - y_1}{x - x_1} = m$$

$$y - y_1 = m(x - x_1) \tag{2}$$

y

(x, y)

Slope = m

(x_1, y_1)

x

FIGURE 3.6   Line through (x_1, y_1) with slope m.

Every point on L satisfies Equation (2). It is also true that *every* point satisfying Equation (2) must lie on L. Thus, Equation (2) is an equation for L and is given a special name:

$$y - y_1 = m(x - x_1)$$

*is a **point-slope form** of an equation of the line through* (x_1, y_1) *with slope* m.

APPLY IT ▸

2. A new applied mathematics program at a university has grown in enrollment by 14 students per year for the last five years. If the program enrolled 50 students in its third year, what is an equation for the number of students S in the program as a function of the number of years T since its inception?

EXAMPLE 2 Point-Slope Form

Find an equation of the line that has slope 2 and passes through $(1, -3)$.

Solution: Using a point-slope form with $m = 2$ and $(x_1, y_1) = (1, -3)$ gives

$$y - y_1 = m(x - x_1)$$
$$y - (-3) = 2(x - 1)$$
$$y + 3 = 2x - 2$$

which can be rewritten as

$$2x - y - 5 = 0$$

Now Work Problem 9 ◁

An equation of the line passing through two given points can be found easily, as Example 3 shows.

APPLY IT ▸

3. Find an equation of the line passing through the given points. A temperature of 41°F is equivalent to 5°C, and a temperature of 77°F is equivalent to 25°C.

EXAMPLE 3 Determining a Line from Two Points

Find an equation of the line passing through $(-3, 8)$ and $(4, -2)$.

Solution:

Strategy First we find the slope of the line from the given points. Then we substitute the slope and one of the points into a point-slope form.

The line has slope

$$m = \frac{-2 - 8}{4 - (-3)} = -\frac{10}{7}$$

Using a point-slope form with $(-3, 8)$ as (x_1, y_1) gives

Choosing $(4, -2)$ as (x_1, y_1) would give the same result.

$$y - 8 = -\frac{10}{7}[x - (-3)]$$
$$y - 8 = -\frac{10}{7}(x + 3)$$
$$7y - 56 = -10x - 30$$
$$10x + 7y - 26 = 0$$

Now Work Problem 13 ◁

Recall that a point $(0, b)$ where a graph intersects the y-axis is called a y-intercept (Figure 3.7). If the slope m and y-intercept b of a line are known, an equation for the line is [by using a point-slope form with $(x_1, y_1) = (0, b)$]

$$y - b = m(x - 0)$$

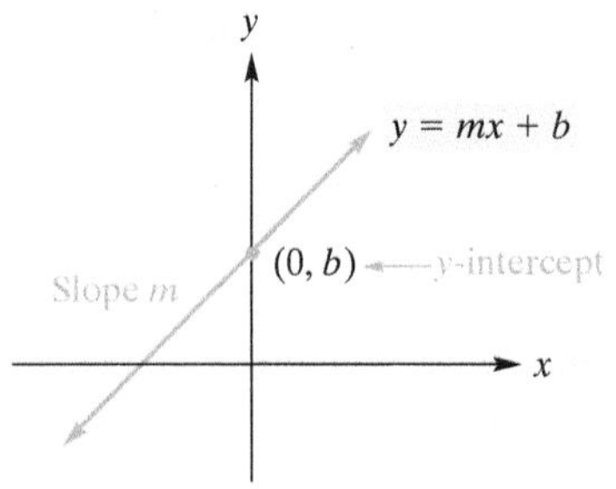

FIGURE 3.7 Line with slope m and y-intercept b.

Solving for y gives $y = mx + b$, called the *slope-intercept form* of an equation of the line:

$$y = mx + b$$

*is the **slope-intercept form** of an equation of the line with slope* m *and* y*-intercept* b.

EXAMPLE 4   Slope-Intercept Form

Find an equation of the line with slope 3 and y-intercept -4.

Solution: Using the slope-intercept form $y = mx + b$ with $m = 3$ and $b = -4$ gives

$$y = 3x + (-4)$$
$$y = 3x - 4$$

Now Work Problem 17 ◁

EXAMPLE 5   Find the Slope and y-Intercept of a Line

APPLY IT ▸

4. One formula for the recommended dosage (in milligrams) of medication for a child t years old is

$$y = \frac{1}{24}(t + 1)a$$

where a is the adult dosage. For an over-the-counter pain reliever, $a = 1000$. Find the slope and y-intercept of this equation.

Find the slope and y-intercept of the line with equation $y = 5(3 - 2x)$.

Solution:

Strategy   We will rewrite the equation so it has the slope-intercept form $y = mx + b$. Then the slope is the coefficient of x and the y-intercept is the constant term.

We have

$$y = 5(3 - 2x)$$
$$y = 15 - 10x$$
$$y = -10x + 15$$

Thus, $m = -10$ and $b = 15$, so the slope is -10 and the y-intercept is 15.

Now Work Problem 25 ◁

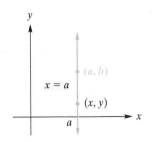

FIGURE 3.8   Vertical line through (a, b).

If a *vertical* line passes through (a, b) (see Figure 3.8), then any other point (x, y) lies on the line if and only if $x = a$. The y-coordinate can have any value. Hence, an equation of the line is $x = a$. Similarly, an equation of the *horizontal* line passing through (a, b) is $y = b$. (See Figure 3.9.) Here the x-coordinate can have any value.

EXAMPLE 6   Equations of Horizontal and Vertical Lines

a. An equation of the vertical line through $(-2, 3)$ is $x = -2$. An equation of the horizontal line through $(-2, 3)$ is $y = 3$.

b. The x-axis and y-axis are horizontal and vertical lines, respectively. Because $(0, 0)$ lies on both axes, an equation of the x-axis is $y = 0$, and an equation of the y-axis is $x = 0$.

Now Work Problems 21 and 23 ◁

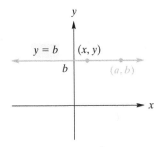

FIGURE 3.9   Horizontal line through (a, b).

From our discussions, we can show that every straight line is the graph of an equation of the form $Ax + By + C = 0$, where A, B, and C are constants and A and B are not both zero. We call this a **general linear equation** (or an *equation of the first degree*) *in the variables x and y,* and x and y are said to be **linearly related.** For example, a general linear equation for $y = 7x - 2$ is $(-7)x + (1)y + (2) = 0$. Conversely, the graph of a general linear equation is a straight line. Table 3.1 gives the various forms of equations of straight lines.

Table 3.1 Forms of Equations of Straight Lines	
Point-slope form	$y - y_1 = m(x - x_1)$
Slope-intercept form	$y = mx + b$
General linear form	$Ax + By + C = 0$
Vertical line	$x = a$
Horizontal line	$y = b$

Example 3 suggests that we could add another entry to the table. For if we know that points (x_1, y_1) and (x_2, y_2) are points on a line, then the slope of that line is $m = \dfrac{y_2 - y_1}{x_2 - x_1}$ and we could say that $y - y_1 = \dfrac{y_2 - y_1}{x_2 - x_1}(x - x_1)$ *is a **two-point form** for an equation of a line passing through points* (x_1, y_1) *and* (x_2, y_2). Whether one chooses to remember many formulas or a few problem-solving principles is very much a matter of individual taste.

APPLY IT ▶

5. Find a general linear form of the Fahrenheit–Celsius conversion equation whose slope-intercept form is $F = \dfrac{9}{5}C + 32$.

EXAMPLE 7 Converting Forms of Equations of Lines

a. Find a general linear form of the line whose slope-intercept form is

$$y = -\frac{2}{3}x + 4$$

Solution: Getting one side to be 0, we obtain

$$\frac{2}{3}x + y - 4 = 0$$

which is a general linear form with $A = \frac{2}{3}$, $B = 1$, and $C = -4$. An alternative general form can be obtained by clearing fractions:

$$2x + 3y - 12 = 0$$

b. Find the slope-intercept form of the line having a general linear form $3x + 4y - 2 = 0$.

Solution: We want the form $y = mx + b$, so we solve the given equation for y. We have

$$3x + 4y - 2 = 0$$
$$4y = -3x + 2$$
$$y = -\frac{3}{4}x + \frac{1}{2}$$

APPLY IT ▶

6. Sketch the graph of the Fahrenheit–Celsius conversion equation that you found in the preceding Apply it. How could you use this graph to convert a Celsius temperature to Fahrenheit?

which is the slope-intercept form. Note that the line has slope $-\frac{3}{4}$ and y-intercept $\frac{1}{2}$.

Now Work Problem 37 ◁

EXAMPLE 8 Graphing a General Linear Equation

Sketch the graph of $2x - 3y + 6 = 0$.

Solution:

Strategy Since this is a general linear equation, its graph is a straight line. Thus, we need only determine two different points on the graph in order to sketch it. We will find the intercepts.

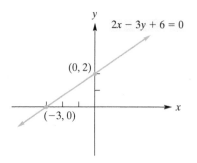

FIGURE 3.10 Graph of $2x - 3y + 6 = 0$.

If $x = 0$, then $-3y + 6 = 0$, so the y-intercept is 2. If $y = 0$, then $2x + 6 = 0$, so the x-intercept is -3. We now draw the line passing through $(0, 2)$ and $(-3, 0)$. (See Figure 3.10.)

Now Work Problem 27 ◁

TECHNOLOGY ▮▮▯▯

To graph the equation of Example 8 with a graphing calculator, we first express y in terms of x:

$$2x - 3y + 6 = 0$$
$$3y = 2x + 6$$
$$y = \frac{1}{3}(2x + 6)$$

Essentially, y is expressed as a function of x; the graph is shown in Figure 3.11.

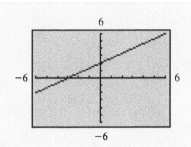

FIGURE 3.11   Calculator graph of $2x - 3y + 6 = 0$.

Parallel and Perpendicular Lines

As stated previously, there is a rule for parallel lines:

> **Parallel Lines**   *Two lines are parallel if and only if they have the same slope or are both vertical.*

It follows that any line is parallel to itself.

There is also a rule for perpendicular lines. Look back to Figure 3.5 and observe that the line with slope $-\frac{1}{2}$ is perpendicular to the line with slope 2. The fact that the slope of either of these lines is the negative reciprocal of the slope of the other line is not a coincidence, as the following rule states.

> **Perpendicular Lines**   *Two lines with slopes m_1 and m_2 are perpendicular to each other if and only if*
>
> $$m_1 = -\frac{1}{m_2}$$
>
> *Moreover, any horizontal line and any vertical line are perpendicular to each other.*

Rather than simply remembering this equation for the perpendicularity condition, observe why it makes sense. For if two lines are perpendicular, with neither vertical, then one will necessarily rise from left to right while the other will fall from left to right. Thus the slopes must have different signs. Also, if one is steep, then the other is relatively flat, which suggests a relationship such as is provided by reciprocals.

APPLY IT ▶

7. Show that a triangle with vertices at $A(0,0)$, $B(6,0)$, and $C(7,7)$ is not a right triangle.

EXAMPLE 9   Parallel and Perpendicular Lines

Figure 3.12 shows two lines passing through $(3, -2)$. One is parallel to the line $y = 3x + 1$, and the other is perpendicular to it. Find equations of these lines.

Solution: The slope of $y = 3x + 1$ is 3. Thus, the line through $(3, -2)$ that is *parallel* to $y = 3x + 1$ also has slope 3. Using a point-slope form, we get

$$y - (-2) = 3(x - 3)$$
$$y + 2 = 3x - 9$$
$$y = 3x - 11$$

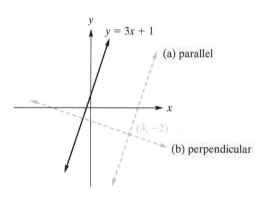

FIGURE 3.12   Lines parallel and perpendicular to $y = 3x + 1$ (Example 9).

The slope of a line *perpendicular* to $y = 3x + 1$ must be $-\frac{1}{3}$ (the negative reciprocal of 3). Using a point-slope form, we get

$$y - (-2) = -\frac{1}{3}(x - 3)$$

$$y + 2 = -\frac{1}{3}x + 1$$

$$y = -\frac{1}{3}x - 1$$

Now Work Problem 55 ◁

PROBLEMS 3.1

In Problems 1–8, find the slope of the straight line that passes through the given points.

1. $(3, 2), (7, 10)$ **2.** $(-2, 10), (5, 3)$

3. $(6, -2), (8, -3)$ **4.** $(2, -4), (3, -4)$

5. $(5, 3), (5, -8)$ **6.** $(0, -4), (3, 6)$

7. $(5, -2), (4, -2)$ **8.** $(1, -7), (9, 0)$

In Problems 9–24, find a general linear equation $(Ax + By + C = 0)$ of the straight line that has the indicated properties, and sketch each line.

9. Passes through $(-1, 7)$ and has slope -5

10. Passes through the origin and has slope 75

11. Passes through $(-5, 5)$ and has slope $-\frac{1}{2}$

12. Passes through $(-\frac{5}{2}, 5)$ and has slope $\frac{1}{3}$

13. Passes through $(-6, 1)$ and $(1, 4)$

14. Passes through $(5, 2)$ and $(6, -4)$

15. Passes through $(-3, -4)$ and $(-2, -8)$

16. Passes through $(0, 0)$ and $(-3, -2)$

17. Has slope 2 and y-intercept 4

18. Has slope 5 and y-intercept -7

19. Has slope $-\frac{1}{2}$ and y-intercept -3

20. Has slope 0 and y-intercept $-\frac{1}{2}$

21. Is horizontal and passes through $(-2, -5)$

22. Is vertical and passes through $(-1, -1)$

23. Passes through $(2, -3)$ and is vertical

24. Passes through the origin and is horizontal

In Problems 25–34, find, if possible, the slope and y-intercept of the straight line determined by the equation, and sketch the graph.

25. $y = 4x - 6$ **26.** $x + 9 = 2$

27. $3x + 5y - 9 = 0$ **28.** $y + 4 = 7$

29. $x = -5$ **30.** $x - 9 = 5y + 3$

31. $y = -2x$ **32.** $y - 7 = 3(x - 4)$

33. $y = 3$ **34.** $6y - 24 = 0$

In Problems 35–40, find a general linear form and the slope-intercept form of the given equation.

35. $2x = 5 - 3y$ **36.** $5x - 2y = 10$

37. $4x + 9y - 5 = 0$ **38.** $3(x - 4) - 7(y + 1) = 2$

39. $-\frac{x}{2} + \frac{2y}{3} = -4\frac{3}{4}$ **40.** $y = \frac{1}{300}x + 8$

In Problems 41–50, determine whether the lines are parallel, perpendicular, or neither.

41. $y = -5x + 7, \ y = -5x - 3$

42. $y = 4x + 3, \ y = 5 + 4x$

43. $y = 5x + 2, \ -5x + y - 3 = 0$

44. $y = x, \ y = -x$

45. $x + 3y + 5 = 0, \ y = -3x$

46. $x + 2y = 0, \ x + 4y - 4 = 0$

47. $y = 3, \ x = -\frac{1}{3}$

48. $x = 3, \ x = -3$

49. $3x + y = 4, \ x - 3y + 1 = 0$

50. $x - 2 = 3, \ y = 2$

In Problems 51–60, find an equation of the line satisfying the given conditions. Give the answer in slope-intercept form if possible.

51. Passing through $(2, 3)$ and parallel to $y = 4x + 3$

52. Passing through $(2, -8)$ and parallel to $x = -4$

53. Passing through $(2, 1)$ and parallel to $y = 2$

54. Passing through $(3, -4)$ and parallel to $y = 3 + 2x$

55. Perpendicular to $y = 3x - 5$ and passing through $(3, 4)$

56. Perpendicular to $3x + 2y - 4 = 0$ and passing through $(3, 1)$

57. Passing through $(5, 2)$ and perpendicular to $y = -3$

58. Passing through $(4, -5)$ and perpendicular to the line
$$3y = -\frac{2x}{5} + 3$$

59. Passing through $(-7, -5)$ and parallel to the line
$2x + 3y + 6 = 0$

60. Passing through $(-4, 10)$ and parallel to the y-axis

61. A straight line passes through $(-1, -2)$ and $(4, 1)$. Find the point on it that has an x-coordinate of 3.

62. A straight line has slope 3 and y-intercept $(0, 1)$. Does the point $(-1, -2)$ lie on the line?

63. Stock In 1996, the stock in a computer hardware company traded for $37 per share. However, the company was in trouble and the stock price dropped steadily, to $8 per share in 2006. Draw a line showing the relationship between the price per share and the year in which it traded for the time interval [1996, 2006], with years on the x-axis and price on the y-axis. Find and interpret the slope.

In Problems 64–65, find an equation of the line describing the following information.

64. Home Runs In one season, a major league baseball player has hit 14 home runs by the end of the third month and 20 home runs by the end of the fifth month.

65. Business A delicatessen owner starts her business with debts of $100,000. After operating for five years, she has accumulated a profit of $40,000.

66. Due Date The length, L, of a human fetus more than 12 weeks old can be estimated by the formula $L = 1.53t - 6.7$, where L is in centimeters and t is in weeks from conception. An obstetrician uses the length of a fetus, measured by ultrasound, to determine the approximate age of the fetus and establish a due date for the mother. The formula must be rewritten to result in an age, t, given a fetal length, L. Find the slope and L-intercept of the equation.

67. Discus Throw A mathematical model can approximate the winning distance for the Olympic discus throw by the

formula $d = 184 + t$, where d is in feet and $t = 0$ corresponds to the year 1948. Find a general linear form of this equation.

68. Campus Map A coordinate map of a college campus gives the coordinates (x, y) of three major buildings as follows: computer center, $(3.5, -1.5)$; engineering lab, $(0.5, 0.5)$; and library $(-1, -2.5)$. Find the equations (in slope-intercept form) of the straight-line paths connecting (a) the engineering lab with the computer center and (b) the engineering lab with the library. Are these two paths perpendicular to each other?

69. Geometry Show that the points $A(0, 0)$, $B(0, 4)$, $C(2, 3)$, and $D(2, 7)$ are the vertices of a parallelogram. (Opposite sides of a parallelogram are parallel.)

70. Approach Angle A small plane is landing at an airport with an approach angle of 45 degrees, or slope of -1. The plane begins its descent when it has an elevation of 3600 feet. Find the equation that describes the relationship between the craft's altitude and distance traveled, assuming that at distance 0 it starts the approach angle. Graph your equation on a graphing calculator. What does the graph tell you about the approach if the airport is 3800 feet from where the plane starts its landing?

71. Cost Equation The average daily cost, C, for a room at a city hospital has risen by $59.82 per year for the years 1990 through 2000. If the average cost in 1996 was $1128.50, what is an equation which describes the average cost during this decade, as a function of the number of years, T, since 1990?

72. Revenue Equation A small business predicts its revenue growth by a straight-line method with a slope of $50,000 per year. In its fifth year, it had revenues of $330,000. Find an equation that describes the relationship between revenues, R, and the number of years, T, since it opened for business.

73. Graph $y = -0.9x + 7.3$ and verify that the y-intercept is 7.3.

74. Graph the lines whose equations are

$$y = 1.5x + 1$$
$$y = 1.5x - 1$$

and

$$y = 1.5x + 2.5$$

What do you observe about the orientation of these lines? Why would you expect this result from the equations of the lines themselves?

75. Graph the line $y = 7.1x + 5.4$. Find the coordinates of any two points on the line, and use them to estimate the slope. What is the actual slope of the line?

76. Show that if a line has x-intercept a and y-intercept b, both different from 0, then $\frac{x}{a} + \frac{y}{b} = 1$ is an equation of the line.

Objective

To develop the notion of demand and supply curves and to introduce linear functions.

3.2 Applications and Linear Functions

Many situations in economics can be described by using straight lines, as evidenced by Example 1.

EXAMPLE 1 Production Levels

Suppose that a manufacturer uses 100 lb of material to produce products A and B, which require 4 lb and 2 lb of material per unit, respectively. If x and y denote the number of units produced of A and B, respectively, then all levels of production are given by the

APPLY IT ▶

8. A sporting-goods manufacturer allocates 1000 units of time per day to make skis and ski boots. If it takes 8 units of time to make a ski and 14 units of time to make a boot, find an equation to describe all possible production levels of the two products.

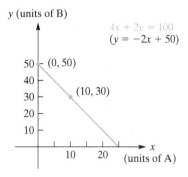

FIGURE 3.13   Linearly related production levels.

CAUTION! ⚠

Typically, a demand curve falls from left to right and a supply curve rises from left to right. However, there are exceptions. For example, the demand for insulin could be represented by a vertical line, since this demand can remain constant regardless of price.

combinations of x and y that satisfy the equation

$$4x + 2y = 100 \qquad \text{where } x,\ y \geq 0$$

Thus, the levels of production of A and B are linearly related. Solving for y gives

$$y = -2x + 50 \qquad \text{slope-intercept form}$$

so the slope is -2. The slope reflects the rate of change of the level of production of B with respect to the level of production of A. For example, if 1 more unit of A is to be produced, it will require 4 more pounds of material, resulting in $\frac{4}{2} = 2$ *fewer* units of B. Accordingly, as x increases by 1 unit, the corresponding value of y decreases by 2 units. To sketch the graph of $y = -2x + 50$, we can use the y-intercept $(0, 50)$ and the fact that when $x = 10, y = 30$. (See Figure 3.13.)

Now Work Problem 21 ◁

Demand and Supply Curves

For each price level of a product, there is a corresponding quantity of that product that consumers will demand (that is, purchase) during some time period. Usually, the higher the price, the smaller is the quantity demanded; as the price falls, the quantity demanded increases. If the price per unit of the product is given by p and the corresponding quantity (in units) is given by q, then an equation relating p and q is called a **demand equation.** Its graph is called a **demand curve.** Figure 3.14(a) shows a demand curve. In keeping with the practice of most economists, the horizontal axis is the q-axis and the vertical axis is the p-axis. We will assume that the price per unit is given in dollars and the period is one week. Thus, the point (a, b) in Figure 3.14(a) indicates that, at a price of b dollars per unit, consumers will demand a units per week. Since negative prices or quantities are not meaningful, both a and b must be nonnegative. For most products, an increase in the quantity demanded corresponds to a decrease in price. Thus, a demand curve typically falls from left to right, as in Figure 3.14(a).

In response to various prices, there is a corresponding quantity of product that *producers* are willing to supply to the market during some time period. Usually, the higher the price per unit, the larger is the quantity that producers are willing to supply; as the price falls, so will the quantity supplied. If p denotes the price per unit and q denotes the corresponding quantity, then an equation relating p and q is called a **supply equation,** and its graph is called a **supply curve.** Figure 3.14(b) shows a supply curve. If p is in dollars and the period is one week, then the point (c, d) indicates that, at a price of d dollars each, producers will supply c units per week. As before, c and d are nonnegative. A supply curve usually rises from left to right, as in Figure 3.14(b). This indicates that a producer will supply more of a product at higher prices.

Observe that a function whose graph either falls from left to right or rises from left to right *throughout its entire domain* will pass the horizontal line test of Section 2.5. Certainly, the demand curve and the supply curve in Figure 3.15 are each cut at most once by any horizontal line. Thus if the demand curve is the graph of a function $p = D(q)$,

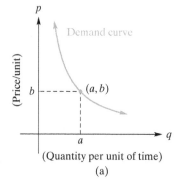

(a)

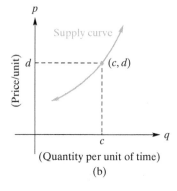

(b)

FIGURE 3.14   Demand and supply curves.

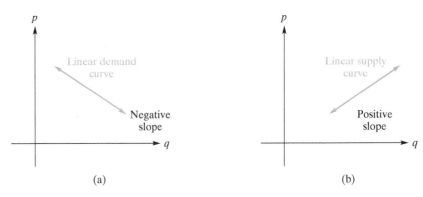

FIGURE 3.15   Linear demand and supply curves.

then D will have an inverse and we can solve for q uniquely to get $q = D^{-1}(p)$. Similarly, if the supply curve is the graph of a function $p = S(q)$, then S is also one-to-one, has an inverse S^{-1}, and we can write $q = S^{-1}(p)$.

We will now focus on demand and supply curves that are straight lines (Figure 3.15). They are called *linear* demand and *linear* supply curves. Such curves have equations in which p and q are linearly related. Because a demand curve typically falls from left to right, a linear demand curve has a negative slope. [See Figure 3.15(a).] However, the slope of a linear supply curve is positive, because the curve rises from left to right. [See Figure 3.15(b).]

EXAMPLE 2   Finding a Demand Equation

Suppose the demand per week for a product is 100 units when the price is \$58 per unit and 200 units at \$51 each. Determine the demand equation, assuming that it is linear.

Solution:

Strategy   Since the demand equation is linear, the demand curve must be a straight line. We are given that quantity q and price p are linearly related such that $p = 58$ when $q = 100$ and $p = 51$ when $q = 200$. Thus, the given data can be represented in a q,p-coordinate plane [see Figure 3.15(a)] by points $(100, 58)$ and $(200, 51)$. With these points, we can find an equation of the line—that is, the demand equation.

The slope of the line passing through $(100, 58)$ and $(200, 51)$ is

$$m = \frac{51 - 58}{200 - 100} = -\frac{7}{100}$$

An equation of the line (point-slope form) is

$$p - p_1 = m(q - q_1)$$

$$p - 58 = -\frac{7}{100}(q - 100)$$

Simplifying gives the demand equation

$$p = -\frac{7}{100}q + 65 \qquad (1)$$

Customarily, a demand equation (as well as a supply equation) expresses p, in terms of q and actually defines a function of q. For example, Equation (1) defines p as a function of q and is called the *demand function* for the product. (See Figure 3.16.)

Now Work Problem 15 ◁

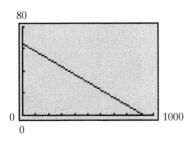

FIGURE 3.16   Graph of demand function $p = -\frac{7}{100}q + 65$.

Linear Functions

A *linear function* was defined in Section 2.2 to be a polynomial function of degree 1. Somewhat more explicitly,

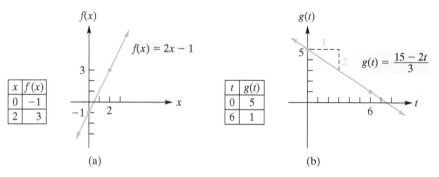

FIGURE 3.17   Graphs of linear functions.

> **Definition**
>
> A function f is a *linear function* if and only if $f(x)$ can be written in the form $f(x) = ax + b$, where a and b are constants and $a \neq 0$.

Suppose that $f(x) = ax + b$ is a linear function, and let $y = f(x)$. Then $y = ax + b$, which is an equation of a straight line with slope a and y-intercept b. Thus, **the graph of a linear function is a straight line that is neither vertical nor horizontal.** We say that the function $f(x) = ax + b$ has slope a.

EXAMPLE 3   Graphing Linear Functions

a. Graph $f(x) = 2x - 1$.

APPLY IT ▶

10. A computer repair company charges a fixed amount plus an hourly rate for a service call. If x is the number of hours needed for a service call, the total cost of a call is described by the function $f(x) = 40x + 60$. Graph the function by finding and plotting two points.

Solution: Here f is a linear function (with slope 2), so its graph is a straight line. Since two points determine a straight line, we need only plot two points and then draw a line through them. [See Figure 3.17(a).] Note that one of the points plotted is the vertical-axis intercept, -1, which occurs when $x = 0$.

b. Graph $g(t) = \dfrac{15 - 2t}{3}$.

Solution: Notice that g is a linear function, because we can express it in the form $g(t) = at + b$.

$$g(t) = \frac{15 - 2t}{3} = \frac{15}{3} - \frac{2t}{3} = -\frac{2}{3}t + 5$$

The graph of g is shown in Figure 3.17(b). Since the slope is $-\frac{2}{3}$, observe that as t increases by 3 units, $g(t)$ *decreases* by 2.

Now Work Problem 3 ◁

EXAMPLE 4   Determining a Linear Function

APPLY IT ▶

11. The height of children between the ages of 6 years and 10 years can be modeled by a linear function of age t in years. The height of one child changes by 2.3 inches per year, and she is 50.6 inches tall at age 8. Find a function that describes the height of this child at age t.

Suppose f is a linear function with slope 2 and $f(4) = 8$. Find f(x).

Solution: Since f is linear, it has the form $f(x) = ax + b$. The slope is 2, so $a = 2$, and we have

$$f(x) = 2x + b \qquad (2)$$

Now we determine b. Since $f(4) = 8$, we replace x by 4 in Equation (2) and solve for b:

$$f(4) = 2(4) + b$$
$$8 = 8 + b$$
$$0 = b$$

Hence, $f(x) = 2x$.

Now Work Problem 7 ◁

APPLY IT ▶

12. An antique necklace is expected to be worth $360 after 3 years and $640 after 7 years. Find a function that describes the value of the necklace after x years.

EXAMPLE 5   Determining a Linear Function

If $y = f(x)$ is a linear function such that $f(-2) = 6$ and $f(1) = -3$, find f(x).

Solution:

Strategy   The function values correspond to points on the graph of f. With these points we can determine an equation of the line and hence the linear function.

The condition that $f(-2) = 6$ means that when $x = -2$, then $y = 6$. Thus, $(-2, 6)$ lies on the graph of f, which is a straight line. Similarly, $f(1) = -3$ implies that $(1, -3)$ also lies on the line. If we set $(x_1, y_1) = (-2, 6)$ and $(x_2, y_2) = (1, -3)$, the slope of the line is given by

$$m = \frac{y_2 - y_1}{x_2 - x_1} = \frac{-3 - 6}{1 - (-2)} = \frac{-9}{3} = -3$$

We can find an equation of the line by using a point-slope form:

$$y - y_1 = m(x - x_1)$$
$$y - 6 = -3[x - (-2)]$$
$$y - 6 = -3x - 6$$
$$y = -3x$$

Because $y = f(x)$, $f(x) = -3x$. Of course, the same result is obtained if we set $(x_1, y_1) = (1, -3)$.

Now Work Problem 9 ◁

In many studies, data are collected and plotted on a coordinate system. An analysis of the results may indicate a functional relationship between the variables involved. For example, the data points may be approximated by points on a straight line. This would indicate a linear functional relationship, such as the one in the next example.

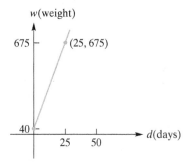

FIGURE 3.18   Linear function describing diet for hens.

EXAMPLE 6   Diet for Hens

In testing an experimental diet for hens, it was determined that the average live weight w (in grams) of a hen was statistically a linear function of the number of days d after the diet began, where $0 \le d \le 50$. Suppose the average weight of a hen beginning the diet was 40 grams and 25 days later it was 675 grams.

a. Determine w as a linear function of d.

Solution: Since w is a linear function of d, its graph is a straight line. When $d = 0$ (the beginning of the diet), $w = 40$. Thus, $(0, 40)$ lies on the graph. (See Figure 3.18.) Similarly, $(25, 675)$ lies on the graph. If we set $(d_1, w_1) = (0, 40)$ and $(d_2, w_2) = (25, 675)$, the slope of the line is

$$m = \frac{w_2 - w_1}{d_2 - d_1} = \frac{675 - 40}{25 - 0} = \frac{635}{25} = \frac{127}{5}$$

Using a point-slope form, we have

$$w - w_1 = m(d - d_1)$$
$$w - 40 = \frac{127}{5}(d - 0)$$
$$w - 40 = \frac{127}{5}d$$
$$w = \frac{127}{5}d + 40$$

which expresses w as a linear function of d.

b. Find the average weight of a hen when $d = 10$.

Solution: When $d = 10, w = \frac{127}{5}(10) + 40 = 254 + 40 = 294$. Thus, the average weight of a hen 10 days after the beginning of the diet is 294 grams.

Now Work Problem 19 ◁

PROBLEMS 3.2

In Problems 1–6, find the slope and vertical-axis intercept of the linear function, and sketch the graph.

1. $y = f(x) = -4x$

2. $y = f(x) = x + 1$

3. $h(t) = 5t - 7$

4. $f(s) = 3(5 - s)$

5. $p(q) = \dfrac{5 - q}{3}$

6. $h(q) = 0.5q + 0.25$

In Problems 7–14, find f(x) if f is a linear function that has the given properties.

7. slope $= 4, f(2) = 8$

8. $f(0) = 3, f(4) = -5$

9. $f(1) = 2, f(-2) = 8$

10. slope $= -5, f(\frac{1}{4}) = 9$

11. slope $= -\frac{2}{3}, f(-\frac{2}{3}) = -\frac{2}{3}$

12. $f(1) = 1, f(2) = 2$

13. $f(-2) = -1, f(-4) = -3$

14. slope $= 0.01, f(0.1) = 0.01$

15. Demand Equation   Suppose consumers will demand 60 units of a product when the price is $15.30 per unit and 35 units when the price is $19.30 each. Find the demand equation, assuming that it is linear. Find the price per unit when 40 units are demanded.

16. Demand Equation   The demand per week for a CD is 26,000 copies when the price is $12 each, and 10,000 copies when the price is $18 each. Find the demand equation for the CD, assuming that it is linear.

17. Supply Equation   A refrigerator manufacturer will produce 3000 units when the price is $940, and 2200 units when the price is $740. Assume that price, p, and quantity, q, produced are linearly related and find the supply equation.

18. Supply Equation   Suppose a manufacturer of shoes will place on the market 50 (thousand pairs) when the price is 35 (dollars per pair) and 35 when the price is 30. Find the supply equation, assuming that price p and quantity q are linearly related.

19. Cost Equation   Suppose the cost to produce 10 units of a product is $40 and the cost of 20 units is $70. If cost, c, is linearly related to output, q, find a linear equation relating c and q. Find the cost to produce 35 units.

20. Cost Equation   An advertiser goes to a printer and is charged $89 for 100 copies of one flyer and $93 for 200 copies of another flyer. This printer charges a fixed setup cost plus a charge for every copy of single-page flyers. Find a function that describes the cost of a printing job, if x is the number of copies made.

21. Electric Rates   An electric utility company charges residential customers 12.5 cents per kilowatt-hour plus a base charge each month. One customer's monthly bill comes to $51.65 for 380 kilowatt-hours. Find a linear function that describes the

total monthly charges for electricity if x is the number of kilowatt-hours used in a month.

22. Radiation Therapy   A cancer patient is to receive drug and radiation therapies. Each cubic centimeter of the drug to be used contains 210 curative units, and each minute of radiation exposure gives 305 curative units. The patient requires 2410 curative units. If d cubic centimeters of the drug and r minutes of radiation are administered, determine an equation relating d and r. Graph the equation for $d \geq 0$, and $r \geq 0$; label the horizontal axis as d.

23. Depreciation   Suppose the value of a mountain bike decreases each year by 10% of its original value. If the original value is $1800, find an equation that expresses the value v of the bike t years after purchase, where $0 \leq t \leq 10$. Sketch the equation, choosing t as the horizontal axis and v as the vertical axis. What is the slope of the resulting line? This method of considering the value of equipment is called *straight-line depreciation*.

24. Depreciation   A new television depreciates $120 per year, and it is worth $340 after four years. Find a function that describes the value of this television, if x is the age of the television in years.

25. Appreciation   A new house was sold for $1,183,000 six years after it was built and purchased. The original owners calculated that the house appreciated $53,000 per year while they owned it. Find a linear function that describes the appreciation of the building, in thousands of dollars, if x is the number of years since the original purchase.

26. Appreciation   A house purchased for $245,000 is expected to double in value in 15 years. Find a linear equation that describes the house's value after t years.

27. Repair Charges   A business-copier repair company charges a fixed amount plus an hourly rate for a service call. If a customer is billed $159 for a one-hour service call and $287 for a three-hour service call, find a linear function that describes the price of a service call, where x is the number of hours of service.

28. Sheep Wool Length   For sheep maintained at high environmental temperatures, respiratory rate, r (per minute), increases as wool length, l (in centimeters), decreases.[2] Suppose sheep with a wool length of 2 cm have an (average) respiratory rate of 160, and those with a wool length of 4 cm have a respiratory rate of 125. Assume that r and l are linearly related. (a) Find an equation that gives r in terms of l. (b) Find the respiratory rate of sheep with a wool length of 1 cm.

29. Isocost Line   In production analysis, an *isocost line* is a line whose points represent all combinations of two factors of production that can be purchased for the same amount. Suppose a farmer has allocated $20,000 for the purchase of x tons of fertilizer (costing $200 per ton) and y acres of land (costing $2000 per acre). Find an equation of the isocost line that describes the

---

[2]Adapted from G. E. Folk, Jr., *Textbook of Environmental Physiology*, 2nd ed. (Philadelphia: Lea & Febiger, 1974).

various combinations that can be purchased for $20,000. Observe that neither x nor y can be negative.

30. Isoprofit Line   A manufacturer produces products X and Y for which the profits per unit are $7 and $8, respectively. If x units of X and y units of Y are sold, then the total profit P is given by $P = P(x, y) = 7x + 8y$, where $x, y \geq 0$. (a) Sketch the graph of this equation for $P = 260$. The result is called an *isoprofit line*, and its points represent all combinations of sales that produce a profit of $260. [It is an example of a *level curve* for the function $P(x, y) = 7x + 8y$ of two variables as introduced in Section 2.8.] (b) Determine the slope for $P = 260$. (c) For $P = 860$, determine the slope. (d) Are isoprofit lines always parallel?

31. Grade Scaling   For reasons of comparison, a professor wants to rescale the scores on a set of test papers so that the maximum score is still 100, but the average is 65 instead of 56. (a) Find a linear equation that will do this. [*Hint:* You want 56 to become 65 and 100 to remain 100. Consider the points (56, 65) and (100, 100) and, more generally, (x, y), where x is the old score and y is the new score. Find the slope and use a point-slope form. Express y in terms of x.] (b) If 62 on the new scale is the lowest passing score, what was the lowest passing score on the original scale?

32. Psychology   The result of Sternberg's psychological experiment[3] on information retrieval is that a person's reaction time R, in milliseconds, is statistically a linear function of memory set size N as follows:

$$R = 38N + 397$$

Sketch the graph for $1 \leq N \leq 5$. What is the slope?

33. Psychology   In a certain learning experiment involving repetition and memory,[4] the proportion, p, of items recalled was estimated to be linearly related to the effective study time, t (in seconds), where t is between 5 and 9. For an effective study time of 5 seconds, the proportion of items recalled was 0.32.

For each 1-second increase in study time, the proportion recalled increased by 0.059. (a) Find an equation that gives p in terms of t. (b) What proportion of items was recalled with 9 seconds of effective study time?

34. Diet for Pigs   In testing an experimental diet for pigs, it was determined that the (average) live weight, w (in kilograms), of a pig was statistically a linear function of the number of days, d, after the diet was initiated, where $0 \leq d \leq 100$. If the weight of a pig beginning the diet was 21 kg, and thereafter the pig gained 6.3 kg every 10 days, determine w as a function of d, and find the weight of a pig 55 days after the beginning of the diet.

35. Cricket Chirps   Biologists have found that the number of chirps made per minute by crickets of a certain species is related to the temperature. The relationship is very close to being linear. At 68°F, the crickets chirp about 124 times a minute. At 80°F, they chirp about 172 times a minute. (a) Find an equation that gives Fahrenheit temperature, t, in terms of the number of chirps, c, per minute. (b) If you count chirps for only 15 seconds, how can you quickly estimate the temperature?

To sketch parabolas arising from quadratic functions.

3.3 Quadratic Functions

In Section 2.2, a *quadratic function* was defined as a polynomial function of degree 2. In other words,

> **Definition**
>
> A function f is a **quadratic function** if and only if $f(x)$ can be written in the form $f(x) = ax^2 + bx + c$, where a, b, and c are constants and $a \neq 0$.

For example, the functions $f(x) = x^2 - 3x + 2$ and $F(t) = -3t^2$ are quadratic. However, $g(x) = \dfrac{1}{x^2}$ is *not* quadratic, because it cannot be written in the form $g(x) = ax^2 + bx + c$.

---

[3]G. R. Loftus and E. F. Loftus, *Human Memory: The Processing of Information* (New York: Lawrence Erlbaum Associates, Inc., distributed by the Halsted Press, Division of John Wiley & Sons, Inc., 1976).

[4]D. L. Hintzman, "Repetition and Learning," in *The Psychology of Learning,* Vol. 10, ed. G. H. Bower (New York: Academic Press, Inc., 1976), p. 77.

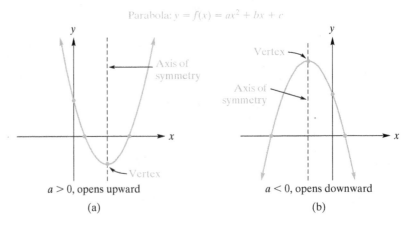

FIGURE 3.19   Parabolas.

The graph of the quadratic function $y = f(x) = ax^2 + bx + c$ is called a **parabola** and has a shape like the curves in Figure 3.19. If $a > 0$, the graph extends upward indefinitely, and we say that the parabola *opens upward* [Figure 3.19(a)]. If $a < 0$, the parabola *opens downward* [Figure 3.19(b)].

Each parabola in Figure 3.19 is *symmetric* about a vertical line, called the **axis of symmetry** of the parabola. That is, if the page were folded on one of these lines, then the two halves of the corresponding parabola would coincide. The axis (of symmetry) is *not* part of the parabola, but is a useful aid in sketching the parabola.

Each part of Figure 3.19 shows a point labeled **vertex,** where the axis cuts the parabola. If $a > 0$, the vertex is the "lowest" point on the parabola. This means that $f(x)$ has a minimum value at this point. By performing algebraic manipulations on $ax^2 + bx + c$ (referred to as *completing the square*), we can determine not only this minimum value, but also where it occurs. We have

$$f(x) = ax^2 + bx + c = (ax^2 + bx) + c$$

Adding and subtracting $\dfrac{b^2}{4a}$ gives

$$f(x) = \left(ax^2 + bx + \frac{b^2}{4a} \right) + c - \frac{b^2}{4a}$$

$$= a \left(x^2 + \frac{b}{a}x + \frac{b^2}{4a^2} \right) + c - \frac{b^2}{4a}$$

so that

$$f(x) = a \left(x + \frac{b}{2a} \right)^2 + c - \frac{b^2}{4a}$$

Since $\left(x + \dfrac{b}{2a} \right)^2 \geq 0$ and $a > 0$, it follows that $f(x)$ has a minimum value when $x + \dfrac{b}{2a} = 0$; that is, when $x = -\dfrac{b}{2a}$. The y-coordinate corresponding to this value of x is $f\left(-\dfrac{b}{2a} \right)$. Thus, the vertex is given by

$$\text{vertex} = \left(-\frac{b}{2a}, f\left(-\frac{b}{2a} \right) \right)$$

This is also the vertex of a parabola that opens downward ($a < 0$), but in this case $f\left(-\dfrac{b}{2a} \right)$ is the maximum value of $f(x)$. [See Figure 3.19(b).]

Observe that a function whose graph is a parabola is not one-to-one, in either the opening upward or opening downward case, since many horizontal lines will cut the graph twice. However, if we restrict the domain of a quadratic function to either

$\left[-\dfrac{b}{2a}, \infty\right)$ or $\left(-\infty, -\dfrac{b}{2a}\right]$, then the restricted function will pass the horizontal line test and therefore be one-to-one. (There are many other restrictions of a quadratic function that are one-to-one; however, their domains consist of more than one interval.) It follows that such restricted quadratic functions have inverse functions.

The point where the parabola $y = ax^2 + bx + c$ intersects the y-axis (that is, the y-intercept) occurs when $x = 0$. The y-coordinate of this point is c, so the y-intercept is c. In summary, we have the following.

Graph of Quadratic Function

The graph of the quadratic function $y = f(x) = ax^2 + bx + c$ is a parabola.

1. If $a > 0$, the parabola opens upward. If $a < 0$, it opens downward.
2. The vertex is $\left(-\dfrac{b}{2a},\ f\left(-\dfrac{b}{2a}\right)\right)$.
3. The y-intercept is c.

We can quickly sketch the graph of a quadratic function by first locating the vertex, the y-intercept, and a few other points, such as those where the parabola intersects the x-axis. These *x-intercepts* are found by setting $y = 0$ and solving for x. Once the intercepts and vertex are found, it is then relatively easy to pass the appropriate parabola through these points. In the event that the x-intercepts are very close to the vertex or that no x-intercepts exist, we find a point on each side of the vertex, so that we can give a reasonable sketch of the parabola. Keep in mind that passing a (dashed) vertical line through the vertex gives the axis of symmetry. By plotting points to one side of the axis, we can use symmetry and obtain corresponding points on the other side.

APPLY IT ▶

13. A car dealership believes that the daily profit from the sale of minivans is given by $P(x) = -x^2 + 2x + 399$, where x is the number of minivans sold. Find the function's vertex and intercepts, and graph the function. If their model is correct, comment on the viability of dealing in minivans.

EXAMPLE 1 Graphing a Quadratic Function

Graph the quadratic function $y = f(x) = -x^2 - 4x + 12$.

Solution: Here $a = -1$, $b = -4$, and $c = 12$. Since $a < 0$, the parabola opens downward and thus has a highest point. The x-coordinate of the vertex is

$$-\frac{b}{2a} = -\frac{-4}{2(-1)} = -2$$

The y-coordinate is $f(-2) = -(-2)^2 - 4(-2) + 12 = 16$. Thus, the vertex is $(-2, 16)$, so the maximum value of $f(x)$ is 16. Since $c = 12$, the y-intercept is 12. To find the x-intercepts, we let y be 0 in $y = -x^2 - 4x + 12$ and solve for x:

$$0 = -x^2 - 4x + 12$$
$$0 = -(x^2 + 4x - 12)$$
$$0 = -(x + 6)(x - 2)$$

Hence, $x = -6$ or $x = 2$, so the x-intercepts are -6 and 2. Now we plot the vertex, axis of symmetry, and intercepts. [See Figure 3.20(a).] Since $(0, 12)$ is *two* units to the *right* of the axis of symmetry, there is a corresponding point *two* units to the *left* of the axis with the same y-coordinate. Thus, we get the point $(-4, 12)$. Through all points, we draw a parabola opening downward. [See Figure 3.20(b).]

Now Work Problem 15 ◁

EXAMPLE 2 Graphing a Quadratic Function

Graph $p = 2q^2$.

Solution: Here p is a quadratic function of q, where $a = 2$, $b = 0$, and $c = 0$. Since $a > 0$, the parabola opens upward and thus has a lowest point. The q-coordinate of the

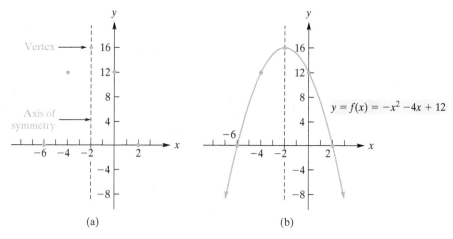

FIGURE 3.20   Graph of parabola $y = f(x) = -x^2 - 4x + 12$.

vertex is

$$-\frac{b}{2a} = -\frac{0}{2(2)} = 0$$

and the p-coordinate is $2(0)^2 = 0$. Consequently, the *minimum* value of p is 0 and the vertex is $(0, 0)$. In this case, the p-axis is the axis of symmetry. A parabola opening upward with vertex at $(0, 0)$ cannot have any other intercepts. Hence, to draw a reasonable graph, we plot a point on each side of the vertex. If $q = 2$, then $p = 8$. This gives the point $(2, 8)$ and, by symmetry, the point $(-2, 8)$. (See Figure 3.21.)

Now Work Problem 13 ◁

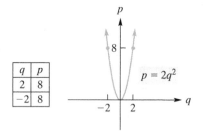

FIGURE 3.21   Graph of parabola $p = 2q^2$.

Example 3 illustrates that finding intercepts may require use of the quadratic formula.

EXAMPLE 3   **Graphing a Quadratic Function**

Graph $g(x) = x^2 - 6x + 7$.

Solution: Here g is a quadratic function, where $a = 1, b = -6$, and $c = 7$. The parabola opens upward, because $a > 0$. The x-coordinate of the vertex (lowest point) is

$$-\frac{b}{2a} = -\frac{-6}{2(1)} = 3$$

and $g(3) = 3^2 - 6(3) + 7 = -2$, which is the minimum value of $g(x)$. Thus, the vertex is $(3, -2)$. Since $c = 7$, the vertical-axis intercept is 7. To find x-intercepts, we set $g(x) = 0$.

$$0 = x^2 - 6x + 7$$

The right side does not factor easily, so we will use the quadratic formula to solve for x:

$$x = \frac{-b \pm \sqrt{b^2 - 4ac}}{2a} = \frac{-(-6) \pm \sqrt{(-6)^2 - 4(1)(7)}}{2(1)}$$

$$= \frac{6 \pm \sqrt{8}}{2} = \frac{6 \pm \sqrt{4 \cdot 2}}{2} = \frac{6 \pm 2\sqrt{2}}{2}$$

$$= \frac{6}{2} \pm \frac{2\sqrt{2}}{2} = 3 \pm \sqrt{2}$$

APPLY IT ▶

14. A man standing on a pitcher's mound throws a ball straight up with an initial velocity of 32 feet per second. The height h of the ball in feet t seconds after it was thrown is described by the function $h(t) = -16t^2 + 32t + 8$, for $t \geq 0$. Find the function's vertex and intercepts, and graph the function.

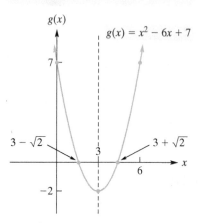

FIGURE 3.22   Graph of parabola $g(x) = x^2 - 6x + 7$.

Therefore, the x-intercepts are $3 + \sqrt{2}$ and $3 - \sqrt{2}$. After plotting the vertex, intercepts, and (by symmetry) the point $(6, 7)$, we draw a parabola opening upward in Figure 3.22.

Now Work Problem 17 ◁

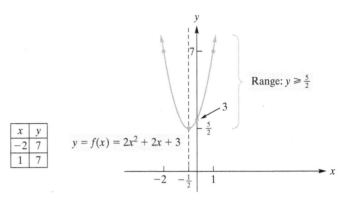

FIGURE 3.23   Graph of $y = f(x) = 2x^2 + 2x + 3$.

EXAMPLE 4   Graphing a Quadratic Function

Graph $y = f(x) = 2x^2 + 2x + 3$ and find the range of f.

Solution: This function is quadratic with $a = 2, b = 2$, and $c = 3$. Since $a > 0$, the graph is a parabola opening upward. The x-coordinate of the vertex is

$$-\frac{b}{2a} = -\frac{2}{2(2)} = -\frac{1}{2}$$

and the y-coordinate is $2(-\frac{1}{2})^2 + 2(-\frac{1}{2}) + 3 = \frac{5}{2}$. Thus, the vertex is $(-\frac{1}{2}, \frac{5}{2})$. Since $c = 3$, the y-intercept is 3. A parabola opening upward with its vertex above the x-axis has no x-intercepts. In Figure 3.23 we plotted the y-intercept, the vertex, and an additional point $(-2, 7)$ to the left of the vertex. By symmetry, we also get the point $(1, 7)$. Passing a parabola through these points gives the desired graph. From the figure, we see that the range of f is all $y \geq \frac{5}{2}$, that is, the interval $[\frac{5}{2}, \infty)$.

Now Work Problem 21 ◁

EXAMPLE 5   Finding and Graphing an Inverse

For the parabola given by the function

$$y = f(x) = ax^2 + bx + c$$

determine the inverse of the restricted function given by $g(x) = ax^2 + bx + c$, for $x \geq -\frac{b}{2a}$. Graph g and g^{-1} in the same plane, in the case where $a = 2, b = 2$, and $c = 3$.

Solution: Following the procedure described in Example 5 of Section 2.4, we begin by solving $y = ax^2 + bx + c$, where $x \geq -\frac{b}{2a}$, for x in terms of y. We do this by applying the quadratic formula to $ax^2 + bx + c - y = 0$, which gives $x = \frac{-b \pm \sqrt{b^2 - 4a(c-y)}}{2a} = \frac{-b}{2a} \pm \frac{\sqrt{b^2 - 4a(c-y)}}{2a}$. Whenever $\sqrt{b^2 - 4a(c-y)}$ is defined (as a real number) it is nonnegative. Therefore, the sign of $\frac{\sqrt{b^2 - 4a(c-y)}}{2a}$ depends on a. It is nonnegative when a is positive, that is, when the parabola opens upward, and nonpositive when a is negative, that is, when the parabola opens downward. Thus, in order to satisfy $x \geq -\frac{b}{2a}$ we must take the $+$ in $\pm$ when $a > 0$ and the parabola opens upward and the $-$ in $\pm$ when $a < 0$ and the parabola opens downward. For definiteness now, let us deal with the case of $a > 0$. It follows, returning to the procedure of Example 5 of 2.4, that $g^{-1}(x) = \frac{-b + \sqrt{b^2 - 4a(c-x)}}{2a}$. The vertex of any paraola has y-coordinate given by $f\left(-\frac{b}{2a}\right) = a\left(-\frac{b}{2a}\right)^2 + b\left(-\frac{b}{2a}\right) + c = -\frac{b^2 - 4ac}{4a}$.

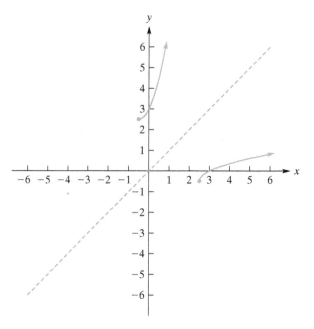

FIGURE 3.24   Graph of g and g^{-1}.

The domain of g is by definition $\left[-\dfrac{b}{2a}, \infty\right)$. It is now apparent that in the upward-opening case, the range of g is $\left[-\dfrac{b^2 - 4ac}{4a}, \infty\right)$. As was stated in Section 2.4, it is a general fact that the domain of g^{-1} is the range of g. Let us verify that claim in this situation by considering the domain of $\dfrac{-b + \sqrt{b^2 - 4a(c - x)}}{2a}$ directly. The domain is the set of all x for which $b^2 - 4a(c - x) \geq 0$. Evidently, this inequality is equivalent to $b^2 - 4ac + 4ax \geq 0$, which in turn is equivalent to $4ax \geq -(b^2 - 4ac)$. In other words, $x \geq -\dfrac{b^2 - 4ac}{4a}$ as required.

To complete the exercise, observe that in Figure 3.23 we have provided the graph of $y = 2x^2 + 2x + 3$. For the task at hand, we redraw that part of the curve which lies to the right of the axis of symmetry. This provides the graph of g. Next we provide a dotted copy of the line $y = x$. Finally, we draw the mirror image of g in the line $y = x$ to obtain the graph of g^{-1} as in Figure 3.24.

Now Work Problem 27 ◁

EXAMPLE 6   Maximum Revenue

APPLY IT ▶

15. The demand function for a publisher's line of cookbooks is $p = 6 - 0.003q$, where p is the price (in dollars) per unit when q units are demanded (per day) by consumers. Find the level of production that will maximize the manufacturer's total revenue, and determine this revenue.

The formula for total revenue is part of the repertoire of relationships in business and economics.

The demand function for a manufacturer's product is $p = 1000 - 2q$, where p is the price (in dollars) per unit when q units are demanded (per week) by consumers. Find the level of production that will maximize the manufacturer's total revenue, and determine this revenue.

Solution:

Strategy   To maximize revenue, we must determine the revenue function, $r = f(q)$. Using the relation

$$\text{total revenue} = (\text{price})(\text{quantity})$$

we have

$$r = pq$$

Using the demand equation, we can express p in terms of q, so r will be a function of q.

We have

$$r = pq$$
$$= (1000 - 2q)q$$
$$r = 1000q - 2q^2$$

Note that r is a quadratic function of q, with $a = -2, b = 1000$, and $c = 0$. Since $a < 0$ (the parabola opens downward), r is maximum at the vertex (q, r), where

$$q = -\frac{b}{2a} = -\frac{1000}{2(-2)} = 250$$

The maximum value of r is given by

$$r = 1000(250) - 2(250)^2$$
$$= 250{,}000 - 125{,}000 = 125{,}000$$

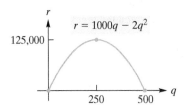

125,000

$r = 1000q - 2q^2$

250   500

Thus, the maximum revenue that the manufacturer can receive is \$125,000, which occurs at a production level of 250 units. Figure 3.25 shows the graph of the revenue function. Only that portion for which $q \geq 0$ and $r \geq 0$ is drawn, since quantity and revenue cannot be negative.

FIGURE 3.25   Graph of revenue function.

Now Work Problem 29 ◁

PROBLEMS 3.3

In Problems 1–8, state whether the function is quadratic.

1. $f(x) = 5x^2$

2. $g(x) = \dfrac{1}{2x^2 - 4}$

3. $g(x) = 7 - 6x$

4. $k(v) = 2v^2(2v^2 + 2)$

5. $h(q) = (3 - q)^2$

6. $f(t) = 2t(3 - t) + 4t$

7. $f(s) = \dfrac{s^2 - 9}{2}$

8. $g(t) = (t^2 - 1)^2$

In Problems 9–12, do not include a graph.

9. (a) For the parabola $y = f(x) = 3x^2 + 5x + 1$, find the vertex. (b) Does the vertex correspond to the highest point or the lowest point on the graph?

10. Repeat Problem 9 if $y = f(x) = 8x^2 + 4x - 1$.

11. For the parabola $y = f(x) = x^2 + x - 6$, find (a) the y-intercept, (b) the x-intercepts, and (c) the vertex.

12. Repeat Problem 11 if $y = f(x) = 5 - x - 3x^2$.

In Problems 13–22, graph each function. Give the vertex and intercepts, and state the range.

13. $y = f(x) = x^2 - 6x + 5$

14. $y = f(x) = 9x^2$

15. $y = g(x) = -2x^2 - 6x$

16. $y = f(x) = x^2 - 4$

17. $s = h(t) = t^2 + 6t + 9$

18. $s = h(t) = 2t^2 + 3t - 2$

19. $y = f(x) = -5 + 3x - 3x^2$

20. $y = H(x) = 1 - x - x^2$

21. $t = f(s) = s^2 - 8s + 14$

22. $t = f(s) = s^2 + 6s + 11$

In Problems 23–26, state whether f(x) has a maximum value or a minimum value, and find that value.

23. $f(x) = 49x^2 - 10x + 17$

24. $f(x) = -7x^2 - 2x + 6$

25. $f(x) = 4x - 50 - 0.1x^2$

26. $f(x) = x(x + 3) - 12$

In Problems 27 and 28, restrict the quadratic function to those x satisfying $x \geq v$, where v is the x-coordinate of the vertex of the parabola. Determine the inverse of the restricted function. Graph the restricted function and its inverse in the same plane.

27. $f(x) = x^2 - 2x + 4$

28. $f(x) = -x^2 + 4x - 3$

29. Revenue   The demand function for a manufacturer's product is $p = f(q) = 100 - 10q$, where p is the price (in dollars) per unit when q units are demanded (per day). Find the level of production that maximizes the manufacturer's total revenue and determine this revenue.

30. Revenue   The demand function for an office supply company's line of plastic rulers is $p = 0.85 - 0.00045q$, where p is the price (in dollars) per unit when q units are demanded (per day) by consumers. Find the level of production that will maximize the manufacturer's total revenue, and determine this revenue.

31. Revenue   The demand function for an electronics company's laptop computer line is $p = 2400 - 6q$, where p is the price (in dollars) per unit when q units are demanded (per week) by consumers. Find the level of production that will maximize the manufacturer's total revenue, and determine this revenue.

32. Marketing   A marketing firm estimates that n months after the introduction of a client's new product, $f(n)$ thousand households will use it, where

$$f(n) = \frac{10}{9}n(12 - n), \quad 0 \leq n \leq 12$$

Estimate the maximum number of households that will use the product.

33. Profit   The daily profit for the garden department of a store from the sale of trees is given by $P(x) = -x^2 + 18x + 144$, where x is the number of trees sold. Find the function's vertex and intercepts, and graph the function.

34. Psychology   A prediction made by early psychology relating the magnitude of a stimulus, x, to the magnitude of a response, y, is expressed by the equation $y = kx^2$, where k is a constant of the experiment. In an experiment on pattern recognition, $k = 3$. Find the function's vertex and graph the equation. (Assume no restriction on x.)

35. Biology Biologists studied the nutritional effects on rats that were fed a diet containing 10% protein.[5] The protein consisted of yeast and corn flour. By varying the percentage, P, of yeast in the protein mix, the group estimated that the average weight gain (in grams) of a rat over a period of time was

$$f(P) = -\frac{1}{50}P^2 + 2P + 20, \quad 0 \le P \le 100$$

Find the maximum weight gain.

36. Height of Ball Suppose that the height, s, of a ball thrown vertically upward is given by

$$s = -4.9t^2 + 62.3t + 1.8$$

where s is in meters and t is elapsed time in seconds. (See Figure 3.26.) After how many seconds will the ball reach its maximum height? What is the maximum height?

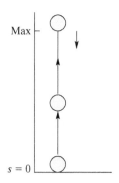

FIGURE 3.26 Ball thrown upward (Problem 36).

37. Archery A boy standing on a hill shoots an arrow straight up with an initial velocity of 85 feet per second. The height, h, of the arrow in feet, t seconds after it was released, is described by the function $h(t) = -16t^2 + 85t + 22$. What is the maximum

height reached by the arrow? How many seconds after release does it take to reach this height?

38. Toy Toss A 6-year-old girl standing on a toy chest throws a doll straight up with an initial velocity of 16 feet per second. The height h of the doll in feet t seconds after it was released is described by the function $h(t) = -16t^2 + 16t + 4$. How long does it take the doll to reach its maximum height? What is the maximum height?

39. Rocket Launch A toy rocket is launched straight up from the roof of a garage with an initial velocity of 90 feet per second. The height, h, of the rocket in feet, t seconds after it was released, is described by the function $h(t) = -16t^2 + 90t + 14$. Find the function's vertex and intercepts, and graph the function.

40. Area Express the area of the rectangle shown in Figure 3.27 as a quadratic function of x. For what value of x will the area be a maximum?

$11 - x$

x

FIGURE 3.27 Diagram for Problem 40.

41. Enclosing Plot A building contractor wants to fence in a rectangular plot adjacent to a straight highway using the highway for one side, which will be left unfenced. (See Figure 3.28.) If the contractor has 500 feet of fence, find the dimensions of the maximum enclosed area.

FIGURE 3.28 Diagram for Problem 41.

42. Find two numbers whose sum is 78 and whose product is a maximum.

[5]Adapted from R. Bressani, "The Use of Yeast in Human Foods," in *Single-Cell Protein,* ed. R. I. Mateles and S. R. Tannenbaum (Cambridge, MA: MIT Press, 1968).

Objective

To solve systems of linear equations in both two and three variables by using the technique of elimination by addition or by substitution. (In Chapter 6, other methods are shown.)

3.4 Systems of Linear Equations

Two-Variable Systems

When a situation must be described mathematically, it is not unusual for a *set* of equations to arise. For example, suppose that the manager of a factory is setting up a production schedule for two models of a new product. Model A requires 4 resistors and 9 transistors. Model B requires 5 resistors and 14 transistors. From its suppliers, the factory gets 335 resistors and 850 transistors each day. How many of each model should the manager plan to make each day so that all the resistors and transistors are used?

It's a good idea to construct a table that summarizes the important information. Table 3.2 shows the number of resistors and transistors required for each model, as well as the total number available.

Suppose we let x be the number of model A made each day and y be the number of model B. Then these require a total of $4x + 5y$ resistors and $9x + 14y$ transistors. Since

Table 3.2

	Model A	Model B	Total Available
Resistors	4	5	335
Transistors	9	14	850

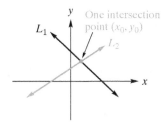

FIGURE 3.29   Linear system (one solution).

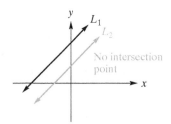

FIGURE 3.30   Linear system (no solution).

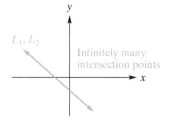

FIGURE 3.31   Linear system (infinitely many solutions).

335 resistors and 850 transistors are available, we have

$$\begin{cases} 4x + 5y = 335 & (1) \\ 9x + 14y = 850 & (2) \end{cases}$$

We call this set of equations a **system** of two linear equations in the variables x and y. The problem is to find values of x and y for which *both* equations are true *simultaneously*. A pair (x, y) of such values is called a *solution* of the system.

Since Equations (1) and (2) are linear, their graphs are straight lines; call these lines L_1 and L_2. Now, the coordinates of any point on a line satisfy the equation of that line; that is, they make the equation true. Thus, the coordinates of any point of intersection of L_1 and L_2 will satisfy both equations. This means that a point of intersection gives a solution of the system.

If L_1 and L_2 are drawn on the same plane, there are three situations that could occur:

1. L_1 and L_2 may intersect at exactly one point, say, (a, b). (See Figure 3.29.) Thus, the system has the solution $x = a$ and $y = b$.

2. L_1 and L_2 may be parallel and have no points in common. (See Figure 3.30.) In this case, there is no solution.

3. L_1 and L_2 may be the same line. (See Figure 3.31.) Here the coordinates of any point on the line are a solution of the system. Consequently, there are infinitely many solutions.

Our main concern in this section is algebraic methods of solving a system of linear equations. We will successively replace the system by other systems that have the same solutions. Generalizing the terminology of Section 0.7, in the subsection titled "Equivalent Equations," we say that two systems are *equivalent* if their sets of solutions are equal. The replacement systems have progressively more desirable forms for determining the solution. More precisely, we seek an equivalent system containing an equation in which one of the variables does not appear. (In this case we say that the variable has been *eliminated*.) In dealing with systems of *linear* equations, our passage from a system to an equivalent system will always be accomplished by one of the following procedures:

1. Interchanging two equations

2. Multiplying one equation by a nonzero constant

3. Replacing an equation by itself plus a multiple of another equation

We will return to these procedures in more detail in Chapter 6. For the moment, since we will also consider nonlinear systems in this chapter, it is convenient to express

CAUTION!

Note that a *single* solution is given by an *ordered pair* of values.

our solutions in terms of the very general principles of Section 0.7 that guarantee equivalence of equations.

We will illustrate the elimination procedure for the system in the problem originally posed:

$$\begin{cases} 4x + 5y = 335 & (3) \\ 9x + 14y = 850 & (4) \end{cases}$$

To begin, we will obtain an equivalent system in which x does not appear in one equation. First we find an equivalent system in which the coefficients of the x-terms in each equation are the same except for their sign. Multiplying Equation (3) by 9 [that is, multiplying both sides of Equation (3) by 9] and multiplying Equation (4) by -4 gives

$$\begin{cases} 36x + 45y = 3015 & (5) \\ -36x - 56y = -3400 & (6) \end{cases}$$

The left and right sides of Equation (5) are equal, so each side can be *added* to the corresponding side of Equation (6). This results in

$$-11y = -385$$

which has only one variable, as planned. Solving gives

$$y = 35$$

so we obtain the equivalent system

$$\begin{cases} 36x + 45y = 3015 & (7) \\ y = 35 & (8) \end{cases}$$

Replacing y in Equation (7) by 35, we get

$$36x + 45(35) = 3015$$
$$36x + 1575 = 3015$$
$$36x = 1440$$
$$x = 40$$

Thus, the original system is equivalent to

$$\begin{cases} x = 40 \\ y = 35 \end{cases}$$

We can check our answer by substituting $x = 40$ and $y = 35$ into *both* of the original equations. In Equation (3), we get $4(40) + 5(35) = 335$, or $335 = 335$. In Equation (4), we get $9(40) + 14(35) = 850$, or $850 = 850$. Hence, the solution is

$$x = 40 \quad \text{and} \quad y = 35$$

Each day the manager should plan to make 40 of model A and 35 of model B. Our procedure is referred to as **elimination by addition.** Although we chose to eliminate x first, we could have done the same for y by a similar procedure.

EXAMPLE 1 Elimination-by-Addition Method

APPLY IT ▶

16. A computer consultant has $200,000 invested for retirement, part at 9% and part at 8%. If the total yearly income from the investments is $17,200, how much is invested at each rate?

Use elimination by addition to solve the system.

$$\begin{cases} 3x - 4y = 13 \\ 3y + 2x = 3 \end{cases}$$

Solution: Aligning the x- and y-terms for convenience gives

$$\begin{cases} 3x - 4y = 13 & (9) \\ 2x + 3y = 3 & (10) \end{cases}$$

To eliminate y, we multiply Equation (9) by 3 and Equation (10) by 4:

$$\begin{cases} 9x - 12y = 39 & (11) \\ 8x + 12y = 12 & (12) \end{cases}$$

Adding Equation (11) to Equation (12) gives $17x = 51$, from which $x = 3$. We have the equivalent system

$$\begin{cases} 9x - 12y = 39 & (13) \\ \qquad\quad x = 3 & (14) \end{cases}$$

Replacing x by 3 in Equation (13) results in

$$9(3) - 12y = 39$$
$$-12y = 12$$
$$y = -1$$

so the original system is equivalent to

$$\begin{cases} y = -1 \\ x = 3 \end{cases}$$

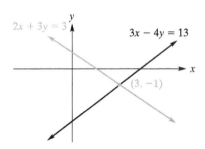

$2x + 3y = 3$ $3x - 4y = 13$

$(3, -1)$

FIGURE 3.32   Linear system of Example 1: one solution.

The solution is $x = 3$ and $y = -1$. Figure 3.32 shows a graph of the system.

Now Work Problem 1 ◁

The system in Example 1,

$$\begin{cases} 3x - 4y = 13 & (15) \\ 2x + 3y = 3 & (16) \end{cases}$$

can be solved another way. We first choose one of the equations—for example, Equation (15)—and solve it for one variable in terms of the other, say x in terms of y. Hence Equation (15) is equivalent to $3x = 4y + 13$, which is equivalent to

$$x = \frac{4}{3}y + \frac{13}{3}$$

and we obtain

$$\begin{cases} x = \dfrac{4}{3}y + \dfrac{13}{3} & (17) \\ 2x + 3y = 3 & (18) \end{cases}$$

Substituting the right side of Equation (17) for x in Equation (18) gives

$$2\left(\frac{4}{3}y + \frac{13}{3}\right) + 3y = 3 \qquad (19)$$

Thus, x has been eliminated. Solving Equation (19), we have

$$\frac{8}{3}y + \frac{26}{3} + 3y = 3$$
$$8y + 26 + 9y = 9 \qquad \text{clearing fractions}$$
$$17y = -17$$
$$y = -1$$

Replacing y in Equation (17) by -1 gives $x = 3$, and the original system is equivalent to

$$\begin{cases} x = 3 \\ y = -1 \end{cases}$$

as before. This method is called **elimination by substitution.**

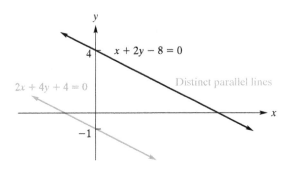

FIGURE 3.33 Linear system of Example 2: no solution.

APPLY IT ▷

17. Two species of deer, A and B, living in a wildlife refuge are given extra food in the winter. Each week, they receive 2 tons of food pellets and 4.75 tons of hay. Each deer of species A requires 4 pounds of the pellets and 5 pounds of hay. Each deer of species B requires 2 pounds of the pellets and 7 pounds of hay. How many of each species of deer will the food support so that all of the food is consumed each week?

EXAMPLE 2 Method of Elimination by Substitution

Use elimination by substitution to solve the system

$$\begin{cases} x + 2y - 8 = 0 \\ 2x + 4y + 4 = 0 \end{cases}$$

Solution: It is easy to solve the first equation for x. Doing so gives the equivalent system

$$\begin{cases} x = -2y + 8 & (20) \\ 2x + 4y + 4 = 0 & (21) \end{cases}$$

Substituting $-2y + 8$ for x in Equation (21) yields

$$2(-2y + 8) + 4y + 4 = 0$$
$$-4y + 16 + 4y + 4 = 0$$

The latter equation simplifies to $20 = 0$. Thus, we have the system

$$\begin{cases} x = -2y + 8 & (22) \\ 20 = 0 & (23) \end{cases}$$

Since Equation (23) is *never* true, there is **no solution** of the original system. The reason is clear if we observe that the original equations can be written in slope-intercept form as

$$y = -\frac{1}{2}x + 4$$

and

$$y = -\frac{1}{2}x - 1$$

These equations represent straight lines having slopes of $-\frac{1}{2}$, but different y-intercepts, namely, 4 and -1. That is, they determine different parallel lines. (See Figure 3.33.)

Now Work Problem 9 ◁

EXAMPLE 3 A Linear System with Infinitely Many Solutions

Solve

$$\begin{cases} x + 5y = 2 & (24) \\ \dfrac{1}{2}x + \dfrac{5}{2}y = 1 & (25) \end{cases}$$

Solution: We begin by eliminating x from the second equation. Multiplying Equation (25) by -2, we have

$$\begin{cases} x + 5y = 2 & (26) \\ -x - 5y = -2 & (27) \end{cases}$$

APPLY IT ▷

18. Two species of fish, A and B, are raised in one pond at a fish farm where they are fed two vitamin supplements. Each day, they receive 100 grams of the first supplement and 200 grams of the second supplement. Each fish of species A requires 15 mg of the first supplement and 30 mg of the second supplement. Each fish of species B requires 20 mg of the first supplement and 40 mg of the second supplement. How many of each species of fish will the pond support so that all of the supplements are consumed each day?

Adding Equation (26) to Equation (27) gives

$$\begin{cases} x + 5y = 2 & (28) \\ 0 = 0 & (29) \end{cases}$$

Because Equation (29) is *always* true, any solution of Equation (28) is a solution of the system. Now let us see how we can express our answer. From Equation (28), we have $x = 2 - 5y$, where y can be any real number, say, r. Thus, we can write $x = 2 - 5r$. The complete solution is

$$x = 2 - 5r$$

$$y = r$$

where r is any real number. In this situation r is called a **parameter,** and we say that we have a one-parameter family of solutions. Each value of r determines a particular solution. For example, if $r = 0$, then $x = 2$ and $y = 0$ is a solution; if $r = 5$, then $x = -23$ and $y = 5$ is another solution. Clearly, the given system has infinitely many solutions.

It is worthwhile to note that by writing Equations (24) and (25) in their slope-intercept forms, we get the equivalent system

$$\begin{cases} y = -\dfrac{1}{5}x + \dfrac{2}{5} \\ y = -\dfrac{1}{5}x + \dfrac{2}{5} \end{cases}$$

in which both equations represent the same line. Hence, the lines coincide (Figure 3.34), and Equations (24) and (25) are equivalent. The solution of the system consists of the coordinate pairs of all points on the line $x + 5y = 2$, and these points are given by our parametric solution.

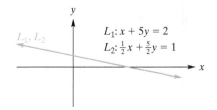

$L_1 : x + 5y = 2$
$L_2 : \frac{1}{2}x + \frac{5}{2}y = 1$

FIGURE 3.34   Linear system of Example 3: infinitely many solutions.

Now Work Problem 13 ◁

TECHNOLOGY ▮▮▮▮

Graphically solve the system

$$\begin{cases} 9x + 4.1y = 7 \\ 2.6x - 3y = 18 \end{cases}$$

Solution: First we solve each equation for y, so that each equation has the form $y = f(x)$:

$$y = \frac{1}{4.1}(7 - 9x)$$

$$y = -\frac{1}{3}(18 - 2.6x)$$

Next we enter these functions as Y_1 and Y_2 and display them on the same viewing rectangle. (See Figure 3.35.)

Finally, either using trace and zoom or using the intersection feature, we estimate the solution to be $x = 2.52$, $y = -3.82$.

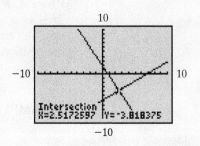

FIGURE 3.35   Graphical solution of system.

EXAMPLE 4   Mixture

A chemical manufacturer wishes to fill an order for 500 liters of a 25% acid solution. (Twenty-five percent by volume is acid.) If solutions of 30% and 18% are available in stock, how many liters of each must be mixed to fill the order?

Solution: Let x and y be the number of liters of the 30% and 18%, solutions respectively, that should be mixed. Then

$$x + y = 500$$

To help visualize the situation, we draw the diagram in Figure 3.36. In 500 liters of a 25% solution, there will be $0.25(500) = 125$ liters of acid. This acid comes from two sources: $0.30x$ liters of it come from the 30% solution, and $0.18y$ liters of it come from the 18% solution. Hence,

$$0.30x + 0.18y = 125$$

These two equations form a system of two linear equations in two unknowns. Solving the first for x gives $x = 500 - y$. Substituting in the second gives

$$0.30(500 - y) + 0.18y = 125$$

Solving this equation for y, we find that $y = 208\frac{1}{3}$ liters. Thus, $x = 500 - 208\frac{1}{3} = 291\frac{2}{3}$ liters. (See Figure 3.37.)

Now Work Problem 25 ◁

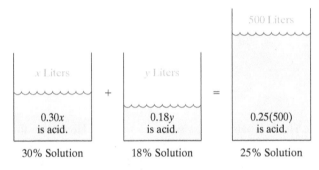

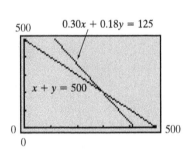

FIGURE 3.36 Mixture problem.   FIGURE 3.37 Graph for Example 4.

Three-Variable Systems

The methods used in solving a two-variable system of linear equations can be used to solve a three-variable system of linear equations. A **general linear equation in the three variables** x, y, **and** z is an equation having the form

$$Ax + By + Cz = D$$

where A, B, C, and D are constants and A, B, and C are not all zero. For example, $2x - 4y + z = 2$ is such an equation. Geometrically, a general linear equation in three variables represents a *plane* in space, and a solution to a system of such equations is the intersection of planes. Example 5 shows how to solve a system of three linear equations in three variables.

APPLY IT ▶

19. A coffee shop specializes in blending gourmet coffees. From type A, type B, and type C coffees, the owner wants to prepare a blend that will sell for $8.50 for a 1-pound bag. The cost per pound of these coffees is $12, $9, and $7, respectively. The amount of type B is to be twice the amount of type A. How much of each type of coffee will be in the final blend?

EXAMPLE 5   Solving a Three-Variable Linear System

Solve

$$\begin{cases} 2x + \ y + \ z = 3 & (30) \\ -x + 2y + 2z = 1 & (31) \\ x - \ y - 3z = -6 & (32) \end{cases}$$

Solution: This system consists of three linear equations in three variables. From Equation (32), $x = y + 3z - 6$. By substituting for x in Equations (30) and (31), we obtain

$$\begin{cases} 2(y + 3z - 6) + y + z = 3 \\ -(y + 3z - 6) + 2y + 2z = 1 \\ \qquad\qquad\qquad x = y + 3z - 6 \end{cases}$$

Simplifying gives

$$\begin{cases} 3y + 7z = 15 & (33) \\ y - z = -5 & (34) \\ x = y + 3z - 6 & (35) \end{cases}$$

Note that x does not appear in Equations (33) and (34). Since any solution of the original system must satisfy Equations (33) and (34), we will consider their solution first:

$$\begin{cases} 3y + 7z = 15 & (33) \\ y - z = -5 & (34) \end{cases}$$

From Equation (34), $y = z - 5$. This means that we can replace Equation (33) by

$$3(z - 5) + 7z = 15 \quad \text{that is,} \quad z = 3$$

Since z is 3, we can replace Equation (34) with $y = -2$. Hence, the previous system is equivalent to

$$\begin{cases} z = 3 \\ y = -2 \end{cases}$$

The original system becomes

$$\begin{cases} z = 3 \\ y = -2 \\ x = y + 3z - 6 \end{cases}$$

from which $x = 1$. The solution is $x = 1$, $y = -2$, and $z = 3$, which you should verify.

Now Work Problem 15 ◁

Just as a two-variable system may have a one-parameter family of solutions, a three-variable system may have a one-parameter or a two-parameter family of solutions. The next two examples illustrate.

EXAMPLE 6 One-Parameter Family of Solutions

Solve

$$\begin{cases} x - 2y = 4 & (35) \\ 2x - 3y + 2z = -2 & (36) \\ 4x - 7y + 2z = 6 & (37) \end{cases}$$

Solution: Note that since Equation (35) can be written $x - 2y + 0z = 4$, we can view Equations (35) to (37) as a system of three linear equations in the variables x, y, and z. From Equation (35), we have $x = 2y + 4$. Using this equation and substitution, we can eliminate x from Equations (36) and (37):

$$\begin{cases} x = 2y + 4 \\ 2(2y + 4) - 3y + 2z = -2 \\ 4(2y + 4) - 7y + 2z = 6 \end{cases}$$

which simplifies to give

$$\begin{cases} x = 2y + 4 & (38) \\ y + 2z = -10 & (39) \\ y + 2z = -10 & (40) \end{cases}$$

Multiplying Equation (40) by -1 gives

$$\begin{cases} x = 2y + 4 \\ y + 2z = -10 \\ -y - 2z = 10 \end{cases}$$

Adding the second equation to the third yields

$$\begin{cases} x = 2y + 4 \\ y + 2z = -10 \\ 0 = 0 \end{cases}$$

Since the equation $0 = 0$ is always true, the system is equivalent to

$$\begin{cases} x = 2y + 4 & (41) \\ y + 2z = -10 & (42) \end{cases}$$

Solving Equation (42) for y, we have

$$y = -10 - 2z$$

which expresses y in terms of z. We can also express x in terms of z. From Equation (41),

$$x = 2y + 4$$
$$= 2(-10 - 2z) + 4$$
$$= -16 - 4z$$

Thus, we have

$$\begin{cases} x = -16 - 4z \\ y = -10 - 2z \end{cases}$$

Since no restriction is placed on z, this suggests a parametric family of solutions. Setting $z = r$, we have the following family of solutions of the given system:

$$x = -16 - 4r$$
$$y = -10 - 2r$$
$$z = r$$

Other parametric representations of the solution are possible.

where r can be any real number. We see, then, that the given system has infinitely many solutions. For example, setting $r = 1$ gives the particular solution $x = -20$, $y = -12$, and $z = 1$. There is nothing special about the name of the parameter. In fact, since $z = r$, we could consider z to be the parameter.

Now Work Problem 19 ◁

EXAMPLE 7   Two-Parameter Family of Solutions

Solve the system

$$\begin{cases} x + 2y + z = 4 \\ 2x + 4y + 2z = 8 \end{cases}$$

Solution: This is a system of two linear equations in three variables. We will eliminate x from the second equation by first multiplying that equation by $-\frac{1}{2}$:

$$\begin{cases} x + 2y + z = 4 \\ -x - 2y - z = -4 \end{cases}$$

Adding the first equation to the second gives

$$\begin{cases} x + 2y + z = 4 \\ 0 = 0 \end{cases}$$

From the first equation, we obtain

$$x = 4 - 2y - z$$

Since no restriction is placed on either y or z, they can be arbitrary real numbers, giving us a two-parameter family of solutions. Setting $y = r$ and $z = s$, we find that the

solution of the given system is

$$x = 4 - 2r - s$$

$$y = r$$

$$z = s$$

where r and s can be any real numbers. Each assignment of values to r and s results in a solution of the given system, so there are infinitely many solutions. For example, letting $r = 1$ and $s = 2$ gives the particular solution $x = 0, y = 1$, and $z = 2$. As in the last example, there is nothing special about the names of the parameters. In particular, since $y = r$ and $z = s$, we could consider y and z to be the two parameters.

Now Work Problem 23 ◁

PROBLEMS 3.4

In Problems 1–24, solve the systems algebraically.

1. $\begin{cases} x + 4y = 3 \\ 3x - 2y = -5 \end{cases}$ **2.** $\begin{cases} 4x + 2y = 9 \\ 5y - 4x = 5 \end{cases}$

3. $\begin{cases} 2x + 3y = 1 \\ x + 2y = 0 \end{cases}$ **4.** $\begin{cases} 2x - y = 1 \\ -x + 2y = 7 \end{cases}$

5. $\begin{cases} u + v = 5 \\ u - v = 7 \end{cases}$ **6.** $\begin{cases} 2p + q = 16 \\ 3p + 3q = 33 \end{cases}$

7. $\begin{cases} x - 2y = -7 \\ 5x + 3y = -9 \end{cases}$ **8.** $\begin{cases} 4x + 12y = 12 \\ 2x + 4y = 12 \end{cases}$

9. $\begin{cases} 4x - 3y - 2 = 3x - 7y \\ x + 5y - 2 = y + 4 \end{cases}$

10. $\begin{cases} 5x + 7y + 2 = 9y - 4x + 6 \\ \frac{21}{2}x - \frac{4}{3}y - \frac{11}{4} = \frac{3}{2}x + \frac{2}{3}y + \frac{5}{4} \end{cases}$

11. $\begin{cases} \frac{2}{3}x + \frac{1}{2}y = 2 \\ \frac{3}{8}x + \frac{5}{6}y = -\frac{11}{2} \end{cases}$ **12.** $\begin{cases} \frac{1}{2}z - \frac{1}{4}w = \frac{1}{6} \\ \frac{1}{2}z + \frac{1}{4}w = \frac{1}{6} \end{cases}$

13. $\begin{cases} 2p + 3q = 5 \\ 10p + 15q = 25 \end{cases}$ **14.** $\begin{cases} 5x - 3y = 2 \\ -10x + 6y = 4 \end{cases}$

15. $\begin{cases} 2x + y + 6z = 3 \\ x - y + 4z = 1 \\ 3x + 2y - 2z = 2 \end{cases}$ **16.** $\begin{cases} x + y + z = -1 \\ 3x + y + z = 1 \\ 4x - 2y + 2z = 0 \end{cases}$

17. $\begin{cases} x + 4y + 3z = 10 \\ 4x + 2y - 2z = -2 \\ 3x - y + z = 11 \end{cases}$ **18.** $\begin{cases} x + 2y + z = 4 \\ 2x - 4y - 5z = 26 \\ 2x + 3y + z = 10 \end{cases}$

19. $\begin{cases} x - 2z = 1 \\ y + z = 3 \end{cases}$ **20.** $\begin{cases} 2y + 3z = 1 \\ 3x - 4z = 0 \end{cases}$

21. $\begin{cases} x - y + 2z = 0 \\ 2x + y - z = 0 \\ x + 2y - 3z = 0 \end{cases}$ **22.** $\begin{cases} x - 2y - z = 0 \\ 2x - 4y - 2z = 0 \\ -x + 2y + z = 0 \end{cases}$

23. $\begin{cases} x - 3y + z = 5 \\ -2x + 6y - 2z = -10 \end{cases}$ **24.** $\begin{cases} 5x + y + z = 17 \\ 4x + y + z = 14 \end{cases}$

25. Mixture   A chemical manufacturer wishes to fill an order for 800 gallons of a 25% acid solution. Solutions of 20% and 35% are in stock. How many gallons of each solution must be mixed to fill the order?

26. Mixture   A gardener has two fertilizers that contain different concentrations of nitrogen. One is 3% nitrogen and the other is 11% nitrogen. How many pounds of each should she mix to obtain 20 pounds of a 9% concentration?

27. Fabric   A textile mill produces fabric made from different fibers. From cotton, polyester, and nylon, the owners want to produce a fabric blend that will cost $3.25 per pound to make. The cost per pound of these fibers is $4.00, $3.00, and $2.00, respectively. The amount of nylon is to be the same as the amount of polyester. How much of each fiber will be in the final fabric?

28. Taxes   A company has taxable income of $758,000. The federal tax is 35% of that portion left after the state tax has been paid. The state tax is 15% of that portion left after the federal tax has been paid. Find the federal and state taxes.

29. Airplane Speed   An airplane travels 900 mi in 2 h, 55 min, with the aid of a tailwind. It takes 3 h, 26 min, for the return trip, flying against the same wind. Find the speed of the airplane in still air and the speed of the wind.

30. Speed of Raft   On a trip on a raft, it took $\frac{1}{2}$ hour to travel 10 miles downstream. The return trip took $\frac{3}{4}$ hour. Find the speed of the raft in still water and the speed of the current.

31. Furniture Sales   A manufacturer of dining-room sets produces two styles: early American and contemporary. From past experience, management has determined that 20% more of the early American styles can be sold than the contemporary styles. A profit of $250 is made on each early American set sold, whereas a profit of $350 is made on each contemporary set. If, in the forthcoming year, management desires a total profit of $130,000, how many units of each style must be sold?

32. Survey   National Surveys was awarded a contract to perform a product-rating survey for Crispy Crackers. A total of

250 people were interviewed. National Surveys reported that 62.5% more people liked Crispy Crackers than disliked them. However, the report did not indicate that 16% of those interviewed had no comment. How many of those surveyed liked Crispy Crackers? How many disliked them? How many had no comment?

33. Equalizing Cost United Products Co. manufactures calculators and has plants in the cities of Exton and Whyton. At the Exton plant, fixed costs are $5000 per month, and the cost of producing each calculator is $5.50. At the Whyton plant, fixed costs are $6000 per month, and each calculator costs $4.50 to produce. Next month, United Products must produce 1000 calculators. How many must be made at each plant if the total cost at each plant is to be the same?

34. Coffee Blending A coffee wholesaler blends together three types of coffee that sell for $2.20, $2.30, and $2.60 per pound, so as to obtain 100 lb of coffee worth $2.40 per pound. If the wholesaler uses the same amount of the two higher-priced coffees, how much of each type must be used in the blend?

35. Commissions A company pays its salespeople on a basis of a certain percentage of the first $100,000 in sales, plus a certain percentage of any amount over $100,000 in sales. If one salesperson earned $8500 on sales of $175,000 and another salesperson earned $14,800 on sales of $280,000, find the two percentages.

36. Yearly Profits In news reports, profits of a company this year (T) are often compared with those of last year (L), but actual values of T and L are not always given. This year, a company had profits of $25 million more than last year. The profits were up 30%. Determine T and L from these data.

37. Fruit Packaging The Ilovetiny.com Organic Produce Company has 3600 lb of Donut Peaches that it is going to package in boxes. Half of the boxes will be loose filled, each containing 20 lb of peaches, and the others will be packed with 8-lb clamshells (flip-top plastic containers), each containing 2.2 lb of peaches. Determine the number of boxes and the number of clamshells that are required.

38. Investments A person made two investments, and the percentage return per year on each was the same. Of the total amount invested, 40% of it minus $1000 was invested in one

venture, and at the end of 1 year the person received a return of $400 from that venture. If the total return after 1 year was $1200, find the total amount invested.

39. Production Run A company makes three types of patio furniture: chairs, rockers, and chaise lounges. Each requires wood, plastic, and aluminum, in the amounts shown in the following table. The company has in stock 400 units of wood, 600 units of plastic, and 1500 units of aluminum. For its end-of-the-season production run, the company wants to use up all the stock. To do this, how many chairs, rockers, and chaise lounges should it make?

	Wood	Plastic	Aluminum
Chair	1 unit	1 unit	2 units
Rocker	1 unit	1 unit	3 units
Chaise lounge	1 unit	2 units	5 units

40. Investments A total of $35,000 was invested at three interest rates: 7, 8, and 9%. The interest for the first year was $2830, which was not reinvested. The second year the amount originally invested at 9% earned 10% instead, and the other rates remained the same. The total interest the second year was $2960. How much was invested at each rate?

41. Hiring Workers A company pays skilled workers in its assembly department $16 per hour. Semiskilled workers in that department are paid $9.50 per hour. Shipping clerks are paid $10 per hour. Because of an increase in orders, the company needs to hire a total of 70 workers in the assembly and shipping departments. It will pay a total of $725 per hour to these employees. Because of a union contract, twice as many semiskilled workers as skilled workers must be employed. How many semiskilled workers, skilled workers, and shipping clerks should the company hire?

42. Solvent Storage A 10,000-gallon railroad tank car is to be filled with solvent from two storage tanks, A and B. Solvent from A is pumped at the rate of 25 gal/min. Solvent from B is pumped at 35 gal/min. Usually, both pumps operate at the same time. However, because of a blown fuse, the pump on A is delayed 5 minutes. Both pumps finish operating at the same time. How many gallons from each storage tank will be used to fill the car?

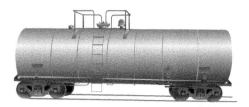

3.5 Nonlinear Systems

A system of equations in which at least one equation is not linear is called a **nonlinear system.** We can often solve a nonlinear system by substitution, as was done with linear systems. The following examples illustrate.

EXAMPLE 1   Solving a Nonlinear System

Solve

$$\begin{cases} x^2 - 2x + y - 7 = 0 & (1) \\ 3x - y + 1 = 0 & (2) \end{cases}$$

Solution:

Strategy   If a nonlinear system contains a linear equation, we usually solve the linear equation for one variable and substitute for that variable in the other equation.

Solving Equation (2) for y gives

$$y = 3x + 1 \qquad (3)$$

Substituting into Equation (1) and simplifying, we have

$$x^2 - 2x + (3x + 1) - 7 = 0$$
$$x^2 + x - 6 = 0$$
$$(x + 3)(x - 2) = 0$$
$$x = -3 \text{ or } x = 2$$

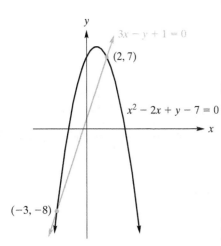

FIGURE 3.38   Nonlinear system of equations.

If $x = -3$, then Equation (3) implies that $y = -8$; if $x = 2$, then $y = 7$. You should verify that each pair of values satisfies the given system. Hence, the solutions are $x = -3$, $y = -8$ and $x = 2$, $y = 7$. These solutions can be seen geometrically in the graph of the system in Figure 3.38. Notice that the graph of Equation (1) is a parabola and the graph of Equation (2) is a line. The solutions correspond to the intersection points $(-3, -8)$ and $(2, 7)$.

Now Work Problem 1 ◁

EXAMPLE 2   Solving a Nonlinear System

CAUTION!

This example illustrates the need for checking all "solutions".

Solve

$$\begin{cases} y = \sqrt{x + 2} \\ x + y = 4 \end{cases}$$

Solution: Solving the second equation, which is linear, for y gives

$$y = 4 - x \qquad (4)$$

Substituting into the first equation yields

$$4 - x = \sqrt{x + 2}$$
$$16 - 8x + x^2 = x + 2 \qquad \text{squaring both sides}$$
$$x^2 - 9x + 14 = 0$$
$$(x - 2)(x - 7) = 0$$

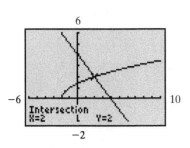

FIGURE 3.39   Nonlinear system of Example 2.

Thus, $x = 2$ or $x = 7$. From Equation (4), if $x = 2$, then $y = 2$; if $x = 7$, then $y = -3$. Since we performed the operation of squaring both sides, we must check our results. Although the pair $x = 2$, $y = 2$ satisfies both of the original equations, this is not the case for $x = 7$ and $y = -3$. Thus, the solution is $x = 2$, $y = 2$. (See Figure 3.39.)

Now Work Problem 13 ◁

TECHNOLOGY ▮▮▮▯

Graphically solve the equation $0.5x^2 + x = 3$, where $x \geq 0$.

Solution: To solve the equation, we could find zeros of the function $f(x) = 0.5x^2 + x - 3$. Alternatively, we can think of this problem as solving the nonlinear system

$$y = 0.5x^2 + x$$

$$y = 3$$

In Figure 3.40, the intersection point is estimated to be $x = 1.65, y = 3$. Note that the graph of $y = 3$ is a horizontal line. The solution of the given equation is $x = 1.65$.

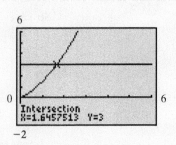

FIGURE 3.40   Solution of $0.5x^2 + x = 3$.

PROBLEMS 3.5

In Problems 1–14, solve the given nonlinear system.

1. $\begin{cases} y = x^2 - 9 \\ 2x + y = 3 \end{cases}$

2. $\begin{cases} y = x^3 \\ x - 2y = 0 \end{cases}$

3. $\begin{cases} p^2 = 5 - q \\ p = q + 1 \end{cases}$

4. $\begin{cases} y^2 - x^2 = 28 \\ x - y = 14 \end{cases}$

5. $\begin{cases} x = y^2 \\ y = x^2 \end{cases}$

6. $\begin{cases} p^2 - q + 1 = 0 \\ 5q - 3p - 2 = 0 \end{cases}$

7. $\begin{cases} y = 4 + 2x - x^2 \\ y = x^2 + 1 \end{cases}$

8. $\begin{cases} x^2 + 4x - y = -4 \\ y - x^2 - 4x + 3 = 0 \end{cases}$

9. $\begin{cases} p = \sqrt{q} \\ p = q^2 \end{cases}$

10. $\begin{cases} z = 4/w \\ 3z = 2w + 2 \end{cases}$

11. $\begin{cases} x^2 = y^2 + 13 \\ y = x^2 - 15 \end{cases}$

12. $\begin{cases} x^2 + y^2 + 2xy = 1 \\ 2x - y = 2 \end{cases}$

13. $\begin{cases} x = y + 1 \\ y = 2\sqrt{x + 2} \end{cases}$

14. $\begin{cases} y = \dfrac{x^2}{x - 1} + 1 \\ y = \dfrac{1}{x - 1} \end{cases}$

15. Decorations   The shape of a paper streamer suspended above a dance floor can be described by the function $y = 0.01x^2 + 0.01x + 7$, where y is the height of the streamer (in feet) above the floor and x is the horizontal distance (in feet) from the center of the room. A rope holding up other decorations touches the streamer and is described by the function $y = 0.01x + 8.0$. Where does the rope touch the paper streamer?

16. Awning   The shape of a decorative awning over a storefront can be described by the function $y = 0.06x^2 + 0.012x + 8$, where y is the height of the edge of the awning (in feet) above the

sidewalk and x is the distance (in feet) from the center of the store's doorway. A vandal pokes a stick through the awning, piercing it in two places. The position of the stick can be described by the function $y = 0.912x + 5$. Where are the holes in the awning caused by the vandal?

▧ **17.** Graphically determine how many solutions there are to the system

$$\begin{cases} y = \dfrac{1}{x^2} \\ y = 2 - x^2 \end{cases}$$

▧ **18.** Graphically solve the system

$$\begin{cases} 2y = x^3 \\ y = 8 - x^2 \end{cases}$$

to one-decimal-place accuracy.

▧ **19.** Graphically solve the system

$$\begin{cases} y = x^2 - 2x + 1 \\ y = x^3 + x^2 - 2x + 3 \end{cases}$$

to one-decimal-place accuracy.

▧ **20.** Graphically solve the system

$$\begin{cases} y = x^3 - x + 1 \\ y = 3x + 2 \end{cases}$$

to one-decimal-place accuracy.

In Problems 21–23, graphically solve the equation by treating it as a system. Round answers to two decimal places.

▧ **21.** $0.8x^2 + 2x = 6$ where $x \geq 0$

▧ **22.** $-\sqrt{x + 3} = 1 - x$ ▧ **23.** $x^3 - 3x^2 = x - 8$

Objective

To solve systems describing equilibrium and break-even points.

3.6 Applications of Systems of Equations

Equilibrium

Recall from Section 3.2 that an equation that relates price per unit and quantity demanded (supplied) is called a *demand equation (supply equation)*. Suppose that, for product Z, the demand equation is

$$p = -\frac{1}{180}q + 12 \tag{1}$$

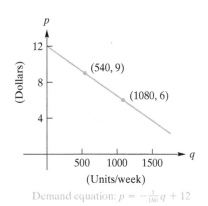

FIGURE 3.41   Demand curve.

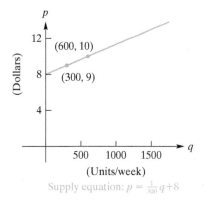

FIGURE 3.42   Supply curve.

and the supply equation is

$$p = \frac{1}{300}q + 8 \qquad (2)$$

where $q, p \geq 0$. The corresponding demand and supply curves are the lines in Figures 3.41 and 3.42, respectively. In analyzing Figure 3.41, we see that consumers will purchase 540 units per week when the price is $9 per unit, 1080 units when the price is $6, and so on. Figure 3.42 shows that when the price is $9 per unit producers will place 300 units per week on the market, at $10 they will supply 600 units, and so on.

When the demand and supply curves of a product are represented on the same coordinate plane, the point (m, n) where the curves intersect is called the **point of equilibrium.** (See Figure 3.43.) The price n, called the **equilibrium price,** is the price at which consumers will purchase the same quantity of a product that producers wish to sell at that price. In short, n is the price at which stability in the producer–consumer relationship occurs. The quantity m is called the **equilibrium quantity.**

To determine precisely the equilibrium point, we solve the system formed by the supply and demand equations. Let us do this for our previous data, namely, the system

$$\begin{cases} p = -\dfrac{1}{180}q + 12 & \text{demand equation} \\[2mm] p = \dfrac{1}{300}q + 8 & \text{supply equation} \end{cases}$$

By substituting $\frac{1}{300}q + 8$ for p in the demand equation, we get

$$\frac{1}{300}q + 8 = -\frac{1}{180}q + 12$$

$$\left(\frac{1}{300} + \frac{1}{180}\right)q = 4$$

$$q = 450 \qquad \text{equilibrium quantity}$$

Thus,

$$p = \frac{1}{300}(450) + 8$$

$$= 9.50 \qquad \text{equilibrium price}$$

and the equilibrium point is (450, 9.50). Therefore, at the price of $9.50 per unit, manufacturers will produce exactly the quantity (450) of units per week that consumers will purchase at that price. (See Figure 3.44.)

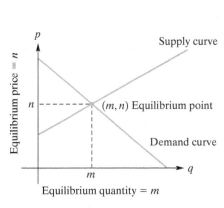

FIGURE 3.43   Equilibrium.

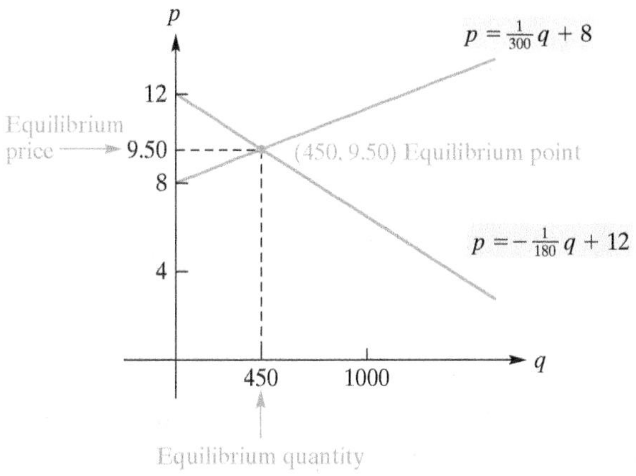

FIGURE 3.44   Equilibrium.

EXAMPLE 1 Tax Effect on Equilibrium

Let $p = \dfrac{8}{100}q + 50$ be the supply equation for a manufacturer's product, and suppose the demand equation is $p = -\dfrac{7}{100}q + 65$.

a. If a tax of \$1.50 per unit is to be imposed on the manufacturer, how will the original equilibrium price be affected if the demand remains the same?

Solution: Before the tax, the equilibrium price is obtained by solving the system

$$\begin{cases} p = \dfrac{8}{100}q + 50 \\[2mm] p = -\dfrac{7}{100}q + 65 \end{cases}$$

By substitution,

$$-\frac{7}{100}q + 65 = \frac{8}{100}q + 50$$

$$15 = \frac{15}{100}q$$

$$100 = q$$

and

$$p = \frac{8}{100}(100) + 50 = 58$$

Thus, \$58 is the original equilibrium price. Before the tax, the manufacturer supplies q units at a price of $p = \dfrac{8}{100}q + 50$ per unit. After the tax, he will sell the same q units for an additional \$1.50 per unit. The price per unit will be $\left(\dfrac{8}{100}q + 50\right) + 1.50$, so the new supply equation is

$$p = \frac{8}{100}q + 51.50$$

Solving the system

$$\begin{cases} p = \dfrac{8}{100}q + 51.50 \\[2mm] p = -\dfrac{7}{100}q + 65 \end{cases}$$

will give the new equilibrium price:

$$\frac{8}{100}q + 51.50 = -\frac{7}{100}q + 65$$

$$\frac{15}{100}q = 13.50$$

$$q = 90$$

$$p = \frac{8}{100}(90) + 51.50 = 58.70$$

The tax of \$1.50 per unit increases the equilibrium price by \$0.70. (See Figure 3.45.) Note that there is also a decrease in the equilibrium quantity from $q = 100$ to $q = 90$, because of the change in the equilibrium price. (In the problems, you are asked to find the effect of a subsidy given to the manufacturer, which will reduce the price of the product.)

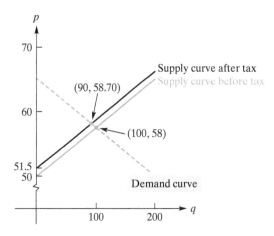

FIGURE 3.45 Equilibrium before and after tax.

Now Work Problem 15 ◁

b. Determine the total revenue obtained by the manufacturer at the equilibrium point both before and after the tax.

Solution: If q units of a product are sold at a price of p dollars each, then the total revenue is given by

$$y_{TR} = pq$$

Before the tax, the revenue at (100, 58) is (in dollars)

$$y_{TR} = (58)(100) = 5800$$

After the tax, it is

$$y_{TR} = (58.70)(90) = 5283$$

which is a decrease.

◁

EXAMPLE 2   Equilibrium with Nonlinear Demand

Find the equilibrium point if the supply and demand equations of a product are $p = \dfrac{q}{40} + 10$ and $p = \dfrac{8000}{q}$, respectively.

Solution: Here the demand equation is not linear. Solving the system

$$\begin{cases} p = \dfrac{q}{40} + 10 \\ p = \dfrac{8000}{q} \end{cases}$$

by substitution gives

$$\frac{8000}{q} = \frac{q}{40} + 10$$

$$320{,}000 = q^2 + 400q \qquad \text{multiplying both sides by } 40q$$

$$q^2 + 400q - 320{,}000 = 0$$

$$(q + 800)(q - 400) = 0$$

$$q = -800 \quad \text{or} \quad q = 400$$

We disregard $q = -800$, since q represents quantity. Choosing $q = 400$, we have $p = (8000/400) = 20$, so the equilibrium point is (400, 20). (See Figure 3.46.)

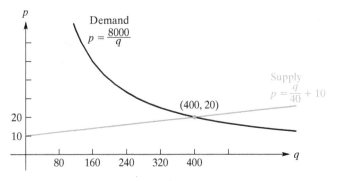

FIGURE 3.46   Equilibrium with nonlinear demand.

Break-Even Points

Suppose a manufacturer produces product A and sells it at $8 per unit. Then the total revenue y_{TR} received (in dollars) from selling q units is

$$y_{TR} = 8q \qquad \text{total revenue}$$

The difference between the total revenue received for q units and the total cost of q units is the manufacturer's profit:

$$\textbf{profit} = \textbf{total revenue} - \textbf{total cost}$$

(If profit is negative, then we have a loss.) **Total cost,** y_{TC}, is the sum of total variable costs y_{VC} and total fixed costs y_{FC}:

$$y_{TC} = y_{VC} + y_{FC}$$

Fixed costs are those costs that, under normal conditions, do not depend on the level of production; that is, over some period of time they remain constant at all levels of output. (Examples are rent, officers' salaries, and normal maintenance.) **Variable costs** are those costs that vary with the level of production (such as the cost of materials, labor, maintenance due to wear and tear, etc.). For q units of product A, suppose that

$$y_{FC} = 5000 \qquad \text{fixed cost}$$

$$\text{and } y_{VC} = \frac{22}{9}q \qquad \text{variable cost}$$

Then

$$y_{TC} = \frac{22}{9}q + 5000 \qquad \text{total cost}$$

The graphs of total cost and total revenue appear in Figure 3.47. The horizontal axis represents the level of production, q, and the vertical axis represents the total dollar value, be it revenue or cost. The **break-even point** is the point at which total revenue equals total cost (TR = TC). It occurs when the levels of production and sales result in neither a profit nor a loss to the manufacturer. In the diagram, called a *break-even chart*, the break-even point is the point (m, n) at which the graphs of $y_{TR} = 8q$ and $y_{TC} = \frac{22}{9}q + 5000$ intersect. We call m the **break-even quantity** and n the **break-even revenue.** When total cost and revenue are linearly related to output, as in this case, for any production level greater than m, total revenue is greater than total cost, resulting in a profit. However, at any level less than m units, total revenue is less than total cost, resulting in a loss. At an output of m units, the profit is zero. In the following example, we will examine our data in more detail.

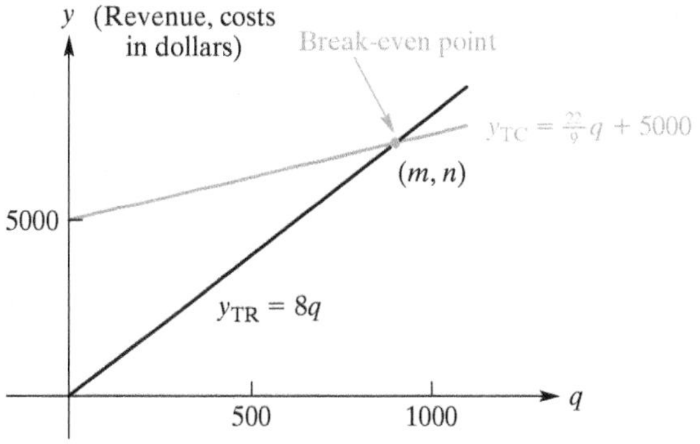

y (Revenue, costs
in dollars)

Break-even point

$y_{TC} = \frac{22}{9}q + 5000$

(m, n)

5000

$y_{TR} = 8q$

500   1000 q

FIGURE 3.47   Break-even chart.

EXAMPLE 3   Break-Even Point, Profit, and Loss

A manufacturer sells a product at $8 per unit, selling all that is produced. Fixed cost is $5000 and variable cost per unit is $\frac{22}{9}$ (dollars).

a. Find the total output and revenue at the break-even point.

Solution: At an output level of q units, the variable cost is $y_{VC} = \frac{22}{9}q$ and the total revenue is $y_{TR} = 8q$. Hence,

$$y_{TR} = 8q$$

$$y_{TC} = y_{VC} + y_{FC} = \frac{22}{9}q + 5000$$

At the break-even point, total revenue equals total cost. Thus, we solve the system formed by the foregoing equations. Since

$$y_{TR} = y_{TC}$$

we have

$$8q = \frac{22}{9}q + 5000$$

$$\frac{50}{9}q = 5000$$

$$q = 900$$

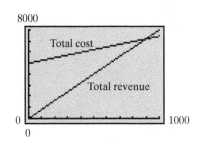

FIGURE 3.48   Equilibrium point (900, 7200).

Hence, the desired output is 900 units, resulting in a total revenue (in dollars) of

$$y_{TR} = 8(900) = 7200$$

(See Figure 3.48.)

b. Find the profit when 1800 units are produced.

Solution: Since profit = total revenue − total cost, when $q = 1800$ we have

$$y_{TR} - y_{TC} = 8(1800) - \left[\frac{22}{9}(1800) + 5000\right]$$

$$= 5000$$

The profit when 1800 units are produced and sold is $5000.

c. Find the loss when 450 units are produced.

Solution: When $q = 450$,

$$y_{TR} - y_{TC} = 8(450) - \left[\frac{22}{9}(450) + 5000\right] = -2500$$

A loss of $2500 occurs when the level of production is 450 units.

d. Find the output required to obtain a profit of $10,000.

Solution: In order to obtain a profit of $10,000, we have

$$\text{profit} = \text{total revenue} - \text{total cost}$$

$$10,000 = 8q - \left(\frac{22}{9}q + 5000\right)$$

$$15,000 = \frac{50}{9}q$$

$$q = 2700$$

Thus, 2700 units must be produced.

Now Work Problem 9 ◁

EXAMPLE 4   Break-Even Quantity

Determine the break-even quantity of XYZ Manufacturing Co., given the following data: total fixed cost, $1200; variable cost per unit, $2; total revenue for selling q units, $y_{TR} = 100\sqrt{q}$.

Solution: For q units of output,

$$y_{TR} = 100\sqrt{q}$$

$$y_{TC} = 2q + 1200$$

Equating total revenue to total cost gives

$$100\sqrt{q} = 2q + 1200$$

$$50\sqrt{q} = q + 600 \qquad \text{dividing both sides by 2}$$

Squaring both sides, we have

$$2500q = q^2 + 1200q + (600)^2$$

$$0 = q^2 - 1300q + 360,000$$

By the quadratic formula,

$$q = \frac{1300 \pm \sqrt{250,000}}{2}$$

$$q = \frac{1300 \pm 500}{2}$$

$$q = 400 \quad \text{or} \quad q = 900$$

Although both $q = 400$ and $q = 900$ are break-even quantities, observe in Figure 3.49 that when $q > 900$, total cost is greater than total revenue, so there will always be a loss. This occurs because here total revenue is not linearly related to output. Thus, producing more than the break-even quantity does not necessarily guarantee a profit.

Now Work Problem 21 ◁

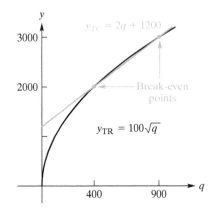

FIGURE 3.49   Two break-even points.

PROBLEMS 3.6

In Problems 1–8, you are given a supply equation and a demand equation for a product. If p represents price per unit in dollars and q represents the number of units per unit of time, find the equilibrium point. In Problems 1 and 2, sketch the system.

1. Supply: $p = \frac{2}{100}q + 3$, Demand: $p = -\frac{3}{100}q + 11$

2. Supply: $p = \frac{1}{1500}q + 4$, Demand: $p = -\frac{1}{2000}q + 9$

3. Supply: $35q - 2p + 250 = 0$, Demand: $65q + p - 537.5 = 0$

4. Supply: $246p - 3.25q - 2460 = 0$, Demand: $410p + 3q - 14,452.5 = 0$

5. Supply: $p = 2q + 20$, Demand: $p = 200 - 2q^2$

6. Supply: $p = (q + 12)^2$, Demand: $p = 644 - 6q - q^2$

7. Supply: $p = \sqrt{q + 10}$, Demand: $p = 20 - q$

8. Supply: $p = \frac{1}{4}q + 6$, Demand: $p = \dfrac{2240}{q + 12}$

In Problems 9–14, y_{TR} represents total revenue in dollars and y_{TC} represents total cost in dollars for a manufacturer. If q represents both the number of units produced and the number of units sold, find the break-even quantity. Sketch a break-even chart in Problems 9 and 10.

9. $y_{TR} = 4q$
   $y_{TC} = 2q + 5000$

10. $y_{TR} = 14q$
    $y_{TC} = \frac{40}{3}q + 1200$

11. $y_{TR} = 0.02q$
    $y_{TC} = 0.5q + 30$

12. $y_{TR} = 0.25q$
    $y_{TC} = 0.16q + 360$

13. $y_{TR} = 90 - \dfrac{900}{q+3}$
    $y_{TC} = 1.1q + 37.3$

14. $y_{TR} = 0.1q^2 + 9q$
    $y_{TC} = 3q + 400$

15. Business Supply and demand equations for a certain product are

$$3q - 200p + 1800 = 0$$

and

$$3q + 100p - 1800 = 0$$

respectively, where p represents the price per unit in dollars and q represents the number of units sold per time period.
(a) Find the equilibrium price algebraically, and derive it graphically.
(b) Find the equilibrium price when a tax of 27 cents per unit is imposed on the supplier.

16. Business A manufacturer of a product sells all that is produced. The total revenue is given by $y_{TR} = 8q$, and the total cost is given by $y_{TC} = 7q + 500$, where q represents the number of units produced and sold.
(a) Find the level of production at the break-even point, and draw the break-even chart.
(b) Find the level of production at the break-even point if the total cost increases by 4%.

17. Business A manufacturer sells a product at $8.35 per unit, selling all produced. The fixed cost is $2116 and the variable cost is $7.20 per unit. At what level of production will there be a profit of $4600? At what level of production will there be a loss of $1150? At what level of production will the break-even point occur?

18. Business The market equilibrium point for a product occurs when 13,500 units are produced at a price of $4.50 per unit. The producer will supply no units at $1, and the consumers will demand no units at $20. Find the supply and demand equations if they are both linear.

19. Business A manufacturer of a children's toy will break even at a sales volume of $200,000. Fixed costs are $40,000, and each unit of output sells for $5. Determine the variable cost per unit.

20. Business The Bigfoot Sandal Co. manufactures sandals for which the material cost is $0.85 per pair and the labor cost is $0.96 per pair. Additional variable costs amount to $0.32 per pair. Fixed costs are $70,500. If each pair sells for $2.63, how many pairs must be sold for the company to break even?

21. Business (a) Find the break-even points for company X, which sells all it produces, if the variable cost per unit is $3, fixed costs are $2, and $y_{TR} = 5\sqrt{q}$, where q is the number of thousands of units of output produced.
(b) Graph the total revenue curve and the total cost curve in the same plane.
(c) Use your answer in (a) to report the quantity interval in which maximum profit occurs.

22. Business A company has determined that the demand equation for its product is $p = 1000/q$, where p is the price per unit for q units produced and sold in some period. Determine the quantity demanded when the price per unit is (a) $4, (b) $2, and (c) $0.50. For each of these prices, determine the total revenue that the company will receive. What will be the revenue regardless of the price? [*Hint:* Find the revenue when the price is p dollars.]

23. Business Using the data in Example 1, determine how the original equilibrium price will be affected if the company is given a government subsidy of $1.50 per unit.

24. Business The Monroe Forging Company sells a corrugated steel product to the Standard Manufacturing Company and is in competition on such sales with other suppliers of the Standard Manufacturing Co. The vice president of sales of Monroe Forging Co. believes that by reducing the price of the product, a 40% increase in the volume of units sold to the Standard Manufacturing Co. could be secured. As the manager of the cost and analysis department, you have been asked to analyze the proposal of the vice president and submit your recommendations as to whether it is financially beneficial to the Monroe Forging Co. You are specifically requested to determine the following:
(a) Net profit or loss based on the pricing proposal
(b) Unit sales volume under the proposed price that is required to make the same $40,000 profit that is now earned at the current price and unit sales volume
Use the following data in your analysis:

	Current Operations	Proposal of Vice President of Sales
Unit price	$2.50	$2.00
Unit sales volume	200,000 units	280,000 units
Variable cost		
Total	$350,000	$490,000
Per unit	$1.75	$1.75
Fixed cost	$110,000	$110,000
Profit	$40,000	?

25. Business Suppose products A and B have demand and supply equations that are related to each other. If q_A and q_B are the quantities produced and sold of A and B, respectively, and p_A and p_B are their respective prices, the demand equations are

$$q_A = 7 - p_A + p_B$$

and

$$q_B = 24 + p_A - p_B$$

and the supply equations are

$$q_A = -3 + 4p_A - 2p_B$$

and

$$q_B = -5 - 2p_A + 4p_B$$

Eliminate q_A and q_B to get the equilibrium prices.

26. Business The supply equation for a product is

$$p = q^2 - 10$$

and the demand equation is

$$p = \frac{20}{q - 2}$$

Here p represents price per unit in dollars and $q > 3.2$ represents number of units (in thousands) per unit time. Graph both equations, and, from your graph, determine the equilibrium price and equilibrium quantity to one decimal place.

27. Business For a manufacturer, the total-revenue equation is

$$y_{TR} = 20.5\sqrt{q + 4} - 41$$

and the total-cost equation is

$$y_{TC} = 0.02q^3 + 10.4,$$

where q represents (in thousands) both the number of units produced and the number of units sold. Graph a break-even chart and find the break-even quantity.

Chapter 3 Review

Important Terms and Symbols   Examples

Summary

The orientation of a nonvertical line is characterized by the slope of the line given by

$$m = \frac{y_2 - y_1}{x_2 - x_1}$$

where (x_1, y_1) and (x_2, y_2) are two different points on the line. The slope of a vertical line is not defined, and the slope of a horizontal line is zero. Lines rising from left to right have positive slopes; lines falling from left to right have negative slopes. Two lines are parallel if and only if they have the same slope or both are vertical. Two lines with non-zero slopes m_1 and m_2 are perpendicular to each other if and only if $m_1 = -\dfrac{1}{m_2}$. Any horizontal line and any vertical line are perpendicular to each other.

Basic forms of equations of lines are as follows:

$y - y_1 = m(x - x_1)$	point-slope form
$y = mx + b$	slope-intercept form
$x = a$	vertical line
$y = b$	horizontal line
$Ax + By + C = 0$	general

The linear function

$$f(x) = ax + b \quad (a \neq 0)$$

has a straight line for its graph.

In economics, supply functions and demand functions have the form $p = f(q)$ and play an important role. Each gives a correspondence between the price p of a product and the number of units q of the product that manufacturers (or consumers) will supply (or purchase) at that price during some time period.

A quadratic function has the form

$$f(x) = ax^2 + bx + c \quad (a \neq 0)$$

The graph of f is a parabola that opens upward if $a > 0$ and downward if $a < 0$. The vertex is

$$\left(-\frac{b}{2a}, f\left(-\frac{b}{2a} \right) \right)$$

and the y-intercept is c. The axis of symmetry and the x- and y-intercepts, are useful in sketching the graph.

A system of linear equations can be solved with the method of elimination by addition or elimination by substitution. A solution may involve one or more parameters. Substitution is also useful in solving nonlinear systems.

Solving a system formed by the supply and demand equations for a product gives the equilibrium point, which indicates the price at which consumers will purchase the same quantity of a product that producers wish to sell at that price.

Profit is total revenue minus total cost, where total cost is the sum of fixed costs and variable costs. The break-even points are the points where total revenue equals total cost.

Review Problems

1. The slope of the line through $(2, 5)$ and $(3, k)$ is 4. Find k.

2. The slope of the line through $(5, 4)$ and $(k, 4)$ is 0. Find k.

In Problems 3–9, determine the slope-intercept form and a general linear form of an equation of the straight line that has the indicated properties.

3. Passes through $(-2, 3)$ and has y-intercept -1

4. Passes through $(-1, -1)$ and is parallel to the line $y = 3x - 4$

5. Passes through $(8, 3)$ and has slope 3

6. Passes through $(3, 5)$ and is vertical

7. Passes through $(-2, 4)$ and is horizontal

8. Passes through $(1, 2)$ and is perpendicular to the line $-3y + 5x = 7$

9. Has y-intercept -3 and is perpendicular to $2y + 5x = 2$

10. Determine whether the point $(3, 11)$ lies on the line through $(2, 7)$ and $(4, 13)$.

In Problems 11–16, determine whether the lines are parallel, perpendicular, or neither.

11. $x + 4y + 2 = 0$, $8x - 2y - 2 = 0$

12. $y - 2 = 2(x - 1)$, $2x + 4y - 3 = 0$

13. $x - 3 = 2(y + 4)$, $y = 4x + 2$

14. $2x + 7y - 4 = 0$, $6x + 21y = 90$

15. $y = 5x + 2$, $10x - 2y = 3$

16. $y = 7x$, $y = 7$

In Problems 17–20, write each line in slope-intercept form, and sketch. What is the slope of the line?

17. $3x - 2y = 4$ **18.** $x = -3y + 4$

19. $4 - 3y = 0$ **20.** $3x - 5y = 0$

In Problems 21–30, graph each function. For those that are linear, give the slope and the vertical-axis intercept. For those that are quadratic, give all intercepts and the vertex.

21. $y = f(x) = 17 - 5x$ **22.** $s = g(t) = 5 - 3t + t^2$

23. $y = f(x) = 9 - x^2$ **24.** $y = f(x) = 3x - 7$

25. $y = h(t) = 3 + 2t + t^2$ **26.** $y = k(t) = -3 - 3t$

27. $p = g(t) = -7t$ **28.** $y = F(x) = (2x - 1)^2$

29. $y = F(x) = -(x^2 + 2x + 3)$ **30.** $y = f(x) = 5x + 2$

In Problems 31–44, solve the given system.

31. $\begin{cases} 2x - y = 6 \\ 3x + 2y = 5 \end{cases}$ **32.** $\begin{cases} 8x - 4y = 7 \\ y = 2x - 4 \end{cases}$

33. $\begin{cases} 7x + 5y = 5 \\ 6x + 5y = 3 \end{cases}$ **34.** $\begin{cases} 2x + 4y = 8 \\ 3x + 6y = 12 \end{cases}$

35. $\begin{cases} \dfrac{1}{2}x - \dfrac{1}{3}y = 2 \\ \dfrac{3}{4}x + \dfrac{1}{2}y = 3 \end{cases}$ **36.** $\begin{cases} \dfrac{1}{3}x - \dfrac{1}{4}y = \dfrac{1}{12} \\ \dfrac{4}{3}x + 3y = \dfrac{5}{3} \end{cases}$

37. $\begin{cases} 3x - 2y + z = -2 \\ 2x + y + z = 1 \\ x + 3y - z = 3 \end{cases}$ **38.** $\begin{cases} 2x + \dfrac{3y + x}{3} = 9 \\ y + \dfrac{5x + 2y}{4} = 7 \end{cases}$

39. $\begin{cases} x^2 - y + 5x = 2 \\ x^2 + y = 3 \end{cases}$ **40.** $\begin{cases} y = \dfrac{3}{x + 2} \\ x + y - 2 = 0 \end{cases}$

41. $\begin{cases} x + 2z = -2 \\ x + y + z = 5 \end{cases}$ **42.** $\begin{cases} x + y + z = 0 \\ x - y + z = 0 \\ x + z = 0 \end{cases}$

43. $\begin{cases} x - y - z = 0 \\ 2x - 2y + 3z = 0 \end{cases}$ **44.** $\begin{cases} 2x - 5y + 6z = 1 \\ 4x - 10y + 12z = 2 \end{cases}$

45. Suppose a and b are linearly related so that $a = 0$ when $b = -3$ and $a = 3$ when $b = -5$. Find a general linear form of an equation that relates a and b. Also, find a when $b = 3$.

46. Temperature and Heart Rate   When the temperature, T (in degrees Celsius), of a cat is reduced, the cat's heart rate, r (in beats per minute), decreases. Under laboratory conditions, a cat at a temperature of 36°C had a heart rate of 206, and at a temperature of 30°C its heart rate was 122.
If r is linearly related to T, where T is between 26 and 38,
(a) determine an equation for r in terms of T, and (b) determine the cat's heart rate at a temperature of 27°C.

47. Suppose f is a linear function such that $f(1) = 5$ and $f(x)$ decreases by four units for every three-unit increase in x. Find $f(x)$.

48. If f is a linear function such that $f(-1) = 8$ and $f(2) = 5$, find $f(x)$.

49. Maximum Revenue   The demand function for a manufacturer's product is $p = f(q) = 200 - 2q$, where p is the price (in dollars) per unit when q units are demanded. Find the level of production that maximizes the manufacturer's total revenue, and determine this revenue.

50. Sales Tax   The difference in price of two items before a 7% sales tax is imposed is $2.00. The difference in price after the sales tax is imposed is allegedly $3.10. Show that this scenario is not possible.

51. Equilibrium Price   If the supply and demand equations of a certain product are $120p - q - 240 = 0$ and $100p + q - 1200 = 0$, respectively, find the equilibrium price.

52. Psychology In psychology, the term *semantic memory* refers to our knowledge of the meaning and relationships of words, as well as the means by which we store and retrieve such information.[6] In a network model of semantic memory, there is a hierarchy of levels at which information is stored. In an experiment by Collins and Quillian based on a network model, data were obtained on the reaction time to respond to simple questions about nouns. The graph of the results shows that, on the average, the reaction time, R (in milliseconds), is a linear function of the level, L, at which a characterizing property of the noun is stored. At level 0, the reaction time is 1310; at level 2, the reaction time is 1460. (a) Find the linear function. (b) Find the reaction time at level 1. (c) Find the slope and determine its significance.

53. Break-Even Point A manufacturer of a certain product sells all that is produced. Determine the break-even point if the product is sold at $16 per unit, fixed cost is $10,000, and variable cost is given by $y_{VC} = 8q$, where q is the number of units produced (y_{VC} expressed in dollars).

54. Temperature Conversion Celsius temperature, C, is a linear function of Fahrenheit temperature, F. Use the facts that 32°F is the same as 0°C and 212°F is the same as 100°C to find this function. Also, find C when $F = 50$.

55. Pollution In one province of a developing nation, water pollution is analyzed using a supply-and-demand model. The

environmental supply equation $L = 0.0183 - \dfrac{0.0042}{p}$ describes the levy per ton, L (in dollars), as a function of total pollution, p (in tons per square kilometer), for $p \geq 0.2295$. The *environmental demand equation,* $L = 0.0005 + \dfrac{0.0378}{p}$, describes the per-ton abatement cost as a function of total pollution for $p > 0$. Find the expected equilibrium level of total pollution to two decimal places.[7]

56. Graphically solve the linear system
$$\begin{cases} 3x + 4y = 20 \\ 7x + 5y = 64 \end{cases}$$

57. Graphically solve the linear system
$$\begin{cases} 0.3x - 0.4y = 2.5 \\ 0.5x + 0.7y = 3.1 \end{cases}$$
Round x and y to two decimal places.

58. Graphically solve the nonlinear system
$$\begin{cases} y = \dfrac{3}{7x} \\ y = x^2 - 9 \end{cases} \quad \text{where } x > 0$$
Round x and y to two decimal places.

59. Graphically solve the nonlinear system
$$\begin{cases} y = x^3 + 1 \\ y = 2 - x^2 \end{cases}$$
Round x and y to two decimal places.

60. Graphically solve the equation
$$x^2 + 4 = x^3 - 3x$$
by treating it as a system. Round x to two decimal places.

Q EXPLORE & EXTEND   Mobile Phone Billing Plans

Selecting a mobile phone plan can be quite difficult. In most urban areas there are many service providers each offering a number of plans. The plans can include monthly access fees, free minutes, charges for additional airtime, regional roaming charges, national roaming charges, peak and off-peak rates, and long-distance charges (not to mention activation fees, cancellation fees, and the like). Even if a consumer has a fairly good knowledge of her typical mobile phone usage, she may have to do dozens of calculations to be absolutely sure of getting the best deal in town.

Mathematical modeling often involves making informed decisions about which factors in a problem are less important. These are then ignored to get a reasonably good approximate solution—in a reasonable amount of time. You may have heard the expression "simplifying assumptions." There are a lot of old jokes about this process. For example, a mathematically minded bookie who

is trying to calculate the attributes of the horses in a given race should probably not assume that all the horses are perfectly spherical. We will simplify our comparison of mobile phone plans by considering just the number of "monthly home airtime minutes" available for the "monthly access fee" and the price per minute of "additional minutes." Many providers offer plans in terms of these basic parameters.

Examining Verizon's offerings for the Saddle River, New Jersey, area, in the spring of 2006, we found these America's Choice monthly plans:

P_1: 450 minutes for $39.99 plus $0.45 per additional minute

P_2: 900 minutes for $59.99 plus $0.40 per additional minute

P_3: 1350 minutes for $79.99 plus $0.35 per additional minute

---

[6]G. R. Loftus and E. F. Loftus, *Human Memory: The Processing of Information* (New York: Lawrence Erlbaum Associates, Inc., distributed by the Halsted Press, Division of John Wiley & Sons, Inc., 1976).

[7]See Hua Wang and David Wheeler, "Pricing Industrial Pollution in China: An Economic Analysis of the Levy System," World Bank Policy Research Working Paper #1644, September 1996.

P_4: 2000 minutes for $99.99 plus $0.25 per additional minute

P_5: 4000 minutes for $149.99 plus $0.25 per additional minute

P_6: 6000 minutes for $199.99 plus $0.20 per additional minute

where we have added the labels P_i, for $i = 1, 2, \ldots, 6$, for our further convenience. Thus, each entry above takes the form

P_i: M_i minutes for $\$C_i$ plus $\$c_i$ per additional minute

where, for plan P_i, M_i is the number of airtime minutes available for the monthly access fee of C_i, with each additional minute costing c_i.

In the spring of 2009, for the same area, we found that Verizon had many new plans. However, there was a grouping that included plans similar to the first three above but with the last three replaced by a single plan:

P_*: unlimited minutes for $99.99

To represent these plans mathematically, we will write total monthly cost as a function of time, for each plan. In

fact, we will write $P_i(t)$ for the monthly cost of t minutes using plan P_i, for $i = 1 \cdots 6$. For each of these plans, the resulting function is a simple case-defined function with just two cases to consider. For these plans, we must consider $t \le M_i$ and $t > M_i$. If $t \le M_i$, then the cost is simply C_i but if $t > M_i$, then the number of additional minutes is $t - M_i$ and, since each of these costs c_i, the additional minutes cost $c_i(t - M_i)$, yielding in this case a total cost of $C_i + c_i(t - M_i)$. We also have $P_*(t)$.

Putting in the numerical values, we have the following six functions:

$$P_1(t) = \begin{cases} 39.99 & \text{if } t \le 450 \\ 39.99 + 0.45(t - 450) & \text{if } t > 450 \end{cases}$$

$$P_2(t) = \begin{cases} 59.99 & \text{if } t \le 900 \\ 59.99 + 0.40(t - 900) & \text{if } t > 900 \end{cases}$$

$$P_3(t) = \begin{cases} 79.99 & \text{if } t \le 1350 \\ 79.99 + 0.35(t - 1350) & \text{if } t > 1350 \end{cases}$$

$$P_4(t) = \begin{cases} 99.99 & \text{if } t \le 2000 \\ 99.99 + 0.25(t - 2000) & \text{if } t > 2000 \end{cases}$$

$$P_5(t) = \begin{cases} 149.99 & \text{if } t \le 4000 \\ 149.99 + 0.25(t - 4000) & \text{if } t > 4000 \end{cases}$$

$$P_6(t) = \begin{cases} 199.99 & \text{if } t \le 6000 \\ 199.99 + 0.20(t - 6000) & \text{if } t > 6000 \end{cases}$$

$$P_*(t) = 99.99$$

The graph of each function is easy to describe. In fact for the generic $P_i(t)$ we have, in the first quadrant, a horizontal line segment starting at $(0, C_i)$ and ending at (M_i, C_i). The graph continues, to the right of (M_i, C_i) as an infinite line segment, starting at (M_i, C_i) with slope c_i. We see also that $P_*(t)$ is a constant function.

However, to see how the functions actually compare, we need to graph them all, in the same plane. We could do this by hand, but this is a good opportunity to use a handy capability of a graphing calculator. We enter the function $P_1(t)$ as

$$Y1 = 39.99 + 0.45(X - 450)(X > 450)$$

The > comes from the TEST menu, and the expression $(X > 450)$ equals either 1 or 0, depending on whether x is, or is not, greater than 450. We enter the other five case-defined functions in similar fashion and the constant function P_* as

$$Y0 = 99.99$$

Graphing them all together, we get the display shown in Figure 3.50.

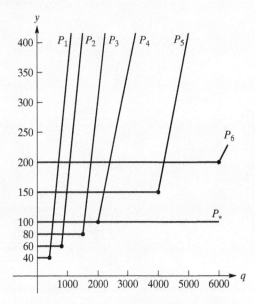

FIGURE 3.50 Costs under different plans.

Which plan is best depends on the amount of calling time: For any given monthly airtime, the best plan is the one whose graph is lowest at that amount. If it were not already clear, the graph makes it obvious why plans P_4, P_5, and P_6 were no longer offered after the introduction of plan P_*.

For very low calling times, the P_1 plan is best, but even at 495 minutes monthly usage it is more expensive than plan P_2 and remains so for any greater monthly usage. To find exactly the usage at which plans P_1 and P_2 cost the same, we of course solve

$$P_1(t) = P_2(t)$$

but because each is a case-defined function we really need the graphs to tell us *where to look for a solution*. From these it is clear that the intersection of the P_1 and P_2 curves occurs when P_1 is defined by its second branch and P_2 is defined by its first branch. Thus we must solve

$$39.99 + 0.45(t - 450) = 59.99$$

for t. To two decimal places this gives $t = 494.44$.

In fact, the graph suggests that it will be instructive to calculate $P_1(900)$ since $P_2(900)$ is still $59.99, although of course the cost of P_2 increases for all $t > 900$. We find

$$P_1(900) = 39.99 + 0.45(900 - 450) = 39.99 + 0.45(450)$$

$$= 39.99 + 202.50 = 242.49$$

To research wireless phone service plans in your area, consult www.point.com.

Problems

1. If a person who actually uses quite a lot of airtime minutes a month, say 1351, is lured by low monthly access fees, calculate how much he will lose by using plan P_1 rather than plan P_*.

2. We have seen that for monthly usage less than 494.44 minutes, plan P_1 is best. Determine the interval of usage for which P_2 is best by finding the value of t for which $P_2(t) = P_3(t)$.

3. Repeat Problem 2 for Plan P_3.

4

Exponential and Logarithmic Functions

EXPLORE & EXTEND

Drug Dosages

Just as biological viruses spread through contact between organisms, so computer viruses spread when computers interact via the Internet. Computer scientists study how to fight computer viruses, which cause a lot of damage in the form of deleted and corrupted files. One thing computer scientists do is devise mathematical models of how quickly viruses spread. For instance, on Friday, March 26, 1999, the first cases of the virus known as Melissa were reported; by Monday, March 29, Melissa had reached over 100,000 computers.

Exponential functions, which this chapter discusses in detail, provide one plausible model. Consider a computer virus that hides in an e-mail attachment and, once the attachment is downloaded, automatically sends a message with a similar attachment to every address in the host computer's e-mail address book. If the typical address book contains 20 addresses, and if the typical computer user retrieves his or her e-mail once a day, then a virus on a single machine will have infected 20 machines after one day, $20^2 = 400$ machines after two days, $20^3 = 8000$ after three days, and, in general, after t days, the number N of infected computers will be given by the exponential function $N(t) = 20^t$.

This model assumes that all the computers involved are linked, via their address book lists, into a single, well-connected group. Exponential models are most accurate for small values of t; this model, in particular, ignores the slowdown that occurs when most e-mails start going to computers already infected, which happens as several days pass. For example, our model tells us that after eight days, the virus will infect $20^8 = 25.6$ billion computers—more computers than actually exist! But despite its limitations, the exponential model does explain why new viruses often infect many thousands of machines before antivirus experts have had time to react.

Objective

To study exponential functions and their applications to such areas as compound interest, population growth, and radioactive decay.

4.1 Exponential Functions

The functions of the form $f(x) = b^x$, for constant b, are important in mathematics, business, economics, science and other areas of study. An excellent example is $f(x) = 2^x$. Such functions are called *exponential functions*. More precisely,

> **Definition**
>
> The function f defined by
>
> $$f(x) = b^x$$
>
> where $b > 0$, $b \neq 1$, and the exponent x is any real number, is called an **exponential function** with base b.[1]

CAUTION!

Do not confuse the exponential function $y = 2^x$ with the *power function* $y = x^2$, which has a variable base and a constant exponent.

Since the exponent in b^x can be any real number, you may wonder how we assign a value to something like $2^{\sqrt{2}}$, where the exponent is an irrational number. Stated simply, we use approximations. Because $\sqrt{2} = 1.41421\ldots$, $2^{\sqrt{2}}$ is approximately $2^{1.4} = 2^{7/5} = \sqrt[5]{2^7}$, which *is* defined. Better approximations are $2^{1.41} = 2^{141/100} = \sqrt[100]{2^{141}}$, and so on. In this way, the meaning of $2^{\sqrt{2}}$ becomes clear. A calculator value of $2^{\sqrt{2}}$ is (approximately) 2.66514.

When you work with exponential functions, it may be necessary to apply rules for exponents. These rules are as follows, where x and y are real numbers and b and c are positive.

TO REVIEW exponents, refer to Section 0.3.

Rules for Exponents

1. $b^x b^y = b^{x+y}$

2. $\dfrac{b^x}{b^y} = b^{x-y}$

3. $(b^x)^y = b^{xy}$

4. $(bc)^x = b^x c^x$

5. $\left(\dfrac{b}{c}\right)^x = \dfrac{b^x}{c^x}$

6. $b^1 = b$

7. $b^0 = 1$

8. $b^{-x} = \dfrac{1}{b^x}$

Some functions that do not appear to have the exponential form b^x can be put in that form by applying the preceding rules. For example, $2^{-x} = 1/(2^x) = (\frac{1}{2})^x$ and $3^{2x} = (3^2)^x = 9^x$.

EXAMPLE 1   Bacteria Growth

APPLY IT ▶

1. The number of bacteria in a culture that doubles every hour is given by $N(t) = A \cdot 2^t$, where A is the number originally present and t is the number of hours the bacteria have been doubling. Use a graphing calculator to plot this function for various values of $A > 1$. How are the graphs similar? How does the value of A alter the graph?

The number of bacteria present in a culture after t minutes is given by

$$N(t) = 300 \left(\frac{4}{3}\right)^t$$

Note that $N(t)$ is a constant multiple of the exponential function $\left(\dfrac{4}{3}\right)^t$.

---

[1] If $b = 1$, then $f(x) = 1^x = 1$. This function is already known to us as a constant function.

a. How many bacteria are present initially?

Solution: Here we want to find $N(t)$ when $t = 0$. We have

$$N(0) = 300 \left(\frac{4}{3}\right)^0 = 300(1) = 300$$

Thus, 300 bacteria are initially present.

b. Approximately how many bacteria are present after 3 minutes?

Solution:

$$N(3) = 300 \left(\frac{4}{3}\right)^3 = 300 \left(\frac{64}{27}\right) = \frac{6400}{9} \approx 711$$

Hence, approximately 711 bacteria are present after 3 minutes.

Now Work Problem 31 ◁

Graphs of Exponential Functions

APPLY IT ▶

2. Suppose an investment increases by 10% every year. Make a table of the factor by which the investment increases from the original amount for 0 to 4 years. For each year, write an expression for the increase as a power of some base. What base did you use? How does that base relate to the problem? Use your table to graph the multiplicative increase as a function of the number of years. Use your graph to determine when the investment will double.

EXAMPLE 2   Graphing Exponential Functions with $b > 1$

Graph the exponential functions $f(x) = 2^x$ and $f(x) = 5^x$.

Solution: By plotting points and connecting them, we obtain the graphs in Figure 4.1. For the graph of $f(x) = 5^x$, because of the unit distance chosen on the y-axis, the points $(-2, \frac{1}{25})$, $(2, 25)$, and $(3, 125)$ are not shown.

We can make some observations about these graphs. The domain of each function consists of all real numbers, and the range consists of all positive real numbers. Each graph has y-intercept $(0, 1)$. Moreover, the graphs have the same general shape. Each *rises* from left to right. As x increases, $f(x)$ also increases. In fact, $f(x)$ increases without bound. However, in quadrant I, the graph of $f(x) = 5^x$ rises more quickly than that of $f(x) = 2^x$ because the base in 5^x is *greater* than the base in 2^x (that is, $5 > 2$). Looking at quadrant II, we see that as x becomes very negative, the graphs of both functions approach the x-axis.[2] This implies that the function values get very close to 0.

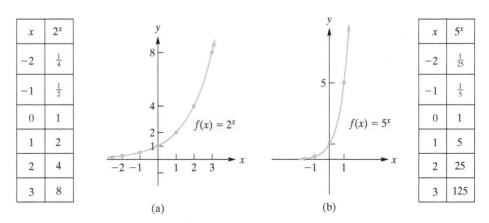

FIGURE 4.1   Graphs of $f(x) = 2^x$ and $f(x) = 5^x$.

Now Work Problem 1 ◁

---

[2]We say that the x-axis is an *asymptote* for each graph.

The observations made in Example 2 are true for all exponential functions whose base b is greater than 1. Example 3 will examine the case for a base between 0 and 1 $(0 < b < 1)$.

APPLY IT ▶

3. Suppose the value of a car depreciates by 15% every year. Make a table of the factor by which the value decreases from the original amount for 0 to 3 years. For each year, write an expression for the decrease as a power of some base. What base did you use? How does that base relate to the problem? Use your table to graph the multiplicative decrease as a function of the number of years. Use your graph to determine when the car will be worth half as much as its original price.

EXAMPLE 3   Graphing Exponential Functions with $0 < b < 1$

Graph the exponential function $f(x) = \left(\frac{1}{2}\right)^x$.

Solution: By plotting points and connecting them, we obtain the graph in Figure 4.2. Notice that the domain consists of all real numbers, and the range consists of all positive real numbers. The graph has y-intercept $(0, 1)$. Compared to the graphs in Example 2, the graph here *falls* from left to right. That is, as x increases, $f(x)$ decreases. Notice that as x becomes very positive, $f(x)$ takes on values close to 0 and the graph approaches the x-axis. However, as x becomes very negative, the function values are unbounded.

Now Work Problem 3 ◁

There are two basic shapes for the graphs of exponential functions, and they depend on the base involved.

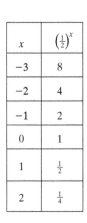

x	$\left(\frac{1}{2}\right)^x$
-3	8
-2	4
-1	2
0	1
1	$\frac{1}{2}$
2	$\frac{1}{4}$

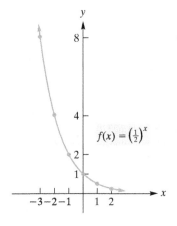

FIGURE 4.2   Graph of $f(x) = \left(\frac{1}{2}\right)^x$.

In general, the graph of an exponential function has one of two shapes, depending on the value of the base b. This is illustrated in Figure 4.3. It is important to observe that in either case the graph passes the horizontal line test. Thus all exponential functions are one-to-one. The basic properties of an exponential function and its graph are summarized in Table 4.1.

Recall from Section 2.7 that the graph of one function may be related to that of another by means of a certain transformation. Our next example pertains to this concept.

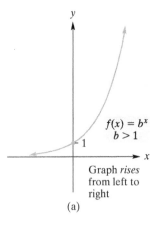
Graph *rises* from left to right
(a)

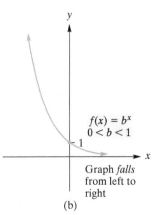
Graph *falls* from left to right
(b)

FIGURE 4.3   General shapes of $f(x) = b^x$.

Table 4.1 Properties of the Exponential Function $f(x) = b^x$

1. The domain of any exponential function is $(-\infty, \infty)$.
   The range of any exponential function is $(0, \infty)$.
2. The graph of $f(x) = b^x$ has y-intercept $(0, 1)$.
   There is no x-intercept.
3. If $b > 1$, the graph *rises* from left to right.
   If $0 < b < 1$, the graph *falls* from left to right.
4. If $b > 1$, the graph approaches the x-axis as x becomes more and more negative.
   If $0 < b < 1$, the graph approaches the x-axis as x becomes more and more positive.

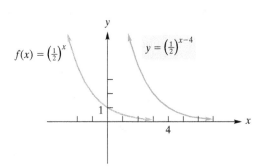

FIGURE 4.4   Graph of $y = 2^x - 3$.

FIGURE 4.5   Graph of $y = \left(\frac{1}{2}\right)^{x-4}$.

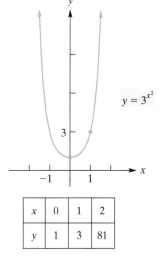

x	0	1	2
y	1	3	81

FIGURE 4.6   Graph of $y = 3^{x^2}$.

Example 4 makes use of transformations
from Table 2.2 of Section 2.7.

APPLY IT ▶

4. After watching his sister's money
grow for three years in a plan with
an 8% yearly return, George started a
savings account with the same plan. If
$y = 1.08^t$ represents the multiplicative increase in his sister's account,
write an equation that will represent
the multiplicative increase in George's
account, using the same time reference.
If George has a graph of the multiplicative increase in his sister's money at
time t years since she started saving,
how could he use the graph to project
the increase in his money?

EXAMPLE 4   Transformations of Exponential Functions

a. Use the graph of $y = 2^x$ to plot $y = 2^x - 3$.

Solution: The function has the form $f(x) - c$, where $f(x) = 2^x$ and $c = 3$. Thus
its graph is obtained by shifting the graph of $f(x) = 2^x$ three units downward. (See
Figure 4.4.)

b. Use the graph of $y = \left(\frac{1}{2}\right)^x$ to graph $y = \left(\frac{1}{2}\right)^{x-4}$.

Solution: The function has the form $f(x - c)$, where $f(x) = \left(\frac{1}{2}\right)^x$ and $c = 4$. Hence,
its graph is obtained by shifting the graph of $f(x) = \left(\frac{1}{2}\right)^x$ four units to the right. (See
Figure 4.5.)

Now Work Problem 7 ◁

EXAMPLE 5   Graph of a Function with a Constant Base

Graph $y = 3^{x^2}$.

Solution: Although this is not an exponential function, it does have a constant base.
We see that replacing x by $-x$ results in the same equation. Thus, the graph is symmetric
about the y-axis. Plotting some points and using symmetry gives the graph in Figure 4.6.

Now Work Problem 5 ◁

TECHNOLOGY ▮▮▮▯

If $y = 4^x$, consider the problem of finding x when $y = 6$.
One way to solve this equation is to find the intersection of
the graphs of $y = 6$ and $y = 4^x$. Figure 4.7 shows that x is
approximately 1.29.

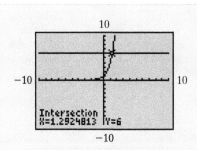

FIGURE 4.7   Solving the equation $6 = 4^x$.

Compound Interest

Exponential functions are involved in **compound interest,** whereby the interest earned by an invested amount of money (or **principal**) is reinvested so that it, too, earns interest. That is, the interest is converted (or *compounded*) into principal, and hence, there is "interest on interest."

For example, suppose that $100 is invested at the rate of 5% compounded annually. At the end of the first year, the value of the investment is the original principal ($100), plus the interest on the principal [100(0.05)]:

$$100 + 100(0.05) = \$105$$

This is the amount on which interest is earned for the second year. At the end of the second year, the value of the investment is the principal at the end of the first year ($105), plus the interest on that sum [105(0.05)]:

$$105 + 105(0.05) = \$110.25$$

Thus, each year the principal increases by 5%. The $110.25 represents the original principal, plus all accrued interest; it is called the **accumulated amount** or **compound amount.** The difference between the compound amount and the original principal is called the **compound interest.** Here the compound interest is $110.25 - 100 = 10.25$.

More generally, if a principal of P dollars is invested at a rate of $100r$ percent compounded annually (for example, at 5%, r is 0.05), the compound amount after 1 year is $P + Pr$, or, by factoring, $P(1 + r)$. At the end of the second year, the compound amount is

$$P(1 + r) + [P(1 + r)]r = P(1 + r)[1 + r] \qquad \text{factoring}$$
$$= P(1 + r)^2$$

Actually, the calculation above using factoring is not necessary to show that the componded amount after two years is $P(1+r)^2$. Since *any* amount P is worth $P(1+r)$ a year later, it follows that the amount of $P(1 + r)$ is worth $P(1 + r)(1 + r) = P(1 + r)^2$ a year later and one year later still the amount of $P(1+r)^2$ is worth $P(1+r)^2(1+r) = P(1+r)^3$.

This pattern continues. After four years, the compound amount is $P(1 + r)^4$. In general, **the compound amount S of the principal P at the end of n years at the rate of r compounded annually** is given by

$$S = P(1 + r)^n \qquad (1)$$

Notice from Equation (1) that, for a given principal and rate, S is a function of n. In fact, S is a constant multiple of the exponential function with base $1 + r$.

APPLY IT ▶

5. Suppose $2000 is invested at 13% compounded annually. Find the value of the investment after five years. Find the interest earned over the first five years.

EXAMPLE 6   Compound Amount and Compound Interest

Suppose $1000 is invested for 10 years at 6% compounded annually.
a. Find the compound amount.

Solution: We use Equation (1) with $P = 1000$, $r = 0.06$, and $n = 10$:

$$S = 1000(1 + 0.06)^{10} = 1000(1.06)^{10} \approx \$1790.85$$

Figure 4.8 shows the graph of $S = 1000(1.06)^n$. Notice that as time goes on, the compound amount grows dramatically.

b. Find the compound interest.

Solution: Using the results from part (a), we have

$$\text{compound interest} = S - P$$
$$= 1790.85 - 1000 = \$790.85$$

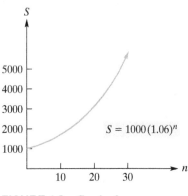

FIGURE 4.8   Graph of
$S = 1000(1.06)^n$.

Now Work Problem 19 ◁

Suppose the principal of $1000 in Example 6 is invested for 10 years as before, but this time the compounding takes place every three months (that is, *quarterly*) at the rate of $1\frac{1}{2}\%$ *per quarter*. Then there are four **interest periods** per year, and in 10 years there are $10(4) = 40$ interest periods. Thus, the compound amount with $r = 0.015$ is now

$$1000(1.015)^{40} \approx \$1814.02$$

and the compound interest is $814.02. Usually, the interest rate per interest period is stated as an annual rate. Here we would speak of an annual rate of 6% compounded quarterly, so that the rate per interest period, or the **periodic rate,** is $6\%/4 = 1.5\%$. This *quoted* annual rate of 6% is called the **nominal rate** or the **annual percentage rate (APR).** Unless otherwise stated, all interest rates will be assumed to be annual (nominal) rates. Thus a rate of 15% compounded monthly corresponds to a periodic rate of $15\%/12 = 1.25\%$.

On the basis of our discussion, we can generalize Equation (1). The formula

$$S = P(1 + r)^n \tag{2}$$

gives **the compound amount S of a principal P at the end of n interest periods at the periodic rate of** r.

We have seen that for a principal of $1000 at a nominal rate of 6% over a period of 10 years, annual compounding results in a compound interest of $790.85, and with quarterly compounding the compound interest is $814.02. It is typical that for a given nominal rate, the more frequent the compounding, the greater is the compound interest. However, while increasing the compounding frequency always increases the amount of interest earned, the effect is not unbounded. For example, with weekly compounding the compound interest is

$$1000 \left(1 + \frac{0.06}{52} \right)^{10(52)} - 1000 \approx \$821.49$$

and with daily compounding it is

$$1000 \left(1 + \frac{0.06}{365} \right)^{10(365)} - 1000 \approx \$822.03$$

Sometimes the phrase "money is worth" is used to express an annual interest rate. Thus, saying that money is worth 6% compounded quarterly refers to an annual (nominal) rate of 6% compounded quarterly.

Population Growth

Equation (2) can be applied not only to the growth of money, but also to other types of growth, such as that of population. For example, suppose the population P of a town of 10,000 is increasing at the rate of 2% per year. Then P is a function of time t, in years. It is common to indicate this functional dependence by writing

$$P = P(t)$$

Here the letter P is used in two ways: On the right side, P represents the function; on the left side, P represents the dependent variable. From Equation (2), we have

$$P(t) = 10,000(1 + 0.02)^t = 10,000(1.02)^t$$

The abbreviation APR is a common one and is found on credit card statements and in advertising.

CAUTION!⚠

A nominal rate of 6% does not necessarily mean that an investment increases in value by 6% in a year's time. The increase depends on the frequency of compounding.

APPLY IT ▶

6. A new company with five employees expects the number of employees to grow at the rate of 120% per year. Find the number of employees in four years.

EXAMPLE 7   Population Growth

The population of a town of 10,000 grows at the rate of 2% per year. Find the population three years from now.

Solution: From the preceding discussion,

$$P(t) = 10,000(1.02)^t$$

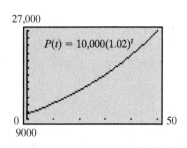

FIGURE 4.9 Graph of population function $P(t) = 10,000(1.02)^t$.

For $t = 3$, we have

$$P(3) = 10,000(1.02)^3 \approx 10,612$$

Thus, the population three years from now will be 10,612. (See Figure 4.9.)

Now Work Problem 15 ◁

The Number e

It is useful to conduct a "thought experiment," based on the discussion following Example 6, to introduce an important number. Suppose that a single dollar is invested for one year with an APR of 100% (remember, this is a thought experiment!) compounded annually. Then the compound amount S at the end of the year is given by

$$S = 1(1 + 1)^1 = 2^1 = 2$$

Without changing any of the other data, we now consider the effect of increasing the number of interest periods per year. If there are n interest periods per year, then the compound amount is given by

$$S = 1\left(1 + \frac{1}{n}\right)^n = \left(\frac{n+1}{n}\right)^n$$

In Table 4.2 we give approximate values for $\left(\dfrac{n+1}{n}\right)^n$ for some values of n.

Table 4.2 Approximations of e	
n	$\left(\dfrac{n+1}{n}\right)^n$
1	$\left(\frac{2}{1}\right)^1 = 2.00000$
2	$\left(\frac{3}{2}\right)^2 = 2.25000$
3	$\left(\frac{4}{3}\right)^3 \approx 2.37037$
4	$\left(\frac{5}{4}\right)^4 \approx 2.44141$
5	$\left(\frac{6}{5}\right)^5 = 2.48832$
10	$\left(\frac{11}{10}\right)^{10} \approx 2.59374$
100	$\left(\frac{101}{100}\right)^{100} \approx 2.70481$
1000	$\left(\frac{1001}{1000}\right)^{1000} \approx 2.71692$
10,000	$\left(\frac{10,001}{10,000}\right)^{10,000} \approx 2.71815$
100,000	$\left(\frac{100,001}{100,000}\right)^{100,000} \approx 2.71827$
1,000,000	$\left(\frac{1,000,001}{1,000,000}\right)^{1,000,000} \approx 2.71828$

Apparently, the numbers $\left(\dfrac{n+1}{n}\right)^n$ increase as n does. However, they do not increase without bound. For example, it is possible to show that for any positive integer n, $\left(\dfrac{n+1}{n}\right)^n < 3$. In terms of our thought experiment, this means that if you start with $1.00 invested at 100%, then, no matter how many interest periods there are per year, you will always have less than $3.00 at the end of a year. There is a smallest real number that is greater than all of the numbers $\left(\dfrac{n+1}{n}\right)^n$. It is denoted by the letter e, in honor of the Swiss mathematician Leonhard Euler (1707–1783). The number e is irrational so that its decimal expansion is nonrepeating, like those of π and $\sqrt{2}$ that we mentioned in Section 0.1. However, each of the numerical values for $\left(\frac{n+1}{n}\right)^n$ can be considered to be a decimal approximation of e. The approximate value $\left(\frac{1,000,001}{1,000,000}\right)^{1,000,000} \approx 2.71828$ gives an approximation of e that is correct to 5 decimal places. The approximation of e correct to 12 decimal places is $e \approx 2.718281828459$.

Exponential Function with Base e

The number e provides the most important base for an exponential function. In fact, the exponential function with base e is called the **natural exponential function** and even *the* **exponential function** to stress its importance.

Although e may seem to be a strange base, the natural exponential function has a remarkable property in calculus (which we will see in a later chapter) that justifies the name. It also occurs in economic analysis and problems involving growth or decay, such as population studies, compound interest, and radioactive decay. Approximate values of e^x can be found with a single key on most calculators. The graph of $y = e^x$ is shown in Figure 4.10. The accompanying table indicates y-values to two decimal places. Of course, the graph has the general shape of an exponential function with base greater than 1.

The graph of the natural exponential function in Figure 4.10 is important.

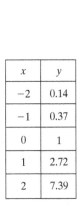

x	y
-2	0.14
-1	0.37
0	1
1	2.72
2	7.39

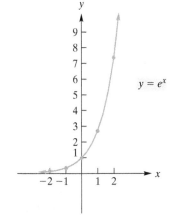

FIGURE 4.10   Graph of natural exponential function.

EXAMPLE 8   Graphs of Functions Involving e

APPLY IT ▷

7. The multiplicative decrease in purchasing power P after t years of inflation at 6% can be modeled by $P = e^{-0.06t}$. Graph the decrease in purchasing power as a function of t years.

a. Graph $y = e^{-x}$.

Solution: Since $e^{-x} = \left(\frac{1}{e}\right)^x$ and $0 < \frac{1}{e} < 1$, the graph is that of an exponential function falling from left to right. (See Figure 4.11.) Alternatively, we can consider the graph of $y = e^{-x}$ as a transformation of the graph of $f(x) = e^x$. Because $e^{-x} = f(-x)$, the graph of $y = e^{-x}$ is simply the reflection of the graph of f about the y-axis. (Compare the graphs in Figures 4.10 and 4.11.)

b. Graph $y = e^{x+2}$.

Solution: The graph of $y = e^{x+2}$ is related to that of $f(x) = e^x$. Since e^{x+2} is $f(x + 2)$, we can obtain the graph of $y = e^{x+2}$ by horizontally shifting the graph of $f(x) = e^x$ two units to the left. (See Figure 4.12.)

◁

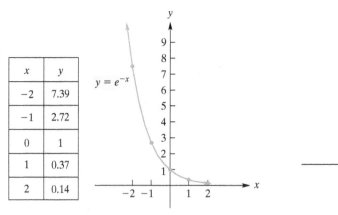

x	y
-2	7.39
-1	2.72
0	1
1	0.37
2	0.14

FIGURE 4.11   Graph of $y = e^{-x}$.

FIGURE 4.12   Graph of $y = e^{x+2}$.

EXAMPLE 9   Population Growth

The projected population P of a city is given by

$$P = 100{,}000e^{0.05t}$$

where t is the number of years after 1990. Predict the population for the year 2010.

Solution: The number of years from 1990 to 2010 is 20, so let $t = 20$. Then

$$P = 100{,}000e^{0.05(20)} = 100{,}000e^1 = 100{,}000e \approx 271{,}828$$

Now Work Problem 35 ◁

In statistics, an important function used to model certain events occurring in nature is the **Poisson distribution function:**

$$f(n) = \frac{e^{-\mu}\mu^n}{n!} \quad n = 0, 1, 2, \ldots$$

The symbol μ (read "mu") is a Greek letter. In certain situations, $f(n)$ gives the probability that exactly n events will occur in an interval of time or space. The constant μ is the average, also called *mean,* number of occurrences in the interval. The next example illustrates the Poisson distribution.

EXAMPLE 10   Hemocytometer and Cells

A hemocytometer is a counting chamber divided into squares and is used in studying the number of microscopic structures in a liquid. In a well-known experiment,[3] yeast cells were diluted and thoroughly mixed in a liquid, and the mixture was placed in a hemocytometer. With a microscope, the number of yeast cells on each square were counted. The probability that there were exactly n yeast cells on a hemocytometer square was found to fit a Poisson distribution with $\mu = 1.8$. Find the probability that there were exactly four cells on a particular square.

Solution: We use the Poisson distribution function with $\mu = 1.8$ and $n = 4$:

$$f(n) = \frac{e^{-\mu}\mu^n}{n!}$$

$$f(4) = \frac{e^{-1.8}(1.8)^4}{4!} \approx 0.072$$

---

[3] R. R. Sokal and F. J. Rohlf, *Introduction to Biostatistics* (San Francisco: W. H. Freeman and Company, 1973).

For example, this means that in 400 squares we would *expect* $400(0.072) \approx 29$ squares to contain exactly 4 cells. (In the experiment, in 400 squares the actual number observed was 30.)

◁

Radioactive Decay

Radioactive elements are such that the amount of the element decreases with respect to time. We say that the element *decays*. It can be shown that, if N is the amount at time t, then

$$N = N_0 e^{-\lambda t} \tag{3}$$

where N_0 and λ (a Greek letter read "lambda") are positive constants. Notice that N involves an exponential function of t. We say that N follows an **exponential law of decay.** If $t = 0$, then $N = N_0 e^0 = N_0 \cdot 1 = N_0$. Thus, the constant N_0 represents the amount of the element present at time $t = 0$ and is called the **initial amount.** The constant λ depends on the particular element involved and is called the **decay constant.**

Because N decreases as time progresses, suppose we let T be the length of time it takes for the element to decrease to half of the initial amount. Then at time $t = T$, we have $N = N_0/2$. Equation (3) implies that

$$\frac{N_0}{2} = N_0 e^{-\lambda T}$$

We will now use this fact to show that over *any* time interval of length T, half of the amount of the element decays. Consider the interval from time t to $t + T$, which has length T. At time t, the amount of the element is $N_0 e^{-\lambda t}$, and at time $t + T$ it is

$$N_0 e^{-\lambda(t+T)} = N_0 e^{-\lambda t} e^{-\lambda T} = (N_0 e^{-\lambda T})e^{-\lambda t}$$

$$= \frac{N_0}{2} e^{-\lambda t} = \frac{1}{2}(N_0 e^{-\lambda t})$$

which is half of the amount at time t. This means that if the initial amount present, N_0, were 1 gram, then at time T, $\frac{1}{2}$ gram would remain; at time $2T$, $\frac{1}{4}$ gram would remain; and so on. The value of T is called the **half-life** of the radioactive element. Figure 4.13 shows a graph of radioactive decay.

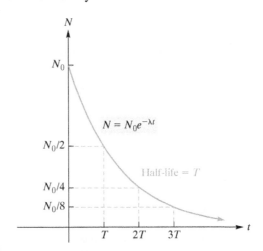

FIGURE 4.13   Radioactive decay.

EXAMPLE 11   **Radioactive Decay**

A radioactive element decays such that after t days the number of milligrams present is given by

$$N = 100e^{-0.062t}$$

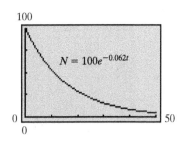

FIGURE 4.14   Graph of radioactive decay function $N = 100e^{-0.062t}$.

a. How many milligrams are initially present?

Solution: This equation has the form of Equation (3), $N = N_0 e^{-\lambda t}$, where $N_0 = 100$ and $\lambda = 0.062$. N_0 is the initial amount and corresponds to $t = 0$. Thus, 100 milligrams are initially present. (See Figure 4.14.)

b. How many milligrams are present after 10 days?

Solution: When $t = 10$,

$$N = 100e^{-0.062(10)} = 100e^{-0.62} \approx 53.8$$

Therefore, approximately 53.8 milligrams are present after 10 days.

Now Work Problem 47 ◁

PROBLEMS 4.1

In Problems 1–12, graph each function.

1. $y = f(x) = 4^x$
2. $y = f(x) = 3^x$
3. $y = f(x) = \left(\frac{1}{3}\right)^x$
4. $y = f(x) = \left(\frac{1}{4}\right)^x$
5. $y = f(x) = 2^{(x-1)^2}$
6. $y = f(x) = 3(2)^x$
7. $y = f(x) = 3^{x+2}$
8. $y = f(x) = 2^{x-1}$
9. $y = f(x) = 3^x - 2$
10. $y = f(x) = 3^{x-1} - 1$
11. $y = f(x) = 3^{-x}$
12. $y = f(x) = \frac{1}{2}(2^{x/2})$

Problems 13 and 14 refer to Figure 4.15, which shows the graphs of $y = 0.4^x$, $y = 2^x$, and $y = 5^x$.

13. Of the curves A, B, and C, which is the graph of $y = 5^x$?

14. Of the curves A, B, and C, which is the graph of $y = 2^x$?

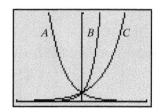

FIGURE 4.15

15. **Population** The projected population of a city is given by $P = 125{,}000(1.11)^{t/20}$, where t is the number of years after 1995. What is the projected population in 2015?

16. **Population** For a certain city, the population P grows at the rate of 1.5% per year. The formula $P = 1{,}527{,}000(1.015)^t$ gives the population t years after 1998. Find the population in (a) 1999 and (b) 2000.

17. **Paired-Associate Learning** In a psychological experiment involving learning,[4] subjects were asked to give particular responses after being shown certain stimuli. Each stimulus was a pair of letters, and each response was either the digit 1 or 2. After each response, the subject was told the correct answer. In this so-called *paired-associate* learning experiment, the theoretical probability P that a subject makes a correct response on the nth trial is given by

$$P = 1 - \frac{1}{2}(1 - c)^{n-1}, \quad n \geq 1, \quad 0 < c < 1$$

where c is a constant. Take $c = \frac{1}{2}$ and find P when $n = 1$, $n = 2$, and $n = 3$.

18. Express $y = 2^{3x}$ as an exponential function in base 8.

In Problems 19–27, find (a) the compound amount and (b) the compound interest for the given investment and annual rate.

19. $2000 for 5 years at 3% compounded annually

20. $5000 for 20 years at 5% compounded annually

21. $700 for 15 years at 7% compounded semiannually

22. $4000 for 12 years at $7\frac{1}{2}$% compounded semiannually

23. $3000 for 16 years at $8\frac{3}{4}$% compounded quarterly

24. $6000 for 2 years at 8% compounded quarterly

25. $5000 for $2\frac{1}{2}$ years at 9% compounded monthly

26. $500 for 5 years at 11% compounded semiannually

27. $8000 for 3 years at $6\frac{1}{4}$% compounded daily. (Assume that there are 365 days in a year.)

28. **Investment** Suppose $900 is placed in a savings account that earns interest at the rate of 4.5% compounded semiannually. (a) What is the value of the account at the end of five years? (b) If the account had earned interest at the rate of 4.5% compounded annually, what would be the value after five years?

29. **Investment** A certificate of deposit is purchased for $6500 and is held for three years. If the certificate earns 2% compounded quarterly, what is it worth at the end of three years?

30. **Population Growth** The population of a town of 5000 grows at the rate of 3% per year. (a) Determine an equation that gives the population t years from now. (b) Find the population three years from now. Give your answer to (b) to the nearest integer.

31. **Bacteria Growth** Bacteria are growing in a culture, and their number is increasing at the rate of 5% an hour. Initially, 400 bacteria are present. (a) Determine an equation that gives the number, N, of bacteria present after t hours. (b) How many bacteria are present after one hour? (c) After four hours? Give your answers to (b) and (c) to the nearest integer.

---

[4]D. Laming, *Mathematical Psychology* (New York: Academic Press, Inc., 1973).

32. Bacteria Reduction   A certain medicine reduces the bacteria present in a person by 10% each hour. Currently, 100,000 bacteria are present. Make a table of values for the number of bacteria present each hour for 0 to 4 hours. For each hour, write an expression for the number of bacteria as a product of 100,000 and a power of $\frac{9}{10}$. Use the expressions to make an entry in your table for the number of bacteria after t hours. Write a function N for the number of bacteria after t hours.

33. Recycling   Suppose the amount of plastic being recycled increases by 30% every year. Make a table of the factor by which recycling increases over the original amount for 0 to 3 years. For each year, write an expression for the increase as a power of some base. What base did you use? How does that base relate to the problem? Use your table to graph the multiplicative increase as a function of years. Use your graph to determine when the recycling will triple.

34. Population Growth   Cities A and B presently have populations of 270,000 and 360,000, respectively. City A grows at the rate of 6% per year, and B grows at the rate of 4% per year. Determine the larger and by how much the populations differ at the end of five years. Give your answer to the nearest integer.

Problems 35 and 36 involve a declining population. If a population declines at the rate of r per time period, then the population after t time periods is given by

$$P = P_0(1 - r)^t$$

where P_0 is the initial population (the population when $t = 0$).

35. Population   Because of an economic downturn, the population of a certain urban area declines at the rate of 1.5% per year. Initially, the population is 350,000. To the nearest person, what is the population after three years?

36. Enrollment   After a careful demographic analysis, a university forecasts that student enrollments will drop by 3% per year for the the next 12 years. If the university currently has 14,000 students, how many students will it have 12 years from now?

In Problems 37–40, use a calculator to find the value (rounded to four decimal places) of each expression.

37. $e^{1.5}$ **38.** $e^{3.4}$ **39.** $e^{-0.8}$ **40.** $e^{-2/3}$

In Problems 41 and 42, graph the functions.

41. $y = -e^{-(x+1)}$ **42.** $y = 2e^x$

43. Telephone Calls   The probability that a telephone operator will receive exactly x calls during a certain period is given by

$$P = \frac{e^{-3}3^x}{x!}$$

Find the probability that the operator will receive exactly three calls. Round your answer to four decimal places.

44. Normal Distribution   An important function used in economic and business decisions is the *normal distribution density function,* which, in standard form, is

$$f(x) = \frac{1}{\sqrt{2\pi}}e^{-\left(\frac{1}{2}\right)x^2}$$

Evaluate $f(0), f(1),$ and $f(2)$. Round your answers to three decimal places.

45. Express e^{kt} in the form b^t.   **46.** Express $\dfrac{1}{e^x}$ in the form b^x.

47. Radioactive Decay   A radioactive element is such that N grams remain after t hours, where

$$N = 12e^{-0.031t}$$

(a) How many grams are initially present? To the nearest tenth of a gram, how many grams remain after (b) 10 hours? (c) 44 hours?

(d) Based on your answer to part (c), what is your estimate of the half-life of this element?

48. Radioactive Decay   At a certain time, there are 75 milligrams of a radioactive substance. The substance decays so that after t years the number of milligrams present, N, is given by

$$N = 75e^{-0.045t}$$

How many milligrams are present after 10 years? Give your answer to the nearest milligram.

49. Radioactive Decay   If a radioactive substance has a half-life of 9 years, how long does it take for 1 gram of the substance to decay to $\frac{1}{8}$ gram?

50. Marketing   A mail-order company advertises in a national magazine. The company finds that, of all small towns, the percentage (given as a decimal) in which exactly x people respond to an ad fits a Poisson distribution with $\mu = 0.5$. From what percentage of small towns can the company expect exactly two people to respond? Round your answer to four decimal places.

51. Emergency-Room Admissions   Suppose the number of patients admitted into a hospital emergency room during a certain hour of the day has a Poisson distribution with mean 4. Find the probability that during that hour there will be exactly two emergency patients. Round your answer to four decimal places.

52. Graph $y = 17^x$ and $y = \left(\frac{1}{17}\right)^x$ on the same screen. Determine the intersection point.

53. Let $a > 0$ be a constant. Graph $y = 2^x$ and $y = 2^a \cdot 2^x$ on the same screen, for constant values $a = 2$ and $a = 3$. It appears that the graph of $y = 2^a \cdot 2^x$ is the graph of $y = 2^x$ shifted a units to the left. Prove algebraically that this is indeed true.

54. For $y = 5^x$, find x if $y = 3$. Round your answer to two decimal places.

55. For $y = 2^x$, find x if $y = 9$. Round your answer to two decimal places.

56. Cell Growth   Cells are growing in a culture, and their number is increasing at the rate of 7% per hour. Initially, 1000 cells are present. After how many full hours will there be at least 3000 cells?

57. Bacteria Growth   Refer to Example 1. How long will it take for 1000 bacteria to be present? Round your answer to the nearest tenth of a minute.

58. Demand Equation   The demand equation for a new toy is

$$q = 10,000(0.95123)^p$$

(a) Evaluate q to the nearest integer when $p = 10$.

(b) Convert the demand equation to the form

$$q = 10,000e^{-xp}$$

(*Hint:* Find a number x such that $0.95123 \approx e^{-x}$.)

(c) Use the equation in part (b) to evaluate q to the nearest integer when $p = 10$. Your answers in parts (a) and (c) should be the same.

59. Investment   If $2000 is invested in a savings account that earns interest at the rate of 9.9% compounded annually, after how many full years will the amount at least double?

Objective

To introduce logarithmic functions and their graphs. Properties of logarithms will be discussed in Section 4.3.

TO REVIEW inverse functions, refer to Section 2.4.

4.2 Logarithmic Functions

Since all exponential functions pass the horizontal line test, they are all one-to-one functions. It follows that each exponential function has an inverse. These functions, inverse to the exponential functions, are called the *logarithmic functions*.

More precisely, if $f(x) = b^x$, the exponential function base b (where $0 < b < 1$ or $1 < b$), then the inverse function $f^{-1}(x)$ is called the *logarithm function base b* and is denoted $\log_b x$. It follows from our general remarks about inverse functions in Section 2.4 that

$$y = \log_b x \quad \text{if and only if} \quad b^y = x$$

and we have the following fundamental equations:

$$\log_b b^x = x \tag{1}$$

and

$$b^{\log_b x} = x \tag{2}$$

where Equation (1) holds for all x in $(-\infty, \infty)$ and Equation (2) holds for all x in $(0, \infty)$. We recall that $(-\infty, \infty)$ is the domain of the exponential function base b and $(0, \infty)$ is the range of the exponential function base b. It follows that $(0, \infty)$ is the domain of the logarithm function base b and $(-\infty, \infty)$ is the range of the logarithm function base b.

Stated otherwise, given positive x, $\log_b x$ is the unique number with the property that $b^{\log_b x} = x$. The generalities about inverse functions also enable us to see immediately what the graph of a logarithmic function looks like.

In Figure 4.16 we have shown the graph of the particular exponential function $y = f(x) = 2^x$, whose general shape is typical of exponential functions $y = b^x$ for which the base b satisfies $1 < b$. We have added a (dashed) copy of the line $y = x$. The graph of $y = f^{-1}(x) = \log_2 x$ is obtained as the mirror image of $y = f(x) = 2^x$ in the line $y = x$.

In Table 4.3 we have tabulated the function values that appear as y-coordinates of the dots in Figure 4.16.

Table 4.3 Selected function values

x	2^x	x	$\log_2 x$
-2	$\frac{1}{4}$	$\frac{1}{4}$	-2
-1	$\frac{1}{2}$	$\frac{1}{2}$	-1
0	1	1	0
1	2	2	1
2	4	4	2
3	8	8	3

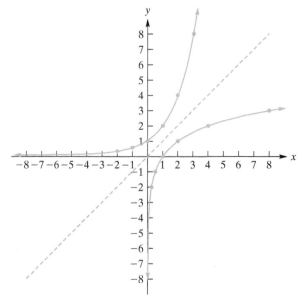

FIGURE 4.16   Graphs of $y = 2^x$ and $y = \log_2 x$.

It is clear that the exponential function base 2 and the logarithm function base 2 *undo* the effects of each other. Thus, for all x in the domain of 2^x [which is $(-\infty, \infty)$], we have

$$\log_2 2^x = x$$

and, for all x in the domain of $\log_2 x$ [which is the range of 2^x, which is $(0, \infty)$], we have

$$2^{\log_2 x} = x$$

It cannot be said too often that

$$y = \log_b x \quad \text{means} \quad b^y = x$$

and conversely

$$b^y = x \quad \text{means} \quad y = \log_b x$$

In this sense, *a logarithm of a number is an exponent:* $\log_b x$ is the power to which we must raise b to get x. For example,

$$\log_2 8 = 3 \quad \text{because} \quad 2^3 = 8$$

We say that $\log_2 8 = 3$ is the **logarithmic form** of the **exponential form** $2^3 = 8$. (See Figure 4.17.)

Logarithmic and
exponential forms

FIGURE 4.17 A logarithm can be considered an exponent.

APPLY IT ▶

8. If bacteria have been doubling every hour and the current amount is 16 times the amount first measured, then the situation can be represented by $16 = 2^t$. Represent this equation in logarithmic form. What does t represent?

APPLY IT ▶

9. An earthquake measuring 8.3 on the Richter scale can be represented by $8.3 = \log_{10}\left(\frac{I}{I_0}\right)$, where I is the intensity of the earthquake and I_0 is the intensity of a zero-level earthquake. Represent this equation in exponential form.

APPLY IT ▶

10. Suppose a recycling plant has found that the amount of material being recycled has increased by 50% every year since the plant's first year of operation. Graph each year as a function of the multiplicative increase in recycling since the first year. Label the graph with the name of the function.

EXAMPLE 1   Converting from Exponential to Logarithmic Form

		Exponential Form		*Logarithmic Form*
a.	Since	$5^2 = 25$	it follows that	$\log_5 25 = 2$
b.	Since	$3^4 = 81$	it follows that	$\log_3 81 = 4$
c.	Since	$10^0 = 1$	it follows that	$\log_{10} 1 = 0$

Now Work Problem 1 ◁

EXAMPLE 2   Converting from Logarithmic to Exponential Form

	Logarithmic Form		*Exponential Form*
a.	$\log_{10} 1000 = 3$	means	$10^3 = 1000$
b.	$\log_{64} 8 = \dfrac{1}{2}$	means	$64^{1/2} = 8$
c.	$\log_2 \dfrac{1}{16} = -4$	means	$2^{-4} = \dfrac{1}{16}$

Now Work Problem 3 ◁

EXAMPLE 3   Graph of a Logarithmic Function with $b > 1$

Examine again the graph of $y = \log_2 x$ in Figure 4.16. This graph is typical for a logarithmic function with $b > 1$.

Now Work Problem 9 ◁

11. Suppose a boat depreciates 20% every year. Graph the number of years the boat is owned as a function of the multiplicative decrease in its original value. Label the graph with the name of the function.

EXAMPLE 4 **Graph of a Logarithmic Function with** $0 < b < 1$

Graph $y = \log_{1/2} x$.

Solution: To plot points, we plot the inverse function $y = \left(\frac{1}{2}\right)^x$ and reflect the graph in the line $y = x$. (See Figure 4.18.)

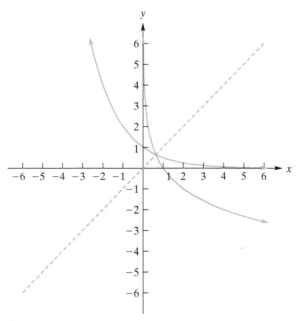

FIGURE 4.18 Graph of $y = \left(\frac{1}{2}\right)^x$ and $y = \log_{1/2} x$.

From the graph, we can see that the domain of $y = \log_{1/2} x$ is the set of all positive reals, for that is the range of $y = \left(\frac{1}{2}\right)^x$ and the range of $y = \log_{1/2} x$ is the set of all real numbers, which is the domain of $y = \left(\frac{1}{2}\right)^x$. The graph falls from left to right. Numbers between 0 and 1 have positive base $\frac{1}{2}$ logarithms, and the closer a number is to 0, the larger is its base $\frac{1}{2}$ logarithm. Numbers greater than 1 have negative base $\frac{1}{2}$ logarithms. The logarithm of 1 is 0, *regardless of the base b,* and corresponds to the x-intercept $(1, 0)$. This graph is typical for a logarithmic function with $0 < b < 1$.

Now Work Problem 11 ◁

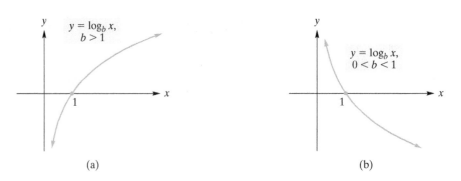

FIGURE 4.19 General shapes of $y = \log_b x$.

Summarizing the results of Examples 3 and 4, we can say that the graph of a logarithmic function has one of two general shapes, depending on whether $b > 1$ or $0 < b < 1$. (See Figure 4.19.) For $b > 1$, the graph rises from left to right; as x gets closer and closer to 0, the function values decrease without bound, and the graph gets closer and closer to the y-axis. For $0 < b < 1$, the graph falls from left to right;

as x gets closer and closer to 0, the function values increase without bound, and the graph gets closer and closer to the y-axis. In each case, note that

1. The domain of a logarithmic function is the interval $(0, \infty)$. Thus, the logarithm of a nonpositive number does not exist.

2. The range is the interval $(-\infty, \infty)$.

3. The logarithm of 1 is 0, which corresponds to the x-intercept $(1, 0)$.

Logarithms to the base 10 are called **common logarithms.** They were frequently used for computational purposes before the calculator age. The subscript 10 is usually omitted from the notation:

$$\log x \quad \text{means} \quad \log_{10} x$$

Important in calculus are logarithms to the base e, called **natural logarithms.** We use the notation "ln" for such logarithms:

$$\ln x \quad \text{means} \quad \log_e x$$

The graph of the natural logarithmic function in Figure 4.20 is important too.

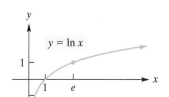

FIGURE 4.20   Graph of natural logarithmic function.

The symbol $\ln x$ can be read "natural log of x." Most calculators give approximate values for natural and common logarithms. For example, verify that $\ln 2 \approx 0.69315$. This means that $e^{0.69315} \approx 2$. Figure 4.20 shows the graph of $y = \ln x$. Because $e > 1$, the graph has the general shape of that of a logarithmic function with $b > 1$ [see Figure 4.19(a)] and rises from left to right. While the conventions about log, with no subscript, and ln are well established in elementary books, be careful when consulting an advanced book. In advanced texts, $\log x$ means $\log_e x$, ln is not used at all, and logarithms base 10 are written explicitly as $\log_{10} x$.

APPLY IT ▶

12. The number of years it takes for an amount invested at an annual rate of r and compounded continuously to quadruple is a function of the annual rate r given by $t(r) = \dfrac{\ln 4}{r}$. Use a calculator to find the rate needed to quadruple an investment in 10 years.

Remember the way in which a logarithm is an exponent.

EXAMPLE 5   Finding Logarithms

a. Find log 100.

Solution: Here the base is 10. Thus, log 100 is the power to which we must raise 10 to get 100. Since $10^2 = 100$, log $100 = 2$.

b. Find ln 1.

Solution: Here the base is e. Because $e^0 = 1$, ln $1 = 0$.

c. Find log 0.1.

Solution: Since $0.1 = \frac{1}{10} = 10^{-1}$, log $0.1 = -1$.

d. Find $\ln e^{-1}$.

Solution: Since $\ln e^{-1}$ is the power to which e must be raised to obtain e^{-1}, clearly $\ln e^{-1} = -1$.

e. Find $\log_{36} 6$.

Solution: Because $36^{1/2} (= \sqrt{36})$ is 6, $\log_{36} 6 = \frac{1}{2}$.

Now Work Problem 17 ◁

Many equations involving logarithmic or exponential forms can be solved for an unknown quantity by first transforming from logarithmic form to exponential form or vice versa. Example 6 will illustrate.

APPLY IT ▶

13. The multiplicative increase m of an amount invested at an annual rate of r compounded continuously for a time t is given by $m = e^{rt}$. What annual percentage rate is needed to triple the investment in 12 years?

EXAMPLE 6   Solving Logarithmic and Exponential Equations

a. Solve $\log_2 x = 4$.

Solution: We can get an explicit expression for x by writing the equation in exponential form. This gives

$$2^4 = x$$

so $x = 16$.

b. Solve $\ln (x + 1) = 7$.

Solution: The exponential form yields $e^7 = x + 1$. Thus, $x = e^7 - 1$.

c. Solve $\log_x 49 = 2$.

Solution: In exponential form, $x^2 = 49$, so $x = 7$. We reject $x = -7$ because a negative number cannot be a base of a logarithmic function.

d. Solve $e^{5x} = 4$.

Solution: We can get an explicit expression for x by writing the equation in logarithmic form. We have

$$\ln 4 = 5x$$
$$x = \frac{\ln 4}{5}$$

Now Work Problem 49 ◁

Radioactive Decay and Half-Life

From our discussion of the decay of a radioactive element in Section 4.1, we know that the amount of the element present at time t is given by

$$N = N_0 e^{-\lambda t} \tag{3}$$

where N_0 is the initial amount (the amount at time $t = 0$) and λ is the decay constant. Let us now determine the half-life T of the element. At time T, half of the initial amount is present. That is, when $t = T, N = N_0/2$. Thus, from Equation (3), we have

$$\frac{N_0}{2} = N_0 e^{-\lambda T}$$

Solving for T gives

$$\frac{1}{2} = e^{-\lambda T}$$
$$2 = e^{\lambda T} \qquad \text{taking reciprocals of both sides}$$

To get an explicit expression for T, we convert to logarithmic form. This results in

$$\lambda T = \ln 2$$
$$T = \frac{\ln 2}{\lambda}$$

Summarizing, we have the following:

If a radioactive element has decay constant λ, then the half-life of the element is given by

$$T = \frac{\ln 2}{\lambda} \tag{4}$$

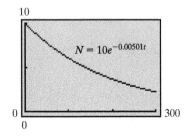

FIGURE 4.21 Radioactive decay function $N = 10e^{-0.00501t}$.

EXAMPLE 7 Finding Half-Life

A 10-milligram sample of radioactive polonium 210 (which is denoted ^{210}Po) decays according to the equation

$$N = 10e^{-0.00501t}$$

where N is the number of milligrams present after t days. (See Figure 4.21.) Determine the half-life of ^{210}Po.

Solution: Here the decay constant λ is 0.00501. By Equation (4), the half-life is given by

$$T = \frac{\ln 2}{\lambda} = \frac{\ln 2}{0.00501} \approx 138.4 \text{ days}$$

Now Work Problem 63 ◁

PROBLEMS 4.2

In Problems 1–8, express each logarithmic form exponentially and each exponential form logarithmically.

1. $10^4 = 10{,}000$
2. $2 = \log_{12} 144$
3. $\log_2 1024 = 10$
4. $8^{2/3} = 4$
5. $e^3 \approx 20.0855$
6. $e^{0.33647} \approx 1.4$
7. $\ln 3 \approx 1.09861$
8. $\log 7 \approx 0.84509$

In Problems 9–16, graph the functions.

9. $y = f(x) = \log_3 x$
10. $y = f(x) = \log_4 2x$
11. $y = f(x) = \log_{1/4} x$
12. $y = f(x) = \log_{1/5} x$
13. $y = f(x) = \log_2 (x + 4)$
14. $y = f(x) = \log_2 (-x)$
15. $y = f(x) = -2 \ln x$
16. $y = f(x) = \ln (x + 2)$

In Problems 17–28, evaluate the expression.

17. $\log_6 36$
18. $\log_2 512$
19. $\log_3 27$
20. $\log_{16} 4$
21. $\log_7 7$
22. $\log 10{,}000$
23. $\log 0.0001$
24. $\log_2 \sqrt[3]{2}$
25. $\log_5 1$
26. $\log_5 \frac{1}{25}$
27. $\log_2 \frac{1}{8}$
28. $\log_3 \sqrt[7]{3}$

In Problems 29–48, find x.

29. $\log_3 x = 4$
30. $\log_2 x = 8$
31. $\log_5 x = 3$
32. $\log_4 x = 0$
33. $\log x = -3$
34. $\ln x = 1$
35. $\ln x = -3$
36. $\log_x 25 = 2$
37. $\log_x 8 = 3$
38. $\log_x 4 = \frac{1}{3}$
39. $\log_x \frac{1}{6} = -1$
40. $\log_x y = 1$
41. $\log_3 x = -3$
42. $\log_x (2x - 3) = 1$
43. $\log_x (12 - x) = 2$
44. $\log_8 64 = x - 1$
45. $2 + \log_2 4 = 3x - 1$
46. $\log_3 (x + 2) = -2$
47. $\log_x (2x + 8) = 2$
48. $\log_x (16 - 4x - x^2) = 2$

In Problems 49–52, find x and express your answer in terms of natural logarithms.

49. $e^{3x} = 2$
50. $0.1e^{0.1x} = 0.5$
51. $e^{2x-5} + 1 = 4$
52. $6e^{2x} - 1 = \frac{1}{2}$

In Problems 53–56, use your calculator to find the approximate value of each expression. Round your answer to five decimal places.

53. $\ln 11$
54. $\ln 4.27$
55. $\ln 7.39$
56. $\ln 9.98$

57. Appreciation Suppose an antique gains 10% in value every year. Graph the number of years it is owned as a function of the multiplicative increase in its original value. Label the graph with the name of the function.

58. Cost Equation The cost for a firm producing q units of a product is given by the cost equation

$$c = (5q \ln q) + 15$$

Evaluate the cost when $q = 12$. (Round your answer to two decimal places.)

59. Supply Equation A manufacturer's supply equation is

$$p = \log \left(10 + \frac{q}{2} \right)$$

where q is the number of units supplied at a price p per unit. At what price will the manufacturer supply 1980 units?

60. Earthquake The magnitude, M, of an earthquake and its energy, E, are related by the equation[5]

$$1.5M = \log \left(\frac{E}{2.5 \times 10^{11}} \right)$$

where M is given in terms of Richter's preferred scale of 1958 and E is in ergs. Solve the equation for E.

61. Biology For a certain population of cells, the number of cells at time t is given by $N = N_0(2^{t/k})$, where N_0 is the number of cells at $t = 0$ and k is a positive constant. (a) Find N when $t = k$. (b) What is the significance of k? (c) Show that the time it takes to have population N_1 can be written

$$t = k \log_2 \frac{N_1}{N_0}$$

62. Inferior Good In a discussion of an inferior good, Persky[6] solves an equation of the form

$$u_0 = A \ln (x_1) + \frac{x_2^2}{2}$$

for x_1, where x_1 and x_2 are quantities of two products, u_0 is a measure of utility, and A is a positive constant. Determine x_1.

63. Radioactive Decay A 1-gram sample of radioactive lead 211 (^{211}Pb) decays according to the equation $N = e^{-0.01920t}$, where N is the number of grams present after t minutes. How long will it take until only 0.25 grams remain? Express the answer to the nearest tenth of a minute.

---

[5] K. E. Bullen, *An Introduction to the Theory of Seismology* (Cambridge, U.K.: Cambridge at the University Press, 1963).

[6] A. L. Persky, "An Inferior Good and a Novel Indifference Map," *The American Economist*, XXIX, no. 1 (Spring 1985).

64. Radioactive Decay   A 100-milligram sample of radioactive actinium 227 (^{227}Ac) decays according to the equation

$$N = 100e^{-0.03194t}$$

where N is the number of milligrams present after t years. Find the half-life of ^{227}Ac to the nearest tenth of a year.

65. If $\log_y x = 3$ and $\log_z x = 2$, find a formula for z as an explicit function of y only.

66. Solve for y as an explicit function of x if

$$x + 3e^{2y} - 8 = 0$$

67. Suppose $y = f(x) = x \ln x$. (a) For what values of x is $y < 0$? (*Hint:* Determine when the graph is below the x-axis.) (b) Determine the range of f.

68. Find the x-intercept of $y = x^3 \ln x$.

69. Use the graph of $y = e^x$ to estimate $\ln 3$. Round your answer to two decimal places.

70. Use the graph of $y = \ln x$ to estimate e^2. Round your answer to two decimal places.

71. Determine the x-values of points of intersection of the graphs of $y = (x - 2)^2$ and $y = \ln x$. Round your answers to two decimal places.

Objective

To study basic properties of logarithmic functions.

4.3 Properties of Logarithms

The logarithmic function has many important properties. For example,

1. $\log_b (mn) = \log_b m + \log_b n$

which says that the logarithm of a product of two numbers is the sum of the logarithms of the numbers. We can prove this property by deriving the exponential form of the equation:

$$b^{\log_b m + \log_b n} = mn$$

Using first a familiar rule for exponents, we have

$$b^{\log_b m + \log_b n} = b^{\log_b m} b^{\log_b n}$$

$$= mn$$

where the second equality uses two instances of the fundamental equation (2) of Section 4.2. We will not prove the next two properties, since their proofs are similar to that of Property 1.

2. $\log_b \dfrac{m}{n} = \log_b m - \log_b n$

That is, the logarithm of a quotient is the difference of the logarithm of the numerator and the logarithm of the denominator.

3. $\log_b m^r = r \log_b m$

That is, the logarithm of a power of a number is the exponent times the logarithm of the number.

Table 4.4 Common Logarithms

x	$\log x$	x	$\log x$
2	0.3010	7	0.8451
3	0.4771	8	0.9031
4	0.6021	9	0.9542
5	0.6990	10	1.0000
6	0.7782	e	0.4343

Table 4.4 gives the values of a few common logarithms. Most entries are approximate. For example, $\log 4 \approx 0.6021$, which means $10^{0.6021} \approx 4$. To illustrate the use of properties of logarithms, we will use this table in some of the examples that follow.

EXAMPLE 1   Finding Logarithms by Using Table 4.4

a. Find $\log 56$.

Solution: Log 56 is not in the table. But we can write 56 as the product $8 \cdot 7$. Thus, by Property 1,

$$\log 56 = \log (8 \cdot 7) = \log 8 + \log 7 \approx 0.9031 + 0.8451 = 1.7482$$

b. Find $\log \frac{9}{2}$.

Solution: By Property 2,

$$\log \frac{9}{2} = \log 9 - \log 2 \approx 0.9542 - 0.3010 = 0.6532$$

c. Find log 64.

Solution: Since $64 = 8^2$, by Property 3,

$$\log 64 = \log 8^2 = 2 \log 8 \approx 2(0.9031) = 1.8062$$

d. Find $\log \sqrt{5}$.

Solution: By Property 3, we have

$$\log \sqrt{5} = \log 5^{1/2} = \frac{1}{2} \log 5 \approx \frac{1}{2}(0.6990) = 0.3495$$

e. Find $\log \dfrac{16}{21}$.

Solution: $\log \dfrac{16}{21} = \log 16 - \log 21 = \log (4^2) - \log (3 \cdot 7)$

$$= 2 \log 4 - [\log 3 + \log 7]$$

$$\approx 2(0.6021) - [0.4771 + 0.8451] = -0.1180$$

Now Work Problem 3 ◁

EXAMPLE 2   **Rewriting Logarithmic Expressions**

a. Express $\log \dfrac{1}{x^2}$ in terms of $\log x$.

Solution: $\log \dfrac{1}{x^2} = \log x^{-2} = -2 \log x$ Property 3

Here we have assumed that $x > 0$. Although $\log (1/x^2)$ is defined for $x \neq 0$, the expression $-2 \log x$ is defined only if $x > 0$. Note that we do have

$$\log \frac{1}{x^2} = \log x^{-2} = -2 \log |x|$$

for all $x \neq 0$.

b. Express $\log \dfrac{1}{x}$ in terms of $\log x$, for $x > 0$.

Solution: By Property 3,

$$\log \frac{1}{x} = \log x^{-1} = -1 \log x = -\log x$$

Now Work Problem 21 ◁

From Example 2(b), we see that $\log (1/x) = -\log x$. Generalizing gives the following property:

4. $\log_b \dfrac{1}{m} = -\log_b m$

That is, the logarithm of the reciprocal of a number is the negative of the logarithm of the number.

For example, $\log \dfrac{2}{3} = -\log \dfrac{3}{2}$.

Manipulations such as those in Example 3 are frequently used in calculus.

EXAMPLE 3 **Writing Logarithms in Terms of Simpler Logarithms**

a. Write $\ln \dfrac{x}{zw}$ in terms of $\ln x$, $\ln z$, and $\ln w$.

Solution:

$$\ln \frac{x}{zw} = \ln x - \ln(zw) \qquad \text{Property 2}$$

$$= \ln x - (\ln z + \ln w) \qquad \text{Property 1}$$

$$= \ln x - \ln z - \ln w$$

b. Write $\ln \sqrt[3]{\dfrac{x^5(x-2)^8}{x-3}}$ in terms of $\ln x$, $\ln(x-2)$, and $\ln(x-3)$.

Solution:

$$\ln \sqrt[3]{\frac{x^5(x-2)^8}{x-3}} = \ln \left[\frac{x^5(x-2)^8}{x-3}\right]^{1/3} = \frac{1}{3}\ln \frac{x^5(x-2)^8}{x-3}$$

$$= \frac{1}{3}\{\ln[x^5(x-2)^8] - \ln(x-3)\}$$

$$= \frac{1}{3}[\ln x^5 + \ln(x-2)^8 - \ln(x-3)]$$

$$= \frac{1}{3}[5\ln x + 8\ln(x-2) - \ln(x-3)]$$

Now Work Problem 29 ◁

APPLY IT ▶

14. The Richter scale measure of an earthquake is given by $R = \log\left(\dfrac{I}{I_0}\right)$, where I is the intensity of the earthquake and I_0 is the intensity of a zero-level earthquake. How much more on the Richter scale is an earthquake with intensity 900,000 times the intensity of a zero-level earthquake than an earthquake with intensity 9000 times the intensity of a zero-level earthquake? Write the answer as an expression involving logarithms. Simplify the expression by combining logarithms, and then evaluate the resulting expression.

EXAMPLE 4 **Combining Logarithms**

a. Write $\ln x - \ln(x+3)$ as a single logarithm.

Solution:

$$\ln x - \ln(x+3) = \ln \frac{x}{x+3} \qquad \text{Property 2}$$

b. Write $\ln 3 + \ln 7 - \ln 2 - 2\ln 4$ as a single logarithm.

Solution:

$$\ln 3 + \ln 7 - \ln 2 - 2\ln 4$$

$$= \ln 3 + \ln 7 - \ln 2 - \ln(4^2) \qquad \text{Property 3}$$

$$= \ln 3 + \ln 7 - [\ln 2 + \ln(4^2)]$$

$$= \ln(3 \cdot 7) - \ln(2 \cdot 4^2) \qquad \text{Property 1}$$

$$= \ln 21 - \ln 32$$

$$= \ln \frac{21}{32} \qquad \text{Property 2}$$

Now Work Problem 37 ◁

Since $b^0 = 1$ and $b^1 = b$, by converting to logarithmic forms we have the following properties:

5. $\log_b 1 = 0$

6. $\log_b b = 1$

APPLY IT ▶

15. If an earthquake is 10,000 times as intense as a zero-level earthquake, what is its measurement on the Richter scale? Write the answer as a logarithmic expression and simplify it. (See the preceding Apply it for the formula.)

EXAMPLE 5   Simplifying Logarithmic Expressions

a. Find $\ln e^{3x}$.

Solution: By the fundamental equation (1) of Section 4.2 with $b = e$, we have $\ln e^{3x} = 3x$.

b. Find $\log 1 + \log 1000$.

Solution: By Property 5, $\log 1 = 0$. Thus,

$$\log 1 + \log 1000 = 0 + \log 10^3$$
$$= 0 + 3 \qquad \text{Fundamental equation (1) of}$$
$$= 3 \qquad \text{Section 4.2 with } b = 10$$

c. Find $\log_7 \sqrt[9]{7^8}$.

Solution:
$$\log_7 \sqrt[9]{7^8} = \log_7 7^{8/9} = \frac{8}{9}$$

d. Find $\log_3 \left(\dfrac{27}{81} \right)$.

Solution:
$$\log_3 \left(\frac{27}{81} \right) = \log_3 \left(\frac{3^3}{3^4} \right) = \log_3 (3^{-1}) = -1$$

e. Find $\ln e + \log \dfrac{1}{10}$.

Solution:
$$\ln e + \log \frac{1}{10} = \ln e + \log 10^{-1}$$
$$= 1 + (-1) = 0$$

Now Work Problem 15 ◁

Do not confuse $\ln x^2$ with $(\ln x)^2$. We have

$$\ln x^2 = \ln (x \cdot x)$$

but

$$(\ln x)^2 = (\ln x)(\ln x)$$

Sometimes $(\ln x)^2$ is written as $\ln^2 x$. This is not a new formula but merely a notation. More generally, some people write $f^2(x)$ for $(f(x))^2$. We recommend avoiding the notation $f^2(x)$.

EXAMPLE 6   Using Equation (2) of Section 4.2

a. Find $e^{\ln x^2}$.

Solution: By (2) with $b = e$, $e^{\ln x^2} = x^2$.

b. Solve $10^{\log x^2} = 25$ for x.

Solution:
$$10^{\log x^2} = 25$$
$$x^2 = 25 \qquad \text{By Equation (2) of Section 4.2}$$
$$x = \pm 5$$

Now Work Problem 45 ◁

EXAMPLE 7   Evaluating a Logarithm Base 5

Use a calculator to find $\log_5 2$.

Solution: Calculators typically have keys for logarithms in base 10 and base e, but not for base 5. However, we can convert logarithms in one base to logarithms in another base. Let us convert from base 5 to base 10. First, let $x = \log_5 2$. Then $5^x = 2$. Taking the common logarithms of both sides of $5^x = 2$ gives

$$\log 5^x = \log 2$$
$$x \log 5 = \log 2$$
$$x = \frac{\log 2}{\log 5} \approx 0.4307$$

If we had taken natural logarithms of both sides, the result would be $x = (\ln 2)/(\ln 5) \approx 0.4307$, the same as before.

◁

Generalizing the method used in Example 7, we obtain the so-called *change-of-base* formula:

Change-of-Base Formula

7. $\log_b m = \dfrac{\log_a m}{\log_a b}$

Some students find the change-of-base formula more memorable when it is expressed in the form

$$(\log_a b)(\log_b m) = \log_a m$$

in which the two instances of b apparently cancel. Let us see how to prove this identity, for the ability to see the truth of such statements greatly enhances one's ability to use them in practical applications. Since $\log_a m = y$ precisely if $a^y = m$, our task is equivalently to show that

$$a^{(\log_a b)(\log_b m)} = m$$

and we have

$$a^{(\log_a b)(\log_b m)} = \left(a^{\log_a b}\right)^{\log_b m}$$
$$= b^{\log_b m}$$
$$= m$$

using a rule for exponents and fundamental equation (2) twice.

The change-of-base formula allows logarithms to be converted from base a to base b.

EXAMPLE 8   Change-of-Base Formula

Express $\log x$ in terms of natural logarithms.

Solution: We must transform from base 10 to base e. Thus, we use the change-of-base formula (Property 7) with $b = 10$, $m = x$, and $a = e$:

$$\log x = \log_{10} x = \frac{\log_e x}{\log_e 10} = \frac{\ln x}{\ln 10}$$

Now Work Problem 49 ◁

TECHNOLOGY ■■■■

Problem: Display the graph of $y = \log_2 x$.

Solution: To enter the function, we must first convert it to base e or base 10. We choose base e. By Property 7,

$$y = \log_2 x = \frac{\log_e x}{\log_e 2} = \frac{\ln x}{\ln 2}$$

Now we graph $y = (\ln x)/(\ln 2)$, which is shown in Figure 4.22.

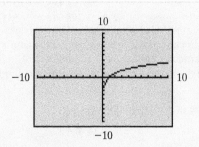

FIGURE 4.22   Graph of $y = \log_2 x$.

PROBLEMS 4.3

In Problems 1–10, let $\log 2 = a$, $\log 3 = b$, and $\log 5 = c$. Express the indicated logarithm in terms of a, b, and c.

1. $\log 30$

2. $\log 1024$

3. $\log \dfrac{2}{3}$

4. $\log \dfrac{5}{2}$

5. $\log \dfrac{8}{3}$

6. $\log \dfrac{6}{25}$

7. $\log 100$

8. $\log 0.00003$

9. $\log_2 3$

10. $\log_3 5$

In Problems 11–20, determine the value of the expression without the use of a calculator.

11. $\log_7 7^{48}$

12. $\log_{11} (11\sqrt[3]{11})^7$

13. $\log 0.0000001$

14. $10^{\log 3.4}$

15. $\ln e^{5.01}$

16. $\ln e$

17. $\ln \dfrac{1}{\sqrt{e}}$

18. $\log_3 81$

19. $\log \frac{1}{10} + \ln e^3$

20. $e^{\ln \pi}$

In Problems 21–32, write the expression in terms of $\ln x$, $\ln (x + 1)$, and $\ln (x + 2)$.

21. $\ln (x(x + 1)^2)$

22. $\ln \dfrac{\sqrt[5]{x}}{(x + 1)^3}$

23. $\ln \dfrac{x^2}{(x + 1)^3}$

24. $\ln (x(x + 1))^3$

25. $\ln \left(\dfrac{x + 1}{x + 2}\right)^4$

26. $\ln \sqrt{x(x + 1)(x + 2)}$

27. $\ln \dfrac{x(x + 1)}{x + 2}$

28. $\ln \dfrac{x^2(x + 1)}{x + 2}$

29. $\ln \dfrac{\sqrt{x}}{(x + 1)^2(x + 2)^3}$

30. $\ln \dfrac{x}{(x + 1)(x + 2)}$

31. $\ln \left(\dfrac{1}{x + 2}\sqrt[5]{\dfrac{x^2}{x + 1}}\right)$

32. $\ln \sqrt[4]{\dfrac{x^2(x + 2)^3}{(x + 1)^5}}$

In Problems 33–40, express each of the given forms as a single logarithm.

33. $\log 6 + \log 4$

34. $\log_3 10 - \log_3 5$

35. $\log_2 (2x) - \log_2 (x + 1)$

36. $2 \log x - \dfrac{1}{2}\log (x - 2)$

37. $7 \log_3 5 + 4 \log_3 17$

38. $5(2 \log x + 3 \log y - 2 \log z)$

39. $2 + 10 \log 1.05$

40. $\dfrac{1}{2}(\log 215 + 8 \log 6 - 3 \log 169)$

In Problems 41–44, determine the values of the expressions without using a calculator.

41. $e^{4 \ln 3 - 3 \ln 4}$

42. $\log_3 (\ln (\sqrt{7 + e^3} + \sqrt{7}) + \ln (\sqrt{7 + e^3} - \sqrt{7}))$

43. $\log_6 54 - \log_6 9$

44. $\log_3 \sqrt{3} - \log_2 \sqrt[3]{2} - \log_5 \sqrt[4]{5}$

In Problems 45–48, find x.

45. $e^{\ln (2x)} = 5$

46. $4^{\log_4 x + \log_4 2} = 3$

47. $10^{\log (x^2 + 2x)} = 3$

48. $e^{3 \ln x} = 8$

In Problems 49–53, write each expression in terms of natural logarithms.

49. $\log_2 (2x + 1)$

50. $\log_3 (x^2 + 2x + 2)$

51. $\log_3 (x^2 + 1)$

52. $\log_7 (x^2 + 1)$

53. If $e^{\ln z} = 7e^y$, solve for y in terms of z.

54. Statistics   In statistics, the sample regression equation $y = ab^x$ is reduced to a linear form by taking logarithms of both sides. Express $\log y$ in terms of x, $\log a$, and $\log b$ and explain what is meant by saying that the resulting expression is linear.

55. Military Compensation   In a study of military enlistments, Brown[7] considers total military compensation C as the sum of basic military compensation B (which includes the value of allowances, tax advantages, and base pay) and educational benefits E. Thus, $C = B + E$. Brown states that

$$\ln C = \ln B + \ln \left(1 + \frac{E}{B}\right)$$

Verify this.

---

[7]C. Brown, "Military Enlistments: What Can We Learn from Geographic Variation?" *The American Economic Review*, 75, no. 1 (1985), 228–34.

56. Earthquake   According to Richter,[8] the magnitude M of an earthquake occurring 100 km from a certain type of seismometer is given by $M = \log(A) + 3$, where A is the recorded trace amplitude (in millimeters) of the quake. (a) Find the magnitude of an earthquake that records a trace amplitude of 10 mm. (b) If a particular earthquake has amplitude A_1 and magnitude M_1, determine the magnitude of a quake with amplitude $10A_1$ in terms of M_1.

57. Display the graph of $y = \log_4 x$.

58. Display the graph of $y = \log_4(x + 2)$.

59. Display the graphs of $y = \log x$ and $y = \dfrac{\ln x}{\ln 10}$ on the same screen. The graphs appear to be identical. Why?

60. On the same screen, display the graphs of $y = \ln x$ and $y = \ln(4x)$. It appears that the graph of $y = \ln(4x)$ is the graph of $y = \ln x$ shifted upward. Determine algebraically the value of this shift.

61. On the same screen, display the graphs of $y = \ln(2x)$ and $y = \ln(6x)$. It appears that the graph of $y = \ln(6x)$ is the graph of $y = \ln(2x)$ shifted upward. Determine algebraically the value of this shift.

4.4 Logarithmic and Exponential Equations

Objective

To develop techniques for solving logarithmic and exponential equations.

Here we solve *logarithmic* and *exponential equations*. A **logarithmic equation** is an equation that involves the logarithm of an expression containing an unknown. For example, $2\ln(x + 4) = 5$ is a logarithmic equation. On the other hand, an **exponential equation** has the unknown appearing in an exponent, as in $2^{3x} = 7$.

To solve some logarithmic equations, it is convenient to use the fact that, for any base b, the function $y = \log_b x$ is one-to-one. This means, of course, that

$$\text{if}\quad \log_b m = \log_b n, \quad \text{then}\quad m = n$$

This follows from the fact that the function $y = \log_b x$ has an inverse and is visually apparent by inspecting the two possible shapes of $y = \log_b x$ given in Figure 4.19. In either event, the function passes the horizontal line test of Section 2.5. Also useful for solving logarithmic and exponential equations are the fundamental equations (1) and (2) in Section 4.2.

EXAMPLE 1   Oxygen Composition

An experiment was conducted with a particular type of small animal.[9] The logarithm of the amount of oxygen consumed per hour was determined for a number of the animals and was plotted against the logarithms of the weights of the animals. It was found that

$$\log y = \log 5.934 + 0.885 \log x$$

where y is the number of microliters of oxygen consumed per hour and x is the weight of the animal (in grams). Solve for y.

Solution: We first combine the terms on the right side into a single logarithm:

$$\log y = \log 5.934 + 0.885 \log x$$
$$= \log 5.934 + \log x^{0.885} \qquad \text{Property 3 of Section 4.3}$$
$$\log y = \log(5.934 x^{0.885}) \qquad \text{Property 1 of Section 4.3}$$

Since log is one-to-one, we have

$$y = 5.934 x^{0.885}$$

Now Work Problem 1 ◁

APPLY IT ▶

16. Greg took a number and multiplied it by a power of 32. Jean started with the same number and got the same result when she multiplied it by 4 raised to a number that was nine less than three times the exponent that Greg used. What power of 32 did Greg use?

EXAMPLE 2   Solving an Exponential Equation

Find x if $(25)^{x+2} = 5^{3x-4}$.

Solution: Since $25 = 5^2$, we can express both sides of the equation as powers of 5:

$$(25)^{x+2} = 5^{3x-4}$$
$$(5^2)^{x+2} = 5^{3x-4}$$
$$5^{2x+4} = 5^{3x-4}$$

---

[8]C. F. Richter, *Elementary Seismology* (San Francisco: W. H. Freeman and Company, 1958).

[9]R. W. Poole, *An Introduction to Quantitative Ecology* (New York: McGraw-Hill, 1974).

Since 5^x is a one-to-one function,

$$2x + 4 = 3x - 4$$
$$x = 8$$

Now Work Problem 7 ◁

Some exponential equations can be solved by taking the logarithm of both sides after the equation is put in a desirable form. The following example illustrates.

APPLY IT ▶

17. The sales manager at a fast-food chain finds that breakfast sales begin to fall after the end of a promotional campaign. The sales in dollars as a function of the number of days d after the campaign's end are given by $S = 800\left(\dfrac{4}{3}\right)^{-0.1d}$. If the manager does not want sales to drop below 450 per day before starting a new campaign, when should he start such a campaign?

EXAMPLE 3   Using Logarithms to Solve an Exponential Equation

Solve $5 + (3)4^{x-1} = 12$.

Solution: We first isolate the exponential expression 4^{x-1} on one side of the equation:

$$5 + (3)4^{x-1} = 12$$
$$(3)4^{x-1} = 7$$
$$4^{x-1} = \frac{7}{3}$$

Now we take the natural logarithm of both sides:

$$\ln 4^{x-1} = \ln 7 - \ln 3$$

Simplifying gives

$$(x - 1)\ln 4 = \ln 7 - \ln 3$$
$$x - 1 = \frac{\ln 7 - \ln 3}{\ln 4}$$
$$x = \frac{\ln 7 - \ln 3}{\ln 4} + 1 \approx 1.61120$$

Now Work Problem 13 ◁

In Example 3, we used natural logarithms to solve the given equation. However, logarithms in any base can be used. If we use common logarithms, we would obtain

$$x = \frac{\log 7 - \log 3}{\log 4} + 1 \approx 1.61120$$

TECHNOLOGY ▮▮▮▮

Figure 4.23 shows a graphical solution of the equation $5 + (3)4^{x-1} = 12$ of Example 3. This solution occurs at the intersection of the graphs of $y = 5 + (3)4^{x-1}$ and $y = 12$.

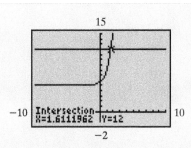

FIGURE 4.23 The solution of $5 + (3)4^{x-1} = 12$ is approximately 1.61120.

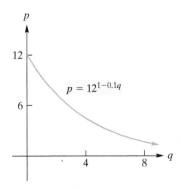

FIGURE 4.24 Graph of the demand equation $p = 12^{1-0.1q}$.

EXAMPLE 4 Demand Equation

The demand equation for a product is $p = 12^{1-0.1q}$. Use common logarithms to express q in terms of p.

Solution: Figure 4.24 shows the graph of this demand equation for $q \geq 0$. As is typical of a demand equation, the graph falls from left to right. We want to solve the equation for q. Taking the common logarithms of both sides of $p = 12^{1-0.1q}$ gives

$$\log p = \log(12^{1-0.1q})$$

$$\log p = (1 - 0.1q)\log 12$$

$$\frac{\log p}{\log 12} = 1 - 0.1q$$

$$0.1q = 1 - \frac{\log p}{\log 12}$$

$$q = 10\left(1 - \frac{\log p}{\log 12}\right)$$

Now Work Problem 43 ◁

To solve some exponential equations involving base e or base 10, such as $10^{2x} = 3$, the process of taking logarithms of both sides can be combined with the identity $\log_b b^r = r$ [Fundamental equation (1) from Section 4.2] to transform the equation into an equivalent logarithmic form. In this case, we have

$$10^{2x} = 3$$

$$2x = \log 3 \qquad \text{logarithmic form}$$

$$x = \frac{\log 3}{2} \approx 0.2386$$

EXAMPLE 5 Predator–Prey Relation

In an article concerning predators and prey, Holling[10] refers to an equation of the form

$$y = K(1 - e^{-ax})$$

where x is the prey density, y is the number of prey attacked, and K and a are constants. Verify his claim that

$$\ln \frac{K}{K - y} = ax$$

Solution: To find ax, we first solve the given equation for e^{-ax}:

$$y = K(1 - e^{-ax})$$

$$\frac{y}{K} = 1 - e^{-ax}$$

$$e^{-ax} = 1 - \frac{y}{K}$$

$$e^{-ax} = \frac{K - y}{K}$$

---

[10]C. S. Holling, "Some Characteristics of Simple Types of Predation and Parasitism," *The Canadian Entomologist*, 91, no. 7 (1959), 385–98.

Now we convert to logarithmic form:

$$\ln \frac{K-y}{K} = -ax$$

$$-\ln \frac{K-y}{K} = ax$$

$$\ln \frac{K}{K-y} = ax \qquad \text{Property 4 of Section 4.3}$$

as was to be shown.

Now Work Problem 9 ◁

Some logarithmic equations can be solved by rewriting them in exponential forms.

EXAMPLE 6   Solving a Logarithmic Equation

APPLY IT ▶

18. The Richter scale measure of an earthquake is given by $R = \log \left(\frac{I}{I_0} \right)$, where I is the intensity of the earthquake, and I_0 is the intensity of a zero-level earthquake. An earthquake that is 675,000 times as intense as a zero-level earthquake has a magnitude on the Richter scale that is 4 more than another earthquake. What is the intensity of the other earthquake?

Solve $\log_2 x = 5 - \log_2 (x + 4)$.

Solution: Here we must assume that both x and $x + 4$ are positive, so that their logarithms are defined. Both conditions are satisfied if $x > 0$. To solve the equation, we first place all logarithms on one side so that we can combine them:

$$\log_2 x + \log_2 (x + 4) = 5$$

$$\log_2 [x(x + 4)] = 5$$

In exponential form, we have

$$x(x + 4) = 2^5$$

$$x^2 + 4x = 32$$

$$x^2 + 4x - 32 = 0 \qquad \text{quadratic equation}$$

$$(x - 4)(x + 8) = 0$$

$$x = 4 \quad \text{or} \quad x = -8$$

Because we must have $x > 0$, the only solution is 4, as can be verified by substituting into the original equation. Indeed, replacing x by 4 in $\log_2 x$ gives $\log_2 4 = \log_2 2^2 = 2$ while replacing x by 4 in $5 - \log_2 (x + 4)$ gives $5 - \log_2 (4 + 4) = 5 - \log_2 (8) = 5 - \log_2 2^3 = 5 - 3 = 2$. Since the results are the same, 4 is a solution of the equation.

In solving a logarithmic equation, it is a good idea to check for extraneous solutions.

Now Work Problem 5 ◁

PROBLEMS 4.4

In Problems 1–36, find x. Round your answers to three decimal places.

1. $\log (5x + 1) = \log (4x + 2)$ **2.** $\log x - \log 5 = \log 7$

3. $\log 7 - \log (x - 1) = \log 4$ **4.** $\log_2 x + 3 \log_2 2 = \log_2 \frac{2}{x}$

5. $\ln (-x) = \ln (x^2 - 6)$ **6.** $\ln (x + 3) + \ln 4 = 2 \ln x$

7. $e^{2x} \cdot e^{5x} = e^{14}$ **8.** $(e^{3x-2})^3 = e^3$ **9.** $(81)^{4x} = 9$

10. $(27)^{2x+1} = \frac{1}{3}$ **11.** $e^{5x} = 7$ **12.** $e^{4x} = \frac{3}{4}$

13. $2e^{5x+2} = 17$ **14.** $5e^{2x-1} - 2 = 23$ **15.** $10^{4/x} = 6$

16. $\frac{2(10)^{0.3x}}{7} = 5$ **17.** $\frac{5}{10^{2x}} = 7$

18. $2(10)^x + (10)^{x+1} = 4$ **19.** $2^x = 5$

20. $7^{2x+3} = 9$ **21.** $5^{7x+5} = 2$

22. $4^{x/2} = 20$ **23.** $2^{-2x/3} = \frac{4}{5}$

24. $5(3^x - 6) = 10$ **25.** $(4)5^{3-x} - 7 = 2$

26. $\frac{5}{2^x} = 11$ **27.** $\log (x - 3) = 3$

28. $\log_2 (x + 1) = 4$ **29.** $\log_4 (9x - 4) = 2$

30. $\log_4 (2x + 4) - 3 = \log_4 3$ **31.** $\ln (x - 2) + \ln (2x + 1) = 5$

32. $\log (x - 3) + \log (x - 5) = 1$

33. $\log_2 (5x + 1) = 4 - \log_2 (3x - 2)$

34. $\log (x + 2)^2 = 2$, where $x > 0$

35. $\log_2 \left(\frac{2}{x} \right) = 3 + \log_2 x$ **36.** $\log (x + 5) = \log (3x + 2) + 1$

37. Rooted Plants In a study of rooted plants in a certain geographic region,[11] it was determined that on plots of size A (in square meters), the average number of species that occurred was S. When log S was graphed as a function of log A, the result was a straight line given by

$$\log S = \log 12.4 + 0.26 \log A$$

Solve for S.

38. Gross National Product In an article, Taagepera and Hayes refer to an equation of the form

$$\log T = 1.7 + 0.2068 \log P - 0.1334(\log P)^2$$

Here T is the percentage of a country's gross national product (GNP) that corresponds to foreign trade (exports plus imports), and P is the country's population (in units of 100,000).[12] Verify the claim that

$$T = 50P^{(0.2068 - 0.1334 \log P)}$$

You may assume that log 50 = 1.7. Also verify that, for any base b, $(\log_b x)^2 = \log_b (x^{\log_b x})$.

39. Radioactivity The number of milligrams of a radioactive substance present after t years is given by

$$Q = 100e^{-0.035t}$$

(a) How many milligrams are present after 0 years?
(b) After how many years will there be 20 milligrams present? Give your answer to the nearest year.

40. Blood Sample On the surface of a glass slide is a grid that divides the surface into 225 equal squares. Suppose a blood sample containing N red cells is spread on the slide and the cells are randomly distributed. Then the number of squares containing no cells is (approximately) given by $225e^{-N/225}$. If 100 of the squares contain no cells, estimate the number of cells the blood sample contained.

41. Population In Springfield the population P grows at the rate of 3% per year. The equation $P = 1,500,000(1.03)^t$ gives the population t years after 2009. Find the value of t for which the population will be 2,000,000. Give your answer to the nearest tenth.

42. Market Penetration In a discussion of market penetration by new products, Hurter and Rubenstein[13] refer to the function

$$F(t) = \frac{q - pe^{-(t+C)(p+q)}}{q[1 + e^{(t+C)(p+q)}]}$$

where p, q, and C are constants. They claim that if $F(0) = 0$, then

$$C = -\frac{1}{p+q} \ln \frac{q}{p}$$

Show that their claim is true.

43. Demand Equation The demand equation for a consumer product is $q = 80 - 2^p$. Solve for p and express your answer in terms of common logarithms, as in Example 4. Evaluate p to two decimal places when $q = 60$.

44. Investment The equation $A = P(1.105)^t$ gives the value A at the end of t years of an investment of P dollars compounded annually at an annual interest rate of 10.5%. How many years will it take for an investment to double? Give your answer to the nearest year.

45. Sales After t years the number of units of a product sold per year is given by $q = 1000\left(\frac{1}{2}\right)^{0.8^t}$. Such an equation is called a *Gompertz equation* and describes natural growth in many areas of study. Solve this equation for t in the same manner as in Example 4, and show that

$$t = \frac{\log\left(\dfrac{3 - \log q}{\log 2}\right)}{\log 0.8}$$

Also, for any A and suitable b and a, solve $y = Ab^{a^x}$ for x and explain how the previous solution is a special case.

46. Learning Equation Suppose that the daily output of units of a new product on the tth day of a production run is given by

$$q = 100(1 - e^{-0.1t})$$

Such an equation is called a *learning equation* and indicates that as time progresses, output per day will increase. This may be due to a gain in a worker's proficiency at his or her job. Determine, to the nearest complete unit, the output on (a) the first day and (b) the tenth day after the start of a production run. (c) After how many days will a daily production run of 80 units be reached? Give your answer to the nearest day.

47. Verify that 4 is the only solution to the logarithmic equation in Example 6 by graphing the function

$$y = 5 - \log_2 (x + 4) - \log_2 x$$

and observing when $y = 0$.

48. Solve $2^{3x+0.5} = 17$. Round your answer to two decimal places.

49. Solve $\ln (x + 2) = 5 - x$. Round your answer to two decimal places.

50. Graph the equation $(3)2^y - 4x = 5$. (*Hint:* Solve for y as a function of x.)

[11]R. W. Poole, *An Introduction to Quantitative Ecology* (New York: McGraw-Hill, 1974).
[12]R. Taagepera and J. P. Hayes, "How Trade/GNP Ratio Decreases with Country Size," *Social Science Research*, 6 (1977), 108–32.

[13]A. P. Hurter, Jr., A. H. Rubenstein et al., "Market Penetration by New Innovations: The Technological Literature," *Technological Forecasting and Social Change*, 11 (1978), 197–221.

Chapter 4 Review

Important Terms and Symbols

Section 4.1 Exponential Functions
exponential function, b^x, for $b > 1$ and for $0 < b < 1$ Ex. 2,3, p. 175,176
compound interest   principal   compound amount   Ex. 6, p. 178
interest period   periodic rate   nominal rate
e natural exponential function, e^x Ex. 8, p. 181
exponential law of decay   initial amount   decay constant   half-life   Ex. 11, p. 183

Section 4.2 Logarithmic Functions
logarithmic function, $\log_b x$ common logarithm, $\log x$ Ex. 5, p. 189
natural logarithm, $\ln x$ Ex. 5, p. 189

Section 4.3 Properties of Logarithms
change-of-base formula   Ex. 8, p. 196

Section 4.4 Logarithmic and Exponential Equations
logarithmic equation   exponential equation   Ex. 1, p. 198

Summary

An exponential function has the form $f(x) = b^x$. The graph of $y = b^x$ has one of two general shapes, depending on the value of the base b. (See Figure 4.3.) The compound interest formula

$$S = P(1 + r)^n$$

expresses the compounded future amount S of a principal P at periodic rate r, as an exponential function of the number of interest periods n.

The irrational number $e \approx 2.71828$ provides the most important base for an exponential function. This base occurs in economic analysis and many situations involving growth of populations or decay of radioactive elements. Radioactive elements follow the exponential law of decay,

$$N = N_0 e^{-\lambda t}$$

where N is the amount of an element present at time t, N_0 is the initial amount, and λ is the decay constant. The time required for half of the amount of the element to decay is called the half-life.

The logarithmic function is the inverse function of the exponential function, and vice versa. The logarithmic function with base b is denoted $\log_b$, and $y = \log_b x$ if and only if $b^y = x$. The graph of $y = \log_b x$ has one of two general shapes, depending on the value of the base b. (See

Figure 4.19.) Logarithms with base e are called natural logarithms and are denoted ln; those with base 10 are called common logarithms and are denoted log. The half-life T of a radioactive element can be given in terms of a natural logarithm and the decay constant: $T = (\ln 2)/\lambda$.

Some important properties of logarithms are the following:

$$\log_b (mn) = \log_b m + \log_b n$$
$$\log_b \frac{m}{n} = \log_b m - \log_b n$$
$$\log_b m^r = r \log_b m$$
$$\log_b \frac{1}{m} = -\log_b m$$
$$\log_b 1 = 0$$
$$\log_b b = 1$$
$$\log_b b^r = r$$
$$b^{\log_b m} = m$$
$$\log_b m = \frac{\log_a m}{\log_a b}$$

Moreover, if $\log_b m = \log_b n$, then $m = n$. Similarly, if $b^m = b^n$, then $m = n$. Many of these properties are used in solving logarithmic and exponential equations.

Review Problems

In Problems 1–6, write each exponential form logarithmically and each logarithmic form exponentially.

1. $3^5 = 243$ **2.** $\log_5 625 = 4$ **3.** $\log_{81} 3 = \frac{1}{4}$

4. $10^5 = 100,000$ **5.** $e^7 \approx 1096.63$ **6.** $\log_9 9 = 1$

In Problems 7–12, find the value of the expression without using a calculator.

7. $\log_5 125$ **8.** $\log_4 16$ **9.** $\log_3 \frac{1}{81}$

10. $\log_{1/5} \frac{1}{625}$ **11.** $\log_{1/3} 9$ **12.** $\log_4 2$

In Problems 13–18, find x without using a calculator.

13. $\log_5 625 = x$ **14.** $\log_x \frac{1}{81} = -4$ **15.** $\log_2 x = -10$

16. $\ln \frac{1}{e} = x$ **17.** $\ln (2x + 3) = 0$ **18.** $e^{\ln (x+4)} = 7$

In Problems 19 and 20, let $\log 2 = a$ and $\log 3 = b$. Express the given logarithm in terms of a and b.

19. $\log 8000$

20. $\log \dfrac{1024}{\sqrt[5]{3}}$

In Problems 21–26, write each expression as a single logarithm.

21. $3 \log 7 - 2 \log 5$

22. $5 \ln x + 2 \ln y + \ln z$

23. $2 \ln x + \ln y - 3 \ln z$

24. $\log_6 2 - \log_6 4 - 9 \log_6 3$

25. $\frac{1}{3} \ln x + 3 \ln (x^2) - 2 \ln (x - 1) - 3 \ln (x - 2)$

26. $4 \log x + 2 \log y - 3(\log z + \log w)$

In Problems 27–32, write the expression in terms of $\ln x$, $\ln y$, and $\ln z$.

27. $\ln \dfrac{x^3 y^2}{z^{-5}}$

28. $\ln \dfrac{\sqrt{x}}{(yz)^2}$

29. $\ln \sqrt[3]{xyz}$

30. $\ln \left(\dfrac{x^4 y^3}{z^2} \right)^5$

31. $\ln \left[\dfrac{1}{x} \sqrt{\dfrac{y}{z}} \right]$

32. $\ln \left[\left(\dfrac{x}{y} \right)^2 \left(\dfrac{x}{z} \right)^3 \right]$

33. Write $\log_3 (x + 5)$ in terms of natural logarithms.

34. Write $\log_2 (7x^3 + 5)$ in terms of common logarithms.

35. We have $\log_2 37 \approx 5.20945$ and $\log_2 7 \approx 2.80735$. Find $\log_7 37$.

36. Use natural logarithms to determine the value of $\log_4 5$.

37. If $\ln 3 = x$ and $\ln 4 = y$, express $\ln (16\sqrt{3})$ in terms of x and y.

38. Express $\log \dfrac{x^2 \sqrt[3]{x + 1}}{\sqrt[5]{x^2 + 2}}$ in terms of $\log x$, $\log (x + 1)$, and $\log (x^2 + 2)$.

39. Simplify $10^{\log x} + \log 10^x + \log 10$.

40. Simplify $\log \dfrac{1}{1000} + \log 1000$.

41. If $\ln y = x^2 + 2$, find y.

42. Sketch the graphs of $y = 3^x$ and $y = \log_3 x$.

43. Sketch the graph of $y = 2^{x+3}$.

44. Sketch the graph of $y = -2 \log_2 x$.

In Problems 45–52, find x.

45. $\log (6x - 2) = \log (8x - 10)$

46. $\log 3x + \log 3 = 2$

47. $3^{4x} = 9^{x+1}$

48. $4^{3-x} = \frac{1}{16}$

49. $\log x + \log (10x) = 3$

50. $\ln \left(\frac{x-5}{x-1} \right) = \ln 6$

51. $\ln (\log_x 3) = 2$

52. $\log_2 x + \log_4 x = 3$

In Problems 53–58, find x. Round your answers to three decimal places.

53. $e^{3x} = 14$

54. $10^{3x/2} = 5$

55. $5(e^{x+2} - 6) = 10$

56. $7e^{3x-1} - 2 = 1$

57. $4^{x+3} = 7$

58. $3^{5/x} = 2$

59. Investment   If \$2600 is invested for $6\frac{1}{2}$ years at 6% compounded quarterly, find (a) the compound amount and (b) the compound interest.

60. Investment   Find the compound amount of an investment of \$2000 for five years and four months at the rate of 12% compounded monthly.

61. Find the nominal rate that corresponds to a periodic rate of $1\frac{1}{6}$% per month.

62. Bacteria Growth   Bacteria are growing in a culture, and their number is increasing at the rate of 5% an hour. Initially, 600 bacteria are present. (a) Determine an equation that gives the number, N, of bacteria present after t hours. (b) How many bacteria are present after one hour? (c) After five hours? Give your answer to (c) to the nearest integer.

63. Population Growth   The population of a small town *grows* at the rate of -0.5% per year because the outflow of people to nearby cities in search of jobs exceeds the birth rate. In 2006 the population was 6000. (a) Determine an equation that gives the population, P, t years from 2006. (b) Find what the population will be in 2016 (be careful to express your answer as an integer).

64. Revenue   Due to ineffective advertising, the Kleer-Kut Razor Company finds that its annual revenues have been cut sharply. Moreover, the annual revenue, R, at the end of t years of business satisfies the equation $R = 200{,}000e^{-0.2t}$. Find the annual revenue at the end of two years and at the end of three years.

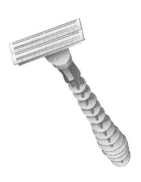

65. Radioactivity   A radioactive substance decays according to the formula

$$N = 10e^{-0.41t}$$

where N is the number of milligrams present after t hours. (a) Determine the initial amount of the substance present. (b) To the nearest tenth of a milligram, determine the amount present after 1 hour and (c) after 5 hours. (d) To the nearest tenth of an hour, determine the half-life of the substance, and (e) determine the number of hours for 0.1 milligram to remain.

66. Radioactivity   If a radioactive substance has a half-life of 10 days, in how many days will $\frac{1}{8}$ of the initial amount be present?

67. Marketing   A marketing-research company needs to determine how people adapt to the taste of a new cough drop. In one experiment, a person was given a cough drop and was asked periodically to assign a number, on a scale from 0 to 10, to the perceived taste. This number was called the *response magnitude*. The number 10 was assigned to the initial taste. After conducting the experiment several times, the company estimated that the response magnitude is given by

$$R = 10e^{-t/40}$$

where t is the number of seconds after the person is given the cough drop. (a) Find the response magnitude after 20 seconds. Give your answer to the nearest integer. (b) After how many seconds does a person have a response magnitude of 5? Give your answer to the nearest second.

68. Sediment in Water   The water in a midwestern lake contains sediment, and the presence of the sediment reduces the transmission of light through the water. Experiments indicate that the intensity of light is reduced by 10% by passage through 20 cm of water. Suppose that the lake is uniform with respect to the amount of sediment contained by the water. A measuring instrument can detect light at the intensity of 0.17% of full sunlight. This measuring instrument is lowered into the lake. At what depth will it first cease to record the presence of light? Give your answer to the nearest 10 cm.

69. Body Cooling   In a discussion of the rate of cooling of isolated portions of the body when they are exposed to low temperatures, there occurs the equation[14]

$$T_t - T_e = (T_t - T_e)_o e^{-at}$$

where T_t is the temperature of the portion at time t, T_e is the environmental temperature, the subscript o refers to the initial temperature difference, and a is a constant. Show that

$$a = \frac{1}{t} \ln \frac{(T_t - T_e)_o}{T_t - T_e}$$

70. Depreciation   An alternative to straight-line depreciation is *declining-balance* depreciation. This method assumes that an item loses value more steeply at the beginning of its life than later on. A fixed percentage of the value is subtracted each month. Suppose an item's initial cost is C and its useful life is N months. Then the value, V (in dollars), of the item at the end of n months is given by

$$V = C\left(1 - \frac{1}{N}\right)^n$$

so that each month brings a depreciation of $\frac{100}{N}$ percent. (This is called *single declining-balance depreciation;* if the annual depreciation were $\frac{200}{N}$ percent, then we would speak of *double-declining-balance depreciation.*) A notebook computer is purchased for $1500 and has a useful life of 36 months. It undergoes double-declining-balance depreciation. After how many months, to the nearest integer, does its value drop below $500?

71. If $y = f(x) = \dfrac{\ln x}{x}$, determine the range of f. Round values to two decimal places.

72. Determine the points of intersection of the graphs of $y = \ln(x + 2)$ and $y = x^2 - 7$. Round your answers to two decimal places.

73. Solve $\ln x = 6 - 2x$. Round your answer to two decimal places.

74. Solve $6^{3-4x} = 15$. Round your answer to two decimal places.

75. Bases   We have seen that there are two kinds of bases b for exponential and logarithmic functions: those b in $(0, 1)$ and those b in $(1, \infty)$. It might be supposed that there are *more* of the second kind but this is not the case. Consider the function $f: (0,1) \longrightarrow (1, \infty)$ given by $f(x) = 1/x$.
(a) Show that the domain of f can be taken to be $(0, 1)$.
(b) Show that with domain $(0, 1)$ the range of f is $(1, \infty)$.
(c) Show that f has an inverse g and determine a formula for $g(x)$.

The exercise shows that the numbers in $(0, 1)$ are in one-to-one correspondence with the numbers in $(1, \infty)$ so that every *base* of either kind corresponds to exactly one of the other kind. Who would have thought it? "$(1, \infty)$—so many numbers; $(0, 1)$—so little space."

76. Display the graph of the equation $(6)5^y + x = 2$. (*Hint:* Solve for y as an explicit function of x.)

77. Graph $y = 3^x$ and $y = \dfrac{3^x}{9}$ on the same screen. It appears that the graph of $y = \dfrac{3^x}{9}$ is the graph of $y = 3^x$ shifted two units to the right. Prove algebraically that this is indeed true.

⊘ EXPLORE & EXTEND   Drug Dosages[1]

Determining and prescribing drug dosages are extremely important aspects of the medical profession. Quite often, caution must be taken because of possible adverse side or toxic effects of drugs.

Many drugs are used up by the human body in such a way that the amount present follows an *exponential law of decay* as studied in Section 4.1. That means, if $N(t)$ is the amount of the drug present in the body at time t, then

$$N = N_0 e^{-kt} \qquad (1)$$

where k is a positive constant and N_0 is the amount present at time $t = 0$. If H is the *half-life* of such a drug, meaning the time H for which $N(H) = N_0/2$, then again from Section 4.2,

$$H = (\ln 2)/k \qquad (2)$$

Note that H completely determines the constant k since we can rewrite Equation (2) as $k = (\ln 2)/H$.

Suppose that you want to analyze the situation whereby equal doses of such a drug are introduced into a patient's system every I units of time until a therapeutic level is attained, and then the dosage is reduced to maintain the therapeutic level. The reason for *reduced* maintenance doses is frequently related to the toxic effects of drugs.

---

[14] R. W. Stacy et al., *Essentials of Biological and Medical Physics* (New York: McGraw-Hill, 1955).

[1] This discussion is adapted from Gerald M. Armstrong and Calvin P. Midgley, "The Exponential-Decay Law Applied to Medical Dosages," *The Mathematics Teacher,* 80, no. 3 (February 1987), 110–13. By permission of the National Council of Teachers of Mathematics.

In particular, assume that

(i) There are d doses of P units each;

(ii) A dose is given at times $t = 0, I, 2I, \ldots,$ and $(d - 1)I$; and

(iii) The therapeutic level, T, is attained at time $t = dI$ (which is one time interval, I, after the last dose is administered).

We now determine a formula that gives the therapeutic level, T. At time $t = 0$ the patient receives the first P units, so the amount of drug in the body is P at $t = 0$. At time $t = I$ the amount present from the first dose is Pe^{-kI} [by Equation (1)]. In addition, at $t = I$ the second P units are given. Thus the *total* amount of the drug present at $t = I$ is

$$P + Pe^{-kI}$$

At time $t = 2I$, the amount remaining from the first dose is Pe^{-2kI}; from the second dose, which has been in the system for only one time interval, the amount present is Pe^{-kI}. Also, at time $t = 2I$ the third dose of P units is given, so the total amount of the drug present at $t = 2I$ is

$$P + Pe^{-kI} + Pe^{-2kI}$$

Continuing, the amount of drug present in the system at time $(d - 1)I$, the time of the last dose, is

$$P + Pe^{-kI} + Pe^{-2kI} + \cdots + Pe^{-(d-1)\cdot kI}$$

Thus, one further time interval later, at time dI, when a dose of P is not administered but the therapeutic level T is reached, we have

$$T = Pe^{-kI} + Pe^{-2kI} + \cdots + Pe^{-dkI} \qquad (3)$$

since each term in the preceding expression decays by a factor of e^{-kI}. This is a good opportunity to use the *summation notation* of Section 1.5 and rewrite Equation (3) as

$$T = P \sum_{i=1}^{d} e^{-ikI} \qquad (4)$$

The sum is actually that of the first d terms of a geometric sequence as studied in Section 1.6. Both the first term of the geometric sequence and its common ratio are given by e^{-kI}. It follows from Equation (16) of Section 1.6 that Equation (4) becomes

$$T = \frac{Pe^{-kI}(1 - e^{-dkI})}{1 - e^{-kI}} \qquad (5)$$

which, after multiplying both numerator and denominator by e^{kI}, gives

$$T = \frac{P(1 - e^{-dkI})}{e^{kI} - 1} \qquad (6)$$

Equation (6) expresses the therapeutic level, T, in terms of the dose, P; the length of the time intervals, I; the number of doses, d; and the half-life, H, of the drug [since $k = (\ln 2)/H$]. It is easy to solve Equation (6) for P if $T, H, I,$ and d are known. It is also possible to solve the equation for d if $T, H, I,$ and P are known. [Solving Equation (6) for either H or I in terms of the other quantities can be quite complicated.]

The objective now is to maintain the therapeutic level in the patient's system. To do this, a reduced dose, R, is given at times $t = dI, (d + 1)I, (d + 2)I,$ and so on. We can determine a formula for R in the following way.

At time $t = (d + 1)I$, but before the second reduced dose is given, the amount of drug in the system from the first reduced dose is Re^{-kI} and the amount that remains from the therapeutic level is Te^{-kI}. Suppose you require that the sum of these amounts be the therapeutic level, T; that is,

$$T = Re^{-kI} + Te^{-kI}$$

Solving for R gives

$$Re^{-kI} = T - Te^{-kI}$$

$$R = T(1 - e^{-kI})e^{kI}$$

Replacing T by the right side of Equation (5) gives

$$R = \frac{Pe^{-kI}(1 - e^{-dkI})}{1 - e^{-kI}}(1 - e^{-kI})e^{kI}$$

which simplifies to

$$R = P(1 - e^{-dkI}) \qquad (7)$$

By continuing the reduced doses at time intervals of length I, we are assured that the drug level in the system never falls below T after time $(d + 1)I$. Furthermore, because $-dkI < 0$, we have $0 < e^{-dkI} < 1$. Consequently, the factor $1 - e^{-dkI}$ in Equation (7) is between 0 and 1. This ensures that R is less than P; hence R is indeed a *reduced* dose.

It is interesting to note that Armstrong and Midgley state that "the therapeutic amount T must be chosen from a range of empirically determined values. Medical discretion and experience are needed to select proper intervals and durations of time to administer the drug. Even the half-life of a drug can vary somewhat among different patients." More on medical drugs and their safe use can be found at `www.fda.gov/cder`.

Problems

1. Solve Equation (6) for (a) P and (b) d.

2. Show that if I is equal to the half-life of the drug, Equation (6) can be written as

$$T = \left(1 - \frac{1}{2^d}\right)P$$

Note that $0 < 1 - (1/2^d) < 1$ for $d > 0$. Hence, the foregoing equation implies that when doses of P units are administered at time intervals equal to the half-life of the drug, it follows that at one time interval after any dose is given, but before the next dose is given, the total level of the drug in a patient's system is less than P.

3. Theophylline is a drug used to treat bronchial asthma and has a half-life of 8 hours in the system of a relatively healthy nonsmoking patient. Suppose that such a patient achieves the desired therapeutic level of this drug in 12 hours when 100 milligrams is administered every 4 hours. Here $d = 3$. Because of toxicity, the dose must be reduced thereafter. To the nearest milligram, determine (a) the therapeutic level and (b) the reduced dose.

4. Use a graphing calculator to generate a drug concentration graph and verify that Equation (7) correctly gives the maintenance dose. On the calculator, enter $0.5 \to K$, $3 \to D$, $1 \to I$ and $1 \to P$. Then enter $Y1 = P(1 - e^{\wedge}(-D*K*I))$ to represent R. Finally, enter $Y2 = P\,e^{\wedge}(-K\,X) + P\,e^{\wedge}(-K(X - I))^{*}(X \geq I) + P\,e^{\wedge}(-K(X - 2I))^{*}(X \geq 2I) + Y1\,e^{\wedge}(-K(X - 3I))^{*}(X \geq 3I) + Y1\,e^{\wedge}(-K(X - 4I))^{*}(X \geq 4I)$. Then select only Y2 to be graphed and graph the function. Experiment with different values for K, D, I, and P. What adjustment is necessary in the expression for Y2 as you change D?

5

Mathematics of Finance

Q EXPLORE & EXTEND
Treasury Securities

For people who like cars and can afford to buy a nice one, a trip to an auto dealership can be a lot of fun. However, buying a car also has a side that many people find unpleasant: the negotiating. The verbal tug-of-war with the salesperson is especially difficult if the buyer is planning to pay on an installment plan and does not understand the numbers being quoted.

How, for instance, does the fact that the salesperson is offering the car for $12,800 translate into a monthly payment of $281.54? The answer is amortization. The term comes via French from the Latin root *mort-,* meaning "dead"; from this we also get *mortal* and *mortified.* A debt that is gradually paid off is eventually "killed," and the payment plan for doing this is called an amortization schedule. The schedule is determined by a formula we give in Section 5.4 and apply in Section 5.5.

Using the formula, we can calculate the monthly payment for the car. If one makes a $900 down payment on a $12,800 car and pays off the rest over four years at 4.8% APR compounded monthly, the monthly payment for principal and interest only should be $272.97. If the payment is higher than that, it may contain additional charges such as sales tax, registration fees, or insurance premiums, which the buyer should ask about since some of them may be optional. Understanding the mathematics of finance can help consumers make more informed decisions about purchases and investments.

Objective

To extend the notion of compound interest to include effective rates and to solve interest problems whose solutions require logarithms.

5.1 Compound Interest

In this chapter we model selected topics in finance that deal with the time value of money, such as investments, loans, and so on. In later chapters, when more mathematics is at our disposal, certain topics will be revisited and expanded.

Let us first review some facts from Section 4.1, where the notion of compound interest was introduced. Under compound interest, at the end of each interest period, the interest earned for that period is added to the *principal* (the invested amount) so that it too earns interest over the next interest period. The basic formula for the value (or *compound amount*) of an investment after n interest periods under compound interest is as follows:

Compound Interest Formula

For an original principal of P, the formula

$$S = P(1 + r)^n \qquad (1)$$

gives the **compound amount** S at the end of n *interest periods* at the *periodic rate* of r.

The compound amount is also called the *accumulated amount,* and the difference between the compound amount and the original principal, $S - P$, is called the *compound interest.*

Recall that an interest rate is usually quoted as an *annual* rate, called the *nominal rate* or the *annual percentage rate* (A.P.R.). The periodic rate (or rate per interest period) is obtained by dividing the nominal rate by the number of interest periods per year.

For example, let us compute the compound amount when $1000 is invested for five years at the nominal rate of 8% compounded quarterly. The rate *per period* is $0.08/4$, and the number of interest periods is 5×4.

From Equation (1), we have

$$S = 1000 \left(1 + \frac{0.08}{4} \right)^{5 \times 4}$$

$$= 1000(1 + 0.02)^{20} \approx \$1485.95$$

A calculator is handy while reading this chapter.

APPLY IT ▶

1. Suppose you leave an initial amount of $518 in a savings account for three years. If interest is compounded daily (365 times per year), use a graphing calculator to graph the compound amount S as a function of the nominal rate of interest. From the graph, estimate the nominal rate of interest so that there is $600 after three years.

EXAMPLE 1   Compound Interest

Suppose that $500 amounted to $588.38 in a savings account after three years. If interest was compounded semiannually, find the nominal rate of interest, compounded semiannually, that was earned by the money.

Solution: Let r be the semiannual rate. There are $2 \times 3 = 6$ interest periods. From Equation (1),

$$500(1 + r)^6 = 588.38$$

$$(1 + r)^6 = \frac{588.38}{500}$$

$$1 + r = \sqrt[6]{\frac{588.38}{500}}$$

$$r = \sqrt[6]{\frac{588.38}{500}} - 1 \approx 0.0275$$

Thus, the semiannual rate was 2.75%, so the nominal rate was $5\frac{1}{2}\%$ compounded semiannually.

◁

EXAMPLE 2   Doubling Money

At what nominal rate of interest, compounded yearly, will money double in eight years?

Solution: Let r be the rate at which a principal of P doubles in eight years. Then the compound amount is $2P$. From Equation (1),

$$P(1 + r)^8 = 2P$$
$$(1 + r)^8 = 2$$
$$1 + r = \sqrt[8]{2}$$
$$r = \sqrt[8]{2} - 1 \approx 0.0905$$

Note that the doubling rate is independent of the principal P.

Hence, the desired rate is 9.05%.

◁

We can determine how long it takes for a given principal to accumulate to a particular amount by using logarithms, as Example 3 shows.

APPLY IT ▸

2. Suppose you leave an initial amount of $520 in a savings account at an annual rate of 5.2% compounded daily (365 days per year). Use a graphing calculator to graph the compound amount S as a function of the interest periods. From the graph, estimate how long it takes for the amount to accumulate to $750.

EXAMPLE 3   Compound Interest

How long will it take for $600 to amount to $900 at an annual rate of 6% compounded quarterly?

Solution: The periodic rate is $r = 0.06/4 = 0.015$. Let n be the number of interest periods it takes for a principal of $P = 600$ to amount to $S = 900$. Then, from Equation (1),

$$900 = 600(1.015)^n \qquad (2)$$
$$(1.015)^n = \frac{900}{600}$$
$$(1.015)^n = 1.5$$

To solve for n, we first take the natural logarithms of both sides:

$$\ln(1.015)^n = \ln 1.5$$
$$n \ln 1.015 = \ln 1.5 \qquad \text{since } \ln m^r = r \ln m$$
$$n = \frac{\ln 1.5}{\ln 1.015} \approx 27.233$$

The number of years that corresponds to 27.233 quarterly interest periods is $27.233/4 \approx 6.8083$, which is about 6 years, $9\frac{1}{2}$ months. Actually, the principal doesn't amount to $900 until 7 years pass, because interest is compounded quarterly.

Now Work Problem 20 ◁

Effective Rate

If P dollars are invested at a nominal rate of 10% compounded quarterly for one year, the principal will earn more than 10% that year. In fact, the compound interest is

$$S - P = P\left(1 + \frac{0.10}{4}\right)^4 - P = [(1.025)^4 - 1]P$$
$$\approx 0.103813P$$

which is about 10.38% of P. That is, 10.38% is the approximate rate of interest compounded *annually* that is actually earned, and that rate is called the **effective rate** of interest. The effective rate is independent of P. In general, the effective interest rate is just the rate of *simple* interest earned over a period of one year. Thus, we have shown that the nominal rate of 10% compounded quarterly is equivalent to an effective rate of 10.38%. Following the preceding procedure, we can generalize our result:

Effective Rate

The **effective rate** r_e that is equivalent to a nominal rate of r compounded n times a year is given by

$$r_e = \left(1 + \frac{r}{n}\right)^n - 1 \qquad (3)$$

APPLY IT ▷

3. An investment is compounded monthly. Use a graphing calculator to graph the effective rate r_e as a function of the nominal rate r. Then use the graph to find the nominal rate that is equivalent to an effective rate of 8%.

EXAMPLE 4   Effective Rate

What effective rate is equivalent to a nominal rate of 6% compounded (a) semiannually and (b) quarterly?

Solution:

a. From Equation (3), the effective rate is

$$r_e = \left(1 + \frac{0.06}{2}\right)^2 - 1 = (1.03)^2 - 1 = 0.0609 = 6.09\%$$

b. The effective rate is

$$r_e = \left(1 + \frac{0.06}{4}\right)^4 - 1 = (1.015)^4 - 1 \approx 0.061364 = 6.14\%$$

Now Work Problem 9 ◁

Example 4 illustrates that, for a given nominal rate r, the effective rate increases as the number of interest periods per year (n) increases. However, in Section 5.3 it is shown that, regardless of how large n is, the maximum effective rate that can be obtained is $e^r - 1$.

EXAMPLE 5   Effective Rate

To what amount will $12,000 accumulate in 15 years if it is invested at an effective rate of 5%?

Solution: Since an effective rate is the rate that is compounded annually, we have

$$S = 12,000(1.05)^{15} \approx \$24,947.14$$

Now Work Problem 15 ◁

EXAMPLE 6   Doubling Money

How many years will it take for money to double at the effective rate of r?

Solution: Let n be the number of years it takes for a principal of P to double. Then the compound amount is $2P$. Thus,

$$2P = P(1 + r)^n$$
$$2 = (1 + r)^n$$
$$\ln 2 = n \ln(1 + r) \qquad \text{taking logarithms of both sides}$$

Hence,

$$n = \frac{\ln 2}{\ln(1 + r)}$$

For example, if $r = 0.06$, the number of years it takes to double a principal is

$$\frac{\ln 2}{\ln 1.06} \approx 11.9 \text{ years}$$

Now Work Problem 11 ◁

We remark that when alternative interest rates are available to an investor, effective rates are used to compare them—that is, to determine which of them is the "best." The next example illustrates.

EXAMPLE 7   Comparing Interest Rates

APPLY IT ▶

4. Suppose you have two investment opportunities. You can invest $10,000 at 11% compounded monthly, or you can invest $9700 at 11.25% compounded quarterly. Which has the better effective rate of interest? Which is the better investment over 20 years?

If an investor has a choice of investing money at 6% compounded daily or $6\frac{1}{8}\%$ compounded quarterly, which is the better choice?

Solution:

Strategy   We determine the equivalent effective rate of interest for each nominal rate and then compare our results.

The respective effective rates of interest are

$$r_e = \left(1 + \frac{0.06}{365}\right)^{365} - 1 \approx 6.18\%$$

and

$$r_e = \left(1 + \frac{0.06125}{4}\right)^{4} - 1 \approx 6.27\%$$

Since the second choice gives the higher effective rate, it is the better choice (in spite of the fact that daily compounding may be psychologically more appealing).

Now Work Problem 21 ◁

PROBLEMS 5.1

In Problems 1 and 2, find (a) the compound amount and (b) the compound interest for the given investment and rate.

1. $6000 for eight years at an effective rate of 8%

2. $750 for 12 months at an effective rate of 7%

In Problems 3–6, find the effective rate that corresponds to the given nominal rate. Round answers to three decimal places.

3. 3% compounded semiannually

4. 5% compounded quarterly

5. 3.5% compounded daily

6. 6% compounded daily

7. Find the effective rate of interest (rounded to three decimal places) that is equivalent to a nominal rate of 10% compounded
(a) yearly,   **(b)** semiannually,
(c) quarterly,   **(d)** monthly,
(e) daily.

8. Find (i) the compound interest (rounded to two decimal places) and (ii) the effective rate (to three decimal places) if $1000 is invested for five years at an annual rate of 7% compounded
(a) quarterly,   **(b)** monthly,
(c) weekly,   **(d)** daily.

9. Over a five-year period, an original principal of $2000 accumulated to $2950 in an account in which interest was compounded quarterly. Determine the effective rate of interest, rounded to two decimal places.

10. Suppose that over a six-year period, $1000 accumulated to $1959 in an investment certificate in which interest was compounded quarterly. Find the nominal rate of interest, compounded quarterly, that was earned. Round your answer to two decimal places.

In Problems 11 and 12, find how many years it would take to double a principal at the given effective rate. Give your answer to one decimal place.

11. 9%   **12.** 5%

13. A $6000 certificate of deposit is purchased for $6000 and is held for seven years. If the certificate earns an effective rate of 8%, what is it worth at the end of that period?

14. How many years will it take for money to triple at the effective rate of r?

15. **University Costs**   Suppose attending a certain university costs $25,500 in the 2009–2010 school year. This price includes tuition, room, board, books, and other expenses. Assuming an effective 3% inflation rate for these costs, determine what the college costs will be in the 2015–2016 school year.

16. College Costs Repeat Problem 15 for an inflation rate of 2% compounded quarterly.

17. Finance Charge A major credit-card company has a finance charge of $1\frac{1}{2}$% per month on the outstanding indebtedness. (a) What is the nominal rate compounded monthly? (b) What is the effective rate?

18. How long would it take for a principal of P to double if money is worth 12% compounded monthly? Give your answer to the nearest month.

19. To what sum will $2000 amount in eight years if invested at a 6% effective rate for the first four years and at 6% compounded semiannually thereafter?

20. How long will it take for $100 to amount to $1000 if invested at 6% compounded monthly? Express the answer in years, rounded to two decimal places.

21. An investor has a choice of investing a sum of money at 8% compounded annually or at 7.8% compounded semiannually. Which is the better of the two rates?

22. What nominal rate of interest, compounded monthly, corresponds to an effective rate of 4.5%?

23. Savings Account A bank advertises that it pays interest on savings accounts at the rate of $4\frac{3}{4}$% compounded daily. Find the effective rate if the bank assumes that a year consists of

(a) 360 days or (b) 365 days in determining the *daily rate*. Assume that compounding occurs 365 times a year, and round your answer to two decimal places.

24. Savings Account Suppose that $700 amounted to $801.06 in a savings account after two years. If interest was compounded quarterly, find the nominal rate of interest, compounded quarterly, that was earned by the money.

25. Inflation As a hedge against inflation, an investor purchased a 1972 Gran Torino in 1990 for $90,000. It was sold in 2000 for $250,000. At what effective rate did the car appreciate in value? Express the answer as a percentage rounded to three decimal places.

26. Inflation If the rate of inflation for certain goods is $7\frac{1}{4}$% compounded daily, how many years will it take for the average price of such goods to double?

27. Zero-Coupon Bond A *zero-coupon bond* is a bond that is sold for less than its face value (that is, it is *discounted*) and has no periodic interest payments. Instead, the bond is redeemed for its face value at maturity. Thus, in this sense, interest is paid at maturity. Suppose that a zero-coupon bond sells for $420 and can be redeemed in 14 years for its face value of $1000. The bond earns interest at what nominal rate, compounded semiannually?

28. Misplaced Funds Suppose that $1000 is misplaced in a non-interest-bearing checking account and forgotten. Each year, the bank imposes a service charge of 1%. After 20 years, how much remains of the $1000? [*Hint:* Consider Equation (1) with $r = -0.01$.]

29. General Solutions Equation (1) can be solved for each of the variables in terms of the other three. Find each of P, r, and n in this way. (There is no need to memorize any of the three new formulas that result. The point here is that by showing the general solutions exist, we gain confidence in our ability to handle any particular cases.)

Objective

To study present value and to solve problems involving the time value of money by using equations of value. To introduce the net present value of cash flows.

5.2 Present Value

Suppose that $100 is deposited in a savings account that pays 6% compounded annually. Then at the end of two years, the account is worth

$$100(1.06)^2 = 112.36$$

To describe this relationship, we say that the compound amount of $112.36 is the *future value* of the $100, and $100 is the *present value* of the $112.36. In general, there are times when we may know the future value of an investment and wish to find the present value. To obtain a formula for doing this, we solve the equation $S = P(1 + r)^n$ for P. The result is $P = S/(1 + r)^n = S(1 + r)^{-n}$.

Present Value

The principal P that must be invested at the periodic rate of r for n interest periods so that the compound amount is S is given by

$$P = S(1 + r)^{-n} \tag{1}$$

and is called the **present value** of S.

EXAMPLE 1 **Present Value**

Find the present value of $1000 due after three years if the interest rate is 9% compounded monthly.

Solution: We use Equation (1) with $S = 1000$, $r = 0.09/12 = 0.0075$, and $n = 3(12) = 36$:

$$P = 1000(1.0075)^{-36} \approx 764.15$$

This means that $764.15 must be invested at 9% compounded monthly to have $1000 in three years.

Now Work Problem 1 ◁

If the interest rate in Example 1 were 10% compounded monthly, the present value would be

$$P = 1000 \left(1 + \frac{0.1}{12}\right)^{-36} \approx 741.74$$

which is less than before. It is typical that the present value for a given future value decreases as the interest rate per interest period increases.

EXAMPLE 2 **Single-Payment Trust Fund**

A trust fund for a child's education is being set up by a single payment so that at the end of 15 years there will be $50,000. If the fund earns interest at the rate of 7% compounded semiannually, how much money should be paid into the fund?

Solution: We want the present value of $50,000, due in 15 years. From Equation (1) with $S = 50,000$, $r = 0.07/2 = 0.035$, and $n = 15(2) = 30$, we have

$$P = 50,000(1.035)^{-30} \approx 17,813.92$$

Thus, $17,813.92 should be paid into the fund.

Now Work Problem 13 ◁

Equations of Value

Suppose that Mr. Smith owes Mr. Jones two sums of money: $1000, due in two years, and $600, due in five years. If Mr. Smith wishes to pay off the total debt now by a single payment, how much should the payment be? Assume an interest rate of 8% compounded quarterly.

The single payment x due now must be such that it would grow and eventually pay off the debts when they are due. That is, it must equal the sum of the present values of the future payments. As shown in the timeline of Figure 5.1, we have

$$x = 1000(1.02)^{-8} + 600(1.02)^{-20} \tag{2}$$

This equation is called an *equation of value*. We find that

$$x \approx 1257.27$$

Thus, the single payment now due is $1257.27. Let us analyze the situation in more detail. There are two methods of payment of the debt: a single payment now or two payments in the future. Notice that Equation (2) indicates that the value *now* of all payments under one method must equal the value *now* of all payments under the other method. In general, this is true not just *now*, but at *any time*. For example, if we multiply both sides of Equation (2) by $(1.02)^{20}$, we get the equation of value

$$x(1.02)^{20} = 1000(1.02)^{12} + 600 \tag{3}$$

Figure 5.1 is a useful tool for visualizing the time value of money. Always draw such a timeline to set up an equation of value.

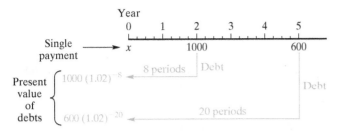

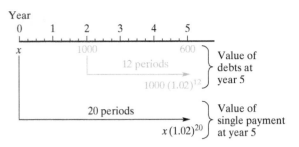

FIGURE 5.1   Replacing two future payments by a single payment now.

FIGURE 5.2   Diagram for equation of value.

The left side of Equation (3) gives the value five years from now of the single payment (see Figure 5.2), while the right side gives the value five years from now of all payments under the other method. Solving Equation (3) for x gives the same result, $x \approx 1257.27$. In general, an **equation of value** illustrates that when one is considering two methods of paying a debt (or of making some other transaction), *at any time*, the value of all payments under one method must equal the value of all payments under the other method.

In certain situations, one equation of value may be more convenient to use than another, as Example 3 illustrates.

EXAMPLE 3   Equation of Value

A debt of $3000 due six years from now is instead to be paid off by three payments: $500 now, $1500 in three years, and a final payment at the end of five years. What would this payment be if an interest rate of 6% compounded annually is assumed?

Solution: Let x be the final payment due in five years. For computational convenience, we will set up an equation of value to represent the situation at the end of that time, for in that way the coefficient of x will be 1, as seen in Figure 5.3. Notice that at year 5 we compute the future values of $500 and $1500, and the present value of $3000. The equation of value is

$$500(1.06)^5 + 1500(1.06)^2 + x = 3000(1.06)^{-1}$$

so

$$x = 3000(1.06)^{-1} - 500(1.06)^5 - 1500(1.06)^2$$

$$\approx 475.68$$

Thus, the final payment should be $475.68.

Now Work Problem 15 ◁

When one is considering a choice of two investments, a comparison should be made of the value of each investment at a certain time, as Example 4 shows.

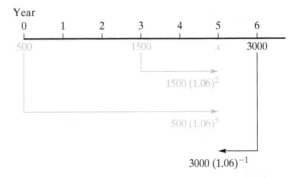

FIGURE 5.3   Time values of payments for Example 3.

EXAMPLE 4   Comparing Investments

Suppose that you had the opportunity of investing $5000 in a business such that the value of the investment after five years would be $6300. On the other hand, you could instead put the $5000 in a savings account that pays 6% compounded semiannually. Which investment is better?

Solution: Let us consider the value of each investment at the end of five years. At that time the business investment would have a value of $6300, while the savings account would have a value of $5000(1.03)^{10} \approx \$6719.58$. Clearly, the better choice is putting the money in the savings account.

Now Work Problem 21 ◁

Net Present Value

If an initial investment will bring in payments at future times, the payments are called **cash flows.** The **net present value,** denoted NPV, of the cash flows is defined to be the sum of the present values of the cash flows, minus the initial investment. If NPV > 0, then the investment is profitable; if NPV < 0, the investment is not profitable.

EXAMPLE 5   Net Present Value

Year	Cash Flow
2	10,000
3	8000
5	6000

Suppose that you can invest $20,000 in a business that guarantees you cash flows at the end of years 2, 3, and 5 as indicated in the table to the left. Assume an interest rate of 7% compounded annually, and find the net present value of the cash flows.

Solution: Subtracting the initial investment from the sum of the present values of the cash flows gives

$$\text{NPV} = 10{,}000(1.07)^{-2} + 8000(1.07)^{-3} + 6000(1.07)^{-5} - 20{,}000$$

$$\approx -457.31$$

Since NPV < 0, the business venture is not profitable if one considers the time value of money. It would be better to invest the $20,000 in a bank paying 7%, since the venture is equivalent to investing only $20,000 − $457.31 = $19,542.69.

Now Work Problem 19 ◁

PROBLEMS 5.2

In Problems 1–10, find the present value of the given future payment at the specified interest rate.

1. $6000 due in 20 years at 5% compounded annually

2. $3500 due in eight years at 6% effective

3. $4000 due in 12 years at 7% compounded semiannually

4. $1950 due in three years at 16% compounded monthly

5. $9000 due in $5\frac{1}{2}$ years at 8% compounded quarterly

6. $6000 due in $6\frac{1}{2}$ years at 10% compounded semiannually

7. $8000 due in five years at 10% compounded monthly

8. $500 due in three years at $8\frac{3}{4}$% compounded quarterly

9. $5000 due in two years at $7\frac{1}{2}$% compounded daily

10. $1250 due in $1\frac{1}{2}$ years at $13\frac{1}{2}$% compounded weekly

11. A bank account pays 5.3% annual interest, compounded monthly. How much must be deposited now so that the account contains exactly $12,000 at the end of one year?

12. Repeat Problem 11 for the nominal rate of 7.1% compounded semiannually.

13. **Trust Fund**   A trust fund for a 10-year-old child is being set up by a single payment so that at age 21 the child will receive $27,000. Find how much the payment is if an interest rate of 6% compounded semiannually is assumed.

14. A debt of $750 due in 10 years and $250 due in 12 years is to be repaid by a single payment now. Find how much the payment is if an interest rate of 8% compounded quarterly is assumed.

15. A debt of $600 due in three years and $800 due in four years is to be repaid by a single payment two years from now. If the interest rate is 8% compounded semiannually, how much is the payment?

16. A debt of $7000 due in five years is to be repaid by a payment of $3000 now and a second payment at the end of five years. How much should the second payment be if the interest rate is 8% compounded monthly?

17. A debt of $5000 due five years from now and $5000 due ten years from now is to be repaid by a payment of $2000 in two years, a payment of $4000 in four years, and a final payment at the end of six years. If the interest rate is 2.5% compounded annually, how much is the final payment?

18. A debt of $3500 due in four years and $5000 due in six years is to be repaid by a single payment of $1500 now and three equal payments that are due each consecutive year from now. If the interest rate is 7% compounded annually, how much are each of the equal payments?

19. Cash Flows An initial investment of $35,000 in a business guarantees the following cash flows:

Year	Cash Flow
5	$13,000
6	$14,000
7	$15,000
8	$16,000

Assume an interest rate of 4% compounded quarterly.
(a) Find the net present value of the cash flows.
(b) Is the investment profitable?

20. Cash Flows Repeat Problem 19 for the interest rate of 6% compounded semiannually.

21. Decision Making Suppose that a person has the following choices of investing $10,000:
(a) placing the money in a savings account paying 6% compounded semiannually;
(b) investing in a business such that the value of the investment after 8 years is $16,000.
Which is the better choice?

22. A owes B two sums of money: $1000 plus interest at 7% compounded annually, which is due in five years, and $2000 plus interest at 8% compounded semiannually, which is due in seven years. If both debts are to be paid off by a single payment at the end of six years, find the amount of the payment if money is worth 6% compounded quarterly.

23. Purchase Incentive A jewelry store advertises that for every $1000 spent on diamond jewelry, the purchaser receives a $1000 bond at absolutely no cost. In reality, the $1000 is the full maturity value of a zero-coupon bond (see Problem 27 of Problems 5.1), which the store purchases at a heavily reduced price. If the bond earns interest at the rate of 7.5% compounded quarterly and matures after 20 years, how much does the bond cost the store?

24. Find the present value of $10,000 due in 10 years at a bank rate of 10% compounded daily. Assume that the bank uses 360 days in determining the daily rate and that there are 365 days in a year; that is, compounding occurs 365 times in a year.

25. Promissory Note A *(promissory) note* is a written statement agreeing to pay a sum of money either on demand or at a definite future time. When a note is purchased for its present value at a given interest rate, the note is said to be *discounted,* and the interest rate is called the *discount rate.* Suppose a $10,000 note due eight years from now is sold to a financial institution for $4700. What is the nominal discount rate with quarterly compounding?

26. Promissory Note **(a)** Repeat Problem 25 with monthly compounding. **(b)** Let r be the nominal discount rate in Problem 25 and let s be the nominal discount rate in part **(a)**. Prove, without reference to the future value and to the present value of the note, that

$$s = 12 \left(\sqrt[3]{1 + \frac{r}{4}} - 1 \right)$$

To extend the notion of compound interest to the situation where interest is compounded continuously. To develop, in this case, formulas for compound amount and present value.

5.3 Interest Compounded Continuously

We have seen that when money is invested at a given annual rate, the interest earned each year depends on how frequently interest is compounded. For example, more interest is earned if it is compounded monthly rather than semiannually. We can successively get still more interest by compounding it weekly, daily, per hour, and so on. However, there is a maximum interest that can be earned, which we now examine.

Suppose a principal of P dollars is invested for t years at an annual rate of r. If interest is compounded k times a year, then the rate per interest period is r/k, and there are kt periods. From Section 4.1, recalled in Section 5.1, the compound amount is given by

$$S = P \left(1 + \frac{r}{k}\right)^{kt}$$

If k, the number of interest periods per year, is increased indefinitely, as we did in the "thought experiment" of Section 4.1 to introduce the number e, then the length of each period approaches 0 and we say that interest is **compounded continuously.** We can make this precise. In fact, with a little algebra we can relate the compound amount to the number e. Let $m = k/r$, so that

$$P \left(1 + \frac{r}{k}\right)^{kt} = P \left(\left(1 + \frac{1}{k/r}\right)^{k/r}\right)^{rt} = P \left(\left(1 + \frac{1}{m}\right)^{m}\right)^{rt} = P \left(\left(\frac{m+1}{m}\right)^{m}\right)^{rt}$$

In Section 4.1 we noted that, for n a positive integer, the numbers $\left(\dfrac{n+1}{n}\right)^n$ increase as n does but they are nevertheless bounded. [For example, it can be shown that all of the numbers $\left(\dfrac{n+1}{n}\right)^n$ are less than 3.] We *defined* e to be the least real number which is greater than all the values $\left(\dfrac{n+1}{n}\right)^n$, where n is a positive integer. It turns out (although it is beyond the scope of this book) that it is not necessary to require that n be an integer. For arbitrary positive m, the numbers $\left(\dfrac{m+1}{m}\right)^m$ increase as m does but they remain bounded and the number e as defined in Section 4.1 is the least real number that is greater than all the values $\left(\dfrac{m+1}{m}\right)^m$.

In the case at hand, for fixed r, the numbers $m = k/r$ increase as k (an integer) does, but the $m = k/r$ are not necessarily integers. However, if one accepts the truth of the preceding paragraph, then it follows that the compound amount $P\left(\left(\dfrac{m+1}{m}\right)^m\right)^{rt}$ approaches the value Pe^{rt} as k, and hence m, is increased indefinitely and we have the following:

> **Compound Amount under Continuous Interest**
>
> The formula
>
> $$S = Pe^{rt} \tag{1}$$
>
> gives the compound amount S of a principal of P dollars after t years at an annual interest rate r compounded continuously.

The interest of $5.13 is the maximum amount of compound interest that can be earned at an annual rate of 5%.

EXAMPLE 1   Compound Amount

If $100 is invested at an annual rate of 5% compounded continuously, find the compound amount at the end of

a. 1 year.

b. 5 years.

Solution:

a. Here $P = 100, r = 0.05$, and $t = 1$, so

$$S = Pe^{rt} = 100e^{(0.05)(1)} \approx 105.13$$

We can compare this value with the value after one year of a $100 investment at an annual rate of 5% compounded semiannually—namely, $100(1.025)^2 \approx 105.06$.

b. Here $P = 100, r = 0.05$, and $t = 5$, so

$$S = 100e^{(0.05)(5)} = 100e^{0.25} \approx 128.40$$

Now Work Problem 1 ◁

We can find an expression that gives the effective rate that corresponds to an annual rate of r compounded continuously. (From Section 5.1, the effective rate is the rate compounded annually that gives rise to the same interest in a year as does the rate and compounding scheme under consideration.) If r_e is the corresponding effective rate, then after one year, a principal P accumulates to $P(1 + r_e)$. This must equal the accumulated amount under continuous interest, Pe^r. Thus, $P(1 + r_e) = Pe^r$, from which it follows that $1 + r_e = e^r$, so $r_e = e^r - 1$.

Effective Rate under Continuous Interest

The effective rate corresponding to an annual rate of r compounded continuously is

$$r_e = e^r - 1$$

EXAMPLE 2   Effective Rate

Find the effective rate that corresponds to an annual rate of 5% compounded continuously.

Solution: The effective rate is

$$e^r - 1 = e^{0.05} - 1 \approx 0.0513$$

which is 5.13%.

Now Work Problem 5 ◁

If we solve $S = Pe^{rt}$ for P, we get $P = S/e^{rt} = Se^{-rt}$. In this formula, P is the principal that must be invested now at an annual rate of r compounded continuously so that at the end of t years the compound amount is S. We call P the **present value** of S.

Present Value under Continuous Interest

The formula

$$P = Se^{-rt}$$

gives the present value P of S dollars due at the end of t years at an annual rate of r compounded continuously.

EXAMPLE 3   Trust Fund

A trust fund is being set up by a single payment so that at the end of 20 years there will be $25,000 in the fund. If interest is compounded continuously at an annual rate of 7%, how much money (to the nearest dollar) should be paid into the fund initially?

Solution: We want the present value of $25,000 due in 20 years. Therefore,

$$P = Se^{-rt} = 25{,}000e^{-(0.07)(20)}$$

$$= 25{,}000e^{-1.4} \approx 6165$$

Thus, $6165 should be paid initially.

Now Work Problem 13 ◁

PROBLEMS 5.3

In Problems 1 and 2, find the compound amount and compound interest if $4000 is invested for six years and interest is compounded continuously at the given annual rate.

1. $6\frac{1}{4}\%$ 2. 9%

In Problems 3 and 4, find the present value of $2500 due eight years from now if interest is compounded continuously at the given annual rate.

3. $1\frac{1}{2}\%$ 4. 8%

In Problems 5–8, find the effective rate of interest that corresponds to the given annual rate compounded continuously.

5. 4%   6. 8%   7. 3%   8. 11%

9. Investment   If $100 is deposited in a savings account that earns interest at an annual rate of $4\frac{1}{2}\%$ compounded continuously, what is the value of the account at the end of two years?

10. Investment   If $1000 is invested at an annual rate of 3% compounded continuously, find the compound amount at the end of eight years.

11. Stock Redemption   The board of directors of a corporation agrees to redeem some of its callable preferred stock in five years. At that time, $1,000,000 will be required. If the corporation can invest money at an annual interest rate of 5% compounded continuously, how much should it presently invest so that the future value is sufficient to redeem the shares?

12. Trust Fund A trust fund is being set up by a single payment so that at the end of 30 years there will be $50,000 in the fund. If interest is compounded continuously at an annual rate of 6%, how much money should be paid into the fund initially?

13. Trust Fund As a gift for their newly born daughter's 21st birthday, the Smiths want to give her at that time a sum of money which has the same buying power as does $21,000 on the date of her birth. To accomplish this, they will make a single initial payment into a trust fund set up specifically for the purpose.
(a) Assume that the annual effective rate of inflation is 3.5%. In 21 years, what sum will have the same buying power as does $21,000 at the date of the Smiths' daughter's birth?
(b) What should be the amount of the single initial payment into the fund if interest is compounded continuously at an annual rate of 3.5%?

14. Investment Presently, the Smiths have $50,000 to invest for 18 months. They have two options open to them:
(a) Invest the money in a certificate paying interest at the nominal rate of 5% compounded quarterly;
(b) Invest the money in a savings account earning interest at the annual rate of 4.5% compounded continuously.
How much money will they have in 18 months with each option?

15. What annual rate compounded continuously is equivalent to an effective rate of 5%?

16. What annual rate r compounded continuously is equivalent to a nominal rate of 6% compounded semiannually?

17. If interest is compounded continuously at an annual rate of 0.07, how many years would it take for a principal P to triple? Give your answer to the nearest year.

18. If interest is compounded continuously, at what annual rate will a principal double in 20 years? Give the answer as a percentage correct to two decimal places.

19. Savings Options On July 1, 2001, Mr. Green had $1000 in a savings account at the First National Bank. This account earns interest at an annual rate of 3.5% compounded continuously. A competing bank was attempting to attract new customers by offering to add $20 immediately to any new account opened with a minimum $1000 deposit, and the new account would earn interest at the annual rate of 3.5% compounded semiannually. Mr. Green decided to choose one of the following three options on July 1, 2001:
(a) Leave the money at the First National Bank;
(b) Move the money to the competing bank;

(c) Leave half the money at the First National Bank and move the other half to the competing bank.

For each of these three options, find Mr. Green's accumulated amount on July 1, 2003.

20. Investment **(a)** On November 1, 1996, Ms. Rodgers invested $10,000 in a 10-year certificate of deposit that paid interest at the annual rate of 4% compounded continuously. When the certificate matured on November 1, 2006, she reinvested the entire accumulated amount in corporate bonds, which earn interest at the rate of 5% compounded annually. To the nearest dollar, what will be Ms. Rodgers's accumulated amount on November 1, 2011?
(b) If Ms. Rodgers had made a single investment of $10,000 in 1996 that matures in 2011 and has an effective rate of interest of 4.5%, would her accumulated amount be more or less than that in part (a) and by how much (to the nearest dollar)?

21. Investment Strategy Suppose that you have $9000 to invest.
(a) If you invest it with the First National Bank at the nominal rate of 5% compounded quarterly, find the accumulated amount at the end of one year.
(b) The First National Bank also offers certificates on which it pays 5.5% compounded continuously. However, a minimum investment of $10,000 is required. Because you have only $9000, the bank is willing to give you a 1-year loan for the extra $1000 that you need. Interest for this loan is at an effective rate of 8%, and both principal and interest are payable at the end of the year. Determine whether or not this strategy of investment is preferable to the strategy in part (a).

22. If interest is compounded continuously at an annual rate of 3%, in how many years will a principal double? Give the answer correct to two decimal places.

23. General Solutions In Problem 29 of Section 5.1 it was pointed out that the *discretely* compounded amount formula, $S = P(1 + r)^n$, can be solved for each of the variables in terms of the other three. Carry out the same derivation for the continuously compounded amount formula, $S = Pe^{rt}$. (Again, there is no need to memorize any of the three other formulas that result, although we have met one of them already. By seeing that the general solutions are easy, we are informed that all particular solutions are easy, too.)

To introduce the notions of ordinary annuities and annuities due. To use geometric series to model the present value and the future value of an annuity. To determine payments to be placed in a sinking fund.

5.4 Annuities

Annuities

It is best to define an **annuity** as any finite sequence of payments made at fixed periods of time over a given interval. The fixed periods of time that we consider will always be of equal length, and we refer to that length of time as the **payment period**. The given interval is the **term** of the annuity. The payments we consider will always be of equal value. An example of an annuity is the depositing of $100 in a savings account every three months for a year.

The word *annuity* comes from the Latin word *annus*, which means "year," and it is likely that the first usage of the word was to describe a sequence of annual payments. We emphasize that the payment period can be of any agreed-upon length. The informal definitions of *annuity* provided by insurance companies in their advertising suggest that an annuity is a sequence of payments in the nature of pension income. However,

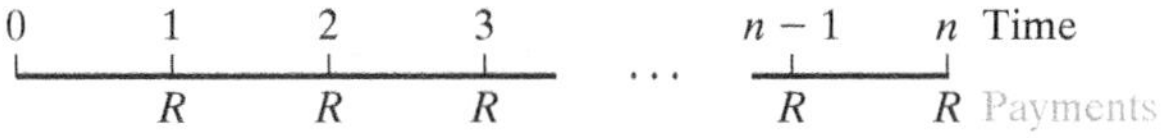

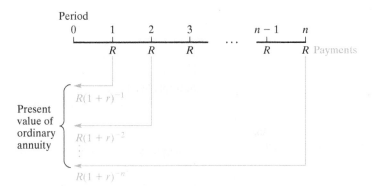

FIGURE 5.4 Ordinary annuity.

FIGURE 5.5 Annuity due.

a sequence of rent, car, or mortgage payments fits the mathematics we wish to describe, so our definition is silent about the purpose of the payments.

When dealing with annuities, it is convenient to mark time in units of payment periods on a line, with time *now*, in other words the present, taken to be 0. Our generic annuity will consist of n payments, each in the amount R. With reference to such a timeline (see Figure 5.4), suppose that the n payments (each of amount R) occur at times $1, 2, 3, \ldots, n$. In this case we speak of an **ordinary annuity**. Unless otherwise specified, an annuity is assumed to be an ordinary annuity. Again with reference to our timeline (see Figure 5.5), suppose now that the n equal payments occur at times $0, 1, 2, \ldots, n - 1$. In this case we speak of an **annuity due**. Observe that in any event, the $n + 1$ different times $0, 1, 2, \ldots, n - 1, n$ define n consecutive time intervals (each of payment period length). We can consider that an ordinary annuity's payments are at the *end* of each payment period while those of an annuity due are at the *beginning* of each payment period. A sequence of rent payments is likely to form an annuity due because most landlords demand the first month's rent when the tenant moves in. By contrast, the sequence of wage payments that an employer makes to a regular full-time employee is likely to form an ordinary annuity because usually wages are for work *done* rather than for work *contemplated*.

We henceforth assume that interest is at the rate of r per payment period. For either kind of annuity, a payment, of amount R, made at time k, for k one of the times $0, 1, 2, \ldots, n - 1, n$, has a value at time 0 and a value at time n. The value at time 0 is the *present value* of the payment made at time k. From Section 5.2 we see that the present value of the payment made at time k is $R(1 + r)^{-k}$. The value at time n is the *future value* of the payment made at time k. From Section 5.1 we see that the future value of the payment made at time k is $R(1 + r)^{n-k}$.

Present Value of an Annuity

The **present value of an annuity** is the sum of the *present values* of all n payments. It represents the amount that must be invested *now* to purchase all n of them. We consider the case of an ordinary annuity and let A be its present value. By the previous paragraph and Figure 5.6, we see that the present value is given by

$$A = R(1 + r)^{-1} + R(1 + r)^{-2} + \cdots + R(1 + r)^{-n}$$

FIGURE 5.6 Present value of ordinary annuity.

From our work in Section 1.6, we recognize this sum as that of the first n terms of the geometric sequence with first term $R(1 + r)^{-1}$ and common ratio $(1 + r)^{-1}$. Hence, from Equation (16) of Section 1.6 we obtain

$$A = \frac{R(1 + r)^{-1}(1 - (1 + r)^{-n})}{1 - (1 + r)^{-1}}$$

$$= \frac{R(1 - (1 + r)^{-n})}{(1 + r)(1 - (1 + r)^{-1})}$$

$$= \frac{R(1 - (1 + r)^{-n})}{(1 + r) - 1}$$

$$= R \cdot \frac{1 - (1 + r)^{-n}}{r}$$

where the main simplification follows by replacing the factor $(1+r)^{-1}$ in the numerator of the first line by $(1 + r)$ in the denominator of the second line.

Present Value of an Annuity

The formula

$$A = R \cdot \frac{1 - (1 + r)^{-n}}{r} \tag{1}$$

gives the **present value** A of an ordinary annuity of R per payment period for n periods at the interest rate of r per period.

The expression $(1 - (1 + r)^{-n})/r$ in Equation (1) is given a somewhat bizarre notation in the mathematics of finance, namely $a_{\overline{n}|r}$, so that we have, *by definition*,

$$a_{\overline{n}|r} = \frac{1 - (1 + r)^{-n}}{r}$$

With this notation, Equation (1) can be written as

$$A = Ra_{\overline{n}|r} \tag{2}$$

If we let $R = 1$ in Equation (2), then we see that $\$a_{\overline{n}|r}$ represents the present value of an annuity of $1 per payment period for n payment periods at the interest rate of r per payment period. The symbol $a_{\overline{n}|r}$ is sometimes read "*a* angle *n* at *r*".

If we write

$$a_{\overline{n}|r} = a(n, r) = \frac{1 - (1 + r)^{-n}}{r}$$

then we see that $a_{\overline{n}|r}$ is just a function of two variables as studied in Section 2.8. Indeed, if we were to write

$$a(x, y) = \frac{1 - (1 + y)^{-x}}{y}$$

Whenever a desired value of $a_{\overline{n}|}$ is not in Appendix A, we will use a calculator to compute it.

then we see that, for fixed y, the function in question is a constant minus a multiple of an *exponential function of x*. For x a fixed positive integer, the function in question is a *rational function of y*.

Of course $a_{\overline{n}|r}$ is not the first deviation from the standard $f(x)$ nomenclature for functions. We have already seen that $\sqrt{x}$, $|x|$, $n!$, and $\log_2 x$ are other creative notations for particular common functions.

Selected values of $a_{\overline{n}|r}$ are given, approximately, in Appendix A.

APPLY IT ▶

5. Given a payment of $500 per month for six years, use a graphing calculator to graph the present value A as a function of the interest rate per month, r. Determine the nominal rate if the present value of the annuity is $30,000.

EXAMPLE 1 Present Value of an Annuity

Find the present value of an annuity of $100 per month for $3\frac{1}{2}$ years at an interest rate of 6% compounded monthly.

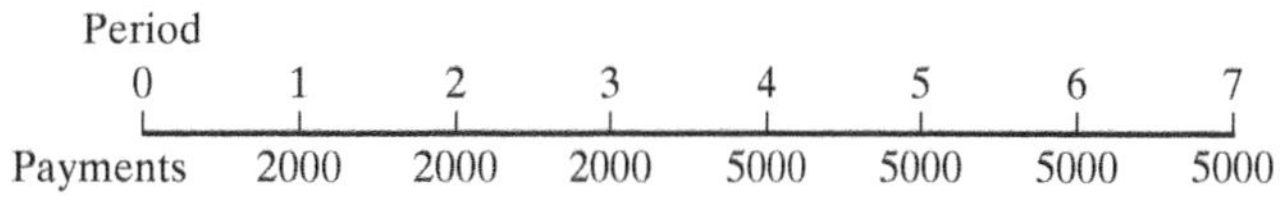

Period

FIGURE 5.7   Annuity of Example 2.

Solution: Substituting in Equation (2), we set $R = 100$, $r = 0.06/12 = 0.005$, and $n = \left(3\frac{1}{2}\right)(12) = 42$. Thus,

$$A = 100a_{\overline{42}|0.005}$$

From Appendix A, $a_{\overline{42}|0.005} \approx 37.798300$. Hence,

$$A \approx 100(37.798300) = 3779.83$$

Thus, the present value of the annuity is $3779.83.

Now Work Problem 5 ◁

APPLY IT ▶

6. Suppose a man purchases a house with an initial down payment of $20,000 and then makes quarterly payments: $2000 at the end of each quarter for six years and $3500 at the end of each quarter for eight more years. Given an interest rate of 6% compounded quarterly, find the present value of the payments and the list price of the house.

EXAMPLE 2   Present Value of an Annuity

Given an interest rate of 5% compounded annually, find the present value of a generalized annuity of $2000, due at the end of each year for three years, and $5000, due thereafter at the end of each year for four years. (See Figure 5.7.)

Solution: The present value is obtained by summing the present values of all payments:

$$2000(1.05)^{-1} + 2000(1.05)^{-2} + 2000(1.05)^{-3} + 5000(1.05)^{-4}$$
$$+ 5000(1.05)^{-5} + 5000(1.05)^{-6} + 5000(1.05)^{-7}$$

Rather than evaluating this expression, we can simplify our work by considering the payments to be an annuity of $5000 for seven years, minus an annuity of $3000 for three years, so that the first three payments are $2000 each. Thus, the present value is

$$5000a_{\overline{7}|0.05} - 3000a_{\overline{3}|0.05}$$
$$\approx 5000(5.786373) - 3000(2.723248)$$
$$\approx 20,762.12$$

Now Work Problem 17 ◁

APPLY IT ▶

7. Given an annuity with equal payments at the end of each quarter for six years and an interest rate of 4.8% compounded quarterly, use a graphing calculator to graph the present value A as a function of the monthly payment R. Determine the monthly payment if the present value of the annuity is $15,000.

EXAMPLE 3   Periodic Payment of an Annuity

If $10,000 is used to purchase an annuity consisting of equal payments at the end of each year for the next four years and the interest rate is 6% compounded annually, find the amount of each payment.

Solution: Here $A = 10,000$, $n = 4$, $r = 0.06$, and we want to find R. From Equation (2),

$$10,000 = Ra_{\overline{4}|0.06}$$

Solving for R gives

$$R = \frac{10,000}{a_{\overline{4}|0.06}} \approx \frac{10,000}{3.465106} \approx 2885.91$$

In general, the formula

$$R = \frac{A}{a_{\overline{n}|r}}$$

gives the periodic payment R of an ordinary annuity whose present value is A.

Now Work Problem 19 ◁

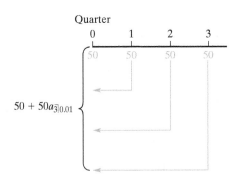

FIGURE 5.8   Annuity due (present value).

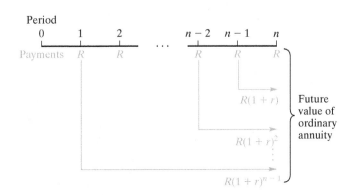

FIGURE 5.9   Future value of ordinary annuity.

EXAMPLE 4   An Annuity Due

8. A man makes house payments of $1200 at the beginning of every month. If the man wishes to pay one year's worth of payments in advance, how much should he pay, provided that the interest rate is 6.8% compounded monthly?

The premiums on an insurance policy are $50 per quarter, payable at the beginning of each quarter. If the policyholder wishes to pay one year's premiums in advance, how much should be paid, provided that the interest rate is 4% compounded quarterly?

Solution: We want the present value of an annuity of $50 per period for four periods at a rate of 1% per period. However, each payment is due at the *beginning* of the payment period so that we have an annuity due. The given annuity can be thought of as an initial payment of $50, followed by an ordinary annuity of $50 for three periods. (See Figure 5.8.) Thus, the present value is

$$50 + 50a_{\overline{3}|0.01} \approx 50 + 50(2.940985) \approx 197.05$$

An example of a situation involving an annuity due is an apartment lease for which the first payment is made immediately.

We remark that the general formula for the **present value of an annuity due** is $A = R + Ra_{\overline{n-1}|r}$; that is,

$$A = R(1 + a_{\overline{n-1}|r})$$

Now Work Problem 9 ◁

Future Value of an Annuity

The **future value of an annuity** is the sum of the *future values* of all n payments. We consider the case of an ordinary annuity and let S be its future value. By our earlier considerations and Figure 5.9, we see that the future value is given by

$$S = R + R(1 + r) + R(1 + r)^2 + \cdots + R(1 + r)^{n-1}$$

Again from Section 1.6, we recognize this as the sum of the first n terms of a geometric sequence with first term R and common ratio $1 + r$. Consequently, using Equation (16) of Section 1.6, we obtain

$$S = \frac{R(1 - (1 + r)^n)}{1 - (1 + r)} = R \cdot \frac{1 - (1 + r)^n}{-r} = R \cdot \frac{(1 + r)^n - 1}{r}$$

Future Value of an Annuity

The formula

$$S = R \cdot \frac{(1 + r)^n - 1}{r} \tag{3}$$

gives the **future value** S of an ordinary annuity of R (dollars) per payment period for n periods at the interest rate of r per period.

The expression $((1 + r)^n - 1)/r$ is written $s_{\overline{n}|r}$ so that we have, *by definition*,

$$s_{\overline{n}|r} = \frac{(1 + r)^n - 1}{r}$$

and some approximate values of $s_{\overline{n}|r}$ are given in Appendix A. Thus,

$$S = Rs_{\overline{n}|r} \qquad (4)$$

It follows that $\$s_{\overline{n}|r}$ is the future value of an ordinary annuity of $1 per payment period for n periods at the interest rate of r per period. Like $a_{\overline{n}|r}$, $s_{\overline{n}|r}$ is also a function of two variables.

APPLY IT ▶

9. Suppose you invest in an IRA by depositing $2000 at the end of every tax year for the next 15 years. If the interest rate is 5.7% compounded annually, how much will you have at the end of 15 years?

EXAMPLE 5   Future Value of an Annuity

Find the future value of an annuity consisting of payments of $50 at the end of every three months for three years at the rate of 6% compounded quarterly. Also, find the compound interest.

Solution: To find the amount of the annuity, we use Equation (4) with $R = 50$, $n = 4(3) = 12$, and $r = 0.06/4 = 0.015$:

$$S = 50s_{\overline{12}|0.015} \approx 50(13.041211) \approx 652.06$$

The compound interest is the difference between the amount of the annuity and the sum of the payments, namely,

$$652.06 - 12(50) = 652.06 - 600 = 52.06$$

Now Work Problem 11 ◁

APPLY IT ▶

10. Suppose you invest in an IRA by depositing $2000 at the beginning of every tax year for the next 15 years. If the interest rate is 5.7% compounded annually, how much will you have at the end of 15 years?

EXAMPLE 6   Future Value of an Annuity Due

At the beginning of each quarter, $50 is deposited into a savings account that pays 6% compounded quarterly. Find the balance in the account at the end of three years.

Solution: Since the deposits are made at the beginning of a payment period, we want the amount of an *annuity due*, as defined in Example 4. (See Figure 5.10.) The given annuity can be thought of as an ordinary annuity of $50 for 13 periods, minus the final payment of $50. Thus, the amount is

$$50s_{\overline{13}|0.015} - 50 \approx 50(14.236830) - 50 \approx 661.84$$

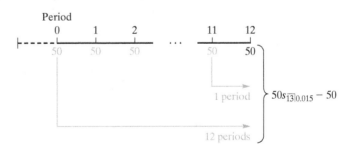

FIGURE 5.10   Future value of annuity due.

The formula for the **future value of an annuity due** is $S = Rs_{\overline{n+1}|r} - R$, which is

$$S = R(s_{\overline{n+1}|r} - 1)$$

Now Work Problem 15 ◁

Sinking Fund

Our final examples involve the notion of a *sinking fund*.

EXAMPLE 7   Sinking Fund

A **sinking fund** is a fund into which periodic payments are made in order to satisfy a future obligation. Suppose a machine costing $7000 is to be replaced at the end of eight years, at which time it will have a salvage value of $700. In order to provide money at that time for a new machine costing the same amount, a sinking fund is set up. The amount in the fund at the end of eight years is to be the difference between the replacement cost and the salvage value. If equal payments are placed in the fund at the end of each quarter and the fund earns 8% compounded quarterly, what should each payment be?

Solution: The amount needed after eight years is $7000 - 700 = \$6300$. Let R be the quarterly payment. The payments into the sinking fund form an annuity with $n = 4(8) = 32$, $r = 0.08/4 = 0.02$, and $S = 6300$. Thus, from Equation (4), we have

$$6300 = Rs_{\overline{32}|0.02}$$

$$R = \frac{6300}{s_{\overline{32}|0.02}} \approx \frac{6300}{44.227030} \approx 142.45$$

In general, the formula

$$R = \frac{S}{s_{\overline{n}|r}}$$

gives the periodic payment R of an annuity that is to amount to S.

Now Work Problem 23 ◁

EXAMPLE 8   Sinking Fund

A rental firm estimates that, if purchased, a machine will yield an annual net return of $1000 for six years, after which the machine would be worthless. How much should the firm pay for the machine if it wants to earn 7% annually on its investment and also set up a sinking fund to replace the purchase price? For the fund, assume annual payments and a rate of 5% compounded annually.

Solution: Let x be the purchase price. Each year, the return on the investment is $0.07x$. Since the machine gives a return of $1000 a year, the amount left to be placed into the fund each year is $1000 - 0.07x$. These payments must accumulate to x. Hence,

$$(1000 - 0.07x)s_{\overline{6}|0.05} = x$$

$$1000s_{\overline{6}|0.05} - 0.07xs_{\overline{6}|0.05} = x$$

$$1000s_{\overline{6}|0.05} = x(1 + 0.07s_{\overline{6}|0.05})$$

$$\frac{1000s_{\overline{6}|0.05}}{1 + 0.07s_{\overline{6}|0.05}} = x$$

$$x \approx \frac{1000(6.801913)}{1 + 0.07(6.801913)}$$

$$\approx 4607.92$$

Another way to look at the problem is as follows: Each year, the $1000 must account for a return of $0.07x$ and also a payment of $\dfrac{x}{s_{\overline{6}|0.05}}$, into the sinking fund. Thus, we have $1000 = 0.07x + \dfrac{x}{s_{\overline{6}|0.05}}$, which, when solved, gives the same result.

Now Work Problem 25 ◁

PROBLEMS 5.4

In Problems 1–4, use Appendix A and find the value of the given expression.

1. $a_{\overline{35}|0.04}$ **2.** $a_{\overline{15}|0.07}$ **3.** $s_{\overline{8}|0.0075}$ **4.** $s_{\overline{12}|0.0125}$

In Problems 5–8, find the present value of the given (ordinary) annuity.

5. $600 per year for six years at the rate of 6% compounded annually

6. $1000 every six months for four years at the rate of 10% compounded semiannually

7. $2000 per quarter for $4\frac{1}{2}$ years at the rate of 8% compounded quarterly

8. $1500 per month for 15 months at the rate of 9% compounded monthly

In Problems 9 and 10, find the present value of the given annuity due.

9. $900 paid at the beginning of each six-month period for seven years at the rate of 8% compounded semiannually

10. $150 paid at the beginning of each month for five years at the rate of 7% compounded monthly

In Problems 11–14, find the future value of the given (ordinary) annuity.

11. $2000 per month for three years at the rate of 15% compounded monthly

12. $600 per quarter for four years at the rate of 8% compounded quarterly

13. $5000 per year for 20 years at the rate of 7% compounded annually

14. $2500 every month for 4 years at the rate of 6% compounded monthly

In Problems 15 and 16, find the future value of the given annuity due.

15. $1200 each year for 12 years at the rate of 8% compounded annually

16. $600 every quarter for $7\frac{1}{2}$ years at the rate of 10% compounded quarterly

17. For an interest rate of 4% compounded monthly, find the present value of an annuity of $150 at the end of each month for eight months and $175 thereafter at the end of each month for a further two years.

18. Leasing Office Space   A company wishes to lease temporary office space for a period of six months. The rental fee is $1500 a month, payable in advance. Suppose that the company wants to make a lump-sum payment at the beginning of the rental period to cover all rental fees due over the six-month period. If money is worth 9% compounded monthly, how much should the payment be?

19. An annuity consisting of equal payments at the end of each quarter for three years is to be purchased for $15,000. If the interest rate is 4% compounded quarterly, how much is each payment?

20. Equipment Purchase   A machine is purchased for $3000 down and payments of $250 at the end of every six months for six

years. If interest is at 8% compounded semiannually, find the corresponding cash price of the machine.

21. Suppose $50 is placed in a savings account at the end of each month for four years. If no further deposits are made, (a) how much is in the account after six years, and (b) how much of this amount is compound interest? Assume that the savings account pays 6% compounded monthly.

22. Insurance Settlement Options   The beneficiary of an insurance policy has the option of receiving a lump-sum payment of $275,000 or 10 equal yearly payments, where the first payment is due at once. If interest is at 3.5% compounded annually, find the yearly payment.

23. Sinking Find   In 10 years, a $40,000 machine will have a salvage value of $4000. A new machine at that time is expected to sell for $52,000. In order to provide funds for the difference between the replacement cost and the salvage value, a sinking fund is set up into which equal payments are placed at the end of each year. If the fund earns 7% compounded annually, how much should each payment be?

24. Sinking Fund   A paper company is considering the purchase of a forest that is estimated to yield an annual return of $60,000 for 8 years, after which the forest will have no value. The company wants to earn 6% on its investment and also set up a sinking fund to replace the purchase price. If money is placed in the fund at the end of each year and earns 4% compounded annually, find the price the company should pay for the forest. Round the answer to the nearest hundred dollars.

25. Sinking Fund   In order to replace a machine in the future, a company is placing equal payments into a sinking fund at the end of each year so that after 10 years the amount in the fund is $25,000. The fund earns 6% compounded annually. After 6 years, the interest rate increases and the fund pays 7% compounded annually. Because of the higher interest rate, the company decreases the amount of the remaining payments. Find the amount of the new payment. Round your answer to the nearest dollar.

26. A owes B the sum of $5000 and agrees to pay B the sum of $1000 at the end of each year for five years and a final payment at the end of the sixth year. How much should the final payment be if interest is at 8% compounded annually?

In Problems 27–35, use the following formulas:

$$a_{\overline{n}|r} = \frac{1 - (1 + r)^{-n}}{r}$$

$$s_{\overline{n}|r} = \frac{(1 + r)^n - 1}{r}$$

$$R = \frac{A}{a_{\overline{n}|r}} = \frac{Ar}{1 - (1 + r)^{-n}}$$

$$R = \frac{S}{s_{\overline{n}|r}} = \frac{Sr}{(1 + r)^n - 1}$$

27. Find $s_{\overline{60}|0.017}$ to five decimal places.

28. Find $a_{\overline{9}|0.052}$ to five decimal places.

29. Find $250a_{\overline{180}|0.0235}$ to two decimal places.

30. Find $1000s_{\overline{120}|0.01}$ to two decimal places.

31. Equal payments are to be deposited in a savings account at the end of each quarter for five years so that at the end of that time there will be $3000. If interest is at $5\frac{1}{2}\%$ compounded quarterly, find the quarterly payment.

32. Insurance Proceeds   Suppose that insurance proceeds of $25,000 are used to purchase an annuity of equal payments at the end of each month for five years. If interest is at the rate of 10% compounded monthly, find the amount of each payment.

33. Lottery   Mary Jones won a state $4,000,000 lottery and will receive a check for $200,000 now and a similar one each year for the next 19 years. To provide these 20 payments, the State Lottery Commission purchased an annuity due at the interest rate of 10% compounded annually. How much did the annuity cost the Commission?

34. Pension Plan Options   Suppose an employee of a company is retiring and has the choice of two benefit options under the company pension plan. Option A consists of a guaranteed payment of $2100 at the end of each month for 20 years. Alternatively, under option B, the employee receives a lump-sum payment equal to the present value of the payments described under option A.
(a) Find the sum of the payments under option A.
(b) Find the lump-sum payment under option B if it is determined by using an interest rate of 6% compounded monthly. Round the answer to the nearest dollar.

35. An Early Start to Investing   An insurance agent offers services to clients who are concerned about their personal financial planning for retirement. To emphasize the advantages of an early start to investing, she points out that a 25-year-old person who saves $2000 a year for 10 years (and makes no more contributions after age 34) will earn more than by waiting 10 years and then saving $2000 a year from age 35 until retirement at age 65 (a total of 30 contributions). Find the net earnings (compound amount minus total contributions) at age 65 for both situations. Assume an effective annual rate of 7%, and suppose that deposits are made at the beginning of each year. Round answers to the nearest dollar.

36. Continuous Annuity   An annuity in which R dollars is paid each year by uniform payments that are payable continuously is called a *continuous annuity*. The present value of a continuous annuity for t years is

$$R \cdot \frac{1 - e^{-rt}}{r}$$

where r is the annual rate of interest compounded continuously. Find the present value of a continuous annuity of $100 a year for 20 years at 5% compounded continuously.

37. Profit   Suppose a business has an annual profit of $40,000 for the next five years and the profits are earned continuously throughout each year. Then the profits can be thought of as a continuous annuity. (See Problem 36.) If money is worth 4% compounded continuously, find the present value of the profits.

To learn how to amortize a loan and set up an amortization schedule.

5.5 Amortization of Loans

Suppose that a bank lends a borrower $1500 and charges interest at the nominal rate of 12% compounded monthly. The $1500 plus interest is to be repaid by equal payments of R dollars at the end of each month for three months. One could say that by paying the borrower $1500, the bank is purchasing an annuity of three payments of R each. Using the formula from Example 3 of the preceding section, we find that the monthly payment is given by

$$R = \frac{A}{a_{\overline{n}|r}} = \frac{1500}{a_{\overline{3}|0.01}} \approx \frac{1500}{2.940985} \approx \$510.0332$$

We will round the payment to $510.03, which may result in a slightly higher final payment. However, it is not unusual for a bank to round *up* to the nearest cent, in which case the final payment may be less than the other payments.

The bank can consider each payment as consisting of two parts: (1) interest on the outstanding loan and (2) repayment of part of the loan. This is called **amortizing**. A loan is **amortized** when part of each payment is used to pay interest and the remaining part is used to reduce the outstanding principal. Since each payment reduces the outstanding principal, the interest portion of a payment decreases as time goes on. Let us analyze the loan just described.

At the end of the first month, the borrower pays $510.03. The interest on the outstanding principal is 0.01($1500) = $15. The balance of the payment, $510.03 − $15 = $495.03, is then applied to reduce the principal. Hence, the principal outstanding is now $1500 − $495.03 = $1004.97. At the end of the second month, the interest is 0.01($1004.97) ≈ $10.05. Thus, the amount of the loan repaid is $510.03 − $10.05 = $499.98, and the outstanding balance is $1004.97 − $499.98 = $504.99. The interest due at the end of the third and final month is 0.01($504.99) ≈ $5.05, so the amount of the loan repaid is $510.03 − $5.05 = $504.98. This would leave an outstanding balance of 504.99 − 504.98 = $0.01, so we take the final payment to be $510.04, and the debt is paid off. As we said earlier, the final payment is adjusted to offset rounding errors. An analysis of how each payment in the loan is handled can be given in a table called an **amortization schedule.** (See Table 5.1.) The total interest paid is $30.10, which is often called the **finance charge.**

Table 5.1 Amortization Schedule

Period	Principal Outstanding at Beginning of Period	Interest for Period	Payment at End of Period	Principal Repaid at End of Period
1	$1500	$15	$510.03	$495.03
2	1004.97	10.05	510.03	499.98
3	504.99	5.05	510.04	504.99
Total		30.10	1530.10	1500.00

When one is amortizing a loan, at the beginning of any period the principal outstanding is the present value of the remaining payments. Using this fact together with our previous development, we obtain the formulas listed in Table 5.2, which describe the amortization of an interest-bearing loan of A dollars, at a rate r per period, by n equal payments of R dollars each and such that a payment is made at the end of each period. In particular, notice that Formula 1 for the periodic payment R involves $a_{\overline{n}|r}$, which, we recall, is defined as $(1 - (1 + r)^{-n})/r$.

Table 5.2 Amortization Formulas

1. Periodic payment: $R = \dfrac{A}{a_{\overline{n}|r}} = A \cdot \dfrac{r}{1 - (1 + r)^{-n}}$

2. Principal outstanding at beginning of kth period:

$$R a_{\overline{n-k+1}|r} = R \cdot \frac{1 - (1 + r)^{-n+k-1}}{r}$$

3. Interest in kth payment: $R r a_{\overline{n-k+1}|r}$

4. Principal contained in kth payment: $R(1 - r a_{\overline{n-k+1}|r})$

5. Total interest paid: $R(n - a_{\overline{n}|r}) = nR - A$

EXAMPLE 1 Amortizing a Loan

A person amortizes a loan of $170,000 for a new home by obtaining a 20-year mortgage at the rate of 7.5% compounded monthly. Find (a) the monthly payment, (b) the total interest charges, and (c) the principal remaining after five years.

Solution:

a. The number of payment periods is $n = 12(20) = 240$, the interest rate per period is $r = 0.075/12 = 0.00625$, and $A = 170,000$. From Formula 1 in Table 5.2, the monthly payment R is $170,000/a_{\overline{240}|0.00625}$. Since $a_{\overline{240}|0.00625}$ is not in Appendix A, we use the following equivalent formula and a calculator:

$$R = 170,000 \left(\frac{0.00625}{1 - (1.00625)^{-240}} \right)$$

$$\approx 1369.51$$

b. From Formula 5, the total interest charges are

$$240(1369.51) - 170,000 = 328,682.40 - 170,000$$

$$= 158,682.40$$

This is almost as much as the loan itself.

c. After five years, we are at the beginning of the 61st period. Using Formula 2 with $n - k + 1 = 240 - 61 + 1 = 180$, we find that the principal remaining is

$$1369.51 \left(\frac{1 - (1.00625)^{-180}}{0.00625} \right) \approx 147{,}733.74$$

Now Work Problem 1 ◁

At one time, a very common type of installment loan involved the "add-on method" of determining the finance charge. With that method, the finance charge is found by applying a quoted annual interest rate under simple (that is, noncompounded) interest to the borrowed amount of the loan. The charge is then added to the principal, and the total is divided by the number of *months* of the loan to determine the monthly installment payment. In loans of this type, the borrower may not immediately realize that the true annual rate is significantly higher than the quoted rate, as the following technology example shows.

TECHNOLOGY ▮▮▮▮

Problem: A $1000 loan is taken for one year at 9% interest under the add-on method. Estimate the true annual interest rate if monthly compounding is assumed.

Solution: Since the add-on method is used, payments will be made monthly. The finance charge for $1000 at 9% simple interest for one year is $0.09(1000) = \$90$. Adding this to the loan amount gives $1000 + 90 = \$1090$. Thus, the monthly installment payment is $1090/12 \approx \$90.83$. Hence, we have a loan of $1000 with 12 equal payments of $90.83. From Formula 1 in Table 5.2,

$$R = \frac{A}{a_{\overline{n}|r}}$$

$$\frac{1090}{12} = \frac{1000}{a_{\overline{12}|r}}$$

$$a_{\overline{12}|r} = \frac{1000(12)}{1090} \approx 11.009174$$

We now solve $a_{\overline{12}|r} = 11.009174$ for the monthly rate r. We have

$$\frac{1 - (1 + r)^{-12}}{r} = 11.009174$$

Graphing

$$Y_1 = (1 - (1 + X) \wedge -12)/X$$

$$Y_2 = 11.009174$$

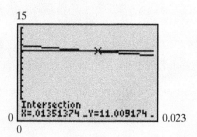

FIGURE 5.11 Solution of $a_{\overline{12}|r} = 11.009174$.

and finding the intersection (see Figure 5.11) gives

$$r \approx 0.01351374$$

which corresponds to an annual rate of

$$12(0.01351374) \approx 0.1622 = 16.22\%$$

Thus, the true annual rate is 16.22%. Federal regulations concerning truth-in-lending laws have made add-on loans virtually obsolete.

The annuity formula

$$A = R \cdot \frac{1 - (1 + r)^{-n}}{r}$$

cannot be solved for r in a simple closed form, and that is why the previous example is given as a technology example. On the other hand, solving the annuity formula for n, to give the number of periods of a loan, is a straightforward matter. We have

$$\frac{Ar}{R} = 1 - (1 + r)^{-n}$$

$$(1 + r)^{-n} = 1 - \frac{Ar}{R} = \frac{R - Ar}{R}$$

$$-n\ln(1 + r) = \ln(R - Ar) - \ln(R) \qquad \text{taking logs of both sides}$$

$$n = -\frac{\ln(R - Ar) - \ln(R)}{\ln(1 + r)}$$

giving

$$n = \frac{\ln(R) - \ln(R - Ar)}{\ln(1 + r)} \tag{1}$$

EXAMPLE 2   Periods of a Loan

Muhammar Smith recently purchased a computer for $1500 and agreed to pay it off by making monthly payments of $75. If the store charges interest at the rate of 12% compounded monthly, how many months will it take to pay off the debt?

Solution: From Equation (1),

$$n = \frac{\ln(75) - \ln(75 - 1500(0.01))}{\ln(1.01)} \approx 22.4$$

Therefore, it will require 23 months to pay off the loan (with the final payment less than $75).

Now Work Problem 11 ◁

PROBLEMS 5.5

1. A person borrows $9000 from a bank and agrees to pay it off by equal payments at the end of each month for two years. If interest is at 13.2% compounded monthly, how much is each payment?

2. A person wishes to make a three-year loan and can afford payments of $50 at the end of each month. If interest is at 12% compounded monthly, how much can the person afford to borrow?

3. **Finance Charge**   Determine the finance charge on a 36-month $8000 auto loan with monthly payments if interest is at the rate of 4% compounded monthly.

4. For a one-year loan of $500 at the rate of 15% compounded monthly, find (a) the monthly installment payment and (b) the finance charge.

5. **Car Loan**   A person is amortizing a 36-month car loan of $7500 with interest at the rate of 4% compounded monthly. Find (a) the monthly payment, (b) the interest in the first month, and (c) the principal repaid in the first payment.

6. **Real-Estate Loan**   A person is amortizing a 48-month loan of $65,000 for a house lot. If interest is at the rate of 7.2% compounded monthly, find (a) the monthly payment, (b) the interest in the first payment, and (c) the principal repaid in the first payment.

In Problems 7–10, construct amortization schedules for the indicated debts. Adjust the final payments if necessary.

7. $5000 repaid by four equal yearly payments with interest at 7% compounded annually

8. $9000 repaid by eight equal semiannual payments with interest at 9.5% compounded semiannually

9. $900 repaid by five equal quarterly payments with interest at 10% compounded quarterly

10. $10,000 repaid by five equal monthly payments with interest at 9% compounded monthly

11. A loan of $1300 is being paid off by quarterly payments of $110. If interest is at the rate of 6% compounded quarterly, how many *full* payments will be made?

12. A loan of $2000 is being amortized over 48 months at an interest rate of 12% compounded monthly. Find

(a) the monthly payment;
(b) the principal outstanding at the beginning of the 36th month;
(c) the interest in the 36th payment;
(d) the principal in the 36th payment;
(e) the total interest paid.

13. A debt of $18,000 is being repaid by 15 equal semiannual payments, with the first payment to be made six months from now. Interest is at the rate of 7% compounded semiannually. However, after two years, the interest rate increases to 8% compounded semiannually. If the debt must be paid off on the original date agreed upon, find the new annual payment. Give your answer to the nearest dollar.

14. A person borrows $2000 and will pay off the loan by equal payments at the end of each month for five years. If interest is at the rate of 16.8% compounded monthly, how much is each payment?

15. **Mortgage**   A $245,000 mortgage for 25 years for a new home is obtained at the rate of 9.2% compounded monthly. Find (a) the monthly payment, (b) the interest in the first payment, (c) the principal repaid in the first payment, and (d) the finance charge.

16. **Auto Loan**   An automobile loan of $23,500 is to be amortized over 60 months at an interest rate of 7.2% compounded monthly. Find (a) the monthly payment and (b) the finance charge.

17. **Furniture Loan**   A person purchases furniture for $2000 and agrees to pay off this amount by monthly payments of $100. If interest is charged at the rate of 18% compounded monthly, how many *full* payments will there be?

18. Find the monthly payment of a five-year loan for $9500 if interest is at 9.24% compounded monthly.

19. Mortgage Bob and Mary Rodgers want to purchase a new house and feel that they can afford a mortgage payment of $600 a month. They are able to obtain a 30-year 7.6% mortgage (compounded monthly), but must put down 25% of the cost of the house. Assuming that they have enough savings for the down payment, how expensive a house can they afford? Give your answer to the nearest dollar.

20. Mortgage Suppose you have the choice of taking out a $240,000 mortgage at 6% compounded monthly for either 15 years or 25 years. How much savings is there in the finance charge if you were to choose the 15-year mortgage?

21. On a $45,000 four-year loan, how much less is the monthly payment if the loan were at the rate of 8.4% compounded monthly rather than at 9.6% compounded monthly?

22. Home Loan The federal government has a program to aid low-income homeowners in urban areas. This program allows certain qualified homeowners to obtain low-interest home improvement loans. Each loan is processed through a commercial bank. The bank makes home improvement loans at an annual rate of $9\frac{1}{4}$% compounded monthly. However, the government subsidizes the bank so that the loan to the homeowner is at the annual rate of 4% compounded monthly. If the monthly payment at the 4% rate is x dollars (x dollars is the homeowner's monthly payment) and the monthly payment at the $9\frac{1}{4}$% rate is y dollars (y dollars is the monthly payment the bank must receive), then the government makes up the difference $y - x$ to the bank each month. From a practical point of view, the government does not want to bother with *monthly* payments. Instead, at the beginning of the loan, the government pays the present value of all such monthly differences, at an annual rate of $9\frac{1}{4}$% compounded monthly.

If a qualified homeowner takes out a loan for $5000 for five years, determine the government's payment to the bank at the beginning of the loan.

Objective

To introduce the notion of perpetuity and simple limits of sequences.

5.6 Perpetuities

Perpetuities

In this section we consider briefly the possibility of an *infinite* sequence of payments. As in Section 5.4, we will measure time in payment periods starting *now*—that is, at time 0—and consider payments, each of amount R, at times $1, 2, \ldots, k, \ldots$. The last sequence of dots is to indicate that the payments are to continue indefinitely. We can visualize this on a timeline as in Figure 5.12. We call such an infinite sequence of payments a **perpetuity**.

0	1	2	3		k	$\cdots$ Time
	R	R	R	$\cdots$	R	$\cdots$ Payments

FIGURE 5.12 Perpetuity.

Since there is no last payment, it makes no sense to consider the future value of such an infinite sequence of payments. However, if the interest rate per payment period is r, we do know that the *present value* of the payment made at time k is $R(1 + r)^{-k}$. If we want to ascribe a present value to the entire perpetuity, we are led by this observation and Figure 5.13 to define it to be

$$A = R(1 + r)^{-1} + R(1 + r)^{-2} + R(1 + r)^{-3} + \cdots + R(1 + r)^{-k} + \cdots$$

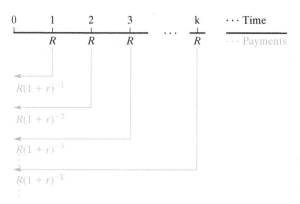

FIGURE 5.13 Present value of perpetuity.

With the benefit of Section 1.6, we recognize this sum as that of an infinite geometric sequence with first term $R(1+r)^{-1}$ and common ratio $(1+r)^{-1}$. Equation (17) of Section 1.6 gives

$$A = \sum_{k=1}^{\infty} R(1+r)^{-k} = \frac{R(1+r)^{-1}}{1-(1+r)^{-1}} = \frac{R}{r}$$

provided that $|(1+r)^{-1}| < 1$. If the rate r is positive, then $1 < 1+r$ so that $0 < (1+r)^{-1} = \dfrac{1}{1+r} < 1$ and the proviso is satisfied.[1]

In practical terms, this means that if an amount R/r is invested at time 0 in an account that bears interest at the rate of r per payment period, then R can be withdrawn at times $1, 2, \ldots, k, \ldots$ indefinitely. It is easy to see that this makes sense because if R/r is invested at time 0, then at time 1 it is worth $(R/r)(1+r) = R/r + R$. If, at time 1, R is withdrawn, then $R/r + R - R = R/r$ remains and this process can be continued indefinitely so that at any time k, the amount after the kth withdrawal is still R/r. In other words, the withdrawals R are such that they consume only the interest earned since the last withdrawal and leave the principal intact. Well-managed endowment funds are run this way. The amount withdrawn each year to fund a scholarship, say, should not exceed the amount earned in interest during the previous year.

EXAMPLE 1   Present Value of a Perpetuity

Dalhousie University would like to establish a scholarship worth \$15,000 to be awarded to the first year Business student who attains the highest grade in MATH 1115, Commerce Mathematics. The award is to be made annually, and the Vice President Finance believes that, for the foreseeable future, the university will be able to earn at least 2% a year on investments. What principal is needed to ensure the viability of the scholarship?

Solution: The university needs to fund a perpetuity with payments $R = 15,000$ and annual interest rate $r = 0.02$. It follows that \$15,000/0.02 = \$750,000 is needed.

Now Work Problem 5 ◁

Limits

An infinite sum, such as $\sum_{k=1}^{\infty} R(1+r)^{-k}$, which has arisen here, derives its meaning from the associated *finite* partial sums. Here the nth partial sum is $\sum_{k=1}^{n} R(1+r)^{-k}$, which we recognize as $Ra_{\overline{n}|r}$, the present value of the annuity consisting of n equal payments of R at an interest rate of r per payment period.

Let $(c_k)_{k=1}^{\infty}$ be an infinite sequence as in Section 1.6. We say that the sequence has **limit** L and write

$$\lim_{k\to\infty} c_k = L$$

if *we can make the values c_k as close as we like to L by taking k sufficiently large.* The equation can be read as "the limit of c_k as k goes to infinity is equal to L". A sequence can fail to have a limit but it can have at most one limit so that we speak of "the limit".

We have already met an important example of this concept. In Section 4.1 we defined the number e as the smallest real number which is greater than all of the real numbers $e_n = \left(\dfrac{n+1}{n}\right)^n$, for n any positive integer. In fact, we have also

$$\lim_{n\to\infty} e_n = e$$

---

[1] The proviso is also satisfied for $r < -2$.

A general infinite sequence $(c_k)_{k=1}^{\infty}$ determines a new sequence $(s_n)_{n=1}^{\infty}$, where $s_n = \sum_{k=1}^{n} c_k$. We define

$$\sum_{k=1}^{\infty} c_k = \lim_{n \to \infty} s_n = \lim_{n \to \infty} \sum_{k=1}^{n} c_k$$

This agrees with what we said about the sum of an infinite geometric sequence in Section 1.6, and it is important to realize that the sums which arise for the present values of annuities and perpetuities are but special cases of sums of geometric sequences.

However, we wish to make a simple observation by combining some of the equalities of this section:

$$\frac{R}{r} = \sum_{k=1}^{\infty} R(1+r)^{-k} = \lim_{n \to \infty} \sum_{k=1}^{n} R(1+r)^{-k} = \lim_{n \to \infty} R a_{\overline{n}|r}$$

and, taking $R = 1$, we get

$$\lim_{n \to \infty} a_{\overline{n}|r} = \frac{1}{r}$$

We can verify this observation directly. In the defining equation

$$a_{\overline{n}|r} = \frac{1 - (1+r)^{-n}}{r}$$

only $(1+r)^{-n} = 1/(1+r)^n$ depends on n. Because $1 + r > 1$, we can make the values $(1+r)^n$ as large as we like by taking n sufficiently large. It follows that we can make the values $1/(1+r)^n$ as close as we like to 0 by taking n sufficiently large. It follows that in the definition of $a_{\overline{n}|r}$, we can make the numerator as close as we like to 1 by taking n sufficiently large and hence that we can make the whole fraction as close as we like to $1/r$ by taking n sufficiently large.

EXAMPLE 2   Limit of a Sequence

Find $\lim\limits_{n \to \infty} \dfrac{2n^2 + 1}{3n^2 - 5}$.

Solution: We first rewrite the fraction $2n^2 + 1/3n^2 - 5$.

$$\lim_{n \to \infty} \frac{2n^2 + 1}{3n^2 - 5} = \lim_{n \to \infty} \frac{\dfrac{2n^2 + 1}{n^2}}{\dfrac{3n^2 - 5}{n^2}}$$

$$= \lim_{n \to \infty} \frac{\dfrac{2n^2}{n^2} + \dfrac{1}{n^2}}{\dfrac{3n^2}{n^2} - \dfrac{5}{n^2}}$$

$$= \lim_{n \to \infty} \frac{2 + \dfrac{1}{n^2}}{3 - \dfrac{5}{n^2}}$$

So far we have only carried along the "limit" notation. We now observe that because we can make the values n^2 as large as we like by taking n sufficiently large, we can make $1/n^2$ and $5/n^2$ as close as we like to 0 by taking n sufficiently large. It follows that we can make the numerator of the main fraction as close as we like to 2 and the denominator of the main fraction as close as we like to 3 by taking n sufficiently large.

In symbols,

$$\lim_{n\to\infty} \frac{2n^2+1}{3n^2-5} = \lim_{n\to\infty} \frac{2+\dfrac{1}{n^2}}{3-\dfrac{5}{n^2}} = \frac{2}{3}$$

Now Work Problem 7 ◁

PROBLEMS 5.6

In Problems 1–4, find the present value of the given perpetuity.

1. $60 per month at the rate of 1.5% monthly

2. $5000 per month at the rate of 0.5% monthly

3. $60,000 per year at the rate of 8% yearly

4. $4000 per year at the rate of 10% yearly

5. Funding a Prize   The Commerce Society would like to endow an annual prize of $120 to the student who is deemed to have exhibited the most class spirit. The Society is confident that it can invest indefinitely at an interest rate of at least 2.5% a year. How much does the Society need to endow its prize?

6. Retirement Planning   Starting a year from now and making 10 yearly payments, Pierre would like to put into a retirement account enough money so that, starting 11 years from now, he can withdraw $30,000 per year until he dies. Pierre is confident that he can earn 8% per year on his money for the next 10 years, but he is only assuming that he will be able to get 5% per year after that. **(a)** How much does Pierre need to pay each year for the first 10 years in order to make the planned withdrawals? **(b)** Pierre's will states that, upon his death, any money left in his retirement account is to be donated to the Princeton Mathematics Department. If he dies immediately after receiving his 17th payment, how much will the Princeton Mathematics Department inherit?

In Problems 7–10, find the limit.

7. $\displaystyle\lim_{n\to\infty} \frac{n^2+3n-6}{n^2+4}$

8. $\displaystyle\lim_{n\to\infty} \frac{n+5}{3n^2+2n-7}$

9. $\displaystyle\lim_{k\to\infty} \left(\frac{k+1}{k}\right)^{2k}$

10. $\displaystyle\lim_{n\to\infty} \left(\frac{n}{n+1}\right)^{n}$

Chapter 5 Review

Important Terms and Symbols

		Examples
Section 5.1	**Compound Interest**	
	effective rate	Ex. 4, p. 211
Section 5.2	**Present Value**	
	present value	Ex. 1, p. 214
	future value equation of value net present value	Ex. 3, p. 215
Section 5.3	**Interest Compounded Continuously**	
	compounded continuously	Ex. 1, p. 218
Section 5.4	**Annuities**	
	annuity ordinary annuity annuity due	Ex. 1, p. 222
	present value of annuity, $a_{\overline{n}|r}$ amount of annuity, $s_{\overline{n}|r}$	Ex. 2, p. 223
Section 5.5	**Amortization of Loans**	
	amortizing amortization schedules finance charge	Ex. 1, p. 229
Section 5.6	**Perpetuities**	
	perpetuity	Ex. 1, p. 233
	limit of a sequence	Ex. 2, p. 234

Summary

The concept of compound interest lies at the heart of any discussion dealing with the time value of money—that is, the present value of money due in the future or the future value of money presently invested. Under compound interest, interest is converted into principal and earns interest itself. The basic compound-interest formulas are

$$S = P(1+r)^n \qquad \text{future value}$$
$$P = S(1+r)^{-n} \qquad \text{present value}$$

where $S = $ compound amount (future value)

$\qquad P = $ principal (present value)

$\qquad r = $ periodic rate

$\qquad n = $ number of interest periods

Interest rates are usually quoted as an annual rate called the nominal rate. The periodic rate is obtained by dividing the nominal rate by the number of interest periods each year. The effective rate is the annual simple-interest rate which is equivalent to the nominal rate of r compounded n times a year and is given by

$$r_e = \left(1 + \frac{r}{n}\right)^n - 1 \qquad \text{effective rate}$$

Effective rates are used to compare different interest rates. If interest is compounded continuously, then

$$S = Pe^{rt} \qquad \text{future value}$$
$$P = Se^{-rt} \qquad \text{present value}$$

where S = compound amount (future value)

P = principal (present value)

r = annual rate

t = number of years

and the effective rate is given by

$$r_e = e^r - 1 \qquad \text{effective rate}$$

An annuity is a sequence of payments made at fixed periods of time over some interval. The mathematical basis for formulas dealing with annuities is the notion of the sum of a geometric sequence—that is,

$$s = \sum_{i=0}^{n-1} ar^i = \frac{a(1 - r^n)}{1 - r} \qquad \text{sum of geometric sequence}$$

where s = sum

a = first term

r = common ratio

n = number of terms

An ordinary annuity is an annuity in which each payment is made at the *end* of a payment period, whereas an annuity due is an annuity in which each payment is made at the *beginning* of a payment period. The basic formulas dealing with ordinary annuities are

$$A = R \cdot \frac{1 - (1 + r)^{-n}}{r} = Ra_{\overline{n}|r} \qquad \text{present value}$$

$$S = R \cdot \frac{(1 + r)^n - 1}{r} = Rs_{\overline{n}|r} \qquad \text{future value}$$

where A = present value of annuity

S = amount (future value) of annuity

R = amount of each payment

n = number of payment periods

r = periodic rate

For an annuity due, the corresponding formulas are

$$A = R(1 + a_{\overline{n-1}|r}) \qquad \text{present value}$$
$$S = R(s_{\overline{n+1}|r} - 1) \qquad \text{future value}$$

A loan, such as a mortgage, is amortized when part of each installment payment is used to pay interest and the remaining part is used to reduce the principal. A complete analysis of each payment is given in an amortization schedule. The following formulas deal with amortizing a loan of A dollars, at the periodic rate of r, by n equal payments of R dollars each and such that a payment is made at the end of each period:

Periodic payment:

$$R = \frac{A}{a_{\overline{n}|r}} = A \cdot \frac{r}{1 - (1 + r)^{-n}}$$

Principal outstanding at beginning of kth period:

$$Ra_{\overline{n-k+1}|r} = R \cdot \frac{1 - (1 + r)^{-n+k-1}}{r}$$

Interest in kth payment:

$$Rra_{\overline{n-k+1}|r}$$

Principal contained in kth payment:

$$R(1 - ra_{\overline{n-k+1}|r})$$

Total interest paid:

$$R(n - a_{\overline{n}|r}) = nR - A$$

A perpetuity is an infinite sequence of payments made at fixed periods of time. The mathematical basis for the formula dealing with a perpetuity is the notion of the sum of an infinite geometric sequence—that is,

$$s = \sum_{i=0}^{\infty} ar^i = \frac{a}{1 - r} \qquad \text{sum of infinite geometric sequence}$$

where s = sum

a = first term

r = common ratio with $|r| < 1$

The basic formula dealing with perpetuities is

$$A = \frac{R}{r} \qquad \text{present value}$$

where A = present value of perpetuity

R = amount of each payment

r = periodic rate

An infinite sum is defined as the limit of the sequence of partial sums.

Review Problems

1. Find the number of interest periods that it takes for a principal to double when the interest rate is r per period.

2. Find the effective rate that corresponds to a nominal rate of 5% compounded monthly.

3. An investor has a choice of investing a sum of money at either 8.5% compounded annually or 8.2% compounded semiannually. Which is the better choice?

4. Cash Flows Find the net present value of the following cash flows, which can be purchased by an initial investment of $7000:

Year	Cash Flow
2	$3400
4	3500

Assume that interest is at 7% compounded semiannually.

5. A debt of $1500 due in five years and $2000 due in seven years is to be repaid by a payment of $2000 now and a second payment at the end of three years. How much should the second payment be if interest is at 3% compounded annually?

6. Find the present value of an annuity of $250 at the end of each month for four years if interest is at 6% compounded monthly.

7. For an annuity of $200 at the end of every six months for $6\frac{1}{2}$ years, find (a) the present value and (b) the future value at an interest rate of 8% compounded semiannually.

8. Find the amount of an annuity due which consists of 13 yearly payments of $150, provided that the interest rate is 4% compounded annually.

9. Suppose $200 is initially placed in a savings account and $200 is deposited at the end of every month for the next year. If interest is at 8% compounded monthly, how much is in the account at the end of the year?

10. A savings account pays interest at the rate of 2% compounded semiannually. What amount must be deposited now so that $350 can be withdrawn at the end of every six months for the next 15 years?

11. Sinking Fund A company borrows $5000 on which it will pay interest at the end of each year at the annual rate of 11%. In addition, a sinking fund is set up so that the $5000 can be repaid at the end of five years. Equal payments are placed in the fund at the end of each year, and the fund earns interest at the effective rate of 6%. Find the annual payment in the sinking fund.

12. Car Loan A debtor is to amortize a $7000 car loan by making equal payments at the end of each month for 36 months. If interest is at 4% compounded monthly, find (a) the amount of each payment and (b) the finance charge.

13. A person has debts of $500 due in three years with interest at 5% compounded annually and $500 due in four years with interest at 6% compounded semiannually. The debtor wants to pay off these debts by making two payments: the first payment now, and the second, which is double the first payment, at the end of the third year. If money is worth 7% compounded annually, how much is the first payment?

14. Construct an amortization schedule for a loan of $3500 repaid by three monthly payments with interest at 16.5% compounded monthly.

15. Construct an amortization schedule for a loan of $15,000 repaid by five monthly payments with interest at 9% compounded monthly.

16. Find the present value of an ordinary annuity of $460 every month for nine years at the rate of 6% compounded monthly.

17. Auto Loan Determine the finance charge for a 48-month auto loan of $11,000 with monthly payments at the rate of 5.5% compounded monthly.

Q EXPLORE & EXTEND   Treasury Securities

The safest single type of investment is in securities issued by the U.S. Treasury. These pay fixed returns on a predetermined schedule, which can span as little as three months or as much as thirty years. The finish date is called the date of maturity.

Although Treasury securities are initially sold by the government, they trade on the open market. Because the prices are free to float up and down, securities' rates of return can change over time. Consider, for example, a six-month Treasury bill, or T-bill, bearing a $10,000 face value and purchased on the date of issue for $9832.84. T-bills pay no interest before maturity but upon maturity are redeemed

by the government at face value. This T-bill, if held the full six months, will pay back $\frac{10,000}{9832.84} \approx 101.7\%$ of the original investment, for an annualized effective annual rate of return of $1.017^2 - 1 \approx 3.429\%$. If the same T-bill, however, is sold at midterm for $9913.75, the new owner has a prospective annualized effective rate of return of $\left(\frac{10,000}{9913.75}\right)^4 - 1 \approx 3.526\%$ over the remaining three months.

Like T-bills, Treasury notes and bonds are redeemed at face value upon maturity. In addition, however, notes and bonds pay interest twice a year according to a fixed nominal rate.[1] A 6.5%, $20,000, seven-year note pays $0.065(20,000) = \$1300$ every six months. At the end of

---

[1] In this context, *nominal rate* does *not* refer to the annual percentage rate. The former is constant, while the latter changes in tandem with the yield.

seven years, the holder receives the final interest payment plus the face value, for a total of $21,300.

Mathematically, it is easier to calculate the present value of a note or bond from an assumed yield than to find the yield given an assumed present value (or price). Notes and bonds differ only in times to maturity: one to ten years for notes, ten to thirty years for bonds. Each note or bond is a guarantee of a lump sum at a future date plus an annuity until then. The present value of the note or bond, then, is the sum of the present value of the future lump sum and the present value of the annuity. We will assume that notes and bonds are evaluated at times when the next interest payment is exactly six months away; that way, we can use the formula for the present value of an annuity in Section 5.4.

With semiannual compounding, an annual yield of r corresponds to an interest payment of $\sqrt{1+r} - 1$ every six months. Making the appropriate substitution in the formulas from Sections 5.2 and 5.4, we obtain the following general formula for the present value of a Treasury note or bond:

$$P = S(1+\sqrt{1+r}-1)^{-2n} + R \cdot \frac{1 - (1+\sqrt{1+r}-1)^{-2n}}{\sqrt{1+r}-1}$$

which simplifies to

$$P = S(1+r)^{-n} + R \cdot \frac{1-(1+r)^{-n}}{\sqrt{1+r}-1}$$

where S is the face value, r is the assumed annual effective rate, and n is the number of years to maturity (so that $2n$ is the number of six-month periods). R is the amount of the semiannual interest payment, which is S times half the bond's nominal rate (for example, $R = 0.03S$ for a 6% bond).

Since we can treat a T-bill as a shorter-term note with a nominal rate of 0%, this formula covers T-bills as well by taking $R = 0$ since there is no annuity component.

To illustrate, if we are seeking a 7.4% effective rate on a new-issue, one-year, $30,000 T-bill (for which $R = 0$), we should be willing to pay

$$30,000(1.074)^{-1} \approx \$27,932.96$$

But if we are seeking a 7.4% effective rate on a 5.5%, $30,000 bond with 17 years left to maturity (here $R = 0.0275 \cdot 30,000 = 825$), we should be willing to pay only

$$30,000(1.074)^{-17} + 825 \cdot \frac{1-(1.074)^{-17}}{\sqrt{1.074}-1} \approx 24,870.66$$

Of course, it may happen that our effective rate expectations are unrealistic and that no bonds are for sale at the price we calculate. In that case, we may need to look at market prices and consider whether we can accept the corresponding effective rates of return. But how do we find a security's effective rate of return r from its market price?

For T-bills, the second term on the right side of the present value formula drops out, and we can solve the simplified formula for r to obtain

$$r = \left(\frac{S}{P}\right)^{1/n} - 1$$

Calculations for three-month and six-month T-bills use $n = \frac{1}{4}$ and $n = \frac{1}{2}$ (as, for example, in the calculations of the second paragraph of this Explore & Extend).

Calculating the effective rate of return on a note or bond, on the other hand, involves solving the complete present value equation for r in terms of S, P, and n—and this cannot be done algebraically. However, it can be done with a graphing calculator. We set Y_1 equal to the left side of the equation, Y_2 equal to the right side, and find where Y_1 and Y_2 are equal. Suppose, for example, that a 6.8%, $26,000 bond is selling at $26,617.50 eleven years from maturity. Each of the 22 interest payments is $R = 0.034(26,000) = 884$. To find the effective rate, set

$$Y_1 = 26,617.50$$

and

$$Y_2 = 26,000(1 + X)^\wedge - 11$$
$$+ 884(1 - (1 + X)^\wedge - 11)/(\sqrt{(1 + X)} - 1)$$

Then graph Y_1 and Y_2, and find where the two graphs intersect (Figure 5.14).

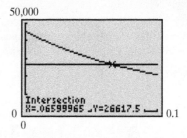

FIGURE 5.14   Finding effective rate.

The graphs intersect for $X \approx 0.0660$, which means that the effective rate is 6.6%.

The graph describing the current effective rates of Treasury securities as a function of time to maturity is called the *yield curve*. Economists keep a daily watch on this curve; you can monitor it yourself on the Web. Most typically, the yield curve looks something like that shown in Figure 5.15 (in which the horizontal time axis has been scaled).

You can see that the longer the time to maturity, the greater the yield. The usual explanation for this pattern is that having money tied up in a long-term investment means a loss of short-term flexibility—of liquidity, as it is called. To attract buyers, long-term securities must generally be priced for slightly higher effective rates than short-term securities.

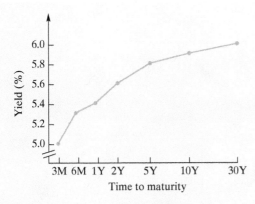

FIGURE 5.15   A typical yield curve.

Problems

1. Find the present value of an 8.5%, 25-year, $25,000 bond, assuming an annual effective rate of 8.25%.

2. Find the effective rate on a 6.5%, $10,000 note that is selling at $10,389 with seven years left to maturity.

3. In late December of 2000, the yield curve for Treasury securities had the atypical shape shown in Figure 5.16.

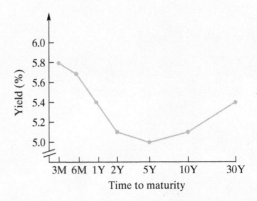

FIGURE 5.16   An atypical yield curve.

T-bills were earning higher yields than five-year notes, contrary to what one would expect. How might investor expectations about future earnings possibilities explain the yield curve?

10 Limits and Continuity

Q EXPLORE & EXTEND

National Debt

The philosopher Zeno of Elea was fond of paradoxes about motion. His most famous one goes something like this: The warrior Achilles agrees to run a race against a tortoise. Achilles can run 10 meters per second and the tortoise only 1 meter per second, so the tortoise gets a 10-meter head start. Since Achilles is so much faster, he should still win. But by the time he has covered his first 10 meters and reached the place where the tortoise started, the tortoise has advanced 1 meter and is still ahead. And after Achilles has covered that 1 meter, the tortoise has advanced another 0.1 meter and is still ahead. And after Achilles has covered that 0.1 meter, the tortoise has advanced another 0.01 meter and is still ahead. And so on. Therefore, Achilles gets closer and closer to the tortoise but can never catch up.

Zeno's audience knew that the argument was fishy. The position of Achilles at time t after the race has begun is $(10 \text{ m/s})t$. The position of the tortoise at the same time t is $(1 \text{ m/s})t + 10 \text{ m}$. When these are equal, Achilles and the tortoise are side by side. To solve the resulting equation

$$(10 \text{ m/s})t = (1 \text{ m/s})t + 10 \text{ m}$$

for t is to find the time at which Achilles pulls even with the tortoise.

The solution is $t = 1\frac{1}{9}$ seconds, at which time Achilles will have run $\left(1\frac{1}{9} \text{ s}\right)(10 \text{ m/s}) = 11\frac{1}{9}$ meters.

What puzzled Zeno and his listeners is how it could be that

$$10 + 1 + \frac{1}{10} + \frac{1}{100} + \cdots = 11\frac{1}{9}$$

where the left side represents an *infinite sum* and the right side is a finite result. The solution to this problem is the concept of a limit, which is the key topic of this chapter. The left side of the equation is the sum of an infinite geometric sequence. Using limit notation, summation notation, and the formula from Section 1.6 for the sum of a finite geometric sequence, we write

$$\lim_{k \to \infty} \sum_{n=0}^{k} 10^{1-n} = \lim_{k \to \infty} \frac{10\left(1 - \left(\frac{1}{10}\right)^{k+1}\right)}{1 - \frac{1}{10}} = \frac{100}{9} = 11\frac{1}{9}$$

and find the sum of this particular infinite geometric sequence. (In Section 1.6 we showed that, for an infinite sequence with first term a and common ratio r, the sum of the infinite sequence exists and is given by $\frac{a}{1-r}$, *provided that $|r| < 1$*.)

459

To study limits and their basic
properties.

10.1 Limits

Perhaps you have been in a parking-lot situation in which you must "inch up" to the
car in front, but yet you do not want to bump or touch it. This notion of getting closer
and closer to something, but yet not touching it, is very important in mathematics and
is involved in the concept of *limit*, which lies at the foundation of calculus. We will let
a variable "inch up" to a particular value and examine the effect this process has on the
values of a function.

For example, consider the function

$$f(x) = \frac{x^3 - 1}{x - 1}$$

Although this function is not defined at $x = 1$, we may be curious about the behavior
of the function values as x gets very close to 1. Table 10.1 gives some values of x that
are slightly less than 1 and some that are slightly greater, as well as their corresponding
function values. Notice that as x takes on values closer and closer to 1, regardless of
whether x approaches it *from the left* $(x < 1)$ or *from the right* $(x > 1)$, the corresponding
values of $f(x)$ get closer and closer to one and only one number, namely 3. This is also
clear from the graph of f in Figure 10.1. Notice there that even though the function is
not defined at $x = 1$ (as indicated by the hollow dot), the function values get closer and
closer to 3 as x gets closer and closer to 1. To express this, we say that the **limit** of $f(x)$
as x approaches 1 is 3 and write

$$\lim_{x \to 1} \frac{x^3 - 1}{x - 1} = 3$$

We can make $f(x)$ as close as we like to 3, and keep it that close, by taking x sufficiently
close to, but different from, 1. The limit exists at 1, even though 1 is not in the domain of f.

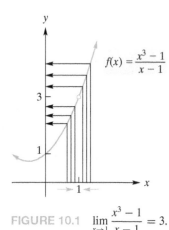

FIGURE 10.1 $\lim_{x \to 1} \dfrac{x^3 - 1}{x - 1} = 3.$

Table 10.1			
$x < 1$		$x > 1$	
x	$f(x)$	x	$f(x)$
0.8	2.44	1.2	3.64
0.9	2.71	1.1	3.31
0.95	2.8525	1.05	3.1525
0.99	2.9701	1.01	3.0301
0.995	2.985025	1.005	3.015025
0.999	2.997001	1.001	3.003001

We can also consider the limit of a function as x approaches a number that is in the
domain. Let us examine the limit of $f(x) = x + 3$ as x approaches 2:

$$\lim_{x \to 2} (x + 3)$$

Obviously, if x is close to 2 (but not equal to 2), then $x + 3$ is close to 5. This is also
apparent from the table and graph in Figure 10.2. Thus,

$$\lim_{x \to 2} (x + 3) = 5$$

Given a function f and a number a, there *may* be two ways of associating a number to the
pair (f, a). One such number is the *evaluation of f at a*, namely $f(a)$. It *exists* precisely
when a is in the domain of f. For example, if $f(x) = \dfrac{x^3 - 1}{x - 1}$, our first example, then
$f(1)$ does not *exist*. Another way of associating a number to the pair (f, a) is *the limit*

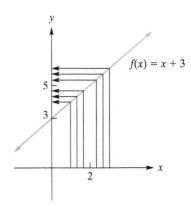

| x < 2 | | x > 2 | |
x	f(x)	x	f(x)
1.5	4.5	2.5	5.5
1.9	4.9	2.1	5.1
1.95	4.95	2.05	5.05
1.99	4.99	2.01	5.01
1.999	4.999	2.001	5.001

FIGURE 10.2 $\lim_{x \to 2} (x + 3) = 5$.

of f(x) as x approaches a, which is denoted $\lim_{x \to a} f(x)$. We have given two examples. Here is the general case.

Definition

The limit of f(x) as x approaches a is the number L, written

$$\lim_{x \to a} f(x) = L$$

provided that we can make the values $f(x)$ as close as we like to L, and keep them that close, by taking x sufficiently close to, but different from, a. If there is no such number, we say that the limit of $f(x)$ as x approaches a *does not exist.*

We emphasize that, when finding a limit, we are concerned not with what happens to $f(x)$ when x equals a, but only with what happens to $f(x)$ when x is close to a. In fact, even if $f(a)$ *exists,* the preceding definition explicitly rules out consideration of it. In our second example, $f(x) = x + 3$, we have $f(2) = 5$ and also $\lim_{x \to 2} (x + 3) = 5$, but it is quite possible to have a function f and a number a for which both $f(a)$ and $\lim_{x \to a} f(x)$ exist and are different. Moreover, a limit must be independent of the way in which x *approaches a,* meaning the way in which x gets close to a. That is, the limit must be the same whether x approaches a from the left or from the right (for $x < a$ or $x > a$, respectively).

EXAMPLE 1 **Estimating a Limit from a Graph**

a. Estimate $\lim_{x \to 1} f(x)$, where the graph of f is given in Figure 10.3(a).

Solution: If we look at the graph for values of x near 1, we see that $f(x)$ is near 2. Moreover, as x gets closer and closer to 1, $f(x)$ appears to get closer and closer to 2.

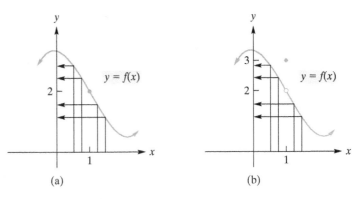

(a) (b)

FIGURE 10.3 Investigation of $\lim_{x \to 1} f(x)$.

Thus, we estimate that

$$\lim_{x \to 1} f(x) = 2$$

b. Estimate $\lim_{x \to 1} f(x)$, where the graph of f is given in Figure 10.3(b).

Solution: Although $f(1) = 3$, this fact has no bearing whatsoever on the limit of $f(x)$ as x approaches 1. We see that as x gets closer and closer to 1, $f(x)$ appears to get closer and closer to 2. Thus, we estimate that

$$\lim_{x \to 1} f(x) = 2$$

Now Work Problem 1 ◁

Up to now, all of the limits that we have considered did indeed exist. Next we look at some situations in which a limit does not exist.

EXAMPLE 2 Limits That Do Not Exist

a. Estimate $\lim_{x \to -2} f(x)$ if it exists, where the graph of f is given in Figure 10.4.

Solution: As x approaches -2 from the left ($x < -2$), the values of $f(x)$ appear to get closer to 1. But as x approaches -2 from the right ($x > -2$), $f(x)$ appears to get closer to 3. Hence, as x approaches -2, the function values do not settle down to one and only one number. We conclude that

$$\lim_{x \to -2} f(x) \text{ does not exist}$$

Note that the limit does not exist even though the function is defined at $x = -2$.

b. Estimate $\lim_{x \to 0} \dfrac{1}{x^2}$ if it exists.

Solution: Let $f(x) = 1/x^2$. The table in Figure 10.5 gives values of $f(x)$ for some values of x near 0. As x gets closer and closer to 0, the values of $f(x)$ get larger and larger without bound. This is also clear from the graph. Since the values of $f(x)$ do not approach a *number* as x approaches 0,

$$\lim_{x \to 0} \dfrac{1}{x^2} \text{ does not exist}$$

Now Work Problem 3 ◁

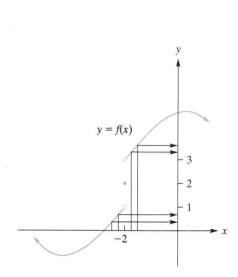

FIGURE 10.4 $\lim_{x \to -2} f(x)$ does not exist.

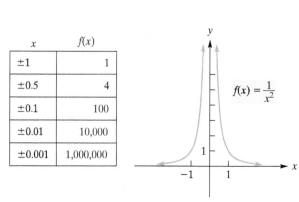

x	$f(x)$
± 1	1
± 0.5	4
± 0.1	100
± 0.01	10,000
± 0.001	1,000,000

FIGURE 10.5 $\lim_{x \to 0} \dfrac{1}{x^2}$ does not exist.

TECHNOLOGY ▮▮▮

Problem: Estimate $\lim_{x \to 2} f(x)$ if

$$f(x) = \frac{x^3 + 2.1x^2 - 10.2x + 4}{x^2 + 2.5x - 9}$$

Solution: One method of finding the limit is by constructing a table of function values $f(x)$ when x is close to 2. From Figure 10.6, we estimate the limit to be 1.57. Alternatively, we can estimate the limit from the graph of f. Figure 10.7 shows the graph of f in the standard window of $[-10, 10] \times [-10, 10]$. First we zoom in several times around $x = 2$ and obtain Figure 10.8. After tracing around $x = 2$, we estimate the limit to be 1.57.

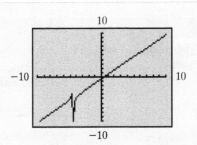

FIGURE 10.7   Graph of $f(x)$ in standard window.

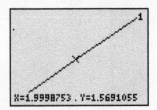

FIGURE 10.8   Zooming and tracing around $x = 2$ gives $\lim_{x \to 2} f(x) \approx 1.57$.

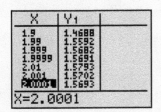

FIGURE 10.6 $\lim_{x \to 2} f(x) \approx 1.57$.

Properties of Limits

To determine limits, we do not always want to compute function values or sketch a graph. Alternatively, there are several properties of limits that we may be able to employ. The following properties may seem reasonable to you:

1. If $f(x) = c$ is a constant function, then

$$\lim_{x \to a} f(x) = \lim_{x \to a} c = c$$

2. $\lim_{x \to a} x^n = a^n$, for any positive integer n

EXAMPLE 3   Applying Limit Properties 1 and 2

a. $\lim_{x \to 2} 7 = 7; \lim_{x \to -5} 7 = 7$
b. $\lim_{x \to 6} x^2 = 6^2 = 36$
c. $\lim_{t \to -2} t^4 = (-2)^4 = 16$

Now Work Problem 9 ◁

Some other properties of limits are as follows:

If $\lim_{x \to a} f(x)$ and $\lim_{x \to a} g(x)$ exist, then

3.
$$\lim_{x \to a} [f(x) \pm g(x)] = \lim_{x \to a} f(x) \pm \lim_{x \to a} g(x)$$

That is, the limit of a sum or difference is the sum or difference, respectively, of the limits.

4.
$$\lim_{x \to a} [f(x) \cdot g(x)] = \lim_{x \to a} f(x) \cdot \lim_{x \to a} g(x)$$

That is, the limit of a product is the product of the limits.

5.
$$\lim_{x \to a} [cf(x)] = c \cdot \lim_{x \to a} f(x), \text{ where } c \text{ is a constant}$$

That is, the limit of a constant times a function is the constant times the limit of the function.

APPLY IT ▶

2. The volume of helium in a spherical balloon (in cubic centimeters), as a function of the radius r in centimeters, is given by $V(r) = \frac{4}{3}\pi r^3$. Find $\lim_{r \to 1} V(r)$.

EXAMPLE 4   Applying Limit Properties

a.
$$\lim_{x \to 2}(x^2 + x) = \lim_{x \to 2} x^2 + \lim_{x \to 2} x \qquad \text{Property 3}$$
$$= 2^2 + 2 = 6 \qquad \text{Property 2}$$

b. Property 3 can be extended to the limit of a finite number of sums and differences. For example,
$$\lim_{q \to -1}(q^3 - q + 1) = \lim_{q \to -1} q^3 - \lim_{q \to -1} q + \lim_{q \to -1} 1$$
$$= (-1)^3 - (-1) + 1 = 1$$

c.
$$\lim_{x \to 2}[(x + 1)(x - 3)] = \lim_{x \to 2}(x + 1) \cdot \lim_{x \to 2}(x - 3) \qquad \text{Property 4}$$
$$= \left(\lim_{x \to 2} x + \lim_{x \to 2} 1\right) \cdot \left(\lim_{x \to 2} x - \lim_{x \to 2} 3\right)$$
$$= (2 + 1) \cdot (2 - 3) = 3(-1) = -3$$

d.
$$\lim_{x \to -2} 3x^3 = 3 \cdot \lim_{x \to -2} x^3 \qquad \text{Property 5}$$
$$= 3(-2)^3 = -24$$

Now Work Problem 11 ◁

APPLY IT ▶

3. The revenue function for a certain product is given by $R(x) = 500x - 6x^2$. Find $\lim_{x \to 8} R(x)$.

EXAMPLE 5   Limit of a Polynomial Function

Let $f(x) = c_n x^n + c_{n-1} x^{n-1} + \cdots + c_1 x + c_0$ define a polynomial function. Then
$$\lim_{x \to a} f(x) = \lim_{x \to a}(c_n x^n + c_{n-1} x^{n-1} + \cdots + c_1 x + c_0)$$
$$= c_n \cdot \lim_{x \to a} x^n + c_{n-1} \cdot \lim_{x \to a} x^{n-1} + \cdots + c_1 \cdot \lim_{x \to a} x + \lim_{x \to a} c_0$$
$$= c_n a^n + c_{n-1} a^{n-1} + \cdots + c_1 a + c_0 = f(a)$$

Thus, we have the following property:

If f is a polynomial function, then
$$\lim_{x \to a} f(x) = f(a)$$

In other words, if f is a polynomial and a is any number, then both ways of associating a number to the pair (f, a), namely formation of the limit and evaluation, exist and are equal.

Now Work Problem 13 ◁

The result of Example 5 allows us to find many limits simply by evaluation. For example, we can find
$$\lim_{x \to -3}(x^3 + 4x^2 - 7)$$

by substituting -3 for x because $x^3 + 4x^2 - 7$ is a polynomial function:
$$\lim_{x \to -3}(x^3 + 4x^2 - 7) = (-3)^3 + 4(-3)^2 - 7 = 2$$

Similarly,
$$\lim_{h \to 3}(2(h - 1)) = 2(3 - 1) = 4$$

We want to stress that we do not find limits simply by evaluating unless there is a rule that covers the situation. We were able to find the previous two limits by evaluation because we have a rule that applies to limits of polynomial functions. However, indiscriminate use of evaluation can lead to errors. To illustrate, in Example 1(b) we have $f(1) = 3$, which is not $\lim_{x \to 1} f(x)$; in Example 2(a), $f(-2) = 2$, which is not $\lim_{x \to -2} f(x)$.

The next two limit properties concern quotients and roots.

If $\lim_{x \to a} f(x)$ and $\lim_{x \to a} g(x)$ exist, then

6.
$$\lim_{x \to a} \frac{f(x)}{g(x)} = \frac{\lim_{x \to a} f(x)}{\lim_{x \to a} g(x)} \quad \text{if} \quad \lim_{x \to a} g(x) \neq 0$$

That is, the limit of a quotient is the quotient of limits, provided that the denominator does not have a limit of 0.

7.
$$\lim_{x \to a} \sqrt[n]{f(x)} = \sqrt[n]{\lim_{x \to a} f(x)} \quad \text{See footnote 1}$$

EXAMPLE 6 Applying Limit Properties 6 and 7

> **CAUTION!**
>
> Note that in Example 6(a) the numerator and denominator of the function are polynomials. In general, we can determine a limit of a rational function by evaluation, provided that the denominator is not 0 at a.

a. $\lim_{x \to 1} \dfrac{2x^2 + x - 3}{x^3 + 4} = \dfrac{\lim_{x \to 1} (2x^2 + x - 3)}{\lim_{x \to 1} (x^3 + 4)} = \dfrac{2 + 1 - 3}{1 + 4} = \dfrac{0}{5} = 0$

b. $\lim_{t \to 4} \sqrt{t^2 + 1} = \sqrt{\lim_{t \to 4} (t^2 + 1)} = \sqrt{17}$

c. $\lim_{x \to 3} \sqrt[3]{x^2 + 7} = \sqrt[3]{\lim_{x \to 3} (x^2 + 7)} = \sqrt[3]{16} = \sqrt[3]{8 \cdot 2} = 2\sqrt[3]{2}$

Now Work Problem 15 ◁

Limits and Algebraic Manipulation

We now consider limits to which our limit properties do not apply and which cannot be determined by evaluation. A fundamental result is the following:

> **CAUTION!**
>
> The condition for equality of the limits does not preclude the possibility that $f(a) = g(a)$. The condition only concerns $x \neq a$.

If f and g are two functions for which $f(x) = g(x)$, for all $x \neq a$, then

$$\lim_{x \to a} f(x) = \lim_{x \to a} g(x)$$

(meaning that if either limit exists, then the other exists and they are equal).

The result follows directly from the definition of *limit* since the value of $\lim_{x \to a} f(x)$ depends only on those values $f(x)$ for x that are close to a. We repeat: The evaluation of f at a, $f(a)$, or lack of its existence, is irrelevant in the determination of $\lim_{x \to a} f(x)$ unless we have a specific rule that applies, such as in the case when f is a polynomial.

EXAMPLE 7 Finding a Limit

APPLY IT ▶

4. The rate of change of productivity p (in number of units produced per hour) increases with time on the job by the function

$$p(t) = \frac{50(t^2 + 4t)}{t^2 + 3t + 20}$$

Find $\lim_{t \to 2} p(t)$.

Find $\lim_{x \to -1} \dfrac{x^2 - 1}{x + 1}$.

Solution: As $x \to -1$, both numerator and denominator approach zero. Because the limit of the denominator is 0, we *cannot* use Property 6. However, since what happens to the quotient when x equals -1 is of no concern, we can assume that $x \neq -1$ and simplify the fraction:

$$\frac{x^2 - 1}{x + 1} = \frac{(x + 1)(x - 1)}{x + 1} = x - 1 \quad \text{for } x \neq -1$$

---

[1] If n is even, we require that $\lim_{x \to a} f(x)$ be nonnegative.

This algebraic manipulation (factoring and cancellation) of the original function $\dfrac{x^2 - 1}{x + 1}$ yields a new function $x - 1$, which is the same as the original function for $x \neq -1$. Thus the fundamental result displayed in the box at the beginning of this subsection applies and we have

$$\lim_{x \to -1} \frac{x^2 - 1}{x + 1} = \lim_{x \to -1} (x - 1) = -1 - 1 = -2$$

Notice that, although the original function is not defined at -1, it *does* have a limit as $x \to -1$.

Now Work Problem 21 ◁

When both $f(x)$ and $g(x)$ approach 0 as $x \to a$, then the limit

$$\lim_{x \to a} \frac{f(x)}{g(x)}$$

is said to have the *form* 0/0. Similarly, we speak of *form* $k/0$, for $k \neq 0$ if $f(x)$ approaches $k \neq 0$ as $x \to a$ but $g(x)$ approaches 0 as $x \to a$.

In Example 7, the method of finding a limit by evaluation does not work. Replacing x by -1 gives 0/0, which has no meaning. When the meaningless form 0/0 arises, algebraic manipulation (as in Example 7) may result in a function that agrees with the original function, except possibly at the limiting value. In Example 7 the new function, $x - 1$, is a polynomial and its limit *can* be found by evaluation.

In the beginning of this section, we found

$$\lim_{x \to 1} \frac{x^3 - 1}{x - 1}$$

by examining a table of function values of $f(x) = (x^3 - 1)/(x - 1)$ and also by considering the graph of f. This limit has the form 0/0. Now we will determine the limit by using the technique used in Example 7.

CAUTION!⚠

There is frequently confusion about which principle is being used in this example and in Example 7. It is this:

If $f(x) = g(x)$ for $x \neq a$,

then $\lim_{x \to a} f(x) = \lim_{x \to a} g(x)$.

EXAMPLE 8   Form 0/0

Find $\displaystyle\lim_{x \to 1} \frac{x^3 - 1}{x - 1}$.

Solution: As $x \to 1$, both the numerator and denominator approach 0. Thus, we will try to express the quotient in a different form for $x \neq 1$. By factoring, we have

$$\frac{x^3 - 1}{x - 1} = \frac{(x - 1)(x^2 + x + 1)}{(x - 1)} = x^2 + x + 1 \qquad \text{for } x \neq 1$$

(Alternatively, long division would give the same result.) Therefore,

$$\lim_{x \to 1} \frac{x^3 - 1}{x - 1} = \lim_{x \to 1} (x^2 + x + 1) = 1^2 + 1 + 1 = 3$$

as we showed before.

Now Work Problem 23 ◁

APPLY IT ▶

5. The length of a material increases as it is heated up according to the equation $l = 125 + 2x$. The rate at which the length is increasing is given by

$$\lim_{h \to 0} \frac{125 + 2(x + h) - (125 + 2x)}{h}$$

Calculate this limit.

EXAMPLE 9   Form 0/0

If $f(x) = x^2 + 1$, find $\displaystyle\lim_{h \to 0} \frac{f(x + h) - f(x)}{h}$.

Solution:

$$\lim_{h \to 0} \frac{f(x + h) - f(x)}{h} = \lim_{h \to 0} \frac{[(x + h)^2 + 1] - (x^2 + 1)}{h}$$

Here we treat x as a constant because h, not x, is changing. As $h \to 0$, both the numerator and denominator approach 0. Therefore, we will try to express the quotient in a different form, for $h \neq 0$. We have

$$\lim_{h \to 0} \frac{[(x + h)^2 + 1] - (x^2 + 1)}{h} = \lim_{h \to 0} \frac{[x^2 + 2xh + h^2 + 1] - x^2 - 1}{h}$$

$$= \lim_{h \to 0} \frac{2xh + h^2}{h}$$

The expression

$$\frac{f(x+h)-f(x)}{h}$$

is called a *difference quotient*. The limit of the difference quotient lies at the heart of differential calculus. We will encounter such limits in Chapter 11.

$$= \lim_{h\to 0} \frac{h(2x+h)}{h}$$

$$= \lim_{h\to 0} (2x+h)$$

$$= 2x$$

Note: It is the fourth equality above, $\lim_{h\to 0} \dfrac{h(2x+h)}{h} = \lim_{h\to 0} (2x+h)$, that uses the fundamental result. When $\dfrac{h(2x+h)}{h}$ and $2x+h$ are considered as *functions of h*, they are seen to be equal, for all $h \neq 0$. It follows that their limits as h approaches 0 are equal.

Now Work Problem 35 ◁

A Special Limit

We conclude this section with a note concerning a most important limit, namely,

$$\lim_{x\to 0} (1+x)^{1/x}$$

Figure 10.9 shows the graph of $f(x) = (1+x)^{1/x}$. Although $f(0)$ does not exist, as $x \to 0$ it is clear that the limit of $(1+x)^{1/x}$ exists. It is approximately 2.71828 and is denoted by the letter e. This, you may recall, is the base of the system of natural logarithms. The limit

This limit will be used in Chapter 12.

$$\lim_{x\to 0} (1+x)^{1/x} = e$$

can actually be considered the definition of e. It can be shown that this agrees with the definition of e that we gave in Section 4.1.

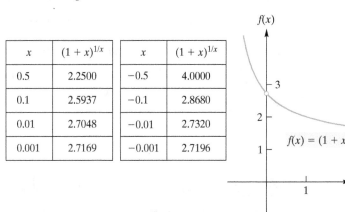

x	$(1+x)^{1/x}$	x	$(1+x)^{1/x}$
0.5	2.2500	-0.5	4.0000
0.1	2.5937	-0.1	2.8680
0.01	2.7048	-0.01	2.7320
0.001	2.7169	-0.001	2.7196

FIGURE 10.9 $\lim_{x\to 0} (1+x)^{1/x} = e$.

PROBLEMS 10.1

In Problems 1–4, use the graph of f to estimate each limit if it exists.

1. Graph of f appears in Figure 10.10.
(a) $\lim_{x\to 0} f(x)$ (b) $\lim_{x\to 1} f(x)$ (c) $\lim_{x\to 2} f(x)$

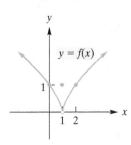

FIGURE 10.10

2. Graph of f appears in Figure 10.11.
(a) $\lim_{x\to -1} f(x)$ (b) $\lim_{x\to 0} f(x)$ (c) $\lim_{x\to 1} f(x)$

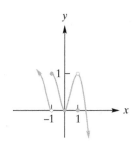

FIGURE 10.11

3. Graph of f appears in Figure 10.12.

(a) $\lim_{x \to -1} f(x)$ **(b)** $\lim_{x \to 1} f(x)$ **(c)** $\lim_{x \to 2} f(x)$

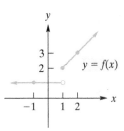

FIGURE 10.12

4. Graph of f appears in Figure 10.13.

(a) $\lim_{x \to -1} f(x)$ **(b)** $\lim_{x \to 0} f(x)$ **(c)** $\lim_{x \to 1} f(x)$

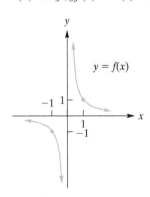

FIGURE 10.13

In Problems 5–8, use your calculator to complete the table, and use your results to estimate the given limit.

5. $\lim_{x \to -1} \dfrac{3x^2 + 2x - 1}{x + 1}$

x	-0.9	-0.99	-0.999	-1.001	-1.01	-1.1
$f(x)$						

6. $\lim_{x \to -3} \dfrac{x^2 - 9}{x + 3}$

x	-3.1	-3.01	-3.001	-2.999	-2.99	-2.9
$f(x)$						

7. $\lim_{x \to 0} |x|^{|x|}$

x	-0.00001	0.00001	0.0001	0.001	0.01	0.1
$f(x)$						

8. $\lim_{h \to 0} \dfrac{\sqrt{1 + h} - 1}{h}$

h	-0.1	-0.01	-0.001	0.001	0.01	0.1
$f(x)$						

In Problems 9–34, find the limits.

9. $\lim_{x \to 2} 16$

10. $\lim_{x \to 3} 2x$

11. $\lim_{t \to -5} (t^2 - 5)$

12. $\lim_{t \to 1/2} (3t - 5)$

13. $\lim_{x \to -2} (3x^3 - 4x^2 + 2x - 3)$

14. $\lim_{r \to 9} \dfrac{4r - 3}{11}$

15. $\lim_{t \to -3} \dfrac{t - 2}{t + 5}$

16. $\lim_{x \to -6} \dfrac{x^2 + 6}{x - 6}$

17. $\lim_{t \to 0} \dfrac{t}{t^3 - 4t + 3}$

18. $\lim_{z \to 0} \dfrac{z^2 - 5z - 4}{z^2 + 1}$

19. $\lim_{p \to 4} \sqrt{p^2 + p + 5}$

20. $\lim_{y \to 15} \sqrt{y + 3}$

21. $\lim_{x \to -2} \dfrac{x^2 + 2x}{x + 2}$

22. $\lim_{x \to -1} \dfrac{x^2 - 1}{x^2 - 1}$

23. $\lim_{x \to 2} \dfrac{x^2 - x - 2}{x - 2}$

24. $\lim_{t \to 0} \dfrac{t^3 + 3t^2}{t^3 - 4t^2}$

25. $\lim_{x \to 3} \dfrac{x^2 - x - 6}{x - 3}$

26. $\lim_{t \to 2} \dfrac{t^2 - 4}{t - 2}$

27. $\lim_{x \to -4} \dfrac{x + 4}{x^2 - 16}$

28. $\lim_{x \to 0} \dfrac{x^2 - 2x}{x}$

29. $\lim_{x \to 4} \dfrac{x^2 - 9x + 20}{x^2 - 3x - 4}$

30. $\lim_{x \to -3} \dfrac{x^4 - 81}{x^2 + 8x + 15}$

31. $\lim_{x \to 2} \dfrac{3x^2 - x - 10}{x^2 + 5x - 14}$

32. $\lim_{x \to 3} \dfrac{x^2 - 2x - 3}{x^2 + 2x - 15}$

33. $\lim_{h \to 0} \dfrac{(2 + h)^2 - 2^2}{h}$

34. $\lim_{x \to 0} \dfrac{(x + 2)^2 - 4}{x}$

35. Find $\lim_{h \to 0} \dfrac{(x + h)^2 - x^2}{h}$ by treating x as a constant.

36. Find $\lim_{h \to 0} \dfrac{3(x + h)^2 + 7(x + h) - 3x^2 - 7x}{h}$ by treating x as a constant.

In Problems 37–42, find $\lim_{h \to 0} \dfrac{f(x + h) - f(x)}{h}$.

37. $f(x) = 5 + 2x$

38. $f(x) = 2x + 3$

39. $f(x) = x^2 - 3$

40. $f(x) = x^2 + x + 1$

41. $f(x) = x^3 - 4x^2$

42. $f(x) = 2 - 5x + x^2$

43. Find $\lim_{x \to 6} \dfrac{\sqrt{x - 2} - 2}{x - 6}$ (*Hint:* First rationalize the numerator by multiplying both the numerator and denominator by $\sqrt{x - 2} + 2$.)

44. Find the constant c so that $\lim_{x \to 3} \dfrac{x^2 + x + c}{x^2 - 5x + 6}$ exists. For that value of c, determine the limit. (*Hint:* Find the value of c for which $x - 3$ is a factor of the numerator.)

45. Power Plant   The maximum theoretical efficiency of a power plant is given by

$$E = \frac{T_h - T_c}{T_h}$$

where T_h and T_c are the absolute temperatures of the hotter and colder reservoirs, respectively. Find (a) $\lim_{T_c \to 0} E$ and (b) $\lim_{T_c \to T_h} E$.

46. Satellite   When a 3200-lb satellite revolves about the earth in a circular orbit of radius r ft, the total mechanical energy E of the earth–satellite system is given by

$$E = -\frac{7.0 \times 10^{17}}{r} \text{ ft-lb}$$

Find the limit of E as $r \to 7.5 \times 10^7$ ft.

In Problems 47–50, use a graphing calculator to graph the functions, and then estimate the limits. Round your answers to two decimal places.

47. $\lim_{x \to 3} \dfrac{x^4 - 2x^3 + 2x^2 - 2x - 3}{x^2 - 9}$

48. $\lim_{x \to 0} x^x$

49. $\lim_{x \to 9} \dfrac{x - 10\sqrt{x} + 21}{3 - \sqrt{x}}$

50. $\lim_{x \to 1} \dfrac{x^3 + x^2 - 5x + 3}{x^3 + 2x^2 - 7x + 4}$

51. Water Purification   The cost of purifying water is given by

$$C = \frac{50{,}000}{p} - 6500,$$ where p is the percent of impurities

remaining after purification. Graph this function on your graphing calculator, and determine $\lim_{p \to 0} C$. Discuss what this means.

52. Profit Function   The profit function for a certain business is given by $P(x) = 225x - 3.2x^2 - 700$. Graph this function on your graphing calculator, and use the evaluation function to determine $\lim_{x \to 40.2} P(x)$, using the rule about the limit of a polynomial function.

Objective

To study one-sided limits, infinite limits, and limits at infinity.

10.2 Limits (Continued)

One-Sided Limits

Figure 10.14 shows the graph of a function f. Notice that $f(x)$ is not defined when $x = 0$. As x approaches 0 *from the right*, $f(x)$ approaches 1. We write this as

$$\lim_{x \to 0^+} f(x) = 1$$

On the other hand, as x approaches 0 *from the left*, $f(x)$ approaches -1, and we write

$$\lim_{x \to 0^-} f(x) = -1$$

Limits like these are called **one-sided limits.** From the preceding section, we know that the limit of a function as $x \to a$ is independent of the way x approaches a. Thus, the limit will exist if and only if both one-sided limits exist and are equal. We therefore conclude that

$$\lim_{x \to 0} f(x) \text{ does not exist}$$

As another example of a one-sided limit, consider $f(x) = \sqrt{x - 3}$ as x approaches 3. Since f is defined only when $x \geq 3$, we can speak of the limit of $f(x)$ as x approaches 3 from the right. If x is slightly greater than 3, then $x - 3$ is a positive number that is close to 0, so $\sqrt{x - 3}$ is close to 0. We conclude that

$$\lim_{x \to 3^+} \sqrt{x - 3} = 0$$

This limit is also evident from Figure 10.15.

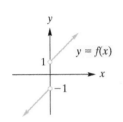

FIGURE 10.14 $\lim_{x \to 0} f(x)$ does not exist.

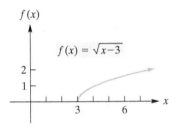

FIGURE 10.15 $\lim_{x \to 3^+} \sqrt{x - 3} = 0$.

Infinite Limits

In the previous section, we considered limits of the form $0/0$—that is, limits where both the numerator and denominator approach 0. Now we will examine limits where the denominator approaches 0, but the numerator approaches a number different from 0. For example, consider

$$\lim_{x \to 0} \frac{1}{x^2}$$

Here, as x approaches 0, the denominator approaches 0 and the numerator approaches 1. Let us investigate the behavior of $f(x) = 1/x^2$ when x is close to 0. The number x^2 is positive and also close to 0. Thus, dividing 1 by such a number results in a very large number. In fact, the closer x is to 0, the larger the value of $f(x)$. For example, see the table of values in Figure 10.16, which also shows the graph of f. Clearly, as $x \to 0$ both from the left and from the right, $f(x)$ increases without bound. Hence, no limit exists at 0. We say that as $x \to 0, f(x)$ becomes positively infinite, and symbolically we express this "infinite limit" by writing

$$\lim_{x \to 0} \frac{1}{x^2} = +\infty = \infty$$

If $\lim_{x \to a} f(x)$ does not exist, it may be for a reason other than that the values $f(x)$ become arbitrarily large as x gets close to a. For example, look again at the situation in Example 2(a) of Section 10.1. Here we have

$$\lim_{x \to -2} f(x) \text{ does not exist but } \lim_{x \to -2} f(x) \neq \infty$$

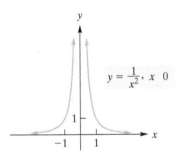

x	$f(x)$
± 1	1
± 0.5	4
± 0.1	100
± 0.01	10,000
± 0.001	1,000,000

FIGURE 10.16 $\lim_{x \to 0} \frac{1}{x^2} = \infty$.

CAUTION!

The use of the "equality" sign in this situation does not mean that the limit exists. On the contrary, it is a way of saying specifically that there is no limit and *why* there is no limit.

Consider now the graph of $y = f(x) = 1/x$ for $x \neq 0$. (See Figure 10.17.) As x approaches 0 from the right, $1/x$ becomes positively infinite; as x approaches 0 from the left, $1/x$ becomes negatively infinite. Symbolically, these infinite limits are written

$$\lim_{x \to 0^+} \frac{1}{x} = \infty \quad \text{and} \quad \lim_{x \to 0^-} \frac{1}{x} = -\infty$$

x	$f(x)$
0.01	100
0.001	1000
0.0001	10,000
−0.01	−100
−0.001	−1000
−0.0001	−10,000

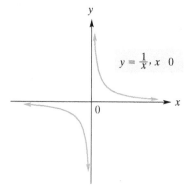

FIGURE 10.17 $\lim_{x \to 0} \dfrac{1}{x}$ does not exist.

Either one of these facts implies that

$$\lim_{x \to 0} \frac{1}{x} \text{ does not exist}$$

EXAMPLE 1   Infinite Limits

Find the limit (if it exists).

a. $\lim\limits_{x \to -1^+} \dfrac{2}{x + 1}$

FIGURE 10.18 $x \to -1^+$.

Solution: As x approaches -1 from the right (think of values of x such as $-0.9, -0.99,$ and so on, as shown in Figure 10.18), $x + 1$ approaches 0 but is always positive. Since we are dividing 2 by positive numbers approaching 0, the results, $2/(x + 1)$, are positive numbers that are becoming arbitrarily large. Thus,

$$\lim_{x \to -1^+} \frac{2}{x + 1} = \infty$$

and the limit does not exist. By a similar analysis, we can show that

$$\lim_{x \to -1^-} \frac{2}{x + 1} = -\infty$$

b. $\lim\limits_{x \to 2} \dfrac{x + 2}{x^2 - 4}$

Solution: As $x \to 2$, the numerator approaches 4 and the denominator approaches 0. Hence, we are dividing numbers near 4 by numbers near 0. The results are numbers that become arbitrarily large in magnitude. At this stage, we can write

$$\lim_{x \to 2} \frac{x + 2}{x^2 - 4} \text{ does not exist}$$

However, let us see if we can use the symbol ∞ or $-\infty$ to be more specific about "does not exist." Notice that

$$\lim_{x \to 2} \frac{x + 2}{x^2 - 4} = \lim_{x \to 2} \frac{x + 2}{(x + 2)(x - 2)} = \lim_{x \to 2} \frac{1}{x - 2}$$

Since

$$\lim_{x \to 2^+} \frac{1}{x - 2} = \infty \quad \text{and} \quad \lim_{x \to 2^-} \frac{1}{x - 2} = -\infty$$

$\lim\limits_{x \to 2} \dfrac{x + 2}{x^2 - 4}$ is neither ∞ nor $-\infty$.

Now Work Problem 31 ◁

Example 1 considered limits of the form $k/0$, where $k \neq 0$. It is important to distinguish the form $k/0$ from the form $0/0$, which was discussed in Section 10.1. These two forms are handled quite differently.

EXAMPLE 2   Finding a Limit

Find $\lim\limits_{t \to 2} \dfrac{t-2}{t^2-4}$.

Solution: As $t \to 2$, *both* numerator and denominator approach 0 (form $0/0$). Thus, we first simplify the fraction, for $t \neq 2$, as we did in Section 10.1, and then take the limit:

$$\lim_{t \to 2} \frac{t-2}{t^2-4} = \lim_{t \to 2} \frac{t-2}{(t+2)(t-2)} = \lim_{t \to 2} \frac{1}{t+2} = \frac{1}{4}$$

Now Work Problem 37 ◁

Limits at Infinity

Now let us examine the function

$$f(x) = \frac{1}{x}$$

We can obtain

$$\lim_{x \to \infty} \frac{1}{x} \quad \text{and} \quad \lim_{x \to -\infty} \frac{1}{x}$$

without the benefit of a graph or a table. Dividing 1 by a large positive number results in a small positive number, and as the divisors get arbitrarily large, the quotients get arbitrarily small. A similar argument can be made for the limit as $x \to -\infty$.

as x becomes infinite, first in a positive sense and then in a negative sense. From Table 10.2, we can see that as x increases without bound through positive values, the values of $f(x)$ approach 0. Likewise, as x decreases without bound through negative values, the values of $f(x)$ also approach 0. These observations are also apparent from the graph in Figure 10.17. There, moving to the right along the curve through positive x-values, the corresponding y-values approach 0 through positive values. Similarly, moving to the left along the curve through negative x-values, the corresponding y-values approach 0 through negative values. Symbolically, we write

$$\lim_{x \to \infty} \frac{1}{x} = 0 \quad \text{and} \quad \lim_{x \to -\infty} \frac{1}{x} = 0$$

Both of these limits are called *limits at infinity*.

Table 10.2 Behavior of $f(x)$ as $x \to \pm\infty$			
x	$f(x)$	x	$f(x)$
1000	0.001	−1000	−0.001
10,000	0.0001	−10,000	−0.0001
100,000	0.00001	−100,000	−0.00001
1,000,000	0.000001	−1,000,000	−0.000001

APPLY IT ▶

6. The demand function for a certain product is given by $p(x) = \dfrac{10,000}{(x+1)^2}$, where p is the price in dollars and x is the quantity sold. Graph this function on your graphing calculator in the window $[0, 10] \times [0, 10,000]$. Use the TRACE function to find $\lim_{x \to \infty} p(x)$. Determine what is happening to the graph and what this means about the demand function.

EXAMPLE 3   Limits at Infinity

Find the limit (if it exists).

a. $\lim\limits_{x \to \infty} \dfrac{4}{(x-5)^3}$

Solution: As x becomes very large, so does $x - 5$. Since the cube of a large number is also large, $(x-5)^3 \to \infty$. Dividing 4 by very large numbers results in numbers near 0. Thus,

$$\lim_{x \to \infty} \frac{4}{(x-5)^3} = 0$$

b. $\lim\limits_{x \to -\infty} \sqrt{4-x}$

Solution: As x gets negatively infinite, $4 - x$ becomes positively infinite. Because square roots of large numbers are large numbers, we conclude that

$$\lim_{x \to -\infty} \sqrt{4-x} = \infty$$

◁

In our next discussion we will need a certain limit, namely, $\lim_{x \to \infty} 1/x^p$, where $p > 0$. As x becomes very large, so does x^p. Dividing 1 by very large numbers results in numbers near 0. Thus, $\lim_{x \to \infty} 1/x^p = 0$. In general,

$$\lim_{x \to \infty} \frac{1}{x^p} = 0 \quad \text{and} \quad \lim_{x \to -\infty} \frac{1}{x^p} = 0$$

for $p > 0$.[2] For example,

$$\lim_{x \to \infty} \frac{1}{\sqrt[3]{x}} = \lim_{x \to \infty} \frac{1}{x^{1/3}} = 0$$

Let us now find the limit of the rational function

$$f(x) = \frac{4x^2 + 5}{2x^2 + 1}$$

as $x \to \infty$. (Recall from Section 2.2 that a rational function is a quotient of polynomials.) As x gets larger and larger, *both* the numerator and denominator of any rational function become infinite in absolute value. However, the form of the quotient can be changed, so that we can draw a conclusion as to whether or not it has a limit. To do this, we divide both the numerator and denominator by the greatest power of x that occurs in the denominator. Here it is x^2. This gives

$$\lim_{x \to \infty} \frac{4x^2 + 5}{2x^2 + 1} = \lim_{x \to \infty} \frac{\dfrac{4x^2 + 5}{x^2}}{\dfrac{2x^2 + 1}{x^2}} = \lim_{x \to \infty} \frac{\dfrac{4x^2}{x^2} + \dfrac{5}{x^2}}{\dfrac{2x^2}{x^2} + \dfrac{1}{x^2}}$$

$$= \lim_{x \to \infty} \frac{4 + \dfrac{5}{x^2}}{2 + \dfrac{1}{x^2}} = \frac{\lim_{x \to \infty} 4 + 5 \cdot \lim_{x \to \infty} \dfrac{1}{x^2}}{\lim_{x \to \infty} 2 + \lim_{x \to \infty} \dfrac{1}{x^2}}$$

Since $\lim_{x \to \infty} 1/x^p = 0$ for $p > 0$,

$$\lim_{x \to \infty} \frac{4x^2 + 5}{2x^2 + 1} = \frac{4 + 5(0)}{2 + 0} = \frac{4}{2} = 2$$

Similarly, the limit as $x \to -\infty$ is 2. These limits are clear from the graph of f in Figure 10.19.

For the preceding function, there is an easier way to find $\lim_{x \to \infty} f(x)$. For *large* values of x, in the numerator the term involving the greatest power of x, namely, $4x^2$, dominates the sum $4x^2 + 5$, and the dominant term in the denominator, $2x^2 + 1$, is $2x^2$. Thus, as $x \to \infty, f(x)$ can be approximated by $(4x^2)/(2x^2)$. As a result, to determine the limit of $f(x)$, it suffices to determine the limit of $(4x^2)/(2x^2)$. That is,

$$\lim_{x \to \infty} \frac{4x^2 + 5}{2x^2 + 1} = \lim_{x \to \infty} \frac{4x^2}{2x^2} = \lim_{x \to \infty} 2 = 2$$

as we saw before. In general, we have the following rule:

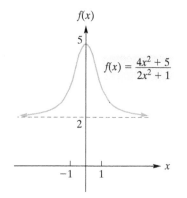

FIGURE 10.19 $\lim_{x \to \infty} f(x) = 2$ and $\lim_{x \to -\infty} f(x) = 2$.

Limits at Infinity for Rational Functions

If $f(x)$ is a *rational function* and $a_n x^n$ and $b_m x^m$ are the terms in the numerator and denominator, respectively, with the greatest powers of x, then

$$\lim_{x \to \infty} f(x) = \lim_{x \to \infty} \frac{a_n x^n}{b_m x^m}$$

and

$$\lim_{x \to -\infty} f(x) = \lim_{x \to -\infty} \frac{a_n x^n}{b_m x^m}$$

---

[2] For $\lim_{x \to -\infty} 1/x^p$, we assume that p is such that $1/x^p$ is defined for $x < 0$.

Let us apply this rule to the situation where the degree of the numerator is greater than the degree of the denominator. For example,

$$\lim_{x \to -\infty} \frac{x^4 - 3x}{5 - 2x} = \lim_{x \to -\infty} \frac{x^4}{-2x} = \lim_{x \to -\infty} \left(-\frac{1}{2} x^3 \right) = \infty$$

(Note that in the next-to-last step, as x becomes very negative, so does x^3; moreover, $-\frac{1}{2}$ times a very negative number is very positive.) Similarly,

$$\lim_{x \to \infty} \frac{x^4 - 3x}{5 - 2x} = \lim_{x \to \infty} \left(-\frac{1}{2} x^3 \right) = -\infty$$

From this illustration, we make the following conclusion:

> If the degree of the numerator of a *rational function* is greater than the degree of the denominator, then the function has no limit as $x \to \infty$ and no limit as $x \to -\infty$.

APPLY IT ▶

7. The yearly amount of sales y of a certain company (in thousands of dollars) is related to the amount the company spends on advertising, x (in thousands of dollars), according to the equation $y(x) = \dfrac{500x}{x + 20}$. Graph this function on your graphing calculator in the window $[0, 1000] \times [0, 550]$. Use TRACE to explore $\lim_{x \to \infty} y(x)$, and determine what this means to the company.

EXAMPLE 4   Limits at Infinity for Rational Functions

Find the limit (if it exists).

a. $\lim_{x \to \infty} \dfrac{x^2 - 1}{7 - 2x + 8x^2}$

Solution:
$$\lim_{x \to \infty} \frac{x^2 - 1}{7 - 2x + 8x^2} = \lim_{x \to \infty} \frac{x^2}{8x^2} = \lim_{x \to \infty} \frac{1}{8} = \frac{1}{8}$$

b. $\lim_{x \to -\infty} \dfrac{x}{(3x - 1)^2}$

Solution:
$$\lim_{x \to -\infty} \frac{x}{(3x - 1)^2} = \lim_{x \to -\infty} \frac{x}{9x^2 - 6x + 1} = \lim_{x \to -\infty} \frac{x}{9x^2}$$
$$= \lim_{x \to -\infty} \frac{1}{9x} = \frac{1}{9} \cdot \lim_{x \to -\infty} \frac{1}{x} = \frac{1}{9}(0) = 0$$

c. $\lim_{x \to \infty} \dfrac{x^5 - x^4}{x^4 - x^3 + 2}$

Solution: Since the degree of the numerator is greater than that of the denominator, there is no limit. More precisely,

$$\lim_{x \to \infty} \frac{x^5 - x^4}{x^4 - x^3 + 2} = \lim_{x \to \infty} \frac{x^5}{x^4} = \lim_{x \to \infty} x = \infty$$

Now Work Problem 21 ◁

CAUTION!⚠

The preceding technique applies only to limits of rational functions at *infinity*.

To find $\lim_{x \to 0} \dfrac{x^2 - 1}{7 - 2x + 8x^2}$, we cannot simply determine the limit of $\dfrac{x^2}{8x^2}$. That simplification applies only in case $x \to \infty$ or $x \to -\infty$. Instead, we have

$$\lim_{x \to 0} \frac{x^2 - 1}{7 - 2x + 8x^2} = \frac{\lim_{x \to 0} x^2 - 1}{\lim_{x \to 0} 7 - 2x + 8x^2} = \frac{0 - 1}{7 - 0 + 0} = -\frac{1}{7}$$

Let us now consider the limit of the polynomial function $f(x) = 8x^2 - 2x$ as $x \to \infty$:

$$\lim_{x \to \infty} (8x^2 - 2x)$$

Because a polynomial is a rational function with denominator 1, we have

$$\lim_{x \to \infty} (8x^2 - 2x) = \lim_{x \to \infty} \frac{8x^2 - 2x}{1} = \lim_{x \to \infty} \frac{8x^2}{1} = \lim_{x \to \infty} 8x^2$$

That is, the limit of $8x^2 - 2x$ as $x \to \infty$ is the same as the limit of the term involving the greatest power of x, namely, $8x^2$. As x becomes very large, so does $8x^2$. Thus,

$$\lim_{x \to \infty} (8x^2 - 2x) = \lim_{x \to \infty} 8x^2 = \infty$$

In general, we have the following:

As $x \to \infty$ (or $x \to -\infty$), the limit of a *polynomial function* is the same as the limit of its term that involves the greatest power of x.

APPLY IT ▶

8. The cost C of producing x units of a certain product is given by $C(x) = 50{,}000 + 200x + 0.3x^2$. Use your graphing calculator to explore $\lim_{x \to \infty} C(x)$ and determine what this means.

EXAMPLE 5 Limits at Infinity for Polynomial Functions

a. $\lim_{x \to -\infty} (x^3 - x^2 + x - 2) = \lim_{x \to -\infty} x^3$. As x becomes very negative, so does x^3. Thus,

$$\lim_{x \to -\infty} (x^3 - x^2 + x - 2) = \lim_{x \to -\infty} x^3 = -\infty$$

b. $\lim_{x \to -\infty} (-2x^3 + 9x) = \lim_{x \to -\infty} -2x^3 = \infty$, because -2 times a very negative number is very positive.

Now Work Problem 9 ◁

The technique of focusing on dominant terms to find limits as $x \to \infty$ or $x \to -\infty$ is valid for *rational functions,* but it is not necessarily valid for other types of functions. For example, consider

Do not use dominant terms when a function is not rational.

$$\lim_{x \to \infty} \left(\sqrt{x^2 + x} - x \right) \qquad (1)$$

Notice that $\sqrt{x^2 + x} - x$ is not a rational function. It is *incorrect* to infer that because x^2 dominates in $x^2 + x$, the limit in (1) is the same as

$$\lim_{x \to \infty} \left(\sqrt{x^2} - x \right) = \lim_{x \to \infty} (x - x) = \lim_{x \to \infty} 0 = 0$$

It can be shown (see Problem 62) that the limit in (1) is not 0, but is $\frac{1}{2}$.

The ideas discussed in this section will now be applied to a case-defined function.

EXAMPLE 6 Limits for a Case-Defined Function

APPLY IT ▶

9. A plumber charges \$100 for the first hour of work at your house and \$75 for every hour (or fraction thereof) afterward. The function for what an x-hour visit will cost you is

$$f(x) = \begin{cases} \$100 & \text{if } 0 < x \leq 1 \\ \$175 & \text{if } 1 < x \leq 2 \\ \$250 & \text{if } 2 < x \leq 3 \\ \$325 & \text{if } 3 < x \leq 4 \end{cases}$$

Find $\lim_{x \to 1} f(x)$ and $\lim_{x \to 2.5} f(x)$.

If $f(x) = \begin{cases} x^2 + 1 & \text{if } x \geq 1 \\ 3 & \text{if } x < 1 \end{cases}$, find the limit (if it exists).

a. $\lim_{x \to 1^+} f(x)$

Solution: Here x gets close to 1 from the right. For $x > 1$, we have $f(x) = x^2 + 1$. Thus,

$$\lim_{x \to 1^+} f(x) = \lim_{x \to 1^+} (x^2 + 1)$$

If x is greater than 1, but close to 1, then $x^2 + 1$ is close to 2. Therefore,

$$\lim_{x \to 1^+} f(x) = \lim_{x \to 1^+} (x^2 + 1) = 2$$

b. $\lim_{x \to 1^-} f(x)$

Solution: Here x gets close to 1 from the left. For $x < 1, f(x) = 3$. Hence,

$$\lim_{x \to 1^-} f(x) = \lim_{x \to 1^-} 3 = 3$$

c. $\lim_{x \to 1} f(x)$

Solution: We want the limit as x approaches 1. However, the rule of the function depends on whether $x \geq 1$ or $x < 1$. Thus, we must consider one-sided limits. The limit as x approaches 1 will exist if and only if both one-sided limits exist and are the same. From parts (a) and (b),

$$\lim_{x \to 1^+} f(x) \neq \lim_{x \to 1^-} f(x) \qquad \text{since } 2 \neq 3$$

Therefore,

$$\lim_{x \to 1} f(x) \qquad \text{does not exist}$$

d. $\lim_{x\to\infty} f(x)$

Solution: For very large values of x, we have $x \geq 1$, so $f(x) = x^2 + 1$. Thus,

$$\lim_{x\to\infty} f(x) = \lim_{x\to\infty} (x^2 + 1) = \lim_{x\to\infty} x^2 = \infty$$

e. $\lim_{x\to-\infty} f(x)$

Solution: For very negative values of x, we have $x < 1$, so $f(x) = 3$. Hence,

$$\lim_{x\to-\infty} f(x) = \lim_{x\to-\infty} 3 = 3$$

All the limits in parts (a) through (c) should be obvious from the graph of f in Figure 10.20.

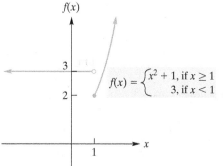

$$f(x) = \begin{cases} x^2 + 1, & \text{if } x \geq 1 \\ 3, & \text{if } x < 1 \end{cases}$$

FIGURE 10.20 Graph of case-defined function.

Now Work Problem 57 ◁

PROBLEMS 10.2

1. For the function f given in Figure 10.21, find the following limits. If the limit does not exist, so state that, or use the symbol ∞ or $-\infty$ where appropriate.

FIGURE 10.21

(a) $\lim_{x\to-\infty} f(x)$ **(b)** $\lim_{x\to-1^-} f(x)$ **(c)** $\lim_{x\to-1^+} f(x)$
(d) $\lim_{x\to-1} f(x)$ **(e)** $\lim_{x\to0^-} f(x)$ **(f)** $\lim_{x\to0^+} f(x)$
(g) $\lim_{x\to0} f(x)$ **(h)** $\lim_{x\to1^-} f(x)$ **(i)** $\lim_{x\to1^+} f(x)$
(j) $\lim_{x\to1} f(x)$ **(k)** $\lim_{x\to\infty} f(x)$

2. For the function f given in Figure 10.22, find the following limits. If the limit does not exist, so state that, or use the symbol ∞ or $-\infty$ where appropriate.

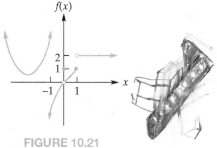

FIGURE 10.22

(a) $\lim_{x\to0^-} f(x)$ **(b)** $\lim_{x\to0^+} f(x)$ **(c)** $\lim_{x\to0} f(x)$
(d) $\lim_{x\to-\infty} f(x)$ **(e)** $\lim_{x\to1} f(x)$ **(f)** $\lim_{x\to\infty} f(x)$
(g) $\lim_{x\to2^+} f(x)$

In each of Problems 3–54, find the limit. If the limit does not exist, so state, or use the symbol ∞ or $-\infty$ where appropriate.

3. $\lim_{x\to3^+} (x-2)$ **4.** $\lim_{x\to-1^+} (1-x^2)$ **5.** $\lim_{x\to-\infty} 5x$

6. $\lim_{x\to-\infty} -6$ **7.** $\lim_{x\to0^-} \frac{6x}{x^4}$ **8.** $\lim_{x\to2} \frac{7}{x-1}$

9. $\lim_{x\to-\infty} x^2$ **10.** $\lim_{t\to\infty} (t-1)^3$ **11.** $\lim_{h\to1^+} \sqrt{h-1}$

12. $\lim_{h\to5^-} \sqrt{5-h}$ **13.** $\lim_{x\to-2^-} \frac{-3}{x+2}$ **14.** $\lim_{x\to0^-} 2^{1/2}$

15. $\lim_{x\to1^+} (4\sqrt{x-1})$ **16.** $\lim_{x\to2^-} (x\sqrt{4-x^2})$ **17.** $\lim_{x\to\infty} \sqrt{x+10}$

18. $\lim_{x\to-\infty} -\sqrt{1-10x}$ **19.** $\lim_{x\to\infty} \frac{3}{\sqrt{x}}$

20. $\lim_{x\to\infty} \frac{-6}{5x\sqrt[3]{x}}$ **21.** $\lim_{x\to\infty} \frac{x-5}{2x+1}$ **22.** $\lim_{x\to\infty} \frac{2x-4}{3-2x}$

23. $\lim_{x\to-\infty} \frac{x^2-1}{x^3+4x-3}$ **24.** $\lim_{r\to\infty} \frac{r^3}{r^2+1}$

25. $\lim_{t\to\infty} \frac{3t^3+2t^2+9t-1}{5t^2-5}$ **26.** $\lim_{x\to\infty} \frac{4x^2}{3x^3-x^2+2}$

27. $\lim_{x\to\infty} \frac{7}{2x+1}$ **28.** $\lim_{x\to-\infty} \frac{2}{(4x-1)^3}$

29. $\lim_{x\to\infty} \frac{3-4x-2x^3}{5x^3-8x+1}$ **30.** $\lim_{x\to-\infty} \frac{3-2x-2x^3}{7-5x^3+2x^2}$

31. $\lim\limits_{x \to 3^+} \dfrac{x + 3}{x^2 - 9}$ **32.** $\lim\limits_{x \to -3^-} \dfrac{3x}{9 - x^2}$ **33.** $\lim\limits_{w \to \infty} \dfrac{2w^2 - 3w + 4}{5w^2 + 7w - 1}$

34. $\lim\limits_{x \to \infty} \dfrac{4 - 3x^3}{x^3 - 1}$ **35.** $\lim\limits_{x \to \infty} \dfrac{6 - 4x^2 + x^3}{4 + 5x - 7x^2}$

36. $\lim\limits_{x \to -\infty} \dfrac{2x - x^2}{x^2 + 19x - 64}$ **37.** $\lim\limits_{x \to -3^-} \dfrac{5x^2 + 14x - 3}{x^2 + 3x}$

38. $\lim\limits_{t \to 3} \dfrac{t^2 - 4t + 3}{t^2 - 2t - 3}$ **39.** $\lim\limits_{x \to 1} \dfrac{x^2 - 3x + 1}{x^2 + 1}$

40. $\lim\limits_{x \to -1} \dfrac{3x^3 - x^2}{2x + 1}$ **41.** $\lim\limits_{x \to 2^-} \left(2 - \dfrac{1}{x - 2} \right)$

42. $\lim\limits_{x \to -\infty} -\dfrac{x^5 + 2x^3 - 1}{x^5 - 4x^2}$ **43.** $\lim\limits_{x \to -7^-} \dfrac{x^2 + 1}{\sqrt{x^2 - 49}}$

44. $\lim\limits_{x \to -2^+} \dfrac{x}{\sqrt{16 - x^4}}$ **45.** $\lim\limits_{x \to 0^+} \dfrac{5}{x + x^2}$

46. $\lim\limits_{x \to -\infty} \left(x^2 + \dfrac{1}{x} \right)$ **47.** $\lim\limits_{x \to 1} x(x - 1)^{-1}$ **48.** $\lim\limits_{x \to 1/2} \dfrac{1}{2x - 1}$

49. $\lim\limits_{x \to 1^+} \left(\dfrac{-5}{1 - x} \right)$ **50.** $\lim\limits_{x \to 3} \left(-\dfrac{7}{x - 3} \right)$ **51.** $\lim\limits_{x \to 1} |x - 1|$

52. $\lim\limits_{x \to 0} \left| \dfrac{1}{x} \right|$ **53.** $\lim\limits_{x \to -\infty} \dfrac{x + 1}{x}$

54. $\lim\limits_{x \to \infty} \left(\dfrac{3}{x} - \dfrac{2x^2}{x^2 + 1} \right)$

In Problems 55–58, find the indicated limits. If the limit does not exist, so state, or use the symbol ∞ or $-\infty$ where appropriate.

55. $f(x) = \begin{cases} 2 & \text{if } x \le 2 \\ 1 & \text{if } x > 2 \end{cases}$

(a) $\lim\limits_{x \to 2^+} f(x)$ **(b)** $\lim\limits_{x \to 2^-} f(x)$ **(c)** $\lim\limits_{x \to 2} f(x)$

(d) $\lim\limits_{x \to \infty} f(x)$ **(e)** $\lim\limits_{x \to -\infty} f(x)$

56. $f(x) = \begin{cases} 2 - x & \text{if } x \le 3 \\ -1 + 3x - x^2 & \text{if } x > 3 \end{cases}$

(a) $\lim\limits_{x \to 3^+} f(x)$ **(b)** $\lim\limits_{x \to 3^-} f(x)$ **(c)** $\lim\limits_{x \to 3} f(x)$

(d) $\lim\limits_{x \to \infty} f(x)$ **(e)** $\lim\limits_{x \to -\infty} f(x)$

57. $g(x) = \begin{cases} x & \text{if } x < 0 \\ -x & \text{if } x > 0 \end{cases}$

(a) $\lim\limits_{x \to 0^+} g(x)$ **(b)** $\lim\limits_{x \to 0^-} g(x)$ **(c)** $\lim\limits_{x \to 0} g(x)$

(d) $\lim\limits_{x \to \infty} g(x)$ **(e)** $\lim\limits_{x \to -\infty} g(x)$

58. $g(x) = \begin{cases} x^2 & \text{if } x < 0 \\ -x & \text{if } x > 0 \end{cases}$

(a) $\lim\limits_{x \to 0^+} g(x)$ **(b)** $\lim\limits_{x \to 0^-} g(x)$ **(c)** $\lim\limits_{x \to 0} g(x)$

(d) $\lim\limits_{x \to \infty} g(x)$ **(e)** $\lim\limits_{x \to -\infty} g(x)$

59. Average Cost If c is the total cost in dollars to produce q units of a product, then the average cost per unit for an output of q units is given by $\bar{c} = c/q$. Thus, if the total cost equation is $c = 5000 + 6q$, then

$$\bar{c} = \dfrac{5000}{q} + 6$$

For example, the total cost of an output of 5 units is $5030, and the average cost per unit at this level of production is $1006. By finding $\lim\limits_{q \to \infty} \bar{c}$, show that the average cost approaches a level of stability if the producer continually increases output. What is the limiting value of the average cost? Sketch the graph of the average-cost function.

60. Average Cost Repeat Problem 59, given that the fixed cost is $12,000 and the variable cost is given by the function $c_v = 7q$.

61. Population The population of a certain small city t years from now is predicted to be

$$N = 40,000 - \dfrac{5000}{t + 3}$$

Find the population in the long run; that is, find $\lim\limits_{t \to \infty} N$.

62. Show that

$$\lim\limits_{x \to \infty} \left(\sqrt{x^2 + x} - x \right) = \dfrac{1}{2}$$

(*Hint:* Rationalize the numerator by multiplying the expression $\sqrt{x^2 + x} - x$ by

$$\dfrac{\sqrt{x^2 + x} + x}{\sqrt{x^2 + x} + x}$$

Then express the denominator in a form such that x is a factor.)

63. Host–Parasite Relationship For a particular host–parasite relationship, it was determined that when the host density (number of hosts per unit of area) is x, the number of hosts parasitized over a period of time is

$$y = \dfrac{900x}{10 + 45x}$$

If the host density were to increase without bound, what value would y approach?

64. If $f(x) = \begin{cases} \sqrt{2 - x} & \text{if } x < 2 \\ x^3 + k(x + 1) & \text{if } x \ge 2 \end{cases}$, determine the value of the constant k for which $\lim\limits_{x \to 2} f(x)$ exists.

In Problems 65 and 66, use a calculator to evaluate the given function when $x = 1, 0.5, 0.2, 0.1, 0.01, 0.001,$ and 0.0001. From your results, speculate about $\lim\limits_{x \to 0^+} f(x)$.

65. $f(x) = x^{2x}$ **66.** $f(x) = e^{1/x}$

67. Graph $f(x) = \sqrt{4x^2 - 1}$. Use the graph to estimate $\lim\limits_{x \to 1/2^+} f(x)$.

68. Graph $f(x) = \dfrac{\sqrt{x^2 - 9}}{x + 3}$. Use the graph to estimate $\lim\limits_{x \to -3^-} f(x)$ if it exists. Use the symbol ∞ or $-\infty$ if appropriate.

69. Graph $f(x) = \begin{cases} 2x^2 + 3 & \text{if } x < 2 \\ 2x + 5 & \text{if } x \ge 2 \end{cases}$. Use the graph to estimate each of the following limits if it exists:

(a) $\lim\limits_{x \to 2^-} f(x)$ **(b)** $\lim\limits_{x \to 2^+} f(x)$ **(c)** $\lim\limits_{x \to 2} f(x)$

Objective

10.3 Continuity

To study continuity and to find points of discontinuity for a function.

Many functions have the property that there is no "break" in their graphs. For example, compare the functions

$$f(x) = x \quad \text{and} \quad g(x) = \begin{cases} x & \text{if } x \ne 1 \\ 2 & \text{if } x = 1 \end{cases}$$

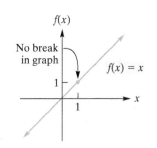

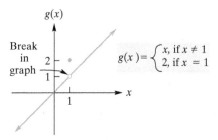

FIGURE 10.23 Continuous at 1.

FIGURE 10.24 Discontinuous at 1.

$$g(x)=\begin{cases} x, & \text{if } x \neq 1 \\ 2, & \text{if } x = 1 \end{cases}$$

whose graphs appear in Figures 10.23 and 10.24, respectively. The graph of f is unbroken, but the graph of g has a break at $x = 1$. Stated another way, if you were to trace both graphs with a pencil, you would have to lift the pencil off the graph of g when $x = 1$, but you would not have to lift it off the graph of f. These situations can be expressed by limits. As x approaches 1, compare the limit of each function with the value of the function at $x = 1$:

$$\lim_{x \to 1} f(x) = 1 = f(1)$$

whereas

$$\lim_{x \to 1} g(x) = 1 \neq 2 = g(1)$$

In Section 10.1 we stressed that given a function f and a number a, there are two important ways to associate a number to the pair (f, a). One is simple evaluation, $f(a)$, which *exists* precisely if a is in the domain of f. The other is $\lim_{x \to a} f(x)$, whose existence and determination can be more challenging. For the functions f and g above, the limit of f as $x \to 1$ is the same as $f(1)$, but the limit of g as $x \to 1$ is *not* the same as $g(1)$. For these reasons, we say that f is *continuous* at 1 and g is *discontinuous* at 1.

Definition

A function f is **continuous** at a if and only if the following three conditions are met:

1. $f(a)$ exists
2. $\lim_{x \to a} f(x)$ exists
3. $\lim_{x \to a} f(x) = f(a)$

If f is not continuous at a, then f is said to be **discontinuous** at a, and a is called a **point of discontinuity** of f.

EXAMPLE 1 Applying the Definition of Continuity

a. Show that $f(x) = 5$ is continuous at 7.

Solution: We must verify that the preceding three conditions are met. First, $f(7) = 5$, so f is defined at $x = 7$. Second,

$$\lim_{x \to 7} f(x) = \lim_{x \to 7} 5 = 5$$

Thus, f has a limit as $x \to 7$. Third,

$$\lim_{x \to 7} f(x) = 5 = f(7)$$

Therefore, f is continuous at 7. (See Figure 10.25.)

b. Show that $g(x) = x^2 - 3$ is continuous at -4.

Solution: The function g is defined at $x = -4 : g(-4) = 13$. Also,

$$\lim_{x \to -4} g(x) = \lim_{x \to -4} (x^2 - 3) = 13 = g(-4)$$

Therefore, g is continuous at -4. (See Figure 10.26.)

Now Work Problem 1 ◁

We say that a function is *continuous on an interval* if it is continuous at each point there. In this situation, the graph of the function is connected over the interval. For example, $f(x) = x^2$ is continuous on the interval $[2, 5]$. In fact, in Example 5 of Section 10.1, we showed that, for *any* polynomial function f, for any number a, $\lim_{x \to a} f(x) = f(a)$. This means that

A polynomial function is continuous at every point.

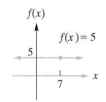

FIGURE 10.25 f is continuous at 7.

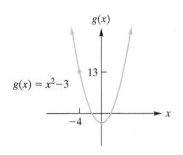

FIGURE 10.26 g is continuous at -4.

It follows that such a function is continuous on every interval. We say that a function is **continuous on its domain** if it is continuous at each point in its domain. If the domain of such a function is the set of all real numbers, we may simply say that the function is continuous.

EXAMPLE 2   Continuity of Polynomial Functions

The functions $f(x) = 7$ and $g(x) = x^2 - 9x + 3$ are polynomial functions. Therefore, they are continuous on their domains. For example, they are continuous at 3.

Now Work Problem 13 ◁

When is a function discontinuous? We can say that a function f defined on an open interval containing a is discontinuous at a if

1. f has no limit as $x \to a$

   or

2. as $x \to a$, f has a limit that is different from $f(a)$

If f is not defined at a, we will say also, in that case, that f is discontinuous at a. In Figure 10.27, we can find points of discontinuity by inspection.

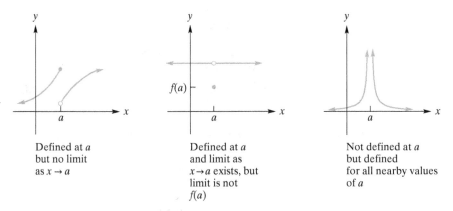

FIGURE 10.27   Discontinuities at a.

EXAMPLE 3   Discontinuities

a. Let $f(x) = 1/x$. (See Figure 10.28.) Note that f is not defined at $x = 0$, but it is defined for all other x nearby. Thus, f is discontinuous at 0. Moreover, $\lim_{x \to 0^+} f(x) = \infty$ and $\lim_{x \to 0^-} f(x) = -\infty$. A function is said to have an **infinite discontinuity** at a when at least one of the one-sided limits is either ∞ or $-\infty$ as $x \to a$. Hence, f has an *infinite discontinuity* at $x = 0$.

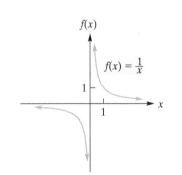

FIGURE 10.28   Infinite discontinuity at 0.

b. Let $f(x) = \begin{cases} 1 & \text{if } x > 0 \\ 0 & \text{if } x = 0 \\ -1 & \text{if } x < 0 \end{cases}$.

(See Figure 10.29.) Although f is defined at $x = 0$, $\lim_{x \to 0} f(x)$ does not exist. Thus, f is discontinuous at 0.

Now Work Problem 29 ◁

The following property indicates where the discontinuities of a rational function occur:

Discontinuities of a Rational Function

A rational function is discontinuous at points where the denominator is 0 and is continuous otherwise. Thus, a rational function is continuous on its domain.

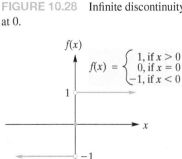

FIGURE 10.29   Discontinuous case-defined function.

The rational function $f(x) = \dfrac{x+1}{x+1}$ is continuous on its domain but it is not defined at -1. It is discontinuous at -1. The graph of f is a horizontal straight line with a "hole" in it at -1.

EXAMPLE 4   **Locating Discontinuities in Rational Functions**

For each of the following functions, find all points of discontinuity.

a. $f(x) = \dfrac{x^2 - 3}{x^2 + 2x - 8}$

Solution: This rational function has denominator

$$x^2 + 2x - 8 = (x + 4)(x - 2)$$

which is 0 when $x = -4$ or $x = 2$. Thus, f is discontinuous only at -4 and 2.

b. $h(x) = \dfrac{x + 4}{x^2 + 4}$

Solution: For this rational function, the denominator is never 0. (It is always positive.) Therefore, h has no discontinuity.

Now Work Problem 19 ◁

EXAMPLE 5   **Locating Discontinuities in Case-Defined Functions**

For each of the following functions, find all points of discontinuity.

a. $f(x) = \begin{cases} x + 6 & \text{if } x \geq 3 \\ x^2 & \text{if } x < 3 \end{cases}$

Solution: The cases defining the function are given by polynomials, which are continuous, so the only possible place for a discontinuity is at $x = 3$, where the separation of cases occurs. We know that $f(3) = 3 + 6 = 9$. So because

$$\lim_{x \to 3^+} f(x) = \lim_{x \to 3^+} (x + 6) = 9$$

and

$$\lim_{x \to 3^-} f(x) = \lim_{x \to 3^-} x^2 = 9$$

we can conclude that $\lim_{x \to 3} f(x) = 9 = f(3)$ and the function has no points of discontinuity. We can reach the same conclusion by inspecting the graph of f in Figure 10.30.

b. $f(x) = \begin{cases} x + 2 & \text{if } x > 2 \\ x^2 & \text{if } x < 2 \end{cases}$

Solution: Since f is not defined at $x = 2$, it is discontinuous at 2. Note, however, that

$$\lim_{x \to 2^-} f(x) = \lim_{x \to 2^-} x^2 = 4 = \lim_{x \to 2^+} x + 2 = \lim_{x \to 2^+} f(x)$$

shows that $\lim_{x \to 2} f(x)$ exists. (See Figure 10.31.)

Now Work Problem 31 ◁

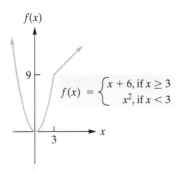

FIGURE 10.30   Continuous case-defined function.

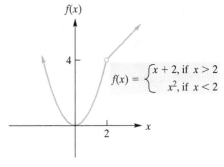

FIGURE 10.31   Discontinuous at 2.

EXAMPLE 6 Post-Office Function

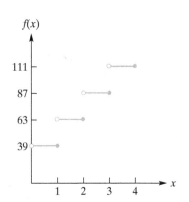

FIGURE 10.32 Post-office function.

The post-office function

$$c = f(x) = \begin{cases} 39 & \text{if } 0 < x \le 1 \\ 63 & \text{if } 1 < x \le 2 \\ 87 & \text{if } 2 < x \le 3 \\ 111 & \text{if } 3 < x \le 4 \end{cases}$$

gives the cost c (in cents) of mailing, first class, an item of weight x (ounces), for $0 < x \le 4$, in July 2006. It is clear from its graph in Figure 10.32 that f has discontinuities at 1, 2, and 3 and is constant for values of x between successive discontinuities. Such a function is called a *step function* because of the appearance of its graph.

Now Work Problem 35 ◁

There is another way to express continuity besides that given in the definition. If we take the statement

$$\lim_{x \to a} f(x) = f(a)$$

and replace x by $a + h$, then as $x \to a$, we have $h \to 0$; and as $h \to 0$ we have $x \to a$. It follows that $\lim_{x \to a} f(x) = \lim_{h \to 0} f(a + h)$, provided the limits exist (Figure 10.33). Thus, the statement

This method of expressing continuity at a is used frequently in mathematical proofs.

$$\lim_{h \to 0} f(a + h) = f(a)$$

assuming both sides exist, also defines continuity at a.

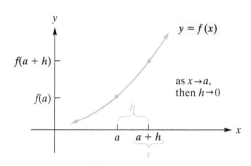

FIGURE 10.33 Diagram for continuity at a.

TECHNOLOGY ▮▮▮▮

By observing the graph of a function, we may be able to determine where a discontinuity occurs. However, we can be fooled. For example, the function

$$f(x) = \frac{x - 1}{x^2 - 1}$$

is discontinuous at ± 1, but the discontinuity at 1 is not obvious from the graph of f in Figure 10.34. On the other hand, the discontinuity at -1 is obvious. Note that f is defined neither at -1 nor at 1.

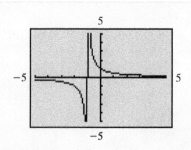

FIGURE 10.34 Discontinuity at 1 is not apparent from graph of $f(x) = \dfrac{x - 1}{x^2 - 1}$.

Often, it is helpful to describe a situation by a continuous function. For example, the demand schedule in Table 10.3 indicates the number of units of a particular product that consumers will demand per week at various prices. This information can be given graphically, as in Figure 10.35(a), by plotting each quantity–price pair as a point.

Table 10.3 Demand Schedule	
Price/Unit, p	Quantity/Week, q
$20	0
10	5
5	15
4	20
2	45
1	95

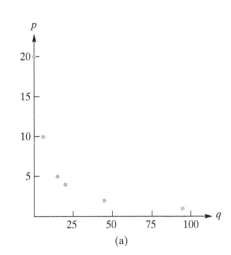

(a)

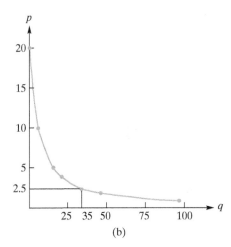

(b)

FIGURE 10.35 Viewing data via a continuous function.

Clearly, the graph does not represent a continuous function. Furthermore, it gives us no information as to the price at which, say, 35 units would be demanded. However, if we connect the points in Figure 10.35(a) by a smooth curve [see Figure 10.35(b)], we get a so-called demand curve. From it, we could guess that at about $2.50 per unit, 35 units would be demanded.

Frequently, it is possible and useful to describe a graph, as in Figure 10.35(b), by means of an equation that defines a continuous function f. Such a function not only gives us a demand equation, $p = f(q)$, which allows us to anticipate corresponding prices and quantities demanded, but also permits a convenient mathematical analysis of the nature and basic properties of demand. Of course, some care must be used in working with equations such as $p = f(q)$. Mathematically, f may be defined when $q = \sqrt{37}$, but from a practical standpoint, a demand of $\sqrt{37}$ units could be meaningless to our particular situation. For example, if a unit is an egg, then a demand of $\sqrt{37}$ eggs make no sense.

We remark that functions of the form $f(x) = x^a$, for fixed a, are continuous on their domains. In particular, (square) root functions are continuous. Also, exponential functions and logarithmic functions are continuous on their domains. Thus, exponential functions have no discontinuities while a logarithmic function has only a discontinuity at 0 (which is an infinite discontinuity). Many more examples of continuous functions are provided by the observation that if f and g are continuous on their domains, then the composite function $f \circ g$, given by $f \circ g(x) = f(g(x))$ is continuous on its domain. For example, the function

$$f(x) = \sqrt{\ln\left(\frac{x^2 + 1}{x - 1}\right)}$$

is continuous on its domain. Determining the domain of such a function may, of course, be fairly involved.

PROBLEMS 10.3

In Problems 1–6, use the definition of continuity to show that the given function is continuous at the indicated point.

1. $f(x) = x^3 - 5x; x = 2$

2. $f(x) = \dfrac{x-3}{5x}; x = -3$

3. $g(x) = \sqrt{2 - 3x}; x = 0$

4. $f(x) = \dfrac{x}{8}; x = 2$

5. $h(x) = \dfrac{x+3}{x-3}; x = -3$

6. $f(x) = \sqrt[3]{x}; x = -1$

In Problems 7–12, determine whether the function is continuous at the given points.

7. $f(x) = \dfrac{x+4}{x-2}; -2, 0$

8. $f(x) = \dfrac{x^2 - 4x + 4}{6}; 2, -2$

9. $g(x) = \dfrac{x-3}{x^2 - 9}; 3, -3$

10. $h(x) = \dfrac{3}{x^2 + 9}; 3, -3$

11. $f(x) = \begin{cases} x + 2 & \text{if } x \geq 2 \\ x^2 & \text{if } x < 2 \end{cases}; 2, 0$

12. $f(x) = \begin{cases} \dfrac{1}{x} & \text{if } x \neq 0 \\ 0 & \text{if } x = 0 \end{cases}; 0, -1$

In Problems 13–16, give a reason why the function is continuous on its domain.

13. $f(x) = 2x^2 - 3$

14. $f(x) = \dfrac{2 + 3x - x^2}{5}$

15. $f(x) = \ln(\sqrt[3]{x})$ **16.** $f(x) = x(1-x)$

In Problems 17–34, find all points of discontinuity.

17. $f(x) = 3x^2 - 3$ **18.** $h(x) = x - 2$

19. $f(x) = \dfrac{3}{x+4}$ **20.** $f(x) = \dfrac{x^2 + 5x - 2}{x^2 - 9}$

21. $g(x) = \dfrac{(2x^2 - 3)^3}{15}$ **22.** $f(x) = -1$

23. $f(x) = \dfrac{x^2 + 6x + 9}{x^2 + 2x - 15}$ **24.** $g(x) = \dfrac{x-3}{x^2 + x}$

25. $h(x) = \dfrac{x-3}{x^3 - 9x}$ **26.** $f(x) = \dfrac{2x-3}{3-2x}$

27. $p(x) = \dfrac{x}{x^2 + 1}$ **28.** $f(x) = \dfrac{x^4}{x^4 - 1}$

29. $f(x) = \begin{cases} 1 & \text{if } x \geq 0 \\ -1 & \text{if } x < 0 \end{cases}$ **30.** $f(x) = \begin{cases} 3x + 5 & \text{if } x \geq -2 \\ 2 & \text{if } x < -2 \end{cases}$

31. $f(x) = \begin{cases} 0 & \text{if } x \leq 1 \\ x - 1 & \text{if } x > 1 \end{cases}$ **32.** $f(x) = \begin{cases} x - 3 & \text{if } x > 2 \\ 3 - 2x & \text{if } x < 2 \end{cases}$

33. $f(x) = \begin{cases} x^2 + 1 & \text{if } x > 2 \\ 8x & \text{if } x < 2 \end{cases}$ **34.** $f(x) = \begin{cases} \dfrac{16}{x^2} & \text{if } x \geq 2 \\ 3x - 2 & \text{if } x < 2 \end{cases}$

35. Telephone Rates Suppose the long-distance rate for a telephone call from Hazleton, Pennsylvania to Los Angeles,

California, is \$0.08 for the first minute or fraction thereof and \$0.04 for each additional minute or fraction thereof. If $y = f(t)$ is a function that indicates the total charge y for a call of t minutes duration, sketch the graph of f for $0 < t \leq 3\frac{1}{2}$. Use your graph to determine the values of t, where $0 < t \leq 3\frac{1}{2}$, at which discontinuities occur.

36. The *greatest integer function*, $f(x) = \lfloor x \rfloor$, is defined to be the greatest integer less than or equal to x, where x is any real number. For example, $\lfloor 3 \rfloor = 3$, $\lfloor 1.999 \rfloor = 1$, $\lfloor \frac{1}{4} \rfloor = 0$, and $\lfloor -4.5 \rfloor = -5$. Sketch the graph of this function for $-3.5 \leq x \leq 3.5$. Use your sketch to determine the values of x at which discontinuities occur.

37. Inventory Sketch the graph of

$$y = f(x) = \begin{cases} -100x + 600 & \text{if } 0 \leq x < 5 \\ -100x + 1100 & \text{if } 5 \leq x < 10 \\ -100x + 1600 & \text{if } 10 \leq x < 15 \end{cases}$$

A function such as this might describe the inventory y of a company at time x. Is f continuous at 2? At 5? At 10?

38. Graph $g(x) = e^{-1/x^2}$. Because g is not defined at $x = 0$, g is discontinuous at 0. Based on the graph of g, is

$$f(x) = \begin{cases} e^{-1/x^2} & \text{if } x \neq 0 \\ 0 & \text{if } x = 0 \end{cases}$$

continuous at 0?

Objective

To develop techniques for solving nonlinear inequalities.

10.4 Continuity Applied to Inequalities

In Section 1.2, we solved linear inequalities. We now turn our attention to showing how the notion of continuity can be applied to solving a nonlinear inequality such as $x^2 + 3x - 4 < 0$. The ability to do this will be important in our study of calculus.

Recall (from Section 2.5) that the x-intercepts of the graph of a function g are precisely the roots of the equation $g(x) = 0$. Hence, from the graph of $y = g(x)$ in Figure 10.36, we conclude that r_1, r_2, and r_3 are roots of $g(x) = 0$ and any other roots will give rise to x-intercepts (beyond what is actually shown of the graph). Assume that in fact all the roots of $g(x) = 0$, and hence all the x-intercepts, are shown. Note further from Figure 10.36 that the three roots determine four open intervals on the x-axis:

$$(-\infty, r_1) \quad (r_1, r_2) \quad (r_2, r_3) \quad (r_3, \infty)$$

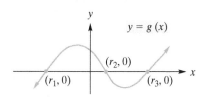

FIGURE 10.36 r_1, r_2, and r_3 are roots of $g(x) = 0$.

To solve $x^2 + 3x - 4 > 0$, we let

$$f(x) = x^2 + 3x - 4 = (x+4)(x-1)$$

Because f is a polynomial function, it is continuous. The roots of $f(x) = 0$ are -4 and 1; hence, the graph of f has x-intercepts $(-4, 0)$ and $(1, 0)$. (See Figure 10.37.) The roots determine three intervals on the x-axis:

$$(-\infty, -4) \quad (-4, 1) \quad (1, \infty)$$

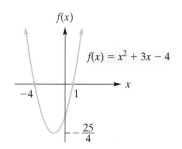

FIGURE 10.37 -4 and 1 are roots of $f(x) = 0$.

Consider the interval $(-\infty, -4)$. Since f is continuous on this interval, we claim that either $f(x) > 0$ or $f(x) < 0$ *throughout* the interval. If this were not the case, then $f(x)$ would indeed change sign on the interval. By the continuity of f, there would be a point where the graph intersects the x-axis—for example, at $(x_0, 0)$. (See Figure 10.38.) But then x_0 would be a root of $f(x) = 0$. However, this cannot be, because there is no root less than -4. Hence, $f(x)$ must be strictly positive or strictly negative on $(-\infty, -4)$. A similar argument can be made for each of the other intervals.

To determine the sign of $f(x)$ on any one of the three intervals, it suffices to determine its sign at *any* point in the interval. For instance, -5 is in $(-\infty, -4)$ and

$$f(-5) = 6 > 0 \qquad \text{Thus, } f(x) > 0 \text{ on } (-\infty, -4)$$

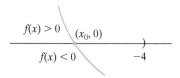

FIGURE 10.38 Change of sign for a continuous function.

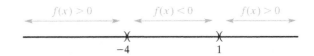

FIGURE 10.39   Simple sign chart for $x^2 + 3x - 4$.

Similarly, 0 is in $(-4, 1)$, and

$$f(0) = -4 < 0 \qquad \text{Thus, } f(x) < 0 \text{ on } (-4, 1)$$

Finally, 3 is in $(1, \infty)$, and

$$f(3) = 14 > 0 \qquad \text{Thus, } f(x) > 0 \text{ on } (1, \infty)$$

(See the "sign chart" in Figure 10.39.) Therefore,

$$x^2 + 3x - 4 > 0 \quad \text{on} \quad (-\infty, -4) \text{ and } (1, \infty)$$

so we have solved the inequality. These results are obvious from the graph in Figure 10.37. The graph lies above the x-axis, meaning that $f(x) > 0$, on $(-\infty, -4)$ and on $(1, \infty)$.

In more complicated examples it will be useful to exploit the multiplicative nature of signs. We noted that $f(x) = x^2 + 3x - 4 = (x + 4)(x - 1)$. Each of $x + 4$ and $x - 1$ has a sign chart that is simpler than that of $x^2 + 3x - 4$. Consider the "sign chart" in Figure 10.40. As before, we placed the roots of $f(x) = 0$ in ascending order, from left to right, so as to subdivide $(-\infty, \infty)$ into three open intervals. This forms the top line of the box. Directly below the top line we determined the signs of $x + 4$ on the three subintervals. We know that for the linear function $x + 4$ there is exactly one root of the equation $x + 4 = 0$, namely -4. We placed a 0 at -4 in the row labeled $x + 4$. By the argument illustrated in Figure 10.38, it follows that the sign of the function $x + 4$ is constant on $(-\infty, -4)$ and on $(-4, \infty)$ and two evaluations of $x + 4$ settle the distribution of signs for $x + 4$. From $(-5) + 4 = -1 < 0$, we have $x + 4$ *negative* on $(-\infty, -4)$, so we entered a $-$ sign in the $(-\infty, -4)$ space of the $x + 4$ row. From $(0) + 4 = 4 > 0$, we have $x + 4$ *positive* on $(-4, \infty)$. Since $(-4, \infty)$ has been further subdivided at 1, we entered a $+$ sign in each of the $(-4, 1)$ and $(1, \infty)$ spaces of the $x + 4$ row. In a similar way we constructed the row labeled $x - 1$.

	$-\infty$	-4	1	∞
$x + 4$	$-$	0	$+$	$+$
$x - 1$	$-$		$-$	0	$+$
$f(x)$	$+$	0	$-$	0	$+$

FIGURE 10.40   Sign chart for $x^2 + 3x - 4$.

Now the bottom row is obtained by taking, for each component, the product of the entries above. Thus we have $(x + 4)(x - 1) = f(x)$, $(-)(-) = +$, $0(\text{any number}) = 0$, $(+)(-) = -$, $(\text{any number})0 = 0$, and $(+)(+) = +$. Sign charts of this kind are useful whenever a continuous function can be expressed as a product of several simpler, continuous functions, each of which has a simple sign chart. In Chapter 13 we will rely heavily on such sign charts.

EXAMPLE 1   **Solving a Quadratic Inequality**

Solve $x^2 - 3x - 10 > 0$.

Solution: If $f(x) = x^2 - 3x - 10$, then f is a polynomial (quadratic) function and thus is continuous everywhere. To find the real roots of $f(x) = 0$, we have

$$x^2 - 3x - 10 = 0$$

$$(x + 2)(x - 5) = 0$$

$$x = -2, 5$$

FIGURE 10.41   Sign chart for $x^2 - 3x - 10$.

The roots -2 and 5 determine three intervals:

$$(-\infty, -2) \quad (-2, 5) \quad (5, \infty)$$

In the manner of the last example, we construct the sign chart in Figure 10.41. We see that $x^2 - 3x - 10 > 0$ on $(-\infty, -2) \cup (5, \infty)$.

Now Work Problem 1 ◁

APPLY IT ▷

10. An open box is formed by cutting a square piece out of each corner of an 8-inch-by-10-inch piece of metal. If each side of the cut-out squares is x inches long, the volume of the box is given by $V(x) = x(8 - 2x)(10 - 2x)$. This problem makes sense only when this volume is positive. Find the values of x for which the volume is positive.

EXAMPLE 2   Solving a Polynomial Inequality

Solve $x(x - 1)(x + 4) \le 0$.

Solution: If $f(x) = x(x - 1)(x + 4)$, then f is a polynomial function and hence continuous everywhere. The roots of $f(x) = 0$ are (in ascending order) -4, 0, and 1 and lead to the sign chart in Figure 10.42.

FIGURE 10.42   Sign chart for $x(x - 1)(x + 4)$.

From the sign chart, noting the endpoints required, $x(x - 1)(x + 4) \le 0$ on $(-\infty, -4] \cup [0, 1]$.

Now Work Problem 11 ◁

The sign charts we have described are certainly not limited to solving polynomial inequalities. The reader will have noticed that we used thicker vertical lines at the endpoints, $-\infty$ and ∞, of the chart. These symbols do not denote real numbers, let alone points in the domain of a function. We extend the thick vertical line convention to single out isolated real numbers that are not in the domain of the function in question. The next example will illustrate.

EXAMPLE 3   Solving a Rational Function Inequality

Solve $\dfrac{x^2 - 6x + 5}{x} \ge 0$.

Solution: Let

$$f(x) = \frac{x^2 - 6x + 5}{x} = \frac{(x - 1)(x - 5)}{x}$$

For a rational function $f = g/h$, we solve the inequality by considering the intervals determined by both the roots of $g(x) = 0$ and the roots of $h(x) = 0$. Observe that the roots of $g(x) = 0$ are the roots of $f(x) = 0$ because the only way for a fraction to be 0 is for its numerator to be 0. On the other hand, the roots of $h(x) = 0$ are precisely

	$-\infty$		0		1		5		∞
$x-1$		$-$		$-$	0	$+$		$+$	
$x-5$		$-$		$-$		$-$	0	$+$	
$1/x$		$-$	×	$+$		$+$		$+$	
$f(x)$		$-$	×	$+$	0	$-$	0	$+$	

FIGURE 10.43   Sign chart for $\dfrac{(x-1)(x-5)}{x}$.

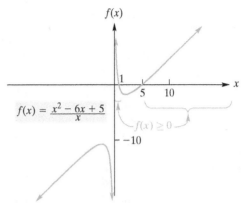

FIGURE 10.44   Graph of $f(x) = \dfrac{x^2 - 6x + 5}{x}$.

the points at which f is not defined and these are also precisely the points at which f is discontinuous. The sign of f may change at a root and it may change at a discontinuity. Here the roots of the numerator are 1 and 5 and the root of the denominator is 0. In ascending order these give us 0, 1, and 5, which determine the open intervals

$$(-\infty, 0) \quad (0, 1) \quad (1, 5) \quad (5, \infty)$$

These, together with the observation that $1/x$ is a *factor* of f, lead to the sign chart in Figure 10.43.

Here the first two rows of the sign chart are constructed as before. In the third row we have placed a $\times$ sign at 0 to indicate that the factor $1/x$ is not defined at 0. The bottom row, as before, is constructed by taking the products of the entries above. Observe that a product is not defined at any point at which any of its factors is not defined. Hence we also have a $\times$ entry at 0 in the bottom row.

From the bottom row of the sign chart we can read that the solution of $\frac{(x-1)(x-5)}{x} \geq 0$ is $(0, 1] \cup [5, \infty]$. Observe that 1 and 5 are in the solution and 0 is not.

In Figure 10.44 we have graphed $f(x) = \frac{x^2-6x+5}{x}$, and we can confirm visually that the solution of the inequality $f(x) \geq 0$ is precisely the set of all real numbers at which the graph lies on or above the x-axis.

Now Work Problem 17 ◁

A sign chart is not always necessary, as the following example shows.

EXAMPLE 4   Solving Nonlinear Inequalities

a. Solve $x^2 + 1 > 0$.

Solution: The equation $x^2 + 1 = 0$ has no real roots. Thus, the continuous function $f(x) = x^2 + 1$ has no x-intercepts. It follows that either $f(x)$ is always positive or $f(x)$ is always negative. But x^2 is always positive or zero, so $x^2 + 1$ is always positive. Hence, the solution of $x^2 + 1 > 0$ is $(-\infty, \infty)$.

b. Solve $x^2 + 1 < 0$.

Solution: From part (a), $x^2 + 1$ is always positive, so $x^2 + 1 < 0$ has no solution, meaning that the set of solutions is Ø, the empty set.

Now Work Problem 7 ◁

We conclude with a nonrational example. The importance of the function introduced will become clear in later chapters.

EXAMPLE 5   Solving a Nonrational Function Inequality

Solve $x \ln x - x \geq 0$.

Solution: Let $f(x) = x \ln x - x = x(\ln x - 1)$, which, being a product of continuous functions, is continuous. From the *factored* form for f we see that the roots of $f(x) = 0$ are 0 and the roots of $\ln x - 1 = 0$. The latter is equivalent to $\ln x = 1$, which is equivalent to $e^{\ln x} = e^1$, since the exponential function is one-to-one. However, the last equality says that $x = e$. The domain of f is $(0, \infty)$ because $\ln x$ is only defined for $x > 0$. The domain dictates the top line of our sign chart in Figure 10.45.

The first row of Figure 10.45 is straightforward. For the second row, we placed a 0 at e, the only root of $\ln x - 1 = 0$. By continuity of $\ln x - 1$, the sign of $\ln x - 1$ on $(0, e)$ and on (e, ∞) can be determined by suitable evaluations. For the first we evaluate at 1 in $(0, e)$ and get $\ln 1 - 1 = 0 - 1 = -1 < 0$. For the second we evaluate at e^2 in (e, ∞) and get $\ln e^2 - 1 = 2 - 1 = 1 > 0$. The bottom row is, as usual, determined by multiplying the others. From the bottom row of Figure 10.45 the solution of $x \ln x - x \geq 0$ is evidently $[e, \infty)$.

Now Work Problem 35 ◁

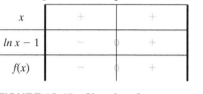

FIGURE 10.45   Sign chart for $x \ln x - x$.

PROBLEMS 10.4

In Problems 1–26, solve the inequalities by the technique discussed in this section.

1. $x^2 - 3x - 4 > 0$
2. $x^2 - 8x + 15 > 0$
3. $x^2 - 3x - 10 \leq 0$
4. $15 - 2x - x^2 \geq 0$
5. $2x^2 + 11x + 14 < 0$
6. $x^2 - 4 < 0$
7. $x^2 + 4 < 0$
8. $2x^2 - x - 2 \leq 0$
9. $(x + 1)(x - 2)(x + 7) \leq 0$
10. $(x + 5)(x + 2)(x - 7) \leq 0$
11. $-x(x - 5)(x + 4) > 0$
12. $(x + 2)^2 > 0$
13. $x^3 + 4x \geq 0$
14. $(x + 3)^2(x^2 - 4) < 0$
15. $x^3 + 8x^2 + 15x \leq 0$
16. $x^3 + 6x^2 + 9x < 0$
17. $\dfrac{x}{x^2 - 9} < 0$
18. $\dfrac{x^2 - 1}{x} < 0$
19. $\dfrac{3}{x + 1} \geq 0$
20. $\dfrac{3}{x^2 - 5x + 6} > 0$
21. $\dfrac{x^2 - x - 6}{x^2 + 4x - 5} \geq 0$
22. $\dfrac{x^2 + 4x - 5}{x^2 + 3x + 2} \leq 0$
23. $\dfrac{3}{x^2 + 6x + 5} \leq 0$
24. $\dfrac{3x + 2}{(x - 1)^2} \leq 0$
25. $x^2 + 2x \geq 2$
26. $x^4 - 16 \geq 0$

27. Revenue   Suppose that consumers will purchase q units of a product when the price of *each* unit is $28 - 0.2q$ dollars. How many units must be sold for the sales revenue to be at least $750?

28. Forest Management   A lumber company owns a forest that is of rectangular shape, 1 mi × 2 mi. The company wants to cut a uniform strip of trees along the outer edges of the forest. At most,

how wide can the strip be if the company wants at least $1\frac{5}{16}$ mi^2 of forest to remain?

29. Container Design   A container manufacturer wishes to make an open box by cutting a 3-in.-by-3-in. square from each corner of a square sheet of aluminum and then turning up the sides. The box is to contain at least 192 cubic inches. Find the dimensions of the smallest square sheet of aluminum that can be used.

30. Workshop Participation   Imperial Education Services (I.E.S.) is offering a workshop in data processing to key personnel at Zeta Corporation. The price per person is $50, and Zeta Corporation guarantees that at least 50 people will attend. Suppose I.E.S. offers to reduce the charge for *everybody* by $0.50 for each person over the 50 who attends. How should I.E.S. limit the size of the group so that the total revenue it receives will never be less than that received for 50 persons?

31. Graph $f(x) = x^3 + 7x^2 - 5x + 4$. Use the graph to determine the solution of

$$x^3 + 7x^2 - 5x + 4 \leq 0$$

32. Graph $f(x) = \dfrac{3x^2 - 0.5x + 2}{6.2 - 4.1x}$. Use the graph to determine the solution of

$$\dfrac{3x^2 - 0.5x + 2}{6.2 - 4.1x} > 0$$

A novel way of solving a nonlinear inequality like $f(x) > 0$ is by examining the graph of $g(x) = f(x)/|f(x)|$, whose range consists only of 1 and −1:

$$g(x) = \dfrac{f(x)}{|f(x)|} = \begin{cases} 1 & \text{if } f(x) > 0 \\ -1 & \text{if } f(x) < 0 \end{cases}$$

The solution of $f(x) > 0$ consists of all intervals for which $g(x) = 1$. Using this technique, solve the inequalities in Problems 33 and 34.

33. $6x^2 - x - 2 > 0$

34. $\dfrac{x^2 + x - 1}{x^2 + x - 6} < 0$

35. Graph $x \ln x - x$. Does the function appear to be continuous? Does the graph support the conclusions of Example 5? At what value does the function appear to have a minimum value?

36. Graph e^{-x^2}. Does the function appear to be continuous? Can the conclusion be confirmed by invoking facts about continuous functions? At what value does the function appear to have a maximum value?

Chapter 10 Review

Important Terms and Symbols   Examples

Section 10.1 **Limits**
$\lim_{x \to a} f(x) = L$ Ex. 8, p. 466

Section 10.2 **Limits (Continued)**
$\lim_{x \to a^-} f(x) = L \qquad \lim_{x \to a^+} f(x) = L \qquad \lim_{x \to a} f(x) = \infty$ Ex. 1, p. 470
$\lim_{x \to \infty} f(x) = L \qquad \lim_{x \to -\infty} f(x) = L$ Ex. 3, p. 471

Section 10.3 **Continuity**
continuous at a discontinuous at a Ex. 3, p. 478
continuous on an interval   continuous on its domain   Ex. 4, p. 479

Section 10.4 **Continuity Applied to Inequalities**
sign chart   Ex. 1, p. 483

Summary

The notion of limit is fundamental for calculus. To say that $\lim_{x \to a} f(x) = L$ means that the values of $f(x)$ can be made as close to the number L as we like by taking x sufficiently close to, but different from, a. If $\lim_{x \to a} f(x)$ and $\lim_{x \to a} g(x)$ exist and c is a constant, then

1. $\lim_{x \to a} c = c$

2. $\lim_{x \to a} x^n = a^n$

3. $\lim_{x \to a} [f(x) \pm g(x)] = \lim_{x \to a} f(x) \pm \lim_{x \to a} g(x)$

4. $\lim_{x \to a} [f(x) \cdot g(x)] = \lim_{x \to a} f(x) \cdot \lim_{x \to a} g(x)$

5. $\lim_{x \to a} [cf(x)] = c \cdot \lim_{x \to a} f(x)$

6. $\lim_{x \to a} \dfrac{f(x)}{g(x)} = \dfrac{\lim_{x \to a} f(x)}{\lim_{x \to a} g(x)}$ if $\lim_{x \to a} g(x) \neq 0$,

7. $\lim_{x \to a} \sqrt[n]{f(x)} = \sqrt[n]{\lim_{x \to a} f(x)}$

8. If f is a polynomial function, then $\lim_{x \to a} f(x) = f(a)$.

Property 8 implies that the limit of a polynomial function as $x \to a$ can be found by simply evaluating the polynomial at a. However, with other functions, f, evaluation at a may lead to the meaningless form $0/0$. In such cases, algebraic manipulation such as factoring and canceling may yield a function g that agrees with f, for $x \neq a$, and for which the limit can be determined.

If $f(x)$ approaches L as x approaches a from the right, then we write $\lim_{x \to a^+} f(x) = L$. If $f(x)$ approaches L as x approaches a from the left, we write $\lim_{x \to a^-} f(x) = L$. These limits are called one-sided limits.

The infinity symbol ∞, which does not represent a number, is used in describing limits. The statement

$$\lim_{x \to \infty} f(x) = L$$

means that as x increases without bound, the values of $f(x)$ approach the number L. A similar statement applies for the situation when $x \to -\infty$, which means that x is decreasing without bound. In general, if $p > 0$, then

$$\lim_{x \to \infty} \frac{1}{x^p} = 0 \quad \text{and} \quad \lim_{x \to -\infty} \frac{1}{x^p} = 0$$

If $f(x)$ increases without bound as $x \to a$, then we write $\lim_{x \to a} f(x) = \infty$. Similarly, if $f(x)$ decreases without bound, we have $\lim_{x \to a} f(x) = -\infty$. To say that the limit of a function is ∞ (or $-\infty$) does not mean that the limit exists. Rather, it is a way of saying that the limit does not exist and tells *why* there is no limit.

There is a rule for evaluating the limit of a rational function (quotient of polynomials) as $x \to \infty$ or $-\infty$. If $f(x)$ is a rational function and $a_n x^n$ and $b_m x^m$ are the terms in the numerator and denominator, respectively, with the greatest powers of x, then

$$\lim_{x \to \infty} f(x) = \lim_{x \to \infty} \frac{a_n x^n}{b_m x^m}$$

and

$$\lim_{x \to -\infty} f(x) = \lim_{x \to -\infty} \frac{a_n x^n}{b_m x^m}$$

In particular, as $x \to \infty$ or $-\infty$, the limit of a polynomial is the same as the limit of the term that involves the greatest power of x. This means that, for a nonconstant polynomial, the limit as $x \to \infty$ or $-\infty$ is either ∞ or $-\infty$.

A function f is continuous at a if and only if

1. $f(a)$ exists
2. $\lim_{x \to a} f(x)$ exists
3. $\lim_{x \to a} f(x) = f(a)$

Geometrically this means that the graph of f has no break at $x = a$. If a function is not continuous at a, then the function is said to be discontinuous at a. Polynomial functions and rational functions are continuous on their domains. Thus polynomial functions have no discontinuities and a rational function is discontinuous only at points where its denominator is zero.

To solve the inequality $f(x) > 0$ (or $f(x) < 0$), we first find the real roots of $f(x) = 0$ and the values of x for which f is discontinuous. These values determine intervals, and on each interval, $f(x)$ is either always positive or always negative. To find the sign on any one of these intervals, it suffices to find the sign of $f(x)$ at any point there. After the signs are determined for all intervals and assembled on a sign chart, it is easy to give the solution of $f(x) > 0$ (or $f(x) < 0$).

Review Problems

In Problems 1–28, find the limits if they exist. If the limit does not exist, so state, or use the symbol ∞ or $-\infty$ where appropriate.

1. $\lim\limits_{x \to -1} (2x^2 + 6x - 1)$

2. $\lim\limits_{x \to 0} \dfrac{2x^2 - 3x + 1}{2x^2 - 2}$

3. $\lim\limits_{x \to 4} \dfrac{x^2 - 16}{x^2 - 4x}$

4. $\lim\limits_{x \to -4} \dfrac{2x + 3}{x^2 - 4}$

5. $\lim\limits_{h \to 0} (x + h)$

6. $\lim\limits_{x \to 2} \dfrac{x^2 - 4}{x^2 - 3x + 2}$

7. $\lim\limits_{x \to -4} \dfrac{x^3 + 4x^2}{x^2 + 2x - 8}$

8. $\lim\limits_{x \to 2} \dfrac{x^2 - 7x + 10}{x^2 + x - 6}$

9. $\lim\limits_{x \to \infty} \dfrac{2}{x + 1}$

10. $\lim\limits_{x \to \infty} \dfrac{x^2 + 1}{2x^2}$

11. $\lim\limits_{x \to \infty} \dfrac{2x + 5}{7x - 4}$

12. $\lim\limits_{x \to -\infty} \dfrac{1}{x^4}$

13. $\lim\limits_{t \to 4} \dfrac{3t - 4}{t - 4}$

14. $\lim\limits_{x \to -\infty} \dfrac{x^6}{x^5}$

15. $\lim\limits_{x \to -\infty} \dfrac{x + 3}{1 - x}$

16. $\lim\limits_{x \to 4} \sqrt[3]{64}$

17. $\lim\limits_{x \to \infty} \dfrac{x^2 - 1}{(3x + 2)^2}$

18. $\lim\limits_{x \to 5} \dfrac{x^2 - 2x - 15}{x - 5}$

19. $\lim\limits_{x \to 3^-} \dfrac{x + 3}{x^2 - 9}$

20. $\lim\limits_{x \to 2} \dfrac{2 - x}{x - 2}$

21. $\lim\limits_{x \to \infty} \sqrt{3x}$

22. $\lim\limits_{y \to 5^+} \sqrt{y - 5}$

23. $\lim\limits_{x \to \infty} \dfrac{x^{100} + (1/x^4)}{e - x^{96}}$

24. $\lim\limits_{x \to -\infty} \dfrac{ex^2 - x^4}{31x - 2x^3}$

25. $\lim\limits_{x \to 1} f(x)$ if $f(x) = \begin{cases} x^2 & \text{if } 0 \le x < 1 \\ x & \text{if } x > 1 \end{cases}$

26. $\lim\limits_{x \to 3} f(x)$ if $f(x) = \begin{cases} x + 5 & \text{if } x < 3 \\ 6 & \text{if } x \ge 3 \end{cases}$

27. $\lim\limits_{x \to 4^+} \dfrac{\sqrt{x^2 - 16}}{4 - x}$ *(Hint: For $x > 4$,*
$\sqrt{x^2 - 16} = \sqrt{x - 4}\sqrt{x + 4}$.)

28. $\lim\limits_{x \to 3^+} \dfrac{x^2 + x - 12}{\sqrt{x - 3}}$ *(Hint: For $x > 3$, $\dfrac{x - 3}{\sqrt{x - 3}} = \sqrt{x - 3}$.)*

29. If $f(x) = 8x - 2$, find $\lim\limits_{h \to 0} \dfrac{f(x + h) - f(x)}{h}$.

30. If $f(x) = 2x^2 - 3$, find $\lim\limits_{h \to 0} \dfrac{f(x + h) - f(x)}{h}$.

31. Host–Parasite Relationship For a particular host–parasite relationship, it was determined that when the host density (number of hosts per unit of area) is x, then the number of hosts parasitized over a certain period of time is

$$y = 23\left(1 - \frac{1}{1 + 2x}\right)$$

If the host density were to increase without bound, what value would y approach?

32. Predator–Prey Relationship For a particular predator–prey relationship, it was determined that the number y of prey consumed by an individual predator over a period of time was a function of the prey density x (the number of prey per unit of area). Suppose

$$y = f(x) = \frac{10x}{1 + 0.1x}$$

If the prey density were to increase without bound, what value would y approach?

33. Using the definition of *continuity*, show that the function $f(x) = x + 3$ is continuous at $x = 2$.

34. Using the definition of *continuity*, show that the function $f(x) = \dfrac{x - 5}{x^2 + 2}$ is continuous at $x = 5$.

35. State whether $f(x) = x^2/5$ is continuous at each real number. Give a reason for your answer.

36. State whether $f(x) = x^2 - 2$ is continuous everywhere. Give a reason for your answer.

In Problems 37–44, find the points of discontinuity (if any) for each function.

37. $f(x) = \dfrac{x^2}{x + 3}$

38. $f(x) = \dfrac{0}{x^2}$

39. $f(x) = \dfrac{x - 1}{2x^2 + 3}$

40. $f(x) = (2 - 3x)^3$

41. $f(x) = \dfrac{4 - x^2}{x^2 + 3x - 4}$

42. $f(x) = \dfrac{2x + 6}{x^3 + x}$

43. $f(x) = \begin{cases} 2x + 3 & \text{if } x > 2 \\ 3x + 5 & \text{if } x \le 2 \end{cases}$

44. $f(x) = \begin{cases} 1/x & \text{if } x < 1 \\ 1 & \text{if } x \ge 1 \end{cases}$

In Problems 45–52, solve the given inequalities.

45. $x^2 + 4x - 12 > 0$

46. $3x^2 - 3x - 6 \le 0$

47. $x^5 \le 7x^4$

48. $x^3 + 9x^2 + 14x < 0$

49. $\dfrac{x+5}{x^2-1} < 0$

50. $\dfrac{x(x+5)(x+8)}{3} < 0$

51. $\dfrac{x^2+3x}{x^2+2x-8} \ge 0$

52. $\dfrac{x^2-9}{x^2-16} \le 0$

53. Graph $f(x) = \dfrac{x^3 + 3x^2 - 19x + 18}{x^3 - 2x^2 + x - 2}$. Use the graph to estimate $\lim_{x \to 2} f(x)$.

54. Graph $f(x) = \dfrac{\sqrt{x+3} - 2}{x - 1}$. From the graph, estimate $\lim_{x \to 1} f(x)$.

55. Graph $f(x) = x \ln x$. From the graph, estimate the one-sided limit $\lim_{x \to 0^+} f(x)$.

56. Graph $f(x) = \dfrac{e^x - 1}{(e^x + 1)(e^{2x} - e^x)}$. Use the graph to estimate $\lim_{x \to 0} f(x)$.

57. Graph $f(x) = x^3 - x^2 + x - 6$. Use the graph to determine the solution of

$$x^3 - x^2 + x - 6 \ge 0$$

58. Graph $f(x) = \dfrac{x^5 - 4}{x^3 + 1}$. Use the graph to determine the solution of

$$\frac{x^5 - 4}{x^3 + 1} \le 0$$

$\mathbb{Q}$ EXPLORE & EXTEND National Debt

The size of the U.S. national debt is of great concern to many people and is frequently a topic in the news. The magnitude of the debt affects the confidence in the U.S. economy of both domestic and foreign investors, corporate officials, and political leaders. There are those who believe that to reduce the debt there must be cuts in government spending, which could affect government programs, or there must be an increase in revenues, possibly through tax increases.

Suppose that it is possible for the debt to be reduced continuously at an annual fixed rate. This is similar to compounding interest continuously, as studied in Chapter 5, except that instead of adding interest to an amount at each instant of time, you would be subtracting from the debt at each instant. Let us see how you could model this situation.

Suppose the debt D_0 at time $t = 0$ is reduced at an annual rate r. Furthermore, assume that there are k time periods of equal length in a year. At the end of the first period, the original debt is reduced by $D_0 \left(\dfrac{r}{k}\right)$, so the new debt is

$$D_0 - D_0 \left(\frac{r}{k}\right) = D_0 \left(1 - \frac{r}{k}\right)$$

At the end of the second period, this debt is reduced by $D_0 \left(1 - \dfrac{r}{k}\right)\dfrac{r}{k}$, so the new debt is

$$D_0 \left(1 - \frac{r}{k}\right) - D_0 \left(1 - \frac{r}{k}\right)\frac{r}{k}$$
$$= D_0 \left(1 - \frac{r}{k}\right)\left(1 - \frac{r}{k}\right)$$
$$= D_0 \left(1 - \frac{r}{k}\right)^2$$

The pattern continues. At the end of the third period the debt is $D_0 \left(1 - \dfrac{r}{k}\right)^3$, and so on. At the end of t years the number of periods is kt and the debt is $D_0 \left(1 - \dfrac{r}{k}\right)^{kt}$. If the debt is to be reduced at each instant of time, then $k \to \infty$.

Thus you want to find

$$\lim_{k \to \infty} D_0 \left(1 - \frac{r}{k}\right)^{kt}$$

which can be rewritten as

$$D_0 \left[\lim_{k \to \infty} \left(1 - \frac{r}{k}\right)^{-k/r}\right]^{-rt}$$

If you let $x = -r/k$, then the condition $k \to \infty$ implies that $x \to 0$. Hence the limit inside the brackets has the form $\lim_{x \to 0} (1 + x)^{1/x}$, which, as we pointed out in Section 10.1, is e. Therefore, if the debt D_0 at time $t = 0$ is reduced continuously at an annual rate r, then t years later the debt D is given by

$$D = D_0 e^{-rt}$$

For example, assume the U.S. national debt of \$11,195 billion (rounded to the nearest billion) in the middle of April 2009 and a continuous reduction rate of 3% annually. Then the debt t years from now is given by

$$D = 11,195 e^{-0.03t}$$

where D is in billions of dollars. This means that in 10 years, the debt will be $11,195 e^{-0.3} \approx \$8293$ billion. Figure 10.46 shows the graph of $D = 11,195 e^{-rt}$ for various rates r. Of course, the greater the value of r, the faster the debt reduction. Notice that for $r = 0.03$, the debt at the end of 30 years is still considerable (approximately $4552 billion).

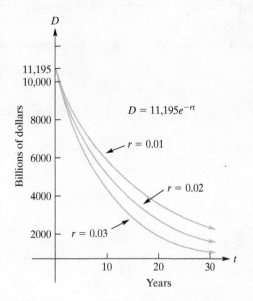

FIGURE 10.46 Budget debt reduced continuously.

It is interesting to note that decaying radioactive elements also follow the model of continuous debt reduction, $D = D_0e^{-rt}$.

To find out where the U.S. national debt currently stands, visit one of the national debt clocks on the Internet. You can find them by looking for "national debt clock" using any search engine.

Problems

In the following problems, assume a current national debt of $11,195 billion.

1. If the debt were reduced to $10,000 billion a year from now, what annual rate of continuous debt reduction would be involved? Give your answer to the nearest percent.

2. For a continuous debt reduction at an annual rate of 3%, determine the number of years from now required for the debt to be reduced by one-half. Give your answer to the nearest year.

3. What assumptions underlie a model of debt reduction that uses an exponential function?

11

Differentiation

Q EXPLORE & EXTEND

Marginal Propensity to Consume

Government regulations generally limit the number of fish taken from a given fishing ground by commercial fishing boats in a season. This prevents overfishing, which depletes the fish population and leaves, in the long run, fewer fish to catch.

From a strictly commercial perspective, the ideal regulations would maximize the number of fish available for the year-to-year fish harvest. The key to finding those ideal regulations is a mathematical function called the reproduction curve. For a given fish habitat, this function estimates the fish population a year from now, $P(n + 1)$, based on the population now, $P(n)$, assuming no external interventions such as fishing or influx of predators.

The figure to the bottom left shows a typical reproduction curve. Also graphed is the line $P(n + 1) = P(n)$, the line along which the populations $P(n + 1)$ and $P(n)$ would be equal. Notice the intersection of the curve and the straight line at point A. This is where, because of habitat crowding, the population has reached its maximum sustainable size. A population that is this size one year will be the same size the next year.

For any point on the horizontal axis, the distance between the reproduction curve and the line $P(n + 1) = P(n)$ represents the sustainable harvest: the number of fish that could be caught, after the spawn have grown to maturity, so that in the end the population is back at the same size it was a year ago.

Commercially speaking, the optimal population size is the one where the distance between the reproduction curve and the line $P(n + 1) = P(n)$ is the greatest. This condition is met where the slopes of the reproduction curve and the line $P(n + 1) = P(n)$ are equal. [The slope of $P(n + 1) = P(n)$ is, of course, 1.] Thus, for a maximum fish harvest year after year, regulations should aim to keep the fish population fairly close to P_0.

A central idea here is that of the slope of a curve at a given point. That idea is the cornerstone concept of this chapter.

Now we begin our study of calculus. The ideas involved in calculus are completely different from those of algebra and geometry. The power and importance of these ideas and their applications will become clear later in the book. In this chapter we introduce the *derivative* of a function and the important rules for finding derivatives. We also show how the derivative is used to analyze the rate of change of a quantity, such as the rate at which the position of a body is changing.

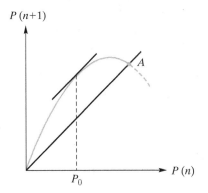

Objective

To develop the idea of a tangent line to a curve, to define the slope of a curve, and to define a derivative and give it a geometric interpretation. To compute derivatives by using the limit definition.

11.1 The Derivative

The main problem of differential calculus deals with finding the slope of the *tangent line* at a point on a curve. In high school geometry a tangent line, or *tangent*, to a circle is often defined as a line that meets the circle at exactly one point (Figure 11.1). However, this idea of a tangent is not very useful for other kinds of curves. For example, in Figure 11.2(a), the lines L_1 and L_2 intersect the curve at exactly one point P. Although we would not think of L_2 as the tangent at this point, it seems natural that L_1 is. In Figure 11.2(b) we intuitively would consider L_3 to be the tangent at point P, even though L_3 intersects the curve at other points.

FIGURE 11.1   Tangent lines to a circle.

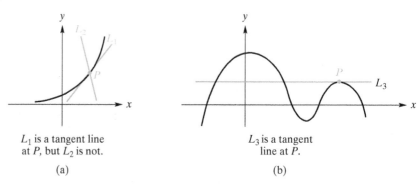

L_1 is a tangent line at P, but L_2 is not.

(a)

L_3 is a tangent line at P.

(b)

FIGURE 11.2   Tangent line at a point.

From these examples, we see that the idea of a tangent as simply a line that intersects a curve at only one point is inadequate. To obtain a suitable definition of tangent line, we use the limit concept and the geometric notion of a *secant line*. A **secant line** is a line that intersects a curve at two or more points.

Look at the graph of the function $y = f(x)$ in Figure 11.3. We wish to define the tangent line at point P. If Q is a different point on the curve, the line PQ is a secant line. If Q moves along the curve and approaches P from the right (see Figure 11.4), typical secant lines are PQ', PQ'', and so on. As Q approaches P from the left, typical secant lines are PQ_1, PQ_2, and so on. *In both cases, the secant lines approach the same limiting position.* This common limiting position of the secant lines is defined to be the **tangent line** to the curve at P. This definition seems reasonable and applies to curves in general, not just circles.

A curve does not necessarily have a tangent line at each of its points. For example, the curve $y = |x|$ does not have a tangent at $(0,0)$. As can be seen in Figure 11.5, a secant line through $(0,0)$ and a nearby point to its right on the curve must always be the line

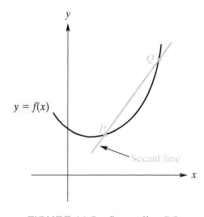

FIGURE 11.3   Secant line PQ.

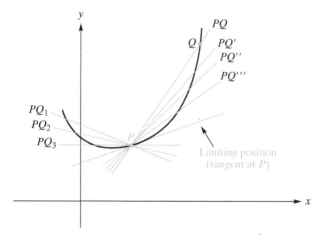

FIGURE 11.4   The tangent line is a limiting position of secant lines.

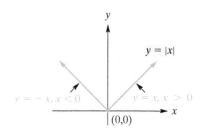

FIGURE 11.5   No tangent line to graph of $y = |x|$ at $(0,0)$.

$y = x$. Thus the limiting position of such secant lines is also the line $y = x$. However, a secant line through $(0,0)$ and a nearby point to its left on the curve must always be the line $y = -x$. Hence, the limiting position of such secant lines is also the line $y = -x$. Since there is no common limiting position, there is no tangent line at $(0,0)$.

Now that we have a suitable definition of a tangent to a curve at a point, we can define the *slope of a curve* at a point.

> **Definition**
>
> The **slope of a curve** at a point P is the slope, if it exists, of the tangent line at P.

Since the tangent at P is a limiting position of secant lines PQ, we consider the slope of the tangent to be the limiting value of the slopes of the secant lines as Q approaches P. For example, let us consider the curve $f(x) = x^2$ and the slopes of some secant lines PQ, where $P = (1, 1)$. For the point $Q = (2.5, 6.25)$, the slope of PQ (see Figure 11.6) is

$$m_{PQ} = \frac{\text{rise}}{\text{run}} = \frac{6.25 - 1}{2.5 - 1} = 3.5$$

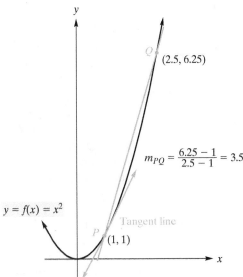

FIGURE 11.6   Secant line to $f(x) = x^2$ through $(1, 1)$ and $(2.5, 6.25)$.

Table 11.1 includes other points Q on the curve, as well as the corresponding slopes of PQ. Notice that as Q approaches P, the slopes of the secant lines seem to approach 2. Thus, we expect the slope of the indicated tangent line at $(1, 1)$ to be 2. This will be confirmed later, in Example 1. But first, we wish to generalize our procedure.

Table 11.1 Slopes of Secant Lines to the Curve $f(x) = x^2$ at $P = (1, 1)$	
Q	Slope of PQ
$(2.5, 6.25)$	$(6.25 - 1)/(2.5 - 1) = 3.5$
$(2, 4)$	$(4 - 1)/(2 - 1) = 3$
$(1.5, 2.25)$	$(2.25 - 1)/(1.5 - 1) = 2.5$
$(1.25, 1.5625)$	$(1.5625 - 1)/(1.25 - 1) = 2.25$
$(1.1, 1.21)$	$(1.21 - 1)/(1.1 - 1) = 2.1$
$(1.01, 1.0201)$	$(1.0201 - 1)/(1.01 - 1) = 2.01$

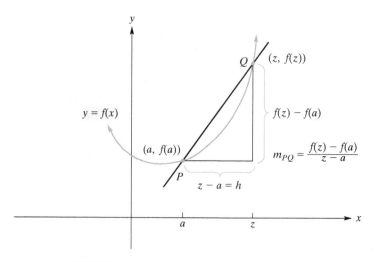

FIGURE 11.7   Secant line through P and Q.

For the curve $y = f(x)$ in Figure 11.7, we will find an expression for the slope at the point $P = (a, f(a))$. If $Q = (z, f(z))$, the slope of the secant line PQ is

$$m_{PQ} = \frac{f(z) - f(a)}{z - a}$$

If the difference $z - a$ is called h, then we can write z as $a + h$. Here we must have $h \neq 0$, for if $h = 0$, then $z = a$, and no secant line exists. Accordingly,

$$m_{PQ} = \frac{f(z) - f(a)}{z - a} = \frac{f(a + h) - f(a)}{h}$$

Which of these two forms for m_{PQ} is most convenient depends on the nature of the function f. As Q moves along the curve toward P, z approaches a. This means that h approaches zero. The limiting value of the slopes of the secant lines—which is the slope of the tangent line at $(a, f(a))$—is

$$m_{\tan} = \lim_{z \to a} \frac{f(z) - f(a)}{z - a} = \lim_{h \to 0} \frac{f(a + h) - f(a)}{h} \qquad (1)$$

Again, which of these two forms is most convenient—which limit is easiest to determine—depends on the nature of the function f. In Example 1, we will use this limit to confirm our previous expectation that the slope of the tangent line to the curve $f(x) = x^2$ at $(1, 1)$ is 2.

EXAMPLE 1   Finding the Slope of a Tangent Line

Find the slope of the tangent line to the curve $y = f(x) = x^2$ at the point $(1, 1)$.

Solution: The slope is the limit in Equation (1) with $f(x) = x^2$ and $a = 1$:

$$\lim_{h \to 0} \frac{f(1 + h) - f(1)}{h} = \lim_{h \to 0} \frac{(1 + h)^2 - (1)^2}{h}$$

$$= \lim_{h \to 0} \frac{1 + 2h + h^2 - 1}{h} = \lim_{h \to 0} \frac{2h + h^2}{h}$$

$$= \lim_{h \to 0} \frac{h(2 + h)}{h} = \lim_{h \to 0} (2 + h) = 2$$

Therefore, the tangent line to $y = x^2$ at $(1, 1)$ has slope 2. (Refer to Figure 11.6.)

Now Work Problem 1 ◁

We can generalize Equation (1) so that it applies to any point $(x, f(x))$ on a curve. Replacing a by x gives a function, called the *derivative* of f, whose input is x and whose output is the slope of the tangent line to the curve at $(x, f(x))$, provided that the tangent line *exists* and *has* a slope. (If the tangent line exists but is *vertical*, then it has no slope.) We thus have the following definition, which forms the basis of differential calculus:

> **Definition**
>
> The **derivative** of a function f is the function denoted f' (read "f prime") and defined by
>
> $$f'(x) = \lim_{z \to x} \frac{f(z) - f(x)}{z - x} = \lim_{h \to 0} \frac{f(x + h) - f(x)}{h} \qquad (2)$$
>
> provided that this limit exists. If $f'(a)$ can be found [while perhaps not all $f'(x)$ can be found] f is said to be **differentiable** at a, and $f'(a)$ is called the derivative of f at a or the derivative of f with respect to x at a. The process of finding the derivative is called **differentiation.**

In the definition of the derivative, the expression

$$\frac{f(z) - f(x)}{z - x} = \frac{f(x + h) - f(x)}{h}$$

where $z = x + h$, is called a **difference quotient.** Thus $f'(x)$ is the limit of a difference quotient.

EXAMPLE 2   Using the Definition to Find the Derivative

If $f(x) = x^2$, find the derivative of f.

Solution: Applying the definition of a derivative gives

$$
\begin{aligned}
f'(x) &= \lim_{h \to 0} \frac{f(x + h) - f(x)}{h} \\
&= \lim_{h \to 0} \frac{(x + h)^2 - x^2}{h} = \lim_{h \to 0} \frac{x^2 + 2xh + h^2 - x^2}{h} \\
&= \lim_{h \to 0} \frac{2xh + h^2}{h} = \lim_{h \to 0} \frac{h(2x + h)}{h} = \lim_{h \to 0} (2x + h) = 2x
\end{aligned}
$$

Observe that, in taking the limit, we treated x as a constant, because it was h, not x, that was changing. Also, note that $f'(x) = 2x$ defines a function of x, which we can interpret as giving the slope of the tangent line to the graph of f at $(x, f(x))$. For example, if $x = 1$, then the slope is $f'(1) = 2 \cdot 1 = 2$, which confirms the result in Example 1.

Now Work Problem 3 ◁

Calculating a derivative via the definition requires precision. Typically, the difference quotient requires considerable manipulation before the limit step is taken. This requires that each written step be preceded by "$\lim_{h \to 0}$" to acknowledge that the limit step is still pending. Observe that after the limit step is taken, h will no longer be present.

Besides the notation $f'(x)$, other common ways to denote the derivative of $y = f(x)$ at x are

$$
\begin{aligned}
&\frac{dy}{dx} && \text{pronounced "dee } y, \text{dee } x \text{" or "dee } y \text{ by dee } x \text{"} \\
&\frac{d}{dx}(f(x)) && \text{"dee } f(x), \text{dee } x \text{" or "dee by dee } x \text{ of } f(x) \text{"} \\
&y' && \text{"} y \text{ prime"} \\
&D_x y && \text{"dee } x \text{ of } y \text{"} \\
&D_x(f(x)) && \text{"dee } x \text{ of } f(x) \text{"}
\end{aligned}
$$

CAUTION!⚠

The notation $\dfrac{dy}{dx}$, which is called *Leibniz notation*, should **not** be thought of as a fraction, although it looks like one. It is a single symbol for a derivative. We have not yet attached any meaning to individual symbols such as dy and dx.

Because the derivative gives the slope of the tangent line, $f'(a)$ is the slope of the line tangent to the graph of $y = f(x)$ at $(a, f(a))$.

Two other notations for the derivative of f at a are

$$\left.\frac{dy}{dx}\right|_{x=a} \quad \text{and} \quad y'(a)$$

EXAMPLE 3   Finding an Equation of a Tangent Line

If $f(x) = 2x^2 + 2x + 3$, find an equation of the tangent line to the graph of f at $(1, 7)$.

Solution:

Strategy   We will first determine the slope of the tangent line by computing the derivative and evaluating it at $x = 1$. Using this result and the point $(1, 7)$ in a point-slope form gives an equation of the tangent line.

In Example 3 it is *not* correct to say that, since the derivative is $4x + 2$, the tangent line at $(1, 7)$ is $y - 7 = (4x + 2)(x - 1)$. (This is not even the equation of a line.) The derivative must be **evaluated** at the point of tangency to determine the slope of the tangent line.

We have

$$f'(x) = \lim_{h \to 0} \frac{f(x+h) - f(x)}{h}$$

$$= \lim_{h \to 0} \frac{(2(x+h)^2 + 2(x+h) + 3) - (2x^2 + 2x + 3)}{h}$$

$$= \lim_{h \to 0} \frac{2x^2 + 4xh + 2h^2 + 2x + 2h + 3 - 2x^2 - 2x - 3}{h}$$

$$= \lim_{h \to 0} \frac{4xh + 2h^2 + 2h}{h} = \lim_{h \to 0} (4x + 2h + 2)$$

So

$$f'(x) = 4x + 2$$

and

$$f'(1) = 4(1) + 2 = 6$$

Thus, the tangent line to the graph at $(1, 7)$ has slope 6. A point-slope form of this tangent is

$$y - 7 = 6(x - 1)$$

which in slope-intercept form is

$$y = 6x + 1$$

Now Work Problem 25 ◁

EXAMPLE 4   Finding the Slope of a Curve at a Point

Find the slope of the curve $y = 2x + 3$ at the point where $x = 6$.

Solution: The slope of the curve is the slope of the tangent line. Letting $y = f(x) = 2x + 3$, we have

$$\frac{dy}{dx} = \lim_{h \to 0} \frac{f(x+h) - f(x)}{h} = \lim_{h \to 0} \frac{(2(x+h) + 3) - (2x + 3)}{h}$$

$$= \lim_{h \to 0} \frac{2h}{h} = \lim_{h \to 0} 2 = 2$$

Since $dy/dx = 2$, the slope when $x = 6$, or in fact at any point, is 2. Note that the curve is a straight line and thus has the same slope at each point.

Now Work Problem 19 ◁

EXAMPLE 5   A Function with a Vertical Tangent Line

Find $\dfrac{d}{dx}(\sqrt{x})$.

Solution: Letting $f(x) = \sqrt{x}$, we have

$$\frac{d}{dx}(\sqrt{x}) = \lim_{h \to 0} \frac{f(x+h) - f(x)}{h} = \lim_{h \to 0} \frac{\sqrt{x+h} - \sqrt{x}}{h}$$

Rationalizing numerators or denominators of fractions is often helpful in calculating limits.

As $h \to 0$, both the numerator and denominator approach zero. This can be avoided by rationalizing the *numerator*:

$$\frac{\sqrt{x+h} - \sqrt{x}}{h} = \frac{\sqrt{x+h} - \sqrt{x}}{h} \cdot \frac{\sqrt{x+h} + \sqrt{x}}{\sqrt{x+h} + \sqrt{x}}$$

$$= \frac{(x+h) - x}{h(\sqrt{x+h} + \sqrt{x})} = \frac{h}{h(\sqrt{x+h} + \sqrt{x})}$$

Therefore,

$$\frac{d}{dx}(\sqrt{x}) = \lim_{h \to 0} \frac{h}{h(\sqrt{x+h} + \sqrt{x})} = \lim \frac{1}{\sqrt{x+h} + \sqrt{x}} = \frac{1}{\sqrt{x} + \sqrt{x}} = \frac{1}{2\sqrt{x}}$$

Note that the original function, $\sqrt{x}$, is defined for $x \geq 0$, but its derivative, $1/(2\sqrt{x})$, is defined only when $x > 0$. The reason for this is clear from the graph of $y = \sqrt{x}$ in Figure 11.8. When $x = 0$, the tangent is a vertical line, so its slope is not defined.

Now Work Problem 17 ◁

In Example 5 we saw that the function $y = \sqrt{x}$ is not differentiable when $x = 0$, because the tangent line is vertical at that point. It is worthwhile to mention that $y = |x|$ also is not differentiable when $x = 0$, but for a different reason: There is *no* tangent line at all at that point. (Refer to Figure 11.5.) Both examples show that the domain of f' may be strictly contained in the domain of f.

To indicate a derivative, Leibniz notation is often useful because it makes it convenient to emphasize the independent and dependent variables involved. For example, if the variable p is a function of the variable q, we speak of the derivative of p with respect to q, written dp/dq.

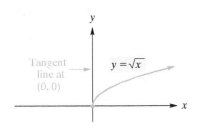

FIGURE 11.8   Vertical tangent line at $(0, 0)$.

Variables other than x and y are often more natural in applied problems. Time denoted by t, quantity by q, and price by p are obvious examples. Example 6 illustrates.

APPLY IT ▶

1. If a ball is thrown upward at a speed of 40 ft/s from a height of 6 feet, its height H in feet after t seconds is given by $H = 6 + 40t - 16t^2$. Find $\dfrac{dH}{dt}$.

| **EXAMPLE 6**   Finding the Derivative of p with Respect to q |

If $p = f(q) = \dfrac{1}{2q}$, find $\dfrac{dp}{dq}$.

Solution: We will do this problem first using the $h \to 0$ limit (the only one we have used so far) and then using $r \to q$ to illustrate the other variant of the limit.

$$\frac{dp}{dq} = \frac{d}{dq}\left(\frac{1}{2q}\right) = \lim_{h \to 0} \frac{f(q+h) - f(q)}{h}$$

$$= \lim_{h \to 0} \frac{\dfrac{1}{2(q+h)} - \dfrac{1}{2q}}{h} = \lim_{h \to 0} \frac{\dfrac{q - (q+h)}{2q(q+h)}}{h}$$

$$= \lim_{h \to 0} \frac{q - (q+h)}{h(2q(q+h))} = \lim_{h \to 0} \frac{-h}{h(2q(q+h))}$$

$$= \lim_{h \to 0} \frac{-1}{2q(q+h)} = -\frac{1}{2q^2}$$

We also have

$$\frac{dp}{dq} = \lim_{r \to q} \frac{f(r) - f(q)}{r - q}$$

$$= \lim_{r \to q} \frac{\dfrac{1}{2r} - \dfrac{1}{2q}}{r - q} = \lim_{r \to q} \frac{\dfrac{q - r}{2rq}}{r - q}$$

$$= \lim_{r \to q} \frac{-1}{2rq} = \frac{-1}{2q^2}$$

We leave it you to decide which form leads to the simpler limit calculation in this case.

Note that when $q = 0$ the function is not defined, so the derivative is also not even defined when $q = 0$.

Now Work Problem 15 ◁

Keep in mind that the derivative of $y = f(x)$ at x is nothing more than a limit, namely

$$\lim_{h \to 0} \frac{f(x+h) - f(x)}{h}$$

equivalently

$$\lim_{z \to x} \frac{f(z) - f(x)}{z - x}$$

whose use we have just illustrated. Although we can interpret the derivative as a function that gives the slope of the tangent line to the curve $y = f(x)$ at the point $(x, f(x))$, this interpretation is simply a geometric convenience that assists our understanding. The preceding limit may exist, aside from any geometric considerations at all. As we will see later, there are other useful interpretations of the derivative.

In Section 11.4, we will make technical use of the following relationship between differentiability and continuity. However, it is of fundamental importance and needs to be understood from the outset.

If f is differentiable at a, then f is continuous at a.

To establish this result, we will assume that f is differentiable at a. Then $f'(a)$ exists, and

$$\lim_{h \to 0} \frac{f(a+h) - f(a)}{h} = f'(a)$$

Consider the numerator $f(a+h) - f(a)$ as $h \to 0$. We have

$$\lim_{h \to 0} (f(a+h) - f(a)) = \lim_{h \to 0} \left(\frac{f(a+h) - f(a)}{h} \cdot h \right)$$

$$= \lim_{h \to 0} \frac{f(a+h) - f(a)}{h} \cdot \lim_{h \to 0} h$$

$$= f'(a) \cdot 0 = 0$$

Thus, $\lim_{h \to 0} (f(a+h) - f(a)) = 0$. This means that $f(a+h) - f(a)$ approaches 0 as $h \to 0$. Consequently,

$$\lim_{h \to 0} f(a+h) = f(a)$$

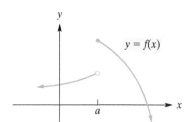

FIGURE 11.9 f is not continuous at a, so f is not differentiable at a.

As stated in Section 10.3, this condition means that f is continuous at a. The foregoing, then, proves that f is continuous at a when f is differentiable there. More simply, we say that **differentiability at a point implies continuity at that point.**

If a function is not continuous at a point, then it cannot have a derivative there. For example, the function in Figure 11.9 is discontinuous at a. The curve has no tangent at that point, so the function is not differentiable there.

EXAMPLE 7   **Continuity and Differentiability**

a. Let $f(x) = x^2$. The derivative, $2x$, is defined for all values of x, so $f(x) = x^2$ must be continuous for all values of x.

b. The function $f(p) = \dfrac{1}{2p}$ is not continuous at $p = 0$ because f is not defined there. Thus, the derivative does not exist at $p = 0$.

◁

The converse of the statement that differentiability implies continuity is *false*. That is, continuity does not imply differentiability. In Example 8, we give a function that is continuous at a point, but not differentiable there.

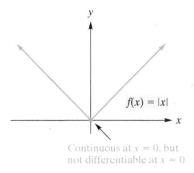

$f(x) = |x|$

Continuous at $x = 0$, but not differentiable at $x = 0$

FIGURE 11.10 Continuity does not imply differentiability.

EXAMPLE 8   Continuity Does Not Imply Differentiability

The function $y = f(x) = |x|$ is continuous at $x = 0$. (See Figure 11.10.) As we mentioned earlier, there is no tangent line at $x = 0$. Thus, the derivative does not exist there. This shows that continuity does *not* imply differentiability.

◁

Finally, we remark that while differentiability of f at a implies continuity of f at a, the derivative function, f', is not necessarily continuous at a. Unfortunately, the classic example is constructed from a function not considered in this book.

PROBLEMS 11.1

In Problems 1 and 2, a function f and a point P on its graph are given.

(a) *Find the slope of the secant line PQ for each point Q = $(x, f(x))$ whose x-value is given in the table. Round your answers to four decimal places.*

(b) *Use your results from part (a) to estimate the slope of the tangent line at P.*

1. $f(x) = x^3 + 3, P = (-2, -5)$

x-value of Q	-3	-2.5	-2.2	-2.1	-2.01	-2.001
m_{PQ}						

2. $f(x) = e^x, P = (0, 1)$

x-value of Q	1	0.5	0.2	0.1	0.01	0.001
m_{PQ}						

In Problems 3–18, use the definition of the derivative to find each of the following.

3. $f'(x)$ if $f(x) = x$

4. $f'(x)$ if $f(x) = 4x - 1$

5. $\dfrac{dy}{dx}$ if $y = 3x + 5$

6. $\dfrac{dy}{dx}$ if $y = -5x$

7. $\dfrac{d}{dx}(3 - 2x)$

8. $\dfrac{d}{dx}\left(1 - \dfrac{x}{2}\right)$

9. $f'(x)$ if $f(x) = 3$

10. $f'(x)$ if $f(x) = 7.01$

11. $\dfrac{d}{dx}(x^2 + 4x - 8)$

12. y' if $y = x^2 + 3x + 2$

13. $\dfrac{dp}{dq}$ if $p = 3q^2 + 2q + 1$

14. $\dfrac{d}{dx}(x^2 - x - 3)$

15. y' if $y = \dfrac{6}{x}$

16. $\dfrac{dC}{dq}$ if $C = 7 + 2q - 3q^2$

17. $f'(x)$ if $f(x) = \sqrt{2x}$

18. $H'(x)$ if $H(x) = \dfrac{3}{x - 2}$

19. Find the slope of the curve $y = x^2 + 4$ at the point $(-2, 8)$.

20. Find the slope of the curve $y = 1 - x^2$ at the point $(1, 0)$.

21. Find the slope of the curve $y = 4x^2 - 5$ when $x = 0$.

22. Find the slope of the curve $y = \sqrt{2x}$ when $x = 18$.

In Problems 23–28, find an equation of the tangent line to the curve at the given point.

23. $y = x + 4; (3, 7)$

24. $y = 3x^2 - 4; (1, -1)$

25. $y = x^2 + 2x + 3; (1, 6)$

26. $y = (x - 7)^2; (6, 1)$

27. $y = \dfrac{4}{x + 1}; (3, 1)$

28. $y = \dfrac{5}{1 - 3x}; (2, -1)$

29. Banking   Equations may involve derivatives of functions. In an article on interest rate deregulation, Christofi and Agapos[1] solve the equation

$$r = \left(\frac{\eta}{1 + \eta}\right)\left(r_L - \frac{dC}{dD}\right)$$

for η (the Greek letter "eta"). Here r is the deposit rate paid by commercial banks, r_L is the rate earned by commercial banks, C is the administrative cost of transforming deposits into return-earning assets, D is the savings deposits level, and η is the deposit elasticity with respect to the deposit rate. Find η.

In Problems 30 and 31, use the numerical derivative feature of your graphing calculator to estimate the derivatives of the functions at the indicated values. Round your answers to three decimal places.

30. $f(x) = \sqrt{2x^2 + 3x}; x = 1, x = 2$

31. $f(x) = e^x(4x - 7); x = 0, x = 1.5$

In Problems 32 and 33, use the "limit of a difference quotient" approach to estimate $f'(x)$ at the indicated values of x. Round your answers to three decimal places.

32. $f(x) = x \ln x - x; x = 1, x = 10$

33. $f(x) = \dfrac{x^2 + 4x + 2}{x^3 - 3}; x = 2, x = -4$

---

[1]A. Christofi and A. Agapos, "Interest Rate Deregulation: An Empirical Justification," *Review of Business and Economic Research*, XX, no. 1 (1984), 39–49.

34. Find an equation of the tangent line to the curve $f(x) = x^2 + x$ at the point $(-2, 2)$. Graph both the curve and the tangent line. Notice that the tangent line is a good approximation to the curve near the point of tangency.

35. The derivative of $f(x) = x^3 - x + 2$ is $f'(x) = 3x^2 - 1$. Graph both the function f and its derivative f'. Observe that there are two points on the graph of f where the tangent line is horizontal. For the x-values of these points, what are the corresponding values of $f'(x)$? Why are these results expected? Observe the intervals where $f'(x)$ is positive. Notice that tangent lines to the graph of f

have positive slopes over these intervals. Observe the interval where $f'(x)$ is negative. Notice that tangent lines to the graph of f have negative slopes over this interval.

In Problems 36 and 37, verify the identity $(z - x)$
$\left(\sum_{i=0}^{n-1} x^i z^{n-1-i}\right) = z^n - x^n$ *for the indicated values of n and calculate the derivative using the $z \to x$ form of the definition of the derivative in Equation (2).*

36. $n = 4, n = 3, n = 2;$ $f'(x)$ if $f(x) = 2x^4 + x^3 - 3x^2$

37. $n = 5, n = 3;$ $f'(x)$ if $f(x) = 4x^5 - 3x^3$

Objective

To develop the basic rules for differentiating constant functions and power functions and the combining rules for differentiating a constant multiple of a function and a sum of two functions.

11.2 Rules for Differentiation

Differentiating a function by direct use of the definition of derivative can be tedious. However, if a function is constructed from simpler functions, then the derivative of the more complicated function can be constructed from the derivatives of the simpler functions. Ultimately, we need to know only the derivatives of a few basic functions and ways to assemble derivatives of constructed functions from the derivatives of their components. For example, if functions f and g have derivatives f' and g', respectively, then $f + g$ has a derivative given by $(f + g)' = f' + g'$. However, some *rules* are less intuitive. For example, if $f \cdot g$ denotes the function whose value at x is given by $(f \cdot g)(x) = f(x) \cdot g(x)$, then $(f \cdot g)' = f' \cdot g + f \cdot g'$. In this chapter we study most such combining rules and some basic rules for calculating derivatives of certain basic functions.

We begin by showing that the derivative of a constant function is zero. Recall that the graph of the constant function $f(x) = c$ is a horizontal line (see Figure 11.11), which has a slope of zero at each point. This means that $f'(x) = 0$ regardless of x. As a formal proof of this result, we apply the definition of the derivative to $f(x) = c$:

$$f'(x) = \lim_{h \to 0} \frac{f(x + h) - f(x)}{h} = \lim_{h \to 0} \frac{c - c}{h}$$

$$= \lim_{h \to 0} \frac{0}{h} = \lim_{h \to 0} 0 = 0$$

Thus, we have our first rule:

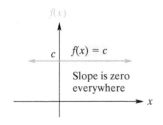

FIGURE 11.11   The slope of a constant function is 0.

BASIC RULE 0   Derivative of a Constant

If c is a constant, then

$$\frac{d}{dx}(c) = 0$$

That is, the derivative of a constant function is zero.

EXAMPLE 1   Derivatives of Constant Functions

a. $\dfrac{d}{dx}(3) = 0$ because 3 is a constant function.

b. If $g(x) = \sqrt{5}$, then $g'(x) = 0$ because g is a constant function. For example, the derivative of g when $x = 4$ is $g'(4) = 0$.

c. If $s(t) = (1{,}938{,}623)^{807.4}$, then $ds/dt = 0$.

Now Work Problem 1 ◁

The next rule gives a formula for the derivative of "x raised to a constant power"— that is, the derivative of $f(x) = x^a$, where a is an arbitrary real number. A function of this form is called a **power function.** For example, $f(x) = x^2$ is a power function. While the rule we record is valid for all real a, we will establish it only in the case where

a is a positive integer, n. The rule is so central to differential calculus that it warrants a detailed calculation—if only in the case where a is a positive integer, n. Whether we use the $h \to 0$ form of the definition of derivative or the $z \to x$ form, the calculation of $\dfrac{dx^n}{dx}$ is instructive and provides good practice with summation notation, whose use is more essential in later chapters. We provide a calculation for each possibility. We must either expand $(x + h)^n$, to use the $h \to 0$ form of Equation (2) from Section 11.1, or factor $z^n - x^n$, to use the $z \to x$ form.

For the first of these we recall the *binomial theorem* of Section 9.2:

$$(x + h)^n = \sum_{i=0}^{n} {}_nC_i x^{n-i} h^i$$

where the ${}_nC_i$ are the binomial coefficients, whose precise descriptions, except for ${}_nC_0 = 1$ and ${}_nC_1 = n$, are not necessary here (but are given in Section 8.2). For the second we have

$$(z - x)\left(\sum_{i=0}^{n-1} x^i z^{n-1-i} \right) = z^n - x^n$$

which is easily verified by carrying out the multiplication using the rules for manipulating summations given in Section 1.5. In fact, we have

$$(z - x)\left(\sum_{i=0}^{n-1} x^i z^{n-1-i} \right) = z \sum_{i=0}^{n-1} x^i z^{n-1-i} - x \sum_{i=0}^{n-1} x^i z^{n-1-i}$$

$$= \sum_{i=0}^{n-1} x^i z^{n-i} - \sum_{i=0}^{n-1} x^{i+1} z^{n-1-i}$$

$$= \left(z^n + \sum_{i=1}^{n-1} x^i z^{n-i} \right) - \left(\sum_{i=0}^{n-2} x^{i+1} z^{n-1-i} + x^n \right)$$

$$= z^n - x^n$$

where the reader should check that the two summations in the second to last line really do cancel as shown.

CAUTION!

There is a lot more to calculus than this rule.

BASIC RULE 1   Derivative of x^a

If a is any real number, then

$$\frac{d}{dx}(x^a) = ax^{a-1}$$

That is, the derivative of a constant power of x is the exponent times x raised to a power one less than the given power.

For n a positive integer, if $f(x) = x^n$, the definition of the derivative gives

$$f'(x) = \lim_{h \to 0} \frac{f(x + h) - f(x)}{h} = \lim_{h \to 0} \frac{(x + h)^n - x^n}{h}$$

By our previous discussion on expanding $(x + h)^n$,

$$f'(x) = \lim_{h \to 0} \frac{\displaystyle\sum_{i=0}^{n} {}_nC_i x^{n-i} h^i - x^n}{h}$$

$$\overset{(1)}{=} \lim_{h \to 0} \frac{\displaystyle\sum_{i=1}^{n} {}_nC_i x^{n-i} h^i}{h}$$

$$\stackrel{(2)}{=} \lim_{h \to 0} \frac{h \sum_{i=1}^{n} {}_nC_i x^{n-i} h^{i-1}}{h}$$

$$\stackrel{(3)}{=} \lim_{h \to 0} \sum_{i=1}^{n} {}_nC_i x^{n-i} h^{i-1}$$

$$\stackrel{(4)}{=} \lim_{h \to 0} \left(nx^{n-1} + \sum_{i=2}^{n} {}_nC_i x^{n-i} h^{i-1} \right)$$

$$\stackrel{(5)}{=} nx^{n-1}$$

where we justify the further steps as follows:

(1) The $i = 0$ term in the summation is ${}_nC_0 x^n h^0 = x^n$ so it cancels with the separate, last, term: $-x^n$.

(2) We are able to extract a common factor of h from each term in the sum.

(3) This is the crucial step. The expressions separated by the equal sign are limits as $h \to 0$ of functions of h that are equal for $h \neq 0$.

(4) The $i = 1$ term in the summation is ${}_nC_1 x^{n-1} h^0 = nx^{n-1}$. It is the only one that does not contain a factor of h, and we separated it from the other terms.

(5) Finally, in determining the limit we made use of the fact that the isolated term is independent of h; while all the others contain h as a factor and so have limit 0 as $h \to 0$.

Now, using the $z \to x$ limit for the definition of the derivative and $f(x) = x^n$, we have

$$f'(x) = \lim_{z \to x} \frac{f(z) - f(x)}{z - x} = \lim_{h \to 0} \frac{z^n - x^n}{z - x}$$

By our previous discussion on factoring $z^n - x^n$, we have

$$f'(x) = \lim_{z \to x} \frac{(z - x)\left(\sum_{i=0}^{n-1} x^i z^{n-1-i} \right)}{z - x}$$

$$\stackrel{(1)}{=} \lim_{z \to x} \sum_{i=0}^{n-1} x^i z^{n-1-i}$$

$$\stackrel{(2)}{=} \sum_{i=0}^{n-1} x^i x^{n-1-i}$$

$$\stackrel{(3)}{=} \sum_{i=0}^{n-1} x^{n-1}$$

$$\stackrel{(4)}{=} nx^{n-1}$$

where this time we justify the further steps as follows:

(1) Here the crucial step comes first. The expressions separated by the equal sign are limits as $z \to x$ of functions of z that are equal for $z \neq x$.

(2) The limit is given by evaluation because the expression is a polynomial in the variable z.

(3) An obvious rule for exponents is used.

(4) Each term in the sum is x^{n-1}, independent of i, and there are n such terms.

EXAMPLE 2   Derivatives of Powers of x

a. By Basic Rule 1, $\dfrac{d}{dx}(x^2) = 2x^{2-1} = 2x$.

b. If $F(x) = x = x^1$, then $F'(x) = 1 \cdot x^{1-1} = 1 \cdot x^0 = 1$. Thus, the derivative of x with respect to x is 1.

c. If $f(x) = x^{-10}$, then $f'(x) = -10x^{-10-1} = -10x^{-11}$.

Now Work Problem 3 ◁

When we apply a differentiation rule to a function, sometimes the function must first be rewritten so that it has the proper form for that rule. For example, to differentiate $f(x) = \dfrac{1}{x^{10}}$ we would first rewrite f as $f(x) = x^{-10}$ and then proceed as in Example 2(c).

EXAMPLE 3   Rewriting Functions in the Form x^a

a. To differentiate $y = \sqrt{x}$, we rewrite $\sqrt{x}$ as $x^{1/2}$ so that it has the form x^n. Thus,

$$\frac{dy}{dx} = \frac{1}{2}x^{(1/2)-1} = \frac{1}{2}x^{-1/2} = \frac{1}{2\sqrt{x}}$$

which agrees with our limit calculation in Example 5 of Section 11.1.

b. Let $h(x) = \dfrac{1}{x\sqrt{x}}$. To apply Basic Rule 1, we must rewrite $h(x)$ as $h(x) = x^{-3/2}$ so that it has the form x^n. We have

$$h'(x) = \frac{d}{dx}(x^{-3/2}) = -\frac{3}{2}x^{(-3/2)-1} = -\frac{3}{2}x^{-5/2}$$

Now Work Problem 39 ◁

CAUTION! ⚠️

In Example 3(b), do not rewrite $\dfrac{1}{x\sqrt{x}}$ as $\dfrac{1}{x^{3/2}}$ and then merely differentiate the denominator.

Now that we can say immediately that the derivative of x^3 is $3x^2$, the question arises as to what we could say about the derivative of a *multiple* of x^3, such as $5x^3$. Our next rule will handle this situation of differentiating a constant times a function.

COMBINING RULE 1   Constant Factor Rule

If f is a differentiable function and c is a constant, then $cf(x)$ is differentiable, and

$$\frac{d}{dx}(cf(x)) = cf'(x)$$

That is, the derivative of a constant times a function is the constant times the derivative of the function.

Proof. If $g(x) = cf(x)$, applying the definition of the derivative of g gives

$$g'(x) = \lim_{h \to 0} \frac{g(x+h) - g(x)}{h} = \lim_{h \to 0} \frac{cf(x+h) - cf(x)}{h}$$

$$= \lim_{h \to 0}\left(c \cdot \frac{f(x+h) - f(x)}{h}\right) = c \cdot \lim_{h \to 0} \frac{f(x+h) - f(x)}{h}$$

But $\displaystyle\lim_{h \to 0} \frac{f(x+h) - f(x)}{h}$ is $f'(x)$; so $g'(x) = cf'(x)$.

EXAMPLE 4   Differentiating a Constant Times a Function

Differentiate the following functions.
a. $g(x) = 5x^3$

Solution: Here g is a constant (5) times a function (x^3). So

$$\frac{d}{dx}(5x^3) = 5\frac{d}{dx}(x^3) \qquad \text{Combining Rule 1}$$

$$= 5(3x^{3-1}) = 15x^2 \qquad \text{Basic Rule 1}$$

b. $f(q) = \dfrac{13q}{5}$

Solution:

Strategy   We first rewrite f as a constant times a function and then apply Basic Rule 1.

Because $\dfrac{13q}{5} = \dfrac{13}{5}q, f$ is the constant $\dfrac{13}{5}$ times the function q. Thus,

$$f'(q) = \frac{13}{5}\frac{d}{dq}(q) \qquad \text{Combining Rule 1}$$

$$= \frac{13}{5} \cdot 1 = \frac{13}{5} \qquad \text{Basic Rule 1}$$

c. $y = \dfrac{0.25}{\sqrt[5]{x^2}}$

Solution: We can express y as a constant times a function:

$$y = 0.25 \cdot \frac{1}{\sqrt[5]{x^2}} = 0.25x^{-2/5}$$

Hence,

$$y' = 0.25\frac{d}{dx}(x^{-2/5}) \qquad \text{Combining Rule 1}$$

$$= 0.25\left(-\frac{2}{5}x^{-7/5}\right) = -0.1x^{-7/5} \qquad \text{Basic Rule 1}$$

Now Work Problem 7 ◁

CAUTION!

In differentiating $f(x) = (4x)^3$, Basic Rule 1 cannot be applied directly. It applies to a power of the variable x, *not* to a power of an expression involving x, such as $4x$. To apply our rules, write $f(x) = (4x)^3 = 4^3x^3 = 64x^3$. Thus,

$$f'(x) = 64\frac{d}{dx}(x^3) = 64(3x^2) = 192x^2.$$

The next rule involves derivatives of sums and differences of functions.

COMBINING RULE 2   Sum or Difference Rule

If f and g are differentiable functions, then $f + g$ and $f - g$ are differentiable, and

$$\frac{d}{dx}(f(x) + g(x)) = f'(x) + g'(x)$$

and

$$\frac{d}{dx}(f(x) - g(x)) = f'(x) - g'(x)$$

That is, the derivative of the sum (difference) of two functions is the sum (difference) of their derivatives.

Proof. For the case of a sum, if $F(x) = f(x) + g(x)$, applying the definition of the derivative of F gives

$$F'(x) = \lim_{h \to 0}\frac{F(x+h) - F(x)}{h}$$

$$= \lim_{h \to 0}\frac{(f(x+h) + g(x+h)) - (f(x) + g(x))}{h}$$

$$= \lim_{h \to 0} \frac{(f(x+h) - f(x)) + (g(x+h) - g(x))}{h} \qquad \text{regrouping}$$

$$= \lim_{h \to 0} \left(\frac{f(x+h) - f(x)}{h} + \frac{g(x+h) - g(x)}{h} \right)$$

Because the limit of a sum is the sum of the limits,

$$F'(x) = \lim_{h \to 0} \frac{f(x+h) - f(x)}{h} + \lim_{h \to 0} \frac{g(x+h) - g(x)}{h}$$

But these two limits are $f'(x)$ and $g'(x)$. Thus,

$$F'(x) = f'(x) + g'(x)$$

The proof for the derivative of a difference of two functions is similar.

Combining Rule 2 can be extended to the derivative of any number of sums and differences of functions. For example,

$$\frac{d}{dx}[f(x) - g(x) + h(x) + k(x)] = f'(x) - g'(x) + h'(x) + k'(x)$$

EXAMPLE 5   Differentiating Sums and Differences of Functions

APPLY IT ▶

2. If the revenue function for a certain product is $r(q) = 50q - 0.3q^2$, find the derivative of this function, also known as the marginal revenue.

Differentiate the following functions.

a. $F(x) = 3x^5 + \sqrt{x}$

Solution: Here F is the sum of two functions, $3x^5$ and $\sqrt{x}$. Therefore,

$$F'(x) = \frac{d}{dx}(3x^5) + \frac{d}{dx}(x^{1/2}) \qquad \text{Combining Rule 2}$$

$$= 3\frac{d}{dx}(x^5) + \frac{d}{dx}(x^{1/2}) \qquad \text{Combining Rule 1}$$

$$= 3(5x^4) + \frac{1}{2}x^{-1/2} = 15x^4 + \frac{1}{2\sqrt{x}} \qquad \text{Basic Rule 1}$$

b. $f(z) = \frac{z^4}{4} - \frac{5}{z^{1/3}}$

Solution: To apply our rules, we will rewrite $f(z)$ in the form $f(z) = \frac{1}{4}z^4 - 5z^{-1/3}$. Since f is the difference of two functions,

$$f'(z) = \frac{d}{dz}\left(\frac{1}{4}z^4\right) - \frac{d}{dz}(5z^{-1/3}) \qquad \text{Combining Rule 2}$$

$$= \frac{1}{4}\frac{d}{dz}(z^4) - 5\frac{d}{dz}(z^{-1/3}) \qquad \text{Combining Rule 1}$$

$$= \frac{1}{4}(4z^3) - 5\left(-\frac{1}{3}z^{-4/3}\right) \qquad \text{Basic Rule 1}$$

$$= z^3 + \frac{5}{3}z^{-4/3}$$

c. $y = 6x^3 - 2x^2 + 7x - 8$

Solution:

$$\frac{dy}{dx} = \frac{d}{dx}(6x^3) - \frac{d}{dx}(2x^2) + \frac{d}{dx}(7x) - \frac{d}{dx}(8)$$

$$= 6\frac{d}{dx}(x^3) - 2\frac{d}{dx}(x^2) + 7\frac{d}{dx}(x) - \frac{d}{dx}(8)$$

$$= 6(3x^2) - 2(2x) + 7(1) - 0$$

$$= 18x^2 - 4x + 7$$

Now Work Problem 47 ◁

In Examples 6 and 7, we need to rewrite the given function in a form to which our rules apply.

EXAMPLE 6 Finding a Derivative

Find the derivative of $f(x) = 2x(x^2 - 5x + 2)$ when $x = 2$.

Solution: We multiply and then differentiate each term:

$$f(x) = 2x^3 - 10x^2 + 4x$$
$$f'(x) = 2(3x^2) - 10(2x) + 4(1)$$
$$= 6x^2 - 20x + 4$$
$$f'(2) = 6(2)^2 - 20(2) + 4 = -12$$

Now Work Problem 75 ◁

EXAMPLE 7 Finding an Equation of a Tangent Line

Find an equation of the tangent line to the curve

$$y = \frac{3x^2 - 2}{x}$$

when $x = 1$.

Solution:

Strategy First we find $\dfrac{dy}{dx}$, which gives the slope of the tangent line at any point. Evaluating $\dfrac{dy}{dx}$ when $x = 1$ gives the slope of the required tangent line. We then determine the y-coordinate of the point on the curve when $x = 1$. Finally, we substitute the slope and both of the coordinates of the point in point-slope form to obtain an equation of the tangent line.

Rewriting y as a difference of two functions, we have

$$y = \frac{3x^2}{x} - \frac{2}{x} = 3x - 2x^{-1}$$

Thus,

$$\frac{dy}{dx} = 3(1) - 2((-1)x^{-2}) = 3 + \frac{2}{x^2}$$

The slope of the tangent line to the curve when $x = 1$ is

$$\frac{dy}{dx}\bigg|_{x=1} = 3 + \frac{2}{1^2} = 5$$

To find the y-coordinate of the point on the curve where $x = 1$, we evaluate $y = \dfrac{3x^2 - 2}{x}$ at $x = 1$. This gives

$$y = \frac{3(1)^2 - 2}{1} = 1$$

CAUTION!⚠

To obtain the y-value of the point on the curve when $x = 1$, evaluate the *original* function at $x = 1$.

Hence, the point $(1, 1)$ lies on both the curve and the tangent line. Therefore, an equation of the tangent line is

$$y - 1 = 5(x - 1)$$

In slope-intercept form, we have

$$y = 5x - 4$$

Now Work Problem 81 ◁

PROBLEMS 11.2

In Problems 1–74, differentiate the functions.

1. $f(x) = \pi$

2. $f(x) = \left(\frac{6}{7}\right)^{2/3}$

3. $y = x^6$

4. $f(x) = x^{21}$

5. $y = x^{80}$

6. $y = x^{2.1}$

7. $f(x) = 9x^2$

8. $y = 4x^3$

9. $g(w) = 8w^7$

10. $v(x) = x^e$

11. $y = \frac{3}{5}x^6$

12. $f(p) = \sqrt{3}p^4$

13. $f(t) = \dfrac{t^7}{25}$

14. $y = \dfrac{x^7}{7}$

15. $f(x) = x + 3$

16. $f(x) = 5x - e$

17. $f(x) = 4x^2 - 2x + 3$

18. $F(x) = 5x^2 - 9x$

19. $g(p) = p^4 - 3p^3 - 1$

20. $f(t) = -13t^2 + 14t + 1$

21. $y = x^4 - \sqrt[3]{x}$

22. $y = -8x^4 + \ln 2$

23. $y = -13x^3 + 14x^2 - 2x + 3$

24. $V(r) = r^8 - 7r^6 + 3r^2 + 1$

25. $f(x) = 2(13 - x^4)$

26. $\psi(t) = e(t^7 - 5^3)$

27. $g(x) = \dfrac{13 - x^4}{3}$

28. $f(x) = \dfrac{5(x^4 - 6)}{2}$

29. $h(x) = 4x^4 + x^3 - \dfrac{9x^2}{2} + 8x$

30. $k(x) = -2x^2 + \dfrac{5}{3}x + 11$

31. $f(x) = \dfrac{5}{7}x^9 + \dfrac{3}{5}x^7$

32. $p(x) = \dfrac{x^7}{7} + \dfrac{2x}{3}$

33. $f(x) = x^{3/5}$

34. $f(x) = 2x^{-14/5}$

35. $y = x^{3/4} + 2x^{5/3}$

36. $y = 4x^2 - x^{-3/5}$

37. $y = 11\sqrt{x}$

38. $y = \sqrt{x^7}$

39. $f(r) = 6\sqrt[3]{r}$

40. $y = 4\sqrt[8]{x^2}$

41. $f(x) = x^{-6}$

42. $f(s) = 2s^{-3}$

43. $f(x) = x^{-3} + x^{-5} - 2x^{-6}$

44. $f(x) = 100x^{-3} + 10x^{1/2}$

45. $y = \dfrac{1}{x}$

46. $f(x) = \dfrac{3}{x^4}$

47. $y = \dfrac{8}{x^5}$

48. $y = \dfrac{1}{4x^5}$

49. $g(x) = \dfrac{4}{3x^3}$

50. $y = \dfrac{1}{x^2}$

51. $f(t) = \dfrac{3}{5t^3}$

52. $g(x) = \dfrac{7}{9x}$

53. $f(x) = \dfrac{x}{7} + \dfrac{7}{x}$

54. $\Phi(x) = \dfrac{x^3}{3} - \dfrac{3}{x^3}$

55. $f(x) = -9x^{1/3} + 5x^{-2/5}$

56. $f(z) = 5z^{3/4} - 6^2 - 8z^{1/4}$

57. $q(x) = \dfrac{1}{\sqrt[3]{8x^2}}$

58. $f(x) = \dfrac{3}{\sqrt[4]{x^3}}$

59. $y = \dfrac{2}{\sqrt{x}}$

60. $y = \dfrac{1}{2\sqrt{x}}$

61. $y = x^3\sqrt[3]{x}$

62. $f(x) = (2x^3)(4x^2)$

63. $f(x) = x(3x^2 - 10x + 7)$

64. $f(x) = x^3(3x^6 - 5x^2 + 4)$

65. $f(x) = x^3(3x)^2$

66. $s(x) = \sqrt{x}(\sqrt[5]{x} + 7x + 2)$

67. $v(x) = x^{-2/3}(x + 5)$

68. $f(x) = x^{3/5}(x^2 + 7x + 11)$

69. $f(q) = \dfrac{3q^2 + 4q - 2}{q}$

70. $f(w) = \dfrac{w - 5}{w^5}$

71. $f(x) = (x - 1)(x + 2)$

72. $f(x) = x^2(x - 2)(x + 4)$

73. $w(x) = \dfrac{x^2 + x^3}{x^2}$

74. $f(x) = \dfrac{7x^3 + x}{6\sqrt{x}}$

For each curve in Problems 75–78, find the slopes at the indicated points.

75. $y = 3x^2 + 4x - 8;\ (0, -8), (2, 12), (-3, 7)$

76. $y = 3 + 5x - 3x^3;\ (0, 3), (\frac{1}{2}, \frac{41}{8}), (2, -11)$

77. $y = 4;$ when $x = -4, x = 7, x = 22$

78. $y = 3x - 4\sqrt{x};$ when $x = 4, x = 9, x = 25$

In Problems 79–82, find an equation of the tangent line to the curve at the indicated point.

79. $y = 4x^2 + 5x + 6;\ (1, 15)$

80. $y = \dfrac{1 - x^2}{5};\ (4, -3)$

81. $y = \dfrac{1}{x^2};\ (2, \frac{1}{4})$

82. $y = -\sqrt[3]{x};\ (8, -2)$

83. Find an equation of the tangent line to the curve

$$y = 3 + x - 5x^2 + x^4$$

when $x = 0$.

84. Repeat Problem 83 for the curve

$$y = \frac{\sqrt{x}(2 - x^2)}{x}$$

when $x = 4$.

85. Find all points on the curve

$$y = \frac{5}{2}x^2 - x^3$$

where the tangent line is horizontal.

86. Repeat Problem 85 for the curve

$$y = \frac{x^6}{6} - \frac{x^2}{2} + 1$$

87. Find all points on the curve

$$y = x^2 - 5x + 3$$

where the slope is 1.

88. Repeat Problem 87 for the curve

$$y = x^4 - 31x + 11$$

89. If $f(x) = \sqrt{x} + \dfrac{1}{\sqrt{x}}$, evaluate the expression

$$\frac{x - 1}{2x\sqrt{x}} - f'(x)$$

90. Economics   Eswaran and Kotwal[2] consider agrarian economies in which there are two types of workers, permanent and casual. Permanent workers are employed on long-term contracts and may receive benefits such as holiday gifts and emergency aid. Casual workers are hired on a daily basis and perform routine and menial tasks such as weeding, harvesting, and threshing. The difference z in the present-value cost of hiring a permanent worker over that of hiring a casual worker is given by

$$z = (1 + b)w_p - bw_c$$

where w_p and w_c are wage rates for permanent labor and casual labor, respectively, b is a constant, and w_p is a function of w_c.

Eswaran and Kotwal claim that

$$\frac{dz}{dw_c} = (1 + b)\left[\frac{dw_p}{dw_c} - \frac{b}{1 + b}\right]$$

Verify this.

91. Find an equation of the tangent line to the graph of $y = x^3 - 2x + 1$ at the point $(1, 0)$. Graph both the function and the tangent line on the same screen.

92. Find an equation of the tangent line to the graph of $y = \sqrt[3]{x}$, at the point $(-8, -2)$. Graph both the function and the tangent line on the same screen. Notice that the line passes through $(-8, -2)$ and the line appears to be tangent to the curve.

Objective

To motivate the instantaneous rate of change of a function by means of velocity and to interpret the derivative as an instantaneous rate of change. To develop the "marginal" concept, which is frequently used in business and economics.

11.3 The Derivative as a Rate of Change

We have given a geometric interpretation of the derivative as being the slope of the tangent line to a curve at a point. Historically, an important application of the derivative involves the motion of an object traveling in a straight line. This gives us a convenient way to interpret the derivative as a *rate of change*.

To denote the change in a variable such as x, the symbol Δx (read "delta x") is commonly used. For example, if x changes from 1 to 3, then the change in x is $\Delta x = 3 - 1 = 2$. The new value of $x(=3)$ is the old value plus the change, which is $1 + \Delta x$. Similarly, if t increases by Δt, the new value is $t + \Delta t$. We will use Δ-notation in the discussion that follows.

Suppose an object moves along the number line in Figure 11.12 according to the equation

$$s = f(t) = t^2$$

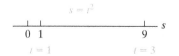

FIGURE 11.12   Motion along a number line.

where s is the position of the object at time t. This equation is called an **equation of motion**, and f is called a *position function*. Assume that t is in seconds and s is in meters. At $t = 1$ the position is $s = f(1) = 1^2 = 1$, and at $t = 3$ the position is $s = f(3) = 3^2 = 9$. Over this two-second time interval, the object has a change in position, or a *displacement*, of $9 - 1 = 8$ m, and the *average velocity* of the object is defined as

$$v_{\text{ave}} = \frac{\text{displacement}}{\text{length of time interval}} \tag{1}$$

$$= \frac{8}{2} = 4 \text{ m/s}$$

To say that the average velocity is 4 m/s from $t = 1$ to $t = 3$ means that, *on the average*, the position of the object changed by 4 m to the right each second during that time interval. Let us denote the changes in s-values and t-values by Δs and Δt, respectively. Then the average velocity is given by

$$v_{\text{ave}} = \frac{\Delta s}{\Delta t} = 4 \text{ m/s} \quad \text{(for the interval } t = 1 \text{ to } t = 3\text{)}$$

The ratio $\Delta s / \Delta t$ is also called the **average rate of change of** s **with respect to** t over the interval from $t = 1$ to $t = 3$.

Now, let the time interval be only 1 second long (that is, $\Delta t = 1$). Then, for the *shorter* interval from $t = 1$ to $t = 1 + \Delta t = 2$, we have $f(2) = 2^2 = 4$, so

$$v_{\text{ave}} = \frac{\Delta s}{\Delta t} = \frac{f(2) - f(1)}{\Delta t} = \frac{4 - 1}{1} = 3 \text{ m/s}$$

[2]M. Eswaran and A. Kotwal, "A Theory of Two-Tier Labor Markets in Agrarian Economies," *The American Economic Review*, 75, no. 1 (1985), 162–77.

Table 11.2

Length of Time Interval Δt	Time Interval $t = 1$ to $t = 1 + \Delta t$	Average Velocity $\dfrac{\Delta s}{\Delta t} = \dfrac{f(1 + \Delta t) - f(1)}{\Delta t}$
0.1	$t = 1$ to $t = 1.1$	2.1 m/s
0.07	$t = 1$ to $t = 1.07$	2.07 m/s
0.05	$t = 1$ to $t = 1.05$	2.05 m/s
0.03	$t = 1$ to $t = 1.03$	2.03 m/s
0.01	$t = 1$ to $t = 1.01$	2.01 m/s
0.001	$t = 1$ to $t = 1.001$	2.001 m/s

More generally, over the time interval from $t = 1$ to $t = 1 + \Delta t$, the object moves from position $f(1)$ to position $f(1 + \Delta t)$. Thus, its displacement is

$$\Delta s = f(1 + \Delta t) - f(1)$$

Since the time interval has length Δt, the object's average velocity is given by

$$v_{\text{ave}} = \frac{\Delta s}{\Delta t} = \frac{f(1 + \Delta t) - f(1)}{\Delta t}$$

If Δt were to become smaller and smaller, the average velocity over the interval from $t = 1$ to $t = 1 + \Delta t$ would be close to what we might call the *instantaneous velocity* at time $t = 1$; that is, the velocity at a *point* in time ($t = 1$) as opposed to the velocity over an *interval* of time. For some typical values of Δt between 0.1 and 0.001, we get the average velocities in Table 11.2, which the reader can verify.

The table suggests that as the length of the time interval approaches zero, the average velocity approaches the value 2 m/s. In other words, as Δt approaches 0, $\Delta s / \Delta t$ approaches 2 m/s. We define the limit of the average velocity as $\Delta t \to 0$ to be the **instantaneous velocity** (or simply the **velocity**), v, at time $t = 1$. This limit is also called the **instantaneous rate of change** of s with respect to t at $t = 1$:

$$v = \lim_{\Delta t \to 0} v_{\text{ave}} = \lim_{\Delta t \to 0} \frac{\Delta s}{\Delta t} = \lim_{\Delta t \to 0} \frac{f(1 + \Delta t) - f(1)}{\Delta t}$$

If we think of Δt as h, then the limit on the right is simply the derivative of s with respect to t at $t = 1$. Thus, the instantaneous velocity of the object at $t = 1$ is just ds/dt at $t = 1$. Because $s = t^2$ and

$$\frac{ds}{dt} = 2t$$

the velocity at $t = 1$ is

$$v = \frac{ds}{dt}\bigg|_{t=1} = 2(1) = 2 \text{ m/s}$$

which confirms our previous conclusion.

In summary, if $s = f(t)$ is the position function of an object moving in a straight line, then the average velocity of the object over the time interval $[t, t + \Delta t]$ is given by

$$v_{\text{ave}} = \frac{\Delta s}{\Delta t} = \frac{f(t + \Delta t) - f(t)}{\Delta t}$$

and the velocity at time t is given by

$$v = \lim_{\Delta t \to 0} \frac{f(t + \Delta t) - f(t)}{\Delta t} = \frac{ds}{dt}$$

Selectively combining equations for v, we have

$$\frac{ds}{dt} = \lim_{\Delta t \to 0} \frac{\Delta s}{\Delta t}$$

which provides motivation for the otherwise bizarre Leibniz notation. (After all, Δ is the [uppercase] Greek letter corresponding to d.)

EXAMPLE 1 Finding Average Velocity and Velocity

Suppose the position function of an object moving along a number line is given by $s = f(t) = 3t^2 + 5$, where t is in seconds and s is in meters.

a. Find the average velocity over the interval $[10, 10.1]$.

b. Find the velocity when $t = 10$.

Solution:

a. Here $t = 10$ and $\Delta t = 10.1 - 10 = 0.1$. So we have

$$
\begin{aligned}
v_{\text{ave}} &= \frac{\Delta s}{\Delta t} = \frac{f(t + \Delta t) - f(t)}{\Delta t} \\
&= \frac{f(10 + 0.1) - f(10)}{0.1} \\
&= \frac{f(10.1) - f(10)}{0.1} \\
&= \frac{311.03 - 305}{0.1} = \frac{6.03}{0.1} = 60.3 \text{ m/s}
\end{aligned}
$$

b. The velocity at time t is given by

$$
v = \frac{ds}{dt} = 6t
$$

When $t = 10$, the velocity is

$$
\left. \frac{ds}{dt} \right|_{t=10} = 6(10) = 60 \text{ m/s}
$$

Notice that the average velocity over the interval $[10, 10.1]$ is close to the velocity at $t = 10$. This is to be expected because the length of the interval is small.

Now Work Problem 1 ◁

Our discussion of the rate of change of s with respect to t applies equally well to *any* function $y = f(x)$. This means that we have the following:

If $y = f(x)$, then

$$
\frac{\Delta y}{\Delta x} = \frac{f(x + \Delta x) - f(x)}{\Delta x} = \begin{cases} \text{average rate of change} \\ \text{of } y \text{ with respect to } x \\ \text{over the interval from} \\ x \text{ to } x + \Delta x \end{cases}
$$

and

$$
\frac{dy}{dx} = \lim_{\Delta x \to 0} \frac{\Delta y}{\Delta x} = \begin{cases} \text{instantaneous rate of change} \\ \text{of } y \text{ with respect to } x \end{cases} \tag{2}
$$

Because the instantaneous rate of change of $y = f(x)$ at a point is a derivative, it is also the *slope of the tangent line* to the graph of $y = f(x)$ at that point. For convenience, we usually refer to the instantaneous rate of change simply as the **rate of change.** The interpretation of a derivative as a rate of change is extremely important.

Let us now consider the significance of the rate of change of y with respect to x. From Equation (2), if Δx (a change in x) is close to 0, then $\Delta y / \Delta x$ is close to dy/dx. That is,

$$
\frac{\Delta y}{\Delta x} \approx \frac{dy}{dx}
$$

Therefore,

$$\Delta y \approx \frac{dy}{dx}\Delta x \tag{3}$$

That is, if x changes by Δx, then the change in y, Δy, is approximately dy/dx times the change in x. In particular,

if x changes by 1, an estimate of the change in y is $\dfrac{dy}{dx}$

APPLY IT ▶

3. Suppose that the profit P made by selling a certain product at a price of p per unit is given by $P = f(p)$ and the rate of change of that profit with respect to change in price is $\dfrac{dP}{dp} = 5$ at $p = 25$. Estimate the change in the profit P if the price changes from 25 to 25.5.

EXAMPLE 2   Estimating Δy by Using dy/dx

Suppose that $y = f(x)$ and $\dfrac{dy}{dx} = 8$ when $x = 3$. Estimate the change in y if x changes from 3 to 3.5.

Solution: We have $dy/dx = 8$ and $\Delta x = 3.5 - 3 = 0.5$. The change in y is given by Δy, and, from Equation (3),

$$\Delta y \approx \frac{dy}{dx}\Delta x = 8(0.5) = 4$$

We remark that, since $\Delta y = f(3.5) - f(3)$, we have $f(3.5) = f(3) + \Delta y$. For example, if $f(3) = 5$, then $f(3.5)$ can be estimated by $5 + 4 = 9$.

◁

APPLY IT ▶

4. The position of an object thrown upward at a speed of 16 feet/s from a height of 0 feet is given by $y(t) = 16t - 16t^2$. Find the rate of change of y with respect to t, and evaluate it when $t = 0.5$. Use your graphing calculator to graph $y(t)$. Use the graph to interpret the behavior of the object when $t = 0.5$.

EXAMPLE 3   Finding a Rate of Change

Find the rate of change of $y = x^4$ with respect to x, and evaluate it when $x = 2$ and when $x = -1$. Interpret your results.

Solution: The rate of change is

$$\frac{dy}{dx} = 4x^3$$

When $x = 2$, $dy/dx = 4(2)^3 = 32$. This means that if x increases, from 2, by a small amount, then y increases approximately 32 times as much. More simply, we say that, when $x = 2$, y is increasing 32 times as fast as x does. When $x = -1$, $dy/dx = 4(-1)^3 = -4$. The significance of the minus sign on -4 is that, when $x = -1$, y is *decreasing* 4 times as fast as x increases.

Now Work Problem 11 ◁

EXAMPLE 4   Rate of Change of Price with Respect to Quantity

Let $p = 100 - q^2$ be the demand function for a manufacturer's product. Find the rate of change of price p per unit with respect to quantity q. How fast is the price changing with respect to q when $q = 5$? Assume that p is in dollars.

Solution: The rate of change of p with respect to q is

$$\frac{dp}{dq} = \frac{d}{dq}(100 - q^2) = -2q$$

Thus,

$$\left.\frac{dp}{dq}\right|_{q=5} = -2(5) = -10$$

This means that when five units are demanded, an *increase* of one extra unit demanded corresponds to a decrease of approximately $10 in the price per unit that consumers are willing to pay.

◁

EXAMPLE 5   Rate of Change of Volume

A spherical balloon is being filled with air. Find the rate of change of the volume of air in the balloon with respect to its radius. Evaluate this rate of change when the radius is 2 ft.

Solution: The formula for the volume V of a ball of radius r is $V = \frac{4}{3}\pi r^3$. The rate of change of V with respect to r is

$$\frac{dV}{dr} = \frac{4}{3}\pi(3r^2) = 4\pi r^2$$

When $r = 2$ ft, the rate of change is

$$\frac{dV}{dr}\bigg|_{r=2} = 4\pi(2)^2 = 16\pi \frac{\text{ft}^3}{\text{ft}}$$

This means that when the radius is 2 ft, changing the radius by 1 ft will change the volume by approximately 16π ft^3.

◁

EXAMPLE 6   Rate of Change of Enrollment

A sociologist is studying various suggested programs that can aid in the education of preschool-age children in a certain city. The sociologist believes that x years after the beginning of a particular program, $f(x)$ thousand preschoolers will be enrolled, where

$$f(x) = \frac{10}{9}(12x - x^2) \quad 0 \le x \le 12$$

At what rate would enrollment change (a) after three years from the start of this program and (b) after nine years?

Solution: The rate of change of $f(x)$ is

$$f'(x) = \frac{10}{9}(12 - 2x)$$

a. After three years, the rate of change is

$$f'(3) = \frac{10}{9}(12 - 2(3)) = \frac{10}{9} \cdot 6 = \frac{20}{3} = 6\frac{2}{3}$$

Thus, enrollment would be increasing at the rate of $6\frac{2}{3}$ thousand preschoolers per year.

b. After nine years, the rate is

$$f'(9) = \frac{10}{9}(12 - 2(9)) = \frac{10}{9}(-6) = -\frac{20}{3} = -6\frac{2}{3}$$

Thus, enrollment would be *decreasing* at the rate of $6\frac{2}{3}$ thousand preschoolers per year.

Now Work Problem 9 ◁

Applications of Rate of Change to Economics

A manufacturer's **total-cost function,** $c = f(q)$, gives the total cost c of producing and marketing q units of a product. The rate of change of c with respect to q is called the **marginal cost.** Thus,

$$\text{marginal cost} = \frac{dc}{dq}$$

For example, suppose $c = f(q) = 0.1q^2 + 3$ is a cost function, where c is in dollars and q is in pounds. Then

$$\frac{dc}{dq} = 0.2q$$

The marginal cost when 4 lb are produced is dc/dq, evaluated when $q = 4$:

$$\frac{dc}{dq}\Big|_{q=4} = 0.2(4) = 0.80$$

This means that if production is increased by 1 lb, from 4 lb to 5 lb, then the change in cost is approximately $0.80. That is, the additional pound costs about $0.80. In general, *we interpret marginal cost as the approximate cost of one additional unit of output.* After all, the difference $f(q + 1) - f(q)$ can be seen as a difference quotient

$$\frac{f(q + 1) - f(q)}{1}$$

(the case where $h = 1$). Any difference quotient can be regarded as an approximation of the corresponding derivative and, conversely, any derivative can be regarded as an approximation of any of its corresponding difference quotients. Thus, for any function f of q we can always regard $f'(q)$ and $f(q + 1) - f(q)$ as approximations of each other. In economics, the latter can usually be regarded as the exact value of the cost, or profit depending upon the function, of the $(q+1)$th item when q are produced. The derivative is often easier to compute than the exact value. [In the case at hand, the actual cost of producing one more pound beyond 4 lb is $f(5) - f(4) = 5.5 - 4.6 = \$0.90$.]

If c is the total cost of producing q units of a product, then the **average cost per unit,** $\bar{c}$, is

$$\bar{c} = \frac{c}{q} \tag{4}$$

For example, if the total cost of 20 units is $100, then the average cost per unit is $\bar{c} = 100/20 = \$5$. By multiplying both sides of Equation (4) by q, we have

$$c = q\bar{c}$$

That is, total cost is the product of the number of units produced and the average cost per unit.

EXAMPLE 7   Marginal Cost

If a manufacturer's average-cost equation is

$$\bar{c} = 0.0001q^2 - 0.02q + 5 + \frac{5000}{q}$$

find the marginal-cost function. What is the marginal cost when 50 units are produced?

Solution:

Strategy   The marginal-cost function is the derivative of the total-cost function c. Thus, we first find c by multiplying $\bar{c}$ by q. We have

$$c = q\bar{c}$$

$$= q\left(0.0001q^2 - 0.02q + 5 + \frac{5000}{q}\right)$$

$$c = 0.0001q^3 - 0.02q^2 + 5q + 5000$$

Differentiating c, we have the marginal-cost function:

$$\frac{dc}{dq} = 0.0001(3q^2) - 0.02(2q) + 5(1) + 0$$

$$= 0.0003q^2 - 0.04q + 5$$

The marginal cost when 50 units are produced is

$$\left.\frac{dc}{dq}\right|_{q=50} = 0.0003(50)^2 - 0.04(50) + 5 = 3.75$$

If c is in dollars and production is increased by one unit, from $q = 50$ to $q = 51$, then the cost of the additional unit is approximately \$3.75. If production is increased by $\frac{1}{3}$ unit, from $q = 50$, then the cost of the additional output is approximately $\left(\frac{1}{3}\right)(3.75) = \$1.25$.

Now Work Problem 21 ◁

Suppose $r = f(q)$ is the **total-revenue function** for a manufacturer. The equation $r = f(q)$ states that the total dollar value received for selling q units of a product is r. The **marginal revenue** is defined as the rate of change of the total dollar value received with respect to the total number of units sold. Hence, marginal revenue is merely the derivative of r with respect to q:

$$\text{marginal revenue} = \frac{dr}{dq}$$

Marginal revenue indicates the rate at which revenue changes with respect to units sold. We interpret it as *the approximate revenue received from selling one additional unit of output.*

EXAMPLE 8   Marginal Revenue

Suppose a manufacturer sells a product at \$2 per unit. If q units are sold, the total revenue is given by

$$r = 2q$$

The marginal-revenue function is

$$\frac{dr}{dq} = \frac{d}{dq}(2q) = 2$$

which is a constant function. Thus, the marginal revenue is 2 regardless of the number of units sold. This is what we would expect, because the manufacturer receives \$2 for each unit sold.

Now Work Problem 23 ◁

Relative and Percentage Rates of Change

For the total-revenue function in Example 8, namely, $r = f(q) = 2q$, we have

$$\frac{dr}{dq} = 2$$

This means that revenue is changing at the rate of \$2 per unit, regardless of the number of units sold. Although this is valuable information, it may be more significant when compared to r itself. For example, if $q = 50$, then $r = 2(50) = 100$. Thus, the rate of change of revenue is $2/100 = 0.02$ *of* r. On the other hand, if $q = 5000$, then $r = 2(5000) = \$10,000$, so the rate of change of r is $2/10,000 = 0.0002$ *of* r.

Although r changes at the same rate at each level, compared to r itself, this rate is relatively smaller when $r = 10,000$ than when $r = 100$. By considering the ratio

$$\frac{dr/dq}{r}$$

we have a means of comparing the rate of change of r with r itself. This ratio is called the *relative rate of change* of r. We have shown that the relative rate of change when $q = 50$ is

$$\frac{dr/dq}{r} = \frac{2}{100} = 0.02$$

and when $q = 5000$, it is

$$\frac{dr/dq}{r} = \frac{2}{10,000} = 0.0002$$

By multiplying relative rates by 100%, we obtain the so-called *percentage rates of change*. The percentage rate of change when $q = 50$ is $(0.02)(100\%) = 2\%$; when $q = 5000$, it is $(0.0002)(100\%) = 0.02\%$. For example, if an additional unit beyond 50 is sold, then revenue increases by approximately 2%.

In general, for any function f, we have the following definition:

> **Definition**
>
> The **relative rate of change** of $f(x)$ is
>
> $$\frac{f'(x)}{f(x)}$$
>
> The **percentage rate of change** of $f(x)$ is
>
> $$\frac{f'(x)}{f(x)} \cdot 100\%$$

CAUTION!⚠

Percentages can be confusing! Remember that *percent* means "per hundred." Thus $100\% = \frac{100}{100} = 1$, $2\% = \frac{2}{100} = 0.02$, and so on.

APPLY IT ▶

5. The volume V enclosed by a capsule-shaped container with a cylindrical height of 4 feet and radius r is given by

$$V(r) = \frac{4}{3}\pi r^3 + 4\pi r^2$$

Determine the relative and percentage rates of change of volume with respect to the radius when the radius is 2 feet.

EXAMPLE 9   Relative and Percentage Rates of Change

Determine the relative and percentage rates of change of

$$y = f(x) = 3x^2 - 5x + 25$$

when $x = 5$.

Solution: Here

$$f'(x) = 6x - 5$$

Since $f'(5) = 6(5) - 5 = 25$ and $f(5) = 3(5)^2 - 5(5) + 25 = 75$, the relative rate of change of y when $x = 5$ is

$$\frac{f'(5)}{f(5)} = \frac{25}{75} \approx 0.333$$

Multiplying 0.333 by 100% gives the percentage rate of change: $(0.333)(100) = 33.3\%$.

Now Work Problem 35 ◁

PROBLEMS 11.3

1. Suppose that the position function of an object moving along a straight line is $s = f(t) = 2t^2 + 3t$, where t is in seconds and s is in meters. Find the average velocity $\Delta s / \Delta t$ over the interval $[1, 1 + \Delta t]$, where Δt is given in the following table:

Δt	1	0.5	0.2	0.1	0.01	0.001
$\Delta s / \Delta t$						

From your results, estimate the velocity when $t = 1$. Verify your estimate by using differentiation.

2. If $y = f(x) = \sqrt{2x+5}$, find the average rate of change of y with respect to x over the interval $[3, 3 + \Delta x]$, where Δx is given in the following table:

Δx	1	0.5	0.2	0.1	0.01	0.001
$\Delta y / \Delta x$						

From your result, estimate the rate of change of y with respect to x when $x = 3$.

In each of Problems 3–8, a position function is given, where t is in seconds and s is in meters.
(a) *Find the position at the given t-value.*
(b) *Find the average velocity over the given interval.*
(c) *Find the velocity at the given t-value.*

3. $s = 2t^2 - 4t; [7, 7.5]; t = 7$

4. $s = \frac{1}{2}t + 1; [2, 2.1]; t = 2$

5. $s = 5t^3 + 3t + 24; [1, 1.01]; t = 1$

6. $s = -3t^2 + 2t + 1; [1, 1.25]; t = 1$

7. $s = t^4 - 2t^3 + t; [2, 2.1]; t = 2$

8. $s = 3t^4 - t^{7/2}; [0, \frac{1}{4}]; t = 0$

9. Income–Education   Sociologists studied the relation between income and number of years of education for members of a particular urban group. They found that a person with x years of education before seeking regular employment can expect to receive an average yearly income of y dollars per year, where

$$y = 5x^{5/2} + 5900 \qquad 4 \le x \le 16$$

Find the rate of change of income with respect to number of years of education. Evaluation the expression when $x = 9$.

10. Find the rate of change of the volume V of a ball, with respect to its radius r, when $r = 1.5$ m. The volume V of a ball as a function of its radius r is given by

$$V = V(r) = \frac{4}{3}\pi r^3$$

11. Skin Temperature   The approximate temperature T of the skin in terms of the temperature T_e of the environment is given by

$$T = 32.8 + 0.27(T_e - 20)$$

where T and T_e are in degrees Celsius.[3] Find the rate of change of T with respect to T_e.

12. Biology   The volume V of a spherical cell is given by $V = \frac{4}{3}\pi r^3$, where r is the radius. Find the rate of change of volume with respect to the radius when $r = 6.3 \times 10^{-4}$ cm.

In Problems 13–18, cost functions are given, where c is the cost of producing q units of a product. In each case, find the marginal-cost function. What is the marginal cost at the given value(s) of q?

13. $c = 500 + 10q; q = 100$

14. $c = 5000 + 6q; q = 36$

15. $c = 0.2q^2 + 4q + 50; q = 10$

16. $c = 0.1q^2 + 3q + 2; q = 3$

17. $c = q^2 + 50q + 1000; q = 15, q = 16, q = 17$

18. $c = 0.04q^3 - 0.5q^2 + 4.4q + 7500; q = 5, q = 25, q = 1000$

In Problems 19–22, $\bar{c}$ represents average cost per unit, which is a function of the number q of units produced. Find the marginal-cost function and the marginal cost for the indicated values of q.

19. $\bar{c} = 0.01q + 5 + \dfrac{500}{q}; q = 50, q = 100$

20. $\bar{c} = 5 + \dfrac{2000}{q}; q = 25, q = 250$

21. $\bar{c} = 0.00002q^2 - 0.01q + 6 + \dfrac{20{,}000}{q}; q = 100, q = 500$

22. $\bar{c} = 0.002q^2 - 0.5q + 60 + \dfrac{7000}{q}; q = 15, q = 25$

In Problems 23–26, r represents total revenue and is a function of the number q of units sold. Find the marginal-revenue function and the marginal revenue for the indicated values of q.

23. $r = 0.8q; q = 9, q = 300, q = 500$

24. $r = q\left(15 - \frac{1}{30}q\right); q = 5, q = 15, q = 150$

25. $r = 240q + 40q^2 - 2q^3; q = 10; q = 15; q = 20$

26. $r = 2q(30 - 0.1q); q = 10, q = 20$

27. Hosiery Mill   The total-cost function for a hosiery mill is estimated by Dean[4] to be

$$c = -10{,}484.69 + 6.750q - 0.000328q^2$$

where q is output in dozens of pairs and c is total cost in dollars. Find the marginal-cost function and the average cost function and evaluate each when $q = 2000$.

28. Light and Power Plant   The total-cost function for an electric light and power plant is estimated by Nordin[5] to be

$$c = 32.07 - 0.79q + 0.02142q^2 - 0.0001q^3 \quad 20 \le q \le 90$$

where q is the eight-hour total output (as a percentage of capacity) and c is the total fuel cost in dollars. Find the marginal-cost function and evaluate it when $q = 70$.

29. Urban Concentration   Suppose the 100 largest cities in the United States in 1920 are ranked according to magnitude (areas of cities). From Lotka,[6] the following relation holds approximately:

$$PR^{0.93} = 5{,}000{,}000$$

Here, P is the population of the city having respective rank R. This relation is called the *law of urban concentration* for 1920. Solve for P in terms of R, and then find how fast the population is changing with respect to rank.

30. Depreciation   Under the straight-line method of depreciation, the value v of a certain machine after t years have elapsed is given by

$$v = 120{,}000 - 15{,}500t$$

where $0 \le t \le 6$. How fast is v changing with respect to t when $t = 2?$ $t = 4?$ at any time?

---

[3]R. W. Stacy et al., *Essentials of Biological and Medical Physics* (New York: McGraw-Hill Book Company, 1955).

[4]J. Dean, "Statistical Cost Functions of a Hosiery Mill," *Studies in Business Administration*, XI, no. 4 (Chicago: University of Chicago Press, 1941).

[5]J. A. Nordin, "Note on a Light Plant's Cost Curves," *Econometrica*, 15 (1947), 231–35.

[6]A. J. Lotka, *Elements of Mathematical Biology* (New York: Dover Publications, Inc., 1956).

31. Winter Moth   A study of the winter moth was made in Nova Scotia (adapted from Embree).[7] The prepupae of the moth fall onto the ground from host trees. At a distance of x ft from the base of a host tree, the prepupal density (number of prepupae per square foot of soil) was y, where

$$y = 59.3 - 1.5x - 0.5x^2 \quad 1 \le x \le 9$$

(a) At what rate is the prepupal density changing with respect to distance from the base of the tree when $x = 6$?
(b) For what value of x is the prepupal density decreasing at the rate of 6 prepupae per square foot per foot?

32. Cost Function   For the cost function

$$c = 0.4q^2 + 4q + 5$$

find the rate of change of c with respect to q when $q = 2$. Also, what is $\Delta c / \Delta q$ over the interval $[2, 3]$?

In Problems 33–38, find **(a)** *the rate of change of y with respect to x and* **(b)** *the relative rate of change of y. At the given value of x, find* **(c)** *the rate of change of y,* **(d)** *the relative rate of change of y, and* **(e)** *the percentage rate of change of y.*

33. $y = f(x) = x + 4; x = 5$ **34.** $y = f(x) = 7 - 3x; x = 6$

35. $y = 2x^2 + 5; x = 10$ **36.** $y = 5 - 3x^3; x = 1$

37. $y = 8 - x^3; x = 1$ **38.** $y = x^2 + 3x - 4; x = -1$

39. Cost Function   For the cost function

$$c = 0.3q^2 + 3.5q + 9$$

how fast does c change with respect to q when $q = 10$? Determine the percentage rate of change of c with respect to q when $q = 10$.

40. Organic Matters/Species Diversity   In a discussion of contemporary waters of shallows seas, Odum[8] claims that in such waters the total organic matter y (in milligrams per liter) is a function of species diversity x (in number of species per thousand individuals). If $y = 100/x$, at what rate is the total organic matter changing with respect to species diversity when $x = 10$? What is the percentage rate of change when $x = 10$?

41. Revenue   For a certain manufacturer, the revenue obtained from the sale of q units of a product is given by

$$r = 30q - 0.3q^2$$

(a) How fast does r change with respect to q? When $q = 10$, **(b)** find the relative rate of change of r, and **(c)** to the nearest percent, find the percentage rate of change of r.

42. Revenue   Repeat Problem 43 for the revenue function given by $r = 10q - 0.2q^2$ and $q = 25$.

43. Weight of Limb   The weight of a limb of a tree is given by $W = 2t^{0.432}$, where t is time. Find the relative rate of change of W with respect to t.

44. Response to Shock   A psychological experiment[9] was conducted to analyze human responses to electrical shocks (stimuli). The subjects received shocks of various intensities. The response R to a shock of intensity I (in microamperes) was to be a number that indicated the perceived magnitude relative to that of a "standard" shock. The standard shock was assigned a magnitude of 10. Two groups of subjects were tested under slightly different conditions. The responses R_1 and R_2 of the first and second groups to a shock of intensity I were given by

$$R_1 = \frac{I^{1.3}}{1855.24} \quad 800 \le I \le 3500$$

and

$$R_2 = \frac{I^{1.3}}{1101.29} \quad 800 \le I \le 3500$$

(a) For each group, determine the relative rate of change of response with respect to intensity.
(b) How do these changes compare with each other?
(c) In general, if $f(x) = C_1 x^n$ and $g(x) = C_2 x^n$, where C_1 and C_2 are constants, how do the relative rates of change of f and g compare?

45. Cost   A manufacturer of mountain bikes has found that when 20 bikes are produced per day, the average cost is \$200 and the marginal cost is \$150. Based on that information, approximate the total cost of producing 21 bikes per day.

46. Marginal and Average Costs   Suppose that the cost function for a certain product is $c = f(q)$. If the relative rate of change of c (with respect to q) is $\dfrac{1}{q}$, prove that the marginal-cost function and the average-cost function are equal.

In Problems 47 and 48, use the numerical derivative feature of your graphing calculator.

47. If the total-cost function for a manufacturer is given by

$$c = \frac{5q^2}{\sqrt{q^2 + 3}} + 5000$$

where c is in dollars, find the marginal cost when 10 units are produced. Round your answer to the nearest cent.

48. The population of a city t years from now is given by

$$P = 250{,}000e^{0.04t}$$

Find the rate of change of population with respect to time t three years from now. Round your answer to the nearest integer.

Objective

To find derivatives by applying the product and quotient rules, and to develop the concepts of marginal propensity to consume and marginal propensity to save.

11.4 The Product Rule and the Quotient Rule

The equation $F(x) = (x^2 + 3x)(4x + 5)$ expresses $F(x)$ as a product of two functions: $x^2 + 3x$ and $4x + 5$. To find $F'(x)$ by using only our previous rules, we first multiply

---

[7] D. G. Embree, "The Population Dynamics of the Winter Moth in Nova Scotia, 1954–1962," *Memoirs of the Entomological Society of Canada*, no. 46 (1965).

[8] H. T. Odum, "Biological Circuits and the Marine Systems of Texas," in *Pollution and Marine Biology*, eds T. A. Olsen and F. J. Burgess (New York: Interscience Publishers, 1967).

[9] H. Babkoff, "Magnitude Estimation of Short Electrocutaneous Pulses," *Psychological Research*, 39, no. 1 (1976), 39–49.

the functions. Then we differentiate the result, term by term:

$$F(x) = (x^2 + 3x)(4x + 5) = 4x^3 + 17x^2 + 15x$$

$$F'(x) = 12x^2 + 34x + 15 \tag{1}$$

However, in many problems that involve differentiating a product of functions, the multiplication is not as simple as it is here. At times, it is not even practical to attempt it. Fortunately, there is a rule for differentiating a product, and the rule avoids such multiplications. Since the derivative of a sum of functions is the sum of their derivatives, you might expect a similar rule for products. However, the situation is rather subtle.

COMBINING RULE 3 The Product Rule

If f and g are differentiable functions, then the product fg is differentiable, and

$$\frac{d}{dx}(f(x)g(x)) = f'(x)g(x) + f(x)g'(x)$$

That is, the derivative of the product of two functions is the derivative of the first function times the second, plus the first function times the derivative of the second.

$$\frac{d}{dx}(\text{product}) = \left(\begin{array}{c}\text{derivative}\\\text{of first}\end{array}\right)(\text{second}) + (\text{first})\left(\begin{array}{c}\text{derivative}\\\text{of second}\end{array}\right)$$

Proof. If $F(x) = f(x)g(x)$, then, by the definition of the derivative of F,

$$F'(x) = \lim_{h \to 0} \frac{F(x+h) - F(x)}{h}$$

$$= \lim_{h \to 0} \frac{f(x+h)g(x+h) - f(x)g(x)}{h}$$

Now we use a "trick." Adding and subtracting $f(x)g(x+h)$ in the numerator, we have

$$F'(x) = \lim_{h \to 0} \frac{f(x+h)g(x+h) - f(x)g(x) + f(x)g(x+h) - f(x)g(x+h)}{h}$$

Regrouping gives

$$F'(x) = \lim_{h \to 0} \frac{(f(x+h)g(x+h) - f(x)g(x+h)) + (f(x)g(x+h) - f(x)g(x))}{h}$$

$$= \lim_{h \to 0} \frac{(f(x+h) - f(x))g(x+h) + f(x)(g(x+h) - g(x))}{h}$$

$$= \lim_{h \to 0} \frac{(f(x+h) - f(x))g(x+h)}{h} + \lim_{h \to 0} \frac{f(x)(g(x+h) - g(x))}{h}$$

$$= \lim_{h \to 0} \frac{f(x+h) - f(x)}{h} \cdot \lim_{h \to 0} g(x+h) + \lim_{h \to 0} f(x) \cdot \lim_{h \to 0} \frac{g(x+h) - g(x)}{h}$$

Since we assumed that f and g are differentiable,

$$\lim_{h \to 0} \frac{f(x+h) - f(x)}{h} = f'(x)$$

and

$$\lim_{h \to 0} \frac{g(x+h) - g(x)}{h} = g'(x)$$

The differentiability of g implies that g is continuous, so, from Section 10.3,

$$\lim_{h \to 0} g(x+h) = g(x)$$

Thus,

$$F'(x) = f'(x)g(x) + f(x)g'(x)$$

EXAMPLE 1   **Applying the Product Rule**

If $F(x) = (x^2 + 3x)(4x + 5)$, find $F'(x)$.

Solution: We will consider F as a product of two functions:

$$F(x) = \underbrace{(x^2 + 3x)}_{f(x)}\underbrace{(4x + 5)}_{g(x)}$$

Therefore, we can apply the product rule:

$$F'(x) = f'(x)g(x) + f(x)g'(x)$$

$$= \underbrace{\frac{d}{dx}(x^2 + 3x)}_{\substack{\text{Derivative} \\ \text{of first}}}\underbrace{(4x + 5)}_{\text{Second}} + \underbrace{(x^2 + 3x)}_{\text{First}}\underbrace{\frac{d}{dx}(4x + 5)}_{\substack{\text{Derivative} \\ \text{of second}}}$$

$$= (2x + 3)(4x + 5) + (x^2 + 3x)(4)$$

$$= 12x^2 + 34x + 15 \qquad\qquad \text{simplifying}$$

> **CAUTION!**
>
> It is worthwhile to repeat that the derivative of the product of two functions is somewhat subtle. Do not be tempted to make up a simpler rule.

This agrees with our previous result. [See Equation (1).] Although there doesn't seem to be much advantage to using the product rule here, there are times when it is impractical to avoid it.

Now Work Problem 1 ◁

EXAMPLE 2   **Applying the Product Rule**

> **APPLY IT** ▷
>
> **6.** A taco stand usually sells 225 tacos per day at \$2 each. A business student's research tells him that for every \$0.15 decrease in the price, the stand will sell 20 more tacos per day. The revenue function for the taco stand is $R(x) = (2 - 0.15x)(225 + 20x)$, where x is the number of \$0.15 reductions in price. Find $\dfrac{dR}{dx}$.

If $y = (x^{2/3} + 3)(x^{-1/3} + 5x)$, find dy/dx.

Solution: Applying the product rule gives

$$\frac{dy}{dx} = \frac{d}{dx}(x^{2/3} + 3)(x^{-1/3} + 5x) + (x^{2/3} + 3)\frac{d}{dx}(x^{-1/3} + 5x)$$

$$= \left(\frac{2}{3}x^{-1/3}\right)(x^{-1/3} + 5x) + (x^{2/3} + 3)\left(\frac{-1}{3}x^{-4/3} + 5\right)$$

$$= \frac{25}{3}x^{2/3} + \frac{1}{3}x^{-2/3} - x^{-4/3} + 15$$

Alternatively, we could have found the derivative without the product rule by first finding the product $(x^{2/3} + 3)(x^{-1/3} + 5x)$ and then differentiating the result, term by term.

Now Work Problem 15 ◁

EXAMPLE 3   **Differentiating a Product of Three Factors**

If $y = (x + 2)(x + 3)(x + 4)$, find y'.

Solution:

> **Strategy**   We would like to use the product rule, but as given it applies only to *two* factors. By treating the first two factors as a single factor, we can consider y to be a product of two functions:
>
> $$y = [(x + 2)(x + 3)](x + 4)$$

The product rule gives

$$y' = \frac{d}{dx}[(x + 2)(x + 3)](x + 4) + [(x + 2)(x + 3)]\frac{d}{dx}(x + 4)$$

$$= \frac{d}{dx}[(x + 2)(x + 3)](x + 4) + [(x + 2)(x + 3)](1)$$

Applying the product rule again, we have

$$y' = \left(\frac{d}{dx}(x+2)(x+3) + (x+2)\frac{d}{dx}(x+3)\right)(x+4) + (x+2)(x+3)$$

$$= [(1)(x+3) + (x+2)(1)](x+4) + (x+2)(x+3)$$

After simplifying, we obtain

$$y' = 3x^2 + 18x + 26$$

Two other ways of finding the derivative are as follows:

1. Multiply the first two factors of y to obtain

$$y = (x^2 + 5x + 6)(x+4)$$

and then apply the product rule.

2. Multiply all three factors to obtain

$$y = x^3 + 9x^2 + 26x + 24$$

and then differentiate term by term.

Now Work Problem 19 ◁

It is sometimes helpful to remember differentiation rules in more streamlined notation. For example,

$$(fg)' = f'g + fg'$$

is a correct equality of functions that expresses the product rule. We can then calculate

$$(fgh)' = ((fg)h)'$$
$$= (fg)'h + (fg)h'$$
$$= (f'g + fg')h + (fg)h'$$
$$= f'gh + fg'h + fgh'$$

It is not suggested that you try to commit to memory derived rules like

$$(fgh)' = f'gh + fg'h + fgh'$$

Because $f'g + fg' = gf' + fg'$, using commutativity of the product of functions, we can express the product rule with the derivatives as second factors:

$$(fg)' = gf' + fg'$$

and using commutativity of addition

$$(fg)' = fg' + gf'$$

Some people prefer these forms.

APPLY IT ▸

7. One hour after x milligrams of a particular drug are given to a person, the change in body temperature $T(x)$, in degrees Fahrenheit, is given approximately by $T(x) = x^2\left(1 - \frac{x}{3}\right)$. The rate at which T changes with respect to the size of the dosage x, $T'(x)$, is called the *sensitivity* of the body to the dosage. Find the sensitivity when the dosage is 1 milligram. Do not use the product rule.

EXAMPLE 4   Using the Product Rule to Find Slope

Find the slope of the graph of $f(x) = (7x^3 - 5x + 2)(2x^4 + 7)$ when $x = 1$.

Solution:

Strategy   We find the slope by evaluating the derivative when $x = 1$. Because f is a product of two functions, we can find the derivative by using the product rule.

We have

$$f'(x) = (7x^3 - 5x + 2)\frac{d}{dx}(2x^4 + 7) + (2x^4 + 7)\frac{d}{dx}(7x^3 - 5x + 2)$$

$$= (7x^3 - 5x + 2)(8x^3) + (2x^4 + 7)(21x^2 - 5)$$

Since we must compute $f'(x)$ when $x = 1$, *there is no need to simplify $f'(x)$ before evaluating it.* Substituting into $f'(x)$, we obtain

$$f'(1) = 4(8) + 9(16) = 176$$

Now Work Problem 49 ◁

Usually, we do not use the product rule when simpler ways are obvious. For example, if $f(x) = 2x(x + 3)$, then it is quicker to write $f(x) = 2x^2 + 6x$, from which $f'(x) = 4x + 6$. Similarly, we do not usually use the product rule to differentiate $y = 4(x^2 - 3)$. Since the 4 is a constant factor, by the constant-factor rule we have $y' = 4(2x) = 8x$.

The next rule is used for differentiating a *quotient* of two functions.

> The product rule (and quotient rule that follows) should not be applied when a more direct and efficient method is available.

COMBINING RULE 4   The Quotient Rule

If f and g are differentiable functions and $g(x) \neq 0$, then the quotient f/g is also differentiable, and

$$\frac{d}{dx}\left(\frac{f(x)}{g(x)}\right) = \frac{g(x)f'(x) - f(x)g'(x)}{(g(x))^2}$$

With the understanding about the denominator not being zero, we can write

$$\left(\frac{f}{g}\right)' = \frac{gf' - fg'}{g^2}$$

That is, the derivative of the quotient of two functions is the denominator times the derivative of the numerator, minus the numerator times the derivative of the denominator, all divided by the square of the denominator.

$$\frac{d}{dx}(\text{quotient})$$

$$= \frac{(\text{denominator})\left(\begin{array}{c}\text{derivative}\\\text{of numerator}\end{array}\right) - (\text{numerator})\left(\begin{array}{c}\text{derivative}\\\text{of denominator}\end{array}\right)}{(\text{denominator})^2}$$

Proof. If $F(x) = \dfrac{f(x)}{g(x)}$, then

$$F(x)g(x) = f(x)$$

By the product rule,

$$F(x)g'(x) + g(x)F'(x) = f'(x)$$

Solving for $F'(x)$, we have

$$F'(x) = \frac{f'(x) - F(x)g'(x)}{g(x)}$$

But $F(x) = f(x)/g(x)$. Thus,

$$F'(x) = \frac{f'(x) - \dfrac{f(x)g'(x)}{g(x)}}{g(x)}$$

Simplifying gives[10]

$$F'(x) = \frac{g(x)f'(x) - f(x)g'(x)}{(g(x))^2}$$

CAUTION!⚠

The derivative of the quotient of two functions is trickier still than the product rule. We must remember where the minus sign goes!

---

[10]The proof given assumes the existence of $F'(x)$. However, the rule can be proved without this assumption.

EXAMPLE 5   Applying the Quotient Rule

If $F(x) = \dfrac{4x^2 + 3}{2x - 1}$, find $F'(x)$.

Solution:

Strategy We recognize F as a quotient, so we can apply the quotient rule.

Let $f(x) = 4x^2 + 3$ and $g(x) = 2x - 1$. Then

$$F'(x) = \frac{g(x)f'(x) - f(x)g'(x)}{(g(x))^2}$$

$$= \frac{\overbrace{(2x-1)}^{\text{Denominator}} \overbrace{\dfrac{d}{dx}(4x^2+3)}^{\substack{\text{Derivative} \\ \text{of numerator}}} - \overbrace{(4x^2+3)}^{\text{Numerator}} \overbrace{\dfrac{d}{dx}(2x-1)}^{\substack{\text{Derivative of} \\ \text{numerator}}}}{\underbrace{(2x-1)^2}_{\substack{\text{Square of} \\ \text{denominator}}}}$$

$$= \frac{(2x-1)(8x) - (4x^2+3)(2)}{(2x-1)^2}$$

$$= \frac{8x^2 - 8x - 6}{(2x-1)^2} = \frac{2(2x+1)(2x-3)}{(2x-1)^2}$$

Now Work Problem 21 ◁

EXAMPLE 6   Rewriting before Differentiating

Differentiate $y = \dfrac{1}{x + \dfrac{1}{x+1}}$.

Solution:

Strategy To simplify the differentiation, we will rewrite the function so that no fraction appears in the denominator.

We have

$$y = \frac{1}{x + \dfrac{1}{x+1}} = \frac{1}{\dfrac{x(x+1)+1}{x+1}} = \frac{x+1}{x^2+x+1}$$

$$\frac{dy}{dx} = \frac{(x^2+x+1)(1) - (x+1)(2x+1)}{(x^2+x+1)^2} \qquad \text{quotient rule}$$

$$= \frac{(x^2+x+1) - (2x^2+3x+1)}{(x^2+x+1)^2}$$

$$= \frac{-x^2 - 2x}{(x^2+x+1)^2} = -\frac{x^2+2x}{(x^2+x+1)^2}$$

Now Work Problem 45 ◁

Although a function may have the form of a quotient, this does not necessarily mean that the quotient rule must be used to find the derivative. The next example illustrates some typical situations in which, although the quotient rule can be used, a simpler and more efficient method is available.

EXAMPLE 7   Differentiating Quotients without Using the Quotient Rule

Differentiate the following functions.

a. $f(x) = \dfrac{2x^3}{5}$

Solution: Rewriting, we have $f(x) = \frac{2}{5}x^3$. By the constant-factor rule,

$$f'(x) = \frac{2}{5}(3x^2) = \frac{6x^2}{5}$$

b. $f(x) = \dfrac{4}{7x^3}$

Solution: Rewriting, we have $f(x) = \frac{4}{7}(x^{-3})$. Thus,

$$f'(x) = \frac{4}{7}(-3x^{-4}) = -\frac{12}{7x^4}$$

c. $f(x) = \dfrac{5x^2 - 3x}{4x}$

Solution: Rewriting, we have $f(x) = \frac{1}{4}\left(\dfrac{5x^2 - 3x}{x}\right) = \frac{1}{4}(5x - 3)$ for $x \neq 0$. Thus,

$$f'(x) = \frac{1}{4}(5) = \frac{5}{4} \qquad \text{for } x \neq 0$$

Since the function f is not defined for $x = 0$, f' is not defined for $x = 0$ either.

Now Work Problem 17 ◁

CAUTION!

To differentiate $f(x) = \dfrac{1}{x^2 - 2}$, we might be tempted first to rewrite the quotient as $(x^2 - 2)^{-1}$. Currently it would be a mistake to do this because we do not yet have a rule for differentiating that form. In short, we have no choice now but to use the quotient rule. However, in the next section we will develop a rule that allows us to differentiate $(x^2 - 2)^{-1}$ in a direct and efficient way.

EXAMPLE 8   Marginal Revenue

If the demand equation for a manufacturer's product is

$$p = \frac{1000}{q + 5}$$

where p is in dollars, find the marginal-revenue function and evaluate it when $q = 45$.

Solution:

> **Strategy** First we must find the revenue function. The revenue r received for selling q units when the price per unit is p is given by
>
> $$\textbf{revenue} = (\textbf{price})(\textbf{quantity}); \quad \text{that is,} \quad r = pq$$
>
> Using the demand equation, we will express r in terms of q only. Then we will differentiate to find the marginal-revenue function, dr/dq.

The revenue function is

$$r = \left(\frac{1000}{q + 5}\right)q = \frac{1000q}{q + 5}$$

Thus, the marginal-revenue function is given by

$$\frac{dr}{dq} = \frac{(q + 5)\dfrac{d}{dq}(1000q) - (1000q)\dfrac{d}{dq}(q + 5)}{(q + 5)^2}$$

$$= \frac{(q + 5)(1000) - (1000q)(1)}{(q + 5)^2} = \frac{5000}{(q + 5)^2}$$

and

$$\left.\frac{dr}{dq}\right|_{q=45} = \frac{5000}{(45+5)^2} = \frac{5000}{2500} = 2$$

This means that selling one additional unit beyond 45 results in approximately $2 more in revenue.

Now Work Problem 59 ◁

Consumption Function

A function that plays an important role in economic analysis is the **consumption function.** The consumption function $C = f(I)$ expresses a relationship between the total national income I and the total national consumption C. Usually, both I and C are expressed in billions of dollars and I is restricted to some interval. The *marginal propensity to consume* is defined as the rate of change of consumption with respect to income. It is merely the derivative of C with respect to I:

$$\text{Marginal propensity to consume} = \frac{dC}{dI}$$

If we assume that the difference between income I and consumption C is savings S, then

$$S = I - C$$

Differentiating both sides with respect to I gives

$$\frac{dS}{dI} = \frac{d}{dI}(I) - \frac{d}{dI}(C) = 1 - \frac{dC}{dI}$$

We define dS/dI as the **marginal propensity to save.** Thus, the marginal propensity to save indicates how fast savings change with respect to income, and

$$\begin{array}{c}\text{Marginal propensity}\\\text{to save}\end{array} = 1 - \begin{array}{c}\text{Marginal propensity}\\\text{to consume}\end{array}$$

EXAMPLE 9   Finding Marginal Propensities to Consume and to Save

If the consumption function is given by

$$C = \frac{5(2\sqrt{I^3} + 3)}{I + 10}$$

determine the marginal propensity to consume and the marginal propensity to save when $I = 100$.

Solution:

$$\frac{dC}{dI} = 5\left(\frac{(I+10)\dfrac{d}{dI}(2I^{3/2}+3) - (2\sqrt{I^3}+3)\dfrac{d}{dI}(I+10)}{(I+10)^2}\right)$$

$$= 5\left(\frac{(I+10)(3I^{1/2}) - (2\sqrt{I^3}+3)(1)}{(I+10)^2}\right)$$

When $I = 100$, the marginal propensity to consume is

$$\left.\frac{dC}{dI}\right|_{I=100} = 5\left(\frac{1297}{12,100}\right) \approx 0.536$$

The marginal propensity to save when $I = 100$ is $1 - 0.536 = 0.464$. This means that if a current income of $100 billion increases by $1 billion, the nation consumes approximately 53.6% (536/1000) and saves 46.4% (464/1000) of that increase.

Now Work Problem 69 ◁

PROBLEMS 11.4

In Problems 1–48, differentiate the functions.

1. $f(x) = (4x + 1)(6x + 3)$ 2. $f(x) = (3x - 1)(7x + 2)$

3. $s(t) = (5 - 3t)(t^3 - 2t^2)$ 4. $Q(x) = (x^2 + 3x)(7x^2 - 5)$

5. $f(r) = (3r^2 - 4)(r^2 - 5r + 1)$

6. $C(I) = (2I^2 - 3)(3I^2 - 4I + 1)$

7. $f(x) = x^2(2x^2 - 5)$ 8. $f(x) = 3x^3(x^2 - 2x + 2)$

9. $y = (x^2 + 5x - 7)(6x^2 - 5x + 4)$

10. $\phi(x) = (3 - 5x + 2x^2)(2 + x - 4x^2)$

11. $f(w) = (w^2 + 3w - 7)(2w^3 - 4)$

12. $f(x) = (3x - x^2)(3 - x - x^2)$

13. $y = (x^2 - 1)(3x^3 - 6x + 5) - 4(4x^2 + 2x + 1)$

14. $h(x) = 5(x^7 + 4) + 4(5x^3 - 2)(4x^2 + 7x)$

15. $F(p) = \frac{3}{2}(5\sqrt{p} - 2)(3p - 1)$

16. $g(x) = (\sqrt{x} + 5x - 2)(\sqrt[3]{x} - 3\sqrt{x})$

17. $y = 7 \cdot \frac{2}{3}$ 18. $y = (x - 1)(x - 2)(x - 3)$

19. $y = (5x + 3)(2x - 5)(7x + 9)$

20. $y = \frac{2x - 3}{4x + 1}$ 21. $f(x) = \frac{5x}{x - 1}$

22. $H(x) = \frac{-5x}{5 - x}$ 23. $f(x) = \frac{-13}{3x^5}$

24. $f(x) = \frac{3(5x^2 - 7)}{4}$ 25. $y = \frac{x + 2}{x - 1}$

26. $h(w) = \frac{3w^2 + 5w - 1}{w - 3}$ 27. $h(z) = \frac{6 - 2z}{z^2 - 4}$

28. $z = \frac{2x^2 + 5x - 2}{3x^2 + 5x + 3}$ 29. $y = \frac{4x^2 + 3x + 2}{3x^2 - 2x + 1}$

30. $f(x) = \frac{x^3 - x^2 + 1}{x^2 + 1}$ 31. $y = \frac{x^2 - 4x + 3}{2x^2 - 3x + 2}$

32. $F(z) = \frac{z^4 + 4}{3z}$ 33. $g(x) = \frac{1}{x^{100} + 7}$

34. $y = \frac{-8}{7x^6}$ 35. $u(v) = \frac{v^3 - 8}{v}$

36. $y = \frac{x - 5}{8\sqrt{x}}$ 37. $y = \frac{3x^2 - x - 1}{\sqrt[3]{x}}$

38. $y = \frac{x^{0.3} - 2}{2x^{2.1} + 1}$ 39. $y = 1 - \frac{5}{2x + 5} + \frac{2x}{3x + 1}$

40. $q(x) = 2x^3 + \frac{5x + 1}{3x - 5} - \frac{2}{x^3}$

41. $y = \frac{x - 5}{(x + 2)(x - 4)}$ 42. $y = \frac{(9x - 1)(3x + 2)}{4 - 5x}$

43. $s(t) = \frac{t^2 + 3t}{(t^2 - 1)(t^3 + 7)}$ 44. $f(s) = \frac{17}{s(4s^3 + 5s - 23)}$

45. $y = 3x - \frac{\frac{2}{x} - \frac{3}{x - 1}}{x - 2}$ 46. $y = 3 - 12x^3 + \frac{1 - \frac{5}{x^2 + 2}}{x^2 + 5}$

47. $f(x) = \frac{a + x}{a - x}$, where a is a constant

48. $f(x) = \frac{x^{-1} + a^{-1}}{x^{-1} - a^{-1}}$, where a is a constant

49. Find the slope of the curve $y = (2x^2 - x + 3)(x^3 + x + 1)$ at $(1, 12)$.

50. Find the slope of the curve $y = \frac{x^3}{x^4 + 1}$ at $(-1, -\frac{1}{2})$.

In Problems 51–54, find an equation of the tangent line to the curve at the given point.

51. $y = \frac{6}{x - 1}$; $(3, 3)$ 52. $y = \frac{x + 5}{x^2}$; $(1, 6)$

53. $y = (2x + 3)[2(x^4 - 5x^2 + 4)]$; $(0, 24)$

54. $y = \frac{x - 1}{x(x^2 + 1)}$; $(2, \frac{1}{10})$

In Problems 55 and 56, determine the relative rate of change of y with respect to x for the given value of x.

55. $y = \frac{x}{2x - 6}$; $x = 1$ 56. $y = \frac{1 - x}{1 + x}$; $x = 5$

57. Motion   The position function for an object moving in a straight line is

$$s = \frac{2}{t^3 + 1}$$

where t is in seconds and s is in meters. Find the position and velocity of the object at $t = 1$.

58. Motion   The position function for an object moving in a straight-line path is

$$s = \frac{t + 3}{t^2 + 7}$$

where t is in seconds and s is in meters. Find the positive value(s) of t for which the velocity of the object is 0.

In Problems 59–62, each equation represents a demand function for a certain product, where p denotes the price per unit for q units. Find the marginal-revenue function in each case. Recall that revenue = pq.

59. $p = 80 - 0.02q$ 60. $p = 500/q$

61. $p = \frac{108}{q + 2} - 3$ 62. $p = \frac{q + 750}{q + 50}$

63. Consumption Function   For the United States (1922–1942), the consumption function is estimated by[11]

$$C = 0.672I + 113.1$$

Find the marginal propensity to consume.

64. Consumption Function   Repeat Problem 63 for $C = 0.836I + 127.2$.

In Problems 65–68, each equation represents a consumption function. Find the marginal propensity to consume and the marginal propensity to save for the given value of I.

65. $C = 3 + \sqrt{I} + 2\sqrt[3]{I}$; $I = 1$

66. $C = 6 + \frac{3I}{4} - \frac{\sqrt{I}}{3}$; $I = 25$

---

[11] T. Haavelmo, "Methods of Measuring the Marginal Propensity to Consume," *Journal of the American Statistical Association*, XLII (1947), 105–22.

67. $C = \dfrac{16\sqrt{I} + 0.8\sqrt{I^3} - 0.2I}{\sqrt{I} + 4}; I = 36$

68. $C = \dfrac{20\sqrt{I} + 0.5\sqrt{I^3} - 0.4I}{\sqrt{I} + 5}; I = 100$

69. Consumption Function   Suppose that a country's consumption function is given by

$$C = \dfrac{9\sqrt{I} + 0.8\sqrt{I^3} - 0.3I}{\sqrt{I}}$$

where C and I are expressed in billions of dollars.

(a) Find the marginal propensity to save when income is $25 billion.

(b) Determine the relative rate of change of C with respect to I when income is $25 billion.

70. Marginal Propensities to Consume and to Save   Suppose that the savings function of a country is

$$S = \dfrac{I - 2\sqrt{I} - 8}{\sqrt{I} + 2}$$

where the national income (I) and the national savings (S) are measured in billions of dollars. Find the country's marginal propensity to consume and its marginal propensity to save when the national income is $150 billion. (*Hint:* It may be helpful to first factor the numerator.)

71. Marginal Cost   If the total-cost function for a manufacturer is given by

$$c = \dfrac{6q^2}{q + 2} + 6000$$

find the marginal-cost function.

72. Marginal and Average Costs   Given the cost function $c = f(q)$, show that if $\dfrac{d}{dq}(\bar{c}) = 0$, then the marginal-cost function and average-cost function are equal.

73. Host–Parasite Relation   For a particular host–parasite relationship, it is determined that when the host density (number of hosts per unit of area) is x, the number of hosts that are parasitized is y, where

$$y = \dfrac{900x}{10 + 45x}$$

At what rate is the number of hosts parasitized changing with respect to host density when $x = 2$?

74. Acoustics   The persistence of sound in a room after the source of the sound is turned off is called *reverberation*. The *reverberation time* RT of the room is the time it takes for the intensity level of the sound to fall 60 decibels. In the acoustical design of an auditorium, the following formula may be used to compute the RT of the room:[12]

$$\mathrm{RT} = \dfrac{0.05V}{A + xV}$$

Here V is the room volume, A is the total room absorption, and x is the air absorption coefficient. Assuming that A and x are positive constants, show that the rate of change of RT with respect to V is always positive. If the total room volume increases by one unit, does the reverberation time increase or decrease?

75. Predator–Prey   In a predator–prey experiment,[13] it was statistically determined that the number of prey consumed, y, by an individual predator was a function of the prey density x (the number of prey per unit of area), where

$$y = \dfrac{0.7355x}{1 + 0.02744x}$$

Determine the rate of change of prey consumed with respect to prey density.

76. Social Security Benefits   In a discussion of social security benefits, Feldstein[14] differentiates a function of the form

$$f(x) = \dfrac{a(1 + x) - b(2 + n)x}{a(2 + n)(1 + x) - b(2 + n)x}$$

where a, b, and n are constants. He determines that

$$f'(x) = \dfrac{-1(1 + n)ab}{(a(1 + x) - bx)^2(2 + n)}$$

Verify this. (*Hint:* For convenience, let $2 + n = c$.) Next observe that Feldstein's function f is of the form

$$g(x) = \dfrac{A + Bx}{C + Dx}, \quad \text{where } A, B, C, \text{ and } D \text{ are constants}$$

Show that $g'(x)$ is a constant divided by a nonnegative function of x. What does this mean?

77. Business   The manufacturer of a product has found that when 20 units are produced per day, the average cost is $150 and the marginal cost is $125. What is the relative rate of change of average cost with respect to quantity when $q = 20$?

78. Use the result $(fgh)' = f'gh + fg'h + fgh'$ to find dy/dx if

$$y = (3x + 1)(2x - 1)(x - 4)$$

---

[12]L. L. Doelle, *Environmental Acoustics* (New York: McGraw-Hill Book Company, 1972).

[13]C. S. Holling, "Some Characteristics of Simple Types of Predation and Parasitism," *The Canadian Entomologist*, XCI, no. 7 (1959), 385–98.

[14]M. Feldstein, "The Optimal Level of Social Security Benefits," *The Quarterly Journal of Economics*, C, no. 2 (1985), 303–20.

Objective

To introduce and apply the chain rule, to derive a special case of the chain rule, and to develop the concept of the marginal-revenue product as an application of the chain rule.

11.5 The Chain Rule

Our next rule, the *chain rule*, is ultimately the most important rule for finding derivatives. It involves a situation in which y is a function of the variable u, but u is a function of x, and we want to find the derivative of y with respect to x. For example, the equations

$$y = u^2 \quad \text{and} \quad u = 2x + 1$$

define y as a function of u and u as a function of x. If we substitute $2x + 1$ for u in the first equation, we can consider y to be a function of x:

$$y = (2x + 1)^2$$

To find dy/dx, we first expand $(2x + 1)^2$:

$$y = 4x^2 + 4x + 1$$

Then

$$\frac{dy}{dx} = 8x + 4$$

From this example, you can see that finding dy/dx by first performing a substitution *could* be quite involved. For instance, if originally we had been given $y = u^{100}$ instead of $y = u^2$, we wouldn't even want to try substituting. Fortunately, the chain rule will allow us to handle such situations with ease.

COMBINING RULE 5   The Chain Rule

If y is a differentiable function of u and u is a differentiable function of x, then y is a differentiable function of x and

$$\frac{dy}{dx} = \frac{dy}{du} \cdot \frac{du}{dx}$$

We can show you why the chain rule is reasonable by considering rates of change. Suppose

$$y = 8u + 5 \quad \text{and} \quad u = 2x - 3$$

Let x change by one unit. How does u change? To answer this question, we differentiate and find $du/dx = 2$. But for *each* one-unit change in u, there is a change in y of $dy/du = 8$. Therefore, what is the change in y if x changes by one unit; that is, what is dy/dx? The answer is $8 \cdot 2$, which is $\dfrac{dy}{du} \cdot \dfrac{du}{dx}$. Thus, $\dfrac{dy}{dx} = \dfrac{dy}{du} \cdot \dfrac{du}{dx}$.

We will now use the chain rule to redo the problem at the beginning of this section. If

$$y = u^2 \quad \text{and} \quad u = 2x + 1$$

then

$$\frac{dy}{dx} = \frac{dy}{du} \cdot \frac{du}{dx} = \frac{d}{du}(u^2) \cdot \frac{d}{dx}(2x + 1)$$
$$= (2u)2 = 4u$$

Replacing u by $2x + 1$ gives

$$\frac{dy}{dx} = 4(2x + 1) = 8x + 4$$

which agrees with our previous result.

APPLY IT ▶

8. If an object moves horizontally according to $x = 6t$, where t is in seconds, and vertically according to $y = 4x^2$, find its vertical velocity $\dfrac{dy}{dt}$.

EXAMPLE 1   Using the Chain Rule

a. If $y = 2u^2 - 3u - 2$ and $u = x^2 + 4$, find dy/dx.

Solution: By the chain rule,

$$\frac{dy}{dx} = \frac{dy}{du} \cdot \frac{du}{dx} = \frac{d}{du}(2u^2 - 3u - 2) \cdot \frac{d}{dx}(x^2 + 4)$$
$$= (4u - 3)(2x)$$

We can write our answer in terms of x alone by replacing u by $x^2 + 4$.

$$\frac{dy}{dx} = [4(x^2 + 4) - 3](2x) = [4x^2 + 13](2x) = 8x^3 + 26x$$

b. If $y = \sqrt{w}$ and $w = 7 - t^3$, find dy/dt.

Solution: Here, y is a function of w and w is a function of t, so we can view y as a function of t. By the chain rule,

$$\frac{dy}{dt} = \frac{dy}{dw} \cdot \frac{dw}{dt} = \frac{d}{dw}(\sqrt{w}) \cdot \frac{d}{dt}(7 - t^3)$$

$$= \left(\frac{1}{2}w^{-1/2}\right)(-3t^2) = \frac{1}{2\sqrt{w}}(-3t^2)$$

$$= -\frac{3t^2}{2\sqrt{w}} = -\frac{3t^2}{2\sqrt{7 - t^3}}$$

Now Work Problem 1 ◁

EXAMPLE 2   Using the Chain Rule

If $y = 4u^3 + 10u^2 - 3u - 7$ and $u = 4/(3x - 5)$, find dy/dx when $x = 1$.

Solution: By the chain rule,

$$\frac{dy}{dx} = \frac{dy}{du} \cdot \frac{du}{dx} = \frac{d}{du}(4u^3 + 10u^2 - 3u - 7) \cdot \frac{d}{dx}\left(\frac{4}{3x - 5}\right)$$

$$= (12u^2 + 20u - 3) \cdot \frac{(3x - 5)\dfrac{d}{dx}(4) - 4\dfrac{d}{dx}(3x - 5)}{(3x - 5)^2}$$

$$= (12u^2 + 20u - 3) \cdot \frac{-12}{(3x - 5)^2}$$

When x is replaced by a, $u = u(x)$ must be replaced by $u(a)$.

Even though dy/dx is in terms of x's and u's, we can evaluate it when $x = 1$ if we determine the corresponding value of u. When $x = 1$,

$$u = \frac{4}{3(1) - 5} = -2$$

Thus,

$$\frac{dy}{dx}\bigg|_{x=1} = [12(-2)^2 + 20(-2) - 3] \cdot \frac{-12}{[3(1) - 5]^2}$$

$$= 5 \cdot (-3) = -15$$

Now Work Problem 5 ◁

The chain rules states that if $y = f(u)$ and $u = g(x)$, then

$$\frac{dy}{dx} = \frac{dy}{du} \cdot \frac{du}{dx}$$

Actually, the chain rule applies to a composite function, because

$$y = f(u) = f(g(x)) = (f \circ g)(x)$$

Thus y, as a function of x, is $f \circ g$. This means that we can use the chain rule to differentiate a function when we recognize the function as a composition. However, we must first break down the function into composite parts.

For example, to differentiate

$$y = (x^3 - x^2 + 6)^{100}$$

we think of the function as a composition. Let

$$y = f(u) = u^{100} \quad \text{and} \quad u = g(x) = x^3 - x^2 + 6$$

Then $y = (x^3 - x^2 + 6)^{100} = (g(x))^{100} = f(g(x))$. Now that we have a composite, we differentiate. Since $y = u^{100}$ and $u = x^3 - x^2 + 6$, by the chain rule we have

$$\frac{dy}{dx} = \frac{dy}{du} \cdot \frac{du}{dx}$$

$$= (100u^{99})(3x^2 - 2x)$$

$$= 100(x^3 - x^2 + 6)^{99}(3x^2 - 2x)$$

We have just used the chain rule to differentiate $y = (x^3 - x^2 + 6)^{100}$, which is a power of a *function* of x, not simply a power of x. The following rule, called the **power rule**, generalizes our result and is a special case of the chain rule:

> The Power Rule $\dfrac{d}{dx}(u^a) = au^{a-1}\dfrac{du}{dx}$

where it is understood that u is a differentiable function of x and a is a real number.
Proof. Let $y = u^a$. Since y is a differentiable function of u and u is a differentiable function of x, the chain rule gives

$$\frac{dy}{dx} = \frac{dy}{du} \cdot \frac{du}{dx}$$

But $dy/du = au^{a-1}$. Thus,

$$\frac{dy}{dx} = au^{a-1}\frac{du}{dx}$$

which is the power rule.

EXAMPLE 3   Using the Power Rule

If $y = (x^3 - 1)^7$, find y'.

Solution: Since y is a power of a *function* of x, the power rule applies. Letting $u(x) = x^3 - 1$ and $a = 7$, we have

$$y' = a[u(x)]^{a-1}u'(x)$$

$$= 7(x^3 - 1)^{7-1}\frac{d}{dx}(x^3 - 1)$$

$$= 7(x^3 - 1)^6(3x^2) = 21x^2(x^3 - 1)^6$$

Now Work Problem 9 ◁

EXAMPLE 4   Using the Power Rule

If $y = \sqrt[3]{(4x^2 + 3x - 2)^2}$, find dy/dx when $x = -2$.

Solution: Since $y = (4x^2 + 3x - 2)^{2/3}$, we use the power rule with

$$u = 4x^2 + 3x - 2$$

and $a = \frac{2}{3}$. We have

$$\frac{dy}{dx} = \frac{2}{3}(4x^2 + 3x - 2)^{(2/3)-1}\frac{d}{dx}(4x^2 + 3x - 2)$$

$$= \frac{2}{3}(4x^2 + 3x - 2)^{-1/3}(8x + 3)$$

$$= \frac{2(8x + 3)}{3\sqrt[3]{4x^2 + 3x - 2}}$$

Thus,

$$\left.\frac{dy}{dx}\right|_{x=-2} = \frac{2(-13)}{3\sqrt[3]{8}} = -\frac{13}{3}.$$

Now Work Problem 19 ◁

EXAMPLE 5   Using the Power Rule

The technique used in Example 5 is frequently used when the numerator of a quotient is a constant and the denominator is not.

If $y = \dfrac{1}{x^2 - 2}$, find $\dfrac{dy}{dx}$.

Solution: Although the quotient rule can be used here, a more efficient approach is to treat the right side as the power $(x^2 - 2)^{-1}$ and use the power rule. Let $u = x^2 - 2$. Then $y = u^{-1}$, and

$$\frac{dy}{dx} = (-1)(x^2 - 2)^{-1-1}\frac{d}{dx}(x^2 - 2)$$

$$= (-1)(x^2 - 2)^{-2}(2x)$$

$$= -\frac{2x}{(x^2 - 2)^2}$$

Now Work Problem 27 ◁

EXAMPLE 6   Differentiating a Power of a Quotient

If $z = \left(\dfrac{2s + 5}{s^2 + 1}\right)^4$, find $\dfrac{dz}{ds}$.

The problem here is to recognize the form of the function to be differentiated. In this case it is a power, not a quotient.

Solution: Since z is a power of a function, we first use the power rule:

$$\frac{dz}{ds} = 4\left(\frac{2s + 5}{s^2 + 1}\right)^{4-1}\frac{d}{ds}\left(\frac{2s + 5}{s^2 + 1}\right)$$

Now we use the quotient rule:

$$\frac{dz}{ds} = 4\left(\frac{2s + 5}{s^2 + 1}\right)^3\left(\frac{(s^2 + 1)(2) - (2s + 5)(2s)}{(s^2 + 1)^2}\right)$$

Simplifying, we have

$$\frac{dz}{ds} = 4 \cdot \frac{(2s + 5)^3}{(s^2 + 1)^3}\left(\frac{-2s^2 - 10s + 2}{(s^2 + 1)^2}\right)$$

$$= -\frac{8(s^2 + 5s - 1)(2s + 5)^3}{(s^2 + 1)^5}$$

Now Work Problem 41 ◁

EXAMPLE 7   Differentiating a Product of Powers

If $y = (x^2 - 4)^5(3x + 5)^4$, find y'.

Solution: Since y is a product, we first apply the product rule:

$$y' = (x^2 - 4)^5\frac{d}{dx}((3x + 5)^4) + (3x + 5)^4\frac{d}{dx}((x^2 - 4)^5)$$

Now we use the power rule:

$$y' = (x^2 - 4)^5(4(3x + 5)^3(3)) + (3x + 5)^4(5(x^2 - 4)^4(2x))$$

$$= 12(x^2 - 4)^5(3x + 5)^3 + 10x(3x + 5)^4(x^2 - 4)^4$$

In differentiating a product in which at least one factor is a power, simplifying the derivative usually involves factoring.

To simplify, we first remove common factors:

$$y' = 2(x^2 - 4)^4(3x + 5)^3[6(x^2 - 4) + 5x(3x + 5)]$$
$$= 2(x^2 - 4)^4(3x + 5)^3(21x^2 + 25x - 24)$$

Now Work Problem 39 ◁

Usually, the power rule should be used to differentiate $y = [u(x)]^n$. Although a function such as $y = (x^2 + 2)^2$ can be written $y = x^4 + 4x^2 + 4$ and differentiated easily, this method is impractical for a function such as $y = (x^2 + 2)^{1000}$. Since $y = (x^2 + 2)^{1000}$ is of the form $y = [u(x)]^n$, we have

$$y' = 1000(x^2 + 2)^{999}(2x)$$

Marginal-Revenue Product

Let us now use our knowledge of calculus to develop a concept relevant to economic studies. Suppose a manufacturer hires m employees who produce a total of q units of a product per day. We can think of q as a function of m. If r is the total revenue the manufacturer receives for selling these units, then r can also be considered a function of m. Thus, we can look at dr/dm, the rate of change of revenue with respect to the number of employees. The derivative dr/dm is called the **marginal-revenue product.** It approximates the change in revenue that results when a manufacturer hires an extra employee.

> **EXAMPLE 8**   **Marginal-Revenue Product**

A manufacturer determines that m employees will produce a total of q units of a product per day, where

$$q = \frac{10m^2}{\sqrt{m^2 + 19}} \tag{1}$$

If the demand equation for the product is $p = 900/(q + 9)$, determine the marginal-revenue product when $m = 9$.

Solution: We must find dr/dm, where r is revenue. Note that, by the chain rule,

$$\frac{dr}{dm} = \frac{dr}{dq} \cdot \frac{dq}{dm}$$

Thus, we must find both dr/dq and dq/dm when $m = 9$. We begin with dr/dq. The revenue function is given by

$$r = pq = \left(\frac{900}{q + 9}\right)q = \frac{900q}{q + 9} \tag{2}$$

so, by the quotient rule,

$$\frac{dr}{dq} = \frac{(q + 9)(900) - 900q(1)}{(q + 9)^2} = \frac{8100}{(q + 9)^2}$$

In order to evaluate this expression when $m = 9$, we first use the given equation $q = 10m^2/\sqrt{m^2 + 19}$ to find the corresponding value of q:

$$q = \frac{10(9)^2}{\sqrt{9^2 + 19}} = 81$$

Hence,

$$\left.\frac{dr}{dq}\right|_{m=9} = \left.\frac{dr}{dq}\right|_{q=81} = \frac{8100}{(81 + 9)^2} = 1$$

Now we turn to dq/dm. From the quotient and power rules, we have

$$\frac{dq}{dm} = \frac{d}{dm}\left(\frac{10m^2}{\sqrt{m^2+19}}\right)$$

$$= \frac{(m^2+19)^{1/2}\dfrac{d}{dm}(10m^2) - (10m^2)\dfrac{d}{dm}[(m^2+19)^{1/2}]}{[(m^2+19)^{1/2}]^2}$$

$$= \frac{(m^2+19)^{1/2}(20m) - (10m^2)[\frac{1}{2}(m^2+19)^{-1/2}(2m)]}{m^2+19}$$

so

$$\left.\frac{dq}{dm}\right|_{m=9} = \frac{(81+19)^{1/2}(20\cdot9) - (10\cdot81)[\frac{1}{2}(81+19)^{-1/2}(2\cdot9)]}{81+19}$$

$$= 10.71$$

A direct formula for the marginal-revenue product is

$$\frac{dr}{dm} = \frac{dq}{dm}\left(p + q\frac{dp}{dq}\right)$$

Therefore, from the chain rule,

$$\left.\frac{dr}{dm}\right|_{m=9} = (1)(10.71) = 10.71$$

This means that if a tenth employee is hired, revenue will increase by approximately $10.71 per day.

Now Work Problem 80 ◁

PROBLEMS 11.5

In Problems 1–8, use the chain rule.

1. If $y = u^2 - 2u$ and $u = x^2 - x$, find dy/dx.

2. If $y = 2u^3 - 8u$ and $u = 7x - x^3$, find dy/dx.

3. If $y = \dfrac{1}{w}$ and $w = 3x - 5$, find dy/dx.

4. If $y = \sqrt[3]{z}$ and $z = x^5 - x^4 + 3$, find dy/dx.

5. If $w = u^3$ and $u = \dfrac{t-1}{t+1}$, find dw/dt when $t = 1$.

6. If $z = u^2 + \sqrt{u} + 9$ and $u = 2s^2 - 1$, find dz/ds when $s = -1$.

7. If $y = 3w^2 - 8w + 4$ and $w = 2x^2 + 1$, find dy/dx when $x = 0$.

8. If $y = 2u^3 + 3u^2 + 5u - 1$ and $u = 3x + 1$, find dy/dx when $x = 1$.

In Problems 9–52, find y'.

9. $y = (3x + 2)^6$

10. $y = (x^2 - 4)^4$

11. $y = (3 + 2x^3)^5$

12. $y = (x^2 + x)^4$

13. $y = 5(x^3 - 3x^2 + 2x)^{100}$

14. $y = \dfrac{(2x^2 + 1)^4}{2}$

15. $y = (x^2 - 2)^{-3}$

16. $y = (2x^3 - 8x)^{-12}$

17. $y = 2(x^2 + 5x - 2)^{-5/7}$

18. $y = 3(5x - 2x^3)^{-5/3}$

19. $y = \sqrt{5x^2 - x}$

20. $y = \sqrt{3x^2 - 7}$

21. $y = \sqrt[4]{2x - 1}$

22. $y = \sqrt[3]{8x^2 - 1}$

23. $y = 4\sqrt[7]{(x^2 + 1)^3}$

24. $y = 7\sqrt[3]{(x^5 - 3)^5}$

25. $y = \dfrac{6}{2x^2 - x + 1}$

26. $y = \dfrac{3}{x^4 + 2}$

27. $y = \dfrac{1}{(x^2 - 3x)^2}$

28. $y = \dfrac{1}{(3 + 5x)^3}$

29. $y = \dfrac{4}{\sqrt{9x^2 + 1}}$

30. $y = \dfrac{3}{(3x^2 - x)^{2/3}}$

31. $y = \sqrt[3]{7x} + \sqrt[3]{7x}$

32. $y = \sqrt{2x} + \dfrac{1}{\sqrt{2x}}$

33. $y = x^3(2x + 3)^7$

34. $y = x(x + 4)^4$

35. $y = 4x^2\sqrt{5x + 1}$

36. $y = 4x^3\sqrt{1 - x^2}$

37. $y = (x^2 + 2x - 1)^3(5x)$

38. $y = x^4(x^4 - 1)^5$

39. $y = (8x - 1)^3(2x + 1)^4$

40. $y = (3x + 2)^5(4x - 5)^2$

41. $y = \left(\dfrac{x-3}{x+2}\right)^{12}$

42. $y = \left(\dfrac{2x}{x+2}\right)^4$

43. $y = \sqrt{\dfrac{x+1}{x-5}}$

44. $y = \sqrt[3]{\dfrac{8x^2 - 3}{x^2 + 2}}$

45. $y = \dfrac{2x - 5}{(x^2 + 4)^3}$

46. $y = \dfrac{(4x - 2)^4}{3x^2 + 7}$

47. $y = \dfrac{(8x - 1)^5}{(3x - 1)^3}$

48. $y = \sqrt[3]{(x-3)^3(x+5)}$

49. $y = 6(5x^2 + 2)\sqrt{x^4 + 5}$

50. $y = 6 + 3x - 4x(7x + 1)^2$

51. $y = 8t + \dfrac{t-1}{t+4} - \left(\dfrac{8t-7}{4}\right)^2$

52. $y = \dfrac{(2x^3 + 6)(7x - 5)}{(2x + 4)^2}$

In Problems 53 and 54, use the quotient rule and power rule to find y'. Do not simplify your answer.

53. $y = \dfrac{(3x + 2)^3(x + 1)^4}{(x^2 - 7)^3}$

54. $y = \dfrac{\sqrt{x + 2}(4x^2 - 1)^2}{9x - 3}$

55. If $y = (5u + 6)^3$ and $u = (x^2 + 1)^4$, find dy/dx when $x = 0$.

56. If $z = 2y^2 - 4y + 5$, $y = 6x - 5$, and $x = 2t$, find dz/dt when $t = 1$.

57. Find the slope of the curve $y = (x^2 - 7x - 8)^3$ at the point $(8, 0)$.

58. Find the slope of the curve $y = \sqrt{x+2}$ at the point $(7, 3)$.

In Problems 59–62, find an equation of the tangent line to the curve at the given point.

59. $y = \sqrt[3]{(x^2-8)^2}$; $(3, 1)$ **60.** $y = (x+3)^3$; $(-1, 8)$

61. $y = \dfrac{\sqrt{7x+2}}{x+1}$; $\left(1, \dfrac{3}{2}\right)$ **62.** $y = \dfrac{-3}{(3x^2+1)^3}$; $(0, -3)$

In Problems 63 and 64, determine the percentage rate of change of y with respect to x for the given value of x.

63. $y = (x^2+1)^4$; $x = 1$ **64.** $y = \dfrac{1}{(x^2-1)^3}$; $x = 2$

In Problems 65–68, q is the total number of units produced per day by m employees of a manufacturer, and p is the price per unit at which the q units are sold. In each case, find the marginal-revenue product for the given value of m.

65. $q = 5m$, $p = -0.4q + 50$; $m = 6$

66. $q = (200m - m^2)/20$, $p = -0.1q + 70$; $m = 40$

67. $q = 10m^2/\sqrt{m^2+9}$, $p = 525/(q+3)$; $m = 4$

68. $q = 50m/\sqrt{m^2+11}$, $p = 100/(q+10)$; $m = 5$

69. Demand Equation   Suppose $p = 100 - \sqrt{q^2+20}$ is a demand equation for a manufacturer's product.

(a) Find the rate of change of p with respect to q.

(b) Find the relative rate of change of p with respect to q.

(c) Find the marginal-revenue function.

70. Marginal-Revenue Product   If $p = k/q$, where k is a constant, is the demand equation for a manufacturer's product and $q = f(m)$ defines a function that gives the total number of units produced per day by m employees, show that the marginal-revenue product is always zero.

71. Cost Function   The cost c of producing q units of a product is given by

$$c = 5500 + 12q + 0.2q^2$$

If the price per unit p is given by the equation

$$q = 900 - 1.5p$$

use the chain rule to find the rate of change of cost with respect to price per unit when $p = 85$.

72. Hospital Discharges   A governmental health agency examined the records of a group of individuals who were hospitalized with a particular illness. It was found that the total proportion that had been discharged at the end of t days of hospitalization was given by

$$f(t) = 1 - \left(\frac{250}{250+t}\right)^3$$

Find $f'(100)$ and interpret your answer.

73. Marginal Cost   If the total-cost function for a manufacturer is given by

$$c = \frac{4q^2}{\sqrt{q^2+2}} + 6000$$

find the marginal-cost function.

74. Salary/Education   For a certain population, if E is the number of years of a person's education and S represents average annual salary in dollars, then for $E \geq 7$,

$$S = 340E^2 - 4360E + 42,800$$

(a) How fast is salary changing with respect to education when $E = 16$?

(b) At what level of education does the rate of change of salary equal $5000 per year of education?

75. Biology   The volume of a spherical cell is given by $V = \frac{4}{3}\pi r^3$, where r is the radius. At time t seconds, the radius (in centimeters) is given by

$$r = 10^{-8}t^2 + 10^{-7}t$$

Use the chain rule to find dV/dt when $t = 10$.

76. Pressure in Body Tissue   Under certain conditions, the pressure p developed in body tissue by ultrasonic beams is given as a function of the beam's intensity via the equation[15]

$$p = (2\rho VI)^{1/2}$$

where ρ (a Greek letter read "rho") is density of the affected tissue and V is the velocity of propagation of the beam. Here ρ and V are constants. (a) Find the rate of change of p with respect to I. (b) Find the relative rate of change of p with respect to I.

77. Demography   Suppose that, for a certain group of 20,000 births, the number of people surviving to age x years is

$$l_x = -0.000354x^4 + 0.00452x^3 + 0.848x^2 - 34.9x + 20,000$$
$$0 \leq x \leq 95.2$$

(a) Find the rate of change of l_x with respect to x, and evaluate your answer for $x = 65$.

(b) Find the relative rate of change and the percentage rate of change of l_x when $x = 65$. Round your answers to three decimal places.

78. Muscle Contraction   A muscle has the ability to shorten when a load, such as a weight, is imposed on it. The equation

$$(P + a)(v + b) = k$$

is called the "fundamental equation of muscle contraction."[16] Here P is the load imposed on the muscle, v is the velocity of the shortening of the muscle fibers, and a, b, and k are positive constants. Express v as a function of P. Use your result to find dv/dP.

79. Economics   Suppose $pq = 100$ is the demand equation for a manufacturer's product. Let c be the total cost, and assume that the marginal cost is 0.01 when $q = 200$. Use the chain rule to find dc/dp when $q = 200$.

80. Marginal-Revenue Product   A monopolist who employs m workers finds that they produce

$$q = 2m(2m+1)^{3/2}$$

units of product per day. The total revenue r (in dollars) is given by

$$r = \frac{50q}{\sqrt{1000 + 3q}}$$

---

[15] R. W. Stacy et al., *Essentials of Biological and Medical Physics* (New York: McGraw-Hill Book Company, 1955).

[16] Ibid.

(a) What is the price per unit (to the nearest cent) when there are 12 workers?
(b) Determine the marginal revenue when there are 12 workers.
(c) Determine the marginal-revenue product when $m = 12$.

81. Suppose $y = f(x)$, where $x = g(t)$. Given that $g(2) = 3, g'(2) = 4, f(2) = 5, f'(2) = 6, g(3) = 7, g'(3) = 8$, $f(3) = 9$, and $f'(3) = 10$, determine the value of $\dfrac{dy}{dt}\Big|_{t=2}$.

82. Business A manufacturer has determined that, for his product, the daily average cost (in hundreds of dollars) is given by

$$\bar{c} = \frac{324}{\sqrt{q^2 + 35}} + \frac{5}{q} + \frac{19}{18}$$

(a) As daily production increases, the average cost approaches a constant dollar amount. What is this amount?
(b) Determine the manufacturer's marginal cost when 17 units are produced per day.
(c) The manufacturer determines that if production (and sales) were increased to 18 units per day, revenue would increase by $275. Should this move be made? Why?

83. If

$$y = (u + 2)\sqrt{u + 3}$$

and

$$u = x(x^2 + 3)^3$$

find dy/dx when $x = 0.1$. Round your answer to two decimal places.

84. If

$$y = \frac{2u + 3}{u^3 - 2}$$

and

$$u = \frac{x + 4}{(2x + 3)^3}$$

find dy/dx when $x = -1$. Round your answer to two decimal places.

Chapter 11 Review

Important Terms and Symbols Examples

Section 11.1	**The Derivative**		
	secant line tangent line slope of a curve		Ex. 1, p. 494
	derivative $\displaystyle\lim_{h\to 0}\frac{f(x+h)-f(x)}{h}$ $\displaystyle\lim_{z\to x}\frac{f(z)-f(x)}{z-x}$		Ex. 2, p. 495
	difference quotient $\quad f'(x) \quad y' \quad \dfrac{d}{dx}(f(x)) \quad \dfrac{dy}{dx}$		Ex. 4, p. 496
Section 11.2	**Rules for Differentiation**		
	power function constant factor rule sum or difference rule		Ex. 5, p. 505
Section 11.3	**The Derivative as a Rate of Change**		
	position function Δx velocity rate of change		Ex. 1, p. 510
	total-cost function marginal cost average cost		Ex. 7, p. 513
	total-revenue function marginal revenue		Ex. 8, p. 514
	relative rate of change percentage rate of change		Ex. 9, p. 515
Section 11.4	**The Product Rule and the Quotient Rule**		
	product rule quotient rule		Ex. 5, p. 522
	consumption function marginal propensity to consume and to save		Ex. 9, p. 524
Section 11.5	**The Chain Rule**		
	chain rule power rule marginal-revenue product		Ex. 8, p. 531

Summary

The tangent line (or tangent) to a curve at point P is the limiting position of secant lines PQ as Q approaches P along the curve. The slope of the tangent at P is called the slope of the curve at P.

If $y = f(x)$, the derivative of f at x is the function $f'(x)$ defined by the limit in the equation

$$f'(x) = \lim_{h\to 0}\frac{f(x+h)-f(x)}{h}$$

Geometrically, the derivative gives the slope of the curve $y = f(x)$ at the point $(x, f(x))$. An equation of the tangent line at a particular point $(a, f(a))$ is obtained by evaluating $f'(a)$,

which is the slope of the tangent line, and using the point-slope form of a line: $y - f(a) = f'(a)(x - a)$. Any function that is differentiable at a point must also be continuous there.

The rules for finding derivatives, discussed so far, are as follows, where we assume that all functions are differentiable:

$\dfrac{d}{dx}(c) = 0$, where c is any constant

$\dfrac{d}{dx}(x^a) = ax^{a-1}$, where a is any real number

$\dfrac{d}{dx}(cf(x)) = cf'(x)$, where c is a constant

$$\frac{d}{dx}(f(x) + g(x)) = f'(x) + g'(x)$$

$$\frac{d}{dx}(f(x) - g(x)) = f'(x) - g'(x)$$

$$\frac{d}{dx}(f(x)g(x)) = f'(x)g(x) + f(x)g'(x)$$

$$\frac{d}{dx}\left(\frac{f(x)}{g(x)}\right) = \frac{g(x)f'(x) - f(x)g'(x)}{(g(x))^2}$$

$$\frac{dy}{dx} = \frac{dy}{du} \cdot \frac{du}{dx}, \text{where } y \text{ is a function of } u \text{ and } u \text{ is a function of } x$$

$$\frac{d}{dx}(u^a) = au^{a-1}\frac{du}{dx}, \text{where } u \text{ is a function of } x \text{ and } a \text{ is any real number}$$

The derivative dy/dx can also be interpreted as giving the (instantaneous) rate of change of y with respect to x:

$$\frac{dy}{dx} = \lim_{\Delta x \to 0} \frac{\Delta y}{\Delta x} = \lim_{\Delta x \to 0} \frac{\text{change in } y}{\text{change in } x}$$

In particular, if $s = f(t)$ is a position function, where s is position at time t, then

$$\frac{ds}{dt} = \text{velocity at time } t$$

In economics, the term *marginal* is used to describe derivatives of specific types of functions. If $c = f(q)$ is a total-cost function (c is the total cost of q units of a product), then the rate of change

$$\frac{dc}{dq} \text{ is called marginal cost}$$

We interpret marginal cost as the approximate cost of one additional unit of output. (Average cost per unit, $\bar{c}$, is related to total cost c by $\bar{c} = c/q$, equivalently, $c = \bar{c}q$.)

A total-revenue function $r = f(q)$ gives a manufacturer's revenue r for selling q units of product. (Revenue r and price p are related by $r = pq$.) The rate of change

$$\frac{dr}{dq} \text{ is called marginal revenue}$$

which is interpreted as the approximate revenue obtained from selling one additional unit of output.

If r is the revenue that a manufacturer receives when the total output of m employees is sold, then the derivative $dr/dm = dr/dq \cdot dq/dm$ is called the marginal-revenue product and gives the approximate change in revenue that results when the manufacturer hires an extra employee.

If $C = f(I)$ is a consumption function, where I is national income and C is national consumption, then

$$\frac{dC}{dI} \text{ is marginal propensity to consume}$$

and

$$1 - \frac{dC}{dI} \text{ is marginal prospensity to save}$$

For any function, the relative rate of change of $f(x)$ is

$$\frac{f'(x)}{f(x)}$$

which compares the rate of change of $f(x)$ with $f(x)$ itself. The percentage rate of change is

$$\frac{f'(x)}{f(x)} \cdot 100\%$$

Review Problems

In Problems 1–4, use the definition of the derivative to find $f'(x)$.

1. $f(x) = 2 - x^2$

2. $f(x) = 5x^3 - 2x + 1$

3. $f(x) = \sqrt{3x}$

4. $f(x) = \dfrac{2}{1 + 4x}$

In Problems 5–38, differentiate.

5. $y = 7^4$

6. $y = ex$

7. $y = \pi x^4 - \sqrt{2}x^3 + 2x^2 + 4$

8. $y = 4(x^2 + 5) - 7x$

9. $f(s) = s^2(s^2 + 2)$

10. $y = \sqrt{x + 3}$

11. $y = \dfrac{x^2 + 1}{5}$

12. $y = -\dfrac{1}{nx^n}$

13. $y = (x^3 + 7x^2)(x^3 - x^2 + 5)$

14. $y = (x^2 + 1)^{100}(x - 6)$

15. $f(x) = (2x^2 + 4x)^{100}$

16. $f(w) = w\sqrt{w} + w^2$

17. $y = \dfrac{c}{ax + b}$

18. $y = \dfrac{5x^2 - 8x}{2x}$

19. $y = (8 + 2x)(x^2 + 1)^4$

20. $g(z) = (2z)^{3/5} + 5$

21. $f(z) = \dfrac{z^2 - 1}{z^2 + 4}$

22. $y = \dfrac{ax + b}{cx + d}$

23. $y = \sqrt[3]{4x - 1}$

24. $f(x) = (1 + 2^3)^{12}$

25. $y = \dfrac{1}{\sqrt{1 - x^2}}$

26. $y = \dfrac{x(x + 1)}{2x^2 + 3}$

27. $h(x) = (ax + b)^m(cx + d)^n$

28. $y = \dfrac{(x + 3)^5}{x}$

29. $y = \dfrac{5x - 4}{x + 6}$

30. $f(x) = 5x^3\sqrt{3 + 2x^4}$

31. $y = 2x^{-3/8} + (2x)^{-3/8}$

32. $y = \sqrt{\dfrac{x}{a}} + \sqrt{\dfrac{a}{x}}$

33. $y = \dfrac{x^2 + 6}{\sqrt{x^2 + 5}}$

34. $y = \sqrt[3]{(7 - 3x^2)^2}$

35. $y = (x^3 + 6x^2 + 9)^{3/5}$

36. $z = 0.4x^2(x + 1)^{-3} + 0.5$

37. $g(z) = \dfrac{-3z}{(z - 2)^{-3}}$

38. $g(z) = \dfrac{-3}{4(z^5 + 2z - 5)^4}$

In Problems 39–42, find an equation of the tangent line to the curve at the point corresponding to the given value of x.

39. $y = x^2 - 6x + 4$, $x = 1$ **40.** $y = -2x^3 + 6x + 1$, $x = 2$

41. $y = \sqrt[3]{x}$, $x = 8$ **42.** $y = \dfrac{x^2}{x - 10}$, $x = 11$

43. If $f(x) = 4x^2 + 2x + 8$, find the relative and percentage rates of change of $f(x)$ when $x = 1$.

44. If $f(x) = x/(x + 4)$, find the relative and percentage rates of change of $f(x)$ when $x = 1$.

45. Marginal Revenue If $r = q(20 - 0.1q)$ is a total-revenue function, find the marginal-revenue function.

46. Marginal Cost If

$$c = 0.0001q^3 - 0.02q^2 + 3q + 6000$$

is a total-cost function, find the marginal cost when $q = 100$.

47. Consumption Function If

$$C = 9 + 0.7I - 0.2\sqrt{I}$$

is a consumption function, find the marginal propensity to consume and the marginal propensity to save when $I = 25$.

48. Demand Equation If $p = \dfrac{q + 12}{q + 5}$ is a demand equation, find the rate of change of price p with respect to quantity q.

49. Demand Equation If $p = -0.1q + 500$ is a demand equation, find the marginal-revenue function.

50. Average Cost If $\bar{c} = 0.03q + 1.2 + \dfrac{3}{q}$ is an average-cost function, find the marginal cost when $q = 100$.

51. Power-Plant Cost Function The total-cost function of an electric light and power plant is estimated by[17]

$$c = 16.68 + 0.125q + 0.00439q^2 \qquad 20 \le q \le 90$$

where q is the eight-hour total output (as a percentage of capacity) and c is the total fuel cost in dollars. Find the marginal-cost function and evaluate it when $q = 70$.

52. Marginal-Revenue Product A manufacturer has determined that m employees will produce a total of q units of product per day, where

$$q = m(60 - m)$$

If the demand function is given by

$$p = -0.02q + 12$$

find the marginal-revenue product when $m = 10$.

53. Winter Moth In a study of the winter moth in Nova Scotia,[18] it was determined that the average number of eggs, y, in a female moth was a function of the female's abdominal width x (in millimeters), where

$$y = f(x) = 14x^3 - 17x^2 - 16x + 34$$

and $1.5 \le x \le 3.5$. At what rate does the number of eggs change with respect to abdominal width when $x = 2$?

54. Host–Parasite Relation For a particular host–parasite relationship, it is found that when the host density (number of hosts per unit of area) is x, the number of hosts that are parasitized is

$$y = 12\left(1 - \dfrac{1}{1 + 3x}\right) \qquad x \ge 0$$

For what value of x does dy/dx equal $\frac{1}{3}$?

55. Bacteria Growth Bacteria are growing in a culture. The time t (in hours) for the number of bacteria to double in number (the generation time) is a function of the temperature T (in degrees Celsius) of the culture and is given by

$$t = f(T) = \begin{cases} \frac{1}{24}T + \frac{11}{4} & \text{if } 30 \le T \le 36 \\ \frac{4}{3}T - \frac{175}{4} & \text{if } 36 < T \le 39 \end{cases}$$

Find dt/dT when (a) $T = 38$ and (b) $T = 35$.

56. Motion The position function of a particle moving in a straight line is

$$s = \dfrac{9}{2t^2 + 3}$$

where t is in seconds and s is in meters. Find the velocity of the particle at $t = 1$.

57. Rate of Change The volume of a ball is given by $V = \frac{1}{6}\pi d^3$, where d is the diameter. Find the rate of change of V with respect to d when $d = 2$ ft.

58. Motion The position function for a ball thrown vertically upward from the ground is

$$s = 218t - 16t^2$$

where s is the height in feet above the ground after t seconds. For what value(s) of t is the velocity 64 ft/s?

59. Find the marginal-cost function if the average-cost function is

$$\bar{c} = 2q + \dfrac{10,000}{q^2}$$

60. Find an equation of the tangent line to the curve

$$y = \dfrac{(x^3 + 2)\sqrt{x + 1}}{x^4 + 2x}$$

at the point on the curve where $x = 1$.

61. A manufacturer has found that when m employees are working, the number of units of product produced per day is

$$q = 10\sqrt{m^2 + 4900} - 700$$

The demand equation for the product is

$$8q + p^2 - 19{,}300 = 0$$

where p is the selling price when the demand for the product is q units per day.

---

[17]J. A. Nordin, "Note on a Light Plant's Cost Curves," *Econometrica*, 15 (1947), 231–55.

[18]D. G. Embree, "The Population Dynamics of the Winter Moth in Nova Scotia, 1954–1962," *Memoirs of the Entomological Society of Canada*, no. 46 (1965).

(a) Determine the manufacturer's marginal-revenue product when $m = 240$.

(b) Find the relative rate of change of revenue with respect to the number of employees when $m = 240$.

(c) Suppose it would cost the manufacturer $400 more per day to hire an additional employee. Would you advise the manufacturer to hire the 241st employee? Why or why not?

62. If $f(x) = xe^{-x}$, use the definition of the derivative ("limit of a difference quotient") to estimate $f'(1)$. Round your answer to three decimal places.

63. If $f(x) = \sqrt[3]{x^2 + 3x - 4}$, use the numerical derivative feature of your graphing calculator to estimate the derivative when $x = 10$. Round your answer to three decimal places.

64. The total-cost function for a manufacturer is given by

$$c = \frac{5q^2 + 4}{\sqrt{q^2 + 6}} + 2500$$

where c is in dollars. Use the numerical derivative feature of your graphing calculator to estimate the marginal cost when 15 units are produced. Round your answer to the nearest cent.

65. Show that Basic Rule 0 is actually a consequence of Combining Rule 1 and the $a = 0$ case of Basic Rule 1.

66. Show that Basic Rule 1 *for positive integers* is a consequence of Combining Rule 3 (the Product Rule) and the $a = 1$ case of Basic Rule 1.

EXPLORE & EXTEND Marginal Propensity to Consume

A consumption function can be defined either for a nation, as in Section 11.4, or for an individual family. In either case, the function relates total consumption to total income. A savings function, similarly, relates total savings to total income, either at the national or at the family level.

Data about income, consumption, and savings for the United States as a whole can be found in the National Income and Product Accounts (NIPA) tables compiled by the Bureau of Economic Analysis, a division of the U.S. Department of Commerce. The tables are downloadable at www.bea.gov. For the years 1959–1999, the national consumption function is indicated by the scatterplot in Figure 11.13.

Notice that the points lie more or less along a straight line. A linear regression gives the equation for this as $y = 0.9314x - 99.1936$.

The marginal propensity to consume derived from this graph is simply the slope of the line, that is, about 0.931 or 93.1%. At the national level, then, an increase of $1 billion in total disposable income produces an increase of $931 million in consumption. And if we assume that the rest is saved, there is an increase of $69 million in total savings.[1]

Perhaps somewhat easier to relate to, because of the smaller numbers involved, is the consumption function for an individual household. This function is documented in Consumer Expenditure Surveys conducted by the Bureau of Labor Statistics, which is part of the U.S. Department of Labor. The survey results for each year can be downloaded at www.bls.gov/cex/.

Each year's survey gives information for five quintiles, as they are called, where a quintile represents one-fifth of American households. The quintiles are ordered by income, so that the bottom quintile represents the poorest 20% of Americans and the top quintile represents the richest 20%.

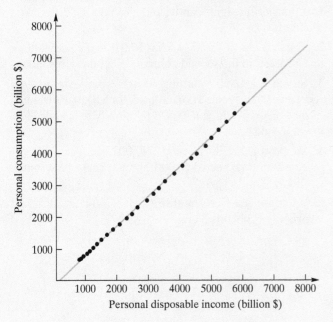

FIGURE 11.13 U.S. national consumption function.

Table 11.3 U.S. Family Income and Expenses, 1999

After-Tax Income	Total Expenses
$7101	$16,766
$17,576	$24,850
$30,186	$33,078
$48,607	$46,015
$98,214	$75,080

For the year 1999, income and consumption are as shown in Table 11.3. The numbers are average values

---

[1] In reality, we must also account for interest payments and other outlays not counted as consumption. But we will ignore this complication from now on.

within each quintile. If these data values are plotted using a graphing calculator, the points lie in a pattern that could be reasonably well approximated by a straight line but could be even better approximated by a curve—a curve shaped, qualitatively, like a square root function (Figure 11.14).

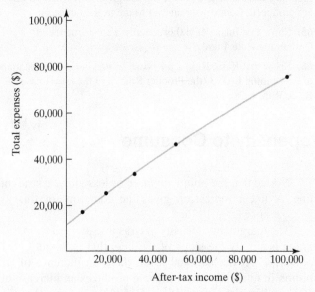

FIGURE 11.14   U.S. family consumption function.

Most graphing calculators do not have a regression function for a square root–type function. They do, however, have a quadratic regression function—and the inverse of a quadratic function is a square root–type function. (Inverse functions were defined in Section 2.4.) So, we proceed as follows. First, using the statistics capabilities of a graphics calculator, enter the numbers in the *second* column in Table 11.3 as x-values and those in the *first* column as y-values. Second, perform a quadratic regression. The function obtained is given by

$$y = (4.4627 \times 10^{-6})x^2 + 1.1517x - 13{,}461$$

Third, swap the lists of x- and y-values in preparation for plotting. Fourth, replace y with x and x with y in the quadratic regression equation and solve the result for y (using the quadratic formula) to obtain the equation

$$y = \frac{-1.1517 \pm \sqrt{\begin{array}{c} 1.1517^2 - 4(4.4627 \times 10^{-6}) \\ (-13{,}461 - x) \end{array}}}{2(4.4627 \times 10^{-6})}$$

or, more simply,

$$y = -129{,}036 \pm \sqrt{1.9667 \times 10^{10} + 224{,}080x}$$

Finally, enter the upper half of the curve (corresponding to the $+$ part of the $\pm$ sign) as a function to be graphed; then display it together with a plot of the data. The result looks as shown in Figure 11.15.

To find the marginal consumption for a given income level, we now use the dy/dx function. To find the marginal consumption at \$50,000, for instance, we select dy/dx, then enter 50000. The calculator returns the value 0.637675, which represents a marginal consumption of about 63.8%. In other words, a family earning \$50,000 per year will, if given an extra \$1000, spend \$638 of it and save the rest.

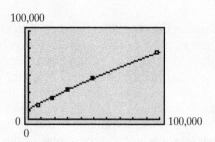

FIGURE 11.15   Graph of regression curve.

Problems

1. Compare the consumption function for Figure 11.13 with the consumption functions in Problems 63 and 64 of Section 11.5. Give two ways that these consumption functions differ significantly, and interpret the differences qualitatively.

2. The first row in Table 11.3 has \$7101 in the first column and \$16,766 in the second column. What does this mean?

3. Suppose a family earning \$25,000 per year in 1999 received an unexpected bonus check for \$1000. How much of that check would you expect the family to spend? How much to save?

4. Suppose a family earning \$90,000 per year in 1999 received an unexpected \$1000 bonus check. How much would the family spend?

5. What are the likely real-life reasons for the different answers in Problems 3 and 4?

12 Additional Differentiation Topics

EXPLORE & EXTEND
Economic Order Quantity

After an uncomfortable trip in a vehicle, passengers sometimes describe the ride as "jerky." But what is jerkiness, exactly? What does it mean for, say, an engineer designing a new transportation system?

Travel in a straight line at a constant speed is called *uniform motion,* and there is nothing jerky about it. But if either the path or the speed changes, the ride may become jerky. Change in velocity over time is the derivative of velocity. Called acceleration, the change in velocity is the *second derivative* of position with respect to time—the derivative of the derivative of position. One of the important concepts covered in this chapter is that of a higher-order derivative, of which acceleration is an example.

But is acceleration responsible for jerkiness? The feeling of being jerked back and forth on a roller coaster is certainly related to acceleration. On the other hand, automotive magazines often praise a car for having *smooth* acceleration. So apparently acceleration has something to do with jerkiness but is not itself the cause.

The derivative of acceleration is the *third* derivative of position with respect to time. When this third derivative is large, the acceleration is changing rapidly. A roller coaster in a steady turn to the left is undergoing steady leftward acceleration. But when the coaster changes abruptly from a hard left turn to a hard right turn, the acceleration changes directions—and the riders experience a jerk. The third derivative of position is, in fact, so apt a measure of jerkiness that it is customarily called the *jerk,* just as the second derivative is called the acceleration.

Jerk has implications not only for passenger comfort in vehicles but also for equipment reliability. Engineers designing equipment for spacecraft, for instance, follow guidelines about the maximum jerk the equipment must be able to survive without damage to its internal components.

To develop a differentiation formula for $y = \ln u$, to apply the formula, and to use it to differentiate a logarithmic function to a base other than e.

12.1 Derivatives of Logarithmic Functions

So far, the only derivatives we have been able to calculate are those of functions that are constructed from power functions using multiplication by a constant, arithmetic operations, and composition. (As pointed out in Problem 65 of Section 11.6, we can calculate the derivative of a constant function c by writing $c = cx^0$; then

$$\frac{d}{dx}(c) = \frac{d}{dx}(cx^0) = c\frac{d}{dx}(x^0) = c \cdot 0x^{-1} = 0$$

Thus, we really have only one *basic* differention formula so far.) The logarithmic functions $\log_b x$ and the exponential functions b^x *cannot* be constructed from power functions using multiplication by a constant, arithmetic operations, and composition. It follows that we will need at least another truly *basic* differentiation formula.

In this section, we develop formulas for differentiating logarithmic functions. We begin with the derivative of $\ln x$, commenting further on the numbered steps at the end of the calculation.

$$\frac{d}{dx}(\ln x) \overset{(1)}{=} \lim_{h \to 0} \frac{\ln(x+h) - \ln x}{h} \qquad \text{definition of derivative}$$

$$\overset{(2)}{=} \lim_{h \to 0} \frac{\ln\left(\dfrac{x+h}{x}\right)}{h} \qquad \text{since } \ln m - \ln n = \ln(m/n)$$

$$\overset{(3)}{=} \lim_{h \to 0} \left(\frac{1}{h}\ln\left(1 + \frac{h}{x}\right)\right) \qquad \text{algebra}$$

$$\overset{(4)}{=} \lim_{h \to 0} \left(\frac{1}{x} \cdot \frac{x}{h}\ln\left(1 + \frac{h}{x}\right)\right) \qquad \text{writing } \frac{1}{h} = \frac{1}{x} \cdot \frac{x}{h}$$

$$\overset{(5)}{=} \lim_{h \to 0} \left(\frac{1}{x}\ln\left(1 + \frac{h}{x}\right)^{x/h}\right) \qquad \text{since } r\ln m = \ln m^r$$

$$\overset{(6)}{=} \frac{1}{x} \cdot \lim_{h \to 0} \left(\ln\left(1 + \frac{h}{x}\right)^{x/h}\right) \qquad \text{by limit property 1 in Section 10.1}$$

$$\overset{(7)}{=} \frac{1}{x} \cdot \ln\left(\lim_{h \to 0} \left(1 + \frac{h}{x}\right)^{x/h}\right) \qquad \ln \text{ is continuous}$$

$$\overset{(8)}{=} \frac{1}{x} \cdot \ln\left(\lim_{h/x \to 0} \left(1 + \frac{h}{x}\right)^{x/h}\right) \qquad \text{for fixed } x > 0$$

$$\overset{(9)}{=} \frac{1}{x} \cdot \ln\left(\lim_{k \to 0} (1 + k)^{1/k}\right) \qquad \text{setting } k = h/x$$

$$\overset{(10)}{=} \frac{1}{x} \cdot \ln(e) \qquad \text{as shown in Section 10.1}$$

$$\overset{(11)}{=} \frac{1}{x} \qquad \text{since } \ln e = 1$$

The calculation is long but following it step by step allows for review of many important ideas. Step (1) is the key definition introduced in Section 11.1. Steps (2), (5), and (11) involve properties found in 4.3. In step (3), labeled simply *algebra*, we use properties of fractions first given in 0.2. Step (4) is admittedly a *trick* that requires experience to discover. Note that necessarily $x \neq 0$ since x is in the domain of ln, which is $(0, \infty)$. To understand the justification for Step (6), we must observe that x, and hence $1/x$, is constant with respect to the limit variable h. We have already remarked in Section 10.3 that logarithmic functions are continuous and this is what allows us to interchange the processes of applying the ln function and taking a limit in (7). In (8) the point is that, for fixed

$x > 0$, h/x goes to 0 when h goes to 0 and conversely h goes to 0 when h/x goes to 0. Thus, we can regard h/x as a new limit variable, k, and this we do in step (9).

In conclusion, we have derived the following:

> **BASIC RULE 2   Derivative of $\ln x$**
>
> $$\frac{d}{dx}(\ln x) = \frac{1}{x} \quad \text{for } x > 0$$

Some care is required with this rule because while the left-hand side is defined only for $x > 0$, the right-hand side is defined for all $x \neq 0$. For $x < 0$, $\ln(-x)$ is defined and by the chain rule we have

$$\frac{d}{dx}(\ln(-x)) = \frac{1}{-x}\frac{d}{dx}(-x) = \frac{-1}{-x} = \frac{1}{x} \quad \text{for } x < 0$$

We can combine the last two equations by using the absolute function to get

$$\frac{d}{dx}(\ln|x|) = \frac{1}{x} \quad \text{for } x \neq 0 \tag{1}$$

EXAMPLE 1   Differentiating Functions Involving $\ln x$

a. Differentiate $f(x) = 5\ln x$.

Solution: Here f is a constant (5) times a function ($\ln x$), so by Basic Rule 2, we have

$$f'(x) = 5\frac{d}{dx}(\ln x) = 5 \cdot \frac{1}{x} = \frac{5}{x} \quad \text{for } x > 0$$

b. Differentiate $y = \dfrac{\ln x}{x^2}$.

Solution: By the quotient rule and Basic Rule 2,

$$y' = \frac{x^2 \dfrac{d}{dx}(\ln x) - (\ln x)\dfrac{d}{dx}(x^2)}{(x^2)^2}$$

$$= \frac{x^2\left(\dfrac{1}{x}\right) - (\ln x)(2x)}{x^4} = \frac{x - 2x\ln x}{x^4} = \frac{1 - 2\ln x}{x^3} \quad \text{for } x > 0$$

Now Work Problem 1 ◁

The chain rule is used to develop the differentiation formula for $\ln|u|$.

We will now extend Equation (1) to cover a broader class of functions. Let $y = \ln|u|$, where u is a differentiable function of x. By the chain rule,

$$\frac{d}{dx}(\ln|u|) = \frac{dy}{du} \cdot \frac{du}{dx} = \frac{d}{du}(\ln|u|) \cdot \frac{du}{dx} = \frac{1}{u} \cdot \frac{du}{dx} \quad \text{for } u \neq 0$$

Thus,

$$\frac{d}{du}(\ln|u|) = \frac{1}{u} \cdot \frac{du}{dx} \quad \text{for } u \neq 0 \tag{2}$$

Of course, Equation (2) gives us $\dfrac{d}{du}(\ln u) = \dfrac{1}{u} \cdot \dfrac{du}{dx}$ for $u > 0$.

APPLY IT ▶

1. The supply of q units of a product at a price of p dollars per unit is given by $q(p) = 25 + 2\ln(3p^2 + 4)$. Find the rate of change of supply with respect to price, $\dfrac{dq}{dp}$.

EXAMPLE 2   Differentiating Functions Involving $\ln u$

a. Differentiate $y = \ln(x^2 + 1)$.

Solution: This function has the form $\ln u$ with $u = x^2 + 1$, and since $x^2 + 1 > 0$, for all x, $y = \ln(x^2 + 1)$ is defined for all x. Using Equation (2), we have

$$\frac{dy}{dx} = \frac{1}{x^2 + 1}\frac{d}{dx}(x^2 + 1) = \frac{1}{x^2 + 1}(2x) = \frac{2x}{x^2 + 1}$$

b. Differentiate $y = x^2 \ln(4x + 2)$.

Solution: Using the product rule gives

$$\frac{dy}{dx} = x^2 \frac{d}{dx}(\ln(4x + 2)) + (\ln(4x + 2))\frac{d}{dx}(x^2)$$

By Equation (2) with $u = 4x + 2$,

$$\frac{dy}{dx} = x^2 \left(\frac{1}{4x + 2}\right)(4) + (\ln(4x + 2))(2x)$$

$$= \frac{2x^2}{2x + 1} + 2x \ln(4x + 2) \quad \text{for } 4x + 2 > 0$$

Since $4x + 2 > 0$ exactly when $x > -1/2$, we have

$$\frac{d}{dx}(x^2 \ln(4x + 2)) = \frac{2x^2}{2x + 1} + 2x \ln(4x + 2) \quad \text{for } x > -1/2$$

c. Differentiate $y = \ln|\ln|x||$.

Solution: This has the form $y = \ln|u|$ with $u = \ln|x|$. Using Equation (2), we obtain

$$y' = \frac{1}{\ln|x|}\frac{d}{dx}(\ln|x|) = \frac{1}{\ln|x|}\left(\frac{1}{x}\right) = \frac{1}{x \ln|x|} \quad \text{for } x, u \neq 0$$

Since $\ln|x| = 0$ when $x = -1, 1$, we have

$$\frac{d}{dx}(\ln|\ln|x||) = \frac{1}{x \ln|x|} \quad \text{for } x \neq -1, 0, 1$$

Now Work Problem 9 ◁

Frequently, we can reduce the work involved in differentiating the logarithm of a product, quotient, or power by using properties of logarithms to rewrite the logarithm *before* differentiating. The next example will illustrate.

EXAMPLE 3   Rewriting Logarithmic Functions before Differentiating

a. Find $\dfrac{dy}{dx}$ if $y = \ln(2x + 5)^3$.

Solution: Here we have the logarithm of a power. First we simplify the right side by using properties of logarithms. Then we differentiate. We have

$$y = \ln(2x + 5)^3 = 3 \ln(2x + 5) \quad \text{for } 2x + 5 > 0$$

$$\frac{dy}{dx} = 3\left(\frac{1}{2x + 5}\right)(2) = \frac{6}{2x + 5} \quad \text{for } x > -5/2$$

Comparing both methods, we note that the easier one is to simplify first and then differentiate.

Alternatively, if the simplification were not performed first, we would write

$$\frac{dy}{dx} = \frac{1}{(2x + 5)^3}\frac{d}{dx}((2x + 5)^3)$$

$$= \frac{1}{(2x + 5)^3}(3)(2x + 5)^2(2) = \frac{6}{2x + 5}$$

b. Find $f'(p)$ if $f(p) = \ln((p + 1)^2(p + 2)^3(p + 3)^4)$.

Solution: We simplify the right side and then differentiate:

$$f(p) = 2 \ln(p + 1) + 3 \ln(p + 2) + 4 \ln(p + 3)$$

$$f'(p) = 2\left(\frac{1}{p + 1}\right)(1) + 3\left(\frac{1}{p + 2}\right)(1) + 4\left(\frac{1}{p + 3}\right)(1)$$

$$= \frac{2}{p + 1} + \frac{3}{p + 2} + \frac{4}{p + 3}$$

Now Work Problem 5 ◁

EXAMPLE 4 **Differentiating Functions Involving Logarithms**

a. Find $f'(w)$ if $f(w) = \ln \sqrt{\dfrac{1+w^2}{w^2-1}}$.

Solution: We simplify by using properties of logarithms and then differentiate:

$$f(w) = \frac{1}{2}(\ln(1+w^2) - \ln(w^2-1))$$

$$f'(w) = \frac{1}{2}\left(\frac{1}{1+w^2}(2w) - \frac{1}{w^2-1}(2w)\right)$$

$$= \frac{w}{1+w^2} - \frac{w}{w^2-1} = -\frac{2w}{w^4-1}$$

b. Find $f'(x)$ if $f(x) = \ln^3(2x+5)$.

Solution: The exponent 3 refers to the cubing of $\ln(2x+5)$. That is,

$$f(x) = \ln^3(2x+5) = [\ln(2x+5)]^3$$

By the power rule,

$$f'(x) = 3(\ln(2x+5))^2 \frac{d}{dx}(\ln(2x+5))$$

$$= 3(\ln(2x+5))^2\left(\frac{1}{2x+5}(2)\right)$$

$$= \frac{6}{2x+5}(\ln(2x+5))^2$$

Now Work Problem 39 ◁

CAUTION!

Do not confuse $\ln^3(2x+5)$ with $\ln(2x+5)^3$, which occurred in Example 3(a). It is advisable to write $\ln^3(2x+5)$ explicitly as $[\ln(2x+5)]^3$ and avoid $\ln^3(2x+5)$.

Derivatives of Logarithmic Functions to the Base b

To differentiate a logarithmic function to a base different from e, we can first convert the logarithm to natural logarithms via the change-of-base formula and then differentiate the resulting expression. For example, consider $y = \log_b u$, where u is a differentiable function of x. By the change-of-base formula,

$$y = \log_b u = \frac{\ln u}{\ln b} \quad \text{for } u > 0$$

CAUTION!

Note that $\ln b$ is just a constant!

Differentiating, we have

$$\frac{d}{dx}(\log_b u) = \frac{d}{dx}\left(\frac{\ln u}{\ln b}\right) = \frac{1}{\ln b}\frac{d}{dx}(\ln u) = \frac{1}{\ln b} \cdot \frac{1}{u}\frac{du}{dx}$$

Summarizing,

$$\frac{d}{dx}(\log_b u) = \frac{1}{(\ln b)u} \cdot \frac{du}{dx} \quad \text{for } u > 0$$

Rather than memorize this rule, we suggest that you remember the procedure used to obtain it.

Procedure to Differentiate $\log_b u$

Convert $\log_b u$ to natural logarithms to obtain $\dfrac{\ln u}{\ln b}$, and then differentiate.

EXAMPLE 5 **Differentiating a Logarithmic Function to the Base** 2

Differentiate $y = \log_2 x$.

Solution: Following the foregoing procedure, we have

$$\frac{d}{dx}(\log_2 x) = \frac{d}{dx}\left(\frac{\ln x}{\ln 2}\right) = \frac{1}{\ln 2}\frac{d}{dx}(\ln x) = \frac{1}{(\ln 2)x}$$

It is worth mentioning that we can write our answer in terms of the original base. Because

$$\frac{1}{\ln b} = \frac{1}{\frac{\log_b b}{\log_b e}} = \frac{\log_b e}{1} = \log_b e$$

we can express $\dfrac{1}{(\ln 2)x}$ as $\dfrac{\log_2 e}{x}$. More generally, $\dfrac{d}{dx}(\log_b u) = \dfrac{\log_b e}{u} \cdot \dfrac{du}{dx}$.

Now Work Problem 15 ◁

APPLY IT ▶

2. The intensity of an earthquake is measured on the Richter scale. The reading is given by $R = \log \dfrac{I}{I_0}$, where I is the intensity and I_0 is a standard minimum intensity. If $I_0 = 1$, find $\dfrac{dR}{dI}$, the rate of change of the Richter-scale reading with respect to the intensity.

EXAMPLE 6 **Differentiating a Logarithmic Function to the Base** 10

If $y = \log(2x + 1)$, find the rate of change of y with respect to x.

Solution: The rate of change is dy/dx, and the base involved is 10. Therefore, we have

$$\frac{dy}{dx} = \frac{d}{dx}(\log(2x + 1)) = \frac{d}{dx}\left(\frac{\ln(2x + 1)}{\ln 10}\right)$$

$$= \frac{1}{\ln 10} \cdot \frac{1}{2x + 1}(2) = \frac{2}{\ln 10(2x + 1)}$$

◁

PROBLEMS 12.1

In Problems 1–44, differentiate the functions. If possible, first use properties of logarithms to simplify the given function.

1. $y = a \ln x$
2. $y = \dfrac{5 \ln x}{9}$
3. $y = \ln(3x - 7)$
4. $y = \ln(5x - 6)$
5. $y = \ln x^2$
6. $y = \ln(5x^3 + 3x^2 + 2x + 1)$
7. $y = \ln(1 - x^2)$
8. $y = \ln(-x^2 + 6x)$
9. $f(X) = \ln(4X^6 + 2X^3)$
10. $f(r) = \ln(2r^4 - 3r^2 + 2r + 1)$
11. $f(t) = t \ln t - t$
12. $y = x^2 \ln x$
13. $y = x^3 \ln(2x + 5)$
14. $y = (ax + b)^3 \ln(ax + b)$
15. $y = \log_3(8x - 1)$
16. $f(w) = \log(w^2 + 2w + 1)$
17. $y = x^2 + \log_2(x^2 + 4)$
18. $y = x^2 \log_2 x$
19. $f(z) = \dfrac{\ln z}{z}$
20. $y = \dfrac{x^2}{\ln x}$
21. $y = \dfrac{x^4 + 3x^2 + x}{\ln x}$
22. $y = \ln x^{100}$
23. $y = \ln(x^2 + 4x + 5)^3$
24. $y = 6 \ln \sqrt[3]{x}$
25. $y = 9 \ln \sqrt{1 + x^2}$
26. $f(t) = \ln\left(\dfrac{t^4}{1 + 6t + t^2}\right)$
27. $f(l) = \ln\left(\dfrac{1 + l}{1 - l}\right)$
28. $y = \ln\left(\dfrac{2x + 3}{3x - 4}\right)$
29. $y = \ln\sqrt[4]{\dfrac{1 + x^2}{1 - x^2}}$
30. $y = \ln\sqrt[3]{\dfrac{x^3 - 1}{x^3 + 1}}$

31. $y = \ln[(ax^2 + bx + c)^p(hx^2 + kx + l)^q]$
32. $y = \ln[(5x + 2)^4(8x - 3)^6]$
33. $y = 13 \ln(x^2\sqrt[3]{5x + 2})$
34. $y = 6 \ln \dfrac{x}{\sqrt{2x + 1}}$
35. $y = (x^2 + 1)\ln(2x + 1)$
36. $y = (ax^2 + bx + c)\ln(hx^2 + kx + l)$
37. $y = \ln x^3 + \ln^3 x$
38. $y = x^{\ln 2}$
39. $y = \ln^4(ax)$
40. $y = \ln^2(2x + 11)$
41. $y = \ln\sqrt{f(x)}$
42. $y = \ln(x^3\sqrt[4]{2x + 1})$
43. $y = \sqrt{4 + 3 \ln x}$
44. $y = \ln(x + \sqrt{1 + x^2})$

45. Find an equation of the tangent line to the curve
$$y = \ln(x^2 - 3x - 3)$$
when $x = 4$.

46. Find an equation of the tangent line to the curve
$$y = x \ln x - x$$
at the point where $x = 1$.

47. Find the slope of the curve $y = \dfrac{x}{\ln x}$ when $x = 3$.

48. **Marginal Revenue** Find the marginal-revenue function if the demand function is $p = 25/\ln(q + 2)$.

49. **Marginal Cost** A total-cost function is given by
$$c = 25 \ln(q + 1) + 12$$
Find the marginal cost when $q = 6$.

50. Marginal Cost   A manufacturer's average-cost function, in dollars, is given by

$$\bar{c} = \frac{500}{\ln{(q + 20)}}$$

Find the marginal cost (rounded to two decimal places) when $q = 50$.

51. Supply Change   The supply of q units of a product at a price of p dollars per unit is given by $q(p) = 27 + 11 \ln{(2p + 1)}$. Find the rate of change of supply with respect to price, $\dfrac{dq}{dp}$.

52. Sound Perception   The loudness of sound L, measured in decibels, perceived by the human ear depends upon intensity levels I according to $L = 10 \log{\dfrac{I}{I_0}}$, where I_0 is the standard threshold of audibility. If $I_0 = 17$, find $\dfrac{dL}{dI}$, the rate of change of the loudness with respect to the intensity.

53. Biology   In a certain experiment with bacteria, it is observed that the relative activeness of a given bacteria colony is described by

$$A = 6 \ln{\left(\frac{T}{a - T} - a \right)}$$

where a is a constant and T is the surrounding temperature. Find the rate of change of A with respect to T.

54. Show that the relative rate of change of $y = f(x)$ with respect to x is equal to the derivative of $y = \ln{f(x)}$.

55. Show that $\dfrac{d}{dx}(\log_b{u}) = \dfrac{1}{u}(\log_b{e})\dfrac{du}{dx}$.

In Problems 56 and 57, use differentiation rules to find $f'(x)$. Then use your graphing calculator to find all roots of $f'(x) = 0$. Round your answers to two decimal places.

56. $f(x) = x^3 \ln{x}$ **57.** $f(x) = \dfrac{\ln{(x^2)}}{x^2}$

Objective

To develop a differentiation formula for $y = e^u$, to apply the formula, and to use it to differentiate an exponential function with a base other than e.

12.2 Derivatives of Exponential Functions

As we pointed out in Section 12.1, the exponential functions cannot be constructed from power functions using multiplication by a constant, arithmetic operations, and composition. However, the functions b^x, for $b > 0$ and $b \neq 1$, are inverse to the functions $\log_b{(x)}$, and if an invertible function f is differentiable, it is fairly easy to see that its inverse is differentiable. The key idea is that the graph of the inverse of a function is obtained by reflecting the graph of the original function in the line $y = x$. This reflection process preserves smoothness so that if the graph of an invertible function is smooth, then so is the graph of its inverse. Differentiating $f(f^{-1}(x)) = x$, we have

$$\frac{d}{dx}(f(f^{-1}(x))) = \frac{d}{dx}(x)$$

$$f'(f^{-1}(x))\frac{d}{dx}(f^{-1}(x)) = 1 \qquad \text{Chain Rule}$$

$$\frac{d}{dx}(f^{-1}(x)) = \frac{1}{f'(f^{-1}(x))}$$

Thus we have

> **COMBINING RULE 6   Inverse Function Rule**
>
> If f is an invertible, differentiable function, then f^{-1} is differentiable and
>
> $$\frac{d}{dx}(f^{-1}(x)) = \frac{1}{f'(f^{-1}(x))}$$

As with the chain rule, Leibniz notation is well suited for inverse functions. Indeed, if $y = f^{-1}(x)$, then $\dfrac{dy}{dx} = \dfrac{d}{dx}(f^{-1}(x))$ and since $f(y) = x$, $f'(y) = \dfrac{dx}{dy}$. When we substitute these in Combining Rule 6, we get

$$\frac{dy}{dx} = \frac{d}{dx}(f^{-1}(x)) = \frac{1}{f'(f^{-1}(x))} = \frac{1}{f'(y)} = \frac{1}{\dfrac{dx}{dy}}$$

so that Combining Rule 6 can be rewritten as

$$\frac{dy}{dx} = \frac{1}{\dfrac{dx}{dy}} \qquad (1)$$

In the immediate case of interest, with $y = e^x$ so that $x = \ln y$ and $dx/dy = 1/y = 1/e^x$, we have

$$\frac{d}{dx}(e^x) = \frac{1}{\dfrac{1}{e^x}} = e^x$$

CAUTION!⚠

The power rule does not apply to e^x and other exponential functions, b^x. The power rule applies to power functions, x^a. Note the location of the variable.

which we record as

$$\frac{d}{dx}(e^x) = e^x \qquad (2)$$

For u a differentiable function of x, an application of the Chain Rule gives

$$\frac{d}{dx}(e^u) = e^u \frac{du}{dx} \qquad (3)$$

EXAMPLE 1   **Differentiating Functions Involving e^x**

a. Find $\dfrac{d}{dx}(3e^x)$. Since 3 is a constant factor,

$$\frac{d}{dx}(3e^x) = 3\frac{d}{dx}(e^x)$$
$$= 3e^x \qquad \text{by Equation (2)}$$

If a quotient can be easily rewritten as a product, then we can use the somewhat simpler product rule rather than the quotient rule.

b. If $y = \dfrac{x}{e^x}$, find $\dfrac{dy}{dx}$.

Solution: We could use first the quotient rule and then Equation (2), but it is a little easier first to rewrite the function as $y = xe^{-x}$ and use the product rule and Equation (3):

$$\frac{dy}{dx} = e^{-x}\frac{d}{dx}(x) + x\frac{d}{dx}(e^{-x}) = e^{-x}(1) + x(e^{-x})(-1) = e^{-x}(1-x) = \frac{1-x}{e^x}$$

c. If $y = e^2 + e^x + \ln 3$, find y'.

APPLY IT ▶

3. When an object is moved from one environment to another, the change in temperature of the object is given by $T = Ce^{kt}$, where C is the temperature difference between the two environments, t is the time in the new environment, and k is a constant. Find the rate of change of temperature with respect to time.

Solution: Since e^2 and $\ln 3$ are constants, $y' = 0 + e^x + 0 = e^x$.

Now Work Problem 1 ◁

EXAMPLE 2   **Differentiating Functions Involving e^u**

a. Find $\dfrac{d}{dx}\left(e^{x^3+3x}\right)$.

Solution: The function has the form e^u with $u = x^3 + 3x$. From Equation (2),

$$\frac{d}{dx}\left(e^{x^3+3x}\right) = e^{x^3+3x}\frac{d}{dx}(x^3 + 3x) = e^{x^3+3x}(3x^2 + 3)$$
$$= 3(x^2 + 1)e^{x^3+3x}$$

$\dfrac{d}{dx}(e^u) = e^u \dfrac{du}{dx}$. Don't forget the $\dfrac{du}{dx}$.

b. Find $\dfrac{d}{dx}(e^{x+1}\ln(x^2 + 1))$.

Solution: By the product rule,

$$\frac{d}{dx}(e^{x+1}\ln(x^2 + 1)) = e^{x+1}\frac{d}{dx}(\ln(x^2 + 1)) + (\ln(x^2 + 1))\frac{d}{dx}(e^{x+1})$$
$$= e^{x+1}\left(\frac{1}{x^2 + 1}\right)(2x) + (\ln(x^2 + 1))e^{x+1}(1)$$
$$= e^{x+1}\left(\frac{2x}{x^2 + 1} + \ln(x^2 + 1)\right)$$

Now Work Problem 3 ◁

EXAMPLE 3   The Normal-Distribution Density Function

An important function used in the social sciences is the **normal-distribution density function**

$$y = f(x) = \frac{1}{\sigma\sqrt{2\pi}}e^{-(1/2)((x-\mu)/\sigma)^2}$$

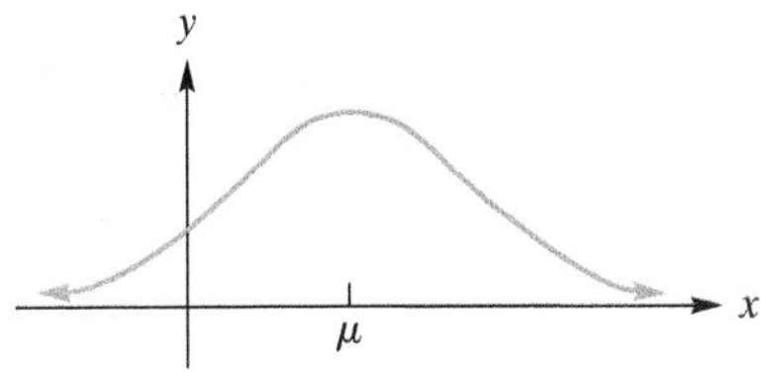

FIGURE 12.1   The normal-distribution density function.

where σ (a Greek letter read "sigma") and μ (a Greek letter read "mu") are constants. The graph of this function, called the normal curve, is bell shaped. (See Figure 12.1.) Determine the rate of change of y with respect to x when $x = \mu + \sigma$.

Solution: The rate of change of y with respect to x is dy/dx. We note that the factor $\frac{1}{\sigma\sqrt{2\pi}}$ is a constant and the second factor has the form e^u, where

$$u = -\frac{1}{2}\left(\frac{x-\mu}{\sigma}\right)^2$$

Thus,

$$\frac{dy}{dx} = \frac{1}{\sigma\sqrt{2\pi}}\left(e^{-(1/2)((x-\mu)/\sigma)^2}\right)\left(-\frac{1}{2}(2)\left(\frac{x-\mu}{\sigma}\right)\left(\frac{1}{\sigma}\right)\right)$$

Evaluating dy/dx when $x = \mu + \sigma$, we obtain

$$\left.\frac{dy}{dx}\right|_{x=\mu+\sigma} = \frac{1}{\sigma\sqrt{2\pi}}\left(e^{-(1/2)((\mu+\sigma-\mu)/\sigma)^2}\right)\left(-\frac{\mu+\sigma-\mu}{\sigma}\right)\left(\frac{1}{\sigma}\right)$$

$$= \frac{1}{\sigma\sqrt{2\pi}}\left(e^{-(1/2)}\right)\left(-\frac{1}{\sigma}\right)$$

$$= \frac{-e^{-(1/2)}}{\sigma^2\sqrt{2\pi}} = \frac{-1}{\sigma^2\sqrt{2\pi e}}$$

◁

Differentiating Exponential Functions to the Base b

Now that we are familiar with the derivative of e^u, we consider the derivative of the more general exponential function b^u. Because $b = e^{\ln b}$, we can express b^u as an exponential function with the base e, a form we can differentiate. We have

$$\frac{d}{dx}(b^u) = \frac{d}{dx}((e^{\ln b})^u) = \frac{d}{dx}(e^{(\ln b)u})$$

$$= e^{(\ln b)u}\frac{d}{dx}((\ln b)u)$$

$$= e^{(\ln b)u}(\ln b)\left(\frac{du}{dx}\right)$$

$$= b^u(\ln b)\frac{du}{dx} \qquad \text{since } e^{(\ln b)u} = b^u$$

Summarizing,

$$\frac{d}{dx}(b^u) = b^u(\ln b)\frac{du}{dx} \tag{4}$$

Note that if $b = e$, then the factor $\ln b$ in Equation (4) is 1. Thus, if exponential functions to the base e are used, we have a simpler differentiation formula with which to work. This is the reason natural exponential functions are used extensively in calculus. Rather than memorizing Equation (4), we advocate remembering the procedure for obtaining it.

Procedure to Differentiate b^u

Convert b^u to a natural exponential function by using the property that $b = e^{\ln b}$, and then differentiate.

The next example will illustrate this procedure.

EXAMPLE 4 Differentiating an Exponential Function with Base 4

Find $\dfrac{d}{dx}(4^x)$.

Solution: Using the preceding procedure, we have

$$
\begin{aligned}
\frac{d}{dx}(4^x) &= \frac{d}{dx}\left((e^{\ln 4})^x\right) \\
&= \frac{d}{dx}\left(e^{(\ln 4)x}\right) \qquad \text{form}: \frac{d}{dx}(e^u) \\
&= e^{(\ln 4)x}(\ln 4) \qquad \text{by Equation (2)} \\
&= 4^x(\ln 4)
\end{aligned}
$$

Verify the result by using Equation (4) directly.

Now Work Problem 15 ◁

EXAMPLE 5 Differentiating Different Forms

Find $\dfrac{d}{dx}\left(e^2 + x^e + 2^{\sqrt{x}}\right)$.

Solution: Here we must differentiate three different forms; do not confuse them! The first (e^2) is a constant base to a constant power, so it is a constant itself. Thus, its derivative is zero. The second (x^e) is a variable base to a constant power, so the power rule applies. The third $(2^{\sqrt{x}})$ is a constant base to a variable power, so we must differentiate an exponential function. Taken all together, we have

$$
\begin{aligned}
\frac{d}{dx}\left(e^2 + x^e + 2^{\sqrt{x}}\right) &= 0 + ex^{e-1} + \frac{d}{dx}\left[e^{(\ln 2)\sqrt{x}}\right] \\
&= ex^{e-1} + \left[e^{(\ln 2)\sqrt{x}}\right](\ln 2)\left(\frac{1}{2\sqrt{x}}\right) \\
&= ex^{e-1} + \frac{2^{\sqrt{x}}\ln 2}{2\sqrt{x}}
\end{aligned}
$$

Now Work Problem 17 ◁

EXAMPLE 6 Differentiating Power Functions Again

We have often used the rule $d/dx(x^a) = ax^{a-1}$, but we have only *proved* it for a a positive integer and a few other special cases. At least for $x > 0$, we can now improve our understanding of power functions, using Equation (2).

For $x > 0$, we can write $x^a = e^{a \ln x}$. So we have

$$
\frac{d}{dx}(x^a) = \frac{d}{dx}e^{a \ln x} = e^{a \ln x}\frac{d}{dx}(a \ln x) = x^a(ax^{-1}) = ax^{a-1}
$$

Now Work Problem 19 ◁

PROBLEMS 12.2

In Problems 1–28, differentiate the functions.

1. $y = 5e^x$

2. $y = \dfrac{ae^x}{b}$

3. $y = e^{2x^2+3}$

4. $y = e^{2x^2+5}$

5. $y = e^{9-5x}$

6. $f(q) = e^{-q^3+6q-1}$

7. $f(r) = e^{4r^3+5r^2+2r+6}$

8. $y = e^{x^2+6x^3+1}$

9. $y = xe^x$

10. $y = 3x^4e^{-x}$

11. $y = x^2e^{-x^2}$

12. $y = xe^{ax}$

13. $y = \dfrac{e^x + e^{-x}}{3}$

14. $y = \dfrac{e^x - e^{-x}}{e^x + e^{-x}}$

15. $y = 5^{2x^3}$

16. $y = 2^x x^2$

17. $f(w) = \dfrac{e^{aw}}{w^2 + w + 1}$

18. $y = e^{x-\sqrt{x}}$

19. $y = e^{1+\sqrt{x}}$

20. $y = (e^{2x} + 1)^3$

21. $y = x^5 - 5^x$

22. $f(z) = e^{1/z}$

23. $y = \dfrac{e^x - 1}{e^x + 1}$

24. $y = e^{2x}(x + 6)$

25. $y = \ln e^x$

26. $y = e^{-x} \ln x$

27. $y = x^x$

28. $y = \ln e^{4x+1}$

29. If $f(x) = ee^x e^{x^2}$, find $f'(-1)$.

30. If $f(x) = 5^{x^2 \ln x}$, find $f'(1)$.

31. Find an equation of the tangent line to the curve $y = e^x$ when $x = -2$.

32. Find an equation of the tangent line to the curve $y = e^x$ at the point $(1, e)$. Show that this tangent line passes through $(0, 0)$ and show that it is the only tangent line to $y = e^x$ that passes through $(0, 0)$.

For each of the demand equations in Problems 33 and 34, find the rate of change of price p with respect to quantity q. What is the rate of change for the indicated value of q?

33. $p = 15e^{-0.001q}; q = 500$ **34.** $p = 9e^{-5q/750}; q = 300$

In Problems 35 and 36, $\bar{c}$ is the average cost of producing q units of a product. Find the marginal-cost function and the marginal cost for the given values of q.

35. $\bar{c} = \dfrac{7000e^{q/700}}{q}; q = 350, q = 700$

36. $\bar{c} = \dfrac{850}{q} + 4000\dfrac{e^{(2q+6)/800}}{q}; q = 97, q = 197$

37. If $w = e^{x^2}$ and $x = \dfrac{t+1}{t-1}$, find $\dfrac{dw}{dt}$ when $t = 2$.

38. If $f'(x) = x^3$ and $u = e^x$, show that

$$\frac{d}{dx}[f(u)] = e^{4x}$$

39. Determine the value of the positive constant c if

$$\frac{d}{dx}(c^x - x^c)\bigg|_{x=1} = 0$$

40. Calculate the relative rate of change of

$$f(x) = 10^{-x} + \ln(8 + x) + 0.01e^{x-2}$$

when $x = 2$. Round your answer to four decimal places.

41. Production Run   For a firm, the daily output on the tth day of a production run is given by

$$q = 500(1 - e^{-0.2t})$$

Find the rate of change of output q with respect to t on the tenth day.

42. Normal-Density Function   For the normal-density function

$$f(x) = \frac{1}{\sqrt{2\pi}}e^{-x^2/2}$$

find $f'(-1)$.

43. Population   The population, in millions, of the greater Seattle area t years from 1970 is estimated by $P = 1.92e^{0.0176t}$. Show that $dP/dt = kP$, where k is a constant. This means that the rate of change of population at any time is proportional to the population at that time.

44. Market Penetration   In a discussion of diffusion of a new process into a market, Hurter and Rubenstein[1] refer to an equation of the form

$$Y = k\alpha^{\beta^t}$$

where Y is the cumulative level of diffusion of the new process at time t and k, α, and β are positive constants. Verify their claim that

$$\frac{dY}{dt} = k\alpha^{\beta^t}(\beta^t \ln \alpha) \ln \beta$$

45. Finance   After t years, the value S of a principal of P dollars invested at the annual rate of r compounded continuously is given by $S = Pe^{rt}$. Show that the relative rate of change of S with respect to t is r.

46. Predator–Prey Relationship   In an article concerning predators and prey, Holling[2] refers to an equation of the form

$$y = K(1 - e^{-ax})$$

where x is the prey density, y is the number of prey attacked, and K and a are constants. Verify his statement that

$$\frac{dy}{dx} = a(K - y)$$

47. Earthquakes   According to Richter,[3] the number of earthquakes of magnitude M or greater per unit of time is given by $N = 10^A 10^{-bM}$, where A and b are constants. Find dN/dM.

[1] A. P. Hurter, Jr., A. H. Rubenstein, et al., "Market Penetration by New Innovations: The Technological Literature," *Technological Forecasting and Social Change*, 11 (1978), 197–221.

[2] C. S. Holling, "Some Characteristics of Simple Types of Predation and Parasitism," *The Canadian Entomologist*, XCI, no. 7 (1959), 385–98.

[3] C. F. Richter, *Elementary Seismology* (San Francisco: W. H. Freeman and Company, Publishers, 1958).

48. Psychology   Short-term retention was studied by Peterson and Peterson.[4] The two researchers analyzed a procedure in which an experimenter verbally gave a subject a three-letter consonant syllable, such as CHJ, followed by a three-digit number, such as 309. The subject then repeated the number and counted backward by 3's, such as 309, 306, 303, ... After a period of time, the subject was signaled by a light to recite the three-letter consonant syllable. The time between the experimenter's completion of the last consonant to the onset of the light was called the *recall interval*. The time between the onset of the light and the completion of a response was referred to as *latency*. After many trials, it was determined that, for a recall interval of t seconds, the approximate proportion of correct recalls with latency below 2.83 seconds was

$$p = 0.89[0.01 + 0.99(0.85)^t]$$

(a) Find dp/dt and interpret your result.
(b) Evaluate dp/dt when $t = 2$. Round your answer to two decimal places.

49. Medicine   Suppose a tracer, such as a colored dye, is injected instantly into the heart at time $t = 0$ and mixes uniformly with blood inside the heart. Let the initial concentration of the tracer in the heart be C_0, and assume that the heart has constant volume V. Also assume that, as fresh blood flows into the heart, the diluted mixture of blood and tracer flows out at the constant positive rate r. Then the concentration of the tracer in the heart at time t is given by

$$C(t) = C_0 e^{-(r/V)t}$$

Show that $dC/dt = (-r/V)C(t)$.

50. Medicine   In Problem 49, suppose the tracer is injected at a constant rate R. Then the concentration at time t is

$$C(t) = \frac{R}{r}\left[1 - e^{-(r/V)t}\right]$$

(a) Find $C(0)$.
(b) Show that $\dfrac{dC}{dt} = \dfrac{R}{V} - \dfrac{r}{V}C(t)$.

51. Schizophrenia   Several models have been used to analyze the length of stay in a hospital. For a particular group of schizophrenics, one such model is[5]

$$f(t) = 1 - e^{-0.008t}$$

where $f(t)$ is the proportion of the group that was discharged at the end of t days of hospitalization. Find the rate of discharge (the proportion discharged per day) at the end of 100 days. Round your answer to four decimal places.

52. Savings and Consumption   A country's savings S (in billions of dollars) is related to its national income I (in billions of dollars) by the equation

$$S = \ln \frac{3}{2 + e^{-I}}$$

(a) Find the marginal propensity to consume as a function of income.
(b) To the nearest million dollars, what is the national income when the marginal propensity to save is $\dfrac{1}{7}$?

In Problems 53 and 54, use differentiation rules to find $f'(x)$. Then use your graphing calculator to find all real zeros of $f'(x)$. Round your answers to two decimal places.

53. $f(x) = e^{2x^3 + x^2 - 3x}$ **54.** $f(x) = x + e^{-x}$

Objective

To give a mathematical analysis of the economic concept of elasticity.

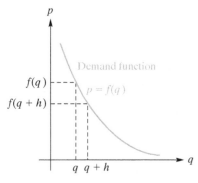

FIGURE 12.2   Change in demand.

12.3 Elasticity of Demand

Elasticity of demand is a means by which economists measure how a change in the price of a product will affect the quantity demanded. That is, it refers to consumer response to price changes. Loosely speaking, elasticity of demand is the ratio of the resulting percentage change in quantity demanded to a given percentage change in price:

$$\frac{\text{percentage change in quantity}}{\text{percentage change in price}}$$

For example, if, for a price increase of 5%, quantity demanded were to decrease by 2%, we would loosely say that elasticity of demand is $-2/5$.

To be more general, suppose $p = f(q)$ is the demand function for a product. Consumers will demand q units at a price of $f(q)$ per unit and will demand $q + h$ units at a price of $f(q + h)$ per unit (Figure 12.2). The *percentage* change in quantity demanded from q to $q + h$ is

$$\frac{(q + h) - q}{q} \cdot 100\% = \frac{h}{q} \cdot 100\%$$

The corresponding percentage change in price per unit is

$$\frac{f(q + h) - f(q)}{f(q)} \cdot 100\%$$

---

[4] L. R. Peterson and M. J. Peterson, "Short-Term Retention of Individual Verbal Items," *Journal of Experimental Psychology,* 58 (1959), 193–98.

[5] W. W. Eaton and G. A. Whitmore, "Length of Stay as a Stochastic Process: A General Approach and Application to Hospitalization for Schizophrenia," *Journal of Mathematical Sociology,* 5 (1977), 273–92.

The ratio of these percentage changes is

$$\frac{\dfrac{h}{q} \cdot 100\%}{\dfrac{f(q+h) - f(q)}{f(q)} \cdot 100\%} = \frac{h}{q} \cdot \frac{f(q)}{f(q+h) - f(q)}$$

$$= \frac{f(q)}{q} \cdot \frac{h}{f(q+h) - f(q)}$$

$$= \frac{\dfrac{f(q)}{q}}{\dfrac{f(q+h) - f(q)}{h}} \qquad (1)$$

If f is differentiable, then as $h \to 0$, the limit of $[f(q+h) - f(q)]/h$ is $f'(q) = dp/dq$. Thus, the limit of (1) is

$$\frac{\dfrac{f(q)}{q}}{f'(q)} = \frac{\dfrac{p}{q}}{\dfrac{dp}{dq}} \qquad \text{since } p = f(q)$$

which is called the *point elasticity of demand*.

> **Definition**
>
> If $p = f(q)$ is a differentiable demand function, the **point elasticity of demand,** denoted by the Greek letter η (eta), at (q, p) is given by
>
> $$\eta = \eta(q) = \frac{\dfrac{p}{q}}{\dfrac{dp}{dq}}$$

CAUTION!

Since p is a function of q, dp/dq is a function of q and thus the ratio that defines η is a function of q. That is why we write $\eta = \eta(q)$.

To illustrate, let us find the point elasticity of demand for the demand function $p = 1200 - q^2$. We have

$$\eta = \frac{\dfrac{p}{q}}{\dfrac{dp}{dq}} = \frac{\dfrac{1200 - q^2}{q}}{-2q} = -\frac{1200 - q^2}{2q^2} = -\left(\frac{600}{q^2} - \frac{1}{2}\right) \qquad (2)$$

For example, if $q = 10$, then $\eta = -\left((600/10^2) - \frac{1}{2}\right) = -5\frac{1}{2}$. Since

$$\eta \approx \frac{\%\ \text{change in demand}}{\%\ \text{change in price}}$$

we have

$$(\%\ \text{change in price})(\eta) \approx \%\ \text{change in demand}$$

Thus, if price were increased by 1% when $q = 10$, then quantity demanded would change by approximately

$$(1\%)\left(-5\frac{1}{2}\right) = -5\frac{1}{2}\%$$

That is, demand would decrease $5\frac{1}{2}\%$. Similarly, decreasing price by $\frac{1}{2}\%$ when $q = 10$ results in a change in demand of approximately

$$\left(-\frac{1}{2}\%\right)\left(-5\frac{1}{2}\right) = 2\frac{3}{4}\%$$

Hence, demand increases by $2\frac{3}{4}\%$.

Note that when elasticity is evaluated, no units are attached to it—it is nothing more than a real number. In fact, the 100%'s arising from the word *percentage* cancel, so that elasticity is really an approximation of the ratio

$$\frac{\text{relative change in quantity}}{\text{relative change in price}}$$

and each of the relative changes is no more than a real number. For usual behavior of demand, an increase (decrease) in price corresponds to a decrease (increase) in quantity. This means that if price is plotted as a function of quantity then the graph will have a negative slope at each point. Thus, dp/dq will typically be negative, and since p and q are positive, η will typically be negative too. Some economists disregard the minus sign; in the preceding situation, they would consider the elasticity to be $5\frac{1}{2}$. We will not adopt this practice.

There are three categories of elasticity:

1. When $|\eta| > 1$, demand is *elastic*.

2. When $|\eta| = 1$, demand has *unit elasticity*.

3. When $|\eta| < 1$, demand is *inelastic*.

For example, in Equation (2), since $|\eta| = 5\frac{1}{2}$ when $q = 10$, demand is elastic. If $q = 20$, then $|\eta| = \left|-\left[(600/20^2) - \frac{1}{2}\right]\right| = 1$ so demand has unit elasticity. If $q = 25$, then $|\eta| = \left|-\frac{23}{50}\right|$, and demand is inelastic.

Loosely speaking, for a given percentage change in price, there is a greater percentage change in quantity demanded if demand is elastic, a smaller percentage change if demand is inelastic, and an equal percentage change if demand has unit elasticity. To better understand elasticity, it is helpful to think of typical examples. Demand for an essential utlity such as electricity tends to be inelastic through a wide range of prices. If electricity prices are increased by 10%, consumers can be expected to reduce their consumption somewhat, but a full 10% decrease may not be possible if most of their electricity usage is for essentials of life such as heating and food preparation. On the other hand, demand for luxury goods tends to be quite elastic. A 10% increase in the price of jewelry, for example, may result in a 50% decrease in demand.

EXAMPLE 1 Finding Point Elasticity of Demand

Determine the point elasticity of the demand equation

$$p = \frac{k}{q}, \quad \text{where } k > 0 \text{ and } q > 0$$

Solution: From the definition, we have

$$\eta = \frac{\dfrac{p}{q}}{\dfrac{dp}{dq}} = \frac{\dfrac{k}{q^2}}{\dfrac{-k}{q^2}} = -1$$

Thus, the demand has unit elasticity for all $q > 0$. The graph of $p = k/q$ is called an *equilateral hyperbola* and is often found in economics texts in discussions of elasticity. (See Figure 2.11 for a graph of such a curve.)

Now Work Problem 1 ◁

If we are given $p = f(q)$ for our demand equation, as in our discussion thus far, then it is usually straightforward to calculate $dp/dq = f'(q)$. However, if instead we are given q as a function of p, then we will have $q = f^{-1}(p)$ and, from Section 12.2,

$$\frac{dp}{dq} = \frac{1}{\dfrac{dq}{dp}}$$

It follows that

$$\eta = \frac{\dfrac{p}{q}}{\dfrac{dp}{dq}} = \frac{p}{q} \cdot \frac{dq}{dp} \tag{3}$$

provides another useful expression for η. Notice too that if $q = g(p)$, then

$$\eta = \eta(p) = \frac{p}{q} \cdot \frac{dq}{dp} = \frac{p}{g(p)} \cdot g'(p) = p \cdot \frac{g'(p)}{g(p)}$$

and thus

elasticity = price $\cdot$ relative rate of change of quantity as a function of price   (4)

EXAMPLE 2   Finding Point Elasticity of Demand

Determine the point elasticity of the demand equation

$$q = p^2 - 40p + 400, \quad \text{where } q > 0$$

Solution: Here we have q given as a function of p and it is easy to see that $dq/dp = 2p - 40$. Thus,

$$\eta(p) = \frac{p}{q} \cdot \frac{dq}{dp} = \frac{p}{q(p)}(2p - 40)$$

For example, if $p = 15$, then $q = q(15) = 25$; hence, $\eta(15) = (15(-10))/25 = -6$, so demand is elastic for $p = 15$.

Now Work Problem 13 ◁

Point elasticity for a *linear* demand equation is quite interesting. Suppose the equation has the form

$$p = mq + b, \quad \text{where } m < 0 \text{ and } b > 0$$

(See Figure 12.3.) We assume that $q > 0$; thus, $p < b$. The point elasticity of demand is

$$\eta = \frac{\dfrac{p}{q}}{\dfrac{dp}{dq}} = \frac{\dfrac{p}{q}}{m} = \frac{p}{mq} = \frac{p}{p - b}$$

By considering $d\eta/dp$, we will show that η is a decreasing function of p. By the quotient rule,

$$\frac{d\eta}{dp} = \frac{(p - b) - p}{(p - b)^2} = -\frac{b}{(p - b)^2}$$

Since $b > 0$ and $(p - b)^2 > 0$, it follows that $d\eta/dp < 0$, meaning that the graph of $\eta = \eta(p)$ has a negative slope. This means that as price p increases, elasticity η decreases. However, p ranges between 0 and b, and at the midpoint of this range, $b/2$,

$$\eta = \eta(b) = \frac{\dfrac{b}{2}}{\dfrac{b}{2} - b} = \frac{\dfrac{b}{2}}{-\dfrac{b}{2}} = -1$$

Therefore, if $p < b/2$, then $\eta > -1$; if $p > b/2$, then $\eta < -1$. Because we typically have $\eta < 0$, we can state these facts another way: When $p < b/2, |\eta| < 1$, and demand is inelastic; when $p = b/2, |\eta| = 1$, and demand has unit elasticity; when $p > b/2, |\eta| > 1$ and demand is elastic. This shows that the slope of a demand curve is not a measure of elasticity. The slope of the line in Figure 12.3 is m everywhere, but elasticity varies with the point on the line. Of course, this is in accord with Equation (4).

Here we analyze elasticity for linear demand.

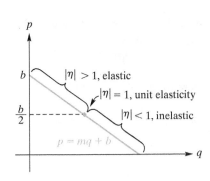

FIGURE 12.3   Elasticity for linear demand.

Elasticity and Revenue

Turning to a different situation, we can relate how elasticity of demand affects changes in revenue (marginal revenue). If $p = f(q)$ is a manufacturer's demand function, the total revenue is given by

$$r = pq$$

To find the marginal revenue, dr/dq, we differentiate r by using the product rule:

$$\frac{dr}{dq} = p + q\frac{dp}{dq}. \tag{5}$$

Factoring the right side of Equation (5), we have

$$\frac{dr}{dq} = p\left(1 + \frac{q}{p}\frac{dp}{dq}\right)$$

But

$$\frac{q}{p}\frac{dp}{dq} = \frac{\dfrac{dp}{dq}}{\dfrac{p}{q}} = \frac{1}{\eta}$$

Thus,

$$\frac{dr}{dq} = p\left(1 + \frac{1}{\eta}\right) \tag{6}$$

If demand is elastic, then $\eta < -1$, so $1 + \dfrac{1}{\eta} > 0$. If demand is inelastic, then $\eta > -1$, so $1 + \dfrac{1}{\eta} < 0$. We can assume that $p > 0$. From Equation (6) we can conclude that $dr/dq > 0$ on intervals for which demand is elastic. As we will soon see, a function is increasing on intervals for which its derivative is positive and a function is decreasing on intervals for which its derivative is negative. Hence, total revenue r is increasing on intervals for which demand is elastic and total revenue is decreasing on intervals for which demand is inelastic.

Thus, we conclude from the preceding argument that as more units are sold, a manufacturer's total revenue increases if demand is elastic, but decreases if demand is inelastic. That is, if demand is elastic, a lower price will increase revenue. This means that a lower price will cause a large enough increase in demand to actually increase revenue. If demand is inelastic, a lower price will decrease revenue. For unit elasticity, a lower price leaves total revenue unchanged.

If we solve the demand equation to obtain the form $q = g(p)$, rather than $p = f(q)$, then a similar analysis gives

$$\frac{dr}{dp} = q(1 + \eta) \tag{7}$$

and the conclusions of the last paragraph follow even more directly.

PROBLEMS 12.3

In Problems 1–14, find the point elasticity of the demand equations for the indicated values of q or p, and determine whether demand is elastic, is inelastic, or has unit elasticity.

1. $p = 40 - 2q$; $q = 5$
2. $p = 10 - 0.04q$; $q = 100$
3. $p = \dfrac{3000}{q}$; $q = 300$
4. $p = \dfrac{500}{q^2}$; $q = 52$
5. $p = \dfrac{500}{q+2}$; $q = 104$
6. $p = \dfrac{800}{2q+1}$; $q = 24$
7. $p = 150 - e^{q/100}$; $q = 100$
8. $p = 250e^{-q/50}$; $q = 50$

9. $q = 1200 - 150p$; $p = 4$
10. $q = 100 - p$; $p = 50$
11. $q = \sqrt{500 - p}$; $p = 400$
12. $q = \sqrt{2500 - p^2}$; $p = 20$
13. $q = (p - 50)^2$; $p = 10$
14. $q = p^2 - 50p + 850$; $p = 20$

15. For the linear demand equation $p = 13 - 0.05q$, verify that demand is elastic when $p = 10$, is inelastic when $p = 3$, and has unit elasticity when $p = 6.50$.

16. For what value (or values) of q do the following demand equations have unit elasticity?

(a) $p = 36 - 0.25q$

(b) $p = 300 - q^2$

17. The demand equation for a product is
$$q = 500 - 40p + p^2$$
where p is the price per unit (in dollars) and q is the quantity of units demanded (in thousands). Find the point elasticity of demand when $p = 15$. If this price of 15 is increased by $\frac{1}{2}\%$, what is the approximate change in demand?

18. The demand equation for a certain product is
$$q = \sqrt{3000 - p^2}$$
where p is in dollars. Find the point elasticity of demand when $p = 40$, and use this value to compute the percentage change in demand if the price of \$40 is increased by 7%.

19. For the demand equation $p = 500 - 2q$, verify that demand is elastic and total revenue is increasing for $0 < q < 125$. Verify that demand is inelastic and total revenue is decreasing for $125 < q < 250$.

20. Verify that $\dfrac{dr}{dq} = p\left(1 + \dfrac{1}{\eta}\right)$ if $p = 50 - 3q$.

21. Repeat Problem 20 for $p = \dfrac{1000}{q^2}$.

22. Suppose $p = mq + b$ is a linear demand equation, where $m \neq 0$ and $b > 0$.

(a) Show that $\lim_{p \to b^-} \eta = -\infty$.

(b) Show that $\eta = 0$ when $p = 0$.

23. The demand equation for a manufacturer's product has the form
$$q = a\sqrt{b - cp^2}$$
where a, b, and c are positive constants.

(a) Show that elasticity does not depend on a.

(b) Determine the interval of prices for which demand is elastic.

(c) For which price is there unit elasticity?

24. Given the demand equation $q^2(1 + p)^2 = p$, determine the point elasticity of demand when $p = 9$.

25. The demand equation for a product is
$$q = \frac{60}{p} + \ln(65 - p^3)$$

(a) Determine the point elasticity of demand when $p = 4$, and classify the demand as elastic, inelastic, or of unit elasticity at this price level.

(b) If the price is lowered by 2% (from \$4.00 to \$3.92), use the answer to part (a) to estimate the corresponding percentage change in quantity sold.

(c) Will the changes in part (b) result in an increase or decrease in revenue? Explain.

26. The demand equation for a manufacturer's product is
$$p = 50(151 - q)^{0.02\sqrt{q+19}}$$

(a) Find the value of dp/dq when 150 units are demanded.

(b) Using the result in part (a), determine the point elasticity of demand when 150 units are demanded. At this level, is demand elastic, inelastic, or of unit elasticity?

(c) Use the result in part (b) to approximate the price per unit if demand decreases from 150 to 140 units.

(d) If the current demand is 150 units, should the manufacturer increase or decrease price in order to increase revenue? (Justify your answer.)

27. A manufacturer of aluminum doors currently is able to sell 500 doors per week at a price of \$80 each. If the price were lowered to \$75 each, an additional 50 doors per week could be sold. Estimate the current elasticity of demand for the doors, and also estimate the current value of the manufacturer's marginal-revenue function.

28. Given the demand equation
$$p = 2000 - q^2$$
where $5 \leq q \leq 40$, for what value of q is $|\eta|$ a maximum? For what value is it a minimum?

29. Repeat Problem 28 for
$$p = \frac{200}{q + 5}$$
such that $5 \leq q \leq 95$.

To discuss the notion of a function defined implicitly and to determine derivatives by means of implicit differentiation.

12.4 Implicit Differentiation

Implicit differentiation is a technique for differentiating functions that are not given in the usual form $y = f(x)$ [nor in the form $x = g(y)$]. To introduce this technique, we will find the slope of a tangent line to a circle. Let us take the circle of radius 2 whose center is at the origin (Figure 12.4). Its equation is
$$x^2 + y^2 = 4$$
$$x^2 + y^2 - 4 = 0 \tag{1}$$

The point $(\sqrt{2}, \sqrt{2})$ lies on the circle. To find the slope at this point, we need to find dy/dx there. Until now, we have always had y given explicitly (directly) in terms of x before determining y'; that is, our equation was always in the form $y = f(x)$ [or in the form $x = g(y)$]. In Equation (1), this is not so. We say that Equation (1) has the form $F(x, y) = 0$, where $F(x, y)$ denotes a function of two variables as introduced in Section 2.8. The obvious thing to do is solve Equation (1) for y in terms of x:
$$x^2 + y^2 - 4 = 0$$
$$y^2 = 4 - x^2$$
$$y = \pm\sqrt{4 - x^2} \tag{2}$$

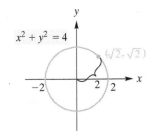

FIGURE 12.4   The circle $x^2 + y^2 = 4$.

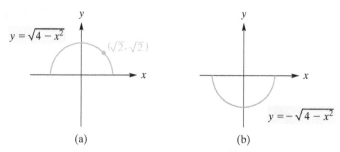

FIGURE 12.5 $x^2 + y^2 = 4$ gives rise to two different functions.

A problem now occurs: Equation (2) may give two values of y for a value of x. It does not define y explicitly as a function of x. We can, however, suppose that Equation (1) defines y as one of two different functions of x,

$$y = +\sqrt{4 - x^2} \quad \text{and} \quad y = -\sqrt{4 - x^2}$$

whose graphs are given in Figure 12.5. Since the point $(\sqrt{2}, \sqrt{2})$ lies on the graph of $y = \sqrt{4 - x^2}$, we should differentiate that function:

$$y = \sqrt{4 - x^2}$$

$$\frac{dy}{dx} = \frac{1}{2}(4 - x^2)^{-1/2}(-2x)$$

$$= -\frac{x}{\sqrt{4 - x^2}}$$

So

$$\left.\frac{dy}{dx}\right|_{x=\sqrt{2}} = -\frac{\sqrt{2}}{\sqrt{4 - 2}} = -1$$

Thus, the slope of the circle $x^2 + y^2 - 4 = 0$ at the point $(\sqrt{2}, \sqrt{2})$ is -1.

Let us summarize the difficulties we had. First, y was not originally given explicitly in terms of x. Second, after we tried to find such a relation, we ended up with more than one function of x. In fact, depending on the equation given, it may be very complicated or even impossible to find an explicit expression for y. For example, it would be difficult to solve $ye^x + \ln(x + y) = 0$ for y. We will now consider a method that avoids such difficulties.

An equation of the form $F(x, y) = 0$, such as we had originally, is said to express y *implicitly* as a function of x. The word *implicitly* is used, since y is not given explicitly as a function of x. However, it is assumed or *implied* that the equation defines y as at least one differentiable function of x. Thus, we assume that Equation (1), $x^2 + y^2 - 4 = 0$, defines some differentiable function of x, say, $y = f(x)$. Next, we treat y as a function of x and differentiate both sides of Equation (1) with respect to x. Finally, we solve the result for dy/dx. Applying this procedure, we obtain

$$\frac{d}{dx}(x^2 + y^2 - 4) = \frac{d}{dx}(0)$$

$$\frac{d}{dx}(x^2) + \frac{d}{dx}(y^2) - \frac{d}{dx}(4) = \frac{d}{dx}(0) \tag{3}$$

We know that $\frac{d}{dx}(x^2) = 2x$ and that both $\frac{d}{dx}(4)$ and $\frac{d}{dx}(0)$ are 0. But $\frac{d}{dx}(y^2)$ is **not** $2y$, because we are differentiating with respect to x, not y. That is, y is not the independent variable. Since y is assumed to be a function of x, y^2 has the form u^n, where y plays the role of u. Just as the power rule states that $\frac{d}{dx}(u^2) = 2u\frac{du}{dx}$, we have $\frac{d}{dx}(y^2) = 2y\frac{dy}{dx}$. Hence, Equation (3) becomes

$$2x + 2y\frac{dy}{dx} = 0$$

Solving for dy/dx gives

$$2y\frac{dy}{dx} = -2x$$

$$\frac{dy}{dx} = -\frac{x}{y} \quad \text{for } y \neq 0 \tag{4}$$

Notice that the expression for dy/dx involves the variable y as well as x. This means that to find dy/dx at a point, both coordinates of the point must be substituted into dy/dx. Thus,

$$\left.\frac{dy}{dx}\right|_{(\sqrt{2},\sqrt{2})} = -\frac{\sqrt{2}}{\sqrt{2}} = -1$$

as before. This method of finding dy/dx is called **implicit differentiation.** We note that Equation (4) is not defined when $y = 0$. Geometrically, this is clear, since the tangent line to the circle at either $(2, 0)$ or $(-2, 0)$ is vertical, and the slope is not defined.

Here are the steps to follow when differentiating implicitly:

Implicit Differentiation Procedure

For an equation that we assume defines y implicitly as a differentiable function of x, the derivative $\dfrac{dy}{dx}$ can be found as follows:

1. Differentiate both sides of the equation with respect to x.

2. Collect all terms involving $\dfrac{dy}{dx}$ on one side of the equation, and collect all other terms on the other side.

3. Factor $\dfrac{dy}{dx}$ from the side involving the $\dfrac{dy}{dx}$ terms.

4. Solve for $\dfrac{dy}{dx}$, noting any restrictions.

EXAMPLE 1   Implicit Differentiation

Find $\dfrac{dy}{dx}$ by implicit differentiation if $y + y^3 - x = 7$.

Solution: Here y is not given as an explicit function of x [that is, not in the form $y = f(x)$]. Thus, we assume that y is an implicit (differentiable) function of x and apply the preceding four-step procedure:

1. Differentiating both sides with respect to x, we have

$$\frac{d}{dx}(y + y^3 - x) = \frac{d}{dx}(7)$$

$$\frac{d}{dx}(y) + \frac{d}{dx}(y^3) - \frac{d}{dx}(x) = \frac{d}{dx}(7)$$

Now, $\dfrac{d}{dx}(y)$ can be written $\dfrac{dy}{dx}$, and $\dfrac{d}{dx}(x) = 1$. By the power rule,

$$\frac{d}{dx}(y^3) = 3y^2\frac{dy}{dx}$$

Hence, we obtain

$$\frac{dy}{dx} + 3y^2\frac{dy}{dx} - 1 = 0$$

2. Collecting all $\dfrac{dy}{dx}$ terms on the left side and all other terms on the right side gives

$$\frac{dy}{dx} + 3y^2\frac{dy}{dx} = 1$$

CAUTION!

The derivative of y^3 with respect to x is $3y^2\dfrac{dy}{dx}$, not $3y^2$.

3. Factoring $\dfrac{dy}{dx}$ from the left side, we have

$$\frac{dy}{dx}(1 + 3y^2) = 1$$

In an implicit-differentiation problem, we are able to find the derivative of a function without knowing the function.

4. We solve for $\dfrac{dy}{dx}$ by dividing both sides by $1 + 3y^2$:

$$\frac{dy}{dx} = \frac{1}{1 + 3y^2}$$

Because step 4 of the process often involves division by an expression involving the variables, the answer obtained must often be restricted to exclude those values of the variables that would make the denominator zero. Here the denominator is always greater than or equal to 1, so there is no restriction.

Now Work Problem 3 ◁

APPLY IT ▶

4. Suppose that P, the proportion of people affected by a certain disease, is described by $\ln\left(\dfrac{P}{1-P}\right) = 0.5t$, where t is the time in months. Find $\dfrac{dP}{dt}$, the rate at which P grows with respect to time.

EXAMPLE 2   Implicit Differentiation

Find $\dfrac{dy}{dx}$ if $x^3 + 4xy^2 - 27 = y^4$.

Solution: Since y is not given explicitly in terms of x, we will use the method of implicit differentiation:

1. Assuming that y is a function of x and differentiating both sides with respect to x, we get

$$\frac{d}{dx}(x^3 + 4xy^2 - 27) = \frac{d}{dx}(y^4)$$

$$\frac{d}{dx}(x^3) + 4\frac{d}{dx}(xy^2) - \frac{d}{dx}(27) = \frac{d}{dx}(y^4)$$

To find $\dfrac{d}{dx}(xy^2)$, we use the product rule:

$$3x^2 + 4\left[x\frac{d}{dx}(y^2) + y^2\frac{d}{dx}(x)\right] - 0 = 4y^3\frac{dy}{dx}$$

$$3x^2 + 4\left[x\left(2y\frac{dy}{dx}\right) + y^2(1)\right] = 4y^3\frac{dy}{dx}$$

$$3x^2 + 8xy\frac{dy}{dx} + 4y^2 = 4y^3\frac{dy}{dx}$$

2. Collecting $\dfrac{dy}{dx}$ terms on the left side and other terms on the right gives

$$8xy\frac{dy}{dx} - 4y^3\frac{dy}{dx} = -3x^2 - 4y^2$$

3. Factoring $\dfrac{dy}{dx}$ from the left side yields

$$\frac{dy}{dx}(8xy - 4y^3) = -3x^2 - 4y^2$$

4. Solving for $\dfrac{dy}{dx}$, we have

$$\frac{dy}{dx} = \frac{-3x^2 - 4y^2}{8xy - 4y^3} = \frac{3x^2 + 4y^2}{4y^3 - 8xy}$$

which gives the value of dy/dx at points (x, y) for which $4y^3 - 8xy \neq 0$.

Now Work Problem 11 ◁

APPLY IT ▶

5. The volume V enclosed by a spherical balloon of radius r is given by the equation $V = \frac{4}{3}\pi r^3$. If the radius is increasing at a rate of 5 inches/minute (that is, $\frac{dr}{dt} = 5$), then find $\frac{dV}{dt}\Big|_{r=12}$, the rate of increase of the volume, when the radius is 12 inches.

EXAMPLE 3   Implicit Differentiation

Find the slope of the curve $x^3 = (y - x^2)^2$ at $(1, 2)$.

Solution: The slope at $(1, 2)$ is the value of dy/dx at that point. Finding dy/dx by implicit differentiation, we have

$$\frac{d}{dx}(x^3) = \frac{d}{dx}[(y - x^2)^2]$$

$$3x^2 = 2(y - x^2)\left(\frac{dy}{dx} - 2x\right)$$

$$3x^2 = 2\left(y\frac{dy}{dx} - 2xy - x^2\frac{dy}{dx} + 2x^3\right)$$

$$3x^2 = 2y\frac{dy}{dx} - 4xy - 2x^2\frac{dy}{dx} + 4x^3$$

$$3x^2 + 4xy - 4x^3 = 2y\frac{dy}{dx} - 2x^2\frac{dy}{dx}$$

$$3x^2 + 4xy - 4x^3 = 2\frac{dy}{dx}(y - x^2)$$

$$\frac{dy}{dx} = \frac{3x^2 + 4xy - 4x^3}{2(y - x^2)} \qquad \text{for } y - x^2 \neq 0$$

For the point $(1, 2)$, $y - x^2 = 2 - 1^2 = 1 \neq 0$. Thus, the slope of the curve at $(1, 2)$ is

$$\frac{dy}{dx}\Big|_{(1,2)} = \frac{3(1)^2 + 4(1)(2) - 4(1)^3}{2(2 - (1)^2)} = \frac{7}{2}$$

Now Work Problem 25 ◁

APPLY IT ▶

6. A 10-foot ladder is placed against a vertical wall. Suppose the bottom of the ladder slides away from the wall at a constant rate of 3 ft/s. (That is, $\frac{dx}{dt} = 3$.) How fast is the top of the ladder sliding down the wall when the top of the ladder is 8 feet from the ground (that is, when $y = 8$)? (That is, what is $\frac{dy}{dt}$?) (Use the Pythagorean theorem for right triangles, $x^2 + y^2 = z^2$, where x and y are the legs of the triangle and z is the hypotenuse.)

EXAMPLE 4   Implicit Differentiation

If $q - p = \ln q + \ln p$, find dq/dp.

Solution: We assume that q is a function of p and differentiate both sides with respect to p:

$$\frac{d}{dp}(q) - \frac{d}{dp}(p) = \frac{d}{dp}(\ln q) + \frac{d}{dp}(\ln p)$$

$$\frac{dq}{dp} - 1 = \frac{1}{q}\frac{dq}{dp} + \frac{1}{p}$$

$$\frac{dq}{dp} - \frac{1}{q}\frac{dq}{dp} = \frac{1}{p} + 1$$

$$\frac{dq}{dp}\left(1 - \frac{1}{q}\right) = \frac{1}{p} + 1$$

$$\frac{dq}{dp}\left(\frac{q - 1}{q}\right) = \frac{1 + p}{p}$$

$$\frac{dq}{dp} = \frac{(1 + p)q}{p(q - 1)} \qquad \text{for } p(q - 1) \neq 0$$

Now Work Problem 19 ◁

PROBLEMS 12.4

In Problems 1–24, find dy/dx by implicit differentiation.

1. $x^2 + 4y^2 = 4$

2. $3x^2 + 6y^2 = 1$

3. $2y^3 - 7x^2 = 5$

4. $5y^2 - 2x^2 = 10$

5. $\sqrt[3]{x} + \sqrt[3]{y} = 3$

6. $x^{1/5} + y^{1/5} = 4$

7. $x^{3/4} + y^{3/4} = 5$

8. $y^3 = 4x$

9. $xy = 36$

10. $x^2 + xy - 2y^2 = 0$

11. $xy - y - 11x = 5$

12. $x^3 - y^3 = 3x^2y - 3xy^2$

13. $2x^3 + y^3 - 12xy = 0$

14. $5x^3 + 6xy + 7y^3 = 0$

15. $x = \sqrt{y} + \sqrt[4]{y}$

16. $x^3y^3 + x = 9$

17. $5x^3y^4 - x + y^2 = 25$

18. $y^2 + y = \ln x$

19. $\ln(xy) = e^{xy}$

20. $\ln(xy) + x = 4$

21. $xe^y + y = 13$

22. $4x^2 + 9y^2 = 16$

23. $(1 + e^{3x})^2 = 3 + \ln(x + y)$ **24.** $e^{x-y} = \ln(x - y)$

25. If $x + xy + y^2 = 7$, find dy/dx at $(1, 2)$.

26. If $x\sqrt{y + 1} = y\sqrt{x + 1}$, find dy/dx at $(3, 3)$.

27. Find the slope of the curve $4x^2 + 9y^2 = 1$ at the point $\left(0, \frac{1}{3}\right)$; at the point (x_0, y_0).

28. Find the slope of the curve $(x^2 + y^2)^2 = 4y^2$ at the point $(0, 2)$.

29. Find equations of the tangent lines to the curve
$$x^3 + xy + y^3 = -1$$
at the points $(-1, -1)$, $(-1, 0)$, and $(-1, 1)$.

30. Repeat Problem 29 for the curve
$$y^2 + xy - x^2 = 5$$
at the point $(4, 3)$.

For the demand equations in Problems 31–34, find the rate of change of q with respect to p.

31. $p = 100 - q^2$

32. $p = 400 - \sqrt{q}$

33. $p = \dfrac{20}{(q + 5)^2}$

34. $p = \dfrac{3}{q^2 + 1}$

35. Radioactivity The relative activity I/I_0 of a radioactive element varies with elapsed time according to the equation
$$\ln\left(\frac{I}{I_0}\right) = -\lambda t$$
where λ (a Greek letter read "lambda") is the disintegration constant and I_0 is the initial intensity (a constant). Find the rate of change of the intensity I with respect to the elapsed time t.

36. Earthquakes The magnitude M of an earthquake and its energy E are related by the equation[6]
$$1.5M = \log\left(\frac{E}{2.5 \times 10^{11}}\right)$$
Here M is given in terms of Richter's preferred scale of 1958 and E is in ergs. Determine the rate of change of energy with respect to magnitude and the rate of change of magnitude with respect to energy.

37. Physical Scale The relationship among the speed (v), frequency (f), and wavelength (λ) of any wave is given by
$$v = f\lambda$$
Find $df/d\lambda$ by differentiating implicitly. (Treat v as a constant.) Then show that the same result is obtained if you first solve the equation for f and then differentiate with respect to λ.

38. Biology The equation $(P + a)(v + b) = k$ is called the "fundamental equation of muscle contraction."[7] Here P is the load imposed on the muscle, v is the velocity of the shortening of the muscle fibers, and a, b, and k are positive constants. Use implicit differentiation to show that, in terms of P,
$$\frac{dv}{dP} = -\frac{k}{(P + a)^2}$$

39. Marginal Propensity to Consume A country's savings S is defined implicitly in terms of its national income I by the equation
$$S^2 + \frac{1}{4}I^2 = SI + I$$
where both S and I are in billions of dollars. Find the marginal propensity to consume when $I = 16$ and $S = 12$.

40. Technological Substitution New products or technologies often tend to replace old ones. For example, today most commercial airlines use jet engines rather than prop engines. In discussing the forecasting of technological substitution, Hurter and Rubenstein[8] refer to the equation
$$\ln\frac{f(t)}{1 - f(t)} + \sigma\frac{1}{1 - f(t)} = C_1 + C_2t$$
where $f(t)$ is the market share of the substitute over time t and C_1, C_2, and σ (a Greek letter read "sigma") are constants. Verify their claim that the rate of substitution is
$$f'(t) = \frac{C_2f(t)[1 - f(t)]^2}{\sigma f(t) + [1 - f(t)]}$$

Objective

To describe the method of logarithmic differentiation and to show how to differentiate a function of the form u^v.

12.5 Logarithmic Differentiation

A technique called **logarithmic differentiation** often simplifies the differentiation of $y = f(x)$ when $f(x)$ involves products, quotients, or powers. The procedure is as

---

[6] K. E. Bullen, *An Introduction to the Theory of Seismology* (Cambridge, U.K.: Cambridge at the University Press, 1963).

[7] R. W. Stacy et al., *Essentials of Biological and Medical Physics* (New York: McGraw-Hill Book Company, 1955).

[8] A. P. Hurter, Jr., A. H. Rubenstein et al., "Market Penetration by New Innovations: The Technological Literature," *Technological Forecasting and Social Change,* 11 (1978), 197–221.

follows:

Logarithmic Differentiation

To differentiate $y = f(x)$,

1. Take the natural logarithm of both sides. This results in

$$\ln y = \ln (f(x))$$

2. Simplify $\ln (f(x))$ by using properties of logarithms.
3. Differentiate both sides with respect to x.
4. Solve for $\dfrac{dy}{dx}$.
5. Express the answer in terms of x only. This requires substituting $f(x)$ for y.

There are a couple of points worth noting. First, irrespective of any simplification, the procedure produces

$$\frac{y'}{y} = \frac{d}{dx}(\ln (f(x))$$

so that

$$\frac{dy}{dx} = y\frac{d}{dx}(\ln (f(x))$$

is a formula that you can memorize, if you prefer. Second, the quantity $\dfrac{f'(x)}{f(x)}$, which results from differentiating $\ln (f(x))$, is what was called the *relative rate of change of* $f(x)$ in Section 11.3.

The next example illustrates the procedure.

EXAMPLE 1   **Logarithmic Differentiation**

Find y' if $y = \dfrac{(2x - 5)^3}{x^2\sqrt[4]{x^2 + 1}}$.

Solution: Differentiating this function in the usual way is messy because it involves the quotient, power, and product rules. Logarithmic differentiation makes the work less of a chore.

1. We take the natural logarithm of both sides:

$$\ln y = \ln \frac{(2x - 5)^3}{x^2\sqrt[4]{x^2 + 1}}$$

2. Simplifying by using properties of logarithms, we have

$$\ln y = \ln (2x - 5)^3 - \ln \left(x^2\sqrt[4]{x^2 + 1}\right)$$
$$= 3\ln (2x - 5) - (\ln x^2 + \ln (x^2 + 1)^{1/4})$$
$$= 3\ln (2x - 5) - 2\ln x - \frac{1}{4}\ln (x^2 + 1)$$

3. Differentiating with respect to x gives

$$\frac{y'}{y} = 3\left(\frac{1}{2x - 5}\right)(2) - 2\left(\frac{1}{x}\right) - \frac{1}{4}\left(\frac{1}{x^2 + 1}\right)(2x)$$
$$= \frac{6}{2x - 5} - \frac{2}{x} - \frac{x}{2(x^2 + 1)}$$

CAUTION!⚠

Since y is a function of x, differentiating $\ln y$ with respect to x gives $\dfrac{y'}{y}$.

4. Solving for y' yields

$$y' = y\left(\frac{6}{2x - 5} - \frac{2}{x} - \frac{x}{2(x^2 + 1)}\right)$$

5. Substituting the original expression for y gives y' in terms of x only:

$$y' = \frac{(2x-5)^3}{x^2\sqrt[4]{x^2+1}}\left[\frac{6}{2x-5} - \frac{2}{x} - \frac{x}{2(x^2+1)}\right]$$

Now Work Problem 1 ◁

Logarithmic differentiation can also be used to differentiate a function of the form $y = u^v$, where both u and v are differentiable functions of x. Because neither the base nor the exponent is necessarily a constant, the differentiation techniques for u^n and a^u do not apply here.

> **EXAMPLE 2** Differentiating the Form u^v

Differentiate $y = x^x$ by using logarithmic differentiation.

Solution: This example is a good candidate for the *formula* approach to logarithmic differentiation.

$$y' = y\frac{d}{dx}(\ln x^x) = x^x\frac{d}{dx}(x\ln x) = x^x\left((1)(\ln x) + (x)\left(\frac{1}{x}\right)\right) = x^x(\ln x + 1)$$

It is worthwhile mentioning that an alternative technique for differentiating a function of the form $y = u^v$ is to convert it to an exponential function to the base e. To illustrate, for the function in this example, we have

$$y = x^x = (e^{\ln x})^x = e^{x\ln x}$$

$$y' = e^{x\ln x}\left(1\ln x + x\frac{1}{x}\right) = x^x(\ln x + 1)$$

Now Work Problem 15 ◁

> **EXAMPLE 3** Relative Rate of Change of a Product

Show that the relative rate of change of a product is the sum of the relative rates of change of its factors. Use this result to express the percentage rate of change in revenue in terms of the percentage rate of change in price.

Solution: Recall that the relative rate of change of a function r is $\dfrac{r'}{r}$. We are to show that if $r = pq$, then $\dfrac{r'}{r} = \dfrac{p'}{p} + \dfrac{q'}{q}$. From $r = pq$ we have $\ln r = \ln p + \ln q$, which, when both sides are differentiated, gives

$$\frac{r'}{r} = \frac{p'}{p} + \frac{q'}{q}$$

as required. Multiplying both sides by 100% gives an expression for the percentage rate of change of r in terms of those of p and q:

$$\frac{r'}{r}100\% = \frac{p'}{p}100\% + \frac{q'}{q}100\%$$

If p is *price* per item and q is *quantity* sold, then $r = pq$ is total *revenue*. In this case we take differentiation to be with respect to p and note that now $\dfrac{q'}{q} = \eta\dfrac{p'}{p}$, where η is the elasticity of demand as in Section 12.3. It follows that in this case we have

$$\frac{r'}{r}100\% = (1 + \eta)\frac{p'}{p}100\%$$

expressing the percentage rate of change in revenue in terms of the percentage rate of change in price. For example, if at a given price and quantity, $\eta = -5$, then a 1% increase in price will result in a $(1 - 5)\% = -4\%$ increase in revenue, which is to say a 4% *decrease* in revenue, while a 3% decrease in price—that is, a -3% *increase* in price—will result in a $(1 - 5)(-3)\% = 12\%$ increase in revenue. It is also clear that at points at which there is unit elasticity ($\eta = -1$), any percentage change in price produces no percentage change in revenue.

Now Work Problem 29 ◁

EXAMPLE 4   Differentiating the Form u^v

Find the derivative of $y = (1 + e^x)^{\ln x}$.

Solution: This has the form $y = u^v$, where $u = 1 + e^x$ and $v = \ln x$. Using logarithmic differentiation, we have

$$\ln y = \ln\left((1 + e^x)^{\ln x}\right)$$

$$\ln y = (\ln x) \ln(1 + e^x)$$

$$\frac{y'}{y} = \left(\frac{1}{x}\right)(\ln(1 + e^x)) + (\ln x)\left(\frac{1}{1 + e^x} \cdot e^x\right)$$

$$\frac{y'}{y} = \frac{\ln(1 + e^x)}{x} + \frac{e^x \ln x}{1 + e^x}$$

$$y' = y\left(\frac{\ln(1 + e^x)}{x} + \frac{e^x \ln x}{1 + e^x}\right)$$

$$y' = (1 + e^x)^{\ln x}\left(\frac{\ln(1 + e^x)}{x} + \frac{e^x \ln x}{1 + e^x}\right)$$

Now Work Problem 17 ◁

Alternatively, we can differentiate even a general function of the form $y = u(x)^{v(x)}$ with $u(x) > 0$ by using the equation

$$u^v = e^{v \ln u}$$

Indeed, if $y = u(x)^{v(x)} = e^{v(x) \ln u(x)}$ for $u(x) > 0$, then

$$\frac{dy}{dx} = \frac{d}{dx}\left(e^{v(x) \ln u(x)}\right) = e^{v(x) \ln u(x)} \frac{d}{dx}(v(x) \ln u(x)) = u^v\left(v'(x) \ln u(x) + v(x)\frac{u'(x)}{u(x)}\right)$$

which could be summarized as

$$(u^v)' = u^v\left(v' \ln u + v\frac{u'}{u}\right)$$

As is often the case, there is no suggestion that the preceding formula should be memorized. The point here is that we have shown that *any* function of the form u^v can be differentiated using the equation $u^v = e^{v \ln u}$. The same result will be obtained from logarithmic differentiation:

$$\ln y = \ln(u^v)$$

$$\ln y = v \ln u$$

$$\frac{y'}{y} = v' \ln u + v\frac{u'}{u}$$

$$y' = y\left(v' \ln u + v\frac{u'}{u}\right)$$

$$(u^v)' = u^v\left(v' \ln u + v\frac{u'}{u}\right)$$

After completing this section, we understand how to differentiate each of the following forms:

$$y = \begin{cases} (f(x))^a & \text{(a)} \\ b^{f(x)} & \text{(b)} \\ (f(x))^{g(x)} & \text{(c)} \end{cases}$$

For type (a), use the power rule. For type (b), use the differentiation formula for exponential functions. [If $b \neq e$, first convert $b^{f(x)}$ to an e^u function.] For type (c), use logarithmic differentiation or first convert to an e^u function. Do not apply a rule in a situation where the rule does not apply. For example, the power rule does not apply to x^x.

PROBLEMS 12.5

In Problems 1–12, find y' by using logarithmic differentiation.

1. $y = (x+1)^2(x-2)(x^2+3)$

2. $y = (3x+4)(8x-1)^2(3x^2+1)^4$

3. $y = (3x^3-1)^2(2x+5)^3$ 4. $y = (2x^2+1)\sqrt{8x^2-1}$

5. $y = \sqrt{x+1}\sqrt{x-1}\sqrt{x^2+1}$ 6. $y = (2x+1)\sqrt{x^3+2}\sqrt[3]{2x+5}$

7. $y = \dfrac{\sqrt{1-x^2}}{1-2x}$ 8. $y = \sqrt{\dfrac{x^2+5}{x+9}}$

9. $y = \dfrac{(2x^2+2)^2}{(x+1)^2(3x+2)}$ 10. $y = \dfrac{x^2(1+x^2)}{\sqrt{x^2+4}}$

11. $y = \sqrt{\dfrac{(x+3)(x-2)}{2x-1}}$ 12. $y = \sqrt[3]{\dfrac{6(x^3+1)^2}{x^6 e^{-4x}}}$

In Problems 13–20, find y'.

13. $y = x^{x^2+1}$ 14. $y = (2x)^{\sqrt{x}}$

15. $y = x^{\sqrt{x}}$ 16. $y = \left(\dfrac{3}{x^2}\right)^x$

17. $y = (3x+1)^{2x}$ 18. $y = (x^2+1)^{x+1}$

19. $y = 4e^x x^{3x}$ 20. $y = (\sqrt{x})^x$

21. If $y = (4x-3)^{2x+1}$, find dy/dx when $x = 1$.

22. If $y = (\ln x)^{\ln x}$, find dy/dx when $x = e$.

23. Find an equation of the tangent line to
$$y = (x+1)(x+2)^2(x+3)^2$$
at the point where $x = 0$.

24. Find an equation of the tangent line to the graph of
$$y = x^x$$
at the point where $x = 1$.

25. Find an equation of the tangent line to the graph of
$$y = x^x$$
at the point where $x = e$.

26. If $y = x^x$, find the relative rate of change of y with respect to x when $x = 1$.

27. If $y = (3x)^{-2x}$, find the value of x for which the *percentage* rate of change of y with respect to x is 60.

28. Suppose $f(x)$ is a positive differentiable function and g is a differentiable function and $y = (f(x))^{g(x)}$. Use logarithmic differentiation to show that
$$\frac{dy}{dx} = (f(x))^{g(x)}\left(f'(x)\frac{g(x)}{f(x)} + g'(x)\ln(f(x))\right)$$

29. The demand equation for a compact disc is
$$q = 500 - 40p + p^2$$
If the price of \$15 is increased by 1/2%, find the corresponding percentage change in revenue.

30. Repeat Problem 29 with the same information except for a 5% *decrease* in price.

Objective

To approximate real roots of an equation by using calculus. The method shown is suitable for calculators.

12.6 Newton's Method

It is easy to solve equations of the form $f(x) = 0$ when f is a linear or quadratic function. For example, we can solve $x^2+3x-2 = 0$ by the quadratic formula. However, if $f(x)$ has a degree greater than 2 (or is not a polynomial), it may be difficult, or even impossible, to find solutions (or roots) of $f(x) = 0$ by the methods to which you are accustomed. For this reason, we may settle for approximate solutions, which can be obtained in a variety of efficient ways. For example, a graphing calculator can be used to estimate the real roots of $f(x) = 0$. In this section, we will study how the derivative can be so used (provided that f is differentiable). The procedure we will develop, called *Newton's method*, is well suited to a calculator or computer.

Newton's method requires an initial estimate for a root of $f(x) = 0$. One way of obtaining this estimate is by making a rough sketch of the graph of $y = f(x)$ and estimating the root from the graph. A point on the graph where $y = 0$ is an x-intercept, and the x-value of this point is a root of $f(x) = 0$. Another way of locating a root is based on the following fact:

> If f is continuous on the interval $[a, b]$ and $f(a)$ and $f(b)$ have opposite signs, then the equation $f(x) = 0$ has at least one real root between a and b.

Figure 12.6 depicts this situation. The x-intercept between a and b corresponds to a root of $f(x) = 0$, and we can use either a or b to approximate this root.

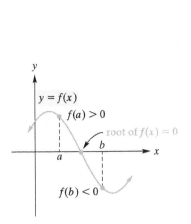

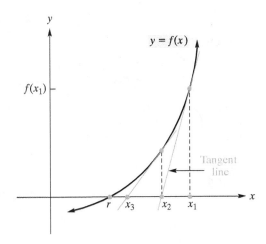

FIGURE 12.6   Root of $f(x) = 0$ between a and b, where $f(a)$ and $f(b)$ have opposite signs.

FIGURE 12.7   Improving approximation of root via tangent line.

Assuming that we have an estimated (but incorrect) value for a root, we turn to a way of getting a better approximation. In Figure 12.7, we see that $f(r) = 0$, so r is a root of the equation $f(x) = 0$. Suppose x_1 is an initial approximation to r (and one that is close to r). Observe that the tangent line to the curve at $(x_1, f(x_1))$ intersects the x-axis at the point $(x_2, 0)$, and x_2 is a better approximation to r than is x_1.

We can find x_2 from the equation of the tangent line. The slope of the tangent line is $f'(x_1)$, so a point-slope form for this line is

$$y - f(x_1) = f'(x_1)(x - x_1) \tag{1}$$

Since $(x_2, 0)$ is on the tangent line, its coordinates must satisfy Equation (1). This gives

$$0 - f(x_1) = f'(x_1)(x_2 - x_1)$$

$$-\frac{f(x_1)}{f'(x_1)} = x_2 - x_1 \qquad \text{if } f'(x_1) \neq 0$$

Thus,

$$x_2 = x_1 - \frac{f(x_1)}{f'(x_1)} \tag{2}$$

To get a better approximation to r, we again perform the procedure described, but this time we use x_2 as our starting point. This gives the approximation

$$x_3 = x_2 - \frac{f(x_2)}{f'(x_2)} \tag{3}$$

Repeating (or *iterating*) this computation over and over, we hope to obtain better approximations, in the sense that the sequence of values

$$x_1, x_2, x_3, \ldots$$

will approach r. In practice, we terminate the process when we have reached a desired degree of accuracy.

Analyzing Equations (2) and (3), we see how x_2 is obtained from x_1 and how x_3 is obtained from x_2. In general, x_{n+1} is obtained from x_n by means of the following general formula, called **Newton's method:**

Newton's Method

$$x_{n+1} = x_n - \frac{f(x_n)}{f'(x_n)} \qquad n = 1, 2, 3, \ldots \tag{4}$$

TO REVIEW recursively defined sequences, see Section 1.6.

A formula, like Equation (4), that indicates how one number in a sequence is obtained from the preceding one is called a **recursion formula,** or an *iteration equation*.

APPLY IT ▶

7. If the total profit (in dollars) from the sale of x televisions is $P(x) = 20x - 0.01x^2 - 850 + 3\ln(x)$, use Newton's method to approximate the break-even quantities. (*Note:* There are two break-even quantities; one is between 10 and 50, and the other is between 1900 and 2000.) Give the x-value to the nearest integer.

In the event that a root lies between a and b and $f(a)$ and $f(b)$ are equally close to 0, choose either a or b as the first approximation.

EXAMPLE 1   Approximating a Root by Newton's Method

Approximate the root of $x^4 - 4x + 1 = 0$ that lies between 0 and 1. Continue the approximation procedure until two successive approximations differ by less than 0.0001.

Solution: Letting $f(x) = x^4 - 4x + 1$, we have

$$f(0) = 0 - 0 + 1 = 1$$

and

$$f(1) = 1 - 4 + 1 = -2$$

(Note the change in sign.) Since $f(0)$ is closer to 0 than is $f(1)$, we choose 0 to be our first approximation, x_1. Now,

$$f'(x) = 4x^3 - 4$$

so

$$f(x_n) = x_n^4 - 4x_n + 1 \quad \text{and} \quad f'(x_n) = 4x_n^3 - 4$$

Substituting into Equation (4) gives the recursion formula

$$x_{n+1} = x_n - \frac{f(x_n)}{f'(x_n)} = x_n - \frac{x_n^4 - 4x_n + 1}{4x_n^3 - 4}$$

$$= \frac{4x_n^4 - 4x_n - x_n^4 + 4x_n - 1}{4x_n^3 - 4}$$

so

$$x_{n+1} = \frac{3x_n^4 - 1}{4x_n^3 - 4} \qquad (5)$$

Since $x_1 = 0$, letting $n = 1$ in Equation (5) gives

$$x_2 = \frac{3x_1^4 - 1}{4x_1^3 - 4} = \frac{3(0)^4 - 1}{4(0)^3 - 4} = 0.25$$

Letting $n = 2$ in Equation (5) gives

$$x_3 = \frac{3x_2^4 - 1}{4x_2^3 - 4} = \frac{3(0.25)^4 - 1}{4(0.25)^3 - 4} \approx 0.25099$$

Letting $n = 3$ in Equation (5) gives

$$x_4 = \frac{3x_3^4 - 1}{4x_3^3 - 4} = \frac{3(0.25099)^4 - 1}{4(0.25099)^3 - 4} \approx 0.25099$$

The data obtained thus far are displayed in Table 12.1. Since the values of x_3 and x_4 differ by less than 0.0001, we take the root to be 0.25099 (that is, x_4).

Now Work Problem 1 ◁

Table 12.1

n	x_n	x_{n+1}
1	0.00000	0.25000
2	0.25000	0.25099
3	0.25099	0.25099

EXAMPLE 2   Approximating a Root by Newton's Method

Approximate the root of $x^3 = 3x - 1$ that lies between -1 and -2. Continue the approximation procedure until two successive approximations differ by less than 0.0001.

Solution: Letting $f(x) = x^3 - 3x + 1$ [we need the form $f(x) = 0$], we find that

$$f(-1) = (-1)^3 - 3(-1) + 1 = 3$$

and

$$f(-2) = (-2)^3 - 3(-2) + 1 = -1$$

(Note the change in sign.) Since $f(-2)$ is closer to 0 than is $f(-1)$, we choose -2 to be our first approximation, x_1. Now,

$$f'(x) = 3x^2 - 3$$

so

$$f(x_n) = x_n^3 - 3x_n + 1 \quad \text{and} \quad f'(x_n) = 3x_n^2 - 3$$

Substituting into Equation (4) gives the recursion formula

$$x_{n+1} = x_n - \frac{f(x_n)}{f'(x_n)} = x_n - \frac{x_n^3 - 3x_n + 1}{3x_n^2 - 3}$$

so

$$x_{n+1} = \frac{2x_n^3 - 1}{3x_n^2 - 3} \tag{6}$$

Since $x_1 = -2$, letting $n = 1$ in Equation (6) gives

$$x_2 = \frac{2x_1^3 - 1}{3x_1^2 - 3} = \frac{2(-2)^3 - 1}{3(-2)^2 - 3} \approx -1.88889$$

Continuing in this way, we obtain Table 12.2. Because the values of x_3 and x_4 differ by 0.00006, which is less than 0.0001, we take the root to be -1.87939 (that is, x_4).

Table 12.2

n	x_n	$x_n + 1$
1	-2.00000	-1.88889
2	-1.88889	-1.87945
3	-1.87945	-1.87939

Now Work Problem 3 ◁

If our choice of x_1 has $f'(x_1) = 0$, then Newton's method will fail to produce a value for x_2. This occurs in Problems 2 and 8 of Problems 12.6. When this happens, the choice of x_1 must be rejected and a different number, close to the desired root, must be chosen for x_1. A graph of f can be helpful in this situation. Finally, there are times when the sequence of approximations does not approach the root. A discussion of such situations is beyond the scope of this book.

TECHNOLOGY ▮▮▮▮

Figure 12.8 gives a short TI-83 Plus program for Newton's method. Before the program is executed, the first approximation to the root of $f(x) = 0$ is stored as X, and $f(x)$ and $f'(x)$ are stored as Y_1 and Y_2, respectively.

When executed, the program computes the first iteration and pauses. Successive iterations are obtained by successively pressing ENTER. Figure 12.9 shows the iterations for the problem in Example 2.

```
PROGRAM:NEWTON
:Lbl A
:X-Y₁(X)/Y₂(X)
:Ans→X
:Disp X
:Pause
:Goto A█
```

FIGURE 12.8   Calculator program for Newton's method.

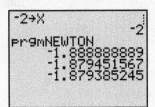

FIGURE 12.9   Iterations for problem in Example 2.

PROBLEMS 12.6

In Problems 1–10, use Newton's method to approximate the indicated root of the given equation. Continue the approximation procedure until the difference of two successive approximations is less than 0.0001.

1. $x^3 - 5x + 1 = 0$;   root between 0 and 1

2. $x^3 + 2x^2 - 1 = 0$;   root between 0 and 1

3. $x^3 - x - 1 = 0$;   root between 1 and 2

4. $x^3 - 9x + 6 = 0$;   root between 2 and 3

5. $x^3 + x + 1 = 0$;   root between -1 and 0

6. $x^3 = 2x + 6$;   root between 2 and 3

7. $x^4 = 3x - 1$;   root between 0 and 1

8. $x^4 + 4x - 1 = 0$;   root between -2 and -1

9. $x^4 - 2x^3 + x^2 - 3 = 0$;   root between 1 and 2

10. $x^4 - x^3 + x - 2 = 0$;   root between 1 and 2

11. Estimate, to three-decimal-place accuracy, the cube root of 73. [*Hint:* Show that the problem is equivalent to finding a root of $f(x) = x^3 - 73 = 0$.] Choose 4 as the initial estimate. Continue the iteration until two successive approximations, rounded to three decimal places, are the same.

12. Estimate $\sqrt[4]{19}$, to two-decimal-place accuracy. Use 2 as your initial estimate.

13. Find, to two-decimal-place accuracy, all real solutions of the equation $e^x = x + 5$. (*Hint:* A rough sketch of the graphs of $y = e^x$ and $y = x + 5$ makes it clear how many solutions there are. Use nearby integer values for your initial estimates.)

14. Find, to three-decimal-place accuracy, all real solutions of the equation $\ln x = 5 - x$.

15. **Break-Even Quantity**   The cost of manufacturing q tons of a certain product is given by

$$c = 250 + 2q - 0.1q^3$$

and the revenue obtained by selling the q tons is given by

$$r = 3q$$

Approximate, to two-decimal-place accuracy, the break-even quantity. (*Hint:* Approximate a root of $r - c = 0$ by choosing 13 as your initial estimate.)

16. **Break-Even Quantity**   The total cost of manufacturing q hundred pencils is c dollars, where

$$c = 50 + 4q + \frac{q^2}{1000} + \frac{1}{q}$$

Pencils are sold for $8 per hundred.

(a) Show that the break-even quantity is a solution of the equation

$$f(q) = \frac{q^3}{1000} - 4q^2 + 50q + 1 = 0$$

(b) Use Newton's method to approximate the solution of $f(q) = 0$, where $f(q)$ is given in part (a). Use 10 as your initial approximation, and give your answer to two-decimal-place accuracy.

17. **Equilibrium**   Given the supply equation $p = 2q + 5$ and the demand equation $p = \dfrac{100}{q^2 + 1}$, use Newton's method to estimate the market equilibrium quantity. Give your answer to three-decimal-place accuracy.

18. **Equilibrium**   Given the supply equation

$$p = 0.2q^3 + 0.5q + 2$$

and the demand equation $p = 10 - q$, use Newton's method to estimate the market equilibrium quantity, and find the corresponding equilibrium price. Use 5 as an initial estimate for the required value of q, and give your answer to two-decimal-place accuracy.

19. Use Newton's method to approximate (to two-decimal-place accuracy) a critical value of the function

$$f(x) = \frac{x^3}{3} - x^2 - 5x + 1$$

on the interval [3, 4].

Objective

To find higher-order derivatives both directly and implicitly.

12.7 Higher-Order Derivatives

We know that the derivative of a function $y = f(x)$ is itself a function, $f'(x)$. If we differentiate $f'(x)$, the resulting function $(f')'(x)$ is called the **second derivative** of f at x. It is denoted $f''(x)$, which is read "f double prime of x." Similarly, the derivative of the second derivative is called the **third derivative,** written $f'''(x)$. Continuing in this way, we get *higher-order derivatives*. Some notations for higher-order derivatives are given in Table 12.3. To avoid clumsy notation, primes are not used beyond the third derivative.

CAUTION!⚠

The symbol d^2y/dx^2 represents the second derivative of y. It is not the same as $(dy/dx)^2$, the square of the first derivative of y.

Table 12.3

First derivative:	y'	$f'(x)$	$\dfrac{dy}{dx}$	$\dfrac{d}{dx}(f(x))$	$D_x y$
Second derivative:	y''	$f''(x)$	$\dfrac{d^2y}{dx^2}$	$\dfrac{d^2}{dx^2}(f(x))$	$D_x^2 y$
Third derivative:	y'''	$f'''(x)$	$\dfrac{d^3y}{dx^3}$	$\dfrac{d^3}{dx^3}(f(x))$	$D_x^3 y$
Fourth derivative:	$y^{(4)}$	$f^{(4)}(x)$	$\dfrac{d^4y}{dx^4}$	$\dfrac{d^4}{dx^4}(f(x))$	$D_x^4 y$

EXAMPLE 1   Finding Higher-Order Derivatives

a. If $f(x) = 6x^3 - 12x^2 + 6x - 2$, find all higher-order derivatives.

Solution: Differentiating $f(x)$ gives

$$f'(x) = 18x^2 - 24x + 6$$

Differentiating $f'(x)$ yields

$$f''(x) = 36x - 24$$

Similarly,

$$f'''(x) = 36$$

$$f^{(4)}(x) = 0$$

All successive derivatives are also 0: $f^{(5)}(x) = 0$, and so on.

b. If $f(x) = 7$, find $f''(x)$.

Solution:

$$f'(x) = 0$$

$$f''(x) = 0$$

Now Work Problem 1 ◁

APPLY IT ▶

8. The height $h(t)$ of a rock dropped off of a 200-foot building is given by $h(t) = 200 - 16t^2$, where t is the time measured in seconds. Find $\dfrac{d^2h}{dt^2}$, the acceleration of the rock at time t.

EXAMPLE 2   Finding a Second-Order Derivative

If $y = e^{x^2}$, find $\dfrac{d^2y}{dx^2}$.

Solution:

$$\frac{dy}{dx} = e^{x^2}(2x) = 2xe^{x^2}$$

By the product rule,

$$\frac{d^2y}{dx^2} = 2(x(e^{x^2})(2x) + e^{x^2}(1)) = 2e^{x^2}(2x^2 + 1)$$

Now Work Problem 5 ◁

APPLY IT ▶

9. If the cost to produce q units of a product is

$$c(q) = 7q^2 + 11q + 19$$

and the marginal-cost function is $c'(q)$, find the rate of change of the marginal cost function with respect to q when $q = 3$.

EXAMPLE 3   Evaluating a Second-Order Derivative

If $y = f(x) = \dfrac{16}{x+4}$, find $\dfrac{d^2y}{dx^2}$ and evaluate it when $x = 4$.

Solution: Since $y = 16(x+4)^{-1}$, the power rule gives

$$\frac{dy}{dx} = -16(x+4)^{-2}$$

$$\frac{d^2y}{dx^2} = 32(x+4)^{-3} = \frac{32}{(x+4)^3}$$

Evaluating when $x = 4$, we obtain

$$\frac{d^2y}{dx^2}\bigg|_{x=4} = \frac{32}{8^3} = \frac{1}{16}$$

The second derivative evaluated at $x = 4$ is also denoted $f''(4)$ or $y''(4)$.

Now Work Problem 21 ◁

EXAMPLE 4   Finding the Rate of Change of $f''(x)$

If $f(x) = x \ln x$, find the rate of change of $f''(x)$.

The rate of change of $f''(x)$ is $f'''(x)$.

Solution: To find the rate of change of any function, we must find its derivative. Thus, we want the derivative of $f''(x)$, which is $f'''(x)$. Accordingly,

$$f'(x) = x\left(\frac{1}{x}\right) + (\ln x)(1) = 1 + \ln x$$

$$f''(x) = 0 + \frac{1}{x} = \frac{1}{x}$$

$$f'''(x) = \frac{d}{dx}(x^{-1}) = (-1)x^{-2} = -\frac{1}{x^2}$$

Now Work Problem 17 ◁

Higher-Order Implicit Differentiation

We will now find a higher-order derivative by means of implicit differentiation. Keep in mind that we will assume y to be a function of x.

EXAMPLE 5 Higher-Order Implicit Differentiation

Find $\dfrac{d^2y}{dx^2}$ if $x^2 + 4y^2 = 4$.

Solution: Differentiating both sides with respect to x, we obtain

$$2x + 8y\frac{dy}{dx} = 0$$

$$\frac{dy}{dx} = \frac{-x}{4y} \tag{1}$$

$$\frac{d^2y}{dx^2} = \frac{4y\dfrac{d}{dx}(-x) - (-x)\dfrac{d}{dx}(4y)}{(4y)^2}$$

$$= \frac{4y(-1) - (-x)\left(4\dfrac{dy}{dx}\right)}{16y^2}$$

$$= \frac{-4y + 4x\dfrac{dy}{dx}}{16y^2}$$

$$\frac{d^2y}{dx^2} = \frac{-y + x\dfrac{dy}{dx}}{4y^2} \tag{2}$$

Although we have found an expression for d^2y/dx^2, our answer involves the derivative dy/dx. It is customary to express the answer without the derivative—that is, in terms of x and y only. This is easy to do. From Equation (1), $\dfrac{dy}{dx} = \dfrac{-x}{4y}$, so by substituting into Equation (2), we have

$$\frac{d^2y}{dx^2} = \frac{-y + x\left(\dfrac{-x}{4y}\right)}{4y^2} = \frac{-4y^2 - x^2}{16y^3} = -\frac{4y^2 + x^2}{16y^3}$$

We can further simplify the answer. Since $x^2 + 4y^2 = 4$ (the original equation),

$$\frac{d^2y}{dx^2} = -\frac{4}{16y^3} = -\frac{1}{4y^3}$$

In Example 5, the simplification of d^2y/dx^2 by making use of the original equation is not unusual.

Now Work Problem 23 ◁

EXAMPLE 6 Higher-Order Implicit Differentiation

Find $\dfrac{d^2y}{dx^2}$ if $y^2 = e^{x+y}$.

Solution: Differentiating both sides with respect to x gives

$$2y\frac{dy}{dx} = e^{x+y}\left(1 + \frac{dy}{dx}\right)$$

Solving for dy/dx, we obtain

$$2y\frac{dy}{dx} = e^{x+y} + e^{x+y}\frac{dy}{dx}$$

$$2y\frac{dy}{dx} - e^{x+y}\frac{dy}{dx} = e^{x+y}$$

$$(2y - e^{x+y})\frac{dy}{dx} = e^{x+y}$$

$$\frac{dy}{dx} = \frac{e^{x+y}}{2y - e^{x+y}}$$

Since $y^2 = e^{x+y}$ (the original equation),

$$\frac{dy}{dx} = \frac{y^2}{2y - y^2} = \frac{y}{2 - y}$$

$$\frac{d^2y}{dx^2} = \frac{(2 - y)\frac{dy}{dx} - y\left(-\frac{dy}{dx}\right)}{(2 - y)^2} = \frac{2\frac{dy}{dx}}{(2 - y)^2}$$

Now we express our answer without dy/dx. Since $\frac{dy}{dx} = \frac{y}{2 - y}$,

$$\frac{d^2y}{dx^2} = \frac{2\left(\frac{y}{2 - y}\right)}{(2 - y)^2} = \frac{2y}{(2 - y)^3}$$

Now Work Problem 31 ◁

PROBLEMS 12.7

In Problems 1–20, find the indicated derivatives.

1. $y = 4x^3 - 12x^2 + 6x + 2$, y'''

2. $y = x^5 + x^4 + x^3 + x^2 + x + 1$, y'''

3. $y = 8 - x$, $\dfrac{d^2y}{dx^2}$

4. $y = -x - x^2$, $\dfrac{d^2y}{dx^2}$

5. $y = x^3 + e^x$, $y^{(4)}$

6. $F(q) = \ln(q + 1)$, $\dfrac{d^3F}{dq^3}$

7. $f(x) = x^3 \ln x$, $f'''(x)$

8. $y = \dfrac{1}{x}$, y'''

9. $f(q) = \dfrac{1}{2q^4}$, $f'''(q)$

10. $f(x) = \sqrt{x}$, $f''(x)$

11. $f(r) = \sqrt{9 - r}$, $f''(r)$

12. $y = e^{ax^2}$, y''

13. $y = \dfrac{1}{2x + 3}$, $\dfrac{d^2y}{dx^2}$

14. $y = (3x + 7)^5$, y''

15. $y = \dfrac{x + 1}{x - 1}$, y''

16. $y = 2x^{1/2} + (2x)^{1/2}$, y''

17. $y = \ln[x(x + a)]$, y''

18. $y = \ln\dfrac{(2x + 5)(5x - 2)}{x + 1}$, y''

19. $f(z) = z^2 e^z$, $f''(z)$

20. $y = \dfrac{x}{e^x}$, $\dfrac{d^2y}{dx^2}$

21. If $y = e^{2x} + e^{3x}$, find $\left.\dfrac{d^5y}{dx^5}\right|_{x=0}$.

22. If $y = e^{2\ln(x^2+1)}$, find y'' when $x = 1$.

In Problems 23–32, find y''.

23. $x^2 + 4y^2 - 16 = 0$

24. $x^2 - y^2 = 16$

25. $y^2 = 4x$

26. $9x^2 + 16y^2 = 25$

27. $a\sqrt{x} + b\sqrt{y} = c$

28. $y^2 - 6xy = 4$

29. $xy + y - x = 4$

30. $x^2 + 2xy + y^2 = 1$

31. $y = e^{x+y}$

32. $e^x + e^y = x^2 + y^2$

33. If $x^2 + 3x + y^2 = 4y$, find d^2y/dx^2 when $x = 0$ and $y = 0$.

34. Show that the equation

$$f''(x) + 4f'(x) + 4f(x) = 0$$

is satisfied if $f(x) = (3x - 5)e^{-2x}$.

35. Find the rate of change of $f'(x)$ if $f(x) = (5x - 3)^4$.

36. Find the rate of change of $f''(x)$ if

$$f(x) = 6\sqrt{x} + \frac{1}{6\sqrt{x}}$$

37. **Marginal Cost**   If $c = 0.2q^2 + 2q + 500$ is a cost function, how fast is marginal cost changing when $q = 97.357$?

38. **Marginal Revenue**   If $p = 400 - 40q - q^2$ is a demand equation, how fast is marginal revenue changing when $q = 4$?

39. If $f(x) = x^4 - 6x^2 + 5x - 6$, determine the values of x for which $f''(x) = 0$.

40. Suppose that $e^y = y^2 e^x$. (a) Determine dy/dx, and express your answer in terms of y only. (b) Determine d^2y/dx^2, and express your answer in terms of y only.

In Problems 41 and 42, determine $f''(x)$. Then use your graphing calculator to find all real roots of $f''(x) = 0$. Round your answers to two decimal places.

41. $f(x) = 6e^x - x^3 - 15x^2$

42. $f(x) = \dfrac{x^5}{20} + \dfrac{x^4}{12} + \dfrac{5x^3}{6} + \dfrac{x^2}{2}$

Chapter 12 Review ━━━━━

Important Terms and Symbols   Examples

Summary

The derivative formulas for natural logarithmic and exponential functions are

$$\frac{d}{dx}(\ln u) = \frac{1}{u}\frac{du}{dx}$$

and

$$\frac{d}{dx}(e^u) = e^u \frac{du}{dx}$$

To differentiate logarithmic and exponential functions in bases other than e, first transform the function to base e and then differentiate the result. Alternatively, differentiation formulas can be applied:

$$\frac{d}{dx}(\log_b u) = \frac{1}{(\ln b)u} \cdot \frac{du}{dx}$$

$$\frac{d}{dx}(b^u) = b^u(\ln b) \cdot \frac{du}{dx}$$

Point elasticity of demand is a function that measures how consumer demand is affected by a change in price. It is given by

$$\eta = \frac{p}{q}\frac{dq}{dp}$$

where p is the price per unit at which q units are demanded. The three categories of elasticity are as follows:

$$|\eta(p)| > 1 \quad \text{demand is elastic}$$

$$|\eta(p)| = 1 \quad \text{unit elasticity}$$

$$|\eta(p)| < 1 \quad \text{demand is inelastic}$$

For a given percentage change in price, if there is a greater (respectively, lesser) percentage change in quantity demanded, then demand is elastic (respectively, inelastic) and conversely.

Two relationships between elasticity and the rate of change of revenue are given by

$$\frac{dr}{dq} = p\left(1 + \frac{1}{\eta}\right) \qquad \frac{dr}{dp} = q(1 + \eta)$$

If an equation implicitly defines y as a function of x [rather than defining it explicitly in the form $y = f(x)$], then dy/dx can be found by implicit differentiation. With this method, we treat y as a function of x and differentiate both sides of the equation with respect to x. When doing this, remember that

$$\frac{d}{dx}(y^n) = ny^{n-1}\frac{dy}{dx}$$

and, more generally, that

$$\frac{d}{dx}(f(y)) = f'(y)\frac{dy}{dx}$$

Finally, we solve the resulting equation for dy/dx.

Suppose that $f(x)$ consists of products, quotients, or powers. To differentiate $y = \log_b(f(x))$, it may be helpful to use properties of logarithms to rewrite $\log_b(f(x))$ in terms of simpler logarithms and then differentiate that form. To differentiate $y = f(x)$, where $f(x)$ consists of products, quotients, or powers, the method of logarithmic differentiation may be used. In that method, we take the natural logarithm of both sides of $y = f(x)$ to obtain $\ln y = \ln(f(x))$. After simplifying $\ln(f(x))$ by using properties of logarithms, we differentiate both sides of $\ln y = \ln(f(x))$ with respect to x

and then solve for y'. Logarithmic differentiation can also be used to differentiate $y = u^v$, where both u and v are functions of x.

Newton's method is the name given to the following formula, which is used to approximate the roots of the equation $f(x) = 0$, provided that f is differentiable:

$$x_{n+1} = x_n - \frac{f(x_n)}{f'(x_n)}, \quad n = 1, 2, 3, \ldots$$

In many cases encountered, the approximation improves as n increases.

Because the derivative $f'(x)$ of a function $y = f(x)$ is itself a function, it can be successively differentiated to obtain the second derivative $f''(x)$, the third derivative $f'''(x)$, and other higher-order derivatives.

Review Problems

In Problems 1–30, differentiate.

1. $y = 3e^x + e^2 + e^{x^2} + x^{e^2}$ **2.** $f(w) = we^w + w^2$

3. $f(r) = \ln(7r^2 + 4r + 5)$ **4.** $y = e^{\ln x}$

5. $y = e^{x^2 + 4x + 5}$ **6.** $f(t) = \log_6 \sqrt{t^2 + 1}$

7. $y = e^x(x^2 + 2)$ **8.** $y = 2^{3x^2}$

9. $y = \sqrt{(x-6)(x+5)(9-x)}$ **10.** $f(t) = e^{1/t}$

11. $y = \dfrac{\ln x}{e^x}$ **12.** $y = \dfrac{e^x + e^{-x}}{x^2}$

13. $f(q) = \ln[(q+a)^m(q+b)^n]$

14. $y = (x+2)^3(x+1)^4(x-2)^2$

15. $y = 2^{2x^2 + 2x - 5}$ **16.** $y = (e + e^2)^0$

17. $y = \dfrac{4e^{3x}}{xe^{x-1}}$ **18.** $y = \dfrac{\ln x}{e^x}$

19. $y = \log_2(8x + 5)^2$ **20.** $y = \ln\left(\dfrac{5}{x^2}\right)$

21. $f(l) = \ln(1 + l + l^2 + l^3)$ **22.** $y = (x^2)^{x^2}$

23. $y = (x^2 + 1)^{x+1}$ **24.** $y = \dfrac{1 + e^x}{1 - e^x}$

25. $\phi(t) = \ln\left(t\sqrt{4 - t^2}\right)$ **26.** $y = (x+3)^{\ln x}$

27. $y = \dfrac{(x^2 + 1)^{1/2}(x^2 + 2)^{1/3}}{(2x^3 + 6x)^{2/5}}$ **28.** $y = (\ln x)\sqrt{x}$

29. $y = (x^x)^x$ **30.** $y = x^{(x^x)}$

In Problems 31–34, evaluate y' at the given value of x.

31. $y = (x+1)\ln x^2, x = 1$ **32.** $y = \dfrac{e^{x^2 + 1}}{\sqrt{x^2 + 1}}, x = 1$

33. $y = (1/x)^x, x = e$

34. $y = \left[\dfrac{2^{5x}(x^2 - 3x + 5)^{1/3}}{(x^2 - 3x + 7)^3}\right]^{-1}, x = 0$

In Problems 35 and 36, find an equation of the tangent line to the curve at the point corresponding to the given value of x.

35. $y = 3e^x, x = \ln 2$ **36.** $y = x + x^2 \ln x, x = 1$

37. Find the y-intercept of the tangent line to the graph of $y = x(2^{2 - x^2})$ at the point where $x = 1$.

38. If $w = 2^x + \ln(1 + x^2)$ and $x = \ln(1 + t^2)$, find w and dw/dt when $t = 0$.

In Problems 39–42, find the indicated derivative at the given point.

39. $y = e^{x^2 - 2x + 1}, y'', (1, 1)$ **40.** $y = x^2 e^x, y''', (1, e)$

41. $y = \ln(2x), y''', (1, \ln 2)$ **42.** $y = x \ln x, y'', (1, 0)$

In Problems 43–46, find dy/dx.

43. $x^2 + 2xy + y^2 = 4$ **44.** $x^3 y^3 = 3$

45. $\ln(xy^2) = xy$ **46.** $y^2 e^{y \ln x} = e^2$

In Problems 47 and 48, find $d^2 y/dx^2$ at the given point.

47. $x + xy + y = 5, (2, 1)$ **48.** $x^2 + xy + y^2 = 1, (0, -1)$

49. If y is defined implicitly by $e^y = (y + 1)e^x$, determine both dy/dx and $d^2 y/dx^2$ as explicit functions of y only.

50. If $\sqrt{x} + \sqrt{y} = 1$, find $\dfrac{d^2 y}{dx^2}$.

51. Schizophrenia   Several models have been used to analyze the length of stay in a hospital. For a particular group of schizophrenics, one such model is[9]

$$f(t) = 1 - (0.8e^{-0.01t} + 0.2e^{-0.0002t})$$

where $f(t)$ is the proportion of the group that was discharged at the end of t days of hospitalization. Determine the discharge rate (proportion discharged per day) at the end of t days.

52. Earthquakes   According to Richter,[10] the number N of earthquakes of magnitude M or greater per unit of time is given by $\log N = A - bM$, where A and b are constants. Richter claims that

$$\log\left(-\dfrac{dN}{dM}\right) = A + \log\left(\dfrac{b}{q}\right) - bM$$

where $q = \log e$. Verify this statement.

53. If $f(x) = e^{x^4 - 10x^3 + 36x^2 - 2x}$, find all real roots of $f'(x) = 0$. Round your answers to two decimal places.

54. If $f(x) = \dfrac{x^5}{10} + \dfrac{x^4}{6} + \dfrac{2x^3}{3} + x^2 + 1$, find all roots of $f''(x) = 0$. Round your answers to two decimal places.

[9] Adapted from W. W. Eaton and G. A. Whitmore, "Length of Stay as a Stochastic Process: A General Approach and Application to Hospitalization for Schizophrenia," *Journal of Mathematical Sociology*, 5 (1977) 273–92.

[10] C. F. Richter, *Elementary Seismology* (San Francisco: W. H. Freeman and Company, Publishers, 1958).

For the demand equations in Problems 55–57, determine whether demand is elastic, is inelastic, or has unit elasticity for the indicated value of q.

55. $p = \dfrac{500}{q}$; $q = 200$

56. $p = 900 - q^2$; $q = 10$

57. $p = 18 - 0.02q$; $q = 600$

58. The demand equation for a product is

$$q = \left(\dfrac{20-p}{2}\right)^2 \quad \text{for } 0 \le p \le 20$$

(a) Find the point elasticity of demand when $p = 8$.

(b) Find all values of p for which demand is elastic.

59. The demand equation of a product is

$$q = \sqrt{2500 - p^2}$$

Find the point elasticity of demand when $p = 30$. If the price of 30 decreases $\frac{2}{3}\%$, what is the approximate change in demand?

60. The demand equation for a product is

$$q = \sqrt{100 - p}, \quad \text{where } 0 < p < 100$$

(a) Find all prices that correspond to elastic demand.

(b) Compute the point elasticity of demand when $p = 40$. Use your answer to estimate the percentage increase or decrease in demand when price is increased by 5% to $p = 42$.

61. The equation $x^3 - 2x - 2 = 0$ has a root between 1 and 2. Use Newton's method to estimate the root. Continue the approximation procedure until the difference of two successive approximations is less than 0.0001. Round your answer to four decimal places.

62. Find, to an accuracy of three decimal places, all real solutions of the equation $e^x = 3x$.

EXPLORE & EXTEND Economic Order Quantity

In inventory management, the economic order quantity is the most cost-efficient size for resupply orders. To find this optimum size, we need to have an idea of how stock depletion and resupply take place, and of how costs accrue.

Here are the classic assumptions:

1. Inventory is depleted through purchases at a constant rate D, which is measured in units per year.

2. Resupply orders are all the same size, and each arrives in a single lump shipment just as stock is running out.

3. Besides the cost per item, each order also involves a fixed cost per order, F.

4. Each unit in stock has a constant value, V, measured in dollars.

5. The cost of inventory storage is a fixed fraction, R, of total current inventory value. This carrying cost factor is measured in dollars per dollar per year.

Assumptions 1 and 2 entail a graph of inventory over time that looks like Figure 12.10.

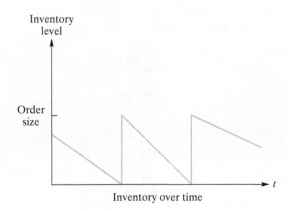

FIGURE 12.10 Inventory over time.

We now wish to minimize the cost, in dollars per year, of managing an inventory in the way Figure 12.10 depicts. If resupply is ordered in lots of q units each, then there are $\dfrac{D}{q}$ orders per year, for an annual ordering cost of $\dfrac{FD}{q}$. (The yearly expense due to the per-item ordering cost cannot be adjusted by changing the order size, so this cost is ignored in our calculations.) With an average inventory level of $\dfrac{q}{2}$, the annual carrying cost is $\dfrac{RVq}{2}$. The annual inventory-related cost, C, is then the sum of the ordering cost and the carrying cost:

$$C = C(q) = \dfrac{FD}{q} + \dfrac{RVq}{2}$$

This function C clearly takes on large values both when q gets large and when q approaches zero. It follows from arguments that we will study in detail in the next chapter that if there is a unique value of q where $\dfrac{dC}{dq}$ equals zero, then this value of q will provide a minimum value of C.

Let us try to find such a q.

$$\frac{dC}{dq} = \frac{-FD}{q^2} + \frac{RV}{2} = 0$$

$$q^2 = \frac{2FD}{RV}$$

$$q = \sqrt{\frac{2FD}{RV}}$$

This formula is called the Wilson lot size formula, after an industry consultant who popularized its use. If we substitute $F = \$10$ per order, $D = 1500$ units per year, $R = \$0.10$ dollars per dollar per year, and $V = \$10$, then q comes out as

$$q = \sqrt{\frac{2(10)(1500)}{(0.10)(10)}} \approx 173.2$$

The most cost-efficient order size is 173 units.

Variations of the Wilson formula relax one or more of the five assumptions on which it is based. One assumption that can be relaxed is assumption 5. Suppose that carrying cost as a percentage of inventory value rises when inventory is low. (Think of a large warehouse sitting nearly empty.) We will model this by replacing R with $R(1 + ke^{-sq})$. R is the per-dollar annual carrying cost for large inventory levels, and the term $ke^{-sq} (k, s > 0)$ raises the cost for low inventory levels. The total annual inventory cost now becomes

$$C = \frac{FD}{q} + \frac{RVq(1 + ke^{-sq})}{2}$$

Again, we wish to minimize this quantity, and again C gets large both as q gets large and as q approaches zero. The minimum is where

$$\frac{dC}{dq} = \frac{-FD}{q^2} + \frac{RV(1 + ke^{-sq} - ksqe^{-sq})}{2} = 0$$

Suppose $k = 1, s = \dfrac{\ln 2}{1000} \approx 0.000693$. Then the per-dollar carrying cost is twice as great for a small inventory as for a very large one and is midway between those two costs at an inventory level of 1000. If we keep F, D, R, and V the same as before and then use a graphing calculator or other numeric solution technique, we find that $\dfrac{dC}{dq} = 0$ when $q \approx 127.9$. The optimum order size is 128 units. Note that even though the assumptions now include economies of scale, the carrying cost is greater at all inventory levels and has led to a lower economic order quantity.

Problems

1. Use the Wilson lot size formula to calculate the economic order quantity for an item that is worth \$36.50, costs 5% of its value annually to store, sells at a rate of 3400 units per year, and is purchased from a supplier that charges a flat \$25 processing fee for every order.

2. Suppose that assumptions 1 and 3–5 are kept but 2 is modified: A manager never allows inventory to drop to zero but instead maintains a safety margin of a certain number of units. What difference does this make to the calculation of the economic order quantity?

3. What other assumptions, besides assumptions 2 and 5, might realistically be relaxed? Explain.

13 Curve Sketching

Q EXPLORE & EXTEND

Population Change over Time

I n the mid-1970s, economist Arthur Laffer was explaining his views on taxes to a politician. To illustrate his argument, Laffer grabbed a paper napkin and sketched the graph that now bears his name: the Laffer curve.

The Laffer curve describes total government tax revenue as a function of the tax rate. Obviously, if the tax rate is zero, the government gets nothing. But if the tax rate is 100%, revenue would again equal zero, because there is no incentive to earn money if it will all be taken away. Since tax rates between 0% and 100% do generate revenue, Laffer reasoned, the curve relating revenue to tax rate must look, qualitatively, more or less as shown in the figure below.

Laffer's argument was not meant to show that the optimal tax rate was 50%. It was meant to show that under some circumstances, namely when the tax rate is to the right of the peak of the curve, it is possible to *raise government revenue by lowering taxes*. This was a key argument made for the tax cuts passed by Congress during the first term of the Reagan presidency.

Because the Laffer curve is only a qualitative picture, it does not actually give an optimal tax rate. Revenue-based arguments for tax cuts involve the claim that the point of peak revenue lies to the left of the current taxation scheme on the horizontal axis. By the same token, those who urge raising taxes to raise government income are assuming either a different relationship between rates and revenues or a different location of the curve's peak.

By itself, then, the Laffer curve is too abstract to be of much help in determining the optimal tax rate. But even very simple sketched curves, like supply and demand curves and the Laffer curve, can help economists describe the causal factors that drive an economy. In this chapter, we will discuss techniques for sketching and interpreting curves.

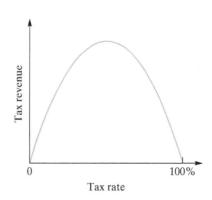

Objective

To find when a function is increasing or decreasing, to find critical values, to locate relative maxima and relative minima, and to state the first-derivative test. Also, to sketch the graph of a function by using the information obtained from the first derivative.

13.1 Relative Extrema

Increasing or Decreasing Nature of a Function

Examining the graphical behavior of functions is a basic part of mathematics and has applications to many areas of study. When we sketch a curve, just plotting points may not give enough information about its shape. For example, the points $(-1, 0), (0, -1)$, and $(1, 0)$ satisfy the equation given by $y = (x + 1)^3(x - 1)$. On the basis of these points, we might hastily conclude that the graph should appear as in Figure 13.1(a), but in fact the true shape is given in Figure 13.1(b). In this chapter we will explore the powerful role that differentiation plays in analyzing a function so that we can determine the true shape and behavior of its graph.

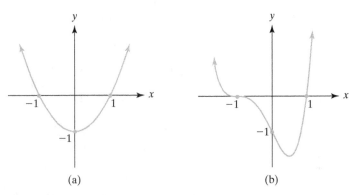

(a)   (b)

FIGURE 13.1   Curves passing through $(-1, 0), (0, -1)$, and $(1, 0)$.

We begin by analyzing the graph of the function $y = f(x)$ in Figure 13.2. Notice that as x increases (goes from left to right) on the interval I_1, between a and b, the values of $f(x)$ increase and the curve is rising. Mathematically, this observation means that if x_1 and x_2 are any two points in I_1 such that $x_1 < x_2$, then $f(x_1) < f(x_2)$. Here f is said to be an *increasing function* on I_1. On the other hand, as x increases on the interval I_2 between c and d, the curve is falling. On this interval, $x_3 < x_4$ implies that $f(x_3) > f(x_4)$, and f is said to be a *decreasing function* on I_2. We summarize these observations in the following definition.

> **Definition**
>
> A function f is said to be **increasing** on an interval I when, for any two numbers x_1, x_2 in I, if $x_1 < x_2$, then $f(x_1) < f(x_2)$. A function f is **decreasing** on an interval I when, for any two numbers x_1, x_2 in I, if $x_1 < x_2$, then $f(x_1) > f(x_2)$.

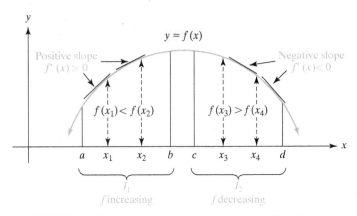

FIGURE 13.2   Increasing or decreasing nature of function.

In terms of the graph of the function, f is increasing on I if the curve rises to the right and f is decreasing on I if the curve falls to the right. Recall that a straight line with positive slope rises to the right while a straight line with negative slope falls to the right.

Turning again to Figure 13.2, we note that over the interval I_1, tangent lines to the curve have positive slopes, so $f'(x)$ must be positive for all x in I_1. A positive derivative implies that the curve is rising. Over the interval I_2, the tangent lines have negative slopes, so $f'(x) < 0$ for all x in I_2. The curve is falling where the derivative is negative. We thus have the following rule, which allows us to use the derivative to determine when a function is increasing or decreasing:

> **Rule 1   Criteria for Increasing or Decreasing Function**
>
> Let f be differentiable on the interval (a, b). If $f'(x) > 0$ for all x in (a, b), then f is increasing on (a, b). If $f'(x) < 0$ for all x in (a, b), then f is decreasing on (a, b).

To illustrate these ideas, we will use Rule 1 to find the intervals on which $y = 18x - \frac{2}{3}x^3$ is increasing and the intervals on which y is decreasing. Letting $y = f(x)$, we must determine when $f'(x)$ is positive and when $f'(x)$ is negative. We have

$$f'(x) = 18 - 2x^2 = 2(9 - x^2) = 2(3 + x)(3 - x)$$

Using the technique of Section 10.4, we can find the sign of $f'(x)$ by testing the intervals determined by the roots of $2(3 + x)(3 - x) = 0$, namely, -3 and 3. These should be arranged in increasing order on the top of a sign chart for f' so as to divide the domain of f into intervals. (See Figure 13.3.) In each interval, the sign of $f'(x)$ is determined by the signs of its factors:

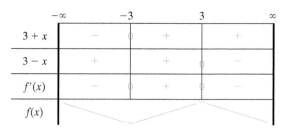

FIGURE 13.3   Sign chart for $f'(x) = 18 - 9x^2$ and its interpretation for $f(x)$.

If $x < -3$, then $\text{sign}(f'(x)) = 2(-)(+) = -$, so f is *decreasing*.

If $-3 < x < 3$, then $\text{sign}(f'(x)) = 2(+)(+) = +$, so f is *increasing*.

If $x > 3$, then $\text{sign}(f'(x)) = 2(+)(-) = -$, so f is *decreasing*.

These results are indicated in the sign chart given by Figure 13.3, where the bottom line is a schematic version of what the signs of f' say about f itself. Notice that the horizontal line segments in the bottom row indicate horizontal tangents for f at -3 and at 3. Thus, f is decreasing on $(-\infty, -3)$ and $(3, \infty)$ and is increasing on $(-3, 3)$. This corresponds to the rising and falling nature of the graph of f shown in Figure 13.4. Indeed, the point of a well-constructed sign chart is to provide a schematic for subsequent construction of the graph itself.

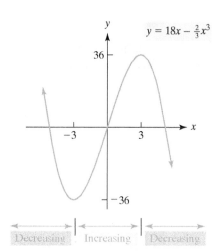

FIGURE 13.4   Increasing/decreasing for $y = 18x - \frac{2}{3}x^3$.

Extrema

Look now at the graph of $y = f(x)$ in Figure 13.5. Some observations can be made. First, there is something special about the points P, Q, and R. Notice that P is *higher* than any other "nearby" point on the curve—and likewise for R. The point Q is *lower* than any other "nearby" point on the curve. Since P, Q, and R may not necessarily be the highest or lowest points on the *entire* curve, we say that the graph

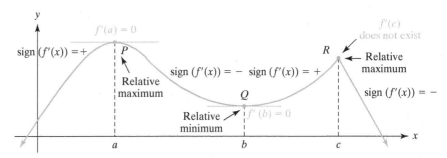

FIGURE 13.5 Relative maxima and relative minima.

CAUTION!

Be sure to note the difference between relative extreme *values* and *where* they occur.

of *f* has relative maxima at *a* and at *c*; and has a relative minimum at *b*. The function *f* has relative maximum values of *f*(*a*) at *a* and *f*(*c*) at *c*; and has a relative minimum value of *f*(*b*) at *b*. We also say that (*a*, *f*(*a*)) and (*c*, *f*(*c*)) are relative maximum points and (*b*, *f*(*b*)) is a relative minimum point on the graph of *f*.

Turning back to the graph, we see that there is an *absolute maximum* (highest point on the entire curve) at *a*, but there is no *absolute minimum* (lowest point on the entire curve) because the curve is assumed to extend downward indefinitely. More precisely, we define these new terms as follows:

> **Definition**
>
> A function *f* has a ***relative maximum*** at *a* if there is an open interval containing *a* on which $f(a) \geq f(x)$ for all *x* in the interval. The relative maximum value is *f*(*a*). A function *f* has a ***relative minimum*** at *a* if there is an open interval containing *a* on which $f(a) \leq f(x)$ for all *x* in the interval. The relative minimum value is *f*(*a*).

If it exists, an absolute maximum value is unique; however, it may occur at more than one value of *x*. A similar statement is true for an absolute minimum.

> **Definition**
>
> A function *f* has an ***absolute maximum*** at *a* if $f(a) \geq f(x)$ for all *x* in the domain of *f*. The absolute maximum value is *f*(*a*). A function *f* has an ***absolute minimum*** at *a* if $f(a) \leq f(x)$ for all *x* in the domain of *f*. The absolute minimum value is *f*(*a*).

We refer to either a relative maximum or a relative minimum as a **relative extremum** (plural: *relative extrema*). Similarly, we speak of **absolute extrema.**

When dealing with relative extrema, we compare the function value at a point with values of nearby points; however, when dealing with absolute extrema, we compare the function value at a point with all other values determined by the domain. Thus, relative extrema are *local* in nature, whereas absolute extrema are *global* in nature.

Referring to Figure 13.5, we notice that at a relative extremum the derivative may not be defined (as when $x = c$). But whenever it is defined at a relative extremum, it is 0 (as when $x = a$ and when $x = b$), and hence the tangent line is horizontal. We can state the following:

> **Rule 2 A Necessary Condition for Relative Extrema**
>
> If *f* has a relative extremum at *a*, then $f'(a) = 0$ or $f'(a)$ does not exist.

The implication in Rule 2 goes in only one direction:

$$\left.\begin{array}{c} \text{relative extremum} \\ \text{at } a \end{array}\right\} \quad \text{implies} \quad \left\{\begin{array}{c} f'(a) = 0 \\ \text{or} \\ f'(a) \text{ does not exist} \end{array}\right.$$

Rule 2 does *not* say that if $f'(a)$ is 0 or $f'(a)$ does not exist, then there must be a relative extremum at *a*. In fact, there may not be one at all. For example, in Figure 13.6(a), $f'(a)$

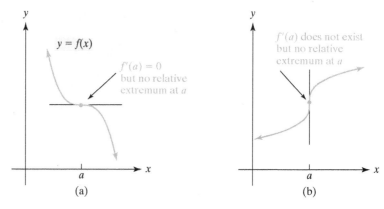

FIGURE 13.6   No relative extremum at a.

is 0 because the tangent line is horizontal at a, but there is no relative extremum there. In Figure 13.6(b), $f'(a)$ does not exist because the tangent line is vertical at a, but again there is no relative extremum there.

But if we want to find all relative extrema of a function—and this is an important task—what Rule 2 *does* tell us is that we can limit our search to those values of x in the domain of f for which *either* $f'(x) = 0$ *or* $f'(x)$ does not exist. Typically, in applications, this cuts down our search for relative extrema from the infinitely many x for which f is defined to a small finite number of *possibilities*. Because these values of x are so important for locating the relative extrema of f, they are called the *critical values* for f, and if a is a critical value for f, then we also say that $(a, f(a))$ is a *critical point* on the graph of f. Thus, in Figure 13.5, the numbers a, b, and c are critical values, and P, Q, and R are critical points.

> **Definition**
>
> For a in the domain of f, if either $f'(a) = 0$ or $f'(a)$ does not exist, then a is called a **critical value** for f. If a is a critical value, then the point $(a, f(a))$ is called a **critical point** for f.

At a critical point, there may be a relative maximum, a relative minimum, or neither. Moreover, from Figure 13.5, we observe that each relative extremum occurs at a point around which the sign of $f'(x)$ is changing. For the relative maximum at a, the sign of $f'(x)$ goes from $+$ for $x < a$ to $-$ for $x > a$, *as long as x is near a*. For the relative minimum at b, the sign of $f'(x)$ goes from $-$ to $+$, and for the relative maximum at c, it again goes from $+$ to $-$. Thus, *around relative maxima, f is increasing and then decreasing, and the reverse holds for relative minima*. More precisely, we have the following rule:

> **Rule 3   Criteria for Relative Extrema**
>
> Suppose f is continuous on an open interval I that contains the critical value a and f is differentiable on I, except possibly at a.
>
> **1.** If $f'(x)$ changes from positive to negative as x increases through a, then f has a relative maximum at a.
>
> **2.** If $f'(x)$ changes from negative to positive as x increases through a, then f has a relative minimum at a.

To illustrate Rule 3 with a concrete example, refer again to Figure 13.3, the sign chart for $f'(x) = 18 - 2x^2$. The row labeled by $f'(x)$ shows clearly that $f(x) = 18x - \frac{2}{3}x^2$ has a relative minimum at -3 and a relative maximum at 3. The row providing the interpretation of the chart for f, labeled $f(x)$, is immediately deduced

CAUTION!

We point out again that not every critical value corresponds to a relative extremum. For example, if $y = f(x) = x^3$, then $f'(x) = 3x^2$. Since $f'(0) = 0$, 0 is a critical value. But if $x < 0$, then $3x^2 > 0$, and if $x > 0$, then $3x^2 > 0$. Since $f'(x)$ does not change sign at 0, there is no relative extremum at 0. Indeed, since $f'(x) \geq 0$ for all x, the graph of f never falls, and f is said to be *nondecreasing*. (See Figure 13.8.)

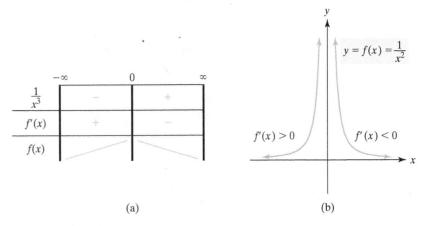

(a)   (b)

FIGURE 13.7 $f'(0)$ is not defined, but 0 is not a critical value because 0 is not in the domain of f.

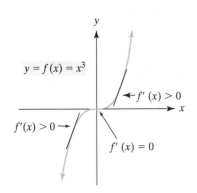

FIGURE 13.8   Zero is a critical value, but does not give a relative extremum.

from the row above it. The significance of the $f(x)$ row is that it provides an intermediate step in actually sketching the graph of f. In this row it stands out, visually, that f has a relative minimum at -3 and a relative maximum at 3.

When searching for extrema of a function f, care must be paid to those a that are not in the domain of f but that are near values in the domain of f. Consider the following example. If

$$y = f(x) = \frac{1}{x^2}, \quad \text{then} \quad f'(x) = -\frac{2}{x^3}$$

Although $f'(x)$ does not exist at 0, 0 is not a critical value, because 0 is not in the domain of f. Thus, a relative extremum cannot occur at 0. Nevertheless, the derivative may change sign around any x-value where $f'(x)$ is not defined, so such values are important in determining intervals over which f is increasing or decreasing. In particular, such values should be included in a sign chart for f'. See Figure 13.7(a) and the accompanying graph in Figure 13.7(b).

Observe that the thick vertical rule at 0 on the chart serves to indicate that 0 is not in the domain of f. Here there are no extrema of any kind.

In Rule 3 the hypotheses must be satisfied, or the conclusion need not hold. For example, consider the case-defined function

$$f(x) = \begin{cases} \dfrac{1}{x^2} & \text{if } x \neq 0 \\ 0 & \text{if } x = 0 \end{cases}$$

Here, 0 is explicitly in the domain of f but f is not continuous at 0. We recall from Section 11.1 that if a function f is not continuous at a, then f is not differentiable at a, meaning that $f'(a)$ does not exist. Thus $f'(0)$ does not exist and 0 is a critical value that must be included in the sign chart for f' shown in Figure 13.9(a). We extend our sign

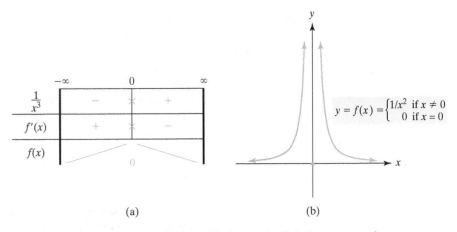

(a)   (b)

FIGURE 13.9   Zero is a critical value, but Rule 3 does not apply.

chart conventions by indicating with a × symbol those values for which f' does not exist. We see in this example that $f'(x)$ changes from positive to negative as x increases through 0 but f does *not* have a relative maximum at 0. Here Rule 3 does not apply because its continuity hypothesis is not met. In Figure 13.9(b), 0 is displayed in the domain of f. It is clear that f has an absolute *minimum* at 0 because $f(0) = 0$ and, for all $x \neq 0, f(x) > 0$.

Summarizing the results of this section, we have the *first-derivative test* for the relative extrema of $y = f(x)$:

First-Derivative Test for Relative Extrema

Step 1. Find $f'(x)$.

Step 2. Determine all critical values of f [those a where $f'(a) = 0$ or $f'(a)$ does not exist] and any a that are not in the domain of f but that are near values in the domain of f, and construct a sign chart that shows for each of the intervals determined by these values whether f is increasing ($f'(x) > 0$) or decreasing ($f'(x) < 0$).

Step 3. For each critical value a at which f is continuous, determine whether $f'(x)$ changes sign as x increases through a. There is a relative maximum at a if $f'(x)$ changes from $+$ to $-$ going from left to right and a relative minimum if $f'(x)$ changes from $-$ to $+$ going from left to right. If $f'(x)$ does not change sign, there is no relative extremum at a.

Step 4. For critical values a at which f is not continuous, analyze the situation by using the definitions of extrema directly.

APPLY IT ▶

1. The cost equation for a hot dog stand is given by $c(q) = 2q^3 - 21q^2 + 60q + 500$, where q is the number of hot dogs sold, and $c(q)$ is the cost in dollars. Use the first-derivative test to find where relative extrema occur.

EXAMPLE 1   First-Derivative Test

If $y = f(x) = x + \dfrac{4}{x+1}$, for $x \neq -1$ use the first-derivative test to find where relative extrema occur.

Solution:

Step 1. $f(x) = x + 4(x+1)^{-1}$, so

$$f'(x) = 1 + 4(-1)(x+1)^{-2} = 1 - \frac{4}{(x+1)^2}$$

$$= \frac{(x+1)^2 - 4}{(x+1)^2} = \frac{x^2 + 2x - 3}{(x+1)^2}$$

$$= \frac{(x+3)(x-1)}{(x+1)^2} \quad \text{for } x \neq -1$$

Note that we expressed $f'(x)$ as a quotient with numerator and denominator fully factored. This enables us in Step 2 to determine easily where $f'(x)$ is 0 or does not exist and the signs of f'.

Step 2. Setting $f'(x) = 0$ gives $x = -3, 1$. The denominator of $f'(x)$ is 0 when x is -1. We note that -1 is not in the domain of f but all values near -1 are in the domain of f. We construct a sign chart, headed by the values $-3, -1$, and 1 (which we have placed in increasing order). See Figure 13.10.

The three values lead us to test four intervals as shown in our sign chart. On each of these intervals, f is differentiable and is not zero. We determine the sign of f' on each interval by first determining the sign of each of its factors on each iterval. For example, considering first the interval $(-\infty, -3)$, it is not easy to see immediately that $f'(x) > 0$ there; but it is easy to see that $x + 3 < 0$ for $x < -3$, while $(x+1)^{-2} > 0$ for all $x \neq -1$, and $x - 1 < 0$ for $x < 1$. These observations account for the signs of the factors in the $(-\infty, -3)$ column of the chart. The sign of $f'(x)$ in that column is obtained by "multiplying signs" (downward): $(-)(+)(-) = +$. We repeat these considerations for the other three intervals. Note that the thick vertical line at -1 in the chart indicates that

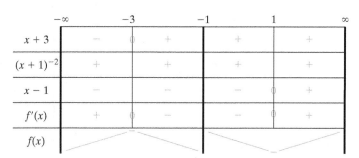

	$-\infty$		-3		-1		1		∞
$x+3$		$-$	0	$+$		$+$		$+$	
$(x+1)^{-2}$		$+$		$+$		$+$		$+$	
$x-1$		$-$		$-$		$-$	0	$+$	
$f'(x)$		$+$	0	$-$		$-$	0	$+$	
$f(x)$									

FIGURE 13.10   Sign chart for $f'(x) = \dfrac{(x+3)(x-1)}{(x+1)^2}$.

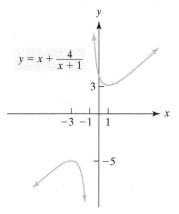

$y = x + \dfrac{4}{x+1}$

FIGURE 13.11   Graph of $y = x + \dfrac{4}{x+1}$.

-1 is not in the domain of f and hence cannot give rise to any extrema. In the bottom row of the sign chart we record, graphically, the nature of tangent lines to $f(x)$ in each interval and at the values where f' is 0.

Step 3. From the sign chart alone we conclude that at -3 there is a relative maximum (since $f'(x)$ changes from $+$ to $-$ at -3). Going beyond the chart, we compute $f(-3) = -3 + (4/-2) = -5$, and this gives the relative maximum value of -5 at -3. We also conclude from the chart that there is a relative minimum at 1 [because $f'(x)$ changes from $-$ to $+$ at 1]. From $f(1) = 1 + 4/2 = 3$ we see that at 1 the relative minimum value is 3.

Step 4. There are no critical values at which f is not continuous, so our considerations above provide the whole story about the relative extrema of $f(x)$, whose graph is given in Figure 13.11. Note that the general shape of the graph was indeed forecast by the bottom row of the sign chart (Figure 13.10).

Now Work Problem 37 ◁

EXAMPLE 2   A Relative Extremum where $f'(x)$ Does Not Exist

Test $y = f(x) = x^{2/3}$ for relative extrema.

Solution: We have

$$f'(x) = \frac{2}{3}x^{-1/3}$$

$$= \frac{2}{3\sqrt[3]{x}}$$

	$-\infty$		0		∞
$(x)^{-1/3}$		$-$	$\times$	$+$	
$f'(x)$		$-$	$\times$	$+$	
$f(x)$					

FIGURE 13.12   Sign chart for $f'(x) = \dfrac{2}{3\sqrt[3]{x}}$.

and the sign chart is given in Figure 13.12. Again, we use the symbol $\times$ on the vertical line at 0 to indicate that the factor $x^{-1/3}$ does not exist at 0. Hence $f'(0)$ does not exist. Since f is continuous at 0, we conclude from Rule 3 that f has a relative minimum at 0 of $f(0) = 0$, and there are no other relative extrema. We note further, by inspection of the sign chart, that f has an *absolute* minimum at 0. The graph of f follows as Figure 13.13. Note that we could have predicted its shape from the bottom line of the sign chart in Figure 13.12, which shows there can be no tangent with a slope at 0. (Of course, the tangent does exist at 0 but it is a vertical line.)

Now Work Problem 41 ◁

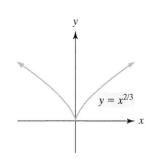

$y = x^{2/3}$

FIGURE 13.13   Derivative does not exist at 0 and there is a minimum at 0.

EXAMPLE 3   Finding Relative Extrema

Test $y = f(x) = x^2 e^x$ for relative extrema.

Solution: By the product rule,

$$f'(x) = x^2 e^x + e^x(2x) = xe^x(x+2)$$

	$-\infty$		-2		0		∞
$x + 2$		$-$	0	$+$		$+$	
x		$-$		$-$	0	$+$	
e^x		$+$		$+$		$+$	
$f'(x)$		$+$	0	$-$	0	$+$	
$f(x)$							

FIGURE 13.14　Sign chart for $f'(x) = x(x+2)e^x$.

APPLY IT ▶

2. A drug is injected into a patient's bloodstream. The concentration of the drug in the bloodstream t hours after the injection is approximated by $C(t) = \dfrac{0.14t}{t^2 + 4t + 4}$. Find the relative extrema for $t > 0$, and use them to determine when the drug is at its greatest concentration.

Noting that e^x is always positive, we obtain the critical values 0 and -2. From the sign chart of $f'(x)$ given in Figure 13.14, we conclude that there is a relative maximum when $x = -2$ and a relative minimum when $x = 0$.

Now Work Problem 49 ◁

Curve Sketching

In the next example we show how the first-derivative test, in conjunction with the notions of intercepts and symmetry, can be used as an aid in sketching the graph of a function.

EXAMPLE 4　Curve Sketching

Sketch the graph of $y = f(x) = 2x^2 - x^4$ with the aid of intercepts, symmetry, and the first-derivative test.

Solution:

Intercepts　If $x = 0$, then $f(x) = 0$ so that the y-intercept is $(0, 0)$. Next note that

$$f(x) = 2x^2 - x^4 = x^2(2 - x^2) = x^2(\sqrt{2} + x)(\sqrt{2} - x)$$

So if $y = 0$, then $x = 0, \pm\sqrt{2}$ and the x-intercepts are $(-\sqrt{2}, 0)$, $(0, 0)$, and $(\sqrt{2}, 0)$. We have the sign chart *for f itself* (Figure 13.15), which shows the intervals over which the graph of $y = f(x)$ is above the x-axis $(+)$ and the intervals over which the graph of $y = f(x)$ is below the x-axis $(-)$.

	$-\infty$		$-\sqrt{2}$		0		$\sqrt{2}$		∞
$\sqrt{2} + x$		$-$	0	$+$		$+$		$+$	
x^2		$+$		$+$	0	$+$		$+$	
$\sqrt{2} - x$		$+$		$+$		$+$	0	$-$	
$f(x)$		$-$	0	$+$	0	$+$	0	$-$	

FIGURE 13.15　Sign chart for $f(x) = (\sqrt{2} + x)x^2(\sqrt{2} - x)$.

Symmetry　Testing for y-axis symmetry, we have

$$f(-x) = 2(-x)^2 - (-x)^4 = 2x^2 - x^4 = f(x)$$

So the graph is symmetric with respect to the y-axis. Because y is a function (and not the zero function), there is no x-axis symmetry and hence no symmetry about the origin.

First-Derivative Test

Step 1.　$y' = 4x - 4x^3 = 4x(1 - x^2) = 4x(1 + x)(1 - x)$.

Step 2.　Setting $y' = 0$ gives the critical values $x = 0, \pm1$. Since f is a polynomial, it is defined and differentiable for all x. Thus the only values to head the sign chart for f' are -1, 0, 1 (in increasing order) and the sign chart is given in Figure 13.16. Since we are interested in the graph, the critical *points* are important to us. By substituting the critical values into the *original* equation, $y = 2x^2 - x^4$,

	$-\infty$		-1		0		1		∞
$1+x$		$-$	0	$+$		$+$		$+$	
$4x$		$-$		$-$	0	$+$		$+$	
$1-x$		$+$		$+$		$+$	0	$-$	
$f'(x)$		$+$	0	$-$	0	$+$	0	$-$	
$f(x)$									

FIGURE 13.16 Sign chart of $y' = (1+x)4x(1-x)$.

we obtain the y-coordinates of these points. We find the critical points to be $(-1, 1)$, $(0, 0)$, and $(1, 1)$.

Step 3. From the sign chart and evaluations in step 2, it is clear that f has relative maxima $(-1, 1)$ and $(1, 1)$ and relative minimum $(0, 0)$. (Step 4 does not apply here.)

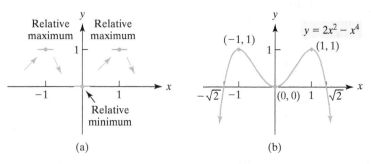

FIGURE 13.17 Putting together the graph of $y = 2x^2 - x^4$.

Discussion In Figure 13.17(a), we have indicated the horizontal tangents at the relative maximum and minimum points. We know the curve rises from the left, has a relative maximum, then falls, has a relative minimum, then rises to a relative maximum, and falls thereafter. By symmetry, it suffices to sketch the graph on one side of the y-axis and construct a mirror image on the other side. We also know, from the sign chart for f, where the graph crosses and touches the x-axis, and this adds further precision to our sketch, which is shown in Figure 13.17(b).

As a passing comment, we note that *absolute* maxima occur at $x = \pm 1$. See Figure 13.17(b). There is no absolute minimum.

Now Work Problem 59 ◁

TECHNOLOGY ▮▮▮▮

A graphing calculator is a powerful tool for investigating relative extrema. For example, consider the function

$$f(x) = 3x^4 - 4x^3 + 4$$

whose graph is shown in Figure 13.18. It appears that there is a relative minimum near $x = 1$. We can locate this minimum by either using "trace and zoom" or (on a TI-83 Plus) using the "minimum" feature. Figure 13.19 shows the latter approach. The relative minimum point is estimated to be $(1.00, 3)$.

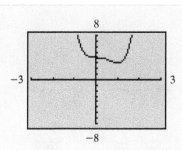

FIGURE 13.18 Graph of $f(x) = 3x^4 - 4x^3 + 4$.

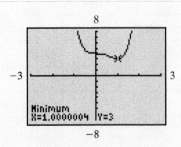

FIGURE 13.19 Relative minimum at (1.00, 3).

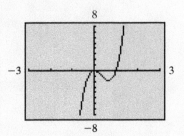

FIGURE 13.20 Graph of $f'(x) = 12x^3 - 12x^2$.

Now let us see how the graph of f' indicates when extrema occur. We have

$$f'(x) = 12x^3 - 12x^2$$

whose graph is shown in Figure 13.20. It appears that $f'(x)$ is 0 at two points. Using "trace and zoom" or the "zero" feature, we estimate the roots of $f' = 0$ (the critical values of f) to be 1 and 0. Around $x = 1$, we see that $f'(x)$ goes from negative values to positive values. (That is, the graph of f' goes from below the x-axis to above it.) Thus, we conclude that f has a relative minimum at $x = 1$, which confirms our previous result.

Around the critical value $x = 0$, the values of $f'(x)$ are negative. Since $f'(x)$ does not change sign, we conclude that there is no relative extremum at $x = 0$. This is also apparent from the graph in Figure 13.18.

It is worthwhile to note that we can approximate the graph of f' without determining $f'(x)$ itself. We make use of the "nDeriv" feature. First we enter the function f as Y_1. Then we set

$$Y_2 = \text{nDeriv}(Y_1, X, X)$$

The graph of Y_2 approximates the graph of $f'(x)$.

PROBLEMS 13.1

In Problems 1–4, the graph of a function is given (Figures 13.21–13.24). Find the open intervals on which the function is increasing, the open intervals on which the function is decreasing, and the coordinates of all relative extrema.

1.

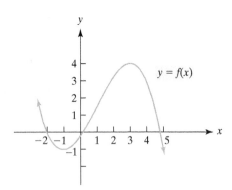

FIGURE 13.21

2.

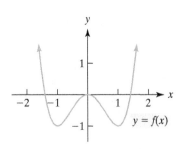

FIGURE 13.22

3.

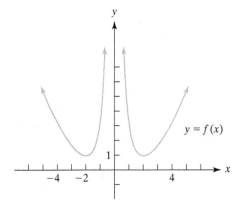

FIGURE 13.23

4.

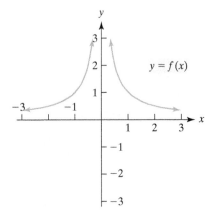

FIGURE 13.24

In Problems 5–8, the derivative of a continuous function f is given. Find the open intervals on which f is **(a)** increasing; **(b)** decreasing; and **(c)** find the x-values of all relative extrema.

5. $f'(x) = (x + 3)(x - 1)(x - 2)$

6. $f'(x) = 2x(x - 1)^3$

7. $f'(x) = (x + 1)(x - 3)^2$ **8.** $f'(x) = \dfrac{x(x + 2)}{x^2 + 1}$

In Problems 9–52, determine where the function is **(a)** increasing; **(b)** decreasing; and **(c)** determine where relative extrema occur. Do not sketch the graph.

9. $y = -x^3 - 1$ **10.** $y = x^2 + 4x + 3$

11. $y = x - x^2 + 2$ **12.** $y = x^3 - \dfrac{5}{2}x^2 - 2x + 6$

13. $y = -\dfrac{x^3}{3} - 2x^2 + 5x - 2$ **14.** $y = -\dfrac{x^4}{4} - x^3$

15. $y = x^4 - 2x^2$ **16.** $y = -3 + 12x - x^3$

17. $y = x^3 - \dfrac{7}{2}x^2 + 2x - 5$ **18.** $y = x^3 - 6x^2 + 12x - 6$

19. $y = 2x^3 - \dfrac{19}{2}x^2 + 10x + 2$ **20.** $y = -5x^3 + x^2 + x - 7$

21. $y = \dfrac{x^3}{3} - 5x^2 + 22x + 1$ **22.** $y = \dfrac{9}{5}x^5 - \dfrac{47}{3}x^3 + 10x$

23. $y = 3x^5 - 5x^3$ **24.** $y = 3x - \dfrac{x^6}{2}$ (Remark: $x^4 + x^3 + x^2 + x + 1 = 0$ has no real roots.)

25. $y = -x^5 - 5x^4 + 200$ **26.** $y = \dfrac{3x^4}{2} - 4x^3 + 17$

27. $y = 8x^4 - x^8$ **28.** $y = \dfrac{4}{5}x^5 - \dfrac{13}{3}x^3 + 3x + 4$

29. $y = (x^2 - 4)^4$ **30.** $y = \sqrt[3]{x}(x - 2)$

31. $y = \dfrac{5}{x - 1}$ **32.** $y = \dfrac{3}{x}$

33. $y = \dfrac{10}{\sqrt{x}}$ **34.** $y = \dfrac{ax + b}{cx + d}$
   (a) for $ad - bc > 0$
   (b) for $ad - bc < 0$

35. $y = \dfrac{x^2}{2 - x}$ **36.** $y = 4x^2 + \dfrac{1}{x}$

37. $y = \dfrac{x^2 - 3}{x + 2}$ **38.** $y = \dfrac{2x^2}{4x^2 - 25}$

39. $y = \dfrac{ax^2 + b}{cx^2 + d}$ for $d/c < 0$ **40.** $y = \sqrt[3]{x^3 - 9x}$
   (a) for $ad - bc > 0$
   (b) for $ad - bc < 0$

41. $y = (x - 1)^{2/3}$ **42.** $y = x^2(x + 3)^4$

43. $y = x^3(x - 6)^4$ **44.** $y = (1 - x)^{2/3}$

45. $y = e^{-\pi x} + \pi$ **46.** $y = x \ln x$

47. $y = x^2 - 9 \ln x$ **48.** $y = x^{-1}e^x$

49. $y = e^x - e^{-x}$ **50.** $y = e^{-x^2/2}$

51. $y = x \ln x - x$ **52.** $y = (x^2 + 1)e^{-x}$

In Problems 53–64, determine intervals on which the function is increasing; intervals on which the function is decreasing; relative extrema; symmetry; and those intercepts that can be obtained conveniently. Then sketch the graph.

53. $y = x^2 - 3x - 10$ **54.** $y = 2x^2 + x - 10$

55. $y = 3x - x^3$ **56.** $y = x^4 - 16$

57. $y = 2x^3 - 9x^2 + 12x$ **58.** $y = 2x^3 - x^2 - 4x + 4$

59. $y = x^4 - 2x^2$ **60.** $y = x^6 - \dfrac{6}{5}x^5$

61. $y = (x - 1)^2(x + 2)^2$ **62.** $y = \sqrt{x}(x^2 - x - 2)$

63. $y = 2\sqrt{x} - x$ **64.** $y = x^{5/3} - 2x^{2/3}$

65. Sketch the graph of a continuous function f such that $f(2) = 2$, $f(4) = 6$, $f'(2) = f'(4) = 0$, $f'(x) < 0$ for $x < 2$, $f'(x) > 0$ for $2 < x < 4$, f has a relative maximum at 4, and $\lim_{x \to \infty} f(x) = 0$.

66. Sketch the graph of a continuous function f such that $f(1) = 2$, $f(4) = 5$, $f'(1) = 0$, $f'(x) \geq 0$ for $x < 4$, f has a relative maximum when $x = 4$, and there is a vertical tangent line when $x = 4$.

67. Average Cost   If $c_f = 25{,}000$ is a fixed-cost function, show that the average fixed-cost function $\overline{c}f = c_f/q$ is a decreasing function for $q > 0$. Thus, as output q increases, each unit's portion of fixed cost declines.

68. Marginal Cost   If $c = 3q - 3q^2 + q^3$ is a cost function, when is marginal cost increasing?

69. Marginal Revenue   Given the demand function

$$p = 500 - 5q$$

find when marginal revenue is increasing.

70. Cost Function   For the cost function $c = \sqrt{q}$, show that marginal and average costs are always decreasing for $q > 0$.

71. Revenue   For a manufacturer's product, the revenue function is given by $r = 240q + 57q^2 - q^3$. Determine the output for maximum revenue.

72. Labor Markets   Eswaran and Kotwal[1] consider agrarian economies in which there are two types of workers, permanent and casual. Permanent workers are employed on long-term contracts and may receive benefits such as holiday gifts and emergency aid. Casual workers are hired on a daily basis and perform routine and menial tasks such as weeding, harvesting, and threshing. The difference z in the present-value cost of hiring a permanent worker over that of hiring a casual worker is given by

$$z = (1 + b)w_p - bw_c$$

where w_p and w_c are wage rates for permanent labor and casual labor, respectively, b is a positive constant, and w_p is a function of w_c.
(a) Show that

$$\frac{dz}{dw_c} = (1 + b)\left[\frac{dw_p}{dw_c} - \frac{b}{1 + b}\right]$$

(b) If $dw_p/dw_c < b/(1 + b)$, show that z is a decreasing function of w_c.

[1] M. Eswaran and A. Kotwal, "A Theory of Two-Tier Labor Markets in Agrarian Economics," *The American Economic Review*, 75, no. 1 (1985), 162–77.

73. Thermal Pollution In Shonle's discussion of thermal pollution,[2] the efficiency of a power plant is given by

$$E = 0.71 \left(1 - \frac{T_c}{T_h}\right)$$

where T_h and T_c are the respective absolute temperatures of the hotter and colder reservoirs. Assume that T_c is a positive constant and that T_h is positive. Using calculus, show that as T_h increases, the efficiency increases.

74. Telephone Service In a discussion of the pricing of local telephone service, Renshaw[3] determines that total revenue r is given by

$$r = 2F + \left(1 - \frac{a}{b}\right)p - p^2 + \frac{a^2}{b}$$

where p is an indexed price per call, and a, b, and F are constants. Determine the value of p that maximizes revenue.

75. Storage and Shipping Costs In his model for storage and shipping costs of materials for a manufacturing process, Lancaster[4] derives the cost function

$$C(k) = 100 \left(100 + 9k + \frac{144}{k}\right) \quad 1 \le k \le 100$$

where $C(k)$ is the total cost (in dollars) of storage and transportation for 100 days of operation if a load of k tons of material is moved every k days.

(a) Find $C(1)$.
(b) For what value of k does $C(k)$ have a minimum?
(c) What is the minimum value?

76. Physiology—The Bends When a deep-sea diver undergoes decompression or a pilot climbs to a high altitude, nitrogen may bubble out of the blood, causing what is commonly called *the bends*. Suppose the percentage P of people who suffer effects of the bends at an altitude of h thousand feet is given by[5]

$$P = \frac{100}{1 + 100,000e^{-0.36h}}$$

Is P an increasing function of h?

In Problems 77–80, from the graph of the function, find the coordinates of all relative extrema. Round your answers to two decimal places.

77. $y = 0.3x^2 + 2.3x + 5.1$ **78.** $y = 3x^4 - 4x^3 - 5x + 1$

79. $y = \dfrac{8.2x}{0.4x^2 + 3}$ **80.** $y = \dfrac{e^x(3 - x)}{7x^2 + 1}$

81. Graph the function

$$f(x) = [x(x - 2)(2x - 3)]^2$$

in the window $-1 \le x \le 3$, $-1 \le y \le 3$. Upon first glance, it may appear that this function has two relative minimum points and one relative maximum point. However, in reality, it has three relative minimum points and two relative maximum points. Determine the x-values of all these points. Round answers to two decimal places.

82. If $f(x) = 3x^3 - 7x^2 + 4x + 2$, display the graphs of f and f' on the same screen. Notice that $f'(x) = 0$ where relative extrema of f occur.

83. Let $f(x) = 6 + 4x - 3x^2 - x^3$. (a) Find $f'(x)$. (b) Graph $f'(x)$. (c) Observe where $f'(x)$ is positive and where it is negative. Give the intervals (rounded to two decimal places) where f is increasing and where f is decreasing. (d) Graph f and f' on the same screen, and verify your results to part (c).

84. If $f(x) = x^4 - x^2 - (x + 2)^2$, find $f'(x)$. Determine the critical values of f. Round your answers to two decimal places.

Objective

To find extreme values on a closed interval.

13.2 Absolute Extrema on a Closed Interval

If a function f is *continuous* on a *closed* interval $[a, b]$, it can be shown that of *all* the function values $f(x)$ for x in $[a, b]$, there must be an absolute maximum value and an absolute minimum value. These two values are called **extreme values** of f on that interval. This important property of continuous functions is called the *extreme-value theorem*.

Extreme-Value Theorem

If a function is continuous on a closed interval, then the function has *both* a maximum value *and* a minimum value on that interval.

For example, each function in Figure 13.25 is continuous on the closed interval $[1, 3]$. Geometrically, the extreme-value theorem assures us that over this interval each graph has a highest point and a lowest point.

In the extreme-value theorem, it is important that we are dealing with

1. a closed interval and
2. a function continuous on that interval

---

[2]J. I. Shonle, *Environmental Applications of General Physics* (Reading, MA: Addison-Wesley Publishing Company, Inc., 1975).

[3]E. Renshaw, "A Note on Equity and Efficiency in the Pricing of Local Telephone Services," *The American Economic Review*, 75, no. 3 (1985), 515–18.

[4]P. Lancaster, *Mathematics: Models of the Real World* (Englewood Cliffs, NJ: Prentice-Hall, Inc., 1976).

[5]Adapted from G. E. Folk, Jr., *Textbook of Environmental Physiology*, 2nd ed. (Philadelphia: Lea & Febiger, 1974).

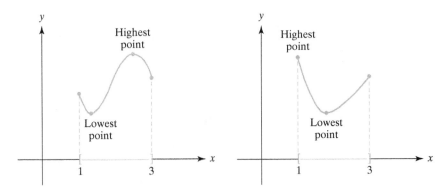

FIGURE 13.25   Illustrating the extreme-value theorem.

If either condition (1) or condition (2) is not met, then extreme values are not guaranteed. For example, Figure 13.26(a) shows the graph of the continuous function $f(x) = x^2$ on the *open* interval $(-1, 1)$. You can see that f has no maximum value on the interval (although f has a minimum value there). Now consider the function $f(x) = 1/x^2$ on the closed interval $[-1, 1]$. Here f is *not continuous* at 0. From the graph of f in Figure 13.26(b), you can see that f has no maximum value (although there is a minimum value).

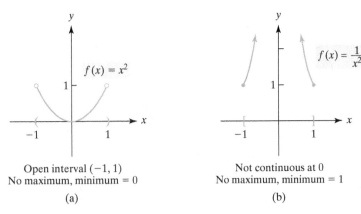

Open interval $(-1, 1)$
No maximum, minimum = 0

(a)

Not continuous at 0
No maximum, minimum = 1

(b)

FIGURE 13.26   Extreme-value theorem does not apply.

In the previous section, our emphasis was on relative extrema. Now we will focus our attention on absolute extrema and make use of the extreme-value theorem where possible. If the domain of a function is a closed interval, to determine *absolute* extrema we must examine the function not only at critical values, but also at the endpoints. For example, Figure 13.27 shows the graph of the continuous function $y = f(x)$ over $[a, b]$. The extreme-value theorem guarantees absolute extrema over the interval. Clearly, the important points on the graph occur at $x = a, b, c,$ and d, which correspond to endpoints

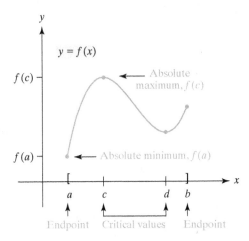

FIGURE 13.27   Absolute extrema.

or critical values. Notice that the absolute maximum occurs at the critical value c and the absolute minimum occurs at the endpoint a. These results suggest the following procedure:

> **Procedure to Find Absolute Extrema for a Function f That Is Continuous on $[a, b]$**
>
> **Step 1.** Find the critical values of f.
>
> **Step 2.** Evaluate $f(x)$ at the endpoints a and b and at the critical values in (a, b).
>
> **Step 3.** The maximum value of f is the greatest of the values found in step 2. The minimum value of f is the least of the values found in step 2.

EXAMPLE 1   Finding Extreme Values on a Closed Interval

Find absolute extrema for $f(x) = x^2 - 4x + 5$ over the closed interval $[1, 4]$.

Solution: Since f is continuous on $[1, 4]$, the foregoing procedure applies.

Step 1. To find the critical values of f, we first find f':

$$f'(x) = 2x - 4 = 2(x - 2)$$

This gives the critical value $x = 2$.

Step 2. Evaluating $f(x)$ at the endpoints 1 and 4 and at the critical value 2, we have

$$\begin{aligned} f(1) &= 2 \\ f(4) &= 5 \end{aligned} \quad \text{values of } f \text{ at endpoints}$$

and

$$f(2) = 1 \quad \text{value of } f \text{ at critical value 2 in } (1, 4)$$

Step 3. From the function values in Step 2, we conclude that the maximum is $f(4) = 5$ and the minimum is $f(2) = 1$. (See Figure 13.28.)

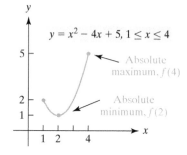

FIGURE 13.28   Extreme values for Example 1.

Now Work Problem 1 ◁

PROBLEMS 13.2

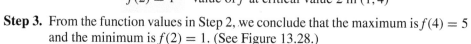

In Problems 1–14, find the absolute extrema of the given function on the given interval.

1. $f(x) = x^2 - 2x + 3$, $[0, 3]$

2. $f(x) = -2x^2 - 6x + 5$, $[-3, 2]$

3. $f(x) = \frac{1}{3}x^3 + \frac{1}{2}x^2 - 2x + 1$, $[-1, 0]$

4. $f(x) = \frac{1}{4}x^4 - \frac{3}{2}x^2$, $[0, 1]$

5. $f(x) = x^3 - 5x^2 - 8x + 50$, $[0, 5]$

6. $f(x) = x^{2/3}$, $[-8, 8]$

7. $f(x) = -3x^5 + 5x^3$, $[-2, 0]$

8. $f(x) = \frac{7}{3}x^3 + 2x^2 - 3x + 1$, $[0, 3]$

9. $f(x) = 3x^4 - x^6$, $[-1, 2]$

10. $f(x) = x^4 - 8x^3 + 22x^2 - 24x + 2$, $[0, 4]$

11. $f(x) = x^4 - 9x^2 + 2$, $[-1, 3]$

12. $f(x) = \dfrac{x}{x^2 + 1}$, $[0, 2]$

13. $f(x) = (x - 1)^{2/3}$, $[-26, 28]$

14. $f(x) = 0.2x^3 - 3.6x^2 + 2x + 1$, $[-1, 2]$

15. Consider the function

$$f(x) = x^4 + 8x^3 + 21x^2 + 20x + 9$$

over the interval $[-4, 9]$.

(a) Determine the value(s) (rounded to two decimal places) of x at which f attains a minimum value.

(b) What is the minimum value (rounded to two decimal places) of f?

(c) Determine the value(s) of x at which f attains a maximum value.

(d) What is the maximum value of f?

Objective

To test a function for concavity and inflection points. Also, to sketch curves with the aid of the information obtained from the first and second derivatives.

13.3 Concavity

The first derivative provides much information for sketching curves. It is used to determine where a function is increasing, is decreasing, has relative maxima, and has relative minima. However, to be sure we know the true shape of a curve, we may need more

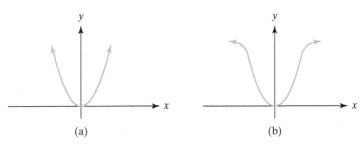

FIGURE 13.29 Two functions with $f'(x) < 0$ for $x < 0$ and $f'(x) > 0$ for $x > 0$.

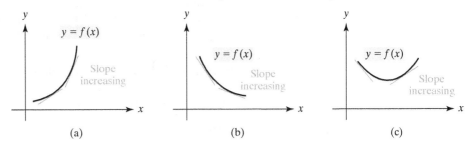

FIGURE 13.30 Each curve is concave up.

information. For example, consider the curve $y = f(x) = x^2$. Since $f'(x) = 2x, x = 0$ is a critical value. If $x < 0$, then $f'(x) < 0$, and f is decreasing; if $x > 0$, then $f'(x) > 0$, and f is increasing. Thus, there is a relative minimum when $x = 0$. In Figure 13.29, both curves meet the preceding conditions. But which one truly describes the curve $y = x^2$? This question will be settled easily by using the second derivative and the notion of *concavity*.

In Figure 13.30, note that each curve $y = f(x)$ "bends" (or opens) upward. This means that if tangent lines are drawn to each curve, the curves lie *above* them. Moreover, the slopes of the tangent lines *increase* in value as x increases: In part (a), the slopes go from small positive values to larger values; in part (b), they are negative and approaching zero (and thus increasing); in part (c), they pass from negative values to positive values. Since $f'(x)$ gives the slope at a point, an increasing slope means that f' must be an increasing function. To describe this property, each curve (or function f) in Figure 13.30 is said to be *concave up*.

In Figure 13.31, it can be seen that each curve lies *below* the tangent lines and the curves are bending downward. As x increases, the slopes of the tangent lines are *decreasing*. Thus, f' must be a decreasing function here, and we say that f is *concave down*.

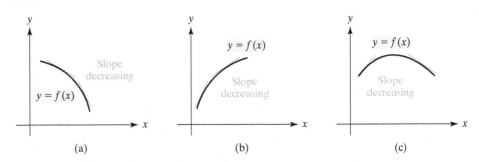

FIGURE 13.31 Each curve is concave down.

CAUTION! ⚠

Concavity relates to whether f', not f, is increasing or decreasing. In Figure 13.30(b), note that f is concave up and decreasing; however, in Figure 13.31(a), f is concave down and decreasing.

Definition

Let f be differentiable on the interval (a, b). Then f is said to be **concave up [concave down]** on (a, b) if f' is increasing [decreasing] on (a, b).

Remember: If f is concave up on an interval, then, geometrically, its graph is bending upward there. If f is concave down, then its graph is bending downward.

Since f' is increasing when its derivative $f''(x)$ is positive, and f' is decreasing when $f''(x)$ is negative, we can state the following rule:

Rule 1 Criteria for Concavity

Let f' be differentiable on the interval (a, b). If $f''(x) > 0$ for all x in (a, b), then f is concave up on (a, b). If $f''(x) < 0$ for all x in (a, b), then f is concave down on (a, b).

A function f is also said to be concave up at a point c if there exists an open interval around c on which f is concave up. In fact, for the functions that we will consider, if $f''(c) > 0$, then f is concave up at c. Similarly, f is concave down at c if $f''(c) < 0$.

EXAMPLE 1 Testing for Concavity

Determine where the given function is concave up and where it is concave down.

a. $y = f(x) = (x - 1)^3 + 1$.

Solution: To apply Rule 1, we must examine the signs of y''. Now, $y' = 3(x - 1)^2$, so

$$y'' = 6(x - 1)$$

Thus, f is concave up when $6(x - 1) > 0$; that is, when $x > 1$. And f is concave down when $6(x - 1) < 0$; that is, when $x < 1$. We now use a sign chart for f'' (together with an interpretation line for f) to organize our findings. (See Figure 13.32.)

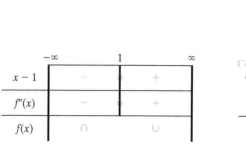
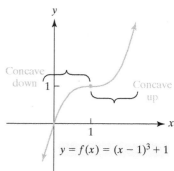

FIGURE 13.32 Sign chart for f'' and concavity for $f(x) = (x - 1)^3 + 1$.

b. $y = x^2$.

Solution: We have $y' = 2x$ and $y'' = 2$. Because y'' is always positive, the graph of $y = x^2$ must always be concave up, as in Figure 13.29(a). The graph cannot appear as in Figure 13.29(b), for that curve is sometimes concave down.

Now Work Problem 1 ◁

A point on a graph where concavity changes from concave down to concave up, or vice versa, such as $(1, 1)$ in Figure 13.32, is called an *inflection point* or a *point of inflection*. Around such a point, the sign of $f''(x)$ goes from $-$ to $+$ or from $+$ to $-$. More precisely, we have the following definition:

Definition

The definition of an inflection point implies that a is in the domain of f.

A function f has an **inflection point** at a if and only if f is continuous at a and f changes concavity at a.

To test a function for concavity and inflection points, first find the values of x where $f''(x)$ is 0 or not defined. These values of x determine intervals. On each interval, determine whether $f''(x) > 0$ (f is concave up) or $f''(x) < 0$ (f is concave down). If concavity changes around one of these x-values and f is continuous there, then f has an inflection point at this x-value. The continuity requirement implies that the x-value must be in the domain of the function. In brief, a *candidate* for an inflection point must satisfy two conditions:

1. f'' must be 0 or fail to exist at that point.
2. f must be continuous at that point.

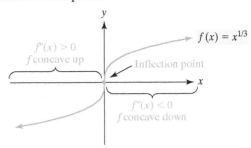

FIGURE 13.33 Inflection point for $f(x) = x^{1/3}$.

The candidate *will be* an inflection point if concavity changes around it. For example, if $f(x) = x^{1/3}$, then $f'(x) = \frac{1}{3}x^{-2/3}$ and

$$f''(x) = -\frac{2}{9}x^{-5/3} = -\frac{2}{9x^{5/3}}$$

Because f'' does not exist at 0, but f is continuous at 0, there is a candidate for an inflection point at 0. If $x > 0$, then $f''(x) < 0$, so f is concave down for $x > 0$; if $x < 0$, then $f''(x) > 0$, so f is concave up for $x < 0$. Because concavity changes at 0, there is an inflection point there. (See Figure 13.33.)

EXAMPLE 2 Concavity and Inflection Points

Test $y = 6x^4 - 8x^3 + 1$ for concavity and inflection points.

Solution: We have

$$y' = 24x^3 - 24x^2$$
$$y'' = 72x^2 - 48x = 24x(3x - 2)$$

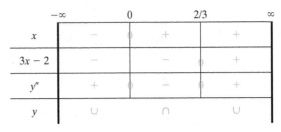

FIGURE 13.34 Sign chart of $y'' = 24x(3x - 2)$ for $y = 6x^4 - 8x^3 + 1$.

To find where $y'' = 0$, we set each factor in y'' equal to 0. This gives $x = 0, \frac{2}{3}$. We also note that y'' is never undefined. Thus, there are three intervals to consider, as recorded on the top of the sign chart in Figure 13.34. Since y is continuous at 0 and $\frac{2}{3}$, these points are candidates for inflection points. Having completed the sign chart, we see that concavity changes at 0 and at $\frac{2}{3}$. Thus these candidates are indeed inflection points. (See Figure 13.35.) In summary, the curve is concave up on $(-\infty, 0)$ and $(\frac{2}{3}, \infty)$ and is concave down on $(0, \frac{2}{3})$. Inflection points occur at 0 and at $\frac{2}{3}$. These points are $(0, y(0)) = (0, 1)$ and $(\frac{2}{3}, y(\frac{2}{3})) = (\frac{2}{3}, -\frac{5}{27})$.

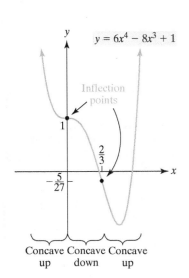

FIGURE 13.35 Graph of $y = 6x^4 - 8x^3 + 1$.

Now Work Problem 13 ◁

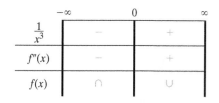

FIGURE 13.36 Sign chart for $f''(x)$.

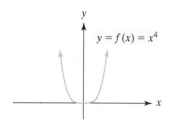

FIGURE 13.37 Graph of $y = \dfrac{1}{x}$.

CAUTION!

A candidate for an inflection point may not necessarily be an inflection point. For example, if $f(x) = x^4$, then $f''(x) = 12x^2$ and $f''(0) = 0$. But $f''(x) > 0$ both when $x < 0$ and when $x > 0$. Thus, concavity does not change, and there are no inflection points. (See Figure 13.38.)

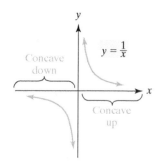

FIGURE 13.38 Graph of $f(x) = x^4$.

As we did in the analysis of increasing and decreasing, so we must in concavity analysis consider also those points a that are not in the domain of f but that are near points in the domain of f. The next example will illustrate.

EXAMPLE 3 A Change in Concavity with No Inflection Point

Discuss concavity and find all inflection points for $f(x) = \dfrac{1}{x}$.

Solution: Since $f(x) = x^{-1}$ for $x \neq 0$,

$$f'(x) = -x^{-2} \quad \text{for } x \neq 0$$
$$f''(x) = 2x^{-3} = \frac{2}{x^3} \quad \text{for } x \neq 0$$

We see that $f''(x)$ is never 0 but it is not defined when $x = 0$. Since f is not continuous at 0, we conclude that 0 is not a candidate for an inflection point. Thus, the given function has no inflection point. However, 0 must be considered in an analysis of concavity. See the sign chart in Figure 13.36; note that we have a thick vertical line at 0 to indicate that 0 is not in the domain of f and cannot correspond to an inflection point. If $x > 0$, then $f''(x) > 0$; if $x < 0$, then $f''(x) < 0$. Hence, f is concave up on $(0, \infty)$ and concave down on $(-\infty, 0)$. (See Figure 13.37.) Although concavity changes around $x = 0$, there is no inflection point there because f is not continuous at 0 (nor is it even defined there).

Now Work Problem 23 ◁

Curve Sketching

EXAMPLE 4 Curve Sketching

Sketch the graph of $y = 2x^3 - 9x^2 + 12x$.

Solution:

Intercepts If $x = 0$, then $y = 0$. Setting $y = 0$ gives $0 = x(2x^2 - 9x + 12)$. Clearly, $x = 0$ is a solution, and using the quadratic formula on $2x^2 - 9x + 12 = 0$ gives no real roots. Thus, the only intercept is $(0, 0)$. In fact, since $2x^2 - 9x + 12$ is a continuous function whose value at 0 is $2 \cdot 0^2 - 9 \cdot 0 + 12 = 12 > 0$, we conclude that $2x^2 - 9x + 12 > 0$ for all x, which gives the sign chart in Figure 13.39 for y.

Note that this chart tells us the graph of $y = 2x^3 - 9x^2 + 12x$ is confined to the third and first quadrants of the xy-plane.

Symmetry None.

Maxima and Minima We have

$$y' = 6x^2 - 18x + 12 = 6(x^2 - 3x + 2) = 6(x - 1)(x - 2)$$

The critical values are $x = 1, 2$, so these and the factors $x - 1$ and $x - 2$ determine the sign chart of y' (Figure 13.40).

From the sign chart for y' we see that there is a relative maximum at 1 and a relative minimum at 2. Note too that the bottom line of Figure 13.40, together with that of Figure 13.39, comes close to determining a precise graph of $y = 2x^3 - 9x^2 + 12x$.

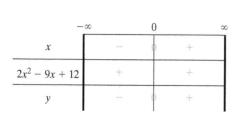

FIGURE 13.39 Sign chart for y.

	$-\infty$		0		∞
x		$-$	0	$+$	
$2x^2 - 9x + 12$		$+$		$+$	
y		$-$	0	$+$	

FIGURE 13.40 Sign chart of $y' = 6(x - 1)(x - 2)$.

	$-\infty$		1		2		∞
$x - 1$		$-$	0	$+$		$+$	
$x - 2$		$-$		$-$	0	$+$	
y'		$+$	0	$-$	0	$+$	
y							

FIGURE 13.41   Sign chart of y''.

Of course, it will help to know the relative maximum $y(1) = 5$, which occurs at 1, and the relative minimum $y(2) = 4$, which occurs at 2, so that in addition to the intercept $(0,0)$ we will actually plot also $(1,5)$ and $(2,4)$.

Concavity

$$y'' = 12x - 18 = 6(2x - 3)$$

Setting $y'' = 0$ gives a possible inflection point at $x = \frac{3}{2}$ from which we construct the simple sign chart for y'' in Figure 13.41.

Since concavity changes at $x = \frac{3}{2}$, at which point f is certainly continuous, there is an inflection point at $\frac{3}{2}$.

Discussion   We know the coordinates of three of the important points on the graph. The only other important point from our perspective is the inflection point, and since $y(3/2) = 2(3/2)^3 - 9(3/2)^2 + 12(3/2) = 9/2$ the inflection point is $(3/2, 9/2)$.

We plot the four points noted above and observe from all three sign charts jointly that the curve increases through the third quadrant and passes through $(0,0)$, all the while concave down until a relative maximum is attained at $(1,5)$. The curve then falls until it reaches a relative minimum at $(2,4)$. However, along the way the concavity changes at $(3/2, 9/2)$ from concave down to concave up and remains so for the rest of the curve. After $(2,4)$ the curve increases through the first quadrant. The curve is shown in Figure 13.42.

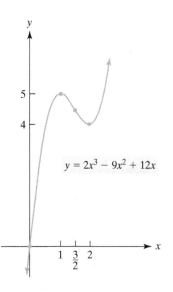

FIGURE 13.42   Graph of $y = 2x^3 - 9x^2 + 12x$.

Now Work Problem 39 ◁

TECHNOLOGY ▮▮▮▮

Suppose that you need to find the inflection points for

$$f(x) = \frac{1}{20}x^5 - \frac{17}{16}x^4 + \frac{273}{32}x^3 - \frac{4225}{128}x^2 + \frac{750}{4}$$

The second derivative of f is given by

$$f''(x) = x^3 - \frac{51}{4}x^2 + \frac{819}{16}x - \frac{4225}{64}$$

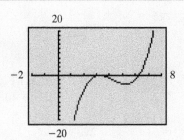

FIGURE 13.43   Graph of f''; roots of of $f'' = 0$ are approximately 3.25 and 6.25.

Here the roots of $f'' = 0$ are not obvious. Thus, we will graph f'' using a graphing calculator. (See Figure 13.43.) We find that the roots of $f'' = 0$ are approximately 3.25 and 6.25. Around $x = 6.25, f''(x)$ goes from negative to positive values. Therefore, at $x = 6.25$, there is an inflection point. Around $x = 3.25, f''(x)$ does not change sign, so no inflection point exists at $x = 3.25$. Comparing our results with the graph of f in Figure 13.44, we see that everything checks out.

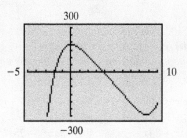

FIGURE 13.44   Graph of f; inflection point at $x = 6.25$, but not at $x = 3.25$.

PROBLEMS 13.3

In Problems 1–6, a function and its second derivative are given. Determine the concavity of f and find x-values where points of inflection occur.

1. $f(x) = x^4 - 3x^3 - 6x^2 + 6x + 1; f''(x) = 6(2x + 1)(x - 2)$

2. $f(x) = \dfrac{x^5}{20} + \dfrac{x^4}{4} - 2x^2; f''(x) = (x - 1)(x + 2)^2$

3. $f(x) = \dfrac{2 + x - x^2}{x^2 - 2x + 1}; f''(x) = \dfrac{2(7 - x)}{(x - 1)^4}$

4. $f(x) = \dfrac{x^2}{(x - 1)^2}; f''(x) = \dfrac{2(2x + 1)}{(x - 1)^4}$

5. $f(x) = \dfrac{x^2 + 1}{x^2 - 2}; f''(x) = \dfrac{6(3x^2 + 2)}{(x^2 - 2)^3}$

6. $f(x) = x\sqrt{a^2 - x^2}; f''(x) = \dfrac{x(2x^2 - 3a^2)}{(a^2 - x^2)^{3/2}}$

In Problems 7–34, determine concavity and the x-values where points of inflection occur. Do not sketch the graphs.

7. $y = -2x^2 + 4x$

8. $y = -74x^2 + 19x - 37$

9. $y = 4x^3 + 12x^2 - 12x$

10. $y = x^3 - 6x^2 + 9x + 1$

11. $y = ax^3 + bx^2 + cx + d$

12. $y = x^4 - 8x^2 - 6$

13. $y = 2x^4 - 48x^2 + 7x + 3$

14. $y = -\dfrac{x^4}{4} + \dfrac{9x^2}{2} + 2x$

15. $y = 2x^{1/5}$

16. $y = \dfrac{a}{x^3}$

17. $y = \dfrac{x^4}{2} + \dfrac{19x^3}{6} - \dfrac{7x^2}{2} + x + 5$

18. $y = -\dfrac{5}{2}x^4 - \dfrac{1}{6}x^3 + \dfrac{1}{2}x^2 + \dfrac{1}{3}x - \dfrac{2}{5}$

19. $y = \dfrac{1}{20}x^5 - \dfrac{1}{4}x^4 + \dfrac{1}{6}x^3 - \dfrac{1}{2}x - \dfrac{2}{3}$

20. $y = \dfrac{1}{10}x^5 - 3x^3 + 17x + 43$

21. $y = \dfrac{1}{30}x^6 - \dfrac{7}{12}x^4 + 6x^2 + 5x - 4$

22. $y = x^6 - 3x^4$

23. $y = \dfrac{x + 1}{x - 1}$

24. $y = 1 - \dfrac{1}{x^2}$

25. $y = \dfrac{x^2}{x^2 + 1}$

26. $y = \dfrac{ax^2}{x + b}$

27. $y = \dfrac{21x + 40}{6(x + 3)^2}$

28. $y = 3(x^2 - 2)^2$

29. $y = 5e^x$

30. $y = e^x - e^{-x}$

31. $y = axe^x$

32. $y = xe^{x^2}$

33. $y = \dfrac{\ln x}{2x}$

34. $y = \dfrac{x^2 + 1}{3e^x}$

In Problems 35–62, determine intervals on which the function is increasing, decreasing, concave up, and concave down; relative maxima and minima; inflection points; symmetry; and those intercepts that can be obtained conveniently. Then sketch the graph.

35. $y = x^2 - x - 6$

36. $y = x^2 + a$ for $a > 0$

37. $y = 5x - 2x^2$

38. $y = x - x^2 + 2$

39. $y = x^3 - 9x^2 + 24x - 19$

40. $y = x^3 - 25x^2$

41. $y = \dfrac{x^3}{3} - 5x$

42. $y = x^3 - 6x^2 + 9x$

43. $y = x^3 - 3x^2 + 3x - 3$

44. $y = 2x^3 + \dfrac{5}{2}x^2 + 2x$

45. $y = 4x^3 - 3x^4$

46. $y = -x^3 + 8x^2 - 5x + 3$

47. $y = -2 + 12x - x^3$

48. $y = (3 + 2x)^3$

49. $y = 2x^3 - 6x^2 + 6x - 2$

50. $y = \dfrac{x^5}{100} - \dfrac{x^4}{20}$

51. $y = 16x - x^5$

52. $y = x^2(x - 1)^2$

53. $y = 3x^4 - 4x^3 + 1$

54. $y = 3x^5 - 5x^3$

55. $y = 4x^2 - x^4$

56. $y = x^2 e^x$

57. $y = x^{1/3}(x - 8)$

58. $y = (x - 1)^2(x + 2)^2$

59. $y = 4x^{1/3} + x^{4/3}$

60. $y = (x + 1)\sqrt{x + 4}$

61. $y = 2x^{2/3} - x$

62. $y = 5x^{2/3} - x^{5/3}$

63. Sketch the graph of a continuous function f such that $f(2) = 4, f'(2) = 0, f'(x) < 0$ if $x < 2$, and $f''(x) > 0$ if $x > 2$.

64. Sketch the graph of a continuous function f such that $f(4) = 4, f'(4) = 0, f''(x) < 0$ for $x < 4$, and $f''(x) > 0$ for $x > 4$.

65. Sketch the graph of a continuous function f such that $f(1) = 1, f'(1) = 0$, and $f''(x) < 0$ for all x.

66. Sketch the graph of a continuous function f such that $f(1) = 1$, both $f'(x) < 0$ and $f''(x) < 0$ for $x < 1$, and both $f(x) > 0$ and $f''(x) < 0$ for $x > 1$.

67. **Demand Equation**   Show that the graph of the demand equation $p = \dfrac{100}{q + 2}$ is decreasing and concave up for $q > 0$.

68. **Average Cost**   For the cost function

$$c = q^2 + 2q + 1$$

show that the graph of the average-cost function $\bar{c}$ is always concave up for $q > 0$.

69. **Species of Plants**   The number of species of plants on a plot may depend on the size of the plot. For example, in Figure 13.45, we see that on 1-m² plots there are three species (A, B, and C on the left plot, A, B, and D on the right plot), and on a 2-m² plot there are four species (A, B, C, and D).

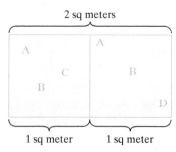

FIGURE 13.45

In a study of rooted plants in a certain geographic region,[6] it was determined that the average number of species, S, occurring on

---

[6]Adapted from R. W. Poole, *An Introduction to Quantitative Ecology* (New York: McGraw-Hill Book Company, 1974).

plots of size A (in square meters) is given by

$$S = f(A) = 12\sqrt[4]{A} \quad 0 \le A \le 625$$

Sketch the graph of f. (*Note:* Your graph should be rising and concave down. Thus, the number of species is increasing with respect to area, but at a decreasing rate.)

70. Inferior Good   In a discussion of an inferior good, Persky[7] considers a function of the form

$$g(x) = e^{(U_0/A)} e^{-x^2/(2A)}$$

where x is a quantity of a good, U_0 is a constant that represents utility, and A is a positive constant. Persky claims that the graph of g is concave down for $x < \sqrt{A}$ and concave up for $x > \sqrt{A}$. Verify this.

71. Psychology   In a psychological experiment involving conditioned response,[8] subjects listened to four tones, denoted 0, 1, 2, and 3. Initially, the subjects were conditioned to tone 0 by receiving a shock whenever this tone was heard. Later, when each of the four tones (stimuli) were heard without shocks, the subjects' responses were recorded by means of a tracking device that measures galvanic skin reaction. The average response to each stimulus (without shock) was determined, and the results were plotted on a coordinate plane where the x- and y-axes represent the stimuli (0, 1, 2, 3) and the average galvanic responses, respectively. It was determined that the points fit a curve that is approximated by the graph of

$$y = 12.5 + 5.8(0.42)^x$$

Show that this function is decreasing and concave up.

72. Entomology   In a study of the effects of food deprivation on hunger,[9] an insect was fed until its appetite was completely satisfied. Then it was deprived of food for t hours (the deprivation period). At the end of this period, the insect was re-fed until its appetite was again completely satisfied. The weight H (in grams) of the food that was consumed at this time was statistically found to be a function of t, where

$$H = 1.00[1 - e^{-(0.0464t+0.0670)}]$$

Here H is a measure of hunger. Show that H is increasing with respect to t and is concave down.

73. Insect Dispersal   In an experiment on the dispersal of a particular insect,[10] a large number of insects are placed at a release point in an open field. Surrounding this point are traps that are placed in a concentric circular arrangement at a distance of 1 m, 2 m, 3 m, and so on from the release point. Twenty-four hours after the insects are released, the number of insects in each trap is counted. It is determined that at a distance of r meters from the release point, the average number of insects contained in a trap is

$$n = f(r) = 0.1 \ln (r) + \frac{7}{r} - 0.8 \quad 1 \le r \le 10$$

(a) Show that the graph of f is always falling and concave up. (b) Sketch the graph of f. (c) When $r = 5$, at what rate is the average number of insects in a trap decreasing with respect to distance?

74. Graph $y = -0.35x^3 + 4.1x^2 + 8.3x - 7.4$, and from the graph determine the number of (a) relative maximum points, (b) relative minimum points, and (c) inflection points.

75. Graph $y = x^5(x - 2.3)$, and from the graph determine the number of inflection points. Now, prove that for any $a \ne 0$, the curve $y = x^5(x - a)$ has two points of inflection.

76. Graph $y = xe^{-x}$ and determine the number of inflection points, first using a graphing calculator and then using the techniques of this chapter. If a demand equation has the form $q = q(p) = Qe^{-Rp}$ for constants Q and R, relate the graph of the resulting revenue function to that of the function graphed above, by taking $Q = 1 = R$.

77. Graph the curve $y = x^3 - 2x^2 + x + 3$, and also graph the tangent line to the curve at $x = 2$. Around $x = 2$, does the curve lie above or below the tangent line? From your observation determine the concavity at $x = 2$.

78. If $f(x) = 2x^3 + 3x^2 - 6x + 1$, find $f'(x)$ and $f''(x)$. Note that where f' has a relative minimum, f changes its direction of bending. Why?

79. If $f(x) = x^6 + 3x^5 - 4x^4 + 2x^2 + 1$, find the x-values (rounded to two decimal places) of the inflection points of f.

80. If $f(x) = \dfrac{x+1}{x^2+1}$, find the x-values (rounded to two decimal places) of the inflection points of f.

13.4 The Second-Derivative Test

Objective

To locate relative extrema by applying the second-derivative test.

The second derivative can be used to test certain critical values for relative extrema. Observe in Figure 13.46 that at a, there is a horizontal tangent; that is, $f'(a) = 0$. Furthermore, around a, the function is concave up [that is, $f''(a) > 0$]. This leads us to conclude that there is a relative minimum at a. On the other hand, around b, the function is concave down [that is, $f''(b) < 0$]. Because the tangent line is horizontal at

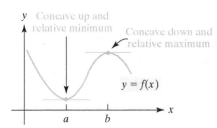

FIGURE 13.46   Relating concavity to relative extrema.

[7]A. L. Persky, "An Inferior Good and a Novel Indifference Map," *The American Economist* XXIX, no. 1 (1985), 67–69.

[8]Adapted from C. I. Hovland, "The Generalization of Conditioned Responses: I. The Sensory Generalization of Conditioned Responses with Varying Frequencies of Tone," *Journal of General Psychology,* 17 (1937), 125–48.

[9]C. S. Holling, "The Functional Response of Invertebrate Predators to Prey Density," *Memoirs of the Entomological Society of Canada,* no. 48 (1966).

[10]Adapted from Poole, op. cit.

b, we conclude that a relative maximum exists there. This technique of examining the second derivative at points where the first derivative is 0 is called the *second-derivative test* for relative extrema.

> **Second-Derivative Test for Relative Extrema**
>
> Suppose $f'(a) = 0$.
>
>   If $f''(a) < 0$, then f has a relative maximum at a.
>
>   If $f''(a) > 0$, then f has a relative minimum at a.

We want to emphasize that *the second-derivative test does* not *apply when* $f''(a) = 0$. If both $f'(a) = 0$ and $f''(a) = 0$, then there may be a relative maximum, a relative minimum, or neither, at a. In such cases, the first-derivative test should be used to analyze what is happening at a. [Also, the second-derivative test does not apply when $f'(a)$ does not exist.]

EXAMPLE 1   Second-Derivative Test

Test the following for relative maxima and minima. Use the second-derivative test, if possible.

a. $y = 18x - \frac{2}{3}x^3$.

Solution:

$$y' = 18 - 2x^2 = 2(9 - x^2) = 2(3 + x)(3 - x)$$

$$y'' = -4x \qquad\qquad \text{taking } \frac{d}{dx} \text{ of } 18 - 2x^2$$

Solving $y' = 0$ gives the critical values $x = \pm 3$.

$$\text{If } x = 3, \quad \text{then } y'' = -4(3) = -12 < 0.$$

There is a relative maximum when $x = 3$.

$$\text{If } x = -3, \quad \text{then } y'' = -4(-3) = 12 > 0.$$

There is a relative minimum when $x = -3$. (Refer to Figure 13.4.)

b. $y = 6x^4 - 8x^3 + 1$.

Solution:

$$y' = 24x^3 - 24x^2 = 24x^2(x - 1)$$

$$y'' = 72x^2 - 48x$$

Solving $y' = 0$ gives the critical values $x = 0, 1$. We see that

$$\text{if } x = 0, \quad \text{then } y'' = 0$$

and

$$\text{if } x = 1, \quad \text{then } y'' > 0$$

By the second-derivative test, there is a relative minimum when $x = 1$. We cannot apply the test when $x = 0$ because $y'' = 0$ there. To analyze what is happening at 0, we turn to the first-derivative test:

$$\text{If } x < 0, \quad \text{then } y' < 0.$$

$$\text{If } 0 < x < 1, \quad \text{then } y' < 0.$$

Thus, no maximum or minimum exists when $x = 0$. (Refer to Figure 13.35.)

Now Work Problem 5 ◁

CAUTION! ⚠

Although the second-derivative test can be very useful, do not depend entirely on it. Not only may the test fail to apply, but also it may be awkward to find the second derivative.

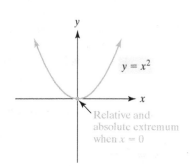

FIGURE 13.47 Exactly one relative extremum implies an absolute extremum.

If a continuous function has *exactly one* relative extremum on an interval, it can be shown that the relative extremum must also be an *absolute* extremum on the interval. To illustrate, in Figure 13.47 the function $y = x^2$ has a relative minimum when $x = 0$, and there are no other relative extrema. Since $y = x^2$ is continuous, this relative minimum is also an absolute minimum for the function.

EXAMPLE 2   Absolute Extrema

If $y = f(x) = x^3 - 3x^2 - 9x + 5$, determine when absolute extrema occur on the interval $(0, \infty)$.

Solution: We have

$$f'(x) = 3x^2 - 6x - 9 = 3(x^2 - 2x - 3)$$
$$= 3(x + 1)(x - 3)$$

The only critical value on the interval $(0, \infty)$ is 3. Applying the second-derivative test at this point gives

$$f''(x) = 6x - 6$$
$$f''(3) = 6(3) - 6 = 12 > 0$$

Thus, there is a relative minimum at 3. Since this is the only relative extremum on $(0, \infty)$ and f is continuous there, we conclude by our previous discussion that there is an *absolute* minimum value at 3; this value is $f(3) = -22$. (See Figure 13.48.)

Now Work Problem 3 ◁

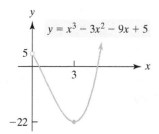

FIGURE 13.48   On $(0, \infty)$, there is an absolute minimum at 3.

PROBLEMS 13.4

In Problems 1–14, test for relative maxima and minima. Use the second-derivative test, if possible. In Problems 1–4, state whether the relative extrema are also absolute extrema.

1. $y = x^2 - 5x + 6$ **2.** $y = 3x^2 + 12x + 14$

3. $y = -4x^2 + 2x - 8$ **4.** $y = 3x^2 - 5x + 6$

5. $y = \frac{1}{3}x^3 + 2x^2 - 5x + 1$ **6.** $y = x^3 - 12x + 1$

7. $y = 2x^3 - 3x^2 - 36x + 17$ **8.** $y = x^4 - 2x^2 + 4$

9. $y = 7 - 2x^4$ **10.** $y = -2x^7$

11. $y = 81x^5 - 5x$ **12.** $y = 15x^3 + x^2 - 15x + 2$

13. $y = (x^2 + 7x + 10)^2$ **14.** $y = -x^3 + 3x^2 + 9x - 2$

Objective

To determine horizontal and vertical asymptotes for a curve and to sketch the graphs of functions having asymptotes.

13.5 Asymptotes

Vertical Asymptotes

In this section, we conclude our discussion of curve-sketching techniques by investigating functions having *asymptotes*. An asymptote is a line that a curve approaches arbitrarily closely. For example, in each part of Figure 13.49, the dashed line $x = a$ is an asymptote. But to be precise about it, we need to make use of infinite limits.

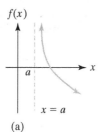
(a)

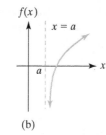
(b)

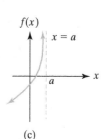
(c)

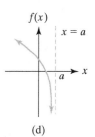
(d)

FIGURE 13.49   Vertical asymptotes $x = a$.

In Figure 13.49(a), notice that as $x \to a^+$, $f(x)$ becomes positively infinite:

$$\lim_{x \to a^+} f(x) = \infty$$

In Figure 13.49(b), as $x \to a^+$, $f(x)$ becomes negatively infinite:

$$\lim_{x \to a^+} f(x) = -\infty$$

In Figures 13.49(c) and (d), we have

$$\lim_{x \to a^-} f(x) = \infty \quad \text{and} \quad \lim_{x \to a^-} f(x) = -\infty$$

respectively.

Loosely speaking, we can say that each graph in Figure 13.49 "blows up" around the dashed vertical line $x = a$, in the sense that a one-sided limit of $f(x)$ at a is either ∞ or $-\infty$. The line $x = a$ is called a *vertical asymptote* for the graph. A vertical asymptote is not part of the graph but is a useful aid in sketching it because part of the graph approaches the asymptote. Because of the explosion around $x = a$, the function is *not* continuous at a.

> **Definition**
>
> The line $x = a$ is a **vertical asymptote** for the graph of the function f if and only if at least one of the following is true:
>
> $$\lim_{x \to a^+} f(x) = \pm\infty$$
>
> or
>
> $$\lim_{x \to a^-} f(x) = \pm\infty$$

To determine vertical asymptotes, we must find values of x around which $f(x)$ increases or decreases without bound. For a rational function (a quotient of two polynomials) *expressed in lowest terms*, these x-values are precisely those for which the denominator is zero but the numerator is not zero. For example, consider the rational function

$$f(x) = \frac{3x - 5}{x - 2}$$

When x is 2, the denominator is 0, but the numerator is not. If x is slightly larger than 2, then $x - 2$ is both close to 0 and positive, and $3x - 5$ is close to 1. Thus, $(3x - 5)/(x - 2)$ is very large, so

$$\lim_{x \to 2^+} \frac{3x - 5}{x - 2} = \infty$$

This limit is sufficient to conclude that the line $x = 2$ is a vertical asymptote. Because we are ultimately interested in the behavior of a function around a vertical asymptote, it is worthwhile to examine what happens to this function as x approaches 2 from the left. If x is slightly less than 2, then $x - 2$ is very close to 0 but negative, and $3x - 5$ is close to 1. Hence, $(3x - 5)/(x - 2)$ is "very negative," so

$$\lim_{x \to 2^-} \frac{3x - 5}{x - 2} = -\infty$$

We conclude that the function increases without bound as $x \to 2^+$ and decreases without bound as $x \to 2^-$. The graph appears in Figure 13.50.

CAUTION!

To see that the proviso about *lowest terms* is necessary, observe that
$$f(x) = \frac{3x - 5}{x - 2} = \frac{(3x - 5)(x - 2)}{(x - 2)^2} \text{ so}$$
that $x = 2$ is a vertical asymptote of
$\dfrac{(3x - 5)(x - 2)}{(x - 2)^2}$, and here 2 makes both
the denominator *and* the numerator 0.

FIGURE 13.50 Graph of $y = \dfrac{3x - 5}{x - 2}$.

In summary, we have a rule for vertical asymptotes.

Vertical-Asymptote Rule for Rational Functions

Suppose that

$$f(x) = \frac{P(x)}{Q(x)}$$

where P and Q are polynomial functions and the quotient is in lowest terms. The line $x = a$ is a vertical asymptote for the graph of f if and only if $Q(a) = 0$ and $P(a) \neq 0$.

[It might be thought here that "lowest terms" rules out the possibility of a value a making *both* denominator *and* numerator 0, but consider the rational function $\dfrac{(3x - 5)(x - 2)}{(x - 2)}$. Here we cannot divide numerator and denominator by $x - 2$, to obtain the polynomial $3x - 5$, because the domain of the latter is not equal to the domain of the former.]

EXAMPLE 1   Finding Vertical Asymptotes

Determine vertical asymptotes for the graph of

$$f(x) = \frac{x^2 - 4x}{x^2 - 4x + 3}$$

Solution: Since f is a rational function, the vertical-asymptote rule applies. Writing

$$f(x) = \frac{x(x - 4)}{(x - 3)(x - 1)} \qquad \text{factoring}$$

makes it clear that the denominator is 0 when x is 3 or 1. Neither of these values makes the numerator 0. Thus, the lines $x = 3$ and $x = 1$ are vertical asymptotes. (See Figure 13.51.)

Now Work Problem 1 ◁

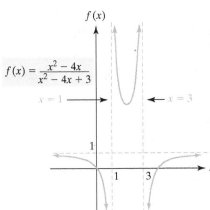

FIGURE 13.51   Graph of $f(x) = \dfrac{x^2 - 4x}{x^2 - 4x + 3}$.

Although the vertical-asymptote rule guarantees that the lines $x = 3$ and $x = 1$ are vertical asymptotes, it does not indicate the precise nature of the "blow-up" around these lines. A precise analysis requires the use of one-sided limits.

Horizontal and Oblique Asymptotes

A curve $y = f(x)$ may have other kinds of asymptote. In Figure 13.52(a), as x increases without bound ($x \to \infty$), the graph approaches the horizontal line $y = b$. That is,

$$\lim_{x \to \infty} f(x) = b$$

In Figure 13.52(b), as x becomes negatively infinite, the graph approaches the horizontal line $y = b$. That is,

$$\lim_{x \to -\infty} f(x) = b$$

In each case, the dashed line $y = b$ is called a *horizontal asymptote* for the graph. It is a horizontal line around which the graph "settles" either as $x \to \infty$ or as $x \to -\infty$.

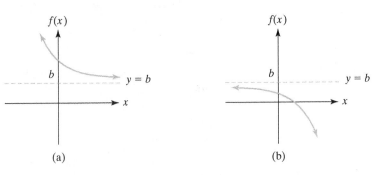

(a)   (b)

FIGURE 13.52   Horizontal asymptotes $y = b$.

In summary, we have the following definition:

> **Definition**
>
> Let f be a function. The line $y = b$ is a **horizontal asymptote** for the graph of f if and only if at least one of the following is true:
> $$\lim_{x \to \infty} f(x) = b \quad \text{or} \quad \lim_{x \to -\infty} f(x) = b$$

To test for horizontal asymptotes, we must find the limits of $f(x)$ as $x \to \infty$ and as $x \to -\infty$. To illustrate, we again consider

$$f(x) = \frac{3x - 5}{x - 2}$$

Since this is a rational function, we can use the procedures of Section 10.2 to find the limits. Because the dominant term in the numerator is $3x$ and the dominant term in the denominator is x, we have

$$\lim_{x \to \infty} \frac{3x - 5}{x - 2} = \lim_{x \to \infty} \frac{3x}{x} = \lim_{x \to \infty} 3 = 3$$

Thus, the line $y = 3$ is a horizontal asymptote. (See Figure 13.53.) Also,

$$\lim_{x \to -\infty} \frac{3x - 5}{x - 2} = \lim_{x \to -\infty} \frac{3x}{x} = \lim_{x \to -\infty} 3 = 3$$

Hence, the graph settles down near the horizontal line $y = 3$ both as $x \to \infty$ and as $x \to -\infty$.

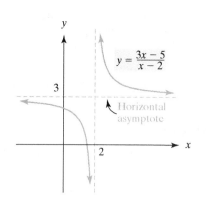

FIGURE 13.53 Graph of $f(x) = \dfrac{3x - 5}{x - 2}$.

EXAMPLE 2 Finding Horizontal Asymptotes

Find horizontal asymptotes for the graph of

$$f(x) = \frac{x^2 - 4x}{x^2 - 4x + 3}$$

Solution: We have

$$\lim_{x \to \infty} \frac{x^2 - 4x}{x^2 - 4x + 3} = \lim_{x \to \infty} \frac{x^2}{x^2} = \lim_{x \to \infty} 1 = 1$$

Therefore, the line $y = 1$ is a horizontal asymptote. The same result is obtained for $x \to -\infty$. (Refer to Figure 13.51.)

Now Work Problem 11 ◁

Horizontal asymptotes arising from limits such as $\lim_{t \to \infty} f(t) = b$, where t is thought of as *time,* can be important in business applications as expressions of long-term behavior. For example, in Section 9.3 we discussed long-term market share.

If we rewrite $\lim_{x \to \infty} f(x) = b$ as $\lim_{x \to \infty} (f(x) - b) = 0$, then another possibility is suggested. For it might be that the long-term behavior of f, while not constant, is linear. This leads us to the following:

> **Definition**
>
> Let f be a function. The line $y = mx + b$ is a **nonvertical asymptote** for the graph of f if and only if at least one of the following is true:
> $$\lim_{x \to \infty} (f(x) - (mx + b)) = 0 \quad \text{or} \quad \lim_{x \to -\infty} (f(x) - (mx + b)) = 0$$

Of course, if $m = 0$, then we have just repeated the definition of horizontal asymptote. But if $m \neq 0$, then $y = mx + b$ is the equation of a nonhorizontal (and nonvertical) line with slope m that is sometimes described as *oblique.* Thus to say that $\lim_{x \to \infty} (f(x) - (mx + b)) = 0$ is to say that for large values of x, the graph settles down near the line $y = mx + b$, often called an *oblique asympote* for the graph.

If $f(x) = \dfrac{P(x)}{Q(x)}$, where the degree of P is one more than the degree of Q, then long divison allows us to write $\dfrac{P(x)}{Q(x)} = (mx + b) + \dfrac{R(x)}{Q(x)}$, where $m \neq 0$ and where either

$R(x)$ is the zero polynomial or the degree of R is strictly less than the degree of Q. In this case, $y = mx + b$ will be an oblique asymptote for the graph of f. The next example will illustrate.

EXAMPLE 3   Finding an Oblique Asymptote

Find the oblique asyptote for the graph of the rational function

$$y = f(x) = \frac{10x^2 + 9x + 5}{5x + 2}$$

Solution: Since the degree of the numerator is 2, one greater than the degree of the denominator, we use long division to express

$$f(x) = \frac{10x^2 + 9x + 5}{5x + 2} = 2x + 1 + \frac{3}{5x + 2}$$

Thus

$$\lim_{x \to \pm\infty} (f(x) - (2x + 1)) = \lim_{x \to \pm\infty} \frac{3}{5x + 2} = 0$$

which shows that $y = 2x + 1$ is an oblique asymptote, in fact the only nonvertical asymptote, as we explain below. On the other hand, it is clear that $x = -\dfrac{2}{5}$ is a vertical asymptote—and the only one. (See Figure 13.54.)

Now Work Problem 35 ◁

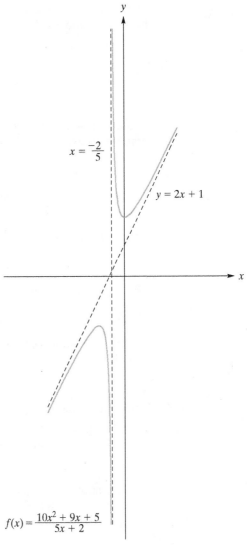

FIGURE 13.54   Graph of $f(x) = \dfrac{10x^2 + 9x + 5}{5x + 2}$ has an oblique asymptote.

A few remarks about asymptotes are appropriate now. With vertical asymptotes, we are examining the behavior of a graph around specific x-values. However, with nonvertical asymptotes we are examining the graph as x becomes unbounded. Although a graph may have numerous vertical asymptotes, it can have at most two different nonvertical asymptotes—possibly one for $x \to \infty$ and possibly one for $x \to -\infty$. If, for example, the graph has two horizontal asymptotes, then there can be no oblique asymptotes.

From Section 10.2, when the numerator of a rational function has degree greater than that of the denominator, no limit exists as $x \to \infty$ or $x \to -\infty$. From this observation, we conclude that *whenever the degree of the numerator of a rational function is greater than the degree of the denominator, the graph of the function cannot have a horizontal asymptote.* Similarly, it can be shown that if the degree of the numerator of a rational function is more than one greater than the degree of the denominator, the function cannot have an oblique asymptote.

EXAMPLE 4 Finding Horizontal and Vertical Asymptotes

Find vertical and horizontal asymptotes for the graph of the polynomial function

$$y = f(x) = x^3 + 2x$$

Solution: We begin with vertical asymptotes. This is a rational function with denominator 1, which is never zero. By the vertical-asymptote rule, there are no vertical asymptotes. Because the degree of the numerator (3) is greater than the degree of the denominator (0), there are no horizontal asymptotes. However, let us examine the behavior of the graph of f as $x \to \infty$ and $x \to -\infty$. We have

$$\lim_{x \to \infty} (x^3 + 2x) = \lim_{x \to \infty} x^3 = \infty$$

and

$$\lim_{x \to -\infty} (x^3 + 2x) = \lim_{x \to -\infty} x^3 = -\infty$$

Thus, as $x \to \infty$, the graph must extend indefinitely upward, and as $x \to -\infty$, the graph must extend indefinitely downward. (See Figure 13.55.)

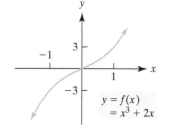

FIGURE 13.55 Graph of $y = x^3 + 2x$ has neither horizontal nor vertical asymptotes.

Now Work Problem 9 ◁

The results in Example 3 can be generalized to any polynomial function:

A polynomial function of degree greater than 1 has no asymptotes.

EXAMPLE 5 Finding Horizontal and Vertical Asymptotes

Find horizontal and vertical asymptotes for the graph of $y = e^x - 1$.

Solution: Testing for horizontal asymptotes, we let $x \to \infty$. Then e^x increases without bound, so

$$\lim_{x \to \infty} (e^x - 1) = \infty$$

Thus, the graph does not settle down as $x \to \infty$. However, as $x \to -\infty$, we have $e^x \to 0$, so

$$\lim_{x \to -\infty} (e^x - 1) = \lim_{x \to -\infty} e^x - \lim_{x \to -\infty} 1 = 0 - 1 = -1$$

Therefore, the line $y = -1$ is a horizontal asymptote. The graph has no vertical asymptotes because $e^x - 1$ neither increases nor decreases without bound around any fixed value of x. (See Figure 13.56.)

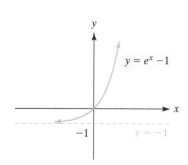

FIGURE 13.56 Graph of $y = e^x - 1$ has a horizontal asymptote.

Now Work Problem 23 ◁

Curve Sketching

In this section we show how to graph a function by making use of all the curve-sketching tools that we have developed.

> **EXAMPLE 6   Curve Sketching**

Sketch the graph of $y = \dfrac{1}{4 - x^2}$.

Solution:

Intercepts   When $x = 0$, $y = \frac{1}{4}$. If $y = 0$, then $0 = 1/(4 - x^2)$, which has no solution. Thus $(0, \frac{1}{4})$ is the only intercept. However, the factorization

$$y = \frac{1}{4 - x^2} = \frac{1}{(2 + x)(2 - x)}$$

allows us to construct the following sign chart, Figure 13.57, for y, showing where the graph lies below the x-axis $(-)$ and where it lies above the the x-axis $(+)$.

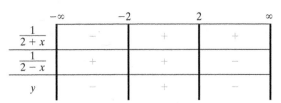

FIGURE 13.57   Sign chart for $y = \dfrac{1}{4 - x^2}$.

Symmetry   There is symmetry about the y-axis:

$$y(-x) = \frac{1}{4 - (-x)^2} = \frac{1}{4 - x^2} = y(x)$$

Since y is a function of x (and not the constant function 0), there can be no symmetry about the x-axis and hence no symmetry about the origin. Since x is not a function of y (and y is a function of x), there can be no symmetry about $y = x$ either.

Asymptotes   From the factorization of y above, we see that $x = -2$ and $x = 2$ are vertical asymptotes. Testing for horizontal asymptotes, we have

$$\lim_{x \to \pm\infty} \frac{1}{4 - x^2} = \lim_{x \to \pm\infty} \frac{1}{-x^2} = -\lim_{x \to \pm\infty} \frac{1}{x^2} = 0$$

Thus, $y = 0$ (the x-axis) is the only nonvertical asymptote.

Maxima and Minima   Since $y = (4 - x^2)^{-1}$,

$$y' = -1(4 - x^2)^{-2}(-2x) = \frac{2x}{(4 - x^2)^2}$$

We see that y' is 0 when $x = 0$ and y' is undefined when $x = \pm 2$. However, only 0 is a critical value, because y is not defined at ± 2. The sign chart for y' follows. (See Figure 13.58.)

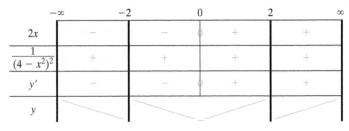

FIGURE 13.58   Sign chart for $y' = \dfrac{2x}{(4 - x^2)^2}$

The sign chart shows clearly that the function is decreasing on $(-\infty, -2)$ and $(-2, 0)$, increasing on $(0, 2)$ and $(2, \infty)$, and that there is a relative minimum at 0.

Concavity

$$y'' = \frac{(4 - x^2)^2(2) - (2x)2(4 - x^2)(-2x)}{(4 - x^2)^4}$$

$$= \frac{2(4 - x^2)[(4 - x^2) - (2x)(-2x)]}{(4 - x^2)^4} = \frac{2(4 + 3x^2)}{(4 - x^2)^3}$$

Setting $y'' = 0$, we get no real roots. However, y'' is undefined when $x = \pm 2$. Although concavity may change around these values of x, the values cannot correspond to inflection points because they are not in the domain of the function. There are three intervals to test for concavity. (See the sign chart in Figure 13.59.)

The sign chart shows that the graph is concave up on $(-2, 2)$ and concave down on $(-\infty, -2)$ and $(2, \infty)$.

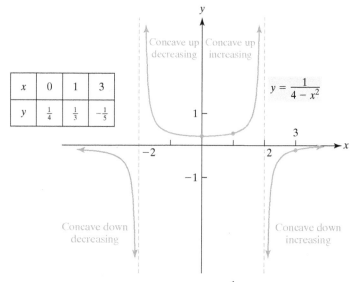

x	0	1	3
y	$\frac{1}{4}$	$\frac{1}{3}$	$-\frac{1}{5}$

	$-\infty$		-2		2		∞
$4 + 3x^2$		$+$		$+$		$+$	
$\dfrac{1}{(4 - x^2)^3}$		$-$		$+$		$-$	
y''		$-$		$+$		$-$	
y		$\cap$		$\cup$		$\cap$	

FIGURE 13.59 Concavity analysis.

FIGURE 13.60 Graph of $y = \dfrac{1}{4 - x^2}$.

Discussion   Only one point on the curve, $(0, 1/4)$, has arisen as a special point that must be plotted (both because it is an intercept and a local minimum). We might wish to plot a few more points as in the table in Figure 13.60, but note that any such extra points are only of value if they are on the same side of the y-axis (because of symmetry). Taking account of all the information gathered, we obtain the graph in Figure 13.60.

Now Work Problem 31 ◁

EXAMPLE 7   **Curve Sketching**

Sketch the graph of $y = \dfrac{4x}{x^2 + 1}$.

Solution:

Intercepts   When $x = 0$, $y = 0$; when $y = 0$, $x = 0$. Thus, $(0, 0)$ is the only intercept. Since the denominator of y is always positive, we see that the sign of y is that of x. Here we dispense with a sign chart for y. From the observations so far it follows that the graph proceeds from the third quadrant (negative x and negative y), through $(0, 0)$ to the positive quadrant (positive x and positive y).

Symmetry   There is symmetry about the origin:

$$y(-x) = \frac{4(-x)}{(-x)^2 + 1} = \frac{-4x}{x^2 + 1} = -y(x)$$

No other symmetry exists.

Asymptotes The denominator of this rational function is never 0, so there are no vertical asymptotes. Testing for horizontal asymptotes, we have

$$\lim_{x \to \pm\infty} \frac{4x}{x^2 + 1} = \lim_{x \to \pm\infty} \frac{4x}{x^2} = \lim_{x \to \pm\infty} \frac{4}{x} = 0$$

Thus, $y = 0$ (the x-axis) is a horizontal asymptote and the only nonvertical asymptote.

Maxima and Minima We have

$$y' = \frac{(x^2 + 1)(4) - 4x(2x)}{(x^2 + 1)^2} = \frac{4 - 4x^2}{(x^2 + 1)^2} = \frac{4(1 + x)(1 - x)}{(x^2 + 1)^2}$$

The critical values are $x = \pm 1$, so there are three intervals to consider in the sign chart. (See Figure 13.61.)

We see that y is decreasing on $(-\infty, -1)$ and on $(1, \infty)$, increasing on $(-1, 1)$, with relative minimum at -1 and relative maximum at 1. The relative minimum is $(-1, y(-1)) = (-1, -2)$; the relative maximum is $(1, y(1)) = (1, 2)$.

	$-\infty$		-1		1		∞
$1 + x$		$-$	0	$+$		$+$	
$1 - x$		$+$		$+$	0	$-$	
$\dfrac{1}{(x^2 + 1)^2}$		$+$		$+$		$+$	
y'		$-$	0	$+$	0	$-$	
y		↘		↗		↘	

FIGURE 13.61 Sign chart for y'.

Concavity Since $y' = \dfrac{4 - 4x^2}{(x^2 + 1)^2}$,

$$y'' = \frac{(x^2 + 1)^2(-8x) - (4 - 4x^2)(2)(x^2 + 1)(2x)}{(x^2 + 1)^4}$$

$$= \frac{8x(x^2 + 1)(x^2 - 3)}{(x^2 + 1)^4} = \frac{8x(x + \sqrt{3})(x - \sqrt{3})}{(x^2 + 1)^3}$$

Setting $y'' = 0$, we conclude that the possible points of inflection are when $x = \pm\sqrt{3}, 0$. There are four intervals to consider in the sign chart. (See Figure 13.62.)

	$-\infty$		$-\sqrt{3}$		0		$\sqrt{3}$		∞
$x + \sqrt{3}$		$-$	0	$+$		$+$		$+$	
x		$-$		$-$	0	$+$		$+$	
$x - \sqrt{3}$		$-$		$-$		$-$	0	$+$	
$\dfrac{1}{(x^2 + 1)^3}$		$+$		$+$		$+$		$+$	
y''		$-$	0	$+$	0	$-$	0	$+$	
y		$\cap$		$\cup$		$\cap$		$\cup$	

FIGURE 13.62 Concavity analysis for $y = \dfrac{4x}{x^2 + 1}$.

Inflection points occur at $x = 0$ and $\pm\sqrt{3}$. The inflection points are

$$(-\sqrt{3}, y(\sqrt{3})) = (-\sqrt{3}, -\sqrt{3}) \quad (0, y(0)) = (0, 0) \quad (\sqrt{3}, y(\sqrt{3})) = (\sqrt{3}, \sqrt{3})$$

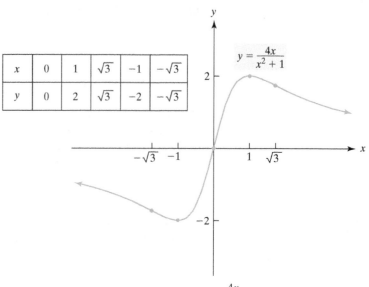

x	0	1	$\sqrt{3}$	-1	$-\sqrt{3}$
y	0	2	$\sqrt{3}$	-2	$-\sqrt{3}$

FIGURE 13.63   Graph of $y = \dfrac{4x}{x^2+1}$.

Discussion   After consideration of all of the preceding information, the graph of $y = 4x/(x^2+1)$ is given in Figure 13.63, together with a table of important points.

Now Work Problem 39 ◁

PROBLEMS 13.5

In Problems 1–24, find the vertical asymptotes and the nonvertical asymptotes for the graphs of the functions. Do not sketch the graphs.

1. $y = \dfrac{x}{x-1}$

2. $y = \dfrac{x+1}{x}$

3. $f(x) = \dfrac{x+5}{2x+7}$

4. $y = \dfrac{2x+1}{2x+1}$

5. $y = \dfrac{4}{x}$

6. $y = 1 - \dfrac{2}{x^2}$

7. $y = \dfrac{1}{x^2-1}$

8. $y = \dfrac{x}{x^2-9}$

9. $y = x^2 - 5x + 5$

10. $y = \dfrac{x^4}{x^3-4}$

11. $f(x) = \dfrac{2x^2}{x^2+x-6}$

12. $f(x) = \dfrac{x^3}{5}$

13. $y = \dfrac{15x^2+31x+1}{x^2-7}$

14. $y = \dfrac{2x^3+1}{3x(2x-1)(4x-3)}$

15. $y = \dfrac{2}{x-3} + 5$

16. $f(x) = \dfrac{x^2-1}{2x^2-9x+4}$

17. $f(x) = \dfrac{3-x^4}{x^3+x^2}$

18. $y = \dfrac{5x^2+7x^3+9x^4}{3x^2}$

19. $y = \dfrac{x^2-3x-4}{1+4x+4x^2}$

20. $y = \dfrac{x^4+1}{1-x^4}$

21. $y = \dfrac{9x^2-16}{2(3x+4)^2}$

22. $y = \dfrac{2}{5} + \dfrac{2x}{12x^2+5x-2}$

23. $y = 5e^{x-3} - 2$

24. $f(x) = 12e^{-x}$

In Problems 25–46, determine intervals on which the function is increasing, decreasing, concave up, and concave down; relative maxima and minima; inflection points; symmetry; vertical and nonvertical asymptotes; and those intercepts that can be obtained conveniently. Then sketch the curve.

25. $y = \dfrac{3}{x}$

26. $y = \dfrac{2}{2x-3}$

27. $y = \dfrac{x}{x-1}$

28. $y = \dfrac{50}{\sqrt{3x}}$

29. $y = x^2 + \dfrac{1}{x^2}$

30. $y = \dfrac{3x^2-5x-1}{x-2}$

31. $y = \dfrac{1}{x^2-1}$

32. $y = \dfrac{1}{x^2+1}$

33. $y = \dfrac{2+x}{3-x}$

34. $y = \dfrac{1+x}{x^2}$

35. $y = \dfrac{x^2}{7x+4}$

36. $y = \dfrac{x^3+1}{x}$

37. $y = \dfrac{9}{9x^2-6x-8}$

38. $y = \dfrac{4x^2+2x+1}{2x^2}$

39. $y = \dfrac{3x+1}{(3x-2)^2}$

40. $y = \dfrac{3x+1}{(6x+5)^2}$

41. $y = \dfrac{x^2-1}{x^3}$

42. $y = \dfrac{3x}{(x-2)^2}$

43. $y = 2x + 1 + \dfrac{1}{x-1}$

44. $y = \dfrac{3x^4+1}{x^3}$

45. $y = \dfrac{-3x^2+2x-5}{3x^2-2x-1}$

46. $y = 3x + 2 + \dfrac{1}{3x+2}$

47. Sketch the graph of a function f such that $f(0) = 0$, there is a horizontal asymptote $y = 1$ for $x \to \pm\infty$, there is a vertical asymptote $x = 2$, both $f'(x) < 0$ and $f''(x) < 0$ for $x < 2$, and both $f'(x) < 0$ and $f''(x) > 0$ for $x > 2$.

48. Sketch the graph of a function f such that $f(0) = -4$ and $f(4) = -2$, there is a horizontal asymptote $y = -3$ for $x \to \pm\infty$,

there is a vertical asymptote $x = 2$, both $f'(x) < 0$ and $f''(x) < 0$ for $x < 2$, and both $f'(x) < 0$ and $f''(x) > 0$ for $x > 2$.

49. Sketch the graph of a function f such that $f(0) = 0$, there is a horizontal asymptote $y = 0$ for $x \to \pm\infty$, there are vertical asymptotes $x = -1$ and $x = 2$, $f'(x) < 0$ for $x < -1$ and $-1 < x < 2$, and $f''(x) < 0$ for $x > 2$.

50. Sketch the graph of a function f such that $f(-2) = 2$, $f(0) = 0$, $f(2) = 0$, there is a horizontal asymptote $y = 1$ for $x \to \pm\infty$, there are vertical asymptotes $x = -1$ and $x = 1$, $f''(x) > 0$ for $x < -1$, and $f'(x) < 0$ for $-1 < x < 1$ and $f''(x) < 0$ for $1 < x$.

51. Purchasing Power In discussing the time pattern of purchasing, Mantell and Sing[11] use the curve

$$y = \frac{x}{a + bx}$$

as a mathematical model. Find the asymptotes for their model.

52. Sketch the graphs of $y = 6 - 3e^{-x}$ and $y = 6 + 3e^{-x}$. Show that they are asymptotic to the same line. What is the equation of this line?

53. Market for Product For a new product, the yearly number of thousand packages sold, y, t years after its introduction is predicted to be given by

$$y = f(t) = 250 - 83e^{-t}$$

Show that $y = 250$ is a horizontal asymptote for the graph. This reveals that after the product is established with consumers, the market tends to be constant.

54. Graph $y = \dfrac{x^2 - 2}{x^3 + \frac{7}{2}x^2 + 12x + 1}$. From the graph, locate any horizontal or vertical asymptotes.

55. Graph $y = \dfrac{6x^3 - 2x^2 + 6x - 1}{3x^3 - 2x^2 - 18x + 12}$. From the graph, locate any horizontal or vertical asymptotes.

56. Graph $y = \dfrac{\ln(x + 4)}{x^2 - 8x + 5}$ in the standard window. The graph suggests that there are two vertical asymptotes of the form $x = k$, where $k > 0$. Also, it appears that the graph "begins" near $x = -4$. As $x \to -4^+$, $\ln(x + 4) \to -\infty$ and $x^2 - 8x + 5 \to 53$. Thus, $\lim_{x \to 4^+} y = -\infty$. This gives the vertical asymptote $x = -4$. So, in reality, there are *three* vertical asymptotes. Use the zoom feature to make the asymptote $x = -4$ apparent from the display.

57. Graph $y = \dfrac{0.34e^{0.7x}}{4.2 + 0.71e^{0.7x}}$, where $x > 0$. From the graph, determine an equation of the horizontal asymptote by examining the y-values as $x \to \infty$. To confirm this equation algebraically, find $\lim_{x \to \infty} y$ by first dividing both the numerator and denominator by $e^{0.7x}$.

13.6 Applied Maxima and Minima

Objective

To model situations involving maximizing or minimizing a quantity.

By using techniques from this chapter, we can solve problems that involve maximizing or minimizing a quantity. For example, we might want to maximize profit or minimize cost. The crucial part is expressing the quantity to be maximized or minimized as a function of some variable in the problem. Then we differentiate and test the resulting critical values. For this, the first-derivative test or the second-derivative test can be used, although it may be obvious from the nature of the problem whether or not a critical value represents an appropriate answer. Because our interest is in *absolute* maxima and minima, sometimes we must examine endpoints of the domain of the function. (Very often the function used to model the situation of a problem will be the restriction to a closed interval of a function that has a large natural domain. Such *real-world* limitations tend to generate endpoints.)

The aim of this example is to set up a cost function from which cost is minimized.

EXAMPLE 1   Minimizing the Cost of a Fence

For insurance purposes, a manufacturer plans to fence in a 10,800-ft^2 rectangular storage area adjacent to a building by using the building as one side of the enclosed area. The fencing parallel to the building faces a highway and will cost \$3 per foot installed, whereas the fencing for the other two sides costs \$2 per foot installed. Find the amount of each type of fence so that the total cost of the fence will be a minimum. What is the minimum cost?

Solution: As a first step in a problem like this, it is a good idea to draw a diagram that reflects the situation. In Figure 13.64, we have labeled the length of the side parallel to the building as x and the lengths of the other two sides as y, where x and y are in feet.

Since we want to minimize cost, our next step is to determine a function that gives cost. The cost obviously depends on how much fencing is along the highway

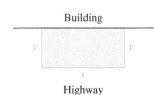

Building

Highway

FIGURE 13.64 Fencing problem of Example 1.

---

[11]L. H. Mantell and F. P. Sing, *Economics for Business Decisions* (New York: McGraw-Hill Book Company, 1972), p. 107.

and how much is along the other two sides. Along the highway the cost per foot is 3 (dollars), so the total cost of that fencing is $3x$. Similarly, along *each* of the other two sides, the cost is $2y$. Thus, the total cost of the fencing is given by the cost function

$$C = 3x + 2y + 2y$$

that is,

$$C = 3x + 4y \qquad (1)$$

We need to find the absolute minimum value of C. To do this, we use the techniques discussed in this chapter; that is, we examine C at critical values (and any endpoints) in the domain. But in order to differentiate, we need to first express C as a function of one variable only. [Equation (1) gives C as a function of *two* variables, x and y.] We can accomplish this by first finding a relationship between x and y. From the statement of the problem, we are told that the storage area, which is xy, must be 10,800:

$$xy = 10,800 \qquad (2)$$

With this equation, we can express one variable (say, y) in terms of the other (x). Then, substitution into Equation (1) will give C as a function of one variable only. Solving Equation (2) for y gives

$$y = \frac{10,800}{x} \qquad (3)$$

Substituting into Equation (1), we have

$$C = C(x) = 3x + 4\left(\frac{10,800}{x}\right)$$

$$C(x) = 3x + \frac{43,200}{x} \qquad (4)$$

From the physical nature of the problem, the domain of C is $x > 0$.

We now find dC/dx, set it equal to 0, and solve for x. We have

$$\frac{dC}{dx} = 3 - \frac{43,200}{x^2} \qquad \frac{d}{dx}(43,200x^{-1}) = -43,200x^{-2}$$

$$3 - \frac{43,200}{x^2} = 0$$

$$3 = \frac{43,200}{x^2}$$

from which it follows that

$$x^2 = \frac{43,200}{3} = 14,400$$

$$x = 120 \qquad \text{since } x > 0$$

Thus, 120 is the *only* critical value, and there are no endpoints to consider. To test this value, we will use the second-derivative test.

$$\frac{d^2C}{dx^2} = \frac{86,400}{x^3}$$

When $x = 120$, $d^2C/dx^2 > 0$, so we conclude that $x = 120$ gives a relative minimum. However, since 120 is the only critical value on the open interval $(0, \infty)$ and C is continuous on that interval, this relative minimum must also be an absolute minimum.

We are not done yet! The questions posed in the problem must be answered. For minimum cost, the number of feet of fencing along the highway is 120. When $x = 120$, we have, from Equation (3), $y = 10,800/120 = 90$. Therefore, the number of feet of fencing for the other two sides is $2y = 180$. It follows that 120 ft of the \$3 fencing and 180 ft of the \$2 fencing are needed. The minimum cost can be obtained from the cost function, Equation (4), and is

$$C(120) = 3x + \frac{43,200}{x}\bigg|_{x=120} = 3(120) + \frac{43,200}{120} = 720$$

Now Work Problem 3 ◁

Based on Example 1, the following guide may be helpful in solving an applied maximum or minimum problem:

> **Guide for Solving Applied Max–Min Problems**
> **Step 1.** When appropriate, draw a diagram that reflects the information in the problem.
> **Step 2.** Set up an expression for the quantity that you want to maximize or minimize.
> **Step 3.** Write the expression in step 2 as a function of one variable, and note the domain of this function. The domain may be implied by the nature of the problem itself.
> **Step 4.** Find the critical values of the function. After testing each critical value, determine which one gives the absolute extreme value you are seeking. If the domain of the function includes endpoints, be sure to also examine function values at these endpoints.
> **Step 5.** Based on the results of step 4, answer the question(s) posed in the problem.

EXAMPLE 2   Maximizing Revenue

This example involves maximizing revenue when a demand equation is known.

The demand equation for a manufacturer's product is

$$p = \frac{80 - q}{4} \quad 0 \le q \le 80$$

where q is the number of units and p is the price per unit. At what value of q will there be maximum revenue? What is the maximum revenue?

Solution: Let r represent total revenue, which is the quantity to be maximized. Since

$$\text{revenue} = (\text{price})(\text{quantity})$$

we have

$$r = pq = \frac{80 - q}{4} \cdot q = \frac{80q - q^2}{4} = r(q)$$

where $0 \le q \le 80$. Setting $dr/dq = 0$, we obtain

$$\frac{dr}{dq} = \frac{80 - 2q}{4} = 0$$
$$80 - 2q = 0$$
$$q = 40$$

Thus, 40 is the only critical value. Now we see whether this gives a maximum. Examining the first derivative for $0 \le q < 40$, we have $dr/dq > 0$, so r is increasing. If $q > 40$, then $dr/dq < 0$, so r is decreasing. Because to the left of 40 we have r increasing, and to the right r is decreasing, we conclude that $q = 40$ gives the *absolute* maximum revenue, namely

$$r(40) = (80(40) - (40)^2)/4 = 400$$

Now Work Problem 7 ◁

EXAMPLE 3   Minimizing Average Cost

This example involves minimizing average cost when the cost function is known.

A manufacturer's total-cost function is given by

$$c = c(q) = \frac{q^2}{4} + 3q + 400$$

where c is the total cost of producing q units. At what level of output will average cost per unit be a minimum? What is this minimum?

Solution: The quantity to be minimized is the average cost $\bar{c}$. The average-cost function is

$$\bar{c} = \bar{c}(q) = \frac{c}{q} = \frac{\dfrac{q^2}{4} + 3q + 400}{q} = \frac{q}{4} + 3 + \frac{400}{q} \tag{5}$$

Here q must be positive. To minimize $\bar{c}$, we differentiate:

$$\frac{d\bar{c}}{dq} = \frac{1}{4} - \frac{400}{q^2} = \frac{q^2 - 1600}{4q^2}$$

To get the critical values, we solve $d\bar{c}/dq = 0$:

$$q^2 - 1600 = 0$$

$$(q - 40)(q + 40) = 0$$

$$q = 40 \qquad \text{since } q > 0$$

To determine whether this level of output gives a relative minimum, we will use the second-derivative test. We have

$$\frac{d^2\bar{c}}{dq^2} = \frac{800}{q^3}$$

which is positive for $q = 40$. Thus, $\bar{c}$ has a relative minimum when $q = 40$. We note that $\bar{c}$ is continuous for $q > 0$. Since $q = 40$ is the only relative extremum, we conclude that this relative minimum is indeed an absolute minimum. Substituting $q = 40$ in Equation (5) gives the minimum average cost $\bar{c}(40) = \dfrac{40}{4} + 3 + \dfrac{400}{40} = 23$.

Now Work Problem 5 ◁

EXAMPLE 4 Maximization Applied to Enzymes

This example is a biological application involving maximizing the rate at which an enzyme is formed. The equation involved is a literal equation.

An enzyme is a protein that acts as a catalyst for increasing the rate of a chemical reaction that occurs in cells. In a certain reaction, an enzyme is converted to another enzyme called the product. The product acts as a catalyst for its own formation. The rate R at which the product is formed (with respect to time) is given by

$$R = kp(l - p)$$

where l is the total initial amount of both enzymes, p is the amount of the product enzyme, and k is a positive constant. For what value of p will R be a maximum?

Solution: We can write $R = k(pl - p^2)$. Setting $dR/dp = 0$ and solving for p gives

$$\frac{dR}{dp} = k(l - 2p) = 0$$

$$p = \frac{l}{2}$$

Now, $d^2R/dp^2 = -2k$. Since $k > 0$, the second derivative is always negative. Hence, $p = l/2$ gives a relative maximum. Moreover, since R is a continuous function of p, we conclude that we indeed have an absolute maximum when $p = l/2$.

◁

Calculus can be applied to inventory decisions, as the following example shows.

EXAMPLE 5 Economic Lot Size

This example involves determining the number of units in a production run in order to minimize certain costs.

A company annually produces and sells 10,000 units of a product. Sales are uniformly distributed throughout the year. The company wishes to determine the number of units to be manufactured in each production run in order to minimize total annual setup costs and carrying costs. The same number of units is produced in each run. This number is referred to as the **economic lot size or economic order quantity.** The production cost of each unit is \$20, and carrying costs (insurance, interest, storage, etc.) are estimated to be 10% of the value of the average inventory. Setup costs per production run are \$40. Find the economic lot size.

Solution: Let q be the number of units in a production run. Since sales are distributed at a uniform rate, we will assume that inventory varies uniformly from q to 0 between production runs. Thus, we take the average inventory to be $q/2$ units. The production costs are \$20 per unit, so the value of the average inventory is $20(q/2)$. Carrying costs are 10% of this value:

$$0.10(20)\left(\frac{q}{2}\right)$$

The number of production runs per year is $10{,}000/q$. Hence, the total setup costs are

$$40\left(\frac{10{,}000}{q}\right)$$

Therefore, the total of the annual carrying costs and setup costs is given by

$$C = 0.10(20)\left(\frac{q}{2}\right) + 40\left(\frac{10{,}000}{q}\right)$$

$$= q + \frac{400{,}000}{q} \qquad q > 0$$

$$\frac{dC}{dq} = 1 - \frac{400{,}000}{q^2} = \frac{q^2 - 400{,}000}{q^2}$$

Setting $dC/dq = 0$, we get

$$q^2 = 400{,}000$$

Since $q > 0$,

$$q = \sqrt{400{,}000} = 200\sqrt{10} \approx 632.5$$

To determine whether this value of q minimizes C, we will examine the first derivative. If $0 < q < \sqrt{400{,}000}$, then $dC/dq < 0$. If $q > \sqrt{400{,}000}$, then $dC/dq > 0$. We conclude that there is an *absolute* minimum at $q = 632.5$. The number of production runs is $10{,}000/632.5 \approx 15.8$. For practical purposes, there would be 16 lots, each having the economic lot size of 625 units.

Now Work Problem 29 ◁

EXAMPLE 6   **Maximizing TV Cable Company Revenue**

The aim of this example is to set up a revenue function from which revenue is maximized over a closed interval.

The Vista TV Cable Co. currently has 100,000 subscribers who are each paying a monthly rate of \$40. A survey reveals that there will be 1000 more subscribers for each \$0.25 decrease in the rate. At what rate will maximum revenue be obtained, and how many subscribers will there be at this rate?

Solution: Let x be the number of \$0.25 decreases. The monthly rate is then $40 - 0.25x$, where $0 \le x \le 160$ (the rate cannot be negative), and the number of *new* subscribers is $1000x$. Thus, the total number of subscribers is $100{,}000 + 1000x$. We want to maximize the revenue, which is given by

$$r = (\text{number of subscribers})(\text{rate per subscriber})$$

$$= (100{,}000 + 1000x)(40 - 0.25x)$$

$$= 1000(100 + x)(40 - 0.25x)$$

$$= 1000(4000 + 15x - 0.25x^2)$$

Setting $r' = 0$ and solving for x, we have

$$r' = 1000(15 - 0.5x) = 0$$

$$x = 30$$

Since the domain of r is the closed interval [0, 160], the absolute maximum value of r must occur at $x = 30$ or at one of the endpoints of the interval. We now compute r at these three points:

$$r(0) = 1000(4000 + 15(0) - 0.25(0)^2) = 4{,}000{,}000$$

$$r(30) = 1000(4000 + 15(30) - 0.25(30)^2) = 4{,}225{,}000$$

$$r(160) = 1000(4000 + 15(160) - 0.25(160)^2) = 0$$

Accordingly, the maximum revenue occurs when $x = 30$. This corresponds to thirty \$0.25 decreases, for a total decrease of \$7.50; that is, the monthly rate is \$40 − \$7.50 = \$32.50. The number of subscribers at that rate is $100{,}000 + 30(1000) = 130{,}000$.

Now Work Problem 19 ◁

EXAMPLE 7 Maximizing the Number of Recipients of Health-Care Benefits

Here we maximize a function over a closed interval.

An article in a sociology journal stated that if a particular health-care program for the elderly were initiated, then t years after its start, n thousand elderly people would receive direct benefits, where

$$n = \frac{t^3}{3} - 6t^2 + 32t \quad 0 \le t \le 12$$

For what value of t does the maximum number receive benefits?

Solution: Setting $dn/dt = 0$, we have

$$\frac{dn}{dt} = t^2 - 12t + 32 = 0$$

$$(t - 4)(t - 8) = 0$$

$$t = 4 \quad \text{or} \quad t = 8$$

Since the domain of n is the closed interval [0, 12], the absolute maximum value of n must occur at $t = 0, 4, 8,$ or 12:

$$n(0) = \frac{0^3}{3} - 6(0^2) + 32(0) = 0$$

$$n(4) = \frac{4^3}{3} - 6(4^2) + 32(4) = \frac{160}{3}$$

$$n(8) = \frac{8^3}{3} - 6(8^2) + 32(8) = \frac{128}{3}$$

$$n(12) = \frac{12^3}{3} - 6(12^2) + 32(12) = \frac{288}{3} = 96$$

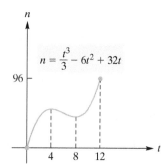

FIGURE 13.65 Graph of $n = \dfrac{t^3}{3} - 6t^2 + 32t$ on [0, 12].

Thus, an absolute maximum occurs when $t = 12$. A graph of the function is given in Figure 13.65.

Now Work Problem 15 ◁

CAUTION! ⚠

The preceding example illustrates that endpoints must not be ignored when finding absolute extrema on a closed interval.

In the next example, we use the word *monopolist*. Under a situation of monopoly, there is only one seller of a product for which there are no similar substitutes, and the seller—that is, the monopolist—controls the market. By considering the demand equation for the product, the monopolist may set the price (or volume of output) so that maximum profit will be obtained.

This example involves maximizing profit when the demand and average-cost functions are known. In the last part, a tax is imposed on the monopolist, and a new profit function is analyzed.

EXAMPLE 8 Profit Maximization

Suppose that the demand equation for a monopolist's product is $p = 400 - 2q$ and the average-cost function is $\bar{c} = 0.2q + 4 + (400/q)$, where q is number of units, and both p and $\bar{c}$ are expressed in dollars per unit.

a. Determine the level of output at which profit is maximized.
b. Determine the price at which maximum profit occurs.
c. Determine the maximum profit.
d. If, as a regulatory device, the government imposes a tax of $22 per unit on the monopolist, what is the new price for profit maximization?

Solution: We know that

$$\text{profit} = \text{total revenue} - \text{total cost}$$

Since total revenue r and total cost c are given by

$$r = pq = 400q - 2q^2$$

and

$$c = q\bar{c} = 0.2q^2 + 4q + 400$$

the profit is

$$P = r - c = 400q - 2q^2 - (0.2q^2 + 4q + 400)$$

so that

$$P(q) = 396q - 2.2q^2 - 400 \quad \text{for } q > 0 \qquad (6)$$

a. To maximize profit, we set $dP/dq = 0$:

$$\frac{dP}{dq} = 396 - 4.4q = 0$$

$$q = 90$$

Now, $d^2P/dq^2 = -4.4$ is always negative, so it is negative at the critical value $q = 90$. By the second-derivative test, then, there is a relative maximum there. Since $q = 90$ is the only critical value on $(0, \infty)$, we must have an absolute maximum there.

b. The price at which maximum profit occurs is obtained by setting $q = 90$ in the demand equation:

$$p = 400 - 2(90) = 220$$

c. The maximum profit is obtained by evaluating $P(90)$. We have

$$P(90) = 396(90) - 2.2(90)^2 - 400 = 17{,}420$$

d. The tax of $22 per unit means that for q units, the total cost increases by $22q$. The new cost function is $c_1 = 0.2q^2 + 4q + 400 + 22q$, and the new profit is given by

$$P_1 = 400q - 2q^2 - (0.2q^2 + 4q + 400 + 22q)$$

$$= 374q - 2.2q^2 - 400$$

Setting $dP_1/dq = 0$ gives

$$\frac{dP_1}{dq} = 374 - 4.4q = 0$$

$$q = 85$$

Since $d^2P_1/dq^2 = -4.4 < 0$, we conclude that, to maximize profit, the monopolist must restrict output to 85 units at a higher price of $p_1 = 400 - 2(85) = \$230$. Since this price is only $10 more than before, only part of the tax has been shifted to the consumer, and the monopolist must bear the cost of the balance. The profit now is $15,495, which is less than the former profit.

Now Work Problem 13 ◁

This discussion leads to the economic principle that when profit is maximum, marginal revenue is equal to marginal cost.

We conclude this section by using calculus to develop an important principle in economics. Suppose $p = f(q)$ is the demand function for a firm's product, where p is price per unit and q is the number of units produced and sold. Then the total revenue is given by $r = qp = qf(q)$, which is a function of q. Let the total cost of producing q units be given by the cost function $c = g(q)$. Thus, the total profit, which is total revenue minus total cost, is also a function of q, namely,

$$P(q) = r - c = qf(q) - g(q)$$

Let us consider the most profitable output for the firm. Ignoring special cases, we know that profit is maximized when $dP/dq = 0$ and $d^2P/dq^2 < 0$. We have

$$\frac{dP}{dq} = \frac{d}{dq}(r - c) = \frac{dr}{dq} - \frac{dc}{dq}$$

Consequently, $dP/dq = 0$ when

$$\frac{dr}{dq} = \frac{dc}{dq}$$

That is, at the level of maximum profit, the slope of the tangent to the total-revenue curve must equal the slope of the tangent to the total-cost curve (Figure 13.66). But dr/dq is the marginal revenue MR, and dc/dq is the marginal cost MC. Thus, under typical conditions, to maximize profit, it is necessary that

$$\text{MR} = \text{MC}$$

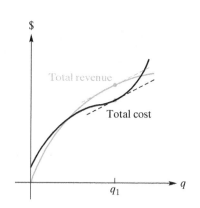

FIGURE 13.66 At maximum profit, marginal revenue equals marginal cost.

For this to indeed correspond to a maximum, it is necessary that $d^2P/dq^2 < 0$:

$$\frac{d^2P}{dq^2} = \frac{d^2}{dq^2}(r - c) = \frac{d^2r}{dq^2} - \frac{d^2c}{dq^2} < 0 \quad \text{equivalently} \quad \frac{d^2r}{dq^2} < \frac{d^2c}{dq^2}$$

That is, when MR = MC, in order to ensure maximum profit, the slope of the marginal-revenue curve must be less than the slope of the marginal-cost curve.

The condition that $d^2P/dq^2 < 0$ when $dP/dq = 0$ can be viewed another way. Equivalently, to have MR = MC correspond to a maximum, dP/dq must go from $+$ to $-$; that is, it must go from $dr/dq - dc/dq > 0$ to $dr/dq - dc/dq < 0$. Hence, as output increases, we must have MR > MC and then MR < MC. This means that at the point q_1 of maximum profit, *the marginal-cost curve must cut the marginal-revenue curve from below* (Figure 13.67). For production up to q_1, the revenue from additional output would be greater than the cost of such output, and the total profit would increase. For output beyond q_1, MC > MR, and each unit of output would add more to total costs than to total revenue. Hence, total profits would decline.

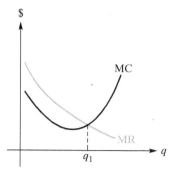

FIGURE 13.67 At maximum profit, the marginal-cost curve cuts the marginal-revenue curve from below.

PROBLEMS 13.6

In this set of problems, unless otherwise specified, p is price per unit (in dollars) and q is output per unit of time. Fixed costs refer to costs that remain constant at all levels of production during a given time period. (An example is rent.)

1. Find two numbers whose sum is 82 and whose product is as big as possible.

2. Find two nonnegative numbers whose sum is 20 and for which the product of twice one number and the square of the other number will be a maximum.

3. Fencing A company has set aside $9000 to fence in a rectangular portion of land adjacent to a stream by using the stream for one side of the enclosed area. The cost of the fencing parallel to the stream is $15 per foot installed, and the fencing for the remaining two sides costs $9 per foot installed. Find the dimensions of the maximum enclosed area.

4. Fencing The owner of the Laurel Nursery Garden Center wants to fence in 1400 ft² of land in a rectangular plot to be used for different types of shrubs. The plot is to be divided into six equal plots with five fences parallel to the same pair of sides, as shown in Figure 13.68. What is the least number of feet of fence needed?

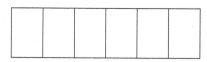

FIGURE 13.68

5. Average Cost A manufacturer finds that the total cost c of producing a product is given by the cost function

$$c = 0.05q^2 + 5q + 500$$

At what level of output will average cost per unit be a minimum?

6. Automobile Expense   The cost per hour (in dollars) of operating an automobile is given by

$$C = 0.12s - 0.0012s^2 + 0.08 \qquad 0 \le s \le 60$$

where s is the speed in miles per hour. At what speed is the cost per hour a minimum?

7. Revenue   The demand equation for a monopolist's product is

$$p = -5q + 30$$

At what price will revenue be maximized?

8. Revenue   Suppose that the demand function for a monopolist's product is of the form

$$q = Ae^{-Bp}$$

for positive constants A and B. In terms of A and B, find the value of p for which maximum revenue is obtained. Can you explain why your answer does not depend on A?

9. Weight Gain   A group of biologists studied the nutritional effects on rats that were fed a diet containing 10% protein.[12] The protein consisted of yeast and cottonseed flour. By varying the percent p of yeast in the protein mix, the group found that the (average) weight gain (in grams) of a rat over a period of time was

$$f(p) = 170 - p - \frac{1600}{p + 15} \qquad 0 \le p \le 100$$

Find (a) the maximum weight gain and (b) the minimum weight gain.

10. Drug Dose   The severity of the reaction of the human body to an initial dose D of a drug is given by[13]

$$R = f(D) = D^2 \left(\frac{C}{2} - \frac{D}{3} \right)$$

where the constant C denotes the maximum amount of the drug that may be given. Show that R has a maximum *rate of change* when $D = C/2$.

11. Profit   For a monopolist's product, the demand function is

$$p = 85 - 0.05q$$

and the cost function is

$$c = 600 + 35q$$

At what level of output will profit be maximized? At what price does this occur, and what is the profit?

12. Profit   For a monopolist, the cost per unit of producing a product is $3, and the demand equation is

$$p = \frac{10}{\sqrt{q}}$$

What price will give the greatest profit?

13. Profit   For a monopolist's product, the demand equation is

$$p = 42 - 4q$$

and the average-cost function is

$$\bar{c} = 2 + \frac{80}{q}$$

Find the profit-maximizing price.

14. Profit   For a monopolist's product, the demand function is

$$p = \frac{50}{\sqrt{q}}$$

and the average-cost function is

$$\bar{c} = \frac{1}{4} + \frac{2500}{q}$$

Find the profit-maximizing price and output.

15. Profit   A manufacturer can produce at most 120 units of a certain product each year. The demand equation for the product is

$$p = q^2 - 100q + 3200$$

and the manufacturer's average-cost function is

$$\bar{c} = \frac{2}{3}q^2 - 40q + \frac{10,000}{q}$$

Determine the profit-maximizing output q and the corresponding maximum profit.

16. Cost   A manufacturer has determined that, for a certain product, the average cost (in dollars per unit) is given by

$$\bar{c} = 2q^2 - 42q + 228 + \frac{210}{q}$$

where $3 \le q \le 12$.

(a) At what level within the interval [3, 12] should production be fixed in order to minimize total cost? What is the minimum total cost?

(b) If production were required to lie within the interval [7, 12], what value of q would minimize total cost?

17. Profit   For XYZ Manufacturing Co., total fixed costs are $1200, material and labor costs combined are $2 per unit, and the demand equation is

$$p = \frac{100}{\sqrt{q}}$$

What level of output will maximize profit? Show that this occurs when marginal revenue is equal to marginal cost. What is the price at profit maximization?

18. Revenue   A real-estate firm owns 100 garden-type apartments. At $400 per month, each apartment can be rented. However, for each $10-per-month increase, there will be two vacancies with no possibility of filling them. What rent per apartment will maximize monthly revenue?

[12]Adapted from R. Bressani, "The Use of Yeast in Human Foods," in *Single-Cell Protein,* eds. R. I. Mateles and S. R. Tannenbaum (Cambridge, MA: MIT Press, 1968).

[13]R. M. Thrall, J. A. Mortimer. K. R. Rebman, and R. F. Baum, eds., *Some Mathematical Models in Biology,* rev. ed., Report No. 40241-R-7. Prepared at University of Michigan, 1967.

19. Revenue A TV cable company has 6400 subscribers who are each paying $24 per month. It can get 160 more subscribers for each $0.50 decrease in the monthly fee. What rate will yield maximum revenue, and what will this revenue be?

20. Profit A manufacturer of a product finds that, for the first 600 units that are produced and sold, the profit is $40 per unit. The profit on each of the units beyond 600 is decreased by $0.05 times the number of additional units produced. For example, the total profit when 602 units are produced and sold is $600(40)+ 2(39.90)$. What level of output will maximize profit?

21. Container Design A container manufacturer is designing a rectangular box, open at the top and with a square base, that is to have a volume of 32 ft^3. If the box is to require the least amount of material, what must be its dimensions?

22. Container Design An open-top box with a square base is to be constructed from 192 ft^2 of material. What should be the dimensions of the box if the volume is to be a maximum? What is the maximum volume?

23. Container Design An open box is to be made by cutting equal squares from each corner of a L-inch-square piece of cardboard and then folding up the sides. Find the length of the side of the square (in terms of L) that must be cut out if the volume of the box is to be maximized. What is the maximum volume? (See Figure 13.69.)

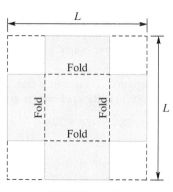

FIGURE 13.69

24. Poster Design A rectangular cardboard poster is to have 720 in^2 for printed matter. It is to have a 5-in. margin on each side and a 4-in. margin at the top and bottom. Find the dimensions of the poster so that the amount of cardboard used is minimized. (See Figure 13.70.)

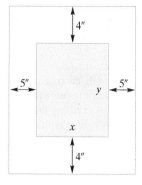

FIGURE 13.70

25. Container Design A cylindrical can, open at the top, is to have a fixed volume of K. Show that if the least amount of material is to be used, then both the radius and height are equal to $\sqrt[3]{K/\pi}$. (See Figure 13.71.)

$$\text{Volume} = \pi r^2 h$$
$$\text{Surface area} = 2\pi rh + \pi r^2$$

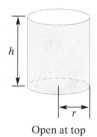

Open at top

FIGURE 13.71

26. Container Design A cylindrical can, open at the top, is to be made from a fixed amount of material, K. If the volume is to be a maximum, show that both the radius and height are equal to $\sqrt{K/(3\pi)}$. (See Figure 13.71.)

27. Profit The demand equation for a monopolist's product is

$$p = 600 - 2q$$

and the total-cost function is

$$c = 0.2q^2 + 28q + 200$$

Find the profit-maximizing output and price, and determine the corresponding profit. If the government were to impose a tax of $22 per unit on the manufacturer, what would be the new profit-maximizing output and price? What is the profit now?

28. Profit Use the *original* data in Problem 27, and assume that the government imposes a license fee of $1000 on the manufacturer. This is a lump-sum amount without regard to output. Show that the profit-maximizing price and output remain the same. Show, however, that there will be less profit.

29. Economic Lot Size A manufacturer has to produce 3000 units annually of a product that is sold at a uniform rate during the year. The production cost of each unit is $12, and carrying costs (insurance, interest, storage, et cetera) are estimated to be 19.2% of the value of average inventory. Setup costs per production run are $54. Find the economic lot size.

30. Profit For a monopolist's product, the cost function is

$$c = 0.004q^3 + 20q + 5000$$

and the demand function is

$$p = 450 - 4q$$

Find the profit-maximizing output.

31. Workshop Attendance Imperial Educational Services (I.E.S.) is considering offering a workshop in resource allocation to key personnel at Acme Corp. To make the offering economically feasible, I.E.S. feels that at least 30 persons must attend at a cost of $50 each. Moreover, I.E.S. will agree to reduce the charge for *everybody* by $1.25 for each person over the 30 who attends. How many people should be in the group for I.E.S. to maximize revenue? Assume that the maximum allowable number in the group is 40.

32. Cost of Leasing Motor The Kiddie Toy Company plans to lease an electric motor that will be used 80,000 horsepower-hours per year in manufacturing. One horsepower-hour is the work done in 1 hour by a 1-horsepower motor. The annual cost to lease a suitable motor is $200, plus $0.40 per horsepower. The cost per horsepower-hour of operating the motor is $0.008/N$, where N is the horsepower. What size motor, in horsepower, should be leased in order to minimize cost?

33. Transportation Cost   The cost of operating a truck on a thruway (excluding the salary of the driver) is

$$0.165 + \frac{s}{200}$$

dollars per mile, where s is the (steady) speed of the truck in miles per hour. The truck driver's salary is $18 per hour. At what speed should the truck driver operate the truck to make a 700-mile trip most economical?

34. Cost   For a manufacturer, the cost of making a part is $30 per unit for labor and $10 per unit for materials; overhead is fixed at $20,000 per week. If more than 5000 units are made each week, labor is $45 per unit for those units in excess of 5000. At what level of production will average cost per unit be a minimum?

35. Profit   Ms. Jones owns a small insurance agency that sells policies for a large insurance company. For each policy sold, Ms. Jones, who does not sell policies herself, is paid a commission of $50 by the insurance company. From previous experience, Ms. Jones has determined that, when she employs m salespeople,

$$q = m^3 - 15m^2 + 92m$$

policies can be sold per week. She pays each of the m salespeople a salary of $1000 per week, and her weekly fixed cost is $3000. Current office facilities can accommodate at most eight salespeople. Determine the number of salespeople that Ms. Jones should hire to maximize her weekly profit. What is the corresponding maximum profit?

36. Profit   A manufacturing company sells high-quality jackets through a chain of specialty shops. The demand equation for these jackets is

$$p = 400 - 50q$$

where p is the selling price (in dollars per jacket) and q is the demand (in thousands of jackets). If this company's marginal-cost function is given by

$$\frac{dc}{dq} = \frac{800}{q + 5}$$

show that there is a maximum profit, and determine the number of jackets that must be sold to obtain this maximum profit.

37. Chemical Production   Each day, a firm makes x tons of chemical A ($x \leq 4$) and

$$y = \frac{24 - 6x}{5 - x}$$

tons of chemical B. The profit on chemical A is $2000 per ton, and on B it is $1000 per ton. How much of chemical A should be

produced per day to maximize profit? Answer the same question if the profit on A is P per ton and that on B is $P/2$ per ton.

38. Rate of Return   To erect an office building, fixed costs are $1.44 million and include land, architect's fees, a basement, a foundation, and so on. If x floors are constructed, the cost (excluding fixed costs) is

$$c = 10x[120,000 + 3000(x - 1)]$$

The revenue per month is $60,000 per floor. How many floors will yield a maximum rate of return on investment? (Rate of return = total revenue/total cost.)

39. Gait and Power Output of an Animal   In a model by Smith,[14] the power output of an animal at a given speed as a function of its movement or *gait*, j, is found to be

$$P(j) = Aj\frac{L^4}{V} + B\frac{V^3L^2}{1 + j}$$

where A and B are constants, j is a measure of the "jumpiness" of the gait, L is a constant representing linear dimension, and V is a constant forward speed.

Assume that P is a minimum when $dP/dj = 0$. Show that when this occurs,

$$(1 + j)^2 = \frac{BV^4}{AL^2}$$

As a passing comment, Smith indicates that "at top speed, j is zero for an elephant, 0.3 for a horse, and 1 for a greyhound, approximately."

40. Traffic Flow   In a model of traffic flow on a lane of a freeway, the number of cars the lane can carry per unit time is given by[15]

$$N = \frac{-2a}{-2at_r + v - \dfrac{2al}{v}}$$

where a is the acceleration of a car when stopping ($a < 0$), t_r is the reaction time to begin braking, v is the average speed of the cars, and l is the length of a car. Assume that a, t_r, and l are constant. To find how many cars a lane can carry at most, we want to find the speed v that maximizes N. To maximize N, it suffices to minimize the denominator

$$-2at_r + v - \frac{2al}{v}$$

[14]J. M. Smith, *Mathematical Ideas in Biology* (London: Cambridge University Press, 1968).

[15]J. I. Shonle, *Environmental Applications of General Physics* (Reading, MA: Addison-Wesley Publishing Co., 1975).

(a) Find the value of v that minimizes the denominator.
(b) Evaluate your answer in part (a) when $a = -19.6 \, (\text{ft/s}^2)$, $l = 20 \, (\text{ft})$, and $t_r = 0.5 \, (\text{s})$. Your answer will be in feet per second.
(c) Find the corresponding value of N to one decimal place. Your answer will be in cars per second. Convert your answer to cars per hour.
(d) Find the relative change in N that results when l is reduced from 20 ft to 15 ft, for the maximizing value of v.

41. Average Cost   During the Christmas season, a promotional company purchases cheap red felt stockings, glues fake white fur and sequins onto them, and packages them for distribution. The total cost of producing q cases of stockings is given by

$$c = 3q^2 + 50q - 18q \ln q + 120$$

Find the number of cases that should be processed in order to minimize the average cost per case. Determine (to two decimal places) this minimum average cost.

42. Profit   A monopolist's demand equation is given by

$$p = q^2 - 20q + 160$$

where p is the selling price (in thousands of dollars) per ton when q tons of product are sold. Suppose that fixed cost is \$50,000 and that each ton costs \$30,000 to produce. If current equipment has a maximum production capacity of 12 tons, use the graph of the profit function to determine at what production level the maximum profit occurs. Find the corresponding maximum profit and selling price per ton.

Chapter 13 Review

Important Terms and Symbols

Summary

Calculus is a great aid in sketching the graph of a function. The first derivative is used to determine when a function is increasing or decreasing and to locate relative maxima and minima. If $f'(x)$ is positive throughout an interval, then over that interval, f is increasing and its graph rises (from left to right). If $f'(x)$ is negative throughout that interval, f is decreasing and its graph is falling.

A point $(a, f(a))$ on the graph at which $f'(a)$ is 0 or is not defined is a candidate for a relative extremum, and a is called a critical value. For a relative extremum to occur at a, the first derivative must change sign around a. The following procedure is the first-derivative test for the relative extrema of $y = f(x)$:

First-Derivative Test for Relative Extrema

Step 1. Find $f'(x)$.

Step 2. Determine all values a where $f'(a) = 0$ or $f'(a)$ is not defined.

Step 3. On the intervals defined by the values in Step 2, determine whether f is increasing ($f'(x) > 0$) or decreasing ($f'(x) < 0$).

Step 4. For each critical value a at which f is continuous, determine whether $f'(x)$ changes sign as x increases through a. There is a relative maximum at a if $f'(x)$ changes from $+$ to $-$, and a relative minimum if $f'(x)$ changes from $-$ to $+$. If $f'(x)$ does not change sign, there is no relative extremum at a.

Under certain conditions, a function is guaranteed to have absolute extrema. The extreme-value theorem states that if f is continuous on a closed interval, then f has an absolute maximum value and an absolute minimum value over the interval. To locate absolute extrema, the following procedure can be used:

> **Procedure to Find Absolute Extrema for a Function** f **Continuous on** $[a, b]$
>
> **Step 1.** Find the critical values of f.
>
> **Step 2.** Evaluate $f(x)$ at the endpoints a and b and at the critical values in (a, b).
>
> **Step 3.** The maximum value of f is the greatest of the values found in Step 2. The minimum value of f is the least of the values found in Step 2.

The second derivative is used to determine concavity and points of inflection. If $f''(x) > 0$ throughout an interval, then f is concave up over that interval, and its graph bends upward. If $f''(x) < 0$ over an interval, then f is concave down throughout that interval, and its graph bends downward. A point on the graph where f is continuous and its concavity changes is an inflection point. The point $(a, f(a))$ on the graph is a possible point of inflection if either $f''(a) = 0$ or $f''(a)$ is not defined and f is continuous at a.

The second derivative also provides a means for testing certain critical values for relative extrema:

> **Second-Derivative Test for Relative Extrema**
>
> Suppose $f'(a) = 0$. Then
>
> If $f''(a) < 0$, then f has a relative maximum at a.
>
> If $f''(a) > 0$, then f has a relative minimum at a.

Asymptotes are also aids in curve sketching. Graphs "blow up" near vertical asymptotes, and they "settle" near horizontal asymptotes and oblique asymptotes. The line $x = a$ is a vertical asymptote for the graph of a function f if $\lim f(x) = \infty$ or $-\infty$ as x approaches a from the right $(x \to a^+)$ or the left $(x \to a^-)$. For the case of a rational function, $f(x) = P(x)/Q(x)$ in lowest terms, we can find vertical asymptotes without evaluating limits. If $Q(a) = 0$ but $P(a) \neq 0$, then the line $x = a$ is a vertical asymptote.

The line $y = b$ is a horizontal asymptote for the graph of a function f if at least one of the following is true:

$$\lim_{x \to \infty} f(x) = b \quad \text{or} \quad \lim_{x \to -\infty} f(x) = b$$

The line $y = mx + b$ is an oblique asymptote for the graph of a function f if at least one of the following is true:

$$\lim_{x \to \infty} (f(x) - (mx + b)) = 0 \quad \text{or} \quad \lim_{x \to -\infty} (f(x) - (mx + b)) = 0$$

In particular, a polynomial function of degree greater than 1 has no asymptotes. Moreover, a rational function whose numerator has degree greater than that of the denominator does not have a horizontal asymptote and a rational function whose numerator has degree more than one greater than that of the denominator does not have an oblique asymptote.

Applied Maxima and Minima

In applied work the importance of calculus in maximization and minimization problems can hardly be overstated. For example, in the area of economics, we can maximize profit or minimize cost. Some important relationships that are used in economics problems are the following:

$$\bar{c} = \frac{c}{q} \quad \text{average cost per unit} = \frac{\text{total cost}}{\text{quantity}}$$

$$r = pq \quad \text{revenue} = (\text{price})(\text{quantity})$$

$$P = r - c \quad \text{profit} = \text{total revenue} - \text{total cost}$$

Review Problems

In Problems 1–4, find horizontal and vertical asymptotes.

1. $y = \dfrac{3x^2}{x^2 - 16}$

2. $y = \dfrac{x + 3}{9x - 3x^2}$

3. $y = \dfrac{5x^2 - 3}{(3x + 2)^2}$

4. $y = \dfrac{4x + 1}{3x - 5} - \dfrac{3x + 1}{2x - 11}$

In Problems 5–8, find critical values.

5. $f(x) = \dfrac{3x^2}{9 - x^2}$

6. $f(x) = 8(x - 1)^2(x + 6)^4$

7. $f(x) = \dfrac{\sqrt[3]{x + 1}}{3 - 4x}$

8. $f(x) = \dfrac{13xe^{-5x/6}}{6x + 5}$

In Problems 9–12, find intervals on which the function is increasing or decreasing.

9. $f(x) = -\frac{5}{3}x^3 + 15x^2 + 35x + 10$

10. $f(x) = \dfrac{3x^2}{(x + 2)^2}$

11. $f(x) = \dfrac{6x^4}{x^2 - 3}$

12. $f(x) = 4\sqrt[3]{5x^3 - 7x}$

In Problems 13–18, find intervals on which the function is concave up or concave down.

13. $f(x) = x^4 - x^3 - 14$

14. $f(x) = \dfrac{x - 2}{x + 2}$

15. $f(x) = \dfrac{1}{3x + 2}$

16. $f(x) = x^3 + 2x^2 - 5x + 2$

17. $f(x) = (2x + 1)^3(3x + 2)$

18. $f(x) = (x^2 - x - 1)^2$

In Problems 19–24, test for relative extrema.

19. $f(x) = 2x^3 - 9x^2 + 12x + 7$

20. $f(x) = \dfrac{ax + b}{x^2}$ for $a > 0$ and $b > 0$

21. $f(x) = \dfrac{x^{10}}{10} + \dfrac{x^5}{5}$

22. $f(x) = \dfrac{x^2}{x^2 - 4}$

23. $f(x) = x^{2/3}(x + 1)$

24. $f(x) = x^3(x - 2)^4$

In Problems 25–30, find the x-values where inflection points occur.

25. $y = 3x^5 + 20x^4 - 30x^3 - 540x^2 + 2x + 3$

26. $y = \dfrac{x^2 + 2}{5x}$

27. $y = 4(3x - 5)(x^4 + 2)$

28. $y = x^2 + 2\ln(-x)$ **29.** $y = \dfrac{x^3}{e^x}$

30. $y = (x^2 - 5)^3$

In Problems 31–34, test for absolute extrema on the given interval.

31. $f(x) = 3x^4 - 4x^3$, $[0, 2]$

32. $f(x) = 2x^3 - 15x^2 + 36x$, $[0, 3]$

33. $f(x) = \dfrac{x}{(5x-6)^2}$, $[-2, 0]$

34. $f(x) = (x+1)^2(x-1)^{2/3}$, $[2, 3]$

35. Let $f(x) = x\ln x$.
(a) Determine the values of x at which relative maxima and relative minima, if any, occur.
(b) Determine the interval(s) on which the graph of f is concave up, and find the coordinates of all points of inflection, if any.

36. Let $f(x) = \dfrac{x}{x^2 - 1}$.

(a) Determine whether the graph of f is symmetric about the x-axis, y-axis, or origin.
(b) Find the interval(s) on which f is increasing.
(c) Find the coordinates of all relative extrema of f.
(d) Determine $\lim_{x\to-\infty} f(x)$ and $\lim_{x\to\infty} f(x)$.
(e) Sketch the graph of f.
(f) State the absolute minimum and absolute maximum values of $f(x)$ (if they exist).

In Problems 37–48, indicate intervals on which the function is increasing, decreasing, concave up, or concave down; indicate relative maximum points, relative minimum points, points of inflection, horizontal asymptotes, vertical asymptotes, symmetry, and those intercepts that can be obtained conveniently. Then sketch the graph.

37. $y = x^2 - 2x - 24$ **38.** $y = 2x^3 + 15x^2 + 36x + 9$

39. $y = x^3 - 12x + 20$ **40.** $y = e^{1/x}$

41. $y = x^3 - x$ **42.** $y = \dfrac{x+2}{x-3}$

43. $f(x) = \dfrac{100(x+5)}{x^2}$ **44.** $y = \dfrac{x^2 - 4}{x^2 - 1}$

45. $y = \dfrac{x}{(x-1)^3}$ **46.** $y = 6x^{1/3}(2x - 1)$

47. $f(x) = \dfrac{e^x + e^{-x}}{2}$ **48.** $f(x) = 1 - \ln(x^3)$

49. Are the following statements true or false?
(a) If $f'(x_0) = 0$, then f must have a relative extremum at x_0.
(b) Since the function $f(x) = 1/x$ is decreasing on the intervals $(-\infty, 0)$ and $(0, \infty)$, it is impossible to find x_1 and x_2 in the domain of f such that $x_1 < x_2$ and $f(x_1) < f(x_2)$.
(c) On the interval $(-1, 1]$, the function $f(x) = x^4$ has an absolute maximum and an absolute minimum.
(d) If $f''(x_0) = 0$, then $(x_0, f(x_0))$ must be a point of inflection.
(e) A function f defined on the interval $(-2, 2)$ with exactly one relative maximum must have an absolute maximum.

50. An important function in probability theory is the standard normal-density function

$$f(x) = \dfrac{1}{\sqrt{2\pi}}e^{-x^2/2}$$

(a) Determine whether the graph of f is symmetric about the x-axis, y-axis, or origin.
(b) Find the intervals on which f is increasing and those on which it is decreasing.
(c) Find the coordinates of all relative extrema of f.
(d) Find $\lim_{x\to-\infty} f(x)$ and $\lim_{x\to\infty} f(x)$.
(e) Find the intervals on which the graph of f is concave up and those on which it is concave down.
(f) Find the coordinates of all points of inflection.
(g) Sketch the graph of f.
(h) Find all absolute extrema.

51. Marginal Cost If $c = q^3 - 6q^2 + 12q + 18$ is a total-cost function, for what values of q is marginal cost increasing?

52. Marginal Revenue If $r = 320q^{3/2} - 2q^2$ is the revenue function for a manufacturer's product, determine the intervals on which the marginal-revenue function is increasing.

53. Revenue Function The demand equation for a manufacturer's product is

$$p = 200 - \dfrac{\sqrt{q}}{5} \quad \text{where } q > 0$$

Show that the graph of the revenue function is concave down wherever it is defined.

54. Contraception In a model of the effect of contraception on birthrate,[16] the equation

$$R = f(x) = \dfrac{x}{4.4 - 3.4x} \quad 0 \le x \le 1$$

gives the proportional reduction R in the birthrate as a function of the efficiency x of a contraception method. An efficiency of 0.2 (or 20%) means that the probability of becoming pregnant is 80% of the probability of becoming pregnant without the contraceptive. Find the reduction (as a percentage) when efficiency is (a) 0, (b) 0.5, and (c) 1. Find dR/dx and d^2R/dx^2, and sketch the graph of the equation.

55. Learning and Memory If you were to recite members of a category, such as four-legged animals, the words that you utter would probably occur in "chunks," with distinct pauses between such chunks. For example, you might say the following for the category of four-legged animals:

dog, cat, mouse, rat,
(pause)
horse, donkey, mule,
(pause)
cow, pig, goat, lamb,
etc.

The pauses may occur because you must mentally search for subcategories (animals around the house, beasts of burden, farm animals, etc.).

---

[16] R. K. Leik and B. F. Meeker, *Mathematical Sociology* (Englewood Cliffs, NJ: Prentice-Hall, Inc., 1975).

The elapsed time between onsets of successive words is called *interresponse time*. A function has been used to analyze the length of time for pauses and the chunk size (number of words in a chunk).[17] This function f is such that

$$f(t) = \begin{cases} \text{the average number of words} \\ \text{that occur in succession with} \\ \text{interresponse times less than } t \end{cases}$$

The graph of f has a shape similar to that in Figure 13.72 and is best fit by a third-degree polynomial, such as

$$f(t) = A t^3 + B t^2 + C t + D$$

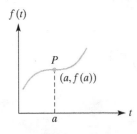

FIGURE 13.72

The point P has special meaning. It is such that the value a separates interresponse times *within* chunks from those *between* chunks. Mathematically, P is a critical point that is also a point of inflection. Assume these two conditions, and show that (a) $a = -B/(3A)$ and (b) $B^2 = 3AC$.

56. Market Penetration   In a model for the market penetration of a new product, sales S of the product at time t are given by[18]

$$S = g(t) = \frac{m(p+q)^2}{p} \left[\frac{e^{-(p+q)t}}{\left(\frac{q}{p} e^{-(p+q)t} + 1 \right)^2} \right]$$

where p, q, and m are nonzero constants.
(a) Show that

$$\frac{dS}{dt} = \frac{\frac{m}{p}(p+q)^3 e^{-(p+q)t} \left[\frac{q}{p} e^{-(p+q)t} - 1 \right]}{\left(\frac{q}{p} e^{-(p+q)t} + 1 \right)^3}$$

(b) Determine the value of t for which maximum sales occur. You may assume that S attains a maximum when $dS/dt = 0$.

In Problems 57–60, where appropriate, round your answers to two decimal places.

57. From the graph of $y = 4x^3 + 5.3x^2 - 7x + 3$, find the coordinates of all relative extrema.

58. From the graph of $f(x) = x^4 - 2x^3 + 3x - 1$, determine the absolute extrema of f over the interval $[-1, 1]$.

59. The graph of a function f has exactly one inflection point. If

$$f''(x) = \frac{x^3 + 3x + 2}{5x^2 - 2x + 4}$$

use the graph of f'' to determine the x-value of the inflection point of f.

60. Graph $y = \dfrac{5x^2 + 2x}{x^3 + 2x + 1}$. From the graph, locate any horizontal or vertical asymptotes.

61. Maximization of Production   A manufacturer determined that m employees on a certain production line will produce q units per month, where

$$q = 80m^2 - 0.1m^4$$

To obtain maximum monthly production, how many employees should be assigned to the production line?

62. Revenue   The demand function for a manufacturer's product is given by $p = 100e^{-0.1q}$. For what value of q does the manufacturer maximize total revenue?

63. Revenue   The demand function for a monopolist's product is

$$p = \sqrt{500 - q}$$

If the monopolist wants to produce at least 100 units, but not more than 200 units, how many units should be produced to maximize total revenue?

64. Average Cost   If $c = 0.01q^2 + 5q + 100$ is a cost function, find the average-cost function. At what level of production q is there a minimum average cost?

65. Profit   The demand function for a monopolist's product is

$$p = 700 - 2q$$

and the average cost per unit for producing q units is

$$\bar{c} = q + 100 + \frac{1000}{q}$$

where p and $\bar{c}$ are in dollars per unit. Find the maximum profit that the monopolist can achieve.

66. Container Design   A rectangular box is to be made by cutting out equal squares from each corner of a piece of cardboard 10 in. by 16 in. and then folding up the sides. What must be the length of the side of the square cut out if the volume of the box is to be maximum?

67. Fencing   A rectangular portion of a field is to be enclosed by a fence and divided equally into three parts by two fences parallel to one pair of the sides. If a total of 800 ft of fencing is to be used, find the dimensions that will maximize the fenced area.

68. Poster Design   A rectangular poster having an area of 500 in^2 is to have a 4-in. margin at each side and at the bottom and

[17]A. Graesser and G. Mandler, "Limited Processing Capacity Constrains the Storage of Unrelated Sets of Words and Retrieval from Natural Categories," *Human Learning and Memory*, 4, no. 1 (1978), 86–100.

[18]A. P. Hurter, Jr., A. H. Rubenstein et al., "Market Penetration by New Innovations: The Technological Literature," *Technological Forecasting and Social Change*, vol. 11 (1978), 197–221.

a 6-in. margin at the top. The remainder of the poster is for printed matter. Find the dimensions of the poster so that the area for the printed matter is maximized.

69. Cost A furniture company makes personal-computer stands. For a certain model, the total cost (in thousands of dollars) when q *hundred* stands are produced is given by

$$c = 2q^3 - 9q^2 + 12q + 20$$

(a) The company is currently capable of manufacturing between 75 and 600 stands (inclusive) per week. Determine the number of stands that should be produced per week to minimize the total cost, and find the corresponding average cost per stand.

(b) Suppose that between 300 and 600 stands must be produced. How many should the company now produce in order to minimize total cost?

70. Bacteria In a laboratory, an experimental antibacterial agent is applied to a population of 100 bacteria. Data indicate that the number of bacteria t hours after the agent is introduced is given by

$$N = \frac{12{,}100 + 110t + 100t^2}{121 + t^2}$$

For what value of t does the maximum number of bacteria in the population occur? What is this maximum number?

EXPLORE & EXTEND   Population Change over Time

Now that we know how to find the derivative of a function, we might ask whether there is a way to run the process in reverse: to find a function, given its derivative. Ultimately, this is what integration (Chapters 14–15) is all about. Meanwhile, however, we can use the derivative of a function to find the function *approximately* even without knowing how to do integration.

To illustrate, suppose we wish to describe the population, over time, of a small town in a frontier area. Let us imagine that the things we know about the town are all facts about how its population, P, changes over time, t, with population measured in people and time in years:

1. Births exceed deaths, so that over the course of a year there is a 25% increase in the population before other factors are accounted for. Thus, the annual change due to the birth/death difference is $0.25P$.

2. Every year, of the travelers passing through, ten decide to stop and settle down. This contributes a constant 10 to the annual change.

3. Loneliness causes some people to leave when the town is too small for them. At the extreme, 99% of people will leave over the course of a year if they are all alone (population = 1). When the population is 100, 10% of the residents leave per year due to loneliness.

Assuming an exponential relationship, we write the likelihood that a given person leaves within a year due to loneliness as Ae^{-kP}, where A and k are positive constants. The numbers tell us that $Ae^{-k\cdot1} = 0.99$ and $Ae^{-k\cdot100} = 0.10$. Solving this pair of equations for A and k yields

$$k = \frac{\ln 9.9}{99} \approx 0.02316$$

and

$$A = 0.99e^{(\ln 9.9)/99} \approx 1.01319$$

And if Ae^{-kP} is the likelihood of a single person's leaving, the population change per year due to loneliness is $-P$ times that, namely $-1.01319Pe^{-0.02316P}$. (The negative sign is due to the fact that the change is downward.)

4. Crowding causes some people to leave when the town is too large for them. Nobody has a crowding problem when they are all alone (population = 1), but when the population is 100, 10% of the residents leave per year due to crowding.

Again assuming an exponential relationship, we write the likelihood that a given person leaves within a year due to crowding as $1 - Ae^{-kP}$. This time, the numbers tell us that $1 - Ae^{-k\cdot1} = 0$ and $1 - Ae^{-k\cdot100} = 0.10$. Solving this pair of equations for A and k yields

$$k = -\frac{\ln 0.9}{99} \approx 0.001064$$

and

$$A = e^{-(\ln 0.9)/99} \approx 1.001065$$

If $1 - Ae^{-kP}$ is the likelihood of a single person's leaving, the population change per year due to crowding is $-P$ times that, namely $-P(1 - 1.001065e^{-0.001064P})$.

The overall rate of change in the population now is the net effect of all these factors added together. In equation form,

$$\frac{dP}{dt} = 0.25P + 10 - 1.01319Pe^{-0.02316P}$$
$$- P(1 - 1.001065e^{-0.001064P})$$

Before we try to reconstruct the function $P(t)$, let us graph the derivative. On a graphing calculator, it looks as shown in Figure 13.73. Note that $\frac{dP}{dt}$ is depicted as a function of P. This is a different graph from what we would get if we knew P as a function of t, found its derivative, and graphed that in the standard manner, namely as a function of t. Nonetheless, this graph reveals some significant facts. First, the derivative is positive from $P = 0$ to $P = 311$; this means that the population will have positive growth in that entire range and thus can be expected to grow from nothing into a substantial community.

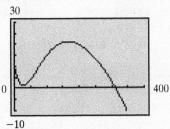

FIGURE 13.73 $\frac{dP}{dt}$ as a function of P.

Growth does fall to near zero at around $P = 30$. Apparently departures due to loneliness nearly bring growth to a halt when the population is still small. But once the town has grown through that phase, its size increases steadily, at one point (around $P = 170$) adding 21 people per year.

Eventually, departures due to crowding start to take a toll. Above 312 the derivative is negative. This means that if the population ever fluctuated above 312, population losses would shrink it back down to that level. In short, the population of this town stabilizes at 311 or 312—not exactly a city, but this is, after all, a frontier environment.

If we now wish to graph the town's population as a function of time, here is how we do this: We approximate the graph with a string of line segments, each of which has a slope given by the expression we obtained for dP/dt. We begin with a known time and population and calculate the initial slope. Let us grow the town from nothing, setting $t = 0$ at $P = 0$. Then $\frac{dP}{dt} = 10$. Now we advance the clock forward by a convenient time interval—let us choose 1 year—and, since the slope at $(0, 0)$ equals 10, we increase

the population from 0 to 10. The new values for t and P are 1 and 10, respectively, so we draw a line segment from $(0, 0)$ to $(1, 10)$. Now, with $t = 1$ and $P = 10$, we recalculate the slope and go through the same steps again, and we repeat this process until we have drawn as much of the curve as we want to see.

Obviously, this would be extremely tedious to do by hand. On a graphing calculator, however, we can use the programming and line-drawing features. For a TI-83 Plus, the following program does the job nicely, after the expression for $\frac{dP}{dt}$ is entered as Y_1 (keeping P as the variable):

```
PROGRAM:POPLTN
:Input "P?",P
:Input "T?", T
:ClrDraw
:T → S
:For(I, S + 1, S + 55)
:Line(T,P,I,P + Y₁)
:I → T
:(P + Y₁) → P
:End
```

Deselect the function Y_1. Set the graphing window to display the coordinate plane from 0 to 55 horizontally and from 0 to 350 vertically. Then run the program and, at the prompt, give initial values for P and t. The program will draw 55 line segments, enough to take the population to its final size from $P = 0, t = 0$. The result is shown in Figure 13.74.

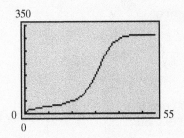

FIGURE 13.74 P as a function of t.

Problems

1. What information does Figure 13.74 give that is not evident from Figure 13.73?

2. What happens when an initial value of 450 is selected for P? (The display should be adjusted to run from 0 to 500 vertically.) Does this seem right?

3. Why is this procedure for obtaining a graph of $P(t)$ only approximate? How could the approximation be improved?

14 Integration

EXPLORE & EXTEND
Delivered Price

Anyone who runs a business knows the need for accurate cost estimates. When jobs are individually contracted, determining how much a job will cost is generally the first step in deciding how much to bid.

For example, a painter must determine how much paint a job will take. Since a gallon of paint will cover a certain number of square feet, the key is to determine the area of the surfaces to be painted. Normally, even this requires only simple arithmetic—walls and ceilings are rectangular, and so total area is a sum of products of base and height.

But not all area calculations are as simple. Suppose, for instance, that the bridge shown below must be sandblasted to remove accumulated soot. How would the contractor who charges for sandblasting by the square foot calculate the area of the vertical face on each side of the bridge?

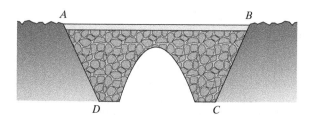

The area could be estimated as perhaps three-quarters of the area of the trapezoid formed by points A, B, C, and D. But a more accurate calculation—which might be desirable if the bid were for dozens of bridges of the same dimensions (as along a stretch of railroad)—would require a more refined approach.

If the shape of the bridge's arch can be described mathematically by a function, the contractor could use the method introduced in this chapter: integration. Integration has many applications, the simplest of which is finding areas of regions bounded by curves. Other applications include calculating the total deflection of a beam due to bending stress, calculating the distance traveled underwater by a submarine, and calculating the electricity bill for a company that consumes power at differing rates over the course of a month. Chapters 11–13 dealt with differential calculus. We differentiated a function and obtained another function, its derivative. *Integral calculus* is concerned with the reverse process: We are given the derivative of a function and must find the original function. The need for doing this arises in a natural way. For example, we might have a marginal-revenue function and want to find the revenue function from it. Integral calculus also involves a concept that allows us to take the limit of a special kind of sum as the number of terms in the sum becomes infinite. This is the real power of integral calculus! With such a notion, we can find the area of a region that cannot be found by any other convenient method.

Objective

To define the differential, interpret it geometrically, and use it in approximations. Also, to restate the reciprocal relationship between dx/dy and dy/dx.

14.1 Differentials

We will soon give a reason for using the symbol dy/dx to denote the derivative of y with respect to x. To do this, we introduce the notion of the *differential* of a function.

> **Definition**
>
> Let $y = f(x)$ be a differentiable function of x, and let Δx denote a change in x, where Δx can be any real number. Then the **differential** of y, denoted dy or $d(f(x))$, is given by
>
> $$dy = f'(x)\,\Delta x$$

TO REVIEW functions of several variables, see Section 2.8.

Note that dy depends on two variables, namely, x and Δx. In fact, dy is a function of two variables.

EXAMPLE 1   Computing a Differential

Find the differential of $y = x^3 - 2x^2 + 3x - 4$, and evaluate it when $x = 1$ and $\Delta x = 0.04$.

Solution: The differential is

$$dy = \frac{d}{dx}(x^3 - 2x^2 + 3x - 4)\,\Delta x$$

$$= (3x^2 - 4x + 3)\,\Delta x$$

When $x = 1$ and $\Delta x = 0.04$,

$$dy = [3(1)^2 - 4(1) + 3](0.04) = 0.08$$

Now Work Problem 1 ◁

If $y = x$, then $dy = d(x) = 1\,\Delta x = \Delta x$. Hence, the differential of x is Δx. We abbreviate $d(x)$ by dx. Thus, $dx = \Delta x$. From now on, it will be our practice to write dx for Δx when finding a differential. For example,

$$d(x^2 + 5) = \frac{d}{dx}(x^2 + 5)\,dx = 2x\,dx$$

Summarizing, we say that if $y = f(x)$ defines a differentiable function of x, then

$$dy = f'(x)\,dx$$

where dx is any real number. Provided that $dx \neq 0$, we can divide both sides by dx:

$$\frac{dy}{dx} = f'(x)$$

That is, dy/dx can be viewed either as the quotient of two differentials, namely, dy divided by dx, or as one symbol for the derivative of f at x. It is for this reason that we introduced the symbol dy/dx to denote the derivative.

EXAMPLE 2   Finding a Differential in Terms of dx

a. If $f(x) = \sqrt{x}$, then

$$d(\sqrt{x}) = \frac{d}{dx}(\sqrt{x})\,dx = \frac{1}{2}x^{-1/2}dx = \frac{1}{2\sqrt{x}}dx$$

b. If $u = (x^2 + 3)^5$, then $du = 5(x^2 + 3)^4(2x)\,dx = 10x(x^2 + 3)^4\,dx$.

Now Work Problem 3 ◁

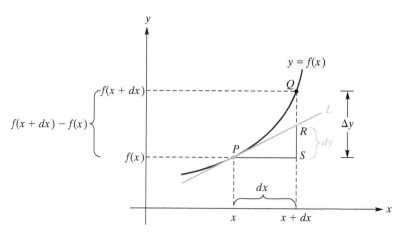

FIGURE 14.1 Geometric interpretation of dy and Δx.

The differential can be interpreted geometrically. In Figure 14.1, the point $P(x, f(x))$ is on the curve $y = f(x)$. Suppose x changes by dx, a real number, to the new value $x + dx$. Then the new function value is $f(x + dx)$, and the corresponding point on the curve is $Q(x + dx, f(x + dx))$. Passing through P and Q are horizontal and vertical lines, respectively, that intersect at S. A line L tangent to the curve at P intersects segment QS at R, forming the right triangle PRS. Observe that the graph of f near P is approximated by the tangent line at P. The slope of L is $f'(x)$ but it is also given by $\overline{SR}/\overline{PS}$ so that

$$f'(x) = \frac{\overline{SR}}{\overline{PS}}$$

Since $dy = f'(x)\,dx$ and $dx = \overline{PS}$,

$$dy = f'(x)\,dx = \frac{\overline{SR}}{\overline{PS}} \cdot \overline{PS} = \overline{SR}$$

Thus, if dx is a change in x at P, then dy is the corresponding vertical change along the **tangent line** at P. Note that for the same dx, the vertical change along the **curve** is $\Delta y = \overline{SQ} = f(x+dx) - f(x)$. Do not confuse Δy with dy. However, from Figure 14.1, the following is apparent:

When dx is close to 0, dy is an approximation to Δy. Therefore,

$$\Delta y \approx dy$$

This fact is useful in estimating Δy, a change in y, as Example 3 shows.

EXAMPLE 3   Using the Differential to Estimate a Change in a Quantity

A governmental health agency examined the records of a group of individuals who were hospitalized with a particular illness. It was found that the total proportion P that are discharged at the end of t days of hospitalization is given by

$$P = P(t) = 1 - \left(\frac{300}{300 + t}\right)^3$$

Use differentials to approximate the change in the proportion discharged if t changes from 300 to 305.

Solution: The change in t from 300 to 305 is $\Delta t = dt = 305 - 300 = 5$. The change in P is $\Delta P = P(305) - P(300)$. We approximate ΔP by dP:

$$\Delta P \approx dP = P'(t)\,dt = -3\left(\frac{300}{300 + t}\right)^2\left(-\frac{300}{(300 + t)^2}\right)dt = 3\frac{300^3}{(300 + t)^4}\,dt$$

When $t = 300$ and $dt = 5$,

$$dP = 3\frac{300^3}{600^4}5 = \frac{15}{2^3 600} = \frac{1}{2^3 40} = \frac{1}{320} \approx 0.0031$$

For a comparison, the true value of ΔP is

$$P(305) - P(300) = 0.87807 - 0.87500 = 0.00307$$

(to five decimal places).

Now Work Problem 11 ◁

We said that if $y = f(x)$, then $\Delta y \approx dy$ if dx is close to zero. Thus,

$$\Delta y = f(x + dx) - f(x) \approx dy$$

Formula (1) is used to approximate a function value, whereas the formula $\Delta y \approx dy$ is used to approximate a change in function values.

so that

$$f(x + dx) \approx f(x) + dy \qquad (1)$$

This formula gives us a way of estimating a function value $f(x + dx)$. For example, suppose we estimate $\ln(1.06)$. Letting $y = f(x) = \ln x$, we need to estimate $f(1.06)$. Since $d(\ln x) = (1/x) dx$, we have, from Formula (1),

$$f(x + dx) \approx f(x) + dy$$

$$\ln (x + dx) \approx \ln x + \frac{1}{x} dx$$

We know the exact value of $\ln 1$, so we will let $x = 1$ and $dx = 0.06$. Then $x + dx = 1.06$, and dx is close to zero. Therefore,

$$\ln (1 + 0.06) \approx \ln (1) + \frac{1}{1}(0.06)$$

$$\ln (1.06) \approx 0 + 0.06 = 0.06$$

The true value of $\ln(1.06)$ to five decimal places is 0.05827.

EXAMPLE 4   **Using the Differential to Estimate a Function Value**

The demand function for a product is given by

$$p = f(q) = 20 - \sqrt{q}$$

where p is the price per unit in dollars for q units. By using differentials, approximate the price when 99 units are demanded.

Solution: We want to approximate $f(99)$. By Formula (1),

$$f(q + dq) \approx f(q) + dp$$

where

$$dp = -\frac{1}{2\sqrt{q}} dq \qquad \frac{dp}{dq} = -\frac{1}{2}q^{-1/2}$$

We choose $q = 100$ and $dq = -1$ because $q + dq = 99$, dq is small, and it is easy to compute $f(100) = 20 - \sqrt{100} = 10$. We thus have

$$f(99) = f[100 + (-1)] \approx f(100) - \frac{1}{2\sqrt{100}}(-1)$$

$$f(99) \approx 10 + 0.05 = 10.05$$

Hence, the price per unit when 99 units are demanded is approximately $10.05.

Now Work Problem 17 ◁

The equation $y = x^3 + 4x + 5$ defines y as a function of x. We could write $f(x) = x^3 + 4x + 5$. However, the equation also defines x implicitly as a function of y. In fact, if we restrict the domain of f to some set of real numbers x so that $y = f(x)$ is a one-to-one function, then in principle we could solve for x in terms of y and get $x = f^{-1}(y)$. [Actually, no restriction of the domain is necessary here. Since $f'(x) = 3x^2 + 4 > 0$, for all x, we see that f is strictly increasing on $(-\infty, \infty)$ and is thus one-to-one on $(-\infty, \infty)$.] As we did in Section 12.2, we can look at the derivative of x with respect to y, dx/dy and we have seen that it is given by

$$\frac{dx}{dy} = \frac{1}{\dfrac{dy}{dx}} \qquad \text{provided that } dy/dx \neq 0$$

Since dx/dy can be considered a quotient of differentials, we now see that it is the reciprocal of the quotient of differentials dy/dx. Thus

$$\frac{dx}{dy} = \frac{1}{3x^2 + 4}$$

It is important to understand that it is not necessary to be able to solve $y = x^3 + 4x + 5$ for x in terms of y, and the equation $\dfrac{dx}{dy} = \dfrac{1}{3x^2 + 4}$ holds for all x.

EXAMPLE 5   Finding dp/dq from dq/dp

Find $\dfrac{dp}{dq}$ if $q = \sqrt{2500 - p^2}$.

Solution:

Strategy   There are a number of ways to find dp/dq. One approach is to solve the given equation for p explicitly in terms of q and then differentiate directly. Another approach to find dp/dq is to use implicit differentiation. However, since q is given explicitly as a function of p, we can easily find dq/dp and then use the preceding reciprocal relation to find dp/dq. We will take this approach.

We have

$$\frac{dq}{dp} = \frac{1}{2}(2500 - p^2)^{-1/2}(-2p) = -\frac{p}{\sqrt{2500 - p^2}}$$

Hence,

$$\frac{dp}{dq} = \frac{1}{\dfrac{dq}{dp}} = -\frac{\sqrt{2500 - p^2}}{p}$$

Now Work Problem 27 ◁

PROBLEMS 14.1

In Problems 1–10, find the differential of the function in terms of x and dx.

1. $y = ax + b$
2. $y = 2$
3. $f(x) = \sqrt{x^4 - 9}$
4. $f(x) = (4x^2 - 5x + 2)^3$
5. $u = \dfrac{1}{x^2}$
6. $u = \sqrt{x}$
7. $p = \ln(x^2 + 7)$
8. $p = e^{x^3 + 2x - 5}$
9. $y = (9x + 3)e^{2x^2 + 3}$
10. $y = \ln\sqrt{x^2 + 12}$

In Problems 11–16, find Δy and dy for the given values of x and dx.

11. $y = ax + b$; for any x and any dx
12. $y = 5x^2$; $x = -1$, $dx = -0.02$

13. $y = 2x^2 + 5x - 7$; $x = -2$, $dx = 0.1$
14. $y = (3x + 2)^2$; $x = -1$, $dx = -0.03$
15. $y = \sqrt{32 - x^2}$; $x = 4$, $dx = -0.05$ Round your answer to three decimal places.
16. $y = \ln x$; $x = 1$, $dx = 0.01$
17. Let $f(x) = \dfrac{x + 5}{x + 1}$.
    (a) Evaluate $f'(1)$.
    (b) Use differentials to estimate the value of $f(1.1)$.
18. Let $f(x) = x^{3x}$.
    (a) Evaluate $f'(1)$.
    (b) Use differentials to estimate the value of $f(0.98)$.

In Problems 19–26, approximate each expression by using differentials.

19. $\sqrt{288}$ (*Hint:* $17^2 = 289$.)   **20.** $\sqrt{122}$

21. $\sqrt[3]{9}$ **22.** $\sqrt[4]{16.3}$

23. $\ln 0.97$ **24.** $\ln 1.01$

25. $e^{0.001}$ **26.** $e^{-0.002}$

In Problems 27–32, find dx/dy or dp/dq.

27. $y = 2x - 1$ **28.** $y = 5x^2 + 3x + 2$

29. $q = (p^2 + 5)^3$ **30.** $q = \sqrt{p + 5}$

31. $q = \dfrac{1}{p^2}$ **32.** $q = e^{4-2p}$

33. If $y = 7x^2 - 6x + 3$, find the value of dx/dy when $x = 3$.

34. If $y = \ln x^2$, find the value of dx/dy when $x = 3$.

In Problems 35 and 36, find the rate of change of q with respect to p for the indicated value of q.

35. $p = \dfrac{500}{q+2}; q = 18$ **36.** $p = 60 - \sqrt{2q}; q = 50$

37. Profit Suppose that the profit (in dollars) of producing q units of a product is

$$P = 397q - 2.3q^2 - 400$$

Using differentials, find the approximate change in profit if the level of production changes from $q = 90$ to $q = 91$. Find the true change.

38. Revenue Given the revenue function

$$r = 250q + 45q^2 - q^3$$

use differentials to find the approximate change in revenue if the number of units increases from $q = 40$ to $q = 41$. Find the true change.

39. Demand The demand equation for a product is

$$p = \dfrac{10}{\sqrt{q}}$$

Using differentials, approximate the price when 24 units are demanded.

40. Demand Given the demand function

$$p = \dfrac{200}{\sqrt{q+8}}$$

use differentials to estimate the price per unit when 40 units are demanded.

41. If $y = f(x)$, then the *proportional change in y* is defined to be $\Delta y/y$, which can be approximated with differentials by dy/y. Use

this last form to approximate the proportional change in the cost function

$$c = f(q) = \dfrac{q^2}{2} + 5q + 300$$

when $q = 10$ and $dq = 2$. Round your answer to one decimal place.

42. Status/Income Suppose that S is a numerical value of status based on a person's annual income I (in thousands of dollars). For a certain population, suppose $S = 20\sqrt{I}$. Use differentials to approximate the change in S if annual income decreases from \$45,000 to \$44,500.

43. Biology The volume of a spherical cell is given by $V = \frac{4}{3}\pi r^3$, where r is the radius. Estimate the change in volume when the radius changes from 6.5×10^{-4} cm to 6.6×10^{-4} cm.

44. Muscle Contraction The equation

$$(P + a)(v + b) = k$$

is called the "fundamental equation of muscle contraction."[1] Here P is the load imposed on the muscle, v is the velocity of the shortening of the muscle fibers, and a, b, and k are positive constants. Find P in terms of v, and then use the differential to approximate the change in P due to a small change in v.

45. Demand The demand, q, for a monopolist's product is related to the price per unit, p, according to the equation

$$2 + \dfrac{q^2}{200} = \dfrac{4000}{p^2}$$

(a) Verify that 40 units will be demanded when the price per unit is \$20.

(b) Show that $\dfrac{dq}{dp} = -2.5$ when the price per unit is \$20.

(c) Use differentials and the results of parts (a) and (b) to approximate the number of units that will be demanded if the price per unit is reduced to \$19.20.

46. Profit The demand equation for a monopolist's product is

$$p = \dfrac{1}{2}q^2 - 66q + 7000$$

and the average-cost function is

$$\bar{c} = 500 - q + \dfrac{80{,}000}{2q}$$

(a) Find the profit when 100 units are demanded.

(b) Use differentials and the result of part (a) to estimate the profit when 101 units are demanded.

[1] R. W. Stacy et al., *Essentials of Biological and Medical Physics* (New York: McGraw-Hill, 1955).

Objective

To define the antiderivative and the indefinite integral and to apply basic integration formulas.

14.2 The Indefinite Integral

Given a function f, if F is a function such that

$$F'(x) = f(x) \tag{1}$$

then F is called an *antiderivative* of f. Thus,

An antiderivative of f is simply a function whose derivative is f.

Multiplying both sides of Equation (1) by the differential dx gives $F'(x)\,dx = f(x)\,dx$. However, because $F'(x)\,dx$ is the differential of F, we have $dF = f(x)\,dx$. Hence, we can think of an antiderivative of f as a function whose differential is $f(x)\,dx$.

Definition

An **antiderivative** of a function f is a function F such that

$$F'(x) = f(x)$$

Equivalently, in differential notation,

$$dF = f(x)\,dx$$

For example, because the derivative of x^2 is $2x$, x^2 is an antiderivative of $2x$. However, it is not the only antiderivative of $2x$: Since

$$\frac{d}{dx}(x^2 + 1) = 2x \qquad \text{and} \qquad \frac{d}{dx}(x^2 - 5) = 2x$$

both $x^2 + 1$ and $x^2 - 5$ are also antiderivatives of $2x$. In fact, it is obvious that because the derivative of a constant is zero, $x^2 + C$ is also an antiderivative of $2x$ for *any* constant C. Thus, $2x$ has infinitely many antiderivatives. More importantly, *all* antiderivatives of $2x$ must be functions of the form $x^2 + C$, because of the following fact:

Any two antiderivatives of a function differ only by a constant.

Since $x^2 + C$ describes all antiderivatives of $2x$, we can refer to it as being the *most general antiderivative* of $2x$, denoted by $\int 2x\,dx$, which is read "the *indefinite integral* of $2x$ with respect to x." Thus, we write

$$\int 2x\,dx = x^2 + C$$

The symbol $\int$ is called the **integral sign,** $2x$ is the **integrand,** and C is the **constant of integration.** The dx is part of the integral notation and indicates the variable involved. Here x is the **variable of integration.**

More generally, the **indefinite integral** of any function f with respect to x is written $\int f(x)\,dx$ and denotes the most general antiderivative of f. Since all antiderivatives of f differ only by a constant, if F is any antiderivative of f, then

$$\int f(x)\,dx = F(x) + C, \quad \text{where } C \text{ is a constant}$$

To *integrate* f means to find $\int f(x)\,dx$. In summary,

$$\int f(x)\,dx = F(x) + C \qquad \text{if and only if} \qquad F'(x) = f(x)$$

Thus we have

$$\frac{d}{dx}\left(\int f(x)\,dx\right) = f(x) \quad \text{and} \quad \int \frac{d}{dx}(F(x))\,dx = F(x) + C$$

which shows the extent to which differentiation and indefinite integration are inverse procedures.

APPLY IT ▶

1. If the marginal cost for a company is $f(q) = 28.3$, find $\int 28.3\,dq$, which gives the form of the cost function.

EXAMPLE 1   Finding an Indefinite Integral

Find $\displaystyle\int 5\,dx$.

Solution:

> **Strategy**   First we must find (perhaps better words are *guess at*) a function whose derivative is 5. Then we add the constant of integration.

CAUTION!

A common mistake is to omit C, the constant of integration.

Since we know that the derivative of $5x$ is 5, $5x$ is an antiderivative of 5. Therefore,

$$\int 5\,dx = 5x + C$$

Now Work Problem 1 ◁

Table 14.1 Elementary Integration Formulas

1. $\displaystyle\int k\,dx = kx + C \qquad k \text{ is a constant}$

2. $\displaystyle\int x^a\,dx = \frac{x^{a+1}}{a+1} + C \qquad a \neq -1$

3. $\displaystyle\int x^{-1}\,dx = \int \frac{1}{x}\,dx = \int \frac{dx}{x} = \ln x + C \qquad \text{for } x > 0$

4. $\displaystyle\int e^x\,dx = e^x + C$

5. $\displaystyle\int kf(x)\,dx = k\int f(x)\,dx \qquad k \text{ is a constant}$

6. $\displaystyle\int (f(x) \pm g(x))\,dx = \int f(x)\,dx \pm \int g(x)\,dx$

Using differentiation formulas from Chapters 11 and 12, we have compiled a list of elementary integration formulas in Table 14.1. These formulas are easily verified. For example, Formula (2) is true because the derivative of $x^{a+1}/(a+1)$ is x^a for $a \neq -1$. (We must have $a \neq -1$ because the denominator is 0 when $a = -1$.) Formula (2) states that the indefinite integral of a power of x, other than x^{-1}, is obtained by increasing the exponent of x by 1, dividing by the new exponent, and adding a constant of integration. The indefinite integral of x^{-1} will be discussed in Section 14.4.

To verify Formula (5), we must show that the derivative of $k\int f(x)\,dx$ is $kf(x)$. Since the derivative of $k\int f(x)\,dx$ is simply k times the derivative of $\int f(x)\,dx$, and the derivative of $\int f(x)\,dx$ is $f(x)$, Formula (5) is verified. The reader should verify the other formulas. Formula (6) can be extended to any number of terms.

EXAMPLE 2   Indefinite Integrals of a Constant and of a Power of x

a. Find $\displaystyle\int 1\,dx$.

Solution: By Formula (1) with $k = 1$

$$\int 1\,dx = 1x + C = x + C$$

Usually, we write $\int 1\,dx$ as $\int dx$. Thus, $\int dx = x + C$.

b. Find $\int x^5\,dx$.

Solution: By Formula (2) with $n = 5$,

$$\int x^5\,dx = \frac{x^{5+1}}{5+1} + C = \frac{x^6}{6} + C$$

Now Work Problem 3 ◁

EXAMPLE 3 Indefinite Integral of a Constant Times a Function

Find $\int 7x\,dx$.

Solution: By Formula (5) with $k = 7$ and $f(x) = x$,

$$\int 7x\,dx = 7\int x\,dx$$

Since x is x^1, by Formula (2) we have

$$\int x^1\,dx = \frac{x^{1+1}}{1+1} + C_1 = \frac{x^2}{2} + C_1$$

where C_1 is the constant of integration. Therefore,

$$\int 7x\,dx = 7\int x\,dx = 7\left(\frac{x^2}{2} + C_1\right) = \frac{7}{2}x^2 + 7C_1$$

Since $7C_1$ is just an arbitrary constant, we will replace it by C for simplicity. Thus,

$$\int 7x\,dx = \frac{7}{2}x^2 + C$$

It is not necessary to write all intermediate steps when integrating. More simply, we write

$$\int 7x\,dx = (7)\frac{x^2}{2} + C = \frac{7}{2}x^2 + C$$

Now Work Problem 5 ◁

EXAMPLE 4 Indefinite Integral of a Constant Times a Function

Find $\int -\frac{3}{5}e^x\,dx$.

Solution:

$$\int -\frac{3}{5}e^x\,dx = -\frac{3}{5}\int e^x\,dx \qquad \text{Formula (5)}$$

$$= -\frac{3}{5}e^x + C \qquad \text{Formula (4)}$$

Now Work Problem 21 ◁

EXAMPLE 5 Finding Indefinite Integrals

a. Find $\int \frac{1}{\sqrt{t}}\,dt$.

Solution: Here t is the variable of integration. We rewrite the integrand so that a basic formula can be used. Since $1/\sqrt{t} = t^{-1/2}$, applying Formula (2) gives

$$\int \frac{1}{\sqrt{t}}\,dt = \int t^{-1/2}\,dt = \frac{t^{(-1/2)+1}}{-\frac{1}{2}+1} + C = \frac{t^{1/2}}{\frac{1}{2}} + C = 2\sqrt{t} + C$$

APPLY IT ▶

2. If the rate of change of a company's revenues can be modeled by $\dfrac{dR}{dt} = 0.12t^2$, then find $\int 0.12t^2\,dt$, which gives the form of the company's revenue function.

CAUTION! ⚠

Only a *constant* factor of the integrand can pass through an integral sign.

APPLY IT ▶

3. Due to new competition, the number of subscriptions to a certain magazine is declining at a rate of $\dfrac{dS}{dt} = -\dfrac{480}{t^3}$ subscriptions per month, where t is the number of months since the competition entered the market. Find the form of the equation for the number of subscribers to the magazine.

b. Find $\int \dfrac{1}{6x^3}\,dx$.

Solution:
$$\int \frac{1}{6x^3}\,dx = \frac{1}{6}\int x^{-3}\,dx = \left(\frac{1}{6}\right)\frac{x^{-3+1}}{-3+1} + C$$

$$= -\frac{x^{-2}}{12} + C = -\frac{1}{12x^2} + C$$

Now Work Problem 9 ◁

APPLY IT ▶

4. The rate of growth of the population of a new city is estimated by $\dfrac{dN}{dt} = 500 + 300\sqrt{t}$, where t is in years. Find

$$\int (500 + 300\sqrt{t})\,dt$$

EXAMPLE 6   Indefinite Integral of a Sum

Find $\int (x^2 + 2x)\,dx$.

Solution: By Formula (6),

$$\int (x^2 + 2x)\,dx = \int x^2\,dx + \int 2x\,dx$$

Now,

$$\int x^2\,dx = \frac{x^{2+1}}{2+1} + C_1 = \frac{x^3}{3} + C_1$$

and

$$\int 2x\,dx = 2\int x\,dx = (2)\frac{x^{1+1}}{1+1} + C_2 = x^2 + C_2$$

Thus,

$$\int (x^2 + 2x)\,dx = \frac{x^3}{3} + x^2 + C_1 + C_2$$

For convenience, we will replace the constant $C_1 + C_2$ by C. We then have

$$\int (x^2 + 2x)\,dx = \frac{x^3}{3} + x^2 + C$$

When integrating an expression involving more than one term, only one constant of integration is needed.

Omitting intermediate steps, we simply integrate term by term and write

$$\int (x^2 + 2x)\,dx = \frac{x^3}{3} + (2)\frac{x^2}{2} + C = \frac{x^3}{3} + x^2 + C$$

Now Work Problem 11 ◁

APPLY IT ▶

5. Suppose the rate of savings in the United States is given by $\dfrac{dS}{dt} = 2.1t^2 - 65.4t + 491.6$, where t is the time in years and S is the amount of money saved in billions of dollars. Find the form of the equation for the amount of money saved.

EXAMPLE 7   Indefinite Integral of a Sum and Difference

Find $\int (2\sqrt[5]{x^4} - 7x^3 + 10e^x - 1)\,dx$.

Solution:

$$\int (2\sqrt[5]{x^4} - 7x^3 + 10e^x - 1)\,dx$$

$$= 2\int x^{4/5}\,dx - 7\int x^3\,dx + 10\int e^x\,dx - \int 1\,dx \quad \text{Formulas (5) and (6)}$$

$$= (2)\frac{x^{9/5}}{\frac{9}{5}} - (7)\frac{x^4}{4} + 10e^x - x + C \quad \text{Formulas (1), (2), and (4)}$$

$$= \frac{10}{9}x^{9/5} - \frac{7}{4}x^4 + 10e^x - x + C$$

Now Work Problem 15 ◁

Sometimes, in order to apply the basic integration formulas, it is necessary first to perform algebraic manipulations on the integrand, as Example 8 shows.

EXAMPLE 8   Using Algebraic Manipulation to Find an Indefinite Integral

Find $\int y^2 \left(y + \dfrac{2}{3} \right) dy$.

Solution: The integrand does not fit a familiar integration form. However, by multiplying the integrand we get

$$\int y^2 \left(y + \frac{2}{3} \right) dy = \int \left(y^3 + \frac{2}{3} y^2 \right) dy$$

$$= \frac{y^4}{4} + \left(\frac{2}{3} \right) \frac{y^3}{3} + C = \frac{y^4}{4} + \frac{2y^3}{9} + C$$

Now Work Problem 41 ◁

CAUTION!⚠

In Example 8, we first multiplied the factors in the integrand. The answer could not have been found simply in terms of $\int y^2 \, dy$ and $\int (y + \frac{2}{3}) \, dy$. There is not a formula for the integral of a general product of functions.

EXAMPLE 9   Using Algebraic Manipulation to Find an Indefinite Integral

a. Find $\int \dfrac{(2x - 1)(x + 3)}{6} \, dx$.

Solution: By factoring out the constant $\frac{1}{6}$ and multiplying the binomials, we get

$$\int \frac{(2x - 1)(x + 3)}{6} \, dx = \frac{1}{6} \int (2x^2 + 5x - 3) \, dx$$

$$= \frac{1}{6} \left((2)\frac{x^3}{3} + (5)\frac{x^2}{2} - 3x \right) + C$$

$$= \frac{x^3}{9} + \frac{5x^2}{12} - \frac{x}{2} + C$$

Another algebraic approach to part (b) is

$\int \dfrac{x^3 - 1}{x^2} \, dx = \int (x^3 - 1) x^{-2} \, dx$

$= \int (x - x^{-2}) \, dx$

and so on.

b. Find $\int \dfrac{x^3 - 1}{x^2} \, dx$.

Solution: We can break up the integrand into fractions by dividing each term in the numerator by the denominator:

$$\int \frac{x^3 - 1}{x^2} \, dx = \int \left(\frac{x^3}{x^2} - \frac{1}{x^2} \right) dx = \int (x - x^{-2}) \, dx$$

$$= \frac{x^2}{2} - \frac{x^{-1}}{-1} + C = \frac{x^2}{2} + \frac{1}{x} + C$$

Now Work Problem 49 ◁

PROBLEMS 14.2

In Problems 1–52, find the indefinite integrals.

1. $\int 7 \, dx$

2. $\int \dfrac{1}{x} \, dx$

3. $\int x^8 \, dx$

4. $\int 5x^{24} \, dx$

5. $\int 5x^{-7} \, dx$

6. $\int \dfrac{z^{-3}}{3} \, dz$

7. $\int \dfrac{5}{x^7} \, dx$

8. $\int \dfrac{7}{x^4 \, dx}$

9. $\int \dfrac{1}{t^{7/4}} \, dt$

10. $\int \dfrac{7}{2x^{9/4}} \, dx$

11. $\int (4 + t) \, dt$

12. $\int (7r^5 + 4r^2 + 1) \, dr$

13. $\int (y^5 - 5y) \, dy$

14. $\int (5 - 2w - 6w^2) \, dw$

15. $\int (3t^2 - 4t + 5) \, dt$

16. $\int (1 + t^2 + t^4 + t^6) \, dt$

17. $\int (\sqrt{2} + e)\, dx$ **18.** $\int (5 - 2^{-1})\, dx$

19. $\int \left(\frac{x}{7} - \frac{3}{4}x^4\right) dx$ **20.** $\int \left(\frac{2x^2}{7} - \frac{8}{3}x^4\right) dx$

21. $\int \pi e^x\, dx$ **22.** $\int (e^x + 3x^2 + 2x)\, dx$

23. $\int (x^{8.3} - 9x^6 + 3x^{-4} + x^{-3})\, dx$

24. $\int (0.7y^3 + 10 + 2y^{-3})\, dy$

25. $\int \frac{-2\sqrt{x}}{3}\, dx$ **26.** $\int dz$

27. $\int \frac{5}{3\sqrt[3]{x^2}}\, dx$ **28.** $\int \frac{-4}{(3x)^3}\, dx$

29. $\int \left(\frac{x^3}{3} - \frac{3}{x^3}\right) dx$ **30.** $\int \left(\frac{1}{2x^3} - \frac{1}{x^4}\right) dx$

31. $\int \left(\frac{3w^2}{2} - \frac{2}{3w^2}\right) dw$ **32.** $\int 7e^{-s}\, ds$

33. $\int \frac{3u - 4}{5}\, du$ **34.** $\int \frac{1}{12}\left(\frac{1}{3}e^x\right) dx$

35. $\int (u^e + e^u)\, du$ **36.** $\int \left(3y^3 - 2y^2 + \frac{e^y}{6}\right) dy$

37. $\int \left(\frac{3}{\sqrt{x}} - 12\sqrt[3]{x}\right) dx$ **38.** $\int 0\, dt$

39. $\int \left(-\frac{\sqrt[3]{x^2}}{5} - \frac{7}{2\sqrt{x}} + 6x\right) dx$

40. $\int \left(\sqrt[3]{u} + \frac{1}{\sqrt{u}}\right) du$ **41.** $\int (x^2 + 5)(x - 3)\, dx$

42. $\int x^3(x^2 + 5x + 2)\, dx$ **43.** $\int \sqrt{x}(x + 3)\, dx$

44. $\int (z + 2)^2\, dz$ **45.** $\int (3u + 2)^3\, du$

46. $\int \left(\frac{2}{\sqrt[5]{x}} - 1\right)^2 dx$ **47.** $\int x^{-2}(3x^4 + 4x^2 - 5)\, dx$

48. $\int (6e^u - u^3(\sqrt{u} + 1))\, du$ **49.** $\int \frac{z^4 + 10z^3}{2z^2}\, dz$

50. $\int \frac{x^4 - 5x^2 + 2x}{5x^2}\, dx$ **51.** $\int \frac{e^x + e^{2x}}{e^x}\, dx$

52. $\int \frac{(x^2 + 1)^3}{x}\, dx$

53. If $F(x)$ and $G(x)$ are such that $F'(x) = G'(x)$, is it true that $F(x) - G(x)$ must be zero?

54. (a) Find a function F such that $\int F(x)\, dx = xe^x + C$.
(b) Is there only one function F satisfying the equation given in part (a), or are there many such functions?

55. Find $\int \frac{d}{dx}\left(\frac{1}{\sqrt{x^2 + 1}}\right) dx$.

Objective

To find a particular antiderivative of a function that satisfies certain conditions. This involves evaluating constants of integration.

14.3 Integration with Initial Conditions

If we know the rate of change, f', of the function f, then the function f itself is an antiderivative of f' (since the derivative of f is f'). Of course, there are many antiderivatives of f', and the most general one is denoted by the indefinite integral. For example, if

$$f'(x) = 2x$$

then

$$f(x) = \int f'(x)\, dx = \int 2x\, dx = x^2 + C. \qquad (1)$$

That is, *any* function of the form $f(x) = x^2 + C$ has its derivative equal to $2x$. Because of the constant of integration, notice that we do not know $f(x)$ specifically. However, if f must assume a certain function value for a particular value of x, then we can determine the value of C and thus determine $f(x)$ specifically. For instance, if $f(1) = 4$, then, from Equation (1),

$$f(1) = 1^2 + C$$
$$4 = 1 + C$$
$$C = 3$$

Thus,

$$f(x) = x^2 + 3$$

That is, we now know the particular function $f(x)$ for which $f'(x) = 2x$ and $f(1) = 4$. The condition $f(1) = 4$, which gives a function value of f for a specific value of x, is called an *initial condition*.

APPLY IT ▶

6. The rate of growth of a species of bacteria is estimated by $\dfrac{dN}{dt} = 800 + 200e^t$, where N is the number of bacteria (in thousands) after t hours. If $N(5) = 40{,}000$, find $N(t)$.

EXAMPLE 1   Initial-Condition Problem

If y is a function of x such that $y' = 8x - 4$ and $y(2) = 5$, find y. [Note: $y(2) = 5$ means that $y = 5$ when $x = 2$.] Also, find $y(4)$.

Solution: Here $y(2) = 5$ is the initial condition. Since $y' = 8x - 4$, y is an antiderivative of $8x - 4$:

$$y = \int (8x - 4)\,dx = 8 \cdot \frac{x^2}{2} - 4x + C = 4x^2 - 4x + C \tag{2}$$

We can determine the value of C by using the initial condition. Because $y = 5$ when $x = 2$, from Equation (2), we have

$$5 = 4(2)^2 - 4(2) + C$$
$$5 = 16 - 8 + C$$
$$C = -3$$

Replacing C by -3 in Equation (2) gives the function that we seek:

$$y = 4x^2 - 4x - 3 \tag{3}$$

To find $y(4)$, we let $x = 4$ in Equation (3):

$$y(4) = 4(4)^2 - 4(4) - 3 = 64 - 16 - 3 = 45$$

Now Work Problem 1 ◁

EXAMPLE 2   Initial-Condition Problem Involving y''

Given that $y'' = x^2 - 6$, $y'(0) = 2$, and $y(1) = -1$, find y.

Solution:

APPLY IT ▶

7. The acceleration of an object after t seconds is given by $y'' = 84t + 24$, the velocity at 8 seconds is given by $y'(8) = 2891$ ft/s, and the position at 2 seconds is given by $y(2) = 185$ ft. Find $y(t)$.

Strategy   To go from y'' to y, two integrations are needed: the first to take us from y'' to y' and the other to take us from y' to y. Hence, there will be two constants of integration, which we will denote by C_1 and C_2.

Since $y'' = \dfrac{d}{dx}(y') = x^2 - 6$, y' is an antiderivative of $x^2 - 6$. Thus,

$$y' = \int (x^2 - 6)\,dx = \frac{x^3}{3} - 6x + C_1 \tag{4}$$

Now, $y'(0) = 2$ means that $y' = 2$ when $x = 0$; therefore, from Equation (4), we have

$$2 = \frac{0^3}{3} - 6(0) + C_1$$

Hence, $C_1 = 2$, so

$$y' = \frac{x^3}{3} - 6x + 2$$

By integration, we can find y:

$$y = \int \left(\frac{x^3}{3} - 6x + 2 \right) dx$$

$$= \left(\frac{1}{3} \right) \frac{x^4}{4} - (6)\frac{x^2}{2} + 2x + C_2$$

so

$$y = \frac{x^4}{12} - 3x^2 + 2x + C_2 \tag{5}$$

Now, since $y = -1$ when $x = 1$, we have, from Equation (5),

$$-1 = \frac{1^4}{12} - 3(1)^2 + 2(1) + C_2$$

Thus, $C_2 = -\frac{1}{12}$, so

$$y = \frac{x^4}{12} - 3x^2 + 2x - \frac{1}{12}$$

Now Work Problem 5 ◁

Integration with initial conditions is applicable to many applied situations, as the next three examples illustrate.

EXAMPLE 3   Income and Education

For a particular urban group, sociologists studied the current average yearly income y (in dollars) that a person can expect to receive with x years of education before seeking regular employment. They estimated that the rate at which income changes with respect to education is given by

$$\frac{dy}{dx} = 100x^{3/2} \quad 4 \le x \le 16$$

where $y = 28{,}720$ when $x = 9$. Find y.

Solution: Here y is an antiderivative of $100x^{3/2}$. Thus,

$$y = \int 100x^{3/2}\,dx = 100 \int x^{3/2}\,dx$$

$$= (100)\frac{x^{5/2}}{\frac{5}{2}} + C$$

$$y = 40x^{5/2} + C \tag{6}$$

The initial condition is that $y = 28{,}720$ when $x = 9$. By putting these values into Equation (6), we can determine the value of C:

$$28{,}720 = 40(9)^{5/2} + C$$

$$= 40(243) + C$$

$$28{,}720 = 9720 + C$$

Therefore, $C = 19{,}000$, and

$$y = 40x^{5/2} + 19{,}000$$

Now Work Problem 17 ◁

EXAMPLE 4   Finding the Demand Function from Marginal Revenue

If the marginal-revenue function for a manufacturer's product is

$$\frac{dr}{dq} = 2000 - 20q - 3q^2$$

find the demand function.

Solution:

Strategy By integrating dr/dq and using an initial condition, we can find the revenue function r. But revenue is also given by the general relationship $r = pq$, where p is the price per unit. Thus, $p = r/q$. Replacing r in this equation by the revenue function yields the demand function.

Since dr/dq is the derivative of total revenue r,

$$r = \int (2000 - 20q - 3q^2)\, dq$$

$$= 2000q - (20)\frac{q^2}{2} - (3)\frac{q^3}{3} + C$$

so that

$$r = 2000q - 10q^2 - q^3 + C \qquad (7)$$

Revenue is 0 when q is 0.

We assume that **when no units are sold, there is no revenue;** that is, $r = 0$ when $q = 0$. This is our initial condition. Putting these values into Equation (7) gives

$$0 = 2000(0) - 10(0)^2 - 0^3 + C$$

Although $q = 0$ gives $C = 0$, this is not true in general. It occurs in this section because the revenue functions are polynomials. In later sections, evaluating at $q = 0$ may produce a nonzero value for C.

Hence, $C = 0$, and

$$r = 2000q - 10q^2 - q^3$$

To find the demand function, we use the fact that $p = r/q$ and substitute for r:

$$p = \frac{r}{q} = \frac{2000q - 10q^2 - q^3}{q}$$

$$p = 2000 - 10q - q^2$$

Now Work Problem 11 ◁

EXAMPLE 5   Finding Cost from Marginal Cost

In the manufacture of a product, fixed costs per week are $4000. (Fixed costs are costs, such as rent and insurance, that remain constant at all levels of production during a given time period.) If the marginal-cost function is

$$\frac{dc}{dq} = 0.000001(0.002q^2 - 25q) + 0.2$$

where c is the total cost (in dollars) of producing q pounds of product per week, find the cost of producing 10,000 lb in 1 week.

Solution: Since dc/dq is the derivative of the total cost c,

$$c(q) = \int [0.000001(0.002q^2 - 25q) + 0.2]\, dq$$

$$= 0.000001 \int (0.002q^2 - 25q)\, dq + \int 0.2\, dq$$

$$c(q) = 0.000001 \left(\frac{0.002q^3}{3} - \frac{25q^2}{2} \right) + 0.2q + C$$

When q is 0, total cost is equal to fixed cost.

Fixed costs are constant regardless of output. Therefore, when $q = 0, c = 4000$, which is our initial condition. Putting $c(0) = 4000$ in the last equation, we find that $C = 4000$, so

Although $q = 0$ gives C a value equal to fixed costs, this is not true in general. It occurs in this section because the cost functions are polynomials. In later sections, evaluating at $q = 0$ may produce a value for C that is different from fixed cost.

$$c(q) = 0.000001 \left(\frac{0.002q^3}{3} - \frac{25q^2}{2} \right) + 0.2q + 4000 \qquad (8)$$

From Equation (8), we have $c(10,000) = 5416\frac{2}{3}$. Thus, the total cost for producing 10,000 pounds of product in 1 week is $5416.67.

Now Work Problem 15 ◁

PROBLEMS 14.3

In Problems 1 and 2, find y subject to the given conditions.

1. $dy/dx = 3x - 4$; $y(-1) = \frac{13}{2}$

2. $dy/dx = x^2 - x$; $y(3) = \frac{19}{2}$

In Problems 3 and 4, if y satisfies the given conditions, find y(x) for the given value of x.

3. $y' = \dfrac{9}{8\sqrt{x}}$, $y(16) = 10$; $x = 9$

4. $y' = -x^2 + 2x$, $y(2) = 1$; $x = 1$

In Problems 5–8, find y subject to the given conditions.

5. $y'' = -3x^2 + 4x$; $y'(1) = 2$, $y(1) = 3$

6. $y'' = x + 1$; $y'(0) = 0$, $y(0) = 5$

7. $y''' = 2x$; $y''(-1) = 3$, $y'(3) = 10$, $y(0) = 13$

8. $y''' = 2e^{-x} + 3$; $y''(0) = 7$, $y'(0) = 5$, $y(0) = 1$

In Problems 9–12, dr/dq is a marginal-revenue function. Find the demand function.

9. $dr/dq = 0.7$

10. $dr/dq = 10 - \dfrac{1}{16}q$

11. $dr/dq = 275 - q - 0.3q^2$

12. $dr/dq = 5{,}000 - 3(2q + 2q^3)$

In Problems 13–16, dc/dq is a marginal-cost function and fixed costs are indicated in braces. For Problems 13 and 14, find the total-cost function. For Problems 15 and 16, find the total cost for the indicated value of q.

13. $dc/dq = 2.47$; {159}

14. $dc/dq = 2q + 75$; {2000}

15. $dc/dq = 0.08q^2 - 1.6q + 6.5$; {8000}; $q = 25$

16. $dc/dq = 0.000204q^2 - 0.046q + 6$; {15,000}; $q = 200$

17. **Diet for Rats**   A group of biologists studied the nutritional effects on rats that were fed a diet containing 10% protein.[2] The protein consisted of yeast and corn flour.

Over a period of time, the group found that the (approximate) rate of change of the average weight gain G (in grams) of a rat with respect to the percentage P of yeast in the protein mix was

$$\frac{dG}{dP} = -\frac{P}{25} + 2 \qquad 0 \le P \le 100$$

If $G = 38$ when $P = 10$, find G.

18. **Winter Moth**   A study of the winter moth was made in Nova Scotia.[3] The prepupae of the moth fall onto the ground from host trees. It was found that the (approximate) rate at which prepupal density y (the number of prepupae per square foot of soil) changes with respect to distance x (in feet) from the base of a host tree is

$$\frac{dy}{dx} = -1.5 - x \quad 1 \le x \le 9$$

If $y = 59.6$ when $x = 1$, find y.

19. **Fluid Flow**   In the study of the flow of fluid in a tube of constant radius R, such as blood flow in portions of the body, one can think of the tube as consisting of concentric tubes of radius r, where $0 \le r \le R$. The velocity v of the fluid is a function of r and is given by[4]

$$v = \int -\frac{(P_1 - P_2)r}{2l\eta}\, dr$$

where P_1 and P_2 are pressures at the ends of the tube, η (a Greek letter read "eta") is fluid viscosity, and l is the length of the tube. If $v = 0$ when $r = R$, show that

$$v = \frac{(P_1 - P_2)(R^2 - r^2)}{4l\eta}$$

20. **Elasticity of Demand**   The sole producer of a product has determined that the marginal-revenue function is

$$\frac{dr}{dq} = 100 - 3q^2$$

Determine the point elasticity of demand for the product when $q = 5$. (*Hint:* First find the demand function.)

21. **Average Cost**   A manufacturer has determined that the marginal-cost function is

$$\frac{dc}{dq} = 0.003q^2 - 0.4q + 40$$

where q is the number of units produced. If marginal cost is $27.50 when $q = 50$ and fixed costs are $5000, what is the *average* cost of producing 100 units?

22. If $f''(x) = 30x^4 + 12x$ and $f'(1) = 10$, evaluate

$$f(965.335245) - f(-965.335245)$$

To learn and apply the formulas for $\int u^a\, du$, $\int e^u\, du$, and $\int \dfrac{1}{u}\, du$.

14.4 More Integration Formulas

Power Rule for Integration

The formula

$$\int x^a\, dx = \frac{x^{a+1}}{n+1} + C \qquad \text{if } a \ne -1$$

---

[2]Adapted from R. Bressani, "The Use of Yeast in Human Foods," in *Single-Cell Protein*, eds. R. I. Mateles and S. R. Tannenbaum (Cambridge, MA: MIT Press, 1968).

[3]Adapted from D. G. Embree,"The Population Dynamics of the Winter Moth in Nova Scotia, 1954–1962," *Memoirs of the Entomological Society of Canada*, no. 46 (1965).

[4]R. W. Stacy et al., *Essentials of Biological and Medical Physics* (New York: McGraw-Hill, 1955).

which applies to a power of x, can be generalized to handle a power of a *function* of x. Let u be a differentiable function of x. By the power rule for differentiation, if $a \neq -1$, then

$$\frac{d}{dx}\left(\frac{(u(x))^{a+1}}{a+1}\right) = \frac{(a+1)(u(x))^a \cdot u'(x)}{a+1} = (u(x))^a \cdot u'(x)$$

Thus,

$$\int (u(x))^a \cdot u'(x)\, dx = \frac{(u(x))^{a+1}}{a+1} + C \quad a \neq -1$$

We call this the *power rule for integration*. Note that $u'(x)dx$ is the differential of u, namely du. In mathematical shorthand, we can replace $u(x)$ by u and $u'(x)\, dx$ by du:

Power Rule for Integration

If u is differentiable, then

$$\int u^a\, du = \frac{u^{a+1}}{a+1} + C \quad \text{if } a \neq -1 \tag{1}$$

It is important to appreciate the difference between the power rule for integration and the formula for $\int x^a\, dx$. In the power rule, u represents a function, whereas in $\int x^a\, dx$, x is a variable.

EXAMPLE 1   Applying the Power Rule for Integration

a. Find $\int (x+1)^{20}\, dx$.

Solution: Since the integrand is a power of the function $x + 1$, we will set $u = x + 1$. Then $du = dx$, and $\int (x+1)^{20}\, dx$ has the form $\int u^{20}\, du$. By the power rule for integration,

$$\int (x+1)^{20}\, dx = \int u^{20}\, du = \frac{u^{21}}{21} + C = \frac{(x+1)^{21}}{21} + C$$

Note that we give our answer not in terms of u, but explicitly in terms of x.

b. Find $\int 3x^2(x^3 + 7)^3\, dx$.

Solution: We observe that the integrand contains a power of the function $x^3 + 7$. Let $u = x^3 + 7$. Then $du = 3x^2\, dx$. Fortunately, $3x^2$ appears as a factor in the integrand and we have

$$\int 3x^2(x^3 + 7)^3\, dx = \int (x^3 + 7)^3[3x^2\, dx] = \int u^3\, du$$

$$= \frac{u^4}{4} + C = \frac{(x^3 + 7)^4}{4} + C$$

After integrating, you may wonder what happened to $3x^2$. We note again that $du = 3x^2\, dx$.

Now Work Problem 3 ◁

In order to apply the power rule for integration, sometimes an adjustment must be made to obtain du in the integrand, as Example 2 illustrates.

EXAMPLE 2   Adjusting for du

Find $\int x\sqrt{x^2 + 5}\, dx$.

Solution: We can write this as $\int x(x^2 + 5)^{1/2}\, dx$. Notice that the integrand contains a power of the function $x^2 + 5$. If $u = x^2 + 5$, then $du = 2x\, dx$. Since the *constant* factor 2 in du does *not* appear in the integrand, this integral does not have the form $\int u^n \, du$. However, from $du = 2x \, dx$ we can write $x \, dx = \dfrac{du}{2}$ so that the integral becomes

$$\int x(x^2 + 5)^{1/2} \, dx = \int (x^2 + 5)^{1/2} [x \, dx] = \int u^{1/2} \frac{du}{2}$$

Moving the *constant* factor $\frac{1}{2}$ in front of the integral sign, we have

$$\int x(x^2 + 5)^{1/2} \, dx = \frac{1}{2} \int u^{1/2} \, du = \frac{1}{2} \left(\frac{u^{3/2}}{\frac{3}{2}} \right) + C = \frac{1}{3} u^{3/2} + C$$

which in terms of x (as is required) gives

$$\int x\sqrt{x^2 + 5} \, dx = \frac{(x^2 + 5)^{3/2}}{3} + C$$

Now Work Problem 15 ◁

CAUTION!

The answer to an integration problem must be expressed in terms of the original variable.

In Example 2, the integrand $x\sqrt{x^2 + 5}$ missed being of the form $(u(x))^{1/2} u'(x)$ by the *constant factor* of 2. In general, if we have $\int (u(x))^a \dfrac{u'(x)}{k} \, dx$, for k a nonzero constant, then we can write

$$\int (u(x))^a \frac{u'(x)}{k} \, dx = \int u^a \frac{du}{k} = \frac{1}{k} \int u^a \, du$$

CAUTION!

We can adjust for constant factors, but not variable factors.

to simplify the integral, but such *adjustments* of the integrand are *not possible for variable factors*.

When using the form $\int u^a \, du$, do not neglect du. For example,

$$\int (4x + 1)^2 \, dx \neq \frac{(4x + 1)^3}{3} + C$$

The correct way to do this problem is as follows. Let $u = 4x + 1$, from which it follows that $du = 4 \, dx$. Thus $dx = \dfrac{du}{4}$ and

$$\int (4x + 1)^2 \, dx = \int u^2 \left[\frac{du}{4} \right] = \frac{1}{4} \int u^2 \, du = \frac{1}{4} \cdot \frac{u^3}{3} + C = \frac{(4x + 1)^3}{12} + C$$

EXAMPLE 3   Applying the Power Rule for Integration

a. Find $\int \sqrt[3]{6y} \, dy$.

Solution: The integrand is $(6y)^{1/3}$, a power of a function. However, in this case the obvious substitution $u = 6y$ can be avoided. More simply, we have

$$\int \sqrt[3]{6y} \, dy = \int 6^{1/3} y^{1/3} \, dy = \sqrt[3]{6} \int y^{1/3} \, dy = \sqrt[3]{6} \frac{y^{4/3}}{\frac{4}{3}} + C = \frac{3\sqrt[3]{6}}{4} y^{4/3} + C$$

b. Find $\int \dfrac{2x^3 + 3x}{(x^4 + 3x^2 + 7)^4} \, dx$.

Solution: We can write this as $\int (x^4 + 3x^2 + 7)^{-4} (2x^3 + 3x) \, dx$. Let us try to use the power rule for integration. If $u = x^4 + 3x^2 + 7$, then $du = (4x^3 + 6x) \, dx$, which is two times the quantity $(2x^3 + 3x) \, dx$ in the integral. Thus $(2x^3 + 3x) \, dx = \dfrac{du}{2}$ and we again illustrate the *adjustment* technique:

$$\int (x^4 + 3x^2 + 7)^{-4} [(2x^3 + 3x) \, dx] = \int u^{-4} \left[\frac{du}{2} \right] = \frac{1}{2} \int u^{-4} \, du$$

$$= \frac{1}{2} \cdot \frac{u^{-3}}{-3} + C = -\frac{1}{6u^3} + C = -\frac{1}{6(x^4 + 3x^2 + 7)^3} + C$$

Now Work Problem 5 ◁

In using the power rule for integration, take care when making a choice for u. In Example 3(b), letting $u = 2x^3 + 3x$ does not lead very far. At times it may be necessary to try many different choices. Sometimes a wrong choice will provide a hint as to what does work. **Skill at integration comes only after many hours of practice and conscientious study.**

EXAMPLE 4   An Integral to Which the Power Rule Does Not Apply

Find $\displaystyle\int 4x^2(x^4 + 1)^2 \, dx$.

Solution: If we set $u = x^4 + 1$, then $du = 4x^3 \, dx$. To get du in the integral, we need an additional factor of the *variable* x. However, we can adjust only for **constant** factors. Thus, we cannot use the power rule. Instead, to find the integral, we will first expand $(x^4 + 1)^2$:

$$\int 4x^2(x^4 + 1)^2 \, dx = 4 \int x^2(x^8 + 2x^4 + 1) \, dx$$

$$= 4 \int (x^{10} + 2x^6 + x^2) \, dx$$

$$= 4 \left(\frac{x^{11}}{11} + \frac{2x^7}{7} + \frac{x^3}{3} \right) + C$$

Now Work Problem 67 ◁

Integrating Natural Exponential Functions

We now turn our attention to integrating exponential functions. If u is a differentiable function of x, then

$$\frac{d}{dx}(e^u) = e^u \frac{du}{dx}$$

CAUTION!

Do not apply the power-rule formula for $\int u^a \, du$ to $\int e^u \, du$.

Corresponding to this differentiation formula is the integration formula

$$\int e^u \frac{du}{dx} \, dx = e^u + C$$

But $\dfrac{du}{dx} \, dx$ is the differential of u, namely, du. Thus,

$$\int e^u \, du = e^u + C \tag{2}$$

APPLY IT ▶

8. When an object is moved from one environment to another, its temperature T changes at a rate given by $\dfrac{dT}{dt} = kCe^{kt}$, where t is the time (in hours) after changing environments, C is the temperature difference (original minus new) between the environments, and k is a constant. If the original environment is $70°$, the new environment is $60°$, and $k = -0.5$, find the general form of $T(t)$.

EXAMPLE 5   Integrals Involving Exponential Functions

a. Find $\displaystyle\int 2xe^{x^2} \, dx$.

Solution: Let $u = x^2$. Then $du = 2x \, dx$, and, by Equation (2),

$$\int 2xe^{x^2} \, dx = \int e^{x^2}[2x \, dx] = \int e^u \, du$$

$$= e^u + C = e^{x^2} + C$$

b. Find $\int (x^2 + 1)e^{x^3+3x}\,dx$.

Solution: If $u = x^3 + 3x$, then $du = (3x^2 + 3)\,dx = 3(x^2 + 1)\,dx$. If the integrand contained a factor of 3, the integral would have the form $\int e^u\,du$. Thus, we write

$$\int (x^2 + 1)e^{x^3+3x}\,dx = \int e^{x^3+3x}[(x^2 + 1)\,dx]$$

$$= \frac{1}{3}\int e^u\,du = \frac{1}{3}e^u + C$$

$$= \frac{1}{3}e^{x^3+3x} + C$$

where in the second step we replaced $(x^2 + 1)\,dx$ by $\frac{1}{3}\,du$ but wrote $\frac{1}{3}$ outside the integral.

Now Work Problem 41 ◁

Integrals Involving Logarithmic Functions

As we know, the power-rule formula $\int u^a\,du = u^{a+1}/(a+1) + C$ does not apply when $a = -1$. To handle that situation, namely, $\int u^{-1}\,du = \int \frac{1}{u}\,du$, we first recall from Section 12.1 that

$$\frac{d}{dx}(\ln|u|) = \frac{1}{u}\frac{du}{dx} \quad \text{for } u \neq 0$$

which gives us the integration formula

$$\int \frac{1}{u}\,du = \ln|u| + C \quad \text{for } u \neq 0 \tag{3}$$

In particular, if $u = x$, then $du = dx$, and

$$\int \frac{1}{x}\,dx = \ln|x| + C \quad \text{for } x \neq 0 \tag{4}$$

APPLY IT ▶

9. If the rate of vocabulary memorization of the average student in a foreign language is given by $\dfrac{dv}{dt} = \dfrac{35}{t+1}$, where v is the number of vocabulary words memorized in t hours of study, find the general form of $v(t)$.

EXAMPLE 6   Integrals Involving $\dfrac{1}{u}\,du$

a. Find $\int \dfrac{7}{x}\,dx$.

Solution: From Equation (4),

$$\int \frac{7}{x}\,dx = 7\int \frac{1}{x}\,dx = 7\ln|x| + C$$

Using properties of logarithms, we can write this answer another way:

$$\int \frac{7}{x}\,dx = \ln|x^7| + C$$

b. Find $\int \dfrac{2x}{x^2 + 5}\,dx$.

Solution: Let $u = x^2 + 5$. Then $du = 2x\,dx$. From Equation (3),

$$\int \frac{2x}{x^2 + 5}\,dx = \int \frac{1}{x^2 + 5}[2x\,dx] = \int \frac{1}{u}\,du$$

$$= \ln|u| + C = \ln|x^2 + 5| + C$$

Since $x^2 + 5$ is always positive, we can omit the absolute-value bars:

$$\int \frac{2x}{x^2 + 5}\,dx = \ln(x^2 + 5) + C$$

Now Work Problem 31 ◁

EXAMPLE 7 An Integral Involving $\dfrac{1}{u}\,du$

Find $\displaystyle \int \frac{(2x^3 + 3x)\,dx}{x^4 + 3x^2 + 7}$.

Solution: If $u = x^4 + 3x^2 + 7$, then $du = (4x^3 + 6x)\,dx$, which is two times the numerator giving $(2x^3 + 3x)\,dx = \dfrac{du}{2}$. To apply Equation (3), we write

$$\int \frac{2x^3 + 3x}{x^4 + 3x^2 + 7}\,dx = \frac{1}{2}\int \frac{1}{u}\,du$$

$$= \frac{1}{2}\ln|u| + C$$

$$= \frac{1}{2}\ln|x^4 + 3x^2 + 7| + C \qquad \text{Rewrite } u \text{ in terms of } x.$$

$$= \frac{1}{2}\ln(x^4 + 3x^2 + 7) + C \qquad x^4 + 3x^2 + 7 > 0 \quad \text{for all } x$$

Now Work Problem 51 ◁

EXAMPLE 8 An Integral Involving Two Forms

Find $\displaystyle \int \left(\frac{1}{(1-w)^2} + \frac{1}{w-1}\right)dw$.

Solution:

$$\int \left(\frac{1}{(1-w)^2} + \frac{1}{w-1}\right)dw = \int (1-w)^{-2}dw + \int \frac{1}{w-1}\,dw$$

$$= -1\int (1-w)^{-2}[-dw] + \int \frac{1}{w-1}\,dw$$

The first integral has the form $\int u^{-2}\,du$, and the second has the form $\int \dfrac{1}{v}\,dv$. Thus,

$$\int \left(\frac{1}{(1-w)^2} + \frac{1}{w-1}\right)dw = -\frac{(1-w)^{-1}}{-1} + \ln|w-1| + C$$

$$= \frac{1}{1-w} + \ln|w-1| + C$$

◁

PROBLEMS 14.4

In Problems 1–80, find the indefinite integrals.

1. $\displaystyle \int (x+5)^7\,dx$

2. $\displaystyle \int 15(x+2)^4\,dx$

3. $\displaystyle \int 2x(x^2+3)^5\,dx$

4. $\displaystyle \int (4x+3)(2x^2+3x+1)\,dx$

5. $\displaystyle \int (3y^2+6y)(y^3+3y^2+1)^{2/3}\,dy$

6. $\displaystyle \int (15t^2 - 6t + 1)(5t^3 - 3t^2 + t)^{17}\,dt$

7. $\displaystyle \int \frac{5}{(3x-1)^3}\,dx$

8. $\displaystyle \int \frac{4x}{(2x^2-7)^{10}}\,dx$

9. $\displaystyle \int \sqrt{7x+3}\,dx$

10. $\displaystyle \int \frac{1}{\sqrt{x-5}}\,dx$

11. $\displaystyle \int (7x-6)^4\,dx$

12. $\displaystyle \int x^2(3x^3+7)^3\,dx$

13. $\displaystyle \int u(5u^2-9)^{14}\,du$

14. $\displaystyle \int x\sqrt{3+5x^2}\,dx$

15. $\displaystyle \int 4x^4(27+x^5)^{1/3}\,dx$

16. $\displaystyle \int (4-5x)^9\,dx$

17. $\displaystyle \int 3e^{3x}\,dx$

18. $\displaystyle \int 5e^{3t+7}\,dt$

19. $\displaystyle \int (3t+1)e^{3t^2+2t+1}\,dt$

20. $\displaystyle \int -3w^2 e^{-w^3}\,dw$

21. $\displaystyle \int xe^{7x^2}\,dx$

22. $\displaystyle \int x^3 e^{4x^4}\,dx$

23. $\displaystyle \int 4e^{-3x}\,dx$

24. $\displaystyle \int 24x^5 e^{-2x^6+7}\,dx$

25. $\displaystyle \int \frac{1}{x+5}\,dx$

26. $\displaystyle \int \frac{12x^2+4x+2}{x+x^2+2x^3}\,dx$

27. $\displaystyle \int \frac{3x^2+4x^3}{x^3+x^4}\,dx$

28. $\displaystyle \int \frac{6x^2-6x}{1-3x^2+2x^3}\,dx$

29. $\displaystyle \int \frac{8z}{(z^2-5)^7}\,dz$

30. $\displaystyle \int \frac{3}{(5v-1)^4}\,dv$

31. $\int \frac{4}{x}\,dx$

32. $\int \frac{3}{1+2y}\,dy$

33. $\int \frac{s^2}{s^3+5}\,ds$

34. $\int \frac{32x^3}{4x^4+9}\,dx$

35. $\int \frac{5}{4-2x}\,dx$

36. $\int \frac{7t}{5t^2-6}\,dt$

37. $\int \sqrt{5x}\,dx$

38. $\int \frac{1}{(3x)^6}\,dx$

39. $\int \frac{x}{\sqrt{ax^2+b}}\,dx$

40. $\int \frac{9}{1-3x}\,dx$

41. $\int 2y^3 e^{y^4+1}\,dy$

42. $\int 2\sqrt{2x-1}\,dx$

43. $\int v^2 e^{-2v^3+1}\,dv$

44. $\int \frac{x^2+x+1}{\sqrt[3]{x^3+\frac{3}{2}x^2+3x}}\,dx$

45. $\int (e^{-5x}+2e^x)\,dx$

46. $\int 4\sqrt[3]{y+1}\,dy$

47. $\int (8x+10)(7-2x^2-5x)^3\,dx$

48. $\int 2ye^{3y^2}\,dy$

49. $\int \frac{6x^2+8}{x^3+4x}\,dx$

50. $\int (e^x+2e^{-3x}-e^{5x})\,dx$

51. $\int \frac{16s-4}{3-2s+4s^2}\,ds$

52. $\int (6t^2+4t)(t^3+t^2+1)^6\,dt$

53. $\int x(2x^2+1)^{-1}\,dx$

54. $\int (45w^4+18w^2+12)(3w^5+2w^3+4)^{-4}\,dw$

55. $\int -(x^2-2x^5)(x^3-x^6)^{-10}\,dx$

56. $\int \frac{3}{5}(v-2)e^{2-4v+v^2}\,dv$

57. $\int (2x^3+x)(x^4+x^2)\,dx$

58. $\int (e^{3.1})^2\,dx$

59. $\int \frac{9+18x}{(5-x-x^2)^4}\,dx$

60. $\int (e^x-e^{-x})^2\,dx$

61. $\int x(2x+1)e^{4x^3+3x^2-4}\,dx$

62. $\int (u^3-ue^{6-3u^2})\,du$

63. $\int x\sqrt{(8-5x^2)^3}\,dx$

64. $\int e^{ax}\,dx$

65. $\int \left(\sqrt{2x}-\frac{1}{\sqrt{2x}}\right)dx$

66. $\int 3\frac{x^4}{e^{x^5}}\,dx$

67. $\int (x^2+1)^2\,dx$

68. $\int \left[x(x^2-16)^2 - \frac{1}{2x+5}\right]dx$

69. $\int \left(\frac{x}{x^2+1}+\frac{x}{(x^2+1)^2}\right)dx$ **70.** $\int \left[\frac{3}{x-1}+\frac{1}{(x-1)^2}\right]dx$

71. $\int \left[\frac{2}{4x+1}-(4x^2-8x^5)(x^3-x^6)^{-8}\right]dx$

72. $\int (r^3+5)^2\,dr$

73. $\int \left[\sqrt{3x+1}-\frac{x}{x^2+3}\right]dx$

74. $\int \left(\frac{x}{7x^2+2}-\frac{x^2}{(x^3+2)^4}\right)dx$

75. $\int \frac{e^{\sqrt{x}}}{\sqrt{x}}\,dx$

76. $\int (e^5-3^e)\,dx$

77. $\int \frac{1+e^{2x}}{4e^x}\,dx$

78. $\int \frac{2}{t^2}\sqrt{\frac{1}{t}+9}\,dt$

79. $\int \frac{4x+3}{2x^2+3x}\ln(2x^2+3x)\,dx$

80. $\int \sqrt[3]{x}e^{\sqrt[3]{8x^4}}\,dx$

In Problems 81–84, find y subject to the given conditions.

81. $y'=(3-2x)^2$; $y(0)=1$ **82.** $y'=\frac{x}{x^2+6}$; $y(1)=0$

83. $y''=\frac{1}{x^2}$; $y'(-2)=3, y(1)=2$

84. $y''=(x+1)^{1/2}$; $y'(8)=19, y(24)=\frac{2572}{3}$

85. Real Estate The rate of change of the value of a house that cost \$350,000 to build can be modeled by $\frac{dV}{dt}=8e^{0.05t}$, where t is the time in years since the house was built and V is the value (in thousands of dollars) of the house. Find $V(t)$.

86. Life Span If the rate of change of the expected life span l at birth of people born in the United States can be modeled by $\frac{dl}{dt}=\frac{12}{2t+50}$, where t is the number of years after 1940 and the expected life span was 63 years in 1940, find the expected life span for people born in 1998.

87. Oxygen in Capillary In a discussion of the diffusion of oxygen from capillaries,[5] concentric cylinders of radius r are used as a model for a capillary. The concentration C of oxygen in the capillary is given by

$$C=\int \left(\frac{Rr}{2K}+\frac{B_1}{r}\right)dr$$

where R is the constant rate at which oxygen diffuses from the capillary, and K and B_1 are constants. Find C. (Write the constant of integration as B_2.)

88. Find $f(2)$ if $f\left(\frac{1}{3}\right)=2$ and $f'(x)=e^{3x+2}-3x$.

Objective

To discuss techniques of handling more challenging integration problems, namely, by algebraic manipulation and by fitting the integrand to a familiar form. To integrate an exponential function with a base different from e and to find the consumption function, given the marginal propensity to consume.

14.5 Techniques of Integration

We turn now to some more difficult integration problems.

When integrating fractions, sometimes a preliminary division is needed to get familiar integration forms, as the next example shows.

---

[5]W. Simon, *Mathematical Techniques for Physiology and Medicine* (New York: Academic Press, Inc., 1972).

EXAMPLE 1 Preliminary Division before Integration

a. Find $\displaystyle\int \frac{x^3 + x}{x^2}\, dx$.

Solution: A familiar integration form is not apparent. However, we can break up the integrand into two fractions by dividing each term in the numerator by the denominator. We then have

$$\int \frac{x^3 + x}{x^2}\, dx = \int \left(\frac{x^3}{x^2} + \frac{x}{x^2} \right) dx = \int \left(x + \frac{1}{x} \right) dx$$

$$= \frac{x^2}{2} + \ln |x| + C$$

Here we split up the integrand.

b. Find $\displaystyle\int \frac{2x^3 + 3x^2 + x + 1}{2x + 1}\, dx$.

Solution: Here the integrand is a quotient of polynomials in which the degree of the numerator is greater than or equal to that of the denominator. In such a situation we first use long division. Recall that if f and g are polynomials, with the degree of f greater than or equal to the degree of g, then long division allows us to find (uniquely) polynomials q and r, where either r is the zero polynomial or the degree of r is strictly less than the degree of g, satisfying

$$\frac{f}{g} = q + \frac{r}{g}$$

Using an obvious, abbreviated notation, we see that

$$\int \frac{f}{g} = \int \left(q + \frac{r}{g} \right) = \int q + \int \frac{r}{g}$$

Since integrating a polynomial is easy, we see that integrating rational functions reduces to the task of integrating *proper rational functions*—those for which the degree of the numerator is strictly less than the degree of the denominator. In this case we obtain

Here we used long division to rewrite the integrand.

$$\int \frac{2x^3 + 3x^2 + x + 1}{2x + 1}\, dx = \int \left(x^2 + x + \frac{1}{2x + 1} \right) dx$$

$$= \frac{x^3}{3} + \frac{x^2}{2} + \int \frac{1}{2x + 1}\, dx$$

$$= \frac{x^3}{3} + \frac{x^2}{2} + \frac{1}{2} \int \frac{1}{2x + 1}\, d(2x + 1)$$

$$= \frac{x^3}{3} + \frac{x^2}{2} + \frac{1}{2} \ln |2x + 1| + C$$

Now Work Problem 1 ◁

EXAMPLE 2 Indefinite Integrals

a. Find $\displaystyle\int \frac{1}{\sqrt{x}(\sqrt{x} - 2)^3}\, dx$.

Solution: We can write this integral as $\displaystyle\int \frac{(\sqrt{x} - 2)^{-3}}{\sqrt{x}}\, dx$. Let us try the power rule for integration with $u = \sqrt{x} - 2$. Then $du = \dfrac{1}{2\sqrt{x}}\, dx$, so that $\dfrac{dx}{\sqrt{x}} = 2\, du$, and

$$\int \frac{(\sqrt{x} - 2)^{-3}}{\sqrt{x}}\, dx = \int (\sqrt{x} - 2)^{-3} \left[\frac{dx}{\sqrt{x}} \right]$$

Here the integral is fit to the form to which the power rule for integration applies.

$$= 2 \int u^{-3}\, du = 2 \left(\frac{u^{-2}}{-2} \right) + C$$

$$= -\frac{1}{u^2} + C = -\frac{1}{(\sqrt{x} - 2)^2} + C$$

b. Find $\int \dfrac{1}{x \ln x} dx$.

Solution: If $u = \ln x$, then $du = \dfrac{1}{x} dx$, and

$$\int \frac{1}{x \ln x} dx = \int \frac{1}{\ln x} \left(\frac{1}{x} dx \right) = \int \frac{1}{u} du$$

$$= \ln |u| + C = \ln | \ln x | + C$$

Here the integral fits the familiar form $\int \dfrac{1}{u} du$.

c. Find $\int \dfrac{5}{w(\ln w)^{3/2}} dw$.

Here the integral is fit to the form to which the power rule for integration applies.

Solution: If $u = \ln w$, then $du = \dfrac{1}{w} dw$. Applying the power rule for integration, we have

$$\int \frac{5}{w(\ln w)^{3/2}} dw = 5 \int (\ln w)^{-3/2} \left[\frac{1}{w} dw \right]$$

$$= 5 \int u^{-3/2} du = 5 \cdot \frac{u^{-1/2}}{-\frac{1}{2}} + C$$

$$= \frac{-10}{u^{1/2}} + C = -\frac{10}{(\ln w)^{1/2}} + C$$

Now Work Problem 23 ◁

Integrating b^u

In Section 14.4, we integrated an exponential function to the base e:

$$\int e^u du = e^u + C$$

Now let us consider the integral of an exponential function with an arbitrary base, b.

$$\int b^u du$$

To find this integral, we first convert to base e using

$$b^u = e^{(\ln b)u} \tag{1}$$

(as we did in many differentiation examples too). Example 3 will illustrate.

EXAMPLE 3 An Integral Involving b^u

Find $\int 2^{3-x} dx$.

Solution:

Strategy We want to integrate an exponential function to the base 2. To do this, we will first convert from base 2 to base e by using Equation (1).

$$\int 2^{3-x} dx = \int e^{(\ln 2)(3-x)} dx$$

The integrand of the second integral is of the form e^u, where $u = (\ln 2)(3 - x)$. Since $du = -\ln 2 \, dx$, we can solve for dx and write

$$\int e^{(\ln 2)(3-x)} dx = -\frac{1}{\ln 2} \int e^u du$$

$$= -\frac{1}{\ln 2} e^u + C = -\frac{1}{\ln 2} e^{(\ln 2)(3-x)} + C = -\frac{1}{\ln 2} 2^{3-x} + C$$

Thus,

$$\int 2^{3-x}\, dx = -\frac{1}{\ln 2} 2^{3-x} + C$$

Notice that we expressed our answer in terms of an exponential function to the base 2, the base of the original integrand.

Now Work Problem 27 ◁

Generalizing the procedure described in Example 3, we can obtain a formula for integrating b^u:

$$\int b^u\, du = \int e^{(\ln b)u}\, du$$

$$= \frac{1}{\ln b} \int e^{(\ln b)u}\, d((\ln b)u) \qquad \ln b \text{ is a constant}$$

$$= \frac{1}{\ln b} e^{(\ln b)u} + C$$

$$= \frac{1}{\ln b} b^u + C$$

Hence, we have

$$\int b^u\, du = \frac{1}{\ln b} b^u + C$$

Applying this formula to the integral in Example 3 gives

$$\int 2^{3-x}\, dx \qquad\qquad b = 2, u = 3 - x$$

$$= -\int 2^{3-x}\, d(3 - x) \qquad -d(3 - x) = dx$$

$$= -\frac{1}{\ln 2} 2^{3-x} + C$$

which is the same result that we obtained before.

Application of Integration

We will now consider an application of integration that relates a consumption function to the marginal propensity to consume.

EXAMPLE 4   Finding a Consumption Function from Marginal Propensity to Consume

For a certain country, the marginal propensity to consume is given by

$$\frac{dC}{dI} = \frac{3}{4} - \frac{1}{2\sqrt{3I}}$$

where consumption C is a function of national income I. Here I is expressed in large denominations of money. Determine the consumption function for the country if it is known that consumption is 10 ($C = 10$) when $I = 12$.

Solution: Since the marginal propensity to consume is the derivative of C, we have

$$C = C(I) = \int \left(\frac{3}{4} - \frac{1}{2\sqrt{3I}} \right) dI = \int \frac{3}{4}\, dI - \frac{1}{2} \int (3I)^{-1/2}\, dI$$

$$= \frac{3}{4} I - \frac{1}{2} \int (3I)^{-1/2}\, dI$$

If we let $u = 3I$, then $du = 3\,dI = d(3I)$, and

$$C = \frac{3}{4}I - \left(\frac{1}{2}\right)\frac{1}{3}\int (3I)^{-1/2}\,d(3I)$$

$$= \frac{3}{4}I - \frac{1}{6}\frac{(3I)^{1/2}}{\dfrac{1}{2}} + K$$

$$C = \frac{3}{4}I - \frac{\sqrt{3I}}{3} + K$$

When $I = 12$, $C = 10$, so

This is an example of an initial-value problem.

$$10 = \frac{3}{4}(12) - \frac{\sqrt{3(12)}}{3} + K$$

$$10 = 9 - 2 + K$$

Thus, $K = 3$, and the consumption function is

$$C = \frac{3}{4}I - \frac{\sqrt{3I}}{3} + 3$$

Now Work Problem 61 ◁

PROBLEMS 14.5

In Problems 1–56, determine the indefinite integrals.

1. $\displaystyle\int \frac{2x^6 + 8x^4 - 4x}{2x^2}\,dx$

2. $\displaystyle\int \frac{9x^2 + 5}{3x}\,dx$

3. $\displaystyle\int (3x^2 + 2)\sqrt{2x^3 + 4x + 1}\,dx$

4. $\displaystyle\int \frac{x}{\sqrt[4]{x^2 + 1}}\,dx$

5. $\displaystyle\int \frac{3}{\sqrt{4 - 5x}}\,dx$

6. $\displaystyle\int \frac{2xe^{x^2}\,dx}{e^{x^2} - 2}$

7. $\displaystyle\int 4^{7x}\,dx$

8. $\displaystyle\int 5^t\,dt$

9. $\displaystyle\int 2x(7 - e^{x^2/4})\,dx$

10. $\displaystyle\int \frac{e^x + 1}{e^x}\,dx$

11. $\displaystyle\int \frac{6x^2 - 11x + 5}{3x - 1}\,dx$

12. $\displaystyle\int \frac{(3x + 2)(x - 4)}{x - 3}\,dx$

13. $\displaystyle\int \frac{5e^{2x}}{7e^{2x} + 4}\,dx$

14. $\displaystyle\int 6(e^{4-3x})^2\,dx$

15. $\displaystyle\int \frac{5e^{13/x}}{x^2}\,dx$

16. $\displaystyle\int \frac{2x^4 - 6x^3 + x - 2}{x - 2}\,dx$

17. $\displaystyle\int \frac{5x^3}{x^2 + 9}\,dx$

18. $\displaystyle\int \frac{5 - 4x^2}{3 + 2x}\,dx$

19. $\displaystyle\int \frac{(\sqrt{x} + 2)^2}{3\sqrt{x}}\,dx$

20. $\displaystyle\int \frac{5e^s}{1 + 3e^s}\,ds$

21. $\displaystyle\int \frac{5(x^{1/3} + 2)^4}{\sqrt[3]{x^2}}\,dx$

22. $\displaystyle\int \frac{\sqrt{1 + \sqrt{x}}}{\sqrt{x}}\,dx$

23. $\displaystyle\int \frac{\ln x}{x}\,dx$

24. $\displaystyle\int \sqrt{t}(3 - t\sqrt{t})^{0.6}\,dt$

25. $\displaystyle\int \frac{r\sqrt{\ln(r^2 + 1)}}{r^2 + 1}\,dr$

26. $\displaystyle\int \frac{9x^5 - 6x^4 - ex^3}{7x^2}\,dx$

27. $\displaystyle\int \frac{3^{\ln x}}{x}\,dx$

28. $\displaystyle\int \frac{4}{x\ln(2x^2)}\,dx$

29. $\displaystyle\int x^2\sqrt{e^{x^3+1}}\,dx$

30. $\displaystyle\int \frac{ax + b}{cx + d}\,dx \quad c \neq 0$

31. $\displaystyle\int \frac{8}{(x + 3)\ln(x + 3)}\,dx$

32. $\displaystyle\int (e^{e^2} + x^e - 2x)\,dx$

33. $\displaystyle\int \frac{x^3 + x^2 - x - 3}{x^2 - 3}\,dx$

34. $\displaystyle\int \frac{4x\ln\sqrt{1 + x^2}}{1 + x^2}\,dx$

35. $\displaystyle\int \frac{12x^3\sqrt{\ln(x^4 + 1)^3}}{x^4 + 1}\,dx$

36. $\displaystyle\int 3(x^2 + 2)^{-1/2}xe^{\sqrt{x^2+2}}\,dx$

37. $\displaystyle\int \left(\frac{x^3 - 1}{\sqrt{x^4 - 4x}} - \ln 7\right)\,dx$

38. $\displaystyle\int \frac{x - x^{-2}}{x^2 + 2x^{-1}}\,dx$

39. $\displaystyle\int \frac{2x^4 - 8x^3 - 6x^2 + 4}{x^3}\,dx$

40. $\displaystyle\int \frac{e^x - e^{-x}}{e^x + e^{-x}}\,dx$

41. $\displaystyle\int \frac{x}{x + 1}\,dx$

42. $\displaystyle\int \frac{2x}{(x^2 + 1)\ln(x^2 + 1)}\,dx$

43. $\displaystyle\int \frac{xe^{x^2}}{\sqrt{e^{x^2} + 2}}\,dx$

44. $\displaystyle\int \frac{5}{(3x + 1)[1 + \ln(3x + 1)]^2}\,dx$

45. $\displaystyle\int \frac{(e^{-x} + 5)^3}{e^x}\,dx$

46. $\displaystyle\int \left[\frac{1}{8x + 1} - \frac{1}{e^x(8 + e^{-x})^2}\right]\,dx$

47. $\displaystyle\int (x^3 + ex)\sqrt{x^2 + e}\,dx$

48. $\displaystyle\int 3^{x\ln x}(1 + \ln x)\,dx \quad [Hint: \frac{d}{dx}(x\ln x) = 1 + \ln x]$

49. $\displaystyle\int \sqrt{x}\sqrt{(8x)^{3/2} + 3}\,dx$

50. $\displaystyle\int \frac{7}{x(\ln x)^\pi}\,dx$

51. $\displaystyle\int \frac{\sqrt{s}}{e^{\sqrt{s^3}}}\,ds$

52. $\displaystyle\int \frac{\ln^3 x}{3x}\,dx$

53. $\displaystyle\int e^{\ln(x^2+1)}\,dx$

54. $\displaystyle\int dx$

55. $\displaystyle\int \frac{\ln\left(\frac{e^x}{x}\right)}{x}\, dx$

56. $\displaystyle\int e^{f(x)+\ln(f'(x))}\, dx$ assuming $f' > 0$

In Problems 57 and 58, dr/dq is a marginal-revenue function. Find the demand function.

57. $\dfrac{dr}{dq} = \dfrac{200}{(q+2)^2}$ **58.** $\dfrac{dr}{dq} = \dfrac{900}{(2q+3)^3}$

In Problems 59 and 60, dc/dq is a marginal-cost function. Find the total-cost function if fixed costs in each case are 2000.

59. $\dfrac{dc}{dq} = \dfrac{20}{q+5}$ **60.** $\dfrac{dc}{dq} = 4e^{0.005q}$

In Problems 61–63, dC/dI represents the marginal propensity to consume. Find the consumption function subject to the given condition.

61. $\dfrac{dC}{dI} = \dfrac{1}{\sqrt{I}};\quad C(9) = 8$

62. $\dfrac{dC}{dI} = \dfrac{1}{2} - \dfrac{1}{2\sqrt{2I}};\quad C(2) = \dfrac{3}{4}$

63. $\dfrac{dC}{dI} = \dfrac{3}{4} - \dfrac{1}{6\sqrt{I}};\quad C(25) = 23$

64. Cost Function   The marginal-cost function for a manufacturer's product is given by

$$\frac{dc}{dq} = 10 - \frac{100}{q+10}$$

where c is the total cost in dollars when q units are produced. When 100 units are produced, the average cost is $50 per unit. To the nearest dollar, determine the manufacturer's fixed cost.

65. Cost Function   Suppose the marginal-cost function for a manufacturer's product is given by

$$\frac{dc}{dq} = \frac{100q^2 - 3998q + 60}{q^2 - 40q + 1}$$

where c is the total cost in dollars when q units are produced.

(a) Determine the marginal cost when 40 units are produced.
(b) If fixed costs are $10,000, find the total cost of producing 40 units.
(c) Use the results of parts (a) and (b) and differentials to approximate the total cost of producing 42 units.

66. Cost Function   The marginal-cost function for a manufacturer's product is given by

$$\frac{dc}{dq} = \frac{9}{10}\sqrt{q}\sqrt{0.04q^{3/4} + 4}$$

where c is the total cost in dollars when q units are produced. Fixed costs are $360.

(a) Determine the marginal cost when 25 units are produced.
(b) Find the total cost of producing 25 units.
(c) Use the results of parts (a) and (b) and differentials to approximate the total cost of producing 23 units.

67. Value of Land   It is estimated that t years from now the value V (in dollars) of an acre of land near the ghost town of Cherokee, California, will be increasing at the rate of

$$\frac{8t^3}{\sqrt{0.2t^4 + 8000}}$$

dollars per year. If the land is currently worth $500 per acre, how much will it be worth in 10 years? Express your answer to the nearest dollar.

68. Revenue Function   The marginal-revenue function for a manufacturer's product is of the form

$$\frac{dr}{dq} = \frac{a}{e^q + b}$$

for constants a and b, where r is the total revenue received (in dollars) when q units are produced and sold. Find the demand function, and express it in the form $p = f(q)$. (*Hint:* Rewrite dr/dq by multiplying both numerator and denominator by e^{-q}.)

69. Savings   A certain country's marginal propensity to save is given by

$$\frac{dS}{dI} = \frac{5}{(I+2)^2}$$

where S and I represent total national savings and income, respectively, and are measured in billions of dollars. If total national consumption is $7.5 billion when total national income is $8 billion, for what value(s) of I is total national savings equal to zero?

70. Consumption Function   A certain country's marginal propensity to save is given by

$$\frac{dS}{dI} = \frac{2}{5} - \frac{1.6}{\sqrt[3]{2I^2}}$$

where S and I represent total national savings and income, respectively, and are measured in billions of dollars.

(a) Determine the marginal propensity to consume when total national income is $16 billion.
(b) Determine the consumption function, given that savings are $10 billion when total national income is $54 billion.
(c) Use the result in part (b) to show that consumption is $\frac{82}{5} = 16.4$ billion when total national income is $16 billion (a deficit situation).
(d) Use differentials and the results in parts (a) and (c) to approximate consumption when total national income is $18 billion.

14.6 The Definite Integral

Figure 14.2 shows the region R bounded by the lines $y = f(x) = 2x$, $y = 0$ (the x-axis), and $x = 1$. The region is simply a right triangle. If b and h are the lengths of the base and the height, respectively, then, from geometry, the area of the triangle is $A = \frac{1}{2}bh = \frac{1}{2}(1)(2) = 1$ square unit. (Henceforth, we will treat areas as pure numbers and write *square unit* only if it seems necessary for emphasis.) We will now find this area by another method, which, as we will see later, applies to more complex regions. This method involves the summation of areas of rectangles.

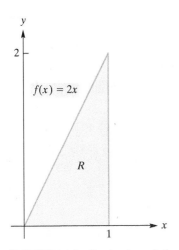

FIGURE 14.2   Region bounded by $f(x) = 2x, y = 0$, and $x = 1$.

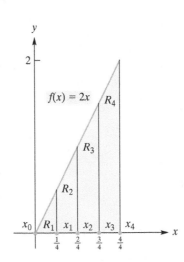

FIGURE 14.3   Four subregions of R.

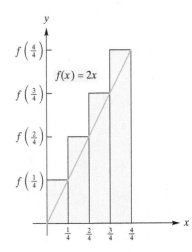

FIGURE 14.4   Four circumscribed rectangles.

Let us divide the interval $[0, 1]$ on the x-axis into four subintervals of equal length by means of the equally spaced points $x_0 = 0, x_1 = \frac{1}{4}, x_2 = \frac{2}{4}, x_3 = \frac{3}{4}$, and $x_4 = \frac{4}{4} = 1$. (See Figure 14.3.) Each subinterval has length $\Delta x = \frac{1}{4}$. These subintervals determine four subregions of R: R_1, R_2, R_3, and R_4, as indicated.

With each subregion, we can associate a *circumscribed* rectangle (Figure 14.4)—that is, a rectangle whose base is the corresponding subinterval and whose height is the *maximum* value of $f(x)$ on that subinterval. Since f is an increasing function, the maximum value of $f(x)$ on each subinterval occurs when x is the right-hand endpoint. Thus, the areas of the circumscribed rectangles associated with regions R_1, R_2, R_3, and R_4 are $\frac{1}{4} f(\frac{1}{4}), \frac{1}{4} f(\frac{2}{4}), \frac{1}{4} f(\frac{3}{4})$, and $\frac{1}{4} f(\frac{4}{4})$, respectively. The area of each rectangle is an approximation to the area of its corresponding subregion. Hence, the sum of the areas of these rectangles, denoted by $\overline{S}_4$ (read "S upper bar sub 4" or "the fourth upper sum"), approximates the area A of the triangle. We have

$$\overline{S}_4 = \tfrac{1}{4} f\left(\tfrac{1}{4}\right) + \tfrac{1}{4} f\left(\tfrac{2}{4}\right) + \tfrac{1}{4} f\left(\tfrac{3}{4}\right) + \tfrac{1}{4} f\left(\tfrac{4}{4}\right)$$
$$= \tfrac{1}{4} \left(2\left(\tfrac{1}{4}\right) + 2\left(\tfrac{2}{4}\right) + 2\left(\tfrac{3}{4}\right) + 2\left(\tfrac{4}{4}\right)\right) = \tfrac{5}{4}$$

You can verify that $\overline{S}_4 = \sum_{i=1}^{4} f(x_i)\Delta x$. The fact that $\overline{S}_4$ is greater than the actual area of the triangle might have been expected, since $\overline{S}_4$ includes areas of shaded regions that are not in the triangle. (See Figure 14.4.)

On the other hand, with each subregion we can also associate an *inscribed* rectangle (Figure 14.5)—that is, a rectangle whose base is the corresponding subinterval, but whose height is the *minimum* value of $f(x)$ on that subinterval. Since f is an increasing function, the minimum value of $f(x)$ on each subinterval will occur when x is the left-hand endpoint. Thus, the areas of the four inscribed rectangles associated with R_1, R_2, R_3, and R_4 are $\frac{1}{4} f(0), \frac{1}{4} f(\frac{1}{4}), \frac{1}{4} f(\frac{2}{4})$, and $\frac{1}{4} f(\frac{3}{4})$, respectively. Their sum, denoted $\underline{S}_4$ (read "S lower bar sub 4" or "the fourth lower sum"), is also an approximation to the area A of the triangle. We have

$$\underline{S}_4 = \tfrac{1}{4} f(0) + \tfrac{1}{4} f\left(\tfrac{1}{4}\right) + \tfrac{1}{4} f\left(\tfrac{2}{4}\right) + \tfrac{1}{4} f\left(\tfrac{3}{4}\right)$$
$$= \tfrac{1}{4} \left(2(0) + 2\left(\tfrac{1}{4}\right) + 2\left(\tfrac{2}{4}\right) + 2\left(\tfrac{3}{4}\right)\right) = \tfrac{3}{4}$$

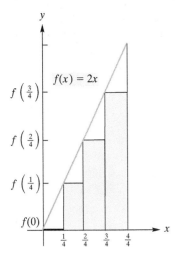

FIGURE 14.5   Four inscribed rectangles.

Using summation notation, we can write $\underline{S}_4 = \sum_{i=0}^{3} f(x_i)\Delta x$. Note that $\underline{S}_4$ is less than the area of the triangle, because the rectangles do not account for the portion of the triangle that is not shaded in Figure 14.5.

Since

$$\frac{3}{4} = \underline{S}_4 \leq A \leq \overline{S}_4 = \frac{5}{4}$$

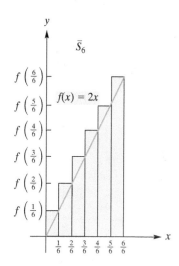

FIGURE 14.6   Six circumscribed rectangles.

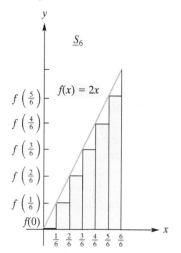

FIGURE 14.7   Six inscribed rectangles.

TO REVIEW summation notation, refer to Section 1.5.

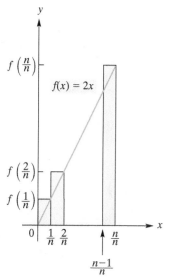

FIGURE 14.8 n circumscribed rectangles.

we say that $\underline{S}_4$ is an approximation to A from *below* and $\overline{S}_4$ is an approximation to A from *above*.

If $[0, 1]$ is divided into more subintervals, we expect that better approximations to A will occur. To test this, let us use six subintervals of equal length $\Delta x = \frac{1}{6}$. Then $\overline{S}_6$, the total area of six circumscribed rectangles (see Figure 14.6), and $\underline{S}_6$, the total area of six inscribed rectangles (see Figure 14.7), are

$$\overline{S}_6 = \tfrac{1}{6} f\left(\tfrac{1}{6}\right) + \tfrac{1}{6} f\left(\tfrac{2}{6}\right) + \tfrac{1}{6} f\left(\tfrac{3}{6}\right) + \tfrac{1}{6} f\left(\tfrac{4}{6}\right) + \tfrac{1}{6} f\left(\tfrac{5}{6}\right) + \tfrac{1}{6} f\left(\tfrac{6}{6}\right)$$

$$= \tfrac{1}{6}\left(2\left(\tfrac{1}{6}\right) + 2\left(\tfrac{2}{6}\right) + 2\left(\tfrac{3}{6}\right) + 2\left(\tfrac{4}{6}\right) + 2\left(\tfrac{5}{6}\right) + 2\left(\tfrac{6}{6}\right)\right) = \tfrac{7}{6}$$

and

$$\underline{S}_6 = \tfrac{1}{6} f(0) + \tfrac{1}{6} f\left(\tfrac{1}{6}\right) + \tfrac{1}{6} f\left(\tfrac{2}{6}\right) + \tfrac{1}{6} f\left(\tfrac{3}{6}\right) + \tfrac{1}{6} f\left(\tfrac{4}{6}\right) + \tfrac{1}{6} f\left(\tfrac{5}{6}\right)$$

$$= \tfrac{1}{6}\left(2(0) + 2\left(\tfrac{1}{6}\right) + 2\left(\tfrac{2}{6}\right) + 2\left(\tfrac{3}{6}\right) + 2\left(\tfrac{4}{6}\right) + 2\left(\tfrac{5}{6}\right)\right) = \tfrac{5}{6}$$

Note that $\underline{S}_6 \le A \le \overline{S}_6$, and, with appropriate labeling, both $\overline{S}_6$ and $\underline{S}_6$ will be of the form $\Sigma f(x)\,\Delta x$. Clearly, using six subintervals gives better approximations to the area than does four subintervals, as expected.

More generally, if we divide $[0, 1]$ into n subintervals of equal length Δx, then $\Delta x = 1/n$, and the endpoints of the subintervals are $x = 0, 1/n, 2/n, \ldots, (n-1)/n$, and $n/n = 1$. (See Figure 14.8.) The endpoints of the kth subinterval, for $k = 1, \ldots n$, are $(k-1)/n$ and k/n and the maximum value of f occurs at the right-hand endpoint k/n. It follows that the area of the kth circumscribed rectangle is $1/n \cdot f(k/n) = 1/n \cdot 2(k/n) = 2k/n^2$, for $k = 1, \ldots, n$. The total area of *all n circumscribed* rectangles is

$$\overline{S}_n = \sum_{k=1}^{n} f(k/n)\Delta x = \sum_{k=1}^{n} \frac{2k}{n^2} \tag{1}$$

$$= \frac{2}{n^2} \sum_{k=1}^{n} k \qquad \text{by factoring } \frac{2}{n^2} \text{ from each term}$$

$$= \frac{2}{n^2} \cdot \frac{n(n+1)}{2} \qquad \text{from Section 1.5}$$

$$= \frac{n+1}{n}$$

(We recall that $\sum_{k=1}^{n} k = 1 + 2 + \cdots + n$ is the sum of the first n positive integers and the formula used above was derived in Section 1.5 in anticipation of its application here.)

For *inscribed* rectangles, we note that the minimum value of f occurs at the left-hand endpoint, $(k-1)/n$, of $[(k-1)/n, k/n]$, so that the area of the kth inscribed rectangle is $1/n \cdot f(k-1/n) = 1/n \cdot 2((k-1)/n) = 2(k-1)/n^2$, for $k = 1, \ldots n$. The total area determined of *all n inscribed* rectangles (see Figure 14.9) is

$$\underline{S}_n = \sum_{k=1}^{n} f((k-1)/n)\,\Delta x = \sum_{k=1}^{n} \frac{2(k-1)}{n^2} \tag{2}$$

$$= \frac{2}{n^2} \sum_{k=1}^{n} k - 1 \qquad \text{by factoring } \frac{2}{n^2} \text{ from each term}$$

$$= \frac{2}{n^2} \sum_{k=0}^{n-1} k \qquad \text{adjusting the summation}$$

$$= \frac{2}{n^2} \cdot \frac{(n-1)n}{2} \qquad \text{adapted from Section 1.5}$$

$$= \frac{n-1}{n}$$

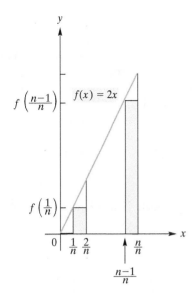

$$f\left(\frac{n-1}{n}\right) \qquad f(x) = 2x$$

$$f\left(\frac{1}{n}\right)$$

$$0 \quad \frac{1}{n} \ \frac{2}{n} \qquad \frac{n}{n}$$

$$\frac{n-1}{n}$$

FIGURE 14.9 n inscribed rectangles.

From Equations (1) and (2), we again see that both $\overline{S}_n$ and $\underline{S}_n$ are sums of the form $\sum f(x)\Delta x$, namely, $\overline{S}_n = \sum_{k=1}^{n} f\left(\frac{k}{n}\right)\Delta x$ and $\underline{S}_n = \sum_{k=1}^{n} f\left(\frac{k-1}{n}\right)\Delta x$.

From the nature of $\overline{S}_n$ and $\underline{S}_n$, it seems reasonable—and it is indeed true—that

$$\underline{S}_n \le A \le \overline{S}_n$$

As n becomes larger, $\underline{S}_n$ and $\overline{S}_n$ become better approximations to A. In fact, let us take the limits of $\underline{S}_n$ and $\overline{S}_n$ as n approaches ∞ through positive integral values:

$$\lim_{n\to\infty} \underline{S}_n = \lim_{n\to\infty} \frac{n-1}{n} = \lim_{n\to\infty}\left(1 - \frac{1}{n}\right) = 1$$

$$\lim_{n\to\infty} \overline{S}_n = \lim_{n\to\infty} \frac{n+1}{n} = \lim_{n\to\infty}\left(1 + \frac{1}{n}\right) = 1$$

Since $\overline{S}_n$ and $\underline{S}_n$ have the same limit, namely,

$$\lim_{n\to\infty} \overline{S}_n = \lim_{n\to\infty} \underline{S}_n = 1 \tag{3}$$

and since

$$\underline{S}_n \le A \le \overline{S}_n$$

we will take this limit to be the area of the triangle. Thus $A = 1$, which agrees with our prior finding. It is important to understand that here we developed a *definition of the notion of area* that is applicable to many different regions.

We call the common limit of $\overline{S}_n$ and $\underline{S}_n$, namely, 1, the *definite integral* of $f(x) = 2x$ on the interval from $x = 0$ to $x = 1$, and we denote this quantity by writing

$$\int_0^1 2x\,dx = 1 \tag{4}$$

The reason for using the term *definite integral* and the symbolism in Equation (4) will become apparent in the next section. The numbers 0 and 1 appearing with the integral sign $\int$ in Equation (4) are called the *limits of integration;* 0 is the *lower limit* and 1 is the *upper limit.*

In general, for a function f defined on the interval from $x = a$ to $x = b$, where $a < b$, we can form the sums $\overline{S}_n$ and $\underline{S}_n$, which are obtained by considering the maximum and minimum values, respectively, on each of n subintervals of equal length Δx.[6] We can now state the following:

The common limit of $\overline{S}_n$ and $\underline{S}_n$ as $n \to \infty$, if it exists, is called the **definite integral** of f over $[a, b]$ and is written

$$\int_a^b f(x)\,dx$$

The numbers a and b are called **limits of integration;** a is the **lower limit** and b is the **upper limit.** The symbol x is called the **variable of integration** and $f(x)$ is the **integrand.**

In terms of a limiting process, we have

$$\sum f(x)\,\Delta x \to \int_a^b f(x)\,dx$$

Two points must be made about the definite integral. First, the definite integral is the limit of a sum of the form $\sum f(x)\,\Delta x$. In fact, we can think of the integral sign as an elongated "S," the first letter of "Summation." Second, for an arbitrary function f

The definite integral is the limit of sums of the form $\sum f(x)\,\Delta x$. This definition will be useful in later sections.

[6]Here we assume that the maximum and minimum values exist.

defined on an interval, we may be able to calculate the sums $\overline{S}_n$ and $\underline{S}_n$ and determine their common limit if it exists. However, some terms in the sums may be negative if $f(x)$ is negative at points in the interval. These terms are not areas of rectangles (an area is never negative), so the common limit may not represent an area. Thus, **the definite integral is nothing more than a real number; it may or may not represent an area.**

As we saw in Equation (3), $\lim_{n \to \infty} \underline{S}_n$ is equal to $\lim_{n \to \infty} \overline{S}_n$. For an arbitrary function, this is not always true. However, for the functions that we will consider, these limits will be equal, and the definite integral will always exist. To save time, we will just use the **right-hand endpoint** of each subinterval in computing a sum. For the functions in this section, this sum will be denoted S_n.

EXAMPLE 1 Computing an Area by Using Right-Hand Endpoints

Find the area of the region in the first quadrant bounded by $f(x) = 4 - x^2$ and the lines $x = 0$ and $y = 0$.

Solution: A sketch of the region appears in Figure 14.10. The interval over which x varies in this region is seen to be $[0, 2]$, which we divide into n subintervals of equal length Δx. Since the length of $[0, 2]$ is 2, we take $\Delta x = 2/n$. The endpoints of the subintervals are $x = 0, 2/n, 2(2/n), \ldots, (n-1)(2/n)$, and $n(2/n) = 2$, which are shown in Figure 14.11. The diagram also shows the corresponding rectangles obtained by using the right-hand endpoint of each subinterval. The area of the kth rectangle, for $k = 1, \ldots n$, is the product of its width, $2/n$, and its height, $f(k(2/n)) = 4 - (2k/n)^2$, which is the function value at the right-hand endpoint of its base. Summing these areas, we get

$$S_n = \sum_{k=1}^{n} f\left(k \cdot \left(\frac{2}{n}\right)\right) \Delta x = \sum_{k=1}^{n} \left(4 - \left(\frac{2k}{n}\right)^2\right) \frac{2}{n}$$

$$= \sum_{k=1}^{n} \left(\frac{8}{n} - \frac{8k^2}{n^3}\right) = \sum_{k=1}^{n} \frac{8}{n} - \sum_{k=1}^{n} \frac{8k^2}{n^3} = \frac{8}{n} \sum_{k=1}^{n} 1 - \frac{8}{n^3} \sum_{k=1}^{n} k^2$$

$$= \frac{8}{n} n - \frac{8}{n^3} \frac{n(n+1)(2n+1)}{6}$$

$$= 8 - \frac{4}{3}\left(\frac{(n+1)(2n+1)}{n^2}\right)$$

The second line of the preceding computations uses basic summation manipulations as discussed in Section 1.5. The third line uses two specific summation formulas, also from Section 1.5: The sum of n copies of 1 is n and the sum of the first n squares is $\frac{n(n+1)(2n+1)}{6}$.

Finally, we take the limit of the S_n as $n \to \infty$:

$$\lim_{n \to \infty} S_n = \lim_{n \to \infty} \left(8 - \frac{4}{3}\left(\frac{(n+1)(2n+1)}{n^2}\right)\right)$$

$$= 8 - \frac{4}{3} \lim_{n \to \infty} \left(\frac{2n^2 + 3n + 1}{n^2}\right)$$

$$= 8 - \frac{4}{3} \lim_{n \to \infty} \left(2 + \frac{3}{n} + \frac{1}{n^2}\right)$$

$$= 8 - \frac{8}{3} = \frac{16}{3}$$

Hence, the area of the region is $\frac{16}{3}$.

Now Work Problem 7 ◁

APPLY IT ▶

10. A company has determined that its marginal-revenue function is given by $R'(x) = 600 - 0.5x$, where R is the revenue (in dollars) received when x units are sold. Find the total revenue received for selling 10 units by finding the area in the first quadrant bounded by $y = R'(x) = 600 - 0.5x$ and the lines $y = 0, x = 0$, and $x = 10$.

In general, over $[a, b]$, we have

$$\Delta x = \frac{b-a}{n}$$

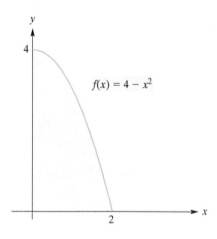

FIGURE 14.10 Region of Example 1.

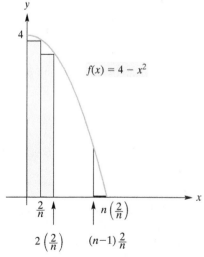

FIGURE 14.11 n subintervals and corresponding rectangles for Example 1.

EXAMPLE 2   Evaluating a Definite Integral

Evaluate $\displaystyle\int_0^2 (4 - x^2)\,dx$.

Solution: We want to find the definite integral of $f(x) = 4 - x^2$ over the interval $[0, 2]$. Thus, we must compute $\lim_{n\to\infty} S_n$. But this limit is precisely the limit $\dfrac{16}{3}$ found in Example 1, so we conclude that

$$\int_0^2 (4 - x^2)\,dx = \frac{16}{3}$$

Now Work Problem 19 ◁

No units are attached to the answer, since a definite integral is simply a number.

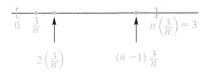

FIGURE 14.12   Dividing $[0, 3]$ into n subintervals.

EXAMPLE 3   Integrating a Function over an Interval

Integrate $f(x) = x - 5$ from $x = 0$ to $x = 3$; that is, evaluate $\int_0^3 (x - 5)\,dx$.

Solution: We first divide $[0, 3]$ into n subintervals of equal length $\Delta x = 3/n$. The endpoints are $0, 3/n, 2(3/n), \ldots, (n - 1)(3/n), n(3/n) = 3$. (See Figure 14.12.) Using right-hand endpoints, we form the sum and simplify

$$S_n = \sum_{k=1}^{n} f\left(k\frac{3}{n}\right)\frac{3}{n}$$

$$= \sum_{k=1}^{n}\left(\left(k\frac{3}{n} - 5\right)\frac{3}{n}\right) = \sum_{k=1}^{n}\left(\frac{9}{n^2}k - \frac{15}{n}\right) = \frac{9}{n^2}\sum_{k=1}^{n}k - \frac{15}{n}\sum_{k=1}^{n}1$$

$$= \frac{9}{n^2}\left(\frac{n(n+1)}{2}\right) - \frac{15}{n}(n)$$

$$= \frac{9}{2}\frac{n+1}{n} - 15 = \frac{9}{2}\left(1 + \frac{1}{n}\right) - 15$$

Taking the limit, we obtain

$$\lim_{n\to\infty} S_n = \lim_{n\to\infty}\left(\frac{9}{2}\left(1 + \frac{1}{n}\right) - 15\right) = \frac{9}{2} - 15 = -\frac{21}{2}$$

Thus,

$$\int_0^3 (x - 5)\,dx = -\frac{21}{2}$$

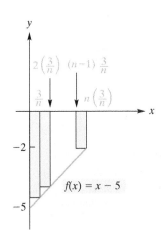

FIGURE 14.13 $f(x)$ is negative at each right-hand endpoint.

Note that the definite integral here is a *negative* number. The reason is clear from the graph of $f(x) = x - 5$ over the interval $[0, 3]$. (See Figure 14.13.) Since the value of $f(x)$ is negative at each right-hand endpoint, each term in S_n must also be negative. Hence, $\lim_{n\to\infty} S_n$, which is the definite integral, is negative.

Geometrically, each term in S_n is the negative of the area of a rectangle. (Refer again to Figure 14.13.) Although the definite integral is simply a number, here we can interpret it as representing the negative of the area of the region bounded by $f(x) = x - 5, x = 0, x = 3$, and the x-axis ($y = 0$).

Now Work Problem 17 ◁

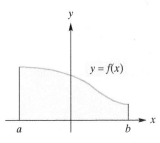

FIGURE 14.14   If f is continuous and $f(x) \geq 0$ on $[a, b]$, then $\int_a^b f(x)\,dx$ represents the area under the curve.

In Example 3, it was shown that *the definite integral does not have to represent an area*. In fact, there the definite integral was negative. However, if f is continuous and $f(x) \geq 0$ on $[a, b]$, then $S_n \geq 0$ for all values of n. Therefore, $\lim_{n\to\infty} S_n \geq 0$, so $\int_a^b f(x)\,dx \geq 0$. Furthermore, this definite integral gives the area of the region bounded by $y = f(x), y = 0, x = a$, and $x = b$. (See Figure 14.14.)

Although the approach that we took to discuss the definite integral is sufficient for our purposes, it is by no means rigorous. **The important thing to remember about the definite integral is that it is the limit of a special sum.**

TECHNOLOGY ▐▐▐

Here is a program for the TI-83 Plus graphing calculator that will estimate the limit of S_n as $n \to \infty$ for a function f defined on $[a, b]$.

PROGRAM:RIGHTSUM
Lbl 1
Input "SUBINTV",N
$(B - A)/N \to H$
$\emptyset \to S$
$A + H \to X$
$1 \to I$
Lbl 2
$Y_1 + S \to S$
$X + H \to X$
$I + 1 \to I$
If $I \le N$
Goto 2
$H^*S \to S$
Disp S
Pause
Goto 1

RIGHTSUM will compute S_n for a given number n of subintervals. Before executing the program, store $f(x)$, a, and b as Y_1, A, and B, respectively. Upon execution of the program, you will be prompted to enter the number of subintervals. Then the program proceeds to display the

```
prgmRIGHTSUM
SUBINTV100
            -10.455
SUBINTV1000
            -10.4955
SUBINTV2000
            -10.49775
■
```

FIGURE 14.15 Values of S_n for $f(x) = x - 5$ on $[0, 3]$.

value of S_n. Each time ENTER is pressed, the program repeats. In this way, a display of values of S_n for various numbers of subintervals may be obtained. Figure 14.15 shows values of $S_n(n = 100, 1000,$ and $2000)$ for the function $f(x) = x - 5$ on the interval $[0, 3]$. As $n \to \infty$, it appears that $S_n \to -10.5$. Thus, we estimate that

$$\lim_{n \to \infty} S_n \approx -10.5$$

Equivalently,

$$\int_0^3 (x - 5)\, dx \approx -10.5$$

which agrees with our result in Example 3.

It is interesting to note that the time required for an older calculator to compute S_{2000} in Figure 14.15 was in excess of 1.5 minutes. The time required on a TI-84 Plus is less than 1 minute.

PROBLEMS 14.6

In Problems 1–4, sketch the region in the first quadrant that is bounded by the given curves. Approximate the area of the region by the indicated sum. Use the right-hand endpoint of each subinterval.

1. $f(x) = x + 1, y = 0, x = 0, x = 1;$ S_4

2. $f(x) = 3x, y = 0, x = 1;$ S_5

3. $f(x) = x^2, y = 0, x = 1;$ S_4

4. $f(x) = x^2 + 1, y = 0, x = 0, x = 1;$ S_2

In Problems 5 and 6, by dividing the indicated interval into n subintervals of equal length, find S_n for the given function. Use the right-hand endpoint of each subinterval. Do not find $\lim_{n\to\infty} S_n$.

5. $f(x) = 4x;$ $[0, 1]$ **6.** $f(x) = 2x + 1;$ $[0, 2]$

In Problems 7 and 8, (a) simplify S_n and (b) find $\lim_{n\to\infty} S_n$.

7. $S_n = \dfrac{1}{n}\left[\left(\dfrac{1}{n} + 1\right) + \left(\dfrac{2}{n} + 1\right) + \cdots + \left(\dfrac{n}{n} + 1\right)\right]$

8. $S_n = \dfrac{2}{n}\left[\left(\dfrac{2}{n}\right)^2 + \left(2 \cdot \dfrac{2}{n}\right)^2 + \cdots + \left(n \cdot \dfrac{2}{n}\right)^2\right]$

In Problems 9–14, sketch the region in the first quadrant that is bounded by the given curves. Determine the exact area of the region by considering the limit of S_n as $n \to \infty$. Use the right-hand endpoint of each subinterval.

9. Region as described in Problem 1

10. Region as described in Problem 2

11. Region as described in Problem 3

12. $y = x^2, y = 0, x = 1, x = 2$

13. $f(x) = 3x^2, y = 0, x = 1$

14. $f(x) = 9 - x^2, y = 0, x = 0$

In Problems 15–20, evaluate the given definite integral by taking the limit of S_n. Use the right-hand endpoint of each subinterval. Sketch the graph, over the given interval, of the function to be integrated.

15. $\displaystyle\int_1^3 5x\, dx$ **16.** $\displaystyle\int_0^a b\, dx$

17. $\displaystyle\int_0^3 -4x\, dx$ **18.** $\displaystyle\int_1^4 (2x + 1)\, dx$

19. $\displaystyle\int_0^1 (x^2 + x)\, dx$ **20.** $\displaystyle\int_1^2 (x + 2)\, dx$

21. Find $\dfrac{d}{dx}\left(\displaystyle\int_0^1 \sqrt{1 - x^2}\, dx\right)$ without the use of limits.

22. Find $\displaystyle\int_0^3 f(x)\, dx$ without the use of limits, where

$$f(x) = \begin{cases} 2 & \text{if } 0 \le x < 1 \\ 4 - 2x & \text{if } 1 \le x < 2 \\ 5x - 10 & \text{if } 2 \le x \le 3 \end{cases}$$

23. Find $\displaystyle\int_{-1}^{3} f(x)\,dx$ without the use of limits, where

$$f(x) = \begin{cases} 1 & \text{if } x \le 1 \\ 2 - x & \text{if } 1 \le x \le 2 \\ -1 + \dfrac{x}{2} & \text{if } x > 2 \end{cases}$$

*In each of Problems 24–26, use a program, such as **RIGHTSUM**, to estimate the area of the region in the first quadrant bounded by the given curves. Round your answer to one decimal place.*

24. $f(x) = x^3 + 1, y = 0, x = 2, x = 3.7$

25. $f(x) = 4 - \sqrt{x}, y = 0, x = 1, x = 9$

26. $f(x) = \ln x, y = 0, x = 1, x = 2$

*In each of Problems 27–30, use a program, such as **RIGHTSUM**, to estimate the value of the definite integral. Round your answer to one decimal place.*

27. $\displaystyle\int_{2}^{5} \frac{x+1}{x+2}\,dx$

28. $\displaystyle\int_{-3}^{-1} \frac{1}{x^2}\,dx$

29. $\displaystyle\int_{-1}^{2} (4x^2 + x - 13)\,dx$

30. $\displaystyle\int_{1}^{2} \ln x\,dx$

Objective

To develop informally the Fundamental Theorem of Integral Calculus and to use it to compute definite integrals.

14.7 The Fundamental Theorem of Integral Calculus

The Fundamental Theorem

Thus far, the limiting processes of both the derivative and definite integral have been considered separately. We will now bring these fundamental ideas together and develop the important relationship that exists between them. As a result, we will be able to evaluate definite integrals more efficiently.

The graph of a function f is given in Figure 14.16. Assume that f is continuous on the interval $[a, b]$ and that its graph does not fall below the x-axis. That is, $f(x) \ge 0$. From the preceding section, the area of the region below the graph and above the x-axis from $x = a$ to $x = b$ is given by $\int_a^b f(x)\,dx$. We will now consider another way to determine this area.

Suppose that there is a function $A = A(x)$, which we will refer to as an area function, that gives the area of the region below the graph of f and above the x-axis from a to x, where $a \le x \le b$. This region is shaded in Figure 14.17. Do not confuse $A(x)$, which is an area, with $f(x)$, which is the height of the graph at x.

From its definition, we can state two properties of A immediately:

1. $A(a) = 0$, since there is "no area" from a to a

2. $A(b)$ is the area from a to b; that is,

$$A(b) = \int_a^b f(x)\,dx$$

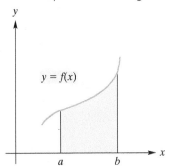

FIGURE 14.16 On $[a, b], f$ is continuous and $f(x) \ge 0$.

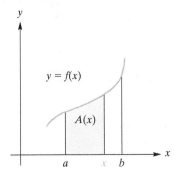

FIGURE 14.17 $A(x)$ is an area function.

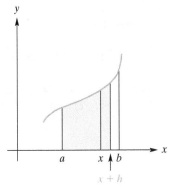

FIGURE 14.18 $A(x + h)$ gives the area of the shaded region.

If x is increased by h units, then $A(x + h)$ is the area of the shaded region in Figure 14.18. Hence, $A(x + h) - A(x)$ is the difference of the areas in Figures 14.18 and 14.17, namely, the area of the shaded region in Figure 14.19. For h sufficiently close to zero, the area of this region is the same as the area of a rectangle (Figure 14.20) whose base is h and whose height is some value $\bar{y}$ between $f(x)$ and $f(x + h)$. Here $\bar{y}$ is a function of h. Thus, on the one hand, the area of the rectangle is $A(x + h) - A(x)$, and, on the other hand, it is $h\bar{y}$, so

$$A(x + h) - A(x) = h\bar{y}$$

Equivalently,

$$\frac{A(x + h) - A(x)}{h} = \bar{y} \qquad \text{dividing by } h$$

Since $\bar{y}$ is between $f(x)$ and $f(x + h)$, it follows that as $h \to 0$, $\bar{y}$ approaches $f(x)$, so

$$\lim_{h \to 0} \frac{A(x + h) - A(x)}{h} = f(x) \tag{1}$$

But the left side is merely the derivative of A. Thus, Equation (1) becomes

$$A'(x) = f(x)$$

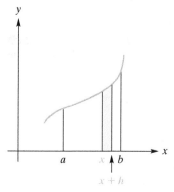

FIGURE 14.19 Area of shaded region is $A(x + h) - A(x)$.

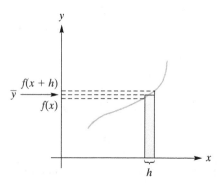

FIGURE 14.20 Area of rectangle is the same as area of shaded region in Figure 14.19.

The definite integral is a number, and an indefinite integral is a function.

We conclude that the area function A has the additional property that its derivative A' is f. That is, A is an antiderivative of f. Now, suppose that F is *any* antiderivative of f. Then, since both A and F are antiderivatives of the same function, they differ at most by a constant C:

$$A(x) = F(x) + C. \tag{2}$$

Recall that $A(a) = 0$. So, evaluating both sides of Equation (2) when $x = a$ gives

$$0 = F(a) + C$$

so that

$$C = -F(a)$$

Thus, Equation (2) becomes

$$A(x) = F(x) - F(a) \tag{3}$$

If $x = b$, then, from Equation (3),

$$A(b) = F(b) - F(a) \tag{4}$$

But recall that

$$A(b) = \int_a^b f(x)\, dx \tag{5}$$

From Equations (4) and (5), we get

$$\int_a^b f(x)\, dx = F(b) - F(a)$$

A relationship between a definite integral and antidifferentiation has now become clear. To find $\int_a^b f(x)\, dx$, it suffices to find an antiderivative of f, say, F, and subtract the value of F at the lower limit a from its value at the upper limit b. We assumed here that f was continuous and $f(x) \geq 0$ so that we could appeal to the concept of an area. However, our result is true for any continuous function[7] and is known as the *Fundamental Theorem of Integral Calculus.*

Fundamental Theorem of Integral Calculus

If f is continuous on the interval $[a, b]$ and F is any antiderivative of f on $[a, b]$, then

$$\int_a^b f(x)\, dx = F(b) - F(a)$$

It is important that you understand the difference between a definite integral and an indefinite integral. The **definite integral** $\int_a^b f(x)\, dx$ is a **number** defined to be the limit of a sum. The Fundamental Theorem states that the **indefinite integral** $\int f(x)\, dx$ (the most general antiderivative of f), which is a **function** of x related to the differentiation process, can be used to determine this limit.

Suppose we apply the Fundamental Theorem to evaluate $\int_0^2 (4 - x^2)\, dx$. Here $f(x) = 4 - x^2$, $a = 0$, and $b = 2$. Since an antiderivative of $4 - x^2$ is $F(x) = 4x - (x^3/3)$, it follows that

$$\int_0^2 (4 - x^2)\, dx = F(2) - F(0) = \left(8 - \frac{8}{3}\right) - (0) = \frac{16}{3}$$

---

[7] If f is continuous on $[a, b]$, it can be shown that $\int_a^b f(x)\, dx$ does indeed exist.

This confirms our result in Example 2 of Section 14.6. If we had chosen $F(x)$ to be $4x - (x^3/3) + C$, then we would have

$$F(2) - F(0) = \left[\left(8 - \frac{8}{3}\right) + C\right] - [0 + C] = \frac{16}{3}$$

as before. Since the choice of the value of C is immaterial, for convenience we will always choose it to be 0, as originally done. Usually, $F(b) - F(a)$ is abbreviated by writing

$$F(b) - F(a) = F(x)\Big|_a^b$$

Since F in the Fundamental Theorem of Calculus is *any* antiderivative of f and $\int f(x)\,dx$ is the most general antiderivative of f, it showcases the notation to write

$$\int_a^b f(x)\,dx = \left(\int f(x)\,dx\right)\Big|_a^b$$

Using the $\Big|_a^b$ notation, we have

$$\int_0^2 (4 - x^2)\,dx = \left(4x - \frac{x^3}{3}\right)\Big|_0^2 = \left(8 - \frac{8}{3}\right) - 0 = \frac{16}{3}$$

APPLY IT ▶

11. The income (in dollars) from a fast-food chain is increasing at a rate of $f(t) = 10{,}000e^{0.02t}$, where t is in years. Find $\int_3^6 10{,}000e^{0.02t}\,dt$, which gives the total income for the chain between the third and sixth years.

EXAMPLE 1 Applying the Fundamental Theorem

Find $\displaystyle\int_{-1}^{3} (3x^2 - x + 6)\,dx$.

Solution: An antiderivative of $3x^2 - x + 6$ is

$$x^3 - \frac{x^2}{2} + 6x$$

Thus,

$$\int_{-1}^{3} (3x^2 - x + 6)\,dx$$

$$= \left(x^3 - \frac{x^2}{2} + 6x\right)\Big|_{-1}^{3}$$

$$= \left[3^3 - \frac{3^2}{2} + 6(3)\right] - \left[(-1)^3 - \frac{(-1)^2}{2} + 6(-1)\right]$$

$$= \left(\frac{81}{2}\right) - \left(-\frac{15}{2}\right) = 48$$

Now Work Problem 1 ◁

Properties of the Definite Integral

For $\int_a^b f(x)\,dx$, we have assumed that $a < b$. We now define the cases in which $a > b$ or $a = b$. First,

$$\text{If } a > b, \quad \text{then} \quad \int_a^b f(x)\,dx = -\int_b^a f(x)\,dx.$$

That is, interchanging the limits of integration changes the integral's sign. For example,

$$\int_2^0 (4 - x^2)\,dx = -\int_0^2 (4 - x^2)\,dx$$

If the limits of integration are equal, we have

$$\int_a^a f(x)\,dx = 0$$

Some properties of the definite integral deserve mention. The first of the properties that follow restates more formally our comment from the preceding section concerning area.

Properties of the Definite Integral

1. If f is continuous and $f(x) \geq 0$ on $[a, b]$, then $\int_a^b f(x)\,dx$ can be interpreted as the area of the region bounded by the curve $y = f(x)$, the x-axis, and the lines $x = a$ and $x = b$.

2. $\int_a^b kf(x)\,dx = k\int_a^b f(x)\,dx,$ where k is a constant

3. $\int_a^b [f(x) \pm g(x)]\,dx = \int_a^b f(x)\,dx \pm \int_a^b g(x)\,dx$

Properties 2 and 3 are similar to rules for indefinite integrals because a definite integral may be evaluated by the Fundamental Theorem in terms of an antiderivative. Two more properties of definite integrals are as follows.

4. $\int_a^b f(x)\,dx = \int_a^b f(t)\,dt$

The variable of integration is a "dummy variable" in the sense that any other variable produces the same result—that is, the same number.

To illustrate property 4, you can verify, for example, that

$$\int_0^2 x^2\,dx = \int_0^2 t^2\,dt$$

5. If f is continuous on an interval I and a, b, and c are in I, then

$$\int_a^c f(x)\,dx = \int_a^b f(x)\,dx + \int_b^c f(x)\,dx$$

Property 5 means that the definite integral over an interval can be expressed in terms of definite integrals over subintervals. Thus,

$$\int_0^2 (4 - x^2)\,dx = \int_0^1 (4 - x^2)\,dx + \int_1^2 (4 - x^2)\,dx$$

We will look at some examples of definite integration now and compute some areas in Section 14.9.

EXAMPLE 2   Using the Fundamental Theorem

Find $\int_0^1 \dfrac{x^3}{\sqrt{1 + x^4}}\,dx$.

Solution: To find an antiderivative of the integrand, we will apply the power rule for integration:

$$\int_0^1 \frac{x^3}{\sqrt{1 + x^4}}\,dx = \int_0^1 x^3(1 + x^4)^{-1/2}\,dx$$

$$= \frac{1}{4}\int_0^1 (1 + x^4)^{-1/2}\,d(1 + x^4) = \left(\frac{1}{4}\right) \frac{(1 + x^4)^{1/2}}{\frac{1}{2}}\Bigg|_0^1$$

CAUTION!⚠

In Example 2, the value of the antiderivative $\frac{1}{2}(1 + x^4)^{1/2}$ at the lower limit 0 is $\frac{1}{2}(1)^{1/2}$. **Do not** assume that an evaluation at the limit zero will yield 0.

$$= \frac{1}{2}(1 + x^4)^{1/2} \Big|_0^1 = \frac{1}{2}\left((2)^{1/2} - (1)^{1/2}\right)$$

$$= \frac{1}{2}(\sqrt{2} - 1)$$

Now Work Problem 13 ◁

EXAMPLE 3   **Evaluating Definite Integrals**

a. Find $\displaystyle\int_1^2 [4t^{1/3} + t(t^2 + 1)^3]\,dt$.

Solution:

$$\int_1^2 [4t^{1/3} + t(t^2 + 1)^3]\,dt = 4\int_1^2 t^{1/3}\,dt + \frac{1}{2}\int_1^2 (t^2 + 1)^3\,d(t^2 + 1)$$

$$= (4)\frac{t^{4/3}}{\frac{4}{3}}\Big|_1^2 + \left(\frac{1}{2}\right)\frac{(t^2 + 1)^4}{4}\Big|_1^2$$

$$= 3(2^{4/3} - 1) + \frac{1}{8}(5^4 - 2^4)$$

$$= 3 \cdot 2^{4/3} - 3 + \frac{609}{8}$$

$$= 6\sqrt[3]{2} + \frac{585}{8}$$

b. Find $\displaystyle\int_0^1 e^{3t}\,dt$.

Solution:

$$\int_0^1 e^{3t}\,dt = \frac{1}{3}\int_0^1 e^{3t}\,d(3t)$$

$$= \left(\frac{1}{3}\right)e^{3t}\Big|_0^1 = \frac{1}{3}(e^3 - e^0) = \frac{1}{3}(e^3 - 1)$$

Now Work Problem 15 ◁

EXAMPLE 4   **Finding and Interpreting a Definite Integral**

Evaluate $\displaystyle\int_{-2}^1 x^3\,dx$.

Solution:

$$\int_{-2}^1 x^3\,dx = \frac{x^4}{4}\Big|_{-2}^1 = \frac{1^4}{4} - \frac{(-2)^4}{4} = \frac{1}{4} - \frac{16}{4} = -\frac{15}{4}$$

The reason the result is negative is clear from the graph of $y = x^3$ on the interval $[-2, 1]$. (See Figure 14.21.) For $-2 \le x < 0$, $f(x)$ is negative. Since a definite integral is a limit of a sum of the form $\Sigma f(x)\,\Delta x$, it follows that $\int_{-2}^0 x^3\,dx$ is not only a negative number, but also the negative of the area of the shaded region in the third quadrant. On the other hand, $\int_0^1 x^3\,dx$ is the area of the shaded region in the first quadrant, since $f(x) \ge 0$ on $[0, 1]$. The definite integral over the entire interval $[-2, 1]$ is the *algebraic* sum of these numbers, because, from property 5,

$$\int_{-2}^1 x^3\,dx = \int_{-2}^0 x^3\,dx + \int_0^1 x^3\,dx$$

Thus, $\int_{-2}^1 x^3\,dx$ does not represent the area between the curve and the x-axis. However, if area is desired, it can be given by

$$\left|\int_{-2}^0 x^3\,dx\right| + \int_0^1 x^3\,dx$$

Now Work Problem 25 ◁

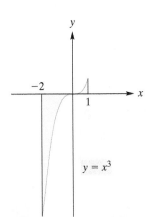

FIGURE 14.21   Graph of $y = x^3$ on the interval $[-2, 1]$.

CAUTION!⚠

Remember that $\int_a^b f(x)\,dx$ is a limit of a sum. In some cases this limit represents an area. In others it does not. When $f(x) \ge 0$ on $[a, b]$, the integral represents the area between the graph of f and the x-axis from $x = a$ to $x = b$.

The Definite Integral of a Derivative

Since a function f is an antiderivative of f', by the Fundamental Theorem we have

$$\int_a^b f'(x)\,dx = f(b) - f(a) \tag{6}$$

But $f'(x)$ is the rate of change of f with respect to x. Hence, if we know the rate of change of f and want to find the difference in function values $f(b) - f(a)$, it suffices to evaluate $\int_a^b f'(x)\,dx$.

APPLY IT ▶

12. A managerial service determines that the rate of increase in maintenance costs (in dollars per year) for a particular apartment complex is given by $M'(x) = 90x^2 + 5000$, where x is the age of the apartment complex in years and $M(x)$ is the total (accumulated) cost of maintenance for x years. Find the total cost for the first five years.

EXAMPLE 5 Finding a Change in Function Values by Definite Integration

A manufacturer's marginal-cost function is

$$\frac{dc}{dq} = 0.6q + 2$$

If production is presently set at $q = 80$ units per week, how much more would it cost to increase production to 100 units per week?

Solution: The total-cost function is $c = c(q)$, and we want to find the difference $c(100) - c(80)$. The rate of change of c is dc/dq, so, by Equation (6),

$$c(100) - c(80) = \int_{80}^{100} \frac{dc}{dq}\,dq = \int_{80}^{100} (0.6q + 2)\,dq$$

$$= \left[\frac{0.6q^2}{2} + 2q\right]\Big|_{80}^{100} = [0.3q^2 + 2q]\Big|_{80}^{100}$$

$$= [0.3(100)^2 + 2(100)] - [0.3(80)^2 + 2(80)]$$

$$= 3200 - 2080 = 1120$$

If c is in dollars, then the cost of increasing production from 80 units to 100 units is \$1120.

Now Work Problem 59 ◁

TECHNOLOGY ▮▮▮

Many graphing calculators have the capability to estimate the value of a definite integral. On a TI-83 Plus, to estimate

$$\int_{80}^{100} (0.6q + 2)\,dq$$

we use the "fnInt(" command, as indicated in Figure 14.22. The four parameters that must be entered with this command are

| function to be integrated | variable of integration | lower limit | upper limit |

We see that the value of the definite integral is approximately 1120, which agrees with the result in Example 5.
Similarly, to estimate

$$\int_{-2}^{1} x^3\,dx$$

FIGURE 14.22 Estimating $\int_{80}^{100} (0.6q + 2)\,dq$.

we enter

$$\text{fnInt}(X^3, X, -2, 1)$$

or, alternatively, if we first store x^3 as Y_1, we can enter

$$\text{fnInt}(Y_1, X, -2, 1)$$

In each case we obtain -3.75, which agrees with the result in Example 4.

PROBLEMS 14.7

In Problems 1–43, evaluate the definite integral.

1. $\int_0^3 5\,dx$

2. $\int_1^5 (e + 3e)\,dx$

3. $\int_1^2 5x\,dx$

4. $\int_2^8 -5x\,dx$

5. $\int_{-3}^1 (2x - 3)\,dx$

6. $\int_{-1}^1 (4 - 9y)\,dy$

7. $\int_1^4 (y^2 + 4y + 4)\,dy$

8. $\int_4^1 (2t - 3t^2)\,dt$

9. $\int_{-2}^{-1} (3w^2 - w - 1)\,dw$

10. $\int_8^9 dt$

11. $\int_1^3 3t^{-3}\,dt$

12. $\int_2^3 \dfrac{3}{x^2}\,dx$

13. $\int_{-8}^8 \sqrt[3]{x^4}\,dx$

14. $\int_{1/2}^{3/2} (x^2 + x + 1)\,dx$

15. $\int_{1/2}^3 \dfrac{1}{x^2}\,dx$

16. $\int_9^{36} (\sqrt{x} - 2)\,dx$

17. $\int_{-2}^2 (z + 1)^4\,dz$

18. $\int_1^8 (x^{1/3} - x^{-1/3})\,dx$

19. $\int_0^1 2x^2(x^3 - 1)^3\,dx$

20. $\int_2^3 (x + 2)^3\,dx$

21. $\int_1^8 \dfrac{4}{y}\,dy$

22. $\int_{-e^{\pi}}^{-1} \dfrac{2}{x}\,dx$

23. $\int_0^1 e^5\,dx$

24. $\int_2^{e+1} \dfrac{1}{x - 1}\,dx$

25. $\int_0^1 5x^2 e^{x^3}\,dx$

26. $\int_0^1 (3x^2 + 4x)(x^3 + 2x^2)^4\,dx$

27. $\int_3^4 \dfrac{3}{(x + 3)^2}\,dx$

28. $\int_{-1/3}^{20/3} \sqrt{3x + 5}\,dx$

29. $\int_{1/3}^2 \sqrt{10 - 3p}\,dp$

30. $\int_{-1}^1 q\sqrt{q^2 + 3}\,dq$

31. $\int_0^1 x^2\sqrt[3]{7x^3 + 1}\,dx$

32. $\int_0^{\sqrt{2}} \left(2x - \dfrac{x}{(x^2 + 1)^{2/3}}\right)dx$

33. $\int_0^1 \dfrac{2x^3 + x}{x^2 + x^4 + 1}\,dx$

34. $\int_a^b (m + ny)\,dy$

35. $\int_0^1 \dfrac{e^x - e^{-x}}{2}\,dx$

36. $\int_{-2}^1 8|x|\,dx$

37. $\int_e^{\sqrt{2}} 3(x^{-2} + x^{-3} - x^{-4})\,dx$

38. $\int_1^2 \left(6\sqrt{x} - \dfrac{1}{\sqrt{2x}}\right)dx$

39. $\int_1^3 (x + 1)e^{x^2 + 2x}\,dx$

40. $\int_1^{95} \dfrac{x}{\ln e^x}\,dx$

41. $\int_0^2 \dfrac{x^6 + 6x^4 + x^3 + 8x^2 + x + 5}{x^3 + 5x + 1}\,dx$

42. $\int_1^2 \dfrac{1}{1 + e^x}\,dx$ (*Hint:* Multiply the integrand by $\frac{e^{-x}}{e^{-x}}$.)

43. $\int_0^2 f(x)\,dx,$ where $f(x) = \begin{cases} 4x^2 & \text{if } 0 \le x < \frac{1}{2} \\ 2x & \text{if } \frac{1}{2} \le x \le 2 \end{cases}$

44. Evaluate $\left(\int_1^3 x\,dx\right)^3 - \int_1^3 x^3\,dx.$

45. Suppose $f(x) = \int_1^x 3\dfrac{1}{t^2}\,dt.$ Evaluate $\int_e^1 f(x)\,dx.$

46. Evaluate $\int_7^7 e^{x^2}\,dx + \int_0^{\sqrt{2}} \dfrac{1}{3\sqrt{2}}\,dx.$

47. If $\int_1^2 f(x)\,dx = 5$ and $\int_3^1 f(x)\,dx = 2,$ find $\int_2^3 f(x)\,dx.$

48. If $\int_1^4 f(x)\,dx = 6,$ $\int_2^4 f(x)\,dx = 5,$ and $\int_1^3 f(x)\,dx = 2,$ find $\int_2^3 f(x)\,dx.$

49. Evaluate $\int_2^3 \left(\dfrac{d}{dx}\int_2^3 e^{x^3}\,dx\right)dx.$ (*Hint:* It is not necessary to find $\int_2^3 e^{x^3}\,dx.$)

50. Suppose that $f(x) = \int_e^x \dfrac{e^t - e^{-t}}{e^t + e^{-t}}\,dt$ where $x > e.$ Find $f'(x).$

51. **Severity Index**   In discussing traffic safety, Shonle[8] considers how much acceleration a person can tolerate in a crash so that there is no major injury. The *severity index* is defined as

$$\text{S.I.} = \int_0^T \alpha^{5/2}\,dt$$

where α (a Greek letter read "alpha") is considered a constant involved with a weighted average acceleration, and T is the duration of the crash. Find the severity index.

52. **Statistics**   In statistics, the mean μ (a Greek letter read "mu") of the continuous probability density function f defined on the interval $[a, b]$ is given by

$$\mu = \int_a^b xf(x)\,dx$$

and the variance σ^2 (σ is a Greek letter read "sigma") is given by

$$\sigma^2 = \int_a^b (x - \mu)^2 f(x)\,dx$$

Compute μ and then σ^2 if $a = 0,$ $b = 1,$ and $f(x) = 6(x - x^2).$

53. **Distribution of Incomes**   The economist Pareto[9] has stated an empirical law of distribution of higher incomes that gives the number N of persons receiving x or more dollars. If

$$\dfrac{dN}{dx} = -Ax^{-B}$$

[8]J. I. Shonle, *Environmental Applications of General Physics* (Reading, MA: Addison-Wesley Publishing Company, Inc., 1975).

[9]G. Tintner, *Methodology of Mathematical Economics and Econometrics* (Chicago: University of Chicago Press, 1967), p. 16.

where A and B are constants, set up a definite integral that gives the total number of persons with incomes between a and b, where $a < b$.

54. Biology In a discussion of gene mutation,[10] the following integral occurs:

$$\int_0^{10^{-4}} x^{-1/2}\, dx$$

Evaluate this integral.

55. Continuous Income Flow The present value (in dollars) of a continuous flow of income of \$2000 a year for five years at 6% compounded continuously is given by

$$\int_0^5 2000 e^{-0.06t}\, dt$$

Evaluate the present value to the nearest dollar.

56. Biology In biology, problems frequently arise involving the transfer of a substance between compartments. An example is a transfer from the bloodstream to tissue. Evaluate the following integral, which occurs in a two-compartment diffusion problem:[11]

$$\int_0^t (e^{-a\tau} - e^{-b\tau})\, d\tau$$

Here, τ (read "tau") is a Greek letter; a and b are constants.

57. Demography For a certain small population, suppose l is a function such that $l(x)$ is the number of persons who reach the age of x in any year of time. This function is called a *life table function*. Under appropriate conditions, the integral

$$\int_a^b l(t)\, dt$$

gives the expected number of people in the population between the exact ages of a and b, inclusive. If

$$l(x) = 1000\sqrt{110 - x} \quad \text{for } 0 \le x \le 110$$

determine the number of people between the exact ages of 10 and 29, inclusive. Give your answer to the nearest integer, since fractional answers make no sense. What is the size of the population?

58. Mineral Consumption If C is the yearly consumption of a mineral at time $t = 0$, then, under continuous consumption, the total amount of the mineral used in the interval $[0, t]$ is

$$\int_0^t C e^{k\tau}\, d\tau$$

where k is the rate of consumption. For a rare-earth mineral, it has been determined that $C = 3000$ units and $k = 0.05$. Evaluate the integral for these data.

59. Marginal Cost A manufacturer's marginal-cost function is

$$\frac{dc}{dq} = 0.2q + 8$$

If c is in dollars, determine the cost involved to increase production from 65 to 75 units.

60. Marginal Cost Repeat Problem 59 if

$$\frac{dc}{dq} = 0.004q^2 - 0.5q + 50$$

and production increases from 90 to 180 units.

61. Marginal Revenue A manufacturer's marginal-revenue function is

$$\frac{dr}{dq} = \frac{2000}{\sqrt{300q}}$$

If r is in dollars, find the change in the manufacturer's total revenue if production is increased from 500 to 800 units.

62. Marginal Revenue Repeat Problem 61 if

$$\frac{dr}{dq} = 100 + 50q - 3q^2$$

and production is increased from 5 to 10 units.

63. Crime Rate A sociologist is studying the crime rate in a certain city. She estimates that t months after the beginning of next year, the total number of crimes committed will increase at the rate of $8t + 10$ crimes per month. Determine the total number of crimes that can be expected to be committed next year. How many crimes can be expected to be committed during the last six months of that year?

64. Hospital Discharges For a group of hospitalized individuals, suppose the discharge rate is given by

$$f(t) = \frac{81 \times 10^6}{(300 + t)^4}$$

where $f(t)$ is the proportion of the group discharged per day at the end of t days. What proportion has been discharged by the end of 700 days?

65. Production Imagine a one-dimensional country of length $2R$. (See Figure 14.23.[12]) Suppose the production of goods for this country is continuously distributed from border to border. If the amount produced each year per unit of distance is $f(x)$, then the country's total yearly production is given by

$$G = \int_{-R}^{R} f(x)\, dx$$

Evaluate G if $f(x) = i$, where i is constant.

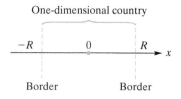

One-dimensional country

FIGURE 14.23

66. Exports For the one-dimensional country of Problem 65, under certain conditions the amount of the country's exports is given by

$$E = \int_{-R}^{R} \frac{i}{2}[e^{-k(R-x)} + e^{-k(R+x)}]\, dx$$

where i and k are constants ($k \ne 0$). Evaluate E.

[10] W. J. Ewens, *Population Genetics* (London: Methuen & Company Ltd., 1969).

[11] W. Simon, *Mathematical Techniques for Physiology and Medicine* (New York: Academic Press, Inc., 1972).

[12] R. Taagepera, "Why the Trade/GNP Ratio Decreases with Country Size," *Social Science Research,* 5 (1976), 385–404.

67. Average Delivered Price   In a discussion of a delivered price of a good from a mill to a customer, DeCanio[13] claims that the average delivered price paid by consumers is given by

$$A = \frac{\displaystyle\int_0^R (m + x)[1 - (m + x)]\, dx}{\displaystyle\int_0^R [1 - (m + x)]\, dx}$$

where m is mill price, and x is the maximum distance to the point of sale. DeCanio determines that

$$A = \frac{m + \dfrac{R}{2} - m^2 - mR - \dfrac{R^2}{3}}{1 - m - \dfrac{R}{2}}$$

Verify this.

In Problems 68–70, use the Fundamental Theorem of Integral Calculus to determine the value of the definite integral. Confirm your result with your calculator.

68. $\displaystyle\int_{2.5}^{3.5} (1 + 2x + 3x^2)\, dx$ **69.** $\displaystyle\int_0^4 \frac{1}{(4x + 4)^2}\, dx$

70. $\displaystyle\int_0^1 e^{3t}\, dt$ Round your answer to two decimal places.

In Problems 71–74, estimate the value of the definite integral. Round your answer to two decimal places.

71. $\displaystyle\int_{-1}^5 \frac{x^2 + 1}{x^2 + 4}\, dx$ **72.** $\displaystyle\int_3^4 \frac{1}{x \ln x}\, dx$

73. $\displaystyle\int_0^3 2\sqrt{t^2 + 3}\, dt$ **74.** $\displaystyle\int_{-1}^1 \frac{6\sqrt{q + 1}}{q + 3}\, dq$

Objective

To estimate the value of a definite integral by using either the trapezoidal rule or Simpson's rule.

14.8 Approximate Integration

Trapezoidal Rule

Any function f constructed from polynomials, exponentials, and logarithms using algebraic operations and composition can be differentiated and the resulting function f' is again of the same kind—one that can be constructed from polynomials, exponentials, and logarithms using algebraic operations and composition. Let us call such functions *elementary* (although the term usually has a slightly different meaning). In this terminology, the derivative of an elementary function is also elementary. Integration is more complicated. If an elementary function f has F as an antiderivative, then F may fail to be elementary. In other words, even for a fairly simple-looking function f it is sometimes impossible to find $\int f(x)\, dx$ in terms of the functions that we consider in this book. For example, there is no elementary function whose derivative is e^{x^2} so that you cannot expect to "do" the integral $\int e^{x^2}\, dx$.

On the other hand, consider a function f that is continuous on a closed interval $[a, b]$ with $f(x) \geq 0$ for all x in $[a, b]$. Then $\int_a^b f(x)\, dx$ is simply the *number* that gives the area of the region bounded by the curves $y = f(x)$, $y = 0$, $x = a$, and $x = b$. It is unsatisfying, and perhaps impractical, not to say anything about the number $\int_a^b f(x)\, dx$ because of an inability to "do" the integral $\int f(x)\, dx$. This also applies when the integral $\int f(x)\, dx$ is merely too difficult for the person who needs to find the number $\int_a^b f(x)\, dx$.

Since $\int_a^b f(x)\, dx$ is defined as a limit of sums of the form $\sum f(x)\, \Delta x$, any particular well-formed sum of the form $\sum f(x)\, \Delta x$ can be regarded as an approximation of $\int_a^b f(x)\, dx$. At least for nonnegative f such sums can be regarded as sums of areas of thin rectangles. Consider, for example, Figure 14.11 in Section 14.6, in which two rectangles are explicitly shown. It is clear that the error that arises from such rectangles is associated with the small side at the top. The error would be reduced if we replaced the rectangles by shapes that have a top side that is closer to the shape of the curve. We will consider two possibilities: using thin trapezoids rather than thin rectangles, the *trapezoidal rule;* and using thin regions surmounted by parabolic arcs, *Simpson's rule.* In each case only a finite number of numerical values of $f(x)$ needs be known and the calculations involved are especially suitable for computers or calculators. In both cases, we assume that f is continuous on $[a, b]$.

In developing the trapezoidal rule, for convenience we will also assume that $f(x) \geq 0$ on $[a, b]$, so that we can think in terms of area. This rule involves approximating the graph of f by straight-line segments.

[13] S. J. DeCanio, "Delivered Pricing and Multiple Basing Point Equationilibria: A Reevaluation," *The Quarterly Journal of Economics,* XCIX, no. 2 (1984), 329–49.

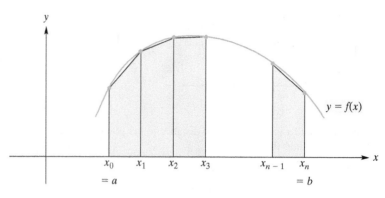

FIGURE 14.24   Approximating an area by using trapezoids.

In Figure 14.24, the interval $[a, b]$ is divided into n subintervals of equal length by the points $a = x_0, x_1, x_2, \ldots,$ and $x_n = b$. Since the length of $[a, b]$ is $b - a$, the length of each subinterval is $(b - a)/n$, which we will call h.

Clearly,

$$x_1 = a + h, x_2 = a + 2h, \ldots, x_n = a + nh = b$$

With each subinterval, we can associate a trapezoid (a four-sided figure with two parallel sides). The area A of the region bounded by the curve, the x-axis, and the lines $x = a$ and $x = b$ is $\int_a^b f(x)\,dx$ and can be approximated by the sum of the areas of the trapezoids determined by the subintervals.

Consider the first trapezoid, which is redrawn in Figure 14.25. Since the area of a trapezoid is equal to one-half the base times the sum of the lengths of the parallel sides, this trapezoid has area

$$\tfrac{1}{2}h[f(a) + f(a + h)]$$

Similarly, the second trapezoid has area

$$\tfrac{1}{2}h[f(a + h) + f(a + 2h)]$$

The area A under the curve is approximated by the sum of the areas of n trapezoids:

$$A \approx \tfrac{1}{2}h[f(a) + f(a + h)] + \tfrac{1}{2}h[f(a + h) + f(a + 2h)]$$
$$+ \tfrac{1}{2}h[f(a + 2h) + f(a + 3h)] + \cdots + \tfrac{1}{2}h[f(a + (n - 1)h) + f(b)]$$

Since $A = \int_a^b f(x)\,dx$, by simplifying the preceding formula we have the trapezoidal rule:

The Trapezoidal Rule

$$\int_a^b f(x)\,dx \approx \frac{h}{2}[f(a) + 2f(a + h) + 2f(a + 2h) + \cdots + 2f(a + (n - 1)h) + f(b)]$$

where $h = (b - a)/n$.

The pattern of the coefficients inside the braces is 1, 2, 2, ... , 2, 1. Usually, the more subintervals, the better is the approximation. In our development, we assumed for convenience that $f(x) \geq 0$ on $[a, b]$. However, the trapezoidal rule is valid without this restriction.

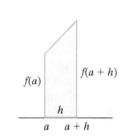

FIGURE 14.25   First trapezoid.

EXAMPLE 1   Trapezoidal Rule

Use the trapezoidal rule to estimate the value of

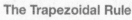

$$\int_0^1 \frac{1}{1 + x^2}\,dx$$

APPLY IT ▶

13. An oil tanker is losing oil at a rate of $R'(t) = \dfrac{60}{\sqrt{t^2 + 9}}$, where t is the time in minutes and $R(t)$ is the radius of the oil slick in feet. Use the trapezoidal rule with $n = 5$ to approximate $\displaystyle\int_0^5 \dfrac{60}{\sqrt{t^2 + 9}}\, dt$, the size of the radius after five seconds.

for $n = 5$. Compute each term to four decimal places, and round the answer to three decimal places.

Solution: Here $f(x) = 1/(1 + x^2), n = 5, a = 0,$ and $b = 1$. Thus,

$$h = \frac{b - a}{n} = \frac{1 - 0}{5} = \frac{1}{5} = 0.2$$

The terms to be added are

$$
\begin{aligned}
f(a) &= f(0) &&= 1.0000 \\
2f(a + h) &= 2f(0.2) &&= 1.9231 \\
2f(a + 2h) &= 2f(0.4) &&= 1.7241 \\
2f(a + 3h) &= 2f(0.6) &&= 1.4706 \\
2f(a + 4h) &= 2f(0.8) &&= 1.2195 \\
f(b) &= f(1) &&= \underline{0.5000} \qquad a + nh = b \\
& && 7.8373 = \text{sum}
\end{aligned}
$$

Hence, our estimate for the integral is

$$\int_0^1 \frac{1}{1 + x^2}\, dx \approx \frac{0.2}{2}(7.8373) \approx 0.784$$

The actual value of the integral is approximately 0.785.

Now Work Problem 1 ◁

Simpson's Rule

Another method for estimating $\int_a^b f(x)\, dx$ is given by Simpson's rule, which involves approximating the graph of f by parabolic segments. We will omit the derivation.

> **Simpson's Rule**
>
> $$\int_a^b f(x)\, dx \approx \frac{h}{3}[f(a) + 4f(a + h) + 2f(a + 2h) + \cdots + 4f(a + (n - 1)h) + f(b)]$$
>
> where $h = (b - a)/n$ and n is even.

The pattern of coefficients inside the braces is $1, 4, 2, 4, 2, \ldots, 2, 4, 1$, which requires that n **be even.** Let us use this rule for the integral in Example 1.

APPLY IT ▶

14. A yeast culture is growing at the rate of $A'(t) = 0.3e^{0.2t^2}$, where t is the time in hours and $A(t)$ is the amount in grams. Use Simpson's rule with $n = 8$ to approximate $\int_0^4 0.3e^{0.2t^2}\, dt$, the amount the culture grew over the first four hours.

EXAMPLE 2   Simpson's Rule

Use Simpson's rule to estimate the value of $\displaystyle\int_0^1 \frac{1}{1 + x^2}\, dx$ for $n = 4$. Compute each term to four decimal places, and round the answer to three decimal places.

Solution: Here $f(x) = 1/(1 + x^2), n = 4, a = 0,$ and $b = 1$. Thus, $h = (b - a)/n = 1/4 = 0.25$. The terms to be added are

$$
\begin{aligned}
f(a) &= f(0) &&= 1.0000 \\
4f(a + h) &= 4f(0.25) &&= 3.7647 \\
2f(a + 2h) &= 2f(0.5) &&= 1.6000 \\
4f(a + 3h) &= 4f(0.75) &&= 2.5600 \\
f(b) &= f(1) &&= \underline{0.5000} \\
& && 9.4247 = \text{sum}
\end{aligned}
$$

Therefore, by Simpson's rule,

$$\int_0^1 \frac{1}{1 + x^2}\, dx \approx \frac{0.25}{3}(9.4247) \approx 0.785$$

This is a better approximation than that which we obtained in Example 1 by using the trapezoidal rule.

Now Work Problem 5 ◁

Both Simpson's rule and the trapezoidal rule can be used if we know only $f(a)$, $f(a + h)$, and so on; we do not need to know $f(x)$ for all x in $[a, b]$. Example 3 will illustrate.

EXAMPLE 3   Demography

In Example 3, a definite integral is estimated from data points; the function itself is not known.

A function often used in demography (the study of births, marriages, mortality, etc., in a population) is the **life-table function,** denoted l. In a population having 100,000 births in any year of time, $l(x)$ represents the number of persons who reach the age of x in any year of time. For example, if $l(20) = 98,857$, then the number of persons who attain age 20 in any year of time is 98,857. Suppose that the function l applies to all people born over an extended period of time. It can be shown that, at any time, the expected number of persons in the population between the exact ages of x and $x+m$, inclusive, is given by

$$\int_x^{x+m} l(t)\, dt$$

The following table gives values of $l(x)$ for males and females in the United States.[14] Approximate the number of women in the 20–35 age group by using the trapezoidal rule with $n = 3$.

Life Table

Age $= x$	$l(x)$ Males	$l(x)$ Females	Age $= x$	$l(x)$ Males	$l(x)$ Females
0	100,000	100,000	45	93,717	96,582
5	99,066	99,220	50	91,616	95,392
10	98,967	99,144	55	88,646	93,562
15	98,834	99,059	60	84,188	90,700
20	98,346	98,857	65	77,547	86,288
25	97,648	98,627	70	68,375	79,926
30	96,970	98,350	75	56,288	70,761
35	96,184	97,964	80	42,127	58,573
40	95,163	97,398			

Solution: We want to estimate

$$\int_{20}^{35} l(t)\, dt$$

We have $h = \dfrac{b - a}{n} = \dfrac{35 - 20}{3} = 5$. The terms to be added under the trapezoidal rule are

$$l(20) = 98,857$$
$$2l(25) = 2(98,627) = 197,254$$
$$2l(30) = 2(98,350) = 196,700$$
$$l(35) = \underline{97,964}$$
$$590,775 = \text{sum}$$

By the trapezoidal rule,

$$\int_{20}^{35} l(t)\, dt \approx \frac{5}{2}(590,775) = 1,476,937.5$$

Now Work Problem 17 ◁

Formulas used to determine the accuracy of answers obtained with the trapezoidal or Simpson's rule can be found in standard texts on numerical analysis.

---

[14]*National Vital Statistics Report*, vol. 48, no. 18, February 7, 2001.

PROBLEMS 14.8

In Problems 1 and 2, use the trapezoidal rule or Simpson's rule (as indicated) and the given value of n to estimate the integral.

1. $\int_{-2}^{4} \dfrac{170}{1+x^2}\,dx$;   trapezoidal rule, $n = 6$

2. $\int_{-2}^{4} \dfrac{170}{1+x^2}\,dx$;   Simpson's rule, $n = 6$

In Problems 3–8, use the trapezoidal rule or Simpson's rule (as indicated) and the given value of n to estimate the integral. Compute each term to four decimal places, and round the answer to three decimal places. In Problems 3–6, also evaluate the integral by antidifferentiation (the Fundamental Theorem of Integral Calculus).

3. $\int_{0}^{1} x^3\,dx$;   trapezoidal rule, $n = 5$

4. $\int_{0}^{1} x^2\,dx$;   Simpson's rule, $n = 4$

5. $\int_{1}^{4} \dfrac{dx}{x^2}$;   Simpson's rule, $n = 4$

6. $\int_{1}^{4} \dfrac{dx}{x}$;   trapezoidal rule, $n = 6$

7. $\int_{0}^{2} \dfrac{x\,dx}{x+1}$;   trapezoidal rule, $n = 4$

8. $\int_{1}^{4} \dfrac{dx}{x}$;   Simpson's rule, $n = 6$

In Problems 9 and 10, use the life table in Example 3 to estimate the given integrals by the trapezoidal rule.

9. $\int_{45}^{70} l(t)\,dt$, males, $n = 5$ **10.** $\int_{35}^{55} l(t)\,dt$, females, $n = 4$

In Problems 11 and 12, suppose the graph of a continuous function f, where $f(x) \geq 0$, contains the given points. Use Simpson's rule and all of the points to approximate the area between the graph and the x-axis on the given interval. Round the answer to one decimal place.

11. $(1, 0.4), (2, 0.6), (3, 1.2), (4, 0.8), (5, 0.5)$; $[1, 5]$

12. $(2, 0), (2.5, 6), (3, 10), (3.5, 11), (4, 14), (4.5, 15), (5, 16)$; $[2, 5]$

13. Using all the information given in Figure 14.26, estimate $\int_{1}^{3} f(x)\,dx$ by using Simpson's rule. Give your answer in fractional form.

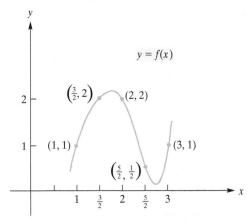

FIGURE 14.26

In Problems 14 and 15, use Simpson's rule and the given value of n to estimate the integral. Compute each term to four decimal places, and round the answer to three decimal places.

14. $\int_{1}^{3} \dfrac{2}{\sqrt{1+x}}\,dx$; $n = 4$ Also, evaluate the integral by the Fundamental Theorem of Integral Calculus.

15. $\int_{0}^{1} \sqrt{1-x^2}\,dx$; $n = 4$

16. Revenue   Use Simpson's rule to approximate the total revenue received from the production and sale of 80 units of a product if the values of the marginal-revenue function dr/dq are as follows:

q (units)	0	10	20	30	40	50	60	70	80
$\dfrac{dr}{dq}$ ($ per unit)	10	9	8.5	8	8.5	7.5	7	6.5	7

17. Area of Pool   Lesley Griffith, who has taken a commerce mathematics class, would like to determine the surface area of her curved, irregularly shaped swimming pool. There is a straight fence that runs along the side of the pool. Lesley marks off points a and b on the fence as shown in Figure 14.27. She notes that the distance from a to b is 8 m and subdivides the interval into eight equal subintervals, naming the resulting points on the fence x_1, x_2, x_3, x_4, x_5, x_6, and x_7. Lesley (L) stands at point x_1, holds a tape measure, and has a friend Chester (C) take the free end of the tape measure to the point P_1 on the far side of the pool. She asks her other friend Willamina (W) to stand at point Q_1 on the near side of the pool and note the distance on the tape measure. See Figure 14.27.

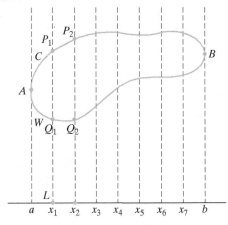

FIGURE 14.27

Lesley then moves to point x_2 and the three friends repeat the procedure. They do this for each of the remaining points x_3 to x_7. Lesley tabulates their measurements in the following table:

Distance along fence (m)	0	1	2	3	4	5	6	7	8
Distance across pool (m)	0	3	4	3	3	2	2	2	0

Lesley says that Simpson's rule now allows them to approximate the area of the pool as

$$\frac{1}{3}(4(3) + 2(4) + 4(3) + 2(3) + 4(2) + 2(2) + 4(2)) = \frac{58}{3}$$

square meters. Chester says that this is not how he remembers Simpson's rule. Willamina thinks that some terms are missing, but Chester gets bored and goes for a swim. Is Lesley's calculation correct? Explain.

18. Manufacturing A manufacturer estimated both marginal cost (MC) and marginal revenue (MR) at various levels of output (q). These estimates are given in the following table:

q(units)	0	20	40	60	80	100
MC ($ per unit)	260	250	240	200	240	250
MR ($ per unit)	410	350	300	250	270	250

(a) Using the trapezoidal rule, estimate the total variable costs of production for 100 units.
(b) Using the trapezoidal rule, estimate the total revenue from the sale of 100 units.
(c) If we assume that maximum profit occurs when MR = MC (that is, when $q = 100$), estimate the maximum profit if fixed costs are $2000.

Objective

To find the area of a region bounded by curves using integration over both vertical and horizontal strips.

14.9 Area between Curves

In Sections 14.6 and 14.7 we saw that the area of a region bounded by the lines $x = a$, $x = b$, $y = 0$, and a curve $y = f(x)$ with $f(x) \geq 0$ for $a \leq x \leq b$ can be found by evaluating the definite integral $\int_a^b f(x)\,dx$. Similarly, for a function $f(x) \leq 0$ on an interval $[a, b]$, the area of the region bounded by $x = a$, $x = b$, $y = 0$, and $y = f(x)$ is given by $-\int_a^b f(x)\,dx = \int_a^b -f(x)\,dx$. Most of the functions f we have encountered, and will encounter, are continuous and have a finite number of roots of $f(x) = 0$. For such functions, the roots of $f(x) = 0$ partition the domain of f into a finite number of intervals on each of which we have either $f(x) \geq 0$ or $f(x) \leq 0$. For such a function we can determine the area bounded by $y = f(x)$, $y = 0$ and *any* pair of vertical lines $x = a$ and $x = b$, with a and b in the domain of f. We have only to find all the roots $c_1 < c_2 < \cdots < c_k$ with $a < c_1$ and $c_k < b$; calculate the integrals $\int_a^{c_1} f(x)\,dx$, $\int_{c_1}^{c_2} f(x)\,dx, \cdots, \int_{c_k}^b f(x)\,dx$; attach to each integral the correct sign to correspond to an area; and add the results. Example 1 will provide a modest example of this idea.

For such an area determination, a rough sketch of the region involved is extremely valuable. To set up the integrals needed, a sample rectangle should be included in the sketch for each individual integral as in Figure 14.28. The area of the region is a limit of sums of areas of rectangles. A sketch helps to understand the integration process and it is indispensable when setting up integrals to find areas of complicated regions. Such a rectangle (see Figure 14.28) is called a **vertical strip**. In the diagram, the width of the vertical strip is Δx. We know from our work on differentials in Section 14.1 that we can consistently write $\Delta x = dx$, for x the independent variable. The height of the vertical strip is the y-value of the curve. Hence, the rectangle has area $y \Delta x = f(x)\,dx$. The area of the entire region is found by summing the areas of all such vertical strips between $x = a$ and $x = b$ and finding the limit of this sum, which is the definite integral. Symbolically, we have

$$\Sigma y \Delta x \rightarrow \int_a^b f(x)\,dx$$

For $f(x) \geq 0$ it is helpful to think of dx as a length differential and $f(x)dx$ as an area differential dA. Then, as we saw in Section 14.7, we have $\dfrac{dA}{dx} = f(x)$ for some area function A and

$$\int_a^b f(x)\,dx = \int_a^b dA = A(b) - A(a)$$

[If our area function A measures area starting at the line $x = a$, as it did in Section 14.7, then $A(a) = 0$ and the area under f (and over 0) from a to b is just $A(b)$.] It is important

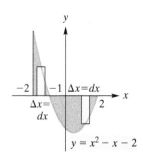

FIGURE 14.28 Diagram for Example 1.

In the figure: $\Delta x = dx$, $y = x^2 - x - 2$, with axes marked at -2, -1, 2.

to understand here that we need $f(x) \geq 0$ in order to think of $f(x)$ as a length and hence $f(x)dx$ as a differential area. But if $f(x) \leq 0$ then $-f(x) \geq 0$ so that $-f(x)$ becomes a length and $-f(x)dx$ becomes a differential area.

EXAMPLE 1   An Area Requiring Two Definite Integrals

Find the area of the region bounded by the curve

$$y = x^2 - x - 2$$

and the line $y = 0$ (the x-axis) from $x = -2$ to $x = 2$.

CAUTION! ⚠

It is wrong to write hastily that the area is $\int_{-2}^{2} y \, dx$, for the following reason: For the left rectangle, the height is y. However, for the rectangle on the right, y is negative, so its height is the positive number $-y$. This points out the importance of sketching the region.

Solution: A sketch of the region is given in Figure 14.28. Notice that the x-intercepts are $(-1, 0)$ and $(2, 0)$.

On the interval $[-2, -1]$, the area of the vertical strip is

$$y dx = (x^2 - x - 2)dx$$

On the interval $[-1, 2]$, the area of the vertical strip is

$$(-y)dx = -(x^2 - x - 2)dx$$

Thus,

$$\text{area} = \int_{-2}^{-1} (x^2 - x - 2) \, dx + \int_{-1}^{2} -(x^2 - x - 2) \, dx$$

$$= \left(\frac{x^3}{3} - \frac{x^2}{2} - 2x \right) \Big|_{-2}^{-1} - \left(\frac{x^3}{3} - \frac{x^2}{2} - 2x \right) \Big|_{-1}^{2}$$

$$= \left[\left(-\frac{1}{3} - \frac{1}{2} + 2 \right) - \left(-\frac{8}{3} - \frac{4}{2} + 4 \right) \right]$$

$$\quad - \left[\left(\frac{8}{3} - \frac{4}{2} - 4 \right) - \left(-\frac{1}{3} - \frac{1}{2} + 2 \right) \right]$$

$$= \frac{19}{3}$$

Now Work Problem 22 ◁

Before embarking on more complicated area problems, we motivate the further study of area by seeing the use of area as a probability in statistics.

EXAMPLE 2   Statistics Application

In statistics, a (probability) **density function** f of a variable x, where x assumes all values in the interval $[a, b]$, has the following properties:

(i) $f(x) \geq 0$

(ii) $\int_{a}^{b} f(x) \, dx = 1$

The probability that x assumes a value between c and d, which is written $P(c \leq x \leq d)$, where $a \leq c \leq d \leq b$, is represented by the area of the region bounded by the graph of f and the x-axis between $x = c$ and $x = d$. Hence (see Figure 14.29),

$$P(c \leq x \leq d) = \int_{c}^{d} f(x) \, dx$$

[In the terminology of Chapters 8 and 9, the condition $c \leq x \leq d$ defines an *event* and $P(c \leq x \leq d)$ is consistent with the notation of the earlier chapters. Note too that the hypothesis **(ii)** above ensures that $a \leq x \leq b$ is the *certain event*.]

For the density function $f(x) = 6(x - x^2)$, where $0 \leq x \leq 1$, find each of the following probabilities.

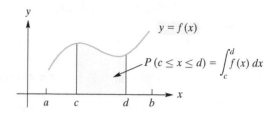

FIGURE 14.29 Probability as an area.

a. $P(0 \leq x \leq \frac{1}{4})$

Solution: Here $[a, b]$ is $[0, 1]$, c is 0, and d is $\frac{1}{4}$. We have

$$P\left(0 \leq x \leq \tfrac{1}{4}\right) = \int_0^{1/4} 6(x - x^2)\,dx = 6\int_0^{1/4} (x - x^2)\,dx$$

$$= 6\left(\frac{x^2}{2} - \frac{x^3}{3}\right)\Bigg|_0^{1/4} = (3x^2 - 2x^3)\Big|_0^{1/4}$$

$$= \left(3\left(\frac{1}{4}\right)^2 - 2\left(\frac{1}{4}\right)^3\right) - 0 = \frac{5}{32}$$

b. $P\left(x \geq \frac{1}{2}\right)$

Solution: Since the domain of f is $0 \leq x \leq 1$, to say that $x \geq \frac{1}{2}$ means that $\frac{1}{2} \leq x \leq 1$. Thus,

$$P\left(x \geq \frac{1}{2}\right) = \int_{1/2}^1 6(x - x^2)\,dx = 6\int_{1/2}^1 (x - x^2)\,dx$$

$$= 6\left(\frac{x^2}{2} - \frac{x^3}{3}\right)\Bigg|_{1/2}^1 = (3x^2 - 2x^3)\Big|_{1/2}^1 = \frac{1}{2}$$

Now Work Problem 27 ◁

Vertical Strips

We will now find the area of a region enclosed by several curves. As before, our procedure will be to draw a sample strip of area and use the definite integral to "add together" the areas of all such strips.

For example, consider the area of the region in Figure 14.30 that is bounded on the top and bottom by the curves $y = f(x)$ and $y = g(x)$ and on the sides by the lines $x = a$ and $x = b$. The width of the indicated vertical strip is dx, and the height is the y-value of the upper curve minus the y-value of the lower curve, which we will write as $y_{\text{upper}} - y_{\text{lower}}$. Thus, the area of the strip is

$$(y_{\text{upper}} - y_{\text{lower}})\,dx$$

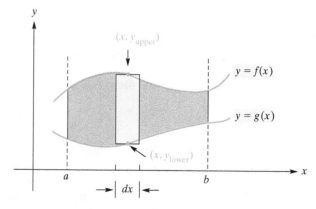

FIGURE 14.30 Region between curves.

which is

$$(f(x) - g(x)) \, dx$$

Summing the areas of all such strips from $x = a$ to $x = b$ by the definite integral gives the area of the region:

$$\sum (f(x) - g(x)) \, dx \rightarrow \int_a^b (f(x) - g(x)) \, dx = \text{area}$$

We remark that there is another way to view this area problem. In Figure 14.30 both f and g are above $y = 0$ and it is clear that the area we seek is also the area under f minus the area under g. That approach tells us that the required area is

$$\int_a^b f(x) \, dx - \int_a^b g(x) \, dx = \int_a^b (f(x) - g(x)) \, dx$$

However, our first approach does not require that either f or g lie above 0. Our usage of y_{upper} and y_{lower} is really just a way of saying that $f \geq g$ on $[a, b]$. This is equivalent to saying that $f - g \geq 0$ on $[a, b]$ so that each differential $(f(x) - g(x)) \, dx$ is meaningful as an area.

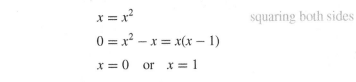

EXAMPLE 3   **Finding an Area between Two Curves**

Find the area of the region bounded by the curves $y = \sqrt{x}$ and $y = x$.

Solution: A sketch of the region appears in Figure 14.31. To determine where the curves intersect, we solve the system formed by the equations $y = \sqrt{x}$ and $y = x$. Eliminating y by substitution, we obtain

$$\sqrt{x} = x$$
$$x = x^2 \qquad\qquad \text{squaring both sides}$$
$$0 = x^2 - x = x(x - 1)$$
$$x = 0 \quad \text{or} \quad x = 1$$

Since we squared both sides, we must check the solutions found with respect to the *original* equation. It is easily determined that both $x = 0$ and $x = 1$ are solutions of $\sqrt{x} = x$. If $x = 0$, then $y = 0$; if $x = 1$, then $y = 1$. Thus, the curves intersect at $(0, 0)$ and $(1, 1)$. The width of the indicated strip of area is dx. The height is the y-value on the upper curve minus the y-value on the lower curve:

$$y_{\text{upper}} - y_{\text{lower}} = \sqrt{x} - x$$

Hence, the area of the strip is $(\sqrt{x} - x) \, dx$. Summing the areas of all such strips from $x = 0$ to $x = 1$ by the definite integral, we get the area of the entire region:

$$\begin{aligned}
\text{area} &= \int_0^1 (\sqrt{x} - x) \, dx \\
&= \int_0^1 (x^{1/2} - x) \, dx = \left(\frac{x^{3/2}}{\frac{3}{2}} - \frac{x^2}{2} \right) \Bigg|_0^1 \\
&= \left(\frac{2}{3} - \frac{1}{2} \right) - (0 - 0) = \frac{1}{6}
\end{aligned}$$

FIGURE 14.31   Diagram for Example 3.

It should be obvious that knowing the points of intersection is important in determining the limits of integration.

Now Work Problem 47 ◁

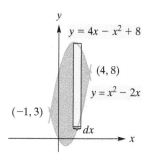

FIGURE 14.32 Diagram for Example 4.

EXAMPLE 4 Finding an Area between Two Curves

Find the area of the region bounded by the curves $y = 4x - x^2 + 8$ and $y = x^2 - 2x$.

Solution: A sketch of the region appears in Figure 14.32. To find where the curves intersect, we solve the system of equations $y = 4x - x^2 + 8$ and $y = x^2 - 2x$:

$$4x - x^2 + 8 = x^2 - 2x,$$
$$-2x^2 + 6x + 8 = 0,$$
$$x^2 - 3x - 4 = 0,$$
$$(x + 1)(x - 4) = 0 \qquad \text{factoring}$$
$$x = -1 \quad \text{or} \quad x = 4$$

When $x = -1$, then $y = 3$; when $x = 4$, then $y = 8$. Thus, the curves intersect at $(-1, 3)$ and $(4, 8)$. The width of the indicated strip is dx. The height is the y-value on the upper curve minus the y-value on the lower curve:

$$y_{\text{upper}} - y_{\text{lower}} = (4x - x^2 + 8) - (x^2 - 2x)$$

Therefore, the area of the strip is

$$[(4x - x^2 + 8) - (x^2 - 2x)]\,dx = (-2x^2 + 6x + 8)\,dx$$

Summing all such areas from $x = -1$ to $x = 4$, we have

$$\text{area} = \int_{-1}^{4} (-2x^2 + 6x + 8)\,dx = 41\tfrac{2}{3}$$

Now Work Problem 51 ◁

EXAMPLE 5 Area of a Region Having Two Different Upper Curves

Find the area of the region between the curves $y = 9 - x^2$ and $y = x^2 + 1$ from $x = 0$ to $x = 3$.

Solution: The region is sketched in Figure 14.33. The curves intersect when

$$9 - x^2 = x^2 + 1$$
$$8 = 2x^2$$
$$4 = x^2$$
$$x = \pm 2 \qquad \text{two solutions}$$

When $x = \pm 2$, then $y = 5$, so the points of intersection are $(\pm 2, 5)$. Because we are interested in the region from $x = 0$ to $x = 3$, the intersection point that is of concern to us is $(2, 5)$. Notice in Figure 14.33 that in the region to the *left* of the intersection point $(2, 5)$, a strip has

$$y_{\text{upper}} = 9 - x^2 \quad \text{and} \quad y_{\text{lower}} = x^2 + 1$$

but for a strip to the *right* of $(2, 5)$ the reverse is true, namely,

$$y_{\text{upper}} = x^2 + 1 \quad \text{and} \quad y_{\text{lower}} = 9 - x^2$$

Thus, from $x = 0$ to $x = 2$, the area of a strip is

$$(y_{\text{upper}} - y_{\text{lower}})\,dx = [(9 - x^2) - (x^2 + 1]\,dx$$
$$= (8 - 2x^2)\,dx$$

but from $x = 2$ to $x = 3$, it is

$$(y_{\text{upper}} - y_{\text{lower}})\,dx = [(x^2 + 1) - (9 - x^2)]\,dx$$
$$= (2x^2 - 8)\,dx$$

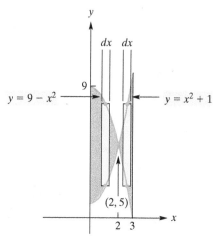

FIGURE 14.33 y_{upper} is $9 - x^2$ on $[0, 2]$ and is $x^2 + 1$ on $[2, 3]$.

Therefore, to find the area of the entire region, we need *two* integrals:

$$\text{area} = \int_0^2 (8 - 2x^2)\, dx + \int_2^3 (2x^2 - 8)\, dx$$

$$= \left(8x - \frac{2x^3}{3}\right)\Big|_0^2 + \left(\frac{2x^3}{3} - 8x\right)\Big|_2^3$$

$$= \left[\left(16 - \frac{16}{3}\right) - 0\right] + \left[(18 - 24) - \left(\frac{16}{3} - 16\right)\right]$$

$$= \frac{46}{3}$$

Now Work Problem 42 ◁

Horizontal Strips

Sometimes area can more easily be determined by summing areas of horizontal strips rather than vertical strips. In the following example, an area will be found by both methods. In each case, the strip of area determines the form of the integral.

EXAMPLE 6 Vertical Strips and Horizontal Strips

Find the area of the region bounded by the curve $y^2 = 4x$ and the lines $y = 3$ and $x = 0$ (the *y*-axis).

Solution: The region is sketched in Figure 14.34. When the curves $y = 3$ and $y^2 = 4x$ intersect, $9 = 4x$, so $x = \frac{9}{4}$. Thus, the intersection point is $(\frac{9}{4}, 3)$. Since the width of the vertical strip is dx, we integrate with respect to the variable x. Accordingly, y_{upper} and y_{lower} must be expressed as functions of x. For the lower curve, $y^2 = 4x$, we have $y = \pm 2\sqrt{x}$. But $y \geq 0$ for the portion of this curve that bounds the region, so we use $y = 2\sqrt{x}$. The upper curve is $y = 3$. Hence, the height of the strip is

$$y_{\text{upper}} - y_{\text{lower}} = 3 - 2\sqrt{x}$$

Therefore, the strip has an area of $(3 - 2\sqrt{x})\,\Delta x$, and we wish to sum all such areas from $x = 0$ to $x = \frac{9}{4}$. We have

$$\text{area} = \int_0^{9/4} (3 - 2\sqrt{x})\, dx = \left(3x - \frac{4x^{3/2}}{3}\right)\Big|_0^{9/4}$$

$$= \left[3\left(\frac{9}{4}\right) - \frac{4}{3}\left(\frac{9}{4}\right)^{3/2}\right] - (0)$$

$$= \frac{27}{4} - \frac{4}{3}\left[\left(\frac{9}{4}\right)^{1/2}\right]^3 = \frac{27}{4} - \frac{4}{3}\left(\frac{3}{2}\right)^3 = \frac{9}{4}$$

Let us now approach this problem from the point of view of a **horizontal strip** as shown in Figure 14.35. The width of the strip is dy. The length of the strip is the *x-value on the rightmost curve minus the x-value on the leftmost curve*. Thus, the area of the strip is

$$(x_{\text{right}} - x_{\text{left}})\, dy$$

We wish to sum all such areas from $y = 0$ to $y = 3$:

$$\sum (x_{\text{right}} - x_{\text{left}})\, dy \rightarrow \int_0^3 (x_{\text{right}} - x_{\text{left}})\, dy$$

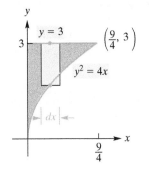

FIGURE 14.34 Vertical strip of area.

CAUTION!⚠

With horizontal strips, the width is dy.

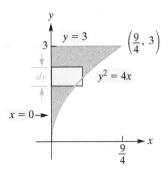

FIGURE 14.35 Horizontal strip of area.

Since the variable of integration is y, we must express x_{right} and x_{left} as functions of y. The rightmost curve is $y^2 = 4x$ so that $x = y^2/4$. The left curve is $x = 0$. Thus,

$$\text{area} = \int_0^3 (x_{\text{right}} - x_{\text{left}})\, dy$$

$$= \int_0^3 \left(\frac{y^2}{4} - 0 \right) dy = \frac{y^3}{12}\Big|_0^3 = \frac{9}{4}$$

Note that for this region, horizontal strips make the definite integral easier to evaluate (and set up) than an integral with vertical strips. In any case, remember that **the limits of integration are limits for the variable of integration.**

Now Work Problem 56 ◁

EXAMPLE 7   Advantage of Horizontal Elements

Find the area of the region bounded by the graphs of $y^2 = x$ and $x - y = 2$.

Solution: The region is sketched in Figure 14.36. The curves intersect when $y^2 - y = 2$. Thus, $y^2 - y - 2 = 0$; equivalently, $(y + 1)(y - 2) = 0$, from which it follows that $y = -1$ or $y = 2$. This gives the intersection points $(1, -1)$ and $(4, 2)$. Let us try vertical strips of area. [See Figure 14.36(a).] Solving $y^2 = x$ for y gives $y = \pm\sqrt{x}$. As seen in Figure 14.36(a), to the *left* of $x = 1$, the upper end of the strip lies on $y = \sqrt{x}$ and the lower end lies on $y = -\sqrt{x}$. To the *right* of $x = 1$, the upper curve is $y = \sqrt{x}$ and the lower curve is $x - y = 2$ (or $y = x - 2$). Thus, with vertical strips, *two* integrals are needed to evaluate the area:

$$\text{area} = \int_0^1 (\sqrt{x} - (-\sqrt{x}))\, dx + \int_1^4 (\sqrt{x} - (x - 2))\, dx$$

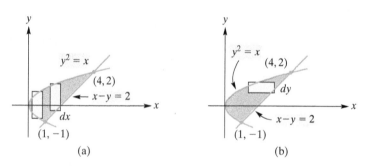

FIGURE 14.36   Region of Example 7 with vertical and horizontal strips.

Perhaps the use of horizontal strips can simplify our work. In Figure 14.36(b), the width of the strip is Δy. The rightmost curve is *always* $x - y = 2$ (or $x = y + 2$), and the leftmost curve is always $y^2 = x$ (or $x = y^2$). Therefore, the area of the horizontal strip is $[(y + 2) - y^2]\, \Delta y$, so the total area is

$$\text{area} = \int_{-1}^2 (y + 2 - y^2)\, dy = \frac{9}{2}$$

Clearly, the use of horizontal strips is the most desirable approach to solving the problem. Only a single integral is needed, and it is much simpler to compute.

Now Work Problem 57 ◁

PROBLEMS 14.9

In Problems 1–24, use a definite integral to find the area of the region bounded by the given curve, the x-axis, and the given lines. In each case, first sketch the region. Watch out for areas of regions that are below the x-axis.

1. $y = 5x + 2$, $x = 1$, $x = 4$

2. $y = x + 5$, $x = 2$, $x = 4$

3. $y = 3x^2$, $x = 1$, $x = 3$

4. $y = x^2$, $x = 2$, $x = 3$

5. $y = x + x^2 + x^3$, $x = 1$

6. $y = x^2 - 2x$, $x = -3$, $x = -1$

7. $y = 3x^2 - 4x$, $x = -2$, $x = -1$

8. $y = 2 - x - x^2$

9. $y = \dfrac{4}{x}, \quad x = 1, \quad x = 2$

10. $y = 2 - x - x^3, \quad x = -3, \quad x = 0$

11. $y = e^x, \quad x = 1, \quad x = 3$

12. $y = \dfrac{1}{(x-1)^2}, \quad x = 2, \quad x = 3$

13. $y = \dfrac{1}{x}, \quad x = 1, \quad x = e$

14. $y = \sqrt{x+9}, \quad x = -9, \quad x = 0$

15. $y = x^2 - 4x, \quad x = 2, \quad x = 6$

16. $y = \sqrt{2x-1}, \quad x = 1, \quad x = 5$

17. $y = x^3 + 3x^2, \quad x = -2, \quad x = 2$

18. $y = \sqrt[3]{x}, \quad x = 2$

19. $y = e^x + 1, \quad x = 0, \quad x = 1$

20. $y = |x|, \quad x = -2, \quad x = 2$

21. $y = x + \dfrac{2}{x}, \quad x = 1, \quad x = 2$

22. $y = x^3, \quad x = -2, \quad x = 4$

23. $y = \sqrt{x-2}, \quad x = 2, \quad x = 6$

24. $y = x^2 + 1, \quad x = 0, \quad x = 4$

25. Given that

$$f(x) = \begin{cases} 3x^2 & \text{if } 0 \le x < 2 \\ 16 - 2x & \text{if } x \ge 2 \end{cases}$$

determine the area of the region bounded by the graph of $y = f(x)$, the x-axis, and the line $x = 3$. Include a sketch of the region.

26. Under conditions of a continuous uniform distribution (a topic in statistics), the proportion of persons with incomes between a and t, where $a \le t \le b$, is the area of the region between the curve $y = 1/(b - a)$ and the x-axis from $x = a$ to $x = t$. Sketch the graph of the curve and determine the area of the given region.

27. Suppose $f(x) = x/8$, where $0 \le x \le 4$. If f is a density function (refer to Example 2), find each of the following.

(a) $P(0 \le x \le 1)$
(b) $P(2 \le x \le 4)$
(c) $P(x \ge 3)$

28. Suppose $f(x) = \frac{1}{3}(1 - x)^2$, where $0 \le x \le 3$. If f is a density function (refer to Example 2), find each of the following.

(a) $P(1 \le x \le 2)$
(b) $P\left(1 \le x \le \frac{5}{2}\right)$
(c) $P(x \le 1)$
(d) $P(x \ge 1)$ using your result from part (c)

29. Suppose $f(x) = 1/x$, where $e \le x \le e^2$. If f is a density function (refer to Example 2), find each of the following.

(a) $P(3 \le x \le 7)$
(b) $P(x \le 5)$
(c) $P(x \ge 4)$
(d) Verify that $P(e \le x \le e^2) = 1$.

30. (a) Let r be a real number, where $r > 1$. Evaluate

$$\int_1^r \frac{1}{x^2}\, dx$$

(b) Your answer to part (a) can be interpreted as the area of a certain region of the plane. Sketch this region.

(c) Evaluate $\displaystyle \lim_{r \to \infty} \left(\int_1^r \frac{1}{x^2}\, dx \right)$.

(d) Your answer to part (c) can be interpreted as the area of a certain region of the plane. Sketch this region.

In Problems 31–34, use definite integration to estimate the area of the region bounded by the given curve, the x-axis, and the given lines. Round your answer to two decimal places.

31. $y = \dfrac{1}{x^2 + 1}, \quad x = -2, \quad x = 1$

32. $y = \dfrac{x}{\sqrt{x+5}}, \quad x = 2, \quad x = 7$

33. $y = x^4 - 2x^3 - 2, \quad x = 1, \quad x = 3$

34. $y = 1 + 3x - x^4$

In Problems 35–38, express the area of the shaded region in terms of an integral (or integrals). Do not evaluate your expression.

35. See Figure 14.37.

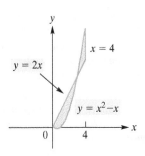

FIGURE 14.37

36. See Figure 14.38.

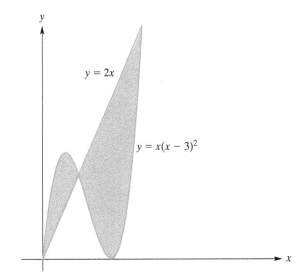

FIGURE 14.38

37. See Figure 14.39.

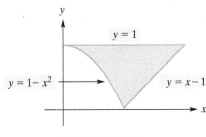

FIGURE 14.39

38. See Figure 14.40.

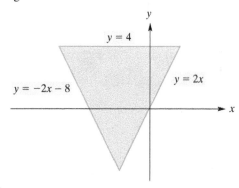

FIGURE 14.40

39. Express, in terms of a single integral, the total area of the region to the right of the line $x = 1$ that is between the curves $y = x^2 - 5$ and $y = 7 - 2x^2$. Do *not* evaluate the integral.

40. Express, in terms of a single integral, the total area of the region in the first quadrant bounded by the x-axis and the graphs of $y^2 = x$ and $2y = 3 - x$. Do *not* evaluate the integral.

In Problems 41–56, find the area of the region bounded by the graphs of the given equations. Be sure to find any needed points of intersection. Consider whether the use of horizontal strips makes the integral simpler than when vertical strips are used.

41. $y = x^2$, $y = 2x$ 42. $y = x$, $y = -x + 3$, $y = 0$

43. $y = 10 - x^2$, $y = 4$ **44.** $y^2 = x + 1$, $x = 1$

45. $x = 8 + 2y$, $x = 0$, $y = -1$, $y = 3$

46. $y = x - 6$, $y^2 = x$ 47. $y^2 = 4x$, $y = 2x - 4$

48. $y = x^3$, $y = x + 6$, $x = 0$.
(*Hint:* The only real root of $x^3 - x - 6 = 0$ is 2.)

49. $2y = 4x - x^2$, $2y = x - 4$

50. $y = \sqrt{x}$, $y = x^2$

51. $y = 8 - x^2$, $y = x^2$, $x = -1$, $x = 1$

52. $y = x^3 + x$, $y = 0$, $x = -1$, $x = 2$

53. $y = x^3 - 1$, $y = x - 1$

54. $y = x^3$, $y = \sqrt{x}$

55. $4x + 4y + 17 = 0$, $y = \dfrac{1}{x}$

56. $y^2 = -x - 2$, $x - y = 5$, $y = -1$, $y = 1$

57. Find the area of the region that is between the curves
$$y = x - 1 \quad \text{and} \quad y = 5 - 2x$$
from $x = 0$ to $x = 4$.

58. Find the area of the region that is between the curves
$$y = x^2 - 4x + 4 \quad \text{and} \quad y = 10 - x^2$$
from $x = 2$ to $x = 4$.

59. Lorenz Curve   A *Lorenz curve* is used in studying income distributions. If x is the cumulative percentage of income recipients, ranked from poorest to richest, and y is the cumulative percentage of income, then equality of income distribution is given by the line $y = x$ in Figure 14.41, where x and y are expressed as decimals. For example, 10% of the people receive

10% of total income, 20% of the people receive 20% of the income, and so on. Suppose the actual distribution is given by the Lorenz curve defined by

$$y = \frac{14}{15}x^2 + \frac{1}{15}x$$

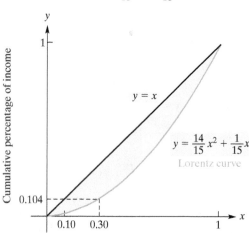

Cumulative percentage of income recipients

FIGURE 14.41

Note, for example, that 30% of the people receive only 10.4% of total income. The degree of deviation from equality is measured by the *coefficient of inequality*[15] for a Lorenz curve. This coefficient is defined to be the area between the curve and the diagonal, divided by the area under the diagonal:

$$\frac{\text{area between curve and diagonal}}{\text{area under diagonal}}$$

For example, when all incomes are equal, the coefficient of inequality is zero. Find the coefficient of inequality for the Lorenz curve just defined.

60. Lorenz curve   Find the coefficient of inequality as in Problem 59 for the Lorenz curve defined by $y = \frac{11}{12}x^2 + \frac{1}{12}x$.

61. Find the area of the region bounded by the graphs of the equations $y^2 = 3x$ and $y = mx$, where m is a positive constant.

62. **(a)** Find the area of the region bounded by the graphs of $y = x^2 - 1$ and $y = 2x + 2$.
(b) What percentage of the area in part (a) lies above the x-axis?

63. The region bounded by the curve $y = x^2$ and the line $y = 4$ is divided into two parts of equal area by the line $y = k$, where k is a constant. Find the value of k.

In Problems 64–68, estimate the area of the region bounded by the graphs of the given equations. Round your answer to two decimal places.

64. $y = x^2 - 4x + 1$, $y = -\dfrac{6}{x}$

65. $y = \sqrt{25 - x^2}$, $y = 7 - 2x - x^4$

66. $y = x^3 - 8x + 1$, $y = x^2 - 5$

67. $y = x^5 - 3x^3 + 2x$, $y = 3x^2 - 4$

68. $y = x^4 - 3x^3 - 15x^2 + 19x + 30$, $y = x^3 + x^2 - 20x$

[15] G. Stigler, *The Theory of Price,* 3rd ed. (New York: The Macmillan Company, 1966), pp. 293–94.

Objective

To develop the economic concepts of consumers' surplus and producers' surplus, which are represented by areas.

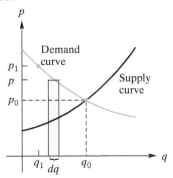

FIGURE 14.42   Supply and demand curves.

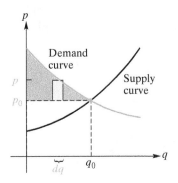

FIGURE 14.43   Benefit to consumers for dq units.

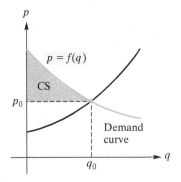

FIGURE 14.44   Consumers' surplus.

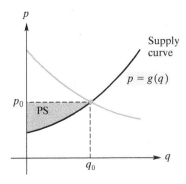

FIGURE 14.45   Producers' surplus.

14.10 Consumers' and Producers' Surplus

Determining the area of a region has applications in economics. Figure 14.42 shows a supply curve for a product. The curve indicates the price p per unit at which the manufacturer will sell (or supply) q units. The diagram also shows a demand curve for the product. This curve indicates the price p per unit at which consumers will purchase (or demand) q units. The point (q_0, p_0) where the two curves intersect is called the *point of equilibrium*. Here p_0 is the price per unit at which consumers will purchase the same quantity q_0 of a product that producers wish to sell at that price. In short, p_0 is the price at which stability in the producer–consumer relationship occurs.

Let us assume that the market is at equilibrium and the price per unit of the product is p_0. According to the demand curve, there are consumers who would be willing to pay *more* than p_0. For example, at the price per unit of p_1, consumers would buy q_1 units. These consumers are benefiting from the lower equilibrium price p_0.

The vertical strip in Figure 14.42 has area $p\,dq$. This expression can also be thought of as the total amount of money that consumers would spend by buying dq units of the product if the price per unit were p. Since the price is actually p_0, these consumers spend only $p_0\,dq$ for the dq units and thus benefit by the amount $p\,dq - p_0\,dq$. This expression can be written $(p - p_0)\,dq$, which is the area of a rectangle of width dq and height $p - p_0$. (See Figure 14.43.) Summing the areas of all such rectangles from $q = 0$ to $q = q_0$ by definite integration, we have

$$\int_0^{q_0} (p - p_0)\,dq$$

This integral, under certain conditions, represents the total gain to consumers who are willing to pay more than the equilibrium price. This total gain is called **consumers' surplus**, abbreviated CS. If the demand function is given by $p = f(q)$, then

$$CS = \int_0^{q_0} [f(q) - p_0]\,dq$$

Geometrically (see Figure 14.44), consumers' surplus is represented by the area between the line $p = p_0$ and the demand curve $p = f(q)$ from $q = 0$ to $q = q_0$.

Some of the producers also benefit from the equilibrium price, since they are willing to supply the product at prices *less* than p_0. Under certain conditions, the total gain to the producers is represented geometrically in Figure 14.45 by the area between the line $p = p_0$ and the supply curve $p = g(q)$ from $q = 0$ to $q = q_0$. This gain, called **producers' surplus** and abbreviated PS, is given by

$$PS = \int_0^{q_0} [p_0 - g(q)]\,dq$$

EXAMPLE 1   **Finding Consumers' Surplus and Producers' Surplus**

The demand function for a product is

$$p = f(q) = 100 - 0.05q$$

where p is the price per unit (in dollars) for q units. The supply function is

$$p = g(q) = 10 + 0.1q$$

Determine consumers' surplus and producers' surplus under market equilibrium.

Solution: First we must find the equilibrium point (p_0, q_0) by solving the system formed by the functions $p = 100 - 0.05q$ and $p = 10 + 0.1q$. We thus equate the two expressions for p and solve:

$$10 + 0.1q = 100 - 0.05q$$

$$0.15q = 90$$

$$q = 600$$

When $q = 600$ then $p = 10 + 0.1(600) = 70$. Hence, $q_0 = 600$ and $p_0 = 70$. Consumers' surplus is

$$CS = \int_0^{q_0} [f(q) - p_0] \, dq = \int_0^{600} (100 - 0.05q - 70) \, dq$$

$$= \left(30q - 0.05\frac{q^2}{2} \right) \Bigg|_0^{600} = 9000$$

Producers' surplus is

$$PS = \int_0^{q_0} [p_0 - g(q)] \, dq = \int_0^{600} [70 - (10 + 0.1q)] \, dq$$

$$= \left(60q - 0.1\frac{q^2}{2} \right) \Bigg|_0^{600} = 18{,}000$$

Therefore, consumers' surplus is $9000 and producers' surplus is $18,000.

Now Work Problem 1 ◁

EXAMPLE 2   Using Horizontal Strips to Find Consumers' Surplus and Producers' Surplus

The demand equation for a product is

$$q = f(p) = \frac{90}{p} - 2$$

and the supply equation is $q = g(p) = p - 1$. Determine consumers' surplus and producers' surplus when market equilibrium has been established.

Solution: Determining the equilibrium point, we have

$$p - 1 = \frac{90}{p} - 2$$

$$p^2 + p - 90 = 0$$

$$(p + 10)(p - 9) = 0$$

Thus, $p_0 = 9$, so $q_0 = 9 - 1 = 8$. (See Figure 14.46.) Note that the demand equation expresses q as a function of p. Since consumers' surplus can be considered an area, this area can be determined by means of horizontal strips of width dp and length $q = f(p)$. The areas of these strips are summed from $p = 9$ to $p = 45$ by integrating with

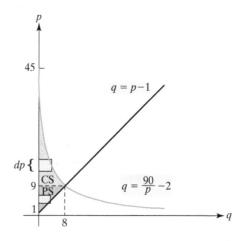

FIGURE 14.46   Diagram for Example 2.

respect to p:

$$\text{CS} = \int_9^{45} \left(\frac{90}{p} - 2 \right) dp = (90 \ln |p| - 2p) \Big|_9^{45}$$

$$= 90 \ln 5 - 72 \approx 72.85$$

Using horizontal strips for producers' surplus, we have

$$\text{PS} = \int_1^9 (p - 1) \, dp = \frac{(p-1)^2}{2} \Big|_1^9 = 32$$

Now Work Problem 5 ◁

PROBLEMS 14.10

In Problems 1–6, the first equation is a demand equation and the second is a supply equation of a product. In each case, determine consumers' surplus and producers' surplus under market equilibrium.

1. $p = 22 - 0.8q$
$p = 6 + 1.2q$

2. $p = 2200 - q^2$
$p = 400 + q^2$

3. $p = \dfrac{50}{q+5}$
$p = \dfrac{q}{10} + 4.5$

4. $p = 900 - q^2$
$p = 10q + 300$

5. $q = 100(10 - 2p)$
$q = 50(2p - 1)$

6. $q = \sqrt{100 - p}$
$q = \dfrac{p}{2} - 10$

7. The demand equation for a product is

$$q = 10\sqrt{100 - p}$$

Calculate consumers' surplus under market equilibrium, which occurs at a price of $84.

8. The demand equation for a product is

$$q = 400 - p^2$$

and the supply equation is

$$p = \frac{q}{60} + 5$$

Find producers' surplus and consumers' surplus under market equilibrium.

9. The demand equation for a product is $p = 2^{10-q}$, and the supply equation is $p = 2^{q+2}$, where p is the price per unit (in hundreds of dollars) when q units are demanded or supplied.

Determine, to the nearest thousand dollars, consumers' surplus under market equilibrium.

10. The demand equation for a product is

$$(p + 10)(q + 20) = 1000$$

and the supply equation is

$$q - 4p + 10 = 0$$

(a) Verify, by substitution, that market equilibrium occurs when $p = 10$ and $q = 30$.
(b) Determine consumers' surplus under market equilibrium.

11. The demand equation for a product is

$$p = 60 - \frac{50q}{\sqrt{q^2 + 3600}}$$

and the supply equation is

$$p = 10 \ln (q + 20) - 26$$

Determine consumers' surplus and producers' surplus under market equilibrium. Round your answers to the nearest integer.

12. Producers' Surplus   The supply function for a product is given by the following table, where p is the price per unit (in dollars) at which q units are supplied to the market:

q	0	10	20	30	40	50
p	25	49	59	71	80	94

Use the trapezoidal rule to estimate the producers' surplus if the selling price is $80.

Chapter 14 Review

Important Terms and Symbols

Examples

Summary

If $y = f(x)$ is a differentiable function of x, we define the differential dy by

$$dy = f'(x)\,dx$$

where $dx = \Delta x$ is a change in x and can be any real number. (Thus dy is a function of two variables, namely x and dx.) If dx is close to zero, then dy is an approximation to $\Delta y = f(x + dx) - f(x)$.

$$\Delta y \approx dy$$

Moreover, dy can be used to approximate a function value using

$$f(x + dx) \approx f(x) + dy$$

An antiderivative of a function f is a function F such that $F'(x) = f(x)$. Any two antiderivatives of f differ at most by a constant. The most general antiderivative of f is called the indefinite integral of f and is denoted $\int f(x)\,dx$. Thus,

$$\int f(x)\,dx = F(x) + C$$

where C is called the constant of integration, if and only if $F' = f$.

Some elementary integration formulas are as follows:

$$\int k\,dx = kx + C \qquad k \text{ a constant}$$

$$\int x^a\,dx = \frac{x^{a+1}}{a+1} + C \qquad a \neq -1$$

$$\int \frac{1}{x}\,dx = \ln x + C \qquad \text{for } x > 0$$

$$\int e^x\,dx = e^x + C$$

$$\int kf(x)\,dx = k\int f(x)\,dx \qquad k \text{ a constant}$$

$$\int [f(x) \pm g(x)]\,dx = \int f(x)\,dx \pm \int g(x)\,dx$$

Another formula is the power rule for integration:

$$\int u^a\,du = \frac{u^{a+1}}{a+1} + C, \quad \text{if } a \neq -1$$

Here u represents a differentiable function of x, and du is its differential. In applying the power rule to a given integral, it is important that the integral be written in a form that precisely matches the power rule. Other integration formulas are

$$\int e^u\,du = e^u + C$$

and

$$\int \frac{1}{u}\,du = \ln |u| + C \qquad u \neq 0$$

If the rate of change of a function f is known—that is, if f' is known—then f is an antiderivative of f'. In addition, if we know that f satisfies an initial condition, then we can find the particular antiderivative. For example, if a marginal-cost function dc/dq is given to us, then by integration, we can find the most general form of c. That form involves a constant of integration. However, if we are also given fixed costs (that is, costs involved when $q = 0$), then we can determine the value of the constant of integration and thus find the particular cost function c. Similarly, if we are given a marginal-revenue function dr/dq, then by integration and by using the fact that $r = 0$ when $q = 0$, we can determine the particular revenue function r. Once r is known, the corresponding demand equation can be found by using the equation $p = r/q$.

It is helpful at this point to review summation notation from Section 1.5. This notation is especially useful in determining areas. For continuous $f \geq 0$, to find the area of the region bounded by $y = f(x)$, $y = 0$, $x = a$, and $x = b$, we divide the interval $[a, b]$ into n subintervals of equal length $dx = (b - a)/n$. If x_i is the right-hand endpoint of an arbitrary subinterval, then the product $f(x_i)\,dx$ is the area of a rectangle. Denoting the sum of all such areas of rectangles for the n subintervals by S_n, we define the limit of S_n as $n \to \infty$ as the area of the entire region:

$$\lim_{n \to \infty} S_n = \lim_{n \to \infty} \sum_{i=1}^{n} f(x_i)\,dx = \text{area}$$

If the restriction that $f(x) \geq 0$ is omitted, this limit is defined as the definite integral of f over $[a, b]$:

$$\lim_{n \to \infty} \sum_{i=1}^{n} f(x_i)\,dx = \int_a^b f(x)\,dx$$

Instead of evaluating definite integrals by using limits, we may be able to employ the Fundamental Theorem of Integral Calculus. Mathematically,

$$\int_a^b f(x)\,dx = F(x)\Big|_a^b = F(b) - F(a)$$

where F is any antiderivative of f.

Some properties of the definite integral are

$$\int_a^b kf(x)\,dx = k\int_a^b f(x)\,dx \qquad k \text{ a constant}$$

$$\int_a^b [f(x) \pm g(x)]\,dx = \int_a^b f(x)\,dx \pm \int_a^b g(x)\,dx$$

and

$$\int_a^c f(x)\,dx = \int_a^b f(x)\,dx + \int_b^c f(x)\,dx$$

If $f(x) \geq 0$ is continuous on $[a, b]$, then the definite integral can be used to find the area of the region bounded by $y = f(x)$, the x-axis, $x = a$, and $x = b$. The definite integral can also be used to find areas of more complicated regions. In these situations, a strip of area should be drawn in the region. This allows us to set up the proper definite integral. In this regard, both vertical strips and horizontal strips have their uses.

One application of finding areas involves consumers' surplus and producers' surplus. Suppose the market for a product is at equilibrium and (q_0, p_0) is the equilibrium point (the point of intersection of the supply curve and the demand curve for the product). Then consumers' surplus, CS, corresponds to the area from $q = 0$ to $q = q_0$, bounded above by the demand curve and below by the line $p = p_0$. Thus,

$$CS = \int_0^{q_0} (f(q) - p_0)\,dq$$

where f is the demand function. Producers' surplus, PS, corresponds to the area from $q = 0$ to $q = q_0$, bounded above by the line $p = p_0$ and below by the supply curve. Therefore,

$$PS = \int_0^{q_0} (p_0 - g(q))\,dq$$

where g is the supply function.

Review Problems

In Problems 1–40, determine the integrals.

1. $\displaystyle\int (x^3 + 2x - 7)\,dx$

2. $\displaystyle\int dx$

3. $\displaystyle\int_0^{12} (9\sqrt{3x} + 3x^2)\,dx$

4. $\displaystyle\int \frac{4}{5 - 3x}\,dx$

5. $\displaystyle\int \frac{6}{(x + 5)^3}\,dx$

6. $\displaystyle\int_3^9 (y - 6)^{301}\,dy$

7. $\displaystyle\int \frac{6x^2 - 12}{x^3 - 6x + 1}\,dx$

8. $\displaystyle\int_0^3 2xe^{5-x^2}\,dx$

9. $\displaystyle\int_0^1 \sqrt[3]{3t + 8}\,dt$

10. $\displaystyle\int \frac{4 - 2x}{7}\,dx$

11. $\displaystyle\int y(y + 1)^2\,dy$

12. $\displaystyle\int_0^1 10^{-8}\,dx$

13. $\displaystyle\int \frac{\sqrt[3]{t} - \sqrt{t}}{\sqrt[3]{t}}\,dt$

14. $\displaystyle\int \frac{(0.5x - 0.1)^4}{0.4}\,dx$

15. $\displaystyle\int_1^3 \frac{2t^2}{3 + 2t^3}\,dt$

16. $\displaystyle\int \frac{4x^2 - x}{x}\,dx$

17. $\displaystyle\int x^2\sqrt{3x^3 + 2}\,dx$

18. $\displaystyle\int (6x^2 + 4x)(x^3 + x^2)^{3/2}\,dx$

19. $\displaystyle\int (e^{2y} - e^{-2y})\,dy$

20. $\displaystyle\int \frac{8x}{3\sqrt[3]{7 - 2x^2}}\,dx$

21. $\displaystyle\int \left(\frac{1}{x} + \frac{2}{x^2}\right)\,dx$

22. $\displaystyle\int_0^2 \frac{3e^{3x}}{1 + e^{3x}}\,dx$

23. $\displaystyle\int_{-2}^2 (y^4 + y^3 + y^2 + y)\,dy$

24. $\displaystyle\int_7^{70} dx$

25. $\displaystyle\int_1^2 5x\sqrt{5 - x^2}\,dx$

26. $\displaystyle\int_0^1 (2x + 1)(x^2 + x)^4\,dx$

27. $\displaystyle\int_0^1 \left[2x - \frac{1}{(x + 1)^{2/3}}\right]\,dx$

28. $\displaystyle\int_0^{18} (2x - 3\sqrt{2x} + 1)\,dx$

29. $\displaystyle\int \frac{\sqrt{t} - 3}{t^2}\,dt$

30. $\displaystyle\int \frac{3z^3}{z - 1}\,dz$

31. $\displaystyle\int_{-1}^0 \frac{x^2 + 4x - 1}{x + 2}\,dx$

32. $\displaystyle\int \frac{(x^2 + 4)^2}{x^2}\,dx$

33. $\displaystyle\int \frac{e^{\sqrt{x}} + x}{2\sqrt{x}}\,dx$

34. $\displaystyle\int \frac{e^{\sqrt{5x}}}{\sqrt{3x}}\,dx$

35. $\displaystyle\int_1^e \frac{e^{\ln x}}{x^2}\,dx$

36. $\displaystyle\int \frac{6x^2 + 4}{e^{x^3 + 2x}}\,dx$

37. $\displaystyle\int \frac{(1 + e^{2x})^3}{e^{-2x}}\,dx$

38. $\displaystyle\int \frac{c}{e^{bx}(a + e^{-bx})^n}\,dx$
  for $n \neq 1$ and $b \neq 0$

39. $\displaystyle\int 3\sqrt{10^{3x}}\,dx$

40. $\displaystyle\int \frac{5x^3 + 15x^2 + 37x + 3}{x^2 + 3x + 7}\,dx$

In Problems 41 and 42, find y, subject to the given condition.

41. $y' = e^{2x} + 3, \quad y(0) = -\frac{1}{2}$ **42.** $y' = \dfrac{x + 5}{x}, \quad y(1) = 3$

In Problems 43–50, determine the area of the region bounded by the given curve, the x-axis, and the given lines.

43. $y = x^3, \quad x = 0, \ x = 2$ **44.** $y = 4e^x, \quad x = 0, \ x = 3$

45. $y = \sqrt{x + 4}, \quad x = 0$

46. $y = x^2 - x - 6, \quad x = -4, \ x = 3$

47. $y = 5x - x^2$ **48.** $y = \sqrt[3]{x}, \quad x = 8, \ x = 16$

49. $y = \dfrac{1}{x} + 2, \quad x = 1, \ x = 4$ **50.** $y = x^3 - 1, \quad x = -1$

In Problems 51–58, find the area of the region bounded by the given curves.

51. $y^2 = 4x$, $x = 0$, $y = 2$ **52.** $y = 3x^2 - 5$, $x = 0$, $y = 4$

53. $y = -x(x - a)$, $y = 0$ for $0 < a$

54. $y = 2x^2$, $y = x^2 + 9$ **55.** $y = x^2 - x$, $y = 10 - x^2$

56. $y = \sqrt{x}$, $x = 0$, $y = 3$

57. $y = \ln x$, $x = 0$, $y = 0$, $y = 1$

58. $y = 3 - x$, $y = x - 4$, $y = 0$, $y = 3$

59. Marginal Revenue   If marginal revenue is given by

$$\frac{dr}{dq} = 100 - \frac{3}{2}\sqrt{2q}$$

determine the corresponding demand equation.

60. Marginal Cost   If marginal cost is given by

$$\frac{dc}{dq} = q^2 + 7q + 6$$

and fixed costs are 2500, determine the total cost of producing six units. Assume that costs are in dollars.

61. Marginal Revenue   A manufacturer's marginal-revenue function is

$$\frac{dr}{dq} = 250 - q - 0.2q^2$$

If r is in dollars, find the increase in the manufacturer's total revenue if production is increased from 15 to 25 units.

62. Marginal Cost   A manufacturer's marginal-cost function is

$$\frac{dc}{dq} = \frac{1000}{\sqrt{3q + 70}}$$

If c is in dollars, determine the cost involved to increase production from 10 to 33 units.

63. Hospital Discharges   For a group of hospitalized individuals, suppose the discharge rate is given by

$$f(t) = 0.007e^{-0.007t}$$

where $f(t)$ is the proportion discharged per day at the end of t days of hospitalization. What proportion of the group is discharged at the end of 100 days?

64. Business Expenses   The total expenditures (in dollars) of a business over the next five years are given by

$$\int_0^5 4000e^{0.05t}\, dt$$

Evaluate the expenditures.

65. Find the area of the region between the curves $y = 9 - 2x$ and $y = x$ from $x = 0$ to $x = 4$.

66. Find the area of the region between the curves $y = 2x^2$ and $y = 2 - 5x$ from $x = -1$ to $x = \frac{1}{3}$.

67. Consumers' and Producers' Surplus   The demand equation for a product is

$$p = 0.01q^2 - 1.1q + 30$$

and the supply equation is

$$p = 0.01q^2 + 8$$

Determine consumers' surplus and producers' surplus when market equilibrium has been established.

68. Consumers' Surplus   The demand equation for a product is

$$p = (q - 4)^2$$

and the supply equation is

$$p = q^2 + q + 7$$

where p (in thousands of dollars) is the price per 100 units when q hundred units are demanded or supplied. Determine consumers' surplus under market equilibrium.

69. Biology   In a discussion of gene mutation,[16] the equation

$$\int_{q_0}^{q_n} \frac{dq}{q - \widehat{q}} = -(u + v)\int_0^n dt$$

occurs, where u and v are gene mutation rates, the q's are gene frequencies, and n is the number of generations. Assume that all letters represent constants, except q and t. Integrate both sides and then use your result to show that

$$n = \frac{1}{u + v}\ln\left|\frac{q_0 - \widehat{q}}{q_n - \widehat{q}}\right|$$

70. Fluid Flow   In studying the flow of a fluid in a tube of constant radius R, such as blood flow in portions of the body, we can think of the tube as consisting of concentric tubes of radius r, where $0 \le r \le R$. The velocity v of the fluid is a function of r and is given by[17]

$$v = \frac{(P_1 - P_2)(R^2 - r^2)}{4\eta l}$$

where P_1 and P_2 are pressures at the ends of the tube, η (a Greek letter read "eta") is the fluid viscosity, and l is the length of the tube. The volume rate of flow through the tube, Q, is given by

$$Q = \int_0^R 2\pi r v\, dr$$

Show that $Q = \dfrac{\pi R^4(P_1 - P_2)}{8\eta l}$. Note that R occurs as a factor to the fourth power. Thus, doubling the radius of the tube has the effect of increasing the flow by a factor of 16. The formula that you derived for the volume rate of flow is called *Poiseuille's law*, after the French physiologist Jean Poiseuille.

71. Inventory   In a discussion of inventory, Barbosa and Friedman[18] refer to the function

$$g(x) = \frac{1}{k}\int_1^{1/x} ku^r\, du$$

---

[16] W. B. Mather, *Principles of Quantitative Genetics* (Minneapolis: Burgess Publishing Company, 1964).

[17] R. W. Stacy et al., *Essentials of Biological and Medical Physics* (New York: McGraw-Hill, 1955).

[18] L. C. Barbosa and M. Friedman, "Deterministic Inventory Lot Size Models—a General Root Law," *Management Science*, 24, no. 8 (1978), 819–26.

where k and r are constants, $k > 0$ and $r > -2$, and $x > 0$. Verify the claim that

$$g'(x) = -\frac{1}{x^{r+2}}$$

(*Hint:* Consider two cases: when $r \neq -1$ and when $r = -1$.)

In Problems 72–74, estimate the area of the region bounded by the given curves. Round your answer to two decimal places.

72. $y = x^3 + 9x^2 + 14x - 24, y = 0$

73. $y = x^3 + x^2 + x + 1, y = x^2 + 2x + 1$

74. $y = x^3 + x^2 - 5x - 3, y = x^2 + 2x + 3$

75. The demand equation for a product is

$$p = \frac{200}{\sqrt{q + 20}}$$

and the supply equation is

$$p = 2 \ln (q + 10) + 5$$

Determine consumers' surplus and producers' surplus under market equilibrium. Round your answers to the nearest integer.

Q EXPLORE & EXTEND   Delivered Price

Suppose that you are a manufacturer of a product whose sales occur within R miles of your mill. Assume that you charge customers for shipping at the rate s, in dollars per mile, for each unit of product sold. If m is the unit price (in dollars) at the mill, then the delivered unit price p to a customer x miles from the mill is the mill price plus the shipping charge sx:

$$p = m + sx \qquad 0 \leq x \leq R \qquad (1)$$

The problem is to determine the average delivered price of the units sold.

Suppose that there is a function f such that $f(t) \geq 0$ on the interval $[0, R]$ and such that the area under the graph of f and above the t-axis from $t = 0$ to $t = x$ represents the total number of units Q sold to customers within x miles of the mill. [See Figure 14.47(a).] You can refer to f as the distribution of demand. Because Q is a function of x and is represented by area,

$$Q(x) = \int_0^x f(t)\,dt$$

In particular, the total number of units sold within the market area is

$$Q(R) = \int_0^R f(t)\,dt$$

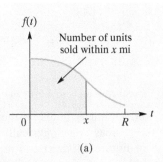

(a)

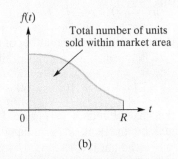

(b)

FIGURE 14.47   Number of units sold as an area.

[see Figure 14.47(b)]. For example, if $f(t) = 10$ and $R = 100$, then the total number of units sold within the market area is

$$Q(100) = \int_0^{100} 10\,dt = 10t\Big|_0^{100} = 1000 - 0 = 1000$$

The average delivered price A is given by

$$A = \frac{\text{total revenue}}{\text{total number of units sold}}$$

Because the denominator is $Q(R)$, A can be determined once the total revenue is found.

To find the total revenue, first consider the number of units sold over an interval. If $t_1 < t_2$ [see Figure 14.48(a)], then the area under the graph of f and above the t-axis from $t = 0$ to $t = t_1$ represents the number of units sold within t_1 miles of the mill. Similarly, the area under the graph of f and above the t-axis from $t = 0$ to $t = t_2$ represents the

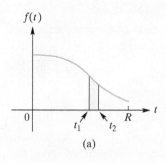

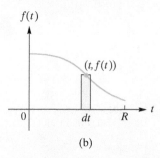

FIGURE 14.48 Number of units sold over an interval.

number of units sold within t_2 miles of the mill. Thus the difference in these areas is geometrically the area of the shaded region in Figure 14.48(a) and represents the number of units sold between t_1 and t_2 miles of the mill, which is $Q(t_2) - Q(t_1)$. Thus

$$Q(t_2) - Q(t_1) = \int_{t_1}^{t_2} f(t)\, dt$$

For example, if $f(t) = 10$, then the number of units sold to customers located between 4 and 6 miles of the mill is

$$Q(6) - Q(4) = \int_4^6 10\, dt = 10t \Big|_4^6 = 60 - 40 = 20$$

The area of the shaded region in Figure 14.48(a) can be approximated by the area of a rectangle [see Figure 14.48(b)] whose height is $f(t)$ and whose width is dt, where $dt = t_2 - t_1$. Thus the number of units sold over the interval of length dt is approximately $f(t)\, dt$. Because the price of each of these units is [from Equation (1)] approximately $m + st$, the revenue received is approximately

$$(m + st)f(t)\, dt$$

The sum of all such products from $t = 0$ to $t = R$ approximates the total revenue. Definite integration gives

$$\sum (m + st)f(t)\, dt \to \int_0^R (m + st)f(t)\, dt$$

Thus,

$$\text{total revenue} = \int_0^R (m + st)f(t)\, dt$$

Consequently, the average delivered price A is given by

$$A = \frac{\displaystyle\int_0^R (m + st)f(t)\, dt}{Q(R)}$$

Equivalently,

$$A = \frac{\displaystyle\int_0^R (m + st)f(t)\, dt}{\displaystyle\int_0^R f(t)\, dt}$$

For example, if $f(t) = 10, m = 200, s = 0.25$, and $R = 100$, then

$$\int_0^R (m + st)f(t)\, dt = \int_0^{100} (200 + 0.25t) \cdot 10\, dt$$

$$= 10 \int_0^{100} (200 + 0.25t)\, dt$$

$$= 10 \left(200t + \frac{t^2}{8} \right) \Big|_0^{100}$$

$$= 10 \left[\left(20{,}000 + \frac{10{,}000}{8} \right) - 0 \right]$$

$$= 212{,}500$$

From before,

$$\int_0^R f(t)\, dt = \int_0^{100} 10\, dt = 1000$$

Thus, the average delivered price is $212{,}500/1000 = \$212.50$.

Problems

1. If $f(t) = 100 - 2t$, determine the number of units sold to customers located (a) within 5 miles of the mill, and (b) between 20 and 25 miles of the mill.

2. If $f(t) = 40 - 0.5t, m = 50, s = 0.20$, and $R = 80$, determine (a) the total revenue, (b) the total number of units sold, and (c) the average delivered price.

3. If $f(t) = 900 - t^2, m = 100, s = 1$, and $R = 30$, determine (a) the total revenue, (b) the total number of units sold, and (c) the average delivered price. Use a graphing calculator if you like.

4. How do real-world sellers of such things as books and clothing generally determine shipping charges for an order? (Visit an online retailer to find out.) How would you calculate average delivered price for their products? Is the procedure fundamentally different from the one discussed in this Explore & Extend?

15 Methods and Applications of Integration

We now know how to find the derivative of a function, and in some cases we know how to find a function from its derivative through integration. However, the integration process is not always straightforward.

Suppose we model the gradual disappearance of a chemical substance using the equations $M' = -0.004t$ and $M(0) = 3000$, where the amount M, in grams, is a function of time t in days. This initial-condition problem is easily solved by integration with respect to t and identifying the constant of integration. The result is $M = -0.002t^2 + 3000$. But what if, instead, the disappearance of the substance were modeled by the equations $M' = -0.004M$ and $M(0) = 3000$? The simple replacement of t in the first equation with M changes the character of the problem. We have not yet learned how to find a function when its derivative is described in terms of the function itself.

In the Explore & Extend in Chapter 13, there was a similar situation, involving an equation with P on one side and the derivative of P on the other. There, we used an approximation to solve the problem. In this chapter, we will learn a method that yields an exact solution for some problems of this type.

Equations of the form $y' = ky$, where k is a constant, are especially common. When y represents the amount of a radioactive substance, $y' = ky$ can represent the rate of its disappearance through radioactive decay. And if y is the temperature of a chicken just taken out of the oven or just put into a freezer, then a related formula, called Newton's law of cooling, can be used to describe the change in the chicken's internal temperature over time. Newton's law, which is discussed in this chapter, might be used to write procedures for a restaurant kitchen, so that food prone to contamination through bacterial growth does not spend too much time in the temperature danger zone (40°F to 140°F). (Bacterial growth, for that matter, also follows a $y' = ky$ law!)

To develop and apply the formula for integration by parts.

15.1 Integration by Parts[1]

Many integrals cannot be found by our previous methods. However, there are ways of changing certain integrals to forms that are easier to integrate. Of these methods, we will discuss two: *integration by parts* and (in Section 15.2) *integration using partial fractions*.

If u and v are differentiable functions of x, we have, by the product rule,

$$(uv)' = uv' + vu'$$

Rearranging gives

$$uv' = (uv)' - vu'$$

Integrating both sides with respect to x, we get

$$\int uv' \, dx = \int (uv)' \, dx - \int vu' \, dx \qquad (1)$$

For $\int (uv)' \, dx$, we must find a function whose derivative with respect to x is $(uv)'$. Clearly, uv is such a function. Hence $\int (uv)' \, dx = uv + C_1$, and Equation (1) becomes

$$\int uv' \, dx = uv + C_1 - \int vu' \, dx$$

Absorbing C_1 into the constant of integration for $\int vu' \, dx$ and replacing $v' \, dx$ by dv and $u' \, dx$ by du, we have the *formula for integration by parts*:

Formula for Integration by Parts

$$\int u \, dv = uv - \int v \, du \qquad (2)$$

This formula expresses an integral, $\int u \, dv$, in terms of another integral, $\int v \, du$, that may be easier to find.

To apply the formula to a given integral $\int f(x) \, dx$, we must write $f(x) \, dx$ as the product of two factors (or *parts*) by choosing a function u and a differential dv such that $f(x) \, dx = u \, dv$. However, for the formula to be useful, we must be able to integrate the part chosen for dv. To illustrate, consider

$$\int xe^x \, dx$$

This integral cannot be determined by previous integration formulas. One way to write $xe^x \, dx$ in the form $u \, dv$ is by letting

$$u = x \quad \text{and} \quad dv = e^x \, dx$$

To apply the formula for integration by parts, we must find du and v:

$$du = dx \quad \text{and} \quad v = \int e^x \, dx = e^x + C_1$$

Thus,

$$\int xe^x \, dx = \int u \, dv$$

$$= uv - \int v \, du$$

$$= x(e^x + C_1) - \int (e^x + C_1) \, dx$$

$$= xe^x + C_1 x - e^x - C_1 x + C$$

$$= xe^x - e^x + C$$

$$= e^x(x - 1) + C$$

---

[1] This section can be omitted without loss of continuity.

The first constant, C_1, does not appear in the final answer. It is easy to prove that the constant involved in finding v from dv will always drop out, so from now on we will not write it when we find v.

When using the formula for integration by parts, sometimes the *best choice* for u and dv is not obvious. In some cases, one choice may be as good as another; in other cases, only one choice may be suitable. Insight into making a good choice (if any exists) will come only with practice and, of course, trial and error.

EXAMPLE 1   Integration by Parts

APPLY IT ▶

1. The monthly sales of a computer keyboard are estimated to decline at the rate of $S'(t) = -4te^{0.1t}$ keyboards per month, where t is time in months and $S(t)$ is the number of keyboards sold each month. If 5000 keyboards are sold now ($S(0) = 5000$), find $S(t)$.

Find $\displaystyle\int \frac{\ln x}{\sqrt{x}}\, dx$ by integration by parts.

Solution: We try

$$u = \ln x \quad \text{and} \quad dv = \frac{1}{\sqrt{x}}\, dx$$

Then

$$du = \frac{1}{x}\, dx \quad \text{and} \quad v = \int x^{-1/2}\, dx = 2x^{1/2}$$

Thus,

$$\int \ln x \left(\frac{1}{\sqrt{x}}\, dx \right) = \int u\, dv = uv - \int v\, du$$

$$= (\ln x)(2\sqrt{x}) - \int (2x^{1/2})\left(\frac{1}{x}\, dx \right)$$

$$= 2\sqrt{x} \ln x - 2 \int x^{-1/2}\, dx$$

$$= 2\sqrt{x} \ln x - 2(2\sqrt{x}) + C \qquad x^{1/2} = \sqrt{x}$$

$$= 2\sqrt{x}[\ln(x) - 2] + C$$

Now Work Problem 3 ◁

EXAMPLE 2   Integration by Parts

Example 2 shows how a poor choice for u and dv can be made. If a choice does not work, there may be another that does.

Evaluate $\displaystyle\int_1^2 x \ln x\, dx$.

Solution: Since the integral does not fit a familiar form, we will try integration by parts. Let $u = x$ and $dv = \ln x\, dx$. Then $du = dx$, but $v = \int \ln x\, dx$ is not apparent by inspection. So we will make a different choice for u and dv. Let

$$u = \ln x \quad \text{and} \quad dv = x\, dx$$

Then

$$du = \frac{1}{x}\, dx \quad \text{and} \quad v = \int x\, dx = \frac{x^2}{2}$$

Therefore,

$$\int_1^2 x \ln x\, dx = (\ln x)\left(\frac{x^2}{2} \right)\Big|_1^2 - \int_1^2 \left(\frac{x^2}{2} \right) \frac{1}{x}\, dx$$

$$= (\ln x)\left(\frac{x^2}{2} \right)\Big|_1^2 - \frac{1}{2} \int_1^2 x\, dx$$

$$= \frac{x^2 \ln x}{2}\Big|_1^2 - \frac{1}{2}\left(\frac{x^2}{2} \right)\Big|_1^2$$

$$= (2\ln 2 - 0) - \left(1 - \tfrac{1}{4} \right) = 2\ln 2 - \frac{3}{4}$$

Now Work Problem 5 ◁

EXAMPLE 3 Integration by Parts where u Is the Entire Integrand

Determine $\int \ln y \, dy$.

Solution: We cannot integrate $\ln y$ by previous methods, so we will try integration by parts. Let $u = \ln y$ and $dv = dy$. Then $du = (1/y) \, dy$ and $v = y$. So we have

$$\int \ln y \, dy = (\ln y)(y) - \int y \left(\frac{1}{y} \, dy \right)$$

$$= y \ln y - \int dy = y \ln y - y + C$$

$$= y[\ln(y) - 1] + C$$

Now Work Problem 37 ◁

Before trying integration by parts, see whether the technique is really needed. Sometimes the integral can be handled by a basic technique, as Example 4 shows.

EXAMPLE 4 Basic Integration Form

Determine $\int x e^{x^2} \, dx$.

Solution: This integral can be fit to the form $\int e^u \, du$.

CAUTION!

Remember the simpler integration forms too. Integration by parts is not needed here.

$$\int x e^{x^2} \, dx = \frac{1}{2} \int e^{x^2}(2x \, dx)$$

$$= \frac{1}{2} \int e^u \, du \qquad \text{where } u = x^2$$

$$= \frac{1}{2} e^u + C = \frac{1}{2} e^{x^2} + C$$

Now Work Problem 17 ◁

Sometimes integration by parts must be used more than once, as shown in the following example.

APPLY IT ▶

2. Suppose a population of bacteria grows at a rate of

$$P'(t) = 0.1t(\ln t)^2$$

Find the general form of $P(t)$.

EXAMPLE 5 Applying Integration by Parts Twice

Determine $\int x^2 e^{2x+1} \, dx$.

Solution: Let $u = x^2$ and $dv = e^{2x+1} \, dx$. Then $du = 2x \, dx$ and $v = e^{2x+1}/2$.

$$\int x^2 e^{2x+1} \, dx = \frac{x^2 e^{2x+1}}{2} - \int \frac{e^{2x+1}}{2}(2x \, dx)$$

$$= \frac{x^2 e^{2x+1}}{2} - \int x e^{2x+1} \, dx$$

To find $\int x e^{2x+1} \, dx$, we will again use integration by parts. Here, let $u = x$ and $dv = e^{2x+1} \, dx$. Then $du = dx$ and $v = e^{2x+1}/2$, and we have

$$\int x e^{2x+1} \, dx = \frac{x e^{2x+1}}{2} - \int \frac{e^{2x+1}}{2} \, dx$$

$$= \frac{x e^{2x+1}}{2} - \frac{e^{2x+1}}{4} + C_1$$

Thus,

$$\int x^2 e^{2x+1}\, dx = \frac{x^2 e^{2x+1}}{2} - \frac{x e^{2x+1}}{2} + \frac{e^{2x+1}}{4} + C \qquad \text{where } C = -C_1$$

$$= \frac{e^{2x+1}}{2}\left(x^2 - x + \frac{1}{2}\right) + C$$

Now Work Problem 23 ◁

PROBLEMS 15.1

1. In applying integration by parts to

$$\int f(x)\, dx$$

a student found that $u = x$, $du = dx$, $dv = (x+5)^{1/2}$, and $v = \frac{2}{3}(x+5)^{3/2}$. Use this information to find $\int f(x)\, dx$.

2. Use integration by parts to find

$$\int x e^{3x+1}\, dx$$

by choosing $u = x$ and $dv = e^{3x+1}\, dx$.

In Problems 3–29, find the integrals.

3. $\displaystyle\int x e^{-x}\, dx$

4. $\displaystyle\int x e^{ax}\, dx \quad \text{for } a \neq 0$

5. $\displaystyle\int y^3 \ln y\, dy$

6. $\displaystyle\int x^2 \ln x\, dx$

7. $\displaystyle\int \ln (4x)\, dx$

8. $\displaystyle\int \frac{t}{e^t}\, dt$

9. $\displaystyle\int x\sqrt{ax+b}\, dx$

10. $\displaystyle\int \frac{12x}{\sqrt{1+4x}}\, dx$

11. $\displaystyle\int \frac{x}{(5x+2)^3}\, dx$

12. $\displaystyle\int \frac{\ln (x+1)}{2(x+1)}\, dx$

13. $\displaystyle\int \frac{\ln x}{x^2}\, dx$

14. $\displaystyle\int \frac{2x+7}{e^{3x}}\, dx$

15. $\displaystyle\int_1^2 4x e^{2x}\, dx$

16. $\displaystyle\int_1^2 2x e^{-3x}\, dx$

17. $\displaystyle\int_0^1 x e^{-x^2}\, dx$

18. $\displaystyle\int \frac{3x^3}{\sqrt{4-x^2}}\, dx$

19. $\displaystyle\int_5^8 \frac{4x}{\sqrt{9-x}}\, dx$

20. $\displaystyle\int (\ln x)^2\, dx$

21. $\displaystyle\int 3(2x-2)\ln (x-2)\, dx$

22. $\displaystyle\int \frac{x e^x}{(x+1)^2}\, dx$

23. $\displaystyle\int x^2 e^x\, dx$

24. $\displaystyle\int_1^4 \sqrt{x}\ln (x^9)\, dx$

25. $\displaystyle\int (x - e^{-x})^2\, dx$

26. $\displaystyle\int x^2 e^{3x}\, dx$

27. $\displaystyle\int x^3 e^{x^2}\, dx$

28. $\displaystyle\int x^5 e^{x^2}\, dx$

29. $\displaystyle\int (e^x + x)^2\, dx$

30. Find $\int \ln (x + \sqrt{x^2+1})\, dx$. *Hint:* Show that

$$\frac{d}{dx}[\ln (x + \sqrt{x^2+1})] = \frac{1}{\sqrt{x^2+1}}$$

31. Find the area of the region bounded by the x-axis, the curve $y = \ln x$, and the line $x = e^3$.

32. Find the area of the region bounded by the x-axis and the curve $y = x^2 e^x$ between $x = 0$ and $x = 1$.

33. Find the area of the region bounded by the x-axis and the curve $y = x^2 \ln x$ between $x = 1$ and $x = 2$.

34. Consumers' Surplus   Suppose the demand equation for a manufacturer's product is given by

$$p = 5(q + 5)e^{-(q+5)/5}$$

where p is the price per unit (in dollars) when q units are demanded. Assume that market equilibrium occurs when $q = 7$. Determine the consumers' surplus at market equilibrium.

35. Revenue   Suppose total revenue r and price per unit p are differentiable functions of output q.

(a) Use integration by parts to show that

$$\int p\, dq = r - \int q\frac{dp}{dq}\, dq$$

(b) Using part (a), show that

$$r = \int \left(p + q\frac{dp}{dq}\right) dq$$

(c) Using part (b), prove that

$$r(q_0) = \int_0^{q_0} \left(p + q\frac{dp}{dq}\right) dq$$

(*Hint:* Refer to Section 14.7.)

36. Suppose f is a differentiable function. Apply integration by parts to $\int f(x)e^x\, dx$ to prove that

$$\int f(x)e^x\, dx + \int f'(x)e^x\, dx = f(x)e^x + C$$

$$\left(\text{Hence, } \int [f(x) + f'(x)]e^x\, dx = f(x)e^x + C\right)$$

37. Suppose that f has an inverse and that $F' = f$. Use integration by parts to develop a useful formula for $\int f^{-1}(x)\, dx$ in terms of F and f^{-1}. [*Hint:* Review Example 3. It used the idea required here, for the special case of $f(x) = e^x$.] If $f^{-1}(a) = c$ and $f^{-1}(b) = d$, show that

$$\int_a^b f^{-1}(x)\, dx = bd - ac - \int_c^d f(x)\, dx$$

For $0 < a < b$ and $f^{-1} > 0$ on $[a, b]$, draw a diagram that illustrates the last equation.

To show how to integrate a proper rational function by first expressing it as a sum of its partial fractions.

15.2 Integration by Partial Fractions[2]

Recall that a *rational function* is a quotient of polynomials $N(x)/D(x)$ and that it is *proper* if N and D have no common polynomial factor and the degree of the numerator N is less than the degree of the denominator D. If N/D is not proper, then we can use long division to divide $N(x)$ by $D(x)$:

$$\begin{array}{r} Q(x) \\ D(x)\overline{\smash{\big)}N(x)} \\ \vdots \\ \overline{R(x)} \end{array} \qquad \text{thus} \qquad \frac{N(x)}{D(x)} = Q(x) + \frac{R(x)}{D(x)}$$

Here the quotient $Q(x)$ and the remainder $R(x)$ are also polynomials and either $R(x)$ is the constant 0-polynomial or the degree of $R(x)$ is less than that of $D(x)$. Thus R/D is a proper rational function. Since

$$\int \frac{N(x)}{D(x)}\,dx = \int \left(Q(x) + \frac{R(x)}{D(x)} \right)dx = \int Q(x)\,dx + \int \frac{R(x)}{D(x)}\,dx$$

and we already know how to integrate a polynomial, it follows that the task of integrating rational functions reduces to that of integrating *proper* rational functions. We emphasize that the technique we are about to explain requires that a rational function be proper so that the long division step is not optional. For example,

$$\int \frac{2x^4 - 3x^3 - 4x^2 - 17x - 6}{x^3 - 2x^2 - 3x}\,dx = \int \left(2x + 1 + \frac{4x^2 - 14x - 6}{x^3 - 2x^2 - 3x} \right)dx$$

$$= x^2 + x + \int \frac{4x^2 - 14x - 6}{x^3 - 2x^2 - 3x}\,dx$$

Distinct Linear Factors

We now consider

$$\int \frac{4x^2 - 14x - 6}{x^3 - 2x^2 - 3x}\,dx$$

It is essential that the denominator be expressed in factored form:

$$\int \frac{4x^2 - 14x - 6}{x(x + 1)(x - 3)}\,dx$$

Observe that in this example the denominator consists only of **linear factors** and that each factor occurs exactly once. It can be shown that, to each such factor $x - a$, there corresponds a *partial fraction* of the form

$$\frac{A}{x - a} \qquad A \text{ a constant}$$

such that the integrand is the sum of the partial fractions. If there are n such *distinct* linear factors, there will be n such partial fractions, each of which is easily integrated. Applying these facts, we can write

$$\frac{4x^2 - 14x - 6}{x(x + 1)(x - 3)} = \frac{A}{x} + \frac{B}{x + 1} + \frac{C}{x - 3} \tag{1}$$

To determine the constants A, B, and C, we first combine the terms on the right side:

$$\frac{4x^2 - 14x - 6}{x(x + 1)(x - 3)} = \frac{A(x + 1)(x - 3) + Bx(x - 3) + Cx(x + 1)}{x(x + 1)(x - 3)}$$

---

[2]This section can be omitted without loss of continuity.

Since the denominators of both sides are equal, we can equate their numerators:

$$4x^2 - 14x - 6 = A(x+1)(x-3) + Bx(x-3) + Cx(x+1) \qquad (2)$$

Although Equation (1) is not defined for $x = 0, x = -1$, and $x = 3$, we want to find values for A, B, and C that will make Equation (2) true for all values of x, so that the two sides of the equality provide equal functions. By successively setting x in Equation (2) equal to any three different numbers, we can obtain a system of equations that can be solved for A, B, and C. In particular, the work can be simplified by letting x be the roots of $D(x) = 0$; in our case, $x = 0, x = -1$, and $x = 3$. Using Equation (2), we have, for $x = 0$,

$$-6 = A(1)(-3) + B(0) + C(0) = -3A, \quad \text{so } A = 2$$

If $x = -1$,

$$12 = A(0) + B(-1)(-4) + C(0) = 4B, \quad \text{so } B = 3$$

If $x = 3$,

$$-12 = A(0) + B(0) + C(3)(4) = 12C, \quad \text{so } C = -1$$

Thus Equation (1) becomes

$$\frac{4x^2 - 14x - 6}{x(x+1)(x-3)} = \frac{2}{x} + \frac{3}{x+1} - \frac{1}{x-3}$$

Hence,

$$\int \frac{4x^2 - 14x - 6}{x(x+1)(x-3)} \, dx = \int \left(\frac{2}{x} + \frac{3}{x+1} - \frac{1}{x-3} \right) dx$$

$$= 2\int \frac{dx}{x} + 3\int \frac{dx}{x+1} - \int \frac{dx}{x-3}$$

$$= 2\ln|x| + 3\ln|x+1| - \ln|x-3| + C$$

For the *original* integral, we can now state that

$$\int \frac{2x^4 - 3x^3 - 4x^2 - 17x - 6}{x^3 - 2x^2 - 3x} \, dx = x^2 + x + 2\ln|x| + 3\ln|x+1| - \ln|x-3| + C$$

An alternative method of determining A, B, and C involves expanding the right side of Equation (2) and combining like terms:

$$4x^2 - 14x - 6 = A(x^2 - 2x - 3) + B(x^2 - 3x) + C(x^2 + x)$$

$$= Ax^2 - 2Ax - 3A + Bx^2 - 3Bx + Cx^2 + Cx$$

$$4x^2 - 14x - 6 = (A + B + C)x^2 + (-2A - 3B + C)x + (-3A)$$

For this last equation to express an equality of functions, the coefficients of corresponding powers of x on the left and right sides must be equal:

$$\begin{cases} 4 = A + B + C \\ -14 = -2A - 3B + C \\ -6 = -3A \end{cases}$$

Solving gives $A = 2, B = 3$, and $C = -1$ as before.

APPLY IT ▶

3. The marginal revenue for a company manufacturing q radios per week is given by $r'(q) = \dfrac{5(q+4)}{q^2 + 4q + 3}$, where $r(q)$ is the revenue in thousands of dollars. Find the equation for $r(q)$.

EXAMPLE 1 Distinct Linear Factors

Determine $\displaystyle\int \frac{2x+1}{3x^2 - 27}\, dx$ by using partial fractions.

Solution: Since the degree of the numerator is less than the degree of the denominator, no long division is necessary. The integral can be written as

$$\frac{1}{3}\int \frac{2x+1}{x^2 - 9}\, dx$$

Expressing $(2x+1)/(x^2 - 9)$ as a sum of partial fractions, we have

$$\frac{2x+1}{x^2 - 9} = \frac{2x+1}{(x+3)(x-3)} = \frac{A}{x+3} + \frac{B}{x-3}$$

Combining terms and equating numerators gives

$$2x + 1 = A(x-3) + B(x+3)$$

If $x = 3$, then

$$7 = 6B, \quad \text{so } B = \frac{7}{6}$$

If $x = -3$, then

$$-5 = -6A, \quad \text{so } A = \frac{5}{6}$$

Thus,

$$\int \frac{2x+1}{3x^2 - 27}\, dx = \frac{1}{3}\left(\int \frac{\frac{5}{6}\, dx}{x+3} + \int \frac{\frac{7}{6}\, dx}{x-3}\right)$$

$$= \frac{1}{3}\left(\frac{5}{6}\ln|x+3| + \frac{7}{6}\ln|x-3|\right) + C$$

Now Work Problem 1 ◁

Repeated Linear Factors

If the denominator of $N(x)/D(x)$ contains only linear factors, some of which are repeated, then, for each factor $(x - a)^k$, where k is the maximum number of times $x - a$ occurs as a factor, there will correspond the sum of k partial fractions:

$$\frac{A}{x - a} + \frac{B}{(x-a)^2} + \cdots + \frac{K}{(x-a)^k}$$

EXAMPLE 2 Repeated Linear Factors

Determine $\displaystyle\int \frac{6x^2 + 13x + 6}{(x+2)(x+1)^2}\, dx$ by using partial fractions.

Solution: Since the degree of the numerator, namely 2, is less than that of the denominator, namely 3, no long division is necessary. In the denominator, the linear factor $x + 2$ occurs once and the linear factor $x + 1$ occurs twice. There will thus be three partial fractions and three constants to determine, and we have

$$\frac{6x^2 + 13x + 6}{(x+2)(x+1)^2} = \frac{A}{x+2} + \frac{B}{x+1} + \frac{C}{(x+1)^2}$$

$$6x^2 + 13x + 6 = A(x+1)^2 + B(x+2)(x+1) + C(x+2)$$

Let us choose $x = -2$, $x = -1$, and, for convenience, $x = 0$. For $x = -2$, we have

$$4 = A$$

If $x = -1$, then

$$-1 = C$$

If $x = 0$, then

$$6 = A + 2B + 2C = 4 + 2B - 2 = 2 + 2B$$

$$4 = 2B$$

$$2 = B$$

Therefore,

$$\int \frac{6x^2 + 13x + 6}{(x+2)(x+1)^2}\, dx = 4\int \frac{dx}{x+2} + 2\int \frac{dx}{x+1} - \int \frac{dx}{(x+1)^2}$$

$$= 4\ln|x+2| + 2\ln|x+1| + \frac{1}{x+1} + C$$

$$= \ln[(x+2)^4(x+1)^2] + \frac{1}{x+1} + C$$

The last line above is somewhat optional (depending on what you need the integral for). It merely illustrates that in problems of this kind the logarithms that arise can often be combined.

Now Work Problem 5 ◁

Distinct Irreducible Quadratic Factors

Suppose a quadratic factor $x^2 + bx + c$ occurs in $D(x)$ and it cannot be expressed as a product of two linear factors with real coefficients. Such a factor is said to be an *irreducible quadratic factor over the real numbers*. To each distinct irreducible quadratic factor that occurs exactly once in $D(x)$, there will correspond a partial fraction of the form

$$\frac{Ax + B}{x^2 + bx + c}$$

Note that even after a rational function has been expressed in terms of partial fractions, it may still be impossible to integrate using only the basic functions we have covered in this book. For example, a very simple irreducible quadratic factor is $x^2 + 1$ and yet

$$\int \frac{1}{x^2 + 1}\, dx = \int \frac{dx}{x^2 + 1} = \tan^{-1} x + C$$

where $\tan^{-1}$ is the inverse of the trigonometric function $\tan$ when $\tan$ is restricted to $(-\pi/2, \pi/2)$. We do not discuss trigonometric functions in this book, but note that any good calculator has a $\tan^{-1}$ key.

EXAMPLE 3 **An Integral with a Distinct Irreducible Quadratic Factor**

Determine $\displaystyle\int \frac{-2x - 4}{x^3 + x^2 + x}\, dx$ by using partial fractions.

Solution: Since $x^3 + x^2 + x = x(x^2 + x + 1)$, we have the linear factor x and the quadratic factor $x^2 + x + 1$, which does not seem factorable on inspection. If it were factorable as $(x - r_1)(x - r_2)$, with r_1 and r_2 real, then r_1 and r_2 would be roots of the equation $x^2 + x + 1 = 0$. By the quadratic formula, the roots are

$$x = \frac{-1 \pm \sqrt{1 - 4}}{2}$$

Since there are no real roots, we conclude that $x^2 + x + 1$ is irreducible. Thus there will be two partial fractions and *three* constants to determine. We have

$$\frac{-2x - 4}{x(x^2 + x + 1)} = \frac{A}{x} + \frac{Bx + C}{x^2 + x + 1}$$

$$-2x - 4 = A(x^2 + x + 1) + (Bx + C)x$$

$$= Ax^2 + Ax + A + Bx^2 + Cx$$

$$0x^2 - 2x - 4 = (A + B)x^2 + (A + C)x + A$$

Equating coefficients of like powers of x, we obtain

$$\begin{cases} 0 = A + B \\ -2 = A + C \\ -4 = A \end{cases}$$

Solving gives $A = -4$, $B = 4$, and $C = 2$. Hence,

$$\int \frac{-2x - 4}{x(x^2 + x + 1)} \, dx = \int \left(\frac{-4}{x} + \frac{4x + 2}{x^2 + x + 1} \right) dx$$

$$= -4 \int \frac{dx}{x} + 2 \int \frac{2x + 1}{x^2 + x + 1} \, dx$$

Both integrals have the form $\int \dfrac{du}{u}$, so

$$\int \frac{-2x - 4}{x(x^2 + x + 1)} \, dx = -4 \ln |x| + 2 \ln |x^2 + x + 1| + C$$

$$= \ln \left[\frac{(x^2 + x + 1)^2}{x^4} \right] + C$$

Now Work Problem 7 ◁

Repeated Irreducible Quadratic Factors

Suppose $D(x)$ contains factors of the form $(x^2 + bx + c)^k$, where k is the maximum number of times the irreducible factor $x^2 + bx + c$ occurs. Then, to each such factor there will correspond a sum of k partial fractions of the form

$$\frac{A + Bx}{x^2 + bx + c} + \frac{C + Dx}{(x^2 + bx + c)^2} + \cdots + \frac{M + Nx}{(x^2 + bx + c)^k}$$

EXAMPLE 4   Repeated Irreducible Quadratic Factors

Determine $\displaystyle\int \frac{x^5}{(x^2 + 4)^2} \, dx$ by using partial fractions.

Solution: Since the numerator has degree 5 and the denominator has degree 4, we first use long division, which gives

$$\frac{x^5}{x^4 + 8x^2 + 16} = x - \frac{8x^3 + 16x}{(x^2 + 4)^2}$$

The quadratic factor $x^2 + 4$ in the denominator of $(8x^3 + 16x)/(x^2 + 4)^2$ is irreducible and occurs as a factor twice. Thus, to $(x^2 + 4)^2$ there correspond two partial fractions and *four* coefficients to be determined. Accordingly, we set

$$\frac{8x^3 + 16x}{(x^2 + 4)^2} = \frac{Ax + B}{x^2 + 4} + \frac{Cx + D}{(x^2 + 4)^2}$$

and obtain

$$8x^3 + 16x = (Ax + B)(x^2 + 4) + Cx + D$$

$$8x^3 + 0x^2 + 16x + 0 = Ax^3 + Bx^2 + (4A + C)x + 4B + D$$

Equating like powers of x yields

$$\begin{cases} 8 = A \\ 0 = B \\ 16 = 4A + C \\ 0 = 4B + D \end{cases}$$

Solving gives $A = 8, B = 0, C = -16$, and $D = 0$. Therefore,

$$\int \frac{x^5}{(x^2 + 4)^2} \, dx = \int \left(x - \left(\frac{8x}{x^2 + 4} - \frac{16x}{(x^2 + 4)^2} \right) \right) dx$$

$$= \int x \, dx - 4 \int \frac{2x}{x^2 + 4} \, dx + 8 \int \frac{2x}{(x^2 + 4)^2} \, dx$$

The second integral on the preceding line has the form $\int \dfrac{du}{u}$, and the third integral has the form $\int \dfrac{du}{u^2}$. So

$$\int \frac{x^5}{(x^2 + 4)^2} = \frac{x^2}{2} - 4 \ln (x^2 + 4) - \frac{8}{x^2 + 4} + C$$

Now Work Problem 27 ◁

From our examples, you may have deduced that the number of constants needed to express $N(x)/D(x)$ by partial fractions is equal to the degree of $D(x)$, if it is assumed that $N(x)/D(x)$ defines a proper rational function. This is indeed the case. Note also that the representation of a proper rational function by partial fractions is unique; that is, there is only one choice of constants that can be made. Furthermore, regardless of the complexity of the polynomial $D(x)$, it can always (theoretically) be expressed as a product of linear and irreducible quadratic factors with real coefficients.

CAUTION!

Be on the lookout for simple solutions too.

APPLY IT ▶

4. The rate of change of the voting population of a city with respect to time t (in years) is estimated to be $V'(t) = \dfrac{300t^3}{t^2 + 6}$. Find the general form of $V(t)$.

EXAMPLE 5   An Integral Not Requiring Partial Fractions

Find $\displaystyle\int \frac{2x + 3}{x^2 + 3x + 1} \, dx$.

Solution: This integral has the form $\displaystyle\int \frac{1}{u} \, du$. Thus,

$$\int \frac{2x + 3}{x^2 + 3x + 1} \, dx = \ln |x^2 + 3x + 1| + C$$

Now Work Problem 17 ◁

PROBLEMS 15.2

In Problems 1–8, express the given rational function in terms of partial fractions. Watch out for any preliminary divisions.

1. $f(x) = \dfrac{10x}{x^2 + 7x + 6}$

2. $f(x) = \dfrac{x + 5}{x^2 - 1}$

3. $f(x) = \dfrac{2x^2}{x^2 + 5x + 6}$

4. $f(x) = \dfrac{2x^2 - 15}{x^2 + 5x}$

5. $f(x) = \dfrac{3x - 1}{x^2 - 2x + 1}$

6. $f(x) = \dfrac{2x + 3}{x^2(x - 1)}$

7. $f(x) = \dfrac{x^2 + 3}{x^3 + x}$

8. $f(x) = \dfrac{3x^2 + 5}{(x^2 + 4)^2}$

In Problems 9–30, determine the integrals.

9. $\displaystyle\int \frac{5x - 2}{x^2 - x} \, dx$

10. $\displaystyle\int \frac{15x + 5}{x^2 + 5x} \, dx$

11. $\displaystyle\int \frac{x + 10}{x^2 - x - 2} \, dx$

12. $\displaystyle\int \frac{2x - 1}{x^2 - x - 12} \, dx$

13. $\displaystyle\int \frac{3x^3 - 3x + 4}{4x^2 - 4} \, dx$

14. $\displaystyle\int \frac{7(4 - x^2)}{(x - 4)(x - 2)(x + 3)} \, dx$

15. $\displaystyle\int \frac{19x^2 - 5x - 36}{2x^3 - 2x^2 - 12x} \, dx$

16. $\displaystyle\int \frac{4 - x}{x^4 - x^2} \, dx$

17. $\displaystyle\int \frac{2(3x^5 + 4x^3 - x)}{x^6 + 2x^4 - x^2 - 2} \, dx$

18. $\displaystyle\int \frac{x^4 - 2x^3 + 6x^2 - 11x + 2}{x^3 - 3x^2 + 2x} \, dx$

19. $\displaystyle\int \frac{2x^2 - 5x - 2}{(x - 2)^2(x - 1)} \, dx$

20. $\displaystyle\int \frac{5x^3 + x^2 + x - 3}{x^4 - x^3} \, dx$

21. $\displaystyle\int \frac{2(x^2 + 8)}{x^3 + 4x} \, dx$

22. $\displaystyle\int \frac{4x^3 - 3x^2 + 2x - 3}{(x^2 + 3)(x + 1)(x - 2)} \, dx$

23. $\displaystyle\int \frac{-x^3 + 8x^2 - 9x + 2}{(x^2 + 1)(x - 3)^2} \, dx$

24. $\displaystyle\int \frac{5x^4 + 9x^2 + 3}{x(x^2 + 1)^2} \, dx$

25. $\displaystyle\int \frac{7x^3 + 24x}{(x^2 + 3)(x^2 + 4)} \, dx$

26. $\displaystyle\int \frac{12x^3 + 20x^2 + 28x + 4}{3(x^2 + 2x + 3)(x^2 + 1)} \, dx$

27. $\displaystyle\int \frac{3x^3 + 8x}{(x^2 + 2)^2} \, dx$

28. $\displaystyle\int \frac{3x^2 - 8x + 4}{x^3 - 4x^2 + 4x - 6} \, dx$

29. $\displaystyle\int_0^1 \frac{2-2x}{x^2+7x+12}\,dx$ **30.** $\displaystyle\int_0^1 \frac{x^2+5x+5}{x^2+3x+2}\,dx$

31. Find the area of the region bounded by the graph of

$$y = \frac{6(x^2+1)}{(x+2)^2}$$

and the x-axis from $x=0$ to $x=1$.

32. Consumers' Surplus Suppose the demand equation for a manufacturer's product is given by

$$p = \frac{200(q+3)}{q^2+7q+6}$$

where p is the price per unit (in dollars) when q units are demanded. Assume that market equilibrium occurs at the point $(q,p) = (10,325/22)$. Determine consumers' surplus at market equilibrium.

Objective

To illustrate the use of the table of integrals in Appendix B.

15.3 Integration by Tables

Certain forms of integrals that occur frequently can be found in standard tables of integration formulas.[3] A short table appears in Appendix B, and its use will be illustrated in this section.

A given integral may have to be replaced by an equivalent form before it will fit a formula in the table. The equivalent form must match the formula exactly. Consequently, the steps performed to get the equivalent form should be written carefully rather than performed mentally. Before proceeding with the exercises that use tables, we recommend studying the examples of this section carefully.

In the following examples, the formula numbers refer to the Table of Selected Integrals given in Appendix B.

EXAMPLE 1   Integration by Tables

Find $\displaystyle\int \frac{x\,dx}{(2+3x)^2}$.

Solution: Scanning the table, we identify the integrand with Formula (7):

$$\int \frac{u\,du}{(a+bu)^2} = \frac{1}{b^2}\left(\ln|a+bu| + \frac{a}{a+bu}\right) + C$$

Now we see if we can exactly match the given integrand with that in the formula. If we replace x by u, 2 by a, and 3 by b, then $du = dx$, and by substitution we have

$$\int \frac{x\,dx}{(2+3x)^2} = \int \frac{u\,du}{(a+bu)^2} = \frac{1}{b^2}\left(\ln|a+bu| + \frac{a}{a+bu}\right) + C$$

Returning to the variable x and replacing a by 2 and b by 3, we obtain

$$\int \frac{x\,dx}{(2+3x)^2} = \frac{1}{9}\left(\ln|2+3x| + \frac{2}{2+3x}\right) + C$$

Note that the answer must be given in terms of x, the *original* variable of integration.

Now Work Problem 5 ◁

EXAMPLE 2   Integration by Tables

Find $\displaystyle\int x^2\sqrt{x^2-1}\,dx$.

Solution: This integral is identified with Formula (24):

$$\int u^2\sqrt{u^2 \pm a^2}\,du = \frac{u}{8}(2u^2 \pm a^2)\sqrt{u^2 \pm a^2} - \frac{a^4}{8}\ln|u+\sqrt{u^2 \pm a^2}| + C$$

In the preceding formula, if the bottommost sign in the dual symbol "$\pm$" on the left side is used, then the bottommost sign in the dual symbols on the right side must also be

---

[3] See, for example, W. H. Beyer (ed.), *CRC Standard Mathematical Tables and Formulae*, 30th ed. (Boca Raton, FL: CRC Press, 1996).

used. In the original integral, we let $u = x$ and $a = 1$. Then $du = dx$, and by substitution the integral becomes

$$\int x^2 \sqrt{x^2 - 1} \, dx = \int u^2 \sqrt{u^2 - a^2} \, du$$

$$= \frac{u}{8}(2u^2 - a^2)\sqrt{u^2 - a^2} - \frac{a^4}{8} \ln |u + \sqrt{u^2 - a^2}| + C$$

Since $u = x$ and $a = 1$,

$$\int x^2 \sqrt{x^2 - 1} \, dx = \frac{x}{8}(2x^2 - 1)\sqrt{x^2 - 1} - \frac{1}{8} \ln |x + \sqrt{x^2 - 1}| + C$$

Now Work Problem 17 ◁

This example, as well as Examples 4, 5, and 7, shows how to adjust an integral so that it conforms to one in the table.

EXAMPLE 3   **Integration by Tables**

Find $\displaystyle\int \frac{dx}{x\sqrt{16x^2 + 3}}$.

Solution: The integrand can be identified with Formula (28):

$$\int \frac{du}{u\sqrt{u^2 + a^2}} = \frac{1}{a} \ln \left| \frac{\sqrt{u^2 + a^2} - a}{u} \right| + C$$

If we let $u = 4x$ and $a = \sqrt{3}$, then $du = 4 \, dx$. Watch closely how, by inserting 4's in the numerator and denominator, we transform the given integral into an equivalent form that matches Formula (28):

$$\int \frac{dx}{x\sqrt{16x^2 + 3}} = \int \frac{(4 \, dx)}{(4x)\sqrt{(4x)^2 + (\sqrt{3})^2}} = \int \frac{du}{u\sqrt{u^2 + a^2}}$$

$$= \frac{1}{a} \ln \left| \frac{\sqrt{u^2 + a^2} - a}{u} \right| + C$$

$$= \frac{1}{\sqrt{3}} \ln \left| \frac{\sqrt{16x^2 + 3} - \sqrt{3}}{4x} \right| + C$$

Now Work Problem 7 ◁

EXAMPLE 4   **Integration by Tables**

Find $\displaystyle\int \frac{dx}{x^2(2 - 3x^2)^{1/2}}$.

Solution: The integrand is identified with Formula (21):

$$\int \frac{du}{u^2\sqrt{a^2 - u^2}} = -\frac{\sqrt{a^2 - u^2}}{a^2 u} + C$$

Letting $u = \sqrt{3}x$ and $a^2 = 2$, we have $du = \sqrt{3} \, dx$. Hence, by inserting two factors of $\sqrt{3}$ in both the numerator and denominator of the original integral, we have

$$\int \frac{dx}{x^2(2 - 3x^2)^{1/2}} = \sqrt{3} \int \frac{(\sqrt{3} \, dx)}{(\sqrt{3}x)^2[2 - (\sqrt{3}x)^2]^{1/2}} = \sqrt{3} \int \frac{du}{u^2(a^2 - u^2)^{1/2}}$$

$$= \sqrt{3} \left[-\frac{\sqrt{a^2 - u^2}}{a^2 u} \right] + C = \sqrt{3} \left[-\frac{\sqrt{2 - 3x^2}}{2(\sqrt{3}x)} \right] + C$$

$$= -\frac{\sqrt{2 - 3x^2}}{2x} + C$$

Now Work Problem 35 ◁

EXAMPLE 5   Integration by Tables

Find $\int 7x^2 \ln(4x)\,dx$.

Solution: This is similar to Formula (42) with $n = 2$:

$$\int u^n \ln u\,du = \frac{u^{n+1}\ln u}{n+1} - \frac{u^{n+1}}{(n+1)^2} + C$$

If we let $u = 4x$, then $du = 4\,dx$. Hence,

$$\int 7x^2 \ln(4x)\,dx = \frac{7}{4^3} \int (4x)^2 \ln(4x)(4\,dx)$$

$$= \frac{7}{64} \int u^2 \ln u\,du = \frac{7}{64}\left(\frac{u^3 \ln u}{3} - \frac{u^3}{9}\right) + C$$

$$= \frac{7}{64}\left(\frac{(4x)^3 \ln(4x)}{3} - \frac{(4x)^3}{9}\right) + C$$

$$= 7x^3 \left(\frac{\ln(4x)}{3} - \frac{1}{9}\right) + C$$

$$= \frac{7x^3}{9}(3\ln(4x) - 1) + C$$

Now Work Problem 45 ◁

EXAMPLE 6   Integral Table Not Needed

Find $\int \frac{e^{2x}\,dx}{7 + e^{2x}}$.

Solution: At first glance, we do not identify the integrand with any form in the table. Perhaps rewriting the integral will help. Let $u = 7 + e^{2x}$, then $du = 2e^{2x}\,dx$. So

$$\int \frac{e^{2x}\,dx}{7 + e^{2x}} = \frac{1}{2}\int \frac{(2e^{2x}\,dx)}{7 + e^{2x}} = \frac{1}{2}\int \frac{du}{u} = \frac{1}{2}\ln|u| + C$$

$$= \frac{1}{2}\ln|7 + e^{2x}| + C = \frac{1}{2}\ln(7 + e^{2x}) + C$$

Thus, we had only to use our knowledge of basic integration forms. [Actually, this form appears as Formula (2) in the table, with $a = 0$ and $b = 1$.]

Now Work Problem 39 ◁

EXAMPLE 7   Finding a Definite Integral by Using Tables

Evaluate $\int_1^4 \frac{dx}{(4x^2 + 2)^{3/2}}$.

Solution: We will use Formula (32) to get the indefinite integral first:

$$\int \frac{du}{(u^2 \pm a^2)^{3/2}} = \frac{\pm u}{a^2 \sqrt{u^2 \pm a^2}} + C$$

Letting $u = 2x$ and $a^2 = 2$, we have $du = 2\,dx$. Thus,

$$\int \frac{dx}{(4x^2 + 2)^{3/2}} = \frac{1}{2}\int \frac{(2\,dx)}{((2x)^2 + 2)^{3/2}} = \frac{1}{2}\int \frac{du}{(u^2 + 2)^{3/2}}$$

$$= \frac{1}{2}\left(\frac{u}{2\sqrt{u^2 + 2}}\right) + C$$

Here we determine the limits of integration with respect to u.

Instead of substituting back to x and evaluating from $x = 1$ to $x = 4$, we can determine the corresponding limits of integration with respect to u and then evaluate the last expression between those limits. Since $u = 2x$, when $x = 1$, we have $u = 2$; when

CAUTION!

When changing the variable of integration x to the variable of integration u, be sure to change the limits of integration so that they agree with u.

$x = 4$, we have $u = 8$. Hence,

$$\int_1^4 \frac{dx}{(4x^2 + 2)^{3/2}} = \frac{1}{2} \int_2^8 \frac{du}{(u^2 + 2)^{3/2}}$$

$$= \frac{1}{2} \left(\frac{u}{2\sqrt{u^2 + 2}} \right) \Big|_2^8 = \frac{2}{\sqrt{66}} - \frac{1}{2\sqrt{6}}$$

Now Work Problem 15 ◁

Integration Applied to Annuities

Tables of integrals are useful when we deal with integrals associated with annuities. Suppose that you must pay out \$100 at the end of each year for the next two years. Recall from Chapter 5 that a series of payments over a period of time, such as this, is called an *annuity*. If you were to pay off the debt now instead, you would pay the present value of the \$100 that is due at the end of the first year, plus the present value of the \$100 that is due at the end of the second year. The sum of these present values is the present value of the annuity. (The present value of an annuity is discussed in Section 5.4.) We will now consider the present value of payments made continuously over the time interval from $t = 0$ to $t = T$, with t in years, when interest is compounded continuously at an annual rate of r.

Suppose a payment is made at time t such that on an annual basis this payment is $f(t)$. If we divide the interval $[0, T]$ into subintervals $[t_{i-1}, t_i]$ of length dt (where dt is small), then the total amount of all payments over such a subinterval is approximately $f(t_i)\, dt$. [For example, if $f(t) = 2000$ and dt were one day, the total amount of the payments would be $2000(\frac{1}{365})$.] The present value of these payments is approximately $e^{-rt_i} f(t_i)\, dt$. (See Section 5.3.) Over the interval $[0, T]$, the total of all such present values is

$$\sum e^{-rt_i} f(t_i)\, dt$$

This sum approximates the present value A of the annuity. The smaller dt is, the better the approximation. That is, as $dt \to 0$, the limit of the sum is the present value. However, this limit is also a definite integral. That is,

$$A = \int_0^T f(t) e^{-rt}\, dt \qquad (1)$$

where A is the **present value of a continuous annuity** at an annual rate r (compounded continuously) for T years if a payment at time t is at the rate of $f(t)$ per year.

We say that Equation (1) gives the **present value of a continuous income stream.** Equation (1) can also be used to find the present value of future profits of a business. In this situation, $f(t)$ is the annual rate of profit at time t.

We can also consider the *future* value of an annuity rather than its present value. If a payment is made at time t, then it has a certain value at the *end* of the period of the annuity—that is, $T - t$ years later. This value is

$$\begin{pmatrix} \text{amount of} \\ \text{payment} \end{pmatrix} + \begin{pmatrix} \text{interest on this} \\ \text{payment for } T - t \text{ years} \end{pmatrix}$$

If S is the total of such values for all payments, then S is called the *accumulated amount of a continuous annuity* and is given by the formula

$$S = \int_0^T f(t) e^{r(T-t)}\, dt$$

where S is the **accumulated amount of a continuous annuity** at the end of T years at an annual rate r (compounded continuously) when a payment at time t is at the rate of $f(t)$ per year.

EXAMPLE 8   Present Value of a Continuous Annuity

Find the present value (to the nearest dollar) of a continuous annuity at an annual rate of 8% for 10 years if the payment at time t is at the rate of t^2 dollars per year.

Solution: The present value is given by

$$A = \int_0^T f(t)e^{-rt}\, dt = \int_0^{10} t^2 e^{-0.08t}\, dt$$

We will use Formula (39),

$$\int u^n e^{au}\, du = \frac{u^n e^{au}}{a} - \frac{n}{a}\int u^{n-1} e^{au}\, du$$

This is called a *reduction formula*, since it reduces one integral to an expression that involves another integral that is easier to determine. If $u = t, n = 2$, and $a = -0.08$, then $du = dt$, and we have

$$A = \frac{t^2 e^{-0.08t}}{-0.08}\Big|_0^{10} - \frac{2}{-0.08}\int_0^{10} te^{-0.08t}\, dt$$

In the new integral, the exponent of t has been reduced to 1. We can match this integral with Formula (38),

$$\int u e^{au}\, du = \frac{e^{au}}{a^2}(au - 1) + C$$

by letting $u = t$ and $a = -0.08$. Then $du = dt$, and

$$A = \int_0^{10} t^2 e^{-0.08t}\, dt = \frac{t^2 e^{-0.08t}}{-0.08}\Big|_0^{10} - \frac{2}{-0.08}\left(\frac{e^{-0.08t}}{(-0.08)^2}(-0.08t - 1)\right)\Big|_0^{10}$$

$$= \frac{100 e^{-0.8}}{-0.08} - \frac{2}{-0.08}\left(\frac{e^{-0.8}}{(-0.08)^2}(-0.8 - 1) - \frac{1}{(-0.08)^2}(-1)\right)$$

$$\approx 185$$

The present value is $185.

Now Work Problem 59 ◁

PROBLEMS 15.3

In Problems 1 and 2, use Formula (19) in Appendix B to determine the integrals.

1. $\int \dfrac{dx}{(6 - x^2)^{3/2}}$

2. $\int \dfrac{dx}{(25 - 4x^2)^{3/2}}$

In Problems 3 and 4, use Formula (30) in Appendix B to determine the integrals.

3. $\int \dfrac{dx}{x^2\sqrt{16x^2 + 3}}$

4. $\int \dfrac{3\, dx}{x^3\sqrt{x^4 - 9}}$

In Problems 5–38, find the integrals by using the table in Appendix B.

5. $\int \dfrac{dx}{x(6 + 7x)}$

6. $\int \dfrac{5x^2\, dx}{(2 + 3x)^2}$

7. $\int \dfrac{dx}{x\sqrt{x^2 + 9}}$

8. $\int \dfrac{dx}{(x^2 + 7)^{3/2}}$

9. $\int \dfrac{x\, dx}{(2 + 3x)(4 + 5x)}$

10. $\int 2^{5x}\, dx$

11. $\int \dfrac{dx}{1 + 2e^{3x}}$

12. $\int x^2\sqrt{1 + x}\, dx$

13. $\int \dfrac{7\, dx}{x(5 + 2x)^2}$

14. $\int \dfrac{dx}{x\sqrt{5 - 11x^2}}$

15. $\int_0^1 \dfrac{x\, dx}{2 + x}$

16. $\int \dfrac{-3x^2\, dx}{2 - 5x}$

17. $\int \sqrt{x^2 - 3}\, dx$

18. $\int \dfrac{dx}{(1 + 5x)(2x + 3)}$

19. $\int_0^{1/12} xe^{12x}\, dx$

20. $\int \sqrt{\dfrac{2 + 3x}{5 + 3x}}\, dx$

21. $\int x^3 e^x\, dx$

22. $\int_1^2 \dfrac{4\, dx}{x^2(1 + x)}$

23. $\int \dfrac{\sqrt{5x^2 + 1}}{2x^2}\, dx$

24. $\int \dfrac{dx}{x\sqrt{2 - x}}$

25. $\int \dfrac{x\, dx}{(1 + 3x)^2}$

26. $\int \dfrac{2\, dx}{\sqrt{(1 + 2x)(3 + 2x)}}$

27. $\int \dfrac{dx}{7 - 5x^2}$

28. $\int 7x^2\sqrt{3x^2 - 6}\, dx$

29. $\int 36x^5 \ln(3x)\, dx$

30. $\int \dfrac{5\, dx}{x^2(3 + 2x)^2}$

31. $\displaystyle\int 5x\sqrt{1+2x}\,dx$

32. $\displaystyle\int 9x^2 \ln x\,dx$

33. $\displaystyle\int \frac{dx}{\sqrt{4x^2-13}}$

34. $\displaystyle\int \frac{dx}{x\ln(2x)}$

35. $\displaystyle\int \frac{2\,dx}{x^2\sqrt{16-9x^2}}$

36. $\displaystyle\int \frac{\sqrt{3-x^2}}{x}\,dx$

37. $\displaystyle\int \frac{dx}{\sqrt{x}(\pi+7e^{4\sqrt{x}})}$

38. $\displaystyle\int_0^1 \frac{3x^2\,dx}{1+2x^3}$

In Problems 39–56, find the integrals by any method.

39. $\displaystyle\int \frac{x\,dx}{x^2+1}$

40. $\displaystyle\int 3x\sqrt{x}e^{x^{5/2}}\,dx$

41. $\displaystyle\int \frac{(\ln x)^3}{x}\,dx$

42. $\displaystyle\int \frac{5x^3-\sqrt{x}}{2x}\,dx$

43. $\displaystyle\int \frac{dx}{x^2-5x+6}$

44. $\displaystyle\int \frac{e^{2x}}{\sqrt{e^{2x}+3}}\,dx$

45. $\displaystyle\int x^3 \ln x\,dx$

46. $\displaystyle\int (9x-6)e^{-30x+20}\,dx$

47. $\displaystyle\int 4x^3 e^{3x^2}\,dx$

48. $\displaystyle\int_1^2 35x^2\sqrt{3+2x}\,dx$

49. $\displaystyle\int \ln^2 x\,dx$

50. $\displaystyle\int_1^e 3x\ln x^2\,dx$

51. $\displaystyle\int_{-2}^1 \frac{x\,dx}{\sqrt{3+x}}$

52. $\displaystyle\int_2^3 x\sqrt{2+3x}\,dx$

53. $\displaystyle\int_0^1 \frac{2x\,dx}{\sqrt{8-x^2}}$

54. $\displaystyle\int_0^{\ln 2} x^2 e^{3x}\,dx$

55. $\displaystyle\int_1^2 x\ln(2x)\,dx$

56. $\displaystyle\int_3^5 dA$

57. Biology   In a discussion about gene frequency,[4] the integral

$$\int_{q_0}^{q_n} \frac{dq}{q(1-q)}$$

occurs, where the q's represent gene frequencies. Evaluate this integral.

58. Biology   Under certain conditions, the number n of generations required to change the frequency of a gene from 0.3 to 0.1 is given by[5]

$$n = -\frac{1}{0.4}\int_{0.3}^{0.1} \frac{dq}{q^2(1-q)}$$

Find n (to the nearest integer).

59. Continuous Annuity   Find the present value, to the nearest dollar, of a continuous annuity at an annual rate of r for T years if the payment at time t is at the annual rate of $f(t)$ dollars, given that

  (a) $r = 0.04$ $T = 9$ $f(t) = 1000$
  (b) $r = 0.06$ $T = 10$ $f(t) = 500t$

60. If $f(t) = k$, where k is a positive constant, show that the value of the integral in Equation (1) of this section is

$$k\left(\frac{1-e^{-rT}}{r}\right)$$

61. Continuous Annuity   Find the accumulated amount, to the nearest dollar, of a continuous annuity at an annual rate of r for T years if the payment at time t is at an annual rate of $f(t)$ dollars, given that

  (a) $r = 0.02$ $T = 10$ $f(t) = 100$
  (b) $r = 0.01$ $T = 10$ $f(t) = 200$

62. Value of Business   Over the next five years, the profits of a business at time t are estimated to be $50{,}000t$ dollars per year. The business is to be sold at a price equal to the present value of these future profits. To the nearest 10 dollars, at what price should the business be sold if interest is compounded continuously at the annual rate of 7%?

Objective

To develop the concept of the average value of a function.

15.4 Average Value of a Function

If we are given the three numbers 1, 2, and 9, then their average value, or *mean*, is their sum divided by 3. Denoting this average by $\bar{y}$, we have

$$\bar{y} = \frac{1+2+9}{3} = 4$$

Similarly, suppose we are given a function f defined on the interval $[a, b]$, and the points $x_1, x_2, \ldots, x_n$ are in the interval. Then the average value of the n corresponding function values $f(x_1), f(x_2), \ldots, f(x_n)$ is

$$\bar{y} = \frac{f(x_1)+f(x_2)+\cdots+f(x_n)}{n} = \frac{\displaystyle\sum_{i=1}^{n} f(x_i)}{n} \tag{1}$$

We can go a step further. Let us divide the interval $[a, b]$ into n subintervals of equal length. We will choose x_i to be the right-hand endpoint of the ith subinterval. Because

---

[4]W. B. Mather, *Principles of Quantitative Genetics* (Minneapolis: Burgess Publishing Company, 1964).

[5]E. O. Wilson and W. H. Bossert, *A Primer of Population Biology* (Stamford, CT: Sinauer Associates, Inc., 1971).

$[a, b]$ has length $b - a$, each subinterval has length $\dfrac{b - a}{n}$, which we will call dx. Thus, Equation (1) can be written

$$\bar{y} = \frac{\displaystyle\sum_{i=1}^{n} f(x_i)\left(\dfrac{dx}{dx}\right)}{n} = \frac{\dfrac{1}{dx}\displaystyle\sum_{i=1}^{n} f(x_i)\,dx}{n} = \frac{1}{n\,dx}\sum_{i=1}^{n} f(x_i)\,dx \qquad (2)$$

Since $dx = \dfrac{b - a}{n}$, it follows that $n\,dx = b - a$. So the expression $\dfrac{1}{n\,dx}$ in Equation (2) can be replaced by $\dfrac{1}{b - a}$. Moreover, as $n \to \infty$, the number of function values used in computing $\bar{y}$ increases, and we get the so-called *average value of the function f*, denoted by $\bar{f}$:

$$\bar{f} = \lim_{n \to \infty}\left[\frac{1}{b - a}\sum_{i=1}^{n} f(x_i)\,dx\right] = \frac{1}{b - a}\lim_{n \to \infty}\sum_{i=1}^{n} f(x_i)\,dx$$

But the limit on the right is just the definite integral $\int_a^b f(x)\,dx$. This motivates the following definition:

> **Definition**
>
> The **_average value of a function_** $f(x)$ over the interval $[a, b]$ is denoted $\bar{f}$ and is given by
>
> $$\bar{f} = \frac{1}{b - a}\int_a^b f(x)\,dx$$

EXAMPLE 1   Average Value of a Function

Find the average value of the function $f(x) = x^2$ over the interval $[1, 2]$.

Solution:

$$\bar{f} = \frac{1}{b - a}\int_a^b f(x)\,dx$$

$$= \frac{1}{2 - 1}\int_1^2 x^2\,dx = \left.\frac{x^3}{3}\right|_1^2 = \frac{7}{3}$$

Now Work Problem 1 ◁

In Example 1, we found that the average value of $y = f(x) = x^2$ over the interval $[1, 2]$ is $\frac{7}{3}$. We can interpret this value geometrically. Since

$$\frac{1}{2 - 1}\int_1^2 x^2\,dx = \frac{7}{3}$$

by solving for the integral we have

$$\int_1^2 x^2\,dx = \frac{7}{3}(2 - 1)$$

However, this integral gives the area of the region bounded by $f(x) = x^2$ and the x-axis from $x = 1$ to $x = 2$. (See Figure 15.1.) From the preceding equation, this area is $\left(\frac{7}{3}\right)(2 - 1)$, which is the area of a rectangle whose height is the average value $\bar{f} = \frac{7}{3}$ and whose width is $b - a = 2 - 1 = 1$.

EXAMPLE 2   Average Flow of Blood

Suppose the flow of blood at time t in a system is given by

$$F(t) = \frac{F_1}{(1 + \alpha t)^2} \qquad 0 \leq t \leq T$$

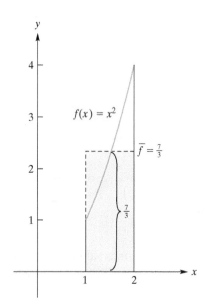

FIGURE 15.1   Geometric interpretation of the average value of a function.

where F_1 and α (a Greek letter read "alpha") are constants.[6] Find the average flow $\overline{F}$ on the interval $[0, T]$.

Solution:

$$\overline{F} = \frac{1}{T - 0} \int_0^T F(t)\, dt$$

$$= \frac{1}{T} \int_0^T \frac{F_1}{(1 + \alpha t)^2}\, dt = \frac{F_1}{\alpha T} \int_0^T (1 + \alpha t)^{-2} (\alpha\, dt)$$

$$= \frac{F_1}{\alpha T} \left(\frac{(1 + \alpha t)^{-1}}{-1} \right) \Bigg|_0^T = \frac{F_1}{\alpha T} \left(-\frac{1}{1 + \alpha T} + 1 \right)$$

$$= \frac{F_1}{\alpha T} \left(\frac{-1 + 1 + \alpha T}{1 + \alpha T} \right) = \frac{F_1}{\alpha T} \left(\frac{\alpha T}{1 + \alpha T} \right) = \frac{F_1}{1 + \alpha T}$$

Now Work Problem 11 ◁

PROBLEMS 15.4

In Problems 1–8, find the average value of the function over the given interval.

1. $f(x) = x^2$; $[-1, 3]$
2. $f(x) = 2x + 1$; $[0, 1]$
3. $f(x) = 2 - 3x^2$; $[-1, 2]$
4. $f(x) = x^2 + x + 1$; $[1, 3]$
5. $f(t) = 2t^5$; $[-3, 3]$
6. $f(t) = t\sqrt{t^2 + 9}$; $[0, 4]$
7. $f(x) = \sqrt{x}$; $[0, 1]$
8. $f(x) = 5/x^2$; $[1, 3]$

9. **Profit**   The profit (in dollars) of a business is given by

$$P = P(q) = 369q - 2.1q^2 - 400$$

where q is the number of units of the product sold. Find the average profit on the interval from $q = 0$ to $q = 100$.

10. **Cost**   Suppose the cost (in dollars) of producing q units of a product is given by

$$c = 4000 + 10q + 0.1q^2$$

Find the average cost on the interval from $q = 100$ to $q = 500$.

11. **Investment**   An investment of \$3000 earns interest at an annual rate of 5% compounded continuously. After t years, its

value S (in dollars) is given by $S = 3000e^{0.05t}$. Find the average value of a two-year investment.

12. **Medicine**   Suppose that colored dye is injected into the bloodstream at a constant rate R. At time t, let

$$C(t) = \frac{R}{F(t)}$$

be the concentration of dye at a location distant (distal) from the point of injection, where $F(t)$ is as given in Example 2. Show that the average concentration on $[0, T]$ is

$$\overline{C} = \frac{R\left(1 + \alpha T + \frac{1}{3}\alpha^2 T^2\right)}{F_1}$$

13. **Revenue**   Suppose a manufacturer receives revenue r from the sale of q units of a product. Show that the average value of the marginal-revenue function over the interval $[0, q_0]$ is the price per unit when q_0 units are sold.

14. Find the average value of $f(x) = \dfrac{1}{x^2 - 4x + 5}$ over the interval $[0, 1]$ using an approximate integration technique. Round your answer to two decimal places.

Objective

To solve a differential equation by using the method of separation of variables. To discuss particular solutions and general solutions. To develop interest compounded continuously in terms of a differential equation. To discuss exponential growth and decay.

15.5 Differential Equations

Occasionally, you may have to solve an equation that involves the derivative of an unknown function. Such an equation is called a **differential equation.** An example is

$$y' = xy^2 \tag{1}$$

More precisely, Equation (1) is called a **first-order differential equation,** since it involves a derivative of the first order and none of higher order. A solution of Equation (1) is any function $y = f(x)$ that is defined on an interval and satisfies the equation for all x in the interval.

---

[6]W. Simon, *Mathematical Techniques for Physiology and Medicine* (New York: Academic Press, Inc., 1972).

To solve $y' = xy^2$, equivalently,

$$\frac{dy}{dx} = xy^2 \tag{2}$$

we think of dy/dx as a quotient of differentials and algebraically "separate variables" by rewriting the equation so that each side contains only one variable and a differential is not in a denominator:

$$\frac{dy}{y^2} = x\,dx$$

Integrating both sides and combining the constants of integration, we obtain

$$\int \frac{1}{y^2}\,dy = \int x\,dx$$

$$-\frac{1}{y} = \frac{x^2}{2} + C_1$$

$$-\frac{1}{y} = \frac{x^2 + 2C_1}{2}$$

Since $2C_1$ is an arbitrary constant, we can replace it by C.

$$-\frac{1}{y} = \frac{x^2 + C}{2} \tag{3}$$

Solving Equation (3) for y, we have

$$y = -\frac{2}{x^2 + C} \tag{4}$$

We can verify that y is a solution to the differential equation (2):
For if y is given by Equation (4), then

$$\frac{dy}{dx} = \frac{4x}{(x^2 + C)^2}$$

while also

$$xy^2 = x\left[-\frac{2}{x^2 + C}\right]^2 = \frac{4x}{(x^2 + C)^2}$$

showing that our y satisfies (2). Note in Equation (4) that, for *each* value of C, a different solution is obtained. We call Equation (4) the **general solution** of the differential equation. The method that we used to find it is called **separation of variables.**

In the foregoing example, suppose we are given the condition that $y = -\frac{2}{3}$ when $x = 1$; that is, $y(1) = -\frac{2}{3}$. Then the *particular* function that satisfies both Equation (2) and this condition can be found by substituting the values $x = 1$ and $y = -\frac{2}{3}$ into Equation (4) and solving for C:

$$-\frac{2}{3} = -\frac{2}{1^2 + C}$$

$$C = 2$$

Therefore, the solution of $dy/dx = xy^2$ such that $y(1) = -\frac{2}{3}$ is

$$y = -\frac{2}{x^2 + 2} \tag{5}$$

We call Equation (5) a **particular solution** of the differential equation.

APPLY IT ▶

5. For a clear liquid, light intensity diminishes at a rate of $\dfrac{dI}{dx} = -kI$, where I is the intensity of the light and x is the number of feet below the surface of the liquid. If $k = 0.0085$ and $I = I_0$ when $x = 0$, find I as a function of x.

EXAMPLE 1   Separation of Variables

Solve $y' = -\dfrac{y}{x}$ if $x, y > 0$.

Solution: Writing y' as dy/dx, separating variables, and integrating, we have

$$\frac{dy}{dx} = -\frac{y}{x}$$

$$\frac{dy}{y} = -\frac{dx}{x}$$

$$\int \frac{1}{y}\, dy = -\int \frac{1}{x}\, dx$$

$$\ln|y| = C_1 - \ln|x|$$

Since $x, y > 0$, we can omit the absolute-value bars:

$$\ln y = C_1 - \ln x \tag{6}$$

To solve for y, we convert Equation (6) to exponential form:

$$y = e^{C_1 - \ln x}$$

So

$$y = e^{C_1} e^{-\ln x} = \frac{e^{C_1}}{e^{\ln x}}$$

Replacing e^{C_1} by C, where $C > 0$, and rewriting $e^{\ln x}$ as x gives

$$y = \frac{C}{x} \qquad C, x > 0$$

Now Work Problem 1 ◁

In Example 1, note that Equation (6) expresses the solution implicitly, whereas the final equation ($y = C/x$) states the solution y explicitly in terms of x. Solutions of certain differential equations are often expressed in implicit form for convenience (or necessity because of the difficulty involved in obtaining an explicit form).

Exponential Growth and Decay

In Section 5.3, the notion of interest compounded continuously was developed. Let us now take a different approach to this topic that involves a differential equation. Suppose P dollars are invested at an annual rate r compounded n times a year. Let the function $S = S(t)$ give the compound amount S (or total amount present) after t years from the date of the initial investment. Then the initial principal is $S(0) = P$. Furthermore, since there are n interest periods per year, each period has length $1/n$ years, which we will denote by dt. At the end of the first period, the accrued interest for that period is added to the principal, and the sum acts as the principal for the second period, and so on. Hence, if the beginning of an interest period occurs at time t, then the increase in the amount present at the end of a period dt is $S(t + dt) - S(t)$, which we write as ΔS. This increase, ΔS, is also the interest earned for the period. Equivalently, the interest earned is principal times rate times time:

$$\Delta S = S \cdot r \cdot dt$$

Dividing both sides by dt, we obtain

$$\frac{\Delta S}{dt} = rS \tag{7}$$

As $dt \to 0$, then $n = \dfrac{1}{dt} \to \infty$, and consequently interest is being *compounded continuously;* that is, the principal is subject to continuous growth at every instant. However, as $dt \to 0$, then $\Delta S/dt \to dS/dt$, and Equation (7) takes the form

$$\frac{dS}{dt} = rS \tag{8}$$

This differential equation means that *when interest is compounded continuously, the rate of change of the amount of money present at time t is proportional to the amount present at time t.* The constant of proportionality is r.

To determine the actual function S, we solve the differential equation (8) by the method of separation of variables:

$$\frac{dS}{dt} = rS$$

$$\frac{dS}{S} = r \, dt$$

$$\int \frac{1}{S} \, dS = \int r \, dt$$

$$\ln |S| = rt + C_1$$

We assume that $S > 0$, so $\ln |S| = \ln S$. Thus,

$$\ln S = rt + C_1$$

To get an explicit form, we can solve for S by converting to exponential form.

$$S = e^{rt+C_1} = e^{C_1} e^{rt}$$

For simplicity, e^{C_1} can be replaced by C (and then necessarily $C > 0$) to obtain the general solution

$$S = Ce^{rt}$$

The condition $S(0) = P$ allows us to find the value of C:

$$P = Ce^{r(0)} = C \cdot 1$$

Hence $C = P$, so

$$S = Pe^{rt} \tag{9}$$

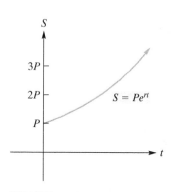

FIGURE 15.2 Compounding continuously.

Equation (9) gives the total value after t years of an initial investment of P dollars compounded continuously at an annual rate r. (See Figure 15.2.)

In our discussion of compound interest, we saw from Equation (8) that the rate of change in the amount present was proportional to the amount present. There are many natural quantities, such as population, whose rate of growth or decay at any time is considered proportional to the amount of that quantity present. If N denotes the amount of such a quantity at time t, then this rate of growth means that

$$\frac{dN}{dt} = kN$$

where k is a constant. If we separate variables and solve for N as we did for Equation (8), we get

$$N = N_0 e^{kt} \tag{10}$$

where N_0 is a constant. In particular, if $t = 0$, then $N = N_0 e^0 = N_0 \cdot 1 = N_0$. Thus, the constant N_0 is simply $N(0)$. Due to the form of Equation (10), we say that the quantity follows an **exponential law of growth** if k is positive and an **exponential law of decay** if k is negative.

EXAMPLE 2 Population Growth

In a certain city, the rate at which the population grows at any time is proportional to the size of the population. If the population was 125,000 in 1970 and 140,000 in 1990, what is the expected population in 2010?

Solution: Let N be the size of the population at time t. Since the exponential law of growth applies,

$$N = N_0 e^{kt}$$

To find the population in 2010, we must first find the particular law of growth involved by determining the values of N_0 and k. Let the year 1970 correspond to $t = 0$. Then

$t = 20$ in 1990 and $t = 40$ in 2010. We have

$$N_0 = N(0) = 125,000$$

Thus,

$$N = 125,000e^{kt}$$

To find k, we use the fact that $N = 140,000$ when $t = 20$:

$$140,000 = 125,000e^{20k}$$

Hence,

$$e^{20k} = \frac{140,000}{125,000} = 1.12$$

Therefore, the law of growth is

$$
\begin{aligned}
N &= 125,000e^{kt} \\
&= 125,000(e^{20k})^{t/20} \\
&= 125,000(1.12)^{t/20}
\end{aligned}
\tag{11}
$$

Setting $t = 40$ gives the expected population in 2010:

$$N = N(40) = 125,000(1.12)^2 = 156,800$$

We remark that from $e^{20k} = 1.12$ we have $20k = \ln(1.12)$ and hence $k = \dfrac{\ln(1.12)}{20} \approx$ 0.0057, which can be placed in $N = 125,000e^{kt}$ to give

$$N \approx 125,000e^{0.0057t} \tag{12}$$

Now Work Problem 23 ◁

In Chapter 4, radioactive decay was discussed. Here we will consider this topic from the perspective of a differential equation. The rate at which a radioactive element decays at any time is found to be proportional to the amount of that element present. If N is the amount of a radioactive substance at time t, then the rate of decay is given by

$$\frac{dN}{dt} = -\lambda N. \tag{13}$$

The positive constant λ (a Greek letter read "lambda") is called the **decay constant,** and the minus sign indicates that N is decreasing as t increases. Thus, we have exponential decay. From Equation (10), the solution of this differential equation is

$$N = N_0 e^{-\lambda t} \tag{14}$$

If $t = 0$, then $N = N_0 \cdot 1 = N_0$, so N_0 represents the amount of the radioactive substance present when $t = 0$.

The time for one-half of the substance to decay is called the **half-life** of the substance. In Section 4.2, it was shown that the half-life is given by

$$\text{half-life} = \frac{\ln 2}{\lambda} \approx \frac{0.69315}{\lambda} \tag{15}$$

Note that the half-life depends on λ. In Chapter 4, Figure 4.13 shows the graph of radioactive decay.

EXAMPLE 3   Finding the Decay Constant and Half-Life

If 60% of a radioactive substance remains after 50 days, find the decay constant and the half-life of the element.

Solution: From Equation (14),

$$N = N_0 e^{-\lambda t}$$

where N_0 is the amount of the element present at $t = 0$. When $t = 50$, then $N = 0.6N_0$, and we have

$$0.6N_0 = N_0 e^{-50\lambda}$$

$$0.6 = e^{-50\lambda}$$

$$-50\lambda = \ln(0.6) \qquad \text{logarithmic form}$$

$$\lambda = -\frac{\ln(0.6)}{50} \approx 0.01022$$

Thus, $N \approx N_0 e^{-0.01022t}$. The half-life, from Equation (15), is

$$\frac{\ln 2}{\lambda} \approx 67.82 \text{ days}$$

Now Work Problem 27 ◁

Radioactivity is useful in dating such things as fossil plant remains and archaeological remains made from organic material. Plants and other living organisms contain a small amount of radioactive carbon 14 (^{14}C) in addition to ordinary carbon (^{12}C). The ^{12}C atoms are stable, but the ^{14}C atoms are decaying exponentially. However, ^{14}C is formed in the atmosphere due to the effect of cosmic rays. This ^{14}C is taken up by plants during photosynthesis and replaces what has decayed. As a result, the ratio of ^{14}C atoms to ^{12}C atoms is considered constant in living tissues over a long period of time. When a plant dies, it stops absorbing ^{14}C, and the remaining ^{14}C atoms decay. By comparing the proportion of ^{14}C to ^{12}C in a fossil plant to that of plants found today, we can estimate the age of the fossil. The half-life of ^{14}C is approximately 5730 years. Thus, if a fossil is found to have a ^{14}C-to-^{12}C ratio that is half that of a similar substance found today, we would estimate the fossil to be 5730 years old.

EXAMPLE 4   Estimating the Age of an Ancient Tool

A wood tool found in a Middle East excavation site is found to have a ^{14}C-to-^{12}C ratio that is 0.6 of the corresponding ratio in a present-day tree. Estimate the age of the tool to the nearest hundred years.

Solution: Let N be the amount of ^{14}C present in the wood t years after the tool was made. Then $N = N_0 e^{-\lambda t}$, where N_0 is the amount of ^{14}C when $t = 0$. Since the ratio of ^{14}C to ^{12}C is 0.6 of the corresponding ratio in a present-day tree, this means that we want to find the value of t for which $N = 0.6N_0$. Thus, we have

$$0.6N_0 = N_0 e^{-\lambda t}$$

$$0.6 = e^{-\lambda t}$$

$$-\lambda t = \ln(0.6) \qquad \text{logarithmic form}$$

$$t = -\frac{1}{\lambda} \ln(0.6)$$

From Equation (15), the half-life is $(\ln 2)/\lambda$, which equals 5730, so $\lambda = (\ln 2)/5730$. Consequently,

$$t = -\frac{1}{(\ln 2)/5730} \ln(0.6)$$

$$= -\frac{5730 \ln(0.6)}{\ln 2}$$

$$\approx 4200 \text{ years}$$

Now Work Problem 29 ◁

PROBLEMS 15.5

In Problems 1–8, solve the differential equations.

1. $y' = 2xy^2$

2. $y' = x^2y^2$

3. $\dfrac{dy}{dx} - 2x \ln(x^2 + 1) = 0$

4. $\dfrac{dy}{dx} = \dfrac{x}{y}$

5. $\dfrac{dy}{dx} = y, \; y > 0$

6. $y' = e^x y^3$

7. $y' = \dfrac{y}{x}, x, y > 0$

8. $\dfrac{dy}{dx} - x \ln x = 0$

In Problems 9–18, solve each of the differential equations, subject to the given conditions.

9. $y' = \dfrac{1}{y^2}; y(1) = 1$

10. $y' = e^{x-y}; y(0) = 0$ *(Hint: $e^{x-y} = e^x/e^y$.)*

11. $e^y y' - x^2 = 0; \quad y = 0$ when $x = 0$

12. $x^2 y' + \dfrac{1}{y^2} = 0; \quad y(1) = 2$

13. $(3x^2 + 2)^3 y' - xy^2 = 0; \quad y(0) = 2$

14. $y' + x^3 y = 0; \quad y = e$ when $x = 0$

15. $\dfrac{dy}{dx} = \dfrac{3x\sqrt{1 + y^2}}{y}; \quad y > 0, y(1) = \sqrt{8}$

16. $2y(x^3 + 2x + 1)\dfrac{dy}{dx} = \dfrac{3x^2 + 2}{\sqrt{y^2 + 9}}; \quad y(0) = 0$

17. $2\dfrac{dy}{dx} = \dfrac{xe^{-y}}{\sqrt{x^2 + 3}}; \quad y(1) = 0$

18. $dy = 2xye^{x^2} dx, \quad y > 0; \quad y(0) = e$

19. **Cost**   Find the manufacturer's cost function $c = f(q)$ given that

$$(q + 1)^2 \dfrac{dc}{dq} = cq$$

and fixed cost is e.

20. Find $f(2)$, given that $f(1) = 0$ and that $y = f(x)$ satisfies the differential equation

$$\dfrac{dy}{dx} = xe^{x-y}$$

21. **Circulation of Money**   A country has 1.00 billion dollars of paper money in circulation. Each week 25 million dollars is brought into the banks for deposit, and the same amount is paid out. The government decides to issue new paper money; whenever the old money comes into the banks, it is destroyed and replaced by new money. Let y be the amount of old money (in millions of dollars) in circulation at time t (in weeks). Then y satisfies the differential equation

$$\dfrac{dy}{dt} = -0.025y$$

How long will it take for 95% of the paper money in circulation to be new? Round your answer to the nearest week. (*Hint:* If money is 95% new, then y is 5% of 1000.)

22. **Marginal Revenue and Demand**   Suppose that a monopolist's marginal-revenue function is given by the differential equation

$$\dfrac{dr}{dq} = (50 - 4q)e^{-r/5}$$

Find the demand equation for the monopolist's product.

23. **Population Growth**   In a certain town, the population at any time changes at a rate proportional to the population. If the population in 1990 was 60,000 and in 2000 was 64,000, find an equation for the population at time t, where t is the number of years past 1990. What is the expected population in 2010?

24. **Population Growth**   The population of a town increases by natural growth at a rate proportional to the number N of persons present. If the population at time $t = 0$ is 50,000, find two expressions for the population N, t years later, if the population doubles in 50 years. Assume that $\ln 2 = 0.69$. Also, find N for $t = 100$.

25. **Population Growth**   Suppose that the population of the world in 1930 was 2 billion and in 1960 was 3 billion. If the exponential law of growth is assumed, what is the expected population in 2015? Give your answer in terms of e.

26. **Population Growth**   If exponential growth is assumed, in approximately how many years will a population double if it triples in 100 years? (*Hint:* Let the population at $t = 0$ be N_0.)

27. **Radioactivity**   If 30% of the initial amount of a radioactive sample remains after 100 seconds, find the decay constant and the half-life of the element.

28. **Radioactivity**   If 20% of the initial amount of a radioactive sample has *decayed* after 100 seconds, find the decay constant and the half-life of the element.

29. **Carbon Dating**   An Egyptian scroll was found to have a ^{14}C-to-^{12}C ratio 0.7 of the corresponding ratio in similar present-day material. Estimate the age of the scroll, to the nearest hundred years.

30. **Carbon Dating**   A recently discovered archaeological specimen has a ^{14}C-to-^{12}C ratio 0.1 of the corresponding ratio found in present-day organic material. Estimate the age of the specimen, to the nearest hundred years.

31. **Population Growth**   Suppose that a population follows exponential growth given by $dN/dt = kN$ for $t \geq t_0$. Suppose also that $N = N_0$ when $t = t_0$. Find N, the population size at time t.

32. **Radioactivity**   Polonium-210 has a half-life of about 140 days. (a) Find the decay constant in terms of $\ln 2$. (b) What fraction of the original amount of a sample of polonium-210 remains after one year?

33. **Radioactivity**   Radioactive isotopes are used in medical diagnoses as tracers to determine abnormalities that may exist in an organ. For example, if radioactive iodine is swallowed, after some time it is taken up by the thyroid gland. With the use of a detector, the rate at which it is taken up can be measured, and a determination can be made as to whether the uptake is normal. Suppose radioactive technetium-99m, which has a half-life of six hours, is to be used in a brain scan two hours from now. What should be its activity now if the activity when it is used is to be 12 units? Give your answer to one decimal place. [*Hint:* In Equation (14), let $N =$ activity t hours from now and $N_0 =$ activity now.]

34. **Radioactivity**   A radioactive substance that has a half-life of eight days is to be temporarily implanted in a hospital patient until three-fifths of the amount originally present remains. How long should the implant remain in the patient?

35. Ecology   In a forest, natural litter occurs, such as fallen leaves and branches, dead animals, and so on.[7] Let $A = A(t)$ denote the amount of litter present at time t, where $A(t)$ is expressed in grams per square meter and t is in years. Suppose that there is no litter at $t = 0$. Thus, $A(0) = 0$. Assume that

(a) Litter falls to the ground continuously at a constant rate of 200 grams per square meter per year.

(b) The accumulated litter decomposes continuously at the rate of 50% of the amount present per year (which is $0.50A$).

The difference of the two rates is the rate of change of the amount of litter present with respect to time:

$$\begin{pmatrix} \text{rate of change} \\ \text{of litter present} \end{pmatrix} = \begin{pmatrix} \text{rate of falling} \\ \text{to ground} \end{pmatrix} - \begin{pmatrix} \text{rate of} \\ \text{decomposition} \end{pmatrix}$$

Therefore,

$$\frac{dA}{dt} = 200 - 0.50A$$

Solve for A. To the nearest gram, determine the amount of litter per square meter after one year.

36. Profit and Advertising   A certain company determines that the rate of change of monthly net profit P, as a function of monthly advertising expenditure x, is proportional to the difference between a fixed amount, $150,000, and $2P$; that is, dP/dx is proportional to $150,000 - 2P$. Furthermore, if no money is spent on monthly advertising, the monthly net profit is $15,000; if $1000 is spent on monthly advertising, the monthly net profit is $70,000. What would the monthly net profit be if $2000 were spent on advertising each month?

37. Value of a Machine   The value of a certain machine depreciates 25% in the first year after the machine is purchased. The rate at which the machine subsequently depreciates is proportional to its value. Suppose that such a machine was purchased new on July 1, 1995, for $80,000 and was valued at $38,900 on January 1, 2006.

(a) Determine a formula that expresses the value V of the machine in terms of t, the number of years after July 1, 1996.

(b) Use the formula in part (a) to determine the year and month in which the machine has a value of exactly $14,000.

Objective

To develop the logistic function as a solution of a differential equation. To model the spread of a rumor. To discuss and apply Newton's law of cooling.

15.6 More Applications of Differential Equations

Logistic Growth

In the previous section, we found that if the number N of individuals in a population at time t follows an exponential law of growth, then $N = N_0 e^{kt}$, where $k > 0$ and N_0 is the population when $t = 0$. This law assumes that at time t the rate of growth, dN/dt, of the population is proportional to the number of individuals in the population. That is, $dN/dt = kN$.

Under exponential growth, a population would get infinitely large as time goes on. In reality, however, when the population gets large enough, environmental factors slow down the rate of growth. Examples are food supply, predators, overcrowding, and so on. These factors cause dN/dt to decrease eventually. It is reasonable to assume that the size of a population is limited to some maximum number M, where $0 < N < M$, and as $N \to M$, $dN/dt \to 0$, and the population size tends to be stable.

In summary, we want a population model that has exponential growth initially but that also includes the effects of environmental resistance to large population growth. Such a model is obtained by multiplying the right side of $dN/dt = kN$ by the factor $(M - N)/M$:

$$\frac{dN}{dt} = kN \left(\frac{M - N}{M} \right)$$

Notice that if N is small, then $(M - N)/M$ is close to 1, and we have growth that is approximately exponential. As $N \to M$, then $M - N \to 0$ and $dN/dt \to 0$, as we wanted in our model. Because k/M is a constant, we can replace it by K. Thus,

$$\frac{dN}{dt} = KN(M - N) \tag{1}$$

This states that the rate of growth is proportional to the product of the size of the population and the difference between the maximum size and the actual size of the population. We can solve for N in the differential equation (1) by the method of separation of

---

[7]R. W. Poole, *An Introduction to Quantitative Ecology* (New York: McGraw-Hill Book Company, 1974).

variables:

$$\frac{dN}{N(M-N)} = K\,dt$$

$$\int \frac{1}{N(M-N)}\,dN = \int K\,dt \qquad (2)$$

The integral on the left side can be found by using Formula (5) in the table of integrals in Appendix B. Thus, Equation (2) becomes

$$\frac{1}{M} \ln \left| \frac{N}{M-N} \right| = Kt + C$$

so

$$\ln \left| \frac{N}{M-N} \right| = MKt + MC$$

Since $N > 0$ and $M - N > 0$, we can write

$$\ln \frac{N}{M-N} = MKt + MC$$

In exponential form, we have

$$\frac{N}{M-N} = e^{MKt+MC} = e^{MKt}\,e^{MC}$$

Replacing the positive constant e^{MC} by A and solving for N gives

$$\frac{N}{M-N} = Ae^{MKt}$$

$$N = (M-N)Ae^{MKt}$$

$$N = MAe^{MKt} - NAe^{MKt}$$

$$NAe^{MKt} + N = MAe^{MKt}$$

$$N(Ae^{MKt} + 1) = MAe^{MKt},$$

$$N = \frac{MAe^{MKt}}{Ae^{MKt} + 1}$$

Dividing numerator and denominator by Ae^{MKt}, we have

$$N = \frac{M}{1 + \dfrac{1}{Ae^{MKt}}} = \frac{M}{1 + \dfrac{1}{A}e^{-MKt}}$$

Replacing $1/A$ by b and MK by c yields the so-called *logistic function:*

Logistic Function

The function defined by

$$N = \frac{M}{1 + be^{-ct}} \qquad (3)$$

is called the **logistic function** or the **Verhulst–Pearl logistic function.**

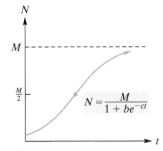

FIGURE 15.3   Logistic curve.

The graph of Equation (3), called a *logistic curve,* is S-shaped and appears in Figure 15.3. Notice that the line $N = M$ is a horizontal asymptote; that is,

$$\lim_{t \to \infty} \frac{M}{1 + be^{-ct}} = \frac{M}{1 + b(0)} = M$$

Moreover, from Equation (1), the rate of growth is

$$KN(M - N)$$

which can be considered a function of N. To find when the maximum rate of growth occurs, we solve $\dfrac{d}{dN}[KN(M-N)] = 0$ for N:

$$\frac{d}{dN}[KN(M-N)] = \frac{d}{dN}[K(MN - N^2)]$$

$$= K[M - 2N] = 0$$

Thus, $N = M/2$. In other words, the rate of growth increases until the population size is $M/2$ and decreases thereafter. The maximum rate of growth occurs when $N = M/2$ and corresponds to a point of inflection in the graph of N. To find the value of t for which this occurs, we substitute $M/2$ for N in Equation (3) and solve for t:

$$\frac{M}{2} = \frac{M}{1 + be^{-ct}}$$

$$1 + be^{-ct} = 2$$

$$e^{-ct} = \frac{1}{b}$$

$$e^{ct} = b$$

$$ct = \ln b \qquad \text{logarithmic form}$$

$$t = \frac{\ln b}{c}$$

Therefore, the maximum rate of growth occurs at the point $((\ln b)/c, M/2)$.

We remark that in Equation (3) we can replace e^{-c} by C, and then the logistic function has the following form:

Alternative Form of Logistic Function

$$N = \frac{M}{1 + bC^t}$$

EXAMPLE 1   Logistic Growth of Club Membership

Suppose the membership in a new country club is to be a maximum of 800 persons, due to limitations of the physical plant. One year ago the initial membership was 50 persons, and now there are 200. Provided that enrollment follows a logistic function, how many members will there be three years from now?

Solution: Let N be the number of members enrolled t years after the formation of the club. Then, from Equation (3),

$$N = \frac{M}{1 + be^{-ct}}$$

Here $M = 800$, and when $t = 0$, we have $N = 50$. So

$$50 = \frac{800}{1 + b}$$

$$1 + b = \frac{800}{50} = 16$$

$$b = 15$$

Thus,

$$N = \frac{800}{1 + 15e^{-ct}} \qquad (4)$$

When $t = 1$, then $N = 200$, so we have

$$200 = \frac{800}{1 + 15e^{-c}}$$

$$1 + 15e^{-c} = \frac{800}{200} = 4$$

$$e^{-c} = \frac{3}{15} = \frac{1}{5}$$

Hence, $c = -\ln\frac{1}{5} = \ln 5$. Rather than substituting this value of c into Equation (4), it is more convenient to substitute the value of e^{-c} there:

$$N = \frac{800}{1 + 15\left(\frac{1}{5}\right)^t}$$

Three years from now, t will be 4. Therefore,

$$N = \frac{800}{1 + 15\left(\frac{1}{5}\right)^4} \approx 781$$

Now Work Problem 5 ◁

Modeling the Spread of a Rumor

Let us now consider a simplified model[8] of how a rumor spreads in a population of size M. A similar situation would be the spread of an epidemic or new fad.

Let $N = N(t)$ be the number of persons who know the rumor at time t. We will assume that those who know the rumor spread it randomly in the population and that those who are told the rumor become spreaders of the rumor. Furthermore, we will assume that each knower tells the rumor to k individuals per unit of time. (Some of these k individuals may already know the rumor.) We want an expression for the rate of increase of the knowers of the rumor. Over a unit of time, each of approximately N persons will tell the rumor to k persons. Thus, the total number of persons who are told the rumor over the unit of time is (approximately) Nk. However, we are interested only in *new* knowers. The proportion of the population that does not know the rumor is $(M - N)/M$. Hence, the total number of new knowers of the rumor is

$$Nk\left(\frac{M - N}{M}\right)$$

which can be written $(k/M)N(M - N)$. Therefore,

$$\frac{dN}{dt} = \frac{k}{M}N(M - N)$$

$$= KN(M - N), \qquad \text{where } K = \frac{k}{M}$$

This differential equation has the form of Equation (1), so its solution, from Equation (3), is a *logistic function*:

$$N = \frac{M}{1 + be^{-ct}}$$

EXAMPLE 2   Campus Rumor

In a large university of 45,000 students, a sociology major is researching the spread of a new campus rumor. When she begins her research, she determines that 300 students know the rumor. After one week, she finds that 900 know it. Estimate the number of students who know it four weeks after the research begins by assuming logistic growth. Give the answer to the nearest thousand.

Solution: Let N be the number of students who know the rumor t weeks after the research begins. Then

$$N = \frac{M}{1 + be^{-ct}}$$

[8]More simplified, that is, than the model described in the Explore and Extend for Chapter 8.

Here M, the size of the population, is 45,000, and when $t = 0, N = 300$. So we have

$$300 = \frac{45,000}{1 + b}$$

$$1 + b = \frac{45,000}{300} = 150$$

$$b = 149$$

Thus,

$$N = \frac{45,000}{1 + 149e^{-ct}}$$

When $t = 1$, then $N = 900$. Hence,

$$900 = \frac{45,000}{1 + 149e^{-c}}$$

$$1 + 149e^{-c} = \frac{45,000}{900} = 50$$

Therefore, $e^{-c} = \frac{49}{149}$, so

$$N = \frac{45,000}{1 + 149\left(\frac{49}{149}\right)^t}$$

When $t = 4$,

$$N = \frac{45,000}{1 + 149\left(\frac{49}{149}\right)^4} \approx 16,000$$

After four weeks, approximately 16,000 students know the rumor.

Now Work Problem 3 ◁

Newton's Law of Cooling

We conclude this section with an interesting application of a differential equation. If a homicide is committed, the temperature of the victim's body will gradually decrease from 37°C (normal body temperature) to the temperature of the surroundings (ambient temperature). In general, the temperature of the cooling body changes at a rate proportional to the difference between the temperature of the body and the ambient temperature. This statement is known as **Newton's law of cooling.** Thus, if $T(t)$ is the temperature of the body at time t and the ambient temperature is a, then

$$\frac{dT}{dt} = k(T - a)$$

where k is the constant of proportionality. Therefore, Newton's law of cooling is a differential equation. It can be applied to determine the time at which a homicide was committed, as the next example illustrates.

EXAMPLE 3 **Time of Murder**

A wealthy industrialist was found murdered in his home. Police arrived on the scene at 11:00 P.M. The temperature of the body at that time was 31°C, and one hour later it was 30°C. The temperature of the room in which the body was found was 22°C. Estimate the time at which the murder occurred.

Solution: Let t be the number of hours after the body was discovered and $T(t)$ be the temperature (in degrees Celsius) of the body at time t. We want to find the value of t for which $T = 37$ (normal body temperature). This value of t will, of course, be negative. By Newton's law of cooling,

$$\frac{dT}{dt} = k(T - a)$$

where k is a constant and a (the ambient temperature) is 22. Thus,

$$\frac{dT}{dt} = k(T - 22)$$

Separating variables, we have

$$\frac{dT}{T - 22} = k\,dt$$

$$\int \frac{dT}{T - 22} = \int k\,dt$$

$$\ln |T - 22| = kt + C$$

Because $T - 22 > 0$,

$$\ln (T - 22) = kt + C$$

When $t = 0$, then $T = 31$. Therefore,

$$\ln (31 - 22) = k \cdot 0 + C$$

$$C = \ln 9$$

Hence,

$$\ln (T - 22) = kt + \ln 9$$

$$\ln (T - 22) - \ln 9 = kt$$

$$\ln \frac{T - 22}{9} = kt \qquad \ln a - \ln b = \ln \frac{a}{b}$$

When $t = 1$, then $T = 30$, so

$$\ln \frac{30 - 22}{9} = k \cdot 1$$

$$k = \ln \frac{8}{9}$$

Thus,

$$\ln \frac{T - 22}{9} = t \ln \frac{8}{9}$$

Now we find t when $T = 37$:

$$\ln \frac{37 - 22}{9} = t \ln \frac{8}{9}$$

$$t = \frac{\ln (15/9)}{\ln (8/9)} \approx -4.34$$

Accordingly, the murder occurred about 4.34 hours *before* the time of discovery of the body (11:00 P.M.). Since 4.34 hours is (approximately) 4 hours and 20 minutes, the industrialist was murdered about 6:40 P.M.

Now Work Problem 9 ◁

PROBLEMS 15.6

1. Population   The population of a city follows logistic growth and is limited to 100,000. If the population in 1995 was 50,000 and in 2000 was 60,000, what will the population be in 2005? Give your answer to the nearest hundred.

2. Production   A company believes that the production of its product in present facilities will follow logistic growth. Presently, 200 units per day are produced, and production will increase to 300 units per day in one year. If production is limited to 500 units per day, what is the anticipated daily production in two years? Give your answer to the nearest unit.

3. **Spread of Rumor**   In a university of 40,000 students, the administration holds meetings to discuss the idea of bringing in a major rock band for homecoming weekend. Before the plans are officially announced, students representatives on the administrative council spread information about the event as a rumor. At the end of one week, 100 people know the rumor. Assuming logistic growth, how many people know the rumor after two weeks? Give your answer to the nearest hundred.

4. Spread of a Fad   At a university with 50,000 students, it is believed that the number of students with a particular ring tone on their mobile phones is following a logistic growth pattern. The student newspaper investigates when a survey reveals that 500 students have the ring tone. One week later, a similar survey reveals that 1500 students have it. The newspaper writes a story about it and includes a formula predicting the number $N = N(t)$ of students who will have the ring tone t weeks after the first survey. What is the formula that the newspaper publishes?

5. Flu Outbreak In a city whose population is 100,000, an outbreak of flu occurs. When the city health department begins its recordkeeping, there are 500 infected persons. One week later, there are 1000 infected persons. Assuming logistic growth, estimate the number of infected persons two weeks after recordkeeping begins.

6. Sigmoid Function A very special case of the logistic function defined by Equation (3) is the *sigmoid function,* obtained by taking $M = b = c = 1$ so that we have

$$N(t) = \frac{1}{1 + e^{-t}}$$

(a) Show directly that the sigmoid function is the solution of the differential equation

$$\frac{dN}{dt} = N(1 - N)$$

and the initial condition $N(0) = 1/2$.

(b) Show that $(0, 1/2)$ is an inflection point on the graph of the sigmoid function.

(c) Show that the function

$$f(t) = \frac{1}{1 + e^{-t}} - \frac{1}{2}$$

is symmetric about the origin.

(d) Explain how (c) above shows that the sigmoid function is *symmetric about the point* $(0, 1/2)$, explaining at the same time what this means.

(e) Sketch the graph of the sigmoid function.

7. Biology In an experiment,[9] five *Paramecia* were placed in a test tube containing a nutritive medium. The number N of *Paramecia* in the tube at the end of t days is given approximately by

$$N = \frac{375}{1 + e^{5.2 - 2.3t}}$$

(a) Show that this equation can be written as

$$N = \frac{375}{1 + 181.27 e^{-2.3t}}$$

and hence is a logistic function.

(b) Find $\lim_{t \to \infty} N$.

8. Biology In a study of the growth of a colony of unicellular organisms,[10] the equation

$$N = \frac{0.2524}{e^{-2.128x} + 0.005125} \qquad 0 \le x \le 5$$

was obtained, where N is the estimated area of the growth in square centimeters and x is the age of the colony in days after being first observed.

(a) Put this equation in the form of a logistic function.

(b) Find the area when the age of the colony is 0.

9. Time of a Murder A murder was committed in an abandoned warehouse, and the victim's body was discovered at 3:17 A.M. by the police. At that time, the temperature of the body was 27°C and the temperature in the warehouse was −5°C. One hour later, the body temperature was 19°C and the warehouse

temperature was unchanged. The police forensic mathematician calculates using Newton's law of cooling. What is the time she reports as the time of the murder?

10. Enzyme Formation An enzyme is a protein that acts as a catalyst for increasing the rate of a chemical reaction that occurs in cells. In a certain reaction, an enzyme A is converted to another enzyme B. Enzyme B acts as a catalyst for its own formation. Let p be the amount of enzyme B at time t and I be the total amount of both enzymes when $t = 0$. Suppose the rate of formation of B is proportional to $p(I - p)$. Without directly using calculus, find the value of p for which the rate of formation will be a maximum.

11. Fund-Raising A small town decides to conduct a fund-raising drive for a fire engine whose cost is $200,000. The initial amount in the fund is $50,000. On the basis of past drives, it is determined that t months after the beginning of the drive, the rate dx/dt at which money is contributed to such a fund is proportional to the difference between the desired goal of $200,000 and the total amount x in the fund at that time. After one month, a total of $100,000 is in the fund. How much will be in the fund after three months?

12. Birthrate In a discussion of unexpected properties of mathematical models of population, Bailey[11] considers the case in which the birthrate per *individual* is proportional to the population size N at time t. Since the growth rate per individual is $\frac{1}{N}\frac{dN}{dt}$, this means that

$$\frac{1}{N}\frac{dN}{dt} = kN$$

so that

$$\frac{dN}{dt} = kN^2 \qquad \text{subject to } N = N_0 \text{ at } t = 0$$

where $k > 0$. Show that

$$N = \frac{N_0}{1 - kN_0 t}$$

Use this result to show that

$$\lim N = \infty \quad \text{as} \quad t \to \left(\frac{1}{kN_0}\right)^{-}$$

This means that over a finite interval of time, there is an infinite amount of growth. Such a model might be useful only for rapid growth over a short interval of time.

13. Population Suppose that the rate of growth of a population is proportional to the difference between some maximum size M and the number N of individuals in the population at time t. Suppose that when $t = 0$, the size of the population is N_0. Find a formula for N.

[9]G. F. Gause, *The Struggle for Existence* (New York: Hafner Publishing Co., 1964).

[10]A. J. Lotka, *Elements of Mathematical Biology* (New York: Dover Publications, Inc., 1956).

[11]N. T. J. Bailey, *The Mathematical Approach to Biology and Medicine* (New York: John Wiley & Sons, Inc., 1967).

To define and evaluate improper integrals.

15.7 Improper Integrals[12]

Suppose $f(x)$ is continuous and nonnegative for $a \le x < \infty$. (See Figure 15.4.) We know that the integral $\int_a^b f(x)\,dx$ is the area of the region between the curve $y = f(x)$ and the x-axis from $x = a$ to $x = b$. As $b \to \infty$, we can think of

$$\lim_{b \to \infty} \int_a^b f(x)\,dx$$

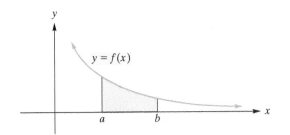

FIGURE 15.4   Area from a to b.

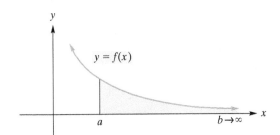

FIGURE 15.5   Area from a to b as $b \to \infty$.

as the area of the unbounded region that is shaded in Figure 15.5. This limit is abbreviated by

$$\int_a^\infty f(x)\,dx \tag{1}$$

and called an **improper integral.** If the limit exists, $\int_a^\infty f(x)\,dx$ is said to be **convergent** and the improper integral *converges* to that limit. In this case the unbounded region is considered to have a finite area, and this area is represented by $\int_a^\infty f(x)\,dx$. If the limit does not exist, the improper integral is said to be **divergent,** and the region does not have a finite area.

We can remove the restriction that $f(x) \ge 0$. In general, the improper integral $\int_a^\infty f(x)\,dx$ is defined by

$$\int_a^\infty f(x)\,dx = \lim_{b \to \infty} \int_a^b f(x)\,dx$$

Other types of improper integrals are

$$\int_{-\infty}^b f(x)\,dx \tag{2}$$

and

$$\int_{-\infty}^\infty f(x)\,dx \tag{3}$$

In each of the three types of improper integrals [(1), (2), and (3)], the interval over which the integral is evaluated has infinite length. The improper integral in (2) is defined by

$$\int_{-\infty}^b f(x)\,dx = \lim_{a \to -\infty} \int_a^b f(x)\,dx$$

APPLY IT ▶

6. The rate at which the human body eliminates a certain drug from its system may be approximated by $R(t) = 3e^{-0.1t} - 3e^{-0.3t}$, where $R(t)$ is in milliliters per minute and t is the time in minutes since the drug was taken. Find $\int_0^\infty (3e^{-0.1t} - 3e^{-0.3t})\,dt$, the total amount of the drug that is eliminated.

If this limit exists, $\int_{-\infty}^b f(x)\,dx$ is said to be convergent. Otherwise, it is divergent. We will define the improper integral in (3) after the following example.

EXAMPLE 1   Improper Integrals of the Form $\int_a^\infty f(x)\,dx$ and $\int_{-\infty}^b f(x)\,dx$

Determine whether the following improper integrals are convergent or divergent. For any convergent integral, determine its value.

---

[12]This section can be omitted if Chapter 16 will not be covered.

a. $\displaystyle\int_1^\infty \frac{1}{x^3}\,dx$

Solution:

$$\int_1^\infty \frac{1}{x^3}\,dx = \lim_{b\to\infty}\int_1^b x^{-3}\,dx = \lim_{b\to\infty} \left.-\frac{x^{-2}}{2}\right|_1^b$$

$$= \lim_{b\to\infty}\left[-\frac{1}{2b^2}+\frac{1}{2}\right] = -0+\frac{1}{2} = \frac{1}{2}$$

Therefore, $\displaystyle\int_1^\infty \frac{1}{x^3}\,dx$ converges to $\dfrac{1}{2}$.

b. $\displaystyle\int_{-\infty}^0 e^x\,dx$

Solution:

$$\int_{-\infty}^0 e^x\,dx = \lim_{a\to-\infty}\int_a^0 e^x\,dx = \lim_{a\to-\infty}\left. e^x\right|_a^0$$

$$= \lim_{a\to-\infty}(1-e^a) = 1-0 = 1 \qquad e^0 = 1$$

(Here we used the fact that as $a \to -\infty$, the graph of $y = e^a$ approaches the a-axis, so $e^a \to 0$.) Therefore, $\int_{-\infty}^0 e^x\,dx$ converges to 1.

c. $\displaystyle\int_1^\infty \frac{1}{\sqrt{x}}\,dx$

Solution:

$$\int_1^\infty \frac{1}{\sqrt{x}}\,dx = \lim_{b\to\infty}\int_1^b x^{-1/2}\,dx = \lim_{b\to\infty}\left. 2x^{1/2}\right|_1^b$$

$$= \lim_{b\to\infty} 2(\sqrt{b}-1) = \infty$$

Therefore, the improper integral diverges.

Now Work Problem 3 ◁

The improper integral $\int_{-\infty}^\infty f(x)\,dx$ is defined in terms of improper integrals of the forms (1) and (2):

$$\int_{-\infty}^\infty f(x)\,dx = \int_{-\infty}^0 f(x)\,dx + \int_0^\infty f(x)\,dx \tag{4}$$

If *both* integrals on the right side of Equation (4) are convergent, then $\int_{-\infty}^\infty f(x)\,dx$ is said to be convergent; otherwise, it is divergent.

EXAMPLE 2 An Improper Integral of the Form $\int_{-\infty}^\infty f(x)\,dx$

Determine whether $\displaystyle\int_{-\infty}^\infty e^x\,dx$ is convergent or divergent.

Solution:

$$\int_{-\infty}^\infty e^x\,dx = \int_{-\infty}^0 e^x\,dx + \int_0^\infty e^x\,dx$$

By Example 1(b), $\displaystyle\int_{-\infty}^0 e^x\,dx = 1$. On the other hand,

$$\int_0^\infty e^x\,dx = \lim_{b\to\infty}\int_0^b e^x\,dx = \lim_{b\to\infty}\left. e^x\right|_0^b = \lim_{b\to\infty}(e^b-1) = \infty$$

Since $\int_0^\infty e^x\,dx$ is divergent, $\int_{-\infty}^\infty e^x\,dx$ is also divergent.

Now Work Problem 11 ◁

EXAMPLE 3   **Density Function**

In statistics, a function f is called a density function if $f(x) \geq 0$ and

$$\int_{-\infty}^{\infty} f(x) \, dx = 1$$

Suppose

$$f(x) = \begin{cases} ke^{-x} & \text{for } x \geq 0 \\ 0 & \text{elsewhere} \end{cases}$$

is a density function. Find k.

Solution: We write the equation $\int_{-\infty}^{\infty} f(x) \, dx = 1$ as

$$\int_{-\infty}^{0} f(x) \, dx + \int_{0}^{\infty} f(x) \, dx = 1$$

Since $f(x) = 0$ for $x < 0$, $\int_{-\infty}^{0} f(x) \, dx = 0$. Thus,

$$\int_{0}^{\infty} ke^{-x} \, dx = 1$$

$$\lim_{b \to \infty} \int_{0}^{b} ke^{-x} \, dx = 1$$

$$\lim_{b \to \infty} -ke^{-x} \Big|_{0}^{b} = 1$$

$$\lim_{b \to \infty} (-ke^{-b} + k) = 1$$

$$0 + k = 1 \qquad \lim_{b \to \infty} e^{-b} = 0$$

$$k = 1$$

Now Work Problem 13 ◁

PROBLEMS 15.7

In Problems 1–12, determine the integrals if they exist. Indicate those that are divergent.

1. $\displaystyle\int_{3}^{\infty} \frac{1}{x^3} \, dx$

2. $\displaystyle\int_{1}^{\infty} \frac{1}{(3x-1)^2} \, dx$

3. $\displaystyle\int_{1}^{\infty} \frac{1}{x} \, dx$

4. $\displaystyle\int_{2}^{\infty} \frac{1}{\sqrt[3]{(x+2)^2}} \, dx$

5. $\displaystyle\int_{37}^{\infty} e^{-x} \, dx$

6. $\displaystyle\int_{0}^{\infty} (5 + e^{-x}) \, dx$

7. $\displaystyle\int_{1}^{\infty} \frac{1}{\sqrt{x}} \, dx$

8. $\displaystyle\int_{4}^{\infty} \frac{x \, dx}{\sqrt{(x^2+9)^3}}$

9. $\displaystyle\int_{-\infty}^{-3} \frac{1}{(x+1)^2} \, dx$

10. $\displaystyle\int_{1}^{\infty} \frac{1}{\sqrt[3]{x-1}} \, dx$

11. $\displaystyle\int_{-\infty}^{\infty} 2xe^{-x^2} \, dx$

12. $\displaystyle\int_{-\infty}^{\infty} (5 - 3x) \, dx$

13. Density Function   The density function for the life x, in hours, of an electronic component in a radiation meter is given by

$$f(x) = \begin{cases} \dfrac{k}{x^2} & \text{for } x \geq 800 \\ 0 & \text{for } x < 800 \end{cases}$$

(a) If k satisfies the condition that $\int_{800}^{\infty} f(x) \, dx = 1$, find k.

(b) The probability that the component will last at least 1200 hours is given by $\int_{1200}^{\infty} f(x) \, dx$. Evaluate this integral.

14. Density Function   Given the density function

$$f(x) = \begin{cases} ke^{-2x} & \text{for } x \geq 1 \\ 0 & \text{elsewhere} \end{cases}$$

find k. (*Hint:* See Example 3.)

15. Future Profits   For a business, the present value of all future profits at an annual interest rate r compounded continuously is given by

$$\int_{0}^{\infty} p(t)e^{-rt} \, dt$$

where $p(t)$ is the profit per year in dollars at time t. If $p(t) = 500{,}000$ and $r = 0.02$, evaluate this integral.

16. Psychology   In a psychological model for signal detection,[13] the probability α (a Greek letter read "alpha") of reporting a signal when no signal is present is given by

$$\alpha = \int_{x_c}^{\infty} e^{-x} \, dx \quad x \geq 0$$

---

[13] D. Laming, *Mathematical Psychology* (New York: Academic Press, Inc., 1973).

The probability β (a Greek letter read "beta") of detecting a signal when it is present is

$$\beta = \int_{x_c}^{\infty} ke^{-kx}\, dx \quad x \geq 0$$

In both integrals, x_c is a constant (called a criterion value in this model). Find α and β if $k = \frac{1}{8}$.

17. Find the area of the region in the third quadrant bounded by the curve $y = e^{3x}$ and the x-axis.

18. Economics In discussing entrance of a firm into an industry, Stigler[14] uses the equation

$$V = \pi_0 \int_0^{\infty} e^{\theta t} e^{-\rho t}\, dt$$

where π_0, θ (a Greek letter read "theta"), and ρ (a Greek letter read "rho") are constants. Show that $V = \pi_0/(\rho - \theta)$ if $\theta < \rho$.

19. Population The predicted rate of growth per year of the population of a certain small city is given by

$$\frac{40{,}000}{(t + 2)^2}$$

where t is the number of years from now. In the long run (that is, as $t \to \infty$), what is the expected change in population from today's level?

Chapter 15 Review

Important Terms and Symbols

Examples

Summary

Sometimes we can easily determine an integral whose form is $\int u\, dv$, where u and v are functions of the same variable, by applying the formula for integration by parts:

$$\int u\, dv = uv - \int v\, du$$

A proper rational function can be integrated by applying the technique of partial fractions (although *some* of the partial fractions that may result have integrals that are beyond the scope of this book). Here we express the rational function as a sum of fractions, each of which is easier to integrate than the original function.

To determine an integral that does not have a familiar form, you may be able to match it with a formula in a table of integrals. However, it may be necessary to transform the given integral into an equivalent form before the matching can occur.

An annuity is a series of payments over a period of time. Suppose payments are made continuously for T years such that a payment at time t is at the rate of $f(t)$ per year. If the annual rate of interest is r compounded continuously, then

---

[14] G. Stigler, *The Theory of Price*, 3rd ed. (New York: Macmillan Publishing Company, 1966), p. 344.

the present value of the continuous annuity is given by

$$A = \int_0^T f(t)e^{-rt}\,dt$$

and the accumulated amount is given by

$$S = \int_0^T f(t)e^{r(T-t)}\,dt$$

The average value $\bar{f}$ of a function f over the interval $[a, b]$ is given by

$$\bar{f} = \frac{1}{b-a}\int_a^b f(x)\,dx$$

An equation that involves the derivative of an unknown function is called a differential equation. If the highest-order derivative that occurs is the first, the equation is called a first-order differential equation. Some first-order differential equations can be solved by the method of separation of variables. In that method, by considering the derivative to be a quotient of differentials, we rewrite the equation so that each side contains only one variable and a single differential in the numerator. Integrating both sides of the resulting equation gives the solution. This solution involves a constant of integration and is called the general solution of the differential equation. If the unknown function must satisfy the condition that it has a specific function value for a given value of the independent variable, then a particular solution can be found.

Differential equations arise when we know a relation involving the rate of change of a function. For example, if a quantity N at time t is such that it changes at a rate proportional to the amount present, then

$$\frac{dN}{dt} = kN, \qquad \text{where } k \text{ is a constant}$$

The solution of this differential equation is

$$N = N_0 e^{kt}$$

where N_0 is the quantity present at $t = 0$. The value of k may be determined when the value of N is known for a given value of t other than $t = 0$. If k is positive, then N follows an exponential law of growth; if k is negative, N follows an exponential law of decay. If N represents a quantity of a radioactive element, then

$$\frac{dN}{dt} = -\lambda N, \qquad \text{where } \lambda \text{ is a positive constant}$$

Thus, N follows an exponential law of decay, and hence

$$N = N_0 e^{-\lambda t}$$

The constant λ is called the decay constant. The time for one-half of the element to decay is the half-life of the element:

$$\text{half-life} = \frac{\ln 2}{\lambda} \approx \frac{0.69315}{\lambda}$$

A quantity N may follow a rate of growth given by

$$\frac{dN}{dt} = KN(M - N), \qquad \text{where } K, M \text{ are constants}$$

Solving this differential equation gives a function of the form

$$N = \frac{M}{1 + be^{-ct}}, \qquad \text{where } b, c \text{ are constants}$$

which is called a logistic function. Many population sizes can be described by a logistic function. In this case, M represents the limit of the size of the population. A logistic function is also used in analyzing the spread of a rumor.

Newton's law of cooling states that the temperature T of a cooling body at time t changes at a rate proportional to the difference $T - a$, where a is the ambient temperature. Thus,

$$\frac{dT}{dt} = k(T - a), \qquad \text{where } k \text{ is a constant}$$

The solution of this differential equation can be used to determine, for example, the time at which a homicide was committed.

An integral of the form

$$\int_a^\infty f(x)\,dx \qquad \int_{-\infty}^b f(x)\,dx \qquad \text{or} \qquad \int_{-\infty}^\infty f(x)\,dx$$

is called an improper integral. The first two integrals are defined as follows:

$$\int_a^\infty f(x)\,dx = \lim_{b\to\infty} \int_a^b f(x)\,dx$$

and

$$\int_{-\infty}^b f(x)\,dx = \lim_{a\to-\infty} \int_a^b f(x)\,dx$$

If $\int_a^\infty f(x)\,dx$ [or $\int_{-\infty}^b f(x)\,dx$] is a finite number, we say that the integral is convergent; otherwise, it is divergent. The improper integral $\int_{-\infty}^\infty f(x)\,dx$ is defined by

$$\int_{-\infty}^\infty f(x)\,dx = \int_{-\infty}^0 f(x)\,dx + \int_0^\infty f(x)\,dx$$

If both integrals on the right side are convergent, $\int_{-\infty}^\infty f(x)\,dx$ is said to be convergent; otherwise, it is divergent.

Review Problems

In Problems 1–22, determine the integrals.

1. $\displaystyle\int x^2 \ln x\,dx$

2. $\displaystyle\int \frac{1}{\sqrt{4x^2 + 1}}\,dx$

3. $\displaystyle\int_0^2 \sqrt{9x^2 + 16}\,dx$

4. $\displaystyle\int \frac{16x}{3 - 4x}\,dx$

5. $\displaystyle\int \frac{15x - 2}{(3x + 1)(x - 2)}\,dx$

6. $\displaystyle\int_{e^a}^{e^b} \frac{1}{x \ln x}\,dx$

7. $\displaystyle\int \frac{dx}{x(x + 2)^2}$

8. $\displaystyle\int \frac{dx}{x^2 - 1}$

9. $\displaystyle\int \frac{dx}{x^2\sqrt{9-16x^2}}$

10. $\displaystyle\int x^3 \ln x^2\, dx$

11. $\displaystyle\int \frac{dx}{x^2 - a^2}$

12. $\displaystyle\int \frac{x}{\sqrt{2+5x}}\, dx$

13. $\displaystyle\int 49xe^{7x}\, dx$

14. $\displaystyle\int \frac{dx}{2+3e^{4x}}$

15. $\displaystyle\int \frac{dx}{2x \ln x^2}$

16. $\displaystyle\int \frac{dx}{x(x+a)}$

17. $\displaystyle\int \frac{2x}{3+2x}\, dx$

18. $\displaystyle\int \frac{dx}{x^2\sqrt{4x^2-9}}$

[15]**19.** $\displaystyle\int \frac{5x^2+2}{x^3+x}\, dx$

[15]**20.** $\displaystyle\int \frac{3x^3+5x^2+4x+3}{x^4+x^3+x^2}\, dx$

[16]**21.** $\displaystyle\int \ln(x+1)\sqrt{x+1}\, dx$

[16]**22.** $\displaystyle\int x^2 e^x\, dx$

23. Find the average value of $f(x) = 3x^2 + 2x$ over the interval $[2, 4]$.

24. Find the average value of $f(t) = t^2 e^t$ over the interval $[0, 1]$.

In Problems 25 and 26, solve the differential equations.

25. $y' = 3x^2 y + 2xy \qquad y > 0$

26. $y' - f'(x)e^{f(x)-y} = 0 \qquad y(0) = f(0)$

In Problems 27–30, determine the improper integrals if they exist.[17] Indicate those that are divergent.

27. $\displaystyle\int_1^\infty \frac{1}{x^{2.5}}\, dx$

28. $\displaystyle\int_{-\infty}^0 e^{2x}\, dx$

29. $\displaystyle\int_1^\infty \frac{1}{2x}\, dx$

30. $\displaystyle\int_{-\infty}^\infty xe^{1-x^2}\, dx$

31. Population The population of a fast-growing city was 500,000 in 1980 and 1,000,00 in 2000. Assuming exponential growth, project the population in 2020.

32. Population The population of a city doubles every 10 years due to exponential growth. At a certain time, the population is 40,000. Find an expression for the number of people N at time t years later. Give your answer in terms of $\ln 2$.

33. Radioactive If 95% of a radioactive substance remains after 100 years, find the decay constant, and, to the nearest percent, give the percentage of the original amount present after 200 years.

34. Medicine Suppose q is the amount of penicillin in the body at time t, and let q_0 be the amount at $t = 0$. Assume that the rate of change of q with respect to t is proportional to q and that q decreases as t increases. Then we have $dq/dt = -kq$, where $k > 0$. Solve for q. What percentage of the original amount present is there when $t = 7/k$?

35. Biology Two organisms are initially placed in a medium and begin to multiply. The number N of organisms that are present after t days is recorded on a graph with the horizontal axis labeled t and the vertical axis labeled N. It is observed that the points lie on a logistic curve. The number of organisms present after 6 days is 300, and beyond 10 days the number approaches a limit of 450. Find the logistic equation.

36. College Enrollment A university believes that its enrollment follows logistic growth. Last year enrollment was 10,000 and this year it is 11,000. If the university can accommodate a maximum of 20,000 students, what is the anticipated enrollment next year?

37. Time of Murder A coroner is called in on a murder case. He arrives at 6:00 P.M. and finds that the victim's temperature is 35°C. One hour later the body temperature is 34°C. The temperature of the room is 25°C. About what time was the murder committed? (Assume that normal body temperature is 37°C.)

38. Annuity Find the present value, to the nearest dollar, of a continuous annuity at an annual rate of 6% for 12 years if the payment at time t is at the annual rate of $f(t) = 10t$ dollars.

[18]**39. Hospital Discharges** For a group of hospitalized individuals, suppose the proportion that has been discharged at the end of t days is given by

$$\int_0^t f(x)\, dx$$

where $f(x) = 0.007e^{-0.01x} + 0.00005e^{-0.0002x}$. Evaluate

$$\int_0^\infty f(x)\, dx$$

[18]**40. Product Consumption** Suppose that $A(t)$ is the amount of a product that is consumed at time t and that A follows an exponential law of growth. If $t_1 < t_2$ and at time t_2 the amount consumed, $A(t_2)$, is double the amount consumed at time t_1, $A(t_1)$, then $t_2 - t_1$ is called a doubling period. In a discussion of exponential growth, Shonle[19] states that under exponential growth, "the amount of a product consumed during one doubling period is equal to the total used for all time up to the beginning of the doubling period in question." To justify this statement, reproduce his argument as follows. The amount of the product used up to time t_1 is given by

$$\int_{-\infty}^{t_1} A_0 e^{kt}\, dt \qquad k > 0$$

where A_0 is the amount when $t = 0$. Show that this is equal to $(A_0/k)e^{kt_1}$. Next, the amount used during the time interval from t_1 to t_2 is

$$\int_{t_1}^{t_2} A_0 e^{kt}\, dt$$

Show that this is equal to

$$\frac{A_0}{k} e^{kt_1}[e^{k(t_2-t_1)} - 1] \qquad (5)$$

If the interval $[t_1, t_2]$ is a doubling period, then

$$A_0 e^{kt_2} = 2A_0 e^{kt_1}$$

Show that this relationship implies that $e^{k(t_2-t_1)} = 2$. Substitute this value into Equation (5); your result should be the same as the total used during all time up to t_1, namely, $(A_0/k)e^{kt_1}$.

---

[15]Problems 19 and 20 refer to Section 15.2.

[16]Problems 21 and 22 refer to Section 15.1.

[17]Problems 27–30 refer to Section 15.7.

---

[18]Problems 39 and 40 refer to Section 15.7.

[19]J. I. Shonle, *Environmental Applications of General Physics* (Reading, MA: Addison-Wesley Publishing Company, Inc., 1975).

41. Revenue, Cost, and Profit   The following table gives values of a company's marginal-revenue (MR) and marginal-cost (MC) functions:

q	0	3	6	9	12	15	18
MR	25	22	18	13	7	3	0
MC	15	14	12	10	7	4	2

The company's fixed cost is 25. Assume that profit is a maximum when MR = MC and that this occurs when $q = 12$. Moreover, assume that the output of the company is chosen to maximize the profit. Use the trapezoidal rule and Simpson's rule for each of the following parts.

(a) Estimate the total revenue by using as many data values as possible.

(b) Estimate the total cost by using as few data values as possible.

(c) Determine how the maximum profit is related to the area enclosed by the line $q = 0$ and the MR and MC curves, and use this relation to estimate the maximum profit as accurately as possible.

◯ EXPLORE & EXTEND   Dieting

Today there is great concern about diet and weight loss. Some people want to lose weight in order to "look good." Others lose weight for physical fitness or for health reasons. In fact, some lose weight because of peer pressure. Advertisements for weight control programs frequently appear on television and in newspapers and magazines. In many bookstores, entire sections are devoted to diet and weight control.

Suppose you want to determine a mathematical model of the weight of a person on a restricted caloric diet.[1] A person's weight depends both on the daily rate of energy intake, say C calories per day, and on the daily rate of energy consumption, which is typically between 15 and 20 calories per day for each pound of body weight. Consumption depends on age, sex, metabolic rate, and so on. For an average value of 17.5 calories per pound per day, a person weighing w pounds expends $17.5w$ calories per day. If $C = 17.5w$, then his or her weight remains constant; otherwise weight gain or loss occurs according to whether C is greater or less than $17.5w$.

How fast will weight gain or loss occur? The most plausible physiological assumption is that dw/dt is proportional to the net excess (or deficit) $C - 17.5w$ in the number of calories per day. That is,

$$\frac{dw}{dt} = K(C - 17.5w) \qquad (1)$$

where K is a constant. The left side of the equation has units of pounds per day, and $C - 17.5w$ has units of calories per day. Hence the units of K are pounds per calorie. Therefore, you need to know how many pounds each excess or deficit calorie puts on or takes off. The commonly used dietetic conversion factor is that 3500 calories is equivalent to one pound. Thus $K = 1/3500$ lb per calorie.

Now, the differential equation modeling weight gain or loss is

$$\frac{dw}{dt} = \frac{1}{3500}(C - 17.5w) \qquad (2)$$

If C is constant, the equation is separable and its solution is

$$w(t) = \frac{C}{17.5} + \left(w_0 - \frac{C}{17.5}\right)e^{-0.005t} \qquad (3)$$

where w_0 is the initial weight and t is in days. In the long run, note that the equilibrium weight (that is, the weight as $t \to \infty$) is $w_{eq} = C/17.5$.

[1]Adapted from A. C. Segal, "A Linear Diet Model," *The College Mathematics Journal,* 18, no. 1 (1987), 44–45. By permission of the Mathematical Association of America.

For example, if someone initially weighing 180 lb adopts a diet of 2500 calories per day, then we have $w_{eq} = 2500/17.5 \approx 143$ lb and the weight function is

$$w(t) \approx 143 + (180 - 143)e^{-0.005t}$$
$$= 143 + 37e^{-0.005t}$$

Figure 15.6 shows the graph of $w(t)$. Notice how long it takes to get close to the equilibrium weight of 143 lb. The half-life for the process is ($\ln 2)/0.005 \approx 138.6$ days, about 20 weeks. (It would take about 584 days, or 83 weeks, to get to 145 lb.) This may be why so many dieters give up in frustration.

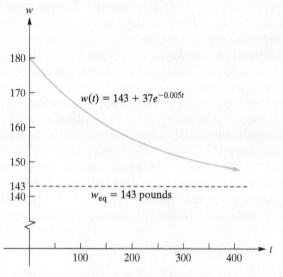

FIGURE 15.6 Weight as a function of time.

Problems

1. If a person weighing 200 lb adopts a 2000-calorie-per-day diet, determine, to the nearest pound, the equilibrium weight w_{eq}. To the nearest day, after how many days will the person reach a weight of 175 lb? Obtain the answer either algebraically or using a graphing calculator.

2. Show that the solution of Equation (2) is given by Equation (3).

3. The weight of a person on a restricted caloric diet at time t is given by $w(t)$. [See Equation (3).] The difference between this weight and the equilibrium weight w_{eq} is $w(t) - w_{eq}$. Suppose it takes d days for the person to lose half of the weight difference. Then

$$w(t + d) = w(t) - \tfrac{1}{2}[w(t) - w_{eq}]$$

By solving this equation for d, show that $d = \dfrac{\ln 2}{0.005}$.

4. Ideally, weight loss goals should be set in consultation with a physician. In general, however, one's ideal weight is related to one's height by the body mass index (BMI), which equals weight in kilograms divided by height in meters squared. The optimal BMI range is 18.5 to 24.9.

How many pounds would a 5'8"-tall, 190-pound woman need to lose to be within the ideal BMI range? (Be mindful of units as you calculate the answer.) To the nearest day, how long would it take for her to lose this much weight on a 2200-calorie-per-day diet?

Further information on weight and dieting can be found at www.consumer.gov/weightloss/set goals.htm.

5. What are the pros and cons of a "crash" diet, one based on drastic changes in eating habits to achieve rapid weight loss?

17

Multivariable Calculus

We know (from Chapter 13) how to maximize a company's profit when both revenue and cost are written as functions of a single quantity, namely the number of units produced. But of course the production level is itself determined by other factors—and, in general, no single variable can represent them.

The amount of oil pumped from an oil field each week, for example, depends on both the number of pumps and the number of hours that the pumps are operated. The number of pumps in the field will depend on the amount of capital originally available to build the pumps as well as the size and shape of the field. The number of hours that the pumps can be operated depends on the labor available to run and maintain the pumps. In addition, the amount of oil that the owner will be willing to have pumped from the oil field will depend on the current demand for oil—which is related to the price of the oil.

Maximizing the weekly profit from an oil field will require a balance between the number of pumps and the amount of time each pump can be operated. The maximum profit will not be achieved by building more pumps than can be operated or by running a few pumps full time.

This is an example of the general problem of maximizing profit when production depends on several factors. The solution involves an analysis of the production function, which relates production output to resources allocated for production. Because, in general, several variables are needed to describe the resource allocation, the most profitable allocation cannot be found by differentiation with respect to a single variable, as in preceding chapters. The more advanced techniques necessary to do the job will be covered in this chapter.

To compute partial derivatives.

functions of several variables, see Section 2.8.

17.1 Partial Derivatives

Throughout this book we have encountered many examples of functions of several variables. We recall, from Section 2.8, that the graph of a function of two variables is a surface. Figure 17.1 shows the surface $z = f(x, y)$ and a plane that is parallel to the x,z-plane and that passes through the point $(a, b, f(a, b))$ on the surface. The equation of this plane is $y = b$. Hence, any point on the curve that is the intersection of the surface $z = f(x, y)$ with the plane $y = b$ must have the form $(x, b, f(x, b))$. Thus, the curve can be described by the equation $z = f(x, b)$. Since b is constant, $z = f(x, b)$ can be considered a function of one variable, x. When the derivative of this function is evaluated at a, it gives the slope of the tangent line to this curve at the point $(a, b, f(a, b))$. (See Figure 17.1.) This slope is called the *partial derivative of f with respect to x at* (a, b) and is denoted $f_x(a, b)$. In terms of limits,

$$f_x(a, b) = \lim_{h \to 0} \frac{f(a + h, b) - f(a, b)}{h} \tag{1}$$

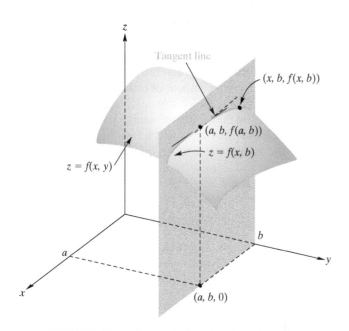

FIGURE 17.1   Geometric interpretation of $f_x(a, b)$.

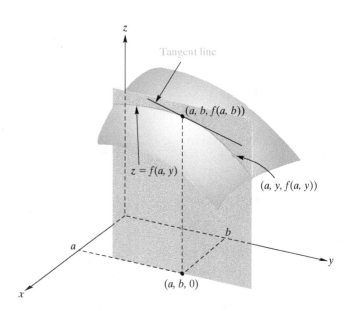

FIGURE 17.2   Geometric interpretation of $f_y(a, b)$.

On the other hand, in Figure 17.2, the plane $x = a$ is parallel to the y,z-plane and cuts the surface $z = f(x, y)$ in a curve given by $z = f(a, y)$, a function of y. When the derivative of this function is evaluated at b, it gives the slope of the tangent line to this curve at the point $(a, b, f(a, b))$. This slope is called the *partial derivative of f with respect to y at* (a, b) and is denoted $f_y(a, b)$. In terms of limits,

$$f_y(a, b) = \lim_{h \to 0} \frac{f(a, b + h) - f(a, b)}{h} \tag{2}$$

This gives us a geometric interpretation of a partial derivative.

We say that $f_x(a, b)$ is the slope of the tangent line to the graph of f at $(a, b, f(a, b))$ *in the x-direction;* similarly, $f_y(a, b)$ is the slope of the tangent line *in the y-direction.*

For generality, by replacing a and b in Equations (1) and (2) by x and y, respectively, we get the following definition.

Definition

If $z = f(x, y)$, the **partial derivative of f with respect to x**, denoted f_x, is the function, of two variables, given by

$$f_x(x, y) = \lim_{h \to 0} \frac{f(x + h, y) - f(x, y)}{h}$$

provided that the limit exists.

The **partial derivative of f with respect to** y, denoted f_y, is the function, of two variables, given by

$$f_y(x, y) = \lim_{h \to 0} \frac{f(x, y + h) - f(x, y)}{h}$$

provided that the limit exists.

By analyzing the foregoing definition, we can state the following procedure to find f_x and f_y:

This gives us a mechanical way to find partial derivatives.

Procedure to Find $f_x(x, y)$ and $f_y(x, y)$

To find f_x, treat y as a constant, and differentiate f with respect to x in the usual way.

To find f_y, treat x as a constant, and differentiate f with respect to y in the usual way.

EXAMPLE 1 Finding Partial Derivatives

If $f(x, y) = xy^2 + x^2y$, find $f_x(x, y)$ and $f_y(x, y)$. Also, find $f_x(3, 4)$ and $f_y(3, 4)$.

Solution: To find $f_x(x, y)$, we treat y as a constant and differentiate f with respect to x:

$$f_x(x, y) = (1)y^2 + (2x)y = y^2 + 2xy$$

To find $f_y(x, y)$, we treat x as a constant and differentiate with respect to y:

$$f_y(x, y) = x(2y) + x^2(1) = 2xy + x^2$$

Note that $f_x(x, y)$ and $f_y(x, y)$ are each functions of the two variables x and y. To find $f_x(3, 4)$, we evaluate $f_x(x, y)$ when $x = 3$ and $y = 4$:

$$f_x(3, 4) = 4^2 + 2(3)(4) = 40$$

Similarly,

$$f_y(3, 4) = 2(3)(4) + 3^2 = 33$$

Now Work Problem 1 ◁

Notations for partial derivatives of $z = f(x, y)$ are in Table 17.1. Table 17.2 gives notations for partial derivatives evaluated at (a, b). Note that the symbol ∂ (not d) is used to denote a partial derivative. The symbol $\partial z/\partial x$ is read "the partial derivative of z with respect to x."

EXAMPLE 2 Finding Partial Derivatives

a. If $z = 3x^3y^3 - 9x^2y + xy^2 + 4y$, find $\dfrac{\partial z}{\partial x}, \dfrac{\partial z}{\partial y}, \dfrac{\partial z}{\partial x}\bigg|_{(1,0)}$ and $\dfrac{\partial z}{\partial y}\bigg|_{(1,0)}$.

Solution: To find $\partial z/\partial x$, we differentiate z with respect to x while treating y as a constant:

$$\frac{\partial z}{\partial x} = 3(3x^2)y^3 - 9(2x)y + (1)y^2 + 0$$

$$= 9x^2y^3 - 18xy + y^2$$

Table 17.1

Partial Derivative of f (or z) with Respect to x	Partial Derivative of f (or z) with Respect to y
$f_x(x,y)$	$f_y(x,y)$
$\dfrac{\partial}{\partial x}(f(x,y))$	$\dfrac{\partial}{\partial y}(f(x,y))$
$\dfrac{\partial z}{\partial x}$	$\dfrac{\partial z}{\partial y}$

Table 17.2

Partial Derivative of f (or z) with Respect to x Evaluated at (a,b)	Partial Derivative of f (or z) with Respect to y Evaluated at (a,b)
$f_x(a,b)$	$f_y(a,b)$
$\left.\dfrac{\partial f}{\partial x}\right|_{(a,b)}$	$\left.\dfrac{\partial f}{\partial y}\right|_{(a,b)}$
$\left.\dfrac{\partial z}{\partial x}\right|_{\substack{x=a\\y=b}}$	$\left.\dfrac{\partial z}{\partial y}\right|_{\substack{x=a\\y=b}}$

Evaluating the latter equation at $(1, 0)$, we obtain

$$\left.\frac{\partial z}{\partial x}\right|_{(1,0)} = 9(1)^2(0)^3 - 18(1)(0) + 0^2 = 0$$

To find $\partial z/\partial y$, we differentiate z with respect to y while treating x as a constant:

$$\frac{\partial z}{\partial y} = 3x^3(3y^2) - 9x^2(1) + x(2y) + 4(1)$$

$$= 9x^3 y^2 - 9x^2 + 2xy + 4$$

Thus,

$$\left.\frac{\partial z}{\partial y}\right|_{(1,0)} = 9(1)^3(0)^2 - 9(1)^2 + 2(1)(0) + 4 = -5$$

b. If $w = x^2 e^{2x+3y}$, find $\partial w/\partial x$ and $\partial w/\partial y$.

Solution: To find $\partial w/\partial x$, we treat y as a constant and differentiate with respect to x. Since $x^2 e^{2x+3y}$ is a product of two functions, each involving x, we use the product rule:

$$\frac{\partial w}{\partial x} = x^2 \frac{\partial}{\partial x}(e^{2x+3y}) + e^{2x+3y}\frac{\partial}{\partial x}(x^2)$$

$$= x^2(2e^{2x+3y}) + e^{2x+3y}(2x)$$

$$= 2x(x+1)e^{2x+3y}$$

To find $\partial w/\partial y$, we treat x as a constant and differentiate with respect to y:

$$\frac{\partial w}{\partial y} = x^2 \frac{\partial}{\partial y}(e^{2x+3y}) = 3x^2 e^{2x+3y}$$

Now Work Problem 27 ◁

We have seen that, for a function of two variables, two partial derivatives can be considered. Actually, the concept of partial derivatives can be extended to functions of more than two variables. For example, with $w = f(x, y, z)$ we have three partial derivatives:

the partial with respect to x, denoted $f_x(x, y, z)$, $\partial w/\partial x$, and so on;
the partial with respect to y, denoted $f_y(x, y, z)$, $\partial w/\partial y$, and so on;
and
the partial with respect to z, denoted $f_z(x, y, z)$, $\partial w/\partial z$, and so on

To determine $\partial w/\partial x$, treat y and z as constants, and differentiate w with respect to x. For $\partial w/\partial y$, treat x and z as constants, and differentiate with respect to y. For $\partial w/\partial z$, treat x and y as constants, and differentiate with respect to z. For a function of n variables, we have n partial derivatives, which are determined in an analogous way.

EXAMPLE 3   Partial Derivatives of a Function of Three Variables

If $f(x, y, z) = x^2 + y^2 z + z^3$, find $f_x(x, y, z), f_y(x, y, z)$, and $f_z(x, y, z)$.

Solution: To find $f_x(x, y, z)$, we treat y and z as constants and differentiate f with respect to x:

$$f_x(x, y, z) = 2x$$

Treating x and z as constants and differentiating with respect to y, we have

$$f_y(x, y, z) = 2yz$$

Treating x and y as constants and differentiating with respect to z, we have

$$f_z(x, y, z) = y^2 + 3z^2$$

Now Work Problem 23 ◁

EXAMPLE 4   Partial Derivatives of a Function of Four Variables

If $p = g(r, s, t, u) = \dfrac{rsu}{rt^2 + s^2 t}$, find $\dfrac{\partial p}{\partial s}, \dfrac{\partial p}{\partial t}$, and $\dfrac{\partial p}{\partial t}\Big|_{(0,1,1,1)}$.

Solution: To find $\partial p / \partial s$, first note that p is a quotient of two functions, each involving the variable s. Thus, we use the quotient rule and treat r, t, and u as constants:

$$\frac{\partial p}{\partial s} = \frac{(rt^2 + s^2 t)\dfrac{\partial}{\partial s}(rsu) - rsu\dfrac{\partial}{\partial s}(rt^2 + s^2 t)}{(rt^2 + s^2 t)^2}$$

$$= \frac{(rt^2 + s^2 t)(ru) - (rsu)(2st)}{(rt^2 + s^2 t)^2}$$

Simplification gives

$$\frac{\partial p}{\partial s} = \frac{ru(rt - s^2)}{t(rt + s^2)^2} \qquad \text{a factor of } t \text{ cancels}$$

To find $\partial p / \partial t$, we can first write p as

$$p = rsu(rt^2 + s^2 t)^{-1}$$

Next, we use the power rule and treat r, s, and u as constants:

$$\frac{\partial p}{\partial t} = rsu(-1)(rt^2 + s^2 t)^{-2}\frac{\partial}{\partial t}(rt^2 + s^2 t)$$

$$= -rsu(rt^2 + s^2 t)^{-2}(2rt + s^2)$$

so that

$$\frac{\partial p}{\partial s} = -\frac{rsu(2rt + s^2)}{(rt^2 + s^2 t)^2}$$

Letting $r = 0, s = 1, t = 1$, and $u = 1$ gives

$$\frac{\partial p}{\partial t}\Big|_{(0,1,1,1)} = -\frac{0(1)(1)(2(0)(1) + (1)^2)}{(0(1)^2 + (1)^2(1))^2} = 0$$

Now Work Problem 31 ◁

PROBLEMS 17.1

In Problems 1–26, a function of two or more variables is given. Find the partial derivative of the function with respect to each of the variables.

1. $f(x, y) = 2x^2 + 3xy + 4y^2 + 5x + 6y - 7$

2. $f(x, y) = 2x^2 + 3xy$

3. $f(x, y) = 2y + 1$

4. $f(x, y) = \ln 2$

5. $g(x, y) = 3x^4 y + 2xy^2 - 5xy + 8x - 9y$

6. $g(x, y) = (x^2 + 1)^2 + (y^3 - 3)^3 + 5xy^3 - 2x^2 y^2$

7. $g(p, q) = \sqrt{pq}$

8. $g(w, z) = \sqrt[3]{w^2 + z^2}$

9. $h(s, t) = \dfrac{s^2 + 4}{t - 3}$

10. $h(u, v) = \dfrac{8uv^2}{u^2 + v^2}$

11. $u(q_1, q_2) = \ln \sqrt{q_1 + 2} + \ln \sqrt[3]{q_2 + 5}$

12. $Q(l, k) = 2l^{0.38}k^{1.79} - 3l^{1.03} + 2k^{0.13}$

13. $h(x, y) = \dfrac{x^2 + 3xy + y^2}{\sqrt{x^2 + y^2}}$

14. $h(x, y) = \dfrac{\sqrt{x + 9}}{x^2 y + y^2 x}$

15. $z = e^{5xy}$

16. $z = (x^3 + y^3)e^{xy + 3x + 3y}$

17. $z = 5x \ln(x^2 + y)$

18. $z = \ln(5x^3 y^2 + 2y^4)^4$

19. $f(r, s) = \sqrt{r + 2s}(r^3 - 2rs + s^2)$

20. $f(r, s) = \sqrt{rs}\, e^{2+r}$

21. $f(r, s) = e^{3-r} \ln(7 - s)$

22. $f(r, s) = (5r^2 + 3s^3)(2r - 5s)$

23. $g(x, y, z) = 2x^3 y^2 + 2xy^3 z + 4z^2$

24. $g(x, y, z) = 2xy^2 z^6 - 4x^2 y^3 z^2 + 3xyz$

25. $g(r, s, t) = e^{s+t}(r^2 + 7s^3)$

26. $g(r, s, t, u) = rs \ln(t)e^u$

In Problems 27–34, evaluate the given partial derivatives.

27. $f(x, y) = x^3 y + 7x^2 y^2$; $\quad f_x(1, -2)$

28. $z = \sqrt{2x^3 + 5xy + 2y^2}$; $\quad \left.\dfrac{\partial z}{\partial x}\right|_{\substack{x=0 \\ y=1}}$

29. $g(x, y, z) = e^x \sqrt{y + 2z}$; $\quad g_z(0, 6, 4)$

30. $g(x, y, z) = \dfrac{3x^2 y^2 + 2xy + x - y}{xy - yz + xz}$, $\quad g_y(1, 1, 5)$

31. $h(r, s, t, u) = (rst^2 u) \ln(1 + rstu)$; $\quad h_t(1, 1, 0, 1)$

32. $h(r, s, t, u) = \dfrac{7r + 3s^2 u^2}{s}$; $\quad h_t(4, 3, 2, 1)$

33. $f(r, s, t) = rst(r^2 + s^3 + t^4)$; $\quad f_s(1, -1, 2)$

34. $z = \dfrac{x^2 + y^2}{e^{x^2 + y^2}}$; $\quad \left.\dfrac{\partial z}{\partial x}\right|_{\substack{x=0 \\ y=0}}$, $\quad \left.\dfrac{\partial z}{\partial y}\right|_{\substack{x=1 \\ y=1}}$

35. If $z = xe^{x-y} + ye^{y-x}$, show that

$$\frac{\partial z}{\partial x} + \frac{\partial z}{\partial y} = e^{x-y} + e^{y-x}$$

36. **Stock Prices of a Dividend Cycle** In a discussion of stock prices of a dividend cycle, Palmon and Yaari[1] consider the

function f given by

$$u = f(t, r, z) = \frac{(1 + r)^{1-z} \ln(1 + r)}{(1 + r)^{1-z} - t}$$

where u is the instantaneous rate of ask-price appreciation, r is an annual opportunity rate of return, z is the fraction of a dividend cycle over which a share of stock is held by a midcycle seller, and t is the effective rate of capital gains tax. They claim that

$$\frac{\partial u}{\partial z} = \frac{t(1 + r)^{1-z} \ln^2(1 + r)}{[(1 + r)^{1-z} - t]^2}$$

Verify this.

37. **Money Demand** In a discussion of inventory theory of money demand, Swanson[2] considers the function

$$F(b, C, T, i) = \frac{bT}{C} + \frac{iC}{2}$$

and determines that $\dfrac{\partial F}{\partial C} = -\dfrac{bT}{C^2} + \dfrac{i}{2}$. Verify this partial derivative.

38. **Interest Rate Deregulation** In an article on interest rate deregulation, Christofi and Agapos[3] arrive at the equation

$$r_L = r + D\frac{\partial r}{\partial D} + \frac{dC}{dD} \tag{3}$$

where r is the deposit rate paid by commercial banks, r_L is the rate earned by commercial banks, C is the administrative cost of transforming deposits into return-earning assets, and D is the savings deposit level. Christofi and Agapos state that

$$r_L = r\left[\frac{1 + \eta}{\eta}\right] + \frac{dC}{dD} \tag{4}$$

where $\eta = \dfrac{r/D}{\partial r/\partial D}$ is the deposit elasticity with respect to the deposit rate. Express Equation (3) in terms of η to verify Equation (4).

39. **Advertising and Profitability** In an analysis of advertising and profitability, Swales[4] considers a function f given by

$$R = f(r, a, n) = \frac{r}{1 + a\left(\dfrac{n - 1}{2}\right)}$$

where R is the adjusted rate of profit, r is the accounting rate of profit, a is a measure of advertising expenditures, and n is the number of years that advertising fully depreciates. In the analysis, Swales determines $\partial R/\partial n$. Find this partial derivative.

Objective

To develop the notions of partial marginal cost, marginal productivity, and competitive and complementary products.

17.2 Applications of Partial Derivatives

From Section 17.1, we know that if $z = f(x, y)$, then $\partial z/\partial x$ and $\partial z/\partial y$ can be geometrically interpreted as giving the slopes of the tangent lines to the surface $z = f(x, y)$ in the x- and y-directions, respectively. There are other interpretations: Because $\partial z/\partial x$ is

---

[1] D. Palmon and U. Yaari, "Taxation of Capital Gains and the Behavior of Stock Prices over the Dividend Cycle," *The American Economist*, XXVII, no. 1 (1983), 13–22.

[2] P. E. Swanson, "Integer Constraints on the Inventory Theory of Money Demand," *Quarterly Journal of Business and Economics*, 23, no. 1 (1984), 32–37.

[3] A. Christofi and A. Agapos, "Interest Rate Deregulation: An Empirical Justification," *Review of Business and Economic Research*, XX (1984), 39–49.

[4] J. K. Swales, "Advertising as an Intangible Asset: Profitability and Entry Barriers: A Comment on Reekie and Bhoyrub," *Applied Economics*, 17, no. 4 (1985), 603–17.

the derivative of z with respect to x when y is held fixed, and because a derivative is a rate of change, we have

$$\frac{\partial z}{\partial x} \text{ is the rate of change of } z \text{ with respect to } x \text{ when } y \text{ is held fixed.}$$

Similarly,

$$\frac{\partial z}{\partial y} \text{ is the rate of change of } z \text{ with respect to } y \text{ when } x \text{ is held fixed.}$$

We will now look at some applications in which the "rate of change" notion of a partial derivative is very useful.

Suppose a manufacturer produces x units of product X and y units of product Y. Then the total cost c of these units is a function of x and y and is called a **joint-cost function.** If such a function is $c = f(x, y)$, then $\partial c / \partial x$ is called the **(partial) marginal cost with respect to** x and is the rate of change of c with respect to x when y is held fixed. Similarly, $\partial c / \partial y$ is the **(partial) marginal cost with respect to** y and is the rate of change of c with respect to y when x is held fixed. It also follows that $\partial c / \partial x(x, y)$ is approximately the cost of producing one more unit of X when x units of X and y units of Y are produced. Similarly, $\partial c / \partial y(x, y)$ is approximately the cost of producing one more unit of Y when x units of X and y units of Y are produced.

For example, if c is expressed in dollars and $\partial c / \partial y = 2$, then the cost of producing an extra unit of Y when the level of production of X is fixed is approximately two dollars.

If a manufacturer produces n products, the joint-cost function is a function of n variables, and there are n (partial) marginal-cost functions.

EXAMPLE 1   Marginal Costs

A company manufactures two types of skis, the Lightning and the Alpine models. Suppose the joint-cost function for producing x pairs of the Lightning model and y pairs of the Alpine model per week is

$$c = f(x, y) = 0.07x^2 + 75x + 85y + 6000$$

where c is expressed in dollars. Determine the marginal costs $\partial c / \partial x$ and $\partial c / \partial y$ when $x = 100$ and $y = 50$, and interpret the results.

Solution: The marginal costs are

$$\frac{\partial c}{\partial x} = 0.14x + 75 \quad \text{and} \quad \frac{\partial c}{\partial y} = 85$$

Thus,

$$\left. \frac{\partial c}{\partial x} \right|_{(100,50)} = 0.14(100) + 75 = 89 \tag{1}$$

and

$$\left. \frac{\partial c}{\partial y} \right|_{(100,50)} = 85 \tag{2}$$

Equation (1) means that increasing the output of the Lightning model from 100 to 101 while maintaining production of the Alpine model at 50 increases costs by approximately \$89. Equation (2) means that increasing the output of the Alpine model from 50 to 51 and holding production of the Lightning model at 100 will increase costs by approximately \$85. In fact, since $\partial c / \partial y$ is a constant function, the marginal cost with respect to y is \$85 at all levels of production.

Now Work Problem 1 ◁

EXAMPLE 2 Loss of Body Heat

On a cold day, a person may feel colder when the wind is blowing than when the wind is calm because the rate of heat loss is a function of both temperature and wind speed. The equation

$$H = (10.45 + 10\sqrt{w} - w)(33 - t)$$

indicates the rate of heat loss H (in kilocalories per square meter per hour) when the air temperature is t (in degrees Celsius) and the wind speed is w (in meters per second). For $H = 2000$, exposed flesh will freeze in one minute.[5]

a. Evaluate H when $t = 0$ and $w = 4$.

Solution: When $t = 0$ and $w = 4$,

$$H = (10.45 + 10\sqrt{4} - 4)(33 - 0) = 872.85$$

b. Evaluate $\partial H/\partial w$ and $\partial H/\partial t$ when $t = 0$ and $w = 4$, and interpret the results.

Solution:
$$\frac{\partial H}{\partial w} = \left(\frac{5}{\sqrt{w}} - 1\right)(33 - t), \quad \left.\frac{\partial H}{\partial w}\right|_{\substack{t=0 \\ w=4}} = 49.5$$

$$\frac{\partial H}{\partial t} = (10.45 + 10\sqrt{w} - w)(-1), \quad \left.\frac{\partial H}{\partial t}\right|_{\substack{t=0 \\ w=4}} = -26.45$$

These equations mean that when $t = 0$ and $w = 4$, increasing w by a small amount while keeping t fixed will make H increase approximately 49.5 times as much as w increases. Increasing t by a small amount while keeping w fixed will make H *decrease* approximately 26.45 times as much as t increases.

c. When $t = 0$ and $w = 4$, which has a greater effect on H: a change in wind speed of 1 m/s or a change in temperature of 1°C?

Solution: Since the partial derivative of H with respect to w is greater in magnitude than the partial with respect to t when $t = 0$ and $w = 4$, a change in wind speed of 1 m/s has a greater effect on H.

Now Work Problem 13 ◁

The output of a product depends on many factors of production. Among these may be labor, capital, land, machinery, and so on. For simplicity, let us suppose that output depends only on labor and capital. If the function $P = f(l, k)$ gives the output P when the producer uses l units of labor and k units of capital, then this function is called a **production function.** We define the **marginal productivity with respect to l** to be $\partial P/\partial l$. This is the rate of change of P with respect to l when k is held fixed. Likewise, the **marginal productivity with respect to k** is $\partial P/\partial k$ and is the rate of change of P with respect to k when l is held fixed.

EXAMPLE 3 Marginal Productivity

A manufacturer of a popular toy has determined that the production function is $P = \sqrt{lk}$, where l is the number of labor-hours per week and k is the capital (expressed in hundreds of dollars per week) required for a weekly production of P gross of the toy. (One gross is 144 units.) Determine the marginal productivity functions, and evaluate them when $l = 400$ and $k = 16$. Interpret the results.

---

[5]G. E. Folk, Jr., *Textbook of Environmental Physiology,* 2nd ed. (Philadelphia: Lea & Febiger, 1974).

Solution: Since $P = (lk)^{1/2}$,

$$\frac{\partial P}{\partial l} = \frac{1}{2}(lk)^{-1/2}k = \frac{k}{2\sqrt{lk}}$$

and

$$\frac{\partial P}{\partial k} = \frac{1}{2}(lk)^{-1/2}l = \frac{l}{2\sqrt{lk}}$$

Evaluating these equations when $l = 400$ and $k = 16$, we obtain

$$\left.\frac{\partial P}{\partial l}\right|_{\substack{l=400 \\ k=16}} = \frac{16}{2\sqrt{400(16)}} = \frac{1}{10}$$

and

$$\left.\frac{\partial P}{\partial k}\right|_{\substack{l=400 \\ k=16}} = \frac{400}{2\sqrt{400(16)}} = \frac{5}{2}$$

Thus, if $l = 400$ and $k = 16$, increasing l to 401 and holding k at 16 will increase output by approximately $\frac{1}{10}$ gross. But if k is increased to 17 while l is held at 400, the output increases by approximately $\frac{5}{2}$ gross.

Now Work Problem 5 ◁

Competitive and Complementary Products

Sometimes two products may be related such that changes in the price of one of them affect the demand for the other. A typical example is that of butter and margarine. If such a relationship exists between products A and B, then the demand for each product is dependent on the prices of both. Suppose q_A and q_B are the quantities demanded for A and B, respectively, and p_A and p_B are their respective prices. Then both q_A and q_B are functions of p_A and p_B:

$$q_A = f(p_A, p_B) \qquad \text{demand function for A}$$
$$q_B = g(p_A, p_B) \qquad \text{demand function for B}$$

We can find four partial derivatives:

$$\frac{\partial q_A}{\partial p_A} \quad \textit{the marginal demand for A with respect to } p_A$$

$$\frac{\partial q_A}{\partial p_B} \quad \textit{the marginal demand for A with respect to } p_B$$

$$\frac{\partial q_B}{\partial p_A} \quad \textit{the marginal demand for B with respect to } p_A$$

$$\frac{\partial q_B}{\partial p_B} \quad \textit{the marginal demand for B with respect to } p_B$$

Under typical conditions, if the price of B is fixed and the price of A increases, then the quantity of A demanded will decrease. Thus, $\partial q_A/\partial p_A < 0$. Similarly, $\partial q_B/\partial p_B < 0$. However, $\partial q_A/\partial p_B$ and $\partial q_B/\partial p_A$ may be either positive or negative. If

$$\frac{\partial q_A}{\partial p_B} > 0 \quad \text{and} \quad \frac{\partial q_B}{\partial p_A} > 0$$

then A and B are said to be **competitive products** or **substitutes**. In this situation, an increase in the price of B causes an increase in the demand for A, if it is assumed that the price of A does not change. Similarly, an increase in the price of A causes an increase in the demand for B when the price of B is held fixed. Butter and margarine are examples of substitutes.

Proceeding to a different situation, we say that if

$$\frac{\partial q_A}{\partial p_B} < 0 \quad \text{and} \quad \frac{\partial q_B}{\partial p_A} < 0$$

then A and B are **complementary products.** In this case, an increase in the price of B causes a decrease in the demand for A if the price of A does not change. Similarly, an increase in the price of A causes a decrease in the demand for B when the price of B is held fixed. For example, cars and gasoline are complementary products. An increase in the price of gasoline will make driving more expensive. Hence, the demand for cars will decrease. And an increase in the price of cars will reduce the demand for gasoline.

EXAMPLE 4 **Determining Whether Products Are Competitive or Complementary**

The demand functions for products A and B are each a function of the prices of A and B and are given by

$$q_A = \frac{50\sqrt[3]{p_B}}{\sqrt{p_A}} \quad \text{and} \quad q_B = \frac{75p_A}{\sqrt[3]{p_B^2}}$$

respectively. Find the four marginal-demand functions, and determine whether A and B are competitive products, complementary products, or neither.

Solution: Writing $q_A = 50p_A^{-1/2}p_B^{1/3}$ and $q_B = 75p_A p_B^{-2/3}$, we have

$$\frac{\partial q_A}{\partial p_A} = 50\left(-\frac{1}{2}\right)p_A^{-3/2}p_B^{1/3} = -25p_A^{-3/2}p_B^{1/3}$$

$$\frac{\partial q_A}{\partial p_B} = 50p_A^{-1/2}\left(\frac{1}{3}\right)p_B^{-2/3} = \frac{50}{3}p_A^{-1/2}p_B^{-2/3}$$

$$\frac{\partial q_B}{\partial p_A} = 75(1)p_B^{-2/3} = 75p_B^{-2/3}$$

$$\frac{\partial q_B}{\partial p_B} = 75p_A\left(-\frac{2}{3}\right)p_B^{-5/3} = -50p_A p_B^{-5/3}$$

Since p_A and p_B represent prices, they are both positive. Hence, $\partial q_A/\partial p_B > 0$ and $\partial q_B/\partial p_A > 0$. We conclude that A and B are competitive products.

Now Work Problem 19 ◁

PROBLEMS 17.2

For the joint-cost functions in Problems 1–3, find the indicated marginal cost at the given production level.

1. $c = 7x + 0.3y^2 + 2y + 900;$ $\quad \dfrac{\partial c}{\partial y}, x = 20, y = 30$

2. $c = 2x\sqrt{x+y} + 6000;$ $\quad \dfrac{\partial c}{\partial x}, x = 70, y = 74$

3. $c = 0.03(x+y)^3 - 0.6(x+y)^2 + 9.5(x+y) + 7700;$ $\dfrac{\partial c}{\partial x}, x = 50, y = 80$

For the production functions in Problems 4 and 5, find the marginal productivity functions $\partial P/\partial k$ and $\partial P/\partial l$.

4. $P = 15lk - 3l^2 + 5k^2 + 500$

5. $P = 2.314l^{0.357}k^{0.643}$

6. **Cobb–Douglas Production Function** In economics, a Cobb–Douglas production function is a production function of the form $P = Al^\alpha k^\beta$, where A, α, and β are constants and $\alpha + \beta = 1$. For such a function, show that

(a) $\partial P/\partial l = \alpha P/l$ (b) $\partial P/\partial k = \beta P/k$

(c) $l\dfrac{\partial P}{\partial l} + k\dfrac{\partial P}{\partial k} = P$. This means that summing the products of the marginal productivity of each factor and the amount of that factor results in the total product P.

In Problems 7–9, q_A and q_B are demand functions for products A and B, respectively. In each case, find $\partial q_A/\partial p_A$, $\partial q_A/\partial p_B$, $\partial q_B/\partial p_A$, $\partial q_B/\partial p_B$ and determine whether A and B are competitive, complementary, or neither.

7. $q_A = 1500 - 40p_A + 3p_B;$ $\quad q_B = 900 + 5p_A - 20p_B$

8. $q_A = 20 - p_A - 2p_B;$ $\quad q_B = 50 - 2p_A - 3p_B$

9. $q_A = \dfrac{100}{p_A\sqrt{p_B}};$ $\quad q_B = \dfrac{500}{p_B\sqrt[3]{p_A}}$

10. Canadian Manufacturing   The production function for the Canadian manufacturing industries for 1927 is estimated by[6] $P = 33.0l^{0.46}k^{0.52}$, where P is product, l is labor, and k is capital. Find the marginal productivities for labor and capital, and evaluate when $l = 1$ and $k = 1$.

11. Dairy Farming   An estimate of the production function for dairy farming in Iowa (1939) is given by[7]

$$P = A^{0.27}B^{0.01}C^{0.01}D^{0.23}E^{0.09}F^{0.27}$$

where P is product, A is land, B is labor, C is improvements, D is liquid assets, E is working assets, and F is cash operating expenses. Find the marginal productivities for labor and improvements.

12. Production Function   Suppose a production function is given by $P = \dfrac{kl}{3k + 5l}$.

(a) Determine the marginal productivity functions.

(b) Show that when $k = l$, the marginal productivities sum to $\dfrac{1}{8}$.

13. M.B.A. Compensation   In a study of success among graduates with master of business administration (M.B.A.) degrees, it was estimated that for staff managers (which include accountants, analysts, etc.), current annual compensation (in dollars) was given by

$$z = 43,960 + 4480x + 3492y$$

where x and y are the number of years of work experience before and after receiving the M.B.A. degree, respectively.[8] Find $\partial z / \partial x$ and interpret your result.

14. Status   A person's general status S_g is believed to be a function of status attributable to education, S_e, and status attributable to income, S_i, where S_g, S_e, and S_i are represented numerically. If

$$S_g = 7\sqrt[3]{S_e}\sqrt{S_i}$$

determine $\partial S_g / \partial S_e$ and $\partial S_g / \partial S_i$ when $S_e = 125$ and $S_i = 100$, and interpret your results.[9]

15. Reading Ease   Sometimes we want to evaluate the degree of readability of a piece of writing. Rudolf Flesch[10] developed a function of two variables that will do this, namely,

$$R = f(w, s) = 206.835 - (1.015w + 0.846s)$$

where R is called the *reading ease score*, w is the average number of words per sentence in 100-word samples, and s is the average number of syllables in such samples. Flesch says that an article for which $R = 0$ is "practically unreadable," but one with $R = 100$ is "easy for any literate person." (a) Find $\partial R / \partial w$ and $\partial R / \partial s$. (b)

Which is "easier" to read: an article for which $w = w_0$ and $s = s_0$, or one for which $w = w_0 + 1$ and $s = s_0$?

16. Model for Voice   The study of frequency of vibrations of a taut wire is useful in considering such things as an individual's voice. Suppose

$$\omega = \frac{1}{bL}\sqrt{\frac{\tau}{\pi\rho}}$$

where ω (a Greek letter read "omega") is frequency, b is diameter, L is length, ρ (a Greek letter read "rho") is density, and τ (a Greek letter read "tau") is tension.[11] Find $\partial\omega / \partial b$, $\partial\omega / \partial L$, $\partial\omega / \partial\rho$, and $\partial\omega / \partial\tau$.

17. Traffic Flow   Consider the following traffic-flow situation. On a highway where two lanes of traffic flow in the same direction, there is a maintenance vehicle blocking the left lane. (See Figure 17.3.) Two vehicles (*lead* and *following*) are in the right lane with a gap between them. The *subject* vehicle can choose either to fill or not to fill the gap. That decision may be based not only on the distance x shown in the diagram, but also on other factors (such as the velocity of the *following* vehicle). A *gap index* g has been used in analyzing such a decision.[12,13] The greater the g-value, the greater is the propensity for the *subject* vehicle to fill the gap. Suppose

$$g = \frac{x}{V_F} - \left(0.75 + \frac{V_F - V_S}{19.2}\right)$$

where x (in feet) is as before, V_F is the velocity of the *following* vehicle (in feet per second), and V_S is the velocity of the *subject* vehicle (in feet per second). From the diagram, it seems reasonable that if both V_F and V_S are fixed and x increases, then g should increase. Show that this is true by applying calculus to the function g. Assume that x, V_F, and V_S are positive.

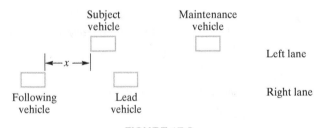

FIGURE 17.3

18. Demand   Suppose the demand equations for related products A and B are

$$q_A = e^{-(p_A + p_B)} \quad \text{and} \quad q_B = \frac{16}{p_A^2 p_B^2}$$

[6] P. Daly and P. Douglas, "The Production Function for Canadian Manufactures," *Journal of the American Statistical Association,* 38 (1943), 178–86.

[7] G. Tintner and O. H. Brownlee, "Production Functions Derived from Farm Records," *American Journal of Agricultural Economics,* 26 (1944), 566–71.

[8] Adapted from A. G. Weinstein and V. Srinivasen, "Predicting Managerial Success of Master of Business Administration (M.B.A.) Graduates," *Journal of Applied Psychology,* 59, no. 2 (1974), 207–12.

[9] Adapted from R. K. Leik and B. F. Meeker, *Mathematical Sociology* (Englewood Cliffs, NJ: Prentice-Hall, Inc., 1975).

[10] R. Flesch, *The Art of Readable Writing* (New York: Harper & Row Publishers, Inc., 1949).

[11] R. M. Thrall, J. A. Mortimer, K. R. Rebman, and R. F. Baum, eds., *Some Mathematical Models in Biology,* rev. ed., Report No. 40241-R-7. Prepared at University of Michigan, 1967.

[12] P. M. Hurst, K. Perchonok, and E. L. Seguin, "Vehicle Kinematics and Gap Acceptance," *Journal of Applied Psychology,* 52, no. 4 (1968), 321–24.

[13] K. Perchonok and P. M. Hurst, "Effect of Lane-Closure Signals upon Driver Decision Making and Traffic Flow," *Journal of Applied Psychology,* 52, no. 5 (1968), 410–13.

where q_A and q_B are the number of units of A and B demanded when the unit prices (in thousands of dollars) are p_A and p_B, respectively.

(a) Classify A and B as competitive, complementary, or neither.

(b) If the unit prices of A and B are $1000 and $2000, respectively, estimate the change in the demand for A when the price of B is decreased by $20 and the price of A is held constant.

19. **Demand** The demand equations for related products A and B are given by

$$q_A = 10\sqrt{\frac{p_B}{p_A}} \quad \text{and} \quad q_B = 3\sqrt[3]{\frac{p_A}{p_B}}$$

where q_A and q_B are the quantities of A and B demanded and p_A and p_B are the corresponding prices (in dollars) per unit.

(a) Find the values of the two marginal demands for product A when $p_A = 9$ and $p_B = 16$.

(b) If p_B were reduced to 14 from 16, with p_A fixed at 9, use part (a) to estimate the corresponding change in demand for product A.

20. **Joint-Cost Function** A manufacturer's joint-cost function for producing q_A units of product A and q_B units of product B is given by

$$c = \frac{q_A^2(q_B^3 + q_A)^{1/2}}{17} + q_A q_B^{1/3} + 600$$

where c is in dollars.

(a) Find the marginal-cost functions with respect to q_A and q_B.

(b) Evaluate the marginal-cost function with respect to q_A when $q_A = 17$ and $q_B = 8$. Round your answer to two decimal places.

(c) Use your answer to part (a) to estimate the change in cost if production of product A is decreased from 17 to 16 units, while production of product B is held constant at 8 units.

21. **Elections** For the congressional elections of 1974, the Republican percentage, R, of the Republican–Democratic vote in a district is given (approximately) by[14]

$$R = f(E_r, E_d, I_r, I_d, N)$$

$$= 15.4725 + 2.5945E_r - 0.0804E_r^2 - 2.3648E_d$$

$$+ 0.0687E_d^2 + 2.1914I_r - 0.0912I_r^2$$

$$- 0.8096I_d + 0.0081I_d^2 - 0.0277E_r I_r$$

$$+ 0.0493E_d I_d + 0.8579N - 0.0061N^2$$

Here E_r and E_d are the campaign expenditures (in units of $10,000) by Republicans and Democrats, respectively; I_r and I_d

are the number of terms served in Congress, *plus one*, for the Republican and Democratic candidates, respectively; and N is the percentage of the two-party presidential vote that Richard Nixon received in the district for 1968. The variable N gives a measure of Republican strength in the district.

(a) In the Federal Election Campaign Act of 1974, Congress set a limit of $188,000 on campaign expenditures. By analyzing $\partial R/\partial E_r$, would you have advised a Republican candidate who served nine terms in Congress to spend $188,000 on his or her campaign?

(b) Find the percentage above which the Nixon vote had a negative effect on R; that is, find N when $\partial R/\partial N < 0$. Give your answer to the nearest percent.

22. **Sales** After a new product has been launched onto the market, its sales volume (in thousands of units) is given by

$$S = \frac{AT + 450}{\sqrt{A + T^2}}$$

where T is the time (in months) since the product was first introduced and A is the amount (in hundreds of dollars) spent each month on advertising.

(a) Verify that the partial derivative of sales volume with respect to time is given by

$$\frac{\partial S}{\partial T} = \frac{A^2 - 450T}{(A + T^2)^{3/2}}$$

(b) Use the result in part (a) to predict the number of months that will elapse before the sales volume begins to decrease if the amount allocated to advertising is held fixed at $9000 per month.

Let f be a demand function for product A and $q_A = f(p_A, p_B)$, where q_A is the quantity of A demanded when the price per unit of A is p_A and the price per unit of product B is p_B. The partial elasticity of demand for A with respect to p_A, denoted η_{p_A}, is defined as $\eta_{p_A} = (p_A/q_A)(\partial q_A/\partial p_A)$. The partial elasticity of demand for A with respect to p_B, denoted η_{p_B}, is defined as $\eta_{p_B} = (p_B/q_A)(\partial q_A/\partial p_B)$. Loosely speaking, η_{p_A} is the ratio of a percentage change in the quantity of A demanded to a percentage change in the price of A when the price of B is fixed. Similarly, η_{p_B} can be loosely interpreted as the ratio of a percentage change in the quantity of A demanded to a percentage change in the price of B when the price of A is fixed. In Problems 23–25, find η_{p_A} and η_{p_B} for the given values of p_A and p_B.

23. $q_A = 1000 - 50p_A + 2p_B$; $p_A = 2, p_B = 10$

24. $q_A = 60 - 3p_A - 2p_B$; $p_A = 5, p_B = 3$

25. $q_A = 100/(p_A\sqrt{p_B})$; $p_A = 1, p_B = 4$

Objective

To find partial derivatives of a function defined implicitly.

17.3 Implicit Partial Differentiation[15]

An equation in x, y, and z does not necessarily define z as a function of x and y. For example, in the equation

$$z^2 - x^2 - y^2 = 0 \tag{1}$$

---

[14] J. Silberman and G. Yochum, "The Role of Money in Determining Election Outcomes," *Social Science Quarterly*, 58, no. 4 (1978), 671–82.

[15] This section can be omitted without loss of continuity.

if $x = 1$ and $y = 1$, then $z^2 - 1 - 1 = 0$, so $z = \pm\sqrt{2}$. Thus, Equation (1) does not define z as a function of x and y. However, solving Equation (1) for z gives

$$z = \sqrt{x^2 + y^2} \quad \text{or} \quad z = -\sqrt{x^2 + y^2}$$

each of which defines z as a function of x and y. Although Equation (1) does not explicitly express z as a function of x and y, it can be thought of as expressing z *implicitly* as one of two different functions of x and y. Note that the equation $z^2 - x^2 - y^2 = 0$ has the form $F(x, y, z) = 0$, where F is a function of three variables. Any equation of the form $F(x, y, z) = 0$ can be thought of as expressing z implicitly as one of a set of possible functions of x and y. Moreover, we can find $\partial z/\partial x$ and $\partial z/\partial y$ directly from the form $F(x, y, z) = 0$.

To find $\partial z/\partial x$ for

$$z^2 - x^2 - y^2 = 0 \tag{2}$$

we first differentiate both sides of Equation (2) with respect to x while treating z as a function of x and y and treating y as a constant:

$$\frac{\partial}{\partial x}(z^2 - x^2 - y^2) = \frac{\partial}{\partial x}(0)$$

$$\frac{\partial}{\partial x}(z^2) - \frac{\partial}{\partial x}(x^2) - \frac{\partial}{\partial x}(y^2) = 0$$

$$2z\frac{\partial z}{\partial x} - 2x - 0 = 0$$

Because y is treated as a constant, $\dfrac{\partial y}{\partial x} = 0$.

Solving for $\partial z/\partial x$, we obtain

$$2z\frac{\partial z}{\partial x} = 2x$$

$$\frac{\partial z}{\partial x} = \frac{x}{z}$$

To find $\partial z/\partial y$, we differentiate both sides of Equation (2) with respect to y while treating z as a function of x and y and treating x as a constant:

$$\frac{\partial}{\partial y}(z^2 - x^2 - y^2) = \frac{\partial}{\partial y}(0)$$

$$2z\frac{\partial z}{\partial y} - 0 - 2y = 0 \qquad\qquad \frac{\partial x}{\partial y} = 0$$

$$2z\frac{\partial z}{\partial y} = 2y$$

Hence,

$$\frac{\partial z}{\partial y} = \frac{y}{z}$$

The method we used to find $\partial z/\partial x$ and $\partial z/\partial y$ is called *implicit partial differentiation*.

EXAMPLE 1   Implicit Partial Differentiation

If $\dfrac{xz^2}{x + y} + y^2 = 0$, evaluate $\dfrac{\partial z}{\partial x}$ when $x = -1, y = 2$, and $z = 2$.

Solution: We treat z as a function of x and y and differentiate both sides of the equation with respect to x:

$$\frac{\partial}{\partial x}\left(\frac{xz^2}{x + y}\right) + \frac{\partial}{\partial x}(y^2) = \frac{\partial}{\partial x}(0)$$

Using the quotient rule for the first term on the left, we have

$$\frac{(x+y)\dfrac{\partial}{\partial x}(xz^2) - xz^2\dfrac{\partial}{\partial x}(x+y)}{(x+y)^2} + 0 = 0$$

Using the product rule for $\dfrac{\partial}{\partial x}(xz^2)$ gives

$$\frac{(x+y)\left[x\left(2z\dfrac{\partial z}{\partial x}\right) + z^2(1)\right] - xz^2(1)}{(x+y)^2} = 0$$

Solving for $\partial z/\partial x$, we obtain

$$2xz(x+y)\frac{\partial z}{\partial x} + z^2(x+y) - xz^2 = 0$$

$$\frac{\partial z}{\partial x} = \frac{xz^2 - z^2(x+y)}{2xz(x+y)} = -\frac{yz}{2x(x+y)} \qquad z \neq 0$$

Thus,

$$\left.\frac{\partial z}{\partial x}\right|_{(-1,2,2)} = 2$$

Now Work Problem 13 ◁

EXAMPLE 2   Implicit Partial Differentiation

If $se^{r^2+u^2} = u\ln(t^2+1)$, determine $\partial t/\partial u$.

Solution: We consider t as a function of r, s, and u. By differentiating both sides with respect to u while treating r and s as constants, we get

$$\frac{\partial}{\partial u}(se^{r^2+u^2}) = \frac{\partial}{\partial u}(u\ln(t^2+1))$$

$$2sue^{r^2+u^2} = u\frac{\partial}{\partial u}(\ln(t^2+1)) + \ln(t^2+1)\frac{\partial}{\partial u}(u) \qquad \text{product rule}$$

$$2sue^{r^2+u^2} = u\frac{2t}{t^2+1}\frac{\partial t}{\partial u} + \ln(t^2+1)$$

Therefore,

$$\frac{\partial t}{\partial u} = \frac{(t^2+1)(2sue^{r^2+u^2} - \ln(t^2+1))}{2ut}$$

Now Work Problem 1 ◁

PROBLEMS 17.3

In Problems 1–11, find the indicated partial derivatives by the method of implicit partial differentiation.

1. $2x^2 + 3y^2 + 5z^2 = 900;$ $\partial z/\partial x$
2. $z^2 - 5x^2 + y^2 = 0;$ $\partial z/\partial x$
3. $3z^2 - 5x^2 - 7y^2 = 0;$ $\partial z/\partial y$
4. $3x^2 + y^2 + 2z^3 = 9;$ $\partial z/\partial y$
5. $x^2 - 2y - z^2 + x^2yz^2 = 20;$ $\partial z/\partial x$
6. $z^3 + 2x^2z^2 - xy = 0;$ $\partial z/\partial x$
7. $e^x + e^y + e^z = 10;$ $\partial z/\partial y$
8. $xyz + xy^2z^3 - \ln z^4 = 0;$ $\partial z/\partial y$
9. $\ln(z) + 9z - xy = 1;$ $\partial z/\partial x$
10. $\ln x + \ln y - \ln z = e^y;$ $\partial z/\partial x$
11. $(z^2 + 6xy)\sqrt{x^3 + 5} = 2;$ $\partial z/\partial y$

In Problems 12–20, evaluate the indicated partial derivatives for the given values of the variables.

12. $xz + xyz - 5 = 0;$ $\partial z/\partial x, x = 1, y = 4, z = 1$
13. $xz^2 + yz^2 - x^2y = 1;$ $\partial z/\partial x, x = 1, y = 0, z = 1$
14. $e^{zx} = xyz;$ $\partial z/\partial y, x = 1, y = -e^{-1}, z = -1$
15. $e^{yz} = -xyz;$ $\partial z/\partial x, x = -e^2/2, y = 1, z = 2$
16. $\sqrt{xz + y^2} - xy = 0;$ $\partial z/\partial y, x = 2, y = 2, z = 6$
17. $\ln z = 4x + y;$ $\partial z/\partial x, x = 5, y = -20, z = 1$
18. $\dfrac{r^2s^2}{s^2+t^2} = \dfrac{t^2}{2};$ $\partial r/\partial t, r = 1, s = 1, t = 1$
19. $\dfrac{s^2+t^2}{rs} = 10;$ $\partial t/\partial r, r = 1, s = 2, t = 4$
20. $\ln(x+y+z) + xyz = ze^{x+y+z};$ $\partial z/\partial x, x = 0, y = 1, z = 0$

21. Joint-Cost Function   A joint-cost function is defined implicitly by the equation

$$c + \sqrt{c} = 12 + q_A\sqrt{9 + q_B^2}$$

where c denotes the total cost (in dollars) for producing q_A units of product A and q_B units of product B.

(a) If $q_A = 6$ and $q_B = 4$, find the corresponding value of c.

(b) Determine the marginal costs with respect to q_A and q_B when $q_A = 6$ and $q_B = 4$.

Objective

To compute higher-order partial derivatives.

17.4 Higher-Order Partial Derivatives

If $z = f(x, y)$, then not only is z a function of x and y, but also f_x and f_y are each functions of x and y, which may themselves have partial derivatives. If we can differentiate f_x and f_y, we obtain **second-order partial derivatives** of f. Symbolically,

$$f_{xx} \text{ means } (f_x)_x \quad f_{xy} \text{ means } (f_x)_y$$
$$f_{yx} \text{ means } (f_y)_x \quad f_{yy} \text{ means } (f_y)_y$$

In terms of ∂-notation,

$$\frac{\partial^2 z}{\partial x^2} \text{ means } \frac{\partial}{\partial x}\left(\frac{\partial z}{\partial x}\right) \qquad \frac{\partial^2 z}{\partial y\,\partial x} \text{ means } \frac{\partial}{\partial y}\left(\frac{\partial z}{\partial x}\right)$$

$$\frac{\partial^2 z}{\partial x\,\partial y} \text{ means } \frac{\partial}{\partial x}\left(\frac{\partial z}{\partial y}\right) \qquad \frac{\partial^2 z}{\partial y^2} \text{ means } \frac{\partial}{\partial y}\left(\frac{\partial z}{\partial y}\right)$$

Note that to find f_{xy}, we first differentiate f with respect to x. For $\partial^2 z/\partial x\,\partial y$, we first differentiate with respect to y.

We can extend our notation beyond second-order partial derivatives. For example, $f_{xxy}\ (= \partial^3 z/\partial y\,\partial x^2)$ is a third-order partial derivative of f, namely, the partial derivative of $f_{xx}\ (= \partial^2 z/\partial x^2)$ with respect to y. The generalization of higher-order partial derivatives to functions of more than two variables should be obvious.

CAUTION!⚠

For $z = f(x, y), f_{xy} = \partial^2 z/\partial y\,\partial x$.

> **EXAMPLE 1   Second-Order Partial Derivatives**
>
> Find the four second-order partial derivatives of $f(x, y) = x^2 y + x^2 y^2$.
>
> **Solution:** Since
>
> $$f_x(x, y) = 2xy + 2xy^2$$
>
> we have
>
> $$f_{xx}(x, y) = \frac{\partial}{\partial x}(2xy + 2xy^2) = 2y + 2y^2$$
>
> and
>
> $$f_{xy}(x, y) = \frac{\partial}{\partial y}(2xy + 2xy^2) = 2x + 4xy$$
>
> Also, since
>
> $$f_y(x, y) = x^2 + 2x^2 y$$
>
> we have
>
> $$f_{yy}(x, y) = \frac{\partial}{\partial y}(x^2 + 2x^2 y) = 2x^2$$
>
> and
>
> $$f_{yx}(x, y) = \frac{\partial}{\partial x}(x^2 + 2x^2 y) = 2x + 4xy$$

Now Work Problem 1 ◁

The derivatives f_{xy} and f_{yx} are called **mixed partial derivatives**. Observe in Example 1 that $f_{xy}(x, y) = f_{yx}(x, y)$. Under suitable conditions, mixed partial derivatives of a function are equal; that is, the order of differentiation is of no concern. You may assume that this is the case for all the functions that we consider.

EXAMPLE 2 **Mixed Partial Derivative**

Find the value of $\dfrac{\partial^3 w}{\partial z\, \partial y\, \partial x}\Big|_{(1,2,3)}$ if $w = (2x + 3y + 4z)^3$.

Solution:

$$\frac{\partial w}{\partial x} = 3(2x + 3y + 4z)^2 \frac{\partial}{\partial x}(2x + 3y + 4z)$$

$$= 6(2x + 3y + 4z)^2$$

$$\frac{\partial^2 w}{\partial y\, \partial x} = 6 \cdot 2(2x + 3y + 4z)\frac{\partial}{\partial y}(2x + 3y + 4z)$$

$$= 36(2x + 3y + 4z)$$

$$\frac{\partial^3 w}{\partial z\, \partial y\, \partial x} = 36 \cdot 4 = 144$$

Thus,

$$\frac{\partial^3 w}{\partial z\, \partial y\, \partial x}\Big|_{(1,2,3)} = 144$$

Now Work Problem 3 ◁

EXAMPLE 3 **Second-Order Partial Derivative of an Implicit Function[16]**

Determine $\dfrac{\partial^2 z}{\partial x^2}$ if $z^2 = xy$.

Solution: By implicit differentiation, we first determine $\partial z / \partial x$:

$$\frac{\partial}{\partial x}(z^2) = \frac{\partial}{\partial x}(xy)$$

$$2z\frac{\partial z}{\partial x} = y$$

$$\frac{\partial z}{\partial x} = \frac{y}{2z} \qquad z \neq 0$$

Differentiating both sides with respect to x, we obtain

$$\frac{\partial}{\partial x}\left(\frac{\partial z}{\partial x}\right) = \frac{\partial}{\partial x}\left(\frac{1}{2}yz^{-1}\right)$$

$$\frac{\partial^2 z}{\partial x^2} = -\frac{1}{2}yz^{-2}\frac{\partial z}{\partial x}$$

Substituting $y/(2z)$ for $\partial z/\partial x$, we have

$$\frac{\partial^2 z}{\partial x^2} = -\frac{1}{2}yz^{-2}\left(\frac{y}{2z}\right) = -\frac{y^2}{4z^3} \qquad z \neq 0$$

Now Work Problem 23 ◁

PROBLEMS 17.4

In Problems 1–10, find the indicated partial derivatives.

1. $f(x, y) = 6xy^2$; $f_x(x, y)$, $f_{xy}(x, y)$, $f_{yx}(x, y)$

2. $f(x, y) = 2x^3y^2 + 6x^2y^3 - 3xy$; $f_x(x, y)$, $f_{xx}(x, y)$

3. $f(x, y) = 7x^2 + 3y$; $f_y(x, y)$, $f_{yy}(x, y)$, $f_{yyx}(x, y)$

4. $f(x, y) = (x^2 + xy + y^2)(xy + x + y)$; $f_x(x, y)$, $f_{xy}(x, y)$

5. $f(x, y) = 9e^{2xy}$; $f_y(x, y)$, $f_{yx}(x, y)$, $f_{yxy}(x, y)$

6. $f(x, y) = \ln(x^2 + y^2) + 2$; $f_x(x, y)$, $f_{xx}(x, y)$, $f_{xy}(x, y)$

7. $f(x, y) = (x + y)^2(xy)$; $f_x(x, y)$, $f_y(x, y)$, $f_{xx}(x, y)$, $f_{yy}(x, y)$

8. $f(x, y, z) = x^2y^3z^4$; $f_x(x, y, z)$, $f_{xz}(x, y, z)$, $f_{zx}(x, y, z)$

9. $z = \ln\sqrt{x^2 + y^2}$; $\dfrac{\partial z}{\partial y}$, $\dfrac{\partial^2 z}{\partial y^2}$

10. $z = \dfrac{\ln(x^2 + 5)}{y}$; $\dfrac{\partial z}{\partial x}$, $\dfrac{\partial^2 z}{\partial y\, \partial x}$

In Problems 11–16, find the indicated value.

11. If $f(x, y, z) = 7$, find $f_{yxx}(4, 3, -2)$.

12. If $f(x, y, z) = z^2(3x^2 - 4xy^3)$, find $f_{xyz}(1, 2, 3)$.

---

[16] Omit if Section 17.3 was not covered.

13. If $f(l, k) = 3l^3k^6 - 2l^2k^7$, find $f_{k\,lk}(2, 1)$.

14. If $f(x, y) = x^3y^2 + x^2y - x^2y^2$, find $f_{xxy}(2, 3)$ and $f_{xyx}(2, 3)$.

15. If $f(x, y) = y^2e^x + \ln(xy)$, find $f_{xyy}(1, 1)$.

16. If $f(x, y) = x^3 - 6xy^2 + x^2 - y^3$, find $f_{xy}(1, -1)$.

17. Cost Function Suppose the cost c of producing q_A units of product A and q_B units of product B is given by

$$c = (3q_A^2 + q_B^3 + 4)^{1/3}$$

and the coupled demand functions for the products are given by

$$q_A = 10 - p_A + p_B^2$$

and

$$q_B = 20 + p_A - 11p_B$$

Find the value of

$$\frac{\partial^2 c}{\partial q_A \, \partial q_B}$$

when $p_A = 25$ and $p_B = 4$.

18. For $f(x, y) = x^4y^4 + 3x^3y^2 - 7x + 4$, show that

$$f_{xyx}(x, y) = f_{xxy}(x, y)$$

19. For $f(x, y) = e^{x^2 + xy + y^2}$, show that

$$f_{xy}(x, y) = f_{yx}(x, y)$$

20. For $f(x, y) = e^{xy}$, show that

$$f_{xx}(x, y) + f_{xy}(x, y) + f_{yx}(x, y) + f_{yy}(x, y)$$
$$= f(x, y)((x + y)^2 + 2)$$

21. For $z = \ln(x^2 + y^2)$, show that $\dfrac{\partial^2 z}{\partial x^2} + \dfrac{\partial^2 z}{\partial y^2} = 0$.

[17]22. If $z^3 - x^3 - x^2y - xy^2 - y^3 = 0$, find $\dfrac{\partial^2 z}{\partial x^2}$.

[17]23. If $z^2 - 3x^2 + y^2 = 0$, find $\dfrac{\partial^2 z}{\partial y^2}$.

[17]24. If $2z^2 = x^2 + 2xy + xz$, find $\dfrac{\partial^2 z}{\partial x \, \partial y}$.

Objective

To show how to find partial derivatives of composite functions by using the chain rule.

17.5 Chain Rule[18]

Suppose a manufacturer of two related products A and B has a joint-cost function given by

$$c = f(q_A, q_B)$$

where c is the total cost of producing quantities q_A and q_B of A and B, respectively. Furthermore, suppose the demand functions for the products are

$$q_A = g(p_A, p_B) \quad \text{and} \quad q_B = h(p_A, p_B)$$

where p_A and p_B are the prices per unit of A and B, respectively. Since c is a function of q_A and q_B, and since both q_A and q_B are themselves functions of p_A and p_B, c can be viewed as a function of p_A and p_B. (Appropriately, the variables q_A and q_B are called *intermediate variables* of c.) Consequently, we should be able to determine $\partial c / \partial p_A$, the rate of change of total cost with respect to the price of A. One way to do this is to substitute the expressions $g(p_A, p_B)$ and $h(p_A, p_B)$ for q_A and q_B, respectively, into $c = f(q_A, q_B)$. Then c is a function of p_A and p_B, and we can differentiate c with respect to p_A directly. This approach has some drawbacks—especially when f, g, or h is given by a complicated expression. Another way to approach the problem would be to use the chain rule (actually *a* chain rule), which we now state without proof.

Chain Rule

Let $z = f(x, y)$, where both x and y are functions of r and s given by $x = x(r, s)$ and $y = y(r, s)$. If f, x, and y have continuous partial derivatives, then z is a function of r and s, and

$$\frac{\partial z}{\partial r} = \frac{\partial z}{\partial x}\frac{\partial x}{\partial r} + \frac{\partial z}{\partial y}\frac{\partial y}{\partial r}$$

and

$$\frac{\partial z}{\partial s} = \frac{\partial z}{\partial x}\frac{\partial x}{\partial s} + \frac{\partial z}{\partial y}\frac{\partial y}{\partial s}$$

---

[17]Omit if Section 17.3 was not covered.

[18]This section can be omitted without loss of continuity.

Note that in the chain rule, the number of intermediate variables of z (two) is the same as the number of terms that compose each of $\partial z/\partial r$ and $\partial z/\partial s$.

Returning to the original situation concerning the manufacturer, we see that if f, q_A, and q_B have continuous partial derivatives, then, by the chain rule,

$$\frac{\partial c}{\partial p_A} = \frac{\partial c}{\partial q_A} \frac{\partial q_A}{\partial p_A} + \frac{\partial c}{\partial q_B} \frac{\partial q_B}{\partial p_A}$$

EXAMPLE 1   Rate of Change of Cost

For a manufacturer of cameras and film, the total cost c of producing q_C cameras and q_F units of film is given by

$$c = 30q_C + 0.015q_C q_F + q_F + 900$$

The demand functions for the cameras and film are given by

$$q_C = \frac{9000}{p_C \sqrt{p_F}} \quad \text{and} \quad q_F = 2000 - p_C - 400p_F$$

where p_C is the price per camera and p_F is the price per unit of film. Find the rate of change of total cost with respect to the price of the camera when $p_C = 50$ and $p_F = 2$.

Solution: We must first determine $\partial c/\partial p_C$. By the chain rule,

$$\frac{\partial c}{\partial p_C} = \frac{\partial c}{\partial q_C} \frac{\partial q_C}{\partial p_C} + \frac{\partial c}{\partial q_F} \frac{\partial q_F}{\partial p_C}$$

$$= (30 + 0.015q_F)\left[\frac{-9000}{p_C^2 \sqrt{p_F}}\right] + (0.015q_C + 1)(-1)$$

When $p_C = 50$ and $p_F = 2$, then $q_C = 90\sqrt{2}$ and $q_F = 1150$. Substituting these values into $\partial c/\partial p_C$ and simplifying, we have

$$\left.\frac{\partial c}{\partial p_C}\right|_{\substack{p_C=50 \\ p_F=2}} \approx -123.2$$

Now Work Problem 1 ◁

The chain rule can be extended. For example, suppose $z = f(v, w, x, y)$ and v, w, x, and y are all functions of r, s, and t. Then, if certain conditions of continuity are assumed, z is a function of r, s, and t, and we have

$$\frac{\partial z}{\partial r} = \frac{\partial z}{\partial v} \frac{\partial v}{\partial r} + \frac{\partial z}{\partial w} \frac{\partial w}{\partial r} + \frac{\partial z}{\partial x} \frac{\partial x}{\partial r} + \frac{\partial z}{\partial y} \frac{\partial y}{\partial r}$$

$$\frac{\partial z}{\partial s} = \frac{\partial z}{\partial v} \frac{\partial v}{\partial s} + \frac{\partial z}{\partial w} \frac{\partial w}{\partial s} + \frac{\partial z}{\partial x} \frac{\partial x}{\partial s} + \frac{\partial z}{\partial y} \frac{\partial y}{\partial s}$$

and

$$\frac{\partial z}{\partial t} = \frac{\partial z}{\partial v} \frac{\partial v}{\partial t} + \frac{\partial z}{\partial w} \frac{\partial w}{\partial t} + \frac{\partial z}{\partial x} \frac{\partial x}{\partial t} + \frac{\partial z}{\partial y} \frac{\partial y}{\partial t}$$

Observe that the number of intermediate variables of z (four) is the same as the number of terms that form each of $\partial z/\partial r$, $\partial z/\partial s$, and $\partial z/\partial t$.

Now consider the situation where $z = f(x, y)$ such that $x = x(t)$ and $y = y(t)$. Then

$$\frac{dz}{dt} = \frac{\partial z}{\partial x} \frac{dx}{dt} + \frac{\partial z}{\partial y} \frac{dy}{dt}$$

Use the partial derivative symbols and the ordinary derivative symbols appropriately.

Here we use the symbol dz/dt rather than $\partial z/\partial t$, since z can be considered a function of *one* variable t. Likewise, the symbols dx/dt and dy/dt are used rather than $\partial x/\partial t$ and $\partial y/\partial t$. As is typical, the number of terms that compose dz/dt equals the number of intermediate variables of z. Other situations would be treated in a similar way.

EXAMPLE 2   **Chain Rule**

a. If $w = f(x, y, z) = 3x^2y + xyz - 4y^2z^3$, where

$$x = 2r - 3s \quad y = 6r + s \quad z = r - s$$

determine $\partial w/\partial r$ and $\partial w/\partial s$.

Solution: Since x, y, and z are functions of r and s, then, by the chain rule,

$$\frac{\partial w}{\partial r} = \frac{\partial w}{\partial x}\frac{\partial x}{\partial r} + \frac{\partial w}{\partial y}\frac{\partial y}{\partial r} + \frac{\partial w}{\partial z}\frac{\partial z}{\partial r}$$

$$= (6xy + yz)(2) + (3x^2 + xz - 8yz^3)(6) + (xy - 12y^2z^2)(1)$$

$$= x(18x + 13y + 6z) + 2yz(1 - 24z^2 - 6yz)$$

Also,

$$\frac{\partial w}{\partial s} = \frac{\partial w}{\partial x}\frac{\partial x}{\partial s} + \frac{\partial w}{\partial y}\frac{\partial y}{\partial s} + \frac{\partial w}{\partial z}\frac{\partial z}{\partial s}$$

$$= (6xy + yz)(-3) + (3x^2 + xz - 8yz^3)(1) + (xy - 12y^2z^2)(-1)$$

$$= x(3x - 19y + z) - yz(3 + 8z^2 - 12yz)$$

b. If $z = \dfrac{x + e^y}{y}$, where $x = rs + se^{rt}$ and $y = 9 + rt$, evaluate $\partial z/\partial s$ when $r = -2$, $s = 5$, and $t = 4$.

Solution: Since x and y are functions of r, s, and t (note that we can write $y = 9 + rt + 0 \cdot s$), by the chain rule,

$$\frac{\partial z}{\partial s} = \frac{\partial z}{\partial x}\frac{\partial x}{\partial s} + \frac{\partial z}{\partial y}\frac{\partial y}{\partial s}$$

$$= \left(\frac{1}{y}\right)(r + e^{rt}) + \frac{\partial z}{\partial y} \cdot (0) = \frac{r + e^{rt}}{y}$$

If $r = -2$, $s = 5$, and $t = 4$, then $y = 1$. Thus,

$$\left.\frac{\partial z}{\partial s}\right|_{\substack{r=-2 \\ s=5 \\ t=4}} = \frac{-2 + e^{-8}}{1} = -2 + e^{-8}$$

Now Work Problem 13 ◁

EXAMPLE 3   **Chain Rule**

a. Determine $\partial y/\partial r$ if $y = x^2 \ln(x^4 + 6)$ and $x = (r + 3s)^6$.

Solution: By the chain rule,

$$\frac{\partial y}{\partial r} = \frac{dy}{dx}\frac{\partial x}{\partial r}$$

$$= \left[x^2 \cdot \frac{4x^3}{x^4 + 6} + 2x \cdot \ln(x^4 + 6)\right][6(r + 3s)^5]$$

$$= 12x(r + 3s)^5\left[\frac{2x^4}{x^4 + 6} + \ln(x^4 + 6)\right]$$

b. Given that $z = e^{xy}, x = r - 4s$, and $y = r - s$, find $\partial z/\partial r$ in terms of r and s.

Solution:

$$\frac{\partial z}{\partial r} = \frac{\partial z}{\partial x}\frac{\partial x}{\partial r} + \frac{\partial z}{\partial y}\frac{\partial y}{\partial r}$$

$$= (ye^{xy})(1) + (xe^{xy})(1)$$

$$= (x + y)e^{xy}$$

Since $x = r - 4s$ and $y = r - s$,

$$\frac{\partial z}{\partial r} = [(r - 4s) + (r - s)]e^{(r-4s)(r-s)}$$

$$= (2r - 5s)e^{r^2 - 5rs + 4s^2}$$

Now Work Problem 15 ◁

PROBLEMS 17.5

In Problems 1–12, find the indicated derivatives by using the chain rule.

1. $z = 5x + 3y, x = 2r + 3s, y = r - 2s$; $\partial z/\partial r, \partial z/\partial s$

2. $z = 2x^2 + 3xy + 2y^2, x = r^2 - s^2, y = r^2 + s^2$; $\partial z/\partial r, \partial z/\partial s$

3. $z = e^{x+y}, x = t^2 + 3, y = \sqrt{t^3}$; dz/dt

4. $z = \sqrt{8x + y}, x = t^2 + 3t + 4, y = t^3 + 4$; dz/dt

5. $w = x^2yz + xy^2z + xyz^2, x = e^t, y = te^t, z = t^2e^t$; dw/dt

6. $w = \ln(x^2 + y^2 + z^2), x = 2 - 3t, y = t^2 + 3, z = 4 - t$; dw/dt

7. $z = (x^2 + xy^2)^3, x = r + s + t, y = 2r - 3s + 8t$; $\partial z/\partial t$

8. $z = \sqrt{x^2 + y^2}, x = r^2 + s - t, y = r - s + t$; $\partial z/\partial r$

9. $w = x^2 + xyz + z^2, x = r^2 - s^2, y = rs, z = r^2 + s^2$; $\partial w/\partial s$

10. $w = \ln(xyz), x = r^2s, y = rs, z = rs^2$; $\partial w/\partial r$

11. $y = x^2 - 7x + 5, x = 19rs + 2s^2t^2$; $\partial y/\partial r$

12. $y = 4 - x^2, x = 2r + 3s - 4t$; $\partial y/\partial t$

13. If $z = (4x + 3y)^3$, where $x = r^2s$ and $y = r - 2s$, evaluate $\partial z/\partial r$ when $r = 0$ and $s = 1$.

14. If $z = \sqrt{2x + 3y}$, where $x = 3t + 5$ and $y = t^2 + 2t + 1$, evaluate dz/dt when $t = 1$.

15. If $w = e^{x+y+z}(x^2 + y^2 + z^2)$, where $x = (r - s)^2, y = (r + s)^2$, and $z = (s - r)^2$, evaluate $\partial w/\partial s$ when $r = 1$ and $s = 1$.

16. If $y = x/(x - 5)$, where $x = 2t^2 - 3rs - r^2t$, evaluate $\partial y/\partial t$ when $r = 0, s = 2$, and $t = -1$.

17. **Cost Function** Suppose the cost c of producing q_A units of product A and q_B units of product B is given by

$$c = (3q_A^2 + q_B^3 + 4)^{1/3}$$

and the coupled demand functions for the products are given by

$$q_A = 10 - p_A + p_B^2$$

and

$$q_B = 20 + p_A - 11p_B$$

Use a chain rule to evaluate $\dfrac{\partial c}{\partial p_A}$ and $\dfrac{\partial c}{\partial p_B}$ when $p_A = 25$ and $p_B = 4$.

18. Suppose $w = f(x, y)$, where $x = g(t)$ and $y = h(t)$.
(a) State a chain rule that gives dw/dt.
(b) Suppose $h(t) = t$, so that $w = f(x, t)$, where $x = g(t)$. Use part (a) to find dw/dt and simplify your answer.

19. (a) Suppose w is a function of x and y, where both x and y are functions of s and t. State a chain rule that expresses $\partial w/\partial t$ in terms of derivatives of these functions.
(b) Let $w = 2x^2 \ln|3x - 5y|$, where $x = s\sqrt{t^2 + 2}$ and $y = t - 3e^{2-s}$. Use part (a) to evaluate $\partial w/\partial t$ when $s = 1$ and $t = 0$.

20. **Production Function** In considering a production function $P = f(l, k)$, where l is labor input and k is capital input, Fon, Boulier, and Goldfarb[19] assume that $l = Lg(h)$, where L is the number of workers, h is the number of hours per day per worker, and $g(h)$ is a labor effectiveness function. In maximizing profit p given by

$$p = aP - whL$$

where a is the price per unit of output and w is the hourly wage per worker, Fon, Boulier, and Goldfarb determine $\partial p/\partial L$ and $\partial p/\partial h$. Assume that k is independent of L and h, and determine these partial derivatives.

Objective

To discuss relative maxima and relative minima, to find critical points, and to apply the second-derivative test for a function of two variables.

17.6 Maxima and Minima for Functions of Two Variables

We now extend the notion of relative maxima and minima (or relative extrema) to functions of two variables.

---

[19]V. Fon, B. L. Boulier, and R. S. Goldfarb, "The Firm's Demand for Daily Hours of Work: Some Implications," *Atlantic Economic Journal*, XIII, no. 1 (1985), 36–42.

A function $z = f(x, y)$ is said to have a ***relative maximum*** at the point (a, b) if, for all points (x, y) in the plane that are sufficiently close to (a, b), we have

$$f(a, b) \geq f(x, y) \qquad (1)$$

For a ***relative minimum***, we replace $\geq$ by $\leq$ in Equation (1).

To say that $z = f(x, y)$ has a relative maximum at (a, b) means, geometrically, that the point $(a, b, f(a, b))$ on the graph of f is higher than (or is as high as) all other points on the surface that are "near" $(a, b, f(a, b))$. In Figure 17.4(a), f has a relative maximum at (a, b). Similarly, the function f in Figure 17.4(b) has a relative minimum when $x = y = 0$, which corresponds to a *low* point on the surface.

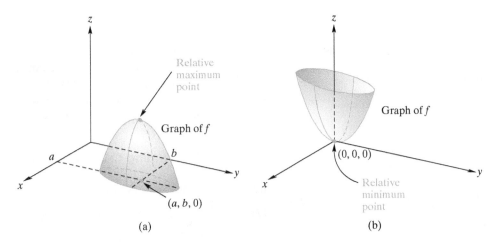

FIGURE 17.4   Relative extrema.

Recall that in locating extrema for a function $y = f(x)$ of one variable, we examine those values of x in the domain of f for which $f'(x) = 0$ or $f'(x)$ does not exist. For functions of two (or more) variables, a similar procedure is followed. However, for the functions that concern us, extrema will not occur where a derivative does not exist, and such situations will be excluded from our consideration.

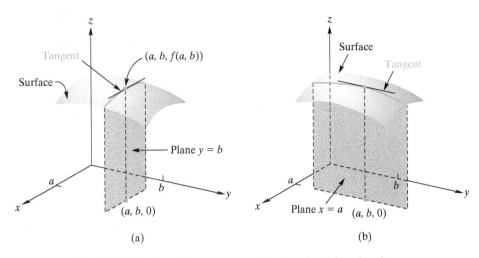

FIGURE 17.5   At relative extremum, $f_x(x, y) = 0$ and $f_y(x, y) = 0$.

Suppose $z = f(x, y)$ has a relative maximum at (a, b), as indicated in Figure 17.5(a). Then the curve where the plane $y = b$ intersects the surface must have a relative maximum when $x = a$. Hence, the slope of the tangent line to the surface in the x-direction must be 0 at (a, b). Equivalently, $f_x(x, y) = 0$ at (a, b). Similarly, on the curve where the plane $x = a$ intersects the surface [Figure 17.5(b)], there must be a relative maximum when $y = b$. Thus, in the y-direction, the slope of the tangent to the surface must be 0 at (a, b). Equivalently, $f_y(x, y) = 0$ at (a, b). Since a similar discussion applies to a relative minimum, we can combine these results as follows:

Rule 1

If $z = f(x, y)$ has a relative maximum or minimum at (a, b), and if both f_x and f_y are defined for all points close to (a, b), it is necessary that (a, b) be a solution of the system

$$\begin{cases} f_x(x, y) = 0 \\ f_y(x, y) = 0 \end{cases}$$

 CAUTION!

Rule 1 does not imply that there must be an extremum at a critical point. Just as in the case of functions of one variable, a critical point can give rise to a relative maximum, a relative minimum, or neither. A critical point is only a *candidate* for a relative extremum.

A point (a, b) for which $f_x(a, b) = f_y(a, b) = 0$ is called a **critical point** of f. Thus, from Rule 1, we infer that, to locate relative extrema for a function, we should examine its critical points.

Two additional comments are in order: First, Rule 1, as well as the notion of a critical point, can be extended to functions of more than two variables. For example, to locate possible extrema for $w = f(x, y, z)$, we would examine those points for which $w_x = w_y = w_z = 0$. Second, for a function whose domain is restricted, a thorough examination for absolute extrema would include a consideration of boundary points.

EXAMPLE 1 Finding Critical Points

Find the critical points of the following functions.

a. $f(x, y) = 2x^2 + y^2 - 2xy + 5x - 3y + 1$.

Solution: Since $f_x(x, y) = 4x - 2y + 5$ and $f_y(x, y) = 2y - 2x - 3$, we solve the system

$$\begin{cases} 4x - 2y + 5 = 0 \\ -2x + 2y - 3 = 0 \end{cases}$$

This gives $x = -1$ and $y = \frac{1}{2}$. Thus, $\left(-1, \frac{1}{2}\right)$ is the only critical point.

b. $f(l, k) = l^3 + k^3 - lk$.

Solution:
$$\begin{cases} f_l(l, k) = 3l^2 - k = 0 & (2) \\ f_k(l, k) = 3k^2 - l = 0 & (3) \end{cases}$$

From Equation (2), $k = 3l^2$. Substituting for k in Equation (3) gives

$$0 = 27l^4 - l = l(27l^3 - 1)$$

Hence, either $l = 0$ or $l = \frac{1}{3}$. If $l = 0$, then $k = 0$; if $l = \frac{1}{3}$, then $k = \frac{1}{3}$. The critical points are therefore $(0, 0)$ and $\left(\frac{1}{3}, \frac{1}{3}\right)$.

c. $f(x, y, z) = 2x^2 + xy + y^2 + 100 - z(x + y - 100)$.

Solution: Solving the system

$$\begin{cases} f_x(x, y, z) = 4x + y - z = 0 \\ f_y(x, y, z) = x + 2y - z = 0 \\ f_z(x, y, z) = -x - y + 100 = 0 \end{cases}$$

gives the critical point $(25, 75, 175)$, as the reader should verify.

Now Work Problem 1 ◁

EXAMPLE 2 Finding Critical Points

Find the critical points of

$$f(x, y) = x^2 - 4x + 2y^2 + 4y + 7$$

Solution: We have $f_x(x, y) = 2x - 4$ and $f_y(x, y) = 4y + 4$. The system

$$\begin{cases} 2x - 4 = 0 \\ 4y + 4 = 0 \end{cases}$$

gives the critical point $(2, -1)$. Observe that we can write the given function as

$$f(x, y) = x^2 - 4x + 4 + 2(y^2 + 2y + 1) + 1$$
$$= (x - 2)^2 + 2(y + 1)^2 + 1$$

and $f(2, -1) = 1$. Clearly, if $(x, y) \neq (2, -1)$, then $f(x, y) > 1$. Hence, a relative minimum occurs at $(2, -1)$. Moreover, there is an *absolute minimum* at $(2, -1)$, since $f(x, y) > f(2, -1)$ for *all* $(x, y) \neq (2, -1)$.

Now Work Problem 3 ◁

Although in Example 2 we were able to show that the critical point gave rise to a relative extremum, in many cases this is not so easy to do. There is, however, a second-derivative test that gives conditions under which a critical point will be a relative maximum or minimum. We state it now, omitting the proof.

Rule 2   Second-Derivative Test for Functions of Two Variables

Suppose $z = f(x, y)$ has continuous partial derivatives $f_{xx}, f_{yy},$ and f_{xy} at all points (x, y) near a critical point (a, b). Let D be the function defined by

$$D(x, y) = f_{xx}(x, y)f_{yy}(x, y) - (f_{xy}(x, y))^2$$

Then

1. if $D(a, b) > 0$ and $f_{xx}(a, b) < 0$, then f has a relative maximum at (a, b);
2. if $D(a, b) > 0$ and $f_{xx}(a, b) > 0$, then f has a relative minimum at (a, b);
3. if $D(a, b) < 0$, then f has a *saddle point* at (a, b) (see Example 4);
4. if $D(a, b) = 0$, then no conclusion about an extremum at (a, b) can be drawn, and further analysis is required.

We remark that when $D(a, b) > 0$, the sign of $f_{xx}(a, b)$ is necessarily the same as the sign of $f_{yy}(a, b)$. Thus, when $D(a, b) > 0$ we can test either $f_{xx}(a, b)$ or $f_{yy}(a, b)$, whichever is easiest, to make the determination required in parts 1 and 2 of the second derivative test.

EXAMPLE 3   Applying the Second-Derivative Test

Examine $f(x, y) = x^3 + y^3 - xy$ for relative maxima or minima by using the second-derivative test.

Solution: First we find critical points:

$$f_x(x, y) = 3x^2 - y \quad f_y(x, y) = 3y^2 - x$$

In the same manner as in Example 1(b), solving $f_x(x, y) = f_y(x, y) = 0$ gives the critical points $(0, 0)$ and $\left(\frac{1}{3}, \frac{1}{3}\right)$. Now,

$$f_{xx}(x, y) = 6x \qquad f_{yy}(x, y) = 6y \qquad f_{xy}(x, y) = -1$$

Thus,

$$D(x, y) = (6x)(6y) - (-1)^2 = 36xy - 1$$

Since $D(0, 0) = 36(0)(0) - 1 = -1 < 0$, there is no relative extremum at $(0, 0)$. Also, since $D\left(\frac{1}{3}, \frac{1}{3}\right) = 36\left(\frac{1}{3}\right)\left(\frac{1}{3}\right) - 1 = 3 > 0$ and $f_{xx}\left(\frac{1}{3}, \frac{1}{3}\right) = 6\left(\frac{1}{3}\right) = 2 > 0$, there is a relative minimum at $\left(\frac{1}{3}, \frac{1}{3}\right)$. At this point, the value of the function is

$$f\left(\tfrac{1}{3}, \tfrac{1}{3}\right) = \left(\tfrac{1}{3}\right)^3 + \left(\tfrac{1}{3}\right)^3 - \left(\tfrac{1}{3}\right)\left(\tfrac{1}{3}\right) = -\tfrac{1}{27}$$

Now Work Problem 7 ◁

EXAMPLE 4   A Saddle Point

Examine $f(x, y) = y^2 - x^2$ for relative extrema.

Solution: Solving

$$f_x(x, y) = -2x = 0 \quad \text{and} \quad f_y(x, y) = 2y = 0$$

we get the critical point $(0, 0)$. Now we apply the second-derivative test. At $(0, 0)$, and indeed at any point,

$$f_{xx}(x, y) = -2 \quad f_{yy}(x, y) = 2 \quad f_{xy}(x, y) = 0$$

The surface in Figure 17.6 is called a hyperbolic paraboloid.

Because $D(0, 0) = (-2)(2) - (0)^2 = -4 < 0$, no relative extremum exists at $(0, 0)$. A sketch of $z = f(x, y) = y^2 - x^2$ appears in Figure 17.6. Note that, for the surface curve cut by the plane $y = 0$, there is a *maximum* at $(0, 0)$; but for the surface curve cut by the plane $x = 0$, there is a *minimum* at $(0, 0)$. Thus, on the *surface*, no relative extremum can exist at the origin, although $(0, 0)$ is a critical point. Around the origin the curve is saddle shaped, and $(0, 0)$ is called a *saddle point* of f.

Now Work Problem 11 ◁

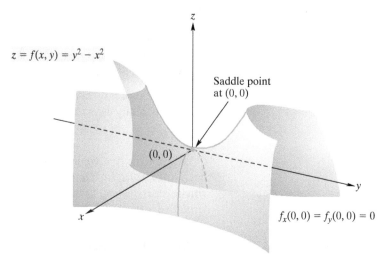

$z = f(x, y) = y^2 - x^2$

Saddle point
at $(0, 0)$

$(0, 0)$

$f_x(0, 0) = f_y(0, 0) = 0$

FIGURE 17.6   Saddle point.

EXAMPLE 5   Finding Relative Extrema

Examine $f(x, y) = x^4 + (x - y)^4$ for relative extrema.

Solution: If we set

$$f_x(x, y) = 4x^3 + 4(x - y)^3 = 0 \tag{4}$$

and

$$f_y(x, y) = -4(x - y)^3 = 0 \tag{5}$$

then, from Equation (5), we have $x - y = 0$, or $x = y$. Substituting into Equation (4) gives $4x^3 = 0$, or $x = 0$. Thus, $x = y = 0$, and $(0, 0)$ is the only critical point. At $(0, 0)$,

$$f_{xx}(x, y) = 12x^2 + 12(x - y)^2 = 0$$
$$f_{yy}(x, y) = 12(x - y)^2 = 0$$

and

$$f_{xy}(x, y) = -12(x - y)^2 = 0$$

Hence, $D(0, 0) = 0$, and the second-derivative test gives no information. However, for all $(x, y) \neq (0, 0)$, we have $f(x, y) > 0$, whereas $f(0, 0) = 0$. Therefore, at $(0, 0)$ the graph of f has a low point, and we conclude that f has a relative (and absolute) minimum at $(0, 0)$.

Now Work Problem 13 ◁

Applications

In many situations involving functions of two variables, and especially in their applications, the nature of the given problem is an indicator of whether a critical point is in fact a relative (or absolute) maximum or a relative (or absolute) minimum. In such cases, the second-derivative test is not needed. Often, in mathematical studies of applied problems, the appropriate second-order conditions are assumed to hold.

EXAMPLE 6   Maximizing Output

Let P be a production function given by

$$P = f(l, k) = 0.54l^2 - 0.02l^3 + 1.89k^2 - 0.09k^3$$

where l and k are the amounts of labor and capital, respectively, and P is the quantity of output produced. Find the values of l and k that maximize P.

Solution: To find the critical points, we solve the system $P_l = 0$ and $P_k = 0$:

$$P_l = 1.08l - 0.06l^2 \qquad P_k = 3.78k - 0.27k^2$$
$$= 0.06l(18 - l) = 0 \qquad = 0.27k(14 - k) = 0$$
$$l = 0, l = 18 \qquad k = 0, k = 14$$

There are four critical points: $(0, 0)$, $(0, 14)$, $(18, 0)$, and $(18, 14)$.

Now we apply the second-derivative test to each critical point. We have

$$P_{ll} = 1.08 - 0.12l \quad P_{kk} = 3.78 - 0.54k \quad P_{lk} = 0$$

Thus,

$$D(l, k) = P_{ll}P_{kk} - [P_{lk}]^2$$
$$= (1.08 - 0.12l)(3.78 - 0.54k)$$

At $(0, 0)$,

$$D(0, 0) = 1.08(3.78) > 0$$

Since $D(0, 0) > 0$ and $P_{ll} = 1.08 > 0$, there is a relative minimum at $(0, 0)$. At $(0, 14)$,

$$D(0, 14) = 1.08(-3.78) < 0$$

Because $D(0, 14) < 0$, there is no relative extremum at $(0, 14)$. At $(18, 0)$,

$$D(18, 0) = (-1.08)(3.78) < 0$$

Since $D(18, 0) < 0$, there is no relative extremum at $(18, 0)$. At $(18, 14)$,

$$D(18, 14) = (-1.08)(-3.78) > 0$$

Because $D(18, 14) > 0$ and $P_{ll} = -1.08 < 0$, there is a relative maximum at $(18, 14)$. Hence, the maximum output is obtained when $l = 18$ and $k = 14$.

Now Work Problem 21 ◁

EXAMPLE 7   Profit Maximization

A candy company produces two types of candy, A and B, for which the average costs of production are constant at $2 and $3 per pound, respectively. The quantities q_A, q_B (in pounds) of A and B that can be sold each week are given by the joint-demand functions

$$q_A = 400(p_B - p_A)$$

and

$$q_B = 400(9 + p_A - 2p_B)$$

where p_A and p_B are the selling prices (in dollars per pound) of A and B, respectively. Determine the selling prices that will maximize the company's profit P.

Solution: The total profit is given by

$$P = \left(\begin{array}{c} \text{profit} \\ \text{per pound} \\ \text{of A} \end{array} \right) \left(\begin{array}{c} \text{pounds} \\ \text{of A} \\ \text{sold} \end{array} \right) + \left(\begin{array}{c} \text{profit} \\ \text{per pound} \\ \text{of B} \end{array} \right) \left(\begin{array}{c} \text{pounds} \\ \text{of B} \\ \text{sold} \end{array} \right)$$

For A and B, the profits per pound are $p_A - 2$ and $p_B - 3$, respectively. Thus,

$$P = (p_A - 2)q_A + (p_B - 3)q_B$$
$$= (p_A - 2)[400(p_B - p_A)] + (p_B - 3)[400(9 + p_A - 2p_B)]$$

Notice that P is expressed as a function of two variables, p_A and p_B. To maximize P, we set its partial derivatives equal to 0:

$$\frac{\partial P}{\partial p_A} = (p_A - 2)[400(-1)] + [400(p_B - p_A)](1) + (p_B - 3)[400(1)]$$
$$= 0$$
$$\frac{\partial P}{\partial p_B} = (p_A - 2)[400(1)] + (p_B - 3)[400(-2)] + 400(9 + p_A - 2p_B)](1)$$
$$= 0$$

Simplifying the preceding two equations gives

$$\begin{cases} -2p_A + 2p_B - 1 = 0 \\ 2p_A - 4p_B + 13 = 0 \end{cases}$$

whose solution is $p_A = 5.5$ and $p_B = 6$. Moreover, we find that

$$\frac{\partial^2 P}{\partial p_A^2} = -800 \quad \frac{\partial^2 P}{\partial p_B^2} = -1600 \quad \frac{\partial^2 P}{\partial p_B \partial p_A} = 800$$

Therefore,

$$D(5.5, 6) = (-800)(-1600) - (800)^2 > 0$$

Since $\partial^2 P / \partial p_A^2 < 0$, we indeed have a maximum, and the company should sell candy A at $5.50 per pound and B at $6.00 per pound.

Now Work Problem 23 ◁

EXAMPLE 8   Profit Maximization for a Monopolist[20]

Suppose a monopolist is practicing price discrimination by selling the same product in two separate markets at different prices. Let q_A be the number of units sold in market

---

[20] Omit if Section 17.5 was not covered.

A, where the demand function is $p_A = f(q_A)$, and let q_B be the number of units sold in market B, where the demand function is $p_B = g(q_B)$. Then the revenue functions for the two markets are

$$r_A = q_A f(q_A) \quad \text{and} \quad r_B = q_B g(q_B)$$

Assume that all units are produced at one plant, and let the cost function for producing $q = q_A + q_B$ units be $c = c(q)$. Keep in mind that r_A is a function of q_A and r_B is a function of q_B. The monopolist's profit P is

$$P = r_A + r_B - c$$

To maximize P with respect to outputs q_A and q_B, we set its partial derivatives equal to zero. To begin with,

$$\frac{\partial P}{\partial q_A} = \frac{dr_A}{dq_A} + 0 - \frac{\partial c}{\partial q_A}$$

$$= \frac{dr_A}{dq_A} - \frac{dc}{dq}\frac{\partial q}{\partial q_A} = 0 \qquad \text{chain rule}$$

Because

$$\frac{\partial q}{\partial q_A} = \frac{\partial}{\partial q_A}(q_A + q_B) = 1$$

we have

$$\frac{\partial P}{\partial q_A} = \frac{dr_A}{dq_A} - \frac{dc}{dq} = 0 \qquad (6)$$

Similarly,

$$\frac{\partial P}{\partial q_B} = \frac{dr_B}{dq_B} - \frac{dc}{dq} = 0 \qquad (7)$$

From Equations (6) and (7), we get

$$\frac{dr_A}{dq_A} = \frac{dc}{dq} = \frac{dr_B}{dq_B}$$

But dr_A/dq_A and dr_B/dq_B are marginal revenues, and dc/dq is marginal cost. Hence, to maximize profit, it is necessary to charge prices (and distribute output) so that the marginal revenues in both markets will be the same and, loosely speaking, will also be equal to the cost of the last unit produced in the plant.

Now Work Problem 25 ◁

PROBLEMS 17.6

In Problems 1–6, find the critical points of the functions.

1. $f(x, y) = x^2 - 3y^2 - 8x + 9y + 3xy$

2. $f(x, y) = x^2 + 4y^2 - 6x + 16y$

3. $f(x, y) = \frac{5}{3}x^3 + \frac{2}{3}y^3 - \frac{15}{2}x^2 + y^2 - 4y + 7$

4. $f(x, y) = xy - x + y$

5. $f(x, y, z) = 2x^2 + xy + y^2 + 100 - z(x + y - 200)$

6. $f(x, y, z, w) = x^2 + y^2 + z^2 + w(x + y + z - 3)$

In Problems 7–20, find the critical points of the functions. For each critical point, determine, by the second-derivative test, whether it corresponds to a relative maximum, to a relative minimum, or to neither, or whether the test gives no information.

7. $f(x, y) = x^2 + 3y^2 + 4x - 9y + 3$

8. $f(x, y) = -2x^2 + 8x - 3y^2 + 24y + 7$

9. $f(x, y) = y - y^2 - 3x - 6x^2$

10. $f(x, y) = 2x^2 + \frac{3}{2}y^2 + 3xy - 10x - 9y + 2$

11. $f(x, y) = x^2 + 3xy + y^2 - 9x - 11y + 3$

12. $f(x, y) = \frac{x^3}{3} + y^2 - 2x + 2y - 2xy$

13. $f(x, y) = \frac{1}{3}(x^3 + 8y^3) - 2(x^2 + y^2) + 1$

14. $f(x, y) = x^2 + y^2 - xy + x^3$

15. $f(l, k) = \frac{l^2}{2} + 2lk + 3k^2 - 69l - 164k + 17$

16. $f(l, k) = l^2 + 4k^2 - 4lk$ 17. $f(p, q) = pq - \frac{1}{p} - \frac{1}{q}$

18. $f(x, y) = (x - 3)(y - 3)(x + y - 3)$

19. $f(x, y) = (y^2 - 4)(e^x - 1)$

20. $f(x, y) = \ln(xy) + 2x^2 - xy - 6x$

21. Maximizing Output Suppose

$$P = f(l, k) = 2.18l^2 - 0.02l^3 + 1.97k^2 - 0.03k^3$$

is a production function for a firm. Find the quantities of inputs l and k that maximize output P.

22. Maximizing Output In a certain office, computers C and D are utilized for c and d hours, respectively. If daily output Q is a function of c and d, namely,

$$Q = 18c + 20d - 2c^2 - 4d^2 - cd$$

find the values of c and d that maximize Q.

In Problems 23–35, unless otherwise indicated, the variables p_A and p_B denote selling prices of products A and B, respectively. Similarly, q_A and q_B denote quantities of A and B that are produced and sold during some time period. In all cases, the variables employed will be assumed to be units of output, input, money, and so on.

23. Profit A candy company produces two varieties of candy, A and B, for which the constant average costs of production are 60 and 70 (cents per lb), respectively. The demand functions for A and B are given by

$$q_A = 5(p_B - p_A) \quad \text{and} \quad q_B = 500 + 5(p_A - 2p_B)$$

Find the selling prices p_A and p_B that maximize the company's profit.

24. Profit Repeat Problem 23 if the constant costs of production of A and B are a and b (cents per lb), respectively.

25. Price Discrimination Suppose a monopolist is practicing price discrimination in the sale of a product by charging different prices in two separate markets. In market A the demand function is

$$p_A = 100 - q_A$$

and in B it is

$$p_B = 84 - q_B$$

where q_A and q_B are the quantities sold per week in A and B, and p_A and p_B are the respective prices per unit. If the monopolist's cost function is

$$c = 600 + 4(q_A + q_B)$$

how much should be sold in each market to maximize profit? What selling prices give this maximum profit? Find the maximum profit.

26. Profit A monopolist sells two competitive products, A and B, for which the demand functions are

$$q_A = 16 - p_A + p_B \quad \text{and} \quad q_B = 24 + 2p_A - 4p_B$$

If the constant average cost of producing a unit of A is 2 and a unit of B is 4, how many units of A and B should be sold to maximize the monopolist's profit?

27. Profit For products A and B, the joint-cost function for a manufacturer is

$$c = \frac{3}{2}q_A^2 + 3q_B^2$$

and the demand functions are $p_A = 60 - q_A^2$ and $p_B = 72 - 2q_B^2$. Find the level of production that maximizes profit.

28. Profit For a monopolist's products A and B, the joint-cost function is $c = 2(q_A + q_B + q_A q_B)$, and the demand functions are $q_A = 20 - 2p_A$ and $q_B = 10 - p_B$. Find the values of p_A and p_B

that maximize profit. What are the quantities of A and B that correspond to these prices? What is the total profit?

29. Cost An open-top rectangular box is to have a volume of 6 ft³. The cost per square foot of materials is \$3 for the bottom, \$1 for the front and back, and \$0.50 for the other two sides. Find the dimensions of the box so that the cost of materials is minimized. (See Figure 17.7.)

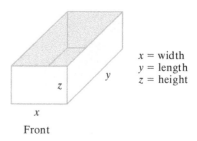

x = width
y = length
z = height

Front

FIGURE 17.7

30. Collusion Suppose A and B are the only two firms in the market selling the same product. (We say that they are *duopolists.*) The industry demand function for the product is

$$p = 92 - q_A - q_B$$

where q_A and q_B denote the output produced and sold by A and B, respectively. For A, the cost function is $c_A = 10q_A$; for B, it is $c_B = 0.5q_B^2$. Suppose the firms decide to enter into an agreement on output and price control by jointly acting as a monopoly. In this case, we say they enter into *collusion*. Show that the profit function for the monopoly is given by

$$P = pq_A - c_A + pq_B - c_B$$

Express P as a function of q_A and q_B, and determine how output should be allocated so as to maximize the profit of the monopoly.

31. Suppose $f(x, y) = x^2 + 3y^2 + 9$, where x and y must satisfy the equation $x + y = 2$. Find the relative extrema of f, subject to the given condition on x and y, by first solving the second equation for y (or x). Substitute the result in the first equation. Thus, f is expressed as a function of one variable. Now find where relative extrema for f occur.

32. Repeat Problem 31 if $f(x, y) = x^2 + 4y^2 + 6$, subject to the condition that $2x - 8y = 20$.

33. Suppose the joint-cost function

$$c = q_A^2 + 3q_B^2 + 2q_A q_B + aq_A + bq_B + d$$

has a relative minimum value of 15 when $q_A = 3$ and $q_B = 1$. Determine the values of the constants a, b, and d.

34. Suppose that the function $f(x, y)$ has continuous partial derivatives f_{xx}, f_{yy}, and f_{xy} at all points (x, y) near a critical point (a, b). Let $D(x, y) = f_{xx}(x, y)f_{yy}(x, y) - (f_{xy}(x, y))^2$ and suppose that $D(a, b) > 0$.

(a) Show that $f_{xx}(a, b) < 0$ if and only if $f_{yy}(a, b) < 0$.
(b) Show that $f_{xx}(a, b) > 0$ if and only if $f_{yy}(a, b) > 0$.

35. Profit from Competitive Products A monopolist sells two competitive products, A and B, for which the demand equations are

$$p_A = 35 - 2q_A^2 + q_B$$

and

$$p_B = 20 - q_B + q_A$$

The joint-cost function is

$$c = -8 - 2q_A^3 + 3q_A q_B + 30q_A + 12q_B + \frac{1}{2}q_A^2$$

(a) How many units of A and B should be sold to obtain a relative maximum profit for the monopolist? Use the second-derivative test to justify your answer.
(b) Determine the selling prices required to realize the relative maximum profit. Also, find this relative maximum profit.

36. Profit and Advertising   A retailer has determined that the number of TV sets he can sell per week is

$$\frac{7x}{2+x} + \frac{4y}{5+y}$$

where x and y represent his weekly expenditures (in dollars) on newspaper and radio advertising, respectively. The profit is $300 per sale, less the cost of advertising, so the weekly profit is given by the formula

$$P = 300\left(\frac{7x}{2+x} + \frac{4y}{5+y}\right) - x - y$$

Find the values of x and y for which the profit is a relative maximum. Use the second-derivative test to verify that your answer corresponds to a relative maximum profit.

37. Profit from Tomato Crop   The revenue (in dollars per square meter of ground) obtained from the sale of a crop of tomatoes grown in an artificially heated greenhouse is given by

$$r = 5T(1 - e^{-x})$$

where T is the temperature (in °C) maintained in the greenhouse and x is the amount of fertilizer applied per square meter. The cost of fertilizer is $20x$ dollars per square meter, and the cost of heating is given by $0.1T^2$ dollars per square meter.

(a) Find an expression, in terms of T and x, for the profit per square meter obtained from the sale of the crop of tomatoes.
(b) Verify that the pairs

$$(T,x) = (20, \ln 5) \quad \text{and} \quad (T,x) = (5, \ln \tfrac{5}{4})$$

are critical points of the profit function in part (a). (*Note:* You need not derive the pairs.)
(c) The points in part (b) are the only critical points of the profit function in part (a). Use the second-derivative test to determine whether either of these points corresponds to a relative maximum profit per square meter.

17.7 Lagrange Multipliers

We will now find relative maxima and minima for a function on which certain *constraints* are imposed. Such a situation could arise if a manufacturer wished to minimize a joint-cost function and yet obtain a particular production level.

Suppose we want to find the relative extrema of

$$w = x^2 + y^2 + z^2 \tag{1}$$

subject to the constraint that x, y, and z must satisfy

$$x - y + 2z = 6 \tag{2}$$

We can transform w, which is a function of three variables, into a function of two variables such that the new function reflects constraint (2). Solving Equation (2) for x, we get

$$x = y - 2z + 6 \tag{3}$$

which, when substituted for x in Equation (1), gives

$$w = (y - 2z + 6)^2 + y^2 + z^2 \tag{4}$$

Since w is now expressed as a function of two variables, to find relative extrema we follow the usual procedure of setting the partial derivatives of w equal to 0:

$$\frac{\partial w}{\partial y} = 2(y - 2z + 6) + 2y = 4y - 4z + 12 = 0 \tag{5}$$

$$\frac{\partial w}{\partial z} = -4(y - 2z + 6) + 2z = -4y + 10z - 24 = 0 \tag{6}$$

Solving Equations (5) and (6) simultaneously gives $y = -1$ and $z = 2$. Substituting into Equation (3), we get $x = 1$. Hence, the only critical point of Equation (1) subject to the constraint represented by Equation (2) is $(1, -1, 2)$. By using the second-derivative test on Equation (4) when $y = -1$ and $z = 2$, we have

$$\frac{\partial^2 w}{\partial y^2} = 4 \quad \frac{\partial^2 w}{\partial z^2} = 10 \quad \frac{\partial^2 w}{\partial z\,\partial y} = -4$$

$$D(-1, 2) = 4(10) - (-4)^2 = 24 > 0$$

Thus w, subject to the constraint, has a relative minimum at $(1, -1, 2)$.

This solution was found by using the constraint to express one of the variables in the original function in terms of the other variables. Often this is not practical, but there is another technique, called the method of **Lagrange multipliers,**[21] that avoids this step and yet allows us to obtain critical points.

The method is as follows. Suppose we have a function $f(x, y, z)$ subject to the constraint $g(x, y, z) = 0$. We construct a new function F of *four* variables defined by the following (where λ is a Greek letter read "lambda"):

$$F(x, y, z, \lambda) = f(x, y, z) - \lambda g(x, y, z)$$

It can be shown that if (a, b, c) is a critical point of f, subject to the constraint $g(x, y, z) = 0$, there exists a value of λ, say, λ_0, such that (a, b, c, λ_0) is a critical point of F. The number λ_0 is called a **Lagrange multiplier.** Also, if (a, b, c, λ_0) is a critical point of F, then (a, b, c) is a critical point of f, subject to the constraint. Thus, to find critical points of f, subject to $g(x, y, z) = 0$, we instead find critical points of F. These are obtained by solving the simultaneous equations

$$\begin{cases} F_x(x, y, z, \lambda) = 0 \\ F_y(x, y, z, \lambda) = 0 \\ F_z(x, y, z, \lambda) = 0 \\ F_\lambda(x, y, z, \lambda) = 0 \end{cases}$$

At times, ingenuity must be used to solve the equations. Once we obtain a critical point (a, b, c, λ_0) of F, we can conclude that (a, b, c) is a critical point of f, subject to the constraint $g(x, y, z) = 0$. Although f and g are functions of three variables, the method of Lagrange multipliers can be extended to n variables.

Let us illustrate the method of Lagrange multipliers for the original situation, namely,

$$f(x, y, z) = x^2 + y^2 + z^2 \quad \text{subject to} \quad x - y + 2z = 6$$

First, we write the constraint as $g(x, y, z) = x - y + 2z - 6 = 0$. Second, we form the function

$$\begin{aligned} F(x, y, z, \lambda) &= f(x, y, z) - \lambda g(x, y, z) \\ &= x^2 + y^2 + z^2 - \lambda(x - y + 2z - 6) \end{aligned}$$

Next, we set each partial derivative of F equal to 0. For convenience, we will write $F_x(x, y, z, \lambda)$ as F_x, and so on:

$$\begin{cases} F_x = 2x - \lambda = 0 & \text{(7)} \\ F_y = 2y + \lambda = 0 & \text{(8)} \\ F_z = 2z - 2\lambda = 0 & \text{(9)} \\ F_\lambda = -x + y - 2z + 6 = 0 & \text{(10)} \end{cases}$$

From Equations (7)–(9), we see immediately that

$$x = \frac{\lambda}{2} \qquad y = -\frac{\lambda}{2} \qquad z = \lambda \qquad \text{(11)}$$

Substituting these values into Equation (10), we obtain

$$-\frac{\lambda}{2} - \frac{\lambda}{2} - 2\lambda + 6 = 0$$
$$-3\lambda + 6 = 0$$
$$\lambda = 2$$

Thus, from Equation (11),

$$x = 1 \quad y = -1 \quad z = 2$$

---

[21] After the French mathematician Joseph-Louis Lagrange (1736–1813).

Hence, the only critical point of f, subject to the constraint, is $(1, -1, 2)$, at which there may exist a relative maximum, a relative minimum, or neither of these. The method of Lagrange multipliers does not directly indicate which of these possibilities occurs, although from our previous work, we saw that $(1, -1, 2)$ is indeed a relative minimum. In applied problems, the nature of the problem itself may give a clue as to how a critical point is to be regarded. Often the existence of either a relative minimum or a relative maximum is assumed, and a critical point is treated accordingly. Actually, sufficient second-order conditions for relative extrema are available, but we will not consider them.

EXAMPLE 1   Method of Lagrange Multipliers

Find the critical points for $z = f(x, y) = 3x - y + 6$, subject to the constraint $x^2 + y^2 = 4$.

Solution: We write the constraint as $g(x, y) = x^2 + y^2 - 4 = 0$ and construct the function

$$F(x, y, \lambda) = f(x, y) - \lambda g(x, y) = 3x - y + 6 - \lambda(x^2 + y^2 - 4)$$

Setting $F_x = F_y = F_\lambda = 0$, we have

$$\begin{cases} 3 - 2x\lambda = 0 & (12) \\ -1 - 2y\lambda = 0 & (13) \\ -x^2 - y^2 + 4 = 0 & (14) \end{cases}$$

From Equations (12) and (13), we can express x and y in terms of λ. Then we will substitute for x and y in Equation (14) and solve for λ. Knowing λ, we can find x and y. To begin, from Equations (12) and (13), we have

$$x = \frac{3}{2\lambda} \quad \text{and} \quad y = -\frac{1}{2\lambda}$$

Substituting into Equation (14), we obtain

$$-\frac{9}{4\lambda^2} - \frac{1}{4\lambda^2} + 4 = 0$$

$$-\frac{10}{4\lambda^2} + 4 = 0$$

$$\lambda = \pm\frac{\sqrt{10}}{4}$$

With these λ-values, we can find x and y. If $\lambda = \sqrt{10}/4$, then

$$x = \frac{3}{2\left(\dfrac{\sqrt{10}}{4}\right)} = \frac{3\sqrt{10}}{5} \qquad y = -\frac{1}{2\left(\dfrac{\sqrt{10}}{4}\right)} = -\frac{\sqrt{10}}{5}$$

Similarly, if $\lambda = -\sqrt{10}/4$,

$$x = -\frac{3\sqrt{10}}{5} \qquad y = \frac{\sqrt{10}}{5}$$

Thus, the critical points of f, subject to the constraint, are $(3\sqrt{10}/5, -\sqrt{10}/5)$ and $(-3\sqrt{10}/5, \sqrt{10}/5)$. Note that the values of λ do not appear in the answer; they are simply a means to obtain the solution.

Now Work Problem 1 ◁

EXAMPLE 2   Method of Lagrange Multipliers

Find critical points for $f(x, y, z) = xyz$, where $xyz \neq 0$, subject to the constraint $x + 2y + 3z = 36$.

Solution: We have

$$F(x, y, z, \lambda) = xyz - \lambda(x + 2y + 3z - 36)$$

Setting $F_x = F_y = F_z = F_\lambda = 0$ gives, respectively,

$$\begin{cases} yz - \lambda = 0 \\ xz - 2\lambda = 0 \\ xy - 3\lambda = 0 \\ -x - 2y - 3z + 36 = 0 \end{cases}$$

Because we cannot directly express x, y, and z in terms of λ only, we cannot follow the procedure in Example 1. However, observe that we can express the products yz, xz, and xy as multiples of λ. This suggests that, by looking at quotients of equations, we can obtain a relation between two variables that does not involve λ. (The λ's will cancel.) Proceeding to do this, we write the foregoing system as

$$\begin{cases} yz = \lambda & (15) \\ \\ xz = 2\lambda & (16) \\ \\ xy = 3\lambda & (17) \\ x + 2y + 3z - 36 = 0 & (18) \end{cases}$$

Dividing each side of Equation (15) by the corresponding side of Equation (16), we get

$$\frac{yz}{xz} = \frac{\lambda}{2\lambda} \quad \text{so} \quad y = \frac{x}{2}$$

This division is valid, since $xyz \neq 0$. Similarly, from Equations (15) and (17), we get

$$\frac{yz}{xy} = \frac{\lambda}{3\lambda} \quad \text{so} \quad z = \frac{x}{3}$$

Now that we have y and z expressed in terms of x only, we can substitute into Equation (18) and solve for x:

$$x + 2\left(\frac{x}{2}\right) + 3\left(\frac{x}{3}\right) - 36 = 0$$

$$x = 12$$

Thus, $y = 6$ and $z = 4$. Hence, $(12, 6, 4)$ is the only critical point satisfying the given conditions. Note that in this situation, we found the critical point without having to find the value for λ.

Now Work Problem 7 ◁

EXAMPLE 3 Minimizing Costs

Suppose a firm has an order for 200 units of its product and wishes to distribute its manufacture between two of its plants, plant 1 and plant 2. Let q_1 and q_2 denote the outputs of plants 1 and 2, respectively, and suppose the total-cost function is given by $c = f(q_1, q_2) = 2q_1^2 + q_1 q_2 + q_2^2 + 200$. How should the output be distributed in order to minimize costs?

Solution: We minimize $c = f(q_1, q_2)$, given the constraint $q_1 + q_2 = 200$. We have

$$F(q_1, q_2, \lambda) = 2q_1^2 + q_1 q_2 + q_2^2 + 200 - \lambda(q_1 + q_2 - 200)$$

$$\begin{cases} \dfrac{\partial F}{\partial q_1} = 4q_1 + q_2 - \lambda = 0 & (19) \\ \\ \dfrac{\partial F}{\partial q_2} = q_1 + 2q_2 - \lambda = 0 & (20) \\ \\ \dfrac{\partial F}{\partial \lambda} = -q_1 - q_2 + 200 = 0 & (21) \end{cases}$$

We can eliminate λ from Equations (19) and (20) and obtain a relation between q_1 and q_2. Then, solving this equation for q_2 in terms of q_1 and substituting into Equation (21), we can find q_1. We begin by subtracting Equation (20) from Equation (19), which gives

$$3q_1 - q_2 = 0 \quad \text{so} \quad q_2 = 3q_1$$

Substituting into Equation (21), we have

$$-q_1 - 3q_1 + 200 = 0$$
$$-4q_1 = -200$$
$$q_1 = 50$$

Thus, $q_2 = 150$. Accordingly, plant 1 should produce 50 units and plant 2 should produce 150 units in order to minimize costs.

Now Work Problem 13 ◁

An interesting observation can be made concerning Example 3. From Equation (19), $\lambda = 4q_1 + q_2 = \partial c/\partial q_1$, the marginal cost of plant 1. From Equation (20), $\lambda = q_1 + 2q_2 = \partial c/\partial q_2$, the marginal cost of plant 2. Hence, $\partial c/\partial q_1 = \partial c/\partial q_2$, and we conclude that, to minimize cost, it is necessary that the marginal costs of each plant be equal to each other.

EXAMPLE 4   Least-Cost Input Combination

Suppose a firm must produce a given quantity P_0 of output in the cheapest possible manner. If there are two input factors l and k, and their prices per unit are fixed at p_l and p_k, respectively, discuss the economic significance of combining input to achieve least cost. That is, describe the least-cost input combination.

Solution: Let $P = f(l, k)$ be the production function. Then we must minimize the cost function

$$c = lp_l + kp_k$$

subject to

$$P_0 = f(l, k)$$

We construct

$$F(l, k, \lambda) = lp_l + kp_k - \lambda[f(l, k) - P_0]$$

We have

$$\begin{cases} \dfrac{\partial F}{\partial l} = p_l - \lambda \dfrac{\partial}{\partial l}[f(l, k)] = 0 & (22) \\[2ex] \dfrac{\partial F}{\partial k} = p_k - \lambda \dfrac{\partial}{\partial k}[f(l, k)] = 0 & (23) \\[2ex] \dfrac{\partial F}{\partial \lambda} = -f(l, k) + P_0 = 0 & \end{cases}$$

From Equations (22) and (23),

$$\lambda = \frac{p_l}{\dfrac{\partial}{\partial l}[f(l, k)]} = \frac{p_k}{\dfrac{\partial}{\partial k}[f(l, k)]} \tag{24}$$

Hence,

$$\frac{p_l}{p_k} = \frac{\dfrac{\partial}{\partial l}[f(l, k)]}{\dfrac{\partial}{\partial k}[f(l, k)]}$$

We conclude that when the least-cost combination of factors is used, the ratio of the marginal productivities of the input factors must be equal to the ratio of their corresponding unit prices.

Now Work Problem 15 ◁

Multiple Constraints

The method of Lagrange multipliers is by no means restricted to problems involving a single constraint. For example, suppose $f(x, y, z, w)$ were subject to constraints $g_1(x, y, z, w) = 0$ and $g_2(x, y, z, w) = 0$. Then there would be two lambdas, λ_1 and λ_2 (one corresponding to each constraint), and we would construct the function $F = f - \lambda_1 g_1 - \lambda_2 g_2$. We would then solve the system

$$F_x = F_y = F_z = F_w = F_{\lambda_1} = F_{\lambda_2} = 0$$

EXAMPLE 5   Method of Lagrange Multipliers with Two Constraints

Find critical points for $f(x, y, z) = xy + yz$, subject to the constraints $x^2 + y^2 = 8$ and $yz = 8$.

Solution: Set

$$F(x, y, z, \lambda_1, \lambda_2) = xy + yz - \lambda_1(x^2 + y^2 - 8) - \lambda_2(yz - 8)$$

Then

$$\begin{cases} F_x = y - 2x\lambda_1 = 0 & (25) \\ F_y = x + z - 2y\lambda_1 - z\lambda_2 = 0 & (26) \\ F_z = y - y\lambda_2 = 0 & (27) \\ F_{\lambda_1} = -x^2 - y^2 + 8 = 0 & (28) \\ F_{\lambda_2} = -yz + 8 = 0 & (29) \end{cases}$$

This appears to be a challenging system to solve. Some ingenuity will come into play. Here is one sequence of operations that will allow us to find the critical points. We can write the system as

$$\begin{cases} \dfrac{y}{2x} = \lambda_1 & (30) \\ x + z - 2y\lambda_1 - z\lambda_2 = 0 & (31) \\ \lambda_2 = 1 & (32) \\ x^2 + y^2 = 8 & (33) \\ z = \dfrac{8}{y} & (34) \end{cases}$$

In deriving Equation (30) we assumed $x \neq 0$. This is permissible because if $x = 0$, then by Equation (25) we have also $y = 0$, which is impossible because the second constraint, $yz = 8$, provides $y \neq 0$. We also used $y \neq 0$ to derive Equations (32) and (34).

Substituting $\lambda_2 = 1$ from Equation (32) into Equation (31) and simplifying gives the equation $x - 2y\lambda_1 = 0$, so

$$\lambda_1 = \frac{x}{2y}$$

Substituting into Equation (30) gives

$$\frac{y}{2x} = \frac{x}{2y}$$

$$y^2 = x^2 \qquad (35)$$

Substituting into Equation (33) gives $x^2 + x^2 = 8$, from which it follows that $x = \pm 2$. If $x = 2$, then, from Equation (35), we have $y = \pm 2$. Similarly, if $x = -2$, then $y = \pm 2$. Thus, if $x = 2$ and $y = 2$, then, from Equation (34), we obtain $z = 4$. Continuing in this manner, we obtain four critical points:

$$(2, 2, 4) \quad (2, -2, -4) \quad (-2, 2, 4) \quad (-2, -2, -4)$$

Now Work Problem 9 ◁

PROBLEMS 17.7

In Problems 1–12, find, by the method of Lagrange multipliers, the critical points of the functions, subject to the given constraints.

1. $f(x, y) = x^2 + 4y^2 + 6$; $2x - 8y = 20$

2. $f(x, y) = 3x^2 - 2y^2 + 9$; $x + y = 1$

3. $f(x, y, z) = x^2 + y^2 + z^2$; $2x + y - z = 9$

4. $f(x, y, z) = x + y + z$; $xyz = 8$

5. $f(x, y, z) = 2x^2 + xy + y^2 + z$; $x + 2y + 4z = 3$

6. $f(x, y, z) = xyz^2$; $x - y + z = 20 \ (xyz^2 \neq 0)$

7. $f(x, y, z) = xyz$; $x + y + z = 1 \ (xyz \neq 0)$

8. $f(x, y, z) = x^2 + y^2 + z^2$; $x + y + z = 3$

9. $f(x, y, z) = x^2 + 2y - z^2$; $2x - y = 0, \ y + z = 0$

10. $f(x, y, z) = x^2 + y^2 + z^2$; $x + y + z = 4, \ x - y + z = 4$

11. $f(x, y, z) = xy^2z$; $x + y + z = 1, \ x - y + z = 0 \ (xyz \neq 0)$

12. $f(x, y, z, w) = x^2 + 2y^2 + 3z^2 - w^2$; $4x + 3y + 2z + w = 10$

13. **Production Allocation**   To fill an order for 100 units of its product, a firm wishes to distribute production between its two plants, plant 1 and plant 2. The total-cost function is given by

$$c = f(q_1, q_2) = 0.1q_1^2 + 7q_1 + 15q_2 + 1000$$

where q_1 and q_2 are the numbers of units produced at plants 1 and 2, respectively. How should the output be distributed in order to minimize costs? (You may assume that the critical point obtained does correspond to the minimum cost.)

14. **Production Allocation**   Repeat Problem 13 if the cost function is

$$c = 3q_1^2 + q_1q_2 + 2q_2^2$$

and a total of 200 units are to be produced.

15. **Maximizing Output**   The production function for a firm is

$$f(l, k) = 12l + 20k - l^2 - 2k^2$$

The cost to the firm of l and k is 4 and 8 per unit, respectively. If the firm wants the total cost of input to be 88, find the greatest output possible, subject to this budget constraint. (You may assume that the critical point obtained does correspond to the maximum output.)

16. **Maximizing Output**   Repeat Problem 15, given that

$$f(l, k) = 20l + 25k - l^2 - 3k^2$$

and the budget constraint is $2l + 4k = 50$.

17. **Advertising Budget**   A computer company has a monthly advertising budget of $20,000. Its marketing department estimates that if x dollars are spent each month on advertising in newspapers and y dollars per month on television advertising, then the monthly sales will be given by $S = 80x^{1/4}y^{3/4}$ dollars. If the profit

is 10% of sales, less the advertising cost, determine how to allocate the advertising budget in order to maximize the monthly profit. (You may assume that the critical point obtained does correspond to the maximum profit.)

18. **Maximizing Production**   When l units of labor and k units of capital are invested, a manufacturer's total production q is given by the Cobb–Douglas production function $q = 6l^{2/5}k^{3/5}$. Each unit of labor costs $25 and each unit of capital costs $69. If exactly $25,875 is to be spent on production, determine the numbers of units of labor and capital that should be invested to maximize production. (You may assume that the maximum occurs at the critical point obtained.)

19. **Political Advertising**   Newspaper advertisements for political parties always have some negative effects. The recently elected party assumed that the three most important election issues, X, Y, and Z, had to be mentioned in each ad, with space x, y, and z units, respectively, allotted to each. The combined bad effect of this coverage was estimated by the party's backroom operative as

$$B(x, y, z) = x^2 + y^2 + 2z^2$$

Aesthetics dictated that the total space for X and Y together must be 20, and realism suggested that the total space allotted to Y and Z together must also be 20 units. What values of x, y, and z in each ad would produce the lowest negative effect? (You may assume that any critical point obtained provides the minimum effect.)

20. **Maximizing Profit**   Suppose a manufacturer's production function is given by

$$16q = 65 - 4(l - 4)^2 - 2(k - 5)^2$$

and the cost to the manufacturer is $8 per unit of labor and $16 per unit of capital, so that the total cost (in dollars) is $8l + 16k$. The selling price of the product is $64 per unit.

(a) Express the profit as a function of l and k. Give your answer in expanded form.

(b) Find all critical points of the profit function obtained in part (a). Apply the second-derivative test at each critical point. If the profit is a relative maximum at a critical point, compute the corresponding relative maximum profit.

(c) The profit may be considered a function of l, k, and q (that is, $P = 64q - 8l - 16k$), subject to the constraint

$$16q = 65 - 4(l - 4)^2 - 2(k - 5)^2$$

Use the method of Lagrange multipliers to find all critical points of $P = 64q - 8l - 16k$, subject to the constraint.

Problems 21–24 refer to the following definition. A utility function is a function that attaches a measure to the satisfaction or utility a consumer gets from the consumption of products per unit of time. Suppose $U = f(x, y)$ is such a function, where x and y are the amounts of two products, X and Y. The marginal utility of X is

$\partial U/\partial x$ and approximately represents the change in total utility resulting from a one-unit change in consumption of product X per unit of time. We define the marginal utility of Y in similar fashion. If the prices of X and Y are p_X and p_Y, respectively, and the consumer has an income or budget of I to spend, then the budget constraint is

$$xp_X + yp_Y = I$$

In Problems 21–23, find the quantities of each product that the consumer should buy, subject to the budget, that will allow maximum satisfaction. That is, in Problems 21 and 22, find values of x and y that maximize $U = f(x, y)$, subject to $xp_X + yp_Y = I$. Perform a similar procedure for Problem 23. Assume that such a maximum exists.

21. $U = x^3 y^3;$ $p_X = 2, p_Y = 3, I = 48$ $(x^3 y^3 \neq 0)$

22. $U = 40x - 8x^2 + 2y - y^2; p_X = 4, p_Y = 6, I = 100$

23. $U = f(x, y, z) = xyz;$ $p_X = p_Y = p_Z = 1, I = 100$ $(xyz \neq 0)$

24. Let $U = f(x, y)$ be a utility function subject to the budget constraint $xp_X + yp_Y = I$, where p_X, p_Y, and I are constants. Show that, to maximize satisfaction, it is necessary that

$$\lambda = \frac{f_x(x, y)}{p_X} = \frac{f_y(x, y)}{p_Y}$$

where $f_x(x, y)$ and $f_y(x, y)$ are the marginal utilities of X and Y, respectively. Show that $f_x(x, y)/p_X$ is the marginal utility of one dollar's worth of X. Hence, maximum satisfaction is obtained when the consumer allocates the budget so that the marginal utility of a dollar's worth of X is equal to the marginal utility per dollar's worth of Y. Performing the same procedure as that for $U = f(x, y)$, verify that this is true for $U = f(x, y, z, w)$, subject to the corresponding budget equation. In each case, λ is called the *marginal utility of income.*

Objective

To develop the method of least squares and introduce index numbers.

Table 17.3

Expenditures x	2	3	4.5	5.5	7
Revenue y		3	6	8	10	11

17.8 Lines of Regression[22]

To study the influence of advertising on sales, a firm compiled the data in Table 17.3. The variable x denotes advertising expenditures in hundreds of dollars, and the variable y denotes the resulting sales revenue in thousands of dollars. If each pair (x, y) of data is plotted, the result is called a **scatter diagram** [Figure 17.8(a)].

From an observation of the distribution of the points, it is reasonable to assume that a relationship exists between x and y and that it is approximately linear. On this basis, we may fit "by eye" a straight line that approximates the given data [Figure 17.8(b)] and, from this line, predict a value of y for a given value of x. The line seems consistent with the trend of the data, although other lines could be drawn as well. Unfortunately, determining a line "by eye" is not very objective. We want to apply criteria in specifying what we will call a line of "best fit." A frequently used technique is called the **method of least squares.**

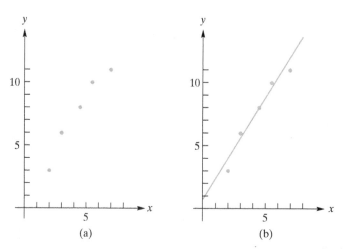

FIGURE 17.8 Scatter diagram and straight line approximation to data points.

To apply the method of least squares to the data in Table 17.3, we first assume that x and y are approximately linearly related and that we can fit a straight line

$$\widehat{y} = a + bx \tag{1}$$

---

[22]This section can be omitted without loss of continuity.

that approximates the given points by a suitable objective choice of the constants a and b. For a given value of x in Equation (1), $\widehat{y}$ is the corresponding predicted value of y, and $(x, \widehat{y})$ will be on the line. Our aim is that $\widehat{y}$ be near y.

When $x = 2$, the observed value of y is 3. Our predicted value of y is obtained by substituting $x = 2$ in Equation (1), which yields $\widehat{y} = a + 2b$. The error of estimation, or vertical deviation of the point $(2, 3)$ from the line, is $\widehat{y} - y$, which is

$$a + 2b - 3$$

This vertical deviation is indicated (although exaggerated for clarity) in Figure 17.9. Similarly, the vertical deviation of $(3, 6)$ from the line is $a + 3b - 6$, as is also illustrated. To avoid possible difficulties associated with positive and negative deviations, we will consider the squares of the deviations and will form the sum S of all such squares for the given data:

$$S = (a + 2b - 3)^2 + (a + 3b - 6)^2 + (a + 4.5b - 8)^2$$
$$+ (a + 5.5b - 10)^2 + (a + 7b - 11)^2$$

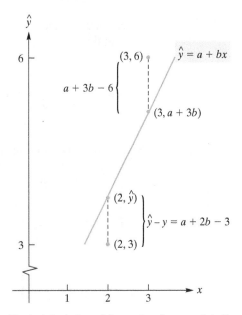

FIGURE 17.9   Vertical deviation of data points from straight line approximation.

The method of least squares requires that we choose as the line of "best fit" the one obtained by selecting a and b so as to minimize S. We can minimize S with respect to a and b by solving the system

$$\begin{cases} \dfrac{\partial S}{\partial a} = 0 \\[2mm] \dfrac{\partial S}{\partial b} = 0 \end{cases}$$

We have

$$\frac{\partial S}{\partial a} = 2(a + 2b - 3) + 2(a + 3b - 6) + 2(a + 4.5b - 8)$$
$$+ 2(a + 5.5b - 10) + 2(a + 7b - 11) = 0$$

$$\frac{\partial S}{\partial b} = 4(a + 2b - 3) + 6(a + 3b - 6) + 9(a + 4.5b - 8)$$
$$+ 11(a + 5.5b - 10) + 14(a + 7b - 11) = 0$$

which, when simplified, give

$$\begin{cases} 10a + 44b = 76 \\ 44a + 225b = 384 \end{cases}$$

Solving for a and b, we obtain

$$a = \frac{102}{157} \approx 0.65 \quad b = \frac{248}{157} \approx 1.58$$

From our calculations of $\partial S/\partial a$ and $\partial S/\partial b$, we see that $S_{aa} = 10 > 0$, $S_{bb} = 225$, and $S_{ab} = 44$. Thus $D = S_{aa}S_{bb} - (S_{ab})^2 = 10 \cdot 225 - 44^2 = 314 > 0$. It follows from the second-derivative test of Section 17.6 that S has a minimum value at the critical point. Hence, in the sense of least squares, the line of best fit $\widehat{y} = a + bx$ is

$$\widehat{y} = 0.65 + 1.58x \tag{2}$$

This is, in fact, the line shown in Figure 17.8(b). It is called the **least squares line of y on x** or the **linear regression line of** y on x. The constants a and b are called **linear regression coefficients.** With Equation (2), we would predict that when $x = 5$, the corresponding value of y is $\widehat{y} = 0.65 + 1.58(5) = 8.55$.

More generally, suppose we are given the following n pairs of observations:

$$(x_1, y_1), (x_2, y_2), \ldots, (x_n, y_n)$$

If we assume that x and y are approximately linearly related and that we can fit a straight line

$$\widehat{y} = a + bx$$

that approximates the data, the sum of the squares of the errors $\widehat{y} - y$ is

$$S = (a + bx_1 - y_1)^2 + (a + bx_2 - y_2)^2 + \cdots + (a + bx_n - y_n)^2$$

Since S must be minimized with respect to a and b,

$$\begin{cases} \dfrac{\partial S}{\partial a} = 2(a + bx_1 - y_1) + 2(a + bx_2 - y_2) + \cdots + 2(a + bx_n - y_n) = 0 \\[2mm] \dfrac{\partial S}{\partial b} = 2x_1(a + bx_1 - y_1) + 2x_2(a + bx_2 - y_2) + \cdots + 2x_n(a + bx_n - y_n) = 0 \end{cases}$$

Dividing both equations by 2 and using summation notation, we have

$$\begin{cases} na + \left(\displaystyle\sum_{i=1}^{n} x_i \right) b - \displaystyle\sum_{i=1}^{n} y_i = 0 \\[4mm] \left(\displaystyle\sum_{i=1}^{n} x_i \right) a + \left(\displaystyle\sum_{i=1}^{n} x_i^2 \right) b - \displaystyle\sum_{i=1}^{n} x_i y_i = 0 \end{cases}$$

which is a system of two linear equations in a and b, the so-called *normal equations:*

$$\begin{cases} na + \left(\displaystyle\sum_{i=1}^{n} x_i \right) b = \displaystyle\sum_{i=1}^{n} y_i \\[4mm] \left(\displaystyle\sum_{i=1}^{n} x_i \right) a + \left(\displaystyle\sum_{i=1}^{n} x_i^2 \right) b = \displaystyle\sum_{i=1}^{n} x_i y_i \end{cases}$$

The coefficients are of course no more than simple sums of values obtained from the observed data. The solution is obtained easily using the techniques of Section 3.4.

$$a = \frac{\left(\displaystyle\sum_{i=1}^{n} x_i^2 \right) \left(\displaystyle\sum_{i=1}^{n} y_i \right) - \left(\displaystyle\sum_{i=1}^{n} x_i \right) \left(\displaystyle\sum_{i=1}^{n} x_i y_i \right)}{n \displaystyle\sum_{i=1}^{n} x_i^2 - \left(\displaystyle\sum_{i=1}^{n} x_i \right)^2} \tag{3}$$

$$b = \frac{n\sum_{i=1}^{n} x_i y_i - \left(\sum_{i=1}^{n} x_i\right)\left(\sum_{i=1}^{n} y_i\right)}{n\sum_{i=1}^{n} x_i^2 - \left(\sum_{i=1}^{n} x_i\right)^2} \qquad (4)$$

Now we have $S_{aa} = 2n > 0$ and $D = S_{aa}S_{bb} - (S_{ab})^2 = (2n)(2\sum x_i^2) - (2\sum x_i)^2$, independent of (a, b). It can be shown that for distinct x_i and $n \geq 2$ that $D > 0$ so a and b, given by Equations (3) and (4), do indeed minimize S. [For example, when $n = 2$, $D > 0$ is provably equivalent to $(x_1 - x_2)^2 > 0$, which is true for distinct x_1 and x_2.]

Computing the linear regression coefficients a and b by the formulas of Equations (3) and (4) gives the linear regression line of y on x, namely, $\widehat{y} = a + bx$, which can be used to estimate y for any given value of x.

In the next example, as well as in the problems, you will encounter **index numbers.** They are used to relate a variable in one period of time to the same variable in another period, called the *base period*. An index number is a *relative* number that describes data that are changing over time. Such data are referred to as *time series*.

For example, consider the time-series data of total production of widgets in the United States for 2002–2006, given in Table 17.4. If we choose 2003 as the base year and assign the index number 100 to it, then the other index numbers are obtained by dividing each year's production by the 2003 production of 900 and multiplying the result by 100. We can, for example, interpret the index 106 for 2006 as meaning that production for that year was 106% of the production in 2003.

Table 17.4

Year	Production (in thousands)	Index (based on 2003)
2002	828	92
2003	900	100
2004	936	104
2005	891	99
2006	954	106

In time-series analysis, index numbers are obviously of great advantage if the data involve numbers of great magnitude. But regardless of the magnitude of the data, index numbers simplify the task of comparing changes in data over periods of time.

EXAMPLE 1   Determining a Linear Regression Line

By means of the linear regression line, use the following table to represent the trend for the index of total U.S. government revenue from 1995 to 2000 (1995 = 100).

Year	1995	1996	1997	1998	1999	2000
Index	100	107	117	127	135	150

Source: Economic Report of the President, 2001, U.S. Government Printing Office, Washington, DC, 2001.

Solution: We will let x denote time and y denote the index and treat y as a linear function of x. Also, we will designate 1995 by $x = 1$, 1996 by $x = 2$, and so on. There are $n = 6$ pairs of measurements. To determine the linear regression coefficients by using Equations (3) and (4), we first perform the arithmetic:

Year	x_i	y_i	$x_i y_i$	x_i^2
1995	1	100	100	1
1996	2	107	214	4
1997	3	117	351	9
1998	4	127	508	16
1999	5	135	675	25
2000	6	150	900	36
Total	21	736	2748	91
	$= \sum\limits_{i=1}^{6} x_i$	$= \sum\limits_{i=1}^{6} y_i$	$= \sum\limits_{i=1}^{6} x_i y_i$	$= \sum\limits_{i=1}^{6} x_i^2$

Hence, by Equation (3),

$$a = \frac{91(736) - 21(2748)}{6(91) - (21)^2} \approx 88.3$$

and, by Equation (4),

$$b = \frac{6(2748) - 21(736)}{6(91) - (21)^2} \approx 9.83$$

Thus, the regression line of y on x is

$$\widehat{y} = 88.3 + 9.83x$$

whose graph, as well as a scatter diagram, appears in Figure 17.10.

Now Work Problem 1 ◁

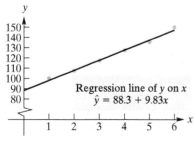

FIGURE 17.10   Linear regression line for government revenue.

TECHNOLOGY ▮▮▮

The TI-83 Plus has a utility that computes the equation of the least squares line for a set of data. We will illustrate by giving the procedure for the six data points (x_i, y_i) of Example 1. After pressing STAT and ENTER, we enter all the x-values and then the y-values. (See Figure 17.11.)

Next, we press STAT and move to CALC. Finally, pressing 8 and ENTER gives the result shown in Figure 17.12. (The number $r \approx 0.99448$ is called the *coefficient of correlation* and is a measure of the degree to which the given data are linearly related.)

FIGURE 17.11   Data of Example 1.

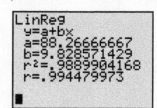

FIGURE 17.12   Equation of least squares line.

PROBLEMS 17.8

In this problem set, use a graphing calculator if your instructor permits you to do so.

In Problems 1–4, find an equation of the least squares linear regression line of y on x for the given data, and sketch both the line and the data. Predict the value of y corresponding to x = 3.5.

1. | x | 1 | 2 | 3 | 4 | 5 | 6 |
   |---|---|---|---|---|---|---|
   | y | 1.5 | 2.3 | 2.6 | 3.7 | 4.0 | 4.5 |

2. | x | 1 | 2 | 3 | 4 | 5 | 6 | 7 |
   |---|---|---|---|---|---|---|---|
   | y | 1 | 1.8 | 2 | 4 | 4.5 | 7 | 9 |

3. | x | 2 | 3 | 4.5 | 5.5 | 7 |
   |---|---|---|---|---|---|
   | y | 3 | 5 | 8 | 10 | 11 |

4. | x | 2 | 3 | 4 | 5 | 6 | 7 |
   |---|---|---|---|---|---|---|
   | y | 2.4 | 2.9 | 3.3 | 3.8 | 4.3 | 4.9 |

5. **Demand**   A firm finds that when the price of its product is p dollars per unit, the number of units sold is q, as indicated in the following table:

Price, p	10	20	40	50	60	70
Demand, q	75	65	56	50	42	34

Find an equation of the regression line of q on p.

6. Water and Crop Yield   On a farm, an agronomist finds that the amount of water applied (in inches) and the corresponding yield of a certain crop (in tons per acre) are as given in the following table:

Water, x	8	16	24	32
Yield, y	5.2	5.7	6.3	6.7

Find an equation of the regression line of y on x. Predict y when $x = 20$.

7. Virus   A rabbit was injected with a virus, and x hours after the injection the temperature y (in degrees Fahrenheit) of the rabbit was measured.[23] The data are given in the following table:

Elapsed Time, x	24	32	48	56
Temperature, y	102.8	104.5	106.5	107.0

Find an equation of the regression line of y on x, and estimate the rabbit's temperature 40 hours after the injection.

8. Psychology   In a psychological experiment, four persons were subjected to a stimulus. Both before and after the stimulus, the systolic blood pressure (in millimeters of mercury) of each subject was measured. The data are given in the following table:

Blood Pressure				
Before Stimulus, x	131	132	135	141
After Stimulus, y	139	139	142	149

Find an equation of the regression line of y on x, where x and y are as defined in the table.

For the time series in Problems 9 and 10, fit a linear regression line by least squares; that is, find an equation of the linear regression line of y on x. In each case, let the first year in the table correspond to $x = 1$.

9.

Production of Product A, 2002–2006 (in thousands of units)	
Year	**Production**
2002	10
2003	15
2004	16
2005	18
2006	21

10. Industrial Production   In the following table, let 1975 correspond to $x = 1$, 1977 correspond to $x = 3$, and so on:

Index of Industrial Production—Electrical Machinery (based on 1977)	
Year	Index
1975	77
1977	100
1979	126
1981	134

Source: Economic Report of the President, 1988, U.S. Government Printing Office, Washington, DC, 1988.

11. Computer Shipments
(a) Find an equation of the least squares line of y on x for the following data (refer to 2002 as year $x = 1$, and so on):

Overseas Shipments of Computers by Acme Computer Co. (in thousands)	
Year	Quantity
2002	35
2003	31
2004	26
2005	24
2006	26

(b) For the data in part (a), refer to 2002 as year $x = -2$, 2003 as year $x = -1$, 2004 as year $x = 0$ and so on. Then $\sum_{i=1}^{5} x_i = 0$. Fit a least squares line and observe how the calculation is simplified.

12. Medical Care   For the following time series, find an equation of the linear regression line that best fits the data (refer to 1983 as year $x = -2$, 1984 as year $x = -1$, and so on):

Consumer Price Index—Medical Care, 1983–1987 (based on 1967)	
Year	Index
1983	357
1984	380
1985	403
1986	434
1987	462

Source: Economic Report of the President, 1988, U.S. Government Printing Office, Washington, DC, 1988.

17.9   Multiple Integrals

Objective

To compute double and triple integrals.

Recall that the definite integral of a function of one variable is concerned with integration over an *interval*. There are also definite integrals of functions of two variables, called (definite) **double integrals.** These involve integration over a *region* in the plane.

---

[23] R. R. Sokal and F. J. Rohlf, *Introduction to Biostatistics* (San Francisco: W. H. Freeman & Company, Publishers, 1973).

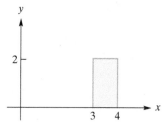

FIGURE 17.13 Region over which $\int_0^2 \int_3^4 xy\, dx\, dy$ is evaluated.

For example, the symbol

$$\int_0^2 \int_3^4 xy\, dx\, dy = \int_0^2 \left(\int_3^4 xy\, dx \right) dy$$

is the double integral of $f(x, y) = xy$ over a region determined by the limits of integration. That region consists of all points (x, y) in the x,y-plane such that $3 \le x \le 4$ and $0 \le y \le 2$. (See Figure 17.13.)

A double integral is a limit of a sum of the form $\sum f(x, y)\, dx\, dy$, where, in this example, the points (x, y) are in the shaded region. A geometric interpretation of a double integral will be given later.

To evaluate

$$\int_0^2 \int_3^4 xy\, dx\, dy = \int_0^2 \left(\int_3^4 xy\, dx \right) dy$$

we use successive integrations starting with the innermost integral. First, we evaluate

$$\int_3^4 xy\, dx$$

by treating y as a constant and integrating with respect to x between the limits 3 and 4:

$$\int_3^4 xy\, dx = \left. \frac{x^2 y}{2} \right|_3^4$$

Substituting the limits for the variable x, we have

$$\frac{4^2 \cdot y}{2} - \frac{3^2 \cdot y}{2} = \frac{16y}{2} - \frac{9y}{2} = \frac{7}{2}y$$

Now we integrate this result with respect to y between the limits 0 and 2:

$$\int_0^2 \frac{7}{2}y\, dy = \left. \frac{7y^2}{4} \right|_0^2 = \frac{7 \cdot 2^2}{4} - 0 = 7$$

Thus,

$$\int_0^2 \int_3^4 xy\, dx\, dy = 7$$

Now consider the double integral

$$\int_0^1 \int_{x^3}^{x^2} (x^3 - xy)\, dy\, dx = \int_0^1 \left(\int_{x^3}^{x^2} (x^3 - xy)\, dy \right) dx$$

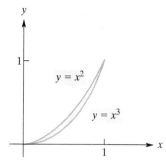

FIGURE 17.14 Region over which $\int_0^1 \int_{x^3}^{x^2} (x^3 - xy)\, dy\, dx$ is evaluated.

Here we integrate first with respect to y and then with respect to x. The region over which the integration takes places is all points (x, y) such that $x^3 \le y \le x^2$ and $0 \le x \le 1$. (See Figure 17.14.) This double integral is evaluated by first treating x as a constant and integrating $x^3 - xy$ with respect to y between x^3 and x^2, and then integrating the result with respect to x between 0 and 1:

$$\int_0^1 \int_{x^3}^{x^2} (x^3 - xy)\, dy\, dx = \int_0^1 \left(\int_{x^3}^{x^2} (x^3 - xy)\, dy \right) dx = \int_0^1 \left. \left(x^3 y - \frac{xy^2}{2} \right) \right|_{x^3}^{x^2} dx$$

$$= \int_0^1 \left[\left(x^3(x^2) - \frac{x(x^2)^2}{2} \right) - \left(x^3(x^3) - \frac{x(x^3)^2}{2} \right) \right] dx$$

$$= \int_0^1 \left(x^5 - \frac{x^5}{2} - x^6 + \frac{x^7}{2} \right) dx = \int_0^1 \left(\frac{x^5}{2} - x^6 + \frac{x^7}{2} \right) dx$$

$$= \left. \left(\frac{x^6}{12} - \frac{x^7}{7} + \frac{x^8}{16} \right) \right|_0^1 = \left(\frac{1}{12} - \frac{1}{7} + \frac{1}{16} \right) - 0 = \frac{1}{336}$$

EXAMPLE 1   Evaluating a Double Integral

Find $\displaystyle\int_{-1}^{1}\int_{0}^{1-x}(2x+1)\,dy\,dx$.

Solution: Here we first integrate with respect to y and then integrate the result with respect to x:

$$\int_{-1}^{1}\int_{0}^{1-x}(2x+1)\,dy\,dx = \int_{-1}^{1}\left(\int_{0}^{1-x}(2x+1)\,dy\right)dx$$

$$= \int_{-1}^{1}(2xy+y)\Big|_{0}^{1-x}dx = \int_{-1}^{1}((2x(1-x)+(1-x))-0)\,dx$$

$$= \int_{-1}^{1}(-2x^2+x+1)\,dx = \left(-\frac{2x^3}{3}+\frac{x^2}{2}+x\right)\Big|_{-1}^{1}$$

$$= \left(-\frac{2}{3}+\frac{1}{2}+1\right)-\left(\frac{2}{3}+\frac{1}{2}-1\right) = \frac{2}{3}$$

Now Work Problem 9 ◁

EXAMPLE 2   Evaluating a Double Integral

Find $\displaystyle\int_{1}^{\ln 2}\int_{e^y}^{2}dx\,dy$.

Solution: Here we first integrate with respect to x and then integrate the result with respect to y:

$$\int_{1}^{\ln 2}\int_{e^y}^{2}dx\,dy = \int_{1}^{\ln 2}\left(\int_{e^y}^{2}dx\right)dy = \int_{1}^{\ln 2}x\Big|_{e^y}^{2}dy$$

$$= \int_{1}^{\ln 2}(2-e^y)\,dy = (2y-e^y)\Big|_{1}^{\ln 2}$$

$$= (2\ln 2 - 2) - (2 - e) = 2\ln 2 - 4 + e$$

$$= \ln 4 - 4 + e$$

Now Work Problem 13 ◁

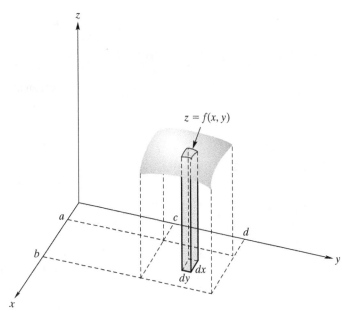

FIGURE 17.15   Interpreting $\int_{a}^{b}\int_{c}^{d}f(x,y)\,dy\,dx$ in terms of volume, where $f(x,y) \geq 0$.

A double integral can be interpreted in terms of the volume of a region between the x,y-plane and a surface $z = f(x,y)$ if $z \geq 0$. In Figure 17.15 is a region whose volume we will consider. The element of volume for this region is a vertical column with height approximately $z = f(x, y)$ and base area $dy\,dx$. Thus, its volume is approximately $f(x, y)\,dy\,dx$. The volume of the entire region can be found by summing the volumes of all such elements for $a \le x \le b$ and $c \le y \le d$ via a double integral:

$$\text{volume} = \int_a^b \int_c^d f(x, y)\,dy\,dx$$

Triple integrals are handled by successively evaluating three integrals, as the next example shows.

EXAMPLE 3   Evaluating a Triple Integral

Find $\displaystyle\int_0^1 \int_0^x \int_0^{x-y} x\,dz\,dy\,dx$.

Solution:

$$\int_0^1 \int_0^x \int_0^{x-y} x\,dz\,dy\,dx = \int_0^1 \int_0^x \left(\int_0^{x-y} x\,dz \right) dy\,dx$$

$$= \int_0^1 \int_0^x (xz)\Big|_0^{x-y} dy\,dx = \int_0^1 \int_0^x (x(x-y) - 0)\,dy\,dx$$

$$= \int_0^1 \int_0^x (x^2 - xy)\,dy\,dx = \int_0^1 \left(\int_0^x (x^2 - xy)\,dy \right) dx$$

$$= \int_0^1 \left(x^2 y - \frac{xy^2}{2} \right)\Big|_0^x dx = \int_0^1 \left[\left(x^3 - \frac{x^3}{2} \right) - 0 \right] dx$$

$$= \int_0^1 \frac{x^3}{2}\,dx = \frac{x^4}{8}\Big|_0^1 = \frac{1}{8}$$

Now Work Problem 21 ◁

PROBLEMS 17.9

In Problems 1–22, evaluate the multiple integrals.

1. $\displaystyle\int_0^3 \int_0^4 x\,dy\,dx$

2. $\displaystyle\int_1^4 \int_0^3 y\,dy\,dx$

3. $\displaystyle\int_0^1 \int_0^1 xy\,dx\,dy$

4. $\displaystyle\int_0^1 \int_0^1 x^2 y^2\,dy\,dx$

5. $\displaystyle\int_1^3 \int_1^2 (x^2 - y)\,dx\,dy$

6. $\displaystyle\int_{-2}^3 \int_0^2 (y^2 - 2xy)\,dy\,dx$

7. $\displaystyle\int_0^1 \int_0^2 (x + y)\,dy\,dx$

8. $\displaystyle\int_0^3 \int_0^x (x^2 + y^2)\,dy\,dx$

9. $\displaystyle\int_2^3 \int_0^{2x} y\,dy\,dx$

10. $\displaystyle\int_1^2 \int_0^{x-1} 2y\,dy\,dx$

11. $\displaystyle\int_0^1 \int_{3x}^{x^2} 14x^2 y\,dy\,dx$

12. $\displaystyle\int_0^2 \int_0^{x^2} xy\,dy\,dx$

13. $\displaystyle\int_0^3 \int_0^{\sqrt{9-x^2}} y\,dy\,dx$

14. $\displaystyle\int_0^1 \int_{y^2}^y x\,dx\,dy$

15. $\displaystyle\int_{-1}^1 \int_x^{1-x} 3(x + y)\,dy\,dx$

16. $\displaystyle\int_0^3 \int_{y^2}^{3y} 5x\,dx\,dy$

17. $\displaystyle\int_0^1 \int_0^y e^{x+y}\,dx\,dy$

18. $\displaystyle\int_0^1 \int_0^1 e^{y-x}\,dx\,dy$

19. $\displaystyle\int_0^1 \int_0^2 \int_0^3 xy^2 z^3\,dx\,dy\,dz$

20. $\displaystyle\int_0^1 \int_0^x \int_0^{x+y} x^2\,dz\,dy\,dx$

21. $\displaystyle\int_0^1 \int_{x^2}^x \int_0^{xy} dz\,dy\,dx$

22. $\displaystyle\int_1^e \int_{\ln x}^x \int_0^y dz\,dy\,dx$

23. **Statistics**   In the study of statistics, a joint density function $z = f(x, y)$ defined on a region in the x, y-plane is represented by a surface in space. The probability that

$$a \le x \le b \quad \text{and} \quad c \le y \le d$$

is given by

$$P(a \le x \le b, c \le y \le d) = \int_c^d \int_a^b f(x, y)\,dx\,dy$$

and is represented by the volume between the graph of f and the rectangular region given by

$$a \le x \le b \quad \text{and} \quad c \le y \le d$$

If $f(x, y) = e^{-(x+y)}$ is a joint density function, where $x \ge 0$ and $y \ge 0$, find

$$P(0 \le x \le 2, 1 \le y \le 2)$$

and give your answer in terms of e.

24. **Statistics**   In Problem 23, let $f(x, y) = 6e^{-(2x+3y)}$ for $x, y \ge 0$. Find

$$P(1 \le x \le 3, 2 \le y \le 4)$$

and give your answer in terms of e.

25. **Statistics**   In Problem 23, let $f(x, y) = 1$, where $0 \le x \le 1$ and $0 \le y \le 1$. Find $P(x \ge 1/2, y \ge 1/3)$.

26. **Statistics**   In Problem 23, let f be the uniform density function $f(x, y) = 1/8$ defined over the rectangle $0 \le x \le 4, 0 \le y \le 2$. Determine the probability that $0 \le x \le 1$ and $0 \le y \le 1$.

Chapter 17 Review

Important Terms and Symbols

Summary

For a function of n variables, we can consider n partial derivatives. For example, if $w = f(x, y, z)$, we have the partial derivatives of f with respect to x, with respect to y, and with respect to z, denoted $f_x, f_y,$ and f_z, or $\partial w/\partial x, \partial w/\partial y,$ and $\partial w/\partial z$, respectively. To find $f_x(x, y, z)$, we treat y and z as constants and differentiate f with respect to x in the usual way. The other partial derivatives are found in a similar fashion. We can interpret $f_x(x, y, z)$ as the approximate change in w that results from a one-unit change in x when y and z are held fixed. There are similar interpretations for the other partial derivatives. A function of several variables may be defined implicitly. In this case, its partial derivatives are found by implicit partial differentiation.

Functions of several variables occur frequently in business and economic analysis, as well as in other areas of study. If a manufacturer produces x units of product X and y units of product Y, then the total cost c of these units is a function of x and y and is called a joint-cost function. The partial derivatives $\partial c/\partial x$ and $\partial c/\partial y$ are called the marginal costs with respect to x and y, respectively. We can interpret, for example, $\partial c/\partial x$ as the approximate cost of producing an extra unit of X while the level of production of Y is held fixed.

If l units of labor and k units of capital are used to produce P units of a product, then the function $P = f(l, k)$ is called a production function. The partial derivatives of P are called marginal productivity functions.

Suppose two products, A and B, are such that the quantity demanded of each is dependent on the prices of both. If q_A and q_B are the quantities of A and B demanded when the prices of A and B are p_A and p_B, respectively, then q_A and q_B are each functions of p_A and p_B. When $\partial q_A/\partial p_B > 0$ and $\partial q_B/\partial p_A > 0$, then A and B are called competitive products (or substitutes). When $\partial q_A/\partial p_B < 0$ and $\partial q_B/\partial p_A < 0$, then A and B are called complementary products.

If $z = f(x, y)$, where $x = x(r, s)$ and $y = y(r, s)$, then z can be considered as a function of r and s. To find, for example, $\partial z/\partial r$, a chain rule can be used:

$$\frac{\partial z}{\partial r} = \frac{\partial z}{\partial x}\frac{\partial x}{\partial r} + \frac{\partial z}{\partial y}\frac{\partial y}{\partial r}$$

A partial derivative of a function of n variables is itself a function of n variables. By successively taking partial derivatives of partial derivatives, we obtain higher-order partial derivatives. For example, if f is a function of x and y, then f_{xy} denotes the partial derivative of f_x with respect to y; f_{xy} is called the second-partial derivative of f, first with respect to x and then with respect to y.

If the function $f(x, y)$ has a relative extremum at (a, b), then (a, b) must be a solution of the system

$$\begin{cases} f_x(x, y) = 0 \\ f_y(x, y) = 0 \end{cases}$$

Any solution of this system is called a critical point of f. Thus, critical points are the candidates at which a relative extremum may occur. The second-derivative test for functions of two variables gives conditions under which a critical point corresponds to a relative maximum or a relative minimum. The test states that if (a, b) is a critical point of f and

$$D(x, y) = f_{xx}(x, y)f_{yy}(x, y) - [f_{xy}(x, y)]^2$$

then

1. if $D(a, b) > 0$ and $f_{xx}(a, b) < 0$, then f has a relative maximum at (a, b);
2. if $D(a, b) > 0$ and $f_{xx}(a, b) > 0$, then f has a relative minimum at (a, b);
3. if $D(a, b) < 0$, then f has a saddle point at (a, b);
4. if $D(a, b) = 0$, no conclusion about an extremum at (a, b) can yet be drawn, and further analysis is required.

To find critical points of a function of several variables, subject to a constraint, we can sometimes use the method of Lagrange multipliers. For example, to find the critical points of $f(x, y, z)$, subject to the constraint $g(x, y, z) = 0$, we first form the function

$$F(x, y, z, \lambda) = f(x, y, z) - \lambda g(x, y, z)$$

By solving the system

$$\begin{cases} F_x = 0 \\ F_y = 0 \\ F_z = 0 \\ F_\lambda = 0 \end{cases}$$

we obtain the critical points of F. If (a, b, c, λ_0) is such a critical point, then (a, b, c) is a critical point of f, subject to the constraint. It is important to write the constraint in the form $g(x, y, z) = 0$. For example, if the constraint is $2x + 3y - z = 4$, then $g(x, y, z) = 2x + 3y - z - 4$. If $f(x, y, z)$ is subject to two constraints, $g_1(x, y, z) = 0$ and $g_2(x, y, z) = 0$, then we would form the function $F = f - \lambda_1 g_1 - \lambda_2 g_2$ and solve the system

$$\begin{cases} F_x = 0 \\ F_y = 0 \\ F_z = 0 \\ F_{\lambda_1} = 0 \\ F_{\lambda_2} = 0 \end{cases}$$

Sometimes sample data for two variables, say, x and y, may be related in such a way that the relationship is approximately linear. When such data points (x_i, y_i), where $i = 1, 2, 3, \ldots, n$, are given to us, we can fit a straight line that approximates them. Such a line is the linear regression line of y on x and is given by

$$\widehat{y} = a + bx$$

where

$$a = \frac{\left(\sum_{i=1}^{n} x_i^2\right)\left(\sum_{i=1}^{n} y_i\right) - \left(\sum_{i=1}^{n} x_i\right)\left(\sum_{i=1}^{n} x_i y_i\right)}{n\sum_{i=1}^{n} x_i^2 - \left(\sum_{i=1}^{n} x_i\right)^2}$$

and

$$b = \frac{n\sum_{i=1}^{n} x_i y_i - \left(\sum_{i=1}^{n} x_i\right)\left(\sum_{i=1}^{n} y_i\right)}{n\sum_{i=1}^{n} x_i^2 - \left(\sum_{i=1}^{n} x_i\right)^2}$$

The $\widehat{y}$-values can be used to predict y-values for given values of x.

When working with functions of several variables, we can consider their multiple integrals. These are determined by successive integration. For example, the double integral

$$\int_1^2 \int_0^y (x + y)\, dx\, dy$$

is determined by first treating y as a constant and integrating $x + y$ with respect to x. After evaluating between the limits 0 and y, we integrate that result with respect to y from $y = 1$ to $y = 2$. Thus,

$$\int_1^2 \int_0^y (x + y)\, dx\, dy = \int_1^2 \left(\int_0^y (x + y)\, dx\right) dy$$

Triple integrals involve functions of three variables and are also evaluated by successive integration.

Review Problems

In Problems 1–12, find the indicated partial derivatives.

1. $f(x, y) = \ln(x^2 + y^2)$; $f_x(x, y), f_y(x, y)$

2. $P = l^3 + k^3 - lk$; $\partial P/\partial l, \partial P/\partial k$

3. $z = \dfrac{x}{x + y}$; $\dfrac{\partial z}{\partial x}, \dfrac{\partial z}{\partial y}$

4. $f(p_A, p_B) = 4(p_A - 10) + 5(p_B - 15)$; $f_{p_B}(p_A, p_B)$

5. $f(x, y) = \ln\sqrt{x^2 + y^2}$; $\dfrac{\partial}{\partial y}[f(x, y)]$

6. $w = \sqrt{x^2 + y^2}$; $\dfrac{\partial w}{\partial y}$ 7. $w = e^{x^2 yz}$; $w_{xy}(x, y, z)$

8. $f(x, y) = xy \ln(xy); \quad f_{xy}(x, y)$

9. $f(x, y, z) = (x + y + z)(x^2 + y^2 + z^2); \quad \dfrac{\partial^2}{\partial z^2}(f(x, y, z))$

10. $z = (x^2 - y)(y^2 - 2xy); \quad \partial^2 z / \partial y^2$

11. $w = e^{x+y+z} \ln(xyz); \quad \partial^3 w / \partial z \partial y \partial x$

12. $P = 100 l^{0.11} k^{0.89}; \quad \partial^2 P / \partial k \partial l$

13. If $f(x, y, z) = \dfrac{x + y}{xz}$, find $f_{xyz}(2, 7, 4)$

14. If $f(x, y, z) = (6x + 1)e^{y^2 \ln(z+1)}$, find $f_{xyz}(0, 1, 0)$

15. If $w = x^2 + 2xy + 3y^2$, $x = e^r$, and $y = \ln(r + s)$, find $\partial w / \partial r$ and $\partial w / \partial s$.

16. If $z = \ln(x/y)$, $x = r^2 + s^2$, and $y = (r + s)^2$, find $\partial z / \partial r - \partial z / \partial s$.

17. If $x^2 + 2xy - 2z^2 + xz + 2 = 0$, find $\partial z / \partial x$.

18. If $z^2 + \ln(yz) + \ln z + x + z = 0$, find $\partial z / \partial y$.

[24]19. Production Function If a manufacturer's production function is defined by $P = 20 l^{0.7} k^{0.3}$, determine the marginal productivity functions.

[24]20. Joint-Cost Function A manufacturer's cost for producing x units of product X and y units of product Y is given by

$$c = 3x + 0.05xy + 9y + 500$$

Determine the (partial) marginal cost with respect to x when $x = 50$ and $y = 100$.

[24]21. Competitive/Complementary Products If $q_A = 100 - p_A + 2p_B$ and $q_B = 150 - 3p_A - 2p_B$, where q_A and q_B are the number of units demanded of products A and B, respectively, and p_A and p_B are their respective prices per unit, determine whether A and B are competitive products or complementary products or neither.

[24]22. Innovation For industry, the following model describes the rate α (a Greek letter read "alpha") at which an innovation substitutes for an established process:[25]

$$\alpha = Z + 0.530P - 0.027S$$

Here, Z is a constant that depends on the particular industry, P is an index of profitability of the innovation, and S is an index of the extent of the investment necessary to make use of the innovation. Find $\partial \alpha / \partial P$ and $\partial \alpha / \partial S$.

23. Examine $f(x, y) = x^2 + 2y^2 - 2xy - 4y + 3$ for relative extrema.

24. Examine $f(w, z) = 2w^3 + 2z^3 - 6wz + 7$ for relative extrema.

25. Minimizing Material An open-top rectangular cardboard box is to have a volume of 32 cubic feet. Find the dimensions of the box so that the amount of cardboard used is minimized.

26. The function

$$f(x, y) = ax^2 + by^2 + cxy - x + y$$

has a critical point at $(x, y) = (0, 1)$, and the second-derivative test is inconclusive at this point. Determine the values of the constants a, b, and c.

27. Maximizing Profit A dairy produces two types of cheese, A and B, at constant average costs of 50 cents and 60 cents per pound, respectively. When the selling price per pound of A is p_A cents and of B is p_B cents, the demands (in pounds) for A and B, are, respectively,

$$q_A = 250(p_B - p_A)$$

and

$$q_B = 32{,}000 + 250(p_A - 2p_B)$$

Find the selling prices that yield a relative maximum profit. Verify that the profit has a relative maximum at these prices.

28. Find all critical points of $f(x, y, z) = xy^2z$, subject to the condition that

$$x + y + z - 1 = 0 \ (xyz \neq 0)$$

29. Find all critical points of $f(x, y, z) = x^2 + y^2 + z^2$, subject to the constraint $3x + 2y + z = 14$.

30. Surviving Infection In an experiment,[26] a group of fish was injected with living bacteria. Of those fish maintained at $28°C$, the percentage p that survived the infection t hours after the injection is given in the following table:

t	8	10	18	20	48
p	82	79	78	78	64

Find the linear regression line of p on t.

31. Equipment Expenditures Find the least squares linear regression line of y on x for the data given in the following table (refer to year 1993 as year $x = 1$, etc.):

Equipment Expenditures of Allied Computer Company, 1993–1998 (in millions of dollars)	
Year	Expenditures
1993	15
1994	22
1995	21
1996	26
1997	27
1998	34

In Problems 32–35, evaluate the double integrals.

32. $\displaystyle \int_1^2 \int_0^y x^2 y^2 \, dx \, dy$ **33.** $\displaystyle \int_0^1 \int_0^{y^2} xy \, dx \, dy$

34. $\displaystyle \int_1^4 \int_{x^2}^{2x} y \, dy \, dx$ **35.** $\displaystyle \int_0^1 \int_{\sqrt{x}}^{x^2} 7(x^2 + 2xy - 3y^2) \, dy \, dx$

---

[24] Problems 19–22 refer to Section 17.3 or Section 17.5.

[25] A. P. Hurter, Jr., A. H. Rubenstein, et al., "Market Penetration by New Innovations: The Technological Literature," *Technological Forecasting and Social Change*, 11 (1978), 197–221.

[26] J. B. Covert and W. W. Reynolds, "Survival Value of Fever in Fish," *Nature*, 267, no. 5606 (1977), 43–45.

$\mathbb{Q}$ EXPLORE & EXTEND Data Analysis to Model Cooling[1]

In Chapter 15 you worked with Newton's law of cooling, which can be used to describe the temperature of a cooling body with respect to time. Here you will determine that relationship in an empirical way via data analysis. This will illustrate how mathematical models are designed in many real-world situations.

Suppose that you want to create a mathematical model of the cooling of hot tea after it is placed in a refrigerator. To do this you place a pitcher containing hot tea and a thermometer in the refrigerator and periodically read and record the temperature of the tea. Table 17.5 gives the collected data, where T is the Fahrenheit temperature t minutes after the tea is placed in the refrigerator. Initially, that is, at $t = 0$, the temperature is 124°F; when $t = 391$, then $T = 47$°F. After being in the refrigerator overnight, the temperature is 45°F. Figure 17.16 gives a graph of the data points (t, T) for $t = 0$ to $t = 391$.

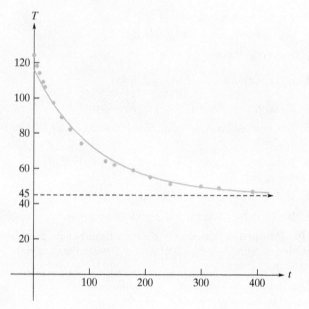

FIGURE 17.16 Data points and exponential approximation.

Table 17.5

Time t	Temperature T	Time t	Temperature T
0 min	124°F	128 min	64°F
5	118	144	62
10	114	178	59
16	109	208	55
20	106	244	51
35	97	299	50
50	89	331	49
65	82	391	47
85	74	Overnight	45

The pattern of these points strongly suggests that they nearly lie on the graph of a decreasing exponential function, such as the one shown in Figure 17.16. In particular, because the overnight temperature is 45°F, this exponential function should have $T = 45$ as a horizontal asymptote. Such a function has the form

$$\widehat{T} = Ce^{at} + 45 \qquad (1)$$

where $\widehat{T}$ gives the predicted temperature at time t, and C and a are constants with $a < 0$. (Note that since $a < 0$, then as $t \to \infty$, you have $Ce^{at} \to 0$, so $Ce^{at} + 45 \to 45$.)

Now the problem is to find the values of C and a so that the curve given by Equation (1) best fits the data. By writing Equation (1) as

$$\widehat{T} - 45 = Ce^{at}$$

and then taking the natural logarithm of each side, we obtain a linear form:

$$\ln(\widehat{T} - 45) = \ln(Ce^{at})$$
$$\ln(\widehat{T} - 45) = \ln C + \ln e^{at}$$
$$\ln(\widehat{T} - 45) = \ln C + at \qquad (2)$$

Letting $\widehat{T}_l = \ln(\widehat{T} - 45)$, Equation (2) becomes

$$\widehat{T}_l = at + \ln C \qquad (3)$$

Because a and $\ln C$ are constants, Equation (3) is a linear equation in $\widehat{T}_l$ and t. This means that for the original data, if you plot the points $(t, \ln(T - 45))$, they should nearly lie on a straight line. These points are shown in Figure 17.17, where T_l represents $\ln(T - 45)$. Thus for the line given by Equation (3) that predicts $T_l = \ln(T - 45)$, you can assume that it is the linear regression line of T_l on t. That is, a and $\ln C$ are linear regression coefficients. By using the formulas for these coefficients and a calculator, you can determine that

$$a = \frac{17\left(\sum_{i=1}^{17} t_i T_{l_i}\right) - \left(\sum_{i=1}^{17} t_i\right)\left(\sum_{i=1}^{17} T_{l_i}\right)}{17\left(\sum_{i=1}^{17} t_i^2\right) - \left(\sum_{i=1}^{17} t_i\right)^2} \approx -0.00921$$

[1]Adapted from Gloria Barrett, Dot Doyle, and Dan Teague, "Using Data Analysis in Precalculus to Model Cooling," *The Mathematics Teacher,* 81, no. 8 (November 1988), 680–84. By permission of the National Council of Teachers of Mathematics.

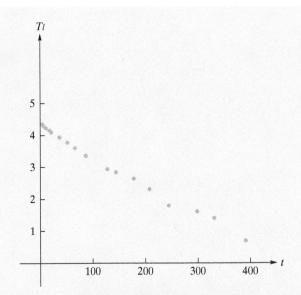

FIGURE 17.17 The points (t, T_l), where $T_l = \ln(T - 45)$, nearly lie on a straight line.

and

$$\ln C = \frac{\left(\displaystyle\sum_{i=1}^{17} t_i^2\right)\left(\displaystyle\sum_{i=1}^{17} T_{l_i}\right) - \left(\displaystyle\sum_{i=1}^{17} t_i\right)\left(\displaystyle\sum_{i=1}^{17} t_i T_{l_i}\right)}{17\left(\displaystyle\sum_{i=1}^{17} t_i^2\right) - \left(\displaystyle\sum_{i=1}^{17} t_i\right)^2}$$

$$\approx 4.260074$$

Since $\ln C \approx 4.260074$, then $C \approx e^{4.260074} \approx 70.82$. Thus from Equation (1),

$$\widehat{T} = 70.82e^{-0.00921t} + 45$$

which is a model that predicts the temperature of the cooling tea. The graph of this function is the curve shown in Figure 17.16.

Problems

1. Plot the following data points on an x,y-coordinate plane:

x	0	1	4	7	10
y	15	12	9	7	6

Suppose that these points nearly lie on the graph of a decreasing exponential function with horizontal asymptote $y = 5$. Use the technique discussed in this Explore and Extend to determine the function.

2. Suppose that observed data follow a relation given by $y = C/x^r$, where $x, y, C > 0$. By taking the natural logarithm of each side, show that $\ln x$ and $\ln y$ are linearly related. Thus, the points $(\ln x, \ln y)$ lie on a straight line.

3. Use Newton's law of cooling (see Section 15.6) and the data points $(0, 124)$ and $(128, 64)$ to determine the temperature T of the tea discussed in this Explore and Extend at time t. Assume that the ambient temperature is 45°F.

4. Try obtaining the final regression equation in this Explore and Extend using the regression capability of a graphing calculator. First use linear regression. How does your result compare with the one in this Explore and Extend Then try skipping the linear-form transformation and perform an exponential regression. What difficulty do you encounter, if any? How could it be overcome?

A

Compound Interest Tables

$r = 0.005$					$r = 0.0075$			
n	$(1+r)^n$	$(1+r)^{-n}$	$a_{\overline{n}|r}$	$s_{\overline{n}|r}$	n	$(1+r)^n$	$(1+r)^{-n}$	$a_{\overline{n}|r}$	$s_{\overline{n}|r}$

n	$(1+r)^n$	$(1+r)^{-n}$	$a_{\overline{n}|r}$	$s_{\overline{n}|r}$	n	$(1+r)^n$	$(1+r)^{-n}$	$a_{\overline{n}|r}$	$s_{\overline{n}|r}$
1	1.005000	0.995025	0.995025	1.000000	1	1.007500	0.992556	0.992556	1.000000
2	1.010025	0.990075	1.985099	2.005000	2	1.015056	0.985167	1.977723	2.007500
3	1.015075	0.985149	2.970248	3.015025	3	1.022669	0.977833	2.955556	3.022556
4	1.020151	0.980248	3.950496	4.030100	4	1.030339	0.970554	3.926110	4.045225
5	1.025251	0.975371	4.925866	5.050251	5	1.038067	0.963329	4.889440	5.075565
6	1.030378	0.970518	5.896384	6.075502	6	1.045852	0.956158	5.845598	6.113631
7	1.035529	0.965690	6.862074	7.105879	7	1.053696	0.949040	6.794638	7.159484
8	1.040707	0.960885	7.822959	8.141409	8	1.061599	0.941975	7.736613	8.213180
9	1.045911	0.956105	8.779064	9.182116	9	1.069561	0.934963	8.671576	9.274779
10	1.051140	0.951348	9.730412	10.228026	10	1.077583	0.928003	9.599580	10.344339
11	1.056396	0.946615	10.677027	11.279167	11	1.085664	0.921095	10.520675	11.421922
12	1.061678	0.941905	11.618932	12.335562	12	1.093807	0.914238	11.434913	12.507586
13	1.066986	0.937219	12.556151	13.397240	13	1.102010	0.907432	12.342345	13.601393
14	1.072321	0.932556	13.488708	14.464226	14	1.110276	0.900677	13.243022	14.703404
15	1.077683	0.927917	14.416625	15.536548	15	1.118603	0.893973	14.136995	15.813679
16	1.083071	0.923300	15.339925	16.614230	16	1.126992	0.887318	15.024313	16.932282
17	1.088487	0.918707	16.258632	17.697301	17	1.135445	0.880712	15.905025	18.059274
18	1.093929	0.914136	17.172768	18.785788	18	1.143960	0.874156	16.779181	19.194718
19	1.099399	0.909588	18.082356	19.879717	19	1.152540	0.867649	17.646830	20.338679
20	1.104896	0.905063	18.987419	20.979115	20	1.161184	0.861190	18.508020	21.491219
21	1.110420	0.900560	19.887979	22.084011	21	1.169893	0.854779	19.362799	22.652403
22	1.115972	0.896080	20.784059	23.194431	22	1.178667	0.848416	20.211215	23.822296
23	1.121552	0.891622	21.675681	24.310403	23	1.187507	0.842100	21.053315	25.000963
24	1.127160	0.887186	22.562866	25.431955	24	1.196414	0.835831	21.889146	26.188471
25	1.132796	0.882772	23.445638	26.559115	25	1.205387	0.829609	22.718755	27.384884
26	1.138460	0.878380	24.324018	27.691911	26	1.214427	0.823434	23.542189	28.590271
27	1.144152	0.874010	25.198028	28.830370	27	1.223535	0.817304	24.359493	29.804698
28	1.149873	0.869662	26.067689	29.974522	28	1.232712	0.811220	25.170713	31.028233
29	1.155622	0.865335	26.933024	31.124395	29	1.241957	0.805181	25.975893	32.260945
30	1.161400	0.861030	27.794054	32.280017	30	1.251272	0.799187	26.775080	33.502902
31	1.167207	0.856746	28.650800	33.441417	31	1.260656	0.793238	27.568318	34.754174
32	1.173043	0.852484	29.503284	34.608624	32	1.270111	0.787333	28.355650	36.014830
33	1.178908	0.848242	30.351526	35.781667	33	1.279637	0.781472	29.137122	37.284941
34	1.184803	0.844022	31.195548	36.960575	34	1.289234	0.775654	29.912776	38.564578
35	1.190727	0.839823	32.035371	38.145378	35	1.298904	0.769880	30.682656	39.853813
36	1.196681	0.835645	32.871016	39.336105	36	1.308645	0.764149	31.446805	41.152716
37	1.202664	0.831487	33.702504	40.532785	37	1.318460	0.758461	32.205266	42.461361
38	1.208677	0.827351	34.529854	41.735449	38	1.328349	0.752814	32.958080	43.779822
39	1.214721	0.823235	35.353089	42.944127	39	1.338311	0.747210	33.705290	45.108170
40	1.220794	0.819139	36.172228	44.158847	40	1.348349	0.741648	34.446938	46.446482
41	1.226898	0.815064	36.987291	45.379642	41	1.358461	0.736127	35.183065	47.794830
42	1.233033	0.811009	37.798300	46.606540	42	1.368650	0.730647	35.913713	49.153291
43	1.239198	0.806974	38.605274	47.839572	43	1.378915	0.725208	36.638921	50.521941
44	1.245394	0.802959	39.408232	49.078770	44	1.389256	0.719810	37.358730	51.900856
45	1.251621	0.798964	40.207196	50.324164	45	1.399676	0.714451	38.073181	53.290112
46	1.257879	0.794989	41.002185	51.575785	46	1.410173	0.709133	38.782314	54.689788
47	1.264168	0.791034	41.793219	52.833664	47	1.420750	0.703854	39.486168	56.099961
48	1.270489	0.787098	42.580318	54.097832	48	1.431405	0.698614	40.184782	57.520711
49	1.276842	0.783182	43.363500	55.368321	49	1.442141	0.693414	40.878195	58.952116
50	1.283226	0.779286	44.142786	56.645163	50	1.452957	0.688252	41.566447	60.394257

		$r = 0.01$					$r = 0.0125$	
n	$(1+r)^n$	$(1+r)^{-n}$	$a_{\overline{n}|r}$	$s_{\overline{n}|r}$	n	$(1+r)^n$	$(1+r)^{-n}$	$a_{\overline{n}|r}$	$s_{\overline{n}|r}$

n	$(1+r)^n$	$(1+r)^{-n}$	$a_{\overline{n}|r}$	$s_{\overline{n}|r}$	n	$(1+r)^n$	$(1+r)^{-n}$	$a_{\overline{n}|r}$	$s_{\overline{n}|r}$
1	1.010000	0.990099	0.990099	1.000000	1	1.012500	0.987654	0.987654	1.000000
2	1.020100	0.980296	1.970395	2.010000	2	1.025156	0.975461	1.963115	2.012500
3	1.030301	0.970590	2.940985	3.030100	3	1.037971	0.963418	2.926534	3.037656
4	1.040604	0.960980	3.901966	4.060401	4	1.050945	0.951524	3.878058	4.075627
5	1.051010	0.951466	4.853431	5.101005	5	1.064082	0.939777	4.817835	5.126572
6	1.061520	0.942045	5.795476	6.152015	6	1.077383	0.928175	5.746010	6.190654
7	1.072135	0.932718	6.728195	7.213535	7	1.090850	0.916716	6.662726	7.268038
8	1.082857	0.923483	7.651678	8.285671	8	1.104486	0.905398	7.568124	8.358888
9	1.093685	0.914340	8.566018	9.368527	9	1.118292	0.894221	8.462345	9.463374
10	1.104622	0.905287	9.471305	10.462213	10	1.132271	0.883181	9.345526	10.581666
11	1.115668	0.896324	10.367628	11.566835	11	1.146424	0.872277	10.217803	11.713937
12	1.126825	0.887449	11.255077	12.682503	12	1.160755	0.861509	11.079312	12.860361
13	1.138093	0.878663	12.133740	13.809328	13	1.175264	0.850873	11.930185	14.021116
14	1.149474	0.869963	13.003703	14.947421	14	1.189955	0.840368	12.770553	15.196380
15	1.160969	0.861349	13.865053	16.096896	15	1.204829	0.829993	13.600546	16.386335
16	1.172579	0.852821	14.717874	17.257864	16	1.219890	0.819746	14.420292	17.591164
17	1.184304	0.844377	15.562251	18.430443	17	1.235138	0.809626	15.229918	18.811053
18	1.196147	0.836017	16.398269	19.614748	18	1.250577	0.799631	16.029549	20.046192
19	1.208109	0.827740	17.226008	20.810895	19	1.266210	0.789759	16.819308	21.296769
20	1.220190	0.819544	18.045553	22.019004	20	1.282037	0.780009	17.599316	22.562979
21	1.232392	0.811430	18.856983	23.239194	21	1.298063	0.770379	18.369695	23.845016
22	1.244716	0.803396	19.660379	24.471586	22	1.314288	0.760868	19.130563	25.143078
23	1.257163	0.795442	20.455821	25.716302	23	1.330717	0.751475	19.882037	26.457367
24	1.269735	0.787566	21.243387	26.973465	24	1.347351	0.742197	20.624235	27.788084
25	1.282432	0.779768	22.023156	28.243200	25	1.364193	0.733034	21.357269	29.135435
26	1.295256	0.772048	22.795204	29.525631	26	1.381245	0.723984	22.081253	30.499628
27	1.308209	0.764404	23.559608	30.820888	27	1.398511	0.715046	22.796299	31.880873
28	1.321291	0.756836	24.316443	32.129097	28	1.415992	0.706219	23.502518	33.279384
29	1.334504	0.749342	25.065785	33.450388	29	1.433692	0.697500	24.200018	34.695377
30	1.347849	0.741923	25.807708	34.784892	30	1.451613	0.688889	24.888906	36.129069
31	1.361327	0.734577	26.542285	36.132740	31	1.469759	0.680384	25.569290	37.580682
32	1.374941	0.727304	27.269589	37.494068	32	1.488131	0.671984	26.241274	39.050441
33	1.388690	0.720103	27.989693	38.869009	33	1.506732	0.663688	26.904962	40.538571
34	1.402577	0.712973	28.702666	40.257699	34	1.525566	0.655494	27.560456	42.045303
35	1.416603	0.705914	29.408580	41.660276	35	1.544636	0.647402	28.207858	43.570870
36	1.430769	0.698925	30.107505	43.076878	36	1.563944	0.639409	28.847267	45.115505
37	1.445076	0.692005	30.799510	44.507647	37	1.583493	0.631515	29.478783	46.679449
38	1.459527	0.685153	31.484663	45.952724	38	1.603287	0.623719	30.102501	48.262942
39	1.474123	0.678370	32.163033	47.412251	39	1.623328	0.616019	30.718520	49.866229
40	1.488864	0.671653	32.834686	48.886373	40	1.643619	0.608413	31.326933	51.489557
41	1.503752	0.665003	33.499689	50.375237	41	1.664165	0.600902	31.927835	53.133177
42	1.518790	0.658419	34.158108	51.878989	42	1.684967	0.593484	32.521319	54.797341
43	1.533978	0.651900	34.810008	53.397779	43	1.706029	0.586157	33.107475	56.482308
44	1.549318	0.645445	35.455454	54.931757	44	1.727354	0.578920	33.686395	58.188337
45	1.564811	0.639055	36.094508	56.481075	45	1.748946	0.571773	34.258168	59.915691
46	1.580459	0.632728	36.727236	58.045885	46	1.770808	0.564714	34.822882	61.664637
47	1.596263	0.626463	37.353699	59.626344	47	1.792943	0.557742	35.380624	63.435445
48	1.612226	0.620260	37.973959	61.222608	48	1.815355	0.550856	35.931481	65.228388
49	1.628348	0.614119	38.588079	62.834834	49	1.838047	0.544056	36.475537	67.043743
50	1.644632	0.608039	39.196118	64.463182	50	1.861022	0.537339	37.012876	68.881790

$r = 0.015$				
n	$(1+r)^n$	$(1+r)^{-n}$	$a_{\overline{n}|r}$	$s_{\overline{n}|r}$
1	1.015000	0.985222	0.985222	1.000000
2	1.030225	0.970662	1.955883	2.015000
3	1.045678	0.956317	2.912200	3.045225
4	1.061364	0.942184	3.854385	4.090903
5	1.077284	0.928260	4.782645	5.152267
6	1.093443	0.914542	5.697187	6.229551
7	1.109845	0.901027	6.598214	7.322994
8	1.126493	0.887711	7.485925	8.432839
9	1.143390	0.874592	8.360517	9.559332
10	1.160541	0.861667	9.222185	10.702722
11	1.177949	0.848933	10.071118	11.863262
12	1.195618	0.836387	10.907505	13.041211
13	1.213552	0.824027	11.731532	14.236830
14	1.231756	0.811849	12.543382	15.450382
15	1.250232	0.799852	13.343233	16.682138
16	1.268986	0.788031	14.131264	17.932370
17	1.288020	0.776385	14.907649	19.201355
18	1.307341	0.764912	15.672561	20.489376
19	1.326951	0.753607	16.426168	21.796716
20	1.346855	0.742470	17.168639	23.123667
21	1.367058	0.731498	17.900137	24.470522
22	1.387564	0.720688	18.620824	25.837580
23	1.408377	0.710037	19.330861	27.225144
24	1.429503	0.699544	20.030405	28.633521
25	1.450945	0.689206	20.719611	30.063024
26	1.472710	0.679021	21.398632	31.513969
27	1.494800	0.668986	22.067617	32.986678
28	1.517222	0.659099	22.726717	34.481479
29	1.539981	0.649359	23.376076	35.998701
30	1.563080	0.639762	24.015838	37.538681
31	1.586526	0.630308	24.646146	39.101762
32	1.610324	0.620993	25.267139	40.688288
33	1.634479	0.611816	25.878954	42.298612
34	1.658996	0.602774	26.481728	43.933092
35	1.683881	0.593866	27.075595	45.592088
36	1.709140	0.585090	27.660684	47.275969
37	1.734777	0.576443	28.237127	48.985109
38	1.760798	0.567924	28.805052	50.719885
39	1.787210	0.559531	29.364583	52.480684
40	1.814018	0.551262	29.915845	54.267894
41	1.841229	0.543116	30.458961	56.081912
42	1.868847	0.535089	30.994050	57.923141
43	1.896880	0.527182	31.521232	59.791988
44	1.925333	0.519391	32.040622	61.688868
45	1.954213	0.511715	32.552337	63.614201
46	1.983526	0.504153	33.056490	65.568414
47	2.013279	0.496702	33.553192	67.551940
48	2.043478	0.489362	34.042554	69.565219
49	2.074130	0.482130	34.524683	71.608698
50	2.105242	0.475005	34.999688	73.682828

$r = 0.02$				
n	$(1+r)^n$	$(1+r)^{-n}$	$a_{\overline{n}|r}$	$s_{\overline{n}|r}$
1	1.020000	0.980392	0.980392	1.000000
2	1.040400	0.961169	1.941561	2.020000
3	1.061208	0.942322	2.883883	3.060400
4	1.082432	0.923845	3.807729	4.121608
5	1.104081	0.905731	4.713460	5.204040
6	1.126162	0.887971	5.601431	6.308121
7	1.148686	0.870560	6.471991	7.434283
8	1.171659	0.853490	7.325481	8.582969
9	1.195093	0.836755	8.162237	9.754628
10	1.218994	0.820348	8.982585	10.949721
11	1.243374	0.804263	9.786848	12.168715
12	1.268242	0.788493	10.575341	13.412090
13	1.293607	0.773033	11.348374	14.680332
14	1.319479	0.757875	12.106249	15.973938
15	1.345868	0.743015	12.849264	17.293417
16	1.372786	0.728446	13.577709	18.639285
17	1.400241	0.714163	14.291872	20.012071
18	1.428246	0.700159	14.992031	21.412312
19	1.456811	0.686431	15.678462	22.840559
20	1.485947	0.672971	16.351433	24.297370
21	1.515666	0.659776	17.011209	25.783317
22	1.545980	0.646839	17.658048	27.298984
23	1.576899	0.634156	18.292204	28.844963
24	1.608437	0.621721	18.913926	30.421862
25	1.640606	0.609531	19.523456	32.030300
26	1.673418	0.597579	20.121036	33.670906
27	1.706886	0.585862	20.706898	35.344324
28	1.741024	0.574375	21.281272	37.051210
29	1.775845	0.563112	21.844385	38.792235
30	1.811362	0.552071	22.396456	40.568079
31	1.847589	0.541246	22.937702	42.379441
32	1.884541	0.530633	23.468335	44.227030
33	1.922231	0.520229	23.988564	46.111570
34	1.960676	0.510028	24.498592	48.033802
35	1.999890	0.500028	24.998619	49.994478
36	2.039887	0.490223	25.488842	51.994367
37	2.080685	0.480611	25.969453	54.034255
38	2.122299	0.471187	26.440641	56.114940
39	2.164745	0.461948	26.902589	58.237238
40	2.208040	0.452890	27.355479	60.401983
41	2.252200	0.444010	27.799489	62.610023
42	2.297244	0.435304	28.234794	64.862223
43	2.343189	0.426769	28.661562	67.159468
44	2.390053	0.418401	29.079963	69.502657
45	2.437854	0.410197	29.490160	71.892710
46	2.486611	0.402154	29.892314	74.330564
47	2.536344	0.394268	30.286582	76.817176
48	2.587070	0.386538	30.673120	79.353519
49	2.638812	0.378958	31.052078	81.940590
50	2.691588	0.371528	31.423606	84.579401

		$r = 0.025$					$r = 0.03$		
n	$(1+r)^n$	$(1+r)^{-n}$	$a_{\overline{n}|r}$	$s_{\overline{n}|r}$	n	$(1+r)^n$	$(1+r)^{-n}$	$a_{\overline{n}|r}$	$s_{\overline{n}|r}$
1	1.025000	0.975610	0.975610	1.000000	1	1.030000	0.970874	0.970874	1.000000
2	1.050625	0.951814	1.927424	2.025000	2	1.060900	0.942596	1.913470	2.030000
3	1.076891	0.928599	2.856024	3.075625	3	1.092727	0.915142	2.828611	3.090900
4	1.103813	0.905951	3.761974	4.152516	4	1.125509	0.888487	3.717098	4.183627
5	1.131408	0.883854	4.645828	5.256329	5	1.159274	0.862609	4.579707	5.309136
6	1.159693	0.862297	5.508125	6.387737	6	1.194052	0.837484	5.417191	6.468410
7	1.188686	0.841265	6.349391	7.547430	7	1.229874	0.813092	6.230283	7.662462
8	1.218403	0.820747	7.170137	8.736116	8	1.266770	0.789409	7.019692	8.892336
9	1.248863	0.800728	7.970866	9.954519	9	1.304773	0.766417	7.786109	10.159106
10	1.280085	0.781198	8.752064	11.203382	10	1.343916	0.744094	8.530203	11.463879
11	1.312087	0.762145	9.514209	12.483466	11	1.384234	0.722421	9.252624	12.807796
12	1.344889	0.743556	10.257765	13.795553	12	1.425761	0.701380	9.954004	14.192030
13	1.378511	0.725420	10.983185	15.140442	13	1.468534	0.680951	10.634955	15.617790
14	1.412974	0.707727	11.690912	16.518953	14	1.512590	0.661118	11.296073	17.086324
15	1.448298	0.690466	12.381378	17.931927	15	1.557967	0.641862	11.937935	18.598914
16	1.484506	0.673625	13.055003	19.380225	16	1.604706	0.623167	12.561102	20.156881
17	1.521618	0.657195	13.712198	20.864730	17	1.652848	0.605016	13.166118	21.761588
18	1.559659	0.641166	14.353364	22.386349	18	1.702433	0.587395	13.753513	23.414435
19	1.598650	0.625528	14.978891	23.946007	19	1.753506	0.570286	14.323799	25.116868
20	1.638616	0.610271	15.589162	25.544658	20	1.806111	0.553676	14.877475	26.870374
21	1.679582	0.595386	16.184549	27.183274	21	1.860295	0.537549	15.415024	28.676486
22	1.721571	0.580865	16.765413	28.862856	22	1.916103	0.521893	15.936917	30.536780
23	1.764611	0.566697	17.332110	30.584427	23	1.973587	0.506692	16.443608	32.452884
24	1.808726	0.552875	17.884986	32.349038	24	2.032794	0.491934	16.935542	34.426470
25	1.853944	0.539391	18.424376	34.157764	25	2.093778	0.477606	17.413148	36.459264
26	1.900293	0.526235	18.950611	36.011708	26	2.156591	0.463695	17.876842	38.553042
27	1.947800	0.513400	19.464011	37.912001	27	2.221289	0.450189	18.327031	40.709634
28	1.996495	0.500878	19.964889	39.859801	28	2.287928	0.437077	18.764108	42.930923
29	2.046407	0.488661	20.453550	41.856296	29	2.356566	0.424346	19.188455	45.218850
30	2.097568	0.476743	20.930293	43.902703	30	2.427262	0.411987	19.600441	47.575416
31	2.150007	0.465115	21.395407	46.000271	31	2.500080	0.399987	20.000428	50.002678
32	2.203757	0.453771	21.849178	48.150278	32	2.575083	0.388337	20.388766	52.502759
33	2.258851	0.442703	22.291881	50.354034	33	2.652335	0.377026	20.765792	55.077841
34	2.315322	0.431905	22.723786	52.612885	34	2.731905	0.366045	21.131837	57.730177
35	2.373205	0.421371	23.145157	54.928207	35	2.813862	0.355383	21.487220	60.462082
36	2.432535	0.411094	23.556251	57.301413	36	2.898278	0.345032	21.832252	63.275944
37	2.493349	0.401067	23.957318	59.733948	37	2.985227	0.334983	22.167235	66.174223
38	2.555682	0.391285	24.348603	62.227297	38	3.074783	0.325226	22.492462	69.159449
39	2.619574	0.381741	24.730344	64.782979	39	3.167027	0.315754	22.808215	72.234233
40	2.685064	0.372431	25.102775	67.402554	40	3.262038	0.306557	23.114772	75.401260
41	2.752190	0.363347	25.466122	70.087617	41	3.359899	0.297628	23.412400	78.663298
42	2.820995	0.354485	25.820607	72.839808	42	3.460696	0.288959	23.701359	82.023196
43	2.891520	0.345839	26.166446	75.660803	43	3.564517	0.280543	23.981902	85.483892
44	2.963808	0.337404	26.503849	78.552323	44	3.671452	0.272372	24.254274	89.048409
45	3.037903	0.329174	26.833024	81.516131	45	3.781596	0.264439	24.518713	92.719861
46	3.113851	0.321146	27.154170	84.554034	46	3.895044	0.256737	24.775449	96.501457
47	3.191697	0.313313	27.467483	87.667885	47	4.011895	0.249259	25.024708	100.396501
48	3.271490	0.305671	27.773154	90.859582	48	4.132252	0.241999	25.266707	104.408396
49	3.353277	0.298216	28.071369	94.131072	49	4.256219	0.234950	25.501657	108.540648
50	3.437109	0.290942	28.362312	97.484349	50	4.383906	0.228107	25.729764	112.796867

		$r = 0.035$		
n	$(1+r)^n$	$(1+r)^{-n}$	$a_{\overline{n}|r}$	$s_{\overline{n}|r}$
1	1.035000	0.966184	0.966184	1.000000
2	1.071225	0.933511	1.899694	2.035000
3	1.108718	0.901943	2.801637	3.106225
4	1.147523	0.871442	3.673079	4.214943
5	1.187686	0.841973	4.515052	5.362466
6	1.229255	0.813501	5.328553	6.550152
7	1.272279	0.785991	6.114544	7.779408
8	1.316809	0.759412	6.873956	9.051687
9	1.362897	0.733731	7.607687	10.368496
10	1.410599	0.708919	8.316605	11.731393
11	1.459970	0.684946	9.001551	13.141992
12	1.511069	0.661783	9.663334	14.601962
13	1.563956	0.639404	10.302738	16.113030
14	1.618695	0.617782	10.920520	17.676986
15	1.675349	0.596891	11.517411	19.295681
16	1.733986	0.576706	12.094117	20.971030
17	1.794676	0.557204	12.651321	22.705016
18	1.857489	0.538361	13.189682	24.499691
19	1.922501	0.520156	13.709837	26.357180
20	1.989789	0.502566	14.212403	28.279682
21	2.059431	0.485571	14.697974	30.269471
22	2.131512	0.469151	15.167125	32.328902
23	2.206114	0.453286	15.620410	34.460414
24	2.283328	0.437957	16.058368	36.666528
25	2.363245	0.423147	16.481515	38.949857
26	2.445959	0.408838	16.890352	41.313102
27	2.531567	0.395012	17.285365	43.759060
28	2.620172	0.381654	17.667019	46.290627
29	2.711878	0.368748	18.035767	48.910799
30	2.806794	0.356278	18.392045	51.622677
31	2.905031	0.344230	18.736276	54.429471
32	3.006708	0.332590	19.068865	57.334502
33	3.111942	0.321343	19.390208	60.341210
34	3.220860	0.310476	19.700684	63.453152
35	3.333590	0.299977	20.000661	66.674013
36	3.450266	0.289833	20.290494	70.007603
37	3.571025	0.280032	20.570525	73.457869
38	3.696011	0.270562	20.841087	77.028895
39	3.825372	0.261413	21.102500	80.724906
40	3.959260	0.252572	21.355072	84.550278
41	4.097834	0.244031	21.599104	88.509537
42	4.241258	0.235779	21.834883	92.607371
43	4.389702	0.227806	22.062689	96.848629
44	4.543342	0.220102	22.282791	101.238331
45	4.702359	0.212659	22.495450	105.781673
46	4.866941	0.205468	22.700918	110.484031
47	5.037284	0.198520	22.899438	115.350973
48	5.213589	0.191806	23.091244	120.388257
49	5.396065	0.185320	23.276564	125.601846
50	5.584927	0.179053	23.455618	130.997910

		$r = 0.04$		
n	$(1+r)^n$	$(1+r)^{-n}$	$a_{\overline{n}|r}$	$s_{\overline{n}|r}$
1	1.040000	0.961538	0.961538	1.000000
2	1.081600	0.924556	1.886095	2.040000
3	1.124864	0.888996	2.775091	3.121600
4	1.169859	0.854804	3.629895	4.246464
5	1.216653	0.821927	4.451822	5.416323
6	1.265319	0.790315	5.242137	6.632975
7	1.315932	0.759918	6.002055	7.898294
8	1.368569	0.730690	6.732745	9.214226
9	1.423312	0.702587	7.435332	10.582795
10	1.480244	0.675564	8.110896	12.006107
11	1.539454	0.649581	8.760477	13.486351
12	1.601032	0.624597	9.385074	15.025805
13	1.665074	0.600574	9.985648	16.626838
14	1.731676	0.577475	10.563123	18.291911
15	1.800944	0.555265	11.118387	20.023588
16	1.872981	0.533908	11.652296	21.824531
17	1.947900	0.513373	12.165669	23.697512
18	2.025817	0.493628	12.659297	25.645413
19	2.106849	0.474642	13.133939	27.671229
20	2.191123	0.456387	13.590326	29.778079
21	2.278768	0.438834	14.029160	31.969202
22	2.369919	0.421955	14.451115	34.247970
23	2.464716	0.405726	14.856842	36.617889
24	2.563304	0.390121	15.246963	39.082604
25	2.665836	0.375117	15.622080	41.645908
26	2.772470	0.360689	15.982769	44.311745
27	2.883369	0.346817	16.329586	47.084214
28	2.998703	0.333477	16.663063	49.967583
29	3.118651	0.320651	16.983715	52.966286
30	3.243398	0.308319	17.292033	56.084938
31	3.373133	0.296460	17.588494	59.328335
32	3.508059	0.285058	17.873551	62.701469
33	3.648381	0.274094	18.147646	66.209527
34	3.794316	0.263552	18.411198	69.857909
35	3.946089	0.253415	18.664613	73.652225
36	4.103933	0.243669	18.908282	77.598314
37	4.268090	0.234297	19.142579	81.702246
38	4.438813	0.225285	19.367864	85.970336
39	4.616366	0.216621	19.584485	90.409150
40	4.801021	0.208289	19.792774	95.025516
41	4.993061	0.200278	19.993052	99.826536
42	5.192784	0.192575	20.185627	104.819598
43	5.400495	0.185168	20.370795	110.012382
44	5.616515	0.178046	20.548841	115.412877
45	5.841176	0.171198	20.720040	121.029392
46	6.074823	0.164614	20.884654	126.870568
47	6.317816	0.158283	21.042936	132.945390
48	6.570528	0.152195	21.195131	139.263206
49	6.833349	0.146341	21.341472	145.833734
50	7.106683	0.140713	21.482185	152.667084

$r = 0.05$				
n	$(1+r)^n$	$(1+r)^{-n}$	$a_{\overline{n}|r}$	$s_{\overline{n}|r}$
1	1.050000	0.952381	0.952381	1.000000
2	1.102500	0.907029	1.859410	2.050000
3	1.157625	0.863838	2.723248	3.152500
4	1.215506	0.822702	3.545951	4.310125
5	1.276282	0.783526	4.329477	5.525631
6	1.340096	0.746215	5.075692	6.801913
7	1.407100	0.710681	5.786373	8.142008
8	1.477455	0.676839	6.463213	9.549109
9	1.551328	0.644609	7.107822	11.026564
10	1.628895	0.613913	7.721735	12.577893
11	1.710339	0.584679	8.306414	14.206787
12	1.795856	0.556837	8.863252	15.917127
13	1.885649	0.530321	9.393573	17.712983
14	1.979932	0.505068	9.898641	19.598632
15	2.078928	0.481017	10.379658	21.578564
16	2.182875	0.458112	10.837770	23.657492
17	2.292018	0.436297	11.274066	25.840366
18	2.406619	0.415521	11.689587	28.132385
19	2.526950	0.395734	12.085321	30.539004
20	2.653298	0.376889	12.462210	33.065954
21	2.785963	0.358942	12.821153	35.719252
22	2.925261	0.341850	13.163003	38.505214
23	3.071524	0.325571	13.488574	41.430475
24	3.225100	0.310068	13.798642	44.501999
25	3.386355	0.295303	14.093945	47.727099
26	3.555673	0.281241	14.375185	51.113454
27	3.733456	0.267848	14.643034	54.669126
28	3.920129	0.255094	14.898127	58.402583
29	4.116136	0.242946	15.141074	62.322712
30	4.321942	0.231377	15.372451	66.438848
31	4.538039	0.220359	15.592811	70.760790
32	4.764941	0.209866	15.802677	75.298829
33	5.003189	0.199873	16.002549	80.063771
34	5.253348	0.190355	16.192904	85.066959
35	5.516015	0.181290	16.374194	90.320307
36	5.791816	0.172657	16.546852	95.836323
37	6.081407	0.164436	16.711287	101.628139
38	6.385477	0.156605	16.867893	107.709546
39	6.704751	0.149148	17.017041	114.095023
40	7.039989	0.142046	17.159086	120.799774
41	7.391988	0.135282	17.294368	127.839763
42	7.761588	0.128840	17.423208	135.231751
43	8.149667	0.122704	17.545912	142.993339
44	8.557150	0.116861	17.662773	151.143006
45	8.985008	0.111297	17.774070	159.700156
46	9.434258	0.105997	17.880066	168.685164
47	9.905971	0.100949	17.981016	178.119422
48	10.401270	0.096142	18.077158	188.025393
49	10.921333	0.091564	18.168722	198.426663
50	11.467400	0.087204	18.255925	209.347996

$r = 0.06$				
n	$(1+r)^n$	$(1+r)^{-n}$	$a_{\overline{n}|r}$	$s_{\overline{n}|r}$
1	1.060000	0.943396	0.943396	1.000000
2	1.123600	0.889996	1.833393	2.060000
3	1.191016	0.839619	2.673012	3.183600
4	1.262477	0.792094	3.465106	4.374616
5	1.338226	0.747258	4.212364	5.637093
6	1.418519	0.704961	4.917324	6.975319
7	1.503630	0.665057	5.582381	8.393838
8	1.593848	0.627412	6.209794	9.897468
9	1.689479	0.591898	6.801692	11.491316
10	1.790848	0.558395	7.360087	13.180795
11	1.898299	0.526788	7.886875	14.971643
12	2.012196	0.496969	8.383844	16.869941
13	2.132928	0.468839	8.852683	18.882138
14	2.260904	0.442301	9.294984	21.015066
15	2.396558	0.417265	9.712249	23.275970
16	2.540352	0.393646	10.105895	25.672528
17	2.692773	0.371364	10.477260	28.212880
18	2.854339	0.350344	10.827603	30.905653
19	3.025600	0.330513	11.158116	33.759992
20	3.207135	0.311805	11.469921	36.785591
21	3.399564	0.294155	11.764077	39.992727
22	3.603537	0.277505	12.041582	43.392290
23	3.819750	0.261797	12.303379	46.995828
24	4.048935	0.246979	12.550358	50.815577
25	4.291871	0.232999	12.783356	54.864512
26	4.549383	0.219810	13.003166	59.156383
27	4.822346	0.207368	13.210534	63.705766
28	5.111687	0.195630	13.406164	68.528112
29	5.418388	0.184557	13.590721	73.639798
30	5.743491	0.174110	13.764831	79.058186
31	6.088101	0.164255	13.929086	84.801677
32	6.453387	0.154957	14.084043	90.889778
33	6.840590	0.146186	14.230230	97.343165
34	7.251025	0.137912	14.368141	104.183755
35	7.686087	0.130105	14.498246	111.434780
36	8.147252	0.122741	14.620987	119.120867
37	8.636087	0.115793	14.736780	127.268119
38	9.154252	0.109239	14.846019	135.904206
39	9.703507	0.103056	14.949075	145.058458
40	10.285718	0.097222	15.046297	154.761966
41	10.902861	0.091719	15.138016	165.047684
42	11.557033	0.086527	15.224543	175.950545
43	12.250455	0.081630	15.306173	187.507577
44	12.985482	0.077009	15.383182	199.758032
45	13.764611	0.072650	15.455832	212.743514
46	14.590487	0.068538	15.524370	226.508125
47	15.465917	0.064658	15.589028	241.098612
48	16.393872	0.060998	15.650027	256.564529
49	17.377504	0.057546	15.707572	272.958401
50	18.420154	0.054288	15.761861	290.335905

		$r = 0.07$					$r = 0.08$		
n	$(1+r)^n$	$(1+r)^{-n}$	$a_{\overline{n}|r}$	$s_{\overline{n}|r}$	n	$(1+r)^n$	$(1+r)^{-n}$	$a_{\overline{n}|r}$	$s_{\overline{n}|r}$
1	1.070000	0.934579	0.934579	1.000000	1	1.080000	0.925926	0.925926	1.000000
2	1.144900	0.873439	1.808018	2.070000	2	1.166400	0.857339	1.783265	2.080000
3	1.225043	0.816298	2.624316	3.214900	3	1.259712	0.793832	2.577097	3.246400
4	1.310796	0.762895	3.387211	4.439943	4	1.360489	0.735030	3.312127	4.506112
5	1.402552	0.712986	4.100197	5.750739	5	1.469328	0.680583	3.992710	5.866601
6	1.500730	0.666342	4.766540	7.153291	6	1.586874	0.630170	4.622880	7.335929
7	1.605781	0.622750	5.389289	8.654021	7	1.713824	0.583490	5.206370	8.922803
8	1.718186	0.582009	5.971299	10.259803	8	1.850930	0.540269	5.746639	10.636628
9	1.838459	0.543934	6.515232	11.977989	9	1.999005	0.500249	6.246888	12.487558
10	1.967151	0.508349	7.023582	13.816448	10	2.158925	0.463193	6.710081	14.486562
11	2.104852	0.475093	7.498674	15.783599	11	2.331639	0.428883	7.138964	16.645487
12	2.252192	0.444012	7.942686	17.888451	12	2.518170	0.397114	7.536078	18.977126
13	2.409845	0.414964	8.357651	20.140643	13	2.719624	0.367698	7.903776	21.495297
14	2.578534	0.387817	8.745468	22.550488	14	2.937194	0.340461	8.244237	24.214920
15	2.759032	0.362446	9.107914	25.129022	15	3.172169	0.315242	8.559479	27.152114
16	2.952164	0.338735	9.446649	27.888054	16	3.425943	0.291890	8.851369	30.324283
17	3.158815	0.316574	9.763223	30.840217	17	3.700018	0.270269	9.121638	33.750226
18	3.379932	0.295864	10.059087	33.999033	18	3.996019	0.250249	9.371887	37.450244
19	3.616528	0.276508	10.335595	37.378965	19	4.315701	0.231712	9.603599	41.446263
20	3.869684	0.258419	10.594014	40.995492	20	4.660957	0.214548	9.818147	45.761964
21	4.140562	0.241513	10.835527	44.865177	21	5.033834	0.198656	10.016803	50.422921
22	4.430402	0.225713	11.061240	49.005739	22	5.436540	0.183941	10.200744	55.456755
23	4.740530	0.210947	11.272187	53.436141	23	5.871464	0.170315	10.371059	60.893296
24	5.072367	0.197147	11.469334	58.176671	24	6.341181	0.157699	10.528758	66.764759
25	5.427433	0.184249	11.653583	63.249038	25	6.848475	0.146018	10.674776	73.105940
26	5.807353	0.172195	11.825779	68.676470	26	7.396353	0.135202	10.809978	79.954415
27	6.213868	0.160930	11.986709	74.483823	27	7.988061	0.125187	10.935165	87.350768
28	6.648838	0.150402	12.137111	80.697691	28	8.627106	0.115914	11.051078	95.338830
29	7.114257	0.140563	12.277674	87.346529	29	9.317275	0.107328	11.158406	103.965936
30	7.612255	0.131367	12.409041	94.460786	30	10.062657	0.099377	11.257783	113.283211
31	8.145113	0.122773	12.531814	102.073041	31	10.867669	0.092016	11.349799	123.345868
32	8.715271	0.114741	12.646555	110.218154	32	11.737083	0.085200	11.434999	134.213537
33	9.325340	0.107235	12.753790	118.933425	33	12.676050	0.078889	11.513888	145.950620
34	9.978114	0.100219	12.854009	128.258765	34	13.690134	0.073045	11.586934	158.626670
35	10.676581	0.093663	12.947672	138.236878	35	14.785344	0.067635	11.654568	172.316804
36	11.423942	0.087535	13.035208	148.913460	36	15.968172	0.062625	11.717193	187.102148
37	12.223618	0.081809	13.117017	160.337402	37	17.245626	0.057986	11.775179	203.070320
38	13.079271	0.076457	13.193473	172.561020	38	18.625276	0.053690	11.828869	220.315945
39	13.994820	0.071455	13.264928	185.640292	39	20.115298	0.049713	11.878582	238.941221
40	14.974458	0.066780	13.331709	199.635112	40	21.724521	0.046031	11.924613	259.056519
41	16.022670	0.062412	13.394120	214.609570	41	23.462483	0.042621	11.967235	280.781040
42	17.144257	0.058329	13.452449	230.632240	42	25.339482	0.039464	12.006699	304.243523
43	18.344355	0.054513	13.506962	247.776496	43	27.366640	0.036541	12.043240	329.583005
44	19.628460	0.050946	13.557908	266.120851	44	29.555972	0.033834	12.077074	356.949646
45	21.002452	0.047613	13.605522	285.749311	45	31.920449	0.031328	12.108402	386.505617
46	22.472623	0.044499	13.650020	306.751763	46	34.474085	0.029007	12.137409	418.426067
47	24.045707	0.041587	13.691608	329.224386	47	37.232012	0.026859	12.164267	452.900152
48	25.728907	0.038867	13.730474	353.270093	48	40.210573	0.024869	12.189136	490.132164
49	27.529930	0.036324	13.766799	378.999000	49	43.427419	0.023027	12.212163	530.342737
50	29.457025	0.033948	13.800746	406.528929	50	46.901613	0.021321	12.233485	573.770156

Table of Selected Integrals

Rational Forms Containing $(a + bu)$

1. $\displaystyle\int u^n \, du = \frac{u^{n+1}}{n+1} + C, \quad n \neq -1$

2. $\displaystyle\int \frac{du}{a+bu} = \frac{1}{b} \ln|a+bu| + C$

3. $\displaystyle\int \frac{u \, du}{a+bu} = \frac{u}{b} - \frac{a}{b^2} \ln|a+bu| + C$

4. $\displaystyle\int \frac{u^2 \, du}{a+bu} = \frac{u^2}{2b} - \frac{au}{b^2} + \frac{a^2}{b^3} \ln|a+bu| + C$

5. $\displaystyle\int \frac{du}{u(a+bu)} = \frac{1}{a} \ln\left|\frac{u}{a+bu}\right| + C$

6. $\displaystyle\int \frac{du}{u^2(a+bu)} = -\frac{1}{au} + \frac{b}{a^2} \ln\left|\frac{a+bu}{u}\right| + C$

7. $\displaystyle\int \frac{u \, du}{(a+bu)^2} = \frac{1}{b^2}\left(\ln|a+bu| + \frac{a}{a+bu}\right) + C$

8. $\displaystyle\int \frac{u^2 \, du}{(a+bu)^2} = \frac{u}{b^2} - \frac{a^2}{b^3(a+bu)} - \frac{2a}{b^3} \ln|a+bu| + C$

9. $\displaystyle\int \frac{du}{u(a+bu)^2} = \frac{1}{a(a+bu)} + \frac{1}{a^2} \ln\left|\frac{u}{a+bu}\right| + C$

10. $\displaystyle\int \frac{du}{u^2(a+bu)^2} = -\frac{a+2bu}{a^2 u(a+bu)} + \frac{2b}{a^3} \ln\left|\frac{a+bu}{u}\right| + C$

11. $\displaystyle\int \frac{du}{(a+bu)(c+ku)} = \frac{1}{bc-ak} \ln\left|\frac{a+bu}{c+ku}\right| + C$

12. $\displaystyle\int \frac{u \, du}{(a+bu)(c+ku)} = \frac{1}{bc-ak}\left[\frac{c}{k} \ln|c+ku| - \frac{a}{b} \ln|a+bu|\right] + C$

Forms Containing $\sqrt{a + bu}$

13. $\displaystyle\int u\sqrt{a+bu} \, du = \frac{2(3bu-2a)(a+bu)^{3/2}}{15b^2} + C$

14. $\displaystyle\int u^2\sqrt{a+bu} \, du = \frac{2(8a^2 - 12abu + 15b^2u^2)(a+bu)^{3/2}}{105b^3} + C$

15. $\displaystyle\int \frac{u \, du}{\sqrt{a+bu}} = \frac{2(bu-2a)\sqrt{a+bu}}{3b^2} + C$

16. $\displaystyle\int \frac{u^2 \, du}{\sqrt{a+bu}} = \frac{2(3b^2u^2 - 4abu + 8a^2)\sqrt{a+bu}}{15b^3} + C$

17. $\displaystyle\int \frac{du}{u\sqrt{a+bu}} = \frac{1}{\sqrt{a}} \ln \left| \frac{\sqrt{a+bu} - \sqrt{a}}{\sqrt{a+bu} + \sqrt{a}} \right| + C, \quad a > 0$

18. $\displaystyle\int \frac{\sqrt{a+bu}\, du}{u} = 2\sqrt{a+bu} + a \int \frac{du}{u\sqrt{a+bu}}$

Forms Containing $\sqrt{a^2 - u^2}$

19. $\displaystyle\int \frac{du}{(a^2 - u^2)^{3/2}} = \frac{u}{a^2\sqrt{a^2 - u^2}} + C$

20. $\displaystyle\int \frac{du}{u\sqrt{a^2 - u^2}} = -\frac{1}{a} \ln \left| \frac{a + \sqrt{a^2 - u^2}}{u} \right| + C$

21. $\displaystyle\int \frac{du}{u^2\sqrt{a^2 - u^2}} = -\frac{\sqrt{a^2 - u^2}}{a^2 u} + C$

22. $\displaystyle\int \frac{\sqrt{a^2 - u^2}\, du}{u} = \sqrt{a^2 - u^2} - a \ln \left| \frac{a + \sqrt{a^2 - u^2}}{u} \right| + C, \quad a > 0$

Forms Containing $\sqrt{u^2 \pm a^2}$

23. $\displaystyle\int \sqrt{u^2 \pm a^2}\, du = \frac{1}{2} \left(u\sqrt{u^2 \pm a^2} \pm a^2 \ln \left| u + \sqrt{u^2 \pm a^2} \right| \right) + C$

24. $\displaystyle\int u^2\sqrt{u^2 \pm a^2}\, du = \frac{u}{8}(2u^2 \pm a^2)\sqrt{u^2 \pm a^2} - \frac{a^4}{8} \ln \left| u + \sqrt{u^2 \pm a^2} \right| + C$

25. $\displaystyle\int \frac{\sqrt{u^2 + a^2}\, du}{u} = \sqrt{u^2 + a^2} - a \ln \left| \frac{a + \sqrt{u^2 + a^2}}{u} \right| + C$

26. $\displaystyle\int \frac{\sqrt{u^2 \pm a^2}\, du}{u^2} = -\frac{\sqrt{u^2 \pm a^2}}{u} + \ln \left| u + \sqrt{u^2 \pm a^2} \right| + C$

27. $\displaystyle\int \frac{du}{\sqrt{u^2 \pm a^2}} = \ln \left| u + \sqrt{u^2 \pm a^2} \right| + C$

28. $\displaystyle\int \frac{du}{u\sqrt{u^2 + a^2}} = \frac{1}{a} \ln \left| \frac{\sqrt{u^2 + a^2} - a}{u} \right| + C$

29. $\displaystyle\int \frac{u^2 du}{\sqrt{u^2 \pm a^2}} = \frac{1}{2} \left(u\sqrt{u^2 \pm a^2} \mp a^2 \ln \left| u + \sqrt{u^2 \pm a^2} \right| \right) + C$

30. $\displaystyle\int \frac{du}{u^2\sqrt{u^2 \pm a^2}} = -\frac{\pm\sqrt{u^2 \pm a^2}}{a^2 u} + C$

31. $\displaystyle\int (u^2 \pm a^2)^{3/2} du = \frac{u}{8}(2u^2 \pm 5a^2)\sqrt{u^2 \pm a^2} + \frac{3a^4}{8} \ln \left| u + \sqrt{u^2 \pm a^2} \right| + C$

32. $\displaystyle\int \frac{du}{(u^2 \pm a^2)^{3/2}} = \frac{\pm u}{a^2\sqrt{u^2 \pm a^2}} + C$

33. $\displaystyle\int \frac{u^2 du}{(u^2 \pm a^2)^{3/2}} = \frac{-u}{\sqrt{u^2 \pm a^2}} + \ln \left| u + \sqrt{u^2 \pm a^2} \right| + C$

Rational Forms Containing $a^2 - u^2$ and $u^2 - a^2$

34. $\displaystyle\int \frac{du}{a^2 - u^2} = \frac{1}{2a} \ln \left| \frac{a + u}{a - u} \right| + C$

35. $\displaystyle\int \frac{du}{u^2 - a^2} = \frac{1}{2a} \ln \left| \frac{u - a}{u + a} \right| + C$

Exponential and Logarithmic Forms

36. $\displaystyle \int e^u\,du = e^u + C$

37. $\displaystyle \int a^u\,du = \frac{a^u}{\ln a} + C, \quad a > 0, a \neq 1$

38. $\displaystyle \int u e^{au}\,du = \frac{e^{au}}{a^2}(au - 1) + C$

39. $\displaystyle \int u^n e^{au}\,du = \frac{u^n e^{au}}{a} - \frac{n}{a}\int u^{n-1} e^{au}\,du$

40. $\displaystyle \int \frac{e^{au}\,du}{u^n} = -\frac{e^{au}}{(n-1)u^{n-1}} + \frac{a}{n-1}\int \frac{e^{au}\,du}{u^{n-1}}, \quad n \neq 1$

41. $\displaystyle \int \ln u\,du = u\ln u - u + C$

42. $\displaystyle \int u^n \ln u\,du = \frac{u^{n+1}\ln u}{n+1} - \frac{u^{n+1}}{(n+1)^2} + C, \quad n \neq -1$

43. $\displaystyle \int u^n \ln^m u\,du = \frac{u^{n+1}}{n+1}\ln^m u - \frac{m}{n+1}\int u^n \ln^{m-1} u\,du, \quad m, n \neq -1$

44. $\displaystyle \int \frac{du}{u \ln u} = \ln\left|\ln u\right| + C$

45. $\displaystyle \int \frac{du}{a + be^{cu}} = \frac{1}{ac}\left(cu - \ln\left|a + be^{cu}\right|\right) + C$

Miscellaneous Forms

46. $\displaystyle \int \sqrt{\frac{a+u}{b+u}}\,du = \sqrt{(a+u)(b+u)} + (a-b)\ln\left(\sqrt{a+u} + \sqrt{b+u}\right) + C$

47. $\displaystyle \int \frac{du}{\sqrt{(a+u)(b+u)}} = \ln\left|\frac{a+b}{2} + u + \sqrt{(a+u)(b+u)}\right| + C$

48. $\displaystyle \int \sqrt{a + bu + cu^2}\,du = \frac{2cu + b}{4c}\sqrt{a + bu + cu^2}$

$$-\frac{b^2 - 4ac}{8c^{3/2}}\ln\left|2cu + b + 2\sqrt{c}\sqrt{a + bu + cu^2}\right| + C, \quad c > 0$$

Answers to Odd-Numbered Problems

Problems 1.1 Numbers

1. (a) six trillion, nine hundred ninety-five billion, 6 hundred fifty-nine million, one hundred fifty-four thousand, three hundred sixty-eight (b) 91,618,984 3. (a) $-\frac{1}{3}$ (b) $-\frac{5}{4}$ (c) $-.237$ (d) -1.451 5. .056373

7. $\frac{5}{8} < \frac{7}{11}$ 9. 8 11. $\frac{97}{60}$ 13. $\frac{17}{4}$ 15. (a) $\frac{502}{100} = \frac{251}{50}$ (b) $\frac{497}{99}$ (c) irrational (d) $\frac{70905}{99000} = \frac{4727}{6600}$ (e) $\frac{1}{8}$

17. (a) $.\overline{074}$ (b) 4.5 (c) $.\overline{012345679}$ (no 8) 19. (a) 459 (b) four hundred fifty-nine

21. Start from 12 o'clock go clockwise $(a+b-c)d$. $(6+6-3)11 = 99$

Problems 1.2 Equations and Series

1. $2a(1+2bc-c)$ 3. Correct: (a), (b), (d) 5. (a) 4 (b) identity (c) $\frac{4}{3}$ 7. $-\frac{7}{4}$ 9. -2 11. 2 13. $i = 24\frac{An-p+r}{n(p+r)}$

15. $\dot{x} = -\frac{x^2 + 2xt + 1/(x+t)}{2x + t^2 + 1/(x+t)}$ 17. $x > 3$ 19. (a) $\frac{22}{7} - \pi$ (b) $3\sqrt{2} - 4$

21. (a) $\{2,3,7,5\}$ gives 72 (b) $\{a,b,d,c\}$: Put d so it is multiplied by the largest of the others. 23. (a) day 11 (b) 143 laps 25. 220 ft

27. (a) 1 (b) Any nonzero number

29. (a) no $|\pi - 2| = 1.14 > 1$ (b) yes $|\pi - 2| = .14 < 1$ (c) yes $|\pi - 4| = .86 < 1$ (d) no $|\pi - 5| = 1.86 > 1$

31. $\frac{3}{4}$ 33. 5 35. $R\frac{1 - 1/(1+i)^n}{i}$ 37. $\frac{1000}{9}$ 39. 6.5% 41. $\frac{8}{5}A$ 43. (a) $2b = a+c$ (b) $b^2 = ac$

Problems 1.3 Introduction to Technology

1. $1 + 2x + 3x^2 + 4x^3 + \cdots + (k-1)x^{k-2} + kx^{k-1}$ 3. (a) $\sum_{j=1}^{50} \frac{(-1)^{j-1}}{2j}$ (b) $\sum_{j=7}^{53}(-1)^{j-1}j^2$ 5. $a = 83, d = -2, n = 40, s = 1760$

7. (a) -7 (b) 1440 (c) 26 (d) 109 (e) 49 9. (a) $\sum_{k=7}^{53} k^2$ (b) 50948 13. $1/(4.7 + 3.6^{\wedge}(1 + \sqrt{(2)})) = 0.0374098$

15. $1/(1 + \sqrt{(2)}) + 1/(1 + \sqrt{(3)}) = 0.780239$ 17. $(\sqrt{(2)} - 3)^{\wedge}(3/5) = -1.31870$ 19. a_{24} 21. (a) =SUM(I*(1/3)^I) (b) $\frac{3}{4}$

23. (a) $\sum_{k=7}^{53} k^2$ (b) 50948 25. [D1]=B1/C1, drag to D7. Select A1:D7, DATA|Sort|By column D, Ascending.

27. =1/(4.7+3.6^(1+SQRT(2))) = 0.0374098 29. =1/(1+SQRT(2))+1/(1+SQRT(3)) = 0.780239

31. =((SQRT(2)-3)^(1/5))^3 = -1.31870 33. =TEXT("1/1"+103,"mmm dd") gives Apr 14 for an ordinary year, Apr 13 for a leap year

Problems 1.4 Percent, Units, Average, Proportion

1. $546\frac{33}{512}$ in 3. (a) 10^{-60} (b) 3.57×10^{-26} (c) 3C 5. (a) 5.260×10 (b) 6.1×10^{-3} (c) 1.72×10^5 (d) 1.720×10^5

9. $|d| < 4.05 \times 10^4$ 11. (a) nearest cm (b) 6 digits=nearest .001 cm 13. 20% 15. $.198 \approx 20\%$ 17. $\frac{2}{3}$ 19. (a) 16.7% (b) 25%

21. (a) 4.35% (b) $11.30 + 1.70 = 13.00$ 23. 27.9% 25. 43.75% GH rounds to 40% 27. (a) $3.00 (b) $2.998 29. 110.3V

31. $w = \sqrt{w_1 w_2}$. Geometric mean 33. 6.7×10^{14} Hz $= 670$ THz 35. 199% 37. 4.58 ton/in² 39. $4731.76

41. (a) 1.424 in (b) $3,068,883.28$ acre-ft 43. (a) 32.2 mi/gal (b) 91 gal saved vs 86 gal 45. $\sqrt{\frac{h}{in} \cdot \frac{w}{lb}}/3125$ 47. R is multiplied by $\frac{1}{16}$.

49. $2123 \approx 2100$ h 51. 11.772 N 53. 555 g 55. $235.87 57. 6.1 h

Problems 1.5 Rational Exponents and Radicals

1. Only (b) 3. $\frac{29}{2}$ 5. -13 7. $\frac{1}{2}$ 9. 100,000 11. $\frac{3}{200}\sqrt{15}$ 13. $6\sqrt{3}$ 15. $40\sqrt{2}$ 17. $17\sqrt{7}$ 19. $x|x|, x \neq 0$

21. (a) $x = -1$ gives $2 = 4$ (b), (c) unconditional (d) $x = -1$ gives undefined $= 1$ 23. Only (a) and (d) are equal. 25. $4x, x \geq 0$

27. $-\frac{3y^2 z^3}{x^2} = -3x^{-2}y^2z^3, y \neq 0, z \neq 0$ 29. $\frac{32}{a^9 b^7} = 32a^{-9}b^{-7}$ 31. $\frac{y}{x^3} = x^{-3}y, x > 0, y \geq 0$ 35. $8x^{20/3} - 56x^{1/3}$ 33. $4a|a|b^{8/3}$ 37. $\pm\frac{2}{3}$

39. $\frac{5}{3}$ 41. $\frac{33}{8}$ 43. 39.14 45. $x = 2m\left(1 - \frac{2}{y^{1/m} + 1}\right)$ 47. $v = \frac{2}{3}\sqrt{2}c$ 49. (a) is a conditional identity (b) is false if $x < 3$

51. (c) is defined at 0 53. 3 55. $\frac{3}{7} - \frac{1}{7}\sqrt{2}$ 57. $-\frac{39}{23} + \frac{29}{23}\sqrt{2}$ 59. $\sqrt{5 + 2\sqrt{5}}$

61. (a) negative to decimal (b) $(-4096)^{903} = -9 \times 10^{3261}$ too big (c) -1684.5 63. $\sqrt{2} + \sqrt{3}$ 65. $3 - \frac{3}{2}\sqrt{2} \approx .879$

67. $\frac{2}{7}\sqrt{14} - \frac{1}{7}\sqrt{7}$ 69. $\frac{1}{4}\left(\sqrt{6} + \sqrt{2}\right)$ 71. (a) $\frac{3}{4}\sqrt{3} + \frac{1}{4}\sqrt{15}$ (b) $\frac{1}{2}\sqrt{3} + \frac{1}{3}\sqrt{6}$ 73. (a) b^d (b) $\frac{b^{3.9} - b^{.3}}{b^{.2} - 1}$ (c) b^{36} 75. (a) 1600 ft (b) $6 + 3\sqrt{2}$

77. (a) $\frac{p_2}{p_1} = \left(\frac{V_1}{V_2}\right)^{1.4}$ (b) $p = 717.9$psi

Problems 1.6 Polynomials

1. $\frac{5}{6}x - \frac{5}{6}x^2$ 3. ab 5. $2x^3 + x^2 - 8x + 21$ 7. $x^5 + 2x^2 - x^3 - 2$ 9. $-4x$ 11. $x^4 - y^4$ 13. $x^4 - 10x^2y + 25y^2$ 15. $8x^2 + 18y^2$

17. $x^4 - 4x^3 + 18x^2 - 28x + 49$ 19. $\frac{15}{2}x - 12$ 21. $x^2 - 2x + 5 - \frac{11}{x+2}$ 23. $x^2 + 2x + \frac{3x+1}{x^2+x-2}$ 25. $x^2 - 2xy + 2y^2$ 27. $2x^2 + x + 2 - \frac{2}{x-1}$

29. $74 + 106(x-3) + 54(x-3)^2 + 12(x-3)^3 + (x-3)^4$ 31. $-\frac{3}{4}, \frac{5}{8}, -\frac{1}{2}$

33. (a) $2 - 2i$ (b) $-2 + 3i$ (c) $-18 + 24i$ 35. (a) $\frac{3}{5} - \frac{4}{5}i$ (b) $\frac{16}{41} + \frac{20}{41}i$ 37. (a) $-\frac{1}{4} - \frac{1}{12}i\sqrt{3}$ (b) $\frac{1}{4} - \frac{1}{12}i\sqrt{3}$

39. $\frac{30}{13}(8 + i)$ 41. (a) $\bar{z} = 3 + 4i$ (b) $|z| = 5$ 43. $3 - 2i$ 45. 1 47. $\sqrt{66} + \sqrt{11}i$

Problems 1.7 Factoring

1. $x^2\left(x - \sqrt{7}\right)\left(x + \sqrt{7}\right), 0, \pm\sqrt{7}$ 3. $(x+4)(x-2), -4, 2$ 5. $(x+2)(2x-3), -2, \frac{3}{2}$ 7. $3(x+4)(x-3), -4, 3$ 9. $2x(x-2)(x+2), 0, 2, -2$

11. $(2x+3)(5x+2), -\frac{3}{2}, -\frac{2}{5}$ 13. $(5x-1)(2x-9), \frac{1}{5}, \frac{9}{2}$ 15. $2x(x-2)^2, 0, 2$ 17. $3x^2(6x-7)^4(16x-7), 0, \frac{7}{6}, \frac{7}{16}$

19. $4(4x+3)^2(5x-2)^3(35x+9), -\frac{3}{4}, \frac{2}{5}, -\frac{9}{35}$ 21. $2^x(2x+1)(3x-2), -\frac{1}{2}, \frac{2}{3}$. 2^x is never 0 23. $(3x+8y)(3x-y)$ 25. $(5x+3y)(2x-21y)$

27. $(2m - n^2)(16m^4 + 8m^3n^2 + 4m^2n^4 + 2mn^6 + n^8)$ 29. $-\frac{1}{2} \pm \frac{1}{2}\sqrt{3}$ 31. $1 \pm \frac{1}{2}\sqrt{10}$ 33. $(a-b)(b-c)(c-a)(a+b+c)$

35. $-\frac{1}{2} \pm \frac{1}{2}i\sqrt{3}$ 37. $5i, 8i$ 39. $\frac{1}{2}\left(\sqrt{5} - 1\right)$ ($|-\frac{1}{2} - \frac{1}{2}\sqrt{5}| > 1$) 41. $\pm 2\sqrt{6}$

43. $\left(y - \left(\sqrt{2} + 1\right)x\right)\left(y + \left(\sqrt{2} + 1\right)x\right)\left(y - \left(\sqrt{2} - 1\right)x\right)\left(y + \left(\sqrt{2} - 1\right)x\right)$ 45. $\left(x^2 + \sqrt{2}x + 1\right)\left(x^2 - \sqrt{2}x + 1\right)$

47. $\left(x^2 + 1 - \sqrt{2 + \sqrt{2}}\,x\right)\left(x^2 + 1 + \sqrt{2 + \sqrt{2}}\,x\right)\left(x^2 + 1 - \sqrt{2 - \sqrt{2}}\,x\right)\left(x^2 + 1 + \sqrt{2 - \sqrt{2}}\,x\right)$

49. $(x^2 + 3x + 1)^2$ The product of 4 consecutive integers plus 1 is a perfect square

51. $1, 1, \frac{1}{2}\left(-3 \pm \sqrt{5}\right)$ 53. $\frac{1}{2}, 4, 6, -2$ 55. 2 57. $\frac{8}{3}$ 59. $\pm\frac{1}{2}\left(\sqrt{y^2 + 4y} \pm \sqrt{y^2 - 4y}\right), y = 0$, or $y \geq 4$ 61. $2, -\frac{1}{2} \pm \frac{1}{2}i\sqrt{3}$

63. $1, -\frac{1}{4} \pm \frac{1}{4}\sqrt{5}$ 65. $\frac{1}{2}, -1 \pm \sqrt{2}$ 67. $0, \frac{2}{3}$ 69. $-1.8319, .0819$ 71. $(x+1)^2(x^2 - x + 1)$ 73. $1/\left[\frac{4E^2(1 - 1/N)}{z^2} + \frac{1}{N}\right]$

Problems 1.8 Algebraic Fractions and Equations

1. $\frac{4cd^4}{9ab}, c \neq 0$ 3. $1, x \neq -3, -4, -\frac{1}{3}$ 5. $\frac{4a - 4}{a(a - 2)}$ 7. $\frac{-x^2 + x + 1}{x + 1}$ 9. $\frac{16a + 15a^2}{12(x + 2)}$ 11. $\frac{79x + 9}{30(x - 2)}$ 13. $\frac{-4y}{(x - 2y)^2(x + 2y)}$ 15. $1, y, x + y \neq 0$

17. $-3 \frac{x + z + 2}{(z+1)^2(x+1)^2}, z \neq x$ 19. $\frac{9x + 4}{(x - 2)(x + 2)(x + 1)}$ 21. $\frac{4(x-y)^2}{(1+x^2)(1+y^2)}$ 23. $3(x + 1/x), x \neq -1$ 25. $\sqrt{\frac{1}{1 - x^2}} = \frac{1}{\sqrt{1 - x^2}}$ 27. $\frac{2}{\sqrt{1 - x^2}}$

29. $\frac{1 - 2x^3}{\sqrt[4]{x(1 + x^3)^7}}$ 31. $p = \frac{16 - x}{x + 8}, p_{max} = 2, x_{max} = 16$

33. To 15 digits: .5 Full accuracy . 499 999 999 999 999 598 08   35. 2.82×10^{-21} 37. -6 or $\frac{6}{23}$ 39. $\frac{11}{2}$ 41. 6

43.   45. 1   47. $Y = \frac{8 - 2s}{s(s - 4)(s + 1)}$ 49. $Y = \frac{4s^4 - 3s^3 + 4}{s^3(s + 2)(s - 3)}$ 51. (a)$\frac{9}{5}, \frac{16}{12}, \frac{25}{21}, \frac{36}{32}, \frac{49}{45}$ (b) $\frac{4(2n+1)}{(n^2-4)(n^2+2n-3)}$
       none

Problems 1.9 Word Problems

1. $\frac{5}{3}$ mi 3. 23 days 5. 2/3 gal 7. 1120 9. 75L 11. 20 s 13. (a) $53,260.87 (b) 10.87% 15. 6   17. 47.3% 19. $\frac{9}{32} \approx 28\%$

21. $x^2 - 2cx + bc + cr - br = 0, x = c - \sqrt{(r - c)(b - c)}$ 23. fast 36mn, slow 45mn or slow fills in 4 mn, fast empties in 5 mn

25. 50ft by 70ft 27. 3 sides 60 yd, 2 sides 90 yd   29. (a) $4x + 300(50 - \sqrt{2500 - x})$ (b) 2275

31. $x \leq 21.6$. 20″ by 20″ by 28″ or 15.84″ by 15.84″ by 44.64″ 33. 4′ by 4′ by 6′ 35. 20″ by 20″ by 10″

Problems 1.10 Inequalities in One Variable

1. $[-\frac{17}{3}, \infty)$ **3.** $(-\frac{2}{3}, \frac{2}{3})$ **5.** $[2, \infty)$ **7.** $\dfrac{s}{1 + z/\sqrt{2n}} < \sigma < \dfrac{s}{1 - z/\sqrt{2n}}$ **9.** $(40, \infty)$ **11.** $6 < w \le 16\,oz$ **13.** $|f(x) - L| < \varepsilon$

15. $[2, 5]$ **17.** $\left(-\frac{11}{3}, -1\right)$ **19.** $(-\infty, -2] \cup \left[\frac{4}{3}, \infty\right)$ **21.** $(-\infty, -1) \cup \left(\frac{1}{7}, \infty\right)$

23. $\dfrac{1}{1 - x}$ **25.** $\left(-\infty, \frac{1}{5}\right) \cup (1, \infty)$ **27.** (a) $|135 - 60t|$ (b) $t = 2, 2.5$

Review Problems for Chapter 1

1. twenty-three quadrillion, one hundred forty-eight trillion, eight hundred fifty-five billion, three hundred eight million, one hundred eighty-four thousand, five hundred dollars

2. (a) $1'7''$ (b) $1'55''$ **3.** (a) $\frac{4}{3}$ (b) $\displaystyle\sum_{j=1}^{40} \frac{1}{3(2)^{j-2}}$ (c) TI:83 sum(seq(1/3/2^(X-2),X,1,40)) Excel =SUM(1/(3*2^(ROW(1:40)-2)))

4. 4.0754 **5.** $1.1 \times 10^6\,cm^3$ **6.** 37.5% **7.** 28.9% **8.** 21.25% **9.** PeopleSoft: $+3.4\%$, Oracle: -24.7%

10. (a) $15\,\Omega$ (arithmetic) (b) $\frac{40}{3}\,\Omega$ (harmonic) **11.** $2704\,lb$ **12.** (a) $20.28\,oz$ (b) $119.5\,kC$ **13.** $813.5W$ **14.** $86\cent$

15. $19.95\,mi$ above, $39.6\,mi$ below **16.** $5.4\,cm$ **17.** $17.118\,\frac{mg}{l}$

18. (a) $6\,706\,166\,29\,mi/h$ (b) $5.878\,4998 \times 10^{12}\,mi$ (c) $.998\,074\,46\,mi \approx 1\,mi$ **19.** $20.32\,micron$ **20.** (a) 2.3% (b) 4.6%

21. $3.596 \times 10^{-8}\,in$ **22.** $11950\,\frac{Btu}{h} \approx 12{,}000\,\frac{Btu}{h}$ **23.** $\$75{,}000$ at 6%, $\$25{,}000$ at 8% **24.** -36 **25.** $\sqrt{2} + \sqrt{3}$ **26.** $\sqrt{10}$

27. (a) $2a^{3/2}b$ (b) $2|a|^{3/2}|b|$ **28.** $\begin{cases} 2y \text{ if } y < x \\ 2x \text{ if } x < y \end{cases} = 2\min(x, y)$ **29.** $-\frac{27}{2}x^{13}y^6, x \ne 0, y \ne 0$ **30.** 5 **31.** $\left(\frac{3}{2}\right)^{27/4}$ **32.** $2x^3 + 3x^2 - 5x - 3$

33. $3x^2 + 7x + 20 + \frac{64}{x-3}$ **34.** $(4x - 3)(2x - 3)$ **35.** $-3(x + 4)(x + 2)$ **36.** $(x + 2y)(x^2 - 2xy + 4y^2)$

37. (a) $\left(x - \sqrt{2}\right)\left(x + \sqrt{2}\right)(x^2 + 2)$ (b) $(x^2 - 2x + 2)(x^2 + 2x + 2)$ **38.** $\left(x^2 - xy + y^2 - \frac{3}{4}\right)\left(x^2 + xy + y^2 - \frac{3}{4}\right)$ **39.** $0, x \ne -1, 0, 1$

40. $\dfrac{2x(1 + 2x^2)}{(1 + x^2 + x)(1 + x^2 - x)}$ **41.** $R_b = 2R \tan^{-1}\left(\dfrac{\sin\theta \cos\theta}{Rg/v^2 - \cos^2\theta}\right)$ if $v \ne 0$ **42.** (c) $\{-4, 4\}$ **43.** $\frac{ar}{a-2}$

44. (i) $\frac{1}{2}(a + c)$ (ii) $\pm\sqrt{ac}$ (iii) $\dfrac{2ac}{a + c} = \dfrac{1}{\frac{1}{2}\left(\frac{1}{a} + \frac{1}{c}\right)}$ **45.** 4 **46.** $a = \pm\sqrt{b^2 - c^2}, c \ge 0$ **47.** $-\frac{2}{5}, 3$ **48.** $-\frac{31}{16}$ **49.** 6

50. $\frac{5}{2} \pm \frac{1}{2}\sqrt{5}$ **51.** $-\frac{7}{3}, 2, -1$ **52.** $(2, 6)$ **53.** $(-\infty, -4] \cup [2, \infty)$ **54.** $x(24 - x), 0 \le x \le 24$ **55.** (a) $\dfrac{1}{2d}\left[d - 2a \pm \sqrt{(d - 2a)^2 + 8sd}\,\right]$ (b) $2, 3$

56. $-\frac{14}{25} + \frac{23}{25}i$ **57.** $\frac{9}{10}d$ **58.** $[700, 900]$ **59.** $\frac{6}{5}h = 1h\,12\min$ **60.** 130; cxxx

Apply It 2.1

1. (a) $a(r) = \pi r^2$ (b) $(-\infty, \infty)$ (c) $r \ge 0$

2. (a) $t(r) = \dfrac{300}{r}$ (b) $(-\infty, \infty) - \{0\}$ (c) $r > 0$

   (d) $t(x) = \dfrac{300}{x}; t\left(\dfrac{x}{2}\right) = \dfrac{600}{x}; t\left(\dfrac{x}{4}\right) = \dfrac{1200}{x}$

   (e) time scaled by a factor of c; $t\left(\dfrac{x}{c}\right) = \dfrac{300c}{x}$

3. (a) 300 (b) $\$21.00$ per pizza   (c) $\$16.00$ per pizza

4. $5500; 8400; 11{,}900; 16{,}000$

Problems 2.1 (page 86)

1. $f \ne g$

3. $h \ne k$

5. $(-\infty, \infty) - \{1\}$

7. $(-\infty, \infty) - \{3\}$

9. $(-\infty, \infty)$

11. $(-\infty, \infty) - \left\{\dfrac{7}{2}\right\}$

13. $(-\infty, \infty) - \{2\}$

15. $(-\infty, \infty) - \left\{-\dfrac{1}{3}, 2\right\}$

17. $1, 7, -7$

19. $-62, 2 - u^2, 2 - u^4$

21. $10, 8v^2 - 2v, 2x^2 + 4ax + 2a^2 - x - a$

23. $4, 0, x^2 + 2xh + h^2 + 2x + 2h + 1$

25. $0, \dfrac{2x - 5}{4x^2 + 1}, \dfrac{x + h - 5}{x^2 + 2xh + h^2 + 1}$ **27.** $0, 256, \dfrac{1}{16}$

29. (a) $4x + 4h - 5$ (b) 4

31. (a) $x^2 + 2hx + h^2 + 2x + 2h$ (b) $2x + h + 2$

33. (a) $3 - 2x - 2h + 4x^2 + 8xh + 4h^2$ (b) $-2 + 8x + 4h$

35. (a) $\dfrac{1}{x+h-1}$　**(b)** $\dfrac{-1}{(x-1)(x+h-1)}$　for $h \neq 0$

37. 5

39. y is a function of x; x is a function of y

41. y is a function of x; x is not a function of y

43. Yes　　**45.** $V(t) = 50,000 + (2300)t$　　**47.** Yes; P; q

49. 402.72; 935.52; supply increases as price increases

51. (a) 4　**(b)** $8\sqrt[3]{2}$　**(c)** $f(2I_0) = 2\sqrt[3]{2}f(I_0)$;
doubling intensity increases response by a factor of $2\sqrt[3]{2}$

53. (a) 3000, 2900, 2300, 2000; 12, 10
　　(b) 10, 12, 17, 20; 3000, 2300

55. (a) -5.13　**(b)** 2.64　**(c)** -17.43

57. (a) 7.89　**(b)** 63.85　**(c)** 1.21

Apply It 2.2

5. (a) $p(n) = \$125$　**(b)** premiums do not change
　(c) constant function

6. (a) quadratic function　**(b)** 2　**(c)** 3

7. $c(n) = \begin{cases} 3.50n & \text{if } n \leq 5 \\ 3.00n & \text{if } 5 < n \leq 10 \\ 2.75n & \text{if } n > 10 \end{cases}$

8. $7! = 5040$

Problems 2.2 (page 90)

1. Yes　　　**3.** No　　　**5.** Yes　　　**7.** No

9. $(-\infty, \infty)$　　**11.** $(-\infty, \infty)$　　**13. (a)** 3　**(b)** 7

15. (a) 7　**(b)** 1　　**17.** 8, 8, 8　　**19.** 2, -1, 0, 2

21. 7, 2, 2, 2　　**23.** 720　　　**25.** 2　　　**27.** n

29. $f(I) = 2.50$, where I is income; constant function

31. (a) $C = 850 + 3q$　**(b)** 250

33. $c(n) = \begin{cases} 9.50n & \text{if } n < 12 \\ 8.75n & \text{if } n \geq 12 \end{cases}$　**35.** $\dfrac{9}{64}$

37. (a) all T such that $30 \leq T \leq 39$　**(b)** 4, $\dfrac{17}{4}$, $\dfrac{33}{4}$

39. (a) 1182.74　**(b)** 4985.27　**(c)** 252.15

41. (a) 2.21　**(b)** 9.98　**(c)** -14.52

Apply It 2.3

9. $c(s(x)) = c(x + 3) = 2(x + 3) = 2x + 6$

10. let side length be $l(x) = x + 3$;
let area of square with side length x be $a(x) = x^2$;
then $g(x) = (x + 3)^2 = (l(x))^2 = a(l(x))$

Problems 2.3 (page 95)

1. (a) $2x + 8$　**(b)** 8　**(c)** -2　**(d)** $x^2 + 8x + 15$
　(e) 3　**(f)** $\dfrac{x+3}{x+5}$　**(g)** $x + 8$　**(h)** 11　**(i)** $x + 8$　**(j)** 11

3. (a) $2x^2 + x - 1$　**(b)** $-x - 1$　**(c)** $-\dfrac{1}{2}$　**(d)** $x^4 + x^3 - x^2 - x$
　(e) $\dfrac{x-1}{x}$ for $x \neq -1$　**(f)** 3　**(g)** $x^4 + 2x^3 + x^2 - 1$
　(h) $x^4 - x^2$　**(i)** 72

5. 6; -32　　**7.** $\dfrac{4}{(t-1)^2} + \dfrac{14}{t-1} + 1; \dfrac{2}{t^2 + 7t}$

9. $\dfrac{1}{v+3}; \sqrt{\dfrac{2v^2 + 3}{v^2 + 1}}$　　**11.** $f(x) = x - 7, g(x) = 11x$

13. $g(x) = x^2 + x + 1$, $f(x) = \dfrac{3}{x}$ is a possibility

$g(x) = x^2 + xf(x) = \dfrac{3}{x+1}$ is another

15. $f(x) = \sqrt[4]{x}$, $g(x) = \dfrac{x^2 - 1}{x + 3}$

17. (a) $r(x) = 9.75x$　**(b)** $e(x) = 4.25x + 4500$
　(c) $(r - e)(x) = 5.5x - 4500$

19. $400m - 10m^2$; revenue from output of m employees

21. (a) 14.05　**(b)** 1169.64　　　**23. (a)** 194.47　**(b)** 0.29

Problems 2.4 (page 98)

1. $f^{-1}(x) = \dfrac{x}{3} - \dfrac{7}{3}$　　　**3.** $F^{-1}(x) = 2x + 14$

5. $r(A) = \sqrt{\dfrac{A}{\pi}}$

7. not one-to-one; for example $g\left(-\dfrac{1}{3}\right) = 9 = g\left(-\dfrac{7}{3}\right)$

9. $h(x) = (5x + 12)^2$, for $x \geq -\dfrac{5}{12}$, is one-to-one

11. $x = \dfrac{\sqrt{23}}{4} + \dfrac{5}{4}$　　　**13.** $q = s\dfrac{1,200,000}{p}, p > 0$

15. Yes, it is one-to-one

Apply It 2.5

11. $y = -600x + 7250$; x-intercept $\left(\dfrac{145}{12}, 0\right)$;
y-intercept $(0, 7250)$

12. $y = 24.95$; horizontal line; no x-intercept;
y-intercept $(0, 24.95)$

13.

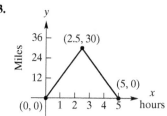

14.

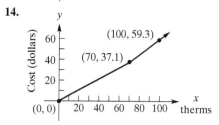

Problems 2.5 (page 106)

1. 3rd, 4th, 2nd, none

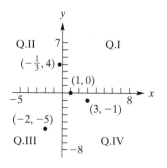

3. (a) 1, 2, 3, 0   **(b)** $(-\infty, \infty)$ **(c)** $(-\infty, \infty)$ **(d)** -2

5. (a) 0, 1, 1   **(b)** $(-\infty, \infty)$ **(c)** $[0, \infty)$ **(d)** 0

7. (0,0); function; one-to-one; $(-\infty, \infty)$; $(-\infty, \infty)$

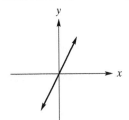

9. $(0, -5), \left(\dfrac{5}{3}, 0\right)$; function; one-to-one; $(-\infty, \infty)$; $(-\infty, \infty)$

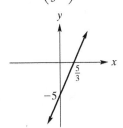

11. $(0, 0)$; y is a function of x; one-to-one; $(-\infty, \infty)$; $(-\infty, \infty)$

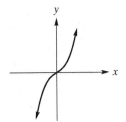

13. every point on y-axis; not a function of x

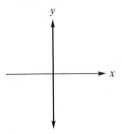

15. (0,0); function; one-to-one; $(-\infty, \infty)$; $(-\infty, \infty)$

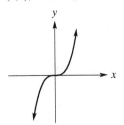

17. $(0, 0)$; not a function of x

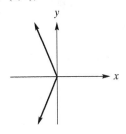

19. (0,2), (1,0); function; one-to-one; $(-\infty, \infty)$; $(-\infty, \infty)$

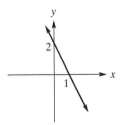

21. $(0, 2)$; $(-\infty, \infty)$; $[2, \infty)$ **23.** $(-\infty, \infty)$; 3; $(0, 3)$

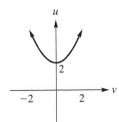 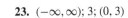

25. $(-\infty, \infty)$; $[-3, \infty)$; $(0, 1)$, $(2 \pm \sqrt{3}, 0)$

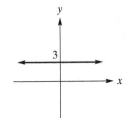

27. $(-\infty, \infty)$; $(-\infty, \infty)$; (0,0)

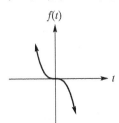

29. $(-\infty, -3] \cup [-3, \infty)$; $[0, \infty)$; $(-3, 0)$, $(3,0)$

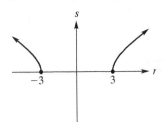

31. $(-\infty, \infty)$; $[0, \infty)$; $\left(-\dfrac{2}{3}, 0\right)$, $(0, 2)$

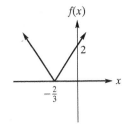

33. $(-\infty, \infty) - \{0\}$; $(0, \infty)$; no intercepts

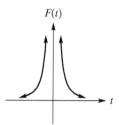

$F(t)$

35. $[0, \infty)$; $[1, 8)$

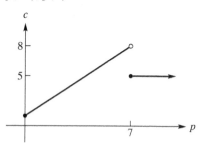

37. $(-\infty, \infty)$; $[0, \infty)$

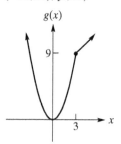

39. (a), (b), (d)

41. $y = 9200 - 325x$; y-intercept is $(0, 9200)$ 9200 is amount owed before any payments x-intercept is $\approx (28.31, 0)$ conclude debt will be paid off after 29 months

43. as price increases, quantity increases; p is a function of q

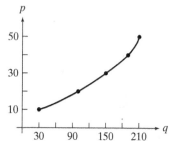

45.

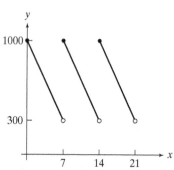

47. 0.39   **49.** $-0.61, -0.04$

51. -1.12 **53.** $-1.70, 0$

55. (a) 19.60   **(b)** -10.86 **57. (a)** 5   **(b)** 4

59. (a) 28   **(b)** $(-\infty, 28]$ **(c)** $-4.02, 0.60$

61. (a) 34.21   **(b)** 18.68   **(c)** $[18.68, 34.21]$ **(d)** none

Problems 2.6 (page 113)

1. $(0,0)$; sym about origin   **3.** $(\pm 2, 0), (0, 8)$; sym. about y-axis

5. $\left(\pm\dfrac{13}{5}, 0\right)$; $\left(0, \pm\dfrac{13}{12}\right)$ sym about x-axis, y-axis, and origin not sym about $y = x$

7. $(-2, 0)$; sym. about x-axis   **9.** sym. about x-axis

11. $(-21, 0), (0, -7), (0, 3)$ **13.** $(1, 0), (0, 0)$

15. $\left(0, \dfrac{2}{27}\right)$; no sym of the given kinds

17. $(3, 0), (0, \pm 3)$; sym. about x-axis

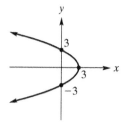

19. $(\pm 2, 0), (0, 0)$; sym about origin

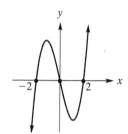

21. $(0,0)$; sym about x-axis, y-axis, origin, $y = x$

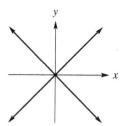

23. $\left(\pm\dfrac{5}{3}, 0\right), \left(0, \pm\dfrac{5}{2}\right)$; sym about x-axis, y-axis, origin

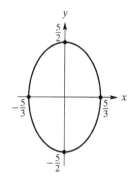

25. (a) $(\pm 0.99, 0)$, $(0, 5)$ (b) 5   (c) $(-\infty, 5]$

27.

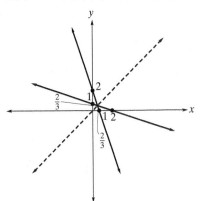

Problems 2.7 (page 115)

1.

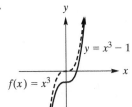

3.

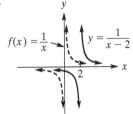

5.

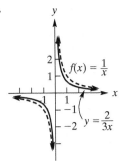

7.

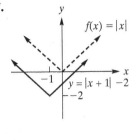

9. shift $y = x^3$ three units left, two units up

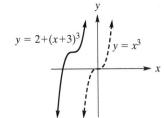

11.

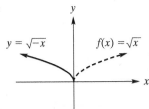

13. translate 3 units left, stretch vertically away from x-axis by a factor of 2, reflect about x-axis, move 2 units up

15. reflect about y-axis, move 5 units down

Apply It 2.8

15. (a) $3260   (b) $4410

Problems 2.8 (page 122)

1. 3   **3.** -6 **5.** -1 **7.** 88   **9.** 3

11. $a^2 + 2ab + b^2 + 2ah + 2bh + h^2$

13. 800   **15.** $y = 2$ **17.** $z = 6$

19.

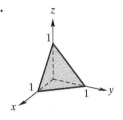

21.

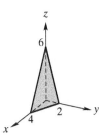

23.

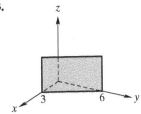

25.

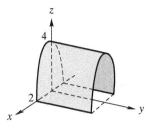

27.

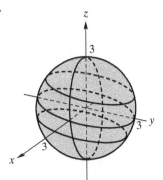

29.

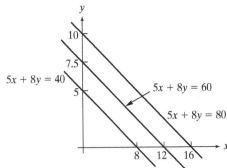

Review Problems—Chapter 2 (page 124)

1. $(-\infty, \infty) - \{1, 5\}$ **3.** $(-\infty, \infty)$

5. $[0, \infty) - \{1\}$ **7.** 5, 19, 40, $2\pi^2 - 3\pi + 5$

9. $0, 2, \sqrt[4]{t-2}, \sqrt[4]{x^3 - 3}$ **11.** $\dfrac{3}{5}, 0, \dfrac{\sqrt{x+4}}{x}, \dfrac{\sqrt{u}}{u-4}$

13. 20, -3, -3, undefined   **15.** (a) $3 - 7x - 7h$ (b) $-7h \neq 0$

17. (a) $3(x + h)^2 + (x + h) - 2$ (b) $6x + 1 + 3h$ for $h \neq 0$

19. (a) $5x + 2$ (b) 22   (c) $x - 4$ (d) $6x^2 + 7x - 3$ (e) 10

  (f) $\dfrac{3x - 1}{2x + 3}$ (g) $6x + 8$ (h) 38   (i) $6x + 1$

21. $\dfrac{1}{(x+1)^2}, \dfrac{1}{x^2} + 1 = \dfrac{1 + x^2}{x^2}$ **23.** $\sqrt{x^3 + 2}, (x + 2)^{3/2}$

25. $(0,0)$, $(\pm\sqrt{3},0)$; sym. about origin

27. $(0, 4)$ only intercept, symmetry about y-axis

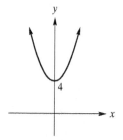

29. $(0,2)$, $(-4,0)$; $[-4,\infty)$; $[0,\infty)$

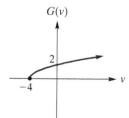

31. $\left(0,\dfrac{1}{2}\right)$; $(-\infty,\infty) - \{4\}$; $[0,\infty)$

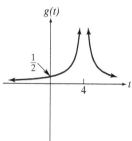

33. $(-\infty,\infty)$; $(-\infty,2]$ **35.**

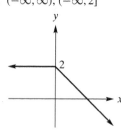

37. (a) and (c)

39. $-0.67, 0.34, 1.73$ **41.** $-1.50, -0.88, -0.11, 1.09, 1.40$

43. (a) $(-\infty,\infty)$ (b) $(1.92,0)$, $(0,7)$ **45.** (a) $0,2,4$ (b) none

47.

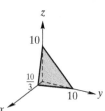

49.

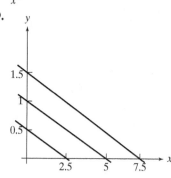

Explore and Extend—Chapter 2 (page 126)

1. $3{,}247.50   **3.** $94{,}229.00   **5.** answers may vary

7. $g(x) = \begin{cases} 0.90x & \text{if } 0 \le x \le 16{,}050 \\ 0.85x + 802.50 & \text{if } 16{,}050 < x \le 65{,}100 \\ 0.75x + 7{,}312.50 & \text{if } 65{,}100 < x \le 131{,}450 \\ 0.72x + 11{,}256 & \text{if } 131{,}450 < x \le 200{,}300 \\ 0.67x + 21{,}271 & \text{if } 200{,}300 < x \le 357{,}700 \\ 0.65x + 28{,}425 & \text{if } x > 357{,}700 \end{cases}$

Apply It 3.1

1. -2000; car depreciated $2000 per year

2. $S = 14T + 8$ **3.** $F = \dfrac{9}{5}C + 32$

4. slope $= \dfrac{125}{3}$; y-intercept $= \dfrac{125}{3}$

5. $9C - 5F + 160 = 0$

6.

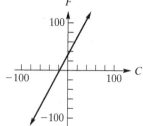

7. slopes of sides are 0, 7, and 1
no pair of which are negative reciprocals
no sides perpendicular so not a right triangle

Problems 3.1 (page 134)

1. 2   **3.** $-\dfrac{1}{2}$ **5.** undefined   **7.** 0

9. $5x + y - 2 = 0$

11. $x + 2y - 5 = 0$

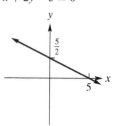

13. $3x - 7y + 25 = 0$ **15.** $4x + y + 16 = 0$

17. $2x - y + 4 = 0$ **19.** $x + 2y + 6 = 0$

21. $y + 5 = 0$ **23.** $x - 2 = 0$

25. $4; -6$ **27.** $-\dfrac{3}{5}; \dfrac{9}{5}$

29. slope undefined; no y-intercept

31. $-2; 0$ **33.** $0; 3$

35. $2x + 3y - 5 = 0$; $y = -\dfrac{2}{3}x + \dfrac{5}{3}$

37. $4x + 9y - 5 = 0$; $y = \dfrac{4}{9}x + \dfrac{5}{9}$

39. $6x - 8y - 57 = 0$; $y = \dfrac{3}{4}x - \dfrac{57}{8}$

41. parallel   **43.** parallel   **45.** neither

47. perpendicular   **49.** perpendicular   **51.** $y = 4x - 5$

53. $y = 1$ **55.** $y = \dfrac{1}{3}x + 5$ **57.** $x = 5$

59. $y = -\dfrac{2}{3}x - \dfrac{29}{3}$ **61.** $\left(3, \dfrac{2}{5}\right)$

63. -2.9; price dropped an average of \$2.90 per year

65. $y = 28{,}000x - 100{,}000$ **67.** $-t + d - 184 = 0$

71. $C = 59.82T + 769.58$ **75.** the slope is 7.1.

Apply It 3.2

8. $x =$ number of skis; $y =$ number of boots; $8x + 14y = 1000$

9. $p = \dfrac{3}{8}q + 1025$

10. answers may vary, two possibilities: $(0, 60)$ and $(2, 140)$

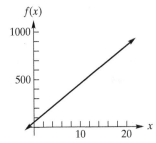

11. $f(t) = 2.3t + 32.2$ **12.** $f(x) = 70x + 150$

Problems 3.2 (page 140)

1. $-4; 0$ **3.** $5; -7$

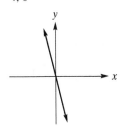 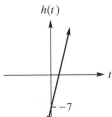

5. $-\dfrac{1}{3}; \dfrac{5}{3}$

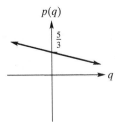

7. $f(x) = 4x$ **9.** $f(x) = -2x + 4$

11. $f(x) = -\dfrac{2}{3}x - \dfrac{10}{9}$ **13.** $f(x) = x + 1$

15. $p = -\dfrac{4}{25}q + 24.90$; \$18.50

17. $p = \dfrac{1}{4}q + 190$ **19.** $c = 3q + 10$; \$115

21. $f(x) = 0.125x + 4.15$

23. $v = -180t + 1800$; slope $= -180$

25. $y = 53x + 865$

27. $f(x) = 64x + 95$

29. $x + 10y = 100$

31. (a) $y = \dfrac{35}{44}x + \dfrac{225}{11}$ (b) 52.2

33. (a) $p = 0.059t + 0.025$ (b) 0.556

35. (a) $t = \dfrac{1}{4}c + 37$ (b) add 37 to # of chirps in 15 seconds

Apply It 3.3

13. vertex: $(1, 400)$; intercepts: $(0, 399)$, $(-19, 0)$, $(21, 0)$

14. vertex: $(1, 24)$; intercepts: $(0, 8)$, $\left(1 \pm \dfrac{\sqrt{6}}{2}, 0\right)$

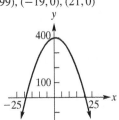 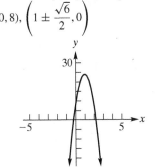

15. 1000 units; \$3000 maximum revenue

Problems 3.3 (page 147)

1. quadratic **3.** not quadratic

5. quadratic **7.** quadratic

9. (a) $\left(-\dfrac{5}{6}, \dfrac{13}{12}\right)$ (b) lowest point

11. (a) -6 (b) $-3, 2$ (c) $\left(-\dfrac{1}{2}, -\dfrac{25}{4}\right)$

13. vertex: $(3, -4)$; $(1,0)$, $(5,0)$, $(0,5)$; range: $[-4, \infty)$

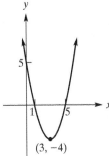

15. vertex: $\left(-\dfrac{3}{2}, \dfrac{9}{2}\right)$; $(0,0)$, $(-3,0)$; range: $\left(-\infty, \dfrac{9}{2}\right]$

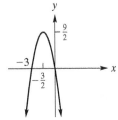

17. vertex: $(-3, 0)$; $(-3, 0)$, $(0, 9)$; range: $[0, \infty)$

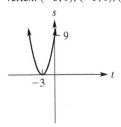

19. vertex: $\left(\dfrac{1}{2}, -\dfrac{17}{4}\right)$; $(0, -5)$; range $\left(-\infty, -\dfrac{17}{4}\right]$

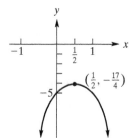

21. vertex: $(4, -2)$; $(0, 14)$ $(4 \pm \sqrt{2}, 0)$; range: $[-2, \infty)$

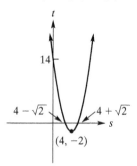

23. minimum; $\dfrac{808}{49}$ **25.** maximum; -10

27. $g^{-1}(x) = 1 + \sqrt{x - 3}, x \geq 3$

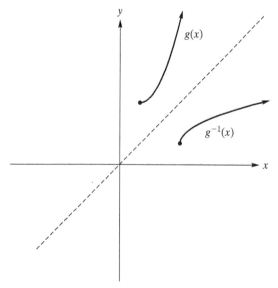

29. max revenue $250 when $q = 5$

31. 200 units; $240,000 maximum revenue

33. vertex: $(9, 225)$; $(0, 144)$, $(-6, 0)$, $(24, 0)$

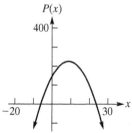

35. 70 grams   **37.** ≈ 134.86 ft; ≈ 2.7 sec

39. vertex $\left(\dfrac{45}{16}, \dfrac{2249}{16}\right)$; h-intercept $(0, 14)$;

for $t \geq 0$, t-intercept $\left(\dfrac{45 + \sqrt{13 \cdot 173}}{16}, 0\right)$

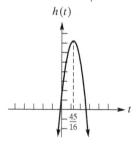

41. 125 ft × 250 ft

Apply It 3.4

16. $120,000 at 9% and $80,000 at 8%

17. 500 of species A and 1000 of species B

18. infinitely many solutions of form $A = \dfrac{20,000}{3} - \dfrac{4}{3}r$, $B = r$, where $0 \leq r \leq 5000$

19. $\dfrac{1}{6}$lb of A; $\dfrac{1}{3}$lb of B; $\dfrac{1}{2}$lb of C

Problems 3.4 (page 157)

1. $x = -1, y = 1$ **3.** $(2, -1)$

5. $u = 6, v = -1$ **7.** $x = -3, y = 2$

9. no solution   **11.** $x = 12, y = -12$

13. $\varnothing$ **15.** $x = \dfrac{1}{2}, y = \dfrac{1}{2}, z = \dfrac{1}{4}$

17. $x = 2, y = -1, z = 4$

19. $x = 1 + 2r, y = 3 - r, z = r$; r in $(-\infty, \infty)$

21. $x = -\dfrac{1}{3}r, y = \dfrac{5}{3}r, z = r$; r in $(-\infty, \infty)$

23. $\{(5 + 3r - s, r, s) \mid r, s \text{ in } (-\infty, \infty)\}$

25. $533\dfrac{1}{3}$gal of 20% soln, $266\dfrac{2}{3}$gal of 35% soln

27. 0.5 lb of cotton; 0.25 lb of polyester; 0.25 lb of nylon

29. ≈ 285mi/h (plane speed in still air), ≈ 23.2mi/h (wind speed)

31. 240 units early American, 200 units contemporary

33. 550 at Exton, 450 at Whyton

35. 4% on first $100,000, 6% on remainder

37. 190 boxes, 760 clamshells

39. 100 chairs, 100 rockers, 200 chaise lounges

41. 10 semiskilled workers, 5 skilled workers, 55 shipping clerks

Problems 3.5 (page 160)

1. $(1 \pm \sqrt{13}, 5 \mp 2\sqrt{13})$ **3.** $(-3, -4)$; $(2, 1)$

5. $(0, 0)$; $(1, 1)$ **7.** $\left(\dfrac{1 \pm \sqrt{7}}{2}, \dfrac{6 \pm \sqrt{7}}{2}\right)$

9. $(0, 0)$; $(1, 1)$ **11.** $(\pm \sqrt{17}, 2)$; $(\pm \sqrt{14}, -1)$

13. $(7, 6)$ **15.** at $(10, 8.1)$ and $(-10, 7.9)$

17. two   **19.** $(-1.3, 5.1)$

21. $x = 1.76$ **23.** $x = -1.46$

Problems 3.6 (page 166)

1. $(160, 6.2)$

3. $(5, 212.50)$

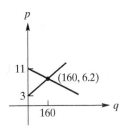

5. $(9, 38)$

7. $(15, 5)$

9. break-even quantity is 2500 units

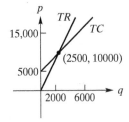

11. cannot break even

13. cannot break even

15. (a) \$12   (b) \$12.18

17. 5840 units; 840 units; 1840 units   **19.** \$4

21. (a) break even at $q = \dfrac{4}{9}$ and at $q = 1$

(b)

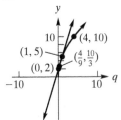

(c) maximum profit for p in interval $\left(\dfrac{4}{9}, 1\right)$

23. decreases by \$0.70   **25.** $P_A = 8; P_B = 10$

27. 2.4 and 11.3

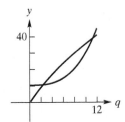

Review Problems—Chapter 3 (page 169)

1. 9

3. $y = -2x - 1; 2x + y + 1 = 0$

5. $y = 3x - 21; 3x - y - 21 = 0$ **7.** $y = 4; y - 4 = 0$

9. $y = \dfrac{2}{5}x - 3; 2x - 5y - 15 = 0$ **11.** perpendicular

13. neither   **15.** parallel, both lines have slope 5

17. $y = \dfrac{3}{2}x - 2; \dfrac{3}{2}$ **19.** $y = \dfrac{4}{3}; 0$

21. $-5; (0, 17)$

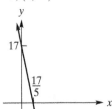
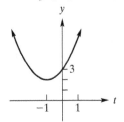

23. $(3, 0), (-3, 0), (0, 9); (0, 9)$

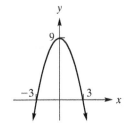

25. intercept $(0, 3)$; vertex $(-1, 2)$

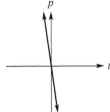

27. $-7; (0, 0)$

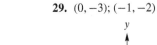

29. $(0, -3); (-1, -2)$

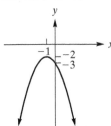

31. $\left(\dfrac{17}{7}, -\dfrac{8}{7}\right)$ **33.** $\left(2, -\dfrac{9}{5}\right)$ **35.** $(4, 0)$ **37.** $(0, 1, 0)$

39. $\left(\dfrac{-5 \pm \sqrt{65}}{4}, \dfrac{-21 \pm 5\sqrt{65}}{8}\right)$

41. $(-2 - 2r, 7 + r, r); r$ in $(-\infty, \infty)$

43. $(r, r, 0); r$ in $(-\infty, \infty)$ **45.** $2a + 3b + 9 = 0; a = -9$

47. $f(x) = -\dfrac{4}{3}x + \dfrac{19}{3}$ **49.** 50 units; \$5000   **51.** ≈ 6.55

53. 1250 units; \$20,000   **55.** 2.36 tons per sq km

57. $x = 7.29, y = -0.78$ **59.** $x = 0.75, y = 1.43$

Explore and Extend—Chapter 3 (page 172)

1. \$345.45

2. usage between 494.44 and 950 minutes

3. usage between 950 and 1407.14 minutes

Apply It 4.1

1. graph shapes are the same
A scales second coordinate by A

2.

Year	Multiplicative Increase	Expression
0	1	1.1^0
1	1.1	1.1^1
2	1.21	1.1^2
3	1.33	1.1^3
4	1.46	1.1^4

1.1; investment increases by 10% every year;
$(1 + 1(0.1) = 1 + 0.1 = 1.1)$

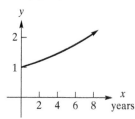

between 7 and 8 years

3.

Year	Multiplicative Decrease	Expression
0	1	0.85^0
1	0.85	0.85^1
2	0.72	0.85^2
3	0.61	0.85^3

0.85; car depreciates by 15% every year;
$(1 - 1(0.15) = 1 - 0.15 = 0.85)$

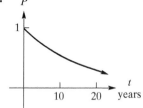

between 4 and 5 years

4. $y = 1.08^{t-3}$; shift graph 3 units right
5. $3684.87; $1684.87   **6.** 117 employees
7.

Problems 4.1 (page 184)

1.

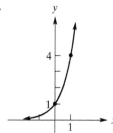

3.

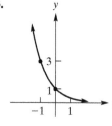

5.

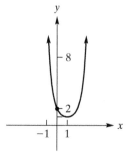

7.

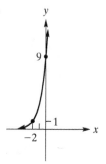

9.

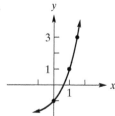

11.

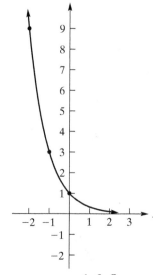

13. B   **15.** 138,750   **17.** $\dfrac{1}{2}, \dfrac{3}{4}, \dfrac{7}{8}$

19. (a) ≈$2318.55   (b) ≈$318.55
21. (a) $1964.76   (b) $1264.76
23. (a) $11,983.37   (b) $8983.37
25. (a) $6256.36   (b) $1256.36   **27.** (a) $9649.69   (b) $1649.69
29. ≈$6900.91   **31.** (a) $N = 400(1.05)^t$ (b) 420   (c) 486

33.

Year	Multiplicative Increase	Expression
0	1	1.3^0
1	1.3	1.3^1
2	1.69	1.3^2
3	2.20	1.3^3

1.3; recycling increases by 30% every year;
$(1 + 1(0.3) = 1 + 0.3 = 1.3)$

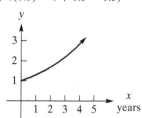

between 4 and 5 years

35. 334,485   **37.** 4.4817   **39.** 0.4493

41.

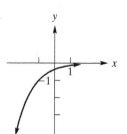

43. 0.2240   **45.** $(e^k)^t$, where $b = e^k$
47. (a) 12   (b) 8.8   (c) 3.1   (d) 22 hr
49. 27 yrs   **51.** 0.1465   **55.** 3.17
57. 4.2 min   **59.** 8 yrs

Apply It 4.2

8. $t = \log_2 16$; number of times the bacteria have doubled

9. $\dfrac{I}{I_0} = 10^{8.3}$ **10.**

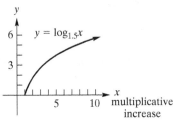

$y = \log_{1.5} x$

multiplicative increase

11.

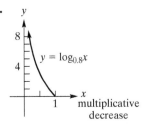

$y = \log_{0.8} x$

multiplicative decrease

12. $\approx 13.9\%$ **13.** $\approx 9.2\%$

Problems 4.2 (page 191)

1. $\log 10{,}000 = 4$ **3.** $2^{10} = 1024$

5. $\ln 20.0855 = 3$ **7.** $e^{1.09861} = 3$

9.

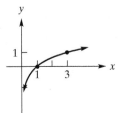

11.

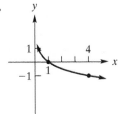

13.

15.

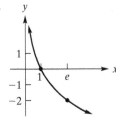

17. 2 **19.** 3 **21.** 1 **23.** -4 **25.** 0 **27.** -3

29. 81 **31.** 125 **33.** $\dfrac{1}{1000}$ **35.** e^{-3} **37.** 2 **39.** 6

41. $\dfrac{1}{27}$ **43.** 3 **45.** $\dfrac{5}{3}$ **47.** 4 **49.** $\dfrac{\ln 2}{3}$ **51.** $\dfrac{5 + \ln 3}{2}$

53. 2.39790 **55.** 2.00013 **57.** $y = \log_{1.10} x$ **59.** 3

61. (a) $2N_0$ **(b)** k is the doubling time

63. ≈ 72.2 minutes **65.** $z = y^{3/2}$

67. (a) $(0, 1)$ **(b)** $[-0.37, \infty)$ **69.** 1.10 **71.** 1.41; 3.06

Apply It 4.3

14. $\log(900{,}000) - \log(9000) = \log\left(\dfrac{900{,}000}{9000}\right) = \log(100) = 2$

15. $\log(10{,}000) = \log(10^4) = 4$

Problems 4.3 (page 197)

1. $a + b + c$ **3.** $a - b$ **5.** $3a - b$ **7.** $2(a + c)$

9. $\dfrac{b}{a}$ **11.** 48 **13.** -7 **15.** 5.01

17. $-\dfrac{1}{2}$ **19.** 2

21. $\ln x + 2\ln(x + 1)$ **23.** $2\ln x - 3\ln(x + 1)$

25. $4[\ln(x + 1) + \ln(x + 2)]$ **27.** $\ln x + \ln(x + 1) - \ln(x + 2)$

29. $\dfrac{1}{2}\ln x - 2\ln(x + 1) - 3\ln(x + 2)$

31. $\dfrac{2}{5}\ln x - \dfrac{1}{5}\ln(x + 1) - \ln(x + 2)$

33. $\log 24$ **35.** $\log_2 \dfrac{2x}{x + 1}$ **37.** $\log_3 (5^7 \cdot 17^4)$

39. $\log(100(1.05)^{10})$ **41.** $\dfrac{81}{64}$ **43.** 1 **45.** $\dfrac{5}{2}$

47. $\{-3, 1\}$ **49.** $\dfrac{\ln(2x + 1)}{\ln 2}$ **51.** $\dfrac{\ln(x^2 + 1)}{\ln 3}$ **53.** $y = \ln\left(\dfrac{z}{7}\right)$

55. $C = B\left(1 + \dfrac{E}{B}\right)$ so $\ln C = \ln B + \ln\left(1 + \dfrac{E}{B}\right)$

57.

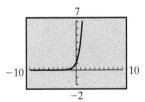

59. $\log x = \dfrac{\ln x}{\ln 10}$ **61.** $\ln 3$

Apply It 4.4

16. 18 **17.** day 20 **18.** 67.5 times as intense

Problems 4.4 (page 201)

1. 1 **3.** 2.75 **5.** -3 **7.** 2

9. 0.125 **11.** $\dfrac{\ln 7}{5} \approx 0.389$ **13.** 0.028 **15.** 5.140

17. -0.073 **19.** 2.322 **21.** $\dfrac{1}{7}\left(\dfrac{\ln 2}{\ln 5} - 5\right) \approx -0.653$ **23.** 0.483

25. 2.496 **27.** 1003 **29.** 2.222 **31.** $\dfrac{3 + \sqrt{9 + 8(2 + e^5)}}{4} \approx 9.45$

33. 1.353 **35.** 0.5 **37.** $S = 12.4A^{0.26}$ **39. (a)** 100 **(b)** 46

41. $\dfrac{\ln 4 - \ln 3}{\ln(1.03)} \approx 9.7$ **43.** $p = \dfrac{\log(80 - q)}{\log 2}$; 4.32 **49.** 3.33

Review Problems—Chapter 4 (page 203)

1. $\log_3 243 = 5$ **3.** $81^{1/4} = 3$ **5.** $\ln 1096.63 \approx 7$

7. 3 **9.** -4 **11.** -2 **13.** 4 **15.** $\dfrac{1}{1024}$

17. -1 **19.** $3(a + 1)$ **21.** $\log\left(\dfrac{7^3}{5^2}\right)$ **23.** $\ln\left(\dfrac{x^2 y}{z^3}\right)$

25. $\ln\left(\dfrac{x^{19/3}}{(x - 1)^2(x - 2)^3}\right)$

27. $3\ln x + 2\ln y + 5\ln z$

29. $\dfrac{1}{3}(\ln x + \ln y + \ln z)$ **31.** $\dfrac{1}{2}(\ln y - \ln z) - \ln x$

33. $\dfrac{\ln(x + 5)}{\ln 3}$ **35.** $\approx \dfrac{5.20945}{2.80735} \approx 1.85565$ n

37. $2y + \dfrac{1}{2}x$ **39.** $2x + 1$ **41.** $y = e^{x^2 + 2}$

43.

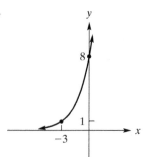

45. 4   **47.** 1   **49.** 10   **51.** $\dfrac{1}{3e^2}$ **53.** 0.880

55. $\ln 8 - 2 \approx 0.07944$ **57.** -1.596

59. (a) $3829.04   **(b)** $1229.04   **61.** 14%

63. (a) $P = 6000(0.995)^t$ **(b)** ≈ 5707

65. (a) 10   **(b)** $10e^{-0.41} \approx 6.6$ **(c)** $10e^{-0.41(5)} \approx 1.3$
(d) $\dfrac{\ln 2}{0.41} \approx 1.7$ **(e)** $\dfrac{\ln(100)}{0.41} \approx 11.2$

67. (a) 6   **(b)** 28

71. $(-\infty, 0.37]$ **73.** 2.53   **75.** $g(x) = \dfrac{1}{x}$

Explore and Extend—Chapter 4 (page 207)

1. (a) $P = \dfrac{T(e^{kI} - 1)}{1 - e^{-dkI}}$ **(b)** $d = \dfrac{1}{kI}\ln\left(\dfrac{P}{P - T(e^{kI} - 1)}\right)$

3. (a) 156   **(b)** 65

Apply It 5.1

1. 4.9%   **2.** 7 years, 16 days   **3.** 7.7208%

4. 11.25% compounded quarterly is better
the $10,000 investment is better over 20 years

Problems 5.1 (page 212)

1. (a) $11,105.58   **(b)** $5105.58
3. 3.023%   **5.** $\approx 3.562\%$

7. (a) 10%   **(b)** 10.25%   **(c)** 10.381%
(d) 10.471%   **(e)** 10.516%

9. 8.08%   **11.** 8.0 years   **13.** $10,282.95

15. $30448.33   **17. (a)** 18%   **(b)** $19.56%

19. $3198.54   **21.** 8% compounded annually

23. (a) 4.93%   **(b)** 4.86%   **25.** 10.757%   **27.** 6.29%

Problems 5.2 (page 216)

1. $2261.34   **3.** $1751.83   **5.** $5821.55
7. $4862.31   **9.** $4303.61   **11.** $11,381.89
13. $14,091.10   **15.** $1238.58   **17.** $3244.63
19. (a) $9669.40   **(b)** yes   **21.** savings account
23. $226.25   **25.** 9.55%

Problems 5.3 (page 219)

1. $5819.97; $1819.97   **3.** $2217.30   **5.** 4.08%

7. 3.05%   **9.** $109.42   **11.** $778,800.78

13. (a) $43,248.06   **(b)** $20,737.68

15. 4.88%   **17.** 16 years

19. (a) $1072.51   **(b)** $1093.30   **(c)** $1072.18

21. (a) $9458.51   **(b)** this is better by $26.90

Apply It 5.4

5. 6.20%   **6.** $101,925; $121,925   **7.** $723.03

8. $13,962.01   **9.** $45,502.06   **10.** $48,095.67

Problems 5.4 (page 227)

1. 18.664613   **3.** 8.213180   **5.** $2950.39

7. $29,984.06   **9.** $9887.08   **11.** $90,231.01

13. $204,977.46   **15.** $24,594.36   **17.** $5106.27

19. $1332.73   **21. (a)** $3048.85   **(b)** $648.85

23. $3474.12   **25.** $1725   **27.** 102.91305

29. 10,475.72   **31.** $131.34   **33.** $1,872,984.02

35. $205,073; $142,146   **37.** $181,269.25

Problems 5.5 (page 231)

1. $428.73   **3.** $502.84

5. (a) $221.43   **(b)** $25   **(c)** $196.43

7.

Period	Prin. Outs. at Beginning	Interest for Period	Pmt. at End	Prin. Repaid at End
1	5000.00	350.00	1476.14	1126.14
2	3873.86	271.17	1476.14	1204.97
3	2668.89	186.82	1476.14	1289.32
4	1379.57	96.57	1476.14	1379.57
Total		904.56	5904.56	5000.00

9.

Period	Prin. Outs. at Beginning	Interest for Period	Pmt. at End	Prin. Repaid at End
1	900.00	22.50	193.72	171.22
2	728.78	18.22	193.72	175.50
3	553.28	13.83	193.72	179.89
4	373.39	9.33	193.72	184.39
5	189.00	4.73	193.73	189.00
Total		68.61	968.61	900.00

11. 13   **13.** $1606

15. (a) $2089.69   **(b)** $1878.33   **(c)** $211.36   **(d)** $381,907

17. 23   **19.** $113,302   **21.** $25.64

Problems 5.6 (page 235)

1. $4000   **3.** $750,000   **5.** $4800   **7.** 1   **9.** e^2

Review Problems—Chapter 5 (page 237)

1. $\dfrac{\ln 2}{\ln(1 + r)}$ **3.** 8.5% compounded annually

5. $1005.41   **7. (a)** $1997.13   **(b)** $3325.37

9. $2506.59   **11.** $886.98   **13.** $314.00

15.

Period	Prin. Outs. at Beginning	Interest for Period	Pmt. at End	Prin. Repaid at End
1	15,000.00	112.50	3067.84	2955.34
2	12,044.66	90.33	3067.84	2977.51
3	9067.15	68.00	3067.84	2999.84
4	6067.31	45.50	3067.84	3022.34
5	3044.97	22.84	3067.81	3044.97
Total		339.17	15,339.17	15,000.00

17. $1279.36

Explore and Extend—Chapter 5 (page 239)

1. $26,102.13

3. when drop in interest rates expected, long-term investments become more attractive

59. 6

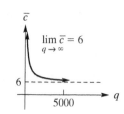

61. 40,000 **63.** 20

65. 1, 0.5, 0.525, 0.631, 0.912, 0.986, 0.998; 1

67. 0 **69.** (a) 11 (b) 9 (c) does not exist

Apply It 10.1

1. exists if and only if a not an integer

2. $\dfrac{4}{3}\pi$ **3.** 3616 **4.** 20 **5.** 2

Problems 10.1 (page 467)

1. (a) 1 (b) 0 (c) 1

3. (a) 1 (b) does not exist (c) 3

5. $f(-0.9) = -3.7; f(-0.99) = -3.97;$
$f(-0.999) = -3.997; f(-1.001) = -4.003;$
$f(-1.01) = -4.03; f(-1.1) = -4.3; -4$

7. $f(-0.00001) \approx 0.99988; f(0.00001) \approx 0.99988;$
$f(0.0001) \approx 0.99908; f(0.001) \approx 0.99312;$
$f(0.01) \approx 0.95499; f(0.1) \approx 0.79433; 1$

9. 16 **11.** 20 **13.** -47 **15.** $-\dfrac{5}{2}$ **17.** 0

19. 5 **21.** -2 **23.** 3 **25.** 5 **27.** $-\dfrac{1}{8}$

29. $-\dfrac{1}{5}$ **31.** $\dfrac{11}{9}$ **33.** 4 **35.** $2x$ **37.** 2

39. $2x$ **41.** $3x^2 - 8x$ **43.** $\dfrac{1}{4}$ **45.** (a) 1 (b) 0

47. $\dfrac{20}{3}$ **49.** 4.00 **51.** does not exist

Apply It 10.2

6. $\lim_{x\to\infty} p(x) = 0$; graph decreases rapidly to 0; demand is a decreasing function of price

7. $\lim_{x\to\infty} y(x) = 500$; even with unlimited advertising sales bounded by $500,000

8. $\lim_{x\to\infty} C(x) = \infty$; cost increases without bound as production increases without bound

9. does not exist; $250

Problems 10.2 (page 475)

1. (a) ∞ (b) ∞ (c) $-\infty$ (d) does not exist (e) 0 (f) 0 (g) 0
(h) 1 (i) 2 (j) does not exist (k) 2

3. 1 **5.** $-\infty$ **7.** $-\infty$ **9.** ∞ **11.** 0

13. ∞ **15.** 0 **17.** ∞ **19.** 0 **21.** $\dfrac{1}{2}$

23. 0 **25.** ∞ **27.** 0 **29.** $\dfrac{2}{5}$ **31.** ∞

33. $\dfrac{2}{5}$ **35.** $-\infty$ **37.** $\dfrac{16}{3}$ **39.** $\dfrac{1}{2}$ **41.** ∞

43. ∞ **45.** ∞ **47.** does not exist **49.** ∞

51. 0 **53.** 1

55. (a) 1 (b) 2 (c) does not exist (d) 1 (e) 2

57. (a) 0 (b) 0 (c) 0 (d) $-\infty$ (e) $-\infty$

Problems 10.3 (page 481)

7. continuous at -2 and 0 **9.** discontinuous at ± 3

11. continuous at 2 and 0 **13.** f is a polynomial function

15. composite of continuous functions

17. none **19.** $x = -4$ **21.** none **23.** $x = -5, 3$

25. $0, \pm 3$ **27.** none **29.** $x = 0$ **31.** none **33.** $x = 2$

35. 1, 2, 3 **37.** yes, no, no

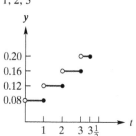 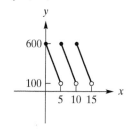

Apply It 10.4

10. $0 < x < 4$

Problems 10.4 (page 486)

1. $(-\infty, -1) \cup (4, \infty)$ **3.** $[-2, 5]$ **5.** $\left(\dfrac{7}{2}, -2\right)$

7. no solution **9.** $(-\infty, -7] \cup [-1, 2]$

11. $(-\infty, -4) \cup (0, 5)$ **13.** $[0, \infty)$

15. $(-\infty, -5] \cup [-3, 0]$ **17.** $(-\infty, -3) \cup (0, 3)$

19. $(-1, \infty)$ **21.** $(-\infty, -5) \cup [-2, 1) \cup [3, \infty$

23. $(-5, -1)$ **25.** $(-\infty, -1-\sqrt{3}] \cup [-1+\sqrt{3}, \infty$

27. integers in $[37, 103]$ **29.** 14in. by 14in.

31. $(-\infty, -7.72]$ **33.** $(-\infty, -0.5) \cup (0.667, \infty)$

Review Problems—Chapter 10 (page 488)

1. -5 **3.** 2 **5.** x **7.** $-\dfrac{8}{3}$ **9.** 0

11. $\dfrac{2}{7}$ **13.** does not exist **15.** -1 **17.** $\dfrac{1}{9}$

19. $-\infty$ **21.** ∞ **23.** $-\infty$ **25.** 1 **27.** $-\infty$ **29.** 8 **31.** 23

35. continuous everywhere; f is a polynomial function

37. $x = -3$ **39.** none **41.** $x = -4, 1$ **43.** $x = 2$

45. $(-\infty, -6) \cup (2, \infty)$ **47.** $(-\infty, 7]$

49. $(-\infty, -5) \cup (-1, 1)$ **51.** $(-\infty, -4) \cup [-3, 0] \cup (2, \infty)$

53. 1.00 **55.** 0 **57.** $[2.00, \infty)$

Explore and Extend—Chapter 10 (page 490)

1. 11.3%

Apply It 11.1

1. $\dfrac{dH}{dt} = 40 - 32t$

Problems 11.1 (page 499)

1. (a)

x-value of Q	-3	-2.5	-2.2	-2.1	-2.01	-2.001
m_{PQ}	19	15.25	13.24	12.61	12.0601	12.0060

(b) estimate $m_{\tan} = 12$

3. 1   **5.** 3   **7.** -2 **9.** 0

11. $2x + 4$ **13.** $6q + 2$ **15.** $\dfrac{6}{x^2}$ **17.** $\dfrac{1}{\sqrt{2x}}$

19. -4 **21.** 0   **23.** $y = x + 4$

25. $y = 4x + 2$ **27.** $y - 1 = -\dfrac{1}{4}(x - 3)$

29. $\dfrac{r}{r_L - r - \dfrac{dC}{dD}}$ **31.** $-3.000, 13.445$

33. $-5.120, 0.038$

35. if tangent at $(a, f(a))$ horizontal then $f'(a) = 0$

37. $20x^4 - 9x^2$

Apply It 11.2

2. $50 - 0.6q$

Problems 11.2 (page 507)

1. 0   **3.** $6x^5$ **5.** $80x^{79}$ **7.** $18x$

9. $56w^6$ **11.** $\dfrac{18}{5}x^5$ **13.** $\dfrac{7}{25}t^6$ **15.** 1

17. $8x - 2$ **19.** $4p^3 - 9p^2$ **21.** $4x^3 - \dfrac{1}{3}x^{-2/3}$

23. $-39x^2 + 28x - 2$ **25.** $-8x^3$ **27.** $\dfrac{4}{3}x^3$

29. $16x^3 + 3x^2 - 9x + 8$ **31.** $\dfrac{45}{7}x^8 + \dfrac{21}{5}x^6$

33. $\dfrac{3}{5}x^{-2/5}$ **35.** $\dfrac{3}{4}x^{-1/4} + \dfrac{10}{3}x^{2/3}$ **37.** $\dfrac{11}{2}x^{-1/2}$

39. $2r^{-2/3}$ **41.** $-6x^{-7}$ **43.** $-3x^{-4} - 5x^{-6} + 12x^{-7}$

45. $-x^{-2}$ **47.** $-40x^{-6}$ **49.** $-4x^{-4}$ **51.** $\dfrac{-9}{5t^4}$

53. $\dfrac{1}{7} - 7x^{-2}$ **55.** $-3x^{-2/3} - 2x^{-7/5}$

57. $-\dfrac{1}{3}x^{-5/3}$ **59.** $-x^{-3/2}$ **61.** $\dfrac{10}{3}x^{7/3}$

63. $9x^2 - 20x + 7$ **65.** $45x^4$ **67.** $\dfrac{1}{3}x^{-2/3} - \dfrac{10}{3}x^{-5/3}$

69. $3 + \dfrac{2}{q^2}$ **71.** $2x + 1$ **73.** 1   **75.** $4, 16, -14$

77. $0, 0, 0$ **79.** $y = 13x + 2$

81. $y - \dfrac{1}{4} = -\dfrac{1}{4}(x - 2)$ **83.** $y = x + 3$

85. $(0, 0), \left(\dfrac{5}{3}, \dfrac{125}{54}\right)$ **87.** $(3, -3)$

89. 0   **91.** $y = x - 1$

Apply It 11.3

3. 2.5 units

4. $\dfrac{dy}{dt} = 16 - 32t$; $\dfrac{dy}{dt}\bigg|_{t=0.5} = 0$;

when $t = 0.5$ object at maximum height

5. 1.2 and 120%

Problems 11.3 (page 515)

1.

Δt	1	0.5	0.2	0.1	0.01	0.001
$\Delta s / \Delta t$	9	8	7.4	7.2	7.02	7.002

estimate and confirm 7 m/s

3. (a) 70 m   (b) 25 m/s   (c) 24 m/s

5. (a) 32   (b) 18.1505   (c) 18

7. (a) 2 m   (b) 10.261 m/s   (c) 9 m/s

9. $\dfrac{dy}{dx} = \dfrac{25}{2}x^{3/2}$; 337.50

11. 0.27   **13.** $dc/dq = 10$; 10

15. $dc/dq = (0.4)q + 4$; 8

17. $dc/dq = 2q + 50$; 80, 82, 84

19. $dc/dq = 0.02q + 5$; 6, 7

21. $dc/dq = 0.00006q^2 - 0.02q + 6$; 4.6, 11

23. $dr/dq = 0.8$; 0.8, 0.8, 0.8

25. $dr/dq = 240 + 80q - 6q^2$; 440; 90; -560

27. $dc/dq = 6.750 - 0.000656q$; 5.438;

$\bar{c} = \dfrac{-10,484.69}{q} + 6.750 - 0.000328q$; 0.851655

29. $P = 5,000,000R^{-0.93}$; $dP/dR = -4,650,000R^{-1.93}$

31. (a) -7.5 (b) 4.5

33. (a) 1   (b) $\dfrac{1}{x+4}$ (c) 1   (d) $\dfrac{1}{9}$ (e) 11.1%

35. (a) $4x$ (b) $\dfrac{4x}{2x^2 + 5}$ (c) 40   (d) $\dfrac{40}{205}$ (e) 19.51%

37. (a) $-3x^2$ (b) $-\dfrac{3x^2}{8 - x^3}$ (c) -3 (d) $-\dfrac{3}{7}$ (e) -42.9%

39. 9.5; 12.8%

41. (a) $dr/dq = 30 - 0.6q$ (b) $\dfrac{4}{45}$ (c) 9%

43. $\dfrac{0.432}{t}$ **45.** \$4150   **47.** \$5.07/unit

Apply It 11.4

6. $\dfrac{dR}{dx} = 6.25 - 6x$

7. $T'(x) = 2x - x^2$; $T'(1) = 1$

Problems 11.4 (page 525)

1. $(4x + 1)(6) + (6x + 3)(4) = 48x + 18 = 6(8x + 3)$

3. $(5 - 3t)(3t^2 - 4t) + (t^3 - 2t^2)(-3) = -12t^3 + 33t^2 - 20t$

5. $(3r^2 - 4)(2r - 5) + (r^2 - 5r + 1)(6r) = 12r^3 - 45r^2 - 2r + 20$

7. $8x^3 - 10x$

9. $(2x + 5)(6x^2 - 5x + 4) + (x^2 + 5x - 7)(12x - 5)$

11. $(w^2 + 3w - 7)(6w^2) + (2w^3 - 4)(2w + 3)$

13. $(x^2 - 1)(9x^2 - 6) + (3x^3 - 6x + 5)(2x) - 4(8x + 2)$

15. $\dfrac{3}{2}\left[(5p^{1/2}-2)(3)+(3p-1)\left(\dfrac{5}{2}p^{-1/2}\right)\right]$

17. 0

19. $(5)(2x-5)(7x+9)+(5x+3)(2)(7x+9)+(5x+3)(2x-5)(7)$

21. $\dfrac{(x-1)(5)-(5x)(1)}{(x-1)^2}$

23. $\dfrac{65}{3x^6}$

25. $\dfrac{(x-1)(1)-(x+2)(1)}{(x-1)^2}$

27. $\dfrac{(z^2-4)(-2)-(6-2z)(2z)}{(z^2-4)^2}$

29. $\dfrac{(3x^2-2x+1)(8x+3)-(4x^2+3x+2)(6x-2)}{(3x^2-2x+1)^2}$

31. $\dfrac{(2x^2-3x+2)(2x-4)-(x^2-4x+3)(4x-3)}{(2x^2-3x+2)^2}$

33. $-\dfrac{100x^{99}}{(x^{100}+7)^2}$

35. $2v+\dfrac{8}{v^2}$

37. $\dfrac{15x^2-2x+1}{3x^{4/3}}$

39. $\dfrac{10}{(2x+5)^2}+\dfrac{(3x+1)(2)-(2x)(3)}{(3x+1)^2}$

41. $\dfrac{[(x+2)(x-4)](1)-(x-5)(2x-2)}{[(x+2)(x-4)]^2}$

43. $\dfrac{[(t^2-1)(t^3+7)](2t+3)-(t^2+3t)(5t^4-3t^2+14t)}{[(t^2-1)(t^3+7)]^2}$

45. $3-\dfrac{2x^3+3x^2-12x+4}{[x(x-1)(x-2)]^2}$

47. $\dfrac{2a}{(a-x)^2}$

49. 25

51. $y=-\dfrac{3}{2}x+\dfrac{15}{2}$

53. $y=16x+24$

55. 1.5

57. 1 m, -1.5 m/s

59. $80-0.04q$

61. $\dfrac{216}{(q+2)^2}-3$

63. $\dfrac{dC}{dI}=0.672$

65. $\dfrac{7}{6};-\dfrac{1}{6}$

67. 0.615; 0.385

69. (a) 0.23 (b) 0.028

71. $\dfrac{dc}{dq}=\dfrac{6q(q+4)}{(q+2)^2}$

73. $\dfrac{9}{10}$

75. $\dfrac{0.7355}{(1+0.02744x)^2}$

77. $-\dfrac{1}{120}$

Apply It 11.5

8. $288t$

Problems 11.5 (page 532)

1. $4x^3-6x^2-2x+2$

3. $\dfrac{-3}{(3x-5)^2}$

5. 0   **7.** 0   **9.** $18(3x+2)^5$

11. $30x^2(3+2x^3)^4$

13. $500(x^3-3x^2+2x)^{99}(3x^2-6x+2)$

15. $-6x(x^2-2)^{-4}$

17. $-\dfrac{10}{7}(2x+5)(x^2+5x-2)^{-12/7}$

19. $\dfrac{1}{2}(10x-1)(5x^2-x)^{-1/2}$

21. $\dfrac{1}{2}(2x-1)^{-3/4}$

23. $\dfrac{12}{7}(x^2+1)^{-4/7}(2x)$

25. $-6(4x-1)(2x^2-x+1)^{-2}$

27. $-2(2x-3)(x^2-3x)^{-3}$

29. $-36x(9x^2+1)^{-3/2}$

31. $\dfrac{7}{3}(7x)^{-2/3}+\sqrt[3]{7}$

33. $3x^2(2x+3)^7+x^3(7)(2x+3)^6(2)$

35. $10x^2(5x+1)^{-1/2}+8x\sqrt{5x+1}$

37. $5(x^2+2x-1)^2(7x^2+8x-1)$

39. $16(8x-1)^2(2x+1)^3(7x+1)$

41. $\dfrac{60(x-3)^{11}}{(x+2)^{13}}$

43. $\dfrac{1}{2}\left(\dfrac{x+1}{x-5}\right)^{-1/2}\dfrac{-6}{(x-5)^2}$

45. $\dfrac{-2(5x^2-15x-4)}{(x^2+4)^4}$

47. $\dfrac{(8x-1)^4(48x-31)}{(3x-1)^4}$

49. $12x(x^4+5)^{-1/2}(10x^4+2x^2+25)$

51. $15-8t+\dfrac{5}{(t+4)^2}$

53. $\dfrac{(x^2-7)^3((3)(3x+2)^2(3)(x+1)^4+(3x+2)^3(4)(x+1)^3)-(3x+2)^3(x+1)^4(3)(x^2-7)^2(2x)}{(x^2-7)^6}$

55. 0   **57.** 0   **59.** $y=4x-11$

61. $y=-\dfrac{1}{6}x+\dfrac{5}{3}$ **63.** 400%   **65.** 130

67. ≈ 13.99

69. (a) $-\dfrac{q}{\sqrt{q^2+20}}$ (b) $-\dfrac{q}{100\sqrt{q^2+20}-q^2-20}$

(c) $100-\dfrac{q^2}{\sqrt{q^2+20}}-\sqrt{q^2+20}$

71. -481.5 **73.** $\dfrac{4q^3+16q}{(q^2+2)^{3/2}}$ **75.** $48\pi(10)^{-19}$

77. (a) $-0.001416x^3+0.01356x^2+1.696x-34.9, -256.238$

(b) $-0.016; -1.578\%$

79. -4 **81.** 40   **83.** 94.03

Review Problems—Chapter 11 (page 535)

1. $-2x$ **3.** $\dfrac{\sqrt{3}}{2\sqrt{x}}$ **5.** 0

7. $4\pi x^3-3\sqrt{2}x^2+4x$ **9.** $4s^3+4s=4s(s^2+1)$

11. $\dfrac{2x}{5}$

13. $6x^5+30x^4-28x^3+15x^2+70x$

15. $400(x+1)(2x^2+4x)^{99}$ **17.** $-\dfrac{ca}{(ax+b)^2}$

19. $2(x^2+1)^3(9x^2+32x+1)$ **21.** $\dfrac{10z}{(z^2+4)^2}$

23. $\dfrac{4}{3}(4x-1)^{-2/3}$ **25.** $x(1-x^2)^{-3/2}$

27. $ma(ax+b)^{m-1}(cx+d)^n+nc(ax+b)^m(cx+d)^{n-1}$

29. $\dfrac{34}{(x+6)^2}$ **31.** $-\dfrac{3}{4}(1+2^{-11/8})x^{-11/8}$

33. $\dfrac{x(x^2+4)}{(x^2+5)^{3/2}}$ **35.** $\dfrac{9}{5}x(x+4)(x^3+6x^2+9)^{-2/5}$

37. $-3(z-2)^3-9z(z-2)^2$ **39.** $y=-4x+3$

41. $y=\dfrac{1}{12}x+\dfrac{4}{3}$ **43.** $\dfrac{5}{7}\approx 0.714; 71.4\%$

45. $dr/dq=20-0.2q$ **47.** 0.68; 0.32

49. $dr/dq=500-0.2q$

51. $dc/dq=0.125+0.00878q; 0.7396$

53. 84 eggs/mm   **55.** (a) $\dfrac{4}{3}$ (b) $\dfrac{1}{24}$ **57.** 2π

59. $4q-\dfrac{10,000}{q^2}$

61. (a) -315.456 (b) -0.00025 (c) no, $dr/dm|_{m=240}<0$

63. 0.305   **65.** -0.32

Explore and Extend—Chapter 11 (page 538)

1. slope is greater; more spent, less saved.

3. spend $705, save $295

5. Answers may vary.

Apply It 12.1

1. $\dfrac{dq}{dp} = \dfrac{12p}{3p^2 + 4}$ **2.** $\dfrac{dR}{dI} = \dfrac{1}{I \ln 10}$

Problems 12.1 (page 544)

1. $\dfrac{a}{x}$ **3.** $\dfrac{3}{3x-7}$ **5.** $\dfrac{2}{x}$ **7.** $-\dfrac{2x}{1-x^2}$ **9.** $\dfrac{3(4X^3+1)}{X(2X^3+1)}$

11. $\ln t$ **13.** $\dfrac{2x^3}{2x+5} + 3x^2 \ln(2x+5)$ **15.** $\dfrac{8}{(\ln 3)(8x-1)}$

17. $2x\left[1 + \dfrac{1}{(\ln 2)(x^2+4)}\right]$ **19.** $\dfrac{1-\ln z}{z^2}$

21. $\dfrac{(\ln x)(4x^3+6x+1) - (x^3+3x+1)}{(\ln x)^2}$

23. $\dfrac{6(x+2)}{x^2+4x+5}$ **25.** $\dfrac{9x}{1+x^2}$ **27.** $\dfrac{2}{1-l^2}$ **29.** $\dfrac{x}{1-x^4}$

31. $\dfrac{p(2ax+b)}{ax^2+bx+c} + \dfrac{q(2hx+k)}{hx^2+kx+l}$ **33.** $\dfrac{26}{x} + \dfrac{65}{3(5x+2)}$

35. $\dfrac{2(x^2+1)}{2x+1} + 2x\ln(2x+1)$ **37.** $\dfrac{3(1+\ln^2 x)}{x}$ **39.** $\dfrac{4\ln^3(ax)}{x}$

41. $\dfrac{f'(x)}{2f(x)}$ **43.** $\dfrac{3}{2x\sqrt{4+3\ln x}}$ **45.** $y = 5x - 20$

47. $\dfrac{\ln(3)-1}{\ln^2 3}$ **49.** $\dfrac{25}{7}$ **51.** $\dfrac{22}{2p+1}$

53. $\dfrac{6a}{(T-a^2+aT)(a-T)}$ **57.** $-1.65, 1.65$

Apply It 12.2

3. $\dfrac{dT}{dt} = Cke^{kt}$

Problems 12.2 (page 549)

1. $5e^x$ **3.** $4xe^{2x^2+3}$ **5.** $-5e^{9-5x}$

7. $(12r^2+10r+2)e^{4r^3+5r^2+2r+6}$ **9.** $x(e^x) + e^x(1) = e^x(x+1)$

11. $2xe^{-x^2}(1-x^2)$ **13.** $\dfrac{e^x - e^{-x}}{3}$ **15.** $(6x^2)5^{2x^3}\ln 5$

17. $\dfrac{(w^2+w+1)ae^{aw} - e^{aw}(2w+1)}{(w^2+w+1)^2}$

19. $\dfrac{e^{1+\sqrt{x}}}{2\sqrt{x}}$ **21.** $5x^4 - 5^x \ln 5$

23. $\dfrac{2e^x}{(e^x+1)^2}$ **25.** 1 **27.** $x^x(\ln x + 1)$ **29.** $-e$

31. $y = e^{-2}x + 3e^{-2}$

33. $dp/dq = -0.015e^{-0.001q}; -0.015e^{-0.5}$

35. $dc/dq = 10e^{q/700}; 10e^{0.5}; 10e$

37. $-12e^9$ **39.** e **41.** $100e^{-2}$ **47.** $-b(10^{A-bM})\ln 10$

51. 0.0036 **53.** $-0.89, 0.56$

Problems 12.3 (page 554)

1. -3 elastic   **3.** -1 unit elasticity   **5.** $-\dfrac{53}{52}$ elastic

7. $-\left(\dfrac{150}{e} - 1\right)$ elastic   **9.** -1 unit elasticity

11. -2 elastic   **13.** $-\dfrac{1}{2}$ inelastic

15. $\eta(10) = -\dfrac{10}{3}; \eta(3) = -\dfrac{3}{10}; \eta(6.5) = -1$

17. $-1.2, 0.6\%$ decrease

23. (a) $\eta = -\dfrac{cp^2}{b-cp^2}$ (b) $\left(\sqrt{\dfrac{b}{2c}}, \sqrt{\dfrac{b}{c}}\right]$ (c) $\sqrt{\dfrac{b}{2c}}$

25. (a) $\eta = -\dfrac{207}{15} = -13.8$ elastic   (b) 27.6%
(c) increase, since demand is elastic

27. $\eta = -1.6; \dfrac{dr}{dq} = 30$

29. maximum at $q = 5$; minimum at $q = 95$

Apply It 12.4

4. $\dfrac{dP}{dt} = 0.5(P - P^2)$

5. $\dfrac{dV}{dt} = 4\pi r^2 \dfrac{dr}{dt}; \dfrac{dV}{dt}\Big|_{r=12} = 2880\pi$ in^3/min

6. $\dfrac{9}{4}$ ft/sec

Problems 12.4 (page 560)

1. $-\dfrac{x}{4y}$ **3.** $\dfrac{7x}{3y^2}$ **5.** $-\dfrac{\sqrt[3]{y^2}}{\sqrt[3]{x^2}}$ **7.** $-\dfrac{y^{1/4}}{x^{1/4}}$

9. $-\dfrac{y}{x}$ for $x \ne 0$ **11.** $\dfrac{11-y}{x-1}$ **13.** $\dfrac{4y-2x^2}{y^2-4x}$ **15.** $\dfrac{4y^{3/4}}{2y^{1/4}+1}$

17. $\dfrac{1-15x^2y^4}{20x^5y^3+2y}$ **19.** $\dfrac{1/x - ye^{xy}}{1/y - xe^{xy}}$ for $1/y - xe^{xy} \ne 0$

21. $-\dfrac{e^y}{xe^y+1}$ **23.** $6e^{3x}(1+e^{3x})(x+y)-1$ **25.** $-\dfrac{3}{5}$

27. $0; -\dfrac{4x_0}{9y_0}$

29. $y+1 = -(x+1); y = 3(x+1); y-1 = -2(x+1)$

31. $\dfrac{dq}{dp} = -\dfrac{1}{2q}$ **33.** $\dfrac{dq}{dp} = -\dfrac{(q+5)^3}{40}$

35. $-\lambda I$ **37.** $-\dfrac{f}{\lambda}$ **39.** $\dfrac{3}{8}$

Problems 12.5 (page 564)

1. $(x+1)^2(x-2)(x^2+3)\left[\dfrac{2}{x+1} + \dfrac{1}{x-2} + \dfrac{2x}{x^2+3}\right]$

3. $(3x^3-1)^2(2x+5)^3\left[\dfrac{18x^2}{3x^3-1} + \dfrac{6}{2x+5}\right]$

5. $\dfrac{1}{2}\sqrt{x+1}\sqrt{x-1}\sqrt{x^2+1}\left(\dfrac{1}{x+1} + \dfrac{1}{x-1} + \dfrac{2x}{x^2+1}\right)$

7. $\dfrac{\sqrt{1-x^2}}{1-2x}\left[\dfrac{x}{x^2-1} + \dfrac{2}{1-2x}\right]$

9. $\dfrac{(2x^2+2)^2}{(x+1)^2(3x+2)}\left[\dfrac{4x}{x^2+1} - \dfrac{2}{x+1} - \dfrac{3}{3x+2}\right]$

11. $\dfrac{1}{2}\sqrt{\dfrac{(x+3)(x-2)}{2x-1}}\left[\dfrac{1}{x+3}+\dfrac{1}{x-2}-\dfrac{2}{2x-1}\right]$

13. $x^{x^2+1}\left(\dfrac{x^2+1}{x}+2x\ln x\right)$ **15.** $x^{\sqrt{x}}\left(\dfrac{2+\ln x}{2\sqrt{x}}\right)$

17. $2(3x+1)^{2x}\left[\dfrac{3x}{3x+1}+\ln(3x+1)\right]$

19. $4e^x x^{3x}(4+3\ln x)$ **21.** 12

23. $y=96x+36$ **25.** $y-e^e=2e^e(x-e)$

27. $\dfrac{1}{3e^{1.3}}$ **29.** 0.1% decrease

Apply It 12.6

7. 43; 1958

Problems 12.6 (page 567)

1. ≈ 0.2016 **3.** 1.32472   **5.** -0.68233 **7.** 0.33767

9. 1.90785   **11.** 4.179   **13.** -4.99 and 1.94

15. 13.33   **17.** 2.880   **19.** 3.45

Apply It 12.7

8. $\dfrac{d^2h}{dt^2}=-32$ ft/sec^2 **9.** $c''(3)=14$ dollars/unit^2

Problems 12.7 (page 571)

1. 24   **3.** 0   **5.** e^x **7.** $6\ln x+11$

9. $-\dfrac{60}{q^7}$ **11.** $-\dfrac{1}{4(9-r)^{3/2}}$ **13.** $\dfrac{8}{(2x+3)^3}$ **15.** $\dfrac{4}{(x-1)^3}$

17. $-\left(\dfrac{1}{x^2}+\dfrac{1}{(x+a)^2}\right)$ **19.** $e^z(z^2+4z+2)$ **21.** 275

23. $-\dfrac{1}{y^3}$ **25.** $-\dfrac{4}{y^3}$ **27.** $\dfrac{a}{b}\sqrt{\dfrac{y}{x}}$

29. $\dfrac{2(y-1)}{(1+x)^2}$ **31.** $\dfrac{y}{(1-y)^3}$ **33.** $\dfrac{25}{32}$

35. $300(5x-3)^2$ **37.** 0.04   **39.** ± 1 **41.** -4.99; 1.94

Review Problems—Chapter 12 (page 573)

1. $3e^x+2xe^{x^2}+e^2 x^{e^2-1}$ **3.** $\dfrac{14r+4}{7r^2+4r+5}$ **5.** $2(x+2)e^{x^2+4x+5}$

7. $e^x(x^2+2x+2)$

9. $\dfrac{\sqrt{(x-6)(x+5)(9-x)}}{2}\left[\dfrac{1}{x-6}+\dfrac{1}{x+5}+\dfrac{1}{x-9}\right]$

11. $\dfrac{1-x\ln x}{xe^x}$ **13.** $\dfrac{m}{x+a}+\dfrac{n}{x+b}$ **15.** $(4x+2)(\ln 2)2^{2x^2+2x-5}$

17. $\dfrac{4e^{2x+1}(2x-1)}{x^2}$ **19.** $\dfrac{16}{(8x+5)\ln 2}$ **21.** $\dfrac{1+2l+3l^2}{1+l+l^2+l^3}$

23. $(x^2+1)^{x+1}\left(\ln(x^2+1)+\dfrac{2x(x+1)}{x^2+1}\right)$ **25.** $\dfrac{1}{t}-\dfrac{t}{4-t^2}$

27. $y\left[\dfrac{x}{x^2+1}+\dfrac{2x}{3(x^2+2)}-\dfrac{6(x^2+1)}{5(x^3+3x)}\right]$ **29.** $(x^x)^x(x+2x\ln x)$

31. 4   **33.** $-2e^{-e}$ **35.** $y=6x+6-\ln 64$ **37.** $(0,4\ln 2)$

39. 2   **41.** 2   **43.** -1 **45.** $\dfrac{xy^2-y}{2x-x^2y}$ **47.** $\dfrac{4}{9}$

49. $\dfrac{dy}{dx}=\dfrac{y+1}{y}$; $\dfrac{d^2y}{dx^2}=-\dfrac{y+1}{y^3}$

51. $f'(t)=0.008e^{-0.01t}+0.00004e^{-0.0002t}$

53. 0.02   **55.** $\eta=-1$ unit elasticity   **57.** $\eta=-0.5$ inelastic

59. $-\dfrac{9}{16}$; $\dfrac{3}{8}$% increase   **61.** 1.7693

Explore and Extend---Chapter 12 (page 575)

1. 305 units   **3.** answers may vary

Apply It 13.1

1. rel max $q=2$; rel min $q=5$ **2.** 2 hours after injection

Problems 13.1 (page 586)

1. dec on $(-\infty,-1)$, $(3,\infty)$; inc on $(-1,3)$; rel min $(-1,-1)$; rel max $(3,4)$

3. dec on $(-\infty,-2)$, $(0,2)$; inc on $(-2,0)$, $(2,\infty)$; rel min $(-2,1)$, $(2,1)$; no rel max

5. inc on $(-3,1)$, $(2,\infty)$; dec on $(-\infty,-3)$, $(1,2)$; rel max $x=1$; rel min $x=-3$, $x=2$

7. dec on $(-\infty,-1)$; inc on $(-1,3)$, $(3,\infty)$; rel min $x=-1$

9. dec on $(-\infty,0)$, $(0,\infty)$; no rel ext

11. inc on $\left(-\infty,\dfrac{1}{2}\right)$; dec on $\left(\dfrac{1}{2},\infty\right)$; rel max $x=\dfrac{1}{2}$

13. dec on $(-\infty,-5)$, $(1,\infty)$; inc on $(-5,1)$; rel min $x=-5$; rel max $x=1$

15. dec on $(-\infty,-1)$, $(0,1)$; inc on $(-1,0)$, $(1,\infty)$; rel max $x=0$; rel min $x=\pm 1$

17. inc on $\left(-\infty,\dfrac{1}{3}\right)$, $(2,\infty)$; dec on $\left(\dfrac{1}{3},2\right)$; rel max $x=\dfrac{1}{3}$; rel min $x=2$

19. inc on $\left(-\infty,\dfrac{2}{3}\right)$, $\left(\dfrac{5}{2},\infty\right)$; dec on $\left(\dfrac{2}{3},\dfrac{5}{2}\right)$; rel max $x=\dfrac{2}{3}$; rel min $x=\dfrac{5}{2}$

21. inc on $(-\infty,5-\sqrt{3})$, $(5+\sqrt{3},\infty)$; dec on $(5-\sqrt{3},5+\sqrt{3})$; rel max $x=5-\sqrt{3}$; rel min $x=5+\sqrt{3}$

23. inc on $(-\infty,-1)$, $(1,\infty)$; dec on $(-1,0)$, $(0,1)$; rel max $x=-1$; rel min $x=1$

25. dec on $(-\infty,-4)$, $(0,\infty)$; inc on $(-4,0)$; rel min $x=-4$; rel max $x=0$

27. inc on $(-\infty,-\sqrt{2})$, $(0,\sqrt{2})$; dec on $(-\sqrt{2},0)$, $(\sqrt{2},\infty)$; rel max $x=\pm\sqrt{2}$; rel min $x=0$

29. inc on $(-2,0)$, $(2,\infty)$; dec on $(-\infty,-2)$, $(0,2)$; rel max $x=0$; rel min $x=\pm 2$

31. dec on $(-\infty,1)$, $(1,\infty)$; no rel ext

33. dec on $(0,\infty)$; no rel ext

35. dec on $(-\infty,0)$, $(4,\infty)$; inc on $(0,2)$, $(2,4)$; rel min $x=0$; rel max $x=4$

37. inc on $(-\infty,-3)$, $(-1,\infty)$; dec on $(-3,-2)$, $(-2,-1)$; rel max $x=-3$; rel min $x=-1$

39. (a) inc on $\left(0,\sqrt{-\dfrac{d}{c}}\right)$, $\left(\sqrt{-\dfrac{d}{c}},\infty\right)$; dec on $\left(-\infty,-\sqrt{-\dfrac{d}{c}}\right)$, $\left(-\sqrt{-\dfrac{d}{c}},0\right)$; rel min $x=0$ (b) as for (a) with "inc" and "dec" interchanged; "min" replaced by "max"

41. inc on $(1, \infty)$; dec on $(-\infty, 1)$; rel min $x = 1$

43. inc on $(-\infty, 0)$, $\left(0, \dfrac{18}{7}\right)$, $(6, \infty)$; dec on $\left(\dfrac{18}{7}, 6\right)$; rel max $x = \dfrac{18}{7}$; rel min $x = 6$

45. dec on $(-\infty, \infty)$; no rel ext

47. dec on $\left(0, \dfrac{3\sqrt{2}}{2}\right)$; inc on $\left(\dfrac{3\sqrt{2}}{2}, \infty\right)$; rel min $x = \dfrac{3\sqrt{2}}{2}$

49. inc on $(-\infty, \infty)$; no rel ext

51. dec on $(0,1)$; inc on $(1, \infty)$; rel min $x = 1$

53. dec on $\left(-\infty, \dfrac{3}{2}\right)$; inc on $\left(\dfrac{3}{2}, \infty\right)$; rel min $x = \dfrac{3}{2}$; int $(-2, 0)$, $(5,0)$, $(0, -10)$

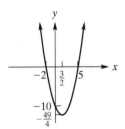

55. dec on $(-\infty, -1)$, $(1, \infty)$; inc on $(-1, 1)$; rel min $x = -1$; rel max $x = 1$; sym about origin; int $(\pm\sqrt{3}, 0)$, $(0,0)$

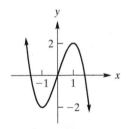

57. inc on $(-\infty, 1)$, $(2, \infty)$; dec on $(1,2)$; rel max $x = 1$; rel min $x = 2$; int $(0,0)$

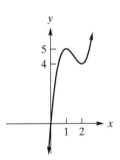

59. inc on $(-1,0)$, $(1, \infty)$; dec on $(-\infty, -1)$, $(0, 1)$; abs min $x = \pm 1$; relative max $x = 0$; sym about $x = 0$; int $(-\sqrt{2}, 0)$, $(0, 0)$, $(\sqrt{2}, 0)$

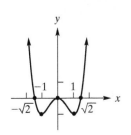

61. dec on $(-\infty, -2)$, $\left(-\dfrac{1}{2}, 1\right)$; inc on $\left(-2, -\dfrac{1}{2}\right)$, $(1, \infty)$; rel min $x = -2$, $x = 1$; rel max $x = -\dfrac{1}{2}$; int $(1,0)$, $(-2, 0)$, $(0,4)$

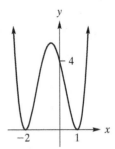

63. dec on $(1, \infty)$; inc on $(0,1)$; rel max $x = 1$; int $(0,0)$, $(4,0)$

65.

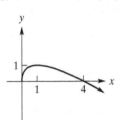

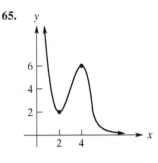

69. $q < 50$

71. 40

75. (a) 25,300   (b) 4   (c) 17,200

77. rel min $(-3.83, 0.69)$

79. rel max $(2.74, 3.74)$; rel min $(-2.74, -3.74)$

81. rel min 0, 1.50, 2.00; rel max 0.57, 1.77

83. (a) $f'(x) = 4 - 6x - 3x^2$ (c) dec on $(-\infty, -2.53)$, $(0.53, \infty)$; inc $(-2.53, 0.53)$

Problems 13.2 (page 590)

1. max $(3, 6)$; min $(1, 2)$

3. max $\left(-1, \dfrac{19}{6}\right)$; min $(0, 1)$

5. max $(0, 50)$; min $(4, 2)$

7. max $(-2, 56)$; min $(-1, -2)$

9. max $(\sqrt{2}, 4)$; min $(2, -16)$

11. max $(0, 2)$, $(3, 2)$; min $\left(\dfrac{3\sqrt{2}}{2}, -\dfrac{73}{4}\right)$

13. max $(-26, 9)$, $(28, 9)$; min $(1, 0)$

15. (a) -3.22, -0.78 (b) 2.75   (c) 9   (d) 14,283

Problems 13.3 (page 596)

1. conc up $\left(-\infty, -\dfrac{1}{2}\right)$, $(2, \infty)$; conc down $\left(-\dfrac{1}{2}, 2\right)$; inf pt $x = -\dfrac{1}{2}$, $x = 2$

3. conc up $(-\infty, 1)$, $(1,7)$; conc down $(7, \infty)$; inf pt $x = 7$

5. conc up $(-\infty, -\sqrt{2})$, $(\sqrt{2}, \infty)$; conc down $(-\sqrt{2}, \sqrt{2})$; no inf pt

7. conc down $(-\infty, \infty)$

9. conc down $(-\infty, -1)$; conc up $(-1, \infty)$; inf pt $x = -1$

11. conc up [down] $\left(-\dfrac{b}{3a}, \infty\right)$ conc down [up] $\left(-\infty, \dfrac{b}{3a}\right)$ for $a > 0$ [$a < 0$]; inf pt $x = \dfrac{b}{3a}$

13. conc up $(-\infty, -2)$, $(2, \infty)$; conc down $(-2, 2)$; inf pt $x = \pm 2$

15. conc up $(-\infty, 0)$; conc down $(0, \infty)$; inf pt $x = 0$

17. conc up $\left(-\infty, -\dfrac{7}{2}\right), \left(\dfrac{1}{3}, \infty\right)$; conc down $\left(-\dfrac{7}{2}, \dfrac{1}{3}\right)$; inf pt $x = -\dfrac{7}{2}, x = \dfrac{1}{3}$

19. conc down $(-\infty, 0)$, $\left(\dfrac{3 - \sqrt{5}}{2}, \dfrac{3 + \sqrt{5}}{2}\right)$; conc up $\left(0, \dfrac{3 - \sqrt{5}}{2}\right), \left(\dfrac{3 + \sqrt{5}}{2}, \infty\right)$; inf pt $x = 0, x = \dfrac{3 \pm \sqrt{5}}{2}$

21. conc up $(-\infty, -2), (-\sqrt{3}, \sqrt{3}), (2, \infty)$; conc down $(-2, -\sqrt{3})$, $(\sqrt{3}, 2)$; inf pt $x = -2, x = -\sqrt{3}, x = \sqrt{3}, x = 2$

23. conc down $(-\infty, 1)$; conc up $(1, \infty)$

25. conc down $(-\infty, -1/\sqrt{3}), (1/\sqrt{3}, \infty)$; conc up $(-1/\sqrt{3}, 1/\sqrt{3})$; inf pt $x = \pm 1/\sqrt{3}$

27. conc down $(-\infty, -3), \left(-3, \dfrac{2}{7}\right)$; conc up $\left(\dfrac{2}{7}, \infty\right)$; inf pt $x = \dfrac{2}{7}$

29. conc up $(-\infty, \infty)$

31. conc down [up] $(-\infty, -2)$ conc up [down] on $(-2, \infty)$ for $a > 0$ $[a < 0]$; inf pt $x = -2$

33. conc down $(0, e^{3/2})$; conc up $(e^{3/2}, \infty)$; inf pt $x = e^{3/2}$

35. int $(-2, 0), (3, 0), (0, -6)$; dec $\left(-\infty, \dfrac{1}{2}\right)$; inc $\left(\dfrac{1}{2}, \infty\right)$; rel min $x = \dfrac{1}{2}$; conc up $(-\infty, \infty)$

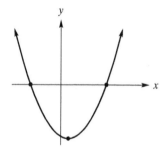

37. int $(0, 0), \left(\dfrac{5}{2}, 0\right)$; inc $\left(-\infty, \dfrac{5}{4}\right)$; dec $\left(\dfrac{5}{4}, \infty\right)$; rel max $x = \dfrac{5}{4}$; conc down $(-\infty, \infty)$

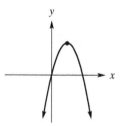

39. int $(0, -19)$; inc $(-\infty, 2), (4, \infty)$; dec $(2, 4)$; rel max $x = 2$; rel min $x = 4$; conc down $(-\infty, 3)$; conc up $(3, \infty)$; inf pt $x = 3$

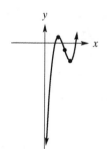

41. inc on $(-\infty, -\sqrt{5}), (\sqrt{5}, \infty)$; dec on $(-\sqrt{5}, \sqrt{5})$; conc down $(-\infty, 0)$; conc up $(0, \infty)$; rel max $\left(-\sqrt{5}, \dfrac{10}{3}(\sqrt{5})\right)$, rel min $\left(\sqrt{5}, -\dfrac{10}{3}(\sqrt{5})\right)$; inf pt $(0, 0)$; sym about $(0, 0)$; int $(\pm \sqrt{15}, 0), (0, 0)$

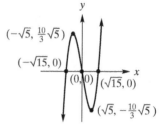

43. int $(0, -3)$; inc on $(-\infty, 1), (1, \infty)$; no rel ext; conc down $(-\infty, 1)$; conc up $(1, \infty)$; inf pt $x = 1$

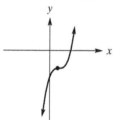

45. int $(0, 0), (4/3, 0)$; inc $(-\infty, 0), (0, 1)$; dec $(1, \infty)$; rel max $x = 1$; conc up $(0, 2/3)$; conc down $(-\infty, 0), (2/3, \infty)$; inf pt $x = 0, x = 2/3$

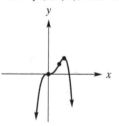

47. int $(0, -2)$; dec $(-\infty, -2), (2, \infty)$; inc $(-2, 2)$; rel min $x = -2$; rel max $x = 2$; conc up $(-\infty, 0)$; conc down $(0, \infty)$; inf pt $x = 0$

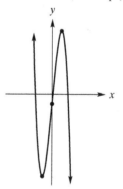

49. int $(0, -2), (1, 0)$; inc on $(-\infty, 1), (1, \infty)$; conc down $(-\infty, 1)$; conc up $(1, \infty)$; inf pt $x = 1$

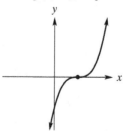

51. dec on $\left(-\infty, -\dfrac{2}{\sqrt[4]{5}}\right)$, $\left(\dfrac{2}{\sqrt[4]{5}}, \infty\right)$; inc on $\left(-\dfrac{2}{\sqrt[4]{5}}, \dfrac{2}{\sqrt[4]{5}}\right)$; conc up $(-\infty, 0)$; conc down $(0, \infty)$; rel min $\left(-\dfrac{2}{\sqrt[4]{5}}, -\dfrac{128}{25}(5)^{3/4}\right)$; rel max $\left(\dfrac{2}{\sqrt[4]{5}}, \dfrac{128}{25}(5)^{3/4}\right)$; inf pt $(0, 0)$; sym about $(0, 0)$; int $(\pm 2, 0), (0, 0)$

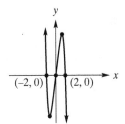

53. int $(0, 1)$, $(1, 0)$; dec $(-\infty, 0)$, $(0, 1)$; inc $(1, \infty)$; rel min $x = 1$; conc up $(-\infty, 0)$, $(2/3, \infty)$; conc down $(0, 2/3)$; inf pt $x = 0$, $x = 2/3$

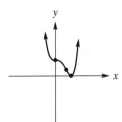

55. int $(0, 0)$, $(\pm 2, 0)$; inc $(-\infty, -\sqrt{2})$, $(0, \sqrt{2})$; dec $(-\sqrt{2}, 0)$, $(\sqrt{2}, \infty)$; rel max $x = \pm\sqrt{2}$; rel min $x = 0$; conc down $(-\infty, -\sqrt{2/3})$, $(\sqrt{2/3}, \infty)$; conc up $(-\sqrt{2/3}, \sqrt{2/3})$; inf pt $x = \pm\sqrt{2/3}$; sym about y-axis

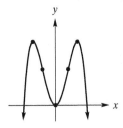

57. int $(0, 0)$, $(8, 0)$; dec $(-\infty, 0)$, $(0, 2)$; inc $(2, \infty)$; rel min $x = 2$; conc up $(-\infty, -4)$, $(0, \infty)$; conc down $(-4, 0)$; inf pt $x = -4$, $x = 0$

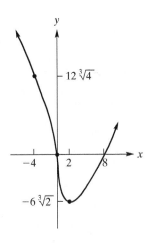

59. int $(0, 0)$, $(-4, 0)$; dec $(-\infty, -1)$; inc on $(-1, 0)$, $(0, \infty)$; rel min $x = -1$; conc up $(-\infty, 0)$, $(2, \infty)$; conc down $(0, 2)$; inf pt $x = 0$, $x = 2$

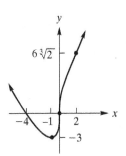

61. dec on $(-\infty, 0)$, $\left(\dfrac{64}{27}, \infty\right)$; inc on $\left(0, \dfrac{64}{27}\right)$; conc down $(-\infty, 0)$, $(0, \infty)$; rel min $(0, 0)$; rel max $\left(\dfrac{64}{27}, \dfrac{32}{27}\right)$; no inf pt; vertical tangent at $(0, 0)$; no sym; $(0, 0)$, $(8, 0)$

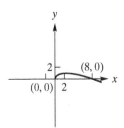

63.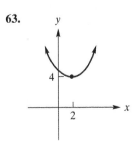

65.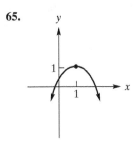

69.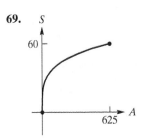

73. **(b)** $f(r)$
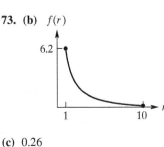

(c) 0.26

75. two

77. above tangent line; concave up

79. -2.61, -0.26

Problems 13.4 (page 599)

1. rel min $x = \dfrac{5}{2}$; abs min

3. rel max $x = \dfrac{1}{4}$; abs max

5. rel max $x = -5$; rel min $x = 1$

7. rel max $x = -2$; rel min $x = 3$

9. test fails, rel max $x = 0$

11. rel max $x = -\dfrac{1}{3}$; rel min $x = \dfrac{1}{3}$

13. rel min $x = -5$, $x = -2$; rel max $x = -\dfrac{7}{2}$

39. int $(0, 20)$, inc on $(-\infty, -2)$, $(2, \infty)$; dec on $(-2, 2)$; rel max $x = -2$; rel min $x = 2$; conc up $(0, \infty)$; conc down $(-\infty, 0)$; inf pt $x = 0$

41. int $(0, 0)$, $(-1, 0)$, $(1, 0)$; inc on $\left(-\infty, -\dfrac{\sqrt{3}}{3}\right)$, $\left(\dfrac{\sqrt{3}}{3}, \infty\right)$; dec on $\left(-\dfrac{\sqrt{3}}{3}, \dfrac{\sqrt{3}}{3}\right)$; conc down $(-\infty, 0)$; conc up $(0, \infty)$; inf pt $x = 0$; sym about origin

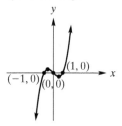

43. int $(-5, 0)$; inc $(-10, 0)$; dec on $(-\infty, -10)$, $(0, \infty)$; rel min $x = -10$; conc up $(-15, 0)$, $(0, \infty)$; conc down $(-\infty, -15)$; inf pt $x = -15$; asymp $y = 0$ $x = 0$

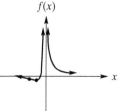

45. inc on $\left(\infty, -\dfrac{1}{2}\right)$; dec on $\left(-\dfrac{1}{2}, 1\right)$, $(1, \infty)$; conc up $(-\infty, -1)$, $(1, \infty)$; conc down $(-1, 1)$; rel max $\left(-\dfrac{1}{2}, \dfrac{4}{27}\right)$; inf pt $\left(-1, \dfrac{1}{8}\right)$; asymp $y = 0$, $x = 1$; no symmetry; int $(0, 0)$

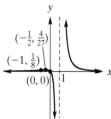

47. int $(0, 1)$; inc on $(0, \infty)$; dec on $(-\infty, 0)$; rel min $x = 0$; conc up $(-\infty, \infty)$; sym about y-axis

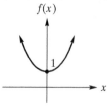

49. (a) false (b) false (c) true (d) false (e) false

51. $q > 2$

57. rel max $(-1.32, 12.28)$; rel min $(0.44, 1.29)$

59. $x \approx -0.60$ **61.** 20   **63.** 200

65. \$29,000   **67.** 100 ft by 200 ft

69. (a) 200 stands at \$120 per stand (b) 300 stands

Explore and Extend—Chapter 13 (page 625)

1. population reaches final size in ≈ 45 days.

3. tangent line will not coincide exactly with curve; smaller time steps could reduce error

Problems 14.1 (page 630)

1. $a\,dx$ **3.** $\dfrac{2x^3}{\sqrt{x^4 - 9}}\,dx$ **5.** $-\dfrac{2}{x^3}\,dx$

7. $\dfrac{2x}{x^2 + 7}\,dx$ **9.** $3e^{2x^2 + 3}(12x^2 + 4x + 3)\,dx$

11. $\Delta y = a\,dx = dy$ **13.** $\Delta y = -0.28$, $dy = -0.3$

15. $\Delta y \approx 0.049$, $dy = 0.050$ **17.** (a) -1 (b) 2.9

19. $\dfrac{577}{34} \approx 16.97$ **21.** $\dfrac{25}{12}$ **23.** -0.03

25. 1.001   **27.** $\dfrac{1}{2}$ **29.** $\dfrac{1}{6p(p^2 + 5)^2}$

31. $-\dfrac{p^3}{2}$ **33.** $\dfrac{1}{36}$ **35.** $-\dfrac{4}{5}$

37. -17; -19.3 **39.** 2.04   **41.** $\dfrac{3}{40} \approx 0.1$

43. $(1.69 \times 10^{-11})\pi$ cm^3 **45.** (c) 42 units

Apply It 14.2

1. $\int 28.3\,dq = 28.3q + C$ **2.** $\int 0.12t^2\,dt = 0.04t^3 + C$

3. $\int -\dfrac{480}{t^3}\,dt = \dfrac{240}{t^2} + C$

4. $\int (500 + 300\sqrt{t})dt = 500t + 200t^{3/2} + C$

5. $S(t) = 0.7t^3 - 32.7t^2 + 491.6t + C$

Problems 14.2 (page 636)

1. $7x + C$ **3.** $\dfrac{x^9}{9} + C$ **5.** $-\dfrac{5}{6x^6} + C$

7. $-\dfrac{5}{6x^6} + C$ **9.** $-\dfrac{4}{3t^{3/4}} + C$ **11.** $4t + \dfrac{t^2}{2} + C$

13. $\dfrac{y^6}{6} - \dfrac{5y^2}{2} + C$ **15.** $t^3 - 2t^2 + 5t + C$

17. $(\sqrt{2} + e)x + C$ **19.** $\dfrac{x^2}{14} - \dfrac{3x^5}{20} + C$

21. $\pi e^x + C$ **23.** $\dfrac{x^{9.3}}{9.3} - \dfrac{9x^7}{7} - \dfrac{1}{x^3} - \dfrac{1}{2x^2} + C$

25. $-\dfrac{4x^{3/2}}{9} + C$ **27.** $5\sqrt[3]{x} + C$ **29.** $\dfrac{x^4}{12} + \dfrac{3}{2x^2} + C$

31. $\dfrac{w^3}{2} + \dfrac{2}{3w} + C$ **33.** $\dfrac{3}{10}u^2 - \dfrac{4}{5}u + C$

35. $\dfrac{u^{e+1}}{e + 1} + e^u + C$ **37.** $6\sqrt{x} - 9\sqrt[3]{x^4} + C$

39. $-\dfrac{3x^{5/3}}{25} - 7x^{1/2} + 3x^2 + C$ **41.** $\dfrac{x^4}{4} - x^3 + \dfrac{5x^2}{2} - 15x + C$

43. $\dfrac{2x^{5/2}}{5} + 2x^{3/2} + C$ **45.** $\dfrac{27}{4}u^4 + 18u^3 + 18u^2 + 8u + C$

47. $x^3 + 4x + \dfrac{5}{x} + C$

49. $\dfrac{z^3}{6} + \dfrac{5z^2}{2} + C$

51. $x + e^x + C$

53. no, $F(x) - G(x) \neq 0$ is possible

55. $\dfrac{1}{\sqrt{x^2+1}} + C$

Apply It 14.3 (page 638)

6. $N(t) = 800t + 200e^t + 6317.37$

7. $y(t) = 14t^3 + 12t^2 + 11t + 3$

Problems 14.3 (page 641)

1. $y = \dfrac{3x^2}{2} - 4x + 1$

3. $\dfrac{31}{4}$

5. $y = -\dfrac{x^4}{4} + \dfrac{2x^3}{3} + x + \dfrac{19}{12}$

7. $y = \dfrac{x^4}{12} + x^2 - 5x + 13$

9. $p = 0.7$

11. $p = 275 - 0.5q - 0.1q^2$

13. $2.47q + 159$

15. \$8079.17

17. $G = -\dfrac{P^2}{50} + 2P + 20$

21. \$80 $(dc/dq|_{q=50} = 27.50$ is not relevant)

Apply It 14.4

8. $T(t) = 10e^{-0.5t} + C$

9. $35 \ln|t+1| + C$

Problems 14.4 (page 646)

1. $\dfrac{(x+5)^8}{8} + C$

3. $\dfrac{(x^2+3)^6}{6} + C$

5. $\dfrac{3}{5}(y^3 + 3y^2 + 1)^{5/3} + C$

7. $-\dfrac{5(3x-1)^{-2}}{6} + C$

9. $\dfrac{2}{21}(7x+3)^{3/2} + C$

11. $\dfrac{(7x-6)^5}{35} + C$

13. $\dfrac{(5u^2-9)^{15}}{150} + C$

15. $\dfrac{3}{5}(27+x^5)^{4/3} + C$

17. $e^{3x} + C$

19. $\dfrac{1}{2}e^{3t^2+2t+1} + C$

21. $\dfrac{1}{14}e^{7x^2} + C$

23. $-\dfrac{4}{3}e^{-3x} + C$

25. $\ln|x+5| + C$

27. $\ln|x^3+x^4| + C$

29. $-\dfrac{2}{3(z^2-5)^6} + C$

31. $4\ln|x| + C$

33. $\dfrac{1}{3}\ln|s^3+5| + C$

35. $-\dfrac{5}{2}\ln|4-2x| + C$

37. $\dfrac{2}{15}(5x)^{3/2} + C = \dfrac{2\sqrt{5}}{3}x^{3/2} + C$

39. $\dfrac{1}{a}\sqrt{ax^2+b} + C$

41. $\dfrac{1}{2}e^{y^4+1} + C$

43. $-\dfrac{1}{6}e^{-2v^3+1} + C$

45. $-\dfrac{1}{5}e^{-5x} + 2e^x + C$

47. $-\dfrac{1}{2}(7 - 2x^2 - 5x)^4 + C$

49. $2\ln|x^3+4x| + C$

51. $2\ln|3 - 2s + 4s^2| + C$

53. $\dfrac{1}{4}\ln(2x^2+1) + C$

55. $\dfrac{1}{27}(x^3 - x^6)^{-9} + C$

57. $\dfrac{1}{4}(x^4 + x^2)^2 + C$

59. $3(5 - x - x^2)^{-3} + C$

61. $\dfrac{1}{6}e^{4x^3+3x^2-4} + C$

63. $-\dfrac{1}{25}(8 - 5x^2)^{5/2} + C$

65. $\dfrac{2\sqrt{2}}{3}x^{3/2} - \sqrt{2}x^{1/2} + C$

67. $\dfrac{x^5}{5} + \dfrac{2x^3}{3} + x + C$

69. $\dfrac{1}{2}(\ln(x^2+1) - (x^2+1)^{-1}) + C$

71. $\dfrac{1}{2}\ln|4x+1| + \dfrac{4}{21}(x^3 - x^6)^{-7} + C$

73. $\dfrac{2}{9}(3x+1)^{3/2} - \dfrac{1}{2}\ln(x^2+3) + C$

75. $2e^{\sqrt{x}} + C$

77. $-\dfrac{1}{4}e^{-x} + \dfrac{1}{4}e^x + C$

79. $\dfrac{1}{2}(\ln(2x^2+3x))^2 + C$

81. $y = -\dfrac{1}{6}(3 - 2x)^3 + \dfrac{11}{2}$

83. $y = \ln|1/x| + \dfrac{5}{2}x - \dfrac{1}{2}$

85. $160e^{0.05t} + 190$

87. $\dfrac{Rr^2}{4K} + B_1 \ln|r| + B_2$

Problems 14.5 (page 651)

1. $\dfrac{1}{5}x^5 + \dfrac{4}{3}x^3 - 2\ln|x| + C$

3. $\dfrac{1}{3}(2x^3 + 4x + 1)^{3/2} + C$

5. $-\dfrac{6}{5}\sqrt{4-5x} + C$

7. $\dfrac{4^{7x}}{7\ln 4} + C$

9. $7x^2 - 4e^{(1/4)x^2} + C$

11. $x^2 - 3x + \dfrac{2}{3}\ln|3x-1| + C$

13. $\dfrac{5}{14}\ln(7e^{2x} + 4) + C$

15. $-\dfrac{5}{13}e^{13/x} + C$

17. $\dfrac{5}{2}x^2 - \dfrac{45}{2}\ln|x^2+9| + C$

19. $\dfrac{2}{9}(\sqrt{x}+2)^3 + C$

21. $3(x^{1/3} + 2)^5 + C$

23. $\dfrac{1}{2}(\ln^2 x) + C$

25. $\dfrac{1}{3}(\ln(r^2+1))^{3/2} + C$

27. $\dfrac{3^{\ln x}}{\ln 3} + C$

29. $\dfrac{2}{3}e^{(x^3+1)/2} + C$

31. $8\ln|\ln(x+3)| + C$

33. $\dfrac{x^2}{2} + x + \ln|x^2-3| + C$

35. $\dfrac{2}{3}(\ln(x^4+1)^3)^{3/2} + C$

37. $\dfrac{\sqrt{x^4-4x}}{2} - (\ln 7)x + C$

39. $x^2 - 8x - 6\ln|x| - \dfrac{2}{x^2} + C$

41. $x - \ln|x+1| + C$

43. $\sqrt{e^{x^2}+2} + C$

45. $-\dfrac{1}{4}(e^{-x}+5)^4 + C$

47. $\dfrac{1}{5}(x^2+e)^{5/2} + C$

49. $\dfrac{1}{36\sqrt{2}}[(8x)^{3/2} + 3]^{3/2} + C$

51. $-\dfrac{2}{3}e^{-\sqrt{s^3}} + C$

53. $\dfrac{x^3}{3} + x + C$

55. $x - \dfrac{1}{2}(\ln x)^2 + C$

57. $p = -\dfrac{200}{q(q+2)}$

59. $c = 20\ln|(q+5)/5| + 2000$

61. $C = 2(\sqrt{I}+1)$

63. $C = \dfrac{3}{4}I - \dfrac{1}{3}\sqrt{I} + \dfrac{71}{12}$

65. (a) 140 per unit   (b) \$14,000   (c) \$14,280

67. $2500 - 800\sqrt{5} \approx$ \$711 per acre   **69.** $I = 3$

Apply It 14.6 (page 656)

10. \$5975

Problems 14.6 (page 658)

1. $\dfrac{13}{8}$

3. $\dfrac{15}{32}$

5. $S_n = \dfrac{1}{n}\left[4\left(\dfrac{1}{n}\right) + 4\left(\dfrac{2}{n}\right) + \cdots + 4\left(\dfrac{n}{n}\right)\right] = \dfrac{2(n+1)}{n}$

7. (a) $S_n = \dfrac{n+1}{2n} + 1$ (b) $\dfrac{3}{2}$ **9.** $\dfrac{3}{2}$

11. $\dfrac{1}{3}$ **13.** 1   **15.** 20   **17.** -18 **19.** $\dfrac{5}{6}$

21. 0   **23.** $\dfrac{11}{4}$ **25.** 14.7   **27.** 2.4   **29.** -25.5

Apply It 14.7

11. $32,830 **12.** $28,750

Problems 14.7 (page 665)

1. 15 **3.** $\dfrac{15}{2}$ **5.** -20 **7.** 63

9. $\dfrac{15}{2}$ **11.** $\dfrac{4}{3}$ **13.** $\dfrac{768}{7}$ **15.** $\dfrac{5}{3}$

17. $\dfrac{244}{5}$ **19.** $-\dfrac{1}{6}$ **21.** $4\ln 8$ **23.** e^5

25. $\dfrac{5}{3}(e-1)$ **27.** $\dfrac{1}{14}$ **29.** $\dfrac{38}{9}$ **31.** $\dfrac{15}{28}$

33. $\dfrac{1}{2}\ln 3$ **35.** $\dfrac{1}{2}\left(e+\dfrac{1}{e}-2\right)$

37. $-\dfrac{5\sqrt{2}+3}{4}+\dfrac{3}{e}+\dfrac{3}{2e^2}-\dfrac{1}{e^3}$

39. $\dfrac{e^3}{2}(e^{12}-1)$ **41.** $6+\ln 19$ **43.** $\dfrac{47}{12}$

45. $6-3e$ **47.** -7 **49.** 0 **51.** $\alpha^{5/2}T$

53. $\int_a^b(-Ax^{-B})dx$ **55.** $8639 **57.** $180,667; 769,126$

59. $220 **61.** $1367.99 **63.** $696;492$ **65.** $2Ri$

69. 0.05 **71.** 3.52 **73.** 14.34

Apply It 14.8 (page 669)

13. 76.90 ft **14.** 5.77 gm

Problems 14.8 (page 671)

1. 413 **3.** $0.26; \dfrac{1}{4}$ **5.** $\approx 0.767; 0.750$

7. $0.883; 2-\ln 3\approx 0.901$ **9.** 2,115,215

11. 3.0 **13.** $\dfrac{8}{3}$ **15.** 0.771 **17.** yes

Problems 14.9 (page 678)

1. $\dfrac{87}{2}$ **3.** 26 **7.** 13 **9.** $\ln 16$

11. e^3-e **13.** 1 **15.** 16 **17.** 16

19. e **21.** $\dfrac{3}{2}+2\ln 2=\dfrac{3}{2}+\ln 4$ **23.** $\dfrac{16}{3}$

25. 19 **27.** (a) $\dfrac{1}{16}$ (b) $\dfrac{3}{4}$ (c) $\dfrac{7}{16}$

29. (a) $\ln\dfrac{7}{3}$ (b) $\ln 5-1$ (c) $2-\ln 4$

31. 1.89 **33.** 11.41

35. $\int_0^3(2x-(x^2-x))dx+\int_3^4((x^2-x)-2x)\,dx$

37. $\int_0^1((y+1)-\sqrt{1-y})\,dy$

39. $\int_1^2((7-2x^2)-(x^2-5))\,dx$

41. $\dfrac{4}{3}$ **43.** $8\sqrt{6}$ **45.** 40 **47.** 9

49. $\dfrac{125}{12}$ **51.** $\dfrac{44}{3}$ **53.** $\dfrac{1}{2}$

55. $\dfrac{255}{32}-4\ln 2$ **57.** 12 **59.** $\dfrac{14}{45}$

61. $\dfrac{3}{2m^3}$ **63.** $2^{4/3}$ **65.** 4.76 **67.** 6.17

Problems 14.10 (page 683)

1. CS $= 25.6$; PS $= 38.4$ **3.** CS $= 50\ln 2-25$; PS $= 1.25$

5. CS $= 225$; PS $= 450$ **7.** $426.67

9. $(q_0,p_0)=(4,64)$; CS$=64\left(\dfrac{15}{\ln 2}-4\right)$ ($100) $\approx$ $113,000

11. CS ≈ 1197; PS ≈ 477

Review Problems—Chapter 14 (page 685)

1. $\dfrac{x^4}{4}+x^2-7x+C$ **3.** 2160 **5.** $-3(x+5)^{-2}+C$

7. $2\ln|x^3-6x+1|+C$ **9.** $\dfrac{11\sqrt[3]{11}}{4}-4$

11. $\dfrac{y^4}{4}+\dfrac{2y^3}{3}+\dfrac{y^2}{2}+C$ **13.** $\dfrac{21}{17}t^{17/21}-\dfrac{6}{7}t^{7/6}+C$

15. $\dfrac{1}{3}\ln\dfrac{57}{5}$ **17.** $\dfrac{2}{27}(3x^3+2)^{3/2}+C$

19. $\dfrac{1}{2}(e^{2y}+e^{-2y})+C$ **21.** $\ln|x|-\dfrac{2}{x}+C$ **23.** $\dfrac{272}{15}$

25. $\dfrac{35}{3}$ **27.** $4-3\sqrt[3]{2}$ **29.** $\dfrac{3}{t}-\dfrac{2}{\sqrt{t}}+C$

31. $\dfrac{3}{2}-5\ln 2$ **33.** $e^{\sqrt{x}}+\dfrac{1}{3}x\sqrt{x}+C$ **35.** 1

37. $\dfrac{(1+e^{2x})^4}{8}+C$ **39.** $\dfrac{2\sqrt{10^{3x}}}{\ln 10}+C$

41. $y=\dfrac{1}{2}e^{2x}+3x-1$ **43.** 4 **45.** $\dfrac{16}{3}$

47. $\dfrac{125}{6}$ **49.** $6+\ln 4$ **51.** $\dfrac{2}{3}$

53. $\dfrac{a^3}{6}$ **55.** $\dfrac{243}{8}$ **57.** $e-1$

59. $p=100-\sqrt{2q}$ **61.** $1483.33

63. $1-e^{-0.7}\approx 0.5034$ **65.** 15

67. CS $=166\dfrac{2}{3}$, PS $=53\dfrac{1}{3}$ **73.** $\dfrac{1}{2}$

75. CS ≈ 1148, PS ≈ 251

Explore and Extend—Chapter 14 (page 688)

1. (a) 475 (b) 275

3. (a) $2,002,500 (b) 18,000 (c) $111.25

Apply It 15.1

1. $S(t)=-40te^{0.1t}+400e^{0.1t}+4600$

2. $P(t)=0.025t^2-0.05t^2\ln t+0.05t^2(\ln t)^2+C$

Problems 15.1 (page 693)

1. $\dfrac{2}{3}x(x+5)^{3/2}-\dfrac{4}{15}(x+5)^{5/2}+C$

3. $-e^{-x}(x+1)+C$ **5.** $\dfrac{y^4}{4}\left[\ln(y)-\dfrac{1}{4}\right]+C$

7. $x[\ln(4x)-1]+C$

9. $\dfrac{2}{3a}x(ax+b)^{3/2}-\dfrac{4}{15a^2}(ax+b)^{5/2}+C$

11. $-\dfrac{x}{10(5x+2)^2}-\dfrac{1}{50(5x+2)}+C$

13. $-\dfrac{1}{x}(1+\ln x)+C$ **15.** $e^2(3e^2-1)$

17. $\dfrac{1}{2}(1-e^{-1})$, parts not needed **19.** $\dfrac{160}{3}$

21. $3x(x-2)\ln(x-2)-\dfrac{3}{2}x^2+C$

23. $e^x(x^2 - 2x + 2) + C$

25. $\dfrac{x^3}{3} + 2e^{-x}(x + 1) - \dfrac{e^{-2x}}{2} + C$ **27.** $\dfrac{e^{x^2}}{2}(x^2 - 1) + C$

29. $\dfrac{1}{2}e^{2x} + 2e^x(x - 1) + \dfrac{1}{3}x^3 + C$

31. $2e^3 + 1$ **33.** $\left[\dfrac{8}{3}\ln(2) - \dfrac{7}{9}\right]$

37. $\int f^{-1}(x)dx = xf^{-1}(x) - F(f^{-1}(x)) + C$

Apply It 15.2

3. $r(q) = \dfrac{5}{2}\ln\left|\dfrac{3(q + 1)^3}{q + 3}\right|$

4. $V(t) = 150t^2 - 900\ln(t^2 + 6) + C$

Problems 15.2 (page 699)

1. $\dfrac{12}{x + 6} - \dfrac{2}{x + 1}$ **3.** $2 + \dfrac{8}{x + 2} - \dfrac{18}{x + 3}$

5. $\dfrac{3}{x - 1} + \dfrac{2}{(x - 1)^2}$ **7.** $\dfrac{3}{x} - \dfrac{2x}{x^2 + 1}$

9. $2\ln|x| + 3\ln|x - 1| + C$

11. $-3\ln|x + 1| + 4\ln|x - 2| + C$

13. $\dfrac{1}{4}\left(\dfrac{3x^2}{2} + 2\ln|x - 1| - 2\ln|x + 1|\right)$

15. $3\ln|x| + \dfrac{5}{2}\ln|x + 2| + 4\ln|x - 3| + C$

17. $\ln|x^6 + 2x^4 - x^2 - 2| + C$, partial fractions not required

19. $\dfrac{4}{x - 2} - 5\ln|x - 1| + 7\ln|x - 2| + C$

21. $4\ln|x| - \ln(x^2 + 4) + C$ **23.** $-\dfrac{1}{2}\ln(x^2 + 1) - \dfrac{2}{x - 3} + C$

25. $\dfrac{3}{2}\ln(x^2 + 3) + 2\ln(x^2 + 4)$ **27.** $\dfrac{3}{2}\ln(x^2 + 2) - \dfrac{1}{x^2 + 2} + C$

29. $18\ln(4) - 10\ln(5) - 8\ln(3)$ **31.** $11 + 24\ln\dfrac{2}{3}$

Problems 15.3 (page 704)

1. $\dfrac{x}{6\sqrt{6 - x^2}} + C$ **3.** $-\dfrac{\sqrt{16x^2 + 3}}{3x} + C$

5. $\dfrac{1}{6}\ln\left|\dfrac{x}{6 + 7x}\right| + C$ **7.** $\dfrac{1}{3}\ln\left|\dfrac{\sqrt{x^2 + 9} - 3}{x}\right| + C$

9. $\dfrac{1}{2}\left(\dfrac{4}{5}\ln|4 + 5x| - \dfrac{2}{3}\ln|2 + 3x|\right) + C$

11. $\dfrac{1}{3}(3x - \ln|1 + 2e^{3x}|) + C$

13. $7\left(\dfrac{1}{5(5 + 2x)} + \dfrac{1}{25}\ln\left|\dfrac{x}{5 + 2x}\right|\right) + C$ **15.** $1 + \ln\dfrac{4}{9}$

17. $\dfrac{1}{2}\left(x\sqrt{x^2 - 3} - 3\ln\left|x + \sqrt{x^2 - 3}\right|\right) + C$

19. $\dfrac{1}{144}$ **21.** $x^3e^x - 3x^2e^x + 6xe^x - 6e^x + C$

23. $\dfrac{\sqrt{5}}{2}\left(-\dfrac{\sqrt{5x^2 + 1}}{\sqrt{5}x} + \ln\left|\sqrt{5}x + \sqrt{5x^2 + 1}\right|\right) + C$

25. $\dfrac{1}{9}\left(\ln|1 + 3x| + \dfrac{1}{1 + 3x}\right) + C$

27. $\dfrac{1}{\sqrt{5}}\left(\dfrac{1}{2\sqrt{7}}\ln\left|\dfrac{\sqrt{7} + \sqrt{5}x}{\sqrt{7} - \sqrt{5}x}\right|\right) + C$

29. $x^6(6\ln(3x) - 1) + C$ **31.** $\dfrac{1}{3}(3x - 1)(1 + 2x)^{3/2} + C$

33. $\dfrac{1}{2}\ln\left|2x + \sqrt{4x^2 - 13}\right| + C$ **35.** $-\dfrac{\sqrt{16 - 9x^2}}{8x} + C$

37. $\dfrac{1}{2\pi}(4\sqrt{x} - \ln|\pi + 7e^{4\sqrt{x}}|) + C$

39. $\dfrac{1}{2}\ln(x^2 + 1) + C$ **41.** $\dfrac{1}{4}(\ln x)^4 + C$

43. $\ln\left|\dfrac{x - 3}{x - 2}\right| + C$ **45.** $\dfrac{x^4}{4}\left[\ln(x) - \dfrac{1}{4}\right] + C$

47. $\dfrac{2}{9}e^{3x^2}(3x^2 - 1) + C$ **49.** $x(\ln x)^2 - 2x\ln(x) + 2x + C$

51. $-\dfrac{4}{3}$ **53.** $2(2\sqrt{2} - \sqrt{7})$ **55.** $\dfrac{7}{2}\ln(2) - \dfrac{3}{4}$

57. $\ln\left|\dfrac{q_n(1 - q_0)}{q_0(1 - q_n)}\right|$ **59. (a)** $7558.09 **(b)** $16,930.75

61. (a) $1107.01 **(b)** $2103.42

Problems 15.4 (page 707)

1. $\dfrac{7}{3}$ **3.** -1 **5.** 0 **7.** $\dfrac{2}{3}$ **9.** $11,050 **11.** $3155.13

Apply It 15.5 (page 709)

5. $I = I_0e^{-0.0085x}$

Problems 15.5 (page 713)

1. $y = -\dfrac{1}{x^2 + C}$

3. $y = (x^2 + 1)\ln(x^2 + 1) - (x^2 + 1) + C$

5. $y = Ce^x, C > 0$ **7.** $y = Cx, C > 0$

9. $y = \sqrt[3]{3x - 2}$ **11.** $y = \ln\dfrac{x^3 + 3}{3}$

13. $y = \dfrac{48(3x^2 + 2)^2}{4 + 23(3x^2 + 2)^2}$ **15.** $y = \sqrt{\left(\dfrac{3x^2}{2} + \dfrac{3}{2}\right)^2 - 1}$

17. $y = \ln\left(\dfrac{1}{2}\sqrt{x^2 + 3}\right)$ **19.** $c = (q + 1)e^{1/(q+1)}$

21. 120 weeks **23.** $P(t) = 60,000e^{\frac{1}{10}(4\ln 2 - \ln 3 - \ln 5)t}$; 68,266

25. $2e^{1.14882}$ billion **27.** 0.01204; 57.57 sec

29. 2900 years **31.** $N = N_0e^{k(t - t_0)}, t \ge t_0$

33. $12(2^{1/3}) \approx 15.1$ **35.** $A = 400(1 - e^{-t/2})$; 157 g/m²

37. (a) $V = 60,000e^{\frac{t}{9.5}\ln(389/600)}$ **(b)** June 2028

Problems 15.6 (page 719)

1. 69,200 **3.** 500 **5.** 1990 **7. (b)** 375

9. 2:20 A.M. **11.** $155,555.56 **13.** $N = M - (M - N_0)e^{-kt}$

Apply It 15.7 (page 721)

6. 20 ml

Problems 15.7 (page 723)

1. $\dfrac{1}{18}$ **3.** divgt **5.** e^{-37} **7.** divgt **9.** $\dfrac{1}{2}$ **11.** 0

13. (a) 800 **(b)** $\dfrac{2}{3}$ **15.** 25,000,000

17. $\dfrac{1}{3}$ **19.** 20,000 increase

1. $\dfrac{1}{3}x^3\left(\ln x - \dfrac{1}{3}\right)$

3. $2\sqrt{13} + \dfrac{8}{3}\ln\left(\dfrac{3+\sqrt{13}}{2}\right)$

5. $\ln|3x + 1| + 4\ln|x - 2| + C$

7. $\dfrac{1}{2(x+2)} + \dfrac{1}{4}\ln\left|\dfrac{x}{x+2}\right| + C$ **9.** $-\dfrac{\sqrt{9-16x^2}}{9x} + C$

11. $\dfrac{1}{2a}(\ln|x - a| - \ln|x + a|) + C$

13. $e^{7x}(7x - 1) + C$

15. $\dfrac{1}{4}\ln|\ln x^2| + C$

17. $x - \dfrac{3}{2}\ln|3 + 2x| + C$

19. $2\ln|x| + \dfrac{3}{2}\ln(x^2 + 1) + C$

21. $\dfrac{2}{3}(x+1)^{3/2}\left(\ln(x+1) - \dfrac{2}{3}\right) + C$

23. 34 **25.** $y = Ce^{x^3 + x^2},\ C > 0$ **27.** $\dfrac{2}{3}$

29. divgt **31.** 2,000,000 **33.** 0.0005; 90%

35. $N = \dfrac{450}{1 + 224e^{-1.02t}}$ **37.** 4:16 P.M. **39.** 0.95

41. (a) 207, 208 (b) 157, 165 (c) 41, 41

1. 114; 69 **5.** answers may vary

1. $f_x(x, y) = 4x + 3y + 5; f_y(x, y) = 3x + 8y + 6$

3. $f_x(x, y) = 0; f_y(x, y) = 2$

5. $g_x(x, y) = 12x^3y + 2y^2 - 5y + 8;$
$g_y(x, y) = 3x^4 + 4xy - 5x - 9$

7. $g_p(p, q) = \dfrac{q}{2\sqrt{pq}}; g_q(p, q) = \dfrac{p}{2\sqrt{pq}}$

9. $h_s(s, t) = \dfrac{2s}{t - 3}; h_t(s, t) = \dfrac{s^2 + 4}{(t - 3)^2}$

11. $\dfrac{\partial u}{\partial q_1} = \dfrac{1}{2(q_1 + 2)}; \dfrac{\partial u}{\partial q_2} = \dfrac{1}{3(q_2 + 5)}$

13. $h_x(x, y) = (x^3 + xy^2 + 3y^3)(x^2 + y^2)^{-3/2};$
$h_y(x, y) = (3x^3 + x^2y + y^3)(x^2 + y^2)^{-3/2}$

15. $\dfrac{\partial z}{\partial x} = 5ye^{5xy}; \dfrac{\partial z}{\partial y} = 5xe^{5xy}$

17. $\dfrac{\partial z}{\partial x} = 5\dfrac{2x^2}{x^2 + y} + \ln(x^2 + y); \dfrac{\partial z}{\partial y} = \dfrac{5x}{x^2 + y}$

19. $f_r(r, s) = \sqrt{r + 2s}\,(3r^2 - 2s) + \dfrac{r^3 - 2rs + s^2}{2\sqrt{r + 2s}}$;

$f_s(r, s) = 2(s - r)\sqrt{r + 2s} + \dfrac{r^3 - 2rs + s^2}{\sqrt{r + 2s}}$

21. $\dfrac{\partial f}{\partial r} = -e^{3-r}\ln(7 - s)$; $\dfrac{\partial f}{\partial s} = -\dfrac{e^{3-r}}{7 - s}$;

23. $g_x(x, y, z) = 6x^2y^2 + 2y^3z$; $g_y(x, y, z) = 4x^3y + 6xy^2z$; $g_z(x, y, z) = 2xy^3 + 8z$

25. $g_r(r, s, t) = 2re^{s+t}$; $g_s(r, s, t) = (7s^3 + 21s^2 + r^2)e^{s+t}$; $g_t(r, s, t) = e^{s+t}(r^2 + 7s^3)$

27. 50   **29.** $\dfrac{1}{\sqrt{14}}$ **31.** 0   **33.** 26

39. $-\dfrac{ra}{2(1 + a(n - 1)/2)^2}$

Problems 17.2 (page 758)

1. 20   **3.** 1374.5

5. $\dfrac{\partial P}{\partial k} = 1.487902\left(\dfrac{l}{k}\right)^{0.357}$; $\dfrac{\partial P}{\partial l} = 0.826098\left(\dfrac{k}{l}\right)^{0.643}$

7. $\partial q_A/\partial p_A = -40$; $\partial q_A/\partial p_B = 3$; $\partial q_B/\partial p_A = 5$; $\partial q_B/\partial p_B = -20$; competitive

9. $\dfrac{\partial q_A}{\partial p_A} = -\dfrac{100}{p_A^2 p_B^{1/2}}$; $\dfrac{\partial q_A}{\partial p_B} = -\dfrac{50}{p_A p_B^{3/2}}$; $\dfrac{\partial q_B}{\partial p_A} = -\dfrac{500}{3 p_B p_A^{4/3}}$;

$\dfrac{\partial q_B}{\partial p_B} = -\dfrac{500}{p_B^2 p_A^{1/3}}$; complementary

11. $\dfrac{\partial P}{\partial B} = 0.01 A^{0.27} B^{-0.99} C^{0.01} D^{0.23} E^{0.09} F^{0.27}$;

$\dfrac{\partial P}{\partial C} = 0.01 A^{0.27} B^{0.01} C^{-0.99} D^{0.23} E^{0.09} F^{0.27}$

13. 4480

15. (a) -1.015; -0.846 **(b)** one with $w = w_0$ and $s = s_0$

17. $\dfrac{\partial g}{\partial x} = \dfrac{1}{V_F} > 0$ for $V_F > 0$; if V_F and V_s fixed and x increases then g increases.

19. (a) $\left.\dfrac{\partial q_A}{\partial p_A}\right|_{p_A=9, p_B=16} = -\dfrac{20}{27}$; $\left.\dfrac{\partial q_A}{\partial p_B}\right|_{p_A=9, p_B=16} = \dfrac{5}{12}$

(b) demand for A decreases by $\approx \dfrac{5}{6}$

21. (a) no   **(b)** 70%

23. $\eta_{p_A} = -\dfrac{5}{46}$, $\eta_{p_B} = \dfrac{1}{46}$ **25.** $\eta_{p_A} = -1$, $\eta_{p_B} = -\dfrac{1}{2}$

Problems 17.3 (page 762)

1. $-\dfrac{2x}{5z}$ **3.** $\dfrac{7y}{3z}$ for $z \neq 0$ **5.** $\dfrac{x(yz^2 + 1)}{z(1 - x^2 y)}$ **7.** $-e^{y-z}$

9. $\dfrac{yz}{1 + 9z}$ **11.** $-\dfrac{3x}{z}$ **13.** $-\dfrac{1}{2}$ **15.** $-\dfrac{4}{e^2}$ **17.** 4

19. $\dfrac{5}{2}$ **21. (a)** 36   **(b)** $c_{q_A} = \dfrac{60}{13}$, $c_{q_B} = \dfrac{288}{65}$

Problems 17.4 (page 764)

1. $6y^2$; $12y$; $12y$ **3.** 3; 0; 0

5. $18xe^{2xy}$; $18e^{2xy}(2xy + 1)$; $72x(1 + xy)e^{2xy}$

7. $3x^2y + 4xy^2 + y^3$; $3xy^2 + 4x^2y + x^3$; $6xy + 4y^2$; $6xy + 4x^2$

9. $\partial z/\partial y = \dfrac{y}{x^2 + y^2}$; $\partial^2 z/\partial y^2 = \dfrac{x^2 - y^2}{(x^2 + y^2)^2}$

11. 0   **13.** 744   **15.** $2e$ **17.** $-\dfrac{1}{8}$

23. $-\dfrac{y^2 + z^2}{z^3} = -\dfrac{3x^2}{z^3}$

Problems 17.5 (page 768)

1. $\dfrac{\partial z}{\partial r} = 13$; $\dfrac{\partial z}{\partial s} = 9$ **3.** $\left(2t + \dfrac{3\sqrt{t}}{2}\right)e^{x+y}$

5. $(2xyz + y^2z + yz^2)(e^t) + (x^2z + 2xyz + xz^2)(e^t + te^t) + (x^2y + xy^2 + 2xyz)(2te^t + t^2e^t)$

7. $3(x^2 + xy^2)^2(2x + y^2 + 16xy)$

9. $-2s(2x + yz) + r(xz) + 2s(xy + 2z)$

11. $19s(2x - 7)$ **13.** 324   **15.** $96e^4$

17. $\left.\dfrac{\partial c}{\partial p_A}\right|_{p_A=25, p_B=4} = -\dfrac{1}{4}$, $\left.\dfrac{\partial c}{\partial p_B}\right|_{p_A=25, p_B=4} = \dfrac{5}{4}$

19. (a) $\dfrac{\partial w}{\partial t} = \dfrac{\partial w}{\partial x}\dfrac{\partial x}{\partial t} + \dfrac{\partial w}{\partial y}\dfrac{\partial y}{\partial t}$ **(b)** $-\dfrac{20}{3\sqrt{2} + 15e}$

Problems 17.6 (page 775)

1. $(1, 2)$ **3.** $(0, -2), (0, 1), (3, -2), (3, 1)$

5. $(50, 150, 350)$ **7.** $\left(-2, \dfrac{3}{2}\right)$ rel min

9. $\left(-\dfrac{1}{4}, \dfrac{1}{2}\right)$ rel max   **11.** $(3, 1)$; $D(3, 1) < 0$ no rel ext

13. $(0, 0)$ rel max; $\left(4, \dfrac{1}{2}\right)$ rel min; $\left(0, \dfrac{1}{2}\right)$, $(4, 0)$, not rel ext

15. $(43, 13)$ rel min   **17.** $(-1, -1)$ rel min

19. $(0, -2), (0, 2)$ not rel ext   **21.** $l = 72.67$, $k = 43.78$

23. $p_A = 80$, $p_B = 85$

25. $q_A = 48$, $q_B = 40$, $p_A = 52$, $p_B = 44$, profit = 3304

27. $q_A = 4$, $q_B = 3$ **29.** 1 ft by 2 ft by 3 ft

31. $\left(\dfrac{3}{2}, \dfrac{1}{2}\right)$ rel min   **33.** $a = -8$, $b = -12$, $d = 33$

35. (a) 2 of A, 3 of B   **(b)** selling price for A is 30, for B is 19, rel max profit is 25

37. (a) $P = 5T(1 - e^{-x}) - 20x - 0.1T^2x$ **(c)** $(20, \ln 5)$ rel max, $\left(5, \ln\dfrac{5}{4}\right)$ not rel ext

Problems 17.7 (page 783)

1. $(2, -2)$ **3.** $\left(3, \dfrac{3}{2}, -\dfrac{3}{2}\right)$ **5.** $\left(0, \dfrac{1}{4}, \dfrac{5}{8}\right)$ **7.** $\left(\dfrac{1}{3}, \dfrac{1}{3}, \dfrac{1}{3}\right)$

9. $\left(\dfrac{2}{3}, \dfrac{4}{3}, -\dfrac{4}{3}\right)$ **11.** $\left(\dfrac{1}{4}, \dfrac{1}{2}, \dfrac{1}{4}\right)$ **13.** 40 at plant 1, 60 at plant 2

15. 74 when $l = 8$, $k = 7$

17. $x = 5,000$ newspaper, $y = 15,000$ TV

19. $x = 5$, $y = 15$, $z = 5$ **21.** $x = 12$, $y = 8$

23. $x = \dfrac{100}{3}$, $y = \dfrac{100}{3}$, $z = \dfrac{100}{3}$

Problems 17.8 (page 788)

1. $\hat{y} = 0.98 + 0.61x$; 3.12   **3.** $\hat{y} = 0.057 + 1.67x$; 5.90

5. $\hat{q} = 80.5 - 0.643p$ **7.** $\hat{y} = 100 + 0.13x$; 105.2

9. $\hat{y} = 8.5 + 2.5x$

11. (a) $\hat{y} = 35.9 - 2.5x$ **(b)** $\hat{y} = 28.4 - 2.5x$

Problems 17.9 (page 792)

1. 18   **3.** $\dfrac{1}{4}$ **5.** $\dfrac{2}{3}$ **7.** 3   **9.** $\dfrac{38}{3}$

11. $-\dfrac{58}{5}$ **13.** 9   **15.** -1 **17.** $\dfrac{e^2}{2} - e + \dfrac{1}{2}$

19. 3   **21.** $\dfrac{1}{24}$ **23.** $e^{-4} - e^{-2} - e^{-3} + e^{-1}$ **25.** $\dfrac{1}{3}$

1. $f_x = \dfrac{2x}{x^2 + y^2}; f_y = \dfrac{2y}{x^2 + y^2}$ **3.** $\dfrac{y}{(x+y)^2}; -\dfrac{x}{(x+y)^2}$

5. $\dfrac{y}{x^2 + y^2}$ **7.** $2xze^{x^2yz}(1 + x^2yz)$

9. $2x + 2y + 6z$ **11.** $e^{x+y+z}(\ln(xyz) + 1/x + 1/y + 1/z)$

13. $\dfrac{1}{64}$ **15.** $2(x+y)e^r + 2\left(\dfrac{x+3y}{r+s}\right); 2\left(\dfrac{x+3y}{r+s}\right)$

17. $\dfrac{2x + 2y + z}{4z - x}$

19. $\dfrac{\partial P}{\partial l} = 14l^{-0.3}k^{0.3}; \dfrac{\partial P}{\partial k} = 6l^{0.7}k^{-0.7}$

21. neither **23.** $(2, 2)$ rel min **25.** 4 ft by 4 ft by 2 ft

27. 89 cents/lb for A; 94 cents/lb for B

29. $(3, 2, 1)$ **31.** $\hat{y} = 12.67 + 3.29x$ **33.** $\dfrac{1}{12}$ **35.** $\dfrac{1}{30}$

1. $y = 9.50e^{-0.22399x} + 5$ **3.** $T = 79e^{-0.01113t} + 45$

Index

Photo Credits